Russian Warships

Russian Warships in the Age of Sail
1696–1860

Design, Construction, Careers and Fates

John Tredrea & Eduard Sozaev

Seaforth
PUBLISHING

Frontispiece: The Russian sailing navy at the height of its power and efficiency: during a state visit to Britain the Russian squadron at Spithead mans the yards in honour of the Duchess of Clarence, 8 August 1827. Drawn with meticulous attention to detail by Henry Moses, all the Russian ships are identified. From left to right, they are: *Sisoi Velikii* (74); *Iezekiil'* (74); *Tsar' Konstantin* (74); *Merkurii* (44); *Kniaz Vladimir* (74); *Gangut* (84), then the British royal yacht *Royal Sovereign* under sail; *Aleksandr Nevskii* (74); *Azov* (74); *Sviatoi Andrei* (74). Elements of this squadron were to fight with distinction a couple of months later at Navarino. (National Maritime Museum PU8013)

To Our Wives and Mothers

Copyright © John Tredrea and Eduard Sozaev 2010

First published in Great Britain in 2010 by Seaforth Publishing
An imprint of Pen & Sword Books Ltd
47 Church Street, Barnsley
S Yorkshire S70 2AS

www.seaforthpublishing.com
Email info@seaforthpublishing.com

British Library Cataloguing in Publication Data
A CIP data record for this book is available from the British Library

ISBN 978-1-84832-058-1

All rights reserved. No part of this publication may be reproduced or transmitted in any form or by any means, electronic or mechanical, including photocopying, recording, or any information storage and retrieval system, without prior permission in writing of both the copyright owner and the above publisher.

The right of John Tredrea and Eduard Sozaev to be identified as the authors of this work has been asserted by them in accordance with the Copyright, Designs and Patents Act 1988

Typeset and designed by Palindrome
Printed and bound in Thailand

Contents

Acknowledgments	viii
The Russian Sailing Navy – Overview	1
Introduction	2
Historical background	4
Sources	4
Transliteration protocols	7
Organization and layout	8
Chronology of Major Events in Russian Naval History 1696–1860	11
Fleet action orders of battle	13
Data Format	18
Ship Types and Classifications	22
Line-of-battle ships	22
Frigates	22
Corvettes and ship sloops	25
Snows and brigs	25
Cutters and schooners	26
Luggers and tenders	26
Bomb vessels	26
Russian Naval Administration	27
Russian naval command structure	27
Naval finance	29
Surveyors, constructors and shipwrights	29
Personnel	31
Russian Shipyards and Naval Bases	33
Baltic fleet shipyards	34
Sea of Azov shipyards	39
Black Sea shipyards	39
Russian Naval Ordnance 1700–1860	41
Edinorogs	41
Cannon, carronades and gunnades	42
Shell guns	42
Naval ordnance tables	43
The Naval Establishments: Force Levels and Ship Armament	46
Russian Naval History 1695–1860	49
Sweden and the Baltic	52
Russia in the Black Sea and the Mediterranean	75
The Caspian flotilla	110
The voyages of exploration	111
Section I The Seagoing Navy	113
The Baltic Fleet	114
The Navy of Peter and His Successors (1696–1761)	114
Ships with 90–100 guns	114
Ships with 70–88 guns	116
Ships with 60–68 guns	120
Ships with 50–58 guns	135
Baltic line of battle ships purchased abroad	138
Baltic frigates	141
Baltic snows	150
Baltic bomb vessels	152
The Navy of Catherine and Paul (1762–1800)	153
Ships with 90–110 guns	153
Ships with 70–78 guns	156
Ships with 60–68 guns	163
Baltic frigates	168
Arkhipelago privateers taken into service	179
Baltic corvettes	182
Baltic brigs	182
Baltic cutters (one- and two-masted)	182
Baltic schooners	184
Baltic lugger purchased abroad	184
Baltic bomb vessels	185
The Navy of Alexander I (1801–24)	186
Baltic ships with 90–110 guns	186
Baltic ships with 80–88 guns	187
Baltic ships with 70–78 guns	188
Baltic ships with 60–68 guns	194
Baltic frigates	196
Baltic sloops	205
Baltic corvettes	208
Baltic brigs	210
Baltic cutters (one- and two-masted)	212
Baltic schooners	215
Baltic luggers	215
Baltic bomb vessels	215

The Navy of Nicholas I and the Creation of the Steam Navy (1825–60)	216
Ships with 90–135 guns	218
Ships with 80–88 guns	220
Ships with 70–78 guns	225
Baltic sailing frigates	235
Baltic sloops	241
Baltic corvettes	241
Baltic brigs	241
Baltic schooners	244
Baltic luggers	246
Baltic one-masted tenders	247
Baltic Prizes (1700–1860)	247
Captured line of battle ships	247
Captured frigates	250
Captured Swedish rowing frigates	252
Captured snows	253
Captured corvettes	254
Captured brigs	255
Captured cutters	255
The Sea of Azov Fleet (1696–1711)	256
Sea of Azov line of battle ships	256
Sea of Azov Barbary ships	259
Sea of Azov bark rigged ships	260
Sea of Azov snows	262
Sea of Azov floating battery	262
Sea of Azov bomb vessels	262
Sea of Azov oared frigates	263
Miscellaneous Azov construction	263
The Black Sea Fleet	264
The Navy of Catherine and Paul (1770–1800)	264
Early square rigged vessels	264
Ships with 110 guns	265
Ships with 80–84 guns	265
Ships with 74 guns	266
Ships with 60–66 guns	268
Black Sea frigates	220
Black Sea schooners	279
Black Sea fleet bomb vessels	280
Black Sea purchased cruising vessels	281
The Navy of Alexander I (1801–1824)	284
Ships of 110 guns	284
Ships of 74–80 guns	285
Frigates	287
Corvettes	289
Sloop	289
Brigs	290
Black Sea schooners	292
Black Sea cutter	293
Black Sea lugger	293
Black Sea single-masted tenders	293
Black Sea bomb vessels	293

The Navy of Nicholas I and the Creation of the Steam Navy (1825–1860)	293
Ships of 110–135 guns	293
Ships of 84 guns	297
Black Sea frigates	302
Black Sea corvettes	305
Black Sea brigs	307
Black Sea schooners	309
Black Sea cutters	310
Black Sea luggers	310
Black Sea single-masted tenders	311
Black Sea fleet bomb vessels	312
Black Sea Prizes (1770–1860)	312
Captured ships of the line	312
Captured frigates	313
Captured corvettes	313
Captured brigs	313
The Caspian flotilla	315
Caspian flotilla two-masted hoeker	315
Caspian flotilla small frigates	315
Caspian flotilla rowing frigate	316
Caspian flotilla corvettes	316
Caspian flotilla ship sloops	316
Caspian flotilla brigs	317
Caspian flotilla schooners	318
Caspian flotilla luggers	319
Caspian flotilla one-masted tenders	319
Caspian flotilla bomb vessels	319
Aral Sea flotilla schooners	320
Sea of Okhotsk ships	321
Far Eastern sloops	321
Okhotsk flotilla brigs	321
Okhotsk flotilla cutters	321
Schooners	322
One-masted tenders	322
Siberian flotilla schooners	322
Section II The Inshore Navy	323
Shebecks (jabeques)	324
War galleys	325
Horse galleys	339
Kayks, kaiks, or half-galleys	340
Baltic secret vessels	341
Rowing brigantines	342
Black Sea lansons	344
Galets	346
Dubbel-shlyupkas	347
Gunboats (*Kanonerskie Lodki*)	350
Yawls	354
Severnye vessesl	355
Caspian flottila gardecotes	355
Prams	355

Floating batteries 358
Bomb cutters 359

Section III Russian Naval Auxiliaries 361
Strugs 362
Galiots 362
Shmaks 366
Buers 367
Fleyts 367
Pilot boats (Lots-bots) 369
Packet boats 371
Shkuts (Shkouts) 373
Pinks 373
Gukors 376
Gekbots 378
Kraers 379
Transports 379
Flashkouts (plashkouts) 398
Gabars 399
Cargo yachts 399
Passenger Boats 400
Miscellaneous Auxiliaries 400

*Section IV The Russian Steam Navy to 1862
(assisted by John Houghton)* 405

Steam-powered Warships: Baltic Fleet 407
Steam screw ship of the line 407
Steam screw frigates 410
Steam paddle frigates 415
Steam screw corvettes 419
Steam screw clippers 421

Steam-powered Sailing Warships: Black Sea Fleet 423
Steam screw ship of the line 423
Steam paddle frigates 423
Captured paddle steamers 424
Steam screw corvettes 424

Steam and Sail Gunboats: All Fleets 425

Postscript: The Russian Navy 1861 428

Appendices 431

A Russian and Swedish fleets in June 1714 431

B Russian fleet on 6 May 1743 431

C Russian and Swedish orders of battle on 13 May 1743 431

D Baltic fleet units dispatched to the Arkhipelago Campaign 1768–74 431

E The Armed Neutrality squadrons 1780–82 432

F Black Sea fleet in 1790 432

G Russian squadron dispatched to England in June, 1795 432

H Russian squadrons dispatched to England in 1798 432

I Admiral Chichagov's squadron to England, September, 1799 433

J Black Sea expeditionary fleet in April, 1798 433

K Ships sssigned to the Mediterranean theatre in 1807 433

L Russian ships evacuated to England in 1812 433

Select Bibliography 435

Indexes of Ship Names

Section I: The Seagoing Navy 436
Section II: The Inshore Navy 441
Section III :Russian Naval Auxiliaries 443
Section IV: The Russian Steam Navy 446

Picture Credits 448

Acknowledgements

This work might never have been followed through to completion were it not for the encouragement of Rif Winfield, who had nothing but encouragement for the American half of the team when the possibility of a study of the Russian sailing navy organized along the lines of the more exhaustively documented studies of the British Royal Navy was nervously broached two years past. Similar praise must also go to Dr Albert C. F. Parker, naval enthusiast, historian, Russian linguist and loyal friend for his endless and patient assistance in helping to obtain research materials and information available only in the Library of Congress – at least on this side of the Atlantic, his careful and exhaustive review of the historical sections of the document for accuracy, his ruthless critiquing of my numerous and inexcusable violations of the rules of grammar and good prose style, as well as for his indispensable proficiency in the Russian language and the mysteries of transliteration from Cyrillic to English. The late Dr Jan Glete also deserves mention for his great kindness in clarifying questions relating to Swedish construction philosophy in the lead up to the 1788 Russo-Swedish War, to Swedish warships involved in the 1807 Russo-Swedish War, and in providing extremely useful information on the economic and political relationships between Sweden, Turkey and France as they related to the financing of the Swedish navy before and during the 1788 Russo-Swedish War. His kind and willing assistance will be greatly missed. Dan O'Dowd was of the greatest assistance in providing perspective from the 'other side' of both the Russo-Swedish conflict and the Russo-Turkish conflict by his help in providing Swedish and German language translations for important studies by Günther Lanitzki, Arnold Munthe and the inestimable Jan Glete as well as a series of highly detailed Turkish battle maps. Bob Legge from Australia succeeded where all other potential avenues had failed in at long last granting the American half of this team access to R. C. Anderson's nearly unobtainable and indispensible 1910 *Naval Wars in the Baltic*, without which any pretence of complete coverage and objectivity would have been impossible. Katherine Hill Reischl, PhD candidate, Slavic Languages and Literatures, University of Chicago, is owed a special debt for her kindness and patience in helping bring over 1,600 Russian ship names into reasonable compliance with the Library of Congress system of transliteration. Thanks also to Ron van Maanen, Dutch archivist and scholar, who brought to our attention a series of fascinating written interchanges between the Dutch ambassador to Constantinople and his superiors in the Netherlands relating to the Turkish side of the Russo-Turkish War or 1788 and to Ottoman attempts to obtain warships from Dutch shipbuilders and the Dutch navy. Special thanks to Teemu Koivumaki of Finland, who operates the most ambitious and comprehensive web site on the subject of sailing warships, for helping clarify an endless number of issues relating to Russian warships and for putting this author in contact with Dr Glete many years ago.

John Houghton of Melbourne, Australia, himself the author of a most excellent work on mid-nineteenth-century steam and sail warships, was indispensable in providing information on the transition of the Russian fleets to steam power in the period between the accession of Nicholas I to the final defeat of the Russian sailing navies of the Baltic and the Black Sea in the Crimean War. He also reviewed the early drafts of the sections on the last quarter century of the Russian sailing navy, uncovering factual errors and helping to fill in a number of gaps in the basic data.

Apologies in advance to any of the many people who have extended themselves towards the completion of this project and who have been inadvertently omitted here. For errors in fact or interpretation, responsibility rests entirely with the American half of this collaboration.

Very special thanks must go to our long-suffering and unsung, but greatly appreciated, editor Paula Turner of Palindrome who, when faced with the enormous challenge of adopting Cyrillic spellings and all the related aspects of this unusual endeavour, rose heroically to the challenge with a positive and cheerful attitude. This book could never have been completed in its present form without her assistance.

Finally, thanks go to my wife Audrey for her patience and understanding and for her frequent assistance in untangling the mysteries of computer technology for her technologically challenged husband.

The Russian Sailing Navy Overview

Introduction

The growth and expansion of Russian naval power between the accession of Peter I ('the Great') in 1696 and effective end of sailing navies in 1860 is a subject that has been poorly understood and little documented by Western naval historians and, most particularly, by scholars interested in the details of naval design and construction. The root causes for this lack of knowledge have been the geographical and linguistic separation of Russian naval discourse from British and Western scholars interested in similar matters, both as a result of the closing off of normal lines of communication with the West during the Communist era from 1917 through 1989, and of the lack of availability of Russian literature on the subject both before and after this period due to language and marketability problems. This separation has been largely one-sided, with Russian scholars being aware of and having a degree of interest in and access to Western thinking that has not been properly reciprocated by the West. There is and has been a treasure trove of Russian interest in and writing about naval developments during the age of sail, much of it finding its ways into articles in periodicals that have been limited in circulation to naval professionals and historians. In contrast, works of substance on naval matters published in the West have generally found their way into Russian libraries and universities, while the unplumbed wealth of similar material published in Russia can only be accessed in the most prestigious Western libraries and then only by those determined few blessed with the patience and capacity to comprehend the very different and difficult Russian language.

The central thesis of this work is the authors' belief that the developmental history of the Russian sailing navy has never been properly understood or appreciated by historians in Western Europe who have dwelt overly much upon the undeniably poor quality of the materiel and workmanship of those Russian warships that came into contact with Western, particularly British, navies in the Mediterranean and the North Sea during the second half of the eighteenth century and the early years of the nineteenth; and who have failed to give due credit to the forward-looking and progressive quality of Russian naval designers and high-ranking naval officers as well as to the systematic and thoughtful manner in which limited Russian fiscal and physical resources were applied to tactical and strategic naval needs in two very different fields of naval conflict, the Baltic and the Black Sea.

Russian warships may have deteriorated rapidly in service according to Western standards, but they also sufficed to defeat their opponents, primarily Swedish and Turkish, in some of the most violent and hard-fought campaigns during the age of sail. Insufficient attention has also been given to the possibility that warships capable of being built and deployed quickly in times of national emergency may well have been a more cost-effective solution for the Russians than investment in the ruggedly constructed, long-lasting and durable – but expensive and maintenance-heavy – ships adopted by the British and other European states, when consideration is given to their very different resource-bases and geographical limitations. The Russian battle fleet accomplished the goals set before it and it did so consistently until overwhelmed by direct confrontation with the world's two largest naval powers during the Crimean War at the very end of the age of sail – and then under highly disadvantageous circumstances resulting from the slight but decisive lead that France and Great Britain had gained in the opening stages of the transition from sail to steam.

Finally, it is our contention that the level of leadership and aggressiveness displayed by Russian admirals of the calibre of Ushakov and Seniavin has never been given due credit in the West. One can only wonder what the result might have been had one of these very aggressive and capable gentlemen faced Horatio Nelson on equal material terms in the Mediterranean, the North Sea, or the Baltic. Whatever the outcome, the confrontation would have been interesting, revealing, and violent.

The most authoritative works on the early history of the Russian navy accessible in the English-speaking world have been R. C. Anderson's highly regarded *Naval Wars in the Baltic* and its companion volume published rather remarkably forty-two years later, *Naval Wars in the Levant*. Obtaining copies of either of these works has been, and remains, a challenge for anyone interested in the subject and not having the great good fortune of being close to a major library fortunate enough to stock one or both copies. This most excellent study of the Russian naval struggles with Turkey and Sweden in the eighteenth century is generally regarded as holy writ among knowledgeable Western scholars and with good cause. It should, of course, also be mentioned that Anderson covers a much wider area than the narrow focus of Russian naval development in the eighteenth and nineteenth centuries, involving himself with navies and conflicts unrelated to our immediate concerns. In spite of the fact that Anderson covered his subject in great detail and in a thoroughly well-researched manner, he has been looked upon by Russian scholars with a degree of muted scepticism. This is not a reflection of any fundamental inaccuracy on his part; but rather a reaction in Russia to what is *felt* to have been his over-reliance upon Western, largely Swedish, sources and his alleged lack of awareness of much of the historical material and differing perspectives available on the Russian side. The Russian perception of Anderson's work is not entirely valid. Anderson did indeed have command of the basic Russian sources available and had even managed to obtain and utilize his very own copy of the encyclopaedic *Materialy dlya istorii Russkogo flota*. Where the truth lies with respect to the even-handedness of his scholarship remains very much open to debate. What is not open to debate, of course, is the great distance between Russian and western perceptions and interpretations of the same historical materials and events.

To those in the West who, like the authors of this work, are primarily interested in the technical details of Russian sailing warships, in construction programmes, classes, ship histories and the like, the well has been dry indeed. While there is and has been a wealth of published material on various specific areas of the subject in both Russian books and periodicals since the end of the sailing ship era in 1860, there have been only three comprehensive surveys of the full range of Russian naval construction along anything approaching the depth of David Lyon and Rif Winfield in Britain, Alain Demerliac in France, and Paul H. Silverstone and Donald L. Canney in the United States. These are Fyodor F. Veselago who published *Spisok Russkich Voennych Sudov, 1668–1860* (St Petersburg, 1872), A. A. Chernyshev who much more recently published *Rossiiskii Parusnyi Flot: Spravochnik*, vols I and II (1997–2002), and A. M. Danilov who published *Lineinye Korabli I Fregaty Russokogo Parusnogo* in 1996.

Veselago's *Spisok* is a chronological listing of Russian naval ships of all types divided first along geographical lines and second into particular classes of ships. His original research grew in large part from his work in compiling much of the material for the above mentioned *Materialy dlya istorii Russkogo flota* (hereafter referred to as the *Materialy* for convenience) and has furnished the basis for all subsequent research on the subject by Russian scholars.

Chernyshev, writing over a century later, does not separate Russian warships geographically into regional fleets, but divides ships solely by type and by the number of guns carried. Although he has derived much of his basic data on the major categories of warships from the earlier scholar, he also avails himself of a century of research by later scholars focusing in greater depth on particular ships, classes and periods in books and periodicals and also covers lesser warship categories in considerably more depth than Veselago. Along with the presentation of basic data, Chernyshev's two books also provide brief operational summaries of individual warships and supplementary attachments including lists of naval wars, information about sails and rigging, glossary material, geographical place names, geographical expeditions and building sites. A minor and unfortunate irritation for those fortunate English and American readers able to obtain copies of volume I or II and to work their way through the mysteries of the Russian language and the Cyrillic alphabet has been Chernyshev's unfortunate, but understandable, conversion of all dimensional data from the feet and inches it was originally recorded in by the Russian naval constructors during the age of sail into the metric system now in use in Russia and elsewhere.

Danilov's work is less highly regarded in Russian naval circles than the other two and, in our opinion, offers no real substitute for Chernyshev's books for those readers having access to both authors. He contents himself with reproducing Veselago's research on capital ships and frigates as originally presented in the *Spisok* in 1872 and excludes consideration of the other lesser ship types that are covered in limited detail by Veselago and in greater detail by Chernyshev in volume II of his work. Danilov redeems himself to some degree by also appending lists of Russian fleets and flotillas, shipbuilding centres, naval ranks, Russian wars, major battles, geographical listings, glossary, and metric conversion tables – subjects also dealt with by Chernyshev.

All three of these works have disadvantages as sources for interested Western readers. The first and most serious, of course, is that they are in Cyrillic script and in the Russian language. The second is that they are difficult to access in all but a handful of Western libraries, and completely out of reach for students and scholars interested in purchasing copies of their own. This problem has been remedied to some degree in recent years by the appearance of various photocopied or digitized versions of both Chernyshev and Veselago (and probably also Danilov) on the internet, but this solution has limited attraction for readers raised in a simpler age and still keen on real books with covers, pages, and illustrations to pore over. The third disadvantage, even for those readers able to overcome the first two, is their *relative* lack of depth as compared to the much greater abundance of detail available in the similar works of British, French, and American authors mentioned above. This is not intended to fault the work of these scholars, most particularly A. A. Chernyshev whom we would very much like to see published in English. It is, rather, a straightforward commentary on the need for further work on the subject, and most particularly on the need for making knowledge of the history and accomplishments of the Russian sailing navies more accessible for English speaking readers with interest in navies and sailing ships.

In very reluctant fairness, mention must also be made of a recently published book in Russian by a Russian popularizer with a history of writing on an extraordinarily wide range of military and non-military subjects and of, shall we say, taking liberties with source accreditation. The book, *200 let parusnogo flota rossii (200 Years of the Russian Sailing Navy)* by A. B. Shirokorad was published in 2007 and is very largely an unaccredited reshuffling of the data presented by A. A. Chernyshev. This would, in itself, discredit it in the eyes of serious students, but Shirokorad has not only lifted his data directly from Chernyshev, he has done so with demonstrable lack of regard for accuracy. As a serious or even as a reliable summary of the subject, Shirokorad's work is not deserving of attention in our opinion, even by those able to read the Russian text. We mention it here to discourage Western readers attracted by its availability (in Russian) on the American market and at a moderate price.

The present work owes an enormous debt to both Veselago and Chernyshev and has the advantages of having been written and transcribed into English (or at least American!) by an avid student of sailing warships living in Chicago, and at the same time of representing a lifetime of research by a Russian scholar and naval enthusiast living in Moscow. It is the product of a collaboration that began via email five years ago and that has expanded gradually and almost inadvertently into the present work. Much of the basic material to be found in the Russian sources cited above has been transcribed directly herein, but with the addition of additional and occasionally contradictory information gleaned from a number of other historical sources along with the inclusion of basic operational information gleaned from the aforementioned *Materialy dlya istorii Russkogo flota*, a 12,000-page collection of Russian eighteenth and early nineteenth century naval documents compiled and published by Captain S. A. Elagin, General F. F. Veselago and S. Ogorodnikov between 1865 and 1904. An attempt has been made to provide the information in a format that will enable English speaking readers to acquire a basic understanding of the organization, history and problems facing the Russian sailing navy as well as the influence of Western naval developments in warship design and technology on the growth and expansion of the Baltic and Black Sea fleets. The authors cheerfully anticipate that their work will be justly criticized for errors and omissions – in spite of their most earnest attempts to avoid them in the process of bridging the linguistic gulf between the English speaking world and the Russian. It is our most sincere hope that this tome will represent the beginning of more extensive research into the subject by Western scholars and enthusiasts.

Historical background

The history of the Russian Navy is most profitably looked upon as the history of two distinctive regional navies, each with its own priorities, problems, and traditions, the Baltic fleet and the Black Sea/Sea of Azov fleets, as well as of the shorter and simpler histories of lesser independent squadrons and flotillas assigned to the Caspian Sea, the White Sea and the Sea of Okhotsk regions. For the Baltic fleet, it is a story of slow but continuous growth and development under Emperors and Empresses both friendly and hostile to naval matters, with the primary focus being on obtaining and maintaining dominance in the closed off world of the Baltic, and with secondary, but significant, attention being given to developing a strategic capability for gradually extending Russian naval capabilities into the larger environments of the Atlantic and the Mediterranean when required by circumstances. For the Black Sea fleet, on the other hand, it has been the story of a false beginning in the form of the aborted Sea of Azov fleet and of a 'poor cousin' of a navy that grew and contracted in response to the problems of controlling a body of water even more effectively cut off from the outside world than the Baltic, and against the challenges presented, not only by the formidable if generally erratic Turkish and Egyptian naval forces of the period, but also against the necessity for developing and expanding Russian amphibious capabilities in the face of the hostility of the various ethnic groups in the areas coming under Russian rule in the Caucasus as a result of the decline of Turkish power.

Western students, nurtured on Mahan and Nelson, will need to adjust their thinking when approaching Russian developments and motivations. Russian naval developments were always conditioned by the desire for securing internal lines of communication within confined coastal waters and upon amphibious preoccupations largely absent in the Western navies. Russian concern with the fleets of France and England during the period of this book was largely passive in nature, and their occasional forays into Atlantic and Mediterranean waters were always related to protecting the flanks of their expanding empire against Western expansionism and never concerned with the kind of sea control, power projection, and colonial expansion concerns that drove the navies of the West.

No discussion of Russian naval growth during this period is possible unless due attention is given to the fact that the Russians were attempting to develop a competitive navy at the same time as the Russian nation state was attempting to close the technological and economic gulf between the largely feudal society that Peter I inherited and the more advanced Western nations. The growth of the Russian navy and the expansion of shipbuilding and maintenance facilities foreshadowed the strikingly similar expansion of Japanese naval power around the turn of the twentieth century. The irony is that naval historians in the West look at the Japanese accomplishment with the greatest respect, while the equally impressive Russian accomplishment during the eighteenth century attracts only condescension when it is noticed at all. The Russian sailing warships that helped maintain British presence in the North Sea during the Great Mutinies of 1797 and that helped to secure British naval dominance in the central and Eastern Mediterranean after the battle of the Nile were as remarkable in their own way as symbols of a nation transitioning to modernity as were Admiral Tojo's warships a century later in the Straits of Tsushima.

Sources

Sources for this study fall into two categories: works in Russian dealing with basic data about Russian naval history and more specifically about the ships of the Russian sailing navy, and works in English dealing with Russian naval and diplomatic history from a Western perspective. Of these, of course, the Russian sources are much the more important, given the nature of the book. Much of the information traditionally available to English historians has come from the accounts of British naval officers and civilians with technical expertise attracted to eighteenth-century Russia by opportunities for advancement and employment not as readily available in their native country and of observations of Russian naval activities made by government officials and naval officers in British service. These reports and accounts, while valuable, reflect the perspectives and prejudices of outside observers often lacking full knowledge of the events and the culture that they are describing.

Russian Source Material

The starting point for any serious study of Russian naval matters between 1700 and 1804 is the oft-cited *Materialy dlya istorii Russkogo flota* (*Materials for the History of Russian Navy*). This remarkable eighteen-volume, 12,000-page document was begun in 1850 at the behest of Grand Duke Konstantin, the younger son of Nicholas I, and published in sections from 1865 to its completion in 1904. Captain S. A. Elagin edited the first four volumes on the Baltic navy under Peter I from 1702 to his death in 1724 and a history of the short-lived Sea of Azov fleet which is found as the final eighteenth volume in the collection. On his death in 1868, General Veselago completed volumes five to fourteen until his death, at which time he was succeeded by S. Ogorodnikov who finished the final four, including volumes seven and fifteen to seventeen. The *Materialy* were drawn entirely from official records and include every conceivable aspect of Russian naval history: official laws, naval regulations, Admiralty orders, ships' journals, minutes on the navigation and movements of warships, Admiralty board meetings, ports, installations, court martials, fiscal matters, as well as commentary by Veselago on the inner workings and social life of the navy. This is the single most indispensable work on Russian naval matters and it is no exaggeration to say that there would be only the scantiest information available on the subject without its having been compiled – at least from the Russian perspective.

Polnoe Sobranie Zakonov Rossiyskoy Imperii (Complete Collection of Laws and Regulations of the Russian Empire) is the source document for information on gun and ship establishments and changes therein. The first series covering the period from 1649 to 1825 consists of 45 volumes edited by M. M. Speranskiy and published in 1830. The second series covering the period from 1830 to 1881 consisting of 55 volumes was published annually. (A third series covering the period from 1881 to 1916 consisting of 33 volumes falls outside of the scope of this work.)

Spisok Russkich Voennych Sudov, 1668–1860 (1872) by General F. F Veselago was the first systematic compilation of data on all of the major sailing warships belonging to the Russian navy. Although it limits itself to a chronological listing of Russian naval ships divided into geographical fleets and classes, with an introductory section dealing with gun armament, it has the virtue of providing a comprehensive and authoritative framework for further study. There are some problems, however, with respect to the dimensions presented in *Spisok*. Veselago makes no attempt to clarify the protocols used to obtain basic dimensions and does not distinguish between the use of English feet and Dutch feet for the ships of Peter I's period.

Rossiiskii Parusnyi Flot: Spravochnik (The Russian Sailing Fleet: An Inquiry) (1997–2002) by A. A. Chernyshev uses the Spisok as its starting point, but involves additional archive work and fleshes out Veselago's work with extensive information on aspects of the subject not covered, including sails and rigging, lists of wars, naval vocabulary, geographical names, voyages of discovery and navigation, and building sites. One problem with the book, if it may be called a problem, is the use of metric measurements in place of the more conventional and familiar feet and inches.

~

Information provided by the *Materialy* is supplemented by a number of other sources dealing with the eighteenth century:

Russkiy Flot pri Konchine Petra Velikogo (The Russian Fleet at the Death of Peter the Great) (Zapiski Gidrograficheskogo Departamenta, vol. VI) by Admiral Sokolov includes the papers of General-Admiral Apraksin (1721), which provide contemporary data on ship dimensions that differ from data recorded by Veselago and also gives detailed data on the Russian navy in 1725 with lists of ships completed and building and listings of commissioned sea-officers.

Russkiy Flot v Tsarstvovanie Imperatritsy Ekateriny II, 1772–1783 (The Russian Navy in the Reign of Empress Catherine II) by A. Krotkov provides data on the armament of Spiridov's ships in 1769.

Nauka Morskoy Artillerii (Science of Naval Ordnance) (1846) by A. A. Ilyin provides coverage for the armament of Baltic fleet ships for the 1780s and 1790s as well as for the period from 1830 to 1846.

Deystviya Russkogo Flota v Voyne so Shvedami 1788–1790 (Operations of the Russian Fleet in the War with Sweden, 1788–1790) (St Petersburg, 1871) by Captain V. F. Golovachev contains historical material on the Russo-Swedish War as well as data on the armament of Russian Baltic warships.

Russkie Flotovodtsy Admiral Ushakov vols 1–3 is one of the primary sources for historical coverage of the Black Sea fleet in its early years and provides documentation of the armaments of ships of the line and frigates earmarked for the expedition to the Mediterranean in April 1798.

The Papers of Admiral Mordvinov provide important historical background material of the early years of the Black Sea fleet.

Istoriya Sevastopolya kak Russkogo Porta (History of Sebastopol as Russian Port) by V. F. Golovachev contains detailed information on the armament and dimensions of Russian warships at the beginning of 1790.

100 Gunned Ships of the 'Victory' Class by G. A. Grebenshchikova is an exhaustive study of the *Ches'ma* class recently published and containing detailed research from archival material at the Main Russian Naval Archives in St Petersburg.

~

Information for the period from 1800 to 1860 is available from a number of sources:

Dokumenty by Lazarev not only contains important letters and papers, but has contemporary dimension data on Black Sea warships that differs from that found in Chernyshev.

Zapiski Uchenogo Komiteta Glavnogo Morskogo Shtaba (1827–45) (Proceedings of the Scientific Committee of the Supreme Naval HQs) contains material on ships put in commission from 1826 to 1844 with voluminous data on the annual composition of the Baltic squadrons, movements of ships, commanders, and the arrival of newly built ships from Arkhangel'sk.

Uchenie Deystviyu Orudiyami (Exercises for Handling Guns) (1837) provides information on the complements of ships, the number of men necessary for guns of different calibres and standard armament establishments for warships.

O Sudakh, Postroennykh so Vremeni Vstupleniya na Prestol Gosudarya Imperatora Nikolaya Pavlovicha (About the Ships

Built Since the Time of Accession to the Throne of His Imperial Majesty Nikolay Pavlovich*) is a compilation of basic data on Russian warships published in 1844 in two volumes, one for the Baltic fleet and one for the Black Sea fleet. A particularly useful source for dimensions with detailed data on LGD, LK, BR, depth, draught with full cargo (by bow and by stern) as determined at the time of launch. For the sake of simplicity, this work will be referred to throughout the text and data presentation simply as O Sudakh.

Pamyatnaya Knizhka Morskogo Vedomstva (Memory book [aide-de-memoire] of the Navy Office) for the years 1853 to 1857 provides data about the armament of Russian warships during the Crimean War period on a year-by-year basis. The 1861 edition is also the source for the list of the fleet as at mid-1861 in the postscript.

English Language and European Source Material
While information on warships, their operational histories and their weapons relied almost entirely on Russian sources and the research of Eduard Sozaev, the historical summary relied heavily on the limited English language studies available on the subject.

R. C. Anderson's studies of naval wars in the Baltic and the Levant remain the essential starting points for any in-depth appreciation of the subject. Although Russian sources differ from Anderson in some of the details of the various naval campaigns described, the essential accuracy of his work has not been challenged, most particularly by Western historians. Readers should be aware in advance that Anderson's approach is entirely descriptive and lacking in any attempt to appreciate or interpret the larger historical context of the naval events that he describes in such great detail.

F. T. Jane, the originator of the iconic *Jane's Fighting Ships*, covers the historical development of the Russian sailing navy in some detail in the opening chapters of *The Imperial Russian Navy*, a work that largely focused on the period leading up to the Russo-Japanese War of 1904. Jane's account makes for fascinating reading and does succeed in providing a useful overview of the subject, so long as the reader keeps in mind the narrow perspectives of Victorian and Edwardian England, with all of their assumptions and smugness.

A more balanced account of Russian naval history by a contemporary historian may be found in David Woodward's *The Russians at Sea: The History of the Russian Navy*. Woodward avoids some of the chauvinistic excesses of F. T. Jane, whom he relies upon heavily by his own statements, along with the more balanced research of R. C. Anderson, and does an excellent job of placing the narrow focus of naval history in the larger context of European historical developments. His characterization of Paul I, however, is overly simplistic and misguided in our opinion and detracts from the otherwise high-quality of his research and writing.

The most learned and insightful modern historian dealing with the subject, in our opinion at least, is Norman Saul, author of a number of works dealing primarily with Russian diplomatic history, but demonstrating a high degree of knowledge of all aspects of Russian naval developments. *Russia and the Mediterranean, 1797–1807* is an excellent study of Russia's attempts to expand into the Mediterranean during the Napoleonic War period and of the personalities of two of Russia's greatest admirals, Fyodor Ushakov and Dmitriy Seniavin. Of even more value to students of the Russian navy, in our opinion, is a paper published by Norman Saul by the United States Naval Institute Press in 1981, *The Russian Navy, 1682–1854: Some Suggestions for Further Study, New Aspects of Naval History*, in which he summarizes the entire subject of Russian naval developments during the age of sail in the most insightful manner that we have come across. He is particularly valuable with respect to the allegedly substandard materials used in the construction of Russian warships and the reasons underlying the Russian rationale for building 'throw-away' warships. His suggestion that Russian combat tactics may have been more aggressive than those of her enemies and her potential rivals in Western Europe precisely because they were so much cheaper to build and operate is particularly telling. The one point at which we would place any distance with Saul is his, to us inexplicable, disregard for Peter I's role in the founding of the Russian navy and his evident feeling that all of his extensive work in both the Baltic and the Sea of Azov was ad hoc and impermanent and related only tangentially to his more serious military and political aims. Characterizing Peter I's Baltic and Azov fleets as 'a motley, makeshift armada that resembled more the Barbary corsairs than a national navy' may be a wonderfully effective rhetorical flourish, but it is so completely divorced from the realities of the mobilization of Russian resources by Peter I and so far removed from his depth of understanding of the later sailing navy that one is left questioning whether there are *two* Norman Sauls at work here.

Mention must be made of an excellent study of the entire course of Russian naval development published in 1974, *A History of Russian and Soviet Sea Power*, by Donald W. Mitchell. Despite the fact that the coverage of the Russian sailing navy makes up only the first 155 pages out of a 555-page history, and some gentle criticism from the above-mentioned Norman Saul for its alleged shortcomings, Mitchell's book provides clarity and depth on the subject, not only of the battles, ships and personnel, but also of the economic and political context in which they operated. In many respects, he is more severely critical of elements relating to incompetence, corruption, and negligence in the command structure of the navy, and of the lack of adequate training of officers and the poor treatment of Russian seamen, as well as of the allegedly poor quality, not only of Russian *materiel*, but of ship design itself, than we feel is fully justified. On the other hand, he balances this severity with an equally generous regard for the difficulties experienced by Peter and his successors and the genuine accomplishments of an organization faced with enormous challenges relating to geographical, economic, and political considerations of a sort not facing the more advanced navies of Western Europe. He is also almost alone among the sources that we have consulted in showing an awareness of and making a sincere effort to present the viewpoints of Russian scholars in instances where they are at variance with those accepted in the West. We recommend this book highly.

A recent study, *The Revolution of Peter the Great* by James Cracraft, has an excellent and compact chapter on Peter I's role in the development of Russian naval power on both administrative and logistical levels.

Of equal value in understanding the formative years under Peter is *Russia in the Age of Peter the Great* by Lindsey Hughes, which provides a fascinating section on the early development of the Russian navy, with particular attention being paid to Peter's importation of foreign talent, the resistance of Russian aristocrats to Peter's reforms and the early development of both the Baltic and Azov fleets.

For those particularly interested in the birth, growth and decline of the Sea of Azov fleet, *The Founding of Russia's Navy: Peter the Great and the Azov Fleet* by Edward J. Phillips is essential, if rather expensive, reading. Phillips not only covers the early career of Peter I up to 1714, but he provides a fully detailed summary of the information available in both Russian and English language sources on this short-lived and poorly understood naval experiment – information not available in the West in any of the published sources we have come across. The title of the work is possibly overly restrictive. The first section deals with Russian maritime development in the millennium before Peter I and the closing section deals in considerable detail with the interplay between the creation of the Sea of Azov fleet and the growth and development of the more successful Baltic fleet. The book is particularly useful in providing background on the enormous logistical, organizational, economic, and human costs involved in lifting Russia from a land-locked semi-feudal state into the semblance of a modern eighteenth-century state.

Readers particularly interested in the subject of British involvement in Russian naval and technological development are referred to *By the Banks of the Neva: Chapters from the Lives and Careers of the British in Eighteenth-century Russia* by Anthony Glenn Cross. The book deals with the entire range of Anglo-Russian cultural and scientific interaction, but the chapter on the importation of British-born shipbuilders and officers into the Russian naval establishment is worth the cost of the book by and of itself.

An insightful look at Russian naval developments of a later period is *Russian Seapower and 'The Eastern Question' 1827–41* by John C. K. Daly. This period deserves more coverage than it has received, but Daly provides a worthy first step in the process.

For readers interested in learning more about the navies and the motivations of Russia's two great opponents, Sweden and Turkey, two important but very different sources should be mentioned. For background on Swedish naval developments, we recommend a paper presented in *Forum Navale* in 1990, by the late Jan Glete, 'Den svenska linjeflottan 1721–1860: En översikt av dess struktur och storlek samt några synpunkter på behovet av ytterligare forskning' ('The Swedish battle fleet, 1721–1860: An overview of its structure and size with some consideration of the need for further research'). Very unfortunately, there has not been an English language translation of this essay, which deals in detail with the theoretical underpinnings of the Swedish naval construction programmes and of Swedish tactical thought in the eighteenth and early nineteenth centuries, with useful sideglances towards Russian naval development. For background on Turkish naval developments, a useful, but sometimes limited, study of the Turkish navy may be found in a recently published book by a Turkish historian, Tuncay Zorlu, *Innovation and Empire in Turkey: Sultam Selim III and the Modernization of the Ottoman Navy*. This book offers little new specific information on Turkish warships built during and before the reign of Sultam Selim III, but it does provide an excellent overview of determined Turkish attempts to modernize their shipbuilding, ordnance, and personnel programmes as a result of their defeat in the 1787–91 war.

Transliteration protocols

Russian names used in this volume, whether personal, geographic or related to particular ships, are English renderings of the Cyrillic alphabet. Students familiar with Russian history may notice departures from the spellings that they are familiar with, but this has unfortunately been unavoidable. Variations in the transliteration of Cyrillic spellings into the Latin (English) alphabet are the result of the difficulties translators have traditionally experienced in rendering Russian phonetic complexities into the straitjacket of the Latin alphabet. The Cyrillic alphabet not only has more characters than the Latin, but there is not always, or even generally, a one-to-one correlation between the pronunciation of Cyrillic characters and Latin characters. As a result, there may be several different 'correct' spellings for a particular Russian word and all are equally 'correct' – and equally 'incorrect', for that matter. Several different international protocols have been developed to deal with the problem – and they are not entirely in agreement.

The system adopted in this work has been that established by the Library of Congress (LoC). Transliterations of ship names have been rendered to the largest degree practicable in compliance with the LoC system and we apologize for any unintentional variations on our part. Having said this, we must immediately qualify ourselves by confessing to four variations we have made from the LoC protocols: Fyodor, Pyotr, Oryol and Tvyordyi. These four words, translating into English respectively as 'Theodore', 'Peter', 'Eagle' and 'Unyielding', are being presented in the text in lieu of the 'proper' LoC transliterations of Fedor, Petr, *orel* and *tverdyi* because the use of the Latin 'e' does not properly reflect the phonetic pronunciation indicated by the Cyrillic 'ё' as well as 'yo' does and because, frankly, the 'yo' transliteration is preferred by the American half of the team on purely aesthetic terms. Other instances of the occurrence of 'ё' in the ship-name list where we have *not* departed from LoC protocols with are: Iozh/Yozh, Otvorennye/Otvoryonnye, Trekh/Tryokh, Legkii/Lyogkii, Razzhennoe/Razzhyonoe and Shchglenok/Shcheglyonok. Of these, only Legkii and Trekh are frequently found, and in both of these the LoC spelling is that most commonly found in most modern texts. We have also made the decision to render the names of well-known historical personages by their normal English renderings in the text while retaining the transliterated version when referencing ships carrying the same name. Accordingly, Catherine II 'the Great') is referred to as Catherine II in the text but as *Ekaterina II* when referring to ships named after her and Alexander I becomes *Aleksandr I*. A further proviso relates to the – to English speaking ears – unusual insertion of an apostrophe in transliterated words. This usage relates to a 'soft sign' that is lost on English readers but of great significance to Russians. The most common example of this in the text is 'Arkhangel'sk' in place of the common English spelling 'Arkhangelsk', but the reader will find numerous instances scattered throughout the text. The reader's patience is requested if our particular rendering of any particular ship name differs from a preferred version. For readers finding themselves hopelessly at sea with all this – as the English-speaking half of this joint effort frequently does – an alphabetically arranged summary of transliterated Russian ship names with English renderings and/or translations in parentheses and Cyrillic originals appended will be found after the appendices.

Organization and layout

Organizing a body of data of the size and complexity of that pertaining to a navy the size of the Russian sailing navy extending over the span of 160 years and four, possibly five, relatively distinct bodies of water has posed a number of problems. The approach adopted here has been to divide the coverage into four general categories and then to treat each of the categories separately according to their own internal logic. The four major subdivisions are: the Seagoing Sailing Navy, the Inshore Navy, Russian Naval Auxiliaries, and the Steam and Sail Navy.

The Russian Sailing Navy
The coverage provided for the seagoing sailing navy is the most extensive and requires the most explanation.
The methodology chosen for section I has been one of adopting geography as the first organizing principle, followed by major time periods as the second, by ship classification as the third and finally by the characteristics and specific histories of the individual ship classes and the ships themselves as the fourth.

The geographical division has centred upon the various wholly and partially enclosed bodies of water that make up the maritime periphery of the Russian nation state. They are, in order of size: the Baltic, the Black Sea, the Sea of Azov, the Caspian and the Sea of Okhotsk. The White Sea flotilla might also be treated as a further separate subdivision, but it is felt that it is most logically included along with the Baltic fleet of which it was an administrative component. It may also, of course, be argued with some justification that the division between the short-lived naval forces of the Sea of Azov created by Peter I and those of the later and larger Black Sea fleet is an arbitrary one and that they should be combined into one. It is our judgement, however, that the extended time period intervening between the *de facto* elimination of the significant naval forces based on the Sea of Azov in 1711 and the later rebirth of a larger and more permanent naval establishment on the Black Sea in 1783 under Catherine II and Prince Potemkin mandates the separation into two fleets. Although Russia did maintain a presence of sorts in the Sea of Azov during the interim, and even constructed a large number of small inshore gunboats and galleys for the 1736–39 war with Turkey, there was nothing approaching a formal fleet or even a permanent flotilla organization until the successful resolution of the 1768–72 war. Finally, even though the smaller flotillas established on the Caspian Sea and in the Sea of Okhotsk were eclipsed by the larger fleets, they stood out clearly as distinct units and merit coverage as interesting examples of very small and self-contained local naval forces created for a narrow range of duties against limited or even non-existant local opposition.

The chronological subdivisions chosen under the various geographical headings have been subdivided into four sections based on a fortuitous and, from our perspective, self-evident convergence of political elements relating to the growth of the Russian state and evolutionary elements relating to the design and evolution of sailing warships. The four periods chosen are 1696–1761, 1762–1800, 1801–24, and 1825–60. Solely for the sake of discourse and convenience, these four eras have been labelled herein respectively as: the Navy of Peter and His Successors, the Navy of Catherine and Paul, the Navy of Alexander I and the Navy of Nicholas I and the Creation of the Steam Navy. It will be noted that the less spectacular accomplishments and policies of no fewer than six emperors and empresses separating the two 'Greats' by over forty years of eventful Russian history have been ignored and overlooked by this artificial division. In self-defence, we can only note that the choice of dates reflects the fact that the transition points selected have been defined not only by the extraordinary influence exercised over the growth of the Russian sailing navy by both Peter I and Catherine II, but also by major developments in the design of warships and in large-scale building programmes. The section on the navy of Catherine and Paul includes the brief reign of her son Paul, whose interest in continued naval growth and imperial expansion mirrored that of his more gifted mother in general tone if not in elegance of execution. There are serious misgivings on our part at the identification of period between 1801 and 1824 with the hostile anti-naval attitudes of Paul's dreamy and ineffectual son Alexander I. Had his career as naval minister begun earlier than 1811 and had he not been a French émigré, this period might have been more appropriately or facetiously deemed the Navy of the Marquis de Traversay in unflattering tribute to his highly destructive role in running the Russian naval forces into the ground by neglect, incompetence and corruption and in undoing much of the good work of the previous century. Nevertheless, Alexander *was* Emperor during this period and it was *his* navy, not Traversay's, even though it was very much a navy in eclipse and decay. The final section on the Navy of Nicholas I and the Creation of the Steam Navy, in contrast, is quite aptly titled because it coincides almost perfectly with his long reign which – only ended in 1855 at the beginning of the Crimean War – and also because his energetic personal involvement in the renaissance in Russian naval affairs and the elevation of the Russian Navy to first-rank status,

The tertiary subdivision into types and classes speaks for itself, but two points of clarification are necessary.

In the infrequent instances in which the construction of specific warship classes spanned two of the major chronological divisions, the practice here has generally been to include the listing and coverage of *all* individual class members within the earlier section, irrespective of their proper temporal placement in both. This has been done with the feeling that all ships belonging to particular classes belong together in this type of work and that the splitting up of what should be a homogeneous group of ships into two different arbitrarily established time periods makes little sense. The most egregious example of a given class overlapping the boundary between two chronological subsections is that of the fifty-nine ship *Slava Rossii* class which was in production from 1733 to 1779, with 28 ships completed under Catherine II. This continued construction of an obsolescent design was both a reflection of the inertia inherent in long-established naval building programmes in Russia as elsewhere and as well as of the essentially artificial nature of all rigid classification systems.

The second point requiring clarification has to do with the treatment of those individual one-off ships belonging to no larger classes. The arrangement of ships is intended to be in order of the dates of their having been authorized, designed and launched. The arbitrary decision has been made to place one-off ships either before or after much larger blocks of ships comprising single classes, depending upon whether their date of launch precedes or follows the laying down date of the *lead ship* of the larger class. In many cases, this has resulted in considerable chronological disruption when large and long-running classes of ships effectively push individual ships and smaller classes of ships out of their properly allotted place based on their date of launching. A case in point is that of the twenty-three-ship *Selafail* class, with its production run from 1802 to 1825, ruthlessly pushing the two-ship *Evstafii* class completed in 1810–11 to the end of the line and depositing them unceremoniously behind members of the larger class whose construction actually began some fourteen years later in 1824. This is unfortunate where it has occurred, but it appears to make more sense to us to group all members of a class together in this manner than to interrupt the continuity of the class with members of other classes. Sometimes there are no simple and tidy solutions.

Two further groups of ships have been included within each of the four major sections and they are treated slightly differently from each other – those of purchased ships and of prize ships. Purchased ships are discussed *within* the type categories to which they logically belong (e.g. frigates or brigs), but they are clearly identified as purchased rather than designed vessels and segregated at the end of each type grouping. Prize ships, on the other hand, are listed *en masse* at the end of each of the four larger chronological sections as aggregate groups containing all captured foreign warships under a single heading. Consideration was given to instead adopting the approach used by David Lyon in *The Sailing Ship List* of having a two-fold division between purpose-built ships built for the Royal Navy followed by a separate and equally large listing of captured ships.

This approach was rejected here for the simple reason that, unlike the case within the British Navy, the size of the Russian prize navy cannot even begin to compare to the size of the Russian purpose-built navy.

The Inshore and Amphibious Navy

Russian naval forces intended for inshore operations in the support of military land operations involved oared warships designed for shallow-water operations and various categories of artillery support vessels. These forces were administratively independent of the seagoing naval forces and comprised very different types of warships intended for very different purposes. Coverage of these vessels has been less comprehensive than that given to the seagoing forces because the amount of material available on them is less extensive and also because inshore vessels were much smaller than seagoing types and, at the same time, were built in very much larger numbers. The division into four time periods given to the seagoing naval forces has been abandoned here in large part because the inshore forces had their greatest importance during the wars of expansion in the eighteenth century and faded in both numbers and significance after 1800, as Russia entered into a more defensive posture with respect to its Baltic and Black Sea holdings, and also because evolutionary design progressions within and between types were less evident. The organization of this section has been fairly straightforward, with the various varieties of highly manoeuvrable shallow-water warships being presented first, organized along geographical lines (Baltic, Black Sea, etc.) and then along chronological lines. Similar coverage has been given to artillery support vessels. Because the information on specifics such as dimensions and armament is very much more fragmentary than that available for seagoing vessels, we have chosen to present data in a more flexible format, with our primary guiding principle being clarity and simplicity.

Russian Naval Auxiliaries

As is the case with all naval organizations, the Russian combat units were supported by a large and diverse collection of auxiliaries involved in the logistical support of seagoing warships and armies. Given the geographically constricted areas of operation prevalent in most of the Russian naval activities, ships assigned to logistical support tended to be smaller and shorter-ranged than those found in the Atlantic navies, and, in many cases, of shallower draft and less dependent on sail power. The ship types developed in Russia were generally straightforward adaptations of European and, in some cases Turkish, types. They were usually given names that were straightforward Russian derivatives taken from a variety of Dutch, French, German, Swedish and Turkish ship classifications. In many respects, this section reads like a descriptive summary of the wide range of eighteenth-century European merchant sailing-ship types, both ship rigged and fore-and-aft rigged.

Organization of Russian auxiliaries has been based on ship type, fleet affiliation, and date of completion. The reader should not be surprised at the mention of various river flotillas, or at the greater prominence given operations in the Caspian, the Sea of

Okhotsk and the White Sea. On the other hand, the experienced reader will note the absence of larger sailing ships devoted to troop transport. For geographical reasons relating to distances travelled, wind and water conditions and water depths, particularly in the Baltic, large troop transports were of little value and the Caspian is the only area in which we find large numbers of sailing ships so employed. This situation explains the Russian use of over-age and temporarily disarmed ships of the line and frigates as ad hoc troop transports for their extended operations in the Mediterranean theatre and the ill-fated operation against the Netherlands at the end of the century. The deliberate purchase of construction of large troop transports was simply not a cost-effective approach.

Detailed data on many of the auxiliaries described here is as sketchy and incomplete as that of the preceding section and for the same reasons. Information on the operational use of many auxiliaries is, however, rather more complete, and a great deal of information on Russian expansion and exploration may be garnered from a study of individual ship's histories.

The Steam and Sail Navy

The development of the Russian steam and sail navy in both the Baltic and the Black Sea is treated separately in the final section of the book. Even though some of the steam powered ships covered were converted from sailing ships while building or after completion, it is felt that the subject requires separate treatment in order to give the process of transformation adequate coverage. Five ships, of necessity, appear in both sections of the book because they began life as sailing ships and only underwent conversion after completion, and in some cases, after extensive careers as pure sailing ships. The basic organizational scheme follows that of the first section with data and operational information being provided for all individual warships.

Chronology of Major Events in Russian Naval History 1696–1860

Gregorian dates are in parentheses

1696 *29 January (8 February)* Peter I becomes the sole ruler of Russia
Capture of Azov by Russia
4 November (14 November) The Russian Duma formally creates the Imperial Russian Navy

1700 *June* War with Sweden (The Great Northern War)
July Thirty-year peace treaty signed with Turkey

1703 *16 May (27 May)* Foundation of St Petersburg

1710 *November* War declared by Turkey

1711 *12 August (23 August)* Peace signed with Turkey (Treaty of Prut). Azov and Taganrog ceded to Turkey. Death of the Sea of Azov Navy.

1714 *27–29 July (7–9 August)* Battle of Gangut. Swedish fleet defeated.

1716 *5 August (16 August)* The Great Armament of 1716 at Copenhagen

1719 *24 May (4 June)* Battle of Osel

1720 *27 July (7 August)* Battle of Grengamn

1721 *30 August (10 September)* Peace with Sweden (Treaty of Nishtadt)

1722–3 Caspian Expedition

1725 *28 January (8 February)* Death of Peter I, accession of Catherine I

1727 *6 May (17 May)* Death of Catherine I, accession of Peter II

1730 *18 Jan. (29 Jan.)* Death of Peter II, accession of Anna Ivanovna

1733 War of the Polish Succession begins

1734 *May–June* Bombardment of Danzig

1735 *October* War of the Polish Succession ends (Treaty of Vienna, November 1738)

1736 War with Turkey. Reconquest of Azov

1739 *7 September (18 September)* Peace signed with Turkey (Treaty of Nissa). Azov retained. Black Sea warships forbidden to Russia.

1740 *17 October (28 October)* Death of Anna Ivanovna, accession of Ivan VI
War of the Austrian Succession begins

1741 *27 October (6 December)* Deposition of Ivan VI, accession of Elizabeth Petrovna
29 July (8 August) War with Sweden begins

1743 *20 May (31 May)* Galley battle of Korpo
4 June (15 June) Battle of Hangö udd
28 July (7 August) Peace with Sweden (Treaty of Turku). Russia obtains the galley port of Fridrikhsgamn

1748 *7 October (18 October)* War of the Austrian Succession ends (Treaty of Aix-la-Chapelle).

1757 *18 June (29 June)* Bombardment of Memel

1761 Bombardment of Kolberg
25 December (5 January) Death of Elizabeth Petrovna, accession of Peter III

1762 *7 July (18 July)* Deposition and assassination of Peter III, Accession of Catherine II

1768 *25 September* War with Turkey

1769 Count Orlov's squadron dispatched from the Baltic to the Mediterranean

1770 *24 June (5 July)* Battle of Chios Strait
26 June (7 July) Battle of Ches'ma. Turkish fleet defeated and burnt.

1772 *28 October (8 November)* Battle of Patras

1774 *21 July (1 August)* Peace with Turkey (Treaty of Kucuk Kaynarca)

1783 Russian annexation of the Crimea

1787 *16 August (27 August)* Turkish declaration of war

1788 *June* Swedish declaration of war
17–18 June (28–29 June) Battle of Ochakov
3 July (14 July) Battle of Fidonisi
6 July (17 July) Battle of Gogland

1789 *15 July (26 July)* Battle of Öland
13 August (24 August) First Battle of Svenskund (Rochensalm)

1790 *2 May (13 May)* Battle of Revel
23–24 May (3–4 June) Battle of Krasnaya Gorka (Styrsudden)
22 June (3 July) Battle of Vyborg Bay
28 June (9 July) Second Battle of Svenskund (Rochensalm). Major defeat for the Russian galley fleet
8 July (19 July) Battle of Kerch. Turkish fleet defeated
3 August (14 August) Peace with Sweden, Treaty of Varala
28–29 August (8–9 September) Battle of Tendra. Turkish fleet defeated

1791 *31 July (11 August)* Battle of Cape Kaliakra. Turkish fleet defeated
29 December (9 January 1792) Peace with Turkey signed (Treaty of Jassy)

1792 First Coalition against France

1793 Russia joins the First Coalition

1795 Squadron of twelve ships of the line sent to England to reinforce the British

1796 *6 November (17 November)* Death of Catherine II, accession of Paul I
British squadron recalled by Paul I

1798 *May* Three squadrons of 27 ships of the line under Admiral Makarov sent to England in sections to reinforce Admiral Duncan
Anglo-Russian blockade of the Dutch coast begun
Squadron under Admiral Ushakov and Seniavin sent to the Mediterranean to co-operate with Royal Navy units in the Levant.

1798 Treaty with Turkey allows for the opening of the Bosporus and reinforcement of Baltic warships by Black Sea units

1799 Second Coalition formed
Capture of Corfu and other Ionic islands by Admiral Ushakov

1801 *11 March (23 March)* Death by assassination of Paul I, accession of Alexander I
Anglo-Russian blockade of the Dutch coast ended
Opening of the Bosporus to Russian warships
1802 *13 March (25 March)* Peace of Amiens signed. Second Coalition ended
1805 *April* Third Coalition formed
1806 *18 December (30 December)* War with Turkey. Bosporus closed
1807 *9 May (21 May)* Battle of the Dardanelles
18 June (30 June) Battle of Mount Athos
26 June (7 July) Peace signed with France (Treaty of Tilsit)
Departure of Russian naval forces from the Mediterranean
1808 *February* War with Sweden. Anglo-Swedish fleet operations against Russia in the Baltic
1809 *September* Peace with Sweden
1812 *12 June (24 June)* Invasion of Russia by Napoleon. Patriotic War of 1812 begins. Russian naval units evacuated to Great Britain from Kronshtadt and Arkhangel'sk
11 June (23 June) Peace with Turkey (Treaty of Bucharest)
1812–14 Operations in North Sea co-operating with British naval units
1815 Defeat of Napoleon
1824 *7 November (19 November)* The Great Flood of 1824 at St Petersburg
1825 *20 November (1 December)* Death of Alexander I, accession of Nicholas I
1827 *8 October (20 October)* Battle of Navarino
1828 *14 April (26 April)* War with Turkey. Dardanelles and Bosporus closed to Russian warships
1829 *2 September (14 September)* Peace with Turkey (Treaty of Adrianople). Caucasus ceded to Russia
1830s and 1840s Amphibious operations against the Caucasus rebels
1833 *February* Turkey requests Russian aid against the Egyptian army that has entered Anatolia. First units of the Black Sea fleet arrive in the Bosporus to deter Egyptian advance on Constantinople.
27 June (8 July) Treaty of Unkiar Skelessi between Russia and Turkey. Russians given right of passage through the Bosporus and Dardanelles
1840 Nicholas cedes right of passage through the Bosporus by Russian naval units
1841 *1 July (13 July)* London Straits Convention formally closes the Bosporus to warships of all nations
1853 *4 October (16 October)* War with Turkey
18 November (30 November) Battle of Sinop
1854 *16 March (28 March)* Crimean War begins
1855 *June* Russian scuttling of the Black Sea fleet at Sevastopol'
18 Feb. (2 March) Death of Nicholas I, accession of Alexander II
1856 *18 March (30 March)* Crimean War ends (Treaty of Paris). Black Sea demilitarized

Fleet Action Orders of Battle

The following is a list of the Russian and opposing Swedish and Turkish vessels that participated in each of the major naval battles of the 1700–1860 period for which detailed information is available. The spelling of Russian proper names for both ships and people follow the protocols described in the section on transliteration. The proper spelling of Turkish names is extremely problematic and the spellings chosen below may deviate widely from those found in other sources.

For reasons of space here and elsewhere in the text, we have adopted the convention of replacing the Russian words for Saint, *Sviatoi* (m) and *Sviataia* (f), with the abbreviation *Sv.*

Key (C) captured, (B) set afire, (S) sunk

1 Battle off island of Osel (Baltic Sea)
24 May (4 June) 1719)
Russian squadron
  6 ships of the line:
  1 x 54 *Portsmut* (Captain 2nd class N. A. Seniavin)
  5 x 52s *Devonshir, Iagudiil, Uriil, Rafail, Varakhail*
  also 1 x 16 snow *Natal'ia*
  Losses: 18 men (killed and wounded)
Swedish squadron
  1 ship of the line
  Wachtmeister (48) (C) (Commodore Wrangel)
  Frigate *Karlskrona Wapen* (30) (C)
  Brigantine *Bernhardus* (10) (C)
  Losses: 50 men killed, 13 wounded, 387 PoW

2 Battle in the Strait of Chios (Aegean Sea)
24 June (5 July) 1770
Russian squadron
  9 ships of the line:
  1 x 80 *Sviatoslav* (flag of Rear-Adm. Elphinston)
  8 x 66 *Trekh Ierarkhov* (flag of General of Horse Count A. G. Orlov), *Sv. Evstafiia Plakida* (flag of Adm. A. G. Spiridov), *Evropa, Trekh Sviatitelei, Ianuarii, Rostislav, Ne Tron' Menia, Saratov*
  1 x 34 *Nadezhda Blagopoluchiia*
  1 x 32 *Afrika*
  1 x 26 *Sv. Nikloai*
  1 x bomb *Grom*
  17 smaller vessels
  Losses: set afire*: *Sv. Evstafiia Plakida* (66)*, 629 men killed
Turkish squadron
  6 ships of the line:
  1 x 86 *Burc-ı Zafer* (B) (flag of Kapudane (Admiral) Cezayirli Hasan Bey)
  2 x 84 *Hisn-i Bahri* (flag of Patrona (Rear-Adm.) Ali Bey), *Ziver-i Bahri* (flag of Riyale (Rear-Adm.) Cafer Bey)
  7 x 70 *Mukaddeme-i Seref, Semend-I Bahri, Mesken-i Bahri, Peleng-I Bahri, Tilsim-i Bahri, Ukaab-i Bahri, Seyf-i Bahri*
  6 x 60 *Rhodos*, 5 unnamed
  6 frigates, 50 smaller vessels
  Losses: set afire: *Burc-i Zafer* about 700 men killed

3 Battle in Ches'ma Bay (Aegean Sea)
26 June (7 July) 1770
General in command Adm. A. G. Spiridov
Russian ships
  4 ships of the line:
  4 x 66 *Rostislav* (broad pennant of Brigadier Greig), *Evropa, Ne Tron' Menia, Saratov*
  1 x 34 *Nadezhda Blagopoluchiia*
  1 x 32 *Afrika*
  1 x bomb *Grom*
  4 x fire ships
  Losses: 11 men
Turkish squadron
  2 x 84 *Hisn-i Bahri* (flag of Patrona (Rear-Admiral) Ali Bey), *Ziver-i Bahri* (flag of Riyale (Rear-Adm.) Cafer Bey)
  7 x 70 *Mukaddeme-i Seref, Semend-I Bahri, Mesken-i Bahri, Peleng-I Bahri, Tilsim-i Bahri, Ukaab-i Bahri, Seyf-i Bahri*
  6 x 60 *Rhodos*, 5 unnamed
  6 frigates, 50 smaller vessels
  Losses: 14 ships of the line, 6 frigates, 45 smaller vessels set afire, *Rhodos*, 5 galleys captured
  Losses: 11,000 killed and wounded

4 Battle in the Bay of Patras (Aegean Sea)
28 October (8 November) 1772
Russian squadron
  2 ships of the line:
  1 x 72 *Ches'ma* (Captain 1st class M. T. Konyaev)
  1 x 66 *Graf Orlov*
  1 x 26 *Sv. Nikloai*
  1 x 16 *Slava*
  Five smaller vessels
  Losses: 1 killed, 7 wounded
Turkish squadron
  9 frigates
  16 shebecks and smaller vessels
  Losses: 8 frigates (B), 8 smaller vessels (B)

5 Battle off the island of Fidonisi (Black Sea)
3 July (14 July) 1788
Russian squadron
2 ships of the line:
2 x 66 *Slava Ekateriny* (flag of Rear-Adm. Voynovich), *Sv. Pavel* (Brigadier Ushakov)
2 x 50 *Sv. Andrei, Sv. Georgii Pobedonosets*
8 x 40 *Berislav, Strela, Pobeda, Perun, Legkii, Kinburn, Fanagoriia, Taganrog*
also 20 smaller vessels
Losses: 5 men wounded
Turkish squadron
17 ships of the line (including 5 x 72–74)
8 frigates
3 bombs
also 21 smaller vessels
Losses: 1 ship of line sunk after battle, 4 ships of the line were seriously damaged

6 Battle off the island of Gogland (Baltic Sea)
6 July (17 July) 1788
Russian squadron
17 ships of the line
1 x 108 *Rostislav* (flag of Adm. S. Greig)
8 x 74 *Vseslav* (flag of Rear-Adm. Kozlyaninov), *Kir Ioann* (flag of Rear-Adm. M. Fondezin), *Sv. Elena* (flag of Rear-Adm. Spiridov), *Ioann Bogoslov, Sv. Pyotr, Mstislav, Vladislav* (C), *Iaroslav*
8 x 66 *Boleslav, Vysheslav, Mecheslav, Rodislav, Iziaslav, Viktor, Pamiat' Evstafiia, Deris'*
2 x 40 *Briachislav, Mstislavets*
5 x 36 *Vozmislav, Premislav, Slava, Nadezhda Blagopoluchiia*
also 8 smaller vessels
Losses: 334 killed, 742 wounded, 477 PoW
Swedish squadron
15 ships of the line, 5 battle frigates
4 x 70 *Gustav III* (flag of Adm.-Gen. Duke of Karl Sydermanland), *Prins Gustav* (B) (flag of Commodore Wachtmeister), *Drottning Sofiia Magdalina* (pennant of Captain Linderstedt), *Enigheten*
10 x 62 *Hedvig Elisabet Charlotta, Omheten, Rättvisan, Dygden, Fäderneslandet, Äran, Forsiktigheten, Prins Karl, Prins Fredrik Adolf, Kronprins Gustav Adolf*
1 x 60 *Vasa*
1 x 44 *Gripen*
4 x 40 *Camilla, Froja, Minerva, Thetis*
1 x 34 *Jaramas*
1 x 32 *Jarislavitz*
2 x 24 *Sprengporten, af Trolle*
1 x 22 *Hector*
also 8 smaller vessels
Losses: 130 killed, 334 wounded, 539 PoW

7 Battle of Öland (Baltic Sea)
15 July 1789 (26 July) 1789
Russian squadron
20 ships of the line
3 x 108 *Rostislav* (flag of Adm. V. Ya. Chichagov), *Kniaz' Vladimir* (flag of Vice-Adm. Musin-Pushkin), *Dvenadtsat' Apostolov* (Rear-Adm. Spiridov)
1 x 78 *Iezekiil'*
8 x 74 *Mstislav, Pobedoslav, Prints Gustav, Kir Ioann, Iaroslav, Sv. Pyotr, Sv. Elena, Vseslav*
8 x 66 *Deris', Vysheslav, Boleslav, Sviatoslav, Rodislav, Viktor, Iziaslav, Pamiat' Evstafiia*
1 x 46 *Briachislav*
1 x 44 *Mstislavets*
1 x 42 *Premislav*
3 x 38 *Slava, Podrazhislav, Nadezhda Blagopoluchiia*
also 9 smaller vessels
Losses: 31 killed, 185 wounded
Swedish squadron
21 ships of the line, 8 battle frigates
1 x 74 *Vladislaff*
6 x 70 *Gustav III* (flag of Adm.-Gen. Duke of Karl Sydermanland), *Drottning Sofiia Magdalina* (flag of Rear-Adm. Liljehorn), *Gota Lejon, Drottning Lovisa Ulrica, Konung Adolf Fredrik, Enigheten*
12 x 62 *Hedvig Elisabet Charlotta* (flag of Commodore Modee), *Dristigheten, Rättvisan, Manligheten, Omheten, Forsiktigheten, Fäderneslandet, Riksens Stander, Dygden, Äran, Tapperheten, Prins Fredrik Adolf*
2 x 60 *Vasa, Prins Karl*
2 x 44 *Uppland, Gripen*
6 x 40 *Zemire, Thetis, Galathee, Minerva, Eurydice, Froja*
1 x 34 *Illerim*
1 x 32 *Jarislavitz*
also 6 smaller vessels
Losses: 3 ships of the line damaged

8 Battle of Revel' (Baltic Sea)
2 May (13 May) 1790
Russian squadron
10 ships of the line, 1 battle frigate:
2 x 108 *Rostislav* (flag of Adm. Chichagov), *Saratov* (flag of Vice-Adm. Musin-Pushkin)
4 x 74 *Sv. Elena* (Rear-Adm. Khanykov), *Iaroslav, Mstislav, Kir Ioann*
4 x 66 *Prokhor, Boleslav, Pobedonosets, Iziaslav*
1 x 44 *Venus*
1 x 42 *Premislav*
3 x 38 *Nadezhda Blagopoluchiia, Slava, Podrazhislav*
also nine smaller
Swedish squadron
20 ships of the line, 6 battle frigates
1 x 74 *Vladislaff*
6 x 70 *Gustav III* (flag of Adm.-Gen. Duke of Karl Sydermanland), *Konung Adolf Fredrik* (flag of Rear-Adm. Modee), *Drottning Sofiia Magdalina* (flag of Lejonankar), *Gota Lejon, Drottning Lovisa Ulrica, , Enigheten*
11 x 62 *Hedvig Elisabet Charlotta, Dristigheten, Rättvisan,*

Omheten, Forsiktigheten, Fäderneslandet, Riksens Stander (B), *Dygden, Äran, Tapperheten, Prins Fredrik Adolf*
2 x 60 *Vasa, Prins Karl* (C)
2 x 44 *Uppland, Gripen*
4 x 40 *Galathee, Eurydice, Froja, Camilla*
1 x 34 *Jaramas*
1 x 32 *Jarislavitz*
also 9 smaller vessels
Losses: 1 ship of line taken, 1 ship of line lost, 150 killed, 520 PoW

9 Battle of Krasnaya Gorka (Styrsudden) (Baltic Sea)
23–24 May (3–4 June) 1790
Russian squadron
17 ships of the line
5 x 108 *Ches'ma* (flag of Vice-Adm. Kruz), *Dvenadtsat' Apostolov* (flag of Vice-Adm. Sukhotin), *Trekh Ierarkhov* (flag of Rear-Adm. Povalishin), *Sv. Kniaz' Vladimir, Sv. Nikolai Chudotvorets*
1 x 78 *Iezekiil'* (flag of Rear-Adm. Spiridov)
7 x 74 *Ioann Bogoslov, Pobedoslav, Prints Gustav, Vseslav, Sisoi Velikii, Sv. Pyotr, Tsar' Konstantin*
4 x 66 *Panteleimon, Ianuarii, Ne Tron' Menia, Amerika*
1 x 46 *Briachislav*
1 x 44 *Mstislavets*
1 x 40 *Pomoshchnyi*
1 x 38 *Arkhangel Gavriil*
8 x 38 (rowing) *Nikloai, Mariia, Aleksandr, Pavel, Ekaterina, Elena, Konstantin, Aleksandra*
also 2 smaller vessels
Losses: 200 killed, 525 wounded
Swedish squadron
21 ships of the line, 8 battle frigates:
1 x 74 *Vladislaff*
6 x 70 *Gustav III* (Commodore Klint), *Konung Adolf Fredrik* (flag of Rear-Adm. Modee), *Drottning Sofiia Magdalina* (flag of Commodore Lejonankar), *Gota Lejon, Drottning Lovisa Ulrica*, , *Enigheten*
12 x 62 *Hedvig Elisabet Charlotta, Dristigheten, Rättvisan, Omheten, Forsiktigheten, Fäderneslandet, Prins Ferdinand, Dygden, Äran, Tapperheten, Prins Fredrik Adolf, Manligheten*
2 x 60 *Vasa, Finland*
2 x 44 *Uppland, Gripen*
6 x 40 *Galathee, Eurydice, Froja, Camilla, Thetis, Zemire*
2 x 34 *Illerim, Jaramas*
1 x 32 *Jarislavitz*
1 x 26 *Hector*
1 x 18 *Ulla Fersen* (flag of Adm.-Gen. Duke of Karl Sydermanland)
also 8 smaller vessels
Losses: 84 killed, 283 wounded

10 Battle of Vyborg (Baltic Sea)
22 June (3 July) 1790
Russian squadron
27 ships of the line
7 x 108 *Rostislav* (flag of Adm. Chichagov), *Ches'ma* (flag of Vice-Adm. Kruz), Saratov (flag of Vice-Adm. Musin-Pushkin), *Sv. Nikolai Chudotvorets* (flag of Rear-Adm. Spiridov), *Dvenadtsat' Apostolov, Trekh Ierarkhov, Sv. Kniaz' Vladimir*
1 x 78 *Iezekiil'*
9 x 74 *Sv. Pyotr* (flag of Rear-Adm. Povalishin), *Pobedoslav, Prints Gustav, Vseslav, Tsar' Konstantin, Iaroslav, Sv. Elena, Mstislav, Kir Ioann*
9 x 66 *Panteleimon, Ianuarii, Ne Tron' Menia, Sviatoslav, Iziaslav, Pobedonosets, Prokhor, Khrabryi, Pobedoslav*
1 x 64 *Prints Karl*
1 x 46 *Briachislav* (flag of Rear-Adm. Khanykov)
2 x 44 *Mstislavets, Venus*
2 x 40 *Pomoshchnyi, Premislav*
5 x 38 *Arkhangel Gavriil, Slava, Podrazhislav, Patrikii, Nadezhda Blagopoluchiia*
2 x 38 (rowing) *Elena, Aleksandra*
also 10 smaller vessels
Losses: 147 killed, 164 wounded
Swedish squadron
21 ships of the line, 8 battle frigates:
1 x 74 *Vladislaff*
6 x 70 *Gustav III* (flag of Adm.-Gen. Duke of Karl Sydermanland), *Konung Adolf Fredrik* (flag of Rear-Adm. Modee), *Drottning Sofiia Magdalina* (C) (flag of Commodore Lejonankar), *Gota Lejon, Drottning Lovisa Ulrica* (C), , *Enigheten* (B)
12 x 62 *Hedvig Elisabet Charlotta* (B), *Dristigheten, Rättvisan* (C), *Omheten* (C), *Forsiktigheten, Fäderneslandet, Prins Ferdinand, Dygden, Äran, Tapperheten, Prins Fredrik Adolf, Manligheten*
2 x 60 *Vasa, Finland* (C)
2 x 44 *Uppland* (C), *Gripen*
6 x 40 *Galathee, Eurydice, Froja, Camilla, Thetis, Zemire* (B)
2 x 34 *Illerim, Jaramas*
1 x 32 *Jarislavitz* (C)
1 x 18 *Ulla Fersen*
also 11 smaller vessels and about 200 vessels of rowing flotilla
Losses: also 54 smaller vessels, sailing and rowing, captured and destroyed; about 7,000 killed, wounded, incl. 4,988 PoW

11 Battle of Kerch Straits (Black Sea)
8 July (19 July) 1790
Russian squadron
5 ships of the line, 5 battle frigates
1 x 78 *Rozhdestvo Khristovo* (flag of Rear-Adm. Ushakov)
4 x 66 *Mariia Magdalina* (flag of Brigadier Golenkin), *Sv. Vladimir, Sv. Pavel, Preobrazhenie Gospodne*
3 x 50 *Sv. Georgii Pobedonosets, Sv. Aleksandr Nevskii, Sv. Andrei*
2 x 46 *Apostol Pyotr, Ioann Bogoslov*
6 x 40 *Pokrov Bogoroditsy, Ioann Voinstvennik, Sv. Ieronim,*

Prepodobnyi Nestor, Sv. Amvrosii Mediolanskii, Kirill Belozerskii
also 16 smaller vessels
Losses: 29 killed, 68 wounded
Turkish squadron
10 ships of the line (including 4 x 72–74), commanded by Kaptan-Pasha Giritli Huseyn-pasha
8 frigates
also 16 smaller vessels
Losses: 1 small vessel

12 Battle of Tendra (Black Sea)
28–29 August (8–9 September) 1790
Russian squadron
5 ships of the line, 5 battle frigates
1 x 78 *Rozhdestvo Khristovo* (flag of Rear-Adm. Ushakov)
4 x 66 *Mariia Magdalina* (flag of Brigadier Golenkin), *Sv. Vladimir, Sv. Pavel, Preobrazhenie Gospodne*
3 x 50 *Sv. Georgii Pobedonosets, Sv. Aleksandr Nevskii, Sv. Andrei*
2 x 46 *Apostol Pyotr, Ioann Bogoslov*
6 x 40 *Pokrov Bogoroditsy, Ioann Voinstvennik, Sv. Ieronim, Prepodobnyi Nestor, Sv. Amvrosii Mediolanskii, Kirill Belozerskii*
also 20 smaller vessels
Losses: 21 killed, 25 wounded
Turkish squadron
14 ships of the line (including 5 x 72–74), commanded by Kaptan-Pasha Giritli Huseyn-pasha
8 frigates
also 23 smaller vessels
Losses: captured 1 x 74 *Kapudaniye*, 1 x 66 *Mulk-i Bahri*, 1 ship of line sunk after action, about 2,000 killed and wounded, Admiral Said-Bey and 733 PoW

13 Battle of Kaliakra (Black Sea)
31 July (11 August) 1791
Russian squadron
6 ships of the line, 10 battle frigates
2 x 78 *Rozhdestvo Khristovo* (flag of Rear-Adm. Ushakov), *Ioann Predtecha* (ex-Turkish *Mulk-i Bahri*)
4 x 66 *Mariia Magdalina* (flag of Brigadier Golenkin), *Sv. Vladimir* (flag of Brigadier Pustoshkin), *Sv. Pavel, Preobrazhenie Gospodne*
3 x 50 *Sv. Georgii Pobedonosets, Sv. Andrei, Sv. Aleksandr Nevskii*
1 x 58 *Muchenik Leontiy* (Turkish prize)
7 x 46 *PyotrApostol, Ioann Bogoslov, Tsar' Konstantin, Fyodr Stratilat, Navarkhiia, Sv. Nikloai*
1 x 40 *Prepodobnyi Nestor*
1 x 36 *Makropleia-Sv. Mark* (Turkish prize)
also 21 smaller vessels
Losses: 17 killed, 28 wounded
Turkish squadron
18 ships of the line commanded by Kaptan-Pasha Giritli Huseyn-pasha and Algerian Admiral Seydi-Ali

10 large and 7 small frigates
also 43 smaller vessels
Losses: many ships including both main flagships were heavily damaged

14 Battle of Mount Athos
18 June (30 June) 1807
Russian Squadron
10 ship of the line 750 guns
3 x 80 *Tverdyi* (flag of Vice-Adm. Seniavin), *Rafail, Uriil*
5 x 74 *Selafail, Iaroslav, Sv. Elena, Moshchnyi, Sil'nyi*
1 x 64 *Retvizan* (flag of Rear-Adm. Greig)
1 x 60 *Skoryi*
Turkish Squadron
10 ship of the line, 5 Heavy frigates, 5 smaller ships 1,200 guns
1 x 120 *Mesudiye* (flag 1 General Admiral (Kaptan-Pasha) Seydi-Ali)
1 x 90 *Sedd-ul Bahr* (flag 2) (C),
5 x 84 *Anka-yi bahri* (flag 3 Vice-Adm. Sheremet-bey), *Taus-i bahri, Tevfik-numa, Besaret-numa* (S), *Kilik-i bahri*
3 x 74 *Sayyad-i bahri, Gulbang-i-Nusrat, Jebel-andaz*
4 x 54 *Meskeni-ghazi, Bedr-i zafar, Fakih-i zafar, Nessim*
1 x 44 *Iskenderiya*
1 x 32 *Metelin, Denyuvet* (?)
1 x 28 *Rahbar-i alam*
2 x 18 *Alamat I Nusrat, Melankai*
Captured: *Sedd-ul Bahr* (90) Sunk: *Besaret-numa* (84), 1 additional ship of the line, 2 frigates

15 Battle of Navarino
8 October (20 October) 1827
Russian contingent
4 ships of the line, 4 frigates
1 x 84 *Gangut*
3 x 74 *Azov* (flag of Rear-Adm. Geiden), *Izekiil', Aleksandr Nevskii*
2 x 44 *Konstantin, Provornyi*
2 x 36 *Elena, Kastor*
British contingent
1 x 84 *Asia* (Fleet Commander Vice-Adm. Codrington)
1 x 76 *Genoa*
1 x 74 *Albion*
1 x 50 *Glasgow*
1 x 48 *Cambrian*
1 x 42 *Dartmouth*
1 x 28 *Talbot*
1 x 18 *Rose*
3 x 10 *Mosquito, Brisk, Philomel*
1 x 6 *Hind*
French contingent
1 x 84 *Breslau*
1 x 80 *Scipio*
1 x 74 *Trident*
1 x 60 *Sirene* (flag Rear-Adm. de Rigny)
1 x 44 *Armide*

1 x 10 *Alcyone*
1 x 6 *Daphne*

Turkish Fleet (including Tunisians)
3 ships of the line, 14 frigates, 16 corvettes, 4 brigs, 5 fireships
1 x 84 *Kuh-i Revân* (flag of Turkish Vice-Adm. Hussein Bey)
2 x 74 *Büruc-u Zafer* (flag of Adm. Tahir Pasha), *Fatih-i Bahrî*
2 x 64 *Fevz-i Nusrat*, *Kaid-i Zafer*
3 x 48 *Keyvan-ý Bahrî*, *Feyz-i Mirâc* (flag of Turkish Rear Adm.), *Mecra-yi Zafer*
9 x 42 *Nusrat-ý Avar*, *Müjde Resan*, *Badi-i Nusrat*, *Beşir-i Zafer*, *Bed-i Nusrat*, *Gurre-i Nusrat*, *Pertev-i Nusrat*, *Menba-i Nusrat*, *Avnilâh-ý Nusrat*
16 x 22 *Gurre-i Fütûh*, *Feyz-i Bahşa*, *Peyk-i Fütûh*, *Mevkib-i Cihâd*, *Kerem-i Bahrî*, *Enver-i Nusrat*, *Id-i Nusrat*, *Talih-i Fütûh*, *Feyz-i Hüda*, *Feyz-i Felek*, *Nâsýr-i Bahrî*, *Muin-i Cihâd*, *Yümn-ü Necâd*, *Mebde-i Nusrat*, *Hilâl-i Zafer*, *Tair-i Bahrî*
4 x 10 *Hençeroōlu Osman Kapidan*, *Bozcaadalý Hüseyin Kapudan*, *Tufan Kapudan*, *Nevruzoōlu Hasan Kapudan*
5 fireships

Egyptian Fleet
4 frigates, 7 corvettes, 7 brigs, 2 schooners, 2 fireships
2 x 64 *Ihsaniye*, *Mürşid-i Cihâd* (flag of Egyptian Vice-Adm. Moharrem-bey)
1 x 60 *Sir-i Cihâd*
1 x 56 *Süreyya*
7 x 22 *Abdullah Helpe Kapudan*, *Ahmet Hoca Kapudan*, *Giritli Mustafa Kapudan* and four unnamed
7 x 10 *Sabur Kapudan*, *Esir Hasan Kapudan*, *Pulaka Mustafa Kapudan*, *Rodoslu Hacý Ibrahim Kapudan* and three unnamed
2 x 6 *Dimyatlý Hacý Mustafa Kapudan*, *Arnavut Hacý Yusuf Kapudan*
2 fireships *Dimyatlý Selim Kapudan*, *Mehmet Yazýcý Kapudan*

Note on Turkish and Egyptian orders of battle: There is considerable disagreement on many details of the numbers, identities and rated armaments of ships present and the degree of damage incurred by them. The above list is based largely, although not exclusively, on research published by Emir Yener on the *Naval History in the Age of Sail (1650–1815)* website. A significant contemporary account is that provided by Jean-Marie Letellier, French advisor to the Egyptian navy, after the battle. Unfortunately, Letellier names few ships and where he does he uses approximate Western translations. His totals for capital ships and frigates are similar to the foregoing but his numbers for smaller ships are much greater. The Turkish fleet comprised two divisions, one which had sailed from Alexandria (1 x 84 [Capitan Bey], 1 x 74, 1 x 54 [razee], 4 x 52, 1 x 44, 12 corvettes) and the other from Constantinople (1 x 60 [ship of the line: Tahir Pasha], 1 x 50, 1 x 48, 4 x 44, 7 corvettes, 6 brigs). Also arrived from Alexandria were the Egyptian division ('*Warrior*' (60) [Moharrem Bey], '*Lion*' (60), 2 x 58, 11 corvettes, 21 brigs, 5 schooners, 6 fireships) and the Tunisians (1 x 42, 1 x 32, 1 brig). Of these, 1 Egyptian brig was absent conveying dispatches at the time of the battle and 3 Egyptian corvettes and 2 Egyptian brigs may have been elsewhere on the coast as they were not damaged. According to Letellier there were afloat after the battle the 60-gun '*Lion*' (*Sir-i Cihâd*), 4 corvettes, 6 brigs and 4 schooners (all Egyptian including those which had been elsewhere). Driven ashore but later refloated were the flagship of the division from Constantinople, 4 frigates (Turkish), 4 corvettes (3 Turkish, 1 Egyptian), 3 brigs (Egyptian) and a fire ship (Egyptian). A number of these proved unserviceable as did a further refloated ship of the line. In more recent literature the surviving ships of the line appear as *Kuh-i Revân* and *Büruc-u Zafer*. Emir Yener places Tahir Pasha on the 84-gun *Kuh-i Revân* as does, for example, R. C. Anderson. Letellier is quite clear, however, that he was on the flagship from Constantinople. Letellier's account is reproduced in Lady Bourchier's *Memoir of the Life of Admiral Sir Edward Codrington* (1873), vol. ii, pp. 600–3.

16 Battle of Sinop
18 November (30 November) 1853

Russian fleet
6 ship of the line, 2 frigates, 2 steamers
3 x 120 *Veliky Kniaz' Constantin*, *Parizh* (flag of Rear Admiral Novosil'skiy), *Tri Sviatitelia*
3 x 84 *Imperatritsa Mariia* (flag of Vice-Adm. Nakhimov), *Rostislav*, *Ches'ma*
1 x 60 *Kulevchik*
1 x 44 *Kagul*
3 steamers *Krym* (4), *Odessa* (4), *Khersones* (4)
Losses: 37 killed, 229 wounded

Turkish fleet
7 frigates, 3 sloops, 2 steamers
1 x 62 *Nizamiye* (flag of Vice-Adm. Osman Pasha)
1 x 60 *Nesim-i Zafer*
1 x 58 *Navek-i Bahri*
1 x 56 *Damiat* (Egyptian)
1 x 54 *Kaid-i Zafer*
2 x 44 *Avnullah* (flag of Rear-Adm.), *Fazilillah*
2 x 24 *Necm-i Fesan*, *Feyz-i Mabud*
1 x 22 *Guh-i Sefid*
2 steamers *Taif* (12), *Eregli* (10)

All Turkish ships destroyed on the day of the battle or the following day except for *Taif* which escaped. Personnel losses in excess of 3,000.

Data Format

Class designations

For our purposes, class names are followed by a parenthesized number including all ships authorized and belonging to a particular class irrespective of whether they were actually laid down or completed. This includes those ships begun but abandoned during construction, several ships launched and fitted out at Arkhangel'sk but lost during the long voyage to St Petersburg and never commissioned or named as a result, as well as those ships separated chronologically from their sisters by extended periods of time The most prominent case in point includes the ninth unnamed First Rate of the *Ches'ma* class whose construction was abandoned on the eve of the Russo-Swedish War of 1788 and the tenth member of the same class, the *Rostislav*, which was laid down and completed during the closing years of the Napoleonic Wars, long after her sisters had been stricken and disposed of. Our justification for this approach lies in the fact that we are as much interested in the *intended* composition of the Russian Navy at any particular point in time as we are in the completed fleet. When ships are abandoned during construction, or when older designs are reinstated at later dates; this often says as much about the problems and priorities faced by decision-makers as do those ships actually completed for service.

Ship names

Russian ship names have origins similar to those of other navies, being comprised of the names of famous battles, naval or land based, geographical locations and cities, famous names in Russian naval and military history, the names of emperors and empresses and members of the Russian nobility, religious names and references, martial adjectives, birds, constellations and classical mythological references. Although Baltic ships were frequently given the names of prominent Russian saints, the names given to Black Sea ships took on a decidedly broader religious tone. Any listing of Black Sea warships overflows with every conceivable religious reference from the Transfiguration to the Twelve Apostles to the Three Holy Prelates to Mary Magdalene. The reasons for this preoccupation with religiosity may lie in the Black Sea fleet's proximity to the seat of the Orthodox Church in Constantinople and to the perceived threat from Islamic nations opposing Russian on its southern land and sea frontiers. One Russian writer has indicated that one reason for the extensive use of religious names lies in the simple and pragmatic fact that, when the Russian navies in both the Baltic and Black Sea fleets were being constructed out of whole cloth in the 1690s and early 1700s, there was no available historical name-pool of famous warships available to draw from. Since Russia in 1700 was a profoundly religious society, the names of prominent prelates and saints and religious events seemed to provide easily recognizable and appropriately prestigious material to draw from. As happened in all navies, a name once used acquired significance and an aura of its own entirely unrelated to its historical origins. For example, a name with deep religious connotations, such as the *Sviatoi Pavel*, no longer had any significance in relation to its pious antecedents, but harked back rather to the histories of the series of similarly named warships that had previously carried the name and acquired fame in historical battles. As a very general rule among the ships of both fleets, religious names and references, national heroes and royal personages were assigned primarily to capital ships and frigates while martial adjectives, constellations, birds, and mythological references were the preserve of smaller vessels such as brigs, sloops, and cutters. Place names and battles seem to have been assigned to both larger and smaller ships on the basis of their relative importance.

As is the case in other navies, well-known ship names recur frequently throughout the age of sail and into the modern era. Popular names were frequently reassigned to ships under construction immediately upon the loss in battle, decommissioning or even the hulking of earlier vessels bearing the same name. Names were rarely assigned to more than one major vessel at a time within either fleet, although there were at least two instances of two ships of the line carrying the same name at the same time. When this occurred, the two ships were often distinguished by sobriquets such as 'the greater' and 'the lesser' or 'the first' and 'the second' (e.g. *Ioann Zlatoust Pervyi* and *Ioann Zlatoust Vtoroi* and *Mariia Magdalina pervaia* and *Mariia Magdalina vtoraia*). It must be emphasized that these comments apply only to major warships. Naval auxiliaries and inshore and amphibious craft were indiscriminately assigned all manner of names without regard to the contemporary presence of ships of different types, or even the same types, being assigned similar names. We have not attempted a survey of duplicate ship names due to the large number of minor ships serving in the various fleets and flotillas, but would not be surprised to find as many as five or six smaller ships carrying popular names such as *Sviatoi Pavel* at any particular time.

Peter I added his personal imprint to the question of ship names, as he did to so many aspects of Russian naval history. He was a great admirer of 'things Dutch' and 'things German'. As a result, many ship and place names of historical import to Russians have German and Dutch names assigned to them. Examples of ship names include *Nord-Adler, Esperans, Fridemaker* and *Ingermanland*. Ingermanland is, of course, also the Germanic name given to the province surrounding St Petersburg which would be rendered as Ingria in Russian. Still other examples of Peter's Teutonic bent include St Petersburg itself, which would be Petrograd in Russian, as well as the great fortresses of Kronshtadt and Shlissel'burg.

As indicated, English, French and German translations of Russian ship names are given in parenthesis. Name changes are also given in parentheses, but these labelled as such, e.g. *Menelai* (*Menelaus*) (renamed *Olivutsa*). In this case, *Menelai* is the English transliteration of the Russian ship name, (*Menelaus*) is the English spelling of the same name, and (renamed *Olivutsa*) alerts the reader to the fact that the ship in question was later renamed *Olivutsa*. Details about the renaming will normally be found in the notes section for the entry. The same logic applies to ships renamed after purchase or capture with the operative prefix being 'ex-' followed by the ship name, e.g. *Ioann Predtecha* (ex-Turkish *Mulk-I Bahri*). In this case, *Ioann Predtecha* is the Russian name given to the captured Turkish *Mulk-I Bahri*. Where the ship name is not followed by a parenthesized name, it should be assumed that the name is either a proper noun not requiring a translation, or that the English version of the name is identical to the Russian. There are, of course, Russian ship names too complicated for a simple parenthesized explanation and these are dealt with in the notes section.

In many cases, particularly with respect to minor warship types and auxiliaries, the reader will find vessels identified by number rather than by name. Some listings will contain mixes of 'named ships' and 'numbered ships' falling within the same categories. In a number of instances, particularly with respect to auxiliaries, there are breaks in the numbering sequences (e.g. no. 1, no. 2, no. 5, etc.). This is not an error, but a reflection of the information obtained by Veselago (in the majority of cases) from available records. It is believed that the missing numbers most probably relate to temporarily hired or requisitioned private vessels.

Numbers of guns
This is the officially designed and rated armament. As was the case in other navies, the number of guns actually carried frequently varied greatly throughout the life of the ship. Where two numbers appear separated by a forward slash (60/64), this may be taken in three different ways, depending on the context:

- the rated armament followed by the actual number of guns carried in service
- the number of conventional cannon carried followed by the total armament including carronades
- the original armament and the armament after reconstruction

When three numbers appear (60/64/68), this should be taken as indicating light armament, normal peacetime armament and maximum armament carried in wartime.

Construction site
This is given as the city where the ship was built, with the shipyard itself specified in parenthesis when appropriate. Information about the specifics of shipyard names and histories is provided below.

Constructor
The name given is generally the individual responsible for overseeing the actual construction of the ship. As was the case with British ships in the eighteenth century, the constructor was frequently also the designer of the vessel, although the degree of overlap between the two functions is not always clear. Whenever possible, the identity of the designer, when separate from that of the constructor, is specified in the notes section. Where a ship is also a member of a larger class, the identity of the designer is generally given in the class notes.

Laid down
This date was consistently recorded and requires no explanation. Dates in the ship data section are all given according to the Julian calendar, which remained in effect in Russia until 1918. Julian dates may be readily converted into Gregorian dates by adding ten days for ships built before 1700, eleven days for ships completed before 1800 and twelve days for ships completed before 1900.

Launched
Launch dates are also consistently recorded in Russian records. The Russian predilection for officially launching ships on dates having religious, historical, or political significance may mean that the recorded dates does not correspond to the actual date on which a given ship entered the water. This will explain the apparently simultaneous launch dates of numbers of ships belonging to given classes. The launch date represents an approximation of the actual date of launch, but the reader can presume that the date was either on or after the actual date of launching. Dates of actual commissioning are indeterminate in many, if not most, cases. One possible reason for the lack of attention given to commissioning dates may relate to the one- to three-month hiatus between the departure of unnamed but manned and fitted out ships from Arkhangel'sk and their formal christening and acceptance into the Russian Baltic fleet at St Petersburg. Those ships that failed to complete the sometimes perilous journey – and there were several – remained forever unnamed.

Dimensions
Russian ships followed British methodology and *avoirdupois* for measuring the dimensions of warships built after 1700. All feet and inches are British unless otherwise indicated. Length and breadth and depth of hold are given with draught and length of keel also being recorded when available. Draught was generally only recorded for steam powered sailing ships, where it frequently replaced depth of hold as the third relevant measure. Basic dimensions are given as length of gun deck/lower deck x breadth x depth of hold. When available, keel length appears between length of gun deck and breadth and is designated by the notation (keel). The draught of the vessel, when available, follows after the depth of hold. This figure may reflect maximum draught or may include figures for draught fore and aft. Examples of both simple and more complicated dimensions are:

144 ft x 35 ft 9 in x 8 ft 6 in
This means 144 ft length x 35 ft 9 in breadth x 8 ft 6 in depth of hold

180 ft 11 in x (151 ft 2 in keel) x 49 ft 6 in x 21 ft 9 in
This means 180 ft 11 in length x 151 ft 2 in length of keel x 49 ft 6 in breadth x 21 ft 9 in depth of hold

242 ft 2 in x 59 ft 6 in (outside plank) x 24 ft 11.2 in
This means 242 ft 2 in length x 59 ft 6 in breadth taken outside the hull x 24 ft 11.2 in depth of hold

70 ft 2 in x (59 ft 5 in keel) x 24 ft x 12 ft 9 in x 14 ft 6 in (max draught)
This means 70 ft 2 in length x 59 ft 5 in length of keel x 24 ft breadth x 12 ft 9 in depth of hold x 14 ft 6 in maximum draught.

206 ft 7 in x (198 ft 8 in keel) x 54 ft 9 in x 22 ft 6 in x 23 ft 8 in/25 ft 8 in (draught fore/aft)
This means 206 ft 7 in length x 198 ft 8 in length of keel x 54 ft 9 in breadth x 22 ft 6 in depth of hold x 23 ft draught forward x 25 ft 8 in draught aft

Russian shipbuilders were apparently uninterested in computing what the British called builder's measurement and accordingly did not normally record the keel length until the 1830s. The reason for this may lie in the fact that, in Great Britain, builder's measure was used in determining the payment due to private British shipyards or awarded for prizes taken into service. This system had no relevance in Russia where the precise economic value of individual warships was neither determined nor of immediate importance owing to the Russian practice of completing almost all of their warships in government shipyards.

Dimensions given generally represent designed class dimensions, unless otherwise indicated. Where a given ship has several different determinations of dimensions recorded by different sources or at different times, these are all included and noted by listing the source and the variant dimensions in brackets. In the majority of cases, the dimensions given here are those specified for the class or the establishment and are followed by the parenthesized notation (establishment). These dimensions may be presumed to have varied somewhat in actuality due to the variability of construction practices relating to wooden ships built by hand out of the most suitable cuts of timber available as well as the degree of creativity exercised by the on-site constructors.

Some of the dimensions for smaller ships have both metric dimensions and their approximations in feet specified. This unfortunate state of affairs is the result of A. A. Chernyshev's having converted the originally recorded English feet and inches found in the records that he consulted into their metric equivalents to serve the needs of a book being published in a nation immersed in the wonders of the metric system and uninterested in the quaint idiosyncratic practices of Great Britain in an earlier age – an action that made perfect sense from his perspective. It has not proved practicable to retrace all of A. A. Chernyshev's conversions, and our apologies must go to readers who are like ourselves in deriving irrational pleasure from seeing the traditional feet and inches and fractions thereof that are *de rigueur* in English naval works. (106 ft 6½ in is much more comforting than 32.47 metres!)

Where either displacement or burthen was available, it is recorded in this section. It should be noted that *displacement* figures (as opposed to measurements of builder's measure) were very approximate numbers in most cases.

Armament
Both the arrangement of information and the abbreviations used here generally follow normal usage as illustrated by the works of Rif Winfield and David Lyon *et al*. Gun decks are abbreviated as follows:

LD for lower gun deck
MD for middle gun deck
UD for upper deck

Where there are only one or two gun decks, MD may be read as an abbreviation for main deck.

Upper works are abbreviated as follows:

FC for forecastle
QD for quarterdeck
RH for roundhouse

Three varieties of ordnance are frequently present on each separate deck of major Russian warships, with the number of each type carried being followed by 'x' and an abbreviated description indicating the type:

Normal ship-borne cannon of the traditional sort specify the weight of shot followed by 'pounder' ('pdr') and 'pounders' ('pdrs'), e.g. '26 x 24pdrs'. This may in turn be followed by a parenthesized description of the subtype, e.g. '26 x 24pdrs (short)'. Carronades are described with 'pdr carr.', e.g. '2 x 32pdr carr.'.
Edinorogs (unicorns in English) appear with a numerical entry specifying the weight of solid ordnance followed by 'u' (for unicorn, the English rendering of the Russian *edinorog*) and with the weight of explosive ordnance listed in parentheses (e.g. 4 x 60 u (1 pood)) If this seems needlessly complicated, the reader is referred to the section on Russian naval ordnance below for clarification.
Shell guns are specified as such and are either described in terms of pounds for 68pdr weapons (e.g. 68pdr shell guns) or in terms of the diameter of the chamber in inches for larger weapons (e.g. 9.65-in shell guns).

When armament listings are followed by parenthesized entries, the reader may still regard the information as reliably determined. Parenthesized entries specifying a particular establishment e.g. (1723 Establishment) always reflect the *intended* armament of a given vessel as built. When a particular ship lies outside of the establishment system, parenthesized entries of 'probable' are based on the time-honoured expedient of 'counting the gun ports' on the various decks and on an awareness of the various gun calibres in use at the time. This too, is a reliable methodology and any deviations are probably limited to the open deck forecastle and quarterdeck guns. In cases where different sources report different armaments, the variations are listed with the names of the alternative sources parenthesized. Where there are no parenthesized comments, it may be safely assumed that the armament has been verified. Where information is available about armament changes in a ship over the course of its service life, the changes are described in separate lines arranged chronologically and with the date of the change in parentheses followed by the armament layout arranged in the normal manner. (e.g. 1856: LD 24 x 24pdrs, etc.) As is the case with dimensions, the source of the information, when known, is indicated in parentheses.

As a note of clarification, actual armament fits for ships built through the end of the eighteenth century are often available as are those for ships built during the reign of Nicholas I. For the period from approximately 1800–25, coinciding roughly with the reign of Alexander I, we have no listings of the actual armaments carried by any Russian warships and must rely on specified gun establishment figures. The reader should keep in mind that this was a period of great stress and transition in Russia owing to the Napoleonic conflict, and in the navy specifically because of to the mandated changeover from long guns to short guns and the formal elimination of edinorogs. This being the case, it is probable that many ships were completed with whatever ordnance may have been available at the time of their fitting out and that significant deviations from the gun establishments were probable and quite possibly the norm rather than the exception.

As an incidental entry in this section and one admittedly unrelated to any sort of logic other than convenience, ship complements are listed here when they are available.

Notes
Where a ship is a member of a larger class, the class name is given in parentheses as the first entry along with the number of ships belonging to the class (see above). For our purposes, a class is defined quite loosely as a group of ships built to common specifications within a given time period and with specified dimensions and armaments. This is an admittedly vague definition intended to include groups of ships built within common parameters and, in theory at least, from a common draught. It is recognized that individual ships may vary significantly from their specified characteristics, but it is noted that the same degree of variability within a class may be found in many twentieth-century ships.

This section is also used for brief commentary on technical issues of significance, most particularly relating to a given ship's relationships with other individual ships or classes.

The primary function of the section is the provision of a brief operational history of each individual ship. This generally includes information pertaining to the working up period, the periods and conditions of active deployment, significant participation in naval campaigns and battles, periods of refit and repair, major conversions, and the conditions of the ship's final departure from full or partial service – when known. It should be born in mind that the final fate and disposition of many Russian warships is a matter of some uncertainty. When ships were determined unsuitable for continued service as seagoing warships, they were generally eased out of service in a phased manner not dissimilar to that existing in other sailing-ship navies. From our observation, it appears that the Russians were rather more retentive of unseaworthy warships than other European navies and we frequently find them, stripped of all or part of their armaments, serving as transports or hospital ships. Others retained their status of potential warships and were kept in reduced commission as 'fire watch ships' retaining some degree of mobility and capable of dealing with fires and other harbour emergencies. In time of war and national emergency, it was not unusual to see some of these ships brought back into full commission as active warships. Other worn-out warships found themselves reduced to harbour hulks similar to those found in the British and other navies, acting as stationary sheer hulks, hospital hulks, prison hulks and the like, but with no hope of ever being returned to active service. The final category here is that of ships listed as serviceable warships in the Russian equivalent of 'ordinary', but which were found to be too seriously deteriorated through the spread of dry rot to hope for recommissioning when called upon. The saddest example here would be the eight ships of the 100-gun *Ches'ma* class, all of whom failed to be found worthy of sea service when examined for recommissioning during the national emergency of 1801. These ships and those in the other categories were frequently retained on the naval 'effective' list for years, quite probably to give the kind of illusory impression of potential naval strength that was commonplace in European navies, including the British, during this period. In still other cases, ships that have actually been formally stricken and sent to be broken up reappear years later as miraculously reincarnated harbour hulks. The reader should keep all of this in mind, but make take solace in the certainty that entries of 'decommissioned in' do mark the effective end of a ship's career as an effective warship. Readers inclined to take all of the above as indicative of Russian sloth and inefficiency should refer to Andrew Lambert's *The Last Sailing Battlefleet* wherein occur a surprising number of wooden British line of battle ships that made their way into the twentieth century as harbour hulks, some even surviving the Second World War and not going to the breakers until the late 1940s.

Ship Types and Classifications

This section only includes major seagoing warships presented in Sections I and IV. Shallow-draught vessels intended solely for inshore and amphibious warfare will be found Section II and naval auxiliaries in Section III. Coverage of the larger oared and rowing frigates has been included here on account of their size and firepower and their seagoing capabilities. The same reasoning applies to bomb vessels which were designed to accompany the battle fleets at sea. The categories covered below are all types familiar to the most casual students of sailing warships and our remarks are largely confined to elements of their construction and utilization unique to Russian conditions and in some degree of variance with normal practice elsewhere.

Line of battle ships

During the formative years of naval development, Russians followed British usage and formally divided their capital ships into four, and later three, Rates. Unlike the British, no attempt was made to assign rates to cruising ships. The following official Rates were in effect prior to the reign of Catherine II:

Inventory of 1727
    First Rate 90–100 guns
    Second Rate 80–88
    Thirrd Rate 66
    Fourth Rate 54

Establishment of 1732
    First Rate   70–100
    Second Rate 66
    Third Rate   54

Establishment of 1750
    First Rate   80–100
    Second Rate 66
    Third Rate   54

It should be noted that these ratings were formal categories and never achieved general circulation in the Russian naval circles of the period. Formal establishments of ships after 1750 describe capital ships solely in terms of the number of guns that they were rated as carrying. The sole exception to this practice was that ships carrying 100 guns or more were always referred to colloquially as First Rates within the fleet. Note also that 'ships of the line' will also be found referenced variously throughout the text as 'line of battle ships', 'line ships' and 'capital ships' solely in the interests of avoiding rhetorical tedium. Ships of the line shared certain basic features with several lesser warship types such as frigates, ship sloops and corvettes. These types were all collectively referred to as 'ships' or 'ship-rigged vessels' and had three square-rigged masts and from one to three continuous gun decks. The feature that distinguishes ships of the line from frigates and the like was their having been designed to 'stand in the line' and withstand the firepower of any and all enemy warships. Some ships of the line were effectively rendered obsolete as ships being built in Russia and elsewhere became larger and more powerfully armed. In the British Royal Navy, these ships, such as 50s and 64s, were usually relegated to colonial service where they could be usefully employed as flagships and prestige ships. Russia lacked significant colonies throughout most of this period and dealt with their older ships of the line by converting them to floating batteries for stationary defence or employing them as troop transports or hospital ships. Many ships designated as frigates were in fact more powerful than some smaller ships of the line, but they were never intended to operate as 'line ships'.

No detailed discussion of capital ship evolution is possible at this point, but the following production table for all Russian purpose-built line of battle ships completed between 1700 and 1860 reflects the overall production of the Russian Navy as well as highlighting the differences in emphasis between the Baltic and Black Sea fleets, with the Black Sea fleet leaning more heavily on larger capital ships, and the Baltic possessing a more balanced mix of types:

Gun ranges	Baltic ship	Black Sea ship	Total*
100–130	24	14	38
80–98	35	26	61
70–78	95	28	123
60–68	109	19	128
50–58	35	10	45
Total	298	97	395

*This total includes Sea of Azov ships for all categories and treats them as components of the Black Sea fleet.

Frigates

Russian frigates were more functionally specialized than those found in Western navies. Readers accustomed to thinking in terms of Fifth Rates and Sixth Rates or 9pdr frigates, 12pdr frigates, 18pdr frigates and the like will need to familiarize themselves here with terms appearing in the body of the text, such as 'battle frigates', 'heavy frigates', 'training frigates', 'small

SHIP TYPES AND CLASSIFICATIONS

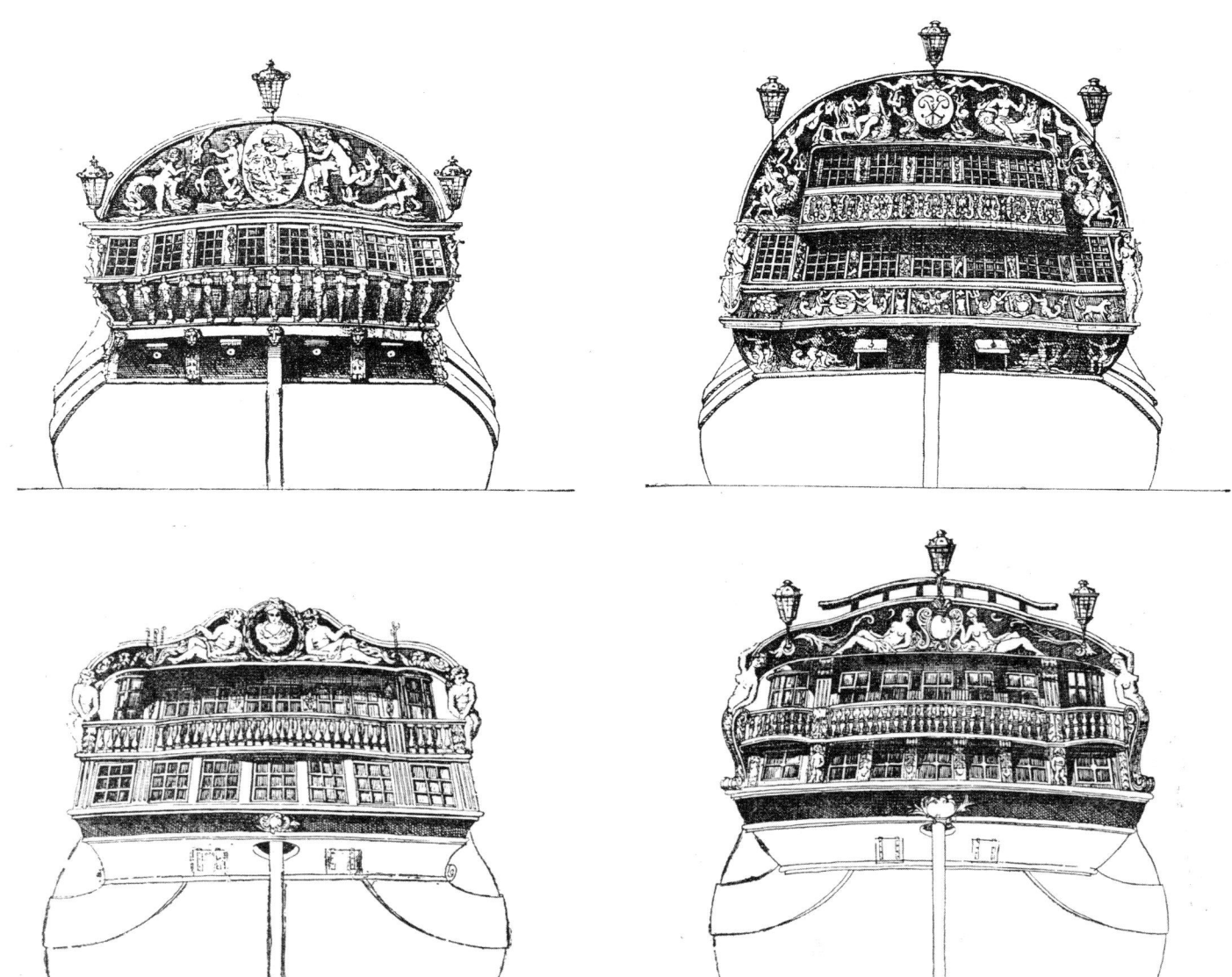

The sterns of four Russian ships of the line built between 1700 and 1763 show in detail the elaborate style of decorative wood carving still in vogue in Russia during the first half of the eighteenth century at a time when the sterns and quarter galleries of other European capital ships were becoming simpler and more utilitarian in the interest of economy and efficiency in battle. As warship design became more functional and less concerned with vulgar (and expensive) display under Catherine II, this level of decoration declined in the Russian navy as it had done so earlier in other European navies: top left, Goto Predestinatsiya *1700; top right,* Ingermanland *1715; below left,* Slava Rossii *1733; below right,* Sviatoi Evstafii Plakida *1763.*

frigates', 'rowing frigates', and even 'newly invented frigates' (*Novoizobretennye Fregaty*). While it is true that standard 12- and 18pdr frigates of the type built in Western European navies were also built in moderate numbers throughout the eighteenth and early nineteenth centuries in Russia, they were steadily eclipsed after 1785 by much heavier 24pdr ships of a type not found elsewhere in significant numbers until the post-Napoleonic period.

Part of the explanation for the Russian predilection for specialized frigate categories lies in the very different and variable operating environments experienced by their regional navies in both the Baltic and the Black Sea. Not only were there differences between the operational demands and expectations placed on cruising vessels in inland sea environments in general, with fewer opportunities for engaging in the traditional scouting, raiding and commerce protection functions of frigates operating in oceanic environments, and greater opportunity for inshore operations of an amphibious nature, there were also significant differences between the requirements imposed by the very different Baltic and the Black Sea environments, both natural and political.

It should be borne in mind that the categories presented below do not necessarily represent formally established categories. They do, however, reflect clearly defined lines of development in the Russian navy, and are being described here for the sake of clarity of communication in the pages that follow. Numerical totals for the frigate category are subject to considerable interpretation and the figures given below should be treated as informed approximations, especially with respect to the smaller and older categories. Many ships classed as frigates by Russia were too small to merit this classification by Royal Navy standards, but most of the ships included here were designed for cruising and scouting purposes, regardless of their size or armament. A total of 274 ships fall within the frigate category in the pages that follow, 190 in the Baltic, 78 in the Black Sea, and 6 in the Caspian.

Battle frigates

A term briefly in vogue in the Black Sea to describe ships falling below the level of line of battle ships, but intended to participate in the line of battle against similar Turkish ships. In practice, this term quickly gave way to the following term:

Heavy frigates

A term applied to large and heavily armed 24-, 30- and 36pdr frigates found in significant numbers in both the Baltic and the Black Sea fleets. These larger ships were more numerous in both theatres than the smaller standard 18pdr frigates; but their respective popularity in the Baltic and the Black Seas arose from rather different tactical requirements and emphases. In the Black Sea, where the type was first introduced, heavy frigates were not regarded as traditional cruisers suited for scouting and raiding, but were rather the direct descendants of the previously described battle frigates and were intended to supplement the line of battle against similar Turkish ships. In the Baltic, on the other hand, heavy frigates were quite ironically the direct design descendants of the captured Swedish heavy frigate *Venus*, specifically designed by af Chapman to take its place in the line of battle, and captured by the Russians during the Russo-Swedish War of 1788–91. Russian heavy frigates built along the lines of the *Venus* were utilized in traditional frigate roles and *not* as battle line adjuncts as was the case with the Black Sea heavies.

During the period between 1770 and 1860, a total of 85 heavy and battle frigates joined the two Russian fleets, almost all of them armed with 24pdr cannon and ranging between 141 ft and 174 ft in length.

Standard frigates

These were similar to frigates found elsewhere in terms of size and capabilities. The same distinction between the older cruising vessels having two fully or partially armed gun decks and the later 'true' or 'classic' frigates of the Revolutionary and Napoleonic War periods, with unarmed lower decks and improved speed and handling characteristics, was found in the Russian Navy as elsewhere. The difference for Russia was that the design transformation that occurred in the 1750s for the navies of France, Spain and Great Britain apparently did not make its way to Russia until the *Vos'moi* class of 12pdr frigates entered service in the late 1770s in the then Sea of Azov flotilla and the *Briachislav* class of 18pdr frigates in the mid-1780s for the Baltic. The inspiration for the first Russian 18pdr frigates of the *Briachislav* class in 1784 probably came from ideas absorbed by Russian students returning from Great Britain in the early 1780s, quite possibly with the plans for the British *Arethusa* class frigates in hand – their armament and dimensions were suspiciously similar. As indicated above, these 'true frigates' were built in smaller numbers proportionally than in other navies where there was an ongoing requirement for large numbers of cruising vessels in scouting and commerce protection (and commerce destruction of course). Russian frigates had smaller areas to patrol in their confined inner seas and very little in the way of merchant ships requiring escort in the navy of a country lacking any significant investment in overseas trade, and so they were never required in the numbers found in the Atlantic navies.

Between 1773 and 1860, only 36 standard or 'classic' frigates armed with 18pdr guns and ranging between 121 ft and 150 ft in length were completed for both the Baltic and Black Sea fleets, less than half the number of 24pdr heavy frigates completed for the two regional fleets during the same general period. In the interests of completeness, it should also be noted that a total of 60 earlier cruising ships, all bearing the multifunctional name of 'frigate' were also completed for service in the Baltic between 1705 and 1785, including 18 obsolescent 12pdr ships of the *Pavel* type constructed between 1773 and 1785, just prior to the introduction of true frigate types.

Small frigates

A descriptive term rather than a formal category, these ships were intermediate in size and power between standard frigate types and corvettes and sloops. In the British Royal Navy, the vessels constructed after 1770 would probably have been rated as ship sloops. Between 1702 and 1761, 17 small ships classed as frigates and ranging between 65 ft and 94 ft in length were completed in the Baltic. Between 1762 and 1845, an additional 38 small frigates of the more classic type with a single gun deck, but ranging between 90 ft and 130 ft were completed, 19 in the Baltic, 13 in the Black Sea and 6 in the Caspian. Armament varied widely in this category, with small frigates carrying between 8 and 32 guns of as little as 6pdr calibre to as much as 30pdr (when rebuilt as 'newly invented frigates'; see below).

Training frigates

These purpose-built ships were limited to the Baltic fleet. They would normally have been rated as sloops or corvettes in most Western navies and are included in the totals given above for the larger 'small frigate' category. These ships were not intended to act as naval combatants, but rather as fully equipped peacetime training ships for young naval recruits. Fourteen ships were formally designated as training frigates during the age of sail.

'Newly invented frigates' (Novoizobretennye Fregaty)

The phrase 'newly invented' does not transfer well from Russian to English and might more readily be rendered as 'rebuilt' or

SHIP TYPES AND CLASSIFICATIONS

'redesigned'. The frigate designation is probably not entirely appropriate for this small collection of short-lived Black Sea ships, five of which originally fell within the category of purpose-built shallow draught frigates, while the others were comprised of a hotch-potch of converted pinks, cutters and merchantmen that were rebuilt as 'frigates'. The purpose-built frigates chosen for the conversion programme were originally shallow-draught ships built in shipyards along the Don River and armed with 12pdrs and generally resembled conventional deep-water frigates. These highly specialized warships were found to be incapable of dealing with more heavily gunned Turkish ships in the opening phases of the Russo-Turkish War of 1788–90 in the Liman. In order to derive some value from their construction when their deficiencies became apparent, they were rebuilt in 1788 with reinforced hulls and enormously powerful (for their size) 30pdr batteries bored out hurriedly from available guns of lesser calibre. The concept of adding very heavy guns to shallow draught vessels in order to use their enhanced combination of firepower and manoeuvrability to compensate for the Russian lack of line of battle ships in the Liman was the result of the fruitful and co-operative relationship that grew up between Samuel Bentham, a British mechanical engineer and later Inspector General of the Royal Navy, and the formidably talented Prince Potemkin. The resulting vessels resembled later nineteenth-century ships armed with gunnades and they proved an effective short-term solution for the Black Sea fleet, although they sacrificed a good deal of their scouting and cruising capabilities in their search for greater short-range firepower, becoming *de facto* coastal defence ships. A total of twelve 'newly invented frigates' of all types were converted in 1788 to meet the demands of the Russo-Turkish War. They were all disposed of in the early 1790s as newer, more carefully thought-out heavy frigate types began entering service in the Black Sea; but they set the tone for future generations of heavily armed Black Sea frigates with their deliberate substitution of heavy ordnance for more conventional cruiser qualities.

Oared or rowing frigates

The shallow coastal waters of the northern Baltic mandated the construction by both Swedes and Russians of large fleets of small rowing vessels similar in function to Western gunboats. These small craft could not operate in deep-water environments, but they could do serious damage to larger sailing ships becalmed in the shallow-water environments of the northern Baltic and made helpless by the vagaries of the Baltic winds. Rowing frigates provided something of a link between the traditional deep-water sailing navy and the gunboat squadrons. They were as large and well armed as true frigates, but were at the same time shallow-draft vessels unsuitable for deep-water use and with sweeps capable of facilitating movement during calms and of manoeuvring successfully against smaller and more agile gunboats. Twenty-six of these handsome and unusual ships were completed between 1773 and 1823, ranging between 130 ft and 144 ft in length. The early ships carried 24pdrs and the final rowing frigates carried 36pdrs, an unprecedented armament for a frigate.

Corvettes and ship sloops

To English-speaking readers, corvette is simply the name used by the French for the British ship sloop and both designations refer (in this time period at least) to three-masted ships similar in layout to frigates but smaller and with fewer and lighter cannon. Both terms were in use in the Russian sailing navy, but they had separate and distinct meanings, although both types were alike in being three-masted ships of generally similar size and armaments.

Corvettes were purely combat ships with sharper lines than corresponding sloops. They were operationally attached to battle groups and employed as scouts, avisos and cruising ships. Corvettes were more popular in the Black Sea where they took on many of the functions reserved to frigates in the Baltic in the absence of adequate numbers of standard frigate types. A total of 15 corvettes entered service in the Black Sea after 1800 as opposed to only 3 for the Baltic and 4 for the Caspian.

Russian ship sloops were broader of beam and better suited for carrying cargo and supplies than corvettes. They retained the capability for assuming scouting and cruising functions if called upon, but were generally employed as armed store ships. After the Napoleonic Wars ended, ship sloops came into their own when they were found to be ideally suited for hydrographic survey work, foreign exploration and global circumnavigation. No sloops are found in the Russian Baltic or Black Sea fleets in the eighteenth century (unless one includes the 'small frigates'), although three were built in Kamchatka. Between 1804 and 1818, 21 ship sloops were built for the Baltic and one lone sloop joined the Black Sea fleet in 1823. Ship sloops were not built in quantity in the Black Sea fleet because the closing of the Bosporus to Russian warships negated their potential for long-range service.

Snows and brigs

Snows and brigs were close cousins. Both had two large square-rigged masts; but the snow in its final incarnation in the second half of the eighteenth century also carried a small, short third mast called a trysail mast immediately abaft the main mast carrying a spanker that could be operated independently of the main mast's sails. The trysail mast was not readily apparent to the uninformed observer due to its close proximity to the main mast and snows were sometimes referred to as 'two-and-a-half mast' ships. Russian snows built in the first quarter of the eighteenth century were originally based upon Dutch designs and were equipped with sweeps for inshore operations. Illustrations indicate that the rig of at least three early snows, two *Lizet*s and the similar *Munker (My Heart)*, all designed by Peter I and named after his daughter Elizabeth, carried traditional three-masted ship rig with a fully developed mizzen mast in place of the trysail. Other contemporary snows, such as *Adler* of 1705, are shown with more traditional snow rig. This may indicate Peter's personal preference for three-masted ships, whatever their size, or it may reflect a variability in the rigging of early snows that would indicate that the designation may have had more to do, at this time, with hull design, size and intended employment than with a particular rig. Russian snows were popular in both the Baltic and Sea of Azov during the first quarter of the eighteenth century, but are not found thereafter. Their decline in popularity in later years mirrors a similar phenomenon in the Royal Navy during the same period and one wonders if there was a connection here, as in other areas, with the Russian employment of large numbers of British shipwrights and officers. A total of 22 snows were completed between 1700 and 1711, 16 in the Baltic and 6 in the Sea of Azov. One final snow was completed for the Baltic in 1723, almost as an afterthought.

Brigs did not begin to appear in the Russian navy until the very close of the eighteenth century, but they became extremely popular during the first half of the nineteenth, gradually edging out the slightly larger corvettes and ship sloops in both the Baltic and Black Sea. The development of the brig as the primary low-end ship best suited for inshore patrol, routine escort and scouting activities parallels a similar process in the British Royal Navy from about 1780 on. To quote Robert Gardiner from *Warships of the Napoleonic Era*, three-masted sloops were 'more seaworthy, more habitable, longer-ranged and better armed than the old two-masted type, and the ship rig must have conferred some advantages in battle – three masts would have made them less vulnerable to damage aloft than two. *But the one quality the new-style sloops did not possess was speed* [author's italics].' Besides having an important edge in speed, brigs required smaller crews as a result of having only two masts to the ship sloop's three. The downside of the two-mast arrangement was a greater vulnerability in battle since the loss of a single mast was of more importance in a two-masted vessel than it was in a ship with three masts.

The nineteenth century saw a flowering of the type, with 37 being built for the Baltic, 26 for the Black Sea, 19 for the Caspian and six for Okhotsk. With few exceptions, brigs were between 90 ft and 105 ft in length and armed with all carronade batteries.

Cutters and schooners

Both cutters and schooners are small ships with largely fore-and-aft rigs, one or two masts, and a very light armament sufficient only for overwhelming the smallest of opponents. The two types developed in the later part of the eighteenth century as highly manoeuverable ships capable of patrolling close inshore and interdicting smugglers and pirates and the like. As a largely self-sufficient nation without much in the way of trade or foreign commerce, Russia in the eighteenth century had relatively little use for vessels of this type. After 1800, and particularly after 1820 as Russian naval horizons expanded, particularly in the areas of coastal surveying and exploration, cutters and schooners found an increasing role in naval affairs. Both types came within the same general size range, although schooners were probably a bit larger on the average. Between 1790 and 1860, the Baltic fleet acquired 27 two-masted schooners ranging between 35 ft and 105 ft, while the Black Sea fleet acquired 24 between 1772 and 1849 ranging between 75 ft and 119 ft. For reasons not immediately apparent, one-masted cutters were decidedly more popular in the Baltic, where there were a total of 42 vessels acquired between 1786 and 1826 as against only four for the Black Sea fleet and two for Okhotsk. Cutters in Russian service were as heterogeneous a group as schooners, with lengths varying between 51 ft and 99 ft and armament between 12 and 32 guns. For reasons that are not entirely clear, the Russians stopped building cutters with the accession of Nicholas I, apparently preferring the slightly larger two-masted schooner.

Luggers and tenders

Luggers and tenders were classified as light warships by the Russians and are included in this section for this reason.

Bomb vessels

Russian naval operations were frequently conducted in support of amphibious objectives and bomb ships, both purpose-built and improvised, were built in some numbers for both major fleets and for the Caspian flotilla. Although designed for shore bombardment, these ships were deep draught vessels, designed to accompany and work with battle fleets at sea, and not for the close-in, shallow water work of prams and gunboats. In appearance, they were clumsy-looking vessels, with heavily reinforced decks to bear the weight of their heavy ordnance.

Seven bombs were built in the closing years of the seventeenth century for the Sea of Azov. The Baltic fleet acquired a total of 18 purpose-built bombs, two converted ships and two ships purchased abroad for a total of 22. The Black Sea built nine, converted eleven and purchased five abroad. Bombs were quite reasonably also found in the Caspian flotilla, where amphibious operations were common, and four ships were launched in 1808.

Russian Naval Administration

Russian naval command structure

Russia was an autocracy under emperors and empresses throughout the period covered by this work. As a result, the command and control structures and the economic underpinnings of the Russian Navy were freed from many of the tensions and conflicts that concerned other European navies. Russia had very little in the way of overseas commerce and was not a participant in the overseas competition for colonies and trade markets that drove the great powers of the west. There was no well-established mercantile class in Russia attempting to drive and control naval policy. The only real naval concerns of the Russian state related to the control of inland seas to facilitate expansion along land routes to the north, the west and the south. Russian battle fleets were designed, built and maintained to prevent foreign powers, primarily Sweden and Turkey, from interfering with landward expansion along the coastlines of the inland seas to the north and south, and from mounting amphibious expeditions of their own against Russian territory. When Russian naval squadrons were employed as instruments of long-range expansion and power projection as was the case in the Mediterranean and the North Sea during the French Revolutionary and Napoleonic Wars, their design unsuitability was evident to all concerned.

Peter I was the sole authority in Russia at the beginning of the eighteenth century and it was his will alone that brought about the formation of naval squadrons in the Baltic and in the Sea of Azov, which was at that time the only Russian outlet to the Black Sea. Had Peter not determined on building a navy, there would not have been a Russian Navy of any significance in the eighteenth century or possibly even later. Because of the exceptionally poor land communications in both the Baltic and the Black Sea areas, the successful deployment of land armies required for territorial expansion against determined opposition would have been highly problematical, if not impossible.

The first steps toward building up Russian naval forces occurred in the 1690s; but the Admiralty Office, initially based in Moscow, was not formally established until 1700 under Count Fyodor Golovin, Field Marshal and Minister of Foreign Affairs. As head of the Russian Navy, Golovin automatically acquired the title of Admiral, as had his predecessor Franz Lefort, a Swiss citizen brought into Russian by Peter I, from 1696 through 1699. His immediate successor was Count F. M. Apraksin who bore the title of admiral from 1706 until 1708 at which time his position was elevated to that of general-admiral until his death in 1728. The title of general-admiral remained in effect thereafter for heads of the new navy. Other prominent general-admirals during this period were Count A. I. Osterman, general-admiral

A part of Peter I's inner circle of friends and advisors from his days as a teenager, F. M. Apraksin (1661–1728) was one of his most competent and loyal assistants. An exceptionally capable general on land, Apraksin proved equally able when he turned to naval matters and served as general-admiral of the navy from 1708 to 1728. Peter I placed himself under Apraksin's command at sea on occasion, an action that not only reflected his respect for the older man, but also a recognition of his abilities as a commander and as a tactician.

and vice-chancellor, in 1740 and 1741; Prince M. M. Golitsyn from 1756 to 1762, and Paul, son of Catherine I and emperor from 1796 on, from 1762 to 1801. The general-admiral, of course, served entirely at the pleasure of the emperor and on at least one occasion (that of Paul) *was* the emperor.

In 1712, the administrative headquarters of the Russian Navy was moved to St Petersburg. The Moscow office continued to remain temporarily in control of naval logistics. In 1715, two new boards were created. The first was placed under the control of a major general and dealt with logistics and supply. (A word of explanation is needed here. Navy officers involved in non-combat roles having to do with construction and logistics, were given military titles commensurate with their command responsibilities in place of the traditional naval titles which were reserved for line officers. These non-combatant officers were still members of the navy and had no connection whatsoever with the Russian army.) The second new office created was charged with the administration of ports and naval construction and this command was headed by a vice-admiral.

In 1718, all of the separate bodies in the administrative sector were consolidated into the Admiralty Board or Collegium which was headed by the general-admiral who also received the title of President of the Board. This system remained in effect until the accession of Alexander I in 1802.

The rebirth of a naval force in the Black Sea area was largely the result of the determination and drive of Prince Potemkin who was determined to push Russian control southward over areas still under the control of Turkey. In 1785, an autonomous Admiralty was established at Kherson (later moved to Sevastopol') and headed by Prince Potemkin until his death in 1791 and then by his successor, Admiral Mordvinov. This Admiralty was accountable, at least in theory, to the Admiralty Board in St Petersburg. In 1802, two new commands were created in the wave of reform that followed Alexander I's coronation. The first was that of Chief Commander of the Fleet and Ports and was an administrative position concerned with logistics. The second was that of Commander of the Black Sea Squadron and was an operational command. In 1816, Samuel Greig, son of the illustrious eighteenth-century admiral, combined the two offices into that of Naval Commander. He remained in this position until he was superseded by one of the great names in Russian naval history, Admiral M. Lazarev, in 1832.

During his brief reign, Paul I instituted a dramatic series of reform, appointing new staffs over both the Baltic and Black Sea fleets, formalizing the size and composition of both fleets, replacing the traditional officers' white dress uniforms with less pretentious dark green, and establishing a uniform white on black colour scheme on all Russian warships. Of possibly greater importance, he established a new system of schools to teach the basics of navigation and opened maritime academies in St Petersburg and Nikolaev for instruction in shipbuilding and design, breaking decisively with past Russian reliance on British guidance, both formal and covert.

In 1802 the old system of command and control was swept aside and replaced by a Ministry of Naval Forces, which was renamed the Naval Ministry after 1815. This was one of the eight

Looking the part of a dissolute French aristocrat, Prince Potemkin (1739–91) as portrayed here gives little indication of his great abilities as an administrator or of the role he played in extending Russian control over the Black Sea or in presiding over the creation of the Black Sea fleet. His interests were wide-ranging and extended to collaboration with the British mechanical engineer Samuel Bentham in the technical side of naval affairs at all levels. He died at the very time when the fleet that he had constructed so diligently was achieving its goal of defeating the navies of the Ottoman Empire.

ministries governing Russia. The four officers serving in the position of First Minister of the Navy until the abolition of the ministry in 1827 were Admirals Mordvinov, Chichagov, Traversay and Moller. During Alexander's reign, the ministry was pursuing a policy of reducing the fleet's function, size and cost. It should be noted that the influence of the Marquis de Traversay was particularly harmful and that his period of formal control over naval affairs during the closing years of Alexander's reign was characterized by decay and neglect at all levels. It was said of Traversay, whether in jest or seriousness, that he was a paid agent of the British government.

The Naval Ministry had been the creation of Alexander I in 1802 and it should come as no surprise that it was abolished in 1827, soon after the accession to power of Alexander's younger brother Nicholas. The Naval Ministry was replaced by the Supreme Naval Staff. This arrangement, in turn, gave way to the creation of an Office of the Supreme Commander on Nicholas I's death in 1855 and the accession of Alexander II. Nicholas' attitudes towards military power in general and naval power in particular were the inverse of his older brother's and his reign through the ending days of the age of sail marked the renaissance and final flowering of the Russian sailing navy.

The major posts in Russian naval administration were always reserved to the emperor himself and to major members of the Russian aristocracy – princes, counts and the like. Lesser administrative positions relating to construction, ordnance, logistics and the like, were open to non-combatant naval officers, who were awarded the titles of generals, colonels and majors to distinguish them from line officers. Operational command at sea was always reserved for upper level aristocrats and the officer corps itself was closed to all non-nobles. The best that a capable member of the Russian middle classes or the peasantry could hope for was commissioning as a warrant officer.

Naval finance

Financing of the navy afloat and the construction of new ships and logistical concerns were entirely in the hands of the Emperor. No legislative assistance or interference was possible for the simple reason that Russia had no legislative bodies at all during the period of our coverage other than the boyar duma which was dissolved in 1711 and replaced by an 11 member Senate composed of Peter's closest advisors acting strictly in an advisory capacity and serving at his pleasure. Taxation of rural estates owned by the landed aristocracy or by the church, of small independent landholders and of towns and villages was by imperial fiat. As a result of the near-medieval conditions that still existed throughout most of rural Russia payment of taxes often took the form of payments in kind. Payments-in-kind frequently took the form of free labour, timber and various other durable goods and this kind of economic *quid pro quo* lay at the heart of much of the Russian shipbuilding activity, at least in the early years.

Sample naval expenditures between 1712 and 1724 were as follows:

1712	400,000 roubles	(£100,000)
1715	700,000	
1721	1,100,000	
1723/24	1,400,000–1,500,000	

The figures for 1723/24 compare to 2,500,000 for the army and a total Russian military budget of 4,000,000. This indicates that naval expenditures represented approximately 60 per cent of the amount spent on the army and 37½ per cent of the total Russian budget. This was during peacetime and does not factor in the worth of the goods and labour paid in lieu of money.

The growth of Russia as a naval power and as a major economic power may be seen by similar figures for the nineteenth century:

1805	12,400,000 roubles
1815	15,000,000
1825	20,700,000
1835	37,500,000
1845	14,500,000
1855	19,100,000

Direct comparisons between early eighteenth century roubles and nineteenth century roubles are, of course, economically questionable, but the trend is clear. Expenditures under Nicholas I rose to a peak in 1839 (37.7 million) and seem to have dropped off dramatically for the remainder of his reign. The apparent drop off in naval expenditures in 1840 is misleading, however, and stems from the fact that state expenditures were measured in paper roubles until 1840 when they converted to silver roubles. The conversion rate of silver roubles to paper roubles varied widely, but the average naval expenditure for the first half of Nicholas I's reign was in the neighbourhood of 12 million silver roubles per year from 1826–39 and 15 million per year from 1840–53, indicating a continuation in the upward trend throughout the first half of the century.

Surveyors, constructors and shipwrights

As a child and as a young man, Peter I (not yet carrying his title of 'the Great') had developed a familiarity with and admiration for Dutch shipbuilding. The shipwrights hired to oversee the construction of the Sea of Azov fleet were, in fact, Dutch hires along with a small number of Venetians. During the first phase of his celebrated Grand Embassy tour of European capitals in 1697–98, he had been apprenticed to Dutch craftsmen and shipwrights in order to familiarize himself personally with the essentials of ship design and construction. While the experience in Dutch shipyards allowed him to develop skills in basic carpentry and the like, Peter was appalled at the lack of scientific method, particularly mathematics, and the traditional hands-on approach of Dutch shipwrights to an endeavour that he felt should be marching in step with the other 'scientific' pursuits of the day. As soon as the young Tsar was made aware of the more mathematically based and rationalistic approach of English shipwrights, he decamped immediately to England in spring 1698. As Edward Phillips points out, there were two additional pluses in replacing Dutch shipbuilding processes with British. Dutch shipbuilding techniques could only be acquired after lengthy apprenticeships under skilled teachers, while English shipbuilding skills could be taught and absorbed more readily in a period of one to two years – provided the student had the necessary intellectual aptitude. Second, as Peter discovered while in England, British shipbuilding was centrally organized and controlled to a degree unknown in the Netherlands and this appealed greatly to Peter's authoritarian nature. An immediate result of his disenchantment with Dutch techniques was seen in his dismissal of Dutch and Venetian shipwrights as they brought their current shipbuilding projects to conclusion, an action that resulted in the Venetians abandoning their in-progress construction and negotiating a financial settlement with the young Tsar.

While visiting England, Peter I visited the shipyard at Deptford and was introduced to John Deane, the son of Anthony Deane, Joseph Nye and Richard Cozens. Impressed by the trio, Peter immediately invited them to Russia as constructors. Deane and Nye accepted at once and left for Russia even before the return of their patron, while Cozens delayed his acceptance and arrival in Russia until 1700. Deane died in 1699 before proving his worth, but Nye and Cozens went on to become Peter's most valued constructors and the trainers of a generation of Russian shipwrights. The subsequent arrivals of Richard Brown in 1705 and Richard Ramsey in 1715 gave Peter I a quartet of highly skilled master constructors that would be rounded up into a sextet with the coming to maturity of two Russians, Fedosey Sklyaev, one of Nye's most able pupils, and G. A. Menshikov. British influence over Russian shipbuilding was again reinforced in 1736–7 with the importation of brothers Alexander and James Sutherland, as well as James Lamb, who came to be known in Russia as 'Lambe Yames' and who had a distinguished career of over fifty years doing design work at St Petersburg and Arkhangel'sk. As late as 1781, he played a major part in the design of the 100-gun *Ches'ma* class, with his revisions of a design based on the draughts of Slade's *Victory* winning approval over those submitted by the younger constructors.

Russian interest in obtaining the services of British and French constructors continued during the second half of the eighteenth century, but salaries had outpaced Russian resources by this time. Jonathan Coleman (Kol'man) was the only British constructor lured to Russia in 1784, and he was hired on at the exorbitant rate of 2,000 roubles for the first year rising to 2,500 roubles after three years and topping out at 3,000 roubles – figures far in excess of the normal salaries paid to Russian shipwrights, which were in the region of 300 to 600 roubles.

Russian lack of success in attracting British shipwrights to Russia did not end the interchanges between the two navies. From 1762 on, the Russian Admiralty began sending skilled Russian assistant constructors to Britain to avail themselves of British expertise. In 1762, 21 Russian officers and midshipmen were sent to Great Britain for study in all areas of naval science. Assistant constructor I. Kutygin was sent in 1776–80 for study and he was followed by F. Ignatyev and D. Masal'skiy in 1778–9. The high point of Anglo-Russian co-operation may well have come in the early 1780s when Admiral Keppel, as First Lord, allowed Russian student shipwrights full access to the facilities of the major British naval shipyards of Plymouth, Portsmouth, and Chatman. D. Masal'skiy was able to obtain the dimensions for HMS *Victory* in 1780, but was unable to obtain her actual plans. Using these specifications in 1782, Russian constructors I. James and A. S. Katsanov prepared plans for the new Russian First Rates of the *Ches'ma* class. Russian access was beginning to dry up as Anglo-Russian relations deteriorated after 1784; but it was in that year that another enterprising Russian student, one Vasily Vlasov, was able to obtain and send complete copies of the original plans for Slade's *Victory* to St Petersburg. As late as 1796, Russian students in Great Britain were still sending British design draughts to St Petersburg for analysis – those of the frigate *Phoebe*, the sloop *Termagant* and the cutter *Dispatch*. The Russians were impressed by *Phoebe* and built a single ship, the *Pospeshnyi*, to her lines, but abandoned further construction of the type in favour of the larger and more effective Swedish-inspired 24pdr, 44-gun frigates of the *Venus* type. Nevertheless, a significant degree of British design influence continued into the first decade of the nineteenth century. The 120-gun First Rate *Khrabryi* is said to have been based on draughts of the British *Caledonia*, a not surprising development as I. V. Kurepanov had studied in England for several years and returned to Russia with the draughts of the British ship in hand. It should be noted that the British ship was beamier and so it is evident that changes were made to suit Russian preferences. The purchase of plans for the 64-gun *Pobedonosets* of 1809 and the simultaneous construction of the seven-ship *Trekh Sviatitelei* class in 1810, based on the draughts of the 'large class' British 74s *Kent* and *Ajax,* are two more prominent examples of British influence.

French shipwrights also had an important, but secondary, role in Russian naval design and construction during the eighteenth century, in spite of the *cachet* attaching to the French 'scientific school'. In 1717, Peter I visited France and obtained the services of the renowned French designer B. Pangalo, but the experiment came to naught as the French designer died after designing and building a single ship, the 66-gun *Panteleimon Viktoria*. In 1731 two Russian shipwrights, G. A. Okunev and I. Ramburg, returned from studying in France to pursue successful careers in Russia under Empress Anna, not a particularly dedicated or knowledgeable naval supporter in the main, who wanted to increase the role played by constructors 'who know French proportions'. The two followed successful careers crowned by their role in the design and construction of the new 100-gun First Rate, the *Sviatoi Dmitrii Rostovskii*, in 1755. At a later date, further attempts at attracting French designers in 1763 fell afoul of the same economic road blocks as had bedevilled attempts at attracting British constructors – the Russian state lacked the capital to compete effectively for their services. Nevertheless, a final French designer appeared on the Russian scene at the turn of the century, Le Brune de St Catherine. After gaining significant experience as an assistant constructor in Toulon, Le Brune first emigrated to Turkey where he did extensive design work, completing or closely overseeing the construction of a very impressive total of one 120, three 80s, five 74s and five 50s and a number of smaller vessels. In 1798, he met Admiral Ushakov in Constantinople while the Russian admiral was taking his squadron into the Mediterranean to assist (and compete with) Russia's erstwhile British allies against the French. Le Brune, no friend of the French Revolution, agreed to work for Russia and cheerfully abandoned his Turkish sponsors. Le Brune's career in Russia lasted from 1799 through his death in 1835. He was appointed a major general and chief constructor in 1811 and given a seat on the Admiralty Board in 1826. A student of Sane, Le Brune's greatest contributions to Russian shipbuilding included his design work on the 120-gun *Khrabryi*, the 88-gun *Smely* of 1808 and on the post-war generation of 84-

gun ships which began to replace the long standard 74s in the Black Sea from 1822 on.

In spite of the influence of British and French design concepts during the eighteenth century, Russian naval construction also developed along its own internal lines and in compliance with Russian national goals. The chief surveyor's office was created in 1717 as a primarily administrative position by Peter I. The first occupant of the new position was Ivan Golovin whose tenure was purely symbolic, with Peter himself being the *de facto* chief constructor. Chief constructors of particular note during the eighteenth century included G. A. Okunev, D. T. Scherbachev, P. Kachalov (a pupil of Cozens), I. Katsanov and ultimately Le Brune in the nineteenth century. Constructors were formally considered naval officers, but held military titles such as colonel, brigadier general, major general and lieutenant general. The six leading constructors at any point in time generally met once monthly under the direction of the chief constructor to exchange information and ideas. Co-operation and openness were the rule at these meetings and secrecy and egotism was discouraged. Individual constructors were allowed to pursue their own projects, the primary restraint being the provision that they be guided by the limits imposed by the Establishments. Innovations were not discouraged, but approval for changes rested ultimately with the Naval Board, which was under the control of line officers and, of course, the Emperor or Empress.

Russian shipbuilding began to come fully into its own after the establishment of formal maritime academies at St Petersburg and Nikolaev in 1798. A new generation of constructors began to reach maturity without having spent some or all of their formative years under British tutelage. The period of neglect under Alexander I may have inhibited this process, but the reforms of Nicholas I stimulated a renaissance in all areas of naval development and it is during this period that many of the technological advances of the final years of sail in Russia were made.

A. M. Kurochkin was probably the most important and influential of the new generation. During his career, he designed and built over 90 large warships and was instrumental in introducing reforms and innovations related to improving the structural strength of Russian warships as well as the material well being of both officers and crews. He was appointed chief constructor at Arkhangel'sk in 1806 and introduced, among other innovations, improved ventilation of lower deck areas, screens to inhibit incoming seawater, improved ship nails designed to avoid tearing ship wood, and the use of iron knees to strengthen hulls. He was particularly known for designing very fast warships, and his line of battleships were said to be capable of 14 knots speed.

Personnel

While it was possible in a completely autocratic nation state like Russia to mandate the construction of a navy or navies as well as the infrastructure required to make them effective, it was not possible to mandate a population base skilled in maritime matters. This was quite possibly the major dilemma facing Peter I and his successors. Seafaring nations dependent on maritime trade, such as Great Britain, Portugal, the Netherlands and the Scandinavian states which had ample human resources to draw upon, still suffered from manpower shortages in times of stress. Less wholly maritime European states, such as France and Spain had much smaller maritime populations to draw upon, and suffered severely in the naval warfare of the eighteenth and early nineteenth Centuries, quite frequently finding themselves with more ships than men to man them. None of these states had problems approaching those of Russia, which was a state almost devoid of fishing or mercantile populations.

In order to overcome these shortages in the realm of command, the Russian Navy turned to qualified naval personnel from other European nations, and even to the United States towards the end of the century. While several Norwegian and Dutch officers rose to prominence at various times, the majority of these officers were unemployed British officers in need of employment or experience abroad while awaiting recall by the British Royal Navy. Norman Saul has pointed out that a majority of these British officers in turn were men of Scottish or Irish nationality with limited opportunities at home in a navy dominated by English families and patronage networks. Most of the British officers attracted to Russian service, such as Samuel Greig, took up permanent residence in Russia, while some, like John Elphinston, returned home after having had distinguished careers in Russia.

The extent of foreign involvement in the Russian naval officer corps may be seen in this snapshot of the situation as it was upon the death of Peter I in 1725:

		non-Russian
Flag officers	11 (incl. three Russian)	72.7%
Commodores	5 (2 Russian)	60%
Captains 1st Class	7 (2 Russian)	71.4%
Captains 2nd Class	9 (2 Russian)	77.7%
Captains 3rd Class	12 (7 Russian)	41.7%
Lieut. Captains	29 (12 Russian)	58.6%
Lieutenants	58 (32 Russian)	44.8%
Junior Lieutenants	112 (108 Russian)	5.3%

All cadets and midshipmen in 1725 were Russian, as were the vast majority of junior lieutenants. The foreign participation in the officer corps gradually decreased as the century wore on; but a significant proportion of the Russian Navy's command positions were still held by foreigners, mostly British, as late as the Russo-Turkish War of 1768–74.

As was only to be expected, there was a degree of friction between these line officers and Russian officers, but the system generally worked well for both the immigrant officers and their host navy. The great and pressing Russian need for qualified command personnel is highlighted by the importation and promotion to flag status of the American John Paul Jones, whose only demonstrated command capabilities at the time of his hire were limited to highly publicized single ship operations. Jones's success or lack thereof as an admiral is still a matter for some debate, but his very presence created a serious strain with British officers in Russian service, the majority of whom regarded him as a pirate and a traitor.

With regards to enlisted personnel, the Russian Navy was made up entirely of Russians in the early years under Peter I. As the size of the Russian Navy increased, the Russian command was increasingly confronted with the unsatisfactory choices of drafting uneducated serfs lacking maritime backgrounds into the navy, or of hiring skilled foreign seamen to make up the shortfall and provide the experience and competence required. Both routes were taken, and Russian landsmen who had never seen the sea, were often forced to learn seamanship in the most stressful of circumstances, while experienced men from Scandinavia and elsewhere entered service with little or no knowledge of the language or customs of their shipmates and officers. The system seemed to work in practice with Swedish sailors fighting willingly alongside Russian sailors in the frequent wars between Russia and Sweden. At least one English officer in Russian service has written that he preferred Russian seamen to British because of their greater hardiness and willingness to accept hardship, as well as their courage in combat. This solution of hiring out seamen from amongst the seafaring ranks of one's potential enemies may have worked well in the Baltic, but the Black Sea was a different environment with a much more restricted manpower pool to draw from because of the impassable gulf between Orthodox Christianity and the Muslim populations to the south. The only readily available Christian resources available to the Black Sea fleet would have come from the Greeks and the other Christian ethnic minorities of the Black Sea region.

Russian Shipyards and Naval Bases

Russian shipyards were state owned and there was very limited contracting out for miscellaneous equipage. The use of private shipbuilders formed by groups of clergy and nobles and consisting of 61 *kumpanstva* (private companies) was originally mandated at the time of the formal creation of the Russian navy by the Duma on four November (14 November) 1696. These groups had been assigned responsibility for the construction of 80 warships at and around Voronezh and the experiment had been such a resounding disaster as to discourage the practice thereafter. The kumpanstvas as they were called were abolished in September 1700 due to lack of organization, corruption and infighting. After their abolition, all ships were built in state owned shipyards, with a single exception noted below. Because of skilled labour shortages in the government yards and the resultant unused capacity, there was always a limited degree of privately owned contractual shipbuilding permitted *within* the state owned shipyards, most particularly those in the Black Sea. Not surprisingly, perhaps, the ships built within government shipyards by private contractors were generally cheaper and of higher quality than the government-built ships.

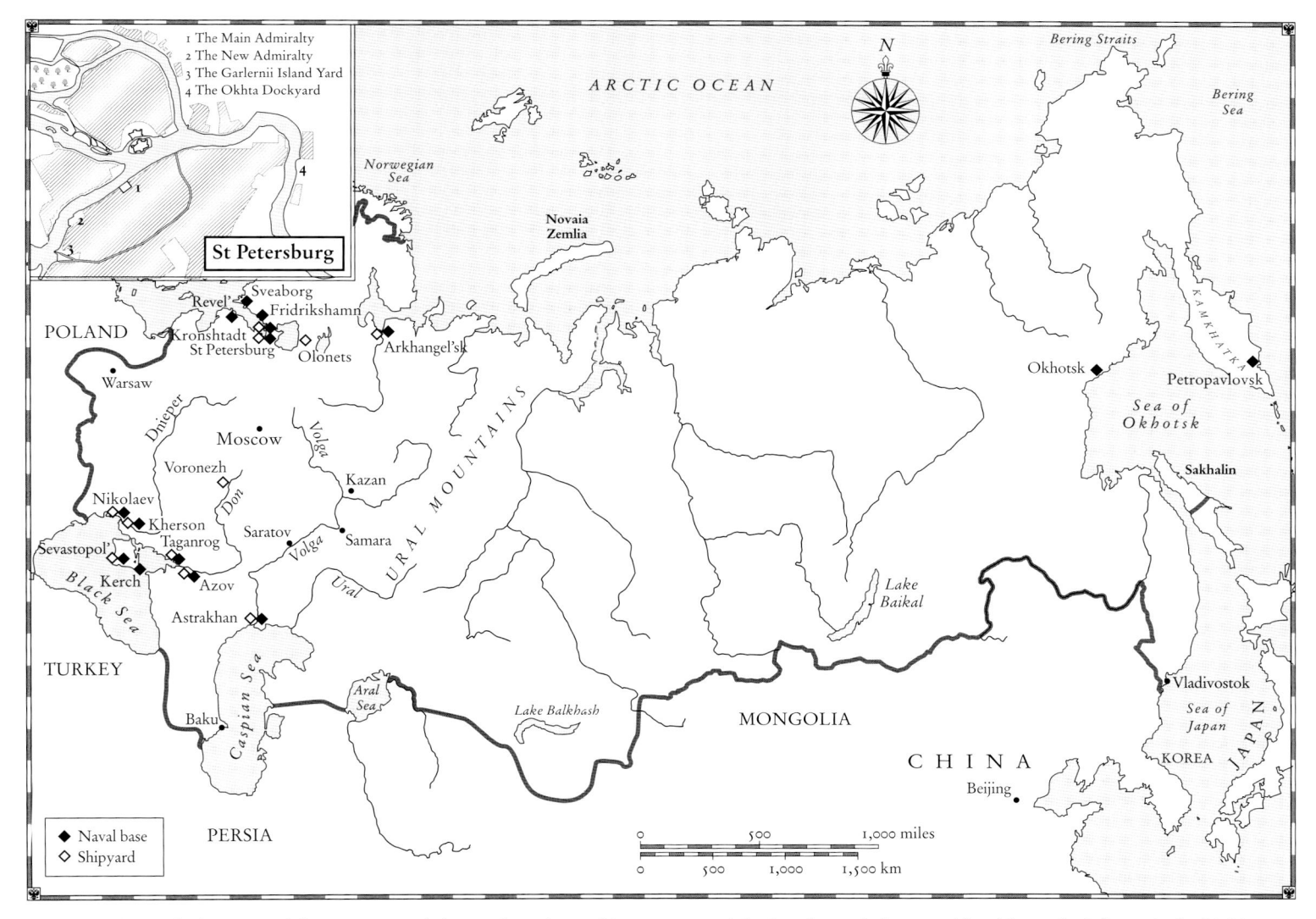

This map shows the location of the major naval shipyards and naval bases operated during the period covered by this work. Of note is the highly concentrated nature of the Russian facilities, a reflection of the geopolitical dilemma confronted by a developing and expanding nation seeking trading opportunities open to European nations and denied to land-locked Russia.

This painting representing Arkhangel'sk in its earliest years by Bonaventura Peeters the Elder gives an excellent idea of the bleak and forbidding nature of Russia's northernmost naval base and shipyard, an effect heightened by the makeshift buildings and the reindeer-drawn sleds on the shoreline. The fortress on the rise in the centre of the picture is Arkhangel'sk itself, the stone walls and six towers (not all visible) dominating the buildings and warehouses at the foot of the hill like a medieval castle. The fort was constructed between 1668 and 1684, but the shipyard was not opened until 1693.

Baltic fleet shipyards

Northern shipyards

Arkhangel'sk

Prior to the completion of St Petersburg on the Gulf of Finland in 1703, Russia's major commercial seaport to the West was Arkhangel'sk at the mouth of the Dvina River on the White Sea facing the bleakness of the Arctic Circle. The shipyard servicing Arkhangel'sk was the Solombala Yard located on the Solombala islands at the mouth of the North Dvina and opened in 1693. Arkhangel'sk was never fully eclipsed by the naval hub of St Petersburg as the major production centre for the Russian sailing navy and did not finally cease operation until 1859 with the launch of the paddle frigate *Solombala*.

Arkhangel'sk had significant advantages as a builder of sailing warships in spite of its wretched climate and its distance from central Russia. The northern larch and pine forests provided an abundant supply of cheap timber and the extensive river network flowing into the Dvina made its transportation to the shipyards easy and cheap. Meaningful price comparisons are difficult during this period, but the cost of the larch used for a Russian 74 in 1805 was worked out at £9,000–9,500 as compared to £48,000 for the cost of properly seasoned timber for a 74 built in England at the same time. Arkhangel'sk had the additional advantage of having ready access to abundant iron ore deposits in the nearby Ural Mountains for the production of ordnance and other warship equipage. The shipyard was also sufficiently remote from the Baltic area as to be free from the likelihood of conquest by land or blockade by sea and the production of warships could continue unabated regardless of unfavourable military events to the south.

Ships completed in the northern yards were only commissioned as warships at St Petersburg after a one to two month working up voyage around the entire extent of the Scandinavian peninsula and then northwards again across the entire length of the Baltic from the straits of Denmark to the naval bases of St Petersburg. This long, arduous, and occasionally dangerous voyage gave Russian commanders a unique two-fold opportunity to work up untrained groups of landsmen with no previous experience with the sea into reasonably competent seamen and also to reveal weaknesses and defects in their newly completed warships.

There was, of course, another side to the coin. Pine and larch were not well suited for use in sailing ships, being liable to rapid dry rot and deterioration in service. The British and other European naval powers turned to the use of pine only during periods of great desperation, and ships so constructed were only expected to have useful service lives of five to seven years. The very ease of transportation of timber by floating it down the Russian waterways leading to the Solombala Yards was in itself a major accelerant to the rapid deterioration of the timber employed by saturating it with moisture at the very point in its life when it was most in need of drying out and seasoning. Floating large quantities of green, newly cut timber on water and then immediately employing it in the construction of warships was the worst possible use of ship timber irrespective of the economic advantages of the process. A one-year seasoning period was specified before the timber was used in construction, but this guideline was not always adhered to, and could not suffice to undo the damage already done. It can only be said at this point that cheapness and ease of construction had a greater priority for the Russia sailing navy than long life and durability in service. The ships produced were still effective warships during their abbreviated service lives and the wisdom of this policy must remain a matter for debate. The situation improved considerably after the accession of Nicholas I with the replacement of the waterborne transportation system by the slower and more expensive method of transportation by road and by rafting. This, in turn, had to await further emergence of Russia from a primitive medieval economic system into one more closely in step with modern European developments.

A final drawback to the use of Arkhangel'sk as a builder of sailing warships lay in the fact that completed ships could only make the long journey to St Petersburg if they were able to leave Arkhangel'sk during a one to three month window early in the season and this, in turn, might be further constricted by a late spring thaw. If the new ships missed the window for departure, they were left to deteriorate through the stresses of yet another arctic winter with increased probabilities of separation of seams and leaking when the voyage became possible in the ensuing year.

The long 2,600-mile voyage from Arkhangel'sk to St Petersburg and the exposure of untried ships early on to severe weather conditions even during summer months may have been beneficial with respect to the working up untrained crews and for uncovering defects in construction, but it was also something of a curse, with warships constructed of poorly prepared materials being subjected to unusually severe hull stresses at the very beginning of their service lives. In addition, the transit through the narrow Straits of Denmark and then along the coast of Sweden was simply not a viable option during wartime at the very time when new construction was most urgently required.

In spite of all of the drawbacks to the use of Arkhangel'sk as a construction centre, some 247 major warships were completed by the Solombala Yards between 1702 and 1855 as against the smaller total of 171 by the more strategically located Main and New Admiralty Yards at St Petersburg between 1706 and 1844 (or 202 if allowance is made to include ships built at Kronshtadt and Okhta). This total for Arkhangel'sk included 64 standard 74s, 78 66s, 21 54s and 84 frigates of all sizes. These figures, both for Arkhangel'sk and the Baltic shipyards, are of course only close approximations and subject to debate on numerous counts. Nevertheless the pattern is clear, Arkhangel'sk built more and smaller ships in all categories while St Petersburg built fewer and larger warships.

No other nation during the sailing ship era was faced with conditions approaching those imposed by this remarkable combination of poor construction materials and long transit from point of production to point of utilization. Arkhangel'sk was unique.

Bykovskaya Yard
The Bykovskaya shipyard located at Byk on the northern Dvina in the vicinity of Arkhangel'sk was the only private shipyard of significance in Russia that was contracted to build warships. Founded in 1734 by a private merchant N. S. Krylov, Bykovskaya was primarily a builder of merchant and fishing vessels but also built a small number of frigates and auxiliary vessels. The yard was finally closed in 1847.

Shipyards located in the St Petersburg Area

This section includes those yards built in and around St Petersburg including Lake Ladoga in the early years and extends to include a complex of shipyards built along the Neva River as well as the island fortress of Kronshtadt outside of St Petersburg. Some of these yards were abandoned at the end of age of sail while others continued in use, sometimes in different forms and under different names, to the present.

Syass'kaya
A short-lived shipyard built in the mouth of the Syas' River which enters Lake Ladoga from the east. Four small frigates were built there between 1702 and 1704.

Lodeynoe Pole (Olonetskaya)
The earliest shipyard in the area, Olonetskaya, or Olonets as she was also called, was built inland on the Svir River which enters Lake Ladoga to the northeast of the future site of St Petersburg. The town serving the shipyard came to be known as Lodeynoe Pole (Boat Field) and the shipyard was known as Olonetskaya until renamed Lodeynopol'skaya Yard in 1785. Completed ships had to cross Lake Ladoga and proceed up the Neva to reach the sea. Between 1703 and 1711, Olonetskaya completed two 52-gun ships, ten snows, two bombs and various other smaller craft. Throughout the eighteenth century, the yard continued to build galleys and small craft. Between 1806 and 1820, an additional twenty additional ships were constructed there including two small frigates. The shipyard formally closed in 1849.

St Petersburg Main Admiralty Yards
The site of the new Russian capital of St Petersburg in 1703 was chosen by Peter I with an eye on its strategic positioning at the head of the Gulf of Finland, with its excellent defensive potentialities and its potential for controlling the entire Baltic to the south. The naval shipyards on the Neva River had access to Russian river waterways for the transportation of timber from

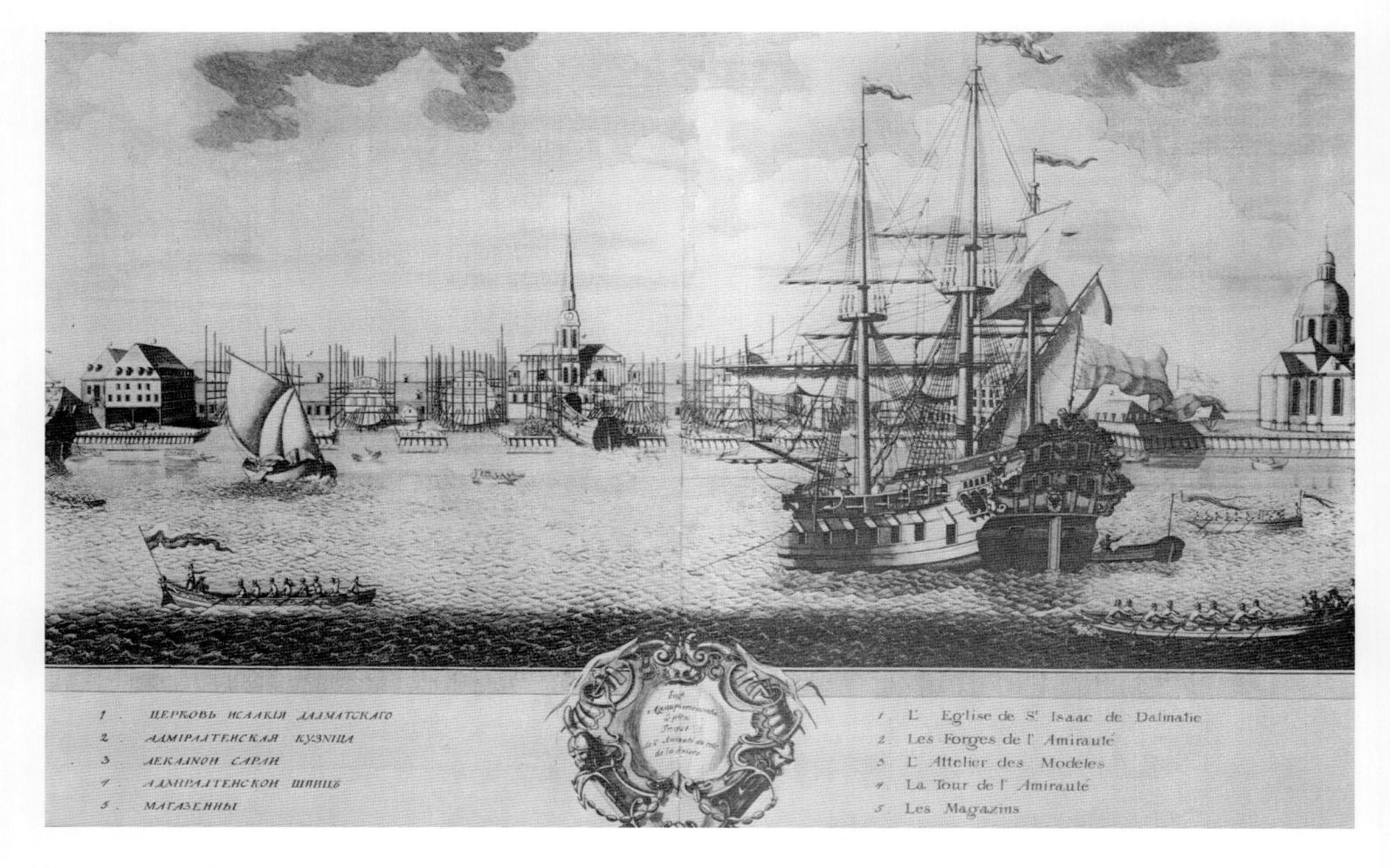

A representation of St Petersburg in 1716 by the contemporary architect Marcelius (no first initial available), showing the administrative and logistical hub of the Baltic fleet in its early years. The view is taken from the banks of the Neva looking across towards the centre of the city, with an unidentified warship anchored to the right and various small craft going about their business on the river. Visible on the opposite bank are the building slips, with a launching under way just beneath the towers of the Admiralty looming in the distance. To the right is the Church of St Isaac of Dalmatia showing the typical features of a Russian Orthodox church. The buildings scattered along the waterfront include the workshops of ship designers, the iron works (smithies) of the navy and the magazines of the fleet.

the interior comparable to that of the Arkhangel'sk shipyards along with the added advantage of readily available supplies of high quality Kazan' oak along with abundant supplies of larch. Fewer warships were completed in the shipyards around St Petersburg than those at Arkhangel'sk, but St Petersburg was entrusted with the honour of constructing the great majority of the Baltic fleet's prestigious First and Second Rates as well as the more important of the heavy frigates. It seems likely that this division of labour between the two yards was a result of the greater durability and life spans that could be hoped for from ships built of higher quality timber than was available to the northern yard, especially when spared the trials of the long transit from Arkhangel'sk. How successful this practice was in actuality in extending the service lives of the most highly valued capital ships and frigates will be a matter for further discussion.

St Petersburg was very nearly as long-lived as its northern compatriot and rival, with the main admiralty yards continuing to build major sailing warships for the Russian Navy from their founding in 1706 to 1844. The total production of both the St Petersburg Main Admiralty and New Admiralty yards taken together (but excluding Okhta and Kronshtadt) was 21 100-gun ships, 30 80-gun ships, 20 70-gun ships, 33 64/66-gun ships, 14 52-gun ships and 53 frigates of all categories.

Galley Yard

Located slightly downriver from the Main Admiralty Yards, the Galley Yard was primarily involved in the production of galleys and other oared craft until it converted to the New Admiralty Yard in 1800 (see below).

Galernyy Island Yards

This site is referred to as Galernyy Ostrovok (Gallerny Island in Russian) throughout the data section. The site was founded in 1719 and built small galleys and sailing ships including 50 Crimean War gunboats, before beginning to construct larger craft from 1858. It was merged with the New Admiralty Yards in 1908.

RUSSIAN SHIPYARDS AND NAVAL BASES

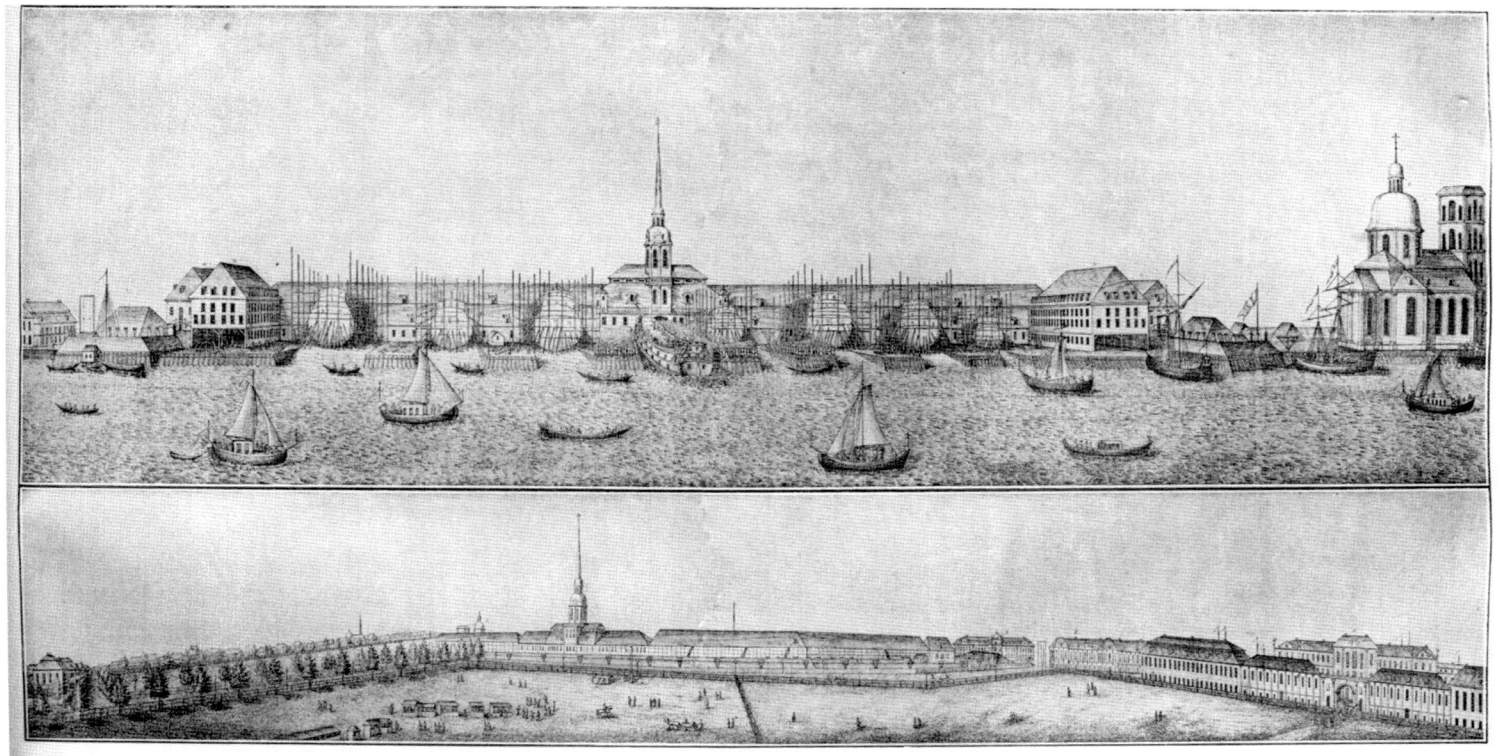

Видъ С.-Петербургскаго адмиралтейства въ 1725 году.
(По рисункамъ того времени Марселиса).

This drawing of St Petersburg in 1725 at the death of its founder Peter I should be compared with that from 1716. Both show the spire of the Admiralty dominating the skyline, but this drawing shows the impressive building from two perspectives. The cleared space in the lower picture is devoted to the drilling and housing of the Russian army and was as much a part of the underpinnings of Russian power as the fleet under construction in the upper. Both drawings show a line of battle ship being launched from the slip immediately below the Admiralty tower, an indication that this artist knew of and was influenced by the 1716 representation. Details are hard to come by, but an observant eye can note that the building slips in the 1725 drawing are occupied by larger warships than those seen the 1716 drawing – a sign of the significant growth in ship size in a single decade.

A portion of a lithograph by K. P. Beggrov showing the Admiralty Yard at St Petersburg in the 1820s. Here we see workers at work on a yard in a scene of orderly activity.

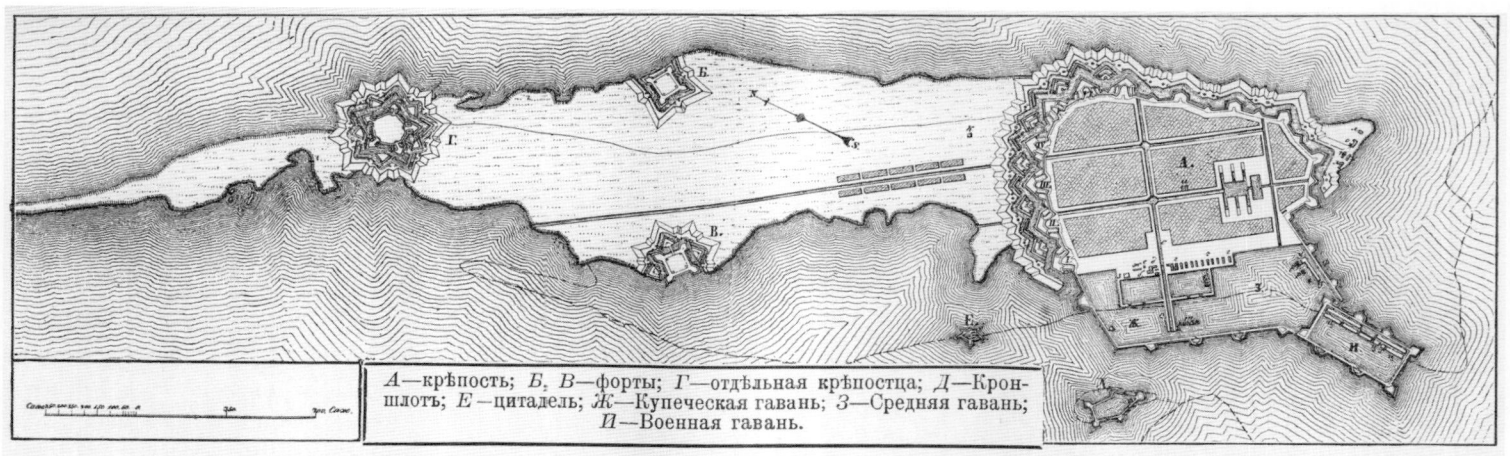

Two plans of the naval base of Kronshtadt completed on Kotlin Island in 1713. The top view depicts the base in 1721 as planned by Peter I. The lower shows the changes made by 1741–3. Both reveal the heavy fortifications that guaranteed its dual status as both the guardian of the Russian capital at St Petersburg and as the major naval base for the Baltic fleet. No serious assault on St Petersburg would have been possible without first reducing this fortress, and the guns of Kronshtadt retained their deterrent value throughout the course of the Napoleonic Wars – and long after.

Kronshtadt

The main naval base for the Russian Baltic fleet was created in 1713 located on the Kotlin Island protecting the approaches to St Petersburg. Both a fortress and a naval base, Kronshtadt was primarily involved with major repairs. Construction activity was largely limited to important larger ships and to specialized prototypes because of the difficulty involved in transporting quantities of timber to the island. With the lonely exception of *Sviatoi Pavel* 86 of 1753, the production of major warships at Kronshtadt began in 1771 with the laying down of the 10-gun bomb *Iupiter* and continued through 1813 with the launching of the 100-gun *Rostislav*. Twenty-two warships ranging in size from First Rates to cutters were constructed there between 1753 and 1813 including four First Rates, one 80, one 66, eight rowing frigates and eight smaller ships.

With the great dry dock facility begun at the order of Peter I and completed in 1752, along with its vast complex of workshops, Kronshtadt has remained the main arsenal, repair and maintenance base for the Russian Baltic fleet to the present day. In 1857 it was determined that Kronshtadt was no longer suitably placed to act as an operational centre for offensive fleet operations. Plans were accordingly made to move fleet operations and the Admiralty headquarters to Rogervik, while retaining Kronshtadt as the armoury and repair centre of the Baltic fleet. Although financial constraints prevented the fulfilment of this project, the harbours serving Kronshtadt were deepened over several years beginning in 1859. A second attempt at providing a more forward operating base for the fleet was undertaken in the 1880s at Libava (now Lithuanian Liepaia), but these were abandoned in their turn in favour of Revel' in 1912.

Okhta Yards

Also known as Okhtenskaya, this yard was located on the Okhta River, a branch of the Neva in the vicinity of St

Petersburg. Builder of small vessels between 1781 and 1794. Between 1810 and 1862, Okhta became a major shipyard, completing eight 74s, nine heavy frigates and 49 smaller ships.

New Admiralty

The New Admiralty yards in St Petersburg were built on the Neva on the site of the former Galley Yard in the final year of the Emperor Paul's short and tragic reign in 1800; 25 major sailing warships were built there between 1806 and 1866, including two First Rates, one completed as a steamship, twelve 80-gun ships, four 74s and three 44-gun heavy frigates. An additional four wooden screw and paddle cruising ships were also completed there between 1844 and 1866. New Admiralty continued to produce iron and steel hulled warships until 1908 when it merged with the Galernyy Island yard.

Sea of Azov Shipyards

With the exception of a single 52-gun ship, *Gerkules*, which was built on the Dnieper, all of the ships built for the short-lived Sea of Azov fleet were constructed in small shipyards situated on the Don in the following order from north to south: Stupino, Ramon, Chertovitskaya wharf, Voronezh, Chizhevka, Tavrov, Korotoyak, Pavlovsk, Khoper and Panshin. The major shipyard, Voronezh, was located in a shallow water tributary of the Don and was initially chosen by the Admiralty for the developing fleet because of its relative accessibility from Moscow, the availability of quantities of timber in the area and the thought that the Don would provide more ready access to the Sea of Azov, some 300 miles to the south, than proved to be the case. Edward Phillips has pointed out that Voronezh was chosen in part because it was in settled Russian territory and hopefully secure from attack, while the provisionally Russian territory to the south was not. This supposed immunity proved to be illusory in 1711 when a revolt by the Crimean Tatars, fomented by Turkey, so threatened Voronezh that urgent attempts were made to relocate the built and building units southward to Azov – attempts that were largely unsuccessful due to navigational problems in attempting to move large seagoing ships across sandbars and shallows. The Admiralty and dockyards had already been transferred to the more advantageously located Tavrov at the confluence of the Voronezh and Don rivers in 1705. Because of its shallow water conditions and its apparent vulnerability to attack, Voronezh had no future as a shipyard and ceased operation after 1711, while Tavrov continued in operation until 1769. During its short life from 1694 through 1711, the yard at Voronezh produced the bulk of the Azov navy, completing a respectable total of one 80, four 70s, nine 60/66s, three 44/46s, thirteen 34/36s and five smaller ships including two galleasses. Most of these ships never reached the open sea and proved to have been a badly thought out misallocation of resources on the part of Peter I.

The only other shipyard to produce significant numbers of ships, Stupino, was also located on the Voronezh River and produced a total of eight 44s and two 36s in 1699. Unfortunately, all ten ships were poorly constructed and failed to see any active service, putting paid to Stupino's future as a shipbuilder. The other shipyards constructed along the Don were all limited from one to three warships apiece.

Black Sea Shipyards

Ships built for the Black Sea fleet were constructed of oak and larch, with oak being generally but not entirely favoured for larger ships of 74 guns and up, while larch was reserved for ships of 66 guns on down. The available oak was more abundant and cheaper than the highly valued Kazan' and Kurlandia oak used by the St Petersburg yards, but it was also of poorer quality. Black Sea fleet ships were subject to problems of rapid deterioration as were the Baltic fleet ships, but the root causes were rather different, being more clearly the result of a lack of ongoing maintenance and supportive infrastructure than of the harsh weather conditions and poor quality timber that led to deterioration in the Baltic. Prior to the accession of Nicholas I and the arrival of the aggressive and capable Admiral Lazarev, no effort was made to provide for the construction of the necessary infrastructure for ongoing ship maintenance. There were no dockyards in the Black Sea prior to 1831 in spite of authorization for their construction having been first signed off on by Alexander I in 1818. Ships were only able to be careened and scraped every two to three years and the predictable result was an average service life of six to seven years. With the reforms instituted by Lazarev and backed by Nicholas I, the material state of the Black Sea fleet improved significantly.

Nikolaev Admiralty Shipyards

Located at the juncture of the Ingul and But rivers and the seat of the Black Sea Admiralty, the Nikolaev shipyard was the longest established and most productive of the Black Sea shipyards. Between 1788 and 1858, 74 major warships were completed at Nikolaev, including eight First Rates of 110 to 135 guns, 20 84s, three 74s, 17 heavy frigates and 26 smaller vessels.

Kherson Shipyard

The only Black Sea builder of line of battle ships besides Nikolaev, Kherson was established as a shipyard in 1781, seven years before Nikolaev. She was quite close geographically to the larger shipyard, being located at the mouth of the Dniepr just to the east. Although Kherson built 37 line of battle ships to Nikolaev's 31, the bulk of her production was comprised of smaller ships in the 66- to 74-gun range, all built before 1825; while Nikolaev built both larger and later, just getting into her stride in the 1820s as Kherson was being phased out. Kherson ceased operation in 1827 after completing six 110-gun First Rates, one 80, twenty 74s, ten 66s, six heavy and nine standard frigates, as well as ten smaller ships.

Sevastopol' Admiralty Shipyard

Located on the southern bay of the city of Sevastopol', this prominent shipyard was primarily employed in repair and

Supporting infrastructure had always been the Achilles heel of the Black Sea fleet, due in large part to its late development as a permanent organization towards the end of the eighteenth century. The first drydock was not completed until 1831. These are the New Sevastopol' docks, opened in the closing years of the Black Sea fleet, with work under way on a three-decker to give perspective on the great size of the dry docks as depicted by L. O. Premazzi in 1850.

maintenance from its opening in 1783 through 1851. Ships were also built there intermittently between 1813 and 1851, with the largest being four 36–60-gun frigates, between 1828 and 1845.

Gnilotonskaya Shipyard
Gnilotonskaya, literally 'rotten channel', was a small shipyard located at the mouth of the Don on a small tributary, Gnilaya Tonya. Besides completing 13 ships in the 26- to 40-gun range she also built store ships and mortar ships between 1778 and 1786.

Novokhoperskaya Shipyard
Novokhoperskaya was located at the town of Novokhopersk on the Khoper. The ships built were all originally commissioned as Sea of Azov ships. Thirteen ships, all called frigates and carrying between 18 and 58 guns were completed between 1771 and 1779.

Rogozhskaya Shipyard
The village of Rogozhskie Khutora was located at the mouth of the Don. Six important heavy frigates, all of the *PyotrApostol* class, were completed there between 1788 and 1791.

Spasskoe Admiralty Shipyard
Spasskoe Admiralty was located on the Yuzhnyy River, a tributary of the Southern Bug at Nikolaev. Ships of all classes, including three transports, were built there between 1825 and 1880.

Russian Naval Ordnance 1700–1860

Russian warships were unique among European sailing navies in employing three distinctive types of ordnance, cannon of the traditional pattern, carronades for close range use against hulls and personnel, and edinorogs as incendiary weapons. Edinorogs are dealt with first, not because of their greater importance, but because English speaking readers are most likely to lack any familiarity with the type.

Edinorogs

Russian naval artillery differed from French and British ordnance in one important respect, the early development and use aboard ships of small numbers of long-barrelled howitzers firing both explosive and solid shot. *Edinorog* translates into English as 'unicorn' and into French as 'licorne'. English-speaking readers may be more familiar with the term 'licorne' but we are retaining the Russian usage here because it became the official designation within Russia. Edinorogs were developed by Field Marshal Shulavo, Chief of Ordnance, and introduced into the Russian army in 1757 and the Russian navy in 1767. They came to be called 'unicorns' because these mythical animals were displayed on his family coat of arms and stamped or cast on all Russian edinorogs thereafter. To our knowledge, edinorogs were limited in their use to the Russian army and navy save only for a brief period in the nineteenth century when they were also manufactured for the Austrian army.

Edinorogs had conical gun chambers and, as a result, were easy to load and could maintain a rate of fire of three to four rounds per minute with a range of 2–2½ miles with a high degree of accuracy for the period. More flexible than standard artillery, they could fire solid shot, grapeshot, bombs or carcasses. Edinorogs began to equip Russian warships in very limited numbers from 1769 on. Their use against both the Turks and Swedes in the wars of the 1770s, 1780s and 1790s produced useful, if debatable, results as well as howls of protest from the Swedes after Gogland, who charged that their opponents were violating the laws of civilized warfare with these barbaric and un-Christian weapons. A source of continuing controversy, they were regarded by their opponents as being of limited value, doubtful reliability, and equally dangerous to friend and foe in battle. Edinorogs were generally mounted on line of battle ships only during time of war, with one or two pairs mounted on each gun deck replacing long guns of approximately equal calibre. Contrary to what one might expect, these guns were not mounted at either the bow or the stern. Instead they were placed amidships. Their use was formally discontinued for a time with the Gun Establishment of 1805, but they were reintroduced in 1826 under Nicholas I and continued in service through the end of sail in 1860.

Most edinorogs fired hollow-core explosive ordnance as well as heavier solid ordnance. The guns were rated in terms of 'poods' rather than pounds and their effectiveness in combat is difficult to compare with more traditional long guns. A Russian 'pood' was a traditional commercial measure of weight consisting of 40 Russian 'trade pounds'. The earliest 1767 model 1-pood guns had a barrel diameter of 7.2 inches and actually fired a 40-pound explosive (bomb) shell, or a 48-pound solid shot, although the early models were too fragile to handle the solid ordnance reliably. These guns were fragile in service and had fearsome recoils. The improved version, introduced in 1780, moved up to 7.7 inches diameter and fired a 44-pound bomb shell and a much heavier 63-pound solid shot. To confuse matters for the uninitiated, these larger guns continued to be

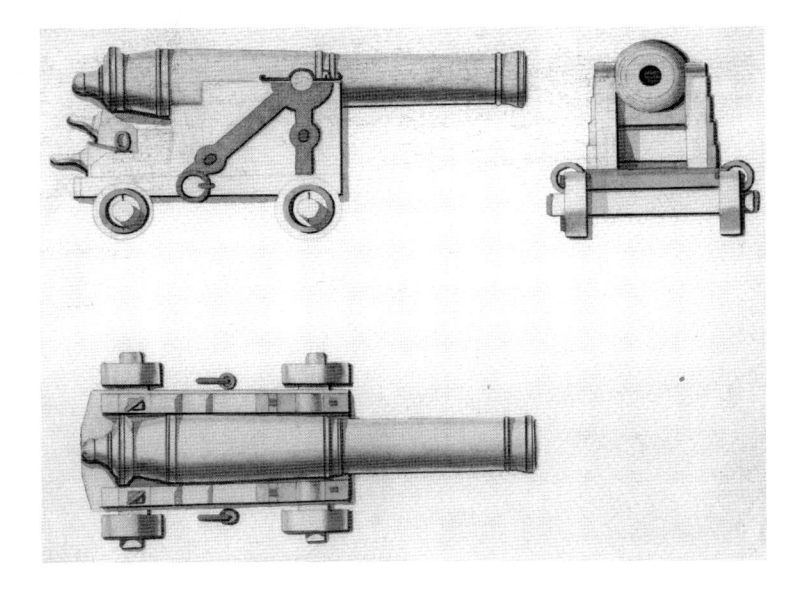

A three-view drawing of a ½-pood edinorog (1780 model) taken from A. S. Katasanov's Album *(1801). The heavily built gun carriage gives evidence of one of the edinorog's primary characteristics – and drawbacks – its fearsome recoil. A ½-pood edinorog would have had a 6.1 in bore and would have fired either a 29 lb (Russian trade pound) solid ball very roughly equivalent to a British 24pdr, or a 22 lb (19.8 pounds British) explosive shell at a greater range and with greater accuracy than its British equivalent, which of course, could not fire explosive ammunition.*

Edinorogs were unique to the Russian army and navy. Aboard ship, they were generally mounted two per gun deck, alongside their nearest conventional cannon equivalents – ½-pood guns alongside Russian 24pdrs and one pood guns alongside 36pdrs.

designated as '1-pood guns'. To confuse matters still further, the Russian 'trade pound' was the traditional pound in use in Russia and weighed 409.5 grams metric and not the 'artillery pound' of 490 grams introduced by Peter I, and in use for both army and navy guns. This was almost precisely equivalent to the French 'pound' of 489.5 grams, but the similarity was entirely fortuitous. To complicate matters still further, edinorogs were not described in terms of the weight of *solid* ordnance fired by the gun as was the case with standard naval artillery, but by the much lighter weight of the hollow-core explosive ordnance. This made sense when the weapon was introduced as the *raison d'être* for the new weapon was the incendiary ordnance and not the solid shot which was of secondary importance. Using poods in place of pounds also made sense because the charges fired by the first weapons fitted neatly into 40 (trade) pound packages. The improved 1-pood guns introduced in 1780 fired hollow shells weighing 44 trade pounds, which converts into 39.6 English pounds or 36.77 artillery pounds; while 1-pood solid shot weighed 63 trade pounds, which converts into 56.7 English pounds and 52.5 artillery pounds. Russian students are quite familiar with this duality, and are frequently given to using one or both measures without clearly indicating which system is in use. Unless otherwise indicated, all references to edinorogs will be made in terms of trade pounds.

Edinorogs were eventually developed in a wide variety of weights, from ¼ pood to 1 pood, with even larger guns being used ashore. Edinorog bombs were spherical hollow devices and should not be confused with more advanced ordnance firing explosive cylindrical shells of the type developed in the 1820s in France.

Cannon, carronades and gunnades

Early Russian iron naval ordnance cast out of iron was said to have been significantly heavier than British cannon of the period, but their quality improved steadily throughout the eighteenth century. During much of the eighteenth century, British foundries were called upon to cast heavier guns in the 30–36pdr range for Russian ships and this may reflect developmental problems in the casting of Russian ordnance of larger calibres, not unlike those being experienced by more technologically advanced countries. In 1772, for example, a consignment of 30pdrs was ordered from Scotland, with the help of Admiral Knowles. Of a total of 267 guns delivered (many of them British 32pdrs instead of the contracted-for 30pdrs!), only 190 were found acceptable by the Russians and approximately 50 guns exploded during proof testing. No comprehensive comparison between quality and reliability of Russian and Western ordnance has been made to our knowledge; but Russian iron ordnance was consistently relatively cheaper to manufacture than comparable Western ordnance, due in part to the difference in the cost of labour as well as to the cheap and abundant supplies of iron ore in the Ural Mountains.

Brass ordnance was frequently specified for prestige warships, but its use declined throughout the century in Russia, as it did elsewhere because of its expense and its tendency to deform when overheated in combat. As late as the 1790s, the prestige value of brass was such that its use was specified for the armament of Admiral Ushakov's flagship and for the most prestigious of the Black Sea heavy frigates.

Carronades were tentatively introduced to the Russian Navy in 1787. Their shipboard use followed the British pattern, with 24pdr carronades being mounted in combination with long 6- and 8pdr guns on the upper works of line of battle ships and frigates, and with many, if not most, of the smaller Russian brigs carrying all carronade batteries.

The Russo-Swedish War of 1789–92 had an unexpectedly significant influence upon the development of Russian naval ordnance. Besides mandating the (temporary) abandonment of edinorogs, the Establishment of 1805 also called for the replacement of long guns of the traditional sort by shorter guns manufactured on the Swedish pattern. These guns required smaller gun crews, fired more rapidly and weighed less than longer guns of the same calibre. Engagements in the confined waters of Baltic and the Black Sea tended to be at short ranges, and the use of the shorter guns with more limited ranges did not carry the same potential dangers that they might have in the more open waters of the North Atlantic and the Mediterranean.

Uniform-calibre guns were introduced as the standard armament for frigates and line of battle ships in the Black Sea fleet in the mid-1830s. Admiral Lazarev was responsible for this transformation, which followed upon similar developments in the British and American navies. Lazarev was a close student of British developments in this and other areas. Acceptance of uniform-calibre armament was more tentative in the Baltic, where the only perceived threat was the somnolent Swedish Navy. One Baltic ship of the line (*Rossiia* 120) was given a uniform armament of massive 48pdrs, a second (*Ne Tron' Menia* 84) received 36pdrs and two others (*Krasnoi* and *Berezino*) received all-30pdr armaments. The bulk of the Baltic battle fleet retained its mixed batteries.

One final Russian innovation was the 'guns-carronade' – to use the Russian term. The English term would be 'gunnade' and will be used hereafter. This ordnance was developed in Russia in the 1830s in response to the increase in battle ranges. They were intended to replace carronades, but in most cases supplemented them aboard ships, most probably because of production and distribution difficulties. Gunnades came in three calibres, 18-, 24- and 36- and all three were 12¼ calibres in length. Because of their similarity to the British intermediate cannon of the period, they were often referred to as 'Russian Congreves'.

The reader is again reminded that Russian naval ordnance was described in terms of 'artillery pounds' weighing 490 grams, or almost exactly the same amount as French ordnance. In practice, this meant that Russian 30pdrs were the equivalent of British 33pdrs, which, of course, did not actually exist, and Russian 36pdrs were equivalent to equally non-existent British 39pdrs.

Shell guns

Shell guns were first introduced experimentally into the Russian navy in 1838 and were in general use as supplements to more traditional types of ordnance by the late 1840s. As was the case with edinorogs, they were described most commonly by the approximate weight of their shells in poods rather than by their barrel diameter in terms of feet and inches. Smoothbore shell guns and edinorogs were similar in concept in that they both could fire spherical hollowbore ammunition containing explosive material. Edinorogs were representative of a much earlier technology, had tapered chambers, and could readily use both solid and hollow-core ammunition (see above). In Russian service, the two terms were largely interchangeable and this can cause confusion. The dividing point between 'true' edinorogs and 'true' shell guns appears to have been with 68-pounder guns, which should always be regarded as shell guns. 60-pounder edinorogs are sometimes described as 'shell guns', but they were actually 1830 model edinorogs on the same pattern as the traditional eighteenth century weapons – but more lightly constructed. Russian technology lagged in this area and most shell guns in service were copies of British and French models.

Russian naval ordnance tables

The following tables give the basic characteristics of Russian naval ordnance in use to 1860. Gun calibre is always expressed in Russian artillery pounds. Specific references to shot weight is always expressed in trade pounds.

Edinorogs
The following table gives the basic characteristics of Russian naval edinorogs in use from 1767 to 1860. (All pounds are trade pounds.)

1-pood 1767
   7.2 in cal. 48 pound (solid shot) 40 pound (bombs)
1-pood 1780
   7.69 in 170 poods 14.31 cal. 63 pound (solid shot) 44 pound (bombs)
1-pood 1830
   7.69 in 164 poods 14.31 cal. 63 pound (solid shot) 44 pound (bombs)
½-pood 1780
   6.1 in 14.5 cal. 88 poods 29 pound (solid shot) 22 pound (bombs)
¼-pood (landing)
   4.8 in 5.62 cal. 22¼ poods 9 pound (solid shot) 6.2 pound (bombs)

Data for early Russian naval guns (1713–16)
(Data for the following tables is from '*Materials for History of Russian Navy*', vol. III):

Guns in 1713
24pdrs	18 calibres	155 poods weight
18pdrs	19.5 calibres	177 poods weight
12pdrs	20 calibres	80 poods weight
8pdrs	20 calibres	not known

(*Note:* Readers interested in comparing the weights of Russian guns and gun carriages to British ordnance may convert poods into hundredweights by multiplying the former by .322.)

Weights of Russian guns cast in 1715
24pdrs	146 poods weight
18pdrs	109 poods weight
12pdrs	76 poods weight
8pdrs	58 poods weight
6pdrs	38 poods weight

Guns in December 1716
30pdrs	18 calibres
24pdrs	19 calibres
18pdrs	20 calibres
12pdrs	21 calibres
8pdrs	23 calibres
6pdrs	23 calibres
4pdrs	22 calibres

Russian brass naval guns at the time of Peter I and Empress Ann (1720–40):
36pdrs	252 poods weight
30pdrs	210 poods weight
18pdrs	126 poods weight
12pdrs	90 poods weight
8pdrs	56 poods weight
6pdrs	54 poods weight

Data for Russian naval guns from the late eighteenth century to 1812:

36pdr long (1786)
   6.87 in   197.75 poods gun wt   38 poods carriage weight
36pdr short (1804, 1807)
   —   171 poods gun wt
30pdr long (1786)
   6.46 in   174.75 poods gun wt   33 poods carriage weight
24pdr long (1786)
   6.00 in   149 poods gun wt   28 poods carriage weight
24pdr short (1804, 1807)
   5.95 in   120 poods gun wt   27.25 poods carriage weight
24pdr frigate (1786)
   —   128 poods gun wt   27.25 poods carriage weight
18pdr long (1786)
   5.46 in   109.75 poods gun wt   22.1 poods carriage weight
18pdr short (1804, 1807)
   5.41 in   88 poods gun wt   21.5 poods carriage weight
12pdr long (1786)
   4.76 in   77.25 poods gun wt   19.25 poods carriage weight
8pdr long (1786)
   4.16 in   53.5 poods gun wt   12.7 poods carriage weight
6pdr (1786)
   3.78 in   41 poods gun wt   11.2 poods carriage weight
3pdr (1794)
   3.00 in   15 poods gun wt   7 poods carriage weight

Data from *Pamyatnaya Knizhka Morskogo Vedomstva (Aide-Memoire of Navy Office)* for 1859 (St Petersburg 1859)

The following small cannons were also carried aboard ships under the Establishment of 1805:

8pdr carronade, 14.5 poods
8pdr brass mortar, 1.5 pood

(*Notes:* The introduction of 'short' guns for weapons in the 18–24pdr range reflects Swedish influence. Note also the considerable savings in weight of the shorter guns. Figures are not available for the short-barrelled 30pdrs.)

Data for Russian nineteenth-century naval ordnance

The data is from Lieutenant Ilyin, *Nauka Morskoy Artillerii* (Science of Naval Gunnery), St Petersburg, 1846 and *Pamyatnaya Knizhka Morskogo Vedomstva (Aide-memoire of Navy Office)* 1869. All guns in the 1848–58 and 1856 groups are from the *Aide-memoire* and are arranged in order of decreasing barrel length. The exact calibre of these guns is unfortunately not available.

The data is given as:
Calibre (artillery pounds, year in parentheses when available)
Muzzle diameter (inches)
Barrel length (in calibres)
Weight without carriage (Russian poods)
Weight of solid shot (trade pounds)

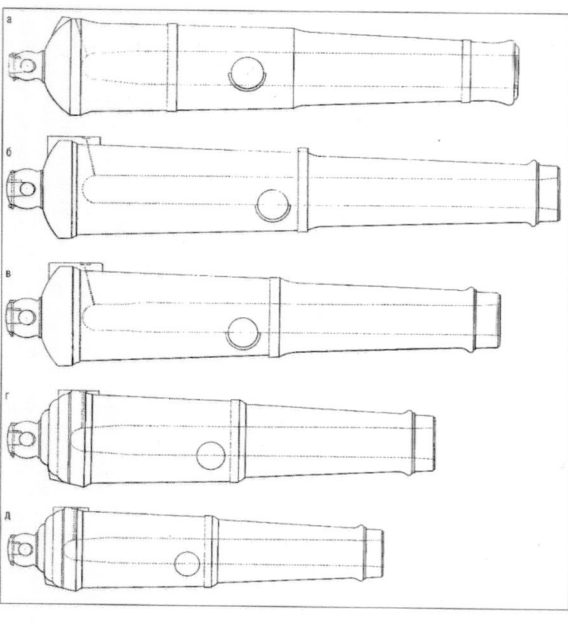

This cross-section of the guns carried aboard the 120-gun Dvenadtsat' Apostolov give an excellent picture of the range of armament carried by Russian line of battle ships under Nicholas I. The massive 68pdr shell guns are actually shorter than the secondary 36pdr long guns just below them – shorter but heavier and with very different ballistic characteristics.

68pdr long
   8 in   — cal.   301 poods gun wt
68pdr short
   8 in   — cal.   195 poods gun wt
60pdr long
   7.7 in   — cal.   300 poods gun wt
60pdr long
   7.7 in   — cal.   196 poods gun wt
Note: Both 60- and 68pdr marks listed above were capable of firing both solid shot and shells.

48pdr long (1836)
   7.7 in   16 cal.   184.20 poods gun wt
48pdr short (1812)
   7.7 in   14 cal.   163 poods gun wt (36pdr bored up)
48pdr demi-gun (1836)
   7.7 in   12.16 cal.   160 poods gun wt
36pdr long (1786)
   6.87 in   16 cal.   197.30 poods gun wt
36pdr long (1833)
   6.81 in   16 cal.   194.20 poods gun wt
36pdr short (1804,1807)
   6.81 in   14 cal.   171 poods gun wt
36pdr
   6.8 in   — cal.   134 poods gun wt (24pdr bored up)
36pdr gunnade (1836–41)
   6.8 in   12.25 cal.   142.20 poods gun wt (Russian Congreves)
36pdr (1848–58)
   6.86 in   — cal.   196 poods gun wt
36pdr (1848–58)
   6.86 in   — cal.   160 poods gun wt
36pdr (1848–58)
   6.86 in   — cal.   128 poods gun wt
36pdr (1848–58)
   6.86 in   — cal.   112–113 poods gun wt
36pdr (1848–58)
   6.86 in   — cal.   90 poods gun wt
30pdr long (1786)
   6.46 in   17 cal.   173.30 poods gun wt
30pdr chambered (1841)
   6.45 in   14.25 cal.   128 poods gun wt
30pdr chambered (1844)
   6.45 in   14.25 cal.   132 poods gun wt
30pdr (1856)
   6.45 in   — cal.   190 poods gun wt
30pdr (1856)
   6.45 in   — cal.   150 poods gun wt
30pdr (1856)
   6.45 in   — cal.   120 poods gun wt
30pdr (1856)
   6.45 in   — cal.   78 poods gun wt
24pdr long (1786)
   6 in   18 cal.   149 poods gun wt
24pdr long (1833)
   5.95 in   18 cal.   140.20 poods gun wt

RUSSIAN NAVAL ORDNANCE 1700–1860

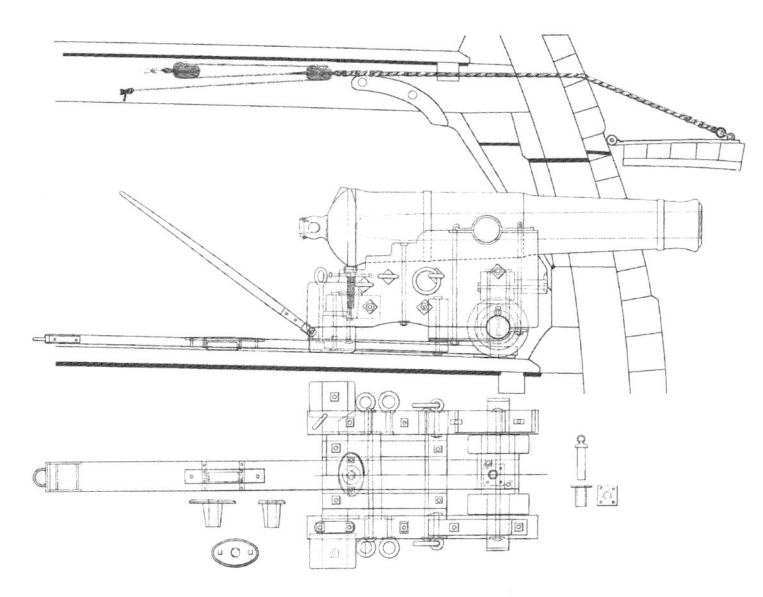

A detailed cross-section and 68-pdr on carriage of Dvenadtsat' Apostolov as completed in 1841. A comparison between this gun carriage and that of a British 68pdr carronade of the Napoleonic era will make clear the degree of technological progress made in just 20 years. Unlike the British gun, which was a carronade firing a solid ball, this squat and massive gun was a shell-firing weapon, albeit a primitive one by later standards.

24pdr frigates (1786)
   6 in   15 cal.   128 poods gun wt
24pdr short (1804/1812)
   5.95 in   15 cal.   120 poods gun wt
24pdr gunnade (1836)
   5.95 in   12.25 cal.   96.20 poods gun wt
18pdr long (1786)
   5.46 in   18 cal.   109 poods gun wt
18pdr short (1804)
   5.41 in   15 cal.   88 poods gun wt
18pdr gunnade (1836)
   5.4 in   12.25 cal.   72 poods gun wt
12pdr long (1786)
   4.76 in   19 cal.   77.10 poods gun wt
12pdr long (1804)
   4.76 in   19 cal.   82 poods gun wt ('Alexander's')
8pdr long (1786)
   4.16 in   20 cal.   55.20 poods gun wt
6pdr long (1786)
   3.78 in   21 cal.   40 poods gun wt
3pdr long (1786)
   3 in   15 cal.   15 poods gun wt

Carronades
96pdr
   9 in   7.44 cal.   146.10 pood gun wt
68pdr
   8 in   7.44 cal.   113.6 pood gun wt
48pdr
   7.7 in   7.44 cal.   93.10 pood gun wt
36pdr
   6.75 in   7.44 cal.   65 pood gun wt
30pdr
   6.4 in   7.44 cal.   56.20 pood gun wt
24pdr
   5.9 in   7.44 cal.   44 pood gun wt
18pdr
   5.35 in   7.44 cal.   31.20 pood gun wt
12pdr
   4.7 in   7.44 cal.   19.20 pood gun wt
8pdr
   4.1 in   7.44 cal.   14.20 pood gun wt
6pdr

Shell-guns
3-pood 1849
   10.75 in 12 cal.   385 pood gun wt   119.39 (bomb) pd
                                                           177 pd (solid shot)
3-pood (1838)
   10.75 in 10 cal.   310 pood gun wt   119 pd (bomb)
                                                           177 pd (solid shot)
—
   10 in   9.57 cal. 262.20 pood gun wt 103.17 pd (bomb)
2-pood
   9.65 in   11.39 cal. 226.20 pood gun wt 91.25 pd (bomb)
1.5-pood
   8.75 in   11.42 cal. 174.30 pood gun wt 66 pd (bomb)
68pdr
   8 in   12.47 cal. 184 (192.20)   51.75 pd (bomb)
                               pood gun wt

Mortars
5-pood 1778
   12.6 in   3.63 cal. 292 pood mortar wt 188 pd (empty bomb)
5-pood 1808
   12.8 in   2.08 cal. 74 pood mortar wt   188 pd
3-pood 1769
   10.72 in 3.63 cal. 157 pood mortar wt 103.5 pd
3-pood 1808
   10.8 in   2.08 cal. 40 pood mortar wt   103.5 pd
2-pood 1812
   9.65 in   2.45 cal. 41 pood mortar wt   77 pd
8pdrs
   4.16 in   2.66 cal. 1.2 pood mortar wt 7 pd

Russian models and French Homers were used. Earlier eighteenth-century ordnance is included here because they were still in use throughout the first half of the century.

The Naval Establishments: Force Levels and Ship Armament

Force levels and armaments were regulated in Russia as in Britain and elsewhere by formal and informal 'establishments'. These attempts at objective setting and regulation were not always adhered to, but are of importance as *indicators* of strategic planning and of perceived limits for growth relating to efficient resource allocation.

New establishments were decided upon by conferences involving the Office of Chief Surveyor, the Office of Ordnance and other relevant parties and the Board of the Admiralty, Naval Ministry or Supreme Naval Staff (depending on the time period). These conferences involved the participation of active admirals as well as retired admirals summoned for the occasion in order to take advantage of their perspective and experience. The Committee brought together to decide on the reforms that became the Establishment of 1803 was noteworthy in breaking with precedent by involving a very few 'damned landsmen', including the Minister of Foreign Affairs in what had been the sole domain of professional naval officers.

The following tables summarize authorize force levels in both the Baltic and the Black Sea fleets and require some discussion. It should be borne in mind that these were *authorized* force levels and are not necessarily reflective of the actual forces available at the point in time specified:

Force level establishments for the Baltic Fleet

1718
   3 x 90, 4 x 80, 3 x 76 (incl. 1 x 3-decker), 12 x 66, 5 x 50, 6 x 32
1732
   4 x 80 *and* larger, 16 x 66, 7 x 54, 6 x 32
1750 (formally confirmed in 1757)
   1 x 100, 8 x 80, 15 x 66, 3 x 54, 6 x 32
1764
   3 x 80, 18 x 66, 4 x 32 (peace); 10 x 80, 22 x 66, 8 x 32 (war); maximum: 10 x 80, 30 x 66, 8 x 32
1777
   8 x 74, 24 x 66, 8 x 32 (peace); 16 x 74, 24 x 66, 12 x 32 (war)
1782
   8 x 100, 8 (war 16) x 74, 24 x 66, 12 (war 16) x 32
1798
   9 x 100, 27 x 74, 9 x 66, 9 x 44, 1 x 40, 9 x 32
1803
   9 x 100, 9 (+2) x 74, 9 (+3) x 66, 8 x 44, 8 x 36, 10 (+2) x 24
1826
   3 x 110, 8 x 84, 16 x 74, 19 x 44

The most obvious point that can be made here is to call attention to the marked expansion in authorized naval strength that followed upon Catherine II's coronation, most particularly with respect to the most powerful class, the First Rate ships, and its continuation to the assassination of Paul. The great contraction in naval strength that came with Alexander I's reign is apparent, but actually understated. No attempt was made under Alexander to replace the eight *Ches'ma*s as they left service prematurely in 1802–3 and the actual decline in strength was even more precipitate than appears from the numbers because nine 100s are kept on the books, even though no effort was made to actually build up to those numbers again. The recovery under Nicholas I is equally apparent, as is the greater reliance on mid-range capital ships (84s and 74s) and heavy frigates. The tenacity of the 66s is of note, as is the slow ascendancy of the 74s.

The changing ratios between capital ships and cruisers were similar to those of the other European navies:

   1718   4.5 to 1
   1732   4.5 to 1
   1750   4.5 to 1
   1764   4 to 1
   1777   3.33 to 1
   1782   4 to 1
   1798   2.36 to 1
   1803   1.14 to 1
   1826   1.42 to 1

Force level establishments for the Black Sea Fleet

1785
   2 x 80, 10 x 66, 8 x 50 (frig.), 6 x 32, 6 x 22
1794
   15 x 74, 6 x 50, 6 x 30, 6 x 28, 3 x 12 (cutters)
1797
   3 x 100, 9 x 74, 3 x 66, 6 x 50, 4 x 36
1803
   3 x 100, six (+3) x 74, 6 (+3) x 64; 3 (+2) x 44, 3 (+2) x 36
1827 (projected)
   5 x 120, 10 x 84, 10 x 60
1832
   3 x 120, 12 x 84, 10 x 60

The most obvious characteristic of the late-born Black Sea fleet is the 'set-in-stone' authorization of the maintenance of 15 capital ships, and the similarly fixed provision for ten cruisers after 1797. The appearance of 100–120-gun First Rates in 1797 was a direct response to similar construction of three-decked line of battle ships in Turkey and Egypt, as was the growing preference by the Russian Black Sea fleet for very heavy 50–60-gun 'battle frigates' able to stand in the line against equally formidable Turkish and Egyptian vessels.

The relative numbers of authorized capital ship totals for the two fleets between 1785 and 1827 is indicative of the relative importance over time of the two regional navies, as well as a commentary on the perceived foreign threat levels in both areas. The force level of the Black Sea fleet remained a constant, while the authorized capital ship level for the Baltic fell from a maximum ratio of three to one over the Black Sea fleet in 1798 to only 1.6 to one in 1832. The Baltic fleet was at its maximum during the long struggle with France, while the Black Sea fleet grew in relative importance with the growing intensity of the struggle against the Turkish and Egyptian navies –and also with the background threat to Russian interests in the Levant by both the British and French fleets.

Formal and informal gun Establishments in the Baltic and Black Sea

Gun establishments are frequently more honoured in theory than practice because of the vagaries of supply and the predilections of commanders. Nevertheless they are of importance as reflections of developments in ordnance and of perceived tactical requirements.

The first formal Establishment was established in the closing years of Peter I's reign, along with establishment mandates for the desired proportions of major warship classes. This initial establishment remained in formal effect for 44 years and in *de facto* force until the accession of Catherine II, the introduction of new capital and cruiser types, and of new types of ordnance brought about significant changes.

1723 Establishments

On 20 May 1723 the Establishment of Russian navy and the 'Table of Ships' Proportions' (breadth x inside plank) was adopted with the following standards for armament. It represents the experience gained by Peter I's fleet during the course of the Great Northern War and exerted its influence on Russian naval growth up to the coronation of Catherine II.

100	28 x 30; 28 x 18; 30 x 12 (brass) or 8 (iron); 14 x 6	178.7 ft x 49.5 ft x 21.9 ft
80	26 x 24; 26 x 16; 26 x 8; 8 x 6	169 ft x 46.4 ft x 20.7 ft
66	26 x 24; 24 x 12; 16 x 6	155.6 ft x 41.6 ft x 18 ft
54	24 x 18; 22 x 8; 8 x 4	143 ft x 38 ft x 16.7 ft
32	20 x 12; 12 x 6	118 ft x 31.6 ft x 14 ft
18	18 x 6	
12	12 x 4	

Of note is the status of the 30pdr as the heaviest weapon in service and its restriction to the largest class of warships, and of the 24pdr as the main armament of the 66- and 80-gun ships that made up the heart of Russian naval power during this period. 16pdr guns were something of an oddity, absent other European navies, although the differential between the Russian artillery pound and the British pound meant in practice that the Russian gun fired very nearly the same weight of shot (17¼ British pounds) as the British 18pdr.

1724 guidelines for shipwrights

The 1723 Establishment was in force until officially superseded by the 1767 Establishment, but it was not followed with respect to the actual armament carried by the 66-gun ships of the *Slava Rossii* class or by the 54-gun ships of the *Pyotr II* class. This has been apparent in the depiction of only 12 lower deck gunports in the builder's model of the *Slava Rossii* at St Petersburg and in the available draughts for members of the *Slava Rossii* class made public over the years, including the two included in this book (*Trekh Ierarkhov* and *Saratov*). A recently discovered document at St Petersburg confirms the change in lower deck armaments, although it gives no background on the reasons behind it – or for the official retention of the previous guidelines. The document in question consists of various precise measurements to be followed by shipwrights for the various ship types covered, including all aspects of construction from keel length to the distance between the ribs to the specified size of various gun ports. In all essentials, it is in agreement with the 1723 Establishment, except for the specified number of lower and upper deck gunports of the 54s and 66s. In the following pages, we are accordingly displaying the probable actual armament as specified by the 1724 amendments reversing the numbers for the lower and upper deck batteries while retaining the number of guns carried, 54 and 66. This revised arrangement is in accordance with the number of available lower and upper deck gunports displayed for these ships in pictures and models, and is a more logical layout and one in compliance with normal practice in other navies, with the number of lighter calibre upper deck guns being greater than the number of lower deck guns.

1767 Establishment of guns

In 1767 a new Establishment of armaments was introduced, together with edinorogs. Very few ships were actually completed to this establishment and the dead hand of the 1723 Establishment continued its dominance. Of note is the replacement of the 30pdr by the 36pdr for First Rates, of the 24pdr by the 30pdr for standard capital ship types, and of 16pdrs (in theory at least) for 12pdr for cruiser types. The continued authorization of smaller brass (12pdr) guns as a substitute for heavier iron 8pdr when available is of interest at this late date.

100	28 x 36; 28 x 18; 30 x 8 (or 12 brass); 14 x 6
80	26 x 30; 26 x 18; 28 x 6
66	12 x 30 + 12 x 24; 26 x 12; 16 x 6

32	20 x 16; 12 x 6
pram	18 x 36; 18 x 18 (previously 18 x 24; 18 x 12)

Baltic fleet armaments in the 1780s and 1790s

The major change during this period was in the introduction of paired edinorogs in calibres proportional to the guns being replaced on various gun deck levels (i.e. 1-pood for 36pdr and ½ pood for 18pdr) and the first appearance of carronades (when available) for placement on the upper open decks.

100	24 x 36 + 4 x 1-pood edinorogs;
	26 x 18 + 4 x ½-pood edinorogs;
	30 x 12; 20 x 6 (later + 2/4 carronades)
74	26 x 30 + 2 x 1-pood; 26 x 18 + 2-pood; 18 x 8
66	24 x 24 + 2 x 1-pood; 22 x 12 + 2-pood; 16 x 6
44	28 x 18; 16 x 6
38	28 x 18; 10v6
32	20 x 16; 12 x 6

1805 Establishment of guns

Two developments are of importance here, the replacement of long guns by short Swedish-style guns for the larger calibres (18pdr and up) and the (temporary) elimination of edinorogs.

100	30 x 36; 32 x 24; 32 x 18; 20 x 6 (or 24-carr.);
	4 x 24-carr. (6 x 3; 6 x 8-carr.; 6 x 8 mortars)
74	28 x 36; 30 x 24; 18 x 8 (or 24-carr.); 6 x 8-carr.; 6 x 3;
	3 x 8 mortars
64	26 x 36; 28 x 24; 18 x 8 (or 24-carr), small guns – as 74s
44	28 x 24; 16 x 8 (or carr.) (2 x 3, 2 x 8-carr., 2 x 8 mortars)
36	26 x 24; 10 x 8 (or carr.) small – same as 44
24	18 x 24, 6 x 8 (or carr.) small – same as 88
corvette	22 x 18 carr.

Establishment of 1830 and 1838

This establishment was introduced in 1830 and officially confirmed in 1838. Note the alternative armaments. Note also the retention of short guns by the 74- and 110-gun ships, and the return to the use of long guns for 84-gun ships. Note finally that the number of guns actually allowed for exceeds the 'rated' armament, a phenomenon shared with other navies of the period.

110	LD 26 x 36pdrs (short); 4 x 60 u (1-pood)
	MD 32 x 24pdrs (short)
	UD 32 x 12pdrs
	FC & QD 24 x 24pdr carr.
110 variant	LD 30 x 36pdrs (short)
	MD 32 x 24pdrs (short)
	UD 32 x 12pdrs
	FC & QD 24 x 24pdr carr.
84	LD 28 x 36pdrs (long); 4 x 60 u (1-pood)
	UD 32 x 24pdrs (long)
	FC & QD 6 x 12pdrs (long); 26 x 24pdr carr.
84 variant	LD 30 x 36pdrs (long)
	UD 32 x 24pdrs (long)
	FC & QD 34 x 12pdrs
84 variant	LD 30 x 36pdrs (long)
	UD 32 x 24pdrs (long)
	FC & QD 4 x 24pdrs (short); 24 x 24pdr carr.
74	LD 24 x 36pdrs (short); 4 x 60 u (1-pood)
	UD 30 x 24pdrs (short)
	FC & QD 16 x 8pdrs (long); 6 x 24pdr carr.
74 variant	LD 28 x 36pdrs (short)
	UD 30 x 24pdrs (short)
	FC & QD 22 x 24pdr carr.
74 variant	LD 28 x 36pdrs (short)
	UD 30 x 24pdrs (short)
	FC & QD 4 x 24pdrs (short); 20 x 24pdr carr.
60	UD 30 x 24pdr (long)
	FC & QD 22 x 24pdr (short)
60 variant	UD 30 x 24pdr (long)
	FC & QD 4 x 24pdr (short); 28 x 24pdr carr
44	UD 30 x 24pdr (short)
	FC & QD 4 x 24pdr (short); 22 x 24pdr carr
44 variant	UD 30 x 24pdr (long)
	FC & QD 2 x 24pdr (short); 22 x 24pdr carr
44 variant	UD 30 x 24pdr (long)
	FC & QD 24 x 24pdr carr
26-gun corvettes	2 12pdr chase 24 x 24pdr carr.
20-gun brigs	2 8pdr chase 18 x 24pdr carr.

Establishment of 1842 (Baltic)

This establishment affected only Baltic ships, and is noteworthy for the introduction of shell guns and the reintroduction of long 36pdrs.

84	LD 26 x 36pdrs (long); 6 x 9.65 in shell guns (2-pood)
	UD 28 24pdrs (long); 4 x 60 u (1-pood)
	FC & QD 6 x 24pdrs (short); 14 x 24pdr carr.
74	LD 24 x 36pdrs (short); 4 x 9.65 in shell guns (2-pood)
	MD 28 x 24pdrs (short); 2 x 60 u (1-pood)
	FC & QD 16 x 24pdr carr.
44	LD 26 x 24pdrs (short); 2 x 60 u (1-pood)
	FC & QD 16 x 24pdr carr.

Russian Naval History 1695–1860

On 4 November (14 November) 1696, the Russian Duma formally created the Imperial Russian Navy. Prior to this moment, nothing resembling an organized military organization intended for combat afloat had existed in this large and almost completely landlocked quasi-feudal state. To a degree unprecedented for those familiar with the gradual and disorderly expansion of small groupings of 'King's Ships' into national navies complete with infrastructure, design and manufacturing facilities, ports, trained officer corps, and some degree of established fiscal underpinning that characterized the process in Western European navies, the creation of a navy in this manner is little short of astonishing. Peter I created his navy out of whole cloth in very much the same manner as he had, as a 16-year-old boy, constructed and operated a 'toy fleet' of two frigates and three yachts on a large lake just outside of Moscow – by royal decree.

There was, of course, more at work than Peter I's fascination with ships and the sea, and the development of the early Russian navy took the rest of his lifetime to realize fully and ultimately brought about his early death. Russia under Peter I and his successors required naval forces not as vehicles for overseas expansion or for the protection of trading empires but rather as facilitators for territorial expansion along the Baltic coast northwards towards Finland and along the coastlines of both the Black Sea and the Caspian against the power of Turkey and Persia. Naval forces could and did act to transport troops and supplies in areas with undeveloped road systems at the same time as they could and did prevent the naval forces of their opponents from doing the same. Without naval forces to support Russian land armies, such expansion would not have been a viable option.

Before Peter I, Russian access to the seas and oceans of the world was limited to Arkhangel'sk in the far north and the Caspian in the south. Arkhangel'sk was indeed an important center of trade with the west, but trade firmly in the hands of England in the guise of the Muscovy Company chartered in 1555. The British monopoly was complete and the Russians had no real reason to challenge it because the benefits derived by the trade were mutual.

The motivation for some degree of naval development in the Caspian was more apparent in the face of Persian domination in the region. As early as 1634, Duke Frederick III of Schleswig-Holstein contracted with Tsar Mikhail Fedorovich to establish trade with Persia through Russian territory. Ten ships were proposed to be built at Niznii Novogorod on the Volga, but only a single ship, the *Frederic*, named after the duke, was actually completed. The builders were supplied by the duke, the construction material was pine, and the dimensions were 36.6 m x 12.2 m x 4 m (about 120 ft x 40 ft x 13 ft). With 3 masts, 12 pairs of oars, 125 men and some light cannon, she was not an inconsequential vessel. Whether she should be considered as a truly Russian ship is, of course, open to debate. Her career was short. After making her way down the Volga to the Caspian, she was wrecked on 14 November (24 November) 1636 off the Dagestan coast.

In 1667, Peter I's father, Tsar Aleksey Mikhailovich, reopened the Caspian trading initiative by establishing shipbuilding facilities on the Oka river at the village of Dedinovo. Five Dutch shipwrights, including L. Gelt, K. van Bukoven, Y. Stark, V. Popkee and V. Vilimson along with experienced artisans were imported to work with and instruct Russian masters, including Y. Poluektov, S. Petrov and F. Koshtunin, on the construction of the first truly Russian naval flotilla centred around the 22-gun *Oryol* supported by a small yacht and three small craft, all armed with 1 or 2 small guns. *Oryol* was laid down on 16 June (26 June) 1667 and launched on 26 May (5 June) 1668. Her initial cruise to Astrakhan' took three months. Little is known of her subsequent career, but she was burnt and severely damaged during the Cossack revolt of Stepan Razin.

The important element here is the apparent deliberate creation by Tsar Aleksey of the beginnings of a shipbuilding infrastructure, however humble, to maintain a naval presence in this inland sea. To this end, Aleksey adopted an approach that foreshadowed that of his more famous son, if on a more modest scale. Substitute Voronezh and St Petersburg for Dedinovo, and the small army of Dutch, Venetian and ultimately English shipwrights that Peter I later brought in to construct the first ships of his proposed navies for the five Dutchmen Aleksey hired, and the parallels are exact right down to the simultaneous effort to use imported foreign talent to train native Russians in advanced European shipbuilding techniques. This brief episode on the shores of an inland sea completely cut off from the open ocean might well have made for the birthing of the Russian navy had it had not fallen prey to ethnic warfare.

A more immediate starting date for the Russian navy might be found in Peter I's visit to Arkhangel'sk in 1693 and his ordering the construction of the 44-gun *Sviatoe Prorochestvo* in the Netherlands and two smaller yachts, the *Sviatoi Pyotr* and *Sviatoi Pavel* at Arkhangel'sk, all by Dutch shipwrights. He cruised briefly in the waters off Arkhangel'sk in 1694 with members of his inner circle, including Patrick Gordon who played a leading role in crushing the Stresny revolt in Moscow three years later. *Sviatoe Prorochestvo* was sold as a merchant ship after Peter I's departure and further naval developments awaited the siege of Azov in 1695.

(For a more detailed discussion of the limited information available on *Oryol* and *Sviatoe Prorochestvo*, please turn to the relevant entries in Section I on pages 315 and 141 respectively.)

Three major themes have predominated in Russian naval history during the period of our coverage:

- the struggle with Sweden for control of both the sea and the littoral of the Baltic as the Russian state extended its holdings and influence on the northern frontier of its growing empire;
- the struggle to neutralize and eventually eliminate the power and holdings of the Ottoman Empire in both the Black Sea and the eastern Mediterranean as Russia expanded to the south;
- the shifting networks of relationships and rivalries that grew up between Russian naval interests and those of the more highly developed powers of France and Great Britain.

Sweden to the north was a smaller, more compact, and more economically and technologically advanced state than Russia until the second quarter of the century. The power balance in 1700 was with the Swedes, but Russia eroded and eliminated these initial advantages during the course of the eighteenth century by virtue of her greater size, larger population base and overall resource base. Even with these advantages, the final neutralization of Swedish power would not have been possible without the systematic and disciplined imposition of more advanced Western technologies upon a society that was barely emerging from its feudal past when Peter I consolidated his shaky hold on the Russian state in the 1690s and began to turn its attentions outwards. Some of the most remarkable and hard-fought naval battles of the eighteenth century marked this progression. Western readers lacking access to R. C. Anderson's *The Naval Wars of the Baltic* have been deprived of much of the inherent interest and drama associated with the great naval battles of Gangut, Ches'ma, Gogland and Vyborg – to name a few – and the leadership of admirals of the calibre of Peter I himself, Fyodor Apraksin, Grigorii Spiridov, Samuel Greig, Fyodor Ushakov, Dmitriy Seniavin and Mikhail Lazarev – to cite only a few of the most prominent names on a long list of aggressive and capable naval leaders, both Russian and British.

Turkey, to the south, was in the early stages of her long decline in the face of the persistent economic and military pressures put upon her by the more technologically developed and organized states of Russia and Western Europe. In spite of internal ethnic divisions and economic backwardness, the Ottoman Empire remained a formidable opponent throughout our period. Its problems were related in large part to the ineffective levels of training and discipline of naval personnel, while its warships were of generally higher quality than Russian warships for much of our period due to French assistance. Very little substantive information is available regarding the actual makeup of the Turkish navy, beyond occasional listings of warship numbers and types gathered by diplomats and naval observers at various points in time. Imported French naval architects appear on the naval scene in Constantinople at various points in the eighteenth century, but very little definitive information has come down to us as to the extent or nature of their contributions to Turkish naval construction with the exception of those provided by the final and most talented of French émigrés to Constantinople, Le Brune de St Catherine. A student of Jacques-Noel Sane, this remarkable designer of warships was responsible for the construction of 14 Turkish ships of the line of between 50 and 120 guns and numerous smaller ships during the 1790s. The Turks were known to have access to excellent timber supplies in Lebanon and elsewhere and to local Mediterranean shipbuilders with considerable experience in the construction of traditional Mediterranean ship types.

Beyond this fragmentary material, we have been largely limited in our assessment of Turkish shipbuilding to apocryphal tales of excessive top heaviness in Turkish warships due to their alleged requirement for high interior deck clearances to allow for the wearing of fezzes below decks, to flattering comments by self-serving French diplomats as to the great beauty of Turkish warships when in formation at sea, to equally unflattering and self-serving comments by British naval officers as to the unsanitary living conditions aboard Turkish warships, and, finally, to R. C. Anderson's exhaustive documentation of their lack of discipline, training and combat effectiveness when tested in combat against the Russians. The only light shed on the subject has come only recently in the form of a recently published work in English on the subject by a Turkish historian, Tuncay Zorlu, *Innovation and Empire in Turkey, Sultan Selim III and the Modernization of the Ottoman Navy*.

Both the Turks and Russians faced similar problems in constructing, maintaining and employing the most highly advanced creations of the eighteenth century – warships – at a time when both nations were attempting to close the gap with the more advanced nations of the west. Both had access to sufficient economic and manpower resources to allow them to build and man sizeable fleets when the political will was present for naval expansion. The Russian advantage in this contest lay in the fact that Russia also had significantly greater access to underemployed and unemployed western naval officers and shipbuilders than the Turks. The cultural gap between Russia and western Europe was large but not impassable for those talented westerners seeking opportunities in Russia not available in their native countries, particularly for those coming from Great Britain, with its overabundance of experienced talent in ship design and construction, the handling of warships in combat, and the training and leadership of both landsmen and seamen. In contrast, the cultural gap between the Ottoman Empire, with its unique amalgam of Islamic and Turkish cultural traditions, and the Christian-based western societies must have been essentially unbridgeable for Europeans.

The third factor in the development of Russian naval power during the age of sail was the interaction between western European nations and navies, with their extensive human and technological resources, and the ships, personnel and infrastructure of the Russian Baltic and Black Sea fleets. As the nation with the largest navy and with the most extensive geographical interests and holdings, Britain was the primary actor in this drama. British naval officers and shipbuilders had a great role to play in the growth and expansion of both the Baltic and Black Sea fleets. British bases and dockyards were essential logistical facilitators for the periodic ventures of the Baltic fleet into North Sea and Eastern Mediterranean waters in the second half of the eighteenth century. On the other hand, relations between the two nations were occasionally unsettled and sometimes openly hostile, as Russia found herself pressured by the course of events into a pattern of alternatively co-operating with and opposing the expansionist policies of monarchical, revolutionary and ultimately Imperial France. The very same Russian and British ships and sailors who acted in close co-operation on many occasions during the various wars during our period of coverage, most particularly during the grim years between 1795 and 1810, found themselves in potential and sometimes real opposition to each other at others. There were few instances of open conflict between the warships of Great Britain and Russia during this period. Those that arose were generally the result of British incursions into the Baltic to insure continued access to the timber and hemp required for her navy and merchant marine, or, on one occasion, of Russian inability to provide logistical support for overly extended Baltic squadrons stranded in the Mediterranean by an unexpected shifting of alliances. The degree of access allowed Russian shipwrights and students to British naval technology was more important to the development of the Russian sailing navy than the occasional confrontations between British and Russian naval forces in the Mediterranean, the North Sea and the Baltic. More will be said about this later, but the availability or unavailability of British technological assistance was of the greatest significance in the growth and development of warship design, construction and maintenance.

These aspects of Russian naval history reflect an essential difference between Russian geopolitical needs and those of the European nations, including Great Britain, that had easy access to the Atlantic and Pacific. Russia was denied the opportunities for trade expansion and acquisition of overseas colonies available to the Atlantic powers. Her need for the development of her own naval power was instead driven by a desire to dominate the restricted environments of the Black Sea and the Baltic in the interests of facilitating her own territorial expansion and of denying similar opportunities to opposing nations.

There were indeed periods when Russia extended its naval power into the north Atlantic and the eastern Mediterranean in support of strategic objectives not dissimilar to those of the French and British, but they were more the exception than the rule. One need only look at Paul I's use of Baltic and Black Sea naval resources in the eastern Mediterranean during the Ionian Campaign, with its goal of establishing permanent Russian bases in the Adriatic and with a more than covert glance in the direction of Malta, to see Russian expansionism beyond its landlocked borders brought to naught when confronted by larger geopolitical realities. Russian expansion beyond her continental borders has always been something of a luxury easily curtailed by events closer to home; and Russian naval involvement in these infrequent enterprises involved the utilization of ships and men in activities for which they were poorly suited in terms of both warship design and personnel training. It was only during the nineteenth century, in the closing years of the age of sail, that we find Russian shipbuilding resources turned purposefully towards the development of true ocean-going ships capable of sustained global exploration. Their success in these endeavours in the Pacific, along the coastline of North America, and in both Arctic and Antarctic waters was both impressive and little noted in the West.

The underpinnings of Russian naval power in both the Baltic and the Black Sea remained those first developed by Peter I: the use of naval power to protect the flanks of Russian territorial expansion and, on occasion, to provide direct gunfire and amphibious support to land armies. Russian naval forces were indeed involved in attacking and destroying enemy fleets in the classic Mahanian manner, but the objective of these attacks was the safeguarding of Russian land forces and bases and the seaborne flanks of advancing Russian land forces and disruption of similar operations by the naval forces of the opposing side. The deliberate and systematic attack on enemy commerce and

---

A note on dating

Reference has been made in the data section under Launch Dates to the use of Julian dates in the data pages. In the following summary of Russian naval history and in other sections as indicated, it has been necessary to provide both Julian and Gregorian dates because English-language historians are generally in the habit of describing events according to the Gregorian calendar, in use in Europe from 1582 and in Great Britain from 1752. The converse applies equally to Russian writers and historians. To the unsuspecting, this can be a source of very great confusion. Many historians either clarify which dating system they are using, or adopt the protocol of providing both dates, identifying Gregorian dates with the suffix NS and Julian with the suffix OS (e.g. 4 July 1776 NS/15 July 1776 OS). Regrettably, some historians give no explanation of the system that they are using. In both the introduction and the historical summary, we have adopted the protocol of listing the Julian date followed by the Gregorian date in parentheses to avoid any unnecessary misunderstandings. All dates in the ship data section are Julian.

American readers should note that the European protocol for dates is being used here with the order of presentation being date/month/year as opposed to the American preference for month/date/year. Accordingly July 4, 1776 will appear as 4 July 1776. In the data sections, the month is not spelled out and 4 July 1776 appears as 4.7.1776.

A note on proper names

In the interest of conforming to common English usage, proper names are presented in the historical section in their accepted English renderings. In the data section, the same name will appear in the properly transliterated spelling. For example, Alexander becomes Aleksandr in the data pages, and Peter becomes Pyotr.

colonial enterprises was not involved in most Russian naval activities in either the Baltic or the Black Sea, although the interdiction of seaborne logistics related to troop transportation or the supply of land forces did occur, most particularly in the Black Sea. Russia, Sweden and Turkey were not dependent on foreign trade for their well being and lacked significant merchant marines vulnerable to naval attack. The only exception to this was the Turkish capital at Constantinople (Istanbul), which was vulnerable to blockade and starvation in the event of the simultaneous closure of the Bosporus and the Dardanelles. This reality goes a long way towards explaining the top heaviness (or high-endedness to use more contemporary language) of much of Russian naval construction in both the preponderance in numbers of capital ships to cruising ships and also that of heavy cruising ships to smaller types. It also helps clarify the chronic over gunning (in British eyes) of Russian warships of all sizes. Russian warships did not normally need to be built to withstand the constant pounding of heavy seas or to provide for the habitability requirements of long overseas deployments. What they did require was firepower for close combat, frequently against enemy squadrons arranged in defensive and stationary formations protecting land-based forces. This kind of naval warfare was not unknown to the western Atlantic based navies – witness British naval attacks at the Nile, Copenhagen, Navarino and Sevastopol' – but it was atypical and of lesser importance than the protection of trade routes and colonies and the destruction of enemy battle fleets at sea. This point should always be borne in mind in appreciating the flow of Russian naval history.

The following is a summary of the major naval confrontations and battles during the period covered by this book with reference, as required, to concurrent developments in Russian political history, and to her developing relationships with the states of Western Europe, including, most especially, Great Britain. The reader should remain aware that Russian naval developments in the Baltic and the Black Sea were always interrelated at a higher level and that nothing occurred within the naval sphere that was not related to the larger issues of Russian and European history. Political and military power in Russia was always centralized in the Russian monarchy and all decision-making arose from the Emperor or Empress and the coterie of close advisors surrounding the royal presence in St Petersburg. This was as true during periods of naval neglect and decay as it was true during times of growth and expansion.

One final proviso is in order. The following brief summary of the major events in Russian naval history does not pretend to be fully comprehensive with respect to the operations and engagements of the various wars described. The major battles described herein were proceeded and followed by a very wide range of lesser naval combat on the small squadron and individual ship levels, all of which is worthy of the reader's further attention and all of which may be found described in fuller detail in the works of R. C. Anderson and Donald W. Mitchell.

Sweden and the Baltic

Russian and Swedish naval forces came into open conflict four times during the period of our coverage: 1700–1721, 1741–3, 1788–90 and 1808–9. The first and third of these were of the greatest importance to both combatants in determining their place in the European hierarchy and their ability to shape events in the Baltic. The second and fourth were on a smaller scale and of lesser import.

A generally overlooked aspect of the struggle between the two great northern powers that has been addressed by a paper presented by Dr Jan Glete in *Forum Navale* magazine in 1990, has been that of the differences that existed between the two combatants with respect to warship construction, maintenance, manning and mobilization, particularly in the second half of the eighteenth century. Sweden after 1700 was limited in the resources that she could bring to bear for naval warfare, in part because she was facing two potential opponents on land and at sea. Denmark, to the west, was more nearly her equal with respect to the size of her naval forces. Russia, to the east, was much the larger opponent and could, once Peter I began his modernization of all levels of Russian society, be relied upon to out-produce any Swedish shipbuilding effort as it had done by 1720, and to bring greater manpower resources to bear in future conflicts. This was the construction strategy followed during the later stages of the Great Northern War as Peter's reforms began to take hold, and again during the 1780s under Catherine II (the Great). It should be noted that a determined Sweden was generally able to maintain numerical parity during the period between the death of Peter I and the accession of Catherine II, but that this was as much a reflection of Russian neglect as of Swedish capabilities. The Swedish monarch Gustav III is frequently regarded as having expanded the Swedish battle fleet during the 1780s. This picture is something of a distortion of actual events prior to the 1788 war. Gustav's construction programmes did not, in fact, increase the size of the Swedish fleet, which remained fairly constant in overall numbers, but replaced obsolescent vessels with more modern ships in line with technological advances taking place throughout Europe after 1750. In contrast, Russia under Catherine II greatly increased not only the overall size of her battle fleet, but also the firepower of individual warships, with the introduction of 74- and 100-gun ships replacing and supplementing the 66- and 80-gun ships which had formed the core of her fleet through most of the century.

In order to deal with this imbalance of resources, the Swedish navy, in Glete's opinion, developed a deliberate policy after 1722 that centred upon maintaining a high degree of peacetime fleet readiness, in order to be able to assail its Russian opponent in her bases within the Gulf of Finland immediately upon the outbreak of war, with a smaller but more capable battle fleet. This strategy could only be economically conducted with a smaller number of warships maintained at a higher degree of readiness than that of their opponents. This, in turn, required higher standards of construction and more frequent periods of refit and maintenance for individual warships. The offensive aspects of this strategy further required that the warships be designed around the conflicting requirements of limited draft in order to deal with the shallow water conditions in the northern Baltic as well as the ability to exhibit a high degree of stiffness. The requirement for stiffness, in turn, related to the need to be able to bring the lower deck batteries of line of battle ships to bear in combat by avoiding the high degrees of heel that generally resulted from their seizing and holding the weather gauge in offensive manoeuvres. The only way to achieve these two conflicting objectives was to limit the size of the capital ships in order to allow for sufficient underwater draft to provide for stiffness even in shallow water conditions. It was this requirement in turn that led to the Swedish predilection for 60-gun line of battle ships at a time when the Russians were building 74- and 100-gun ships. The marriage of these various requirements produced a battle fleet of warships that had useful lifespans on the order of twice those of British and French ships and four times those of contemporary Russian ships.

The Russian approach throughout the eighteenth century was the reverse of the coin. With an abundance of low-quality timber resources in the area around Arkhangel'sk – and higher quality resources around St Petersburg – and with abundant human resources in the form of untrained peasant recruits, the Russians were motivated to rely upon large numbers of rapidly built warships with relatively limited life expectancies, manned by minimally qualified seamen who would be trained in service. The rapid mobilization of these naval resources was not a priority with the Russians, who could rely on mass and attrition to wear down their smaller opponent.

In the end, the Russian approach won out over the Swedish because the disparity in size between the two powers was too great, because the Russian naval strategy and tactical performance was more aggressive than the Swedes had expected, and finally because the line officers commanding the Swedish navy, for debatable reasons, proved neither able nor willing to effectively implement the policies of rapid mobilization and preemptive attack that had been developed by higher authorities.

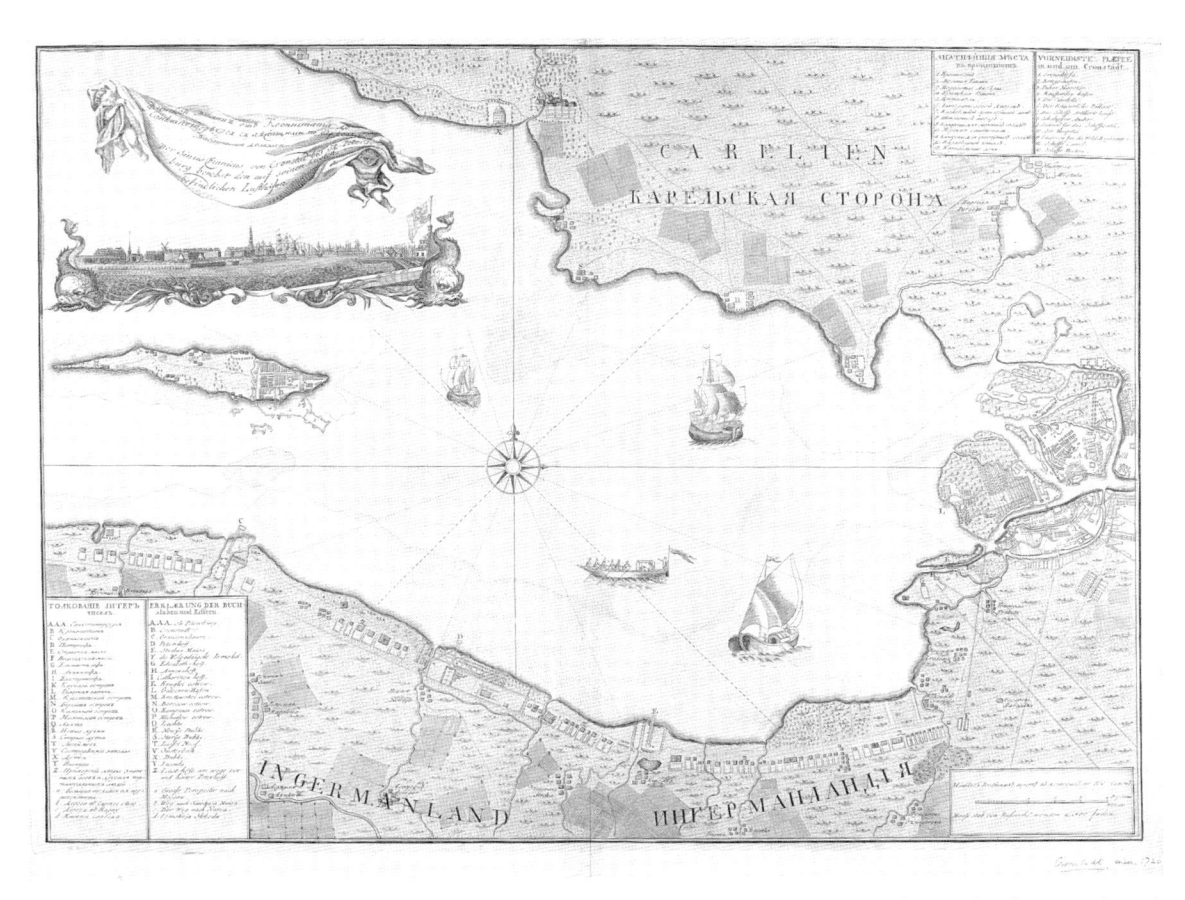

A highly detailed overhead view of the eastern Gulf of Finland showing the recently completed fortress of Kronshtadt on Kotlin Island and the capital of St Petersburg around 1720. The strategic importance of the fortress as a safeguard against attack on the capital from the sea is quite clear, as is the fact that the capital has been built on what is essentially the natural delta serving the Neva River to the east – hardly a rational choice except for its value as a base for Russian naval and land-based operations against Finland. Any attempt by Sweden to recapture Ingermanland on the southern shore of the Gulf of Finland would require advancing an army against the capital through Karelia on the northern shore. Swedish armies would depend on logistical support from naval forces, owing to the sparsely populated nature of southern Finland and its lack of roads and cities. This, in its turn, would mandate the capture or neutralization of the fortress of Kronshtadt. Peter I knew exactly what he was doing here, and the fortuitous placement of Kotlin Island determined the course of Russo-Swedish conflict for the next century.

The Great Northern War 1700–21

The Great Northern War of 1700–21 was one of the formative events of Russian history, bringing a new and major presence onto the European stage, and giving the Russian people and aristocracy a sense of mission and assurance previously absent from what had been a feudal assemblage of quarrelling aristocrats. There was a great deal of amphibious naval activity associated with the attempts of a determined Swedish state under an aggressive and determined monarch, Charles XII, to counter the territorial expansion of an equally aggressive and determined emperor, Peter I, and to capture the newly created Russian capital of St Petersburg. The majority of the naval combat during the war occurred in shallow coastal waters and involved combined, but not always well co-ordinated, actions on the part of large square rigged sailing ships operating or attempting to operate, in combination with smaller oared vessels ranging in size from small gunboats to well-armed galleys. The Swedish fleet had had over a century of combat experience against the Danes. Their fleet comprised warships designed according to Swedish experience with the range of environmental conditions existing in the Baltic. They were particularly adept at shallow water galley operations. In contrast, the Russian fleet was in its infancy, lacked any sort of combat experience and was a composite of foreign built purchases and of untried ships built in Russian shipyards by imported British shipwrights. Peter I fought the war with severely limited financial and manpower resources and, on at least one occasion at the battle of Gangut, was forced to shift his limited store of seamen and officers from galley fleet to sailing fleet and back again in response to the demands of the moment.

Early clashes between the technologically advanced and well disciplined Swedish armies and the disorganized and poorly equipped armies of semi-feudal Russia went Charles XII's way, most notably at Narva in 1700 where a Swedish army (of between 8,500 according to Western sources and 32,500 according to Russian) was able to rout a larger Russian force of between 35,000 and 37,000 men. Casualty figures for the Russians ranged from 8,000 to 16,000, once again according to differing sources, and 143 cannons out of 173 were destroyed or captured by the Swedes. Swedish casualties were in the neighbourhood of 3,000. In the wake of this defeat, Peter I was able to use the greater resources of the Russian state to recoup his early losses and to rebuild his army into a capable and efficient force able to face his initially more advanced opponent as a qualitative equal. The great land battle of the Great Northern War took place in 1708 at Poltava and involved the destruction of Swedish land power. Although the Great Northern War dragged on (with Turkish encouragement) for thirteen more years, Poltava effectively ended Charles XII's hopes for expansion into Russian territory and signalled the eclipse of Sweden as a power of the first order.

A preliminary skirmish between elements of the two navies occurred off Gogland in 1713 and involved the pursuit of three unfortunate Swedish ships of the line caught reconnoitring the Russian naval base at Revel' and forced to flee by the unexpected appearance of the entire Russian battle fleet. During the pursuit, the two fastest of seven Russian ships of the line, *Vyborg* and *Riga*, both grounded on a sandbank along with *Esperans*, allowing for the escape of the Swedish ships. *Vyborg* broke her back upon grounding and had to be burnt in place. *Riga* worked her way free, but was unable to continue the pursuit. Both commanding officers, one an admiral, were initially sentenced to death and subsequently pardoned by Peter I with the proviso that they be given no further seagoing commands. The difficulties involved in operating large warships in shallow Baltic waters becomes apparent in this incident. Of greater importance, perhaps, was the establishment of future command expectations by Peter I. Aggressiveness and competence at higher levels of command were expected and rewarded. Failure was summarily punished. The decision maker here and throughout later Russian naval history was, of course, the Tsar.

The Battle of Gangut (Hangö udd) 27–29 July (7–9 August) 1714

The great naval battle of Gangut (Hangö udd in Swedish) took place over three days between 27–29 July (7–9 August) in 1714 and was fought almost entirely by oared galleys and smaller sailing ships on both sides operating in shallow coastal waters inaccessible to capital ships. Hangö udd was a headland so situated as to act as a choke point for any oared vessels trying to move into the Gulf of Finland from the north or out of the gulf from Revel' and St Petersburg to the east. Although Russia had the makings of a viable seagoing battle fleet formed up at Revel' consisting of 16 ships of the line and eight frigates, these ships were not deployed in the coming campaign due to a severe shortage of trained seamen throughout both the sailing and galley fleets. All available trained seamen serving with the sailing fleet had been transferred to the galley fleet by Peter, leaving the battle fleet at Revel' immobilized with crews composed almost entirely of untrained landsmen and soldiers. This decision was well thought out, given the circumstances, but it left Peter with a force comprised entirely of shallow-water warships facing a Swedish fleet made up of oared craft for inshore work and a deep-water fleet of 15 ships of the line and five frigates.

In 1714, General Admiral Apraksin was in command of the Russian galley fleet, but Peter, apparently feeling that his own tactical skills were superior to those of his most trusted and capable assistant, took the unusual step of placing Apraksin in charge of the entire Russian navy – as a face-saving measure, no doubt – while theoretically subordinating himself and taking personal charge of the galleys as a rear-admiral. In late July, the fleet found its progress out of the Gulf of Finland in support of military operations to the north in Finland, blocked at the head of the cape by the combined Swedish battle fleet consisting of 15 ships of the line and large numbers of supporting rowing craft under the command of Admiral Wattrang. Hangö udd was the one point in the North Baltic at which it was possible for sailing warships to come close enough inshore to use their superior firepower to block oared vessels moving in either direction

The battle of Hangö (Gangut) as seen through the eyes of A. P. Bogolyubov in 1875–7. Shown here is the climactic final assault on Admiral Ehrensköld's flagship Elefant, *said by some to have been led by Peter I in person. This was the first great victory of the Russian Baltic fleet over the Swedish enemy and was the subject of innumerable paintings in the coming century.*

around the cape and would figure in numerous future naval actions in the coming century.

Peter had very limited options in the situation facing him. He first attempted to transfer galleys across the isthmus of Hangö udd to outflank the Swedish forces blocking his passage. This action proved unsuccessful, but succeeded in forcing the detachment of a small Swedish force consisting of an 18-gun rowing frigate, several cutters and six galleys under the control of Wattrang's second in command Admiral S. Ehrensköld in an attempt to block the transfer at the end point of the portage. Peter was forced to abandon the attempt at moving a significant portion of his fleet over land, but on the next morning he was able to isolate Ehrensköld's small squadron by moving a force of 34 Russian galleys in two groups around the outer deep-water flank of the main Swedish battle fleet at Hangö udd. Under normal circumstances, this move would have been suicidal and the galleys could have easily been destroyed by the overwhelming firepower of the sailing ships operating in their normal environment. Unfortunately for Wattrang, his battle fleet was immobilized by extremely light wind conditions and unable to take any action to block the passage of the Russian galleys. Wattrang moved his battle fleet away from the shore to counter any similar moves by the Russians the next morning. That evening, Peter reversed the previous day's operation, and sent an additional 60 Russian galleys rounding Hangö udd to the *inside* of the Swedish battle fleet. On the third day, with the main Swedish fleet unable to intervene, the now isolated Ehrensköld refused to surrender his squadron and the ensuing extremely bloody battle was fought in a narrow bay over a very narrow front. Russia suffered personnel losses of 124 killed and 342 wounded. Sweden suffered losses of 361 killed and 580 taken prisoner, including 350 wounded. Peter I is said to have personally led the final attack against the heroic Swedish admiral, but there is some disagreement about this. Ehrensköld survived the battle to be greeted not only as a national hero by the Swedes, but by Peter himself.

The immediate result of the battle was the withdrawal from the Gulf of Finland of the Swedish fleet enabling the Russian fleet to provide amphibious and logistical support for the further advance of the Russian army into Swedish territory. The Russian victory has been enshrined in Russian history beside the land victory at Poltava. Its importance here is to show the unique interrelatedness between deep water and shallow water naval operations in the conditions prevailing in the northern Baltic, to highlight the manpower problems that faced the Russian sailing navy throughout its history, and to show the tactical brilliance and adaptability of Peter I in finding his way out of what most commanders might have found an irresoluble problem. Hangö udd itself may have been the prime actor in the battle. Very few geographical features figure so prominently in naval history and the name Hangö udd will reappear frequently in later Russian naval history.

Although the Great Northern War lasted until 1721, the much larger War of the Spanish Succession, of which it was a small part, came to an end in 1715. The temporary elimination of the French threat to European stability allowed Great Britain and

The battle of Grengamn in 1720 as seen in a contemporary illustration. Russian galleys are swarming around the four soon-to-be-captured Swedish frigates, themselves unable to manoeuvre or escape in the rock-strewn shallows. In the distance pursued by more Russian galleys is the Swedish flagship Pommern *successfully making her escape.*

the Netherlands to turn their attention to the ongoing interruption of Baltic trade by Swedish privateers and to gather an allied coalition at Copenhagen in 1716 consisting of 18 British and 12 Dutch ships of the line under the command of British Admiral John Norris joining up with the Danish battle fleet of 21 ships. Denmark and Russia were at that time allied against Sweden and it was only natural for Peter I to add a Russian squadron of 15 ships to the coalition. The combined squadron of 59 ships belonging to four nations (19 British, 19 Danish, 15 Russian and six Dutch) was placed, rather surprisingly, under the command of Peter I himself, rather than under the command of the more experienced British admiral.

The Swedish battle fleet had not been touched at Gangut and was still a formidable element in 1716, but quite reasonably refrained from battle during the three-year period (1716–18) during which the combined squadron continued to patrol the Baltic. Charles XII died in battle in 1718, ending one of the great monarchical rivalries of the period, but the conflict he had initiated dragged on for three more years.

The Battle of Osel 24 May (4 June) 1719

The battle of Osel in 1719 would be of comparatively minor importance here except for the fact that it represented the first fleet action undertaken by Russia at sea without the concurrent involvement of rowing vessels or galleys of any sort. The battle was a one sided affair, with six Russian ships of the line engaging and capturing a single Swedish ship of the line, the unfortunate *Wachtmeister* accompanied by a frigate and a brigantine.

In 1720, Great Britain reversed alliances and took the side of Sweden against Russia in an attempt to restore equilibrium to Baltic affairs and to prevent any single Baltic power, whether Swedish, Danish, or Russian, from gaining anything approaching the monopolization of commerce in an area so vital to British naval and mercantile logistics. Russian warships refrained from directly challenging the combined strength of the Anglo-Swedish coalition of 20 British and 49 Swedish ships at sea in the closing year of the war; but Russian naval forces were still able to engage in operations against Swedish coastal towns and installations with impunity and to defeat the Swedish galley fleet at the battle of Grengamn in July of that year.

Grengamn 27 July (7 August) 1720

The battle of Grengamn was the final major confrontation between Swedish and Russian naval forces during the Great Northern War. Although not a large-scale confrontation, it enhanced Russian self-confidence and was not lost upon the British naval forces operating in the area under Admiral Norris. The battle was precipitated by the retreat of General Prince M.

Golitsyn from his position in the Aland Islands to the security of Helsingfors and by Peter's reprimand of Golitsyn and his insistence that he immediately reoccupy the islands. The chastened admiral returned to the Alands with a rowing squadron made up of 52 galleys and half-galleys and 14 smaller boats, where he encountered a Swedish squadron under the command of Vice-Admiral Shoblad consisting of the 52-gun *Pommern*, four frigates and nine smaller vessels on 26 July. In the absence of suitable winds, the Russian flotilla retreated to Grengam Island awaiting more favourable conditions on the 27th. That day the Swedish forces attacked and forced Golitsyn to retreat, a move that led the Swedish sailing ships to make the mistake of entering a narrow passage, severely limiting their freedom of manoeuvre. The Russian galleys responded by attacking the Swedish ships, forcing the four frigates to ground where they were taken after savage fighting which resulted in Russian casualties of 82 dead and 246 wounded against Swedish losses of 103 dead and 407 taken prisoner. The Swedish admiral succeeded in extracting the *Pommern* and the smaller vessels, but lost *Stora Phoenix* (34), *Vainqueur* (30), *Kiskin* (22) and *Danska Orn* (18).

As indicated at the beginning of this section the Great Northern War was of seminal importance in bringing about the emergence of Russia as a great European power and in unifying the heterogeneous elements of the vast nation. Of equal importance was the confirmation of permanent Russian control of the eastern and southern shores of the Gulf of Finland and the eastern shore of the Baltic. Although Sweden resisted the implications of its defeat by the larger Russian state and sought to re-establish its former position on two subsequent occasions in the coming century, her status as a great power had been lost not only in the eyes of her Russian opponents, but in the eyes of the other European states.

The period between the end of the Great Northern War in 1721 and the death of Peter I in 1725 was marked by his plans for future orderly naval expansion based on the evaluation of the lessons of the naval war that had just ended and exemplified by the formation of the previously alluded to Admiralty Collegium of 1718, the codification of Navy Regulations similar to the British Fighting Instructions in 1720, the Table of Ranks of 1722 regularizing and defining the structure of the officer corps, and the ship and gunnery establishments of 1723. The impetus for orderly naval growth and expansion died with Peter and would not be fully revived until the German-born Catherine II took the throne from her feckless Russian husband, Peter III, in 1762.

An interesting closing commentary on the state of the Russian navy in the closing years of Peter I's life and on the ambivalence that always existed between Great Britain and Russia on the subject of Russian naval growth is provided by Lindsey Hughes in his study of Peter I: 'The British rated the Russian fleet quite highly [in 1723], regretting their own contribution to its creation despite the fact that the Russian and British fleets were not strictly comparable, the former relying more on shallow-draught galleys and vessels, the latter on deep-draught ocean-going ships.' Jeffereys is reported as saying, 'If we do not take measures against the development of the Russian fleet we shall live to regret it.'

The Interregnum between Peter I and Catherine II

A period of instability accompanied by general neglect of naval matters followed Peter I's unexpected death in 1725. The throne was occupied first by Peter's second wife Catherine I from 1725 to her death in 1727, and then by his grandson Peter II until his untimely death from smallpox in 1730. A degree of order and stability was restored during the next decade by Peter I's niece Anna Ivanovna, who had some interest in naval affairs but whose foreign policy has been described as cautious and primarily concerned with blocking French influence in Poland. It must be noted that real political power during this power rested with the Russian gentry and landowners rather than with

Empress Anna Ivanovna (1693–1740) ruled Russia from 1730 to 1740. Her record as empress was decidedly mixed, with the effective direction of the nation in the hands of the Boyars until she found her footing in the middle years of her reign and was gradually able to reassert a measure of the kind of unquestioned control exercised by previous Tsars and emperors. For the Russian navy this was a time of general decay and decline, although Anna's overall record in this area is a matter of some dispute and is belied by Russian victories against both Poland and Turkey.

the monarchy. The reassertion of even the basic elements of monarchical control would not begin in earnest until the accession of Peter I's daughter Elizabeth in 1742.

On the naval side, the most significant activity during the period before the accession of Anna had involved the intervention in 1726 of a combined Anglo-Danish squadron under the command of Vice-Admiral Wager consisting of 20 British and six Danish ships of the line which had cruised provocatively off the Kronshtadt naval base inviting combat. The Russian fleet of 16 effective line of battle ships remained passively (and prudently) in harbour under the protection of the guns of Kronshtadt, but the ability of the British Royal Navy to disrupt Russia's hard-won suzerainty in the Baltic for the second time in ten years must not have been lost on its commanders, both naval and political.

Two naval conflicts of limited size, duration and importance occurred during Anna's ten year reign. The first involved Russian intervention in the War of the Polish Succession in 1733–5 and is dealt with here. The second took place in the Black Sea against the Turks between 1737 and 1739, and will be dealt with in the section on the Black Sea fleet.

The War of the Polish Succession 1733–5

For our purposes, this brief conflict is of importance because it involved the successful employment of Russian naval forces in amphibious operations of a type that would come to characterize much of the future application of Russian naval power in both the Baltic and the Black Seas. After years of neglect following the death of Peter I, the Russian battle fleet was in relatively poor material condition. There were only 16 ships considered worthy of standing in line of battle and available for service. Two of them, *Viktoriia* and *Devonshire*, had been reduced to an armament of 12pdrs on the lower deck due to their fragile condition; and two, *Arondel'* and *Esperance*, were actually frigates. There was a shortage of experienced officers, but adequate numbers of enlisted men as a result of the decision not to mobilize the galley flotilla in 1734 and an abundance of raw recruits. In spite of these shortcomings, the Baltic fleet proved up to the task of successfully blockading and bombarding the port of Danzig and bringing about the victory of the Russian side of a dynastic dispute involving conflicting Russian and French interests. Neither the besieged Poles supporting the pretender Stanislaus, nor Russia's allies amongst the Saxons and Poles opposing him, had anything in the way of naval forces able to affect events. The only real potential for naval action was provided by a small French squadron operating in the Baltic. With a lack of available intelligence, rumors exaggerated the size of the French squadron sent to the Baltic and they were credited with as many as three 74s, five 60s and four frigates. The Russian commander, Admiral Gordon, was more subdued in his assessment, estimating French strength at five warships and six auxiliaries. The actual size of the French squadron was three ships of the line and two frigates. Given his limited assets, the French commander avoided contact with the Russian fleet maintaining the blockade of Danzig.

This episode represents an early and important instance of successful Russian avoidance of conflict with larger western naval forces in the Baltic by the deployment of locally superior naval assets. The French Navy of the period could have overwhelmed the Russian Navy with superior forces had it so desired, but Polish dynastic disputes were not worth the expenditure and diversion of naval assets from the Atlantic where Great Britain had 30 active ships of the line to counter the French 14. A further factor inhibiting more aggressive naval action on the part of France was the open opposition of the British government to a naval confrontation in the Baltic. So long as Russian naval dominance in the Baltic did not appear to threaten the flow of timber and hemp to the great Atlantic naval powers, Russian pre-eminence in the area was acceptable to both France and Great Britain and not worth challenging.

War with Sweden 1741–3

Anna Ivanovna died in 1740. Her immediate successor, Ivan VI, was her nephew and Peter I's grandnephew. Ivan VI was two months old at his accession. Beyond the declaration of war with Sweden, very little was accomplished during his one-year reign before his deposition by Peter's daughter Elizabeth Petrovna. Empress Elizabeth was more aggressive than Anna had been, and was primarily involved during this period with supporting Austria against Prussia during the War of the Austrian Succession. The conflict with Sweden was of secondary importance, although the new Tsarina managed to surprise her erstwhile Swedish supporters among the Hat faction by refusing to surrender Russian territorial gains in the eventual peace negotiations. This second brief encounter between Sweden and Russia led to the fall of Helsinki in 1742, and the capitulation of a Swedish army of 17,000 to a Russian army of 17,500. Although there was a minimum of actual combat between the two navies, there was a degree of indecisive manoeuvering, and it was the persistent Russian naval presence that allowed for the supplying of Russian land forces in an area with sparse population and extremely scanty road networks.

At sea, the verdict was mixed, in part due to a lack of aggressiveness on either side. Although the Russian fleet was possibly in poorer material condition than the Swedish, both fleets were hampered throughout the conflict by illness. Serious conflict between the two fleets was deferred until 1743, and was, predictably, related to Swedish attempts to interrupt Russian amphibious support for their land armies. A decisive victory was won by the Russian galley fleet over the Swedish galleys at Korpo on 20 May (31 May) 1743. The unique nature of Russian naval operations and their close ties to military operations ashore was clearly demonstrated by this battle in which a Russian galley fleet under the commander of an *army general* (General Keith, a British-born officer who would later achieve fame as one of Frederick the Great's field marshals) commanded a naval division of seven galleys and two prams, and forced a larger Swedish flotilla of one pram and eighteen galleys to retreat after a two hour battle. The positive effect of this victory was very

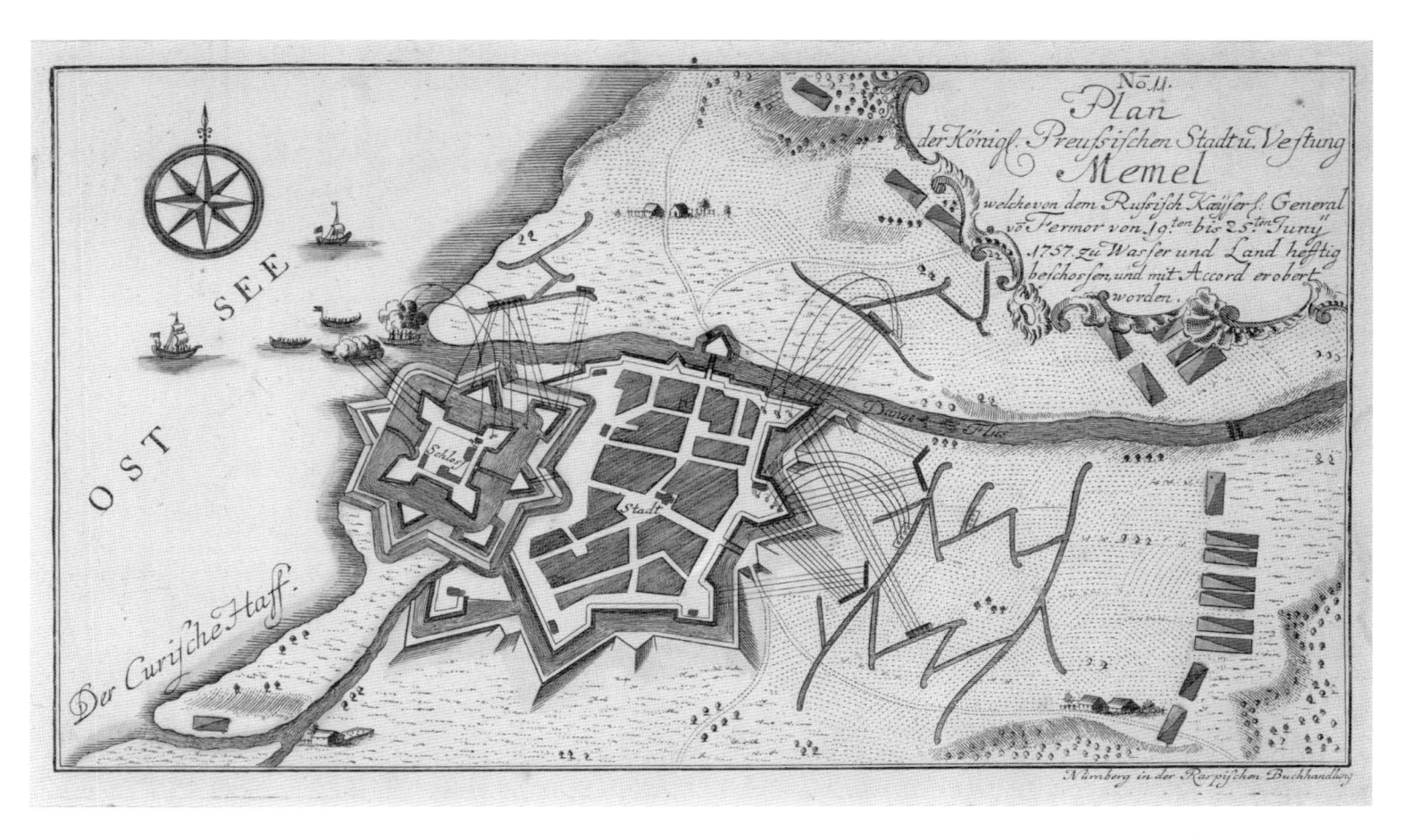

Russian naval participation in the Seven Years War was minor, since Prussia lacked naval resources of any sort. Action was limited to amphibious support operations, and the assault on Memel (now Klaipeda in Lithuania) on 18 June 1757 (29th NS) was one of the largest. This overhead view is of interest in showing the nature of eighteenth-century fortifications and the systematic manner in which diagonal trench lines were used to advance against them. The city is being attacked on three sides by a combination of flat trajectory and plunging artillery, with the fleet units covering one of the flanks with both conventional fire from warships and mortar fire from bomb vessels. How many warships involved themselves in this bombardment is uncertain, but eleven ships of the line and four frigates are known to have been involved in the blockade at various times.

quickly offset by an indecisive confrontation between Swedish and Russian naval forces at Hangö udd on 4 June (15 June) 1743. Facing a Swedish fleet of 17 ships of the line – including a three-decker – with 14 Russian ships, the Russian commander, Admiral Gollovin, embarrassed himself and his country by retreating to the shelter of Revel' after a very brief and inconsequential exchange of fire with the Swedes, who in turn held the weather gauge and failed to press the issue. In a manner not dissimilar to that of less-than-acceptably-aggressive British admirals falling back upon the Fighting Instructions to justify their timidity, Gollovin later defended himself against subsequent criticism by falling back upon Peter I's much earlier written instructions that the Russian fleet was only to engage Swedish forces when in possession of a three to two advantage. What Peter would have thought of Gollovin's performance may easily be imagined.

Russian territorial gains in the war involved a small expansion of Russian territory into Finland, including the galley port of Fridrikhshamn (now Kotka). Russian political gains were of more importance, as Elizabeth's candidate for the Swedish throne was confirmed. An essential point that needs to be made about the Russo-Swedish War of 1741–3 was that it was of secondary importance to events taking place between Russia and Austria, both seeking to limit the growing power of Frederick the Great's Prussia. Russia's commitment of ground troops to the conflict with Sweden was perforce limited by commitments elsewhere to the struggle with Prussia, and the ability of the Baltic fleet to provide logistical support was of decisive importance in balancing the situation ashore in Finland. Had the Swedish Navy been able to engage and defeat the Russian; or had the Russian Navy been forced to counter moves by (nonexistent) Prussian naval forces to the south, the successful outcome of the struggle would not have been possible.

The Seven Years War 1756–63

Russian involvement in the Seven Years War related to the conflict between Russian and Austrian interests and those of a determinedly land-based, but rapidly growing, power, Frederick the Great's Prussia. It is of interest here because Russia was once again able to successfully employ its moderately sized naval forces in the imposition of a blockade upon the Baltic coastline of Prussia, the bombardment of Prussian (now Polish) cities, and the supplementation and enhancement of the power and mobility of the Russian land army. At the time, and in an interesting suspension of traditional rivalries in the presence of a common threat from the emergence of Prussia, a Swedish naval squadron served annually under Russian command. It was also of importance because the threat of British naval intervention in the Baltic in support of Prussia in 1757 led to the full mobilization of Russian naval resources to block the passage of British warships through the straits of Denmark. Two 80s, ten 66s and two 54s were sent to patrol the sound off Copenhagen in 1758, a force sufficient to have at the least bloodied any British squadron seeking to force entry into the Baltic. Whether the threat of British naval intervention for the third time in the eighteenth century was in the nature of a considered bluff, or a serious undertaking disrupted only by the urgency of British naval commitments elsewhere and the Russian show of force, the Russian response was determined and aggressive and stands in contrast to its earlier pattern of withdrawal to the security of Kronshtadt and Revel' in the face of overwhelming British superiority.

The death of Empress Elizabeth in 1761 and the assumption of the Russian throne by Catherine II in 1762, after her deposition and apparent assassination of her pro-Prussian husband Peter III, was of the greatest importance, not only to the acceleration of Russian political and economic growth, but also in its stimulation of a naval renaissance, first in the Baltic and later in the Black Sea. The size and quality of the Russian Baltic fleet was enhanced by the construction of more and larger warships and by the deliberate importation of highly skilled naval officers, particularly British, and marked most prominently by Catherine's willingness to project Russian naval power beyond the confines of the Baltic and into the Atlantic and the Mediterranean.

Under Catherine II, Russian attention was initially directed towards the conflict with Turkey to the south in the Russo-Turkish war of 1768–74. The naval side of this conflict was fought by units of the Baltic fleet transferred to the eastern Mediterranean, with British assistance in the provision of bases and repair facilities in Great Britain and in the Mediterranean. The Russian show of audacity and determination in this remarkable extension of their naval power well beyond their normal sphere of influence has received inadequate attention in the West. What attention has been given by Western writers generally focuses on the alleged deficiencies of Russian naval personnel and the reportedly poor construction of Russian ships during their layover in Great Britain, as well as on the participation of naval officers on leave from the British Royal Navy and serving with the Russian navy with the tacit approval of the British government. There was probably a good deal of validity to these claims of Russian inadequacies and the overwhelming importance of British assistance and advice on all levels, but they may also have been overstated to a greater or lesser degree by British naval and shipyard personnel for reasons more germane to British naval history than to Russian. Irrespective of the occasionally less-than-stellar performance of Russian warships and seamen, the fact remains that Russia was at this point a *developing* naval power dealing on a scale unprecedented in its history with the strategic extension of its forces into environments for which they had not been designed or trained. How well the more established navies of the West might have done in similar circumstance must remain a matter of conjecture. The details of Russian naval participation in the Russo-Turkish War will be dealt with in the next section where it appropriately belongs, even though undertaken by the Baltic units dispatched to the theatre, and not the-then nonexistent-Black Sea fleet.

The Armed Neutrality Patrols

The Armed Neutrality alliance between Russia, Austria, Sweden and Portugal from 1779 to the end of the American War of Independence in 1783 was an attempt by the minor European powers and Russia to protect neutral shipping against French, Spanish and British interference. It warrants attention here because the alliance was initiated by Catherine II and marked another step in the progressive expansion of Russian prestige and importance on the European stage. On a strictly naval level, the alliance provided for the stationing of Russian squadrons totalling 22 ships of the line and four frigates in four squadrons in the North Sea, the Atlantic, the Barents Sea and the Mediterranean over a period of four years, and presented the opportunity for much needed experience and training outside of the peaceful and predictable Baltic. As may be expected, the alliance was the source for considerable friction between Russia and Great Britain. Fred T. Jane goes so far as to suggest that the lack of aggressive Russian enforcement of the Alliance's provisions traces back directly to the presence of British naval officers at all levels of the Russian officer corps.

The Russo-Swedish War 1788–90

Hostilities with Sweden resumed in 1788 as a result of the unrealistic ambitions of the Swedish monarch Gustav III who thought to take advantage of Russian preoccupation with its war with Turkey and the expected transfer of fifteen ships from the Baltic to the Mediterranean, to recover Finnish territory lost in previous wars. In going to war with a nation that was, by this time, significantly more powerful than his own, the Swedish monarch relied on a mistaken view of British intentions towards Russia at the time, and on the optimistic belief that he would receive their support in the coming hostilities. With the war under way in 1789, Gustav III also received a Turkish promise of financial subsidies in the amount of 2 million piastres a year. In the event, the Ottoman Empire only provided a single year's subsidy as a result of Sweden's withdrawal from the conflict in 1790. For its part, the British government contented itself with applying diplomatic pressure on the Danes to refrain from fulfilling their treaty obligations with Russia in the event of war between Russia and Sweden.

The Swedish Navy of the period was smaller than the Russian Baltic fleet in both the absolute number and size of its ships; but the Swedes built and maintained their available warships with greater care than the Russians and had the benefit of the design skills of Frederick af Chapman along with what was arguably among the most highly advanced naval ordnance in Europe at the time, using casting techniques that compared favourably with those of Great Britain. Although the expected departure of a major part of the Baltic fleet to the Mediterranean theatre was successfully delayed by the premature outbreak of war, the ships themselves were trapped at Copenhagen for the first year of the war. This eventuality gave the Swedes something approaching equality in the Baltic theatre during the opening phases of the conflict. Because of its economic limitations, Sweden was forced to fight the war entirely with the naval assets that they had available in 1788, while the Russians demonstrated the capacity for continuing to increase the size of their Baltic fleet during the war with new construction. From 1788 to 1790, Russian shipyards completed four 100s, six 74s, six 66s, six 44-gun heavy frigates and eight 38-gun rowing frigates along with a host of cutters. During the same period, Sweden managed to complete only a single 18-gun sloop, *Ulla Fersen*, in 1789.

Looked at objectively, the Swedish confidence and aggressiveness at this point of the war is difficult to account for given that the advantage between the two navies was, even then, with the Russians. As was to become increasingly evident during the next three years, the Russian ships were, on the average, larger and more heavily armed than their Swedish opposites, and the Russian fleet would only increase its material lead as hostilities continued due to the significantly greater resource base of the Russian state, even in the face of its simultaneous conflict with Turkey in the south.

As had been the case during the earlier Russo-Swedish wars, naval warfare revolved around control of the Gulf of Finland and the Russian defence of St Petersburg against attack from both land and sea. In contrast with the Great Northern War of 1700–21, this war was fought over a compressed time period of only three years and marked by more frequent and intense naval confrontations between the opposing battle fleets – one fleet action in each of the first two years, plus one at sea and two at anchor in the third year.

Russian and Swedish naval forces met in five major sea and two major galley engagements during the three years of the war. Although the naval forces involved tended to be evenly matched in terms of numbers of both ships of the line and frigates, Russian forces edged out their Swedish opposition in five of the battles by virtue of their having the larger and more heavily armed warships.

The following is a brief summary of the major naval actions of the war. For more detailed breakdowns of the ships and personnel involved, the reader is referred to the Orders of Battle section at the beginning of this introduction.

An excellent portrait of Samuel Greig (1736–88), a Scotsman who is regarded as Russia's most brilliant British-born flag officer. He first attracted notice as a young officer at Ches'ma in 1770 and was placed in charge of the Russian Baltic fleet in 1788, where he won the first major battle of the Russo-Swedish War of 1788–90 at Hogland. He became ill and died under unusual circumstances shortly after the battle while he was in the middle of planning an assault on the Swedish naval base at Sveaborg, and his death is sometimes attributed – solely based on circumstantial evidence – to Swedish malfeasance. In contrast to a slightly older, but equally talented, British import during the earlier Russo-Turkish War, John Elphinston, Samuel Greig got on well with his Russian peers and subordinates, remained in Russia, and sired Alexii Greig, who himself became a flag officer of considerable note.

Gogland 6 July (17 July) 1788

The first meeting of the two navies resulted from a Swedish attempt to force entry into the Gulf of Finland and attack the Russian capital at St Petersburg at the very outset of the war. The Russian fleet was under the command of the British born Samuel Greig whose reputation for aggressiveness, leadership and competence had been established earlier at Ches'ma against the Turks. The Swedish sailing fleet was under the nominal command of Duke Karl of Sodermanland, brother to the king; while command of the galley fleet remained in the hands of

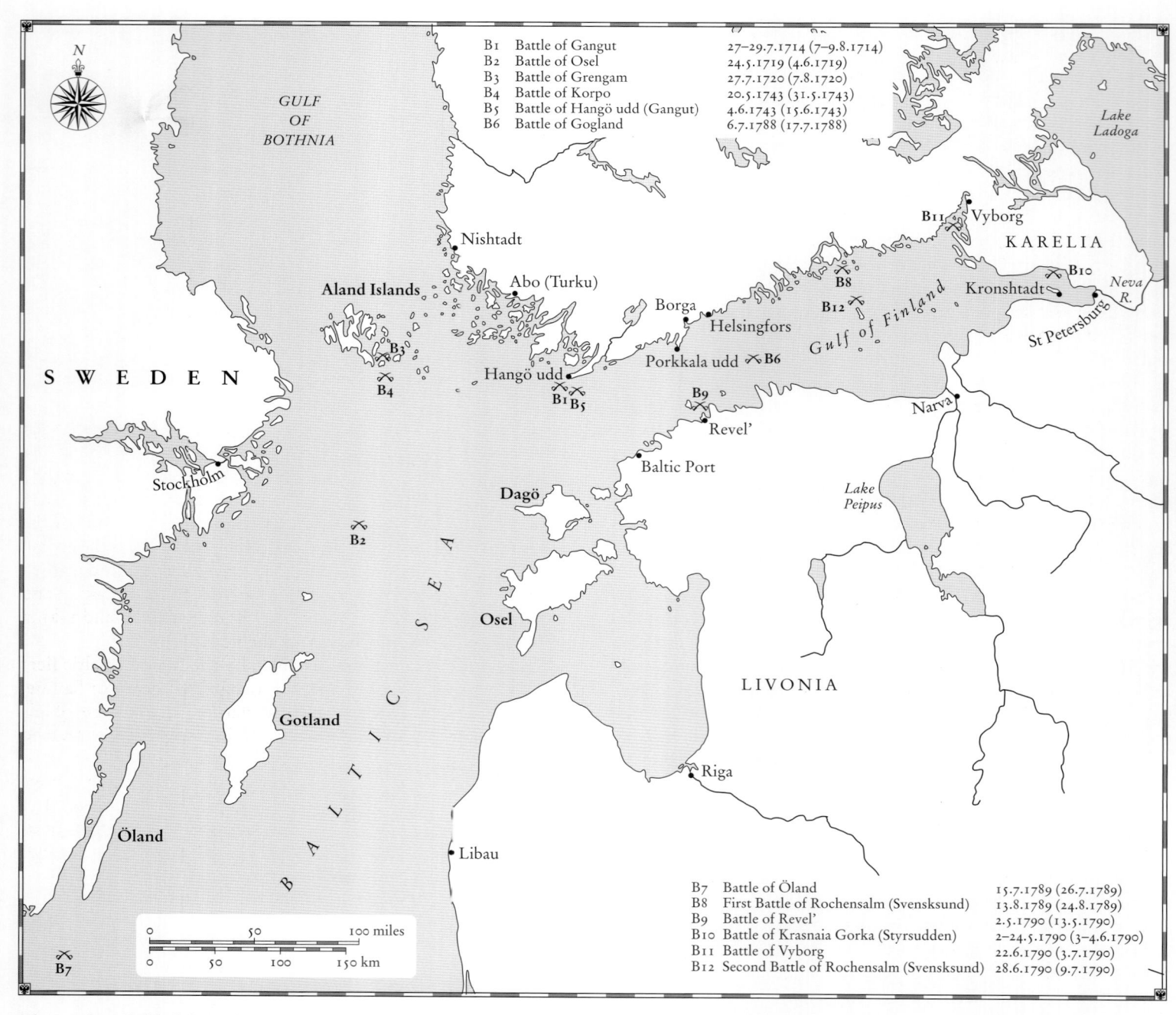

B1	Battle of Gangut	27–29.7.1714 (7–9.8.1714)
B2	Battle of Ösel	24.5.1719 (4.6.1719)
B3	Battle of Grengam	27.7.1720 (7.8.1720)
B4	Battle of Korpo	20.5.1743 (31.5.1743)
B5	Battle of Hangö udd (Gangut)	4.6.1743 (15.6.1743)
B6	Battle of Gogland	6.7.1788 (17.7.1788)

B7	Battle of Öland	15.7.1789 (26.7.1789)
B8	First Battle of Rochensalm (Svensksund)	13.8.1789 (24.8.1789)
B9	Battle of Revel'	2.5.1790 (13.5.1790)
B10	Battle of Krasnaia Gorka (Styrsudden)	2–24.5.1790 (3–4.6.1790)
B11	Battle of Vyborg	22.6.1790 (3.7.1790)
B12	Second Battle of Rochensalm (Svensksund)	28.6.1790 (9.7.1790)

The northern half of the Baltic sea was the site for twelve major naval confrontations between Sweden and Russian during the eighteenth century. As the map here shows, the Gulf of Finland was the site for eight of the twelve actions, with the prizes being control of Finland to the north and the safety of the Russian capital of St Petersburg.

Gustav III, the monarch. The two fleets at Gogland were fairly evenly balanced numerically, with Russia disposing of seventeen ships of the line and eight standard frigates against a Swedish fleet of fifteen ships of the line and five heavy and two light frigates (see the Order of Battle section for precise details).

The potential size of the Russian Baltic fleet would have been greater than these figures indicate, but ten of their best ships of the line (including three of the eight 100s completed and under construction) had been caught up unexpectedly in Denmark by the outbreak of war, while preparing for passage to the Mediterranean to operate against the Turks. This deployment would have duplicated the earlier deployment to that theatre in 1768. Its disruption was of the greatest value to the Turks and helps account for their promises of financial support to Sweden. The ships, prevented from fulfilling their intended purpose, and blocked from returning to St Petersburg, were forced to winter in Copenhagen, missing the first year's combat entirely. Denmark was bound to Russia by a defensive treaty and the Russian squadron operated with elements of the Danish battle fleet during 1788, deterring any attack by Sweden until events

> ### Roman Crown
>
> The spring of 1789 was marked by two single-ship actions on the part of a young Irish-born Lieutenant, Commander Roman Crown, that were to have long-term consequences for Russian naval history. As commander of the 22-gun two-masted cutter *Merkurii*, Brown captured a 12-gun Swedish tender, ironically named *Snapupp,* on 29 April (10 May), a useful but unremarkable feat. He then performed the remarkable feat of surprising, engaging and capturing the much more powerful Swedish heavy frigate, the 40-gun *Venus*, on 21 May (1 June) of the same year. Crown would rise to become a Russian admiral in the coming years, with a record of proven valour and high accomplishment that extended into the 1820s. The captured *Venus* would be taken into the Russian navy under the command of the heroic young officer who had captured her. In Russian service under Crown's command, she would accomplish great deeds against her nation of origin, fighting at Revel' in 1789 and Vyborg in 1790 and then assisting in the capture of the Swedish 64-gun *Rättvisan* in the immediate aftermath of the battle. Her stout construction and excellent design characteristics would be incorporated into the designs of nearly two score Russian heavy frigates built during the nineteenth century. As for Lieutenant Commander Crown's first command, the *Merkurii*, she lent her name to a 20-gun brig built in 1820 and destined for even greater fame than her name-ship by single-handedly engaging a Turkish 120 and a 74 in a four-hour battle in 1829 and emerging heavily damaged but intact.

allowed for their return to Russia in the second year of the war.

The Swedish inferiority in ships of the line at Gogland was balanced in part by the participation of five of their heavy 24pdr frigates. These ships had been designed specifically for standing in line of battle, when called upon to do so, by Frederick Chapman. Even though they largely failed in their intended role as suitable supplements to the overmatched Swedish battle line, they exercised great influence on the future course of Russian naval construction in terms of both their design excellence and of the unique (for the period) nature of their heavy-calibre short-barrelled cannon.

A major determinant of the course of the six-hour battle of Gogland was the prevalence of light wind conditions throughout the conflict. This goes some way, at least, towards explaining the failure of supporting elements of the Russian line to come to the assistance of Admiral Greig in the 100-gun *Rostislav*, accompanied by a single 74-gun ship, when the aggressive admiral opened the hostilities by engaging the Swedish flagship, the *Gustav III* in close combat. The Swedish flagship was supported by three 60-gun ships, *Vasa*, *Äran* and *Fäderneslandet*, and the fiercest action and heaviest casualties of the battle centred around this engagement between two Russian and four Swedish ships that ended with the withdrawal of the Swedish flagship. Depending on sources, the exchanges between the two fleets at other points of the conflict were either perfunctory or intense, but all of the Russian combatants took casualties and suffered damage. Two of the combatants, one on either side, – the Swedish *Prince Gustav* and the Russian *Vladislav* – were caught up by circumstances, isolated from the support of other friendly ships, and forced to surrender (*Prince Gustav* to the apparently omnipresent *Rostislav*) after putting up respectable resistance against superior odds.

The majority of the casualties on both sides were sustained during the ferocious combat circling about the two flagships. Russian casualties totaled 334 men killed with an additional 742 wounded and 477 taken prisoner. Swedish casualties were 130 men killed with 334 men wounded and 539 taken prisoner. Based on the respective casualty lists, the Swedes claimed a tactical victory of sorts, but their attempt to force entry into the Gulf of Finland and assault St Petersburg from the sea was a failure on the strategic level. After the battle, the Swedish fleet was forced to retreat to the security of their naval base at Sveaborg where they lacked the wherewithal to quickly repair the damage they had sustained in the battle. The Russians under Admiral Greig, on the other hand, were able to send four damaged ships of the line to Kronshtadt for repairs, recoup their losses with the arrival of four additional ships of the line, lay siege to the damaged Swedish warships at Sveaborg on 26 July (6 August), taking and burning the *Kronprins Gustav Adolf* in the process, and taking control of the Baltic for the rest of the year.

Possibly the greatest loss sustained by the Russian Baltic fleet in 1788 came with the sudden and unexpected death of Samuel Greig within weeks of his greatest battle. At the time of his death, Greig had been involved in preparations for a combined operations attack against the Swedish naval base and fortress at Sveaborg. The operation would have involved landing troops supported by mortar vessels and fire ships. Had it succeeded, it would have brought the war to an end in 1788. The preparations were abandoned with his death and the war dragged on for two more years.

Battle of Öland 15 July (26 July) 1789

Vasily Chichagov was placed in command of the Baltic fleet upon the death of Samuel Greig. The Swedes, still under the command of Duke Karl (who had allegedly spent most of the battle of Gogland in his cabin drinking), again sought out combat with the Russians, almost exactly a year after their combat at Gogland. This second engagement took place at Öland on the Swedish side of the Baltic and away from the normal locus of combat in the Gulf of Finland. Once again, the two fleets were well matched on paper, with the Russians having 20 ships of the line and six frigates against 21 Swedish line of battle ships and ten frigates. Once again, the Swedes had the edge in frigates, deploying eight of their nine remaining heavy frigates; but the Russians now had three 100-gun three-deckers, as well as a clear superiority in the total firepower carried by her smaller line of battle ships.

Admiral Vasiley Y. Chichagov (1726–1809) assumed command of the Russian Baltic fleet upon the death of Vice-Admiral Greig and led it to victory in major engagements at Öland in 1789 and also at Revel' and Vyborg in 1790. Although he has been criticized for allowing a portion of the Swedish fleet to escape timely pursuit at Vyborg, he is regarded as a competent, if not brilliant, commander.

In contrast to Gogland, the conflict between the two fleets was indecisive, with the Swedes engaging in long range gunfire and refusing to close with the Russians, who were themselves assuming a defensive posture and awaiting the arrival of reinforcements from Copenhagen, where their squadron of ships originally bound for the Mediterranean had wintered with Danish consent. Any possibility of a Swedish victory in the engagement was effectively negated by the unwillingness or inability of Rear-Admiral Lilljehorn to bring the Swedish rear into the combat. Lilljehorn had previously established a record for bravery and the reasons for his apparent cowardice at Öland must remain a mystery. Three subsequent days of manoeuvring between the two battle lines ensued after the engagement was finally broken off by the Swedes and this was followed by a further Swedish retreat to Karlskrona. On 22 July (2 August), the long awaited arrival of the Copenhagen squadron under Vice-Admiral Koslanianov, with an additional 11 ships of the line and four frigates, secured the Russian blockade of the Swedish battle fleet and once again asserted her control over events in the Baltic for the second year of the war.

1st Battle of Svensksund 13 August (24 August) 1789

The persistent and prominent participation of rowing vessels of all sizes in the Russo-Swedish wars of the eighteenth and early nineteenth centuries may appear anachronistic to readers unfamiliar with conditions in the Baltic. Nevertheless the shallow water conditions and amphibious nature of much of the naval combat along the Finnish coast insured that shallow water operations, conducted by rowing vessels up to galley size, would continue to play a major part in the prosecution of the war. It was these conditions that made possible the Swedish movement of 40 vessels including one sailing and 11 rowing frigates as well as five galleys and 23 gunboats along the northern shore of the Gulf of Finland in support of land operations to the vicinity of Svensksund (Ruochensaalmi in Finnish), where they were driven to seek shelter by a superior Russian force of 61 rowing ships on 4 August (15 August). On 13 August (24 August), the Russian force divided into two sections totalling 86 vessels, including 11 large galleys, attacked the Swedish squadron on either flank. Although the attack was poorly co-ordinated, it succeeded in spite of determined Swedish opposition. Swedish casualties totalled 1,400 men and 21 vessels. Russian losses totalled 1,010 casualties and a single gun sloop. As a result of this defeat, Sweden was forced to abandon its land campaign against St Petersburg for the year.

Battle of Revel' 2 May (13 May) 1790

In spite of two successive years of failure in advancing its goal of dominating the Gulf of Finland and capturing St Petersburg against determined Russian resistance, the Swedish monarchy committed to yet a third attempt in 1790. As had been previously the case, Gustav III commanded the galley fleet and his brother Duke Karl the sailing fleet. The Swedes had one significant advantage over the Russians in the war – the earlier breakup of the ice in the southern Baltic which enabled the Swedish navy to mobilize at an earlier date, while the Russian ships were still ice bound in their bases at Kronshtadt and Revel'. It was this factor that enabled Duke Karl to appear off Revel' and attack that portion of the Russian Baltic fleet based there on 2 May (13 May). With 20 ships of the line, six heavy frigates and two light frigates, Duke Karl had a clear advantage over his Russian opponents for the first and only time in the war. The anchored Russian squadron under Admiral Chichagov consisted of only ten ships of the line, four standard frigates – and the recently captured *Venus*. Unfortunately for the Swedes, two of the Russian line of battle ships were 100-gun *Ches'ma* class three-deckers and the Russian line was also supported by shore batteries. The attacking ships were hindered in their attack by high westerly winds making control difficult and quite probably causing excessive heeling, making it difficult or impossible for them to bring their lower deck batteries into action. The Russian ships, on the other hand, had the advantage of being at anchor with furled sails and would have been relatively stable gun platforms. The Russian ships sustained relatively little damage

The better part of the Russian battle fleet in action against the Swedish fleet making its most determined and final bid at capturing Vyborg and laying the Russian capital of St Petersburg open to direct attack. This may have been Catherine II's navy at its moment of greatest power and glory, with five 100-gun First Rates of the Ches'ma class, twelve lesser line of battle ships and eight heavily armed rowing frigates arrayed in a two-layered defensive formation that proved unassailable by the more numerous but smaller ships of the Swedish line of battle. By M. V. Petrov-Maslakov, 2001.

and this would have been the expected outcome had the Swedish ships been so disadvantaged. Had the Swedes had the benefit of lighter winds, they might well have been able to double the Russian line, taking advantage of their numerical superiority and making proper use of their lower deck batteries. As it was, they were driven off in a state of disorder and with heavy losses – the 60-gun *Prince Karl* being forced to surrender and the 62-gun *Riksens Stander* having to be set afire to prevent her capture after grounding in the panicky Swedish retreat. Swedish personnel losses were 150 killed and 520 taken prisoner. Russian losses were insignificant.

Battle of Krasnaya Gorka (Styrsudden) 23–24 May (3–4 June) 1790

The Swedish army, reinforced by 10,000 seamen from the rowing forces, had failed in its attempt at taking the fortress of Fridrikshamn in the face of determined Russian resistance, forcing Gustav III to seek temporary shelter for his still considerable naval and land forces in Vyborg Bay while he awaited the planned reinforcement by the sailing navy under Duke Karl in order to continue his drive towards St Petersburg.

In spite of his losses at Revel', Duke Karl succeeded in expeditiously refitting his damaged warships and reinforcing them with two additional ships of the line and a frigate. With 21 ships of the line and eight battle frigates representing the total effective strength of the Swedish sailing navy in the third and final year of the war, he was intercepted *en route* to Vyborg Bay by Vice-Admiral Kruz leading the Kronshtadt squadron of 17 ships of the line, four standard sailing frigates and eight heavily gunned 38-gun 18pdr rowing frigates fresh from the dockyards. Kruz's squadron had not been engaged at Revel', but comprised the larger portion of the Russian Baltic battle fleet seeking to link up with the smaller Revel' squadron and deny the Swedish battle fleet access to St Petersburg. As had been the case in earlier battles, the numbers of capital ships engaged in this confrontation told only part of the tale. Kruz had at his disposal no fewer than five of the *Ches'ma* class 100-gun ships. These ships, reinforced by newly completed 38-gun rowing frigates armed with 18pdrs firing between the gaps in the larger ships' battle line, gave the Russian fleet a decisive firepower advantage in spite

The battle of Vyborg on 22 June 1790 (OS) with the Russian line of battle seen dominating the centre of the picture firing upon the Swedish line to the right which is attempting to make its way around the head of the Russian line to escape into the Gulf of Finland. The explosion seen in the distance to the left of the Russian line may represent the collision between the Swedish Engheiten, her fireship, and the frigate Zemire, an event that destroyed the cohesion of the Swedish line and led to chaos. In reality of course, none of this action would have been visible beyond the flash of the cannons and the flames from the burning Swedish ships since the action took place at night. By M.V. Petrov-Maslakov 1996.

of their apparent numerical inferiority. The rowing frigates were of particular value due to the extremely light wind conditions prevailing on the day of the battle. These conditions made movement difficult for the sailing vessels on both sides and at the same time allowed the rowing frigates to not only prevent Swedish ships of the line from attempting to double the shorter Russian line but also to discourage gunboats from attempting the same manoeuvre. The Russian advantage in firepower was counterbalanced in part by personnel shortages of the sort that had formed a background to Russian naval operations from the earliest years (see Gangut 1714). In order to man the ships of his squadron fully, Vice-Admiral Kruz had had to draft guards, fortress soldiers, militia men, invalids, non-combatants and dockyard workers. The shortages were so severe that the fortress commandant, Vice-Admiral M. Pushkin was deprived of his secretarial staff and was forced to write out his own orders personally.

Both sides suffered heavy casualties in the fighting on the 23rd without a clear decision being reached. The battle resumed the next morning, with Duke Karl discretely controlling the action from behind the Swedish line in the newly completed 18-gun 'frigate' *Ulla Fersen*. The Duke broke off action upon learning of the long anticipated approach of Chichagov's Revel' squadron of 11 ships of the line and one frigate and retreated into Vyborg Bay to achieve the sought for linkup with the Swedish rowing fleet and auxiliaries albeit under less than optimal conditions. The combined Russian Baltic fleet now at its full strength of 30 ships of the line and 15 frigates took up station outside of the harbour, awaiting events.

Battle of Vyborg 22 June (3 July) 1790

By retreating to the shelter of Vyborg Bay, Duke Karl had ironically achieved the long sought for unification of all available Swedish land and naval forces within striking distance of St Petersburg, but in the unsought for and undesired positioning of those forces in a long and narrow bay at the mercy of the combined strength of the fully mobilized Russian battle fleet, and with no means for supplying either his land based or his naval forces. The Swedish battle fleet had been inadequately provisioned at the onset of the campaign, and the combined naval and land forces reached a point of desperation after a month of blockade. It would appear that the Swedish command had been anticipating a degree of control over the flow of supplies in the gulf that did not materialize in the face of Russian naval superiority. When matters reached a crisis, the Swedish armada attempted to force its way out of the harbour at night and with the deployment of four fire ships intended to throw the Russians into confusion. The plan was not without its merits, but the Swedish battle line, while succeeding in penetrating the Russian line, came under heavy fire from the Russian ships as it emerged from the harbour and was thrown into chaotic disorder when the 70-gun *Enigheten* was accidentally rammed by its own assigned fire ship. The unfortunate ship of the line then compounded its problems by colliding with the 40-gun heavy frigate, *Zemire*, resulting in the spectacular explosion of all three. The rest of the night was a compound of chaos and disaster for the Swedes. The 64-gun *Hedvig Elisabet Charlotta* ran on to the rocks in the confusion and sank. Three other ships of the line – *Drotting Louisa Ulrica* (70), *Omheten* (62), and *Finland* (62), and two frigates, *Uppland* (44) and *Jarislavets* (32) (the former Russian *Iaroslavets*) – were all forced to surrender after grounding. *Sofiia Magdalina*, flagship of one of the Swedish division commanders, was also captured during the attempted breakout. The day after the battle, the 62-gun *Rättvisan* was captured by the newly promoted Captain Crown in the recently captured *Venus* – with an assist from the 66-gun *Iziaslav*. This brought the total Swedish losses in the breakout to seven capital ships, two heavy and one light frigates. Total Swedish losses after the 90-minute breakout had ended included over 250 smaller vessels, including 16 troop transports, approximately 7,000 dead sailors and soldiers, and 4,988 prisoners. Russian losses were 147 killed and 164 wounded.

Admiral Chichagov has been criticized for failing to anticipate the breakout attempt and for and for failing to immediately order the pursuit of those ships and boats that had succeeded in running the Russian gauntlet. The Swedes claimed a strategic victory in spite of their considerable losses and the elimination of their battle fleet's capacity to further challenge Russian domination of the northern Baltic. Had the Russian fleet succeeded in destroying the Swedish transport fleet and the accompanying rowing warships and possibly capturing the Swedish monarch in the process, Russia would have been able to annex all of Finland had she so chosen. The disastrous 2nd battle of Svensksund would have been avoided entirely.

2nd Battle of Svensksund 28 June (9 July) 1790

In the aftermath of Vyborg, Gustav III was able to escape with the bulk of his galley fleet of 196 vessels intact and took refuge at Svensksund (Rochensalm in Russian). The forces available to the Swedes included five 'coast frigates', a pair of brigs and 16 galleys, with the remainder being comprised of smaller gunboats. The Russians had a clear material advantage in the larger types of rowing warships, with 134 vessels including seven 38-gun rowing frigates and numerous smaller oared vessels including shebecks, galleys and gun sloops, along with a small number of sailing ships in the form of cutters and ketches. The Swedes had an edge in small, highly manoeuvrable gunboats and these may have made the difference in the battle. Long, fast moving galleys of the sort so well suited for the Mediterranean were no longer built in any quantity by the Russians after this battle. The Swedes had abandoned their construction, but not their use, after 1749. The Russian galley commander was the feckless Prince Nassau-Ziegen, fresh from his mediocre performance in the Liman campaign and his rivalry with John Paul Jones. His lackluster performance in the battle may well have been as great a factor in the Russian defeat as their overreliance on galleys.

The Russian forces drove into the middle of the Swedish line – as desired by the Swedes – only to be enveloped on both flanks by the fire of the strongest units in the Swedish fleet. The ensuing battle lasted for a full 24 hours, involved repeated clashes between the two fleets, and resulted in one of the worst defeats in Russian naval history, with the loss of 52 vessels and casualties of between 7,000 and 9,500 men. The debacle, following the victory at Vyborg, has been traditionally blamed upon the overconfidence of Prince Nassau-Ziegen, who began the attack without adequate preparation. In spite of the scale of the losses, the Russian rowing flotilla was rapidly restored to its former level with new construction. The humiliated, but unchastened, Nassau-Ziegen pushed for a resumption of hostilities, only to be blocked by Chichagov and Catherine herself, who wanted an end to the war with Sweden in order to concentrate her limited military resources on the struggle with Turkey to the south. The Treaty of Varala restoring the *status quo ante* between Russia and Sweden was quickly patched together and signed on 3 August (14 August) 1790, just a month after the defeat.

Two vital foreign policy elements were resolved by the Russo-Turkish War of 1788–90. The first was the clear inability of Sweden to ever effectively challenge Russian power for control of the Baltic and the disputed territory in Finland in the future. The second was the reversal of Russian priorities since the beginning of the eighteenth century. Russian expansion to the south had become the greater priority and any future difficulties with Sweden a sideshow.

The Russian Armament of 1791

During 1791, British concerns with Russian successes in the Black Sea led to the mobilization of a major battle fleet intended for operations against the Baltic fleet. The British fleet included 36 ships of the line under the command of Admiral Howe in the *Victory*. Russia responded by mobilizing and arming its entire Baltic fleet at Kronshtadt and Revel' under Admiral Kruz in *Ches'ma*. The Russian fleet assembled included all 8 *Ches'ma* class 100s, 1 x 78, 14 x 74s, 10 x 64/66s (including 3 Swedish ships captured during the recent war) and 13 frigates. How this experienced Russian fleet might have fared against a slightly larger British fleet must remain a matter for conjecture. Neither nation had any serious interest in hostilities and both sides compromised with the result that Russia sacrificed some, but not all, of her gains against Turkey in the Black Sea with the signing of the Treaty of Jassy in January 1791. Four years later, Russia's entry into the First Coalition against revolutionary France would relegate this brief moment of potential conflict to the status of a minor footnote in the naval interrelationships of the two powers.

Russia in the English Channel and the North Sea 1795–1800

The British role in nurturing and occasionally challenging and inhibiting the development of Russian naval power is a constant undercurrent in the study of Russian naval history from 1700 to 1860. In most instances, the traffic between Britain and Russia was unidirectional, with British assistance being given when beneficial to British interests, whether in the employment and development of otherwise surplus British officers and naval constructors, or in the use of the Russian navy as a pawn and surrogate in areas on the periphery of British interests such as the Eastern Mediterranean and the Baltic.

The period associated with the First and Second Coalitions against Revolutionary France, most particularly that between 1795 and 1800, marked a significant and generally disregarded reversal of roles, with Russian naval forces extending themselves into the English Channel, the North Sea and the Eastern Mediterranean to provide direct assistance to the Royal Navy in areas of the greatest importance to Great Britain, and of little immediate import to Russia. The Russian expansion into the Mediterranean in the campaign against France is dealt with in the section on the Black Sea fleet, but attention is given here to the Russian dispatch of significant naval forces to assist directly in North Sea waters in the defence of the British Isles and the struggle against the French in the Netherlands. How great a role was played by the Russian squadrons dispatched, first by Catherine II and then by her son Paul I, is a matter of perspective and debate. Russian historians stress and perhaps overplay the significance of Russian involvement in what were essentially British affairs during this period. For their part, British historians have done their best to ignore the Russian ships off their shores during the Great Mutinies of 1797, their participation in the capture of Dutch warships in the Texel, and the abortive invasion of Holland – or to trivialize the issue by providing anecdotal accounts of drunken Russian sailors and

Vice Admiral Khanykov's squadron consisting of four 74s and eight 66s was a largely unsung Russian contribution to British operations against the French during the troublesome years of the First Coalition. Here we see two unnamed Russian 66s at rest off Sheerness in 1795 and surrounded by the usual scattering of small craft. This was the first of three Russian deployments to British waters during the French Revolutionary and Napoleonic Wars between 1795 and 1814. Khanykov's ships operated in the North Sea with British fleet units in 1795 and 1796 and attracted a degree of scornful comment from many British officers, driven by an uncharitable combination of higher performance expectations and traditional British chauvinism and reinforced at time by the boisterous excesses of Russian seamen on liberty in a strange and foreign environment. Save only for a token squadron under Rear-Admiral Makarov, Khanykov's ships were recalled to Russia on the death of Catherine II. For all of the British grumblings against their Russian allies, the return of an even larger Russian squadron in 1798 was more than welcomed by the British naval command.

soldiers cavorting through peaceful British seaports and drinking the oil out of the street lamps, or descriptions of sluggish and poorly trained Russian warships slowing up their more highly trained British betters in joint manoeuvres off the Dutch coast. The truth of the matter undoubtedly lies somewhere between these two positions, but the participation of Russian Baltic warships in operations outside of the Baltic was, if of marginal importance to the British, of the greatest importance to the Russian navy, providing it with operational experience unobtainable in home waters.

Russian naval involvement with the First Coalition was originally limited to operations in the southern Baltic in 1793. The first extension of Russian naval forces beyond the Baltic was limited to a two-week cruise into the North Sea by nine ships of the line and three frigates under Admiral Alexander Kruz. In 1795, the formal declaration of war between France and Russia led to the basing at the Nore of a major battle squadron under Vice-Admiral Khanykov consisting of 12 ships of the line supported by eight frigates, under the operational control of Vice-Admiral Duncan. Although there were predictable tensions and problems of communication between officers from both nations, the Russian squadron successfully co-operated with the British in maintaining the North Sea blockade until the autumn of 1796, when they returned first to Copenhagen and then to Russia for refit.

Rear-Admiral Makarov's contingent of three ships of the line and four frigates did not return to Russia with the rest of Khanykov's squadron. On 24 October (4 November 1796) Makarov's detached squadron departed Copenhagen to return to the Nore where it anchored on the 15th (26th), shortly after the death of Catherine II on 6 November (17 November). The new Emperor Paul I had recalled the rest of the squadron to Russia upon taking the throne, in order to mark his accession to power with a fleet review involving almost the entire Baltic fleet and including 27 capital ships. This recall has been generally attributed to his coolness towards Great Britain as a result of growing tensions between Russia and Britain. This may indeed be the case, but the recall, which was reversed within the year, may also have simply been a reflection of Paul's egotism and desire to assert his accession and symbolically place himself on a par with his domineering mother who had held similar reviews to mark important events in her long and prosperous reign. At any rate, Makarov's squadron was exempted from attending the review and allowed to remain passively anchored in the Nore, without going to sea in active support of British fleet units. Makarov is alleged to have played a part in the suppression of the Nore mutiny in May of the following year by virtue of his quiet presence in the harbour as an unspoken ally of the British government and rebuke to the mutineers. Whatever the actual degree of Makarov's participation in the suppression of the mutiny at the Nore, his squadron did spend several weeks in June operating in direct support of Admiral Duncan in his lonely vigil off the Dutch coast aboard the Venerable before proceeding on its way back to Russia.

The spring of 1798 witnessed the most ambitious deployments of Russian naval power into foreign waters to date, with the nearly simultaneous dispatch of major naval forces from the Black Sea to the eastern Mediterranean under Vice-Admiral Ushakov, and from the Baltic to the North Sea under the newly promoted Vice-Admiral Makarov. The assignment of Makarov's squadron had been requested by the British government in order to allow for the assignment of additional British warships from home waters to the Mediterranean theatre, an action that called into some question the earlier assertions by some British officers about the incompetence of the Russians at sea in the deployment of 1795-6. Ushakov's slightly earlier deployment of Black Sea fleet units into the Mediterranean – with unprecedented Turkish compliance in allowing them to transit the Bosporus – will be dealt with in the coverage of the Black Sea fleet. Suffice it to say here that he deployed seven ships of the line and five heavy frigates in April to support – and compete with – British warships in the area operating under Horatio Nelson, fresh from his victory at the Nile.

Vice-Admiral Makarov's deployment was a more ambitious undertaking than either Vice-Admiral Ushakov's deployment of ships from the Black Sea to the Mediterranean, or the earlier deployment of Baltic ships under Vice-Admiral Khanykov to the North Sea. Beginning in May 1798 with the spring thaw in the Baltic and White Sea, a force of 15 ships of the line supported by four frigates was ordered to reinforce the British fleet units stationed at the Nore, with an eye towards co-operating in amphibious operations against the Dutch coast. The Russian deployment was in three stages. Vice-Admiral Makarov left

---

Health in the Russian navy

The complaints of British officers during this period about the allegedly poor quality of Russian seamanship may be attributed, in part at least, to the normal tensions that arise between allies unused to co-operating with each other and separated by language and culture. Complaints about the poor health of Russian seamen, the inadequacies of their diet and the poor material conditions of Russian warships are of a more objective nature. They are based on the one hand upon the recorded observations of British doctors, well versed in the maintenance of the health of seamen and concerned about the prevalence of fever and scurvy in the lower decks of Russian warships and, on the other, upon the amount of dockyard repair work required to keep the ships of the Russian squadron at sea. Russian problems in these areas can be attributed to their inexperience with long deployments, the conditions of the North Sea environment and the high proportion of untrained and inadequately clothed landsmen making up a large part of their ship complements. It should also be borne in mind that the ships and the men of Khanykov's squadron were being judged according to the rigorous standards of health and maintenance established by the Royal Navy of Great Britain at the height of its power, standards that did not apply to most other navies.

Kronshtadt in May with five line of battle ships, one frigate and a cutter. He arrived at the Nore in July without incident, and placed himself once again under the command of Vice-Admiral Duncan with his ten ships of the line, two frigates and a single brig. The second squadron under Vice-Admiral Thate left Arkhangel'sk with a contingent of five ships of the line and two frigates, all virtually new ships, and also arrived safely at the Nore in August. The third squadron, also from Kronshtadt, under Rear-Admiral Kartsev was comprised of five ships of the line and a single frigate. All of the ships in Kartsev's squadron were older vessels, and included two Swedish prizes taken in 1788. The squadron did not leave Revel' until 20 August and ran into a severe weather system off Skagen, Norway. *Prints Gustav*, the flag, was sunk in the storm, and her consort *Sviatoi Pyotr* was so heavily damaged that she had to return to Revel' for repairs. All four of the other squadron members suffered severe damage and required extensive repairs in Danish and Norwegian ports before finally linking up with Makarov's squadron.

In May of 1799 three lines of battleships and a frigate were detached from the North Sea squadron to reinforce Russian Black Sea forces operating in the eastern Mediterranean under Vice-Admiral Ushakov. Two capital ships and a frigate were detached back to the Baltic in June, and the remaining ships were deployed on the blockade of the Dutch coastline. Three of Makarov's ships of the line participated in the attack upon, and seizure of, eight Dutch capital ships on the Vleiter. This Russian squadron was reinforced in September by five ships of the line and five frigates under Admiral Chichagov escorting 17,000 troops intended for the projected invasion of the Netherlands. The Anglo-Russian invasion of the Netherlands came to a quick end in the face of superior French reinforcements, poor planning and co-operation between the British and Russian officers involved in the operation, and the failure of the local population to provide the anticipated support. Amidst contradictory charges of inept performance and incompetence by the ranking British and Russian officers involved, the Russian troops were withdrawn and garrisoned in the Channel islands until they could be returned to Russia, the end to an episode that marked one of the low points of Anglo-Russian co-operation. The debacle in the Netherlands occurred at the same time as Field Marshall Suvorov was extricating his troops from Switzerland, as a result of Austrian withdrawal from the war and the two misadventures combined to mark the beginning of a decisive cooling off of relations between Paul I and the British government.

With the withdrawal of Russia from the Second Coalition in 1800, Russian warships were recalled from Britain, ending the longest period of friendly (and occasionally not-so-friendly) collaboration between the two nations to date. The extent of the Russian commitment to the North Sea deployment is best shown by the fact that no fewer than 16 ships of the line were deployed in British waters at the time of their final withdrawal, at a time when the total effective strength of the Baltic fleet was officially 48 ships. Due to the inevitable deterioration of ships held in ordinary, this figure in itself gives a somewhat understated picture of the real level of Russian commitment. When Paul I ordered a review of the readiness of the 45 Baltic 'effectives' mandated by the Establishment of 1797 in October, 1800, the resulting survey found only 25 fit for active service, including only two of nine three-decker ships. This would place the Russian deployment of Baltic ships to the North Sea campaign on the order of two-thirds of the effective strength of the Baltic fleet at the time.

Nelson and Armed Neutrality

The formation of the Armed Neutrality Pact between Russia, Prussia, Sweden and Denmark in 1800 led to the dispatch of Admiral Sir Hyde Parker with a fleet of 20 ships of the line to the Baltic to protect British interests, which were primarily tied to maintaining access to timber and hemp sources. After the successful neutralization of Danish naval power at the battle of Copenhagen, it was the intent of the British to attack and destroy the Russian Baltic fleet in its bases at Revel' and Kronshtadt as necessary. Hyde Parker's replacement by Admiral Horatio Nelson led to the very real prospect of a confrontation in the Gulf of Finland in May of that year between Nelson's twelve ships consisting of two 98s, eight 74s and two 64s and the Russian Baltic fleet which consisted of 18 ships of the line including the 130-gun *Blagodat'*, three 100s, 11 74s, two 66s and a single 62. Had hostilities between the former allies actually occurred at this time, it seems most likely that the Russians would have awaited the British under the cover of the formidable defences of Kronshtadt, which also included two additional unrigged ships of the line, nine frigates, two bomb vessels, four bomb cutters and 23 floating batteries. Even with Nelson in command and in spite of British confidence, the outcome of a direct attack on fixed Russian defences as formidable as these would have been very much in question and a prolonged blockade could not have been easily sustained. The new Russian Emperor Alexander I, having nothing to gain and a great deal to lose from hostilities with Great Britain, very quickly reached a diplomatic solution ending both the Armed Neutrality coalition and the threat of pointless hostilities between the two nations.

The Russo-Swedish War 1808–9

The final stage of the century long rivalry between Sweden and Russia for control of the Baltic was a minor component in the struggle between Great Britain and Napoleonic France and was as much a phase in the long term development of Anglo-Russian relationships as it was the final stage in the long running rivalry between Sweden and Russia. Hostilities were precipitated between Russia and Sweden by the Russian invasion of Finland and the successful capture of the Swedish fortress of Sveaborg along with a considerable portion of the painfully reconstructed Swedish rowing fleet. Russia was at the time allied with France, and Sweden was not unexpectedly on the other side of the conflict as a member of the Third Coalition. In addition, the better part of the Baltic fleet was stranded in the Mediterranean as a result of Russia's withdrawal from the Third Coalition,

> ### *Lieutenant Nevelskoy and the* Opyt
>
> As had been the case before the battle of Öland in 1789, a junior officer, commanding a small warship and acting independently against heavy odds, provided an inspiring prelude to the main action about to unfold between the opposing battle fleets. On 11 June (23 June) 1808, a Russian cutter, the *Opyt* armed with fourteen 12pdr carronades was overtaken by a 42-gun British frigate, the *Salsette*, in weather conditions favourable to the larger ship. The cutter's commander, Lieutenant Nevelskoy, refused to surrender to the overwhelmingly more powerful British frigate. In the four-hour action that followed, the British frigate fired two full broadsides into the much smaller warship and caused extremely heavy casualties among the cutter's 53-man crew. After doing more to satisfy Russian honour than reason required, Lieutenant Nevelskoy surrendered his heavily damaged cutter to the British commander, Captain Bathurst, only to have his sword returned by the astounded and admiring British captain, who had him landed ashore along with his surviving crew members.

leaving her naval presence in the Baltic greatly reduced. Britain was motivated by a desire to prevent French subversion of the Swedish government and by her traditional objective of preventing any single Baltic state from achieving unchallenged dominance in the Baltic.

Britain dispatched Vice-Admiral Saumerez with a naval squadron built around the *Victory* 100, eight 74s, two 64s, five frigates, supporting craft and 10,000 troops to secure Sweden against an anticipated Russian invasion. Although Sweden had only added a single new line of battle ship and a single frigate to her fleet since her defeat at Vyborg in 1790, preferring instead to concentrate her limited resources on her inshore galley and gunboat fleet, she had rebuilt the seagoing survivors of that conflict in the late 1790s to mollify that portion of the Swedish navy that still had traditional battle fleet loyalties. As a result she could still deploy a shrunken, but still respectable, fleet of 11 active ships of the line and six frigates against the Russian Baltic fleet, and accordingly remained a formidable if diminished presence in the Baltic, particularly in view of the loss of the Russian Mediterranean squadron.

Two months later, on 12 August (24 August) 1808, the combined Anglo-Swedish squadron under the overall command of the Swedish Admiral Cederstrom, consisting of two British 74s under Rear-Admiral Hood and ten Swedish ships of the line in company with five frigates, deployed to Hangö udd to intercept any attempt on the part of the Russian fleet to cross into Swedish waters. The next day, on 13 August (25 August), the combined squadron came into contact with a Russian squadron consisting of nine ships of the line, including the massive 130-gun *Blagodat'* and the 100-gun *Gavriil*, under Admiral Peter Khanykov. Although the Anglo-Swedish

Although he fought with distinction in a secondary command role during the Russo-Swedish War of 1788–90, Vice-Admiral Pyotr Khanykov's (?–1813) chief historical plaudits were garnered for his skilful handling of both the naval and the political problems arising during the stationing of a Russian battle squadron at the Nore in 1795–6. His claim to some notoriety came in 1808 when he avoided conflict with an Anglo-Swedish squadron of roughly equal force and then refused to come to the aid of the heavily engaged Russian 74 Vsevolod which had fallen behind the retreating Russian squadron and was successfully attacked and taken by two British 74s – a failure of nerve that sullied a previously honourable record and led to his court-martial. He was broken to a common seaman but Alexander I intervened and allowed him to retire honourably because of his 'past deeds'.

squadron outnumbered the Russian squadron, the presence of two Russian three-deckers greatly evened the odds, as did the relatively heavier armament of the Russian 74s. On sighting the Anglo-Swedish squadron, Khanykov, who had had a long and honourable career in the Russian Navy, reversed course and made for the shelter of Rogerswick (Swedish Rågerwik). In the ensuing pursuit, the two British 74s easily outran the Swedish ships, which were lacking in either seamanship or commitment, and closed with 74-gun *Vsevolod*, which was bringing up the rear of the Russian squadron. The *Vsevolod* was caught and engaged by the *Implacable* and heavily damaged in the ensuing exchange of fire. The two British ships were then forced to retreat some distance by the approach of the entire Russian squadron returning to the aid of *Vsevolod*. The unfortunate Russian 74 was then taken in tow by the Russian frigate *Poluks* while the rest of the Russian squadron made its way into the shelter of Rogerswick. *Poluks* was forced to abandon her tow by the return of the two British 74s who were quick to take advantage of the Russian squadron's premature and unseemly abandonment of one of its major components. Both *Centaur* and *Vsevolod* grounded in the ensuing exchanges, and both British 74s took their Russian opponent under fire just six miles outside of the harbour in full view of her squadron mates, forcing her surrender, and setting her afire the next morning. Russian casualties were 303 men, British casualties 62. Although the *Vsevolod* had performed heroically in the battle, Khanykov was broken to a common seaman for a day and dismissed from the service for his failure to accept battle with an opponent of equal or lesser strength or to come to the assistance of his unlucky subordinate. The Anglo-Swedish squadron was joined the next day by Vice-Admiral Saumerez with his entire squadron, making any Russian sortie suicidal. The combined fleet blockaded Khanykov's disgraced squadron for several months, after which time they abandoned the blockade and Khanykov's ships were able to retreat to Kronshtadt.

The final Russo-Swedish war ended in September 1809 and with it a rivalry between two peoples that had lasted for over a century. Neither the Swedish nor Russian naval forces gave the appearance of being greatly interested in contesting this final round of their long naval dispute – at least at sea – and the brief war is primarily of interest in that it witnessed the only significant incidents of actual naval conflict between Russia and Great Britain prior to the Crimean War in 1853. By 1812, Sweden had temporarily entered the French sphere with the accession of Marshall Bernadotte to the Swedish throne; while Napoleon had invaded his erstwhile Russian ally, forcefully the reestablishment co-operative relations between the Russians and the British at sea and on the land and laying the groundwork for his final defeat.

The final phase of Anglo-Russian naval co-operation

The invasion of Russia by Napoleon in 1812 was fraught with unintended consequences, not the least of which was the decision to transfer the entire active Kronshtadt and Arkhangel'sk battle fleets to British ports. The movement of the main fleet at Kronshtadt was motivated in large part by fears on the part of the Russian government that St Petersburg would fall to the invading French armies. The movement of the Arkhangel'sk 'squadron' of newly completed warships resulted from the simple need to provide them with an alternative destination to their normal basing at Kronshtadt and Revel'. The willingness of the British government to commit to the logistical support of 18 ships of the line and six frigates cannot be overstated, especially at a time when their own financial resources were severely strained and their naval forces in a position of unchallenged domination over the scattered remnants of the French navy.

The transfer of the Kronshtadt fleet of one 120, one 88, eight 74s, five frigates and a single brig, all under the command of Admiral George Thate, was accomplished without incident, with the departure of a final small frigate being delayed until the next year. The transfer of the Arkhangel'sk squadron under Roman Crown of *Venus* fame, now a Vice-Admiral, was rather more difficult. Vice-Admiral Crown was placed in command of five 74s, two 66s and a single British-designed 64, all of recent construction and prey to the usual range of problems experienced by Arkhangel'sk ships undertaking their maiden voyages around the Scandinavian peninsula. Through no fault of his own, Crown first took his squadron to Sveaborg, having left Arkhangel'sk prior to receipt of new orders redirecting him to England. One 66, the *Vsevolod*, whose name commemorates the 74 lost to the British in 1808, became detached from the squadron, wintered in Norway and arrived in England in 1813. The second 66, *Saratov*, grounded at Sveaborg and had to be destroyed. The rest of Vice-Admiral Crown's squadron completed their roundabout odyssey to Great Britain successfully in the autumn of 1812.

Russian naval forces operated with the British Navy in the North Sea from 1812 to 1814, at which time they became involved in the repatriation of victorious Russian troops from France to St Petersburg. British officers who had had experience with the earlier Russian deployment under Vice-Admiral Makarov in the 1790s are said to have been pleasantly surprised at improvements in Russian seamanship and professionalism during this final Russian deployment to Great Britain. Future friendly close contact between Russian and British warships during the remaining years of the age of sail would be largely limited thereafter to peacetime contacts in the eastern Mediterranean and to co-operation against the Turkish navy at Navarino in 1827. Sadly enough, the final contacts between the two navies during the age of sail would be of a less co-operative nature during the Crimean War in 1853.

The post-Napoleonic Baltic fleet under Alexander I and Nicholas I

With defeat of Napoleon in 1815, Russian naval attention began to shift towards developments in the Black Sea where Turkey and Egypt and ultimately France and Great Britain began to threaten Russian interests and hopes for further southward expansion. The Russians continued to maintain the Baltic fleet as the larger of the two major components of their navy, but the absence of a clear cut threat to Russian suzerainty in northern waters after the final elimination of the Swedish threat could not help but dull growth and innovation in what had traditionally been the more important of the two great Russian fleets.

The downward trend in the effectiveness of the Baltic fleet during the last decade of Alexander I's reign was highlighted by the sale of five ships of the line and three frigates to Spain in 1817 in exchange for badly needed revenue for the Russian state, which was still recovering from the devastation of the Napoleonic Wars. These ships were of fairly recent construction

Four prominent Russian Admirals during the great crisis in 1812 – three fleet commanders and one administrator – seen here clockwise from top right: Admiral George Thate (Tate), commander-in-chief of the Baltic fleet; Vice-Admiral Roman Crown (Cronin, of Venus fame) commander of the Arkhangel'sk squadron; Rear-Admiral von Moller, commander of the rowing flotilla besieging Danzig; and Admiral Alexandr Shishkov – advisor to Emperor Alexander I and the writer of his laws and directives throughout the war.

and of sound design, although the quality of their construction *may* have been below the level of the quality of their design. Had they been properly maintained, they would have served as useful military assets for the Russians. In reality, all of the ships were already showing serious signs of deterioration at the time of their sale due to the inattentive maintenance practices that had become the norm for Russian warships, particularly during Marquis Traversay's tenure in office.

A further and even more telling commentary on Russian naval neglect during the closing years of Alexander I's reign was provided by the investigations initiated into the poor state of the ships of Baltic fleet in the aftermath of the Great Flood of 1824 (see p. 216). Instead of taking the expedient step of attributing the extensive damage the Baltic fleet experienced to the flood itself, the investigators chose to dwell upon the obvious material neglect of the fleet. Ships that might have survived being knocked about and grounded during the enormous tidal surge were determined to have fallen to pieces due to dry rot and similar maladies that should have been avoided.

As already indicated, Alexander's younger brother Nicholas, who assumed the throne in 1825, had entirely different attitudes towards the proper maintenance and employment of the Russian navy and initiated reforms at all levels to insure the future material readiness of Russian warships. His reforms were not entirely successful, but quality control and training within the Russian sailing navy during its final quarter century was of a very different order than had heretofore been the case. During Nicholas's reign, Russia was alone among European nations in commissioning two-thirds of its battle fleet on a rotating basis annually in order to ensure the adequate maintenance of ships in reserve. On the basis of these and other reforms, the Russians under Nicholas, with some justification, considered their ships to be more nearly the equals of their opposite numbers in the French and British navies than had been the case at earlier periods of their naval development. During his reign, the Russian Navy was generally rated as the second largest fleet in the world after Great Britain, ahead of both France and the United States. Whether British naval officers recognized or credited the qualitative improvements made during this period is unclear.

While the Baltic fleet was forced by circumstances into a largely passive role during the final years of sail, its potential value as an asset to Russian power projection was made clear by two unrelated episodes, the Allied intervention against Turkey in 1827 and the Russian intervention in the Schleswig-Holstein crisis of 1848–50.

For the third time since Count Orlov's Baltic squadron had originally been dispatched to the Mediterranean in 1768, Baltic warships provided a necessary vehicle for Russian naval intervention into a theatre outside of its normal range of operation with the deployment of Rear-Admiral Login Petrovich Geiden's squadron to the Mediterranean where it participated in the final fleet engagement of the age of sail at Navarino in 1827. In what can only be described as an assertion of Russian naval pride, eight Russian ships of the line deployed to Portsmouth in August of 1827. Four of the capital ships in the squadron then returned to Kronshtadt after having provided a largely symbolic escort for Rear-Admiral Login Petrovich Geiden's Mediterranean squadron of four ships of the line, three heavy frigates and four brigs.

Navarino and the Closing Years of Sail in the Baltic

Geiden's ships joined the Anglo-French fleet in October and the combined armada easily annihilated a smaller Turkish fleet at Navarino on 8 October (20 October) 1827, assuring Greek independence, providing an opportunity for charges and countercharges about the relative importance of the Russian contribution to the preordained outcome, and laying the groundwork for further multi-national competition over domination of the eastern Mediterranean and ultimately the Black Sea. While Britain and France withdrew from further conflict with either Turkey or Egypt after Navarino, formal warfare between Russia and Turkey broke out in 1828 and lasted until 1830. Evidence for Russian commitment to the Mediterranean theatre and her capacity for sustained power projection was provided by the dispatch of a second squadron to reinforce Geiden's squadron, which departed Kronshtadt in June of 1828 with an additional four ships of the line and two brigs under Rear-Admiral Rikord, bringing the total number of Baltic fleet units committed to the eastern Mediterranean to eight ships of the line, three heavy frigates and six brigs. This would have been considered as a fairly limited deployment in the Napoleonic era and earlier. By the standards of the post-Napoleonic era, it represented a major commitment of force. Peace between Russia and Turkey in 1830, their alliance against the growing power of Egypt, and the opening of the Bosporus to Russian warships based in the Black Sea (until 1841) made the further involvement of Baltic warships in this theatre moot. Further developments in the Mediterranean theatre will be found in the section on the Black Sea fleet.

The war between Denmark and Prussia over Schleswig-Holstein between 1848 and 1850 provided an opportunity for the deployment of the Russian Baltic fleet on a scale not seen since the Russo-Swedish wars of the previous century. Russian involvement in the resolution of the conflict receives almost no attention in Western histories. On the other hand, Russian sources sometimes go to the opposite extreme of attributing the favourable outcome for Denmark entirely to the presence of Russian warships. Whatever the truth of the matter, Russia deployed virtually its entire active battle fleet to Danish waters between 1848 and 1850 with a total participation of 26 ships of the line, five heavy frigates, four brigs, two schooners and a corvette. This was naval intervention on a scale that could not be matched by any possible combination of Baltic naval forces and one that would have required a major commitment on the part of one or both of the major Atlantic naval powers, Great Britain or France to equal.

The Crimean War of 1853 marks the effective end of the Russian sailing navy in both the Black Sea and the Baltic. Great Britain expanded a conflict that related entirely to the collapse of Turkish power in the Black Sea and Mediterranean to Baltic

This aerial view showing the allied naval forces advancing against the Turkish naval units at Navarino in 1827 offers a clear perspective on the battle, but fails to make clear the disparity in force levels between the combatants. Although the numbers of major combatants appear to be well balanced, the Turks have only three line of battle ships to match ten Allied ships. As was customary, the Turkish naval units are at anchor passively awaiting their opponents, with their line anchored by the arms of the bay and further reinforced by shore batteries. The fortress at the bottom of the picture was known as 'New Navarino' and is protected by the Turkish army encampment surrounding it. The ranges involved here were too great for the land-based artillery to offer any effective support and the Turkish ships were left to face the overwhelming firepower advantage possessed by the Allies alone and without any freedom of movement to avoid destruction. The illustration was done by William Innes Pocock, the son of the famous marine painter Nicholas, who was a young naval officer present at the battle.

waters in 1854 with the dispatch of nine steam ships of the line and six obsolescent sail powered ships of the line under the command of Sir Charles Napier. The Russian Baltic fleet at that time numbered 27 capital ships, but was only in the earliest stages of converting to steam and had no realistic recourse beyond seeking the shelter of the guns of Kronshtadt for the duration of the war, as it had in response to Nelson's deployment a half century earlier. A heroic sortie of the Russian Baltic fleet would have accomplished nothing favourable to Russian interests, even assuming a Russian victory – an assumption with no possible basis in reality, given the ability of steam powered warships to manoeuvre in ways impossible for sail powered warships. Nicholas I died in 1855 and with his death, the history of the Russian sailing navy came to an ending sadly muted by the terms of its final demise.

Russia in the Black Sea and the Mediterranean

As Turkey was a larger nation with greater population and financial resources than Sweden, the struggle between Russia and Turkey was of greater duration and intensity than that between Russia and Sweden. The struggle with Turkey antedates the Great Northern War, and the Crimean War marking its climatic resolution – at least during the age of sail – was fought nearly a full half century after the last brief and anti-climactic conflict between the two Baltic rivals ended in 1809. Eight declared wars took place between Russia and Turkey during the age of sail: 1686–1700, 1710–11, 1735–9, 1768–74, 1787–92, 1806–12, 1828–9 and 1853–6, with two further wars taking place in 1878 and during the First World War. While Turkey was the loser in the

Bomarsund was a Russian fortress erected in 1832 on the Aland Islands, much fought over and strategically placed in the Gulf of Bothnia midway between Finland and Sweden. The fortress was attacked and taken on 18 August 1854 by Anglo-French forces in the Crimean War after a fierce defence by its outnumbered Russian garrison. In this overhead depiction, the Anglo-French fleet is bombarding the central fortress, which is responding as vigorously as possible. The Russian Baltic fleet is conspicuously absent from the battle, paralyzed at Kronshtadt by the logic of numbers and its almost complete lack of steam powered warships.

An overhead view of the city of Helsingfors and her defending fortress of Sveaborg during the Crimean War. Sveaborg had been fought over repeatedly during the Russo-Swedish wars of the preceding century and was still the site of the massive fortifications seen in the foreground. In August 1855 both city and fortress were heavily shelled by mortar firing gunboats of the Anglo-French fleet able to deal with the shallow approaches, unnavigable for the majority of the deep draught warships in allied service. Two dozen ships were sunk in the harbour by the 17,000 shells expended, and the garrison at Sveaborg suffered heavy casualties of 2000 dead or wounded. The ship of the line Rossiia *may be seen anchored at the bottom of the picture in the channel just to the right of the fortress.*

majority of the land and sea engagements of these wars, she began and ended the period as a determined and formidable opponent, in spite of her technological and economic backwardness.

Besides the larger scale of the conflict, the struggle along Russia's southern frontier differed from that in the Baltic in that circumstances and necessity forced Russia to attack Turkey on both of her flanks – the Black Sea to the north and the Mediterranean to the south. The use of the Mediterranean as a point of attack against Turkey was in large part driven by difficulties that Russia had had in creating and maintaining a naval presence on the Black Sea and would not have been possible without the active assistance of Great Britain at critical junctures. The final *denouement* of the struggle was to Russia's disadvantage, not because of the strength of Turkish arms, but because the struggle for control of the straits and the Black Sea in 1853 involved a simultaneous confrontation with the two major European powers of the period, both enjoying economic and technological superiority over Russia – France and Great Britain.

The Sea of Azov fleet

Once Peter I had consolidated his control in Russia and begun to turn his eyes towards territorial expansion, it was apparent that any southward expansion of the Russian state, in furtherance of its long term goal of capturing Constantinople from the Turks and gaining access to the Mediterranean, would be conditional upon gaining control of the Black Sea and its coastline. Any furtherance of this goal, in turn, was conditional upon establishing a sea port on the northern shore of the Baltic and creating adequate naval facilities for the construction and maintenance of a fleet to challenge Turkish dominance and to provide logistical support for Russian land armies. This was the background for the conquest of the seaport and fortress of Azov by Russia in 1696, a conquest doomed to initial failure as a result of the simultaneous struggle with Sweden and later success a full generation after Peter I's death.

Given its strategic location at the mouth of the Don, Azov was the natural target for Peter I's first attempt at pushing Russian frontiers southward into Turkish territory. His initial attempt at besieging and taking Azov in 1695 failed in spite of the commitment of over 30,000 troops due to the inability of the Russians to prevent Turkey from supplying the fortress by sea. The only realistic hope for taking Azov lay in establishing an effective seaborne blockade and this required ships, or at least galleys and gunboats, to intercept merchant ships attempting to reach the city and to block Turkish warships from safely escorting them. Peter had the will and the resources to create the first makings of a navy, but he lacked an adequate seaport for the construction of seagoing sailing ships. What he did have, instead, was the Don River and its tributaries.

With remarkable speed, considering the undeveloped nature of southern Russia, Peter set about creating a fleet of two 36-gun rowing frigates, four fire ships and 22 galleys. The two frigates were built at Voronezh on the Don some 800 miles north of Azov, while the lesser vessels had been prefabricated at Moscow

A highly romanticized depiction of the final assault on Azov in 1696 by the early nineteenth-century artist R. K. Porter. For the first time in Russian history, the Russian navy is engaged in action alongside the Russian army. Peter I, still untested as a warrior or as a ruler, is seen here dominating the action and leading the assault. The future emperor had seen the need for a fleet able to further his ambitions in the Black Sea and had created one within the space of a single year capable of a major offensive against a powerful and determined enemy, a remarkable accomplishment for a remarkable man.

and then moved in sections to Voronezh for completion. Peter faced two major obstacles in his first attempt at constructing a significant naval force. The first lay in the shallow conditions of the Don which limited the allowable draft of the ships being built and accordingly their size, and which frequently prevented their passage down river upon completion. The second was the initial decision to assign the fiscal responsibility for building the new fleet to aristocrats and ecclesiastical powers throughout Russia and then allow them to contract out the work to private contractors of questionable integrity and limited experience in the construction of warships – the *kumpanstva*. The first problem would ultimately be resolved by capturing the port of Azov. This was accomplished in 1696 with the imposition of the blockade and with the refusal of a marginally superior Turkish fleet of six ships and 17 galleys to accept combat with the available Russian naval forces. The second problem would not be resolved until 1700, with the elimination of the *kumpanstva* and their permanent replacement in the Sea of Azov and elsewhere

Looking every inch a dour Dutchman, this is Vice-Admiral Cruys (1657–1727), a Dutch naval officer recruited during Peter I's European tour and a rare example of Dutch influence in a navy increasingly dependent on the British connections developed by the young Tsar while on his European tour. Cruys was in command during the first exchange of fire between Russian and Swedish warships in 1705 and again in the failed defence of Azov in 1711. In 1713 he attracted Peter I's wrath by running his ship aground when in pursuit of fleeing Swedish warships. Condemned to death, his sentence was remanded and he was allowed to return to service, but only in an administrative capacity ashore. By P. P. Bruks 1870.

by state operated shipyards (see Shipyards for further details).

With the exception of the 36-gun rowing frigates *Apostl Pyotr* and *Sviatoi Pavel*, the initial 'fleet' of ships was little more than a collection of shallow water galleys and it quickly deteriorated into unserviceability after the conquest of Azov. The vessels that successfully blockaded the Turkish port were essentially river craft and hardly merit description as a prototypical battle fleet. Nevertheless, they were a beginning, and one that convincingly demonstrated what would be the amalgamation of river, naval and land forces that would characterize Russian naval operations in the future in the Black Sea, the Baltic and the Caspian.

Seizing Azov was not the same as holding Azov, and Peter I began constructing a true seagoing fleet in earnest after his victory, bringing in human and material resources from throughout Russia, establishing a network of shipyards along the length of the Don and her tributaries in the process, and hiring skilled designers and shipwrights from all over Europe, most particularly Venice and the Netherlands. The Turks continued to maintain pressure on Azov until 1698, when a two years' truce was agreed upon. Peter did not return to Azov from his travels throughout the capitals of Europe and his suppression of an incipient rebellion in his own capital until June of 1699. In July of that year, the newly formed fleet left for exercises and manoeuvres under Admiral Golovin and Vice-Admiral Kruys, with the Tsar travelling under his assumed title as Captain Pyotr Mikhailov. This fleet was of respectable size and comprised ten ships – all formally, if optimistically, designated as ships of the line carrying 36 to 52 guns apiece – and two galleys. It should be noted that this squadron represented the *successful* products of the construction programme of the late 1690s and did not include the eleven ships that had been rejected on delivery due to shoddy construction by the aforementioned *Kumpanstva*. The cruise terminated at the end of August at the Turkish fortress of Kerch, where the squadron left the 52-gun *Krepost'* to conduct the Russian ambassador with a Turkish escort to Constantinople. The negotiations culminated in the signing of a 30-year peace treaty between Russia and Turkey in July of 1700. The 'thirty years' lasted until 1710 when war broke out again, due, in part at least, to the machinations of the exiled Charles XII of Sweden.

Peter's construction programme expanded with the signing of peace and, as R. C. Anderson notes, a further 15 'line of battleships' were completed by 1702, and armed with 36 to 66 guns. Had war with Turkey not broken out again in 1710, these ships would have shortly included a number of 70- and 80-gun ships (see data section on the Sea of Azov fleet for details). There can be no question about the seriousness of Peter I's commitment to the construction of a viable battle fleet capable of challenging the Turkish domination of the Black Sea, in spite of suggestions by some historians that it was merely a temporary expedient. Unfortunately, when war with Turkey broke out again in 1710, the vast majority of the ships already completed were found to be unserviceable due to the combined effects of the severe Russian winters, heavy ice build-up along the Don, and inadequate maintenance practices of the sort that would bedevil the Russians over the coming century. The 70- and 80-gun ships that were at the heart of the programme were well advanced in their construction, but could not make the passage to the Sea of Azov for fitting out due to unusually low water conditions. Only four of 19 of the officially designated 'battleships', two galleys and five smaller ships could be commissioned for service to face the Turkish battle fleet of 18 capital ships and 14 galleys that appeared off Azov in July 1711. In spite of this overwhelming disparity of force, a squadron of seven Turkish galleys was successfully driven off by a tiny Russian force made up of the 30-gun *Unia* and three 14-gun snows in the very brief interval before the end of hostilities saved Admiral Kruys's tiny squadron from probable destruction in the face of overwhelming Turkish material superiority.

Peter I has been called 'the Great' with good cause, but his involvement in a two-front war with Sweden to the north and Turkey to the south exceeded even his resources. At this point in

Russian history, the struggle against Sweden was of greater consequence than the struggle against Turkey, and the Russian state was forced to cut its losses in the southern theatre by signing the Treaty of Prut on 12 August (23 August) 1711. Azov and Taganrog were returned to Turkey and the survivors of the painfully constructed Sea of Azov fleet were consigned to the Turks, with the exception of a very few ships built and building along the Don.

In retrospect, the short-lived Sea of Azov fleet served a useful purpose for the Russians in spite of its untimely demise. By building and operating a full-fledged naval force in very short order and with little preparation, Russia and Peter I gained essential experience with the wide range of human, material, economic, political and organizational elements necessary for the creation of an effective navy. The experience gained was transferred to the Baltic upon the loss of Azov, as were the human resources including shipwrights and skilled craftsmen who were transferred directly from Azov to the shipyards of St Petersburg, abandoning their work underway in the process. Without the experience gained in the Sea of Azov, Russia could not have created the infrastructure and the naval forces that ultimately seized control of the Gulf of Finland from the experienced and sophisticated naval forces deployed against it by Charles XII.

The Russo-Turkish War 1736–9

The Sea of Azov fleet had died a premature death in 1711 as had ambitious Russian plans for its further growth and expansion. The first tentative steps towards the rebirth of a fleet capable of challenging Turkey for domination in the Black Sea were not taken until 1769. The little remarked Russo-Turkish War of 1735–9, undertaken by the Empress Anna and marking the resumption of Russian southward expansion, falls almost precisely in the middle of these two periods. R. C. Anderson describes the flotilla of galleys, prams and gunboats constructed on the Don before and during this brief war as the Second Black Sea fleet. Labelling the half-born Sea of Azov flotilla of 1696–1711 as the First Black Sea fleet *may have been* allowable overstatement on Anderson's part. Calling the ad hoc assemblage of shallow water craft created on the Don and on the Dniepr for the 1735–9 war – nine 44-gun prams, six 8-gun prams, 92 galleys and over a thousand small craft – a 'fleet' in any sense of the word is unwarranted hyperbole. The forces involved in the capture of the Turkish fortress in 1736 were a purpose-built and short-lived collection of shallow bottomed river craft designed for the narrowest of military purposes – the reduction of a fortified port – and not a seagoing navy in any real sense. Although the Russian flotilla under Rear-Admiral Bredal, of Norwegian descent, was successful in insuring the early recapture of Azov, the Turkish navy demonstrated the superiority of *balanced* naval power by using a combination of galleys and sailing ships to neutralize and devastate the Russian inshore flotillas in the Sea of Azov in every subsequent encounter during the war. Similar amphibious operations involving large Russian flotillas of galleys, prams and gunboats taking place around the port and fortress of Ochakov to the west, were similarly dealt with by the Turkish navy.

The peace treaty negotiated and signed in 1739 returned Ochakov to Turkey, but gave Russia possession of two important ports with access to the Black Sea, Azov and Taganrog, at the cost of their demilitarization and the prohibition of Russian naval forces in either the Sea of Azov or the Black Sea. In spite of these restrictions, the Treaty of Constantinople did at last give Russian merchant ships access to the Black Sea and laid the groundwork for the creation of a true navy under Catherine II.

The Turkish Problem

The following discussion of naval warfare between Russia and Turkey between 1700 and 1860 will stand in marked contrast to our earlier discussion of warfare between Russia and Sweden during the same time period. Although the Ottoman Empire was organized on very different cultural, administrative and bureaucratic lines than European nations, it is difficult to imagine that an organization of the size of the Turkish navy could have functioned without some form of organized record keeping relating to construction programmes, personnel and command matters, fleet listings and dispositions, operational instructions and battle reports. While these records very possibly are extant in Turkish government archives, they have not been made available for researchers to the best of our knowledge. It is however, reasonable to assume a relative lack of structure, organization and accountability along European lines in the period leading up to the reforms instituted by Selim III in 1789 by the fact that formal log keeping in Turkish warships was not formally mandated until 1796. The information that we do have on the performance of the Turkish Navy during this period accordingly comes essentially from two sources: Russian naval records and histories, primarily the oft-mentioned *Materialy* on the one hand, and the writings of Western, primarily British, officers who served in the Russian navy in either the Mediterranean or the Black Sea during this period, on the other. Both of these sources require careful handling, because their authors were affected, not only by own quite natural nationalistic biases against an alien culture, that of Islamic Turkey, but also by the infighting that also took place between Russian and foreign officers in Russian service, primarily British, over the significance of their respective contributions to the conflict.

Not only are we left in the dark about the motivations and decision making processess of the Turkish commanders, we are frequently forced to estimate the strength and composition of Turkish squadrons participating in various battles. While we generally have a very good idea of the Russian warships involved in various fleet actions, their positioning in battle squadrons and their armaments and types, we are just as often left with only the vaguest estimates for the numbers and types of Turkish ships. Turkish warships were sometimes referred to by their commander's names, which could vary from one campaign to the next, or by their function, such as 'Primary Flagship' or 'Secondary Flagship'. When formal ship names are known, foreign transliterations of Arabic spellings, especially those involving multiple recasting (e.g. from Arabic to German to English), can exhibit such great variability as to make recognition of even the simplest ship names a matter for conjecture for the confused Westerner. Nor is the rating by armament of much use, as a ship may appear in one context as an '80' and in another as a '110'. Finally, the number of guns carried by Turkish warships may have very limited value for drawing comparisons with Russian ships, because many of the ships involved in major battles are thought to have been hired merchantmen with lighter batteries and scantlings than purpose-built warships with the same number of guns (see Anderson for examples).

Even the reported figures for ships lost and casualties sustained are very much open to debate. For the Russians, we have precise and exact information and no good cause for doubting its general validity. For the Turks, we only have estimates made by the Russians after the fact and without solid information from the Turkish side to provide balance, confirmation, or contradiction. There should be little doubt that the Russian figures for Turkish casualties are overstated to an indeterminate degree. This is no particular reflection on the integrity of the Russians, since this type of exaggeration is inevitable in all forms of warfare as conducted by all nationalities at all times. The problem here is that there was no mechanism to balance out the exaggerations of the victorious Russians with less extravagant Turkish figures. If there are reliable casualty figures buried somewhere in the government archives in Constantinople, they are likely to remain so for the foreseeable future.

A very recent publication by a Turkish historian, Tuncay Zorlu, has gone some considerable distance towards shedding some useful light on Turkish naval matters. It is clear from Zorlu's account that the Turkish navy prior to and during the 1787–92 war was technologically inferior in most respects to Russian and European navies. According to Zorlu, the technological disparity between the Turkish navy and the Russian navy was highlighted by their shortcomings in naval ordnance. The quality of iron manufacture is said to have lagged behind that of Russia and Western Europe. Not only were Turkish guns said to have been poorly manufactured by Western standards, the metal fittings and braces on the gun carriages were also of poor quality, making for instability and unreliability in combat. Cannon balls were generally said to have been manufactured of marble and granite instead of iron, and this was still purported to have been the case during the 1807–12 war.

It must be noted that this information runs directly counter to contemporary Russian reports. Battle reports filed by Russian artillery officers during this entire period make no mention of the presence of any naval ordnance other than iron shot, although the large bombards defending the Straits were indeed known to be limited to stone shot due to their enormous size. As for the alleged poor quality of Turkish ordnance, this also runs counter to the very high regard that European observers had for Turkish artillery throughout the sixteenth and seventeenth centuries. On the other hand, the reported poor quality of Turkish ordnance and ammunition comes from a Turkish historian with no particular motivation for calling attention to his own country's shortcomings. The matter clearly requires further investigation.

Regardless of the debate over the quality of Turkish ordnance, there was an unquestioned shortage of trained gunnery personnel aboard Turkish warships, and similar shortages in skilled manpower in other technologically important areas. To make matters worse, the gun batteries carried aboard ships were generally said by Zorlu to have been made up of random collections of whatever ordnance was available at the time of their fitting out, with little regard for uniformity of type or calibre. Different guns require not only different shot sizes, but different amounts of gunpowder for effective use in battle. The difficulties this chaos must have presented to ship commanders trying to maintain high rates of fire in action can only be imagined. In contrast, the quality of Turkish gunpowder was said to be fairly good, and British ships operating in the Levant after the Nile had no problems with accepting Turkish supplies. The Turks also were rather surprisingly ahead of the Russians in their adoption of coppering for their line ships and frigates in the early 1790s, a situation which allowed for greater speed and ease of handling, and provided protection against hull deterioration.

After the defeat at Ches'ma in 1770, and most particularly in the period after Selim III assumed the throne in 1789, intense efforts were made to rebuild and modernize the Ottoman navy, to eliminate corruption and incompetence among the naval officers, and to import large numbers of skilled ship builders, artisans and workmen from France and elsewhere in Europe. The real problems facing the Turks were the lack of technological depth in their overall economy, the corresponding lack of an educated and educable officer corps and competent candidates for the various noncommissioned specialties. Although loyalty and motivation may have been a problem for the Turks because of ethnic and religious problems, there was never a shortage in the potential supply of skilled seamen from various subject ethnicities, particularly Greek. Recruitment and retention were serious problems, however, because of the extremely poor habitability of Turkish warships and the inadequacy and infrequency of pay.

All of these factors should be borne in mind in the following discussion. The situation improves over time and we do have a far better picture of events occurring after 1800, but a fog remains over the entire subject of Turkish fleet composition, readiness, training and performance. The reader should remember that the events described in the following have been presented almost entirely from the perspective of the winning side.

The Russo-Turkish War 1768–74

War broke out again between Turkey and Russia in 1768 over events in Poland that had no direct relationship with events in either the Black Sea or the Mediterranean. Catherine II had no means of striking directly at Turkey through the most direct water route, the Black Sea, because she had no naval forces there. She accordingly made the unprecedented decision to strike at

Turkey from an unexpected quarter by sending the better part of the Baltic fleet around the entire European peninsula and through the Mediterranean to Turkish controlled waters in and around the Greek Archipelago, a move that involved serious logistical risks and one that left her Baltic naval forces dangerously short of warships. Her purpose in doing so was to divert Turkish naval and ground resources from the Black Sea to the Mediterranean by threatening Turkish lines of maritime communication and by encouraging Greek nationalists to intensify their efforts at the liberation of Greek territories in Greece itself and in the Aegean. The Empress was only able to consider such an audacious move because of the willingness of Great Britain to make available the facilities and resources of her naval bases at Portsmouth, Gibraltar and Port Mahon on the isle of Minorca. Great Britain, of course, had her own very selfish reasons for wishing to undermine Turkey at the time, and her friendship with Russia was conditional and tentative. On other occasions, the two nations would find themselves very much at odds over 'the Turkish Question', but Catherine had the advantage at this point in European history.

Even with British assistance, the transfer of Baltic fleet units to the Aegean was a move of extraordinary daring. The other Mediterranean powers were opposed to the Russian presence in the Levant and offered neither assistance nor comfort. The Russian Baltic fleet had never had experience with this type of long-range deployment, and its ships were not designed for Mediterranean conditions. Problems related to strenuous employment and a lack of adequate maintenance facilities would become increasingly severe as the campaign continued for several years. Finally, stripping Russia of most of her Baltic naval resources left her potentially vulnerable at home in the Baltic, even allowing for the comparative weakness of the other Baltic states at the time. Nevertheless Catherine took the gamble, giving the Baltic fleet invaluable operational experience in distant waters, and opening the way for some of the greatest victories in Russian naval history.

The initial Russian deployment to the Baltic was planned for the summer of 1769 and was to have involved the sequential transfer of two squadrons, the first under the command of Admiral Grigorii Spiridov, and the second under the command of Rear-Admiral John Elphinston, a newly appointed Scotsman on approved leave from the Royal Navy. Elphinston had accumulated a solid record of accomplishment – and of independence and untoward initiative occasionally bordering on insubordination and both aspects of his personality would manifest themselves during his service in the Russian Navy. The original intent of the deployment was to have Spiridov depart from Kronshtadt in July with seven ships of the line, a single frigate, the bomb vessel *Grom* and five smaller craft. Elphinston was to follow thereafter with three additional capital ships and two frigates, leaving the Baltic fleet with only five capital ships and four frigates left to deal with unexpected contingencies at home. The two squadrons were to proceed to Port Mahon in the Mediterranean, where they would reunite and be placed under the overall command of Count Aleksei Orlov, an experienced military officer, but lacking in naval experience. Orlov was the

John Elphinston (1722–85) was one of a very large number of experienced British naval officers recruited by Russia during the reign of Catherine II as a result of a deliberate policy aimed at upgrading Russian naval skills in preparation for renewed war with Turkey. A brilliant and aggressive officer, he was given command of one of the two squadrons operating in the Mediterranean against the Turks in the 1768–74 war under the overall command of Count Orlov. As the highest-ranking British officer serving with Russia, he found himself in a position that required tact and good judgment as well as tactical proficiency. During his tenure under Count Orlov, he accomplished all that could have been asked of him as a flag officer in combat with the Turks, at the same time as he clashed repeatedly with his nominal superior, Admiral Spiridov as well as the Russian officers under his authority. By the time that he ran his 80-gun flagship Sviatoslav *aground at Lemnos on 6 July 1770, he was already operating under a cloud of disapproval and his dismissal from Russian service four months later was almost an afterthought.*

brother to Grigorii Orlov, Catherine's current court favourite, and a man of considerable ability in his own right.

Neither the ships nor the weather conditions co-operated with the planned schedule of operations, and the progress of both squadrons from Kronshtadt to Port Mahon was filled with misadventures and calamities, along with extensive periods of

The siege and bombardment of the Greek fortress town of Coron (modern Koroni) by the Russian fleet in 1770.

refit and repair at the British naval bases at Portsmouth and Gibraltar. Spiridov's squadron left Kronshtadt in August; but Elphinston's smaller squadron did not set sail until October. Both groups ran into problems relating to weather conditions and to the sometimes inadequate material condition of their ships. Spiridov's ships did not begin arriving at Port Mahon until November 1769. Elphinston's group was delayed at Portsmouth until May of 1770 by adverse weather conditions and by the need for refit after the journey from the Baltic. One of his ships, the *Tver'* (66), was so badly damaged by severe weather conditions that she was forced to return to Revel'. A second 66, the *Severnyi Oryol* – originally assigned to Spiridov's group and forced to turn back to Portsmouth due to leaks – was in such bad condition that she had to be cut down to a 32 by the Portsmouth dockyard and then sent on her way to the Mediterranean as a hospital ship. Two of the smaller escorts were lost in the long transit to the Mediterranean. As for Spiridov's intended flagship, the 80-gun *Sviatoslav*, she was sidelined twice for repairs. As a result of these delays, she ended up in Elphinston's Second Squadron, where became his unexpectedly prestigious flagship until her loss to grounding at the approaches to Constantinople.

After refitting at Port Mahon, Spiridov sent a small squadron to pick up Count Orlov at Leghorn in February as planned. The squadron then began a systematic campaign of bombarding Greek ports under Turkish control and of landing small contingents of troops to stir up resistance against the Turks and to draw out the Turkish battle fleet. The port of Navarino was taken by Orlov in April and became the primary Russian base of operations pending the arrival of Elphinston's squadron. Elphinston finally arrived with his squadron in May, began landing troops at Rupino and then received reports that the Turkish fleet was concentrating at Nafplion. With only three ships of the line and two frigates under his command, he located and pursued the much larger Turkish squadron, of ten to 13 ships of the line with supporting units. Elphinston has been criticized for attacking the larger Turkish squadron without waiting for support from Spiridov's squadron, but his action reveals the confidence felt by the Russians in their first major engagement with the Turks at sea as well as the aggressiveness and independence of their Scottish commander. Part of Elphinston's confidence may also have been based on his use of edinorogs and related explosive ordnance in combat at sea for the first time. These explosive shells created great consternation amongst the Turks, as much by their novelty as by their effectiveness.

The Turkish fleet sought shelter under the guns of the fortress at Nafplion. Elphinston initially entered the harbour in pursuit and engaged the Turks under the guns of Turkish shore batteries, doing serious damage before being forced to withdraw in the face of the superior numbers. He then imposed a blockade of sorts with his smaller force and sent a courier overland to request reinforcements of Orlov. When the Turkish fleet finally set sail three days into the standoff, Elphinston was unable to take action to engage or pursue them, due to the refusal of one of his subordinates to obey his direct orders. He was forced instead to retreat, with the Turkish squadron now in pursuit of their

RUSSIAN NAVAL HISTORY 1695–1860

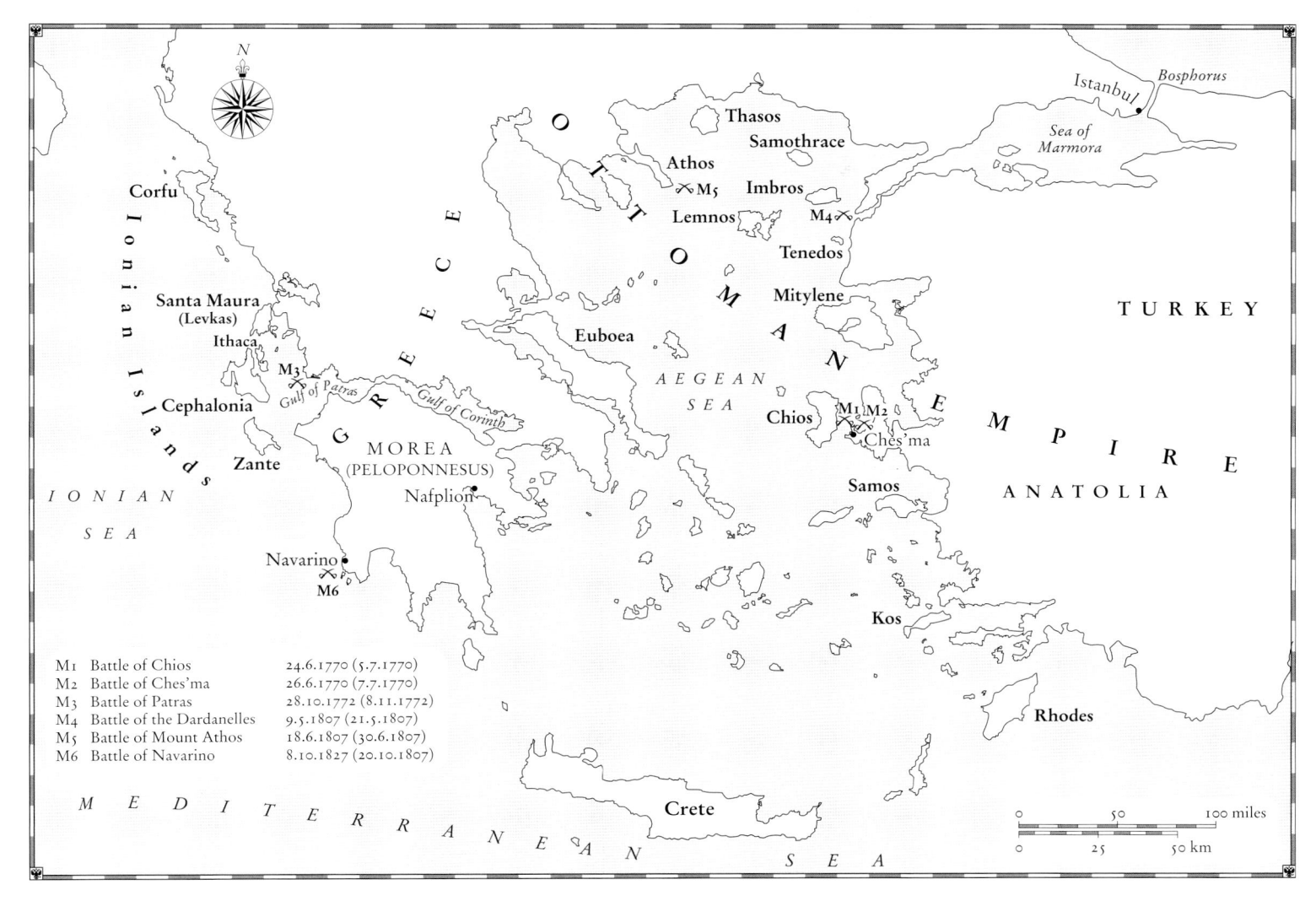

Given the early weakness of Russian naval power in the Black Sea, the Aegean to the south of Istanbul offered a point of attack for Baltic warships able to redeploy to the Mediterranean. Between 1770 and 1827, six major battles were fought in and around the Aegean and the Adriatic.

M1 Battle of Chios 24.6.1770 (5.7.1770)
M2 Battle of Ches'ma 26.6.1770 (7.7.1770)
M3 Battle of Patras 28.10.1772 (8.11.1772)
M4 Battle of the Dardanelles 9.5.1807 (21.5.1807)
M5 Battle of Mount Athos 18.6.1807 (30.6.1807)
M6 Battle of Navarino 8.10.1827 (20.10.1807)

erstwhile pursuers. The recalcitrant officer, Commodore Barsh of the *Saratov* (66), later fell back on Peter I's instructions from the previous half-century regarding the acceptable conditions for accepting combat – a three to two ratio of superiority being required – and the British officer could do nothing to remedy his Russian subordinate's insubordination and apparent cowardice beyond removing him from his command – incidentally alienating many of the Russian officers in his squadron, who were already resentful over having to accept a foreign born commander.

Elphinston and Spiridov finally linked up at the beginning of June and immediately began quarrelling over the question of leadership and seniority, with the recently appointed Scotsman maintaining that Catherine II had expressly placed himself in overall command of the two squadrons – an assertion that seems unlikely given Spiridov's seniority and the larger size of his squadron. The issue of command was not resolved until Count Orlov, having evacuated Navarino under pressure from the Turkish army, joined the two squadrons on the 22nd at Paros with his single line of battle ship, the *Trekh Ierakhov* (66) and the bomb vessel *Grom*. The combined Russian fleet now consisted of nine ships of the line and three frigates and Orlov decided to seek out the Turkish battle fleet, which comprised 14 to 17 capital ships and supporting frigates.

The Battles of Chios and Ches'ma 24–26 June (5–7 July) 1770

The combined squadrons found the Turkish battle fleet at anchor off the isle of Chios on 24 June (5 July) 1770. The resulting three-day series of battles was anticlimactic in its outcome, if spectacular in its fury. On the face of it, the odds should have been strongly with the Turkish side. The Russian battle line consisted of a single 80-gun ship and eight 66s, while the Turks had three 80-gun ships, seven 70-gun ships and six 60s according to Orlov's report (According to Anderson, Hammer Purgstall and Samuel Greig give slightly different figures of 15 and 17

The battle at Chios Straits in 1770. To the left is the bow of a Russian frigate. In the middle distance are the two flagships locked in mortal combat just minutes before exploding. In the centre are Russian boats either fleeing the conflagration or picking up survivors. P. J. Volaire's painting of 1771 can be regarded as more accurately detailed than most such after-battle paintings – he was a participant and a survivor.

ships of the line, a salient example of the uncertainty surrounding Turkish force levels). In spite of the material advantage possessed by the Turks, the real advantage lay with the Russians, based on their higher level of training and discipline – and their possession of an untried new weapons system in the form of explosive ordnance fired from mortars, edinorogs and occasionally from conventional cannon.

The American born Ottoman historian Stanford Shaw has noted that Turkish warships, in this period before the reforms instituted by Selim III, 'were invariably massive and bulky, with excessively high poops, superstructures and riggings, with widths almost as great as their lengths and with unusually deep drafts, which denied them access to any but the deepest harbours. These ships were extremely difficult to manoeuvre in the ordinary course of sailing, let alone in battle; and were prone to capsize as a result of sudden movements by inexperienced hands during storms or battles.' Shaw is clearly overstating matters, especially with respect to the alleged beaminess of Turkish ships, but his point is clear, even if his credentials as an authority on warship design are open to question. The size of the

Turkish fleet was no indication of its quality, and this should be borne in mind in considering the debacle that followed However one wishes to evaluate the allegedly fragile material condition of the Russian combatants at Chios and Ches'ma, they were modern ships, with excellent ordnance, and with crews hardened and disciplined by their long voyage from Kronshtadt. The odds were with the Russians.

During its approach to the Turkish line, the Russian fleet was divided into the traditional centre, van and rear, with three ships in each group and with Spiridov in the van, Orlov the centre and Elphinston the rear. The Turkish fleet contented itself with waiting passively for the Russian attack, with their fleet disposed in two lines arranged to allow the second line to provide support by firing through the intervals in the first line, which was made up of the heaviest ships, an arrangement of somewhat limited utility for a fleet manoeuvring at sea as opposed to that it offered to a fleet at anchor. This refusal by the Turks to attempt to actively manoeuvre against a numerically weaker opponent, not only revealed the inadequacies of both their training and leadership; it allowed the attacking Russians, who had the wind on their side, complete control of the course of the initial battle.

Rather than approaching and engaging the Turkish line in the traditional manner on the morning of the 24 June (5 July) wearing in succession and passing down the entire length of the longer Turkish line: the Russians chose to approach in a somewhat uneven line abreast, with each ship wearing individually while maintaining its proper station in line. This tactic was unorthodox and required a degree of skill to execute properly; but it allowed them to close more rapidly and engage an equal number of Turkish warships and to avoid exposing the leading elements of the Russian line to the disproportionate punishment that would have resulted from their passing down the entire length of the longer Turkish line to seek out their 'proper' opponents. The two lines became fully engaged, with Spiridov's flagship, *Sviatoi Evstafii (66)* taking fire from five other Turkish ships before engaging the Turkish flagship, the 84-gun *Burc-i Zafer (Real Mustafa* in some sources*)* and setting her afire with carcasses (explosive fused spherical ordnance) fired from her edinorogs. The Turkish flagship was successfully boarded, but both ships were destroyed by the spread of the fire to the *Evstafii* and by the resulting explosion of the Russian flagship. Both Spiridov and the Turkish commander Hassan Pasha escaped the simultaneous loss of their flagships. The Turkish fleet was thrown into panic by this catastrophe and cut its cables *en masse*, drifting in an unorganized and undignified mass into the harbour of Ches'ma south of the battle site.

25 June (6 July) found the Turkish fleet of 70 to 80 warships of all sizes and over 100 other smaller craft forced into close proximity within the congested harbour and exposed throughout the day to long range shelling by the bomb vessel *Grom*, supported during the night by *Sviatoslav, Rostislav* and *Evropa* and the next day by *Trekh Ierarkhov* and *Sviatoslav*. The Turkish fleet was intact if demoralized, contenting itself with once again forming an in-depth defensive line with eight of the strongest ships blocking entrance to the harbour, and having the advantage of being covered on either flank by the arms of the bay and of being further protected by shore batteries. For its part, the Russian fleet was in a more difficult position than it had been the previous day when it had first sighted the Turkish fleet in the open waters between Chios and the mainland. Its only apparent options included establishing a blockade with all its attendant logistical problems, launching a risky frontal attack on the Turkish position, or withdrawing to its available bases in the Aegean and awaiting combat on a later date. The option to attack was chosen and the assault was launched late on the 25th over a narrow front with four ships of the line, two frigates and the *Grom*, all under the command of Samuel Greig, a Scotsman on leave from the Royal Navy and Count Orlov's flag captain under more normal circumstances.

The resulting battle of Ches'ma devolved quickly into an outright slaughter when an explosive shell from the *Grom* set fire to one of the Turkish ships of the line and the resulting conflagration began to spread throughout the congested harbour. The Russian victory has frequently been attributed to the use of fire ships, but it should be noted that the four ships so employed were not sent into action until *after* the *Grom* had done her damage and started fires that were already spreading on their own throughout the Turkish fleet. It should also be noted that only one of the four fire ships was able to accomplish its mission by starting a fire on a Turkish ship – an action that only added to the conflagration already under way. The Russian success should be attributed to the successful use of explosive ordnance in conjunction with the use of fire ships, along with the passivity and incompetence of the Turkish commanders. When the fires had died down by eight o'clock the morning of the 26 June (7 July), Turkish losses included 14 ships of the line, six frigates, 45 lesser craft and an appalling total of 11,000 men killed. In addition the Russians succeeded in rescuing a single Turkish line of battle ship and five galleys from the disaster by towing them out of the harbour before they could be consumed in the conflagration.

The back-to-back battles of Chios and Ches'ma are dealt with in such detail here, not only because they are regarded quite rightly by the Russians as one of their most decisive victories, but also because they bring together the interplay between the advantages possessed by the Russians with respect to training and discipline, their successful introduction of a new type of weaponry – edinorogs firing explosive shells – the determined aggressiveness of the Russian naval commanders and both the positive and negative aspects of the Russian reliance on British officers released by the Royal Navy for temporary – and in some cases, permanent – service with the Russian navy. John Elphinston stands out as a talented and aggressive officer who managed to accomplish much that was of value to the campaign, at the same time as he alienated and at times infuriated his peers and superiors by his headstrong independence. In contrast, Samuel Greig, while junior to Elphinston at the time, showed equal talent as an officer and as a tactician, at the same time as he proved able to establish warm and friendly relationships with his Russian superiors, peers and subordinates.

The British government had one of its not infrequent changes of heart shortly after the battle of Ches'ma and recalled British officers serving on detached duty with the Russians to British service. Elphinston and many of his fellow officers returned to Great Britain and to useful and productive careers in the Royal Navy. Samuel Greig stands out as the most famous, but hardly the only, British officer to elect to remain with the Russian Navy and to live out their lives in Russia.

In the immediate aftermath of the destruction of the Turkish battle fleet at Ches'ma, the Russian Archipelago Squadron found itself in search of a mission. The hoped for expansion of long simmering Greek hostility to Turkish rule into a major uprising on the Greek mainland had failed to materialize, due to the forceful and effective response of the Turkish army to Russian amphibious operations. In contrast, there was very little Turkish naval opposition left to deal with in either the Aegean or the Eastern Mediterranean. Russian naval attention turned naturally to Constantinople and the Dardanelles, long the objective of Russian policy. With the destruction of the Turkish battle fleet, the islands of the Archipelago all revolted against the Turks. The only apparent obstacles remaining to achieving the Russian objective of forcing the Dardanelles were the forts protecting them. The condition of the forts has been a source of some controversy, with some authors suggesting that they were in a state of ineffectual decrepitude and with others holding that they presented a real obstacle to Russian warships. The defences of the Dardanelles and Constantinople itself were never tested, however, because the Turks responded to the Russian seizure of Lemnos by retaking it immediately with 3,500 Turkish troops and forcing a Russian evacuation – hardly the actions of a defeated and cowed opponent. Spiridov and Elphinston were forced to content themselves with imposing a blockade of the Straits, an action that caused panics and rioting in the Turkish capital. Elphinston brought an end to his contentious career with the Russians by grounding and losing his flagship, the *Sviatoslav*, during these operations. He was dismissed from Russian service four months later, for reasons quite probably as much related to his willful recalcitrance as to his grounding and losing his flagship.

The remainder of the war was involved with Russian consolidation of her holdings in the Archipelago, in shutting down Turkish maritime communications and in raids against Turkish bases throughout the eastern Mediterranean. Strong reinforcements were sent from the Baltic in 1770, 1772 and 1773, consisting of a total of nine ships of the line and two frigates and lesser craft. These ships helped make good the losses from attrition experienced by ships separated from adequate maintenance facilities and driven severely by the exigencies of combat. The only further naval combat of any consequence occurred on 28 October (8 November) 1772 at the battle of Patras and involved the destruction of nine Turkish 30-gun frigates and ten xebecs by two Russian ships of the line and two frigates at the entrance to the Gulf of Corinth. This series of engagements extended over three days and the Turkish ships were protected on the final day by shore batteries, but to no avail. Only six xebecs were able to escape down the Gulf of Corinth, while the Russians suffered insignificant casualties of only one dead and seven injured.

Although the dispatch of the better part of the Baltic fleet to the Aegean had succeeded in drawing the Turkish battle fleet out of the Black Sea and into the Mediterranean, the lack of an organized naval force in the Black Sea itself made military operations in the Ukraine against Turkish coastal cities and fortifications difficult for the Russians and gave Turkey the potential ability to move and supply her armies without interference. To remedy this situation, the Azov Squadron was reborn after a lapse of 30 years with the completion in 1770 of ten heavily armed, shallow draught 14/16-gun 'battleships' and two bomb vessels constructed by I. I. Afanasyev. Four additional 30/32-gun frigates of considerably larger size, but still shallow draught vessels unsuitable for deep-water operations, were also completed before the end of hostilities. This modest force, under the leadership of an enterprising and aggressive group of young officers destined for greater things, including Vice-Admiral Aleksi Seniavin, son and father of a famous naval dynasty, Rear Admiral Pavel Chichagov, Captain M. Sukhotin and a Dutch-born officer Captain H. Kinsbergen, successfully and repeatedly engaged the significantly larger fleet of Turkish warships still operating in the Black Sea after the disaster at Ches'ma, breaking up attempted landings and forcing the withdrawal of superior Turkish forces. A further dozen 'frigates' of similar design were laid down in shipyards feeding into the Don during the 1770s, but the problem that had faced the Sea of Azov fleet earlier in the century remained – the impracticability of attempting to build seaworthy deep water warships in shallow water shipyards along the Don.

Peace was signed between Russia and Turkey on 21 July (1 August) 1774. Russia was awarded the ports of Azov, Taganrog, Kerch and Kinburn and much of the Ukraine in exchange for the surrender of the Aegean islands taken in the war. In addition, Russia now was allowed passage through the Straits for mercantile purposes and was ceded the right to build and operate naval forces in the Black Sea. The Crimea was initially given its independence from Turkey as a Russian protectorate and formally annexed in 1783.

Donald W. Mitchell puts the Russian accomplishment in the following perspective: 'The Russian squadrons gradually returned to the Baltic. The battleships were in such poor condition that of the 13 in the first three Mediterranean squadrons only six got back to Russia. Several were lost and three were sold for firewood. In all, the Russians had sent 20 battleships, five frigates and eight lesser vessels to the Aegean and bought 11 frigates and two bombs. Of these, 13 battleships and all the frigates returned to Russia. Of the 12,200 men sent to the Aegean, 4,516 did not return. Considering the achievements of the Russian fleets, these were extremely modest.' Modest indeed. Catherine II had risked the better part of her naval resources as well as the credibility of Russia as an emerging Great Power in a naval and amphibious deployment at a distance from its home bases that beggared description at the time. She did so with an untried assembly of ships and men faced with problems and challenges at all levels and, in doing so, completed the process interrupted by the early and untimely death of Peter I a half century earlier.

The Russo-Turkish War 1787–92

The opening of a major naval base at Sevastopol' and the provocative visit of Catherine II to the new city of Kherson precipitated the Turkish declaration of war on 16 August (27 August) 1787 and the opening phases of a conflict that would not be finally resolved by the signing of the Treaty of Jassy until 29 December 1791 (9 January 1792). The initial Russian plan of operations involved the transfer of the better portion of the Baltic fleet to the eastern Mediterranean in a repeat of its successful employment in the 1768–74 war. Whether this would have been a practicable deployment, given the absence of British diplomatic and logistical support and the hostility of all of the Mediterranean states with the sole exception of Genoa, is a matter for debate. As it was, the battle squadron bound for the Turkish theatre was held up *en route* at Copenhagen by the outbreak of the unexpected and unplanned for war with Sweden, and prevented from returning to the Gulf of Finland by the interposition of the Swedish battle fleet between Copenhagen and St Petersburg, reducing effective Russian naval strength in both theatres during the opening phases of both wars.

In the absence of the kind of naval diversion provided by Baltic warships operating in the Aegean that had proved so beneficial to Russian amphibious operations in the Sea of Azov theatre in the earlier war, the Turkish Navy was free to bring all of its resources to bear against Russian naval forces in the Black Sea. The total Turkish naval strength at the beginning of the war – according to R. C. Anderson and based on the report of a Greek in Turkish service – consisted of 15 serviceable ships of the line and eight frigates in the Black Sea and an additional seven ships of the line in the Mediterranean. Fortunately for Russia, considerable progress towards the establishment of an effective naval force in the Black Sea had been made during the nine years of peace under the direction of the competent and energetic Prince Potemkin. Shipbuilding facilities had been established at the naval base of Kherson on the Dnieper and naval bases constructed or improved at Sevastopol' in the Crimea and Taganrog in the Sea of Azov. Total Russian naval forces available at the outbreak of war included a single 80- and four 66-gun ships of the line, three 50-gun 24-pounder heavy frigates able to stand in the line of battle if needed, as well as the 13 surviving 12-pounder shallow-draught ships built during the 1770s for the Azov flotilla. An additional three 66-gun ships of the line and nine 46-gun battle frigates would join this fleet during the course of the war, but its overall size never approached that of the Turks.

It was, however, a fleet designed for deep-water operations in contrast to its immediate predecessor, the Azov flotilla, which had only ventured into open water at considerable peril due to the shallow draft construction of its ships and the unpredictable weather conditions prevailing in the Black Sea. The major problem facing the newborn Black Sea fleet during the war lay in the inadequacy of the logistical backup available at the three Russian naval bases, none of which were able to adequately support more than a portion of the entire battle fleet for any extended period of time. Those forces built and building at Kherson found themselves effectively bottled up in the Liman, a narrow 30-mile body of water ending at its western end in an easily blockaded channel, guarded on the southern shore by the Russian fortress of Kinburn and by the Turkish fortress of Ochakov on the northern. Passage through the narrows was further complicated by the presence of shallow sandbanks on the northern, or Turkish, side.

Freedom of movement for Russian land armies seeking to extend Russian control along the western side of the Black Sea was contingent upon elimination of Ochakov and, as a result, the major naval combat during the first three years of the war involved attempts by both combatants to invest and capture the opposing fortresses. These military undertakings ashore, in turn, required the close support of inshore rowing squadrons by conventional sailing ships on both sides operating within the narrow confines of the Liman, and the maintenance or elimination of the Turkish blockade outside of the bay. The capture of the fortress of Kinburn by Turkey would have made further Russian expansion to the south difficult in the extreme. The capture of Ochakov, on the other, would make possible the unification of Russian naval forces and the mounting of a direct challenge to Turkish control along both the eastern and western shores of the Black Sea.

The conflict opened in August of 1787, with Turkey taking the initiative by declaring war and attempting to capture the Russian fortress at Kinburn by direct assault. The Turks were initially able to bring three ships of the line, a frigate and supporting amphibious and rowing forces to bear on the campaign. The Russians, for their part, had two ships of the line and two operational frigates with supporting forces available up river at the naval base at Kherson. Unfortunately, they had been caught unprepared by the outbreak of war and were initially able to provide only minimal support for the garrison at Kinburn in the form of a single galley, the *Desna*, armed with a single one pood edinorog under the command of an aggressive and capable commander. Sublieutenant Lombard harried and intimidated the overwhelmingly superior Turkish amphibious forces, single handedly forcing their withdrawal on both 16 and 19 (27 and 30) September, earning a solid place in the pantheon of Russian naval heroes and winning time for Russian mobilization. On hearing that the main Russian fleet at Kherson under the command of Rear-Admiral Mordvinov was finally on the move into the Liman, the Turkish army attempted an all out assault on Kinburn on 1 October (12 October), only to be repulsed by the garrison forces under the command of Alexander Suvorov with the loss of 5,000 troops out of 5,300 committed to the assault. Mordvinov finally reached the mouth of the Dniepr on the 14th, where he found the numerically superior Turkish fleet of three ships of the line and five frigates blocking passage into the Black Sea and providing cover for their inshore vessels. Several days of indecisive fighting ensued between xebecs, galleys, bombs and gunboats on both sides and resulting in the capture of the heroically aggressive Sublieutenant Lombard. The year ended with the departure of the blockading Turkish battle fleet on 6 October (17 October) to its winter quarters in Constantinople.

Not all naval operations in 1787 were confined to the

Although the details of this painting are difficult to determine, this depiction of the action on 12 October 1787 (23rd NS) would appear to show Russian forces in the last stages of their repulse of the final Turkish assault on Kinburn, during the course of which 4,500 of the 5,000 Turkish troops assailing the Russian fortress were killed and the 500 survivors driven back to their ships in confusion. The vessel exploding to the left of the picture would appear to be the Turkish xebec mentioned in the Life of Ushakov *and cited by R. C. Anderson. The Turkish fortress of Otchakov is visible across the Liman. It would fall to the Russians a year later on 6 December 1788 (17th NS). This painting gives a very good impression of the confused nature of the fighting in the Liman and of the interrelatedness of the naval and military sides of the conflict.*

amphibious struggle in the Liman. On 1 September (11 September), the main Russian fleet at Sevastopol' under Rear-Admiral Count Voinovich set sail for a raid on the Turkish naval base at Varna, to the south of the Liman. Voinovich had three ships of the line, two heavy and four light frigates in his fleet. The operation would have represented the first extended deployment of Black Sea warships in a non-amphibious operation – had it succeeded. The northern Black Sea is subject to severe weather conditions in the autumn and winter, and a violent storm struck the fleet on 8 September (19 September) off Cape Kaliakra. The *Mariia Magdalina* (66) grounded in the storm and was subsequently captured by the Turks, while the frigate *Krym* (44) was lost with all hands. The remaining ships all suffered severe damage in the storm and the squadron returned to Sevastopol' having accomplished nothing of value. The attempted sortie served not only to show the instability of weather conditions in the Black Sea, but also made clear shortcomings in the design of Black Sea warships and the inexperience of both crews and officers.

In the autumn of the 1787 campaign year, Prince Potemkin restructured the Russian command, placing Alexander Suvorov in charge of an army of 30,000 between the mouth of the Bug and the fortress of Kinburn, Prince Charles of Nassau-Siegen in command of the Dnieper rowing flotilla, and the American Revolutionary War hero John Paul Jones in command of the sailing vessels of the Liman flotilla and technically junior to Prince Charles. This three-fold division of command responsibilities was similar to that had been found useful for Baltic operations and was adopted for similar reasons. The arrangement would depend for its success on close communication and

ism RUSSIAN NAVAL HISTORY 1695–1860

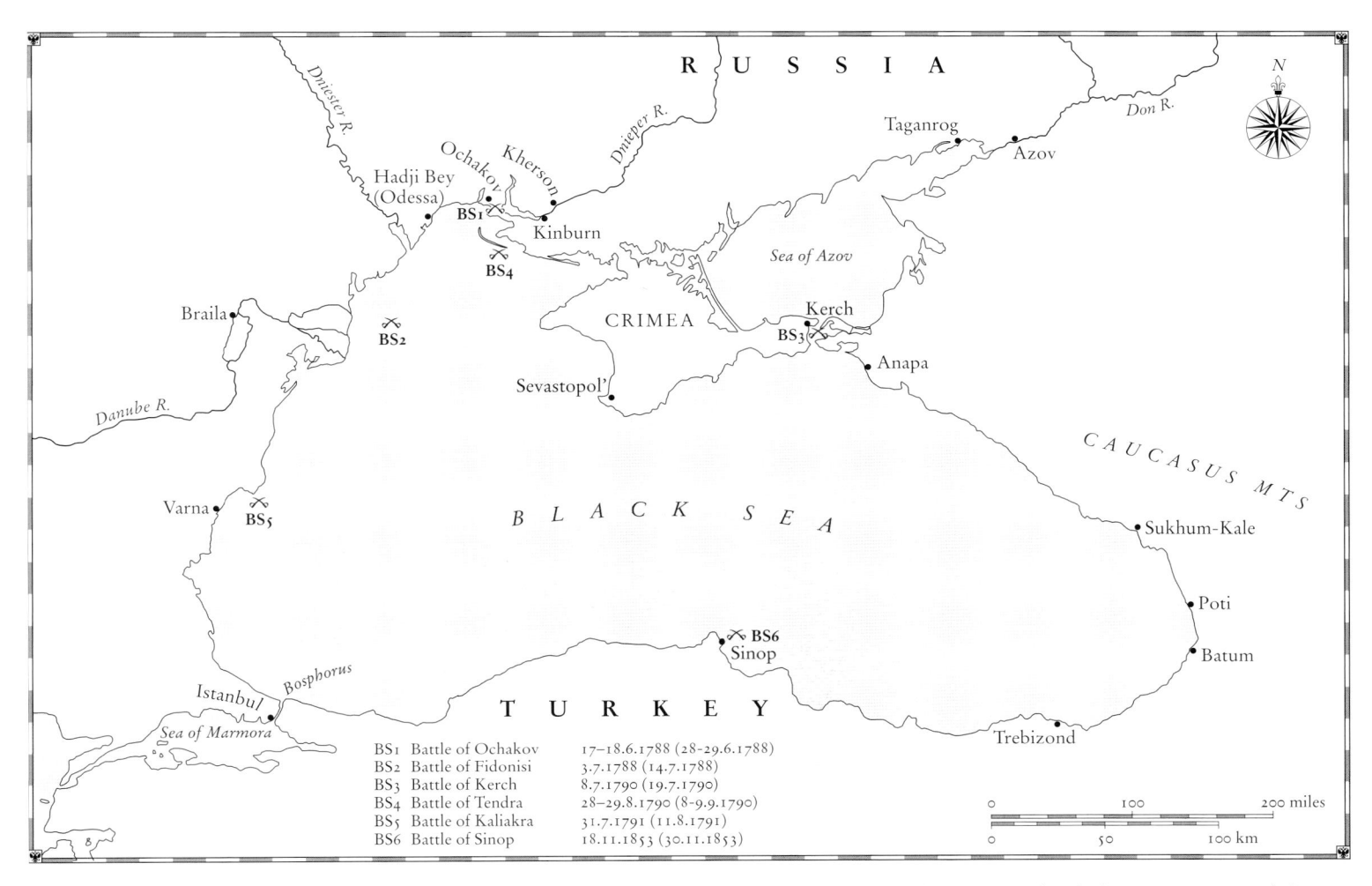

BS1	Battle of Ochakov	17–18.6.1788 (28–29.6.1788)
BS2	Battle of Fidonisi	3.7.1788 (14.7.1788)
BS3	Battle of Kerch	8.7.1790 (19.7.1790)
BS4	Battle of Tendra	28–29.8.1790 (8–9.9.1790)
BS5	Battle of Kaliakra	31.7.1791 (11.8.1791)
BS6	Battle of Sinop	18.11.1853 (30.11.1853)

For most of the eighteenth century, Russia was the weaker naval power in the Black Sea. Five major battles were fought between Russia and the Ottoman Empire between 1788 and 1791. By 1792 Russia, the nominally weaker naval power, had wrested control of the inland sea from the Turks. The battle of Sinope in 1853, also shown here, was a much later finale to the rivalry and the prelude to French and British intervention and the temporary destruction of Russian naval power in the area.

co-operation between all three parties, and this would be found lacking in the coming months between the two naval commanders who spent nearly as much time in casting aspersions upon each others' performance as they did in attacking their common enemy. For his part, Suvorov would be promoted to the rank of field marshal for his achievements in the campaign and rise to become one of Russia's greatest generals. John Paul Jones and Prince Charles would have less rosy future prospects as a result of their unseemly rivalry.

1787 had been marked by the Turkish attempt to capture Kinburn. 1788 would see the Russians taking the offensive against the Turkish fortress of Ochakov, in the face of renewed and determined Turkish attempts at capturing the fortress of Kinburn. The Turkish naval commander was once again Hassan Pasha, the former Algerian galley slave who had risen to command the Turkish Navy in the previous war by retaking Lemnos from the Russians at a moment of great crisis for the Ottoman Empire. The Turkish fleet, numbering 98 ships, including ten to 14 ships of the line and six to 15 frigates, entered the bay on 18 May (29 May) and set the stage for one of the great moments of self-

sacrificing heroism in Russian naval history. Captain Reingold Saken, in command of a Russian sloop found himself attacked by 11 to 13 Turkish galleys, ordered his crew to abandon ship, allowed his small warship to be surrounded by four Turkish galleys, and then blew his powder magazine, destroying all four of the Turkish vessels and – of course – himself.

The Battle of Ochakov 17–18 June (28–29 June) 1788

Turkish forces failed in their attempt to launch an offensive against Kinburn and instead found Ochakov under siege by Russian land forces and a combined squadron of 58 Russian ships divided into inshore forces under Nassau-Siegen and seagoing forces under Jones. The forces available to Jones included two ships of the line operating with only 40–48 guns because of the shallowness of the waters of the bay, and seven ships rated loosely as frigates with 24 to 40 guns apiece. The Russian ships were the first of the 'newly invented frigates' and were heavily armed in the pattern established by Samuel

Bentham and approved by Prince Potemkin. Because of their heavy calibre cannon, these vessels were more formidable than their more numerous but lightly gunned Turkish counterparts. It should also be noted that the Turkish 'battleships' were, in part or entirety, composed of armed merchantmen carrying approximately 40 guns apiece.

The two Russian flotillas failed to provide effective mutual support during the ensuing two days' battle, but nonetheless succeeded in inflicting a serious defeat on the nominally more powerful Turkish squadron. As the Turkish ships attempted to withdraw from the Liman after being severely punished on the first day, nine of their ships grounded on the sandy shallows of the northern shore while attempting to avoid a shore battery that Jones had had the foresight to install on the southern shore against just such an eventuality. The grounded ships were quickly destroyed or captured. Total Turkish losses over the two days of fighting in the bay included 2,000 seamen killed and 1,673 taken prisoner. There is considerable variation in the claims for Turkish ships destroyed and captured, with figures ranging from two to three ships of the line and two to five frigates, but with total losses in the neighborhood of 15 large vessels of all types. In contrast, the Russian losses were light, with the loss of 18 men killed and 67 wounded, and with ship losses of only a single floating battery.

In the period immediately following the battle of Ochakov, Nassau-Siegel and Jones concentrated on consolidating their control of the Liman, with the final attack on the remaining Turkish ships inside the bay occurring on 1 July (12 July), while the Russian army continued its pressure on the fortress itself. Hassan Pasha and the Turkish battle fleet had been compelled by the threat of Jones' strategically sited shore battery to remain outside the bay unable to render any further assistance to the fortress. Three days earlier, on 29 June (9 July), news of the approach of the main Russian fleet from Sevastopol' had compelled the Turkish commander to set sail to intercept this larger threat under the command of Rear-Admiral Voinovich, seconded by the rapidly rising Captain-Brigadier Fyodor Ushakov.

The Battle of Fidonisi 3 July (14 July) 1788

The Russian and Turkish fleets met south of the island of Tendra and manoeuvred for three days until they finally engaged off Fidonisi, a small island east of the Danube delta. Anderson puts the Russian strength as two 66-gun ships of the line, two 50-gun battle frigates armed with 24pdrs and eight lighter 40-gun frigates, still armed with 12pdrs although they would be up gunned to 18pdrs after the battle. All were expected to take their place in the line of battle if needed because of the lack of adequate numbers of true capital ships. On the other side, the Turkish fleet had been heavily reinforced since the previous month's battle and consisted of 15 ships of the line, eight frigates, three bombs and 21 xebecs. Once again, it is difficult to evaluate the effective strength of the Turkish warships. Nevertheless, the presence of five ships, rated variously as either 74s or 80s, each nominally superior to Rear-Admiral Voinovich's two 66s, would seem to indicate that the Turks had committed their most modern and capable ships to the relief of Ochakov.

The Turkish fleet had the windward position and opened the action on 3 July with Hassan Pasha closing the Russian vanguard with six ships of the line nearly cutting off two of the leading Russian 40-gun frigates, *Berislav* and *Strela*. What might have been a disaster for the Russians was averted by the independent decision of Voinovich's second in command, Brigadier-Captain Fyodor Ushakov, to come to their support with his flagship *Sviatoi Pavel*, in spite of Voinovich's apparent unwillingness to do so himself. After three hours of combat in which the *Sviatoi Pavel* was heavily engaged by the Turkish flagship, the Turkish commander broke off the action and retreated. Russian losses were extremely light with only five to seven men injured or killed (sources vary). No ships were lost on either side during or immediately after the battle, but Greek spies working for the Russians in Constantinople later reported that one ship of the line was lost during the return to Constantinople due to a combination of battle damage and heavy weather, while an additional four ships were seriously damaged by the battle and the weather.

Nothing of great immediate importance resulted from Fidonisi other than the temporary frustration of the Turkish battle fleet in its goal of re-establishing control over the approaches to the Liman and delaying or preventing the loss of Ochakov – and the eclipse of Voinovich as commander in chief by Ushakov's decisive leadership at the critical moment in the battle. The Russian main fleet retired to Sevastopol' after the battle and played no direct part in operations for the rest of the year. A final sortie by Voinovich in November found only that the Turkish fleet had already retired for the year to its base in Constantinople. The battle is of note, however, as the first fully naval operation undertaken by the newborn Black Sea fleet. It had involved a successful standoff between a greatly inferior Russian line of battle and a Turkish line that, in theory at least, was far superior in numbers and firepower. The fortress of Ochakov finally fell to the Russian army in November, but a linkup between the Kherson squadron and the other Black Sea elements would have to await the coming year's campaign.

Another even younger Russian officer destined for greater stature in the future first came to prominence during the period following Fidonisi. Dmitriy Seniavin was given independent command of a group of four small ships and turned loose on what was essentially a mission of commerce raiding and disruption of Turkish communications. Before the 1788 campaign ended in November, Seniavin had established a reputation for daring and leadership by capturing nine Turkish transports.

Although the Russian navy had performed credibly against a numerically superior opponent in 1788, the Turkish Navy retained command of the Black Sea throughout the spring and summer of 1789 by virtue of its overwhelming numerical strength. Russian naval activity during the year was largely limited to raids by privateers on Turkish installations and shipping in the Black Sea. In the face of the continuing Turkish control of the intervening waters between the two major bases of Kherson and Sevastopol', the two Russian squadrons were unable to combine their naval resources throughout the better part of the year. This failure was due in part to the continuing reluctance towards risking combat on the part of Rear-Admiral Voinovich who continued to command the Sevastopol' squadron throughout the coming campaign season, but more largely a reflection of the relative exhaustion of the Russian forces at Kherson and the overwhelming superiority of the Turkish battle fleet. The Turkish fleet under Hussein Pasha is estimated by Anderson as having consisted of 57 warships, including 17 ships of the line and ten frigates, a force superior to the potential combined strength of both Russian squadrons and overwhelmingly superior to that of either unit attempting to fight separately. The mounting of an effective challenge against the Turks for control of the Black Sea would have to await the coming year with the completion and fitting out of a new *Mariia Magdalina* 66 and of the two new battle frigates building at Kherson, along with that of an additional six battle frigates under construction at a new facility on the Don at Rogozhskaya. A large-scale naval confrontation might have taken place in June of 1789 when the Turkish fleet sorteed in force in support of the final Turkish attempt at retaking Ochakov. The Turkish attack failed on land, but the Turkish battle fleet challenged battle on 12 June (23 June) at Ochakov and the challenge was prudently refused by the outnumbered Kherson squadron. At the beginning of October, the fall of Odessa to the Russian armies under Alexander Suvorov finally forced the withdrawal of the Turkish battle fleet, making possible the long sought for combination of the two Russian squadrons. The united fleet wintered in the Liman where adequate facilities now existed, not only at the established base at Kherson, but also at the newly constructed facilities at Nikolaev. Anderson estimates the strength of the combined Russian fleet at 11 ships of the line and battle frigates supported by nine to ten smaller 40-gun frigates. While this respectable force was still outweighed by the Turkish battle fleet, the basis for an effective Russian challenge to Turkish control in 1790 was now in place.

In October of 1789, Prince Potemkin finally dismissed Prince Charles of Nassau-Siegen and John Paul Jones for poor combat performance. The dismissals reflected the growing confidence of the Russian high command in the capacity of their own native born officers as well as its disgust at the infighting of the two foreign imports. Historian Anthony Cross has estimated that during the reign of Catherine II about 150 British officers joined the Russian navy, 40 in 1783 alone. Russian officers would still be sent to Great Britain for training with the Royal Navy during periods of good relations between the two nations, but Paul I was no Anglophile and did not continue his mother Catherine's programme of active recruitment of British officers. In spite of the growing reliance upon Russian officers in command positions, a place would continue to be found for competent foreign-born officers of the calibre of Samuel Greig and Roman Crown, who were already in Russian service at the time of Catherine's death. Fourteen of the British officers hired originally by Catherine II rose to the rank of admiral in the nineteenth century; but after 1790 the future lay increasingly with Russian born officers, two of whom, Fyodor Ushakov and Dmitriy Seniavin, were themselves the products of the 1787–92 conflict.

Ushakov was given overall command of the entire Black Sea fleet in 1790 and began his command by organizing and personally leading a flying squadron of three battle and five standard frigates, supported by 11 privateers for raids on Turkish bases and lines of communication in late May and June. These were similar to, but on a larger scale than, the privateering forays of Dmitriy Seniavin the previous year. (As a point of clarification it should be noted that the ships described as 'privateers' appear to have been under the direct operational control of the Russian naval command. They might be more properly described as hired mercenaries than as privateers in the genuinely accepted western sense.) Although the raids had significant military value in and of themselves, the organization of the squadron also allowed for much needed operational training for a fleet that was still lacking in experience and cohesiveness.

The Battle of Kerch 8 July (19 July) 1790

Surprisingly enough, in spite of their repeated defeats on land and at sea in the first two years of the war, the Turks initiated a campaign in June to recapture the Crimea and, presumably, bring the smaller Russian fleet to decisive battle. Ushakov now had under his command the 84-gun *Rozhdestvo Khristovo*, four 66s, five battle frigates and six frigates and smaller supporting craft. The Turkish fleet, under a new commander, Hussein Pasha, consisted of ten line of battle ships including four 72/74-gun ships and eight frigates, with the usual supporting craft. Ushakov intercepted the Turkish fleet off Kerch and engaged in an indecisive three hour running battle, which began with the Turks to the windward and ended with the Russians capturing the windward position with a change in the wind from ENE to NNE. When two of the Turkish line of battle ships suffered damage to their sails and rigging in the disorderly manoeuvring following upon the change in wind direction, the Turkish fleet broke off the action and retreated to the south, effectively abandoning their original objective of invading the Crimea. The retreating Ottoman fleet was said to have been able to outrun the pursuing Russians because they possessed the advantage of having coppered hulls. Turkish sources, on the contrary, indicate that the adoption of copper sheathing was only in the experimental stage at this date and could not have explained the superior sailing performance of the Turkish ships. The relatively slow speed of Russian warships in this and subsequent engagements *may* have instead been the result of the absence of adequate maintenance facilities for cleaning the bottoms of their warships. Adequate dockyard facilities did not appear in the Black Sea until the reign of Nicholas I. The difficult and risky process of careening warships for scraping of underwater hulls was the only available method available to the Russians in this period. For obvious reasons, this was an unlikely type of maintenance during wartime when readiness was a premium concern.

An important tactical development during the confrontation of the two battle lines at Kerch had been Ushakov's detachment of the six lighter frigates to a position behind his line of battle

The opening phase of indecisive battle of Kerch on 8 July 1790 (OS), as seen by eyewitness Cadet Depal'do. Depal'do was a Greek in Russian service with formal artistic training and the progenitor of a series of prominent artists in the nineteenth century. The Turks are here in a disorganized gaggle, with the Russians approaching in line ahead with frigates following in line with the larger ships.

The second phase of the battle of Kerch on 8 July 1790 as seen by Cadet Depal'do. Rear-Admiral Ushakov has now stationed his reserve squadron of six lighter frigates behind his battle line consisting of five heavy frigates and five ships of the line. The Turkish line is beginning to break contact as shown by the angle of their stern galleries in the drawing and the battle would shortly degenerate into headlong flight.

acting as a mobile reserve capable of intervening where needed and as a stopgap to any attempt by the longer Turkish battle line to double the Russian line. He would further develop the concept of maintaining a mobile reserve made up of lighter units in coming battles.

The Battle of Tendra 28–29 August (8–9 September) 1790

Tendra was the decisive naval battle of the war. Ushakov had previously demonstrated aggressiveness and skill at manoeuvre, but the battle of Kerch had been a strategically defensive affair involving the disruption of a Turkish invasion of the Crimea. The next confrontation with Hussein Pasha and the Turkish battle fleet occurred in the waters just south of Tendra and saw the Russian fleet clearly taking the offensive in the open sea against the Turks for the first time in the war. The forces available to Ushakov were essentially the same as he had had at Kerch, but the Turkish fleet had been augmented by new construction and their line of battle now included 14 ships, five of which were 72/74-gun ships and eight frigates.

Ushakov happened upon the Turkish battle fleet while he was *en route* from Sevastopol' to Kherson to convoy several new and 'newly built' frigates back to Sevastopol'. The Russian fleet was proceeding in three parallel columns and there was some delay in closing with the Turkish fleet's line of battle while the Russian columns reformed into battle order, with the weather gauge to their advantage. Once again, Ushakov detached a squadron of 40-gun frigates as an independent squadron able to intervene where needed – but with a difference. At Kerch, the intent had been, in part, to relieve the lighter 40-gun frigates from the necessity of standing in line against heavier Turkish ships by positioning them *behind* the battle line. At Tendra, the three ships selected were stationed to the windward and in the van of the Russian line with the specific intent of their being available to prevent any Turkish attempt at doubling the Russian line or of breaking off action prematurely. Ushakov's thoughts on their deployment are a matter for conjecture, but some Russian historians hold that he had planned to use them to break through the Turkish line and isolate the leading ships in a manner that would have anticipated Nelson's tactics at Trafalgar.

In contrast to previous encounters, the two lines fought at close range (less than 300 metres). As had been his previous practice, Ushakov personally engaged the Turkish admiral's flagship. The firing continued for some five hours from 3:00 p.m. to 8:00 p.m., with the Turkish ships breaking off the action as the day ended. The next day saw a repeat of the previous month's battle, with the majority of the Turkish ships drawing away from their Russian pursuers, allegedly by virtue of their coppered hulls. Two of the less fortunate Turkish ships had been so heavily damaged by the previous day's fighting as to be easily run down by the pursuing Russian ships. *Mulk-i Bahri* (66) surrendered to three Russian ships, but the 74-gun Kapudaniye (i.e. flagship – a descriptive term and not a ship name) of the Turkish second in command, put up a determined fight against three Russian ships for four hours until Ushakov's flagship, the *Rozhdestvo Khristovo*, raked her at point blank range, finally compelling her surrender. The *Mulk-i Bahri* was repaired and taken into the Russian Black fleet as *Ioann Predtecha*, but the heroic Kapudaniye caught fire and exploded after her surrender, taking nearly 800 men with her. Total Turkish losses were 2,000 men killed and wounded and 733 taken prisoner. Russian losses were 25 killed and 25 wounded.

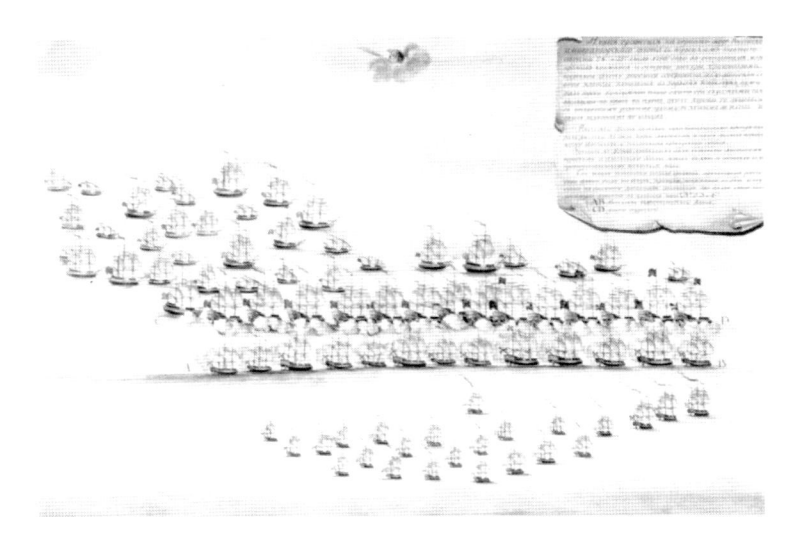

The battle of Tendra on 28–29 August 1790, again seen through the eyes of Cadet A. N Depal'do. The drawing may represent either the first day's combat or that on the second day before the Turkish line broke up and fled. On this day, Ushakov is again varying his pattern of using his lighter, faster frigates to cover his van and discourage the Turks from using their longer line and greater speed to double the Russian vanguard. Three of the six smaller frigates are bringing up the rear, while three may be seen moving into position on the starboard windward side of the Russian van to intercept any attempt by the faster Turkish line to double the Russian van. A risky assignment for frigates, but Ushakov knew his enemy well by now.

The Battle of Kaliakra 31 July (11 August) 1791

The Turkish navy had been seriously degraded as an effective and organized force by the battles of Kerch and Tendra in 1790. By calling in naval forces from throughout the Mediterranean, including Albania and the semi-autonomous Barbary states of Algeria, Tunis and Tripoli, Hussein Pasha was able to cobble together a numerically impressive force consisting of 18 ships of the line, ten large and seven smaller frigates for the 1791 campaign. This was, however, a heterogeneous collection of ships lacking any sort of cohesiveness and bereft of morale after the unbroken series of defeat suffered by the Turks in the previous years of combat. Attempts were made at this very late hour to obtain assistance in the form of experienced officers from Great Britain to provide badly needed training and discipline, but the British government was unwilling to back a losing cause, even in the face of their increasing coolness towards Russia as a result of Catherine II's successful expansionism.

The Russian Black Sea fleet was at the height of its power in 1791, with seven ships of the line, ten of the well tried battle frigates, as well as two standard frigates, two of the capital ships and one of the standard frigates were former Turkish prizes repaired and brought into Russian service. Fyodor Ushakov was in command and at the peak of his prestige. He can only have looked upon the coming campaign season with optimism and confidence.

It was evident by 1791 that Russia had assumed the strategic

The climactic battle of Tendra on 28–29 August 1790. The ship burning in the centre between two Russian ships may represent the Turkish flagship, which was run down and engaged by three Russian warships on the day after the battle. After a four-hour fight which gained her the respect of her Russian opponents, the Kapudaniye (flagship) surrendered shortly before exploding and taking the majority of her crew with her. Of particular interest are the Turkish warship's elaborate and highly decorated stern galleries. Depictions of Turkish warships are rare and, when available, highly stylized. It would be interesting to know whether the artist, A. A. Blinkov in 1955, was working from a model or from his imagination.

The battle of Cape Kaliakra on 31 July 1791 (OS) as seen by Cadet A. N. Depal'do. The Cape is to the north and the Russian line, having driven the larger Turkish fleet from its moorings in a state of disorder, has reversed tack and reorganized its line in good order, while the Turkish battle fleet is desperately attempting to form a coherent battle line. The disorganized clusters of ships above and below the two battle lines are the normal clusters of auxiliaries and scouts attached to battle squadrons at the time.

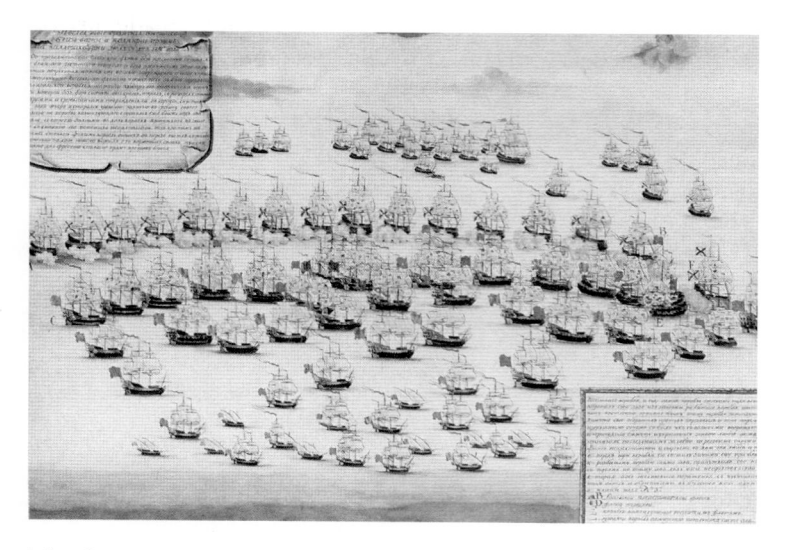

The climactic moment of the battle of Kaliakra 31 July 1791 as seen by Cadet Depal'do. Vice-Admiral Ushakov's flagship Rozhdestvo Khristovo *has left the Russian line to intercept an attempt by the Algerian van to double the Russian line and may be seen here single-handedly turning the Turkish van and saving the day for the Russians. The two lines would continue to engage, but the Turkish and Algerian ships would shortly begin to follow their common practice of breaking off in small groups and using their speed to escape their tormentors.*

offensive at sea and that Turkey could do little more than defend what was left of their holdings in the Black Sea. Ushakov spent the month of June unsuccessfully attempting to intercept a Turkish squadron dispatched from Varna on the western shore of the Black Sea to provide assistance to Anapa on the eastern shore, which the Russian army was attacking. As had been the case previously, the Russian fleet found itself incapable of running down the faster Turkish ships and Ushakov was forced to return to Sevastopol' empty-handed.

At the end of July, Ushakov once again took the offensive and sought out the Turkish fleet, which was anchored to the northeast of Varna, just south of Cape Kaliakra. The larger Turkish fleet was at anchor and protected by land based gun emplacements. The Turks fully expected the Russians to pass to the south of their line in order to place the Turkish ships between their line and the potentially dangerous covering fire of the Turkish shore batteries. In an action that in some respects anticipated Nelson's actions at the Nile six years later, Ushakov chose to pass *between* the Turkish line and the shore batteries, throwing the Turkish line into chaos as ships of the line desperately cut their cables in an attempt to gain the open sea and avoid the point blank Russian attack. Before Hussein Pasha could restore order and form a line of battle heading to the east of Kaliakra, two of his ships had succeeded in colliding and rendering themselves *hors de combat*. As the two lines of battle finally closed in the late afternoon, Hussein Pasha's Algerian subordinate, Said Ali, attempted to use his squadron of fast Algerian frigates to double the slower Russian battle line. As he had done in previous actions, Ushakov left his own line with his flagship to intercept and frustrate the Algerians, saving his command from potential disaster. The two lines engaged from 4:45 to 8:30 p.m. and the combat gradually petered out as the Turkish ships broke out of line one by one and again used their greater speed to avoid further combat. No ships were lost in this final battle of the war and Russian casualties were 17 killed and 28 wounded. One Russian battle frigate, the *Aleksandr Nevskii*, sustained heavy damage. The Turkish ships were heavily damaged aloft, but casualty figures are not available.

Beyond providing Fyodor Ushakov yet another opportunity to demonstrate his skill at introducing innovative tactics and his penchant for aggressiveness in battle, Kaliakra accomplished very little of substance. Although neither side was aware of the ending of the war, Turkey had agreed to an armistice prior to the engagement and active combat should have come to an end. As they had done previously, Great Britain and Prussia placed joint pressure on Russia to abandon its territorial gains in the war. Russia had to give up its recent conquest of Anapa in the process but did succeed in retaining the port and fortress of Ochakov along with the territory that they had captured between the Bug and the Dniester. The peace was formally signed on 29 December 1791 (9 January 1792).

The most lasting Russian gain in the war was the morale ascendancy that its unbroken string of naval victories gave the newly established Black Sea fleet over the once dominant Turkish Navy. Russian naval construction in the Black Sea continued and expanded throughout the 1790s, with additional battle frigates being added as well as a new 84 and a class of 74s in a programme designed to insure continued Russian dominance. For his part, an equally determined Selim III obtained the services of French ship designers, including Le Brune de St Catherine, and began rebuilding the Ottoman Navy into a larger, more modern and more formidable fleet with every intention of challenging Russia at the appropriate moment and regaining its former ascendancy.

Russian in the Mediterranean 1798–1807

Mention has been made in the section on the Baltic fleet of Catherine II and Paul's expansion of the operations of the Baltic fleet into Atlantic waters during the opening stages of the French Revolutionary and Napoleonic wars at the request of Great Britain. Paul also used the shifting alliances brought about by French expansion into the central and eastern Mediterranean to obtain permission from the Turks, who were for the moment greatly concerned about French expansionism, for the passage of Black Sea warships through the Bosporus into the Mediterranean in September 1798. Once in the Mediterranean, the Russian squadron, under the command of Fyodor Ushakov, now a Vice-Admiral, combined for the first time with Turkish warships and joined with the command of Horatio Nelson, fresh from his victory at the Nile. Ushakov was senior to Nelson and the issue of overall command was never resolved, although the much younger British admiral clearly considered himself the senior member of the uneasy partnership. The unified campaign developed and expanded into the Adriatic with the systematic capture and liberation of the Greek Ionic Islands from French control. At the same time, Russian troops under the command of another Russian veteran and hero of the recently concluded Russo-Turkish War, Field Marshall Alexander Suvorov, moved into northern Italy by way of Austria and succeeded in defeating, at least temporarily, the French armies in the northern half of the peninsula. Paul's ambitions in the area, particularly with respect to Malta, expanded with the success of Russian arms in Italy and the Ionian Islands. The mixed motives of both Great Britain and Russia gave rise to an undercurrent of growing hostility and mistrust between their governments and navies and left Ushakov, newly promoted to full Admiral, with diplomatic headaches marching in unison with the demands of naval command.

Horatio Nelson's not-so-veiled contempt for the naval capabilities of British allies in the Mediterranean and elsewhere is a matter of historical record, and his casual attempt to relegate the sizeable Russo-Turkish squadron to secondary patrol and convoy duties quickly brought him into conflict with Ushakov, whose age, experience and credentials as a commander and as a skilled tactician merited better treatment from the younger and less experienced British admiral. In addition, the Russo-Turkish expeditionary fleet under Ushakov's overall command was a formidable force in its own right, comprised of six Russian ships of the line, six battle frigates and two standard frigates along with an equally balanced and frequently troublesome Turkish squadron of six ships of the line and eight frigates. Ushakov's squadron was, in the words of Norman Saul, 'made up of officers and crews, who were probably among the best seamen

The bombardment of Ancona by Russian warships under Vice Admiral Ushakov's command in 1799 would stand as a fairly typical amphibious exercise – except for the presence of Turkish warships acting in the unusual role of allies to their traditional enemies. The polyglot aspect of this phase of the war in Italy is made even clearer by the fact that the troops that besieged and ultimately captured the town from the French forces holding it were a mix of Russians, Austrians, Turks and Italian insurgents. The cannonballs descending on the town are likely a stylized attempt to represent the use of high trajectory explosive ordnance by the assailing parties.

A portrait of Admiral Ushakov (1745–1817), arguably Russia's greatest admiral, painted in 1912 by P. N. Bazhanov and hardly showing the 'Russian bear' so scornfully described by Britain's greatest admiral, Horatio Nelson. Despite the gulf in age between the two men, both thought alike on matters of tactics and strategy and it is an irony of history that they were brought together only as rivals in the contest for control in the central Mediterranean.

Ushakov and Nelson

In contrast to Ushakov's affability and tact, Nelson could only bring a degree of arrogance to the relationship that sadly stands in marked contrast to the kind of warm-hearted leadership skills that he demonstrated throughout his career towards officers and seamen *within* the Royal Navy. His infamous characterization of Ushakov as 'a blackguard' and 'polished outside, but the bear is close to the skin' says little for the British half of *this* particular partnership. For all of his many great and positive qualities, Great Britain's greatest admiral had human weaknesses and his Anglocentricity blinded him to the qualities of a man who was probably closer to being his peer than any other living naval officer, British or otherwise.

We are again indebted to Donald W. Mitchell for this summary of Ushakov's naval philosophy and for his calling much needed attention to the similarities that existed between the two admirals' approach to their professions:

'Key points in his (Ushakov's) naval doctrine were (1) good care of material was essential; (2) it was excellent strategy to

As a young officer on half pay in the late 1780s with a wife to support, Horatio Nelson seriously considered offering his then-untested talents to the Russian navy in much the same manner as very many other unemployed British officers had done during that century. He chose otherwise, sadly for the Russians, and his future contact with the Russians would be largely hostile and combative, whether as an 'ally' to Vice Admiral Ushakov in the eastern Mediterranean in the closing years of the eighteenth century or as the head of a potentially hostile battle fleet at the gates of St Petersburg in the early years of the nineteenth. His distaste for foreigners is well known, and it remains one of the unanswered questions of history whether his career as a British officer in Russian service would have been combative and disruptive as was the case with John Elphinston, or warm and accommodating as was the case with Samuel Greig.

concentrate all of one's strength on a portion of the enemy's forces; (3) the unexpected action was of inestimable value in breaking the enemy's formation; (4) faithful support of injured Russian ships was a necessity; (5) avid exploitation of enemy weaknesses was essential to victory. He was opposed to extremely long lines of battle, believing them to be difficult to maintain and not conducive to decisive victories. Like Nelson, he left considerable initiative to his captains once he had trained them in his own philosophy of naval warfare.'

For all the gulf that existed between the two men in background, education, nationality and age, they might have been brothers. Nelson failed to recognize Ushakov's genius. On the other hand, it may well have been an intuitive recognition of their likenesses that led to his not-so-subdued hostility.

Russia had yet produced.' Although the highly regarded Russian admiral was lacking in formal education and polish and could only speak his native language, he had shown a natural talent for diplomacy as evidenced by the excellent relations that he immediately established with his newfound Turkish allies upon his arrival in Constantinople.

A major problem experienced by the Russian fleet throughout the Ionian campaign was the premature deterioration of its warships as a result of the rigours of the campaign, the lack of adequate maintenance facilities outside the Black Sea, and the absence of underwater coppering to prevent the accelerated progress of the Teredo worm in the warm waters of the Mediterranean. Russian problems with upkeep and maintenance attracted little sympathy from Nelson, who on one occasion responded to Ushakov's unwillingness to operate his ships during winter weather by suggesting privately that there was some question as to the Russian ability to operate effectively, even during summer weather.

While the British concentrated on operations on the western side of the Italian peninsula during the spring and summer of 1799; the Russo-Turkish squadrons liberated the various Ionian islands from French domination and disrupted French lines of communication and commerce in the Adriatic. The most difficult operation for the Russians was the four-month siege of Corfu, the taking of which resulted, among other things, in the recapture of the British veteran of the Nile, the *Leander*, and the return of the ship – after some hesitation on the part of the Russians – to the British. The next phase of the war for the Russians – the Turks having abandoned the campaign – would have been their participation in the siege and conquest of Malta, a situation that would have brought Anglo-Russian rivalries to a head. As was so frequently the case during this period of unexpectedly shifting alliances, Ushakov found himself unexpectedly recalled to the Black Sea by the unanticipated withdrawal of Russia from the war with France. The assassination of Paul followed in 1801 and the next phase of Anglo-Russian co-operation in the Mediterranean would await the accession of Paul's son, Alexander I, the Treaty of Amiens in 1802, the formation of the Third Coalition against France in 1805 and the arrival of a new commander with strong reinforcements from the Baltic for the greatly diminished Russian Mediterranean squadron – Vice-Admiral Dmitriy Seniavin.

Although the Greek Ionian Islands had been granted formal independence after the withdrawal of Russia from the war with France, they remained de facto Russian colonies. A small squadron of Russian warships made up of two ships of the line, a single battle frigate, three corvettes and two brigs remained stationed at Corfu after Ushakov's departure. The heavy ships were veterans of Ushakov's campaign and the small craft were all captured or converted vessels picked up in and about the Adriatic. In order to reinforce this squadron in the face of growing problems with the French, a moderately sized squadron was dispatched from the Baltic in 1804 under the command of Commodore Aleksei Greig, son of Samuel Greig. Greig's squadron was comprised of a single Russian-built 74 and three elderly Swedish veterans of the 1788–92 war, the 62-gun

Count Alexander Suvorov (1729–1800). Russia's greatest general, he was a major participant in the siege of Ochakov in the Russo-Turkish War of 1787–92 and later played a crucial supporting role in supporting Vice-Admiral Ushakov's Ionian campaign by driving the French out of Italy. With the Russian withdrawal from the 2nd Coalition, Suvorov conducted a brilliant retreat through the Alps against heavy French resistance and brought his battered army through intact. He was shunned by the Emperor Paul I (himself soon to be assassinated) and died a broken man in 1800, having never lost a battle against a foreign army.

Retvizan, the 44-gun *Venus* and the 24-gun rowing frigate *Avtroil*. It is unclear whether these Swedish veterans were sent because of their excellent and sturdy construction or because they were simply odd numbers in the Russian Baltic fleet. Regardless of their advancing age, they all served with distinction through the coming campaigns, with *Venus* acquiring the highest honours and suffering the most unusual fate.

Upon renewal of hostilities between Russia and France, Vice-Admiral Seniavin was dispatched from Kronshtadt on 10 September (22 September) 1805 with an 80-gun flagship and four 74s, all recently completed warships. In 1806, a second squadron under Commodore Ignatyev, made up of two 80s, one 74, one 66 and one 60 accompanied by a 32-gun frigate was dispatched to further reinforce the Russian squadron.

Seniavin's mission was the protection of the Russian protectorate in the Ionian Islands and the undermining of the

> ## Dmitriy Seniavin
>
> Seniavin, member of a distinguished naval family and son of a famous father, Admiral A. N. Seniavin, had served with considerable distinction in the Russo-Turkish War of 1787–92. While serving as aide-de-camp to Prince Potemkin in 1788–9, he had been placed under house arrest for his independence and insubordination by Ushakov. This unseemly *contretemps* between the two strong-willed officers had required the intervention of Potemkin himself to resolve. Potemkin reportedly told Ushakov that this quarrelsome and independent young officer would, in the course of time, become one of Russia's greatest admirals. In spite of their earlier and largely unresolved history of personal antagonism, Ushakov unhesitatingly recommended Seniavin as the most highly qualified Russian officer available to command the new expeditionary squadron to the Mediterranean in 1806. Although Alexander I detested him and unjustly short-circuited his career at the end of the Russo-Turkish War of 1806–12, Seniavin was later rehabilitated in 1826 by Nicholas I. Today he ranks among the greatest of Russian admirals for his skilful handling of an enormously difficult diplomatic and military situation in the Mediterranean during his period of command there and for his decisive defeat of the Turkish fleet at Mount Athos in 1807.

French occupation of the Dalmatian coast. He faced little in the way of organized naval opposition from the French and his major concerns were amphibious operations along the coastline involving the deployment of various small combinations of warships, supported by troops as required. Political infighting among the various ethnic groups ashore was a constant problem for the Russian admiral as were the uncertain policies of Alexander I. At the beginning of the campaign, Seniavin's naval assets included nine ships of the line, six frigates, six corvettes, seven brigs and a schooner, a formidable force and one that was in generally good material condition and of recent construction. When Commodore Ignatyev's reinforcements arrived a year later, the Russians were in an unassailable position in the Adriatic, at least from a naval point of view.

Seniavin made considerable use of an enterprising Irish officer, one Captain Belli (originally Baillie), who had distinguished himself earlier as a lieutenant under Ushakov. During the earlier campaign, Belli had led a commando operation that had climaxed in the joint liberation of Naples by Russian, Portuguese and British troops. In the current operation, he was given command of a ship of the line, a frigate and a schooner and allowed free rein to conduct operations against the French in the northern Adriatic while Seniavin operated to the south from his base in Corfu. It was Belli's initiative that enabled the Russians to occupy the fortified port of Catarro at the invitation of the inhabitants, who were unwilling to accept French control. On the other hand, it was Belli's commander, Seniavin, who risked his career by refusing to follow instructions from Alexander to cease operations in the area due to protests from the Austrians – who were themselves under pressure from the French to intervene on their behalf in their former possession. Seniavin was very quickly justified in his actions once his successful occupation of Catarro and Montenegro became known to St Petersburg. He faced almost precisely the same situation a few months later in July of 1805 when he again received instructions to cease hostilities and withdraw due to a pending peace treaty with France. Once again, Seniavin acted upon his own judgment and refused to surrender Catarro to the French, and once again he was supported by the course of events when Alexander failed to ratify the peace treaty. How successful further Russian involvement in the Adriatic might have been in establishing and extending Russian influence is an open question, because Seniavin was forced to abandon Corfu and take the better part of his fleet east on 10 February 1807 upon learning that Turkey and Russia were, once again, at war. Four 74s, three frigates, a sloop and three brigs were left in the Adriatic to protect Russian interests, but it was clear that further offensive operations against the French were at an end, pending resolution of the war with Turkey.

War with Turkey 1806–12

Turkey had been seduced into declaring war on Russia by French assurances of support and by news of the Prussian defeat at Jena, and entered enthusiastically upon a war that it had little realistic hope of winning without a greater commitment of military forces in the theatre than the French proved interested in providing. The Turkish navy had been rebuilt with considerable French assistance in the design and construction of warships and in the upgrading of naval infrastructure. Bilateral agreements had been signed between the two nations and aid missions were sent to Constantinople in 1784 and 1787. With a downturn in relations, these missions had been recalled in 1788, but many French engineers and artisans chose to remain in Turkish employ. The most illustrious of the French engineers in Turkish service was Jacques Le Brun who designed the great majority of new Turkish warships of all sizes during the 1790s, until he was lured away into Russian service by Fyodor Ushakov in 1798. By 1800, the Ottoman navy had been rebuilt into a respectable force consisting of at least ten modern and well designed ships of the line – including two 3-deckers – supported by five heavy and two light frigates, all under the command of Said Ali, the Algerian commander who had so ably seconded Hassan Pasha at Kaliakra. Although there were still problems with personnel training and discipline, considerable progress had been made during the 1790s as a result of Selim III's determined efforts at upgrading standards and training for officers and seamen alike. Ordnance was still a problem with poorly manufactured cannon and gun carriages making for indifferent and sporadic gunnery in combat. Previous inefficient and disruptive practices, such as the scattered presence of cook stoves on the gun decks and the catch-as-catch-can arrangement of whatever cannon were available, were problems that had been largely corrected. Although there were still problems, the Turkish battle fleet of 1806 was altogether a more credible force than the fleet of 1787, or the even less capable fleet of 1770.

As for the Russian Mediterranean squadron, Seniavin had some of the most modern and well designed ships ever deployed by Russia in the Mediterranean or elsewhere, not to mention the value of the experience gained by his officers and men in their deployment in the Adriatic. The situation was not as rosy for the Black Sea fleet under Rear-Admiral Pustoshkin. Although his ships were numerically and qualitatively well matched against their potential Turkish opponents, their readiness and training was well below the level of Seniavin's Baltic fleet ships, and the Black Sea still lacked adequate infrastructure for extended naval warfare. Fortunately they would not be seriously challenged in the coming war by the Turks, whose entire attention was turned to the threat to their southern flank by Seniavin's fleet.

In previous conflicts, the Turks had faced the prospect of Russian naval attack from either the Mediterranean with ships transferred from the Baltic, or from the Black Sea – but never from both quarters at the same time. The Russian high command, under the Naval Minister Admiral Paul Chichagov, hoped to launch simultaneous land and sea attacks against the Straits and Constantinople itself, with assistance from Great Britain on the Mediterranean side. This ambitious plan might, in fact, have exceeded Russian military resources, particularly with respect to the availability of adequate land forces. It was quickly abandoned upon the outbreak of war due to the lack of readiness of the Black Sea fleet. Unspoken Russian designs on the Straits unfortunately ran parallel to and in potential conflict with those of her British ally. As had proven to be the case with joint Russo-British operations in the Ionian Campaign, the alliance was fraught with undercurrents of distrust and bedeviled by uncoordinated naval operations that often inhibited the attainment of the larger common objective, the neutralization and defeat of Turkey.

Although tentative plans for Anglo-Russian co-operation had been formulated by Lord Collingwood, veteran of Trafalgar and British commander in the Mediterranean, a sizeable force under Sir John Duckworth, consisting of two 3-deckers, six 2-deckers and two frigates, passed largely unchallenged through the Dardanelles in February 1807 without waiting for the arrival of the Russian squadron as originally agreed upon. Upon clearing the forts guarding the Dardanelles, Duckworth engaged and destroyed or captured a small and luckless Turkish squadron consisting of a 64-gun ships of the line, four frigates and eight smaller ships. Having passed through the southern defences to the capital with minimal losses, Duckworth anchored outside Constantinople, making futile demands for the surrender of the outgunned Turkish fleet, which was securely protected by the shore batteries of the capital. When his demands were rejected, Duckworth had no options beyond withdrawing from the Turkish capital empty-handed and attempting to renegotiate the Dardanelles – which were now fully alerted and mobilized to the British presence. The British fleet took heavy casualties on the way out, suffering losses of 29 killed and 138 wounded (Russian sources give the figure as 600) and serious damage to the ships which were struck repeatedly by Turkish cannon and mortars firing stone balls weighing up to 800 pounds.

Four days after the British humiliation, the Russians arrived and Seniavin proposed another attempt on the Dardanelles, this time with a combined Anglo-British squadron as originally envisioned. Duckworth had had enough of the Turkish shore batteries and, although he was no Nelson, proved his equal in at least one respect – tactless arrogance with foreign allies – replying when pressed by Seniavin 'that where a British squadron had failed, no other was likely to succeed.' The British fleet left for Malta a week later, taking nine Turkish prizes on the return journey. Seniavin stayed on the scene and established a blockade outside the Dardanelles, while also exerting pressure on the Turkish fortress at Tenedos, which surrendered in March providing the Russian Mediterranean fleet with a badly needed forward base.

The Battle of the Dardanelles 9 May (21 May) 1807

In spite of the disruptive effect of the simultaneous blockade of both sides of the Straits upon the population of Constantinople, the Turkish fleet of nine ships of the line and six frigates remained at anchor until 7 May (19 May), when it moved into the Aegean. The Turkish objective appears to have been the recapture of Tenedos and the drawing off of Russian naval forces from their blockade. Seniavin chose to trust in the ability of Russian troops on Tenedos to hold out against the expected Turkish attack and positioned his fleet to intercept the Turkish battle fleet when it attempted to return to Constantinople. Although Russian troops were able to repulse the Turkish amphibious attack, adverse winds prevented Seniavin from achieving an optimal position for intercepting the retreating Turkish fleet. On 9 May, he was forced to order a general chase after the Turkish warships running for the security of the forts protecting the Dardanelles, sacrificing control of his fleet to the exigencies of the situation. The well-tried veteran *Venus* (44) was the first of the pursuing Russian ships to overtake the Turkish ships at 6:00 p.m. In company with *Selafail* (74), she engaged the Turkish 120-gun flagship, both ships manoeuvring off the quarters of the more powerful three-decker. Fighting between scattered elements of both fleets continued sporadically until 9:00 p.m. The chase resumed on the following morning, until the Turks succeeded in gaining the shelter of the Dardanelles' fortifications. Three Turkish ships failed to reach the Straits and ran themselves aground during the pursuit. While the Russians later maintained that these ships had been destroyed by battle damage and grounding, it is also alleged that they were later salvaged and returned to Turkish service – yet another example of the uncertainties that surrounded all Russo-Turkish engagements. 26 Russians were killed in the fighting and 56 wounded. Turkish casualties are indeterminate – as usual – but the Russians state that they were heavy.

The largely unsuccessful pursuit of Turkish naval forces

attempting to relieve Tenedos was a repeat of all too common Russian experience in previous conflicts. Seniavin was unhappy with the result, because his objective was the destruction of the Turkish fleet and not its neutralization. A month later at the battle of Mount Athos, he remedied the problem decisively by adopting what might be best described as Nelsonian tactics tailored to Russian needs.

The Battle of Mount Athos (Lemnos) 18–19 June (30 June–1 July) 1807

Russian historians maintain that it was the effectiveness of their naval blockades at both ends of the Straits and the resulting shortages and food riots in the Turkish capital that led to the revolt of the Janissaries on 19 May (31 May) and the deposition of Selim III in favour of his son Mustapha. Whether this interpretation of the situation in the capital is correct or not, it is a fact that the Turkish fleet finally emerged from the shelter of the Dardanelles three weeks later on 10 June to make a second attempt at recapturing Tenedos and depriving the Russians of the forward basing that they needed to maintain a close blockade on the southern approaches to Constantinople. The Turks succeeded in sidestepping the Russian fleet for a second time, this time landing 6,000 troops on the island, but Seniavin then succeeded in driving the Turkish fleet away from the beachhead, reinforcing the Russian garrison and closing off the Turkish battle fleet's line of retreat by occupying a strategic position between Mount Athos and Lemnos, forcing the battle that he had sought unsuccessfully a month earlier.

In the ensuing battle, which began between 8:00 and 9:00 a.m. on the 18 June (30 June), both sides had ten ships of the line. The weight of metal was clearly with the Turks, whose capital ships were more heavily gunned, with a 128-gun flagship, the *Selimiye*, the 90-gun *Sedd-ul bahr*, five 84s and three 74s, backed up by six heavy frigates forming a second line providing supporting fire between the gaps in the main line. The heaviest ships on the Russian side were three 80-gun ships, supported by five 74s and two 60/64s. The Russians had no frigates. Readers consulting a map of the opening phases of the battle may be forgiven for thinking that they are looking at a replay of Trafalgar, with Seniavin's ten ships approaching the Turkish line in two closely

A view of the battle at Athos in 1807 as depicted by A. P. Bogolyubov in 1852. On display here is the Russian sailing battle line in its final fleet action during the age of sail. To the right we see Vice-Admiral Seniavin's flagship Tvordyi *engaging the Turkish* Sedd-ul Bahr. *The battle ended with the Turkish flagship striking to* Tvordyi *and the rest of the Turkish battle fleet followed tradition by breaking off action and retreating in disorder at the end of the day.*

The battered Turkish flagship in tow after the battle of Athos in 1807. Although her sails are badly shot up, she still has her masts and most of her spars.

spaced parallel columns aimed directly at the centre of the Turkish line. Seniavin was undoubtedly familiar with Nelson's innovative tactics in the earlier battle and quite possibly inspired by them, but his intent was *not* to break the Turkish line. Rather, his aim was to throw six ships of the line against the three extremely powerful Turkish flagships in the centre of their line, while his four remaining ships, including his flagship, the *Tvyordyi* (80) and Rear-Admiral Greig's flagship, the *Retvizan* (64), dealt with the Turkish vanguard ships and any unforeseen eventualities in the centre of the line. The Turkish flagships were not distributed along the Turkish line in order to provide command and control, the customary role of flagships; instead they were clustered for mutual support in the centre of the line and this would be their undoing. As for the Turkish rear, Seniavin had sufficient confidence in his own ships' ability to deal with the leading elements of their line expeditiously and, one might suspect, sufficient disregard for his opponents' aggressiveness and initiative to risk the possibility of their coming to the assistance of their flagships before he was ready to deal with them with his vanguard ships.

The leading ship in the starboard line, the 80-gun *Rafail*, took heavy fire during the approach from the 120-gun *Mesudiye*, the 90-gun *Sedd-ul bahr* and two of the supporting second line frigates. She lost control of her movements, lurching through the Turkish line – unintentionally imitating the *Victory* at Trafalgar, but without being followed by her fellows, who formed up abreast the Turkish flagships on the windward side of the line as planned. *Rafail*'s dead included her captain and 66 Russian sailors, and she was only able to repair her damage and join the pursuit of the Turkish fleet during the latter stages of the battle. In spite of having lost their most powerful ship at the outset of the battle, the five remaining Russian ships accomplished their intended mission and succeeded in engaging and forcing both the *Mesudiye* and the *Sedd-ul bahr* to break off the action and retreat, signalling the dissolution of the Turkish line.

In the meantime, Seniavin and Greig had attacked the Turkish van with their remaining four ships as planned. These four ships included the two flagships and two supporting ships of the line. They had originally represented the rearmost elements of the two attacking five-ship columns, with Seniavin and his flagship *Tvyordyi* in the starboard column and Greig and his flagship *Retvizan* in the port column. These two two-ship mini-columns disengaged from their original columns and turned to starboard to halt the advance of the Turkish van, while the five leading ships of the two original columns (minus the unfortunate *Rafail*) engaged the three flagships. Taking the lead in *Tvyordyi* (74) and supported by *Skoryi* (64), Seniavin moved to engage the two leading Turkish ships of the line and an accompanying frigate, achieving his objective of bringing the forward progress of the Turkish line to a halt. Greig in *Retvizan* (64) supported by *Sviataia Elena* (74) formed up behind Seniavin's ships, but ahead of the five ships engaging the Turkish flagships in the centre of the line. The end result of these manoeuvres had the originally trailing ships of the two Russian columns at the head of the reformed line, with the five ships originally in the lead (minus the unfortunate *Rafail*) were now massed against the Turkish centre. All of the Russian ships were heavily engaged, with the exception of the badly damaged *Rafail*, and the entire Turkish line, including the four-ship rear-guard which had very belatedly joined the fight, was in retreat by 10:00 a.m. after less than two hours of fighting. Intermittent Russian pursuit continued throughout the day as wind conditions allowed and the heavily damaged *Sedd-ul bahr* was abandoned by her fellows and surrendered to the *Selafail* that evening.

The pursuit of the Turks fleeing for the shelter of the Dardanelles, picked up again the next morning and one ship of the line and two frigates were driven ashore and wrecked. On 20 June (2 July), the Turks set fire to another severely damaged ship of the line and frigate, and then had two more frigates or sloops sink from damage incurred in the battle before reaching the safety of the Dardanelles. The fleet that the deposed Selim III had so painfully rebuilt over two decades had been effectively destroyed in just two days of fighting.

In the tradition of genial and not-so-genial condescension towards their Russian allies established by his fellow flag officers, Lord Nelson and Sir John Duckworth, Lord Collingwood dismissed Mount Athos as 'a sort of a battle' – a dismissal so entirely unwarranted in its overweening arrogance as to prompt the normally unemotional R. C. Anderson to respond a century later by writing that 'there was little reason to sneer'. (In fairness to Collingwood, he is said by Russian sources to have related well on a personal level with Russian officers to and to have developed high regard for his Russian ally during their short period of personal interaction.) Indeed, Mount Athos ranks as one of the more important Russian victories during the age of sail and certainly as one of the most brilliantly planned and executed. It may be argued that the Russian qualitative superiority over their Turkish opponents was so overwhelming as to have made victory inevitable, but this disregards the tactical creativity of Seniavin's plan of attack on the Turkish line and his ability to find and fix an opponent with a long history of successfully breaking off action and running for shelter. Seniavin should have returned to Russia a hero on a par with Orlov, Greig and Ushakov. Instead, as a result of circumstances beyond his control in the larger Mediterranean theatre as well as the petty spitefulness of his emperor, he found himself shamed and rejected upon his eventual return to Russia.

The disgraceful treatment of Rear-Admiral Seniavin was still in the future after the victory at Mount Athos, but the downturn in the fortunes of the Russian Mediterranean fleet came about almost immediately with the negotiation of the Treaty of Tilsit, putting an end to war with France and establishing a cease fire with Turkey for the next two years. Seniavin is said to have broken into tears when learning of the treaty and its implications. The victor of Mount Athos found himself deprived of a mission at the same time as he was stripped of his base at Tenedos which was returned to Turkey by the treaty along with his backup base at Corfu, which was ceded to France with the rest of the Ionic islands that had been so painstakingly won by Ushakov a decade earlier. The Russian Mediterranean fleet, comprised of the most powerful and highly trained ships and crews available to Russia at the time, was orphaned and left to wander the Mediterranean in search of a viable route back to the Baltic in the face of growing British hostility. Elements of his fleet were surrendered to France at Toulon and the famed veteran of the Russo-Swedish War, *Venus*, was handed over to Naples, while Seniavin himself was forced to negotiate the internment of the main body of his fleet by Great Britain after they were penned into the Tagus outside Lisbon by overwhelmingly superior British forces (15 ships of the line and ten frigates). Nine ships of the line and a frigate were impounded at Portsmouth until they were officially 'purchased' by Great Britain with the renewal of warfare between Russia and France in 1812. Alexander I, whose shortcomings and policies had doomed Seniavin and his fleet, blamed the unfortunate admiral, relegated him to insignificant duties in Russia and left him in poverty and disgrace.

With Turkish attention and resources focused on the joint

British attitudes towards the Russian navy

Before moving on, it should be mentioned that the abrasiveness shown by Nelson, Duckworth and Collingwood, while not uncommon in the Royal Navy during this period, does not represent a complete picture of Anglo-Russian naval interactions. Many British officers had better opinions of the Russians at sea. No better evidence of this duality of opinion is evidenced than the report made by Captain Troubridge to his mentor Nelson on the state of Ushakov's fleet at Corfu in 1798: 'They are for the most part very fine ships, and all carry very heavy metal' (Norman Saul) or the report of a British naval surgeon in 1814: 'The Russian sailors possess all the requisites for becoming the first among their profession – courage, fortitude, patience, obedience, hardihood, and activity. A little experience makes them very smart in doing duty aloft in fine weather . . . No men can be better behaved' (Norman Saul). Many British officers before, during and after the period of complete British naval ascendancy during the final decade of the Napoleonic Wars, established warm and cordial relations with their Russian counterparts. The Royal Navy not only supplied numbers of qualified officers who remained in Russian service, such as Samuel Greig, it also served as a training ground for a significant number of young Russian officers who later rose to positions of command and influence, Dmitriy Seniavin being a case in point.

threat of British and Russian naval concentrations in the Aegean, the Russian Black Sea fleet had little to contend with during the war beyond the notoriously treacherous weather of the Black Sea itself and the not inconsequential threat of Turkish shore batteries. The withdrawal of major naval forces from the Black Sea by Turkey made sense from their perspective because of the more formidable fortifications guarding the Bosporus approaches to Constantinople and the much greater strength of the Russian and British naval forces threatening the Dardanelles. Once mobilized, the Black Sea fleet under Rear-Admiral Pustoshkin could muster two 3-deckers, four 2-deckers, five frigates and three brigs. In the absence of Turkish naval opposition, Pustoshkin was free to use his resources to support Russian land forces advancing to the south of Odessa, and to attack and harass Turkish positions on the southern shore or the Black Sea. Anapa surrendered in May to the combined force of the Russian battle fleet and troops landed to assault the Turkish positions. A month later at Trebizond, however, Turkish shore batteries at succeeded in driving off Russian naval forces operating in the absence of supporting land forces. The Treaty of Tilsit signed that same month put a temporary end to conflict between Russia and France. While it did not end hostilities between Turkey and Russia, it did provide for a two-year ceasefire that allowed the Turks to recover somewhat from their losses sustained in the Aegean and to reposition their remaining naval assets in the Black Sea with the departure of the Baltic fleet from the Mediterranean.

When hostilities resumed in 1809, the Russian Black Sea fleet, now under Rear-Admiral Sarytchev, faced a Turkish fleet composed, at its height, of three 3-deckers, six 2-deckers and six frigates (Anderson). It is unclear how much of this considerable concentration consisted of veterans of Mount Athos and how much was new construction. The Turkish level of training and leadership is equally indeterminate, but what is clear is that it was a fleet determined to avoid confrontation with the Russian battle fleet – and one that quite successfully accomplished its goal by repeatedly declining battle during the next three years. Russian forces available during this final phase of the war reached a peak of three 110s, five 74s and two 66s, with supporting frigates, once again achieving nearly perfect numerical equivalency with their opposite numbers. Sarytchev was successful in 1810 in his primary mission of providing cover for Russian land forces advancing on Varna on the coast of present day Bulgaria. He was not successful, however, when a second attempt was made upon Trebizond – this time with supporting troops – only to be repulsed with heavy casualties. Nor was he successful in bringing the Turkish fleet to battle. He was replaced in 1811 by yet another Englishman in Russian service, Vice-Admiral Robert Hall (Gall to the Russians, who have no 'H' as such), who was equally unsuccessful in pinning down the Turks prior to the end of the war.

When Napoleon invaded Russia in 1812, Alexander I wasted no time in negotiating an end to the war with Turkey. The Black Sea fleet was not in a position to influence directly the remaining years of the twenty year struggle with France, but it continued to be maintained as an effective counterweight to the Turkish navy.

The post-Napoleonic years under Alexander I 1815–24

Mention has been made of the malaise affecting the development of Russian naval power in the Baltic as a result of the indifference of Alexander I, the policies of the Marquis de Traversay, the French émigré whose policies and retrenchments as Navy Minister did severe damage to the morale and effectiveness of the Russian navy, and to the near bankruptcy of the Russian government in the wake of the Napoleonic Wars. Similar conditions prevailed in the Black Sea, aggravated by the lack of logistical support and infrastructure in the form of shipyard facilities and dry docks. In one important respect, however, the 'poor relation' of the more powerful Baltic fleet was in an advantageous position – the presence of credible potential enemies. All of Russia's traditional Baltic rivals were in eclipse after the Napoleonic Wars, and none were likely to reassert themselves as naval rivals to Russian dominance in northern waters in the foreseeable future. In the south, on the other hand, the Russians not only faced the continuing threat of a revival of Turkish naval power, they were also presented with the growth of a new and virtually independent naval power, Egypt, nominally a vassal state of the Ottoman Empire.

Aleksei Greig, son of Samuel Greig, and able second in command to Dmitriy Seniavin in the Ionian Campaign and the Russo-Turkish War of 1807–12, took command of the Black Sea fleet in 1815. Besides being an exceptionally capable naval commander with an established record of accomplishment, Greig proved to be a reformer, an innovator and a humanitarian who did as much as was possible to preserve his command from the mediocrity and corruption prevalent throughout the Russian fleet during the ministry of the Marquis de Traversay. During his tenure, the shipbuilding facilities of Nikolaev were upgraded and expanded at the expense of those at Kherson, the use of underwater coppering and iron reinforcement of ship frames became the norm rather than the exception, and the firepower of warships was increased by the installation of more and heavier cannon, disregarding the provisions of the Gun Establishment of 1803. Not only did he outlaw flogging and minimize corporal punishment, but he insisted upon adequate standards of training for common seamen, and became famous for the determined instillation of his own high standards of leadership among his frequently resistant subordinates. Although his successor, Mikhail Lazarev, would find much to complain about in the Black Sea fleet, there is little question that Aleksei Greig left it in far better shape than he had found it.

War with Turkey 1827–9

The combined application of French, British and Russian naval power to restrain and limit Ottoman power and ostensibly to assist in the Greek independence movement is discussed in the Baltic section of this summary. Suffice it to say here that the Russian ships that fought at Navarino represented the final attempt to extend the reach of the Baltic fleet into the Levant.

Admiral Aleksei S. Greig (1775–1845) was the accomplished son of a famous father and a second-generation Scottish immigrant to Russia. He established his credentials by serving with distinction under Vice-Admiral Ushakov in the Mediterranean and later under Vice-Admiral Dmitri Seniavin before going on to command of the Black Sea fleet after the Napoleonic Wars. As commander in the Black Sea, he did much to overcome the neglect and damage wrought under Alexander and his naval minister Marquis de Traversay and to bring an element of humanity into the lives of the sailors in his command. Unknown artist.

Henceforth, the projection and utilization of sea power on the southern frontiers of the Russian state would be left to the ships of the Black Sea fleet. This being the case, the accessibility or inaccessibility of the Straits and the quality of the relations with the declining Ottoman Empire would become a factor of increasing importance. The allied intervention against Turkey in 1827 was conditioned by mutual rivalries and suspicions among the three great powers, who were all allegedly interested in promoting Greek democracy and independence against the allegedly barbaric and non-Christian Turks. There is no evidence that Russia was at this time interested in any sort of serious confrontation with Great Britain or France on its southern frontier or elsewhere, but it is clear, in retrospect, that the time would come when these two European powers would be as interested in limiting Russian expansionism as they were already interested in undermining what was left of the Ottoman Empire. When this conflict matured, the point of contact would be through the Black Sea and, accordingly, through whatever naval resources the Russians had available in the area.

Although the French and British naval forces departed from Greece and the Aegean after Navarino, Russia and Turkey remained at war for two more years, providing the opportunity for Russia to continue its southward drive along the Black Sea coastline.

Admiral Greig was still in command of the Black Sea fleet and conducted operations along the western shore of the Black Sea, providing naval support necessary for the taking of Anapa (for the third time) and Varna, and supporting Russian troops in their southward advance, insuring against the intervention by the remaining effective elements of the Turkish Navy. The Turkish navy spent most of this period avoiding contact with the greatly superior Black Sea fleet, but in May of 1829 it emerged from the shelter of Constantinople long enough to skirmish with a 20-gun brig headed for heroism and glory and to capture a 36-gun frigate doomed to disgrace and humiliation.

The heroism and glory was provided on 14 May (26 May) 1829 by Lieutenant Alexander Kazarskii in command of the 20-gun *Merkurii*, a brig that had inherited the name of the equally famous schooner that had captured the Swedish heavy frigate *Venus* in 1788. This tiny ship ran afoul of the 122-gun Turkish flagship *Mesudiye* accompanied by an 84-gun escort in very light winds and succeeded in manoeuvring off the larger ships' quarters and exchanging fire with them for four hours before escaping with a change in the wind conditions. This incident is understandably one of the most revered events in Russian naval history and such a remarkable example of seamanship and coolness under fire as to have caused open skepticism among some British historians, including F. T. Jane, who dismisses it out of hand, and R. C. Anderson, who assumed a more guarded but not entirely skeptical point of view. While acknowledging the apparent improbability of *Merkurii*'s managing to evade the larger ships' fire for such an extended period, Anderson does note the deplorable quality of Turkish gunnery and gives the reported incident his conditional support. Russian historians do not question the incident and it is accepted here as correct and true in its essentials.

The humiliation and disgrace that was swept aside by *Merkurii*'s near miraculous engagement, had already occurred three days earlier on 11 May (23 May) 1829, and involved the surrender of the frigate *Rafail* when she found herself becalmed and surrounded by no fewer than six Turkish ships of the line, two frigates, five corvettes and two brigs. After consulting with his fellow officers, Captain Stroynikov had taken the only sensible course of action, and surrendered his ship to overwhelmingly superior force without attempting to make a fight of it. Nicholas I had more rigorous ideas of personal honour – at least with the lives of his subjects – and thought the only honourable course of action would have been for Stroynikov to have blown up his ship in a repeat of Captain Reingold Saken's heroic self-destruction in somewhat different circumstances in 1788. All of the officers involved with Stroynikov were broken to common seamen and the unfortunate captain himself was forbidden to ever marry in order to preserve Russia from the off-

A painting by I. K. Ayvazovskiy of the tiny Russian brig Merkurii *in combat with two Turkish ships of the line. To the left in the painting is the 128-gun Turkish flagship* Selimye, *and to the right is 74-gun* Rivale. *The painting shows her pinned between her two colossal opponents with little hope of escape is for dramatic effect. In actuality the Russian captain is said to have survived the four-hour battle by taking advantage of the prevailing light winds and manoeuvring off the quarters of his foes to avoid their broadside guns.* Merkurii *did take a number of hull hits, but the majority of the damage was to her rigging. Turkish ships were traditionally reputed to 'shoot high' and this, along with the fact that they may have been unable to depress their guns sufficiently to target the much smaller ship, may further explain her survival.*

spring of a 'coward and traitor'. It is not known whether Stroynikov faithfully obeyed his emperor's harsh directive in later years . . .

Admiral Lazarev and the Black Sea fleet

Mikhail Lazarev succeeded to command of the Black Sea fleet in 1833 after an extraordinary early career that had involved three circumnavigations of the globe, the discovery of the Antarctic mainland, combat at Navarino as commander of Rear-Admiral Login Petrovich Geiden's flagship *Azov*, and command of the blockade of the Dardanelles in the 1828–9 war. He was a ruthless critic of what he considered to have been the shoddy construction standards of Russian Black Sea warships and did much to upgrade infrastructure and quality control during his tenure as commander. During his earlier years, Lazarev had established close relations with British officers serving in the Mediterranean and he introduced uniform calibre gun establishments along lines established in the Royal Navy in the 1820s at a time when the less progressive Baltic fleet remained tied to mixed batteries, with the exception of a very small number of experimental ship of the line and frigates. Lazarev was intensely interested in technological progress of all sorts and pushed for the introduction of steam power in advance of its acceptance and feasibility in a Russia that was only slowly entering into the beginning stages of the Industrial Revolution. Had his determination and dynamism been sufficient in and of itself to bring about the modernization and reconstruction of Russian warships, the Russian navy might well have been in a position to give a better account of itself in 1853. As it was, his legacy was carried on by two of his pupils, Vice Admiral Pavel Nakhimov and Vice Admiral Vladimir Kornilov, both of whom insured the continuation of his standards of excellence and both of whom died heroically during the siege of Sevastopol during the Crimean War.

Admiral Lazarev (1788–1851) drove many of the reforms that helped mould Russia into the world's second naval power by the 1830s. An explorer in his early days as an officer, he formed close relationships with officers of the Royal Navy when serving in the Mediterranean, keeping abreast of new developments in ship design and ordnance developments in the process. He remained open to change throughout his life, and promoted improvements in ordnance and the adoption of steam propulsion, working to overcome the complacency and lethargy of a peacetime navy. His greatest gifts were as an administrator, and his two most accomplished subordinates were Vice-Admirals Pavel Nakhimov and Vladimir Kornilov, both of whom died in the siege of Sevastopol'. Painted by L. D. Blinov 1885, after Karl Briullov's portrait.

Turkey and the Caucasus Campaign 1830–40

In the wake of the Russo-Turkish War of 1827–9, the Ottoman Empire found itself in the unlikely position of having to enter into friendly relations with its ancient enemy, Russia. The rise of Egyptian power was of more moment to Constantinople than the threat of further Russian expansion to the south. While the Egyptians had fought alongside the Turks at Navarino, the Egyptian Pasha Mehmed Ali was clearly on a collision course with his Turkish overlord, the Sultan. By the early 1830s, both Egypt and Turkey were engaged in massive shipbuilding programmes, and the former vassal state was in the lead. By 1837, the Egyptian fleet included ten ships of the line with over 100 guns, two with 88–92 guns and six in the 60-gun range – for a total of 18 capital ships, a remarkable accomplishment in itself and one little noted by most naval historians. Three of the 100-gun ships were under construction, but all had been launched by 1838, although one of these was accidentally burnt while fitting out. Against this, only two 126-gun ships, six with 74–80 guns and seven heavy frigates with 52 guns were active at Constantinople out of a total Turkish strength of three 126-gun ships, 12 of 74–90 and ten heavy frigates of 50–60 guns including one still under construction. The Turkish fleet was in poor condition in contrast to the Egyptian. The only available counterweight to the Egyptian navy was alliance with Russia and this carried a price tag: opening of the Straits to Russian naval movements, the closing of the Black Sea to non-Russian warships and the ceding of the Caucasus to Russian control. In 1833, Admiral Lazarev entered the Bosporus at Turkish invitation with the Black Sea fleet and 12,000 Russian troops and saved Constantinople from almost certain capture by the Egyptians, who were by this time in open revolt and approaching the heart of the Empire with an army that had successfully defeated the Ottoman forces sent against it. For their assistance in containing Mehmed Ali, Russia was awarded with *de facto* control over the Straits until 1841 at which time the combined power of France and Great Britain brought about a return to previous restrictions on the movement of naval forces in either direction.

The subjection of the independent tribal groups in the Caucasus became a major focus for the Russians from 1836 on and through the early 1840s. While the rebellious ethnic groups presented no naval threat to Russian control of the Black Sea, the elements of the Black Sea fleet – from the lightest to the heaviest – were all extensively involved in the full range of amphibious support activities, from transportation of troops and supplies, to shore bombardment, to patrol and escort activities, and to the landing, establishment, and protection of beachheads and forts. While these activities must have been tedious in the extreme, one can only surmise that the level of training, readiness and seamanship of the ships involved must have been of a high order – especially under Admiral Lazarev's demanding leadership.

Sinop and the Crimean War 1853–6

The Russian Black Sea fleet had approached the highest standards of efficiency during the closing years of the age of sail and its warships and commanders were well regarded by informed British and French observers. By mid-century, technological change was transforming military and naval weapons and tactical systems at a rate that often left even the most advanced European powers struggling to keep up. The Ottoman Empire was quickly left behind by improvements in ordnance and the introduction of steam propulsion, while their Russian rivals were at the same time attempting with only limited success to keep abreast of European powers possessing even more fully matured industrial and scientific resources. One effect of the industrial revolution would be the Russian destruction of Turkish naval forces at Sinop by means of their more advanced ordnance, their more highly trained manpower resources and their overwhelming materiel superiority. In a similar manner, Russian naval power would in its turn be eclipsed very shortly thereafter at the siege of Sevastopol'

RUSSIAN NAVAL HISTORY 1695–1860

This portrayal of the landing of Russian and Georgian troops at Subashi (now Abhasia) in 1838, by I. K. Ayvazovskiy is typical of the long struggle to subdue rebellious local tribes after Russia was awarded the Caucasus by Turkey in the 1830s. In the foreground irregular native troops fire on orderly columns of regulars emerging from landing boats. In the centre ships of the line and frigates of the Russian Black Sea fleet give fire support to the landings, unchallenged by shore batteries or any sort of naval opposition. An omen of things to come is evidenced by the small steam paddle ship bravely polluting the Black Sea sky with a line of smoke from its stack.

Russia's final victory during the age of sail is shown here in A. P. Bogolyubov's 1860 treatment of the battle of Sinop in 1853. With shell-firing Russian line of battle ships facing Turkish frigates firing solid shot, there was never any doubt about the outcome. Given the disparity in firepower, there would have been little chance for the Turkish squadron even had the Russians been limited to solid shot weapons. An interesting aspect of the painting is the degree to which it resembles depictions of earlier and more traditional eighteenth-century warfare, except possibly for the spectacular damage being inflicted upon the Turkish ships by exploding shells. The ships themselves are clearly post-Napoleonic, but there are no tell-tale funnels or paddle wheels in sight to advertise the very late date of a battle that took place in the closing years of the age of sail. Funnels and paddle wheels would be very much in evidence just a year later when the French and British invaded both the Black Sea and the Baltic.

An unprepossessing picture of one of Russia's greatest admirals, Pavel. S. Nakhimov (1803–55). A veteran of Navarino, student of Admiral Mikhail Lazarev and an advocate of technical change in an age of transition, he was a firm disciplinarian with a great love for the sailors serving under him. The victory at Sinop was of his making and his capacity for leadership by example was shown two years later by his willingness to die for his country at the side of his sailors at the fall of Sevastopol' in 1855. Artist unknown.

A handsome portrayal of one of the great Russian heroes of the Crimean War, Vice-Admiral Kornilov (1806–1854). He and Vice-Admiral Nakhimov had both pushed for the modernization of the Russian fleet in the years before the Crimean War, both agitated for a more active involvement of the Black Sea fleet during the war and both died heroically in the defence of Sevastopol'. Portrait by A. F. Pershakov, 1900.

by British and French naval forces operating with even more highly developed technological sophistication acting similarly in tandem with equally overwhelming materiel superiority.

For westerners unaccustomed to the highly developed interrelatedness of Russian naval and military operations, the decision of Emperor Nicholas I, acting upon the advice of Prince Menshikov, to order Admiral Nakhimov to scuttle the major elements of the Black Sea fleet at the harbour entrance and send his sailors ashore along with their artillery to aid in the defence of Sevastopol' seems an act of craven cowardice or incredibly poor judgment. Many of Nakhimov's officers are said to have held similar viewpoints, holding that the honour of Russia required a fight to the death against an overwhelmingly powerful Anglo-French armada in the open waters of the Black Sea. If real military effectiveness is deemed the criterion in place of self-serving posturing by officers imbued with an excess of nineteenth-century romanticism, the practical contribution of the Russian sailors to the defence of Sevastopol' clearly outweighed whatever propaganda value the heroic sacrifice of the certainly doomed Russian battle fleet at sea by the superior Anglo-French forces might have had in the eyes of history and naval tradition. If, on the other hand, real courage and sacrifice were to become the criteria, the death of Admirals Kornilov, Istomin and Nakhimov along with 15,000 seamen and officers during the siege and the survival of a mere 600 speaks for itself.

Official Russian records credit the warship losses during the siege of Sevastopol at 12 line of battle ships, two frigates, five corvettes and brigs and five steam warships. This was the fleet built so carefully over a quarter century by the will of Nicholas I and the skill and leadership of Admiral Lazarev. It was unquestionably the most efficient and well-trained fleet ever put into service by the Russian Navy during the age of sail. Its inability to mount an effective challenge to the combined fleets of two of the most powerful and technologically advanced great powers of the period is no reflection on its standing in this regard. The Treaty of Paris signed in March of 1856 ended the Crimean War and forbade (temporarily as events were to prove) the future operation of Russian naval forces in the Black Sea. Sailing ships would hang on in the Baltic until 1860, but the death by scuttling of the Black Sea fleet at Sevastopol marked the real end for the Russian sailing navy.

RUSSIAN NAVAL HISTORY 1695–1860

Vice-Admiral Nakhimov directing the action at the battle of Sinop in 1853. A protégé of Mikhail Lazarev and a brilliant and courageous officer in his own right, he never had the opportunity to show his worth against an opponent of equal stature. The Turks, here being systematically destroyed, were too weak an opponent and the Anglo-French armada that assailed Sevastopol' two years later, too strong a one for a realistic appraisal to be made of his full potential. Note the Russian seamen at work on their deck gun, wearing uniforms in contrast to enlisted men during earlier eras.

Admiral and General A. S. Menshikov (1787–1869) acted as naval minister under Nicholas I from 1827 to 1855. A gifted administrator and a vocal and sarcastic critic of his contemporaries, in the Crimean War, Menshikov organized the defence of Sevastopol' and had the great misfortune of overseeing the destruction of Russian naval power. Undated, artist unknown.

Right: An idealizing picture showing Russian gunners preparing to go into action in the 1850s, an interesting contrast with the more realistic portrayal in the painting above. The rolled hammocks lining the top of the barricades were intended to provide some degree of added protection against shrapnel and gunfire. Portrayals of Russian common seamen are relatively rare. The dog is apparently a ship's mascot, unconcerned by the coming engagement.

A photograph of Emperor Alexander II 1818–81. The eldest of Nicholas I's sons, he is of interest here as the Russian emperor in charge of the Russian sailing navy in its final days during and immediately following the Crimean War. Alexander II presided over the reconstruction of a country and a navy devastated by war, and is remembered in history for this and as the Emperor who freed the serfs.

The Caspian flotilla

The Caspian Sea is an entirely landlocked body of water of low salinity and considerable extent. The northern half is quite shallow, but the southern is extremely deep for an inland body of water, reaching depths in excess of 3,000 feet.

The Caspian served both as a buffer between Russia and the Persian Empire and as a channel for trade. Russian presence on the northern shore goes back to the early 1600s and any southward expansion towards the Indian Ocean had to take place along its eastern and western coastlines in a manner similar to the Russian movement along the littoral of the Black Sea to the west. There were, of course, differences between events in the Black Sea and the Caspian. Turkey had a long history as a Mediterranean naval power and could readily transfer all or part of its navy from the Mediterranean to the Black Sea as required to counter Russian expansionism. The Persians, on the other hand, had no maritime traditions to draw upon and no means for transferring non-existent warships into the Caspian from other areas – even had they chosen to challenge the Russians at sea. In addition, the conflict between Persia and Russia was intermittent and of low intensity until the nineteenth century, with the result that the Caspian remained largely a conduit for peaceful trade throughout most of the period of our coverage.

The first attempt to establish a Russian naval presence in the Caspian dates to 1667, with the construction of the short-lived gukor *Oryol* at the Russian port of Astrakhan' on the northern shore. Any further plans for this area came to an abrupt end in 1670 with the burning of Russia's first purpose-built warship during the Cossack rebellion under Stenka (Stepan) Razin.

A second ill-fated attempt at establishing a permanent base on the eastern coast under Peter I's personal representative, the Caucasian Prince Alexander Bekovich-Cherkasskiy, came to an even more abrupt end in 1715, with the massacre of the entire party by local Turkmen tribesmen. Two years later in 1717, a second expedition, including the Prince himself and 5,000 troops, was ruthlessly massacred by the Khan of Khivan.

With the end of the Great Northern War freeing Russian resources for southern expansion, a third and more substantial attempt was made by Peter I in 1722. Astrakhan' was established as a naval port and an expeditionary force of 22,000 troops transported by eight naval and 79 cargo vessels along with about 200 small boats, all under the command of Count Apraksin, was sent against the Persians to the south. The Persians at this time had nothing afloat capable of challenging this large-scale amphibious endeavour, but Russian interest in the Caspian evaporated with Peter I's death.

The Caspian flotilla was allowed to languish and had shrunk to only three vessels by 1740. In the early 1750s, the Persian government, at the instigation of a British trading company, attempted to construct a small fleet of its own to counter Russian dominance in the area. One ship was completed and several more laid down. This half-hearted attempt by the Persians to create a navy of sorts, was brushed aside by a Russian expedition to Derbent in 1752 led by a Lieutenant Tolmachev, operating with a single ship. During the raid, the young lieutenant fired the completed Persian ship, bloodied the local merchants and compelled a formal gun salute from the local garrison – unintentionally anticipating what would become standard British operating procedure in the coming century of unrestrained imperial expansion.

The establishment of a permanent Russian naval presence in the Caspian took place under Catherine II at virtually the same time as did the birth of the Black Sea fleet under Prince Potemkin and for the same reasons – a renewed Russian interest in southern expansion. By 1780, Captain Voynovich already had three sloops of 20 guns apiece, one bomb ship and two boats. The Caspian flotilla was formally created in 1783 and was maintained thereafter on a permanent basis.

Russia had had considerable experience in the uses of sea power as an adjunct to territorial expansion in earlier warfare

Located on the present day site of Sitka in the Alaskan archipelago, Novo Arkhangels'k was established in 1804 and became the centre for exploration and trade in Russian America prior to the US's Alaskan Purchase after the American Civil War. The grim and forbidding nature of life here, or anywhere in the Russian Pacific network is readily apparent. By I. P. Pshenichnyy, 1989.

with Turkey and Sweden, and the amphibious applications of naval forces were almost inbred by the late eighteenth century. Warships could transport and provide cover for the transport of troops, use their firepower to support military operations ashore, intimidate recalcitrant trading powers, and in general engage in the kind of gunboat diplomacy made famous by the Royal Navy during the nineteenth century, even in the absence of opposing naval forces. This is precisely what happened in the Caspian during the course of the Russo-Persian wars of 1803–13 and 1826–8. The warships and forces available for these campaigns were small compared to the larger scale of Russian amphibious operations in the Mediterranean, the Black Sea, or the Baltic. Nevertheless, they were successful in bringing about the reduction of a series of towns and fortresses in both wars, with two notable exceptions in 1805, the attack on Resht and the first unsuccessful attack on Baku in the same year.

The Caspian flotilla never faced any significant naval opposition and never operated ships larger than small frigates – actually ship sloops by European standards. These diminutive 'capital ships' armed with 6pdrs and/or 24pdr carronades were backed up by the normal array of supporting craft, including bomb vessels, imitating the Black Sea and Baltic fleets in structure and organization, if not in size.

The Voyages of Exploration

There has been little awareness outside Russia of the extensive involvement of the Russian navy in the systematic and deliberate exploration of the Pacific basin even as far as Antarctica. Mention has been made of Mikhail Lazarev's three circumnavigations before his service as Rear-Admiral Login Petrovich Geiden's flag captain at Navarino. These voyages were representative of the large-scale programme of systematic exploration begun in 1803 and continuing until 1855, by which time 41 trips from Kronshtadt to Kamchatka and back had been successfully completed.

Before most other European explorers, Russian brigs and sloops had

- explored Arctic waters north of their settlements in the Kamchatka peninsula
- sailed down the western coast of North America from Russian settlements in Alaska as far as San Francisco
- visited Hawaii, Japan and the islands of the South Pacific, and
- penetrated the previously unexplored waters of Antarctica.

Those Westerners inclined to condescension towards the seamanship of Russian sailors and contempt for the quality of construction of Russian ships would be well served to consider the record of these explorers in their modestly proportioned sloops and brigs operating in the face of extremes of climate, adverse weather conditions and personal privation that bear comparison to the best and most heroic efforts of the Atlantic sailing nations.

Section I
The Seagoing Navy

The Baltic Fleet

The Navy of Peter and His Successors (1696–1761)

A contemporary portrait of Peter I at the height of his power and prestige as seen by A. Caravac in 1720. This painting gives a realistic picture of the Russian Tsar in his middle years shortly before he was proclaimed emperor. Peter is standing in front of symbols of Russian naval and military power in the form of a line of battleships surrounded by land-based fortresses. A determined autocrat, he would nevertheless end his life by heroically going into the icy waters of the Baltic to rescue common seamen from drowning.

Ships with 90–100 guns (7 built 1696–1761)

Seven three-decked First Rates were completed between 1718 and 1758. When Peter I was in England, he visited and was greatly impressed with the then new English 90-gun ship, *Triumph*. The dimensions of these ships closely parallel those of British 90s and it appears likely that they were deliberately patterned after them, even allowing for a delay of 20 years. They were primarily intended as prestige ships and saw limited active service and no significant combat. First Rates absorbed inordinate amounts of money to operate and maintain and were equally expensive in terms of manpower.

Lesnoe 90 St Petersburg
Constructor Peter I
Laid down 7.11.1714   *Launched* 29.7.1718
Dimensions 161 ft x 46 ft x 21 ft 6 in
Armament   LD 26/28 x 24pdrs
              MD 28 x 18pdrs
              UD 28 x 8pdrs
              FC & QD 6/8 x 4pdrs (conjecture)

First Russian three-decked warship. Name commemorates a major land victory against the Swedes in 1708, and her design was credited to Peter I himself. Drifted ashore and sunk in Kronshtadt Roads on 23.5.1719. Raised and repaired and returned to service in 7.1720. Cruised in the Baltic in 1721 and 1723–4. Plans for commissioning her in 1728 in response to tensions arising out of the Holstein Question were never acted upon. Restricted to short cruises after 1730 and to stationary duty in Kronshtadt Roads in 1732. Surveyed and determined 'likely to sink at anchor' in 1733. Listed until 1740 for prestige purposes until she was broken apart by a storm on 9.10.1741.

Gangut 90/92 St Petersburg
Constructor R. Kosentz (Richard Cozens)
Laid Down 9.8.1714   *Launched* 28.4.1719
Dimensions 164 ft x (139 ft 8 in) x 47 ft 4 in x 19 ft 6 in (Veselago)
             165 ft 10 in x 47 ft 11 in x 19 ft (Apraksin)
Armament   LD 26/28 x 24pdrs
              MD 28 x 18pdrs
              UD 28 x 8pdrs
              FC & QD 6/8 x 4pdrs (conjecture)

Name commemorates the naval battle of Gangut in 1714, one of the decisive battles of the Great Northern War. Cruised in the Baltic in 1721 and 1723–4. In 1723–4, France unsuccessfully negotiated for her purchase for 92,000 roubles. Restricted to short cruises after 1728 due to deterioration. Ordered broken up in 1736. (Note the differences in dimensions between Veselago and Apraksin.)

Fridrikhshtadt 90/96 St Petersburg
Constructor O. Nye (Joseph Noy)
Laid Down 22.1.1716   *Launched* 1.5.1720
Dimensions 163 ft x 47 ft 10 in x 20 ft (Veselago)
             165 ft 8 in x 48 ft 3 in x19 ft 6 in (Apraksin)
Armament   LD 26/28 x 24pdrs

Lesnoe (90) of 1718, Russia's first three-decker as depicted by A. A. Tron, 2001–2. Noteworthy here is the retention of a spritsail topmast at this comparatively late date. Although replaced by a fore and aft jib in most smaller craft, spritsail topmasts were retained in the largest ships as an aid in manoeuvring the massive and unresponsive vessels. Named after the site of a great military victory on land against the Swedes in 1708, she was said to been designed by Peter I himself. Although Lesnoe managed to ground herself soon after commissioning, she was repaired and cruised several times in the years before Peter's premature death in 1725. Thereafter, she suffered the fate of most prestige ships in the early years of the eighteenth century – harbour duty and gradual deterioration until she was wrecked in a storm in 1740.

```
              MD 28 x 18pdrs
              UD 28 x 8pdrs
              FC & QD 12/14 x 6pdrs
```
Trials in 7.1720. Name commemorates Peter I's victory over the Swedish army in Poland (then Germany) on 30.1.1713. Cruised in the Baltic in 1721 and 1723–4. Broken up after 1736. (Note differences in dimensions between Veselago and Apraksin)

Pyotr I i II 100 St Petersburg
Constructors Peter I et al.
Laid Down 29.6.1723 *Launched* 29.6.1727
Dimensions 181 ft x 49 ft 6 in x 21 ft 9 in (Peter I's designed draught)
            180 ft 2 in x 49 ft 2 in x 18 ft 10 in (Veselago)
            180 ft 11 in x (151 ft 2 in keel) x 49 ft 6 in x 21 ft 9 in
              as completed with Palchikov's alterations
Armament LD 28 x 30pdrs
           MD 28 x 18pdrs
           UD 30 x 8pdrs
           FC & QD 14 x 6pdrs (1723 Establishment)

Russia's first First Rate 100-gun 3-decker. Main armament increased from 24pdrs to 30pdrs, an armament more in keeping with practices abroad at the time. Originally named *Pyotr Pervyi i Vtoroi*. Begun by Peter I and completed after his death at the order of Empress Catherine I by the co-operative endeavour of all active constructors (O. Nye, G. Ramz, F. M. Sklyaev, G. A. Menshikov, R. Brown and F. P. Palchikov). The original intent was to follow the British Establishments of 1706 and 1719, details of which are to be found in Peter I's personal papers. Peter's papers also included plans for a French First Rate, possibly provided by the French designer B. Pangalo (see *Pantelemon-Viktoriia* (66)) and French influence may have been incorporated in the final design. There was said to have been considerable infighting over details of the construction, with the chief constructor altering Peter I's original dimensions and restricting access to the building site. F. M. Sklyaev is believed to have had the major role in completing the project.

Cruised in the Baltic in 1729. Stationed in Kronshtadt Roads in 1732. Participated in the Danzig expedition of 1734. Damaged by lightning in 1736. In service until 1739. Harbour service 1739–44. Preserved on a floating dock 1744–52 due to her status and historical significance. Broken up after 1752.

Imperatritsa Anna 110/114 St Petersburg
Constructor R. Brown
Laid Down 9.5.1732 *Launched* 13.5.1737
Dimensions 186 ft x 49 ft 10 in x 21 ft 9 in
Armament LD 28 x 36pdrs
           MD 28 x 16pdrs
           LD 30 x 12pdrs
           FC & QD 14 x 6pdrs (brass, as designed)
           LD 28 x 24pdrs,
           MD 30 x 16/18pdrs
           UD 30 x 8pdrs
           FC & QD 16 x 6pdrs, 10 x 3pdrs

The original 181 ft design was prepared by R. Brown in 1730 at the direction of Empress Anna for whom the ship was named. Construction was to have been of the highest-quality oak imported from Kazan' and Kurlandia and coated with pitch for improved protection against rot. The original armament was to have been all brass and to have included 28 x 36pdrs, 28 x 16pdrs, 30 x 12pdrs and 14 x pdrs. Considerable debate over the alleged inadequacy of a 181 ft design resulted in the expansion of the design to 186 ft and an increase in armament to 110 guns. It would appear that 36pdrs were unobtainable and were replaced by 24pdrs.

Cruised in the Baltic in 1739–40. Stationed in harbour at Kronshtadt in 1741–4 because of a shortage of seamen. Cruised in the Baltic in 1746 and reassigned to Revel'. Later returned to Kronshtadt where she was decommissioned in 1749 and broken up after 1752.

Zakharii i Elisavet 99/100 St Petersburg
Constructor D. T. Scherbachov
Laid Down 26.5.1745 *Launched* 1.10.1747
Dimensions 181 ft x 51 ft x 21 ft 9 in
Armament LD 28 x 30pdrs
           MD 28 x 18pdrs
           UD 30 x 12pdrs
           FC & QD 14 x 6pdrs (1723 Establishment)

The least successful Russian First Rate built during the eighteenth century, owing to shoddy construction standards and poor material. Her design followed closely that of the *Pyotr I*. During her trials in 7.1748 she was the fastest ship in her squadron, but deteriorated very quickly in service. In ordinary at Kronshtadt from 1748 to 1757, being preserved solely 'for the glory of Russia'. Inspected and found unfit for service and beyond repair in 1757. Broken up in 1759.

Sviatoi Dmitrii Rostovskii 100 St Petersburg
Constructor A. Sutherland
Laid down 11.4.1756   *Launched* 12.6.1758
Dimensions 180 ft 11 in x 49 ft 6 in x 21 ft 9 in
Armament   LD 28 x 30pdrs
             MD 28 x 18pdrs
             UD 30 x 8pdrs iron/12pdrs brass
             FC & QD 14 x 6pdrs (1723 Establishment)

Alexander Sutherland's design was chosen from among plans submitted by Ivan S. Ramburg, Gavrila Okunev, Dmitriy Shcherbachev, and Potap Kachalov. Sutherland submitted two alternate plans and the final design incorporated changes ordered personally by Empress Elisabeth, drawing upon the successful lines of *Pyotr I*. She was built from high-quality Kazan' and Kurlandia oak and contained furniture and decorations removed from the earlier ship.

As the flag of Adm. Mishukov, carried troops to Kolberg in 1760. Transported troops to Kolberg in 1761, landing 150 marines. Cruised in the Baltic in 1764. Decommissioned in 1764. Condemned in 1771. Broken up in 1772.

Ships with 70–88 guns (12 built 1696–1761)

When the Inventory of 1727 established the first Russian rating system for ships of which we have a record, there were no intermediate steps specified between the Second Rate of 80- to 88-gun ships, the Third Rate of 66-gun ships, and the Fourth Rate of 54-gun ships. In contrast with the British and French rating systems which were based on ranges of guns carried for each rate, the Russian system specified one specific number of guns carried within each of the lower ratings, 66 and 54 guns respectively. This implied a degree of order which certainly did not exist within the Russian Navy as it had developed under Peter I. The Establishment of 1732 was even more explicitly constricted, placing all ships with 70 or more guns in the First Rate, 66-gun ships in the Second Rate and 54-gun ships in the Third Rate, again with no apparent allowances for ships with intermediate armaments. In the Establishment of 1750, which was the last formal establishment to be enacted before the Russians abandoned formal rates entirely, the gap was even more pronounced between 66-gun ships and 80-gun ships. It seems evident from this that the Russians conceived a clear cut distinction between two categories of ships, those ships capable of standing in the line of battle, and those ships capable not only of taking their place in line, but also of acting as command and control ships. To a very marked degree, Russian building programmes adhered to these guidelines and it was only during the closing years of the eighteenth century that the gap between 80-gun flagships and 66-gun line of battle ships began to be blurred by the introduction of the 74, a two-decker ship of considerably greater force than a 66, but one neither intended nor well suited to command and control.

Two-decker 70-gun ships

Only two 70-gun ships having two complete gun decks were built during this early period. They were larger and more heavily armed than contemporary British 70-gun Establishment ships and had dimensions very nearly identical to those of the overloaded British three-decker 80s. Based on their having immediately preceded the first of the Russian 80-gun ships in point of time, as well as on dimensions which closely anticipate those of the three-deckers, and finally upon the fact that *Sviatoi Aleksandr*, the first ship was actually rebuilt as a three-decked ship in 1727, they are being placed here as part of a logical progression in warship size and power.

A slightly damaged draught of Sviatoi Dmitrii Rostovskii (100) of 1758. She was the third and last ship of the line patterned after Pyotr I *and* II *of 1727. As was customary with all European First Rates during the early years of the eighteenth century, she was primarily a prestige ship and saw limited active service. Comparisons between this draught and that of Rostislav, completed just a quarter of a century later, reveals a great deal about warship evolution during the intervening years.*

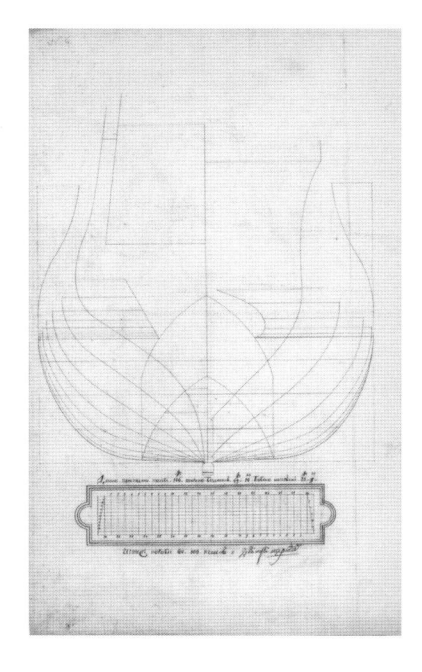

Sviatoi Aleksandr 70/76 St Petersburg
Constructor R. Brown
Laid down 8.11.1714   *Launched* 13.10.1717
Dimensions 155 ft x 43 ft x 17 ft 6 in (Veselago)
             155 ft 9½ in x 43 ft 6¼ in x 17 ft 7½ in (Apraksin)
Armament   1717 LD 26 x 24pdrs
                  UD 24 x 18pdrs
                  FC & QD 16 x 6pdrs (conjecture)
             1721 LD 26 x 24pdrs
                  UD 24 x 12pdrs
                  FC & QD 16 x 6pdrs (conjecture)
             1726 LD 26 x 18pdrs
                  UD 24 x 12pdrs
                  FC & QD 16 x 6pdrs (conjecture)
             1732 LD 26 x 24pdrs
                  MD 24 x 18pdrs
                  UD 24 x 6pdrs (conjecture)

Cruised in the Baltic in 1718–19 and 1721–5. Progressively down-gunned due to poor condition in 1721 and again in 1726. Stationed in Kronshtadt Roads as a guard ship against Wager's squadron. Found unserviceable in 1727. Completely rebuilt in a covered slip from 1729–32, emerging as a 3-deck 76 with an unarmed quarterdeck. Cruised in the Baltic, taking part in the Danzig expedition in 1733–4. Took part in the war with Sweden in 1741–3 with a complement of 693. Cruised in the Baltic in 1744 and 1746. Replaced by a new ship of the same name in 1747 and decommissioned in 1746–7. (Note differences in dimensions between Veselago and Apraksin.)

Neptunus 70/72 St Petersburg
Constructor R. Kosentz (Richard Cozens)
Laid down 9.8.1715   *Launched* 15.6.1718
Dimensions 153 ft x (122 ft k) x 43 ft x 17 ft (Veselago)

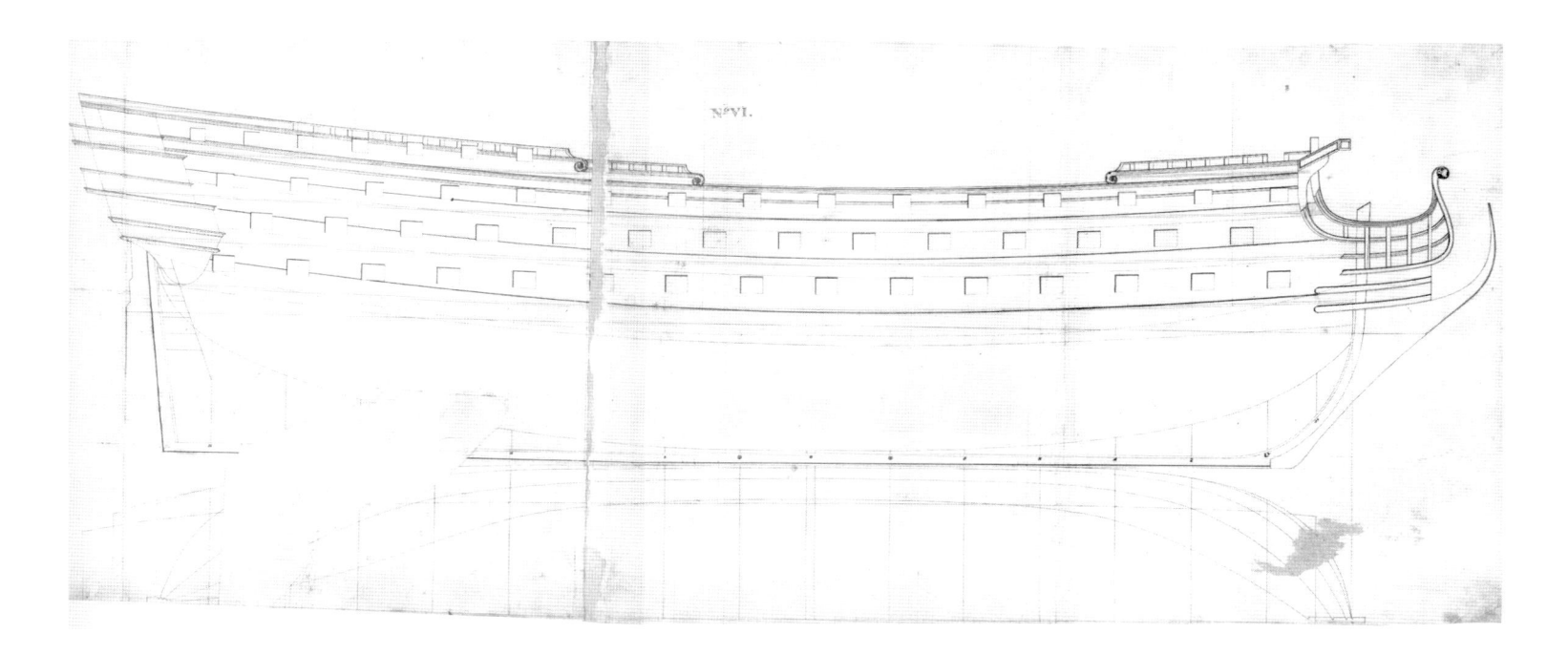

THE BALTIC FLEET 1696–1761

Armament 153 ft ½ in x 43 ft 3½ in x 16 ft 10 in (Apraksin)
1718 LD 26 x 24pdrs
UD 26 x 18pdrs
FC & QD 16 x 6pdrs (conjecture)
1726 LD 26 x 18pdrs
UD 24 x 12pdrs
FC & QD 16 x 6pdrs (being in a poor state)
1732 LD 26 x 24pdrs
UD 24 x 18pdrs
FC & QD 24 x 6pdrs (after reconstruction)

Cruised in the Baltic in 1719 and 1721–5. Down gunned due to poor condition in 1726. Guard ship in Kronshtadt Roads against Wager's squadron in 1726. Ordered to be repaired in 1727, but hulked instead from 1728–32. Condemned in 1732 and ordered to be broken up. (Note differences in dimensions between Veselago and Apraksin.)

Three-decker 80-gun ships (1696–1761)

Three-decker 80-gun ships were very probably imitative of contemporary British designs. The other European naval powers had long since abandoned the undersized and top heavy three-decker 80s due to their very poor handling characteristics and problems experienced with operating the main battery guns due to inadequate lower deck clearance in any sort of rough weather. The British and the Russians were alone in their continued reliance on the type as an intermediate sort of capital ship assuming the functions of a First Rate without entailing its costs in production, manpower and maintenance.

Nord-Adler class (3 ships)

Not surprisingly, the first Russian class of 80-gun ships followed the British Establishment of 1706 quite closely in general characteristics as may be seen by comparing the British establishment standard of 156 ft x 43 ft 6 in x 17 ft 8 in to the Russian design dimensions of 157 ft x 44 ft 8 in x 19 ft. Given British influence over the Russian shipbuilding programme at the time, it appears likely that the Russians were following British protocols for basic hull dimensions, although the discrepancies between Veselago and Apraksin for the dimensions of *Fridemaker* are interesting. It would appear that the Russian 80s were simultaneously beamier and deeper than the British ships. This could only have aggravated the tendency towards instability and leewardiness already evident in the British ships.

None of the *Nord-Adler* class were ever tested in combat and all came to peaceful ends at the breakers in the late 1730s and early 1740s.

Nord-Adler 78/80/88 St Petersburg
Constructor R. Ramz (R. Ramsay)
Laid down 29.6.1716 *Launched* 5.6.1720
Dimensions 157 ft x 44 ft 8 in x 19 ft
Armament LD 26 x 24pdrs
MD 26 x 16pdrs
UD 26 x 8pdrs
FC & QD 10 x 4pdrs

Nord-Adler class. Cruised in the Baltic in 1721 and 1723. Prepared in 1725–7 for arming and commissioning in 1728 in response to the Holstein Question. Rearmament plans aborted in 4.1728. Broken up after 1740.

Sviatoi Andrei 78/80/88 St Petersburg
Constructor O. Nye (Joseph Noy)
Laid down 3.4.1716 *Launched* 3.2.1721
Dimensions 157 ft x 44 ft 8 in x 19 ft
Armament LD 26 x 24pdrs
MD 26 x 16pdrs
UD 26 x 8pdrs
FC & QD 10 x 4pdrs (probable)

Nord-Adler class. Cruised in the Baltic in 1721 and 1723. Prepared in 1725–7 for arming and commissioning in 1728 in response to the Holstein Question. Rearmament plans aborted. Broken up after 1740.

Fridemaker 80/88/90 St Petersburg
Constructor F. M. Sklyaev
Laid down 8.7.1716 *Launched* 5.3.1721

A builder's model of Sviatoi Andrei *(88) of 1721 showing her basic lines with underwater framing exposed, said to have been made by her builder, R. Ramsay, who is otherwise credited with building her sister Nord-Adler,* with Sviatoi Andrei *credited to Joseph Nye. The model may actually be of the later ship – or intended to represent all three members of the class.*

Dimensions 157 ft x 43 ft 6 in x 20 ft 8 in (Veselago)
  157 ft 8 in x 45 ft 7½ in x 18 ft 8 in (Apraksin)
Armament LD 26 x 24pdrs
  MD 26 x 16pdrs
  UD 26 x 8pdrs
  FC & QD 10 x 4pdrs (probable)

Nord-Adler class. Cruised in the Baltic in 1721 and 1723. Prepared in 1725–7 for arming and commissioning in 1728 in response to the Holstein Question. Rearmament plans aborted. Broken up after 1736. (Note the differences in dimensions between Veselago and Apraksin)

Sviatoi Pyotr 80/88 St Petersburg
Constructor R. Kosentz (Richard Cozens)
Laid down 15.4.1716   *Launched* 5.10.1720
Dimensions 160 ft x (138 ft k) x 45 ft x 18 ft 8 in (Veselago)
  162 ft 1 in x 46 ft 10½ in x 18 ft 9½ in (Apraksin)
Armament LD 26 x 24pdrs
  MD 26 x 18pdrs
  UD 26 x 8pdrs
  FC & QD 10 x 4pdrs
  650 men

Cruised in the Baltic in 1721 and 1723. Prepared in 1725–7 for arming and commissioning in 1728 in response to the Holstein Question. Rearmament plans aborted. Broken up after 1736. (Note differences in dimensions between Veselago and Apraksin.)

Sviatoi Pavel class (10 ships)

Ten 80-gun three-deckers were built to a common design specification between 1743 and 1770. The final four class members fall chronologically within the reign of Catherine II, but are included here for reasons of continuity. They followed the specified dimensions of the Establishment of 1723 and were significantly longer and beamier than British 80s of the Establishment era. In spite of their greater size, they suffered from the same problems with excessive crankness experienced by the British three-decker 80s and were an obsolescent design concept for the period entering service at the same time that the type was being abandoned by its only remaining European advocate, the British, in favour of the more capable and powerful two-decker 74. The gentler weather conditions prevailing in the Baltic may have allowed the Russian 80s to avoid the recurrent problems that British 80s experienced of having to close their lower-deck batteries in combat to avoid taking on water in heavy and even moderate seas. The stability problems experienced by *Sviatoslav* during her Mediterranean deployment gives testimony to the inherent weakness of three-decker 80s when exposed to the stress of employment in deep water environments. In service in the Baltic, they were frequently employed in transport duties and none were lost in combat against enemy ships, although *Sviatoslav* grounded accidentally while operating against the Turks and had to be set afire as unsalvageable. The problems experienced by *Sviatoslav* very probably was the motivation for the decision to raze the three remaining 80-gun ships, *Sviatoi Andrei Pervozvannyy*, *Sviatoi Kliment Papa Rimskii* and *Ches'ma*, into 72-gun two-deckers in 1772.

Sviatoi Pavel 80/86 St Petersburg
Constructor F. Osokin
Laid down 2.9.1741   *Launched* 17.4.1743
Dimensions 169 ft x 46 ft 4 in x 20 ft 7 in (1723 Establishment)
Armament LD 26 x 24pdrs
  MD 26 x 16pdrs
  UD 26 x 8pdrs
  FC & QD 8 x 6pdrs
  674 men (actual)

Sviatoi Pavel class. Joined the Russian battle fleet on 28.6.1743 too late to participate in the war with Sweden. Cruised in the Baltic in June and September of 1743 but began leaking. Attempted to cruise again in 1746, but again developed leaks. Decommissioned in 1746. Broken up in 1756 due to a lack of suitable available timber for repairs.

Ioann Zlatoust Pervyi 80/86 St Petersburg
Constructor F. Osokin
Laid down 18.5.1749   *Launched* 8.9.1751
Dimensions 169 ft x 46 ft 4 in x 20 ft 7 in (1723 Establishment)
Armament LD 26 x 24pdrs

THE BALTIC FLEET 1696–1761

MD 26 x 16pdrs
UD 26 x 8pdrs
FC & QD 8 x 6pdrs (1723 Establishment)

Sviatoi Pavel class. Named '*Pervyi*' to distinguish her from her similarly named and slightly earlier Baltic contemporary, *Ioann Zlatoust* (66) which was renamed *Ioann Zlatoust Vtoroi* upon the larger ship's completion. Cruised on trials in the Baltic in 1752. Cruised off Memel, Pillau, and Danzig in 1757. Cruised in the Sound off Copenhagen to block the expected intervention of the British navy in 1759. Repaired in 1759. Transported troops to Kolberg in 1760 and acted as the test bed for newly developed edinorogs. Transported troops to Kolberg in 1761, landing 150 marines, and later suffering storm damage. Decommissioned in 1764. Broken up in 1769.

Sviatoi Nikolai 80/86 St Petersburg
Constructor G. Okunev
Laid down 18.6.1752 *Launched* 12.9.1754
Dimensions 169 ft x 46 ft 4 in x 20 ft 7 in
Armament LD 26 x 24pdrs
MD 26 x 16pdrs
UD 26 x 8pdrs
FC & QD 8 x 6pdrs (1723 Establishment)

Sviatoi Pavel class. Cruised to Gottland in 1756. Blockaded Memel, Pillau, and Danzig in 1757. Cruised in the Sound off Copenhagen to block the expected intervention of the British navy in 1758. Transported troops to Danzig in 1759. Transported troops to Kolberg and blockaded Kolberg in 1760. Transported troops to Kolberg, blockaded Kolberg, and landed 150 marines in 1761. Decommissioned in 1764. Broken up after 1769.

Sviatoi Pavel 80/86 Kronshtadt
Constructor A. Sutherland
Laid down 3.6.1753 *Launched* 10.7.1755
Dimensions 169 ft x 46 ft 4 in x 20 ft 7 in
Armament LD 26 x 24pdrs
MD 26 x 16pdrs
UD 26 x 8pdrs
FC & QD 8 x 6pdrs (1723 Establishment)

Sviatoi Pavel class. Cruised to Gottland in 1756. Blockaded Memel, Pillau, and Danzig, in 1757. Cruised in the Sound off Copenhagen to block the expected intervention of the British navy in 1758. Transported troops to Kolberg and blockaded Kolberg in 1760. Transported troops to Kolberg, blockaded Kolberg, and landed 150 marines in 1761. Decommissioned in 1764. Broken up after 1769.

Sviatoi Andrei Pervozvannyy 80/86 St Petersburg
Constructor A. Sutherland
Laid down 1.8.1756 *Launched* 20.5.1758
Dimensions 169 ft x 46 ft 4 in x 20 ft 7 in
Armament LD 26 x 24pdrs
MD 26 x 16pdrs
UD 26 x 8pdrs
FC & QD 8 x 6pdrs (1723 Establishment)

Sviatoi Pavel class. Transported troops to Kolberg, blockaded Kolberg, and carried sick and injured from Kolberg to Kronshtadt in 1760. Under Capt. Spiridov, transported troops to Kolberg and landed 150 marines in 1761. Repaired in 1770. Cruised in the Baltic in 1771. Reduced to 72 guns in 1772 and assigned to training duties at Kronshtadt Roads. Cruised in the Baltic in 1773. Decommissioned in 1777. Broken up in 1780.

Sviatoi Kliment Papa Rimskii 80/86 St Petersburg
Constructor P. G. Kachalov
Laid down 20.7.1756 *Launched* 28.9.1758
Dimensions 169 ft x 46 ft 4 in x 20 ft 7 in
Armament LD 26 x 24pdrs
MD 26 x 16pdrs
UD 26 x 8pdrs
FC & QD 8 x 6pdrs (1723 Establishment)

Sviatoi Pavel class. Transported troops to Kolberg, blockaded Kolberg, and carried sick and injured from Kolberg to Revel' in 1760. As flag for Vice-Adm. Polyanskiy, transported troops to Kolberg and landed 150 marines in 1761. As flag for Rear-Adm. Spiridov, transported troops from Kolberg to Revel' in 1762. As flag for Adm. Polyanskiy carried Catherine II from Revel' to Rogervik in 1764. Transferred from Revel' to Kronshtadt to Revel' in 1766. Repaired in 1770 and reduced to a 72. Cruised to Gottland in 1771. Reduced to a 72 in 1772. Decommissioned in 1777. Broken up in 1780.

The four following *Sviatoi Pavel* class members fall chronologically within section II, but are included here for reasons of class continuity.

Kir Ioann (ex-*Fridrikhh reks*) 80/86 St Petersburg
Constructor I. S. Ramburg
Laid down 11.1.1759 *Launched* 6.5.1762
Dimensions 169 ft x 46 ft 4 in x 20 ft 7 in
Armament LD 26 x 24pdrs
MD 26 x 16pdrs
UD 26 x 8pdrs
FC & QD 8 x 6pdrs (1723 Establishment)

Sviatoi Pavel class. Originally to have been named *Fridrikhh reks* after Frederick the Great in accordance with Peter III's foreign policy, but renamed prior to completion to commemorate Catherine II's coup on 28.6.1762 on the Day of the Miracle Workers, Kir and Ioann, and to repudiate the alliance with Frederick. Cruised in the Baltic in 1764. Escorted Adm. Spiridov's First Arkhipelago Squadron to Copenhagen in 1769. Wintered in Revel' in 1769–70. In ordinary in 1770–2. Condemned in 1773.

Sviataia Ekaterina (ex-*Prints Georg*) 80/86 St Petersburg
Constructor A. Sutherland
Laid down 16.12.1758 *Launched* 6.5.1762
Dimensions 169 ft x 46 ft 4 in x 20 ft 7 in
Armament LD 26 x 24pdrs
MD 26 x 16pdrs
UD 26 x 8pdrs
FC & QD 8 x 6pdrs (1723 Establishment)

Sviatoi Pavel class. Originally *Prints Georg*, renamed in honour of Catherine's accession to power on 28.6.1762. Cruised in the Baltic in 1764. Escorted Adm. Spiridov's 1st Arkhipelago Squadron to Copenhagen in 1769. Wintered in Revel' in 1769/70. Condemned in 1773.

Sviatoslav 80/86 St Petersburg
Constructor I. V. James
Laid down 18.6.1766 *Launched* 7.5.1769
Dimensions 169 ft x 46 ft 4 in x 20 ft 7 in
Armament LD 24 x 24pdrs, 2 x 48u (1 pood)
MD 24 x 18pdrs, 2 x 24u (½ pood)
UD 26 x 8pdrs
FC & QD 8 x 6pdrs (1723 Establishment) modified

Sviatoi Pavel class. Left Kronshtadt in 27.7.1769 with Rear-Adm.

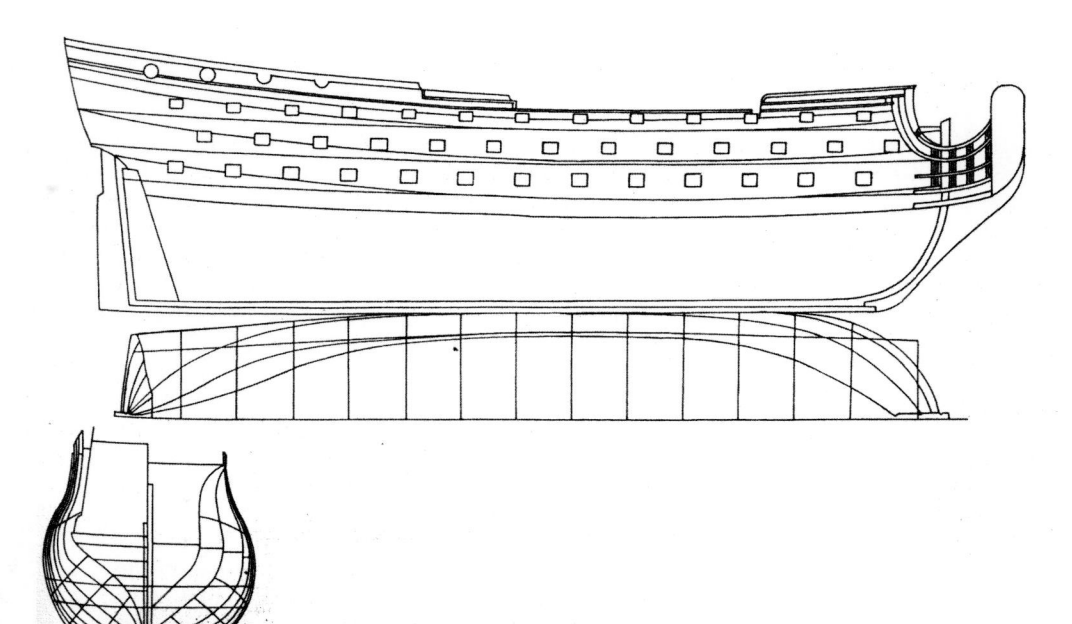

A member of the 10-strong Sviatoi Pavel *class,* Fridrikh Rex *of 1762 was given the name of Frederick the Great of Prussia while building, but became* Kir Ioann *at launching.* Kir Ioann *was one of the last of the notorious 80-gun three-deckers adopted by the Russian navy in imitation of the equally unsuccessful British 80s. The drawing is in the French style, without quarter galleries or bowsprit or anything beyond the most essential details and proportions of the ship being displayed. Nevertheless, the high-sidedness that made this type so dangerously leewardly and difficult to handle in any sort of weather is clearly evident here.*

Spiridov's First Arkhipelago Squadron. Repaired leak at Revel' on 24.11.1769, while the First Arkhipelago Squadron continued on to Copenhagen and England. Rejoined Rear-Adm. Elphinston's 2nd Arkhipelago Squadron at Copenhagen. Docked at Portsmouth for extensive repairs on 27.12.1769. Rear-Adm. Elphinston reported that she replaced her two experimental 48pdr edinorogs with two 24pdrs taken from *Ne Tron' Menia* because of weight problems in 1770. Elphinston considered razeeing her because of her excessive crankness, but this was not followed through with as reported in other sources. On 16–17.5.1770, she attacked the Turkish battle squadron without success. Joined Elphinston's 2nd Squadron off Cerigo on 22.5.1770. Fought at Chios on 26.6.1770. Operated off the Dardanelles on 16.7.1770. Grounded off Lemnos on 6.9.1770. Determined unsalvageable and set afire on 27.9.1770.

Ches'ma (ex-*Sviatoi Ioann Krestitel'*) 80/86 St Petersburg
Constructor I. V. James
Laid down   13.6.1766   Launched 9.10.1770
Dimensions 169 ft x 46 ft 4 in x 20 ft 7 in
Armament   LD 24 x 24pdrs, 2 x 48u (1 pood)
            MD 24 x 18pdrs, 2 x 24u (½ pood)
            UD 26 x 8pdrs
            FC & QD 8 x 6pdrs (1723 Establishment) modified
Sviatoi Pavel class. Originally to have been named *Sviatoi Ioann Krestitel'*, but renamed *Ches'ma* in honour of the victory over the Turks. Cruised to Gottland in 1771. Departed Revel' on 8.5.1772 as flag to Rear-Adm. I. Chichagov's 4th Arkhipelago Squadron. Chichagov left the squadron at Livorno and Capt. Konyaev took command of the 4th Arkhipelago Squadron. On 28.10.1772, in company with *Graf Orlov*, 2 frigates, and 3 smaller ships mounting a total of 224 guns; she attacked a Turkish–North African squadron in the Bay of Patras comprised of 9 frigates and xebecs and 16 smaller vessels mounting 630 guns and intent on attacking the Russians at Auza. The squadron destroyed all 9 frigate/xebecs as well as 8 of the smaller vessels. Operated in the Arkhipelago in 1772–5. Returned to Revel' on 9.10.1775. Participated in the Imperial Review in honour of Catherine II in 1776. Decommissioned in 1777. Repaired in 1780 and reduced to a 72. Broken up in 1781.

Ships with 60–68 guns (44 built 1700–79)

A single extra pair of open-deck guns was all that separated the Russian 66-gun ship from the 64s that were being built in goodly numbers in the French, Spanish and British navies during the middle years of the eighteenth century. The real distinction between the Russian 66s and the French, British and Spanish 64s lay in their greater relative importance to the Russian navy where they served as the standard capital ship, with no fewer than 72 60–66 gun ships being completed between 1713 and 1779. For the Atlantic navies, the 64 was always a low-end line of battle ship and one whose place in the line was always less certain than that of 70s and then 74s, ships which carried not only more, but heavier guns in both their main and upper deck batteries. For the Russian navy, the 66 was the standard line of battleship and more resistance was shown to its elimination than was shown by the navies of the Atlantic powers to the obsolescence of the generally comparable 64-gun ship. The reason for this, of course, was that the Russians were not competing against the Atlantic powers with their rapidly spiralling requirements with respect to size, range and firepower for their capital ships, but against the Swedes and the Turks in more confined waters, where range and endurance was not of the greatest import and where firepower needed only to be sufficient to the task of overcoming similarly armed warships.

Sviataia Ekaterina class (3 ships)

One of the earliest Russian purpose-built classes of line of battle ships. None were lost in combat, but *Narva* was one of four Russian ships known to have been struck by lightning while in harbour and the only to have been destroyed as a result.

Sviataia Ekaterina (renamed *Vyborg*) 60/64 St Petersburg
Constructor R. Brown
Laid down 29.6.1711   Launched 8.10.1713
Dimensions 145 ft x (118 ft 6 in k) x 41 ft x 17 ft 4 in (Veselago)
           145 ft x 42 ft 1 in x 17 ft 2 in (Apraksin)
Armament   1715 LD 26 x 24pdrs
                 HD 26 x 12pdrs

THE BALTIC FLEET 1696–1761

FC & QD 12 x 6pdrs
456 men (1714)
1722 LD 26 x 18pdrs
HD 26 x 8pdrs
FC & QD 12 x 4pdrs

Sviatoi Ekaterina class. Cruised in the Baltic 1714–15. To Copenhagen in 1716 to participate in the 'Great Armament of 1716'. Cruised in the Baltic in 1717–19. Renamed *Vyborg* in 1721. Cruised in the Baltic in 1721. Rearmed with lighter guns in 1722 due to poor condition. Cruised in the Baltic in 1722–4. Reduced to a pram in 1727. Last listed in 1729. (Note differences in dimensions between Veselago and Apraksin.)

Shlissel'burg 60/64/66 St Petersburg
Constructor R. Brown
Laid down 29.6.1712   *Launched* 28.9.1714
Dimensions 145 ft x (118 ft 6 in k) x 41 ft x 17 ft 4 in
Armament   1715 LD 26 x 24pdrs
                     UD 26 x 12pdrs
                     FC & QD 12 x 6pdrs (*Materialy*)
               1734 LD 26 x 24pdrs
                     UD 24 x 12pdrs
                     FC & QD 16 x 6pdrs (1723 Establishment)

Sviatoi Ekaterina class. Presented by Peter I to his favourite, Aleksandr Menshikov, who was responsible for her maintenance and upkeep (see also *Prints Aleksandr* pink). Cruised in the Baltic in 1715–19 and 1721–2. Repaired and lengthened 1723–8. (Chernyshev has her incorrectly participating in the campaign of 1724 and being repaired in 1725.) Cruised in the Baltic in 1732–4. Carried cargo from Riga to Kronshtadt in 1735. Condemned in 1736, but listed to 1740.

Narva 60/64 St Petersburg
Constructor F. M. Sklyaev
Laid down 20.3.1712   *Launched* 26.10.1714
Dimensions 145 ft x (118 ft 6 in k) x 41 ft x 17 ft 4 in
Armament   1715 LD 26 x 24pdrs
                     UD 26 x 12pdrs
                     FC & QD 12 x 6pdrs (*Materialy*)

Sviatoi Ekaterina class. Blown up by lightning in Kronshtadt Roads on 27.6.1715 with approximately 400 dead and 15 saved.

Ingermanland class (2 ships)
The *Ingermanland* class formed the basis for all successive classes of 66-gun ships built during the eighteenth century.
The successive *Slava Rossii* and *Aziia* classes would gradually reduce sheer lines fore and aft and increase their length over *Ingermanland* by about 5 ft, but breadth and armament would remain essentially the same.

Ingermanland 64/68 St Petersburg
Constructor R. Kosentz (Richard Cozens)
Laid down 30.10.1712   *Launched* 1.5.1715
Dimensions 151 ft x 42 ft x 18 ft 3 in (Veselago)
              155 ft (lower deck) x 41 ft 10 in (inside plank)
              x 19 ft 7 in 1992 tons bm (A. A. Popov)
Armament   1715 LD 26 x 24pdrs
                     UD 26 x 12pdrs
                     FC & QD 16 x 6pdrs
                     470 men (*Materialy*)
               1715 LD 24 x 30pdrs
                     UD 24 x 12/16pdrs
                     FC & QD 16 x 4pdrs (A. A. Popov)

Ingermanland class. Named after the province that served as the site for St Petersburg, *Ingermanland* was Peter I's much beloved flagship. Cruised in the Baltic in 1715. Peter I's flagship at the 'Great Armament of 1716'. Described by Peter I as 'running faster than all other ships' and as 'one of the best sailing ships ever'. Cruised in the Baltic in 1716–19, 1721–2 and 1724. Peter I ordered her preservation and she was repaired in 1727 but not returned to service. Found unfit for sea duty in 1731. Rotted out and beached in 1738. Broken up after 1739, but listed until 1741. (Note that A. A. Popov and Veselago differed significantly with respect to dimensions and armament. 30pdrs were officially introduced in 1716.)

Moskva 64/68 St Petersburg
Constructor R. Kosentz (Richard Cozens)
Laid down 30.10.1712   *Launched* 27.6.1715
Dimensions 151 ft x 42 ft x 18 ft 3 in
Armament   LD 26 x 24pdrs
              UD 24/26 x 12pdrs
              FC & QD 14/16 x 6pdrs (probable)

Ingermanland class. Cruised in the Baltic in 1716–19 and 1721–3. Training ship in Kronshtadt Roads in 1724. Cruised in the Baltic in 1725. Stationed at Kronshtadt Roads in 1726 as defence against Wager's squadron. Decommissioned in 1727. Hulked until 1732.

Revel' 68 St Petersburg
Constructor F. M. Sklyaev
Laid down 18.8.1712   *Launched* 21.10.1717
Dimensions 145 ft x 41 ft x 17 ft 4 in (Veselago)
              151 ft 6½ in x 42 ft 5 in x 17 ft 2¼ in (Apraksin)
Armament   1717 LD ? x 24pdrs
                     UD ? x 12pdrs
                     FC & QD ? x 6pdrs
                     500 men
               1725 LD ? x 18pdrs
                     UD ? x 8pdrs
                     FC & QD ? x 3pdrs

Cruised in the Baltic in 1718–19 and 1721–5. Down gunned in 1725

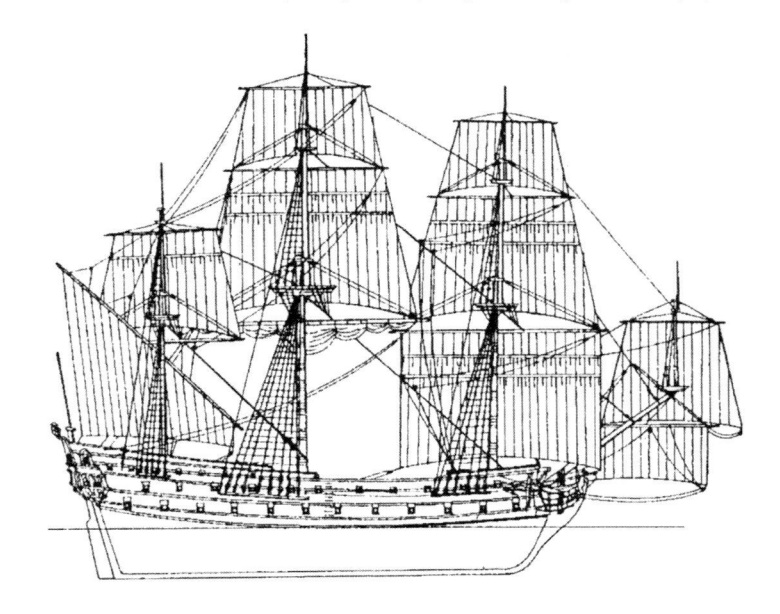

A representation of Peter I's flagship Ingermanland *(64) of 1715, concentrating on the details of sail plan and ignoring her underwater lines.*

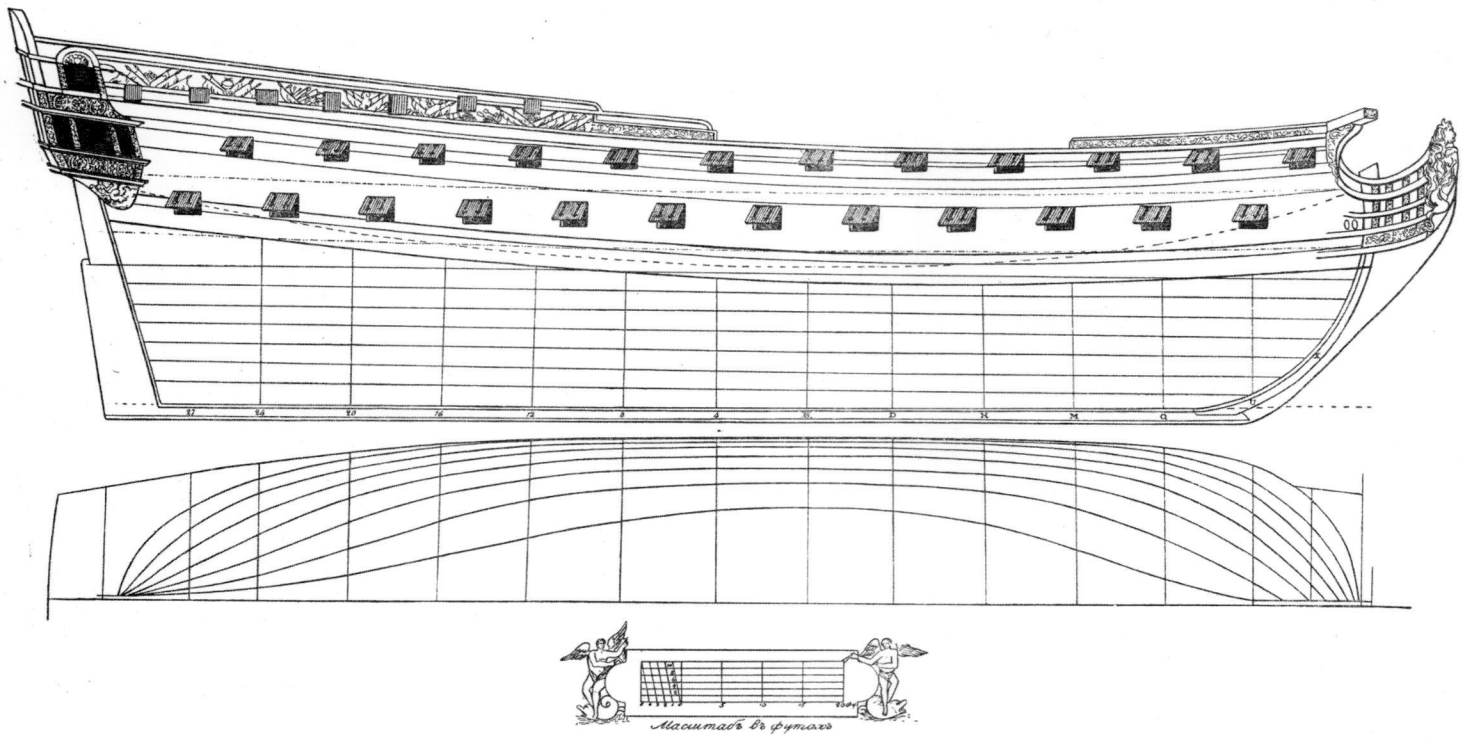

A very early draught of Peter I's flagship Ingermanland, *done in the quasi-naturalistic style featuring raised gunport lids and details of her decorative carving that antedates the more stylized appearance of later eighteenth-century draughts. Named after the province surrounding St Petersburg, the 64-gun* Ingermanland *of 1715 was the effective prototype for the 66-gun ships of the line that comprised the heart of the Russian battlefleet for most of the eighteenth century. Save only for the more pronounced sheer forward and aft, the ornate carving still favoured in 1715, and her retention of a spritsail topmast (not shown),* Ingermanland *might very easily have stood in the Russian line at Chios or even later without attracting undue notice.*

due to poor condition. Guard ship in Kronshtadt Roads against Wager's squadron in 1726. Ordered to be repaired in drydock in 1727, but hulked from 1728–32 and ordered to be broken up. (Note the differences in dimensions between Veselago and Apraksin.)

Isaak-Viktoriia class (2 ships)
Isaak-Viktoriia 64/66 St Petersburg
Constructor O. Nye (Joseph Noy)
Laid down 15.7.1716   Launched 30.5.1719
Dimensions 151 ft x 42 ft x 17 ft 6 in
Armament LD 26 x 24pdrs
UD 24 x 12pdrs
FC & QD 14/16 x 6pdrs (probable)
Isaak-Viktoriia class. Trials in 7.1720. Cruised in the Baltic in 1721–5. Commissioned and armed in Kronshtadt Roads in 1726–8 although her rigging was removed and used to equip new ships. Broken up after 1739.

Astrakhan' 62/66 St Petersburg
Constructor O. Nye (Joseph Noy)
Laid down 26.12.1716   Launched 2.10.1720
Dimensions 151 ft x 42 ft x 17 ft 6 in (Veselago)
152 ft 4½ in x 42 ft 5½ in x 17 ft ¼ in (Apraksin)
Armament LD 26 x 24pdrs
MD 24 x 12pdrs
FC & QD 16 x 6pdrs (probable)
Isaak-Viktoriia class. Cruised in the Baltic in 1721–3. Commissioned and armed in Kronshtadt Roads in 1724. Cruised in the Baltic in 1725. Commissioned and armed in Kronshtadt Roads in 1726–7. Rigging removed for use in new ships in 1733. Broken up after 1736. (Note the differences in dimensions between Veselago and Apraksin.)

Sviataia Ekaterina 66/70/74 St Petersburg
Constructor R. Brown
Laid down 28.9.1718   Launched 16.3.1721
Dimensions 153 ft x 42 ft x 18 ft 6 in (Veselago)
153 ft 4½ in x 43 ft ¼ in x 17 ft 10½ in (Apraksin)
Armament LD 26 x 24pdrs
UD 26 x 12pdrs
FC & QD 14/18 x 6pdrs (probable)
Cruised in the Baltic in 1721–3 as Peter I's new flagship and named after his second wife. Commissioned in Kronshtadt Roads in 1726–8 and 1732. Harbour service in 1733. Listed until 1740, but possibly broken up after 1736.

Panteleimon-Viktoriia 66 St Petersburg
Constructor B. Pangalo
Laid down 22.3.1719   Launched 27.7.1721
Dimensions 151 ft x 40 ft x 18 ft 10 in
Armament LD 26 x 24pdrs
UD 24 x 12pdrs
FC & QD 16 x 6pdrs (1723 Establishment)
Built to the plans of B. Pangalo, a French designer brought to Russia in 1717 by Peter I. Narrower than other Russian 66s and probably reflective of French design influences and philosophies. Cruised in the Baltic in 1722–3. Commissioned in Kronshtadt Roads in 1726. Cruised in the Baltic in 1727. Transferred from Kronshtadt to Revel'. Broken up in 1736 or thereafter.

THE BALTIC FLEET 1696–1761

Narva 64/66 St Petersburg
Constructor G. A. Menshikov
Laid down 7.12.1718 *Launched* 11.10.1725
Dimensions 155 ft x 43 ft x 18 ft 11 in
Armament LD 26 x 24pdrs
            UD 24 x 12pdrs
            FC & QD 16 x 6pdrs (1723 Establishment)
Stationed in Kronshtadt Roads in 1726. Cruised in the Baltic in 1727. Stationed in Kronshtadt Roads in 1728–31. Cruised in the Baltic in 1732–3. Participated in the Danzig expedition of 1734. Broken up after 1739, but listed to 1740.

Sviataia Natal'ia 66 St Petersburg
Constructor R. Kosentz (Richard Cozens)
Laid down 17.5.1719 *Launched* 17.9.1727
Dimensions 155 ft 8 in x 43 ft x 18 ft
Armament LD 26 x 24pdrs
            UD 24 x 12pdrs
            FC & QD 16 x 6pdrs (1723 Establishment)
Named after Peter I's mother. Cruised in the Baltic in 1729, 1732 and 1733. Participated in the Danzig expedition of 1734. Decommissioned after 1734. Broken up after 1739, but listed until 1740.

Derbent 64/66 St Petersburg
Constructor R. Kosentz (Richard Cozens)
Laid down 11.1.1719 *Launched* 27.7.1724
Dimensions 151 ft 6 in x 42 ft x 17 ft
Armament LD 26 x 24pdrs
            UD 24 x 12pdrs
            FC & QD 16 x 6pdrs
Cruised in the Baltic in 1725. Damaged by lightning in Kronshtadt Roads and repaired in 1726. Escorted the Duke of Holstein and Tsarina Ann to Kiel in 1727. Stationed in Kronshtadt Roads in 1732. Broken up after 1732, but listed to 1740.

Slava Rossii **class** (59 ships)
Based on the Establishment of 1723, with the initial design having been prepared by Joseph Noy, the dimensions of the *Slava Rossii* class closely resemble those of *Ingermanland* of 1715, if A. A. Popov's measurements are correct. Fifty-nine ships of this class were completed between 1733 and 1779. They comprised the largest single class of line of battle ships ever completed for Russia during the age of sail and were succeeded during the 1770s by the generally similar but slightly larger 28-ship *Aziia* class. No fewer than 28 members of the *Slava Rossii* class fall chronologically within the reign of Catherine II. They are included here for reasons of class continuity. The *Slava Rossii* class represented a type that continued to remain an important component of Russian battle fleets in both the Baltic and Black Sea until the early years of the nineteenth century. While 74-gun ships of the sort preferred by the Atlantic powers Great Britain, France and Spain after 1750, began to be built in increasing numbers in Russia during the 1770s; the 66-gun ship was still well suited to Baltic and Black Sea conditions because of its relative economies of cost and operation, and because of its shallow draught and handiness. Even though Russia under Catherine II was rapidly developing Great Power pretensions, 60–64 gun 24pdr line of battle ships remained the norm for the lesser European navies of the period. The *Slava Rossii*'s proved to be well suited for use against both Sweden and Turkey, whose battle lines were largely made up of similar 60-gun ships and who were equally disinclined towards building larger ships.

In accordance with recent findings discussed in the Introduction, the armament of *Slava Rossii* and her sister ships was not in complete compliance with the Establishment of 1723. The actual armament was prescribed by the informally established 'Establishment of 1724' and is presented here for all class members and consisted of the elimination of two lower deck 24pdrs and the addition of two middle deck 12pdrs. The total rated armament remained 66.

A comparison between the design specifications of these Russian 66-gun ships and comparable 64-gun ships built towards the end of the period by the other Great Powers is instructive:

Russia
Slava Rossii class   155 ft 6 in x 41 ft 6 in x 18 ft
                       24 x 24pdrs, 26 x 12pdrs, 16 x 6pdrs
Great Britain
Intrepid class   159 ft x 44 ft x 19 ft
                       26 x 24pdrs, 26 x 18pdrs, 12 x 9pdrs
France
Indien class   157 ft x 40 ft x 17 ft 6 in
                       26 x 24pdrs, 28 x 12pdrs, 10 x 6pdrs
Spain
San Fernando   158 ft x 40 ft x19 ft
                       26 x 24pdrs, 28 x 12pdrs, 10 x 8pdrs

It is unclear how much latitude of design was allowed to individual constructors during the class's 46-year production run; but breadth was formally increased to 43 ft 6 in on five ships completed after 1755. Their only major armament change came after 1763 with the introduction of edinorogs into the Russian navy. Two of the lower-deck 24pdrs were replaced in ships entering service by two 48pdr edinorogs and two of the open-deck 6pdrs were replaced by 24pdr edinorogs.

That the class was successful in service is evidenced by its

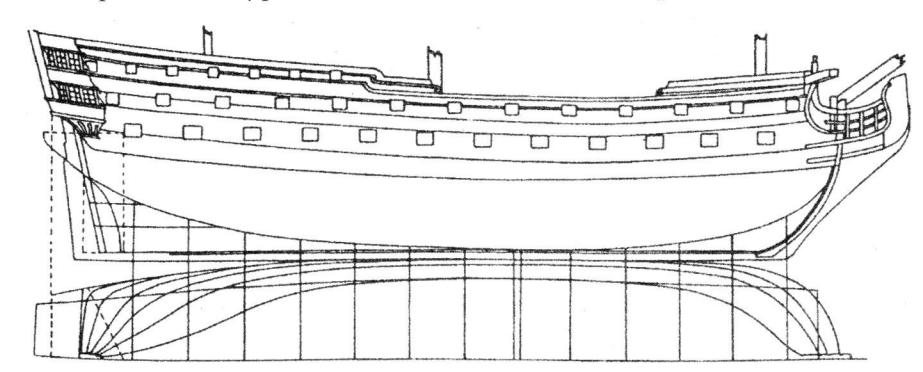

The virtues of standardization are apparent in this drawing of Saratov *of 1765 showing a typical 66 of the 59-ship strong* Slava Rossii *class. She bears a close relationship to the* Ingermanland *of 1715, the differences being largely stylistic and reflective of the slow pace of technological change of the period.*

lengthy production run. Seven *Slava Rossii*s were sent to the Mediterranean in 1769 for the conflict with Turkey. They played a major part in the battles of Chios and Ches'ma, and *Evropa* achieved great fame by single-handedly engaging the entire Turkish battle fleet during the opening stages of the battle of Ches'ma.

As might be expected with such a large class, seven ships came to violent ends. *Evstafii Plakida* blew up at the battle of Chios. *Vsevolod*, *Aleksandr Nevskii* and *Sviatoi Pyotr* were all destroyed by fire. Three others were wrecked: *Moskva* and *Astrakhan'* while in active service, and one unfortunate and forever unnamed ship while in transit to St Petersburg for commissioning.

Slava Rossii 66 St Petersburg
Constructor O. Nye (Joseph Noy)
Laid down 28.1.1731 *Launched* 30.4.1733
Dimensions 155 ft 6 in x 41 ft 6 in x 18 ft (1723 Establishment)
Armament LD 24 x 24pdrs
UD 26 x 12pdrs
FC & QD 16 x 6pdrs (1724 'Establishment')
Slava Rossii class. Cruised in the Baltic in 1733. Participated in the Danzig expedition of 1734. Carried supplies in 1735 from Riga to Kronshtadt. Repaired in 1738. Stationed in Kronshtadt Roads in 1741. Took part in the war with Sweden in 1741–3. Cruised in the Baltic in 1744. Converted into a hospital ship 1746–9. Broken up after 1752.

Severnyi Oryol 66 St Petersburg
Constructor O. Nye (Joseph Noy)
Laid down 4.10.1733 *Launched* 1.6.1735
Dimensions 155 ft 6 in x 41 ft 6 in x 18 ft (1723 Establishment)
Armament LD 24 x 24pdrs
UD 26 x 12pdrs
FC & QD 16 x 6pdrs (1724 'Establishment')
Slava Rossii class. Carried supplies from Riga to Kronshtadt in 1735. Stationed in Kronshtadt Roads in 1736. Repaired in 1738. Stationed in Kronshtadt Roads in 1741. Took part in the war with Sweden in 1741–3. Cruised in the Baltic in 1744 and 1746. Great repair in 1749–51. Cruised in the Baltic in 1752–6. Participated in the blockade of Danzig in 1757. Stationed off Copenhagen in 1758. Operated off Kolberg and Bornholm in 1759. Sprang a leak while deploying to Kolberg in 1760 and forced to return to Russia. Decommissioned and broken up in 1763.

Revel' 66 St Petersburg
Constructor R. Devenport (Robert Davenport)
Laid down 12.2.1732 *Launched* 28.6.1735
Dimensions 155 ft 6 in x 41 ft 6 in x 18 ft (1723 Establishment)
Armament LD 24 x 24pdrs
UD 26 x 12pdrs
FC & QD 16 x 6pdrs (1724 'Establishment')
Slava Rossii class. Cruised in the Baltic in 1736. Repaired in 1738. Commissioned in Kronshtadt Roads in 1741. Took part in the war with Sweden in 1741–3. Cruised in the Baltic in 1744–6. Collided with *Schastie* (54) in 1746, suffering damage to her stern. In service until 1749. Broken up after 1752.

Ingermanland 66 St Petersburg
Constructor G. A. Menshikov
Laid down 14.6.1733 *Launched* 17.8.1735
Dimensions 155 ft 6 in x 41 ft 6 in x 18 ft (1723 Establishment)
Armament LD 24 x 24pdrs
UD 26 x 12pdrs
FC & QD 16 x 6pdrs (1724 'Establishment')
Slava Rossii class. Cruised in the Baltic in 1736. Took part in the war with Sweden in 1741–3. Cruised in the Baltic in 1744 and 1746. In service until 1749. Listed to 1752.

Osnovanie Blagopoluchiia 66 St Petersburg
Constructor R. Brown
Laid down 1.6.1735 *Launched* 29.5.1735
Dimensions 155 ft 6 in x 41 ft 6 in x 18 ft (1723 Establishment)
Armament LD 24 x 24pdrs
UD 26 x 12pdrs
FC & QD 16 x 6pdrs (1724 'Establishment')
Slava Rossii class. Cruised in the Baltic in 1736. Repaired in 1738. Cruised in the Baltic in 1739. Stationed in Kronshtadt Roads in 1741. Took part in the war with Sweden in 1741–3. Cruised in the Baltic in 1744–7. Transferred to Kronshtadt in 1747. Broken up after 1752.

Leferm 62/66 Arkhangel'sk
Constructor I. V. James
Laid down 24.5.1737 *Launched* 10.5.1739
Dimensions 155 ft 6 in x 41 ft 6 in x 18 ft (Veselago)
Armament LD 24 x 24pdrs
UD 26 x 12pdrs
FC & QD 16 x 6pdrs (1724 'Establishment')
Slava Rossii class. Commissioned in 1739 for passage to the Baltic, but her departure was delayed due to the arrival at Stockholm of the French squadron under Lieut Gen. d'Antin with four ships of the line. Later that year, State Secretary Osterman left several ships including *Leferm* at Arkhangel'sk for a possible diversion against Sweden. In 7.1741, she sailed from Arkhangel'sk to the bay of Kola and wintered at Catherine Bay. On 22.6.1742 she returned to Arkhangel'sk to become the flagship of Vice-Adm. Bredal. On 19.7.1742 she left Arkhangel'sk for the Baltic in company with five ships of the line and five frigates. On 10–11.8.1742, the squadron encountered a severe storm off Nordcap and was dispersed and damaged, but was still able to proceed minus its damaged flagship which was left behind with Vice-Adm. Bredal. The damaged *Leferm* returned to Catherine Bay (Ekaterininskaya gavan) on 20.8.1742, where she wintered. On 6.8.1743 she again put to sea (under a new commander, Capt. Lewis). She again met with storms on 10–21.8.1743 and was once again forced to return to Catherine Bay. On 6–7.1744, she managed to pass to Kronshtadt. Cruised in the Baltic in 1745–6, taking part in tactical fleet exercises off Revel' on 22–23.7.1746. Cruised in the Baltic in 1748 and 1751. Listed to 1755. Broken up at Kronshtadt in 1756.)

Schastie (ex-*Generalissimus Rossiiskii*) 66 Arkhangel'sk
Constructor V. Batakov
Laid down 11.7.1740 *Launched* 12.5.1741
Dimensions 155 ft 6 in x 41 ft 6 in x 18 ft (1723 Establishment)
Armament LD 24 x 24pdrs
UD 26 x 12pdrs
FC & QD 16 x 6pdrs (1724 'Establishment')
Slava Rossii class. Completed as *Generalissimus Rossiiskii* and renamed *Schastie* before 25.11.1741, possibly reflecting the change in dynasty. Remained in port with *Leferm* due to the presence of a French squadron at Stockholm. Left Arkhangel'sk with Vice-Adm. Bredal's squadron on 19.7.1742, separated from the squadron on 23.7.1742 off Kildin, lost her mainmast in the storm on 21.8.1742, but proceeded on to Kronshtadt. Remained in service until 1746. Listed to 1756.

Blagopoluchie (ex-*Pravitel'nitsa Rossiiskaia*) 66 Arkhangel'sk
Constructor I. V. James

Laid down 13.6.1740 *Launched* 16.5.1741
Dimensions 155 ft 6 in x 41 ft 6 in x 18 ft (1723 Establishment)
Armament LD 24 x 24pdrs
            UD 26 x 12pdrs
            FC & QD 16 x 6pdrs (1724 'Establishment')
Slava Rossii class. Commissioned as *Pravitel'nitsa Rossiiskaia* and renamed *Blagopoluchie* before 25.11.1741. Grounded in 6.1742 while crossing the mouth of the Severnaya Dvina and returned to Arkhangel'sk for repairs. Left Arkhangel'sk in 1744, but again forced to return to port due to leaks. Converted to a sheer hulk and broken up in 1744.

Sviatoi Pyotr (ex-*Ioann*) 66 Arkhangel'sk
Constructor D. T. Scherbachov
Laid down 4.11.1740 *Launched* 12.8.1741
Dimensions 155 ft 6 in x 41 ft 6 in x 18 ft (1723 Establishment)
Armament LD 24 x 24pdrs
            UD 26 x 12pdrs
            FC & QD 16 x 6pdrs (1724 'Establishment')
Slava Rossii class. Commissioned as *Ioann*, but renamed *Sviatoi Pyotr* before 25.11.1741. *Sviatoi Pyotr* was a special case. Although formally a member of the *Slava Rossii* class, she incorporated a number of French design influences, introduced the use of iron knees to the Russian navy, and was carefully constructed of high-quality oak. Took part in the war with Sweden in 1741–3. Cruised in the Baltic in 1744, and 1747–8. Carried baggage of Russian troops being evacuated from Danzig to Revel' in 1749. Cruised in the Baltic from 1750–2. Decommissioned in 1752, but listed to 1756.

Sviataia Ekaterina 66 St Petersburg
Constructor V. Batakov
Laid down 1.7.1741 *Launched* 16.6.1742
Dimensions 155 ft 6 in x 41 ft 6 in x 18 ft (1723 Establishment)
Armament LD 24 x 24pdrs
            UD 26 x 12pdrs
            FC & QD 16 x 6pdrs (1724 'Establishment')
Slava Rossii class. Sailed from Arkhangel'sk to Kronshtadt in 7–11.1741. Cruised in the Baltic in 1744 and 1746. Grounded and damaged off Nargen while cruising in 1748. Carried the baggage of Russian troops being evacuated from Danzig to Revel' in 1749. Cruised in the Baltic in 1750. Decommissioned in 1750, but listed to 1756.

Fridemaker 66 Arkhangel'sk
Constructor I. V. James
Laid down 7.7.1741 *Launched* 8.7.1742
Dimensions 155 ft 6 in x 41 ft 6 in x 18 ft (1723 Establishment)
Armament LD 24 x 24pdrs
            UD 26 x 12pdrs
            FC & QD 16 x 6pdrs (1724 'Establishment')
Slava Rossii class. Departed Arkhangel'sk for the Baltic on 15.7.1742 with Vice-Adm. Bredal's squadron. Severely damaged in the storm of 10–21.8.1742 and forced to winter in the Gulf of Kola at Catherine Bay (Ekaterininskaya gavan) on the White Sea. Sailed from the Gulf of Kola to Kronshtadt from 4–7.1744. Commissioned and armed for training in Kronshtadt Roads in 1745. Cruised in the Baltic in 1746 and 1748. Decommissioned in 1748. Broken up in 1756.

Lesnoe 66 Arkhangel'sk
Constructor A. Sutherland
Laid down 31.7.1741 *Launched* 5.5.1743
Dimensions 155 ft 6 in x 41 ft 6 in x 18 ft (1723 Establishment)
Armament LD 24 x 24pdrs
            UD 26 x 12pdrs
            FC & QD 16 x 6pdrs (1724 'Establishment')
Slava Rossii class. Name commemorates one of Peter I's major land battle victories over the Swedes in 1708. Left Arkhangel'sk for the Baltic on 14.6.1744, but returned from Bergen. 7–9.1744 sailed from Arkhangel'sk to Kronshtadt. Cruised in the Baltic in 1746. In commission until 1756. Repaired in 1756, but still found to be leaking in 1757. Broken up in 1759. (Veselago incorrectly has her as having been wrecked in 1759.)

Poltava 66 Arkhangel'sk
Constructor P. G. Kachalov
Laid down 5.8.1741 *Launched* 15.5.1743
Dimensions 155 ft 6 in x 41 ft 6 in x 18 ft (1723 Establishment)
Armament LD 24 x 24pdrs
            UD 26 x 12pdrs
            FC & QD 16 x 6pdrs (1724 'Establishment')
Slava Rossii class. Name commemorates the land battle in 1709 that broke the military power of Sweden. Sailed from Arkhangel'sk to Kronshtadt 6–8.1744. Commissioned in Kronshtadt Roads for training in 1745. Cruised in the Baltic in 1745 and 1748, and to Gottland in 1750. Decommissioned in 1750. Broken up in 1756 due to a lack of suitable timber for repairs.

Arkhangel Rafail 66 Arkhangel'sk
Constructor V. Batakov
Laid down 4.6.1744 *Launched* 15.5.1745
Dimensions 155 ft 6 in x 41 ft 6 in x 18 ft (1723 Establishment)
Armament LD 24 x 24pdrs
            UD 26 x 12pdrs
            FC & QD 16 x 6pdrs (1724 'Establishment')
Slava Rossii class. 7–9.1745 sailed from Arkhangel'sk to Kronshtadt. Cruised in the Baltic in 1746 to Rogervik and Revel'. Carried the baggage of Russian troops being evacuated from Danzig to Revel' in 1749. Cruised in the Baltic in 1751. Participated in the blockade of the Prussian coast and Danzig in 1757, losing her mainmast in a storm on 18.8.1757. Determined unfit for service in 1758 and paid off. Broken up in 1759.

Sviataia Velikomuchenitsa Varvara 66 St Petersburg
Constructor A. Sutherland
Laid down 3.5.1743 *Launched* 26.5.1745
Dimensions 155 ft 6 in x 41 ft 6 in x 18 ft (1723 Establishment)
Armament LD 24 x 24pdrs
            UD 26 x 12pdrs
            FC & QD 16 x 6pdrs (1724 'Establishment')
Slava Rossii class. Participated in the naval procession on the Neva River in the shadow of the Winter Palace commemorating the Great Northern War of 1700–21 in 1745. Cruised in the Baltic in 1746–8 and off Gottland in 1750. Broken up in 1755 due to a lack of adequate timber to effect repairs.

Sviatoi Sergii 66 Arkhangel'sk
Constructor P. G. Kachalov
Laid down 21.8.1746 *Launched* 26.8.1747
Dimensions 155 ft 6 in x 41 ft 6 in x 18 ft (1723 Establishment)
Armament LD 24 x 24pdrs
            UD 26 x 12pdrs
            FC & QD 16 x 6pdrs (1724 'Establishment')
Slava Rossii class. Sailed from Arkhangel'sk to Kronshtadt in

7–10.1747. Grounded and repaired during cruise in the Baltic in 1750. Cruised off Pilau and Danzig in 1757. Cruised in the sound off Copenhagen to block the expected intervention of the British navy in 1758. Transported troops to Danzig in 1759. Cruised off Kolberg in 1760. Decommissioned in 1760. Broken up in 1763.

Sviatoi Aleksandr Nevskii 66 St Petersburg
Constructor G. Okunev
Laid down 1.10.1747   *Launched* 18.5.1749
Dimensions 155 ft 6 in x 41 ft 6 in x 18 ft (1723 Establishment)
Armament   LD 24 x 24pdrs
             UD 26 x 12pdrs
             FC & QD 16 x 6pdrs (1724 'Establishment')
Slava Rossii class. Alexander Nevskiy routed the Swedes in 1240 and the Lithuanians in 1242 and stands as one of the great heroes of Russian history. Cruised on trials in 1749. Cruised in the Baltic in 1750–6. Cruised off Memel and Danzig in 1757. Cruised in the sound off Copenhagen to block the expected intervention of the British navy in 1758, Transported troops to Danzig in 1759. Transported 160 troops to Kolberg in 1760. Decommissioned in 1760. Broken up in 1763.

Ioann Zlatoust Vtoroi 66 St Petersburg
Constructor I. S. Ramburg
Laid down 1.10.1747   *Launched* 18.5.1749
Dimensions 155 ft 6 in x 41 ft 6 in x 18 ft (1723 Establishment)
Armament   LD 24 x 24pdrs
             UD 26 x 12pdrs
             FC & QD 16 x 6pdrs (1724 'Establishment')
Slava Rossii class. Cruised in the Baltic on trials in 1749. Renamed *Ioann Zlatoust Vtoroi* (i.e. the Second) on 9.9.1751 upon the completion of *Ioann Zlatoust Pervyi* (80). Cruised in the Baltic in 1750–6. Cruised off Pillau and Danzig in 1757. Condemned and paid off in 1758. Broken up in 1759.

Arkhangel Gavriil 66 Arkhangel'sk
Constructor P. G. Kachalov
Laid down 23.8.1748   *Launched* 13.9.1749
Dimensions 155 ft 6 in x 41 ft 6 in x 18 ft (1723 Establishment)
Armament   LD 24 x 24pdrs
             UD 26 x 12pdrs
             FC & QD 16 x 6pdrs (1724 'Establishment')
Slava Rossii class. Sailed from Arkhangel'sk to Kronstadt in 6–8.1750. Cruised in the Baltic in 1751. Cruised off Memel during the war with Prussia, damaged in a storm, repaired at Revel', and returned to the fleet off Danzig in 1757. Cruised in the sound off Copenhagen to block the expected intervention of the British navy in 1758. Carried troops to Danzig in 1759. Carried troops to Kolberg in 1760. Participated in the blockade of Kolberg and damaged in a storm in 1761. Decommissioned in 1761. Broken up in 1763.

Arkhangel Uriil 66 Arkhangel'sk
Constructor I. V. James
Laid down 28.8.1748   *Launched* 21.8.1749
Dimensions 155 ft 6 in x 41 ft 6 in x 18 ft (1723 Establishment)
Armament   LD 24 x 24pdrs
             UD 26 x 12pdrs
             FC & QD 16 x 6pdrs (1724 'Establishment')
Slava Rossii class. Sailed from Arkhangel'sk to Kronstadt in 7–8.1750. Cruised in the Baltic in 1750. Cruised off Danzig and Pillau in 1757. Cruised in the Sound off Copenhagen to block the expected intervention of the British navy in 1758. Transported troops to Danzig in 1759 and to Kolberg in 1760. Converted to a hospital ship off Kolberg in 1761. Broken up in 1763.

Moskva 66 Arkhangel'sk
Constructor A. Sutherland
Laid down 24.8.1749   *Launched* 19.4.1750
Dimensions 155 ft 6 in x 41 ft 6 in x 18 ft (1723 Establishment)
Armament   LD 24 x 24pdrs
             UD 26 x 12pdrs
             FC & QD 16 x 6pdrs (1724 'Establishment')
Slava Rossii class. Departed Arkhangel'sk on 19.7.1750 and forced to return by storm on 23.7.1750. Departed a second time on 1.8.1750 and arrived at Revel' on 10.10.1750. Cruised in the Baltic in 1751–6. Cruised off Memel and Danzig in 1757. Cruised in the Sound off Copenhagen to block the expected intervention of the British navy in 1758. Wrecked off Livava 26.9.1758 with a loss of 98 men.

Ingermanland 66 Arkhangel'sk
Constructor A. Sutherland
Laid down 4.6.1751   *Launched* 30.4.1752
Dimensions 155 ft 6 in x 41 ft 6 in x 18 ft (1723 Establishment)
Armament   LD 24 x 24pdrs
             UD 26 x 12pdrs
             FC & QD 16 x 6pdrs (1724 'Establishment')
Slava Rossii class. Sailed from Arkhangel'sk to Kronstadt in 7–8.1752. Blockaded Danzig and cruised off the Swedish coasts in 1757. Cruised in the Sound off Copenhagen to block the expected intervention of the British navy in 1758. Transported troops to Danzig in 1759 and to Kolberg in 1760. Transported troops to Kolberg and blockaded it in 1761. Transported sick and wounded and army baggage from Pillau to Kronshtadt in 1762. Decommissioned in 1764. Broken up in 1765.

Poltava 66 Arkhangel'sk
Constructor I. V. James
Laid down 15.4.1753   *Launched* 26.4.1754
Dimensions 155 ft 6 in x 41 ft 6 in x 18 ft (1723 Establishment)
Armament   LD 24 x 24pdrs
             UD 26 x 12pdrs
             FC & QD 16 x 6pdrs (1724 'Establishment')
Slava Rossii class. Sailed from Arkhangel'sk to Kronstadt in 6–10.1754. Blockaded Memel and Danzig in 1757. Cruised in the Sound off Copenhagen to block the expected intervention of the British navy in 1758. Transported troops to Danzig in 1759. Blockaded Kolberg in 1760. Transported troops to Kolberg and blockaded Kolberg in 1761. Cruised to Rogervik in 1764. Decommissioned in 1764. Sank at Kronshtadt on 30.4.1770 due to rotten trenail pins in the planking. Broken up in place.

Natal'ia 66 Arkhangel'sk
Constructor A. Sutherland
Laid down 15.4.1753   *Launched* 26.4.1754
Dimensions 155 ft 6 in x 41 ft 6 in x 18 ft (1723 Establishment)
Armament   LD 24 x 24pdrs
             UD 26 x 12pdrs
             FC & QD 16 x 6pdrs (1724 'Establishment')
Slava Rossii class. The name Natal'ia commemorates the mother of Peter I. Sailed from Arkhangel'sk to Kronstadt in 6–8.1754. Cruised to Gottland in 1756. Blockaded Memel, Danzig, and the Swedish coast in 1757. Cruised in the Sound off Copenhagen to block the expected intervention of the British navy in 1758. Cruised off Kiel, Pillau, Danzig, Öland and Svenskzund in 1759. Bombarded Kolberg and

transported sick and injured from Kolberg to Revel' in 1760. Transported troops to Kolberg, bombarded Kolberg, and transported sick and injured from Kolberg to Revel' in 1761. Transported troops from Kolberg to Revel' in 1762. Cruised to Rogervik to attend the visit of Catherine II in 1764. Decommissioned in 1764. Broken up in 1771.

Revel' 66 Arkhangel'sk
Constructor I. V. James
Laid down 26.4.1755   *Launched* 12.5.1756
Dimensions 155 ft 6 in x 41 ft 6 in x 18 ft (1723 Establishment)
Armament   LD 24 x 24pdrs
             UD 26 x 12pdrs
             FC & QD 16 x 6pdrs (1724 'Establishment')
Slava Rossii class. Sailed from Arkhangel'sk to Kronshtadt in 7–8.1756. Carried the flag of Rear-Adm. Lewis in 1757 while blockading the Prussian coasts and transporting sick and injured from Danzig to Revel'. Cruised in the sound off Copenhagen to block the expected intervention of the British navy in 1758. Cruised off Kolberg, returned to Danzig with over 200 sailors down with scurvy, and transported troops from Revel' to Danzig in 1759. Blockaded Kolberg in 1760. Transported troops to Kolberg and blockaded Kolberg in 1761. Transported troops from Kolberg to Revel'. Cruised in the Baltic in 1762 after the war. Attended the visit of Catherine II in 1764. Decommissioned in 1767. Broken up after 1771.

Astrakhan' 66 Arkhangel'sk
Constructor A. Sutherland
Laid down 26.4.1755   *Launched* 12.5.1756
Dimensions 155 ft 6 in x 43 ft 6 in x 17 ft 6 in
Armament   LD 24 x 24pdrs
             UD 26 x 12pdrs
             FC & QD 16 x 6pdrs (1724 'Establishment')
Slava Rossii class. Note the increase in breadth, applied to *Astrakhan'* and four other *Slava Rossii* class members. Sailed from Arkhangel'sk to Kronshtadt in 6–9.1756. Cruised as flag of Adm. Mishukov and blockaded Danzig in 1757. Cruised in the sound off Copenhagen to block the expected intervention of the British navy in 1758. Escorted ammunition ships to Pillau and rejoined the fleet off Öland in 1759. Bombarded Kolberg and transported sick and injured to Kronshtadt in 1760. Grounded while transporting troops to Kolberg in 1761. Relieved by *Rafail*, rejoining the fleet and landing marines at Kolberg. Damaged by counter-battery while bombarding Kolberg. Damaged in a storm off Gottland, drifted ashore and grounded at Dago on 10.11.1761 as a total loss on 10.11.1761 but without casualties.

Rafail 66 Arkhangel'sk
Constructor I. V. James
Laid down 29.4.1757   *Launched* 20.5.1758
Dimensions 155 ft 6 in x 41 ft 6 in x 18 ft (1723 Establishment)
Armament   LD 24 x 24pdrs
             UD 26 x 12pdrs
             FC & QD 16 x 6pdrs (1724 'Establishment')
Slava Rossii class. Sailed from Arkhangel'sk to Revel' in 7–9.1759. Bombarded Kolberg and transported sick and injured from Kolberg to Revel' in 1760. Transported troops to Kolberg and bombarded Kolberg in 1761. Arrived at Kolberg to transport troops to Russia, but developed a leak and returned to Revel'. Cruised in the Baltic in 1764 and 1766. Decommissioned in 1766. Broken up after 1771.

Unnamed 66 Arkhangel'sk
Constructor A. Sutherland & I. V. James
Laid down 29.4.1757   *Launched* 20.5.1758
Dimensions 155 ft 6 in x 41 ft 6 in x 18 ft (1723 Establishment)
Armament   LD 24 x 24pdrs
             UD 26 x 12pdrs
             FC & QD 16 x 6pdrs (1724 'Establishment')
Slava Rossii class. Left Arkhangel'sk in 7.1758. Dismasted during a storm on 11–13.8.1758 and forced into Bergen for repairs. On completion of repairs, she was wrecked on Skagen Reef with the loss of 16 sailors on 19.9.1758. Hull cracked on 22.9.1758 and she was declared a total loss on 26.9.1758 without having been named or commissioned.

Moskva 66 Arkhangel'sk
Constructor I. V. James
Laid down 25.9.1758   *Launched* 25.4.1760
Dimensions 155 ft 6 in x 43 ft 6 in x 17 ft 6 in
Armament   LD 24 x 24pdrs
             UD 26 x 12pdrs
             FC & QD 16 x 6pdrs (1724 'Establishment')
Slava Rossii class. Note the increase in breadth, applied to *Astrakhan'* and four other *Slava Rossii* class members. Sailed from Arkhangel'sk to Revel' in 7–9.1760. Transported troops to Kolberg and blockaded Kolberg in 1761. Transported troops from Kolberg to Revel' in 1762. Cruised in the Baltic in 1764 and 1767. Cruised between Dagdrort and Gottland in 1769. Broken up in 1771.

Sviatoi Pyotr 66 Arkhangel'sk
Constructor I. V. James
Laid down 25.9.1758   *Launched* 25.4.1760
Dimensions 155 ft 6 in x 43 ft 6 in x 17 ft 6 in
Armament   LD 24 x 24pdrs
             UD 26 x 12pdrs
             FC & QD 16 x 6pdrs (1724 'Establishment')
Slava Rossii class. Note the increase in breadth, applied to *Astrakhan'* and four other *Slava Rossii* class members. Sailed from Arkhangel'sk to Revel' in 7–9.1760. Transported troops to Kolberg and blockaded and bombed Kolberg in 1761. Again transported troops from Kolberg to Revel' in 1762. Attended Catherine II's visit to Rogervik in 1764 and returned to Revel'. Fire in her magazine on 4.8.1764 caused her complete destruction along with the *Sviatoi Aleksandr Nevskii* and the loss of 6 sailors. *Moskva*, *Rafail* and *Sviatoi Kliment Papa Rimskii* were endangered but escaped harm.

Sviatoi Iakov 66 Arkhangel'sk
Constructor I. V. James
Laid down 25.5.1760   *Launched* 17.5.1761
Dimensions 155 ft 6 in x 43 ft 6 in x 17 ft 6 in
Armament   LD 24 x 24pdrs
             UD 26 x 12pdrs
             FC & QD 16 x 6pdrs (1724 'Establishment')
Slava Rossii class. Note the increase in breadth, applied to *Astrakhan'* and four other *Slava Rossii* class members. 2.7.1761 departed Arkhangel'sk, but forced to winter in Bergen due to storm damage. Arrived at Kronshtadt in 6.1762. Transported sick and injured and army baggage from Pillau to Kronshtadt in 7–9.1762. Cruised in the Baltic in 1764, 1766, and 1773. Decommissioned in 1773. Broken up in 1774.

The final 28 members following of the *Slava Rossii* class fall chronologically within the reign of Catherine II. They are included here for reasons of class continuity.

Sviatoi Aleksandr Nevskii 66 Arkhangel'sk
Constructor I. V. James
Laid down 3.7.1760   *Launched* 3.5.1762
Dimensions 155 ft 6 in x 43 ft 6 in x 17 ft 6 in
Armament LD 24 x 24pdrs
      UD 26 x 12pdrs
      FC & QD 16 x 6pdrs (1724 'Establishment')

Slava Rossii class. Note the increase in breadth, applied to *Astrakhan'* and four other *Slava Rossii* class members. Sailed from Arkhangel'sk to Revel' in 7–9.1762. Cruised in the Baltic in 1764. Set on fire by the burning *Sviatoi Pyotr* and burnt to the waterline with a loss of 5 sailors after being towed out of the harbour and grounded.

Severnyi Oryol 66 Arkhangel'sk
Constructor I. V. James
Laid down 20.7.1762   *Launched* 20.5.1763
Dimensions 155 ft 6 in x 41 ft 6 in x 18 ft (1723 Establishment)
Armament LD 24 x 24pdrs
      UD 26 x 12pdrs
      FC & QD 16 x 6pdrs (1724 'Establishment')

Slava Rossii class. Sailed from Arkhangel'sk to Kronshtadt in 7–9.1765. Cruised in the Baltic in 1768. Assigned to Adm. Spiridov's First Arkhipelago Squadron to Copenhagen in 1769 and proceeded with the squadron to Hull. Suffered damage while leaving the Channel, developed a serious leak off Finisterre, and returned to Portsmouth for repairs on 28.10.1769. Joined Rear-Adm. Elphinston's 2nd Arkhipelago Squadron as a hospital ship with armament reduced to 50 and then 32, 6pdrs and 12pdrs. Departed Portsmouth on 2.4.1770 with the 2nd Arkhipelago Squadron, developed another leak on 10.4.1770, and returned to Portsmouth on 16.4.1770. Moved to the Thames in 6.1770 where she was sold for scrap in 8.1770.

Ne Tron' Menia 66 Arkhangel'sk
Constructor V. A. Selyaninov
Laid down 30.8.1762   *Launched* 20.5.1763
Dimensions 155 ft 6 in x 41 ft 6 in x 18 ft (1723 Establishment)
Armament 1763 LD 24 x 24pdrs
         UD 26 x 12pdrs
         FC & QD 16 x 6pdrs (1724 'Establishment')
      1770 LD 22 x 24pdrs, 2 x 48u (1 pood)
         UD 24 x 12pdrs, 2 x 24u (½ pood)
         FC & QD 16 x 6pdrs (1724 'Establishment' modified)

Slava Rossii class. Sailed from Arkhangel'sk to Kronshtadt in 7–9.1765. Cruised in the Baltic in 1769. Departed Kronshtadt as flag for Rear-Adm. Elphinston's 2nd Arkhipelago Squadron on 9.10.1769. In compliance with the decision to rearm all ships of the line from 1770 onwards, she landed two 24pdrs and two 12pdrs and replaced them with two 1 pood and two ½ pood edinorogs. Stopped at Copenhagen and docked at Portsmouth 22.12.1769–2.4.1770. Transited to the Mediterranean, stopping at Finisterre, Gibraltar, Sicily and Malta. Landed troops at Rupino (Morea) on 11.5.1770. In action with the Turks off Spetsai on 16–17.5.1770. Joined Adm. Spiridov's Division on 22.5.1770 and pursued the Turks on 24.5.1770. Fought at Chios and Ches'ma on 24–26.6.1770. Blockaded the Dardanelles in 7–9.1770. Cruised in the Arkhipelago in the autumn and winter 1770/1771. Razeed to a frigate in 1772. Stationed at Auza as a floating battery in 1772–5. Unable to return to the Baltic due to her poor material condition and refused access to the Black Sea by Turkey. Sold for scrap at Livorno on 7.9.1775.

Sviatoi Evstafii Plakida 66 St Petersburg
Constructor V. A. Selyaninov
Laid down 30.7.1762   *Launched* 20.8.1763
Dimensions 155 ft 6 in x 41 ft 6 in x 18 ft (1723 Establishment)
Armament 1763 LD 24 x 24pdrs
         UD 26 x 12pdrs
         FC & QD 16 x 6pdrs (1724 'Establishment')
      1770 LD 22 x 24pdrs, 2 x 48u (1 pood)
         UD 24 x 12pdrs, 2 x 24u (½ pood)
         FC & QD 16 x 6pdrs (1724 'Establishment' modified)

Slava Rossii class. The name *Sviatoi Evstafii Plakida* was chosen to commemorate Peter I's birthday which fell on this saint's day. Cruised in the Baltic in 1764 and 1766–8. Left Kronshtadt as flag of Adm. Spiridov and the First Arkhipelago Squadron on 26.7.1769. Damaged at Revel' on 26.12.1769. Rejoined her squadron at Copenhagen and proceeded to Hull. Separated from her squadron again and proceeded to Cape St Vincent, Gibraltar and Port Mahon where she was rejoined by the rest of the squadron between 18.11.1769 and 23.1.1770. Proceeded to Malta and arrived at Vistulo (Morea) on 18.2.1770. Landed troops and bombarded Koron on 1–3.8.1770. At Navarino on 18.4.1770. Met up with the 2nd Arkhipelago Squadron at Cerigo on 22.5.1770. Blew up in action at the battle of Chios on 26.7.1770 with only 70 survivors including Adm. Spiridov and Capt. Kruz. One of the most highly revered of Russian warships in later years.

Sviatoi Ianuarii 66 St Petersburg
Constructor V. A. Selyaninov
Laid down 30.7.1762   *Launched* 20.8.1763
Dimensions 155 ft 6 in x 41 ft 6 in x 18 ft (1723 Establishment)
Armament 1763 LD 24 x 24pdrs
         UD 26 x 12pdrs
         FC & QD 16 x 6pdrs (1724 'Establishment')
      1770 LD 22 x 24pdrs, 2 x 48u (1 pood)
         UD 24 x 12pdrs, 2 x 24u (½ pood)
         FC & QD 16 x 6pdrs (1724 'Establishment' modified)

Slava Rossii class. The name *Sviatoi Ianuarii* was chosen to commemorate Catherine II's birthday which fell on this saint's day. Cruised in the Baltic in 1764 and 1766–8. Left Kronshtadt as part of Adm. Spiridov's First Arkhipelago Squadron on 26.7.1769. Stopped at Copenhagen, Hull, Gibraltar, and Malta, arriving at Vitullo Bay (Morea) on 18.2.1770. In action against Koron and Navarino. Fought in the battles of Chios and Ches'ma on 24–26.6.1770 and bombarded Pelari on the island of Lemnos. Operated off Patmos and blockaded Turkey in 1771–2. Cruised off Morea in 1773 and developed a serious leak. Unsuccessful attempt at repair failed due to lack of funds and available timber. Decommissioned in 1774. Sold for scrap at Auza in 1775.

Tver' 66 Arkhangel'sk
Constructor I. V. James
Laid down 20.8.1762   *Launched* 30.4.1765
Dimensions 155 ft 6 in x 41 ft 6 in x 18 ft (1723 Establishment)
Armament 1765 LD 24 x 24pdrs
         UD 26 x 12pdrs
         FC & QD 16 x 6pdrs (1724 'Establishment')
      1770 LD 22 x 24pdrs, 2 x 48u (1 pood)
         UD 24 x 12pdrs, 2 x 24u (½ pood)
         FC & QD 16 x 6pdrs (1724 'Establishment' modified)

Slava Rossii class. Sailed from Arkhangel'sk to Kronshtadt in 7–10.1765.

A rendering of the climactic moment of the battle of Chios as portrayed by A. A. Tron (2001–2) that shows a high degree of attention to detail, and is an excellent portrayal of the Russian flagship Sviatoi Evstafii. *Here the Turkish flagship* Burc-i Zafer *is burning fiercely and the conflagration is just beginning to spread to the doomed* Sviatoi Evstafii *dominating the centre of the picture. Note the artist's contrast between the panicky Turkish sailors seen leaping from the bows of* Burc-i Zafer *and the long boats pulling away rapidly but in good order from* Sviatoi Evstafii.

Repaired in 1769. Departed Kronshtadt with the 2nd Arkhipelago Squadron of Adm. Elphinston on 9.10.1769, but forced to return to Revel' due to storm damage. Her captain was dismissed and her officers were broken to common seamen for their alleged negligence. Cruised to Gottland in 1770. Transferred from Kronshtadt to Revel' in 1772. In harbour in sea pay status in 1773. Cruised in the Baltic in 1774, but developed a leak. Decommissioned in 1774. Broken up in 1776.

Saratov 66 Arkhangel'sk
Constructor V. A. Selyaninov
Laid down 20.8.1762 *Launched* 30.4.1765
Dimensions 155 ft 6 in x 41 ft 6 in x 18 ft (1723 Establishment)
Armament 1765 LD 24 x 24pdrs
UD 26 x 12pdrs
FC & QD 16 x 6pdrs (1724 'Establishment')
1770 LD 22 x 24pdrs, 2 x 48u (1 pood)
UD 24 x 12pdrs, 2 x 24u (½ pood)
FC & QD 16 x 6pdrs (1724 'Establishment' modified)
Slava Rossii class. Sailed from Arkhangel'sk to Kronshtadt in 7.10.1765. Cruised in the Baltic in 1768. Departed Kronshtadt with Adm. Elphinston's 2nd Arkhipelago Squadron on 9.10.1769. Arrived at Vitullo Bay (Morea) on 18.2.1770. In action against Koron and Navarino. Fought in the battles of Chios and Ches'ma on 24–26.6.1770. Cruised off Patmos and blockaded Turkey. Burnt a Turkish 66 that had run aground on 12.1770. Bombarded Metelino in 1771. Repaired at Malta in 1772. Cruised in the Arkhipelago in 1773–4, bombarding Budrum and Stancio in 1773. Cruised off the Dardanelles in 1774. Departed for Russia on 16.12.1774, stopping at Malta, Elba, Leghorn, Gibraltar, Portsmouth, Copenhagen and Revel' en route. Arrived at Kronshtadt on 19.8.1775. Participated in the Imperial Review in honour of Catherine II in 1776. Decommissioned in 1777. Listed until 1786. Ordered broken up in 1786, but still extant in 1791.

Trekh Sviatitelei 66 St Petersburg
Constructor P. G. Kachalov
Laid down 13.11.1763 *Launched* 30.4.1765
Dimensions 155 ft 6 in x 41 ft 6 in x 18 ft (1723 Establishment)
Armament 1765 LD 24 x 24pdrs
UD 26 x 12pdrs
FC & QD 16 x 6pdrs (1724 'Establishment')
1770 LD 22 x 24pdrs, 2 x 48u (1 pood)
UD 24 x 12pdrs, 2 x 24u (½ pood)
FC & QD 16 x 6pdrs (1724 'Establishment' modified)
Slava Rossii class. The complete Russian name is *Trekh Sviatitelei – Petra, Aleksaya, Iony*. This was shortened in common usage to *Trekh Sviatitelei*. Cruised in the Baltic in 1767–8. Assigned to Adm. Spiridov's First Arkhipelago Squadron and transited to the Mediterranean in 1769–70. Fought at Chios and Ches'ma on 24–26.6.1770. Blockaded the Dardanelles in 1771–2. Bombarded Budrum and Stancio in 1773. Cruised in the Arkhipelago in 1774. Condemned at Auza in 1775, guns removed to other ships, and broken up.

Trekh Ierarkhov 66 St Petersburg
Constructor D. Ul'fov
Laid down 13.11.1763 *Launched* 30.6.1765
Dimensions 155 ft 6 in x 41 ft 6 in x 18 ft (1723 Establishment)

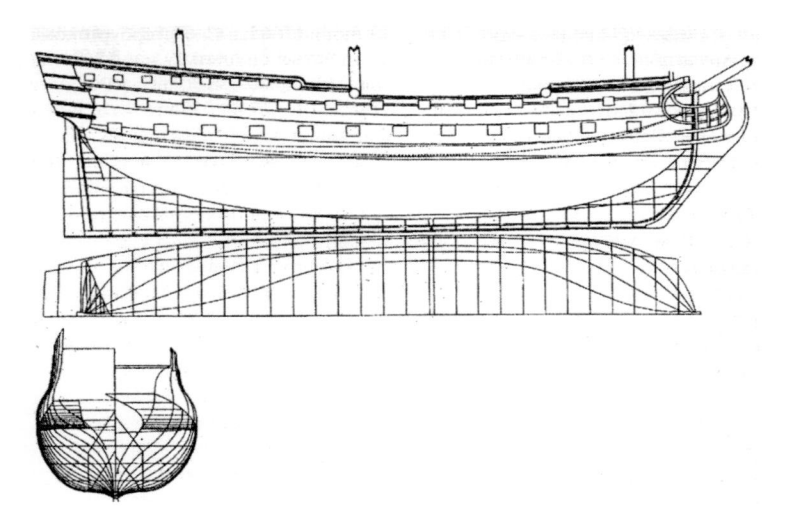

Trekh Ierarkhov (1766) closely resembles Saratov *(1765) and this should come as no great surprise as they are sisters. A look at the two ships' underwater lines, however, reveals the variability that existed during the age of sail for even nominally standardized designs.* Saratov *was built at Arkhangel'sk by Selyaninov and* Trekh Ierarkhov *in St Petersburg by Kachalov. Both constructors had their own ideas about desirable underwater lines for a large ship of this type and both were also limited to a degree by their need to use the timber available to them. These two ships may have* looked *like twins, but it is a good bet to say that they did not* sail *like twins.*

A fully rigged model of Trekh Ierarkhov *(1766) showing the appearance of the standard Russian 66 to good advantage.* Trekh Ierarkhov *served as Count Orlov's flagship at both Chios and Ches'ma in 1770.*

Armament   1765   LD 24 x 24pdrs
                  UD 26 x 12pdrs
                  FC & QD 16 x 6pdrs (1724 'Establishment')
           1770   LD 22 x 24pdrs, 2 x 48u (1 pood)
                  UD 24 x 12pdrs, 2 x 24u (½ pood)
                  FC & QD 16 x 6pdrs (1724 'Establishment' modified)

Slava Rossii class. The complete Russian name is *Trekh Ierarkhov – Vasiliia Velikogo, Grigoriia Bogoslova, Ioanna Zlatousta*. This was shortened in common usage to *Trekh Ierarkhov* to distinguish her from the contemporary *Trekh Sviatitelei* named after three major church saints. Cruised in the Baltic in 1767–8. Assigned to Adm. Spiridov's First Arkhipelago Squadron and transited to the Mediterranean in 1769–70. Arrived at Port Mahon on 2.12.1769. Separated from the squadron in company with frigate *Nadezhda Blagopoluchiia* and arrived at Livorno on 3.2.1770. Assigned as flag to Count Orlov on 1.4.1770. Bombarded Modon. Fought at Chios and Ches'ma on 24–26.6.1770. Blockaded Morea and the Dardanelles in 1771. Repaired at Livorno 1772–3. Bombarded Budrum and Stancio in 1773. Bombarded Patmos and Samos and blockaded Turkey in 1774. Returned to Kronshtadt on 19.10.1775. Took part in the Imperial Review in honour of Catherine II in 1776. Decommissioned in 1777. Ordered broken up in 1786, but still extant in 1791.

Evropa 66 Arkhangel'sk
Constructor I. Davydov
Laid down 1.11.1767   *Launched* 13.5.1768
Dimensions 155 ft 6 in x 41 ft 6 in x 18 ft (1723 Establishment)
Armament   1768 LD 24 x 24pdrs
                   UD 26 x 12pdrs
                   FC & QD 16 x 6pdrs (1724 'Establishment')
             1770 LD 22 x 24pdrs, 2 x 48u (1 pood)
                   UD 24 x 12pdrs, 2 x 24u (½ pood)
                   FC & QD 16 x 6pdrs (1724 'Establishment' modified)

Slava Rossii class. Sailed from Arkhangel'sk to Kronshtadt in 7–9.1768. Assigned to Adm. Spiridov's First Arkhipelago Squadron, but damaged off the isle of Wight on 28.10.1769. Repaired at Portsmouth in 1–2.1770 and rejoined Spiridov off Koron on 25.3.1770. Faced the entire Turkish fleet alone for 30 minutes at the onset of the battle of Ches'ma on 26.6.1770, expending over 100 bombs and carcasses and taking 9 casualties. Acted as Adm. Spiridov's flag during the blockade of the Dardanelles and the bombardment of Mitileno in 1771. Repaired at Auza in 1772. Cruised in the Arkhipelago and off the Dardanelles in 1772–4. Repaired again at Auza in 1772. Returned to Russia on 9.10.1775. Participated in the Imperial Review in honour of Catherine II in 1776. Great repair at Kronshtadt in 1780. Returned to the Mediterranean as part of Rear-Adm. Sukhotin's Armed Neutrality Squadron in 1781–2. Cruised in the Baltic to Gottland and Bornholm in 1783–4. Part of Vice-Adm. Kruz's Reserve Squadron in defence of Kronshtadt in 8–9.1788 during the Russo-Swedish War. Escorted six store ships to Revel' in 6.1789 as part of the Reserve Squadron. Successfully repulsed six Swedish rowing ships off Porkkala-udd on 17.8.1789. Decommissioned in 1789. Broken up after 1791.

Rostislav 66 Arkhangel'sk
Constructor I. Davydov
Laid down 28.8.1768   *Launched* 13.5.1768
Dimensions 155 ft 6 in x 41 ft 6 in x 18 ft (1723 Establishment)
Armament   LD 22 x 24pdrs, 2 x 48u (1 pood)
             UD 24 x 12pdrs, 2 x 24u (½ pood)
             FC & QD 16 x 6pdrs (1724 'Establishment' modified)

Slava Rossii class. Introduced edinorogs to Russian 66s. Sailed from Arkhangel'sk to Copenhagen in 16.7-13.8.1769 to join Adm. Spiridov's First Arkhipelago Squadron as replacement for the damaged *Sviatoslav* (80). On 12.9.1769, proceeded to the Mediterranean, becoming separated from Spiridov's squadron in fog. Damaged in storm off Minorca on 11.1.1770 and finally rejoined Spiridov on 11.6.1770. Fought in the battles of Chios and Ches'ma on 24–26.6.1770. Operated in the Arkhipelago in 1770–5. Returned to Kronshtadt on 19.8.1775. Participated in the Imperial Review in honour of Catherine II in 1776. Decommissioned in 1776. Repaired in 1780. Condemned in 1782, but still extant in 1791.

Vsevolod 66 Arkhangel'sk
Constructor I. Davydov
Laid down 1.11.1767   *Launched* 7.5.1769
Dimensions 155 ft 6 in x 41 ft 6 in x 18 ft (1723 Establishment)
Armament LD 22 x 24pdrs, 2 x 48u (1 pood)
UD 24 x 12pdrs, 2 x 24u (½ pood)
FC & QD 16 x 6pdrs (1724 'Establishment' modified)
Slava Rossii class. Sailed from Arkhangel'sk to Revel' in 7–10.1769. Left for the Mediterranean on 30.6.1770 as part of the 3rd Arkhipelago Squadron under Rear-Adm. Arf. Repaired at Port Mahon in 1770. Cruised in the Arkhipelago in 1771–5. Returned to Kronshtadt on 24.5.1775. Repaired in 1777. Cruised in the Baltic in 1778. Accidentally destroyed by fire in Revel' in 8.3.1779, forcing other ships to cut their way out of ice to flee the harbour.

Sviatoi Georgii Pobedonosets 66 Arkhangel'sk
Constructor I. Davydov
Laid down 28.5.1769   *Launched* 28.4.1770
Dimensions 155 ft 6 in x 41 ft 6 in x 18 ft (1723 Establishment)
Armament LD 22 x 24pdrs, 2 x 48u (1 pood)
UD 24 x 12pdrs, 2 x 24u (½ pood)
FC & QD 16 x 6pdrs (1724 'Establishment' modified)
Slava Rossii class. Arrived at Revel' from Arkhangel'sk on 17.6.1770. 16 x 6pdrs were removed at Revel' to improve stability. Departed Revel' on 30.6.1770 as part of Rear-Adm. Arf's 3rd Arkhipelago Squadron. Operated in the Arkhipelago in 1771–5. Returned to Revel' on 9.10.1775. Participated in the Imperial Review in honour of Catherine II in 1776. Decommissioned in 1776. Repaired in 1778 and reduced to a 50. Broken up in 1780.

Pobeda 66 Arkhangel'sk
Constructor I. Davydov
Laid down 7.5.1769   *Launched* 3.5.1770
Dimensions 155 ft 6 in x 41 ft 6 in x 18 ft (1723 Establishment)
Armament LD 22 x 24pdrs, 2 x 48u (1 pood)
UD 24 x 12pdrs, 2 x 24u (½ pood)
FC & QD 16 x 6pdrs (1724 'Establishment' modified)
Slava Rossii class. Sailed from Arkhangel'sk to Revel' in 7–9.1770. Cruised to Gottland in 1771. Departed Revel' on 8.5.1772 as part of Rear-Adm. I. Chichagov's 4th Arkhipelago Squadron. Operated in the Arkhipelago in 1772–5. Returned to Revel' on 9.10.1775. Participated in the Imperial Review in honour of Catherine II in 1776. Decommissioned in 1776. Stricken in 1780, but still extant in 1791.

Graf Orlov 66 Arkhangel'sk
Constructor I. Davydov
Laid down 7.5.1769   *Launched* 3.5.1770
Dimensions 155 ft 6 in x 41 ft 6 in x 18 ft (1723 Establishment)
Armament LD 22 x 24pdrs, 2 x 48u (1 pood)
UD 24 x 12pdrs, 2 x 24u (½ pood)
FC & QD 16 x 6pdrs (1724 'Establishment' modified)
Slava Rossii class. Named after Count Aleksei Orlov, the victor at Ches'ma and brother to Grigorii Orlov, Catherine II's favourite at the time. Sailed from Arkhangel'sk to Revel' in 6–9.1770. Transited to the Mediterranean as part of Rear-Adm. I. Chichagov's 4th Arkhipelago Squadron. Operated in the Arkhipelago in 1772–5. Returned to Kronshtadt on 19.8.1775. Participated in the Imperial Review in honour of Catherine II in 1776. Cruised in the Baltic in 1778. Decommissioned in 1778, Broken up in 1791.

Pamiat' Evstafii 66 Arkhangel'sk
Constructor I. Davydov
Laid down 29.9.1769   *Launched* 3.5.1770
Dimensions 155 ft 6 in x 41 ft 6 in x 18 ft (1723 Establishment)
Armament LD 22 x 24pdrs, 2 x 48u (1 pood)
UD 24 x 12pdrs, 2 x 24u (½ pood)
FC & QD 16 x 6pdrs (1724 'Establishment' modified)
Slava Rossii class. The name commemorates the *Evstafii Plakida*, the Russian flagship lost at the battle of Chios. Sailed from Arkhangel'sk to Revel' in 6–7.1770. Cruised in the Baltic to Gottland in 1771–5. Repaired in 1780. Deployed to the Mediterranean in 1781–2 as part of Rear-Adm. Sukhotin's Armed Neutrality Squadron. Cruised in the Baltic to Gottland in 1783. Withdrew prematurely from the battle of Gogland on 6.7.1788, after taking minor personnel losses of 4 killed and 13 wounded out of 607 crewmen and with no shot holes in the hull. Adm. Greig dismissed her captain immediately. On 26.7.1788, cooperated with two other ships of the line to force *Gustav-Adol'f* to beach herself and surrender. Fought at the battle of Öland on 15.7.1789. Returned to Kronshtadt on 15.10.1789. Decommissioned in 1789. Broken up in 1791.

Viktor 66 Arkhangel'sk
Constructor I. Davydov
Laid down 24.11.1769   *Launched* 17.5.1771
Dimensions 155 ft 6 in x 41 ft 6 in x 18 ft (1723 Establishment)
Armament LD 22 x 24pdrs, 2 x 48u (1 pood)
UD 24 x 12pdrs, 2 x 24u (½ pood)
FC & QD 16 x 6pdrs (1724 'Establishment' modified)
Slava Rossii class. Sailed from Arkhangel'sk to Kronshtadt in 1772. Training ship in Kronshtadt Roads in 1772. Cruised in the Baltic in 1773–5. Repaired in 1780. In the Mediterranean as part of Rear-Adm. Sukhotin's Armed Neutrality Squadron in 1781–2. Cruised to Gottland in 1783. Cruised to Bornholm in 1786. Fought at Gogland on 6.7.1788 with 10 killed, 25 wounded and 25 shot holes. Fought at the battle of Öland on 15.7.1789 with only a single death. Decommissioned in 1789. Broken up after 1791.

Viacheslav 66 Arkhangel'sk
Constructor I. Davydov
Laid down 21.9.1770   *Launched* 17.5.1771
Dimensions 155 ft 6 in x 41 ft 6 in x 18 ft (1723 Establishment)
Armament LD 22 x 24pdrs, 2 x 48u (1 pood)
UD 24 x 12pdrs, 2 x 24u (½ pood)
FC & QD 16 x 6pdrs (1724 'Establishment' modified)
Slava Rossii class. Departed Arkhangel'sk on 13.7.1771, separated from the squadron, grounded, and forced to winter at Karlshamn. Arrived at Kronshtadt on 23.6.1772. Cruised to Copenhagen in 1773–4 and in 1778–9. Part of the Armed Neutrality squadron under Rear-Adm. Khmetevskiy in 1779. Forced to winter at Copenhagen in 1779–80 due to major leak. Decommissioned in 1780. Broken up after 1784.

Dmitrii Donskoi 66 Arkhangel'sk
Constructor I. Davydov
Laid down 21.9.1770   *Launched* 17.5.1771

Dimensions 155 ft 6 in x 41 ft 6 in x 18 ft (1723 Establishment)
Armament LD 22 x 24pdrs, 2 x 48u (1 pood)
UD 24 x 12pdrs, 2 x 24u (½ pood)
FC & QD 16 x 6pdrs (1724 'Establishment' modified)

Slava Rossii class. Dmitrii Donskoi routed the Golden Horde at Kulikovskoe Pole in 1380 and was one of the great heroes of Russian history. Sailed from Arkhangel'sk to Kronstadt in 7–10.1771. Training duties in Kronshtadt Roads in 1772. Departed for the Mediterranean on 21.19.1773 as part of Rear-Adm. Greig's 5th Squadron. Arrived at Auza on 6.9.1774 after hostilities had ended. Returned to Kronshtadt on 24.5.1775. Decommissioned in 1777, but not broken up until 1791.

Sviatoi Kniaz' Vladimir 66 St Petersburg
Constructors M. D. Portnov & Aksengam
Laid down 28.9.1770 *Launched* 28.8.1771
Dimensions 155 ft 6 in x 41 ft 6 in x 18 ft (1723 Establishment)
Armament LD 22 x 24pdrs, 2 x 48u (1 pood)
UD 24 x 12pdrs, 2 x 24u (½ pood)
FC & QD 16 x 6pdrs (1724 'Establishment' modified)

Slava Rossii class. Cruised to Gottland in 1772. Cruised to Copenhagen in 1773–4. Operated off Portugal as part of Rear-Adm. Palibin's Armed Neutrality squadron in 1780–81. Returned to Kronshtadt on 15.7.1781. Decommissioned in 1781. Broken up after 1791.

Sviatyk Zhen Mironosits 66 St Petersburg
Constructor I. V. James
Laid down 28.5.1769 *Launched* 28.8.1771
Dimensions 155 ft 6 in x 41 ft 6 in x 18 ft (1723 Establishment)
Armament LD 22 x 24pdrs, 2 x 48u (1 pood)
UD 24 x 12pdrs, 2 x 24u (½ pood)
FC & QD 16 x 6pdrs (1724 'Establishment' modified)

Slava Rossii class. Named by Catherine II who was colloquially referred to as 'Mironosits' (The Lord's Anointed). Cruised to Gottland in 1772. Joined Rear-Adm. Greig's 5th Arkhipelago Squadron at Copenhagen en route to the Mediterranean in 1773. Cruised in the Arkhipelago in 1773–4. Returned to Kronshtadt on 24.5.1775. Participated in the Imperial Review in honour of Catherine II in 1776. Decommissioned in 1777. Broken up in 1791.

Aleksandr Nevskii 66 Arkhangel'sk
Constructors I. Davydov & G. Maltsev
Laid down 21.9.1770 *Launched* 1.5.1772
Dimensions 155 ft 6 in x 41 ft 6 in x 18 ft (1723 Establishment)
Armament LD 22 x 24pdrs, 2 x 48u (1 pood)
UD 24 x 12pdrs, 2 x 24u (½ pood)
FC & QD 16 x 6pdrs (1724 'Establishment' modified)

Slava Rossii class. Sailed from Arkhangel'sk to Revel' in 7–9.1772. Joined Rear-Adm. Greig's 5th Arkhipelago Squadron at Copenhagen en route to the Mediterranean in 1773. Cruised in the Arkhipelago in 1773–4. Returned to Kronshtadt on 24.5.1775. Operated in the North Sea in 1780 with Rear-Adm. Kruz's Armed Neutrality Squadron. Decommissioned in 1780. Broken up in 1784.

Boris i Gleb 66 Arkhangel'sk
Constructors I. Davydov & G. Maltsev
Laid down 1.11.1771 *Launched* 6.5.1772
Dimensions 155 ft 6 in x 41 ft 6 in x 18 ft (1723 Establishment)
Armament LD 22 x 24pdrs, 2 x 48u (1 pood)
UD 24 x 12pdrs, 2 x 24u (½ pood)
FC & QD 16 x 6pdrs (1724 'Establishment' modified)

Slava Rossii class. Sailed from Arkhangel'sk to Revel' in 7–10.1772. Cruised to Gottland. Cruised in the Baltic in 1774–5 and 1777–8. Damaged in collision in 1778 and in need of repair. Listed until 1789 without having been repaired. Broken up after 1789.

Preslava 66 Arkhangel'sk
Constructors I. Davydov & G. Maltsev
Laid down 1.11.1771 *Launched* 6.5.1772
Dimensions 155 ft 6 in x 41 ft 6 in x 18 ft (1723 Establishment)
Armament LD 22 x 24pdrs, 2 x 48u (1 pood)
UD 24 x 12pdrs, 2 x 24u (½ pood)
FC & QD 16 x 6pdrs (1724 'Establishment' modified)

Slava Rossii class. Sailed from Arkhangel'sk to Revel' in 7–10.1772. Training duties in Revel' Roads in 1773. Cruised in the Baltic in 1774–6 and 1778. Operated with Rear-Adm. Khmetevskiy's Armed Neutrality squadron in the Barents Sea in 1779. Decommissioned in 1779. Broken up after 1791.

Deris' 66 Arkhangel'sk
Constructor V. Gunion
Laid down 4.10.1771 *Launched* 19.5.1772
Dimensions 155 ft 6 in x 41 ft 6 in x 18 ft (1723 Establishment)
Armament LD 22 x 24pdrs, 2 x 48u (1 pood)
UD 24 x 12pdrs, 2 x 24u (½ pood)
FC & QD 16 x 6pdrs (1724 'Establishment' modified)

Slava Rossii class. Sailed from Arkhangel'sk to Revel' as flag to Rear-Adm. Seniavin in 7–10.1772. Cruised to Copenhagen in 1773–4. Cruised in the Baltic in 1778. Operated off Portugal as part of Brigadier Palibin's Armed Neutrality Squadron in 1780–81. Repaired in 1782. Present at Gogland on 6.7.1788 but avoided conflict and failed to assist *Vladislav*, leading to the court-martial and breaking of her captain by Adm. Greig. Fought at Öland on 15.7.1788 and suffered severe damage as a result of the explosion of three of her guns causing 15 deaths and 98 injuries. She was saved from a magazine explosion by the heroism of a lone midshipman. Escorted to Revel' after the battle and decommissioned in 1789. Broken up after 1791.

Ingermanlandiia 66 Arkhangel'sk
Constructors I. Davydov & G. Maltsev
Laid down 1.11.1771 *Launched* 14.5.1773
Dimensions 155 ft 6 in x 41 ft 6 in x 18 ft (1723 Establishment)
Armament LD 22 x 24pdrs, 2 x 48u (1 pood)
UD 24 x 12pdrs, 2 x 24u (½ pood)
FC & QD 16 x 6pdrs (1724 'Establishment' modified)

Slava Rossii class. Sailed from Arkhangel'sk to Kronshtadt in 6–10.1775. Participated in the Imperial Review in honour of Catherine II in 1776. Cruised in the Baltic in 1777–8. Operated in the North Sea in 1780 with Rear-Adm. Kruz's Armed Neutrality squadron. Decommissioned in 1780. Broken up in 1784.

Spiridon 66 St Petersburg
Constructor ?
Laid down 24.4.1770 *Launched* 24.6.1779
Dimensions 155 ft 6 in x 41 ft 6 in x 18 ft (1723 Establishment)
Armament LD 22 x 24pdrs, 2 x 48u (1 pood)
UD 24 x 12pdrs, 2 x 24u (½ pood)
FC & QD 16 x 6pdrs (1724 'Establishment' modified)

Slava Rossii class. Construction and completion delayed for two years on the slip. Operated in Brigadier Palibin's Armed Neutrality squadron off Portugal in 1780–81. Cruised to Bornholm in the Baltic in 1787. Decommissioned in 1787. Broken up after 1791.

THE BALTIC FLEET 1696–1761

David Selunskii 66 St Petersburg
Constructors   Aksengam & V. A. Selyaninov
Laid down 9.10.1770/15.11.1773   *Launched* 24.6.1779
Dimensions 159 ft x 44 ft 4½ in x 18 ft
Armament   LD 22 x 24pdrs, 2 x 48u (1 pood)
             UD 24 x 12pdrs, 2 x 24u (½ pood)
             FC & QD 16 x 6pdrs (1724 'Establishment' modified)
Slava Rossii class. Due to the dilapidated condition of her building slip, she was laid down a second time on 15.11.1773, greatly delaying her completion. Note atypical dimensions as completed. Operated in Brigadier Palibin's Armed Neutrality Squadron off Portugal in 1780–81. Operated in Vice-Adm. I.Chichagov's Mediterranean squadron in 1782–4. Decommissioned in 1784. Broken up after 1786.

Ships with 50–58 Guns (34 built 1696–1761)

50-gun ships were the first Russian line of battle ships. Although they were subsequently built in smaller numbers than the 66s, 52/54-gun ships armed with 18pdrs were still considered to be of value in secondary roles. They were officially dropped from force level establishments after 1750 but continued to be built in small numbers. A total of 34 were built between 1710 and 1761 and a final unit was completed during Catherine II's reign.

Vyborg class (4 ships)
An important prototypical class of line of battle ships. *Vyborg* was lost to grounding while in pursuit of Swedish ships in 1713. The fourth and final unit of the class was never christened, having been lost to grounding while en route to St Petersburg for commissioning.

Vyborg 50 ?
Constructor R. Brown
Laid down 8.1708   *Launched* 1710
Dimensions ?
Armament   1715 LD 20 x 18pdrs
                   UD 20 x 8pdrs
                   FC & QD 10 x 4pdrs (probable)
Vyborg class. Named in honour of the capture of Vyborg by the Russian army on 13.7.1710. Arrived at St Petersburg on 6.1710 and proceeded to Kronshtadt. Cruised in the Baltic in 1710–13, acting as Peter I's flagship in 1710. Grounded on 11.7.1712 while in pursuit of three Swedish ships of the line and the captured Russian ship of the line *Bulinbruk*. Unlike *Riga*, which was similarly grounded in the pursuit, she broke her back and had to be set afire 12.7.1719. Her captain was sentenced to death, but pardoned and allowed only shore commands thereafter.

Riga 50 Nova Ladoga
Constructor R. Brown
Laid down 8.1708   *Launched* 1710
Dimensions ?
Armament   1715 LD 20 x 18pdrs
                   UD 20 x 8pdrs
                   FC & QD 10 x 4pdrs
                   323 men (1714) (*Materialy*)
Vyborg class. Named in honour of the capture of Riga from Sweden on 4.7.1710. Arrived at Kotlin (Kronshtadt) in 8.1710. Commissioned from 1710–18. Cruised with the Baltic fleet in 1710–15. Temporarily grounded on 11.7.1713 while acting as the flagship of Vice-Adm. Kruys in pursuit three Swedish Ships of the line and the captured Russian ship of the line *Bulinbruk*. This action led to the court martial of Vice-Adm.

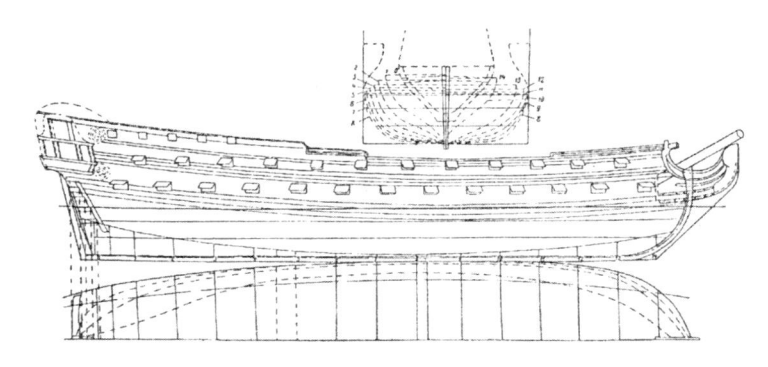

The design for the 50-gun Vyborg, Riga and Pernov of 1710 was the work of one of Peter I's imported British shipwrights, Richard Brown. Armed with 18pdr lower deck guns, they were more heavily armed than similar ships being built for the Royal Navy at the time which were armed with 12pdrs and would not move up to the heavier guns until the Establishment of 1716. Fourth Rates by British standards, these ships nevertheless marked the coming of age of Peter's Baltic fleet. They would be followed in a very few years by 66-gun ships and even 90-gun ships by 1720. The drawing is rather problematic since the number of gunports exceeds the armament as reported in the Materialy. *Nevertheless it may be accurate since ships of the period did not always carry guns to fill all their available gunports.*

Kruys. He was initially sentenced to death, but pardoned by Peter I and reduced to shore commands thereafter. Stationed in Kronshtadt Roads in 1716–17. Cruised again in 1718. Last mentioned in 1721.

Pernov 50/52 Olonetskaya
Constructor G. A. Menshikov
Laid down 10.1708   *Launched* 1710
Dimensions ?
Armament   1715 LD 20 x 18pdrs
                   UD 20 x 8pdrs
                   FC & QD 10 x 4pdrs
                   323 men (1714) (*Materialy*)
Vyborg class. Named in honour of the capture of Pernoy by the Russian army on 14.8.1710. Arrived in St Petersburg in 9.1710. Commissioned 1712–17. Cruised in the Baltic in 1712–15. Stationed in Kronshtadt 1716–17. Broken up in 1721.

Unnamed 50 Olonetskaya
Constructor Bent & Graf
Laid down 11.1708   *Launched* 7.1711
Dimensions ?
Armament   1715 LD 20 x 18pdrs
                   UD 20 x 8pdrs
                   FC & QD 10 x 4pdrs (probable planned
                   armament)
Vyborg class. Wrecked in Lake Ladoga in 1712 while en route to St Petersburg after being launched. Never named or commissioned.

Poltava 52/54 St Petersburg
Constructor Peter I
Laid down 5.12.1709   *Launched* 15.6.1712
Dimensions 130 ft 8 in x 38 ft 4½ in x 15 ft 2½ in (Veselago)
              131 ft 6 in x 39 ft 4½ in x 14 ft 11 in (Apraksin)
Armament   1715 LD 22 x 18pdrs
                   UD 20 x 12pdrs
                   FC & QD 12 x 6pdrs

The construction of Poltava *(54) of 1712 was personally overseen by Peter I at St Petersburg. Her name commemorates the great Russian land victory over Sweden in 1709. Of interest in this stern perspective is the unusual recess in the stern galleries. The artist of this work, Peter Picart, was yet another of Peter I's imports from Europe, arriving in Russia in 1702 and remaining for 35 years, during which time he created very many engravings and etchings for his adopted country.*

351 men (1714)

The first warship built at St Petersburg. Named in honour of the Russian victory on 27.6.1709. Cruised in the Baltic 1713–17. Grounded off Sweden in 8.1717. Great repair completed in 1718–19. Cruised in the Baltic in 1721–3. Declared surplus to naval requirements in 1725 and decommissioned in 1727. Broken up in 1732. (Note the differences in dimensions between Veselago and Apraksin.)

Arkhangel Gavriil class (3 ships)
Arkhangel Gavriil 52/54   Arkhangel'sk
Constructor V. Gerens
Laid down   1712   *Launched* 6.1713
Dimensions 127 ft x 35 ft x 15 ft 6 in
Armament   1715   LD 22 x 18pdrs
                     UD 22 x 8pdrs
                     FC & QD 8 x 4pdrs
              323 men (1714)

Arkhangel Gavriil class. Delayed by ice at Arkhangel'sk until 17.10.1713 at which time she departed for the Baltic with her sisters *Mikhail* and *Rafail*. Wintered in the gulf of Kola in 1713–14. Arrived at Revel' in 6.1713. Cruised in the Baltic in 1714–15. Cruised to Copenhagen in 1716 and participated in the 'Great Armament of 1716'. Cruised in the Baltic in 1717. Cargo service in 1719. Broken up in 1721.

Arkhangel Mikhail 52   Arkhangel'sk
Constructor V. Gerens
Laid down   1712   *Launched* 6.1713
Dimensions 127 ft x 35 ft x 15 ft 6 in
Armament   1716   LD 22 x 18pdrs
                     UD 22 x 8pdrs
                     FC & QD 8 x 3pdrs
              323 men (1714)/400 men (*Materialy*)

Arkhangel Gavriil class. Delayed by ice at Arkhangel'sk until 17.10.1713 at which time she departed for the Baltic with her sisters *Gavriil* and *Rafail*. Arrived at Revel' in 1714. Cruised in the Baltic in 1715. To Copenhagen in 1716 to participate in the 'Great Armament of 1716'. Cruised in the Baltic in 1717–18. Decommissioned in 1718. Broken up in 1722.

Arkhangel Rafail 52/54   Arkhangel'sk
Constructor V. Gerens
Laid down   1712   *Launched* 7.1713
Dimensions 127 ft x 35 ft x 15 ft 6 in
Armament   1715   LD 22 x 18pdrs
                     UD 22 x 8pdrs
                     FC & QD 8 x 4pdrs
              323 men (1714)/404 men (*Materialy*)

Arkhangel Gavriil class. Delayed by ice at Arkhangel'sk until 17.10.1713 at which time she departed for the Baltic with her sisters *Gavriil* and *Mikhail*. Wintered in the gulf of Kola in 1713-14. Arrived at Revel' in 4.1714. Cruised in the Baltic in 1715. To Copenhagen in 1716 to participate in the 'Great Armament of 1716'. Cruised in the Baltic in 1717–19. In action with Swedish ships on 24.5.1719, capturing *Wachtmeister* with assistance from *Iagudiil*. Cruised in the Baltic in 1721. Heavily damaged in a storm off Dagerort on 9.5.1721 and taken in tow by *Samson*. Arrived at Revel' minus her mainmast on 20.5.1721. Decommissioned in 1721. Sunk at Revel' as a foundation in 1724.

Uriil class (4 ships)

As was the case with the preceding *Arkhangel Gavriil* class, the four *Uriil*s were all named after biblical archangels. For reasons that are not clear, V. Gerens's trio carried 'Arkhangel' as part of their formally assigned names, while P. Vybe's quartet apparently did not.

Uriil 52   Arkhangel'sk
Constructor P. Vybe
Laid down   1713   *Launched* 6.1715
Dimensions 130 ft x 35 ft x 15 ft 6 in
Armament   1720   LD 22 x 18pdrs
                     UD 22 x 8pdrs
                     FC & QD 8 x 4pdrs
              317 men (*Materialy*)

Uriil class. Left Arkhangel'sk in company with *Varakhail*, *Selafail* and *Iagudiil* on 24.8.1715 Arrived in Copenhagen in 11.1715 to participate in the 'Great Armament of 1716'. Cruised in the Baltic in 1717–20, participating in the pursuit and capture of a Swedish ship of the line, frigate, and brigantine off Osel on 24.5.1719. Escorted merchant ships to Amsterdam in 1721 and was severely damaged by ice off Denmark in February. Temporarily repaired at Copenhagen and condemned and sold at Amsterdam in 6.1722. Guns and fittings were removed for use in newly purchased ships.

Selafail 50/52   Arkhangel'sk
Constructor P. Vybe
Laid down   20.6.1714   *Launched* 6.1715
Dimensions 130 ft x 35 ft x 15 ft 6 in
Armament   1720   LD 22 x 18pdrs
                     UD 22 x 8pdrs
                     FC & QD 8 x 4pdrs
              309 men (*Materialy*)

Uriil class. Left Arkhangel'sk in company with *Uriil*, *Varakhail* and

Iagudiil on 24.8.1715 Arrived in company with *Uriil* in 11.1715 to participate in the 'Great Armament of 1716'. Cruised in the Baltic in 1717–21. Decommissioned in 1721. Listed until 1724.

Varakhail 50/52 Arkhangel'sk
Constructor P. Vybe
Laid down 20.6.1714   *Launched* 6.1715
Dimensions 130 ft x 35 ft x 15 ft 6 in
Armament   1720 LD 20 x 18pdrs
                   UD 22 x 8pdrs
                   FC & QD 8 x 4pdrs
             330 men (*Materialy*)

Uriil class. Left Arkhangel'sk in company with *Uriil*, *Selafail* and *Iagudiil* on 24.8.1715. Damaged en route with a loss of 107 men and forced to winter at Christiansand. Arrived at Copenhagen in the spring of 1716 and joined the 'Great Armament of 1716'. Cruised in the Baltic 1717–21. Decommissioned in 1721. Listed until 1724.

Iagudiil 50/52 Arkhangel'sk
Constructor P. Vybe
Laid down 1713   *Launched* 6.1715
Dimensions 130 ft x 35 ft x 15 ft 6 in
Armament   1720 LD 20 x 18pdrs
                   UD 22 x 8pdrs
                   FC & QD 8 x 4pdrs
             330 men (*Materialy*)

Uriil class. Left Arkhangel'sk in company with *Uriil*, *Selafail* and *Varakhail* on 24.8.1715. Returned to Arkhangel'sk due to damage sustained. Departed a second time on 17.10.1715 and again damaged, taking in 4 ft of water. Wintered at Ramsund, Norway with 36 men lost and 47 severely frostbitten. Arrived at Copenhagen in 5.1716 to join the 'Great Armament of 1716'. Remained at Copenhagen for needed repairs upon departure of the Russian squadron. Sailed to the Texel in 1717 and returned to Revel' in 5.1718 in company with the Danish squadron. Fought at the battle of Osel on 24.5.1719 and joined with *Rafail* to force the surrender of *Wachtmeister*. Cruised in the Baltic in 1720–1. Arrived at Amsterdam in 11.1721 where she was determined to be rotten. Sold in 6.1722.

Sankt Mikhail class (4 ships)
Sankt Mikhail 54 St Petersburg
Constructor R. Brown
Laid down 24.9.1721   *Launched* 26.5.1723
Dimensions 142 ft x 38 ft x 16 ft 6 in
Armament   LD 22 x 18pdrs
             UD 24 x 8pdrs
             FC & QD 8 x 4pdrs

Sankt Mikhail class. Planned as a flagship and intended to operate performing command and control functions behind the line of battle in a role later assumed by frigates. Cruised in the Baltic in 1723 and 1725. At Revel' in 1726. Escorted the Tsarina Anna to Kiel in 1727 in company with *Derbent*. Stationed at Revel' in 1728 and 1729. Transferred to Kronshtadt in 1730. Harbour service 1731–3. Broken up after 1739 but still listed to 1740.

Rafail 54 St Petersburg
Constructor R. Ramz (R. Ramsay)
Laid down 17.9.1721   *Launched* 19.7.1724
Dimensions 142 ft x 38 ft x 16 ft 6 in
Armament   LD 22 x 18pdrs
             UD 24 x 8pdrs
             FC & QD 8 x 4pdrs

Sankt Mikhail class. Cruised in the Baltic in 1725–6. Returned the body of Tsarina Ann to Russia in 1728. Cruised in the Baltic in 1730. Found unfit for service in 1731. Broken up after 1739.

Ne Tron' Menia 54 St Petersburg
Constructor R. Brown
Laid down 15.10.1722   *Launched* 25.4.1725
Dimensions 142 ft x 38 ft 4 in x 16 ft 6 in
Armament   LD 22 x 18pdrs
             UD 24 x 8pdrs
             FC & QD 8 x 4pdrs

Sankt Mikhail class. Laid down as *Varakhail*, completed as *Ne Tron' Menia*. Renamed in this unusual manner by Catherine I before launch. '*Ne tron' menia*' means 'Don't touch me', and is a common name for various northern Russian plants that call to mind Christ's admonition to Mary Magdalene after the Resurrection. This unusual play on words was assigned to four later Russian ships of the line, the last in 1832. Cruised in the Baltic in 1725. Stayed in harbour with the Revel' squadron in 1726. Cruised in the Baltic in 1727. Stayed in harbour with the Revel' squadron in 1728 and 1729. Transferred to Kronshtadt in 7.1731. Broken up after 1739, but listed to 1740.

Riga 54 St Petersburg
Constructor R. Brown
Laid down 3.3.1724   *Launched* 6.7.1729
Dimensions 142 ft x 38 ft 4 in x 16 ft 6 in

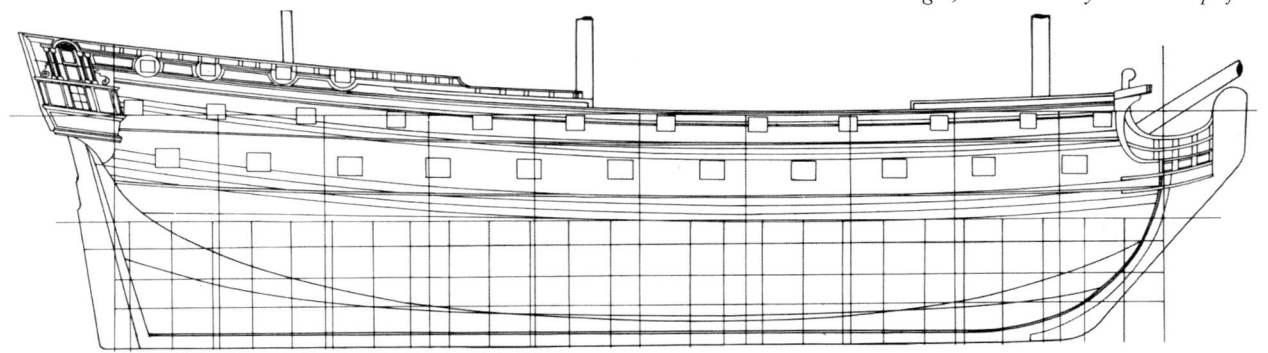

Sankt Mikhail (54) of 1723 was built at St Petersburg as an unexceptional representative of a class of warship that barely merited a place in the battle-lines in the Atlantic navies by the 1720s. Slightly larger and more heavily armed representatives of the type would continue to be found useful for secondary service in the Baltic until the early years of Catherine II's reign (as similar ships in fact continued to serve the Royal Navy in specialist roles). Thereafter, they were finally declared obsolete and larger, more heavily armed ships found favour.

Armament 1729 LD 22 x 18pdrs
UD 24 x 8pdrs
FC & QD 8 x 4pdrs
1736 LD 22 x 12pdrs
UD 28 x 6pdrs
FC & QD 8 3pdrs

Sankt Mikhail class. Cruised in the Baltic in 1730 and 1732 and to Copenhagen and the Skagerrak in 1733. Participated in the Danzig expedition of 1734. Carried supplies in 1735. Cruised in the Baltic in 1738 and determined to be rotten. Broken up after 1739, but listed to 1747.

Pyotr II class (19 ships)
Nineteen ships were built to a common design between 1728 and 1766, based upon the Establishment of 1723, and closely resembling the preceding *Sankt Mikhail* class but with a slightly heavier armament. Although the 50-gun ship was approaching obsolescence in Europe; they still rated as line of battle ships by Baltic standards. The ships of the *Pyotr II* class were widely employed in service in secondary roles as escort, transport and supply duties in a manner that closely paralleled British practice with their Fourth Rates. None were lost in combat, but *Varakhail* capsized in harbour for unknown reasons and *Aziia*, the final unit, was lost at sea.

In accordance with recent findings discussed in the introduction, the armament of *Pyotr II* and her sister ships was not in complete compliance with the Establishment of 1723. The actual armament was prescribed by the informally established 'Establishment of 1724' and is presented here for all class members and consisted of the elimination of two lower deck 18pdrs and the addition of two middle deck 8pdrs. The total rated armament remained 54.

Pyotr II 54 St Petersburg
Constructor O. Nye (Joseph Noy)
Laid down 10.3.1724 *Launched* 22 or 29.5.1728
Dimension 143 ft x 38 ft x 16 ft 7 in (1723 Establishment)
Armament LD 22 x 18pdrs
UD 24 x 8pdrs
FC & QD 8 x 4pdrs (1724 'Establishment')

Pyotr II class. Named after Peter I's grandson, whose brief reign began in 1727. Cruised in the Baltic in 1729, 1732, and 1733. Participated in the Danzig expedition of 1734. Carried supplies from Riga to Kronshtadt in 1735. Cruised in the Baltic in 1736 and determined to be rotten. Broken up after 1739, but listed till 1747.

Vyborg 54 St Petersburg
Constructor R. Brown
Laid down 24.10.1725 *Launched* 19.10.1729
Dimensions 142 ft x 38 ft 4 in x 16 ft 6 in
Armament LD 22 x 18pdrs
UD 24 x 8pdrs
FC & QD 8 x 4pdrs (1724 'Establishment')

Pyotr II class. Cruised in the Baltic in 1730 and 1732 and to Copenhagen and the Skagerrak in 1733. Participated in the Danzig expedition of 1734. Carried supplies in 1735. Cruised in the Baltic in 1736 and 1738. Broken up after 1739.

Novaia Nadezhda 54 St Petersburg
Constructor G. A. Menshikov
Laid down 23.1.1726 *Launched* 9.6.1730
Dimensions 143 ft x 38 ft x 16 ft 7 in (1723 Establishment)
Armament LD 22 x 18pdrs
UD 24 x 8pdrs
FC & QD 8 x 4pdrs (1724 'Establishment')

Pyotr II class. Cruised in the Baltic in 1730 in the Baltic and in 1733 to Copenhagen and the Skagerrak. Participated in the Danzig expedition of 1734. Carried supplies in 1735 from Riga to Kronshtadt. Cruised in the Baltic in 1738. Stationed in Kronshtadt Roads in 1741. Served as a hospital hulk from 1742–3. No further mention.

Gorod Arkhangel'sk 54 Arkhangel'sk
Constructor R. Kosentz (Richard Cozens)
Laid down 2.6.1734 *Launched* 22.6.1735
Dimensions 143 ft x 38 ft x 16 ft 7 in (1723 Establishment)
Armament LD 22 x 18pdrs
UD 24 x 8pdrs
FC & QD 8 x 4pdrs (1724 'Establishment')

Pyotr II class. Arrived at Kronshtadt in 1735. Cruised in the Baltic in 1736 and 1740. Commissioned and armed in Kronshtadt Roads in 1741. Took part in the war with Sweden in 1741–3. Cruised in the Baltic in 1744–8. Broken up after 1749.

Severnaia Zvezda 54 Arkhangel'sk
Constructor R. Kosentz (Richard Cozens)
Laid down 22.7.1734 *Launched* 15.7.1735
Dimensions 143 ft x 38 ft x 16 ft 7 in (1723 Establishment)
Armament LD 22 x 18pdrs
UD 24 x 8pdrs
FC & QD 8 x 4pdrs (1724 'Establishment')

Pyotr II class. Scheduled departure from Arkhangel'sk in 8.1735 delayed by the early onset of winter. Arrived at Kronshtadt in 9.1736. Cruised in the Baltic in 1737 and 1740. Commissioned and armed in Kronshtadt Roads in 1741. Took part in the war with Sweden in 1741–3. Cruised in the Baltic in 1744, 1746, and 1748. Broken up after 1749.

Neptunus 54 Arkhangel'sk
Constructor Ya. Brant
Laid down 29.3.1735 *Launched* 29.6.1736
Dimensions 143 ft x 38 ft x 16 ft 7 in (1723 Establishment)
Armament LD 22 x 18pdrs
UD 24 x 8pdrs
FC & QD 8 x 4pdrs (1724 'Establishment')

Pyotr II class. Sailed from Arkhangel'sk in 6.7.1737. Cruised in the Baltic in 1740. Took part in the war with Sweden in 1741–3. Cruised in the Baltic in 1744 and 1746–8. In 1749 repatriated Russian troops that had been sent to assist Austria in 1748, transporting them from Danzig to Russia. Cruised in the Baltic in 1750. Last listed in 1752.

Astrakhan' 54 St Petersburg
Constructor G. Okunev
Laid down 10.9.1734 *Launched* 31.10.1736
Dimensions 143 ft x 38 ft x 16 ft 7 in (1723 Establishment)
Armament LD 22 x 18pdrs
UD 24 x 8pdrs
FC & QD 8 x 4pdrs (1724 'Establishment')

Pyotr II class. Cruised in the Baltic in 1737 and 1739. Took part in the war with Sweden in 1741–3. Cruised in the Baltic in 1744–6 and 1748. Carried equipment of Russian troops from Danzig to Revel' in 1749. Last listed in 1752.

Azov 54 St Petersburg
Constructor I. S. Ramburg
Laid down 24.3.1734 *Launched* 31.10.1736

Dimensions 143 ft x 38 ft x 16 ft 7 in (1723 Establishment)
Armament   LD 22 x 18pdrs
             UD 24 x 8pdrs
             FC & QD 8 x 4pdrs (1724 'Establishment')
Pyotr II class. Cruised in the Baltic in 1737 and 1739. Took part in the war with Sweden in 1741–3. Cruised in 1744–6 and 1748. Broken up in 1752.

Sviatoi Andrei 54   Arkhangel'sk
Constructors R. Kosentz (Richard Cozens) and V. Batakov
Laid down   10.9.1735   *Launched*   12.5.1737
Dimensions 143 ft x 38 ft x 16 ft 7 in (1723 Establishment)
Armament   LD 22 x 18pdrs
             UD 24 x 8pdrs
             FC & QD 8 x 4pdrs (1724 'Establishment')
Pyotr II class. Sailed from Arkhangel'sk to Kronshtadt in 1737. Repaired in 1738. Cruised in the Baltic in 1740. Took part in the war with Sweden in 1741–3. Cruised in the Baltic in 1744–6 and 1748. Carried equipment of Russian troops from Danzig to Revel' in 1749. Found unserviceable and converted into a sheer hulk at Revel' in 1750. Broken up after 1752.

Kronshtadt 54   Arkhangel'sk
Constructor R. Kosentz (Richard Cozens) and V. Batakov
Laid down   5.8.1737   *Launched*   21.5.1738
Dimensions 143 ft x 38 ft x 16 ft 7 in (1723 Establishment)
Armament   LD 22 x 18pdrs
             UD 24 x 8pdrs
             FC & QD 8 x 4pdrs (1724 'Establishment')
Pyotr II class. Construction begun under R. Kozents and completed by V. Batakov upon his death. Sailed from Arkhangel'sk to Kronshtadt in 1738, temporarily grounded in the Skagerrak. Cruised in the Baltic in 1739. Took part in the war with Sweden in 1741–3. Cruised in the Baltic in 1744, 1746 and 1748. Carried baggage of Russian troops being evacuated from Danzig to Revel' in 1749. Cruised in the Baltic in 1750 and 1751. Decommissioned in 1752. Broken up in 1755.

Sviatoi Panteleimon 54   Arkhangel'sk
Constructor V. Batakov
Laid down   3.5.1739   *Launched*   11.5.1740
Dimensions 143 ft x 38 ft x 16 ft 7 in
Armament   LD 22 x 18pdrs
             UD 24 x 8pdrs
             FC & QD 8 x 4pdrs (1724 'Establishment')
Pyotr II class. *Sviatoi Panteleimon* is the saint's day upon which the battle of Gangut was won. Wintered in the Gulf of Kola with Vice-Adm. Bredal's squadron in 1741/42. Sailed to Kronshtadt in 8–11.1743. Cruised in the Baltic in 1744–8. Carried baggage of Russian troops being evacuated from Danzig to Revel' in 1749. Cruised in the Baltic in 1750–1. Decommissioned in 1751. Broken up in 1756.

Sviatoi Isakii 54   Arkhangel'sk
Constructor V. Batakov
Laid down   10.7.1739   *Launched*   18.5.1740
Dimensions 143 ft x 38 ft x 16 ft 7 in
Armament   LD 22 x 18pdrs
             UD 24 x 8pdrs
             FC & QD 8 x 4pdrs (1724 'Establishment')
Pyotr II class. Wintered in the Gulf of Kola with Vice-Adm. Bredal's squadron in 1741/42. Sailed to Kronshtadt in 8–11.1743. Cruised in the Baltic in 1744. Searched off Gottland for a French corsair and then carried the Russian ambassador to Lübeck in 1745. Cruised in the Baltic in 1746–8. Carried baggage of Russian troops being evacuated from Danzig to Revel' in 1749. Cruised in the Baltic in 1750–1. Decommissioned in 1751. Broken up in 1756.

Sviatoi Nikolai 54   Arkhangel'sk
Constructor I. V. James
Laid down   16.6.1747   *Launched*   8.5.1748
Dimensions 143 ft x 38 ft x 16 ft 7 in
Armament   LD 22 x 18pdrs
             UD 24 x 8pdrs
             FC & QD 8 x 4pdrs (1724 'Establishment')
Pyotr II class. Sailed from Arkhangel'sk to Revel' in 7–10.1748. Carried baggage of Russian troops being evacuated from Danzig to Revel' in 1749. Cruised in the Baltic in 1750–3. Converted into a hospital ship in 1757, participated in the blockade of Prussia off Memel, transported 216 sick and injured to Revel', returned to the blockade, cruised off Sweden, and suffered storm damage. Sent to operate off the Sound off Copenhagen in 1758 as part of the Russo-Swedish squadron awaiting the expected arrival of the British fleet and then assigned to transport sick and injured soldiers to Revel'. Operated off Danzig in 1759 and off Kolberg in 1761. Determined to be in poor condition in 1762. Broken up after 1763.

Varakhail 54   Arkhangel'sk
Constructor A. Sutherland
Laid down   27.4.1748   *Launched*   15.5.1749
Dimensions 143 ft x 38 ft x 16 ft 7 in
Armament   LD 22 x 18pdrs
             UD 24 x 8pdrs
             FC & QD 8 x 4pdrs (1724 'Establishment')
Pyotr II class. Crossed the mouth of the North Dvina and capsized while anchoring for indeterminate reasons on 7.6.1749. 28 men were lost and 349 were saved.

Shlissel'burg 54   Arkhangel'sk
Constructor I. V. James
Laid down   24.8.1749   *Launched*   28.4.1751
Dimensions 143 ft x 38 ft x 16 ft 7 in
Armament   LD 22 x 18pdrs
             UD 24 x 8pdrs
             FC & QD 8 x 4pdrs (1724 'Establishment')
Pyotr II class. Sailed from Arkhangel'sk to Revel' in 6–8.1751. Cruised in the Baltic in 1752–6. Blockaded Memel, Danzig, and Pillau in 1757. Cruised in the Sound off Copenhagen to block the expected intervention of the British navy in 1758. Transported troops to Danzig in 1759. Bombarded Kolberg in 1760. Carried troops to Kolberg and participated in the siege of Kolberg in 1761. Carried sick and supplies from Pillau to Kronshtadt in 1762. Participated in the visit of Catherine II in 1764. Decommissioned in 1764. Broken up in 1765.

Varakhail 54   Arkhangel'sk
Constructor I. V. James
Laid down   4.6.1751   *Launched*   30.4.1752
Dimensions 143 ft x 38 ft x 16 ft 7 in
Armament   LD 22 x 18pdrs
             UD 24 x 8pdrs
             FC & QD 8 x 4pdrs (1724 'Establishment')
Pyotr II class. Name commemorates the previous *Varakhail* that capsized in 1749. Sailed from Arkhangel'sk to Kronshtadt in 7–9.1752. Cruised in the Baltic in 1754 and 1756. Blockaded Danzig, Memel and

Pillau in 1757. Cruised in the Sound off Copenhagen to block the expected intervention of the British navy in 1758. Escorted store ships to Pillau and transported troops to Danzig in 1759. Bombarded Kolberg in 1760. Transported troops to Kolberg and bombarded Kolberg in 1761. Escorted store ships from Revel' to Kronshtadt in 1762. Broken up in 1763.

Neptunus 54 Arkhangel'sk
Constructor I. V. James
Laid down 29.4.1757   *Launched* 20.5.1758
Dimensions 143 ft x 40 ft x 16 ft 7 in
Armament   LD 22 x 18pdrs
             UD 24 x 8pdrs
             FC & QD 8 x 4pdrs (1724 'Establishment')

Pyotr II class. Note increase in breadth for *Neptunus* and *Gorod Arkhangel'sk*. Sailed from Arkhangel'sk to Revel' in 7–8.1757. Transported troops from Revel' to Danzig in 1759. Bombarded Kolberg and transported sick and injured to Revel' and Kronhshtadt in 1760. Transported troops to Kolberg and escorted supplies from Pillau to Kolberg. In 1761. Transported troops from Kolberg to Revel' in 1762. Cruised in the Baltic in 1764. Decommissioned in 1764. Broken up after 1771.

Gorod Arkhangel'sk 54 Arkhangel'sk
Constructor I. V. James
Laid down 25.5.1760   *Launched* 29.5.1761
Dimensions 143 ft x 40 ft x 16 ft 7 in
Armament   LD 22 x 18pdrs
             UD 24 x 8pdrs
             FC & QD 8 x 4pdrs (1724 'Establishment')

Pyotr II class. Note increase in breadth for *Neptunus* and *Gorod Arkhangel'sk*. Sailed from Arkhangel'sk to Kronshtadt in 7–9.1762. Cruised to Norway with naval cadets in 1763. Cruised in the Baltic in 1764. Cruised to Copenhagen in 1769. Cruised the Baltic in 1770 and 1773. Decommissioned in 1773. Broken up after 1774.

The final member of the *Pyotr II* class falls chronologically within the reign of Catherine II. It is included here for reasons of class continuity

Aziia 54 Arkhangel'sk
Constructor I. V. James
Laid down 27.2.1764   *Launched* 13.6.1766
Dimensions 143 ft x 38 ft x 16 ft 7 in
Armament 1766 LD 22 x 18pdrs
                  UD 24 x 8pdrs
                  FC & QD 8 x 4pdrs (1724 'Establishment')
            1770 LD 20 x 18pdrs, 2 x 48u (1 pood)
                  UD 22 x 8pdrs, 2 x 24u (½ pood)
                  FC & QD 8 x 4pdrs

Pyotr II class. Sailed from Arkhangel'sk to Kronshtadt 7–10.1768. Cruised in the Baltic in 1769 and escorted the First Arkhipelago Squadron to Copenhagen. Rearmed with two 48pdr edinorogs and two 24pdr edinorogs in 1770 taken from *Tver'* (66). On 15.6.1770 left Revel' as part of Rear-Adm. Arf's 3rd Arkhipelago Squadron proceeding to the Mediterranean by way of Copenhagen, the English Channel, Gibraltar, Port Mahon, and Sicily. Arrived at Auza on 25.12.1770. Bombarded Mitileno and landed troops in 1771. Blockaded the Dardanelles and underwent repairs at Auza in 1772. Departed the island of Mikono on 7.2.1773 en route to the Imbros peninsula. Lost with all 439 crew members off Mikono on 9.2.1773.

Baltic line of battle ships purchased abroad (18 purchased 1696–1761)

During the early years of Russian naval expansion, when Russian shipbuilding was in its developmental period, Peter I augmented limited domestic warship construction with the purchase of a heterogeneous collection of foreign warships available on the open market in Europe. Between 1711 and 1721, a total of eighteen newly built and second-hand line of battle ships were acquired by Russia from friendly and neutral European nations. With one exception, the French-built *Leferm*, these ships were of limited size and firepower by the prevailing standards of the day. Nine of these ships came from England, six from the Netherlands, two from France and one from Hamburg. Five of the Dutch ships were actually purpose-built for Russia, but the remaining thirteen acquired ships were a mixed bag of second-hand castoffs of sometimes dubious value. It had been the original intent of Peter I and his representative, Prince Kurakin, to have *Portsmut*, *Devonshir* and *Marl'burg* built in England, but lower construction costs in the Netherlands led to their being built there – even while retaining their British names. Only 15 of the purchased ships actually saw useful service under the Russian flag. One unfortunate, *Bulinbruk* (ex-*Sussex*), was captured by Sweden while still in transit to join the Baltic fleet, while the final purchased ship, *Nishtadt*, was wrecked prior to even reaching Russian waters. Four of the ships that did enter Russian service were wrecked, while one particularly unfortunate vessel, *Oksford*, was found to be unsound and unfit for active service during the course of her maiden voyage and sold without accomplishing anything to recoup the cost of her purchase.

Sviatoi Antonii (*Paduanskiy*) 50/52 Hamburg
Laid down ?   *Launched* ?
Purchased 1711
Dimensions 113 ft 6 in x 43 ft 11 in x 13 ft 3 in
Armament ?
            323 men (1714)

Purchased in Hamburg in 1711 and originally known as *Antonio di Padua*. Arrived at Revel' in 3.1713 after transit from Copenhagen. Cruised in the Baltic 1713–15. Converted into a store ship in 1716. Lost in a storm off Revel' on 10.11.1716.

Randol'f 50 England
Laid down ?   *Launched* ?
Purchased 1712
Dimensions 127 ft 6 in x 32 ft x 13 ft 2½ in
Armament 1715 LD 20 x 18pdrs
                  UD 20 x 6pdrs
                  FC & QD 10 x 3pdrs
                  320 men (1714) (*Materialy*)
            1720 LD 10 x 18pdrs, 10 x 12pdrs
                  UD 20 x 6pdrs
                  FC & QD 8 x 3pdrs
                  250 men (*Materialy*)

Purchased in England in 1712. Arrived at Revel' on 2.3.1713 after transit from Copenhagen. Cruised in the Baltic 1713–15. Training ship in Kronshtadt Roads in 1717. At Hamburg in 1718–19. Cruised 1720–4. Ordered to be broken up in 1725, but listed to 1728.

Bulinbruk (ex-*Sussex*) 46/50 England
Laid down ?   *Launched* 1704
Purchased 1712

Dimensions 120 ft x (95 ft k.) x 29 ft 6 in x ?
Armament ?
Former *Sussex*, purchased in England in 1712. Captured by Sweden in 1713 while transiting unarmed to Russia.

Viktoriia (ex-*Vainqueur*) 40/60 Bristol
Laid down ?   *Launched* ?
Purchased 1712
Dimensions 127 ft 6 in x 35 ft 8 in x 14 ft
Armament Actual 10 x 12pdrs, 24 x 6pdrs, 6 x 4pdrs
450 men (1714) (*Materialy*)
Planned 24 x 12pdrs, 28 x 6pdrs, 12 4pdrs

Former *Vainqueur*, purchased in Bristol in 1712. Arrived at Revel' on 23.5.1713. Cruised in the Baltic in 1713–15. Reduced to a store ship in 1716, cruising as such in 1717 and 1719. Converted to a pram in 1719. Transported cargo and passengers to Revel' and Rogervik in 1725 and to Kiel in 1731. Nominally reclassified as a ship of the line in 1734 and used to carry powder and ammunition to Danzig. Transported supplies to Kronshtadt in 1735–6. Listed to 1740 but broken up after 1739.

Oksford (ex-*Tankerville*) 50 England
Laid down ?   *Launched* ?
Purchased 1712
Dimensions 114 ft x 30 ft 1 in x 14 ft
Armament Planned LD 18 x 12pdrs, 4 x 9pdrs
MD 20 x 8pdrs
FC & QD 8 x 3pdrs
Actual 4 x 9pdrs, 20 x 6pdrs, 8 x 3pdrs
320 men (1714) (*Materialy*)

Former *Tankerville* (32) of 450 tons, purchased in England in 1712. Cruised in the Baltic in 1713–14. Sent to London in 10.1715 to escort newly purchased ships to Russia. Found unfit for the return journey in 1716 and sold in London in 1717.

Straford (ex-*Wintworth*) 50 England
Laid down ?   *Launched* 1701
Purchased 1712
Dimensions 104 ft x 28 ft 1 in x 12 ft
Armament 1713 18 x 6pdrs, 6 x 3pdrs (*Materialy*)
1714 13 x 8pdrs, 20 x 6pdrs
Planned 20 x 9pdrs, 18 x 6pdrs, 8 x 3pdrs

Former *Wintworth* purchased in England in 1712. Arrived at Revel' in 1.6.1713. Cruised in the Baltic in 1713–14. Travelled to England, Holland and Germany between 8.1715 and 7.1716 to transport purchased munitions to Russia. Converted into a hospital ship in 1717. Converted into a 30-gun pram in 1719. Converted a second time into a hospital ship in 1721. Converted into a fire ship in 1727. Broken up after 1732.

Leferm (ex-*Le Ferme*) 62/66/70/74 Rochefort, France
Constructors   H. Malet & P. Masson
Laid down 1698   *Launched* 6.1700
Purchased 11.1713
Dimensions 1714 151 ft (lgd) x (136 ft keel) x 39 ft x 18 ft (British measure)
154 ft 1 in x 44 ft 2¼ in x 17 ft 11¼ in
154 ft 10 in x 44 ft x 17 ft 11 in (Veselago)
147 ft 4 in x (130 ft k) x 40 ft 9 in x 16 ft 6 in (French measure (Demerliac)
Armament (1714 as purchased)   LD 26 x 24pdrs
UD 28 x 12pdrs

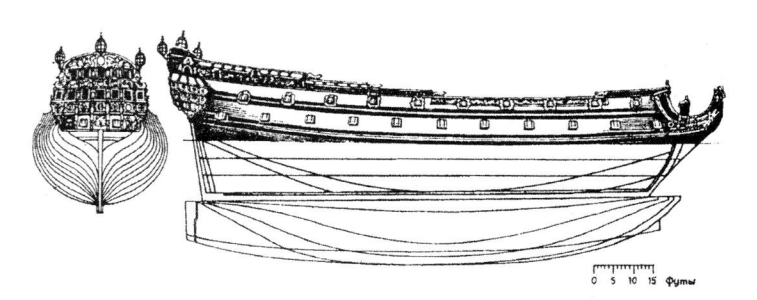

This is a drawing of Straford, *the former British* Wintworth, *built in 1701 and purchased in 1712, one of a grab bag of 50-gun ships purchased on the European market by a ship-hungry Peter I locked in combat with Charles XII of Sweden. Her mercantile origins are revealed in her armament as delivered: 18 x 6pdrs and 6 x 3pdrs, hardly worthy for a ship rated as a 50. She never reached her officially rated armament of 50 guns, carrying only 33 in 1714, still well short of the proposed armament of 46.*

FC & QD 20 x 6pdrs
518 men
1715 LD 14 x 24pdrs, 12 x 18pdrs
UD 28 x 12pdrs
FC & QD 12 x 6pdrs
518 men (1714) (*Materialy*)

Former French *Le Ferme*, with the distinction of being the only foreign purchase to carry her original name into Russian service. Captured by England at Vigo in 10.1702 and sold to Russia in 11.1713. The largest of the 1713 war purchases. Arrived at Revel' on 9.6.1714. Cruised in the Baltic in 1714–15. Commissioned in Kronshtadt Roads in 1716. Cruised in the Baltic in 1717–18. Repaired and resheathed in 1719–23. Based on the testimony of her commander in 1734, she emerged from her great repair as a 74. Training duty in Kronshtadt Roads in 1723. Cruised in the Baltic in 1725. Defensive duty at Kronshtadt against the combined Anglo-Danish squadron under Adm. Wagner in 1726. In Kronshtadt Roads in 1728. Cruised in the Baltic in 1729, 1732, and 1733. Cruised to Danzig in 1734. Condemned in 1736. Ordered broken up in 1737, but still listed to 1740.

Fortuna (ex-*Fortune*) 48/50 Toulon/France
Constructor F. Coulomb
Laid down 1695   *Launched* 1696
Purchased 1713
Dimensions 126 ft x (105 ft k) x 31 ft x 13 ft 6 in

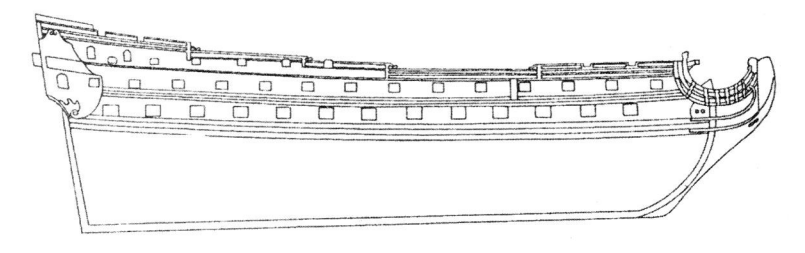

The French Leferm, *(70) of 1700, was the largest of the 1713 war purchases and, for several years the most powerful capital ship in the Baltic fleet. She was highly regarded in Russian service and was rebuilt as a 74 at the end of the Great Northern War, managing to soldier on through the early 1730s.*

108 ft x (80 ft k) x 29 ft x 12 ft 6 in French measure (Demerliac)
Armament 1716 18pdrs/8pdrs/3pdrs
300 men (323 in 1714)

Former French *Fortune* (36), sold to England in 1700, purchased by Russia in England in 1713. Arrived at Revel' on 30.4.1714. Cruised in the Baltic in 1714–16. At Copenhagen in July and August 1716 as part of the 'Great Armament of 1716' comprising 15 Russian ships of the line, 19 British, 19 Danish and 6 Dutch. Wrecked in a storm at Revel' on 11.11.1716.

Armont (ex-*Ormonde*) 44/48/50 England
Laid down ?   *Launched* ?
Purchased 1713
Dimensions 112 ft 7 in x 30 ft 4 in x 13 ft 7 in
Armament 1715   LD 20 x 12pdrs
UD 20 x 6pdrs
FC & QD 8 x 3pdrs (*Materialy*)
330 men (1714)

Former *Ormonde*, constructed in England but purchased in the Hague in 1713. Arrived at Revel' on 30.4.1714. Cruised in the Baltic in 1714–16. Stationed as a training ship in Kronshtadt Roads in 1716. Transported cargo to Venice in 9.1719. Wintered at Bergen in 1718–19 and returned to Kronshtadt in.5.1719. Cruised in the Baltic in 1720–3 and 1725. Commissioned in Kronshtadt Roads in 1726. Cruised in the Baltic in 1727. Disarmed at Revel' 1728–33. Moved to Kronshtadt in 7.1733. Participated in the Danzig expedition in 1734. Carried supplies from Riga to Kronshtadt in 1735. Broken up in 1747.

Arondel' (ex-*Arundel*) 44/48/50 England
Laid down ?   *Launched* ?
Purchased 1713
Dimensions 113 ft 6 in x 30 ft 1 in x 13 ft 6½ in
Armament 1713   LD 22 x 12pdrs
UD 22 x 6pdrs 8 x 3pdrs
200 men (*Materialy*)
1715   LD 20 x 12pdrs
UD 20 x 6pdrs
FC & QD 8 x 3pdrs

Former *Arundel*, purchased in England in 1713. Arrived at Revel' on 30.4.1714. Cruised in the Baltic 1714–16. At Copenhagen in July and August 1716 as part of the 'Great Armament of 1716' comprising 15 Russian Ships of the line, 19 British, 19 Danish, and 6 Dutch. At Copenhagen in 1717. Cruised in the Baltic in 1718–22. In 1722, she was involved in an unsuccessful attempt at refloating the grounded *Nishtadt*, but managed to salvage her guns. Cruised in the Baltic in

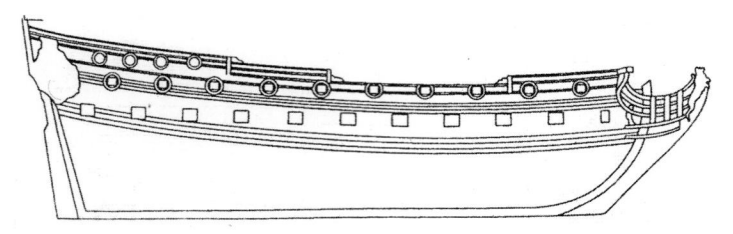

A profile of Fortuna, *50, purchased 1713. Completed for the French navy in 1696 by the accomplished French shipwright F. Coulomb, sold to England in 1700, and finally resold to Russia when in her dotage. Her history speaks volumes about the urgency of Peter I's need to acquire useful warships to fill the void while his own building programmes were still gaining momentum.*

1723, 1725 and 1726. Reclassified as a frigate in 1727. Carried the Duke of Holstein and his wife, Peter I's daughter Ann, to Kiel in 1727. Experienced problems with leaking during voyage to Kiel and returned to Russia in 1728. Cruised in the Baltic in 1731 and 1733. Cruised to Danzig in 1734. Carried supplies in 1735. Cruised in the Baltic in 1737 and 1738. Determined to be rotten in 1738. Broken up in 1747.

Perl (ex-*Groote Perel*) 48/50 Holland
Laid down ?   *Launched* 1706
Purchased 1713
Dimensions 120 ft x 36 ft 2 in x 13 ft 10½ in
Armament 1715   LD 20 x 18pdrs
UD 20 x 8pdrs
FC & QD 10 x 4pdrs
226 men (330 men in 1714) (*Materialy*)
1720   LD 24 x 12pdrs
UD 24 x 6pdrs
FC & QD 4 x 4pdrs
300 men (*Materialy*)

Former Dutch *Groote Perel*, purchased in Holland in 1713. Arrived at Revel' in 7.1714. Cruised in the Baltic in 1714–15. To Holland in 8.1715. Escorted *Iagudiil* to Norway in 1716, wintering in Copenhagen. Cruised in the Baltic in 1717–27. Disarmed at Kronshtadt 1728–33. Participated in the Danzig expedition in 1734 and converted into a hospital hulk.

London 54 England
Laid down ?   *Launched* 1707
Purchased 1714
Dimensions ?
Armament ?

Purchased in England in 1714. Arrived at Revel' 19.6.1715. Cruised in the Baltic in 1715 and 1717–19. Wrecked off the island of Kotlin in a storm on 1.10.1719. The site of her loss has been since known as Londonskaya Bank.

Marl'burg 60/64 Amsterdam
Laid down 6.1714   *Launched* 11.1714
Dimensions 145 ft 8 in x 42 ft 8 in x 16 ft 2 in (Veselago)
145 ft 10 in x 43 ft 2 in x 17 ft (Apraksin)
Armament 1716   LD 26 x 24pdrs
UD 24 x 12pdrs
FC & QD 12 x 6pdrs
450 men (*Materialy*)

Built for Russia in Amsterdam. Wintered in England in 1715–16. Arrived at Copenhagen on 31.5.1716 to participate in the 'Great Armament of 1716'. Cruised in the Baltic in 1717–19 and 1721–5. Training duty in Kronshtadt Roads in 1728. Disarmed from 1728–33. Participated in the Danzig expedition of 1734. Reduced to a harbour hulk in 1735. Hospital ship from 1739–47. Broken up in 1747. (Note the differences in dimensions between Veselago and Apraksin.)

Britaniia 44/50 England
Laid down ?   *Launched* 1707
Purchased 1714
Dimensions 118 ft 3 in x 31 ft x 13 ft 3½ in
Armament 1720   LD 20 x 12pdrs
UD 22 x 6pdrs
FC & QD 8 x 4pdrs
250 men (*Materialy*)

Former *Great Allen*, purchased in England in 1714. Arrived at Revel'

THE BALTIC FLEET 1696–1761

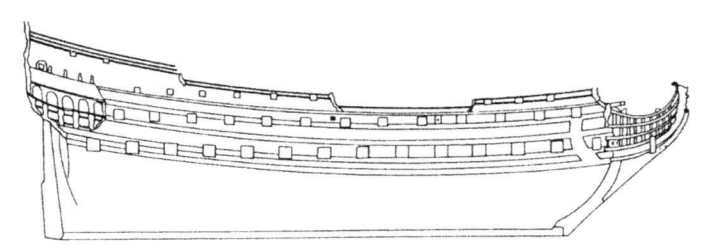

A ship built on order for Russia in the Netherlands, with the name of one of Great Britain's finest generals, Marl'burg (60) of 1714 has a look that reveals her Dutch ancestry. Her English name reflects the fact that the original intent was that she be built in English shipyards. The transfer of the contract for this ship and other Dutch-built Russian warships with British names reflects the urgency of the Russian need for quickly produced hulls at this time. While Dutch ship design had fallen behind that of Great Britain, they were still able to build sturdy ships quickly and cheaply.

on 19.6.1715. Cruised in the Baltic in 1715 and in 1717–20. Escorted four captured Swedish frigates to Kronshtadt in 1720. Cruised in the Baltic in 1722 and 1724. At Revel' in 1726 as a defence against the Anglo-Danish squadron under Adm. Wagner. Converted to a pram in 1728. Last listed in 1729.

Portsmut 54 Amsterdam
Laid down 6.1714 *Launched* 11.1714
Dimensions ?
Armament 1716 LD 18pdrs
              UD 8pdrs
              FC & QD 3pdrs (probable conjecture)
Built for Russia in Amsterdam. Arrived at Copenhagen on 31.5.1716 with *Devonshir* as part of the 'Great Armament of 1716'. Cruised in the Baltic in 1717–19. Wrecked in company with *London* on 1.10.1719.

Devonshir 52 Amsterdam
Constructor O. Solovyov
Laid down 6.1714 *Launched* 11.1714
Dimensions 128 ft x 37 ft 10 in x 14 ft 6 in
Armament 1716 LD 18pdrs
              UD 8pdrs
              FC & QD 3pdrs
              305 men
Built for Russia in Amsterdam. Arrived at Copenhagen on 31.5.1716 with *Portsmut* as part of the 'Great Armament of 1716'. Cruised in the Baltic in 1717–19 and 1721–3. Prepared in 1724 for expedition to Spain and Portugal. Departed Revel' on the 'Spanish Expedition' in 1726, arriving at Cadiz in 18.8.1726 and at Lisbon on 16.11.1726. Left Santander on 11.3.1726 and arrived at Kronshtadt on 14.5.1726. Repaired in 1727. Transferred to Kiel in 1731. Participated in the Danzig expedition of 1734 but was considered too weak by this time to stand in line of battle. Carried cargo between Riga and Kronshtadt in 1735–6. Decommissioned in 1737, but listed until 1740.

Prints Evgenii 50 Amsterdam
Constructor R. Devenport (Robert Davenport)
Laid down 3.1720 *Launched* 1721
Dimensions 133 ft 2 in x 37 ft 6 in x 15 ft 4 in
Armament LD 18pdrs
            UD 8pdrs
            FC & QD 3/4pdrs (probable)

Built in Amsterdam by order of Prince Kurakin. Arrived at Revel' from Amsterdam in 1722. Cruised in the Baltic in 1723. Prepared in 1724 for aborted expedition to Madagascar. Cruised in the Baltic in 1725–6. To Kiel as escort for the Duke of Holstein and his wife, Tsarina Ann in 1727. Stationed in the Revel' Roads in 1728. Cruised to Kiel in 1731. Stationed in the Revel' Roads in 1732. Transferred to Kronshtadt in 1733 and condemned. Rigging removed to outfit new ships. Broken up after 1739 and listed to 1740.

Nishtadt 56 Rotterdam
Constructor ?
Laid down 1720 *Launched* 1721
Dimensions 133 ft x 36 ft x 15 ft 4 in
Armament LD 18pdrs
            UD 8pdrs
            FC & QD 3pdrs (probable)
Built in Amsterdam by order of Prince Kurakin. Purpose-built at Rotterdam, but grounded off Esel in transit to Russia on 12.11.1721. Guns and rigging salvaged in 1722 after unsuccessful attempts at freeing her were abandoned.

Baltic frigates (40 built, purchased 1696–1761)

Prototype

Sviatoe Prorochestvo 44 Rotterdam
Laid down 1694 *Launched* 1694
Dimensions ?
Armament ?
A small frigate built at the order of Peter I at Rotterdam in 1694 with 44 guns on the upper deck and falling outside of the proper scope of this book. Included here for the sake of complete coverage and as the first warship authorized for what developed into Peter I's navy after 1696. Arrived at Arkhangel'sk in 8.1694. Local escort of merchant ships. Converted to a merchant ship after 1695.

Standard frigates

During the first half of the eighteenth century, the term frigate was loosely applied to any armed three-masted square rigged warship of significant size and intended for cruising, scouting, and escort work as distinct from battle line employment. The Russians completed a heterogeneous collection of 37 frigates prior to 1761, ranging from 65 ft to 136 ft in length. Ships built after 1720 were armed with 12pdrs, but the earliest ships carried 6- and 8pdrs.

Frigate no. 1 Unnamed (later *Etna*) 18 Syass'kaya
Constructor W. Waterson
Laid down 5.1702 *Launched* 9.1702
Dimensions 65 ft x 18 ft 9 in x 8 ft 6 in
Armament 18 light guns in an open battery
Built of green timber and difficult to steer. Converted to a fire ship and renamed *Etna* in 1705. Cruised to Kronshlot in 1705–7. Participated in the defence of Kronshtadt against the Swedish fleet in 6–7.1705.

Frigate no. 2 Unnamed (later *Vesuvii*) 18 Syass'kaya
Constructor W. Waterson
Laid down 5.1702 *Launched* 9.1702
Dimensions 65 ft x 18 ft 9 in x 8 ft 6 in
Armament 18 light guns in an open battery
Built of green timber and difficult to steer. Converted to a fire ship and renamed *Vesuvii* in 1705. Cruised to Kronshlot in 1705–7. Participated

Although a minor warship by British standards, the frigate Shtandart *seen here off St Petersburg in 1703 giving and receiving salutes was the capital ship of the young Russian navy. Of interest are the carved wreaths around the upper and lower gunports and the presence of a spritsail topmast, common features for the period, but in the process of being phased out elsewhere. The use of oak-leaf wreaths was officially eliminated in 1703 in England by the Admiralty, but remained popular even in the face of official disapproval, particularly among modelmakers of the period who have added an element of confusion to later generations of naval enthusiasts by placing them on ships that, in actuality, never carried them! The ships behind* Shtandart *in this modern painting can only have been the smaller and earlier Frigate 1 and Frigate 2, soon to be converted into fireships and appropriately named (or renamed)* Etna *and* Vesiviy. Shtandart *would find herself in action against Swedish warships just two years later in 1705, while the first true 50-gun line of battle ships would not be laid down for the Baltic fleet until 1708.*

in the defence of Kronshtadt against the Swedish fleet in 6–7.1705.

Shtandart 28 Olononetskaya

Constructor V. Gerens
Laid down 24.3.1703 Launched 22.8.1703
Dimensions 90 ft x 24 ft x 9 ft (Dutch measurements)
83.5 ft x 22.3 ft x 8.35 ft (English measurements)
Armament MD 18/20 x 6pdrs
FC & QD 10/8 x 3pdrs (conjecture based on gun calibres carried)

Built of green timber. Gun deck believed to have been covered. Sailed to St Petersburg in 9.1703. Cruised in the Baltic in 1705–9. Operated with Vice-Adm. Kruys' squadron in 5–10.6.1705 and exchanged fire with Swedish ships in defence of Kronshtadt. Found unfit in 1709. Repaired in 1709–11. Relaunched on 4.7.1711. Cruised in the Baltic in 1712–13. Harbour service in 1714. Brought ashore as a memorial in 1725. Broken up in 1730.

Mikhail Arkhangel class (2 ships)
Mikhail Arkhangel 28 Syass'kaya
Constructor W. Waterson
Laid down 11.1702 Launched 1704
Dimensions 94 ft x 24 ft 6 in x 11 ft 5 in
Armament MD 18/20 x 6pdrs
FC & QD 10/8 x 3pdrs (conjecture based on gun calibres carried)

Mikhail Arkhangel class. Sailed to St Petersburg in 1704. Cruised in the Baltic in 1705–10. Operated with Vice-Adm. Kruys's squadron in 5–10.6.1705 and exchanged fire with Swedish ships in defence of Kronshtadt. Escorted transports to Biork-e zund in 1710. Broken up after 1710.

Ivan-Gorod 28 Syass'kaya
Constructor W. Waterson
Laid down 31.10.1702 Launched 24.5.1705
Dimensions 94 ft x 24 ft 6 in x 11 ft 5 in
Armament MD 18/20 x 6pdrs
FC & QD 10/8 3pdrs (conjecture based on gun calibres carried)

Mikhail Arkhangel class. Sailed to St Petersburg in 1705. Cruised in the Baltic in 1706–10 and wintered in the Neva River. Escorted transports to Biork-e zund in 1710. Broken up after 1710.

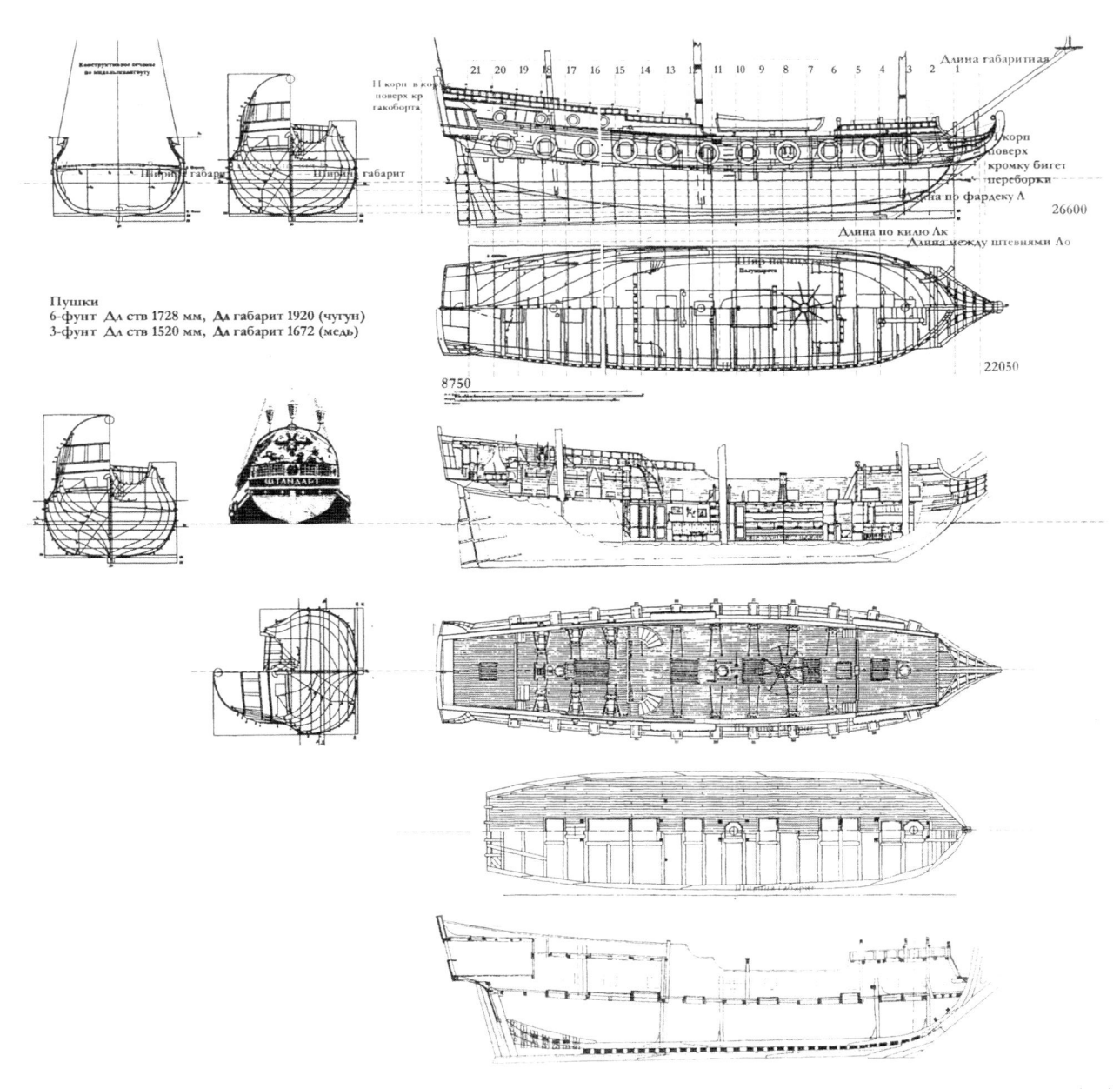

THE BALTIC FLEET 1696–1761

A highly detailed series of profiles and sections for Shtandart, *as completed for the Baltic fleet in 1703. The drawing shows not only the underwater lines of the ship, but also the layout and arrangement of the interior decks. The main deck guns are here shown exposed to the weather amidships, but there is some controversy over whether this was actually the case or whether they were in fact completely decked over.*

Shlissel'burg class (7 ships)
These small and lightly armed cruising ships represent Russia's first venture into the series production of warships. They accomplished little during their short service lives and none remained in commission after 1711, although three were designated as fire ships in 1710.

Shlissel'burg 28 Olononetskaya
Constructor V. Gerens
Laid down 18.10.1703 *Launched* 27.7.1704
Dimensions 92 ft x 22 ft x 9 ft 5 in
Armament MD 18/20 x 6pdrs
FC & QD 10/8 x 3pdrs (conjecture based on gun calibres carried)
Shlissel'burg class. Wintered at Lake Ladoga in 1704–5. Arrived at St Petersburg in 1705. Cruised in the Baltic in 1705–10. Escorted transports to Biork-e zund. Broken up after 1710.

Peterburg 28 Olononetskaya
Constructor V. Gerens
Laid down 12.11.1703 *Launched* 6.8.1704
Dimensions 92 ft x 22 ft x 9 ft 5 in
Armament MD 18/20 x 6pdrs
FC & QD 10/8 x 3pdrs (conjecture based on gun calibres carried)
Shlissel'burg class. Sailed to St Petersburg in 1704. Cruised in the Baltic in 1705–10. Operated with Vice-Adm. Kruys's squadron in 5–10.6.1705 and exchanged fire with Swedish ships in defence of Kronshtadt. Escorted transports to Biork-e zund in 1710. Broken up after 1710.

Kronshlot 28 Olononetskaya
Constructors P. Kornilisen & Emb
Laid down 8.10.1703 *Launched* 6.8.1704
Dimensions 92 ft x 22 ft x 9 ft 5 in
Armament MD 18/20 x 6pdrs
FC & QD 10/8 x 3pdrs (conjecture based on gun calibres carried)
Shlissel'burg class. Named after a fort near the island of Kotlin. Sailed to St Petersburg in 1704. Cruised in the Baltic in 1705–10. Operated with Vice-Adm. Kruys's squadron in 5–10.6.1705 and exchanged fire with Swedish ships in defence of Kronshtadt. Escorted transports to Biork-e zund in 1710. Broken up after 1710.

Triumf 28 Olononetskaya
Constructor K. Bureing
Laid down 12.11.1703 *Launched* 4.8.1704
Dimensions 92 ft x 22 ft x 9 ft 5 in
Armament MD 18/20 x 6pdrs
FC & QD 10/8 x 3pdrs (conjecture based on gun calibres carried)
Shlissel'burg class. Sailed to St Petersburg in 1704. Cruised in the Baltic in 1705–10. Operated with Vice-Adm. Kruys's squadron in 5–10.6.1705 and exchanged fire with Swedish ships in defence of Kronshtadt. Converted into a fire ship in 1710.

Derpt 28 Olononetskaya
Constructors P. Kornilisen & Emb
Laid down 8.10.1703 *Launched* 13.8.1704
Dimensions 92 ft x 22 ft x 9 ft 5 in
Armament MD 18/20 x 6pdrs
FC & QD 10/8 x 3pdrs (conjecture based on gun calibres carried)
Shlissel'burg class. Named after a city taken from Sweden in 1704. Sailed to St Petersburg in 1704. Cruised in the Baltic in 1705-10. Operated with Vice-Adm. Kruys's squadron in 5–10.6.1705 and exchanged fire with Swedish ships in defence of Kronshtadt. Converted into a fire ship in 1710.

Narva 28 Olononetskaya
Constructor K. Bureing
Laid down 8.10.1703 *Launched* 13.8.1704
Dimensions 92 ft x 22 ft x 9 ft 5 in
Armament MD 18/20 x 6pdrs
FC & QD 10/8 x 3pdrs (conjecture based on gun calibres carried)
Shlissel'burg class. Named after a Swedish fortress taken in 1704. Sailed to St Petersburg in 1704. Cruised in the Baltic in 1705–10. Operated with Vice-Adm. Kruys's squadron in 5–10.6.1705 and exchanged fire with Swedish ships in defence of Kronshtadt. Broken up after 1710.

Fligel'-Fam (*Fligel' De Fam*) 28 Olononetskaya
Constructor F. S. Saltykov
Laid down 18.10.1703 *Launched* 24.9.1704
Dimensions 92 ft x 22 ft x 9 ft 5 in
Armament MD 18/20 x 6pdrs
FC & QD 10/8 x 3pdrs (conjecture based on gun calibres carried)
Shlissel'burg class. Sailed to St Petersburg. Cruised in the Baltic in 1705–9. Operated with Vice-Adm. Kruys's squadron in 5–10.6.1705 and exchanged fire with Swedish ships in defence of Kronshtadt. Converted into a fire ship in 1710.

Olifant 32 Olononetskaya
Constructor Peter I and V. Gerens
Laid down 2.10.1704 *Launched* 4.6.1705
Dimensions 109 ft 8 in x 28 ft 7 in x 10 ft 6 in or 116 ft x 30 ft x 9 ft
Armament MD 18/20 x 12pdrs
FC & QD 12/14 x 6pdrs (conjecture)
Designed by Peter I. Sailed to St Petersburg in 1705. Cruised in 1706–10 in the Baltic and wintered in the Neva River. Served as the flagship of the Baltic fleet in 1706–7. Escorted transports to Biork-e zund in 1710. Broken up after 1712.

Unnamed ? Olononetskaya
Constructor Varfolomeev
Laid down 12.4.1705 *Launched* ?
Dimensions 80 ft x (70 ft keel) x 34 ft x 9 ft
Armament ?
The builder died in 6.1705 and this ship was broken up incomplete due to the refusal of other builders to complete her.

Dumkrakht 32 Olononetskaya
Constructor V. Gerens
Laid down 9.7.1706 *Launched* 8.6.1707
Dimensions 110 ft x 32 ft 10 in x 13 ft
Armament MD 18/20 x 8pdrs
FC & Q 14/12 4/6pdrs (Conjecture)
Sailed to St Petersburg in 1704. Cruised in the Baltic in 1708–11. Replaced *Olifant* as flagship of the Baltic fleet in 1708. Escorted troopships to Biork-e zund in 5.1710. Broken up in 1713.

Sviatoi Pavel 32 Arkhangel'sk
Constructor V. Gerens
Laid down 1708 *Launched* 1710
Dimensions 105 ft x 29 ft x 13 ft 6 in
Armament MD 18/20 x 8pdrs
FC & QD 14/12 x 4/6pdrs (conjecture)
200 men (1714)
Departed Arkhangel'sk and forced to return due to storm damage. Arrived at Copenhagen in 1711. Cruised in the North Sea in 1711 and wintered at Copenhagen. Arrived at Riga in 9.1712. Cruised in the Baltic in 1713 and provided cover for the galley flotilla. Operated off Gogland in 1714 and carried Peter I from Revel' to Helsingfors. Carried troops to Gottland in 1715. Departed for Holland, forced into Copenhagen by a leak, and condemned there. Broken up in 1716.

Sviatoi Pyotr 32 Arkhangel'sk
Constructor V. Gerens
Laid down 1708 *Launched* 1710
Dimensions 105 ft x 29 ft x 13 ft 6 in
Armament MD 18/20 x 8pdrs
FC & QD 14/12 x 4/9pdrs (conjecture)
200 men
Sailed from Arkhangel'sk to Copenhagen in 1710. Cruised in the North Sea from Copenhagen in 1710–12. Arrived at Riga in 9.1712. Cruised in the Baltic in 1713 and provided cover for the galley flotilla. Operated off Gogland in 1714. Landed troops at Gottland in 1715. Cruised to Danzig in 1716. Broken up in 1719.

Sviatoi Il'ia 26 Arkhangel'sk
Constructor O. Nye (Joseph Noy)
Laid down 5.1702 *Launched* 1703
Dimensions 79 ft 9 in x 20 ft 4 in x 8 ft 2 in

Armament ?

Some sources have her as being laid down in 1708. Arrived at Copenhagen in 9.1710. Cruised in the North Sea from Copenhagen in 1710–12. Appointed flag to Peter I in 8.1712. Wrecked in 9.1712 en route to Riga.

Sviatoi Il'ia 30/32 St Petersburg
Constructor F. M. Sklyaev
Laid down 16.8.1713 *Launched* 06.5.1714
Dimensions ?
Armament 1715 12pdrs/6pdrs/3pdrs
170 men (200 in 1714)
18/20 x 12pdrs, 12/14 x 6pdrs (conjecture)

Replacement for the ship of the same name wrecked in 1712. Cruised in the Baltic in 1714–19. To Copenhagen in 1716 to participate in the 'Great Armament of 1716'. Landed troops at Gottland in 1717. Landed troops at Osel in 1719. Found unfit for service in 1720. Broken up in 1721.

Kreiser class (3 ships)

Kreiser (*Kruyser*) 32 St Petersburg
Constructor O. Nye (Joseph Noy)
Laid down 9.11.1721 *Launched* 23.6.1723
Dimensions 113 ft x 32 ft x 13 ft
Armament LD 20 x 12pdrs
UD 12 x 6pdrs (1723 Establishment)

Kreiser class. Sailed to Revel' in 1723. Cruised in the Baltic with the Revel' Squadron in 1724–30. Carried Count N. F. Golovin as ambassador to Stockholm in 1725. In company with *Rafail*, transported the body of Princess Anne, deceased eldest daughter of Peter I, from Holstein to Kronshtadt in 1728. Broken up in 1732.

Iakht-Khund 32 St Petersburg
Constructor O. Nye (Joseph Noy)
Laid down 2.11.1721 *Launched* 2.8.1724
Dimensions 113 ft x 32 ft x 13 ft
Armament LD 20 x 12pdrs
UD 12 x 6pdrs (1723 Establishment)

Kreiser class. Sailed to Kronshtadt in 1724. Cruised in the Baltic in 1725–6. Visited Stockholm in 1727. Cruised in the Baltic in 1728 and 1731. Sailed from Revel' to Kronshtadt in 1732. Found unfit in 1733. Ordered to be broken up in 1736. Last mentioned in 1740.

Vind-Hund 32 St Petersburg
Constructor R. Ramz
Laid down ? *Launched* 28.9.1724
Dimensions 113 ft x 32 ft x 13 ft
Armament LD 20 x 12pdrs
UD 12 x 6pdrs (1723 Establishment)

Kreiser class. Cruised in the Baltic in 1725–7. Transported Princess Anne and the Duke of Holstein to Kiel in Rear-Adm. Seniavin's squadron in 1727. Departed Kronshtadt for Arkhangel'sk in the company of frigate *Rossiia* in 1730. Forced into Copenhagen with a severe leak and returned to Kronshtadt after being repaired. Found unfit in 1731. Ordered to be broken up in 1736. Last mentioned in 1740.

Rossiia 32 St Petersburg
Constructor R. Brown
Laid down 20.12.1724 *Launched* 2.5.1728
Dimensions 118 ft x 31 ft 6 in x 14 ft (1723 Establishment)
Armament LD 20 x 12pdrs
UD 12 x 6pdrs (1723 Establishment)

Prototype for the *Gektor* class. Built at St Petersburg and completed with 20 lower deck guns in contrast to the later ships of the type which were all built at Arkhangel'sk with only 18 lower deck guns. Cruised in the Baltic as flag to Adm. Sivers in 1729. To Arkhangel'sk in company with *Vind-Khund* in 1730 and forced to return due to *Vind-Khund*'s having developed a leak. To Arkhangel'sk and back in 1731. Cruised in the Baltic in 1732–3 and involved in a collision with *Shlissel'burg*, requiring repair of damage sustained. Participated in the Expedition to Danzig in 1734, during which she captured French privateer *Brilliant*. To Arkhangel'sk in 1735–6 during the course of which she wintered in Bergen. Repaired at the Solombala Yard at Arkhangel'sk in 1736–7. Operated against the Swedish fleet in 1741–3. Escorted store ships from Revel' to Stockholm in 1744. Searched for French capers off Gottland and Öland in 1745. Cruised in the Baltic in 1746–7. Carried the Duke of Holstein to Kiel in 1747. Broken up in 1752.

Vakhmeister 32/46 St Petersburg
Constructor R. Kosentz (Richard Cozens)
Laid down 1.1.1729 *Launched* 16.7.1732
Dimensions 120 ft x 32 ft x 14 ft 2 in
Armament LD 22 x 12pdrs
UD 14 x 6pdrs

French designed two-decker with 46 guns. Considered a failure as built and reduced to a 32-gun ship. Training duty in Kronshtadt Roads in 1732. To Arkhangel'sk and back in company with frigate *Dekrondelivde* in 1733–4. Carried supplies from Riga to Kronshtadt in 1735. Stationed in Kronshtadt Roads in 1736. Cruised in the Baltic in 1737. Repaired in 1738–9. Sailed from Revel' to Arkhangel'sk in 1741. Departed Arkhangel'sk en route to the Baltic with Vice-Adm. Bredal's squadron in 1742, but driven back due to a storm off Nordcap. Found unfit for further service in 1743. Condemned at Arkhangel'sk in 4.1744.

Mitau 32 St Petersburg
Constructor G. A. Okunev and I. S. Ramburg
Laid down 23.12.1731 *Launched* 28.5.1733
Dimensions 121 ft 6 in x 31 ft 4 in x 15 ft 2 in
Armament ?

French design. Cruised in the Baltic in 1733. Departed Kronshtadt for Danzig in 1734. Intercepted by a French squadron consisting of two ships of the line and three other ships under Barrailh and forced to surrender in 1734. Returned to Russia later that year with the resolution of the Danzig conflict. Repaired in 1738. Converted into a fire ship during the Russo-Swedish War of 1741–3, but retained the rigging and appearance of a frigate. Broken up in 1747.

Gektor class (16 ships)

Sixteen ships were laid down and completed to a common design at Arkhangel'sk between 1735 and 1768. The final five members of the *Gektor* class fall chronologically within the reign of Catherine II. They are included here for reasons of class continuity. They were patterned after *Rossiia* of 1728 and had similar dimensions, but apparently the early units were pierced for only 18 guns in contrast to the 20 carried by the *Rossiia* and the final 6 *Gektor*s. Both Russian Admiralty documents and the extant model of *Gektor* are in agreement that the first 5 ships at least were completed with only 18 x 12pdrs and 14 x 6pdrs in contrast to *Rossiia*'s slightly heavier armament. This may have been the case with the remaining class members, but certainty in this regards is lacking.

Although not in true frigates in in the manner of the French and British frigates with their unarmed lower decks, lower freeboards, and superior speed and weatherliness that began entering service after 1740, these ships represented the first large class of homogeneous cruising vessels to be built by the Russians and proved well suited for the duties assigned them. All sixteen had active service lives, being widely employed in typical cruiser roles involving cruising, escort work, amphibious support activities, blockade work, surveying, and occasional transport duties. None were lost in combat, but four were wrecked in active service *Vakhmeister*, *Arkhangel Mikhail*, *Merkurius* and *Gektor*.

Gektor 32 Arkhangel'sk
Constructor R. Kosentz (Richard Cozens)
Laid down 7.10.1735   *Launched* 30.5.1736
Dimensions 118 ft x 31 ft 6 in x 14 ft (1723 Establishment)
Armament   Planned LD 20 x 12pdrs
              UD 12 x 6pdrs (1723 Establishment)
              Probable as completed LD 18 x 12pdrs
              UD 14 x 6pdrs

Gektor class. Sailed from Arkhangel'sk to Kronshtadt in 1736. Cruised in the Baltic in 1737. Repaired in 1738. Cruised in the Baltic in 1739. Active in the Russo-Swedish war of 1741–2. Wrecked without casualties on an unknown reef off Gogland on 29.7.1742.

Voin 32 Arkhangel'sk
Constructor Ya. Brant
Laid down 1.9.1736   *Launched* 24.5.1737
Dimensions 118 ft x 31 ft 6 in x 14 ft (1723 Establishment)
Armament   Planned LD 20 x 12pdrs
              UD 12 x 6pdrs (1723 Establishment)
              Probable as completed LD 18 x 12pdrs
              UD 14 x 6pdrs

Gektor class. Sailed from Arkhangel'sk to Kronshtadt in 1737. Cruised in the Baltic in 1738 and 1739. Active in the Russo-Swedish war of 1741–2. Cruised in the Baltic in 1744. Cruised to Danzig in 1745. Cruised in the Baltic in 1746–8 and 1750. Broken up in 1755.

Kavaler 32 Arkhangel'sk
Constructor V. Batakov
Laid down 6.11.1736   *Launched* 5.7.1737
Dimensions 118 ft x 31 ft 6 in x 14 ft (1723 Establishment)
Armament   Planned LD 20 x 12pdrs
              UD 12 x 6pdrs (1723 Establishment)
              Probable as completed LD 18 x 12pdrs
              UD 14 x 6pdrs

Gektor class. Sailed from Arkhangel'sk to Kronshtadt in 1737. Cruised in the Baltic in 1738 and 1740. Sailed from Revel' to Arkhangel'sk in 5–7.1741. Departed for the Baltic in 1742 with Vice-Adm. Bredal's squadron, but forced back to Arkhangel'sk by bad weather. Returned to Kronshtadt in 11.1743. Cruised in the Baltic in 1744–8. Broken up in 1755.

Merkurius 32 Arkhangel'sk
Constructor A. Sutherland
Laid down 17.7.1739   *Launched* 11.5.1740
Dimensions 118 ft x 31 ft 6 in x 14 ft (1723 Establishment)
Armament   Planned LD 20 x 12pdrs
              UD 12 x 6pdrs (1723 Establishment)
              Probable as completed LD 18 x 12pdrs
              UD 14 x 6pdrs

Gektor class. Active in the Russo-Swedish war of 1741–3. Departed for the Baltic with Vice-Adm. Bredal's squadron in 1742, but forced back to Arkhangel'sk by bad weather. Departed again for the Baltic on 15.7.1743. Wrecked during a storm off Nordcap, Norway without casualties in 13.9.1743.

Apollon (Apollo) 32 Arkhangel'sk
Constructor I. V. James
Laid down 3.5.1739   *Launched* 18.5.1740
Dimensions 118 ft x 31 ft 6 in x 14 ft (1723 Establishment)
Armament   Planned LD 20 x 12pdrs
              UD 12 x 6pdrs (1723 Establishment)
              Probable as completed LD 18 x 12pdrs
              UD 14 x 6pdrs

Gektor class. Sailed from Arkhangel'sk to the Gulf of Kola in 7.1741 and wintered there. Prevented by storms from proceeding to the Baltic in both 1742 and 1743. Finally reached Kronstadt in 1744. Cruised in the Baltic in 1745–8. Cruised to Danzig in 1749. Hydrographic survey of the Baltic coastline in 1750–1. Broken up in 1756.

Iagudiil 32 Arkhangel'sk
Constructor I. V. James
Laid down 30.9.1745   *Launched* 21.5.1746
Dimensions 118 ft x 31 ft 6 in x 14 ft (1723 Establishment)
Armament   LD 20 x 12pdrs
              UD 12 x 6pdrs (1723 Establishment)
              Probable as completed LD 18 x 12pdrs
              UD 14 x 6pdrs

Gektor class. Sailed from Arkhangel'sk to Kronshtadt in 1746. Cruised in the Baltic in 1747–8. To Danzig in 1749. Cruised in the Baltic in 1750–3. Cruised to the North Sea to Skagen in 1755. Blockaded Memel with Adm. Mishukov's squadron in 1757. Blockaded the Sound off Copenhagen and Amager Island to prevent the Royal Navy from entering the Baltic in 1758. Broken up in 1760.

Selafail 32 Arkhangel'sk
Constructor P. G. Kachalov
Laid down 30.9.1745   *Launched* 21.5.1746
Dimensions 118 ft x 31 ft 6 in x 14 ft (1723 Establishment)
Armament   Planned LD 20 x 12pdrs
              UD 12 x 6pdrs (1723 Establishment)
              Probable as completed LD 18 x 12pdrs
              UD 14 x 6pdrs

Gektor class. Sailed from Arkhangel'sk to Kronshtadt in 7–10.1746. Cruised in the Baltic in 1747–8. To Danzig in 1749. Cruised in the Baltic in 1750–4. Cruised in the Kattegat in 1755. Blockaded Memel with Adm. Mishukov's squadron in 1757. Blockaded the Sound off Copenhagen and Amager Island to prevent the Royal Navy from entering the Baltic in 1758. Broken up in 1760.

Arkhangel Mikhail 32 Arkhangel'sk
Constructor A. Sutherland
Laid down 22.9.1747   *Launched* 8.8.1748
Dimensions 118 ft x 31 ft 6 in x 14 ft (1723 Establishment)
Armament   Planned LD 20 x 12pdrs
              UD 12 x 6pdrs (1723 Establishment)
              Probable as completed LD 18 x 12pdrs
              UD 14 x 6pdrs

Gektor class. Sailed from Arkhangel'sk to Kronshtadt in 7–9.1748. To Danzig in 1749. Hydrographic survey of the Gulf of Finland in 1750–1. Cruised in the Baltic in 1754–6. Cruised to Copenhagen and Danzig in 1757. Cruised off Amager Island and the Sound off Copenhagen to block the possible intervention of the Royal Navy in 1758. Transported troops to Danzig in 6–7.1759. Escorted 30 galiots to

Danzig in 1760 and returned to Kronshtadt. Departed Kronshtadt with another 26 galiots in 8.1759. Wrecked off Gogland in.5.8.1760 with no casualties. The abandoned frigate broke up on 20.8.1760.

Kreiser 32 Arkhangel'sk
Constructor I. V. James
Laid down 24.8.1749   *Launched* 28.4.1751
Dimensions 118 ft x 31 ft 6 in x 14 ft (1723 Establishment)
Armament   Planned LD 20 x 12pdrs
             UD 12 x 6pdrs (1723 Establishment)
             Probable as completed LD 18 x 12pdrs
             UD 14 x 6pdrs
Gektor class. Sailed from Arkhangel'sk to Kronshtadt in 6–9.1751. Cruised in the Baltic in 1754–5. Carried the Russian ambassador to Stockholm in 1756. Cruised in the Baltic in 1756–7 and participated in the blockade of Prussia. Cruised off Amager Island and the Sound off Copenhagen to block the possible intervention of the Royal Navy in 1758. Cruised off Pillau, escorted supply ships to Danzig, and carried wounded from Danzig to Revel' in 1759. Bombarded Kolberg in 1760. Broken up in 1763.

Rossiia 32 Arkhangel'sk
Constructor I. V. James
Laid down 25.4.1753   *Launched* 26.4.1754
Dimensions 118 ft x 31 ft 6 in x 14 ft (1723 Establishment)
Armament   Planned LD 20 x 12pdrs
             UD 12 x 6pdrs (1723 Establishment)
             Probable as completed LD 18 x 12pdrs
             UD 14 x 6pdrs
Gektor class. Replacement for the first *Rossiia*. Sailed from Arkhangel'sk to Kronshtadt in 6–8.1754. Cruised in the North Sea in 1755 and 1756. Participated in the blockade of Prussia and went to Stockholm in 1757. Cruised off Amager Island and the Sound off Copenhagen to block the possible intervention of the Royal Navy in 1758. Operated off Pilau and escorted supply ships to Danzig in 1759. Bombarded Kolberg in 1760. Carried troops to Kolberg and bombarded the city in 1761. Operated off the Kolberg Roads and escorted store ships from Riga to Revel' in 1762. Cruised in the Baltic in 1764–5 during the visit of Catherine II. Transported German settlers invited into Russia by Catherine II from Lübeck to Kronshtadt in 1766. Stationed in Kronshtadt Roads in 1767–8. Broken up in 1771.

Vakhmeister 32 Arkhangel'sk
Constructor A. Sutherland
Laid down 23.5.1753   *Launched* 26.4.1754
Dimensions 118 ft x 31 ft 6 in x 14 ft (1723 Establishment)
Armament   Planned LD 20 x 12pdrs
             UD 12 x 6pdrs (1723 Establishment)
             Probable as completed LD 18 x 12pdrs
             UD 14 x 6pdrs
Gektor class. Sailed from Arkhangel'sk to Kronshtadt. Cruised in the North Sea in 1755. Cruised in the Baltic in 1756. Blockaded Memel in 1757. Wrecked off Wulf Island during a storm on 3.10.1757 with a loss of 14 men drowned while proceeding from Revel' to Kronshtadt. The wreck was the result of unruly crew members, having been instigated by a midshipman, taking advantage of their captain's severe illness to invade his cabin and become hopelessly intoxicated on his liquor stores.

Sviatoi Mikhail 32 Arkhangel'sk
Constructors A. Sutherland & I. V. James
Laid down 24.4.1757   *Launched* 20.5.1758
Dimensions 118 ft x 31 ft 6 in x 14 ft (1723 Establishment)
Armament   Planned LD 20 x 12pdrs
             UD 12 x 6pdrs (1723 Establishment)
             Probable as completed LD 18 x 12pdrs
             UD 14 x 6pdrs
Gektor class. Sailed from Arkhangel'sk to Revel' in 7–10.1758. Cruised off Prussia in 1759. Bombarded Kolberg in 1760–61. Stationed in Kolberg Roads in 1762. Fire watch ship at Revel' in 1764. Cruised in the Baltic in 1765 and 1769. Broken up in 1771.

Sviatoi Sergii 32 Arkhangel'sk
Constructor I. V. James
Laid down 18.7.1760   *Launched* 17.5.1761
Dimensions 118 ft x 31 ft 6 in x 14 ft (1723 Establishment)
Armament   Planned LD 20 x 12pdrs
             UD 12 x 6pdrs (1723 Establishment)
             Probable as completed LD 18 x 12pdrs
             UD 14 x 6pdrs
Gektor class. Departed Arkhangel'sk for the Baltic in 7.1761. Damaged in transit with 11 men killed and forced to winter in Copenhagen. Arrived at Revel' in 1762 and sent to Kolberg to operate with Rear-Adm. Spiridov's squadron. Cruised in the Baltic in 1764–6. Carried Catherine II's imperial baggage to Lübeck in 1768. Cruised in the Baltic in 1769. Broken up in 1771.

The final three members of the *Gektor* class fall chronologically within the reign of Catherine II. They are included here for reasons of class continuity

Gremiashchii 32 Arkhangel
Constructor I. V. James
Laid down 20.8.1761   *Launched* 20.5.1762
Dimensions 118 ft x 31 ft 6 in x 14 ft (1723 Establishment)
Armament   Planned LD 20 x 12pdrs
             UD 12 x 6pdrs (1723 Establishment)
             Probable as completed LD 18 x 12pdrs
             UD 14 x 6pdrs
Gektor class. Sailed from Arkhangel'sk to Kronshtadt in 7–9.1765. Cruised in the Baltic in 1766–8, 1770 and 1773. Fire watch ship in Kronshtadt Roads in 1774–5. Reduced to a harbour hulk in 1778.

Nadezhda 32 Arkhangel'sk
Constructor A. Sutherland
Laid down 20.8.1760   *Launched* 20.5.1762
Dimensions 118 ft x 31 ft 6 in x 14 ft (1723 Establishment)
Armament   Planned LD 20 x 12pdrs
             UD 12 x 6pdrs (1723 Establishment)
             Probable as completed LD 18 x 12pdrs
             UD 14 x 6pdrs
Gektor class. Sailed from Arkhangel'sk to Kronshtadt in 7–10.1765. Cruised in the Baltic in 1767–9. To the Mediterranean with Rear-Adm. Elphinston's 2nd Arkhipelago Squadron in 1769. Fought in the battles of Chios and Ches'ma on 24–26.6.1770. Operated in the Mediterranean in 1770–5. Departed Auza on 13.3.1775 and returned to Kronshtadt on 15.10.1775. Attended the Imperial Review in Kronshtadt Roads in 1776. Carried cargo between Kronshtadt and Revel' in 1778–9. Converted to a store ship in 1780.

Afrika 32 Arkhangel'sk
Constructors V. A. Selyaninov & I. Davydov
Laid down 17.2.1764   *Launched* 13.5.1768

Dimensions 118 ft x 31 ft 6 in x 14 ft (1723 Establishment)
Armament Planned LD 20 x 12pdrs
UD 12 x 6pdrs (1723 Establishment)
Probable as completed LD 18 x 12pdrs
UD 14 x 6pdrs

Gektor class. Sailed from Arkhangel'sk to Kronshtadt in 7–9.1768. Cruised in the Baltic in 1769. To the Mediterranean with Rear-Adm. Elphinston's 2nd Arkhipelago Squadron in 1769. Fought in the battles of Chios and Ches'ma on 24–26.6.1770. Operated in the Arkhipelago in 1770–5. Returned to Revel' with Vice-Adm. Elmanov's squadron on 18.10.1775. Participated in the Imperial Review at Kronshtadt in 1776. Broken up in 1790.

Small frigates (3 built 1696–1761)

Small ship-rigged ships in Russian service were referred to as frigates and frequently employed as training ships. In most other European navies, they would have been classed as sloops or corvettes.

Sviatoi Il'ia 12/26 Arkhangel'sk, Solombala
Constructor O. Nye (Joseph Noy)
Laid down 5.1702 *Launched* 1703
Dimensions approx. 80 ft x 20 ft x 8 ft
24.3 m x 6.2 m x 2.5 m (Chernyshev)
Armament ?
Small frigate. Sailed to Copenhagen in 9.1710. Cruised in the North Sea in 1710–12. Wrecked in 9.1712 en route to Riga.

Kur'er class (2 ships)
Kur'er 12 Arkhangel'sk
Constructor ?
Laid down 1.1702 *Launched* 24.5.1702
Dimensions approx. 65 ft x 17 ft x 8½ ft
19.8 m x 5.1 m x 2.6 m (Chernyshev)
Armament ?
Kur'er class. Small frigate. Hauled overland and then floated down the Svir' River from Arkhangel'sk to Lake Ladoga from 17–27.8.1702. Assisted in the capture of Noteburg fortress (later renamed *Shlissel'burg*). No further mention.

Svyatogo Dukha 12 Arkhangel'sk
Constructor ?
Laid down 1.1702 *Launched* 24.5.1702
Dimensions approx. 65 ft x 17 ft x 8½ ft
19.8 m x 5.1 m x 2.6 m (Chernyshev)
Armament ?
Kur'er class. Small frigate. Hauled overland and then floated down the Svir' River from Arkhangel'sk to Lake Ladoga from 17–27.8.1702. Assisted in the capture of Noteburg fortress (later renamed *Shlissel'burg*). No further mention.

Printsessa Anna (renamed *Svyatov Iakov*) 12 St Petersburg
Constructor R. Brown
Laid down ? *Launched* 1733
Dimensions ?
Armament 12 x 4pdrs (1723 Establishment)
Small frigate, purpose-built as a fire watch ship. Commissioned as *Printsessa Anna*, but renamed *Sviatoi Iakov* in 1746. Sailed from Kronshtadt to Revel' in 10.1733. Fire watch ship at Revel' Roads from 1733 to 1755. Performed reconnaissance to Pillau in.4.1734. To Gottland to recall frigates *Kavaler*, *Rossiia* and *Voin* in 7.1745. Broken up after 1755.

A painting showing the portaging of the two small frigates Kur'er *and* Sviatogo Dukha *overland from Arkhangel'sk on the White Sea to the Lake of Onega in 1702 for use on Lake Ladoga in the taking of the Swedish fort of Noteburg. Peter I is directing the action in person, of course, and the work is being accomplished by the brute strength of both men and horses pitted against the forbidding forests and marshes of northern Russia. The road hacked out of the wilderness was known as 'The Royal Way'. The symbolism of the rainbow in the background hardly requires comment.*

Baltic frigates purchased abroad (9 purchased 1696–1761)
Nine ships rated as frigates were purchased from neutral and friendly European nations during the early formative years of the Baltic fleet. Seven came from the Netherlands, one by way of purchase from Dunkirk privateers, and two from England. The English purchases were older ships, as was the ship purchased second hand from Dunkirk privateers. All six of the directly purchased Dutch ships were newly built. One ship was wrecked in service and another captured by Sweden. The others all came to quiet ends after being relegated to harbour service.

Samson 32/34 Saardam
Constructor ?
Laid down 1.11.1710 *Launched* 16.1.1711
Dimensions 107 ft 7 in x 31 ft 11 in x 13 ft 4 in
Armament Projected 18 x 12pdrs, 14 x 6pdrs
 1720 18 x 8pdrs, 12 x 6pdrs
 180 men (200 in 1714) (*Materialy*)
Built at Holland by order of A. Menshikov and presented to Peter I. The name *Samson* is based on the Samson Fountain at Petergof with a statue of Samson representing Russia slaying a lion representing Sweden. Arrived at Revel' in 1711 and departed for Kronshtadt escaping from two Swedish ships. Cruised in the Baltic in 1712–23 and 1725. Captured three Swedish capers and landed troops at Gottland in 1715. To England in 1715 to escort newly purchased warships to Copenhagen in 1716 to participate in the 'Great Armament of 1716'. Captured eight prizes in 1718. Sent to the Sound off Copenhagen in 1719 for negotiations with Adm. Norris. Cruised to Gottland in 1720. Towed the damaged *Rafail* to Revel' in 1721. Transported the Russian ambassador from Copenhagen to Kronshtadt in 1723. Stationed at Kronshtadt in 1728. Determined unfit in 1728 and her rigging distributed to new ships. Last mentioned in 1740.

Sviatoi Iakov 16/32 Holland
Constructor ?
Laid down ? *Launched* 1711
Purchased 1711
Dimensions 80 ft 11 in x 29 ft 5 in x 10 ft 9 in
Armament 1715 12 x 4pdrs, 4 x 2pdrs (*Materialy*)
A small frigate purchased in Holland in 1711. Eighteen gun ports on the gun deck and four on the quarterdeck. Arrived at Revel' in 4.1712. Cruised with the fleet in the Baltic in 1713 in pursuit of Swedish warships. Cruised in the Baltic in 1714 and forced to return to St Petersburg to repair a leak. Cruised in the Baltic in 1715. Transported General Adm. Apraksin to Helsingfors in 1716. Cruised in the Baltic in 1718 and took six prizes. Stationed in Kronshtadt Roads in 1721. Cruised in the Baltic in 1722–3. Served as a packet between Kronshtadt, Lübeck, and Danzig in 1725–30. Broken up in 1732.

Esperans 40/50 Amsterdam
Constructor ?
Laid down ? *Launched* 1698
Purchased 1712
Dimensions 127 ft x (114 ft k) x 33 ft x 11 ft 9 in (English measure)
 139 ft x 37.5 ft x 14.75 ft (Dutch measure)
Armament 1715 18 x 12pdrs, 18 x 6pdrs, 4 x 3pdrs
 268 men (320 in 1714) (*Materialy*)
 1720 18 x 12pdrs, 18 x 6pdrs, 4 x 4pdrs
 230 men (*Materialy*)
Dutch *Hardenbroek* (50), captured by two Dunkirk capers in 1709 and purchased by Russia in 1712. Originally named *Gardenbruk* in Russian service and renamed *Esperans*. Arrived at Revel' in 3.1713. Cruised in the Baltic in 1713–15. Stationed in Kronshtadt Roads in 1716. Cruised in the Baltic in 1717–20. Unsuccessfully attempted to refloat the grounded *Nishtadt* with *Arondel*'s assistance in 1722, but managed to salvage her guns and rigging. Repaired in 1723–5. To Bordeaux in 1726 where she wintered. Returned to Kronshtadt in 1727. To Kiel in Schoutbijnacht Seniavin's squadron with the Duke of Holstein in 1727. Cruised in the Baltic in 1731–2. To Danzig with Adm. Gordon's squadron in 1734. Determined to be in poor condition in 1735. Broken up after 1739. Last mentioned in 1740.

Sviatoi Nikolai 42/50 Holland
Constructor ?
Laid down ? *Launched* ?
Purchased 1712
Dimensions 118 ft x (102 ft keel) x 28 ft x 11 ft
 118 ft x (102 ft keel) x 30 ft 6 in x 12 ft 8 (in alternate measure
Armament 1715 20 x 12pdrs, 20 x 8pdrs, 10 x 3pdrs
 200 men (*Materialy*)
Projected armament was unrealistically large for her size and may have not been mounted in service. Sailed from Amsterdam to Revel' in 5.1713. Transferred to Kronshtadt in 7.1713. Converted to a store ship with armament reduced to 32 guns in 1716. Broken up in 1721.

Landsdou (ex-*Noris*) 32/44 England
Constructor ?
Laid down ? *Launched* ?
Purchased 1713
Dimensions 107 ft x 29 ft 10 in x 12 ft 6 in (Veselago)
 109 ft x 30 ft 5½ in x 12 ft 10 in (Apraksin)
Armament 1720 MD 20 x 6pdrs
 FC & QD 4 x 4pdrs
 150 men (200 in 1714) (*Materialy*)
Former *Noris*, purchased from England. Arrived at Kronshtadt in 7.1713. Cruised in the Baltic in 1714–15. To Copenhagen in 1716 to participate in the 'Great Armament of 1716'. Cruised in the Baltic in 1718–19. Cruised to Copenhagen in 1720. Cruised in the Baltic in 1721 and 1723–4. Found unfit in 1726. Converted to a fire ship in 1727. Broken up in 1728. (Note the differences in dimensions between Veselago and Apraksin.)

Richmond (ex-*Svivsten*) 44 England
Constructor ?
Laid down ? *Launched* ?
Purchased 1714.
Dimensions ?
Armament ?
Former *Svivsten*, purchased in England in 1714. Arrived at Revel' in 6.1715 with the Anglo-Dutch fleet under Adm. Norris. Cruised in the Baltic in 1716–17. Determined to be unfit for service in 1717 due to rot. Broken up in 1721.

Amsterdam Galey 32 Amsterdam
Constructor ?
Laid down 1719 *Launched* 1720
Purchased 1721
Dimensions 108 ft x 34 ft 4 in x 13 ft 2 in
Armament 12pdrs/6pdrs (conjecture)
Arrived at Revel' as a merchant ship on 18.10.1721. Transported Swedish PoWs to Stockholm in 1722. Departed for Madagascar with

Dekrondelivde in 12.1723. Forced to return for repairs in 1.1724 due to leaks. To Cadiz via Norway in.5.1725. Returned to Russia in.5.1726. Repaired in 1727. Cruised to Kildin Island in the Barents Sea in 1728–9. To Arkhangel'sk in 1731. Severely damaged by storm on return to Kronhshtadt in 1732. Cruised to Memel in 1733. Departed for Arkhangel'sk in 1734, but forced to return to Revel' owing to the outbreak of hostilities between Danzig and France over the Polish succession. To Arkhangel'sk in 1735. Returned to Kronstadt in 1736. Repaired in 1738. Departed for Arkhangel'sk with naval cadets in 1739, but forced to return due to the arrival of a French squadron at Stockholm. Departed Revel' for Arkhangel'sk in.5.1740 and wrecked on the coast of Pomerania with a loss of 3 crewmen due to navigational error.

Dekrondelivde (De Kroon de Liefde) 32 Amsterdam
Constructor ?
Laid down 1719 *Launched* 1720
Purchased 1721
Dimensions 105 ft 5 in x 31 ft 10 in x 13 ft 7½ in
Armament 12pdrs/6pdrs (conjecture)
Arrived at Revel' as a merchant ship on 19.10.1721. Transported Swedish PoWs to Stockholm in 1722. Sent to Stockholm with instructions for the Russian ambassador in 1723. Departed for Madagascar with *Amsterdam Galey* in 12.1723, and returned due to storm in 1.1724. Expedition cancelled in 2.1724. Cruised in the Baltic in 1724. Took part in the Spanish expedition to Cadiz with *Amsterdam Galey* in 1725. Repaired in 1727. Cruised to Kildin Island in the Barents Sea in 1782–9. Cruised to the North Sea in company with the frigate *Vakhtmeister* and then to Arkhangel'sk. Returned to Kronstadt in 1734. Transported supplies from Riga to Kronstadt in 1735. Transferred to Arkhangel'sk in 1736. Returned to Kronstadt in 1737. Repaired in 1738. Transferred to Revel' in 1740. Transferred to Arkhangel'sk in 1741. Departed Arkhangel'sk for the Baltic in 1742 but forced to return due to a storm. In poor condition and reduced to a fire guard ship at Arkhangel'sk in 1743. Last mentioned in 1744.

Endrakht 32 Amsterdam
Constructor ?
Laid down ? *Launched* 1719
Purchased 1720
Dimensions ?
Armament 12pdrs/6pdrs (conjecture)
Purchased in Amsterdam in 1720. Captured by Swedish frigate *Santa Ern* in 1720 and renamed *Erns Pris*.

Baltic snows (17 built 1696–1761)

The Russians made extensive use of snow-rigged vessels during the first half of the eighteenth century, with 16 being built and disposed of prior to 1721. One final but long-lived vessel, *Favoritka*, was added in 1723. Their place would be taken by brigs during the latter years of the century.

Sant Iakim class (10 ships)
Sant Iakim 14 Olonetskaya
Constructor Y. Rulovs
Laid down 1703 *Launched* 1704
Dimensions 72 ft x 18 ft 6 in x 8 ft
Armament ?
   70 men
Sant Iakim class. Purpose-built snow. Sailed from Olonetskaya to St Petersburg in 1704. Operations in the Baltic in 1705–10. Broken up after 1710.

Unnamed 14 Olonetskaya
Constructors Peter I & I. Nemtsov
Laid down 1703 *Launched* 24.9.1704
Dimensions 72 ft x 18 ft 6 in x 8 ft
Armament ? 70 men
Sant Iakim class. Purpose-built snow. Operations in the Baltic in 1704-13. Converted into a floating hospital in 1714–15. Preserved as a monument in St Petersburg until 1732.

Degas 14 Olonetskaya
Constructors G. Meybou & Y. Rulovs
Laid down 12.11.1703 *Launched* 18.7.1704
Dimensions 72 ft x 18 ft 6 in x 8 ft
Armament ? 70 men
Sant Iakim class. Purpose-built snow. Sailed from Olonetskaya to St Petersburg in 9–10.1704. Operations in the Baltic in 1705–10. Broken up after 1710.

Kopor'e 14 Olonetskaya
Constructor V. Graf
Laid down 15.10.1703 *Launched* 18.7.1704
Dimensions 72 ft x 18 ft 6 in x 8 ft
Armament ?
   70 men
Sant Iakim class. Purpose-built snow. Named after a Swedish fortress taken on 27.5.1703. Sailed from Olonetskaya to St Petersburg in 9–10.1704. Operations in the Baltic in 1705–10. Broken up after 1710.

Iamburg 14 Olonetskaya
Constructor V. Graf
Laid down 15.10.1703 *Launched* 20.7.1704
Dimensions 72 ft x 18 ft 6 in x 8 ft
Armament ?
   70 men
Sant Iakim class. Purpose-built snow. Named after a Swedish fortress taken on 27.5.1703. Sailed from Olonetskaya to St Petersburg in 9–10.1704. Operations in the Baltic in 1705–10. Broken up after 1710.

Luks 14 Olonetskaya
Constructor V. Graf
Laid down 1.11.1704 *Launched* 7.6.1705
Dimensions 72 ft x 18 ft 6 in x 8 ft
Armament ?
   70 men
Sant Iakim class. Purpose-built snow. Sailed from Olonetskaya to St Petersburg in 6–7.1705. Operations in the Baltic in 1706–10. Broken up after 1710.

Falk 14 Olonetskaya
Constructors P. Kornilisn and Y. Starn
Laid down 1.11.1704 *Launched* 7.6.1705
Dimensions 72 ft x 18 ft 6 in x 8 ft
Armament ?
   70 men
Sant Iakim class . Purpose-built snow. Sailed from Olonetskaya to St Petersburg in 6–7.1705.Operations in the Baltic in 1706–9. Sent to the Swedish fleet under flag of truce in 4.1709, but treacherously captured by Swedish Adm. Ankarstiern's squadron.

Snuk 14 Olonetskaya
Constructor V. Graf
Laid down 1.11.1704   *Launched* 17.6.1705
Dimensions 72 ft x 18 ft 6 in x 8 ft
Armament ?
          70 men
Sant Iakim class. Purpose-built snow. Sailed from Olonetskaya to St Petersburg in 6–7.1705. Operations in the Baltic in 1706–10. Broken up after 1710.

Feniks 14 Olonetskaya
Constructor P. Bas
Laid down 1.11.1704   *Launched* 17.6.1705
Dimensions 72 ft x 18 ft 6 in x 8 ft
Armament ?
          70 men
Sant Iakim class. Purpose-built snow. Sailed from Olonetskaya to St Petersburg in 6–7.1705. Operations in the Baltic in 1706–10. Broken up after 1710.

Roza 14 Olonetskaya
Constructor P. Kornilisen
Laid down 12.11.1704   *Launched* 19.6.1705
Dimensions 72 ft x 18 ft 6 in x 8 ft
Armament ?
          70 men
Sant Iakim class. Purpose-built snow. Sailed from Olonetskaya to St Petersburg in 6–7.1705. Operations in the Baltic in 1706–10. Broken up after 1710.

Adler class (2 ships)
Adler ? Selitskiy Ryadok
Constructor V. Graf
Laid down 1705   *Launched* 1705
Dimensions 65 ft x 17 ft x ?
Armament ?
Adler class Purpose-built snow. Operations in the Baltic in 1706–11. Broken up after 1711.

Beber ? Selitskiy Ryadok
Constructor V. Graf
Laid down 1705   *Launched* 1705
Dimensions 65 ft x 17 ft x ?
Armament ?
Adler class Purpose-built snow. Operations in the Baltic in 1706–11. Broken up after 1710.

Lizet *(Munker)* 16/18 St Petersburg
Constructors   Peter I & F. M. Sklyaev
Laid down 30.11.1706   *Launched* 1708
Dimensions 76 ft x 22 ft x 12 ft 6 in
Armament 1715   20 x 3pdrs (*Materialy*)
          1715   18 x 6pdrs
          94 men
Three-masted ship, nominally rated as a 'snow'. Highly regarded and frequently used by Peter I. Name is the diminutive for Elizabeth, Peter I's daughter. For a similar three-masted design, see the similarly named *Lizet* in the Sea of Azov fleet. Operations in the Baltic in 1709–16. Stationed at Copenhagen in 1716. Wrecked and lost off Denmark on 20.10.1716. No casualties, guns and equipment successfully salvaged.

A drawing of Peter I's beloved snow Munker *as completed in 1708. 'Munker' originates from the French* mon coeur, *'my heart', and refers to Peter's daughter Elizabeth. Features of particular interest are the retention of a spritsail and the rigging. Readers more familiar with late eighteenth-century British terminology, will not regard this ship as 'snow-rigged', given the clear separation between the main and mizzenmasts, but ship nomenclature changes from country to country and over time.*

Diana class (2 ships)
Diana 18 Novoladozhskaya
Constructors   F. S. Saltykov & G. A. Menshikov
Laid down 1710   *Launched* 1711
Dimensions ?
Armament 1715   18 x 6pdrs
          80–110 men
Diana class. Purpose-built snow. Operations in the Baltic in 1713–18. Broken up in 1721.

Natal'ia 18 Novoladozhskaya
Constructors F. S. Saltykov & G. A. Menshikov
Laid down 1710   *Launched* 1711
Dimensions ?
Armament 1715   18 x 6pdrs
          80–110 men
Diana class. *Natal'ia* commemorates the name of Peter I's mother. Purpose-built snow. Operations in the Baltic in 1713–21. Broken up in 1721.

Printsessa 18/20 St Petersburg
Constructor F. M. Sklyaev
Laid down 17.11.1711   *Launched* 27.4.1714
Dimensions 89 ft x 24 ft x 10 ft
Armament 1715   14 x 6pdrs, 4 smaller
          111 men (100 in 1714) (*Materialy*)
Purpose-built snow. Operations in the Baltic in 1714–16. Wrecked off Jutland on 1.12.1716 while en route to Holland.

Favoritka 16 St Petersburg
Constructor G. A. Menshikov
Laid down 1721   *Launched* 28.9.1723
Dimensions 71 ft x 18 ft x 6 ft 10 in
Armament ?
         80 men
Purpose-built snow. Cruised in the Baltic in 1725–6, 1733–4 and 1741–5. Broken up after 1745.

Baltic bomb vessels (10 purpose-built, 2 converted 1700–61)

Because of Russia's amphibious activities and interests, bomb vessels were extensively employed during this early period with twelve being built or converted prior to 1761.

Purpose-built

Khobot 14 Olonetakaya
Constructor R. Brown
Laid down 4.3.1707   *Launched* 6.1708
Dimensions approx. 90 ft x ? x ?; 27.4 m x ? x ? (Chernyshev)
Armament 12 x 20pdrs, 2 x 3 pood howitzers
         150 men
Purpose-built bomb vessel. Cruised in the Baltic with the fleet in 1710–13. No further mention.

Iupiter 6 St Petersburg
Constructor O. Nye (Joseph Noy)
Laid down 21.7.1714   *Launched* 27.4.1715
Dimensions 80 ft (lgd) x 27 ft x 10 ft (Veselago)
Armament 4 cannon, 2 mortars
         50 men
Purpose-built bomb vessel. In commission at Kronshtadt Roads with occasional Baltic cruises from 1715–26. Transferred to Revel' from 1727–32. Transferred to Kronshtadt in 1733. Participated in the bombardment of Danzig with Adm. Gordon's squadron in 1734. Broken up after 1735.

Donder (*Grom*) 6 St Petersburg
Constructor O. Nye (Joseph Noy)
Laid down 11.7.1715   *Launched* 5.6.1716
Dimensions 85 ft (lgd) x 27 ft (LK) x 27¼ ft x 10 ft 2 in (Veselago)
Armament 4 cannon, 2 mortars
         50 men
Purpose-built bomb vessel. Commissioned in the Baltic from 1718–24. Repaired in 1725. Transferred to Kronshtadt from 1726–34. Participated in the bombardment of Danzig with Adm. Gordon's squadron in 1734. Wintered at Vyborg in 1734/35. Transferred to Kronshtadt in 1735. No further mention.

Samson 6 St Petersburg
Constructor R. Kosentz (Richard Cozens)
Laid down ?   *Launched* 27.6.1727
Dimensions approx. 85 ft x 27¼ ft x 10 ft
         25.9 m x 8.3 m x 3 m (Chernyshev)
Armament 4 cannon, 2 mortars
         50 men
Purpose-built bomb vessel. Stationed in Kronshtadt. Never at sea. Broken up after 1735.

Etna 6 St Petersburg
Constructor ?
Laid down ?   *Launched* 21.9.1727
Dimensions ?
Armament 4 cannon, 2 mortars
Purpose-built bomb vessel. Stationed in Kronshtadt. Never at sea. Broken up after 1735.

Samson class (2 ships)
Samson 10/14   St Petersburg
Constructor R. Ramzay
Laid down 27.6.1739   *Launched* 1.7.1740
Dimensions 102 ft x 27 ft 4 in x 12 ft 6 in (Veselago)
Armament 10 x 6pdrs, 2 x 5 pood mortars, 2–3 pood howitzers
Samson class Purpose-built bomb vessel. Trials in 9.1740. Active during the war with Sweden in 1741–3. Commissioned until 1751. Broken up in 1751.

Iupiter 10/14   St Petersburg
Constructor R. Ramzay
Laid down 27.6.1739   *Launched* 1.7.1740
Dimensions 102 ft x 27 ft 4 in x 12 ft 6 in (Veselago)
Armament 10 x 6pdrs, 2 x 5 pood mortars, 2 x 3 pood howitzers
Samson class Purpose-built bomb vessel. Trials in 9.1740. Active during the war with Sweden in 1741–3. Commissioned until 1751. Broken up in 1751.

Donder class 1st group (3 ships)
Six purpose-built bomb vessels, designed by D. Sutherland and built by various constructors. The first three were built at St Petersburg between 1751 and 1758 and belong to this section. The final three were built at Kronshtadt in 1771 and may be found in the next section.

Donder 10 St Petersburg
Constructor D. Sutherland
Laid down 1.12.1751   *Launched* 23.9.1752
Dimensions 95 ft x 27 ft x 11 ft x 12 ft (Veselago)
Armament 6 cannon, 2 mortars, 2 howitzers
         100 men
Donder class. Purpose-built bomb vessel. Active during the war with Prussia in 1757–61. Broken up in 1763.

Iupiter 10 St Petersburg
Constructor Kronong
Laid down 18.10.1754   *Launched* 7.7.1755
Dimensions 95 ft x 27 ft x 11 ft x 12 ft (Veselago)
Armament 6 cannon, 2 mortars, 2 howitzers
         100 men
Donder class. Purpose-built bomb vessel. Active during the war with Prussia in 1757–61. Stationed at Kronshtadt in 1762–4. Participated in the Imperial Review of 1765. Broken up in 1769.

Samson 10 St Petersburg
Constructor I. Ilyin
Laid down 17.11.1757   *Launched* 16.5.1758
Dimensions 95 ft x 27 ft x 11 ft x 12 ft (draft) (Veselago)
Armament 6 cannon, 2 mortars, 2 howitzers
         100 men
Donder class. Purpose-built bomb vessel. Active during the war with Prussia in 1758–61. Stationed at Kronshtadt in 1762–4. Participated in the Imperial Review of 1765. Broken up in 1769.

Converted

Bir-Drager class (2 ships)
Bir-Drager 3 Olonetskaya
Constructor ?
Laid down ?   Launched 1703
Dimensions approx. 80 ft x 24 ft x 9 ft
           24.4 m x 7.3 m x 2.7 m (Chernyshev)
Armament 3 x 3 pood mortars
Bir-Drager class Bomb vessel converted from buer. Cruised in the Baltic in 1705–9. Broken up after 1710. (See also under Baltic buers.)

Vein-Drager 3 Olonetskaya
Constructor ?
Laid down ?   Launched 1703
Dimensions approx. 80 ft x 24 ft x 9 ft
           24.4 m x 7.3 m x 2.7 m (Chernyshev)
Armament 3 x 3 pood mortars
Bir-Drager class Bomb vessel converted from buer. Cruised in the Baltic in 1705–9. Broken up after 1710. (See also under Baltic buers.)

The Navy of Catherine and Paul 1762–1800

Ships with 90–110 guns
(9 Built 1762–1800)

Ches'ma class 100/108/110 guns (10 ships)

This class was intended to be the centrepiece of the expanding Russian Baltic fleet taking shape in the 1780s as the primary instrument of Catherine I's drive to consolidate Russian control over the Baltic and to reassert Russia's status as one of the European Great Powers. The *Ches'ma*s represented the first class of 100 gun three-decked line of battle ships laid down for Russia. They were ordered at a time when the French and Spanish were also moving in the direction of series production for a type of warship that had previously been largely confined to the completion of 'one-off' prestige ships. In contrast to earlier Russian First Rates, these ships were intended from the start for active duty as combatants and this was the role they fulfilled in the Russo-Swedish War that began in 1788.

During the period of close naval cooperation between Britain and Russia from 1777–84, Russian constructors and students were allowed considerable access to the major British dockyards at Portsmouth, Plymouth, and Chatham at the instruction of Adm. Keppel. A visiting Russian student, D. Masal'skiy, had been able to obtain the dimensions for HMS *Victory* in 1780, but he was unable to obtain her actual plans. Using these specifications in 1782, Russian constructors I. James and A. S. Katsanov prepared competitive plans for the new Russian First Rates. I. James generally receives credit for the final class design, although there is some indication that the Russian Board actually regarded the plans submitted by Katasanov as superior after comparing the two designers' proposals, and Katsanov was made responsible for the detailed design work on *Rostislav*. In 1784, a second Russian student, Vasilii Vlasov, obtained exact copies of *Victory*'s plans at considerable expense, and sent them to Russia in 1784. Jonathan Coleman (Kol'man) is said to have designed the final four ships, although the entire in class in fell within the

Catherine II in her later years, standing in front of a portrait of warships locked in combat and pointing imperiously at a globe to her left. The symbolism is obvious, and Catherine's role in developing the Russian navy into a first rate force for the expansion of Russian territory and prestige is equally apparent. Her role in broader Russian history is a bit murkier. Initially giving verbal support to liberal enlightenment thinking and attempting to improve the lot of the serfs, she ultimately sided with the Russian aristocracy, removing their obligations of service to the state (initiated by Peter I) and refusing to emancipate the serfs.

same overall parameters and traces its ultimate origins to *Victory*.

With prospects for war with Sweden growing, there were originally to have been nine ships in this class. Only eight were completed, with the final vessel being cancelled as superfluous to Russian requirements as a result of the favorable outcome of the conflict with Sweden. It is not clear how closely the actual details of construction followed the *Victory*'s draught with respect to framing and fittings, but the dimensions of the completed ships followed closely upon those of the highly regarded British ship.

In 1789, three Russian *Ches'ma*s participated in the battle of Öland (*Rostislav*, *Dvenadstat Apostolov* and *Sviatoi Ravnoapostol'nyi Kniaz' Vladimir*) while three more (*Ches'ma*, *Trekh Ierarkhov* and *Saratov*) were held up at Copenhagen and did not rejoin the main fleet until 7.1789. The seventh class member, *Sviatoi Nikolai*, was launched in July 1789, included in July in the reserve squadron under Vice-Adm. Kruz, and finally joined the main fleet in August 1789. No fewer than five *Ches'ma*s (*Ches'ma*, *Dvenadstat Apostolov*, *Tri Ierakhov*, *Sviatoi Vladimir*

A beautifully preserved draught of Rostislav *(100) of 1784, from the Central Naval Archive collection at St Petersburg. She was considered the best of the* Ches'ma *class ships. Interested readers are invited to compare this draught to that of Slade's* Victory *and to draw their own conclusions as to the alleged relationship between the two ships.*

and *Sviatoi Nikolai*) took part in the battle of Styrsudden in 1790, one of the heaviest concentrations of First Rates in naval history before Trafalgar. The eighth *Ches'ma*, *Sviatoi Evsevii*, was launched in July 1790, too late for her to take an active part in the war.

After 1800, with the threat of war with France growing again, the condition of the *Ches'ma*s was formally evaluated at the order of Paul I. The entire class was found to have deteriorated to the point of unserviceability due to cheap construction materials and inadequate maintenance. By the end of 1801, all had been retired from active service, being reduced to duty as hulks and floating batteries.

As an afterward, in 1813, a tenth member of the class was laid down and completed as the *Rostislav*, an interesting commentary on the quality of the original concept and a belated and unintentional tribute to the genius of Thomas Slade in 1765.

Ioann Krestitel' (*Ches'ma*) 100/108 St Petersburg
Constructors   I. James and V. A. Selyaninov
Laid down   26.7.1782   Launched   16.9.1783
Dimensions   186 ft x 50 ft (51 ft 10 in outside plank) x 21 ft 6 in
Armament   Designed LD 26 x 36pdrs, 2 x 60 u (1 pood)
            MD 26 x 18pdrs, 2 x 24u (½ pood)
            UD 30 x 8pdrs
            FC & QD 10 x 6pdrs, 6 x 24pdr carr.
         1788   LD 24 x 36pdrs, 4 x 60 u (1 pood)
            MD 26 x 18pdrs, 4 x 24u (½ pood)
            UD 30 x 12pdrs
            FC & QD 20 x 6pdrs (2 x 68pdr carr. in 1789)

Ches'ma class. Commissioned as *Ioann Krestitel'*, but always known as *Ches'ma* in commemoration of the great victory over the Turks in 1770. James did the basic design work for *Ches'ma*, but Selyaninov supervised much of the actual construction, while James was involved in supervising work on *Trekh Ierarkhov*. In service, she is reported to have carried 11 officers and 550 men. Draught astern was 21 ft 3 in and 20 ft 10 in at the bow. The lower deck gun ports had a respectable clearance of 7 ft 1½ in over the waterline.

Left Kronshtadt with sister ships *Trekh Ierarkhov* and *Saratov* en route to Copenhagen as flag to Vice-Adm. Fondesin on 5.6.1788. Avoided conflict with a Swedish squadron prior to the declaration of war, and arrived at Copenhagen on 28.6.1788. Cruised in the Kattegat blockading Karlskrona in 7–10.1788. Joined the Russian fleet under Adm. I Chichagov on 22.7.1789. Fought at Krasnaia Gorka on 23–24.5.1790 as flag to Vice-Adm. Kruz taking casualties of 5 killed, 13 wounded, and 2 shot holes. Fought at Vyborg on 22.6.1790. Stationed at Kronshtadt Roads in 1791. Blockaded the Sound off Copenhagen in 1793. Visited by Emperor Paul I in 1797. Cruised to Bornholm in 1798. Decommissioned in 1798. Found unfit for sea duty in 1801. Ordered to be broken up in 12.1802. Transferred from Kronshtadt to Revel' in 1803 as a floating battery. Broken up after 1806.

Trekh Ierarkhov 100/108 St Petersburg
Constructor   I. V. James
Laid down   26.6.1782   Launched   26.9.1783
Dimensions   186 ft x 50 ft (51 ft 10 in outside plank) x 21 ft 6 in
Armament   Designed LD 26 x 36pdrs, 2 x 60 u (1 pood)
            MD 26 x 18pdrs, 2 x 24u (½ pood)
            UD 30 x 8pdrs
            FC & QD 10 x 6pdrs, 6 x 24pdr carr.
         1788   LD 24 x 36pdrs, 4 x 60 u (1 pood)
            MD 26 x 18pdrs, 4 x 24u (½ pood)
            UD 30 x 12pdrs
            FC & QD 20 x 6pdrs

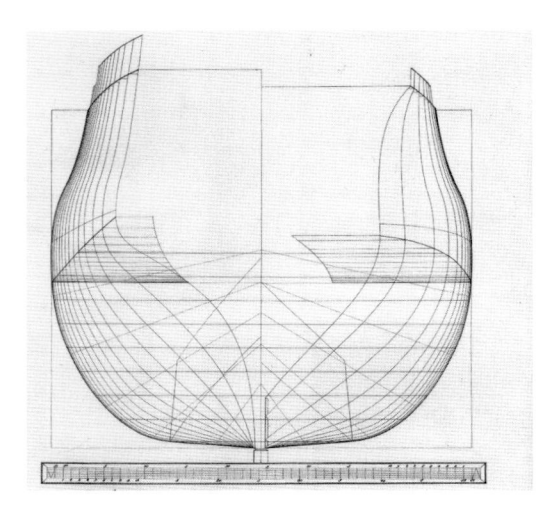

Ches'ma class. Left Kronshtadt with sister ships *Ches'ma* and *Saratov* in Vice-Adm. Fondesin's squadron en route to Copenhagen on 5.6.1788. Avoided conflict with a Swedish squadron prior to the declaration of war, and arrived at Copenhagen on 28.6.1788. Assigned as flag to Vice-Adm. Kozlyaninov under Adm. I. Chichagov on 22.7.1789. Fought at the battle of Krasnaia Gorka on 23–24.5.1790 with casualties of 15 killed and 14 wounded. Fought at the battle of Vyborg on 22.6.1790. Cruised in the Baltic in 1791. Cruised in the Sound off Copenhagen in 1793. Assigned to training duties in Revel' Roads in 1795. Cruised in the Baltic in 1796. Decommissioned in 1796. Found unfit for sea duty in 1797. Broken up after 1802.

Rostislav 100/108 Kronshtadt
Constructors   Katasonov and G. Ignatyev
Laid down   2.7.1782   Launched   23.5.1784
Dimensions   186 ft x 51 ft 6 in (52 ft 3 in outside plank) x 21 ft 4 in
Armament   Designed LD 24 x 36pdrs, 4 x 60 u (1 pood)
            MD 26 x 18pdrs, 2 x 24u (½ pood)
            UD 30 x 8pdrs
            FC & QD 10 x 6pdrs, 6 x 24pdr carr.
         1788   LD 24 x 36pdrs, 4 x 60 u (1 pood)
            MD 26 x 18pdrs, 4 x 24u (½ pood)
            UD 30 x 12pdrs
            FC & QD 20 x 6pdrs (4 x 24pdr carr. added in 1789)

Ches'ma class. Rated as a 110-gun ship by Chernyshev, but as a 100 in other sources. A. S. Katsanov is credited with the design work on *Rostislav* with G. Ignatyev assisting in the actual construction. '*Rostislav* was a crack ship, and for a long time was object of admiration of sailors.' In 1785, she out-sailed her sister ship *Trekh Ierarkhov* in calm weather, although she was found to be crank in heavier weather and unable to carry all of her sails safely. As a result, later class members had their sterns cut down and their masts lowered. Fought at Gogland on 6.7.1788 as flag of Adm. Greig, captured *Prins-*

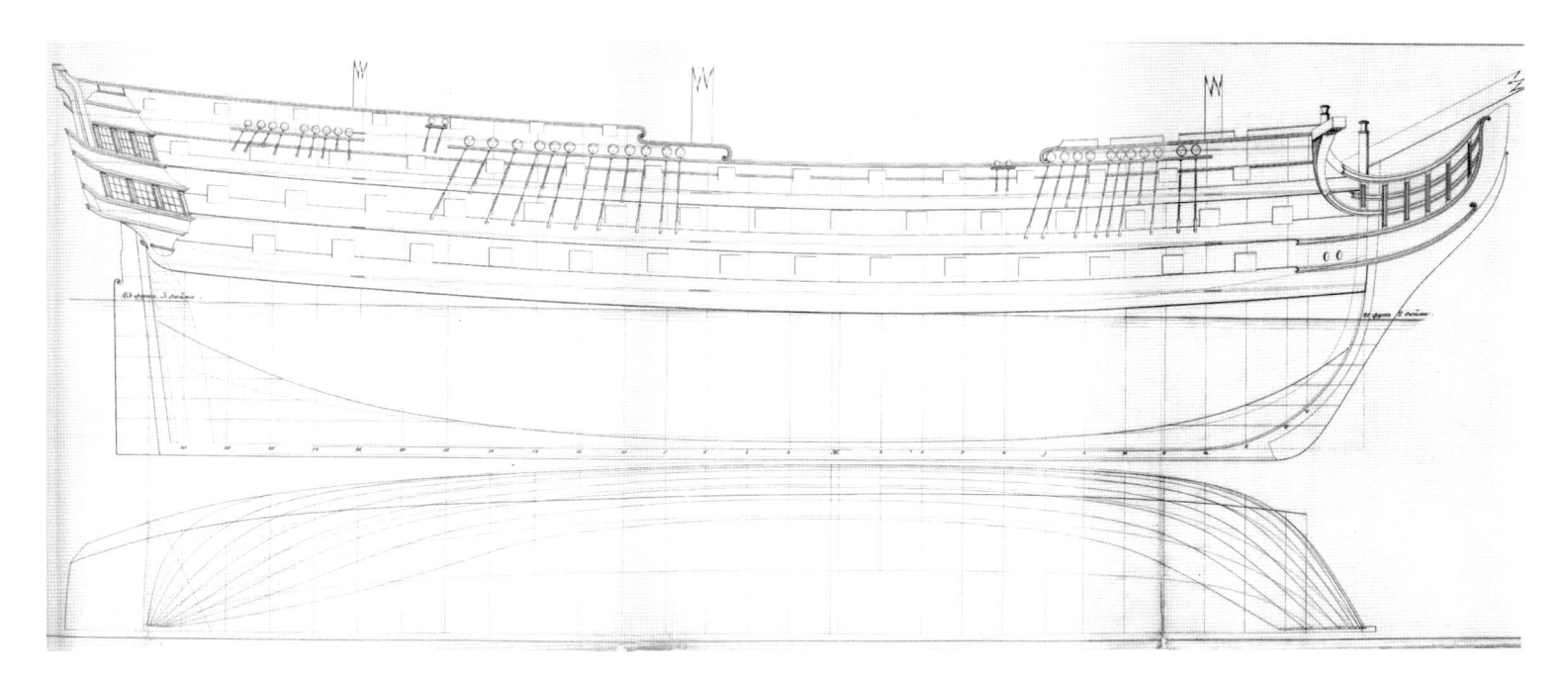

Gustaf, the Swedish second-in-command, and suffered casualties of 17 killed, 43 wounded while taking 121 shot holes. Fought at Öland on 15.7.1789 as flag of Adm. I. Chichagov. Patrolled between Bornholm, Gottland and Dagerort during the rest of the year. Fought at Revel' on 2.5.1790 expending 1,207 rounds and capturing *Prins Karl* 62. Fought at Vyborg on 22.6.1790. Cruised in the Baltic in 1791. Cruised in the Sound off Copenhagen in 1793. Served in training duties in Revel' Road in 1794–5. Cruised in the Baltic in 1796–8 and 1800–1. Reduced to harbour service in 1801. Floating battery in the Revel' Roads with the middle deck guns removed in 1803. Hulked as a hospital ship in 1804, paid off in 1805. Broken up in 1808.

Saratov 100/108 Kronshtadt
*Constructor*s Jonathan Coleman (Kol'man) and G. Ignatyev
Laid down 22.2.1784   *Launched* 15.10.1785
Dimensions 186 ft x 51 ft (51 ft 6 in outside plank) x 21 ft 6 in
Armament   Designed LD 24 x 36pdrs, 4 x 60 u (1 pood)
             MD 26 x 18pdrs, 2 x 24u (½ pood)
             UD 30 x 8pdrs
             FC & QD 10 x 6pdrs, 6 x 24pdr carr.
             1788 LD 24 x 36pdrs, 4 x 60 u (1 pood)
             MD 26 x 18pdrs, 4 x 24u (½ pood)
             UD 30 12pdrs
             FC & QD 20 x 6pdrs (2 x 68pdr carr. added in 1789)

Ches'ma class. Jonathan Coleman (Kol'man) did the design work and G. Ignatyev supervised the actual construction. Left Kronshtadt with First Rates *Ches'ma* and *Trekh Ierarkhov* in Vice-Adm. Fondesin's squadron en route to Copenhagen on 5.6.1788. Avoided conflict with a Swedish squadron prior to the declaration of war, and arrived at Copenhagen on 28.6.1788. Operated in Vice-Adm. Fondesin's squadron and cruised in the Kattegat and blockaded Karlskrona in the summer and autumn of 1788. Became Vice-Adm. Musin-Pushkin's permanent flagship in 1789 and throughout the remainder of her active service life. Joined Adm. I.Chichagov's fleet off Bornholm on 22.7.1789 and cruised between Bornholm, Gottland, and Dagerort and then into the Gulf of Finland. Fought at Revel' on 2.5.1790 and expended 1809 rounds. Fought at Vyborg on 22.6.1790. Cruised in the Baltic in 1791.

Blockaded the Sound off Copenhagen in 1793. Cruised in the Baltic in 1794. Training duty in Revel' Roads in 1795. Cruised in the Baltic in 1797 and 1801. Decommissioned in 1801 and relegated to harbour service. Ordered to be broken up in 12.1782, but employed as a floating battery at Kronshtadt in 1803 with the middle deck battery removed. Reduced to a hospital hulk in 1804.

Dvu-na-desat' Apostolov 100/108/112 St Petersburg
Constructor Jonathan Coleman (Kol'man)
Laid down 15.5.1785   *Launched* 2.8.1788
Dimensions 186 ft x 51 ft (51 ft 10 in outside plank) x 21 ft 6 in
             2,208 x 60/94 tons bm
Armament   Designed LD 24 x 36pdrs, 4 x 60 u (1 pood)
             MD 26 x 18pdrs, 2 x 24u (½ pood)
             UD 30 x 8pdrs
             FC & QD 10 x 6pdrs, 6 x 24pdr carr.
             1788 LD 24 x 36pdrs, 4 x 60 u (1 pood)
             MD 26 x 18pdrs, 4 x 24u (½ pood)
             UD 30 x 12pdrs
             FC & QD 20 x 6pdrs (4 x 24pdr carr. added in 1789)

Ches'ma class. Spelling of the name is the archaic version of *Dvenadtsat' Apostolov* still in use at the time of her completion and used hereafter. Jonathan Coleman (Kol'man) did the design work and supervised the actual construction. Fought at Öland on 15.7.1789. Cruised in the Baltic in the remainder of 1789. Led the attack at Krasnaia Gorka on 23–24.1790 as flag to Vice-Adm. Sukhotin who was mortally wounded along with other casualties of 10 killed and 22 wounded. Fought at Vyborg on 22.6.1790. Cruised in the Baltic in 1793, 1794, 1797 and in 1799 as flag to Adm. Khanykov. Decommissioned in 1799. Ordered to be broken up in 1802.

Sviatoi Ravnoapostol'nyi Kniaz' Vladimir 100/112 St Petersburg
*Constructor*s Jonathan Coleman (Kol'man) and D. Masal'skiy
Laid down 6.9.1785   *Launched* 2.8.1788
Dimensions 186 ft x 51 ft (51 ft 10 in outside plank) x 21 ft 6 in
             2,208 x 60/94 tons bm
Armament   Designed LD 24 x 36pdrs, 4 x 60 u (1 pood)

           MD 26 x 18pdrs, 2 x 24u(½ pood)
           UD 30 x 8pdrs
           FC & QD 10 x 6pdrs, 6 x 24pdr carr.
      1788 LD 24 x 36pdrs, 4 x 60 u (1 pood)
           MD 26 x 18pdrs, 4 x 24u (½ pood)
           UD 30 x 12pdrs
           FC & QD 20 x 6pdrs (4 x 24pdr carr. added 1789)

Ches'ma class. Jonathan Coleman (Kol'man) did the design work and D. Masal'skiy supervised the actual construction. Fought at Öland on 15.7.1789 and patrolled in the Baltic for the remainder of the year. Fought at Krasnaia Gorka on 23–24.5.1790 with casualties of 7 killed and 34 wounded. Fought at Vyborg on 22.6.1790. Cruised in the Baltic in 1791, 1793, 1795 and 1797. Decommissioned in 1797. Broken up after 1802.

Sviatoi Nikolai Chudotvorets 100/108/112 Kronshtadt
Constructor Jonathan Coleman (Kol'man) and G. Ignatyev
Laid down 19.9.1785 *Launched* 13.5.1789
Dimensions 186 ft x 51 ft (51 ft 10 in outside plank) x 21 ft 6 in
           2,208 x 60/94 tons bm
Armament Designed LD 24 x 36pdrs, 4 x 60 u (1 pood)
           MD 26 x 18pdrs, 2 x 24u (½ pood)
           UD 30 x 8pdrs
           FC & QD 10 x 6pdrs, 6 x 24pdr carr.
      1788 LD 24 x 36pdrs, 4 x 60 u (1 pood)
           MD 26 x 18pdrs, 4 x 24u (½ pood)
           UD 30 x 12pdrs
           FC & QD 20 x 6pdrs (4 x 24pdr carr. added 1789)

Ches'ma class. Jonathan Coleman (Kol'man) did the design work and G. Ignatyev supervised the construction. Fought at Öland on 15.7.1789 and patrolled in the Baltic for the remainder of the year. Fought at Krasnaia Gorka on 23–24.5.1790 with casualties of 1 killed and 2 wounded. Fought at Vyborg on 22.6.1790. Cruised in the Baltic in 1791, 1793, 1794–7 and 1800. Decommissioned in 1801. Training duties in Kronshtadt Roads in 1803. Employed as a floating battery at Kronshtadt with the middle deck battery removed in 1803. Hospital ship until 1808. The last ship of her class to be disposed of in 1808.

Sviatoi Evsevii 100/108/112 St Petersburg
Constructor Jonathan Coleman (Kol'man)
Laid down 3.1.1788 *Launched* 6.7.1790
Dimensions 186 ft x 51 ft (51 ft 10 in outside plank) x 21 ft 6 in
           2208 x 60/94 tons bm
Armament Designed LD 24 x 36pdrs, 4 x 60 u (1 pood)
           MD 26 x 18pdrs, 2 x 24u (½ pood)
           UD 30 x 8pdrs
           FC & QD 10 x 6pdrs, 6 x 24pdr carr.
      1788 LD 24 x 36pdrs, 4 x 60 u (1 pood)
           MD 26 x 18pdrs, 4 x 24u (½ pood)
           UD 30 x 12pdrs
           FC & QD 20 x 6pdrs (4 x 24pdr carr. added 1789)

Ches'ma class. Name taken from the saint whose saint's day falls on the same date as the battle of Ches'ma. Cruised in Kronshtadt Roads in 1791. Operated in the Sound off Copenhagen in 1793. Cruised in the Baltic in 1795–7. Decommissioned in 1799. Condemned in 1800. Moved from Revel' to Kronshtadt in 1801. Ordered to be broken up in 12.1802. Employed as a floating battery at Kronshtadt with the middle deck battery removed in 1803. Broken up in 1803.

Unnamed 100/108/112 ?
Laid down 1790 *Launched* broken up prior to launch
Dimensions 186 ft x 51 ft x 21 ft 6 in

Armament Designed LD 24 x 36pdrs, 4 x 60 u (1 pood)
           MD 26 x 18pdrs, 2 x 24u (½ pood)
           UD 30 x 8pdrs
           FC & QD 10 x 6pdrs, 6 x 24pdr carr.

Ches'ma class. Building postponed due to the end of the war with Sweden. Broken up due to dry rot and deterioration.

Blagodat' 130 St Petersburg
Constructor A. S. Katasonov
Laid down 25.2.1799 *Launched* 3.8.1800
Dimensions 198 ft x 52 ft (outside plank) x 21 ft 8 in
Armament   LD 26 x 36pdrs, 4 x 60 u (1 pood)
           MD 28 x 24pdrs, 4 x 24u (½ pood)
           UD 32 x 12pdrs
           FC & QD 24 x 8pdrs, 12 x 3pdrs (probable)

Design commissioned by Paul I to A. S. Katasonov for a ship comparable in force to the Spanish *Santisima Trinidad* but suitable for shallow Baltic conditions. A copy of the original plans for the *Santisma Trinidad* has recently been discovered in the St Petersburg archives and a representation of the Russian ship shows what appears to have been a smaller copy of the Spanish ship. On the other hand, *Blagodat'*'s dimensions were also close to those of French 110-gun ships of the 1780s. While acting as general admiral of the Russian navy in 1782, the future Paul I had reportedly been presented with their plans during his visit to Brest and the design of *Blagodat'* may have been influenced directly or indirectly by the French ships. The name *Blagodat'* itself was a reference to Paul I's beloved mistress Anna Lopukhina, something of a departure from normal protocols for choosing ship names. Coppered on completion. Cruised in the Baltic to Gottland in 1801. Struck by lightning off Dagerort with severe fire damage. Cruised in the Baltic to Bornholm in 1802. Sailed from Revel' to Kronshtadt in 1803. Transported troops to Pomerania in 1805. Storm damaged and forced to winter in Karlskrona. Operated as Adm. Khanykov's flag in 1808. Khanykov encountered the Anglo-Swedish squadron on 13.8.1808 and was forced to retreat to Rogervik (Baltiyskiy). Stationed in Kronshtadt Roads in 1809. Rearmed en flute and used to transport troops from Sveaborg to Revel' in 1812. Decommissioned in 1812. Broken up in 1814.

Ships with 70–78 guns (27 built 1762–1800, excluding the problematic *Ioann Bogoslov*)

The 74-gun ship in Russian service

The Russians were well behind the other major European naval powers in adopting the 74-gun ship as the standard capital ship for their Baltic and Black Sea battle fleets. Unlike the other great powers with access to and heavy commitments in Atlantic waters, there was no corresponding pressure placed on the Russians to move up to the 74 from their well-established 66-gun line of battle ships, both because of the shallow and restricted nature of the Baltic and because of the concurrent retention of similar, moderately sized 60–64-gun ships by their potential rivals, most particularly the Swedes in the Baltic and the Turks in the Levant.

In the absence of direct competion with the Atlantic naval powers, pressure for the adoption of the larger and more capable 74 was a more gradual process for the Russians than it was for the larger French, British and Spanish navies – all of whom were already in possession of significant numbers of 70-gun ships generally armed with guns heavier than the 24pdrs mounted on their own 60-gun ships. For the Western European navies, the

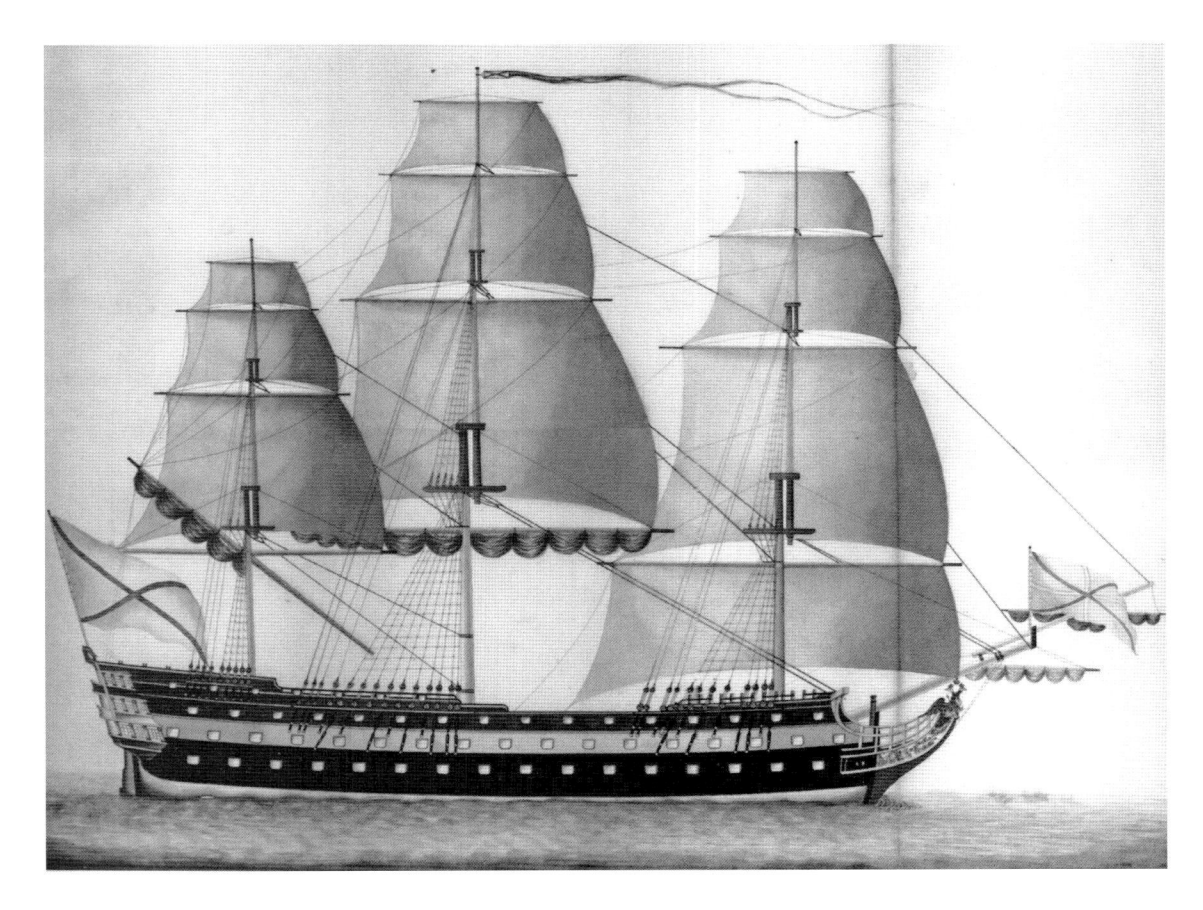

The 130-gun Blagodat *of 1800 was the Emperor Paul's great prestige ship. Although there are suggestions that her design was influenced by the French 110s, this painting from A. S. Katasanov's* Album *of 1801 shows unmistakable Spanish influence. This is reinforced by the recent discovery of plans for the Spanish* Santisima Trinidad *as she appeared after her 1795 reconstruction held in the Central Naval Archive at St Petersburg.*

60–64-gun ship had represented a lower end capital ship most useful for secondary duty in secondary theaters since the Anglo-Dutch wars of the preceeding century had demonstrated the need for maximizing concentrated fire power in line of battle confrontations, and one only useful for inclusion in the line of battle as a supplement for the larger ships. For the Russians, on the other hand, the 66-gun ship remained the standard line of battle ship for much of the eighteenth century. Russia eventually completed a total of fifty 74s and sixty-five 60/66s between 1762 and 1815, and continued to find the less capable 66-gun type useful as a fleet unit, even though it was gradually assuming less importance within their battle fleet. In this regard, it is instructive to recall that when the British chose to penetrate into Baltic waters during the Napoleonic period, they relied largely on their remnant 64s for reasons of their excellent suitability for Baltic conditions as well as because of their lack of value as battle fleet units in the Atlantic and Mediterranean.

When they did adopt to the larger type in 1770, Russian designs compared to contemporary European 74s as follows:

Arranged by length:
Spain
  San Miguel   1773   182 ft x 48 ft x 20 ft
France
  Pegase   1781   178 ft x 47 ft x 21 ft
Denmark
  Pr. Sofia Frederica   1773   175 ft x 47 ft x 19 ft
Sweden
  Sofiia Magdalina   1774   171 ft x 44 ft x 19 ft
Russia
  Sv. Velikomuchenik Isidor   1772   169 ft x 46 ft x 20 ft
Great Britain
  Elizabeth   1769   168 ft x 46 ft x 19 ft
Netherlands
  Jupiter   1782   167 ft x 46 ft x 18 ft

As arranged by calibre of lower deck main armaments:
France
  Pegase   1781   28 x 36, 30 x 18, 16 x 8
Russia
  Sv. Velikomuchenik Isidor   1772   26 x 30, 2 x 48 u, 26 x 18,
                                         2 x 24 u, 18 x 8
Great Britain
  Elizabeth   1769   28 x 32, 28 x 18, 18 x 9
Netherlands
  Jupiter   1782   28 x 30, 28 x 18, 18 x 12
Spain
  San Miguel   1773   28 x 24, 30 x 18, 16 x 8
Denmark
  Pr. Sofia Frederica   1773   28 x 24, 28 x 18, 18 x 8
Sweden
  Sofiia Magdalina   1774   28 x 24, 26 x 18, 16 x 6

All of these ships are typical of the 74s operated by their nations of origin during this period. With the exceptions of the Swedish *Sofiia Magdalina* and the Russian *Sviatoi Velikomuchenik*, they had all been captured and measured by the Royal Navy prior to inclusion therein, thus fortuitously insuring a uniformity of recorded dimensions for purposes of comparison. For historical reasons already cited relating to the early importation of British constructors by Peter I and his successors, the Russians also adopted British standards of measurement and British avoirdupois for their ships. Of the sample ships listed above, this leaves only the Swedish *Sofiia Magdalina* as having been measured by different protocols, and her dimensions are being included here because of the great importance of Swedish naval developments to Russian naval planning. The reader should bear in mind that the dimensions given for *Sofiia Magdalina* are those determined by Swedish naval protocol and are only approximations of what they might have been had this ship been captured and surveyed by the British.

In contrast to this degree of uniformity of measurement, the armaments of the various 74s reflect the differing avoirdupois of their countries of origin and their comparative values are more difficult to interpret. The primary armament for the Russian 74-gun ship was actually heavier in total weight of broadside than that of all the other ships except for the French and Dutch ships. This becomes clear when the weight of broadsides for the various lower deck main armaments are converted from national 'pounds' into grams to establish a common standard of comparison:

French	36pdr	17,622 g	(489.5g/lb)
Dutch	30pdr	14,823g	(494.1g/lb)
Russian	30pdr	14,700g	(490g/lb)
British	32pdr	14,528g	(454g/lb)
Swedish	24pdr	12,000g	(500g/lb)
Danish	24pdr	11,904g	(496g/lb)
Spanish	24pdr	11,748g	(489.5g/lb)

The Russian 30pdr lower deck guns would actually have been equivalent in weight of metal to British 32.4pdrs – had the British actually possessed such a weapon. In a similar manner, the French *Pegase* would have carried the equivalent of British 38.8pdr guns – again assuming that the British had had such weapons in their inventory.

From these tables, it is apparent that Russian 74s were rather on the smaller side of the spectrum for standard European 74s of the period and quite close in fact to the much criticized British 'common class' ships of which *Elizabeth* was a typical example. French and Spanish ships, on the other hand, were significantly larger than their opposite numbers in Russia and elsewhere. It is also apparent that the Russian ships carried heavier lower deck guns than their potential rivals (when various national 'pounds' are uniformly converted into metric terms). This is what might be expected, given the Russian practice of relying on the milder Baltic weather and hydrographic conditions as well as the shorter anticipated service lives of their warships to load their gun decks down with heavier ordnance than would have been acceptable in other navies. In this respect, it is interesting that the Russian *Vladislav*, after being captured by Sweden, was rearmed with very much lighter Swedish 24pdrs in place of the larger Russian 30pdrs.

Sviatoi Velikomuchenik Isidor class (2 ships)
Two prototypes laid down in 1769 established the pattern for subsequent Russian 74s with respect to both dimensions and armament. The introduction of 74s to the Russian navy fortuitously coincided with the introduction of edinorogs and the new ships carried two different calibres of the new type of ordnance. Both ships participated in the Armed Neutrality patrols, but they were withdrawn in the early 1780s and were never tested in combat.

Sviatoi Velikomuchenik Isidor 74 St Petersburg
Constructor I. V. James
Laid down 28.9.1769 *Launched* 17.9.1772
Dimensions 169 ft x 46 ft 4 in x 20 ft
Armament LD 26 x 30pdrs, 2 x 48u (1 pood)
            UD 26 x 18pdrs, 2 x 24u (½ pood)
            FC & QD 18 x 8pdrs

Sviatoi Velikomuchenik Isidor class. The first Russian 74. Assigned as the flag to Rear-Adm. Greig's 5th Arkhipelago Squadron on 21.10.1773. Operated in the Arkhipelago in 1773–4. Returned to Kronshtadt on 24.5.1775 carrying Princess Tarakanova, a pretender to the throne of Russia lured on board at Livorno and taken prisoner by a ruse on the part of Russian Count Orlov and Spanish Grand Duke de Ribas on 12.2.1775. Participated in the Imperial Review in honour of Catherine II in 1776. Returned to the Mediterranean in 1780–1 as flag to Rear-Adm. Borisov on Armed Neutrality Squadron. Decommissioned in 1781. Broken up in 1784.

Sviatoi Velikomuchenik Panteleimon 74 St Petersburg
Constructor V. A. Selyaninov
Laid down 28.9.1769 *Launched* 17.9.1772
Dimensions 169 ft x 47 ft x 20 ft 10 in
Armament LD 26 x 30pdrs, 2 x 48u (1 pood)
            UD 26 x 18pdrs, 2 x 24u (½ pood)
            FC & QD 18 x 8pdrs

Sviatoi Velikomuchenik Isidor class. *Sviatoi Panteleimon* is the saint day on which the battle of Gangut was won. Cruised in the Baltic in 1773, 1775, and 1777. Operated in the North Sea in 1780 as flag to Rear-Adm. Kruz. Operated in the Mediterranean on Armed Neutrality Patrol as the flag of Rear-Adm. Sukhotin in 1781–2. Decommissioned in 1782. Broken up in 1784.

Iezekiil 78 St Petersburg
Constructor V. A. Selyaninov
Laid down 5.12.1772 *Launched* 22.8.1773
Dimensions 178 ft x 48 ft 8 in x 20 ft 3 in
Armament LD 30 x 30pdrs
            UD 30 x 18pdrs, 18 x 8pdrs (conjecture based on known gun port arrangement)

A one-off ship designed by Adm. Knowles and constructed by Adm. Seniavin. Believed to have introduced the use of iron knees to Russian ships. She may have been something of a prototypical two-decker 80, but even this is uncertain in spite of her being sometimes rated as an 80/84. Cruised in the Baltic in 1774 and 1776–7. Operated off Portugal in 1780–1 as the flag to Brigadier Palibin's Armed Neutrality Squadron. Repaired in 1782–3. Cruised in the Baltic in 1784–5 and 1787. Cruised in the Baltic 8–10.1788. Fought at the battle of Öland in 15.7.1789. Fought at the battle of Krasnaia Gorka on 23–24.5.1790 with casualties of 4 killed and 5 wounded. Fought at the battle of Vyborg on 22.6.1790. In Kronshtadt Roads for training in 1791. Repaired in 1793. Broken up after 1797.

Tsar' Konstantin class (4 ships)

The four ships of the *Tsar' Konstantin* class were laid down at a leisurely rate over a seventeen-year period between 1770 and 1786. Armament was identical to that of the *Isidor* class on a hull that was 1 ft longer and 1 ft beamier. Three of the four were built at St Petersburg, and they were all apparently more solidly constructed than subsequent Russian 74s as evidenced by their long careers in active service, averaging out at 18½ years, well ahead of the service life averages of successive classes of Russian 74s. All four were involved in the Russo-Swedish War of 1788–90 and three fought in two or more of the major battles of the war. Three were retired before 1800, but *Sviataia Elena* was actively employed in the Mediterranean through 1807 after undergoing an extensive repair from 1798–1804.

Tsar' Konstantin 74 St Petersburg
Constructors   M. D. Portnov and I. V. James
Laid down 24.4.1770   *Launched* 24.6.1779
Dimensions 170 ft x 48 ft x 20 ft
Armament   LD 26 x 30pdrs, 2 x 48u (1 pood)
             UD 26 x 18pdrs, 2 x 24u (½ pood)
             FC & QD 18 x 8pdrs

Tsar' Konstantin class. Cruised in the Mediterranean in 1782–4 as flag to Vice-Adm. I. Chichagov. Cruised in the Baltic to Bornholm in 1785–6. Joined the Baltic fleet on 21.7.1788 and cruised until 11.1788. Fought at the battle of Krasnaia Gorka on 23.5.1790 and suffered casualties of 2 killed and 16 wounded with 10 shot holes and 11 guns blown up. Fought at the battle of Vyborg on 22–23.6.1790. Stationed in Kronshtadt Roads in training status in 1791. Cruised in the Baltic in 1792 and 1795–7. Decommissioned in 1797. Broken up after 1799.

Pobedoslav 74 St Petersburg
Constructors   V. A. Selyaninov and I. V. James
Laid down 26.1.1777   *Launched* 26.6.1782
Dimensions 170 ft x 48 in x 20 ft
Armament   LD 26 x 30pdrs, 2 x 60 u (1 pood)
             UD 26 x 18pdrs, 2 x 24u (½ pood)
             FC & QD 18 x 8pdrs

Tsar' Konstantin class. Cruised in the Baltic in 1783 and 1785. Operated in 8–9.1788 in Vice-Adm. Kruz's reserve squadron for the defence of Kotlin. Fought at Öland on 15.7.1789 (where she is reported to have been armed with 12pdrs in place of 18pdrs on the upper deck) with casualties of 2 killed and 17 wounded. Fought at Krasnaia Gorka on 23–24.5.1790 with casualties of 4 killed and 7 wounded. Fought at Vyborg on 22.6.1790. Commissioned in 1791 for training. Cruised in the Baltic in 1794–5 and 1797. Decommissioned in 1797. Broken up in 1804.

Sviataia Elena 74 St Petersburg
Constructors   I. V. James and G. Ivanov
Laid down 1.7.1780   *Launched* 6.9. 1785
Dimensions 170 ft x 48 ft x 20 ft
Armament   LD 26 x 30pdrs, 2 x 60 u (1 pood)
             UD 26 x 18pdrs, 2 x 24u (½ pood)
             FC & QD 18 x 8pdrs, 2 x 32pdr carr.

Tsar' Konstantin class. Fought at Gogland in 6.7.1788 with casualties of 6 killed and 10 wounded and 35 shot holes. Fought off Öland on 15.7.1789 and then patrolled off Bornholm, Gottland, and Dagerort for the rest of the year. Fought at Revel' on 2.5.1790 with 518 rounds expended. Fought at Vyborg on 22.6.1790. Cruised in the Baltic in 1791. Blockaded the sound off Copenhagen in 1793. Cruised in the Baltic in 1794. Operated with the squadron of Rear-Adm. Khanykov in Great Britain in 1795–6. Underwent a long repair in 1798–1804. Operated in the Mediterranean with a consignment of marines in 1804 under Commodore Greig (son of Adm. Greig). Stationed at Corfu in 1805 and transported troops to Naples. Escorted British troopships to Malta in 1806, proceeded to Trieste, blockaded Venice, and participated in the capture of Curzalo. Fought in the battle off the Dardanelles on 10–11.5.1807, at the battle of Athos on 19.6.1807, and arrived at Lisbon on 28.10.1807 where the Russian squadron was blockaded by the British. Repaired at Lisbon in 1808. Arrived at Portsmouth on 26.9.1808 and interned. Purchased by Great Britain in 1813.

Aleksandr Nevskii 74 Arkhangel'sk
Constructor M. D. Portnov
Laid down 11.5.1786   *Launched* 9.5.1787
Dimensions 170 ft x 48 ft x 20 ft
Armament   LD 26 x 30pdrs, 2 x 60 u (1 pood)
             UD 26 x 18pdrs, 2 x 24u (½ pood)
             FC & QD 18 x 8pdrs

Tsar' Konstantin class. Left Arkhangel'sk with Rear-Adm. Povalishin's squadron on 5.7.1788. Arrived at Copenhagen on 29.8.1788. Joined Adm. I. Chichagov's fleet on 22.7.1789 and cruised between Bornholm, Gottland, and Dagerort. Returned to Revel' and then Kronshtadt on 6.8.1790 after developing a leak. Repaired at Kronshtadt in 1790. Transferred to Revel' on 29.8.1790. Blockaded the Sound off Copenhagen as part of Adm. Chichagov's squadron in 7.1793. Cruised in the Baltic in 5–9.1794. Repaired at Kronshtadt in 1795–8. Joined Vice-Adm. Kruz's squadron and blockaded the Sound off Copenhagen in 1798. Armed en flute as part of Rear-Adm. P. Chichagov's squadron in 1799, and deployed to Great Britain for the Dutch Expedition. Damaged in a storm in the North Sea and repaired at Yarmouth. Landed troops in the Texel on 6.1800 and returned to the Baltic. Arrived at Kronshtadt on 21.7.1800. Decommissioned in 1801. Converted into a receiving ship in 1804. Broken up in 1814. (See *Aleksandr Nevskii* (74), commissioned in the Black Sea from 1787–1801 for a rare instance of two major Russian warships with the same name being in commission during the same time period.)

Ioann Bogoslov 74 ?
Constructor ?
Laid down ?   *Launched* 1783
Dimensions ?
Armament ?

This highly problematic ship is not listed in Veselago's *Spisok*, but is thought with some certitude to have existed. The Admiralty Board issued instructions to cover the 'new ship' *Ioann Bogoslov* with an experimental in white metal in of unknown composition to observe its effectiveness in resisting hull corrosion and to compare it with a similar coppering of *Trekh Ierarkhov* (100). It is unclear whether this experiment was actually implemented or what happened to this mystery ship.

Iaroslav class (19 ships)

The *Iaroslav*s became the standard 74-gun class of ships for the Baltic fleet prior to the major changes brought about by the Establishment of 1805. M. D. Portnoy who had worked on the preceding *Tsar' Konstantin* class, was constructor for the first eleven ships of the new class, while G. Ignatyev was responsible for the final six. All were built at Arkhangel'sk which had by now become the primary builder of Russian Baltic warships. The *Iaroslav*s were marginally less beamy than their predecessors and it is assumed that this was in the interest of improving their speed. Excluding the two combat losses, the *Iaroslav*s had average active service lives of 12.58 years, a poor showing when placed against the average of 18.5 for the four *Konstantin*s. The markedly shorter lifespans of these ships may have been the result of inferior materials and construction standards being employed at Arkhangel'sk, their more arduous and eventful service careers, or a combination of the two.

Eight of the early ships were actively involved in the War with Sweden in 1788–90. *Vladislav* suffered the misfortune of being captured by the Swedes in a conflict that went entirely in favor of the Russians in most other respects. She remained in Swedish service until 1819, a tribute to the intensive Swedish standards of ship maintenance and an interesting indication of what the Russians might have accomplished with their ships had their priorities with regards to preventative maintenance been different. After 1800, four of the newer *Iaroslav*s made their way to the Mediterranean where a lack of maintenance opportunities and intense operational activity resulted in three being reduced to unserviceability within a few years, while the fourth ship, *Isidor*, successfully made her way to Sevastopol' where she was absorbed into the Black Sea fleet and where she survived as a hulk until 1812. A second member of the class, *Vsevolod*, was also lost in combat, being destroyed in 1808 by two British 74s during the final Russo-Swedish War.

In common with other Russian line of battle ships, *Iaroslav*s completed after 1780 were armed with 7.7-in. 60pdr 1 pood edinorogs in place of the earlier 7.2-in 48pdr 1 pood guns.

Iaroslav 74 Arkhangel'sk
Constructor M. D. Portnov
Laid down 13.1.1783   *Launched* 12.5.1784
Dimensions 170 ft x 46 ft 8 in x 20 ft 8 in
Armament   LD 26 x 30pdrs, 2 x 60 u (1 pood)
             UD 26 x 18pdrs, 2 x 24u (½ pood)
             FC & QD 18 x 8pdrs, 2 x 42pdr carr.

Iaroslav class. Introduced carronades to 74s. Sailed from Arkhangel'sk to Kronstadt in 6–8.1784. Cruised in the Baltic to Bornholm in 1785. Fought at Gogland on 6.7.1788 with casualties of 7 killed and 29 wounded and 20 shot holes. Attacked and captured *Gustav-Adol'f* on 26.7.1788. Fought at Öland on 15.7.1789 and patrolled between Bornholm, Gottland, and Daterort for the rest of the year. Fought at Revel' on 2.5.1790 with casualties of 1 killed, 3 wounded, and 1330 rounds expended. Fought at Vyborg on 22.6.1790 and patrolled between Porkkala-udd, Sveaborg, and Baresund for the rest of the year. Cruised in the Baltic in 1791. Blockaded the Sound off Copenhagen in 1793. Transferred from Revel' to Kronstadt and decommissioned in 1795. Broken up in 1798.

Vladislav 74 Arkhangel'sk
Constructor M. D. Portnov
Laid down 19.9.1782   *Launched* 12.5.1784
Dimensions 170 ft x 48 ft 8 in x 20 ft
Armament   LD 26 x 30pdrs, 2 x 60 u (1 pood)
             UD 26 x 18pdrs, 2 x 24u (½ pood)
             FC & QD 18 x 8pdrs, 2 x 42pdr carr.

Iaroslav class. Sailed from Arkhangel'sk to Kronstadt in 6–8.1784. Cruised in the Baltic to Bornholm in 1785. Fought at Gogland on 6.7.1788 and forced to surrender with casualties of 257–9 killed and wounded, 34 underwater shot holes, and 3 guns destroyed. (The failure of *Deris'* 66 to come to her support led to the court-martial and disgrace of her captain – see *Deris'*). Extant in Swedish service as *Vladislaff* (the Swedish spelling of Vladislav) until 1819.

Vseslav 74 Arkhangel'sk
Constructor M. D. Portnov
Laid down 1.5.1784   *Launched* 13.5.1785
Dimensions 170 ft x 46 ft 8 in x 20 ft
Armament   LD 26 x 30pdrs, 2 x 60 u (1 pood)
             UD 26 x 18pdrs, 2 x 24u (½ pood)
             FC & QD 18 x 8pdrs, 2 x 42pdr carr.

Iaroslav class. Sailed from Arkhangel'sk to Kronstadt on 20.12.1787. Included in Greig's Mediterranean Squadron in 1787. Fought at Gogland on 6.7.1788 as flag to Rear-Adm. Kozlyaninov; engaging and routing two Swedish ships of the line, suffering casualties of 35 killed and 13 wounded and 40 shot holes and severe damage to the rigging. Forced to return to Kronstadt for repairs after the battle. Fought at Osel in 1789 without taking casualties. On 24.9.1789 damaged in a storm and forced to return to Revel' and then Kronstadt for repairs. Fought at Krasnaia Gorka on 23–24.5.1790 with casualties of 1 killed and 13 wounded. Heavily engaged at Vyborg on 22.6.1790, engaged simultaneously on both broadsides and then forced to evade several fire-ships. Training duty in Kronstadt Roads in 1791. Operated in Adm. I. Chichagov's squadron blockading the Sound off Copenhagen in 1793. Cruised in the Baltic in 1794 as part of Rear-Adm. Makarov's squadron in 1794. Sailed from Revel' to Kronstadt in 7.1795 and decommissioned. Broken up in 1798 at Kronstadt.

Mstislav 74 Arkhangel'sk
Constructor M. D. Portnov
Laid down 1.5.1784   *Launched* 13.5.1785
Dimensions 170 ft x 46 ft 8 in x 20 ft
Armament   LD 26 x 30pdrs, 2 x 60 u (1 pood)
             UD 26 x 18pdrs, 2 x 24u (½ pood)
             FC & QD 18 x 8pdrs, 2 x 32pdr carr.
             672 men

Iaroslav class. Sailed from Arkhangel'sk to Kronstadt in 7–8.1785. Fought at Gogland on 6.7.1788 with 23 killed, 47 wounded and 116 shot holes. Cruised in the Gulf of Finland during the rest of the year. Fought at Öland on 15.7.1789 with casualties of 2 killed, including Capt. Mulovskiy, and 16 wounded. Fought at Revel' on 2.5.1790 with casualties of 3 wounded and with 793 rounds expended. Cruised in the Baltic in 1791. Blockaded the Sound off Copenhagen in 1793. Left Kronstadt in.5.1798 with the First Division of Vice-Adm. Makarov's squadron and from 7.1798 operated under the overall command of British Vice-Adm. Duncan in North Sea waters in 1798–1800. Participated in the surrender of the Dutch fleet. on 19–20.8.1799 under the command of Adm. Mitchell. Cruised in the Baltic in 1802. Training duties in Kronstadt Roads in 1803. Decommissioned in 1804. Hulked in 1805. Broken up in 1811.

Sviatoi Pyotr 74 Arkhangel'sk
Constructor M. D. Portnov
Laid down 20.7.1785   *Launched* 14.5.1786
Dimensions 170 ft x 46 ft 8 in x 20 ft
Armament   LD 26 x 30pdrs, 2 x 60 u (1 pood)
             UD 26 x 18pdrs, 2 x 24u (½ pood)
             FC & QD 18 x 8pdrs, 2 x 42pdr carr.   656 men

Iaroslav class. Sailed from Arkhangel'sk to Kronstadt in 7–8.1787. Fought at Gogland on 6.7.1788 with casualties of 22 dead and 66 wounded and 76 shot holes. Fought at Öland on 15.7.1789 with casualties of 5 dead and 22 wounded. Patrolled between Bornholm,

Gottland, and Dagerort and then in the Gulf of Finland during the remainder of 1789. Fought at Krasnaia Gorka on 23–24.5.1790 with casualties of 12 dead and 13 wounded. Fought at Vyborg on 22.6.1790 where she sustained serious damage and was forced to return to Kronshtadt for repair. Assigned to training duties in Kronshtadt Roads in 1791. Cruised in the Sound off Copenhagen in 1793. Cruised in the Baltic in 1794. Cruised in the Baltic in 1795 and transferred from Revel' to Kronshtadt. Repaired in 1796. Departed Revel' for England with Rear-Adm. Kartsov's 3rd Division on 20.8.1798. Damaged in storm off Skagen and repaired at Mandal, Norway. Arrived at Yarmouth on 8.11.1798. Returned to Kronshtadt on 21.7.1800. Cruised in the Baltic in 1800. Decommissioned in 1802. Hulked in 1803.

Kir Ioann 74 Arkhangel'sk
Constructor M. D. Portnov
Laid down 20.6.1785 *Launched* 16.5.1786
Dimensions 170 ft x 46 ft 8 in x 20 ft 8 in
Armament LD 26 x 30pdrs, 2 x 60 u (1 pood)
UD 26 x 18pdrs, 2 x 24u (½ pood)
FC & QD 18 x 8pdrs, 2 x 42pdr carr.
Iaroslav class. Sailed from Arkhangel'sk to Kronshtadt in 7–8.1787. Fought at Gogland on 6.7.1788 with casualties of 7 killed and 22 wounded and 67 shot holes. Fought at Öland on 15.7.1789 and patrolled between Bornholm, Gottland, Dagerort and in the Gulf of Finland during the remainder of the year. Fought at Revel' on 5.5.1790, expending 800 rounds and taking no casualties. Fought at Vyborg on 22.6.1790. Cruised in the Baltic in 1791. Operated under Vice-Adm. Kruz in the Sound off Copenhagen and then in the North Sea in 1793. Decommissioned in 1793. Broken up in 1798.

Sysoi Velikii 74 Arkhangel'sk
Constructor M. D. Portnov
Laid down 10.6.1787 *Launched* 7.5.1788
Dimensions 170 ft x 46 ft 8 in x 20 ft 8 in
Armament LD 26 x 30pdrs, 2 x 60 u (1 pood)
UD 26 x 18pdrs, 2 x 24u (½ pood)
FC & QD 18 x 8pdrs
Iaroslav class. Departed Arkhangel'sk with Rear-Adm. Povalishin's squadron on 5.7.1788. Grounded, damaged, repaired and forced to winter at Christiansand, Norway in 1788–9. Joined Adm. I. Chichagov's fleet on 22.7.1789 and patrolled between Bornholm, Gottland, and Dagerort. Damaged and returned to Revel' and then Kronshtadt. Fought at Krasnaia Gorka on 2.5.1790 and suffered 41 wounded when a 30pdr exploded. Fought at Biork-e zund off Copenhagen on 20.16.1790. Fought at Vyborg on 23.6.1790. Training duty at Kronshtadt Roads in 1791. Cruised in the Baltic in 1794–5, 1797–8 and 1801. Decommissioned in 1801. Broken up in 1804.

Maksim Ispovednik 74 Arkhangel'sk
Constructor M. D. Portnov
Laid down 10.6.1787 *Launched* 8.5.1788
Dimensions 170 ft x 46 ft 8 in x 20 ft 8 in
Armament LD 26 x 30pdrs, 2 x 60 u (1 pood)
UD 26 x 18pdrs, 2 x 24u (½ pood)
FC & QD 18 x 8pdrs
Iaroslav class. Sailed from Arkhangel'sk to Copenhagen with Rear-Adm. Povalishin's squadron from 5.7.1788 to 29.8.1788. Joined Adm. Fondesin's squadron at Copenhagen and blockaded Karlskrona. Joined Adm. Chichagov's squadron on 22.7.1789 and cruised in the Baltic until forced to return for a long refit after storm damage. Patrolled off Gogland in 7–8.1790. Cruised in the Baltic in 1791–3 and 1795–8.

In.4.1801 sailed from Revel' to Kronshtadt with 17 other ships of the line anticipating the arrival of Horatio Nelson's Baltic squadron. Decommissioned in 1801. Broken up in 1804.

Boris 74 Arkhangel'sk
Constructor M. D. Portnov
Laid down 1.7.1788 *Launched* 16.5.1789
Dimensions 170 ft x 46 ft 8 in x 20 ft 8 in
Armament LD 26 x 30pdrs, 2 x 60 u (1 pood)
UD 26 x 18pdrs, 2 x 24u (½ pood)
FC & QD 18 x 8pdrs
Iaroslav class. Sailed from Arkhangel'sk to Kronshtadt in 7–9.1792. Cruised in the North Sea in 1793. Cruised on training duties in 1794–5. Cruised in the Baltic in 1798–1800. Decommissioned in 1800. Floating battery off Kotlin in 1801. Hulked after 1802.

Gleb 74 Arkhangel'sk
Constructor M. D. Portnov
Laid down 25.7.1788 *Launched* 16.5.1789
Dimensions 170 ft x 46 ft 8 in x 20 ft 8 in
Armament LD 26 x 30pdrs, 2 x 60 u (1 pood)
UD 26 x 18pdrs, 2 x 24u (½ pood)
FC & QD 18 x 8pdrs
Iaroslav class. Sailed from Arkhangel'sk to Kronshtadt in 7–9.1792. Cruised in the North Sea in 1793. To England in 1795, operating in the North Sea, and participating in the blockade of Holland. Returned to Kronshtadt in 1796. Repaired in 1798. Cruised in the Baltic in 1799–1801. Decommissioned in 1801. Receiving ship in 1802. Floating battery at Revel' in 1803. Hospital ship 1805–9. Hulked after 1809.

Pyotr 74 Arkhangel'sk
Constructor M. D. Portnov
Laid down 26.6.1789 *Launched* 22.5.1790
Dimensions 170 ft x 46 ft 8 in x 20 ft 8 in
Armament LD 26 x 30pdrs, 2 x 60 u (1 pood)
UD 26 x 18pdrs, 2 x 24u (½ pood)
FC & QD 18 x 8pdrs
Iaroslav class. Sailed from Arkhangel'sk to Kronshtadt in 7–9.1792. Cruised in the North Sea in 1793. Cruised in the Baltic in 1794. Operated as flag for Rear-Adm. Thate in the squadron of Vice-Adm. Khanykov in England in 1795–6. Operated off Copenhagen and then again in England under Rear-Adm. Makarov in 1796–7. Operated off the Prussian coast under Rear-Adm. Khanykov in 1799. Cruised in the Baltic in 1800 and 1803. Decommissioned in 1804. Condemned in 1805. Broken up in 1821.

Aleksei 74 Arkhangel'sk
Constructor M. D. Portnov
Laid down 26.6.1789 *Launched* 22.5.1790
Dimensions 170 ft x 46 ft 8 in x 20 ft 8 in
Armament LD 26 x 30pdrs, 2 x 60 u (1 pood)
UD 26 x 18pdrs, 2 x 24u (½ pood)
FC & QD 18 x 8pdrs
624 men
Iaroslav class. Sailed from Arkhangel'sk to Kronshtadt as flag to Rear-Adm. Thate from 30.6–27.9.1794. Cruised in the Baltic in 1795–7. Left for England with Rear-Adm. Kartsov's 3rd Squadron on 20.8.1798. Delayed in transit by a severe storm off Skagen, Norway. Operated in the North Sea in 1798–9 as part of Rear-Adm. Kartsov's 3rd Squadron. Cruised in the Baltic in 1800–2. Decommissioned in 1804. Condemned in 1805. Floating battery in the north freeway of Kotlin from 1807–12. Broken up in 1815.

Pamiat' Evstafii 74 Arkhangel'sk
Constructor M. D. Portnov
Laid down 14.7.1790 *Launched* 24.5.1791
Dimensions 170 ft x 46 ft 8 in x 20 ft 8 in
Armament LD 26 x 30pdrs, 2 x 60 u (1 pood)
UD 26 x 18pdrs, 2 x 24u (½ pood)
FC & QD 18 x 8pdrs

Iaroslav class. Name commemorates the *Evstafii Plakida*, the Russian flagship lost at the battle of Chios. Sailed from Arkhangel'sk to Kronshtadt as flag to Rear-Adm. Povalishin in 30.6–27.9.1794. To England with Vice-Adm. Khanykov's squadron in 1795–6. Cruised to Bornholm with Vice-Adm. Kruz's squadron in 1798. Cruised in the Baltic in 1800. Decommissioned in 1800. Harbour service in 1801. Sailed from Kronshtadt to Revel' for service as a floating battery in 1803. Broken up in 1817.

Isidor 74 Arkhangel'sk
Constructor G. Ignatyev
Laid down 10.10.1792 *Launched* 1795
Dimensions 170 ft x 46 ft 8 in x 20 ft 8 in
Armament LD 26 x 30pdrs, 2 x 60 u (1 pood)
UD 26 x 18pdrs, 2 x 24u (½ pood)
FC & QD 18 x 8pdrs
613 men

Iaroslav class. Left Arkhangel'sk as part of Vice-Adm. Thate's 2nd Division on 3.7.1798. Arrived at Nore on 8.8.1798. On 2.6.1799, left for the Mediterranean as flag to Vice-Adm. Kartsov's squadron sent to reinforce Adm. Ushakov. Arrived at Palermo on 3.8.1799 and at Corfu on 7.1.1800. Returned to Sevastopol' and the Black Sea fleet with Adm. Ushakov's squadron on 26.10.1800. In 1804, transported troops from Sevastopol' to Poti in the Caucasus. Transported troops to Corfu in 1805 and returned to Sevastopol'. Landed troops at the siege of Anapa in 1807. Decommissioned and hulked in 1809. Broken up in 1812.

Vsevolod 74 Arkhangel'sk
Constructor G. Ignatyev
Laid down 21.9.1794 *Launched* 24.8.1796
Dimensions 170 ft x 46 ft 8 in x 20 ft 8 in
Armament LD 26 x 30pdrs, 2 x 60 u (1 pood)
UD 26 x 18pdrs, 2 x 24u (½ pood)
FC & QD 18 x 8pdrs
640 men

Iaroslav class. Left Arkhangel'sk with the 2nd Division as flag to Vice-Adm. Thate on 3.7.1798. Arrived at Nore on 8.8.1798 and operated in the North Sea and off the Texel in 1798–00. Returned to Kronshtadt on 21.7.1800. Carried supplies to Revel' in 1800. Cruised in the Baltic in 1801 and 1803. Repaired in 1804. Transported troops to Pomerania as part of Adm. Thate's squadron in 9.1805. Operated in Adm. Khanykov's squadron in 1808. Khanykov encountered the superior Anglo-Swedish squadron on 13.8.1808 and was forced to retreat to Rogervik (Baltiyskiy). On 14.8.1808, *Vsevolod* was heavily damaged by gunfire while three nearby Russian ships failed to render assistance. While under tow by the frigate *Poluks*, she grounded 6 miles outside of Rogervik where she was attacked, raked, looted and fired by *Centaur* and *Implacable* with the loss of 303 men. She was blown up on 15.8.1808. Khanykov was dismissed for his failure to properly assist her.

Severnyi Oryol 74 Arkhangel'sk
Constructor G. Ignatyev
Laid down 21.9.1794 *Launched* 2.5.1797
Dimensions 170 ft x 46 ft 8 in x 20 ft 8 in
Armament LD 26 x 30pdrs, 2 x 60 u (1 pood)
UD 26 x 18pdrs, 2 x 24u (½ pood)
FC & QD 18 x 8pdrs
636 men

Iaroslav class. Departed Arkhangel'sk in Vice-Adm. Thate's 2nd Division on 3.7.1798. Arrived at Nore on 8.8.1798. Operated in the North Sea in 1798–1800, and transported troops to Holland. Returned to Kronshtadt on 21.7.1800. Carried supplies to Revel' in 1800. Cruised in the Baltic in 1801 and 1803. Decommissioned in 1804. Hulked after 1805. Reduced to a floating battery in the northern freeway of Kotlin (Kronshtadt) in 1808. Broken up in 1809.

Moskva 74 Arkhangel'sk
Constructor G. Ignatyev
Laid down 21.8.1798 *Launched* 22.5.1799
Dimensions 170 ft x 46 ft 8 in x 20 ft 8 in
Armament LD 26 x 30pdrs, 2 x 60 u (1 pood)
UD 26 x 18pdrs, 2 x 24u (½ pood)
FC & QD 18 x 8pdrs (Morskoi Sbornik)

Iaroslav class. Departed Arkhangel'sk for England in Vice-Adm. Baratynskiy's squadron on 8.9.1799. Cruised in the North Sea in 1798–1800. Arrived at Kronshtadt on 26.9.1800. Cruised in the Baltic in 1801 and 1803. Departed Kronshtadt for the Mediterranean in Vice-Adm. Seniavin's squadron on 10.9.1805. Operated in the Mediterranean in 1806–7. Storm damaged between Sicily and Sardinia in 9.1807 while returning to Russia in company with *Sviatoi Pyotr*. and forced into Elba for repairs. Arrived at Toulon in 1808 where she remained for 22 months prior to being sold to France in a dilapidated state on 27.9.1809.

Iaroslav 74 Arkhangel'sk
Constructor G. Ignatyev
Laid down 21.8.1798 *Launched* 22.5.1799
Dimensions 170 ft x 46 ft 8 in x 20 ft 8 in
Armament LD 26 x 30pdrs, 2 x 60 u (1 pood)
UD 26 x 18pdrs, 2 x 24u (½ pood)
FC & QD 18 x 8pdrs (Morskoi Sbornik)

Iaroslav class. Departed Arkhangel'sk for England in Vice-Adm. Baratynskiy's squadron on 8.9.1799. Severely damaged in a storm off Norway, taken in tow by a British store ship and then by the British frigate HMS *Champion*. Repaired in England and returned to Kronshtadt in Vice-Adm. Baratynskiy's squadron on 26.9.1800. Cruised in the Baltic in 1801 and 1803. Transported troops in 1804 in Rear-Adm. Crown's squadron and then repaired and coppered. Departed Kronshtadt for the Mediterranean in Vice-Adm. Seniavin's squadron on 10.9.1805. Operated in the Mediterranean in 1806–7. In combat in the Dardanelles in 10–11.5.1807. Fought at Athos in 19.6.1807. Arrived at Lisbon on 30.10.1807. Escorted to Great Britain for internment in 1809. Abandoned due to her poor condition and sold to Great Britain in 1813.

Sviatoi Pyotr (*Sankt Pyotr*) 74 Arkhangel'sk
Constructor G. Ignatyev
Laid down 12.11.1798 *Launched* 22.7.1799
Dimensions 170 ft x 46 ft 8 in x 20 ft 8 in
Armament LD 26 x 30pdrs, 2 x 60 u (1 pood)
UD 26 x 18pdrs, 2 x 24u (½ pood)
FC & QD 18 x 8pdrs (Morskoi Sbornik)

Iaroslav class. Usually referred to as *Sankt Pyotr* to distinguish her from Black Sea contemporary *Sviatoi Pyotr*. Departed Arkhangel'sk for England in Vice Baratynskiy's squadron on 8.9.1799. Severely damaged in a storm, losing masts and bowsprit and taking 3–4 ft of water. Spent two winters at Bergen, Norway before returning to Kronshtadt on 19.9.1801. Cruised in the Baltic in 1802–4, carrying troops in Rear-Adm. Crown's squadron. Repaired and coppered in 1804. Departed Kronshtadt for the Mediterranean in Vice-Adm. Seniavin's squadron on 10.9.1805. Operated in the Mediterranean in 1806–7. Arrived in company with her sister ship *Moskva* (74) at Toulon after the Peace of Tilsit. Sold to France in 1809, by which time she was incapable of putting to sea.

Elisaveta 74 St Petersburg
*Constructor*s Jonathan Coleman (Kol'man) and M. Sarychev
Laid down 22.11.1788   *Launched* 6.9.1795
Dimensions 176 ft x 48 ft 8 in x 19 ft 6 in
Armament   LD 26 x 30pdrs, 2 x 60 u (1 pood)
              UD 26 x 18pdrs, 2 x 24u (½ pood)
              FC & QD 18 x 8pdrs
              672 men

Another one-off design built at St Petersburg at a time when the construction of 74s had largely passed to Arkhangel'sk. Significantly larger than the ships of the *Iaroslav* class. Cruised in the Baltic in 1796–7. Departed Kronshtadt in 5.1798 as flagship of the First Division to Vice-Adm. Makarov. Operated from 7.1798 under the overall command of British Vice-Adm. Duncan in North Sea waters in 1798–1800, landing troops in the Netherlands. Cruised in the Baltic in 1802. Decommissioned in 1802. Assigned as fireguard at Revel' in 1803–12. Broken up in 1817.

Ships with 60–68 guns (59 built 1762–1800 including 28 *Slava Rossii*s from the previous section)

Aziia class (28 ships)
The *Aziia* class was a straightforward enlargement of the earlier *Slava Rossii* class with the same armament being carried on an additional 4½ ft of length and 3 ft of beam. The additional 4½ feet would appear to have been utilized in part at least to accommodate an additional pair of lower deck guns, bringing their armament into compliance with the original requirements of the 1723 Establishment (see notes for the *Slava Rossii* class). As was the case with the earlier class, there appears to have been a degree of variability in some individual class members, with individual designers making alterations to suit their own concepts in at least seven class members. How great a degree of variability from the designed draught and specified dimensions resulted from this practice is a matter for conjecture. The *Aziia*s were theoretically armed as per the 1723 Establishment, but actual armament generally involved replacing two of the lower deck 24pdrs with a pair of one-pood edinorogs and two of the upper deck 12pdrs with a pair of ½-pood edinorogs. Twenty-eight ships were built to this design between 1773 and 1797. With the completion of the final class member, *Pobeda*, in 1797, the 66-gun ship had effectively ceased to be a front-line fleet unit and the future belonged to 74s and even larger 84s. A further eight ships in the 60–66-gun range would be built for the Russian fleet in the Baltic after 1800. None of these ships was developments of earlier designs; they were rather a hotchpotch of derivative Swedish designs, experimental Russian designs, and a single unique 64-gun design purchased from Great Britain.

Slava Rossii II was one of nine *Aziia*s sent to the Mediterranean as part of the Armed Neutrality squadron in 1780–4. She was wrecked off Toulon in 1780. A total of thirteen *Aziia*s were later employed against Sweden in 1788–90 and they played a major part in combat operations along with the newer and more capable 74s. *Rodislav* and *Vysheslav* were both lost to grounding during the war, while *Severnyi Oryol* was the only combat fatality, being deliberately grounded and set afire to avoid capture by the Swedish rowing flotilla.

As was the case with the 74-gun *Iaroslav*s, those *Aziia*s completed after 1780 were armed with 60-pdr 1-pood edinorogs in place of the earlier standard 48pdr weapons.

Aziia 66 Arkhangel'sk
Constructor G. Maltsev
Laid down 19.8.1772   *Launched* 20.9.1773
Dimensions 160 ft x 44 ft 6 in x 19 ft
Armament   LD 24 x 24pdrs, 2 x 48u (1 pood)
              UD 24 x 12pdrs, 2 x 24u (½ pood)
              FC & QD 14 x 6pdrs (1723 Establishment) modified

Aziia class. Successor to the *Slava Rossii* class. Sailed from Arkhangel'sk to Kronshtadt in 6–10.1775. Cruised in the Baltic in 1776–8. Operated in the Mediterranean in Rear-Adm. Borisov's Armed Neutrality Squadron. Decommissioned in 1780. Repaired in 1782. Broken up after 1791.

Amerika 66 Arkhangel'sk
Constructor G. Maltsev
Laid down 19.8.1772   *Launched* 20.9.1773
Dimensions 160 ft x 44 ft 6 in x 19 ft
Armament   LD 24 x 24pdrs, 2 x 48u (1 pood)
              UD 22 x 12pdrs, 2 x 24u (½ pood)
              FC & QD 16 x 6pdrs (1723 Establishment) modified

Aziia class (28 ships). Name makes reference to Russian settlements along the Pacific coastline of North America. Sailed from Arkhangel'sk to Revel' in 6–9.1775. Transferred to Kronshtadt in 1777. Operated in the Mediterranean as part of Rear-Adm. Borisov's Armed Neutrality Squadron in 1780–1. Cruised in the Baltic in 1787. Fought at Krasnasya Gorka (Styrsudden) on 23–24.5.1790 and took casualties of 10 killed and 26 wounded. Escorted the galley flotilla of Nassau-Siegen to Biorke-e Sound on 13.6.1790. Fought at the battle of Vyborg on 21–22.6.1790. Returned to Kronshtadt with damages on 23.6.1790. Decommissioned in 1790. Broken up after 1791.

Slava Rossii 66 Arkhangel'sk
*Constructor*s   V. Gunion and M. D. Portnov
Laid down 20.9.1773   *Launched* 18.5.1774
Dimensions 160 ft x 44 ft 6 in x 19 ft
Armament   LD 24 x 24pdrs, 2 x 48u (1 pood)
              UD 22 x 12pdrs, 2 x 24u (½ pood)
              FC & QD 16 x 6pdrs (1723 Establishment) modified

Aziia class. Remained at Arkhangel'sk until 1778. Sailed to Kronshtadt in 6–8.1778. Operated in Rear-Adm. Borisov's Armed Neutrality squadron in the Mediterranean in 1780 until she was wrecked on 23.10.1780 eight miles outside of Toulon with a loss of 11 men drowned and 446 saved.

Blagopoluchie 66 Arkhangel'sk
*Constructor*s   V. Gunion and M. D. Portnov
Laid down 20.9.1773   *Launched* 18.5.1774
Dimensions 160 ft x 44 ft 6 in x 19 ft
Armament   LD 24 x 24pdrs, 2 x 48u (1 pood)
              UD 22 x 12pdrs, 2 x 24u (½ pood)
              FC & QD 16 x 6pdrs (1723 Establishment) modified

Aziia class (28 ships). Remained at Arkhangel'sk until 1778. Sailed to Kronshstadt in 6–8.1778. Operated in Rear-Adm. Kruz's Armed Neutrality squadron in the North Sea in 1780 and 1782. Decommissioned in 1782. Broken up in 1793.

Tvyordyi 66 Arkhangel'sk
Constructors   V. Gunion and M. D. Portnov
Laid down 20.9.1773   *Launched* 21.5.1774
Dimensions 160 ft x 44 ft 6 in x 19 ft
Armament   LD 24 x 24pdrs, 2 x 48u (1 pood)
             UD 22 x 12pdrs, 2 x 24u (½ pood)
             FC & QD 16 x 6pdrs (1723 Establishment) modified
Aziia class. Remained at Arkhangel'sk until 1778. Sailed to Kronshstadt in 6–8.1778. Operated in Rear-Adm. Borisov's Armed Neutrality Squadron in the Mediterranean in 1780–1. Operated in Rear-Adm. Kruz's Armed Neutrality squadron in the North Sea in 1782. Cruised in the Baltic to Bornholm in 1787. Decommissioned in 1787. Broken up in 1791.

Sviatoi Nikolai 66 Arkhangel'sk
Constructors   V. Gunion and M. D. Portnov
Laid down 12.11.1773   *Launched* 21.5.1774
Dimensions 160 ft x 44 ft 6 in x 19 ft
Armament   LD 24 x 24pdrs, 2 x 48u (1 pood)
             UD 22 x 12pdrs, 2 x 24u (½ pood)
             FC & QD 16 x 6pdrs (1723 Establishment) modified
Aziia class. Remained at Arkhangel'sk until 1779. Arrived at Kronshtadt on 17.10.1779. Operated in Rear-Adm. Kruz's Armed Neutrality squadron in the North Sea in 1780 and 1782. Decommissioned in 1782. Broken up in 1790.

Khrabryi 66 Arkhangel'sk
Constructors   V. Gunion and M. D. Portnov
Laid down 12.11.1773   *Launched* 21.5.1774
Dimensions 160 ft x 44 ft 6 in x 19 ft
Armament   LD 24 x 24pdrs, 2 x 48u (1 pood)
             UD 22 x 12pdrs, 2 x 24u (½ pood)
             FC & QD 16 x 6pdrs (1723 Establishment) modified
Aziia class. Remained at Arkhangel'sk until 1779. Severely damaged on passage to the Baltic in 1779, suffering the loss of 43 sailors, being dismasted and forced to winter in Norway. Arrived at Kronshtadt in 6.1780. Cruised to Bornholm in 1787. Fought at the battle of Vyborg on 22–23.6.1790 where she and *Mstislav* combined to capture the *Sofiia Magdalina*. Decommissioned in 1790. Repaired in 1793. Found unfit for further service in 1796.

Ne Tron' Menia 66 Arkhangel'sk
Constructor M. D. Portnov
Laid down 1.12.1776   *Launched* 12.5.1780
Dimensions 160 ft x 44 ft 6 in x 19 ft
Armament   LD 24 x 24pdrs, 2 x 60 u (1 pood)
             UD 22 x 12pdrs, 2 x 24u (½ pood)
             FC & QD 16 x 6pdrs (1723 Establishment) modified
Aziia class. Built by M. D. Portnov to a plan by I. V. James. Sailed from Arkhangel'sk to Kronshtadt in 7–10.1780. Operated in the Mediterranean in 1781–2 in Rear-Adm. Sukhotin's Armed Neutrality Squadron. Cruised in the Baltic to Gottland in 1783. Repaired in 1788. Cruised in the Baltic in 6–9.1789. Fought at the battle of Krasnaia Gorka on 23–24.5.1790 with casualties of 1 killed, 2 wounded, one gun destroyed and a single hull hole. Fought at the battle of Vyborg on 22.6.1790 with the loss of the captain and severely damaged rigging. Cruised in the Baltic in 1792 and off Prussia in 1796–1801. Decommissioned in 1801. Stationed in the Revel' Roads as a floating battery in 1803. Hulked in the autumn of 1803.

Sviatoi Ianuarii 66 Arkhangel'sk
Constructor M. D. Portnov
Laid down 1.12.1776   *Launched* 12.5.1780
Dimensions 160 ft x 44 ft 6 in x 19 ft
Armament   LD 24 x 24pdrs, 2 x 60 u (1 pood)
             UD 22 x 12pdrs, 2 x 24u (½ pood)
             FC & QD 16 x 6pdrs (1723 Establishment) modified
Aziia class. The name *Sviatoi Ianuarii* was chosen to commemorate Catherine II's birthday which fell on this saint's day. Built by M. D. Portnov to a plan by I. V. James. Left Arkhangel'sk in the squadron under Brigadier V. Fondesin on 10.7.1780. Separated from squadron in a storm and severely damaged and forced to winter in Bergen. Arrived at Kronshtadt in 6.1781. Operated in the Mediterranean as part of Vice-Adm. I.Chichagov's squadron in 1782–4. Escorted 6 store ships from Kronshtadt to Revel' and blockaded Porkkala-udd in 1789. On 15 and 17.8.1789 repulsed attacks by the Swedish rowing flotilla. Fought at the battle of Krasnaia Gorka on 23–24.5.1790 suffering casualties of 6 killed and 20 wounded. Fought at the battle of Vyborg on 22.6.1790. Repaired in 1796–8. Departed Revel' for Holland as part of Rear-Adm. P. Chichagov's squadron on 21.7.1799. Returned to Russia in 1800. Cruised in the Baltic in 1801 and 1803–4. Transported troops to Pommerania in 1805. Cruised in the Baltic in 1806. Decommissioned in 1806. Stationed in Kronshtadt Roads in 1807–10 as a floating battery for the defence of Kotlin. Broken up in 1815.

Sviatoi Georgii Pobedonosets 66 Kronshtadt
Constructor A. S. Kasatonov
Laid down 9.7.1778   *Launched* 16.9.1780
Dimensions 160 ft x 44 ft 6 in x 19 ft
Armament   LD 24 x 24pdrs, 2 x 60 u (1 pood)
             UD 22 x 12pdrs, 2 x 24u (½ pood)
             FC & QD 16 x 6pdrs (1723 Establishment) modified
Aziia class. Built experimentally of baked timber with pitch and proved highly resistant to dry rot and deterioration. Operated in the Mediterranean in 1782–4 under Vice-Adm. I. Chichagov. Cruised in the Gulf of Finland in 1788 and joined V. Fondesin's squadron at Copenhagen on 12.11.1788. Transferred to Adm. I. Chichagov's squadron, also at Copenhagen, on 22.7.1789. Returned to Revel' with both squadrons on 16.8.1789. Fought at Revel' on 2.5.1790 with 5 wounded and 1430 rounds expended. Fought at Vyborg on 22–23.6.1790, capturing and towing away the grounded *Finland* on the 23rd. Cruised in the Baltic in 1791, 1793, and 1794. Stationed in Kronshtadt Roads in 1795. Cruised in the Baltic in 1797. Decommissioned in 1797. Employed as a floating battery in the defence of Kotlin in 1801. Broken up in 1807–8.

Sviatoslav 66 Arkhangel'sk
Constructor M. D. Portnov
Laid down 1.12.1776   *Launched* 22.5.1781
Dimensions 160 ft x 44 ft 6 in x 19 ft
Armament   LD 24 x 24pdrs, 2 x 60 u (1 pood)
             UD 22 x 12pdrs, 2 x 24u (½ pood)
             FC & QD 16 x 6pdrs (1723 Establishment) modified
Aziia class. Sailed from Arkhangel'sk to Kronshtadt in 7–9.1781. Operated in the Mediterranean as part of Vice-Adm. I. Chichagov's squadron in 1782–4. Cruised to Bornholm in 1785. Cruised in the Gulf of Finland in 7–10.1788. Fought at Öland on 15.7.1789. Fought at

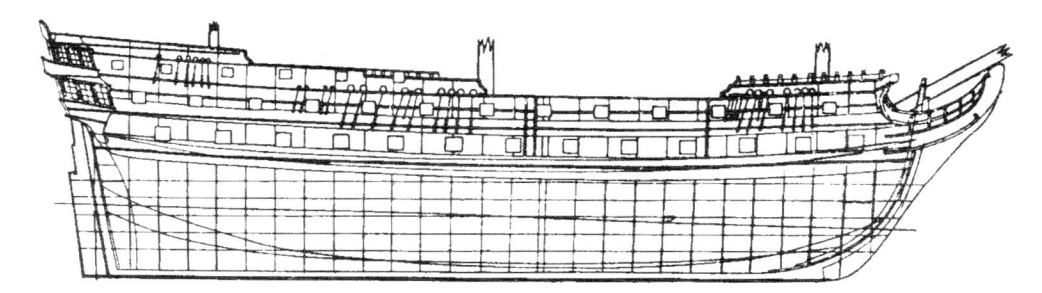

The Aziia class 66-gun Pobedonosets of 1780 was very nearly the only major warship completed at the naval dockyard of Kronshtadt during the eighteenth century. The reason for choosing Kronshtadt as her construction site had to do with the experimental nature of her construction, involving the use of experimentally treated timber intended to prevent the onset of the dry rot that was the bane of all wooden ships. The treatment given to Pobedonosets *was successful, as evidenced by her very long lifespan (for a Russian ship of the line) of 27 years, but never repeated, probably due to its expense. In other aspects of her design, she was a typical member of the 28-ship* Aziia *class and her great moment of glory came when she captured the Swedish ship of the line* Finland *at Vyborg in 1790.*

Vyborg on 22.6.1790. Cruised in the Baltic in 1794–5. Decommissioned in 1795. Broken up after 1800.

Trekh Sviatitelei 66 Arkhangel'sk
Constructor M. D. Portnov
Laid down 27.8.1778   *Launched* 22.5.1781
Dimensions 160 ft x 44 ft 6 in x 19 ft
Armament   LD 24 x 24pdrs, 2 x 60 u (1 pood)
             UD 22 x 12pdrs, 2 x 24u (½ pood)
             FC & QD 16 x 6pdrs (1723 Establishment) modified

Aziia class. Sailed from Arkhangel'sk to Kronshtadt in 7–8.1781. Operated in the North Sea as part of Rear-Adm. Kruz's squadron in 1782. Cruised in the Baltic to Bornholm in 1785. Cruised to the Sound off Copenhagen and the North Sea in 1793. Decommissioned in 1793. Broken up in 1801.

Vysheslav 66 Arkhangel'sk
Constructor M. D. Portnov
Laid down 27.8.1778   *Launched* 22.5.1781
Dimensions 160 ft x 44 ft 6 in x 19 ft
Armament   LD 24 x 24pdrs, 2 x 60 u (1 pood)
             UD 22 x 12pdrs, 2 x 24u (½ pood)
             FC & QD 16 x 6pdrs (1723 Establishment) modified

Aziia class. Sailed from Arkhangel'sk to Kronshtadt in 7–8.1782. Cruised in the Baltic to Bornholm in 1784–5. Fought with great distinction at Gogland in 6.7.1788, suffering severe damage and taking casualties of 52 killed and 82 wounded. Fought at Öland on 15.7.1789 with casualties of 1 killed and 11 wounded. Grounded off Rodsher on 20.10.1789 while in transit from Revel' to Kronshtadt. Unable to be salvaged and burnt in place on 23.10.1789.

Rodislav 66 Arkhangel'sk
Constructor M. D. Portnov
Laid down 6.10.1778   *Launched* 21.5.1782
Dimensions 160 ft x 44 ft 6 in x 19 ft
Armament   LD 24 x 24pdrs, 2 x 60 u (1 pood)
             UD 22 x 12pdrs, 2 x 24u (½ pood)
             FC & QD 16 x 6pdrs (1723 Establishment) modified

Aziia class. Sailed from Arkhangel'sk to Kronshtadt in 7–8.1782. Cruised in the Baltic in 1784–6. Fought at Gogland on 6.7.1788 with casualties of 24 killed and 27 wounded. Fought at Öland on 15.7.1789. Grounded and wrecked on 15.10.1789. Destroyed in place on 24.10.1789.

Mecheslav 66 Arkhangel'sk
Constructor M. D. Portnov
Laid down 19.9.1781   *Launched* 16.5.1783
Dimensions 160 ft x 44 ft 6 in x 19 ft
Armament 1783 LD 24 x 24pdrs, 2 x 60 u (1 pood)
                  UD 22 x 12pdrs, 2 x 24u (½ pood)
                  FC & QD 16 x 6pdrs (1723 Establishment) modified
            1788 LD 24 x 24pdrs, 2 x 60 u (1 pood)
                  UD 22 x 12pdrs, 2 x 24u (½ pood)
                  FC & QD 16 x 6pdrs 2 x 24pdr carr.

Aziia class. Sailed from Arkhangel'sk to Kronshtadt in 7–9.1783. Cruised in the Baltic to Bornholm in 1784–6. Two 24pdr carronades were added in 1788. Fought at Gogland on 6.7.1788 with casualties of 29 killed, 84 wounded and 84 shot-holes. Serious leaking forced her return to Kronshtadt for repairs. Returned to service and cruised in Vice-Adm. Kruz's squadron. Arrived at Copenhagen on 12.11.1788 and joined Vice-Adm. Fondesin's squadron. Joined Adm. I. Chichagov's fleet on 22.7.1789. Assigned to training duties in Kronshtadt Roads in 1791. Cruised in the Baltic in 1794. Decommissioned in 1794. Broken up before 1797.

Boleslav 66 Arkhangel'sk
Constructor M. D. Portnov
Laid down 19.9.1781   *Launched* 16.5.1783
Dimensions 160 ft x 44 ft 6 in x 19 ft
Armament 1783 LD 24 x 24pdrs, 2 x 60 u (1 pood)
                  UD 22 x 12pdrs, 2 x 24u (½ pood)
                  FC & QD 16 x 6pdrs (1723 Establishment) modified
                  552 men
            1788 LD 24 x 24pdrs, 2 x 60 u (1 pood)
                  UD 22 x 12pdrs, 2 x 24u (½ pood)
                  FC & QD 16 x 6pdrs 2 x 32pdr carr.

Aziia class. Sailed from Arkhangel'sk to Kronshtadt in 7–9.1783. Cruised in the Baltic to Bornholm in 1784–6. Fought at Gogland on 6.7.1788 with casualties of 58 killed, 72 wounded and numerous shot-holes. Repaired and cruised in the Gulf of Finland. Engaged the Swedish rowing flotilla off Porkkala-udd in 1789. Fought at Öland on 15.7.1789 with 7 wounded. Patrolled between Bornholm, Gottland, and Dagerort during the remainder of 1789. Fought at Revel' on 2.5.1790 with 2100 rounds expended and casualties of 1 killed and 5 wounded. Fought at Vyborg on 22.6.1790 and captured several

Swedish oared warships. Cruised in the Baltic in 1791. Repaired in 1796–8. Left Kronshtadt in.5.1798 as part of Vice-Adm. Makarov's First Division and arrived in Britain in 7.1798. Operated in Britain in 1798–1800 cooperating with Vice-Adm. Onslow's squadron. Assigned to training in Kronshtadt Roads in 1813. Cruised in the Baltic in 1804–5. Decommissioned in 1805. Broken up in 1808.

Panteleimon 66 Arkhangel'sk
Constructor M. D. Portnov
Laid down 7.9.1784   *Launched* 14.5.1786
Dimensions 160 ft x 44 ft 6 in x 19 ft
Armament   LD 24 x 24pdrs, 2 x 60 u (1 pood)
             UD 24 x 12pdrs, 2 x 24u (½ pood)
             FC & QD 14 x 6pdrs (1723 Establishment) modified
Aziia class. *Sviatoi Panteleimon* is the saint day on which the battle of Gangut was won. Sailed from Arkhangel'sk to Kronshtadt in 7–8.1787. Cruised in the Gulf of Finland for the remainder of the year. Arrived at Copenhagen on 6.11.1788. Cruised in the Kattegat, and blockaded Karlskrona during the remainder of the year. Joined Adm. I. Chichagov's fleet off Bornholm on 22.7.1789, and patrolled between Bornholm, Gottland, and Dagerort, and engaged the Swedish rowing flotilla off Porkkala-udd. Fought at Krasnaia Gorka on 23–24.5.1790 with casualties of 9 killed and 19 wounded inflicted largely by her own exploding cannons. Fought at Vyborg on 22.6.1790 and incurred heavy damage. Stationed in Kronshtadt Roads for training in 1791. Repaired in 1795. Cruised off Bornholm in 1796–8 and participated in the blockade of the Sound off Copenhagen. Operated in the Squadron of Rear-Adm. P. Chichagov in 1799, transporting troops to Great Britain for the planned landing in Holland. Lost her main mast and 29 sailors during a storm on 27.9.1799. Cruised in the Baltic in 1800 and 1803. Hulked at the end of 1803. Assigned to harbour service in 1804.

Severnyi Oryol 66 Arkhangel'sk
Constructor M. D. Portnov
Laid down 11.5.1786   *Launched* 9.5.1787
Dimensions 160 ft x 44 ft 6 in x 19 ft
Armament   LD 24 x 24pdrs, 2 x 60 u (1 pood)
             UD 24 x 12pdrs, 2 x 24u (½ pood)
             FC & QD 14 x 6pdrs (1723 Establishment) modified
Aziia class. Left Arkhangel'sk on 5.7.1788 under Rear-Adm. Povalishin. Joined Vice-Adm. Fondesin at Copenhagen on 29.8.1788 and blockaded Karlsrona. Joined Adm. I. Chichagov's squadron off Bornholm on 22.7.1789 and patrolled between Bornholm, Gottland, and Dagerort. Engaged the Swedish rowing flotilla off Porkkala-udd. Grounded and lost on 13.9.1789.

Prokhor 66 Arkhangel'sk
Constructor M. D. Portnov
Laid down 10.6.1787   *Launched* 7.5.1788
Dimensions 160 ft x 44 ft 6 in x 19 ft
Armament   LD 24 x 24pdrs, 2 x 60 u (1 pood)
             UD 24 x 12pdrs, 2 x 24u (½ pood)
             FC & QD 14 x 6pdrs (1723 Establishment) modified
Aziia class. Built to a plan of I. V. James. Sailed from Arkhangel'sk to Copenhagen in 1788. Joined Adm. Fondesin's squadron on 29.8.1788 and blockaded Karlskrona. Joined Adm. Chichagov's squadron on 22.7.1789 and cruised in the Baltic. Fought at Revel' on 2.5.1790 with a single casualty after expending 1177 rounds. Fought at Vyborg on 22.5.1790 and captured a Swedish gun boat. Cruised in the Baltic in 1791–3. Training duties in 1795. Decommissioned in 1795. Stricken before 1797.

Parmen 66 Arkhangel'sk
Constructor M. D. Portnov
Laid down 28.8.1788   *Launched* 15.5.1789
Dimensions 160 ft x 44 ft 4 in x 19 ft
Armament   LD 24 x 24pdrs, 2 x 60 u (1 pood)
             UD 24 x 12pdrs, 2 x 24u (½ pood)
             FC & QD 14 x 6pdrs (1723 Establishment) modified
Aziia class. Notice 2-in decrease in beam. Sailed from Arkhangel'sk to Kronshtadt in 7–9.1792. Cruised in the Baltic in 1792–3 and 1795. Cruised in the North Sea in 1796. Decommissioned in 1796. Broken up in 1798.

Nikanor 66 Arkhangel'sk
Constructor M. D. Portnov
Laid down 1.7.1788   *Launched* 16.5.1789
Dimensions 160 ft x 44 ft 4 in x 19 ft
Armament   LD 24 x 24pdrs, 2 x 60 u (1 pood)
             UD 24 x 12pdrs, 2 x 24u (½ pood)
             FC & QD 14 x 6pdrs (1723 Establishment) modified
Aziia class. Sailed from Arkhangel'sk to Kronshtadt in 7–9.1792. Cruised in the North Sea in 1793. Stationed in England in 1795–6. Decommissioned in 1796. Stricken by 1797.

Pimen 66 Arkhangel'sk
Constructor M. D. Portnov
Laid down 25.7.1788   *Launched* 16.5.1789
Dimensions 160 ft x 44 ft 4 in x 19 ft
Armament   LD 24 x 24pdrs, 2 x 60 u (1 pood)
             UD 24 x 12pdrs, 2 x 24u (½ pood)
             FC & QD 14 x 6pdrs (1723 Establishment) modified
Aziia class. Built to plans of Adm. Greig. Sailed from Arkhangel'sk to Kronshtadt in 7–9.1792. Cruised in the North Sea in 1793. To England in 1795–6. Decommissioned in 1796. Broken up in 1798.

Iona 66 Arkhangel'sk
Constructor M. D. Portnov
Laid down 26.6.1789   *Launched* 22.5.1790
Dimensions 160 ft x 44 ft 4 in x 19 ft
Armament   LD 24 x 24pdrs, 2 x 60 u (1 pood)
             UD 24 x 12pdrs, 2 x 24u (½ pood)
             FC & QD 14 x 6pdrs (1723 Establishment) modified
Aziia class. Sailed from Arkhangel'sk to Kronshtadt from 30.06–27.9.1794. In England with Vice-Adm. Khanykov's squadron in 1795–6. Cruised to Bornholm, Denmark in 1798. To Yarmouth with Rear-Adm. P. Chichagov's squadron in 1799. Landed troops at the Texel in 9.1799. Returned to Kronshtadt on 21.7.1800 for decommissioning. Harbour hulk 1801–3. Transferred to Revel' in 1803. Broken up in 1803.

Filipp 66 Arkhangel'sk
Constructor M. D. Portnov
Laid down 9.7.1789   *Launched* 22.5.1790
Dimensions 160 ft x 44 ft 4 in x 19 ft
Armament   LD 24 x 24pdrs, 2 x 60 u (1 pood)
             UD 24 x 12pdrs, 2 x 24u (½ pood)
             FC & QD 14 x 6pdrs (1723 Establishment) modified
Aziia class. Sailed from Arkhangel'sk to Kronshtadt with the squadron of Rear-Adm. Thate from 30.06–27.9.1794. To England under Vice-Adm. Khanykov in 1795–7. To Bornholm and the Sound off Copenhagen with Adm. Kruz's squadron in 1798. Operated off the Prussian coast in the squadron of Adm. Khanykov in 1798,

experiencing storm damage. Cruised in the Gulf of Finland in 1800. Decommissioned in 1800. Condemned in 1801. Broken up in 1803.

Graf Orlov (renamed Mikhail) 66 Arkhangel'sk
Constructor M. D. Portnov
Laid down 14.7.1790   *Launched* 24.5.1791
Dimensions 160 ft x 44 ft 4 in x 19 ft
Armament   LD 24 x 24pdrs, 2 x 60 u (1 pood)
             UD 24 x 12pdrs, 2 x 24u (½ pood)
             FC & QD 14 x 6pdrs (1723 Establishment) modified

Aziia class. Named after Graf Orlov, the Russian commander at Ches'ma. Sailed from Arkhangel'sk to Kronshtadt with Rear-Adm. Thate's squadron in 30.6–27.9.1794. To England with Vice-Adm. Khanykov's squadron in 1795–6. Renamed *Mikhail* in 1796 after the death of Catherine II. Repaired in 1798. To England with Rear-Adm. P. Chichagov's squadron in 1799–1800 during which deployment she landed troops in the Texel. Training duties in Kronshtadt Roads in 1803. Cruised in the Baltic in 1804. Decommissioned in 1804. Floating battery defending Kotlin in the northern freeway in 1808. Broken up in 1809.

Evropa 66 Arkhangel'sk
Constructor G. Ignatyev
Laid down 19.7.1791   *Launched* 15.5.1793
Dimensions 160 ft x 44 ft 4 in x 19 ft
Armament   LD 24 x 24pdrs, 2 x 60 u (1 pood)
             UD 24 x 12pdrs, 2 x 24u (½ pood)
             FC & QD 14 x 6pdrs (1723 Establishment) modified
             534 men

Aziia class. Sailed from Arkhangel'sk to Kronshtadt with Rear-Adm. Thate's squadron in 30.6–27.9.1794. To England and the North Sea under Vice-Adm. Khanykov in 1795–6. Cruised in the North Sea under Rear-Adm. Makarov in 1796–7. Departed Kronshtadt with Vice-Adm. Makarov's First Division in.5.1798 and arrived in Great Britain in 7.1798. Operated in the North Sea under the overall command of Vice-Adm. Duncan in 1798–1800. Landed troops at Gelder, Holland as part of Adm. Mitchell's allied squadron. Witnessed the surrender of the Dutch fleet in 1799. Repaired at Portsmouth in 1800. Decommissioned and hulked in 1806. Floating battery in the northern freeway at Kotlin in 1809. Broken up in 1811.

Aziia 66 Arkhangel'sk
Constructor G. Ignatyev
Laid down 21.9.1794   *Launched* 24.8.1796
Dimensions 160 ft x 44 ft 4 in x 19 ft
Armament   LD 24 x 24pdrs, 2 x 60 u (1 pood)
             UD 24 x 12pdrs, 2 x 24u (½ pood)
             FC & QD 14 x 6pdrs (1723 Establishment) modified
             526 men

Aziia class. Departed Arkhangel'sk in Vice-Adm. Thate's 2nd Division on 3.7.1798. Arrived at Nore on 8.8.1798 and cruised in the North Sea. Departed Portsmouth in Rear-Adm. Kartsov's squadron on 2.6.1799 to join Adm. Ushakov's squadron in the Mediterranean, escorting British troopships to Gibraltar en route. Joined Adm. Ushakov's squadron at Palermo on 22.8.1799. Operated in the Mediterranean and off Malta through.5.1800. Transferred to Sevastopol' for repairs on 26.10.1800 with Adm. Ushakov's squadron. Transported troops to Corfu in 1804. Transported troops with Rear-Adm. Sorokin's squadron from Corfu to Naples in 1805. Operated in the Adriatic in 1806 with Vice-Adm. Seniavin's squadron. Operated off Lepanto, Zante, and Patras and transported troops to Ancona in 1807. Blockaded in Trieste by the British as part of Commodore Saltanov's squadron in 1808. Ceded to France on 20.10.1809.

Pobeda 66 Arkhangel'sk
Constructor G. Ignatyev
Laid down 11.9.1795   *Launched* 26.5.1797
Dimensions 160 ft x 44 ft 4 in x 19 ft
Armament   LD 24 x 24pdrs, 2 x 60 u (1 pood)
             UD 24 x 12pdrs, 2 x 24u (½ pood)
             FC & QD 14 x 6pdrs (1723 Establishment) modified
             530 men

Aziia class. Built to plans of Adm. Greig. Departed Arkhangel'sk in Vice-Adm. Thate's 2nd Division on 3.7.1798. Arrived at Nore on 8.8.1798 and cruised in the North Sea. Left Portsmouth on 2.6.1799 with Rear-Adm. Kartsov's squadron to join Adm. Ushakov's Mediterranean Squadron, escorting British troops to Gibraltar en route. Joined Adm. Ushakov's squadron at Palermo on 22.8.1799. Recalled to Corfu from Messina where she had been preparing to carry troops to Malta on 24.12.1799 by order of Paul I. Cruised off Sicily and Malta in 1800. To Sevastopol' and service with the Black Sea fleet on 20.10.1800. Transported troops to Corfu in 1804. Storm damaged and forced to return to Sevastopol' for repairs in.4.1807 while heading for Anapa with Rear-Adm. Pustoshkin's squadron. Landed troops at Anapa in 1809. Unsuccessfully pursued the Turkish battle squadron off Varna on 17.8.1810 while part of Rear-Adm. Sarychev's squadron. Cruised with Vice-Adm. Hull's squadron between Varna and the Bosporus in 1811. Transported troops from Anapa to Sevastopol' in 1812. Decommissioned in 1812. Broken up after 1816.

Iziaslav 66 Arkhangel'sk
Constructor M. D. Portnov
Laid down 19.9.1782   *Launched* 16.5.1784
Dimensions 160 ft x 44 ft 6 in x 19 ft
Armament   LD 24 x 24pdrs, 2 x 60 u (1 pood)
             UD 24 x 12pdrs, 2 x 24u (½ pood)
             FC & QD 14 x 6pdrs, 2 x 24pdr carr. (1723
                Establishment) modified
             534 men

An experimental design, built to the plan of Adm. Greig. Sailed from Arkhangel'sk to Kronshtadt in 6–8.1784. Cruised in the Baltic to Bornholm in 1785. Fought at Gogland on 6.7.1788 with casualties of 10 killed, 41 wounded and 108 shot–holes. Cruised in the Gulf of Finland for the rest of the year. Fought at Öland on 15.7.1789 with casualties of with casualties of 5 killed and 5 wounded. Patrolled between Bornholm, Gottland and Dagerort during the rest of the year. Fought at Revel' on 2.5.1790 without casualties after having expended 744 rounds. Fought at Vyborg on 22.6.1790. On 23.6.1790, in company with *Venus*, captured the Swedish *Rättvisan* (64). Training duty in Kronshtadt Roads in 1791. Cruised in the Baltic in 1792 and 1796–7. Departed Revel' for Great Britain on 20.8.1798 as part of Rear-Adm. Kartsov's 3rd Division. Encountered a severe storm off Skagen, Norway on 19.9.1798 and forced to make repairs to leak in Christiansand. On.4.11.1798, she rescued the crew of the sinking Russian flagship *Prints Gustav*. Repaired in dock in Great Britain in 5–6.1799. Returned to Kronshtadt as part of Rear-Adm. Borisov's squadron on 14.8.1799. Repaired and rebuilt temporarily as a 74 in 1800. Cruised in the Baltic in 1801 and 1803–4. Decommissioned in 1804. Hulked in 1805. Broken up in 1808.

Zachatie Sviatoi Anny 66/74 St Petersburg
Constructor M. Sarychev

Laid down 25.2.1799 *Launched* 3.5.1800
Dimensions 162 ft x 45 ft x 18 ft 6 in
Armament LD 24 x 30pdrs, 2 x 60 u (1 pood)
 UD 24 x 18pdrs, 2 x 24u (½ pood)
 FC & QD 16 x 6pdrs, 6 x 24pdr carr. (conjecture)

Built to the lines of the captured Swedish *Rättvisan*. Cruised in the Baltic to Bornholm in 1801–4. Transported troops to Pomerania in 1805. Operated in Adm. Khanykov's squadron in 1808. Forced to retreat to Rogervik (Baltiyskiy) when the squadron encountered a marginally superior Anglo-Swedish squadron on 13.8.1808. Decommissioned in 1809. Broken up in 1810.

Arkhistratig Mikhail 64/72 St Petersburg
Constructor A. S. Katasonov
Laid down 25.2.1799 *Launched* 3.5.1800
Dimensions 162 ft x 45 ft x 18 ft 6 in
Armament 1800 LD 24 x 30pdrs, 2 x 60 u (1 pood)
 UD 24 x 18pdrs, 2 x 24u (½ pood)
 FC & QD 14 x 6pdrs, 6 x 24pdr carr. (conjecture)
 1812 LD 24 x 18/24pdrs (short), 2 x 60 u (1 pood)
 UD 24 x 12pdrs (long)
 FC & QD 14 x 6pdrs, 6 x 24pdr carr. (conjecture)

Built to the lines of the captured Swedish *Omheten*. Cruised in the Baltic to Skafgen in 1801–4. Transported troops to Pomerania in 1805. Operated in Adm. Khanykov's squadron in 1808. Forced to retreat to Rogervik (Baltiyskiy) when the squadron encountered a marginally superior Anglo-Swedish squadron on 13.8.1808. Stationed in the northern freeway of Kotlin for the defence of Kronshtadt in 1809. In Kronshtadt Roads in 1810. Reduced to a transport, carrying troops from Sveaborg to Revel' in 1812 and rearmed as above. Decommissioned in 1812. Converted to a store ship in 1812–13. Broken up in 1817.

Baltic frigates (59 built 1762–1800)

With the exception of 5 12pdr frigates completed in the early years of Catherine II's reign during the 1760s and representing the completion of programmes begun under Elizabeth, Russian frigate production and development was largely sidelined and did not resume in meaningful numbers until the decade of the 1770s, with the authorization of the first units of the *Pavel* class of 12pdr ships. A total of 18 *Pavels* were completed by the mid-1780s, but they in their turn represented the continuation of a style of frigate that had been superseded in the Atlantic navies in the late 1740s. When 'true' frigates of the type that became universal in the Atlantic and Mediterranean navies of the French Revolutionary and Napoleonic War period were first introduced in Russia in the middle 1780s, they took the form of 18pdr ships skipping over the 9pdr and 12pdr 'true' frigates that had typified the first generation of frigates in the French and British navies. By the 1790s, the Russians were beginning to augment their 18pdr frigates with even larger 24pdr ships, quite probably in reaction to Swedish designs introduced under Fredrik af Chapman in the 1780s.

24pdr heavy frigates (5 built 1762–1800)

After the Russo-Swedish War of 1788–90, the Russians followed the Swedish lead in developing a series of heavy frigates armed with short-barrelled 24pdrs based on af Chapman's designs for frigates capable of standing in line of battle as needed. Five of these generally successful and formidable Russian ships entered service in the 1790s, followed by another quintet during the next decade. *Arkhangel Mikhail*, the name ship of the group, was wrecked off Finland in 1796 while returning home from deployment to England in 1795–6. The other four were all deployed to Great Britain for operations in the North Sea in the 1790s. The final three heavy frigates built during this period continued to be actively involved in naval operations during the first decade of the nineteenth century.

The French, British, and American navies all commissioned small numbers of very large 24pdr frigates during this same period, but these ships differed from the Russian heavy frigates by being armed with long 24pdrs rather than with the short-barrelled 24pdrs adopted by both Russian and Swedish ships and by being designed for a wider range of duties in the less forgiving waters of the North Atlantic.

Arkhangel Mikhail **class** (3 ships)
Arkhangel Mikhail 44 Arkhangel'sk
Constructor M. D. Portnov
Laid down 14.7.1790 *Launched* 24.5.1791
Dimensions 151 ft 6 in x 38 ft 10 in x 15 ft 9 in
Armament LD 28 x 24pdrs (short frigate guns)
 FC & QD 16 x 6pdrs + carrs
 398 men

Arkhangel Mikhail class. Based on the design of the captured Swedish heavy frigate *Venus*. Departed Arkhangel'sk on 8.7.1792. Damaged and forced to winter at Bergen. Joined Adm. Kruz's squadron in the summer of 1793 and cruised in the North Sea. Arrived at Kronshtadt on 15.9.1793. To England in 1795–6. Wrecked while returning home on 25.10.1796 off Porkkala-udd on the coast of Finland. No casualties.

Arkhangel Rafail 44 Arkhangel'sk
Constructor M. D. Portnov
Laid down 14.7.1790 *Launched* 24.5.1791
Dimensions 151 ft 6 in x 38 ft 10 in x 15 ft 9 in
Armament LD 28 x 24pdrs (short frigate guns)
 FC & QD 16 x 6pdrs + carrs
 398 men

Arkhangel Mikhail class. Based on the design of the captured Swedish heavy frigate *Venus*. Sailed to Kronshtadt in 1794. To England in 1795–6. Operated off Holstein in 1797. Repaired in 1798. To Holland with troops with Rear-Adm. Chichagov's squadron in 1799. Returned to Kronshtadt on 26.9.1800. Carried cargo between Baltic ports in 1802–3. Broken up in 1804.

Schastlivyi 44 Arkhangel'sk
Constructor G. Ignatyev
Laid down 19.12.1796 *Launched* 19.5.1798
Dimensions 151 ft 6 in x 38 ft 10 in x 15 ft 9 in
Armament LD 28 x 24pdrs (short frigate guns)
 FC & QD 16 x 6pdrs + carrs
 256/398 men

Arkhangel Mikhail class. Based on the design of the captured Swedish heavy frigate *Venus*. To England with Vice-Adm. Thate's 2nd Division on 3.7.1798, arriving at the Nore on 8.8.1798. Operated in the North Sea 1798–1800. Returned to Kronshtadt on 21.7.1800. Cruised in the Baltic with naval cadets in 1801–3. Cruised to Dogger Bank with Rear-Adm. Lomen's squadron in 1804. Participated in Vice-Adm. Thate's landing of over 20,000 troops on the German coast in 1805. Training duties in Kronshtadt Roads in 1806. Cruised with Adm. Khanykov's squadron in 1808 and returned to Kronshtadt in 10.1808. Stationed in Kronshtadt Roads as a guard ship in 1809. Blockship in Kronshtadt Roads in 1810–12.

***Feodosii Totemskii* class** (2 ships)
Feodosii Totemskii 44 Arkhangel'sk
Constructor G. Ignatyev
Laid down 9.8.1798   *Launched* 24.9.1798
Dimensions 150 ft x 39 ft x 16 ft
Armament   LD 28 x 24pdrs (short frigate guns)
            FC & QD 16 x 6pdrs + carrs

Feodosii Totemskii class. Based on an amended design of the captured Swedish heavy frigate *Venus*. Departed Arkhangel'sk for England with Vice-Adm. Baratynskiy's squadron in 9.1799. Returned to Revel' in 9.1800. Cruised in the Baltic in 1803–4. Landed troops on the German coast with Adm. Thate's squadron in 1805. Cruised in the Baltic with Adm. Khanykov's squadron in 1808 and returned to Kronshtadt in 10.1808. Floating battery in Kronshtadt Roads in 1809–11. Broken up in 1819.

Tikhvinskaya Bogoroditsa 44 Arkhangel'sk
Constructor G. Ignatyev
Laid down 19.8.1798   *Launched* 22.7.1799
Dimensions 150 ft x 39 ft x 16 ft
Armament   LD 28 x 24pdrs (short frigate guns)
            FC & QD 16 x 6pdrs + carrs

Feodosii Totemskii class. Based on an amended design of the captured Swedish heavy frigate *Venus*. Departed Arkhangel'sk for England with Vice-Adm. Baratynskiy's squadron in 9.1799. Returned to Kronshtadt in 9.1800. Cruised in the Baltic with naval cadets in 1801–3. Cruised to Dogger Bank in 1804. Landed troops on the German coast with Adm. Thate's squadron in 1805. Fire watch ship at Revel' in 1807. Cruised with Adm. Khanykov's squadron in 1808. Returned to Kronshtadt in 10.1808. Stationed in Kronshtadt Roads in 1809. Fire watch ship at Riga in 1812. Broken up in 1819.

18pdr frigates (11 laid down, 10 completed 1762–1800)

As previously noted, Russia lagged behind the other major European naval powers in adopting in true in frigates of the sort that came to characterize the second half of the eighteenth century in European navies involved in the French Revolutionary and Napoleonic wars. These more advanced types were distinguished from earlier two-decked frigate designs by having unarmed lower 'gun decks' converted into berthing spaces with reduced overhead clearance, and by the re-positioning of the main armament from the lower gun deck to what had previously been the upper gun deck. This arrangement had the two-fold advantage of improving the command of the main armament by raising it by one full deck over the waterline and at the same time of reducing the lateral area exposed to the wind by reducing the total height of the lower deck by 1–2 ft. The result of these changes was a faster, more weatherly ship capable of operating its primary armament in all weather conditions.

Russian delay in adopting what had become the standard frigate type of the Atlantic navies by the mid-1750s (with the notable exception of the conservative Dutch) for its Baltic frigates, may be explained at least in part by the milder weather conditions of the Baltic as contrasted to the more stressful environment of the North Atlantic. Milder weather conditions made it possible to avoid the problem experienced by ships operating in stormier Atlantic waters of being unable to open their lower deck gun ports in combat without risking taking in water and capsizing, and also lessened the probability of ships being driven against lee shores as a result of the pressure of wind on the higher exposed freeboards of the less advanced designs. The late 1770s and early 1780s were characterized by the acquisition of the latest developments in British naval technology by young Russian constructors training in Great Britain at the invitation of the British government during a period of close co-operation between the two nations. It should come as no surprise that the first Russian class of 18pdr frigates, the eight *Briachislav*s, laid down and launched between 1784 and 1790 show evidence of having been near duplicates of one of the first of the British 18pdr classes, the *Arethusa*s of 1780. (The *Briachislav*s may have been the first 'true' Baltic 18pdr frigates, but they appear to have been preceeded into service by the series of 12pdr 'true' frigates that began entering service in the then Sea of Azov flotilla in the early 1770s. The reader is referred to the Black Sea section on early frigate types for more details.)

Mstislavets 44 Arkhangel'sk
Constructor M. D. Portnov
Laid down 23.6.1783   *Launched* 17.5.1784
Dimensions 150 ft 2 in x 39 ft 6 in (outside plank) x 10 ft 8 in
Armament   LD 28/30 18pdrs
            FC & QD 12/14 x 6pdrs (conjecture)

Believed to have been the first Russian example of an 18pdr 'true' frigate design. Sailed from Arkhangel'sk to Kronshtadt in 6–8.1784. Cruised in the Baltic in 1786. Cruised in the Baltic in 1787 with naval cadets. Located the Swedish fleet on 13.6.1788 and returned to inform Adm. Greig's squadron. Fought at Gogland in 6.7.1788. Fought at Öland on 15.7.1789. Fought at the Krasnaia Gorka/Styrsudden battle on 23–24.5.1790. Returned to Revel' for repairs. Cruised in the Baltic in 1793. No further mention.

***Briachislav* class** (8 ships)
The first full class of 18pdr frigates built in Russia. Their armament and dimensions are virtual duplicates of those of the British *Arethusa* class of 1780. The first three ships were heavily involved in the Russo-Swedish War of 1788–90. The final five were all deployed to England with Adm. Khanykov's Squadron between 1794 and 1797.

Briachislav 38/46 Arkhangel'sk
Constructor M. D. Portnov
Laid down 18.6.1784   *Launched* 13.5.1785
Dimensions 141 ft x 38 ft 4 in (inside plank) x 13 ft 9 in
Armament   LD 28 x 18pdrs
            FC & QD 10 x 6pdrs, 8 x carr.

Briachislav class (8 ships). Sailed from Arkhangel'sk to Kronshtadt in 7–8.1785. Cruised in the Baltic in 1786–7 with naval cadets. Fought at Gogland on 6.7.1788 and sent to Copenhagen with orders for Vice-Adm. V. Fondesin. Fought at Öland on 15.7.1790. Fought at the battle of Krasnaia Gorka on 23–24.5.1790. Fought at Vyborg on 22.6.1790. Stationed in Kronshtadt Roads in 1791. Cruised in the Baltic in 1793 and 1795–7. Broken up in 1804.

Arkhangel Gavriil 38 Arkhangel'sk
Constructor M. D. Portnov
Laid down 11.5.1786   *Launched* 9.5.1787
Dimensions 141 ft x 38 ft 4 in (inside plank) x 13 ft 9 in
Armament   LD 28 x 18pdrs
            FC & QD 10 x 6pdrs, 8 x carr.

Briachislav class (8 ships). Departed Arkhangel'sk with Rear-Adm. Povalishin's squadron on 5.7.1788. Joined Vice-Adm. V. Fondesin's squadron at Copenhagen on 29.8.1788. Blockaded Karlskrona on

22.9–22.10.1788. Cruised in the Kattegat and the Skagerrak in 5–7.1789. Joined Adm. Chichagov's fleet off Bornholm on 22.7.1789. Spotted the Swedish fleet headed for St Petersburg on 21.5.1790. Fought in the battle of Krasnaia Gorka/Styrsudden on 22–23.5.1790. Fought at Vyborg on 22.6.1790 where she captured *Omheten* (64) and escorted her to Kronshtadt. Cruised in the Baltic in 1791 and 1794–5. Broken up after 1799.

Pomoshchnyi 38/40   Arkhangel'sk
Constructor M. D. Portnov
Laid down 10.6.1787   *Launched* 7.5.1788
Dimensions 141 ft x 38 ft 4 in (inside plank) x 13 ft 9 in
Armament   LD 28 x 18pdrs
         FC & QD 10 x 6pdrs, 8 x carr.
Briachislav class (8 ships). Departed Arkhangel'sk with Rear-Adm. Povalishin's squadron on 5.7.1788. Joined Rear-Adm. Povalishin's squadron at Copenhagen on 22.9.1788. Blockaded Karlskrona on 22.9–22.10.1788. Cruised in the Kattegat and the Skagerrak in 5–7.1789. Joined Adm. Chichagov's fleet off Bornholm on 22.7.1789. Located the Swedish fleet headed for St Petersburg on 21.5.1790. Fought in the battle of Krasnaia Gorka/Styrsudden on 22–23.5.1790. Fought at Vyborg on 22.6.1790. Escorted Swedish prizes to Revel' after the battle. Cruised in the Baltic in 1791. Cruised in the North Sea in 1793 and transferred to Kronshtadt. Broken up after 1799.

Kronshtadt 38/46   Arkhangel'sk
Constructor M. D. Portnov
Laid down 28.8.1788   *Launched* 15.5.1789
Dimensions 141 ft x 128 ft 6 in (keel) x 38 ft 4 in (inside plank)
         x 13 ft 9 in
Armament   LD 28 x 18pdrs
         FC & QD 10 x 6pdrs, 8 x carr.
Briachislav class (8 ships). Stationed in Arkhangel'sk Roads as a guard ship in 1790. Sailed from Arkhangel'sk to Kronshtadt in 7–9.1792. Cruised in the Baltic in 1794. To England with Vice-Adm. Khanykov's squadron in 1795–6. Returned to Kronshtadt in 1796. Broken up after 1800.

Arkhipelag 38/46   Arkhangel'sk
Constructor M. D. Portnov
Laid down 1.7.1788   *Launched* 16.5.1789
Dimensions 141 ft x 38 ft 4 in (inside plank) x 13 ft 9 in
Armament   LD 28 x 18pdrs
         FC & QD 10 x 6pdrs, 8 x carr.
Briachislav class (8 ships). Stationed in Arkhangel'sk Roads as a guard ship in 1790. Sailed from Arkhangel'sk to Kronshtadt in 7–9.1792. Cruised in the North Sea with Adm. Kruz's squadron in 1793. To England in 1795–7 with Vice-Adm. Khanykov's squadron. Cruised to Norway with naval cadets in 1800–2. Stationed in Kronshtadt Roads in 1803–6. Broken up in 1809.

Revel' 38/46   Arkhangel'sk
Constructor M. D. Portnov
Laid down 26.6.1789   *Launched* 21.5.1790
Dimensions 141 ft x 38 ft 4 in (inside plank) x 13 ft 9 in
Armament   LD 28 x 18pdrs
         FC & QD 10 x 6pdrs, 8 x carr.
Briachislav class (8 ships). Stationed in Arkhangel'sk Roads as a guard ship in 1790. Cruised in the White Sea in 1791. Sailed to Kronshtadt in 6–9.1794. To England with Vice-Adm. Khanykov's squadron in 1795–6. Cruised in the Baltic in 1798. Departed Revel' for England with troops for the Holland expedition in 1799 but forced back to Revel' with a leak. Fire watch ship in Kronshtadt Roads in 1801–4. Broken up after 1805.

Narva 38/46   Arkhangel'sk
Constructor M. D. Portnov
Laid down 9.7.1789   *Launched* 21.5.1790
Dimensions 141 ft x 38 ft 4 in (inside plank) x 13 ft 9 in
Armament   LD 28 x 18pdrs
         FC & QD 10 x 6pdrs, 8 x carr.
         326 men
Briachislav class (8 ships). Stationed at Arkhangel'sk until 1794. Left Arkhangel'sk on 30.6.1794, with Vice-Adm. Povalishin's squadron of 6 ships of the line and 4 frigates. Separated from the squadron in order to receive intelligence from the Russian ambassador to London, Vorontsov, as to continued Swedish neutrality. Rejoined Povalishin at Edinburgh on 14.8.1794 and arrived at Kronshtadt on 27.9.1794. To England with Vice-Adm. Khanykov's squadron in 1794–6. While returning to Russia on 24.10.1796, she was recalled to England from Copenhagen, this time in company with Rear-Adm. Makarov's squadron. Returned to Kronshtadt on 16.7.1797. Departed Kronshtadt with Vice-Adm. Makarov's First Division in 5.1798 and arrived in Britain in 7.1798. Operated in the North Sea under Vice-Adm. Duncan's overall control in 1798–9. Cruised in the Baltic in 1800–2. Fire watch ship at Revel' in 1803–6. Broken up in 1815.

Riga 38/46   Arkhangel'sk
Constructor M. D. Portnov
Laid down 9.7.1789   *Launched* 22.5.1790
Dimensions 141 ft x 38 ft 4 in (inside plank) x 13 ft 9 in
Armament   LD 28 x 18pdrs
         FC & QD 10 x 6pdrs, 8 x carr.
         304 men
Briachislav class (8 ships). Stationed at Arkhangel'sk in 1790. Sailed to Kronshtadt in 6–10.1794. To England with Vice-Adm. Khanykov's squadron in 1794–6. Cruised in the Baltic in 1798. Departed from Revel' for England with Rear-Adm. Kartsov's 3rd Division on 20.8.1798. Delayed in transit by a severe storm off Skagen, Norway on 19.9.1798. Arrived at Yarmouth on 2.11.1798. Returned to the Baltic in 1800. Converted into a transport in 1801. Converted into a magazine in 1805. Broken up in 1811.

Unnamed ?   St Petersburg
Constructor ?
Laid down 7.3.1795   *Launched* never
Dimensions ?
Armament ?
Unnamed vessel, characteristics indeterminate. Never launched and broken up in 1799.

Pospeshnyi 36/38   Arkhangel'sk (Solombala)
Constructor G. Ignatiev
Laid down 19.19.1796   *Launched* 19.5.1798
Dimensions 142 ft 6 in x 31 ft 6 in x 13 ft 5 in
Armament ?
         282 men
Experimental larch-built ship with very fine lines, based in part on comparative analysis made between the draughts of HMS *Phoebe*, obtained in 1796, and the contemporary Russian frigate *Briachislav*. Armament is not known, but she is rated hers as an 18pdr frigate based on her dimensions. Left Arkhangel'sk with Vice-Adm. That's 2nd

Division on 3.7.1798 and arrived at the Nore on 8.8.1798. Departed Yarmouth on 29.4.1799 for the Mediterranean with Rear-Adm. Kartsov's squadron. Arrived at Sevastopol' with Adm. Ushakov's squadron on 26.10.1800 and formally transferred from the Baltic to the Black Sea fleet. Cruised in the Black Sea in 1802–3. Carried troops to Corfu in 1804. Returned to Sevastopol' in 1805. Carried powder to Corfu in 1806 and escorted 10 Russian store ships to the Black Sea. To Anapa and Trabzon in 1807. Fire watch ship at Sevastopol' in 1808–9. Broken up after 1809. No further Russian frigates were based on this design and she remained a one-off design.

12/16pdr frigates (30 built 1762–1800)

Sviatoi Fyodor 32 Arkhangel'sk
Constructor I. V. James
Laid down 1.8.1761 *Launched* 8.5.1762
Dimensions 130 ft x 36 ft x 14 ft
Armament Planned LD 20 x 12pdrs
UD 12 x 6pdrs (1723 Establishment)
Completed LD 18 x 12pdrs
UD 14 x 6pdrs

This ship served as prototype for the later *Sviatoi Pavel* class of frigates. Sailed from Arkhangel'sk to Kronshtadt in 7–10.1762. Cruised in the North sea with naval cadets in 1763. Cruised in the Baltic in 1764–6, 1768, 1770–1 and 1773. Broken up in 1774.

Nadezhda Blagopoluchiia 34 St Petersburg
Constructor I. I. Afanasyev
Laid down ? *Launched* 4.6.1764
Dimensions 136 ft x 36 ft 3 in x 16 ft 1 in
Armament LD 20 x 12pdrs
UD 12/14 x 6pdrs

Purpose-built for service in the Mediterranean. To Livonro and back under merchant colours in 1764–5. To the Mediterranean with Adm. Spiridov's First Arkhipelago Squadron in 1769. Operated in the Mediterranean in 1770–3. Developed a serious leak in 3.1773 and forced to return to Auza. Condemned in 1774 due to hull deterioration. Guns salvaged.

Pavel class group I (5 ships)

Design based on that of *Sviatoi Fyodor* of 1762 and representative of a type that was largely obsolescent in the Atlantic navies by this time. Nonetheless, both groups of *Pavel*s were successfully employed in a variety of traditional cruiser roles during the 1780s. Although the specification was for 16pdr guns, most members of the class are believed to have been armed with 12 pdrs. Some were rearmed with 18 pdrs by 1786.

Natal'ia and *Pavel* were the most widely travelled members of the first group, having been sent to Istanbul in 1776–7 in an unsuccessful attempt to pass into the Black Sea to reinforce the developing Russian naval forces there on the brink of renewed war with Turkey by posing as merchantmen with reduced crews and with their armament concealed as ballast. *Natal'ia* was also the only member of the class to come to a violent end, being wrecked in the North Sea in 1779.

Pavel 32 Arkhangel'sk
Constructors Mal'tsev and V. Gunion
Laid down 19.8.1772 *Launched* 14.5.1773
Dimensions 130 ft x 32 ft x 14 ft
Armament LD 20 x 12/16pdrs
UD 12 x 6pdrs

Pavel class Group I (5 ships). Sailed from Arkhangel'sk to Kronshtadt in 7–9.1773. To the Arkhipelago with Rear-Adm. Greig's 5th Arkhipelago Squadron on 21.10.1773. Returned to Kronshtadt on 24.5.1775. Departed Kronshtadt on 15.6.1776 with *Natal'ia*, both disguised as 8-gun cargo ships en route to the Black Sea with half-strength complements, commercial cargos and the remaining guns carried covertly in sand ballast. Arrived at Istanbul on 6.2.1777 and refused admittance to the Black Sea. Returned to Livorno. At Tangiers in 1778. Joined Kozlyaninov's division off Gibraltar and returned to Livorno. Arrived at Kronshtadt on 14.5.1779. Broken up in 1791.

Evstafii 32 Arkhangel'sk
Constructor Mal'tsev
Laid down 19.8.1772 *Launched* 14.5.1773
Dimensions 130 ft x 32 ft x 14 ft
Armament LD 20 x 12/16pdrs
UD 12 x 6pdrs

Pavel class Group I (5 ships). Sailed from Arkhangel'sk to Kronshtadt in 7–9.1773. Cruised in the Baltic in 1774–5 and 1778. To Arkhangel'sk with Rear-Adm. Khmetevskiy's squadron in 1779. Returned to Kronshtadt on 17.10.1779. Broken up in 1793.

Natal'ia 32 Arkhangel'sk
Constructor V. Gunion
Laid down 1772 *Launched* 18.5.1773
Dimensions 130 ft x 32 ft x 14 ft
Armament LD 20 x 12/16pdrs
UD 12 x 6pdrs

Pavel class Group I (5 ships). Sailed from Arkhangel'sk to Kronshtadt in 7–9.1773. To the Mediterranean with Rear-Adm. Greig's 5th Arkhipelago Squadron on 21.10.1773. Operated in the Arkhipelago in 1774–5. Returned to Kronshtadt on 26.10.1775 with Vice-Adm. Elmanov's squadron. Departed Kronshtadt on 15.6.1776 with *Pavel*, both disguised as 8-gun cargo ships en route to the Black Sea with half-strength complements, commercial cargos and the remaining guns carried covertly in sand ballast. Arrived at Istanbul on 6.2.1777 and refused admittance to the Black Sea. Returned to Livorno. Departed for Russia but forced back to Livorno due to storm damage. Returned to Kronshtadt on 14.4.1779 (one day ahead of *Pavel*). To England with 370 tons of cargo in 8.1779. Grounded and wrecked in the North Sea on 22.9.1779. No casualties.

Legkii 32 Arkhangel'sk
Constructor V. Gunion
Laid down 5.12.1772 *Launched* 21.7.1773
Dimensions 130 ft x 32 ft x 14 ft
Armament LD 20 x 12/16pdrs
UD 12 x 6pdrs

Pavel class Group. I (5 ships). Sailed from Arkhangel'sk to Kronshtadt in 6–8.1776. Cruised in the Baltic in 1777. Cruised between Revel' and Kronshtadt in 1779. To Spain as a cargo ship with frigate *Sviatoi Mikhail* in 1781. Arrived at Cadiz on 19.7.1782. Returned to Kronshtadt on 22.7.1782. Sailed to Arkhangel'sk with guns and ammunition for newly completed ships in 1783. Returned to Kronshtadt in 1784. Broken up in 1793.

Schastlivyi 32 Arkhangel'sk
Constructor V. Gunion
Laid down 5.12.1772 *Launched* 18.8.1774
Dimensions 130 ft x 32 ft x 14 ft
Armament LD 20 x 12/16pdrs
UD 12 x 6pdrs

Pavel class Group I (5 ships). Sailed from Arkhangel'sk to Kronshtadt in 6–8.1776. Cruised in the Baltic in 1777–8 and 1783. Broken up in 1793.

Pavel class group II (13 ships)

This second group closely resembled their half-sisters, but were built with an extra 4 ft of beam, presumably in the interest of improving stability and internal capacity. At least nine of the class had six 24pdr carronades added between 1788 and 1790.

Seven group II ships participated in the Armed Neutrality Squadron in 1780–4. *Nadezhda* was the farthest-ranging class member, being employed against the Turks in the Arkhipelago in 1788. The class was extensively employed during the Russo-Swedish war of 1788–90 and nine ships saw combat. *Vozmislav* was wrecked in 1788 one month after participating in the battle of Gogland.

Sviatoi Mikhail 32 Arkhangel'sk
Constructor V. Gunion
Laid down 10.11.1772   *Launched* 31.5.1774
Dimensions 130 ft x 36 ft x 14 ft
Armament LD 20 x 12/16pdrs
                  UD 12 x 6pdrs

Pavel class Group II (13 ships). Sailed from Arkhangel'sk to Revel' in 6–8.1776. Cruised in the Baltic in 1778. Cruised to the Barents Sea and back in 1779. Cruised to Spain with the frigate *Legkii* in 1781 and underwent repair at Ferrol, arriving at Lisbon on 29.5.1782. Returned to Revel' on 29.8.1782. Transferred to Kronshtadt in 1783. Broken up in 1796.

Pospeshnyi 32 Arkhangel'sk
Constructors V. Gunion and M. D. Portnov
Laid down 5.12.1772   *Launched* 26.7.1774
Dimensions 130 ft x 36 ft x 13 ft
Armament LD 20 x 12/16pdrs
                  UD 12 x 6pdrs

Pavel class Group II (13 ships). Sailed from Arkhangel'sk to Revel' in 6–8.1776. Transferred to Kronshtadt in 1777. This ship was apparently defective and was broken up in 1791 after spending 14 years in harbour.

Aleksandr 32/38 Arkhangel'sk
Constructors V. Gunion and M. D. Portnov
Laid down 23.11.1773   *Launched* 15.5.1778
Dimensions 130 ft x 36 ft x 13 ft
Armament LD 20 x 12/16pdrs
                  UD 12 x 6pdrs
                  LD 20 x 12/16pdrs
                  UD 12 x 6pdrs, 6 x 24pdr carr. (1788–90)

Pavel class Group II (13 ships). Designed by Adm. Knowles. Sailed from Arkhangel'sk to Kronshtadt in 7–8.1778. To Portugal in 1780 with Brigadier Palibin's Armed Neutrality Squadron. Returned to Kronshtadt on 15.7.1781. Cruised in the Baltic in 1783, and 1785. Repaired in 1788–9. Took part in the pursuit of the Swedish fleet on 23.6.1790 after Vyborg. Cruised in the Baltic in 1792. Escorted troops bound for England to Copenhagen in 6.1796. Cruised in the Baltic in 1797–8. Broken up in 1804.

Voin 32/38 Arkhangel'sk
Constructors V. Gunion and M. D. Portnov
Laid down 23.11.1773   *Launched* 15.5.1778
Dimensions 130 ft x 36 ft x 13 ft
Armament LD 20 x 12/16pdrs
                  UD 12 x 6pdrs
                  LD 20 x 12/16pdrs
                  UD 12 x 6pdrs, 6 x 24pdr carr. (1788–90)

Pavel class Group II (13 ships). Sailed from Arkhangel'sk to Kronshtadt in 7–8.1778. To the Mediterranean with Rear-Adm. Sukhotin's Armed Neutrality Squadron in 1781. Returned to Kronshtadt on 2.7.1782. Transported guns and ammunition for new ships in 1784. Returned to Kronshtadt in 1785. Fought at Vyborg on 22.6.1790. Cruised in the Baltic in 1792 and 1794. Fire watch ship in Kronshtadt Roads in 1795–1800. Floating battery in the northern freeway off Kotlin in 1801. Broken up in 1804.

Mariia 32 Arkhangel'sk
Constructors V. Gunion and M. D. Portnov
Laid down 23.11.1773   *Launched* 21.5.1778
Dimensions 130 ft x 36 ft x 14 ft
Armament LD 20 x 12/16pdrs
                  UD 12 x 6pdrs

Pavel class Group II (13 ships). Sailed from Arkhangel'sk to Kronshtadt in 6–8.1778. To the North Sea with Rear-Adm. Kruz's squadron on 11.6.1780. To the Mediterranean with Rear-Adm. Sukhotin's squadron in 1781–2. Broken up in 1796.

Patrikii 32/38 Arkhangel'sk
Constructor M. D. Portnov
Laid down 3.2.1778   *Launched* 14.5.1779
Dimensions 130 ft x 36 ft x 14 ft
Armament LD 20 x 12/16pdrs
                  UD 12 x 6pdrs
                  LD 20 x 12pdrs
                  UD 12 x 6pdrs, 6 x 24pdr carr. (1788–90)

Pavel class Group II (13 ships). Left Arkhangel'sk and joined Rear-Adm. Khmetevskiy's squadron off Nordcap on 21.6.1779. To the Mediterranean with Rear-Adm. Borisov's Armed Neutrality Squadron in 1780–1. In the Mediterranean with Vice-Adm. Chichagov's squadron in 1782–4. Cruised in the Baltic in 1785. Repaired in 1788. Said to have carried 12pdrs in place of the 16pdrs in 1788–90. Operated in Vice-Adm. Kruz's Reserve Squadron in 1789. Fought at the battle of Rochensalm on 13–21.1789 and captured several Swedish rowing vessels. Fought at Vyborg with Capt. Crown's division on 22.6.1790. Cruised off the Danish and Swedish coasts in 1795–8. Attended the Imperial Review of 1800. Converted into a store ship in 1801.

Simion 32/38 Arkhangel'sk
Constructor M. D. Portnov
Laid down 5.10.1778   *Launched* 16.5.1779
Dimensions 130 ft x 36 ft x 14 ft
Armament LD 20 x 12/16pdrs
                  UD 12 x 6pdrs
                  LD 20 x 12pdrs
                  UD 12 x 6pdrs, 6 x 24pdr carr. (1788–90)

Pavel class Group II (13 ships). Left Arkhangel'sk and joined Rear-Adm. Khmetevskiy's squadron off Nordcap on 21.6.1779. To the Mediterranean with Rear-Adm. Borisov's Armed Neutrality Squadron in 1780–1. To the North Sea with Rear-Adm. Kruz's Reserve Squadron in 1782. Cruised in the Baltic in 1785. Repaired in 1788. Participated in the battle of Rochensalm against Swedish rowing flotillas on 13–21.8.1789 and captured several Swedish rowing vessels. Cruised in the Baltic in 1792, 1795–6 and 1797. Fire watch ship at Revel' in 1798–1802. Broken up in 1803.

Slava 32/38 Arkhangel'sk
Constructor M. D. Portnov

THE BALTIC FLEET 1762–1800

This painting of the 1st battle of Rochensalm on 8 May 1789 portrays the southern Russian rowing squadron heavily pressed by the Swedish rowing flotilla in the early stages of the battle. At the centre of the picture, both preceded and followed by Russian shebecks, is the frigate Simion *(32) holding the outnumbered Russians together against superior numbers of Swedish rowing vessels and awaiting for the arrival of the northern arm of the planned pincer movement. Prince Nassau-Siegen, the discredited veteran of the Liman campaign and the future architect of the disastrous defeat at the 2nd battle of Rochensalm, failed to bring his heavier forces stationed to the north of the Swedish flotillas into action for three hours, almost dooming the southern flotilla to defeat. Once the northern half of the Russian pincer did finally come into action, the Swedes were quickly put to flight, no thanks to the politically connected German mercenary.*

Laid down 27.8.1778   *Launched* 22.5.1781
Dimensions 130 ft x 36 ft x 14 ft
Armament LD 20-12/16pdrs
            UD 12 x 6pdrs
            LD 20 x 12pdrs
            UD 12 x 6pdrs, 6 x 24pdr carr. (1788–90)

Pavel class Group II (13 ships). Sailed from Arkhangel'sk to Kronshtadt in 7–9.1781. To the Mediterranean with Vice-Adm. Chichagov's squadron in 1782–4. Cruised in the Baltic in 1786. Fought at Gogland on 6.7.1788, escorted damaged ships to Kronshtadt, and cruised off Sveaborg. Fought at Öland on 15.7.1789. Fought at Revel' on 2.5.1790, expending 300 rounds and suffering casualties of 1 dead and 2 wounded. Fought at Vyborg and captured 2 Swedish galleys on 22.6.1790. Cruised in the Baltic in 1791, 1793, and 1797. Converted to a harbour vessel at Kronshtadt in 1799.

Nadezhda 32 Arkhangel'sk
Constructor M. D. Portnov
Laid down 27.8.1778   *Launched* 22.5.1781
Dimensions 130 ft x 36 ft x 14 ft
Armament LD 20 x 12/16pdrs
            UD 12 x 6pdrs

Pavel class Group II (13 ships). Sailed from Arkhangel'sk to Kronshtadt in 7–9.1781. To the North Sea with Rear-Adm. Kruz's squadron in 1782. Cruised in the Baltic in 1783 and 1785–7. To the Arkhipelago with Vice-Adm. V. Fondesin's squadron in 1788. Stationed at Copenhagen in 1788–9. Cruised off Bornholm and Gottland in 1789. Fire watch ship at Kronshtadt in 1790–4. Broken up in 1799.

Vozmislav 32/38 Arkhangel'sk
Constructor M. D. Portnov
Laid down 18.11.1781   *Launched* 16.5.1783
Dimensions 130 ft x 36 ft x 14 ft
Armament LD 20 x 12/16pdrs
            UD 12 x 6pdrs
            LD 20 x 12pdrs
            UD 12 x 6pdrs, 6 x 24pdr carr. (1788–90)

Pavel class Group II (13 ships). Sailed from Arkhangel'sk to Kronshtadt in 7–9.1783. Hydrographic survey work in the Kattegat in 1784. Cruised in the Baltic in 1785–6. Fought at Gogland on 6.7.1788. Departed Revel' on 10.8.1788 and grounded and wrecked off Nargen with 1 man drowned.

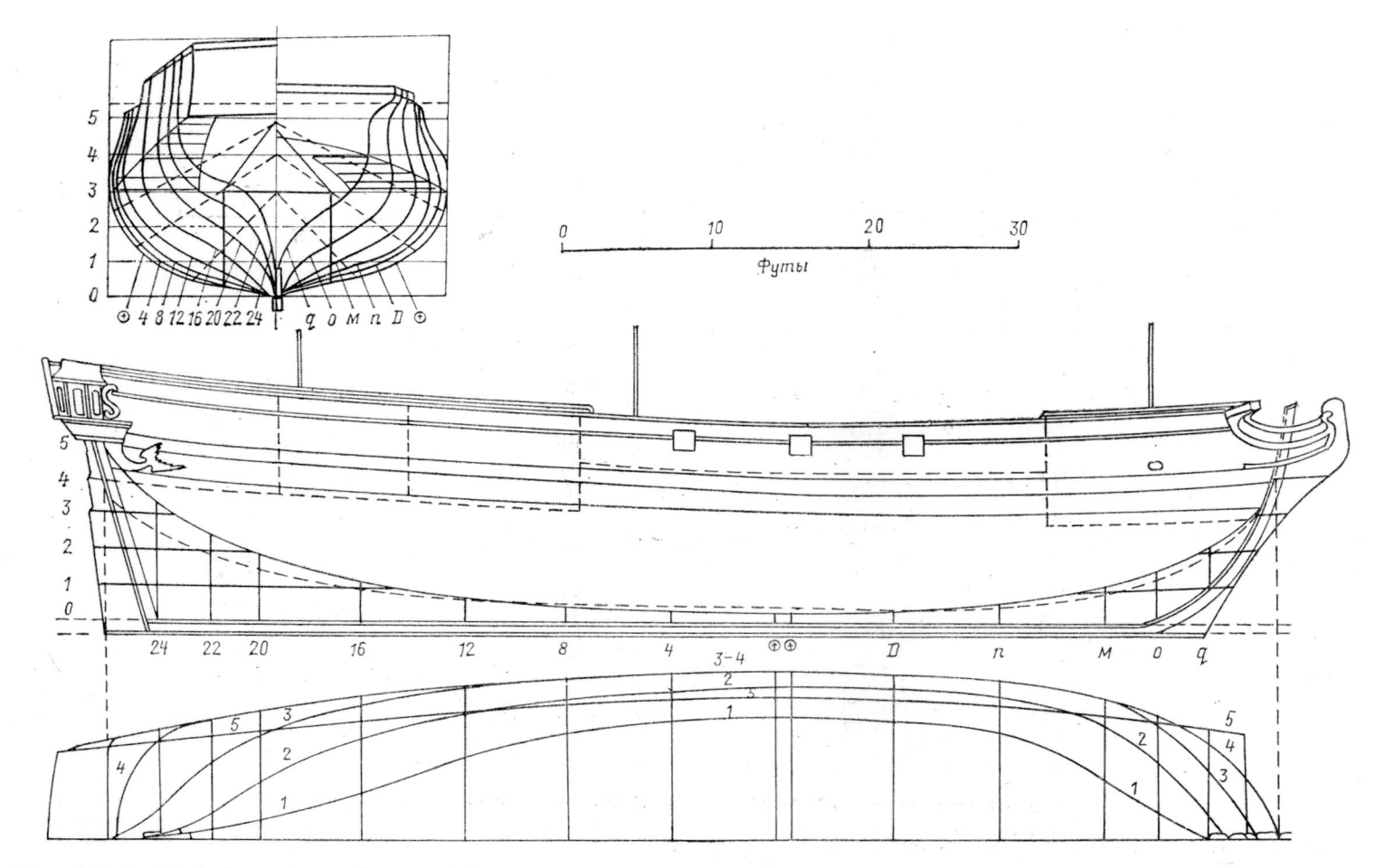

Although Nadezhda *had a single tier of guns and three square rigged masts, her classification as a frigate might have raised a few eyebrows in the Atlantic navies of the period. With 2 men and 25 cadets, this 77-foot ship was one of the earliest Russian examples of a type that continued to be built in small numbers to the end of sail. Classified as 'training frigates' and armed with 8–20 small cannon, these ships were never intended for or employed in combat operations.*

Podrazhislav 32/38 Arkhangel'sk
Constructor M. D. Portnov
Laid down 27.8.1778 *Launched* 22.5.1781
Dimensions 130 ft x 36 ft x 14 ft
Armament LD 20 x 12/16pdrs
            UD 12 x 6pdrs
            LD 20 x 12pdrs
            UD 12 x 6pdrs, 6 x 24pdr carr. (1788–90)
Pavel class Group II (13 ships). Sailed from Arkhangel'sk to Kronshtadt in 7–9.1783. Cruised in the Baltic in 1784–5. Fought at Gogland on 6.7.1788. Fought at Öland on 15.7.1789. Fought at Revel' on 2.5.1790 with 120 rounds expended and 1 man killed. On 3.5.1790, attacked the grounded Swedish ship of the line *Riksen Stander* (64) resulting in that ship's being fired by her crew. Fought at Vyborg on 22.6.1790. Stationed in Kronshtadt Roads in 1791. Cruised in the Baltic in 1793. Stationed in Kronshtadt Roads in 1795. Escorted troopships bound for England to Copenhagen in 1796. No further mention.

Premislav 34/42 Arkhangel'sk
Constructor M. D. Portnov
Laid down 18.6.1784 *Launched* 13.5.1785
Dimensions 130 ft x 36 ft(inside plank) x 14 ft
Armament LD 20 x 12/16pdrs
            UD 12 x 6pdrs (as designed)
            LD 20 x 18pdrs
            UD 12 x 6pdrs, 6 x 24pdr carr. (as rearmed 1788–90)
Pavel class Group II (13 ships). *Premislav* is known to have been re-armed with lower deck 18pdrs during the 1788–90 conflict. Whether this change was applied to other class members is unclear. Sailed from Arkhangel'sk to Kronshtadt in 7–8.1785. Fought at Gogland on 6.7.1788. Fought at Öland on 15.7.1789. Fought at Revel' on 2.5.1790. Fought at Vyborg on 22.6.1790 and captured a gunboat and 2 transports. Cruised in the Baltic in 1791–2. Stationed in Kronshtadt Roads in 1793. Determined to be in poor condition in 1796–7. No further mention.

Nadezhda Blagopoluchiia 32/38 Arkhangel'sk
Constructor M. D. Portnov
Laid down 17.5.1785 *Launched* 17.5.1786
Dimensions 130 ft x 36 ft(inside plank) x 14 ft
Armament LD 20 x 12/16pdrs
            UD 12 x 6pdrs
            LD 20 x 12/16pdrs
            UD 12 x 6pdrs, 6 x 24pdr carr. (1788–90)
Pavel class Group II (13 ships). Sailed from Arkhangel'sk to

Kronshtadt in 7–8.1787. First Russian ship to make contact with the Swedish fleet at Gogland on 6.7.1788. Took the Swedish prize *Prins Gustav* in tow after the battle and brought her back to Kronshtadt. Fought at Öland on 15.7.1789. Fought at Revel' on 2.5.1790. Fought at Vyborg on 22.6.1790 where she captured 4 Swedish gun boats. Proceeded to Copenhagen after the battle. Cruised in the Baltic in 1791. Fire watch ship in Revel' Roads in 1793–8. No further mention.

Training frigates (2 built 1762–1800)

Gektor 26 St Petersburg
Constructor I. V. James
Laid down 9.7.1774 *Launched* 4.11.1781
Dimensions 130 ft 9 in x 33 ft 6 in x 10 ft 9 in
Armament ?
Training frigate. Completed in 1777 but allowed to remain on the slip for 4 years. Surveyed the Gulf of Finland in 1784. Cruised to Bornholm in 1787. Caught unawares on 27.6.1788 and captured by the Swedish fleet in the Gulf of Finland upon the outbreak of war.

Iaroslavets 36 Arkhangel'sk
Constructor M. D. Portnov
Laid down 23.6.1783 *Launched* 12.5.1784
Dimensions 135 ft 4 in x 35 ft 6 in (inside plank) x 10 ft 10 in
Armament LD 26 x 12pdrs
             FC & QD 10 x 4pdrs (in Swedish service)
Training frigate. Sailed from Arkhangel'sk to Kronshtadt in 7–8.1784. Cruised in the Baltic with naval cadets in 1786–7. Sent on a reconnaissance mission in 6.1788 and driven by a squall into the centre of the Swedish fleet where she was forced to surrender. Recaptured at Vyborg on 22.6.1790. Fire watch ship at Kronshtadt in 1791. Transferred to Revel' as a fire watch ship in 1792–4. Returned to Kronshtadt in 1794. Broken up at Kronshtadt in 1799.

Small frigates (5 built 1762–1800)

Vestovoi 8 ?
Constructor ?
Laid down ? *Launched* ?
Purchased 1763
Dimensions 76 ft x 22 ft 11 in x ?
Armament ?
Purchased small frigate. Repaired in 1764. Cruised in the Baltic with naval cadets in 1765. Transferred to Riga in 1765. Fire watch ship off Riga near the mouth of the Dvina in 1766–75. Transferred to Kronshtadt in 1775. Broken up at Kronshtadt in 1776.

Sviatoi Aleksandr 8 St Petersburg
Constructor I. V. James
Laid down 23.12.1765 *Launched* 4.6.1766
Dimensions 88 ft 6 in x 23 ft x 9 ft 6 in
Armament ?
Small frigate. Cruised to Copenhagen in 1773. Transferred to Riga as a fire watch ship in 1775. Broken up in 1776.

Nadezhda 10 St Petersburg
Constructor I. V. James
Laid down 23.12.1765 *Launched* 4.6.1766
Dimensions 77 ft x 22 ft x 9 ft 3 in   270 tons
Armament ?
             24 men and 25 cadets
Small purpose-built training frigate. Cruised annually in the Gulf of Finland in 1766–74. Broken up in 1774.

Vtoraia Ekaterina 20 ?
Constructor ?
Laid down ? *Launched* 9.8.1773
Dimensions 90 ft x 25 ft 3 in x 11 ft
Armament ?
Converted yacht. Cruised in the Baltic in 1773–4 and 1776. Harbour service in 1777. Broken up in 1782.

Unnamed 16 Olonetskaya
Constructor I. I. Afanasyev
Laid down 3.10.1783 *Launched* 9.5.1784
Dimensions 90 ft x 26 ft 6 in (inside plank) x 12 ft 6 in
Armament ?
Frigate rigged ship, purpose-built as a fire watch ship at Riga. Broken up in 1791.

Rowing frigates (20 laid down, 18 completed 1762–1800)

After the disastrous defeats suffered by Sweden during the 1741–3 war, it was decided by the Swedes to create a local force in Finland for self-defence. From the 1760s, cyclopean ramparts were erected by the Swedes at Sveaborg, and a supporting fleet of powerful sailing/rowing ships was built, consisting of flat-bottomed shebeck-type vessels armed with heavy guns. At the outbreak of hostilities in 1788, the entire Russian rowing fleet consisted of only 8 half-galleys; but a building programme consisting of hundreds of rowing vessels of various types was immediately put into effect to counter the Swedish advantage. The largest of these ships were classed as rowing frigates, and they were intended solely for use in shallow coastal waters with no thought of wider employment even within the Baltic. Although intended for a narrow range of duties, they were formidably armed ships and might, in the right circumstances, have been reasonable matches for true seagoing frigates.

Evangelist Mark class (2 ships)

Evangelist Mark (*Sviatoi Mark*) 20/22 St Petersburg
Constructor I. V. James
Laid down 22.10.1772 *Launched* 24.4.1773
Dimensions 124 ft 4 in x 26 ft x 9 ft
Armament 20 x 8pdrs, 2 x 8pdr mortars
             2 x 24pdrs, 6 x 12pdrs, 12 x 6pdrs (later armament)
Evangelist Mark class. Rowing frigate employed tactically with the sailing fleet. Transported the future bride of the future Paul I from Lübeck to Russia in 1773. Cruised in the Baltic in 1774 to Petergof. Cruised in the Baltic in 1776 to Lübeck and Danzig. Escorted the personal galley of the Swedish King Gustav III to St Petersburg for an incognito visit in 1777. Transported household goods for Catherine II from Lübeck in 1780. Test bed for coppering in 1782. Set fire to 14 Swedish rowing vessels off Sveaborg in 10.1788. Successfully engaged Swedish oared flotillas in 1789. Cruised to Revel' in 1790. Cruised in the Baltic in 1791–3. Broken up in 1794.

Provornyi 20/22 St Petersburg
Constructor I. V. James
Laid down 27.1.1776 *Launched* 4.11.1781
Dimensions 124 ft 4 in x 26 ft x 9 ft
Armament 20 x 8pdrs, 2 x 6pdr mortars
Evangelist Mark class Rowing frigate. Cruised as a test bed for sheathing materials including 'white metal', an alloy of tin and lead. Stationed in the Kotlin Roads. Broken up in 1789.

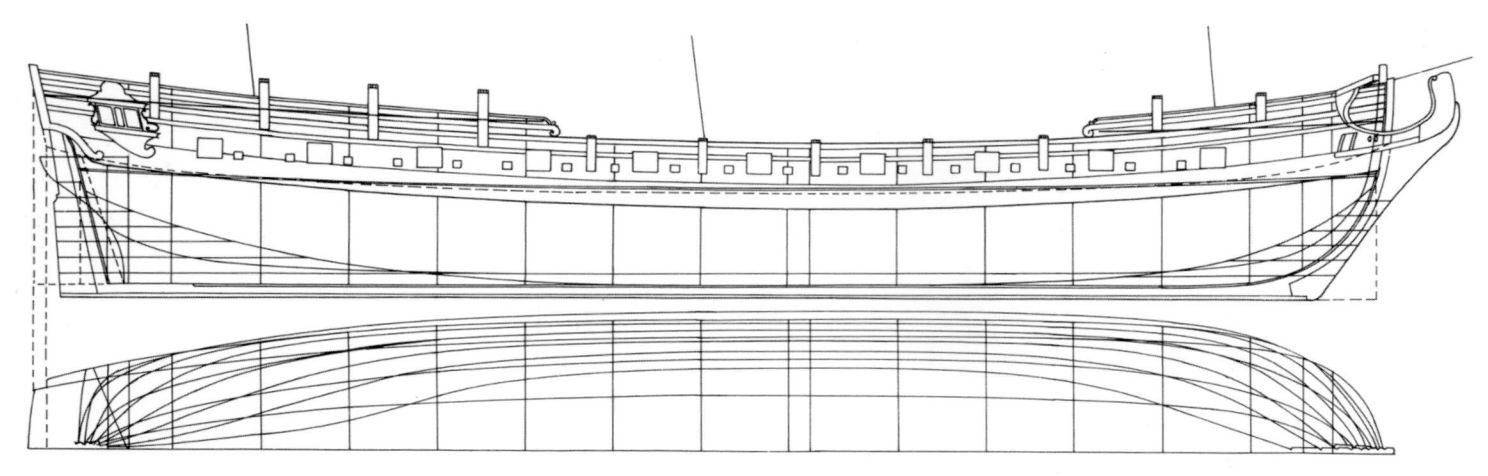

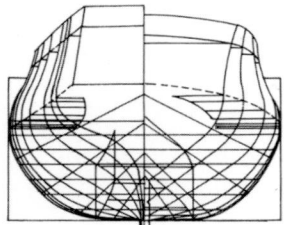

A draught of the first Russian rowing frigate, Evangelist Mark (20) of 1773, showing her external appearance and underwater lines. With only 8pdrs in her broadside, she was hardly suited for backing line of battle ships and firing through intervals in the line as was one of the functions of later rowing frigates, but she could wreak havoc when turned loose on gunboat squadrons, as she did on at least two occasions in 1788 and 1789.

Aleksandr class (18 laid down, 16 completed)
In January 1790 a class initially consisting of eight frigates similar in concept to the earlier *Evangelist Mark* and *Provornyi*, but larger and more heavily armed, were laid down at Kronstadt and launched 23.4.1790 by D. Masal'skiy and I. Kutygin. In spite of their heavy losses at the 2nd battle of Rochensalm (Svenskund), they had been successfully employed during the closing stages of the Russo-Swedish War, most particularly at Styrsudden where they provided a de facto mobile reserve for the line of battle which found itself nearly immobilized by light wind conditions. They were followed by ten duplicates, this time laid down at St Petersburg rather than at Kronstadt, between 1794 and 1796, although only eight of the second group were completed. The three survivors of the battle of Rochensalm later had their main deck 18pdrs replaced by 24pdrs and the final eight ships all completed with the heavier armament.

All eight ships of the initial group took part in the battle of Krasnaia Gorka 23–4.5.1790 under the command of Capt. Dennison (a British officer on Russian service), where they fired at Swedish ships from the intervals between the Russian ships of the line and were used as a reserve to prevent the Swedish warships from doubling the shorter Russian line. On 22–23.6.1790 they took part in the battle of Vyborg and on 28.6.1790 in the disastrous 2nd battle of Rochensalm, when five of them were lost due to the premature and inadequately planned attack of the Russian rowing fleet commander Vice-Adm. Nassau-Siegen, (who had recently been transferred from the Black Sea due to poor performance while in charge of rowing forces in the Liman). These ships were colloquially referred to by name only, but were formally known by their saint names as *Sviatoi Aleksandr*, *Sviataia Elena*, etc.

Sviatoi Aleksandr 38 Kronstadt
Constructors   D. Masal'skiy and I. Kutygin
Laid down   1.1790   Launched   23.4.1790
Dimensions   130 ft x 32 ft x 11 ft   9 pairs of oars
            720 tons standard
Armament   1790 LD 2 x 24pdrs, 20 x 18pdrs
            FC & QD 2 x 18pdrs, 14 x 6pdrs
            250 men
Aleksandr class. Rowing frigate. Lost during the 2nd battle of Rochensalm on 28.6.1790. 46 men saved.

Sviataia Aleksandra 34/38 Kronstadt
Constructors   D. Masal'skiy and I. Kutygin
Laid down   1.1790   Launched   23.4.1790
Dimensions   130 ft x 32 ft x 11 ft   9 pairs of oars
            720 tons standard
Armament   1790 LD 2 x 24pdrs, 20 x 18pdrs
            FC & QD 2 x 18pdrs, 14 x 6pdrs
            250 men
            1791 LD 22 x 24pdrs
            FC & QD 2 x 18pdrs, 10 x 12pdrs
Aleksandr class. Rowing frigate. Captured 4 galleys, 2 gunboats and 6 transports at Vyborg on 22–23.6.1790. Repaired at Kronstadt, fortuitously missing the 2nd battle of Rochensalm. Cruised in the Baltic in 1791–4 and employed in the hydrographic survey of the Finnish coastline. Stationed in Kronstadt Roads in 1801. Broken up in 1804.

Sviataia Ekaterina 38 Kronstadt
Constructors   D. Masal'skiy and I. Kutygin
Laid down   1.1790   Launched   23.4.1790
Dimensions   130 ft x 32 ft x 11 ft, 9 pairs of oars
            720 tons standard
Armament   1790 LD 2 x 24pdrs, 20 x 18pdrs
            FC & QD 2 x 18pdrs, 14 x 6pdrs
            250 men
Aleksandr class. Rowing frigate. Disabled, grounded and set afire by her crew at the 2nd battle of Rochensalm on 28.6.1790. 84 men saved.

Sviataia Elena 34/38 Kronstadt
Constructors   D. Masal'skiy and Kutygin
Laid down   1.1790   Launched   23.4.1790
Dimensions   130 ft x 32 ft x 11 ft 9 pairs of oars

THE BALTIC FLEET 1762–1800

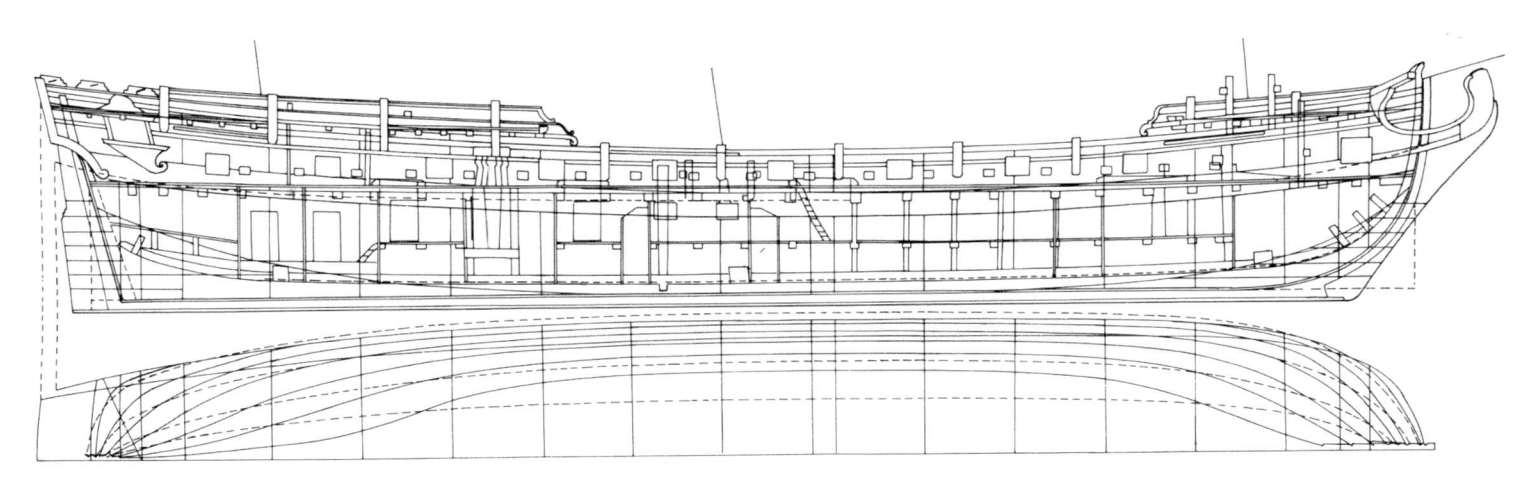

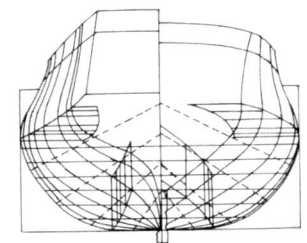

A sheer and longitudinal profile of Evangelist Mark, *showing her internal arrangements. The contrast between this drawing and the more highly developed* Sviatoi Pavel *rowing frigates is striking.*

720 tons standard
Armament 1790 LD 2 x 24pdrs, 20 x 18pdrs
FC & QD 2 x 18pdrs, 14 x 6pdrs
250 men
1791 LD 22 x 24pdrs
FC & QD 2 x 18pdrs, 10 x 12pdrs
Aleksandr class. Rowing frigate. Under repair at Kronshtadt after Vyborg and absent from the 2nd battle of Rochensalm on 28.6.1790. Cruised in the Baltic in 1791–9. Broken up in 1802.

Sviatoi Konstantin 38 Kronshtadt
Constructors   D. Masal'skiy and I. Kutygin
Laid down 1.1790   *Launched* 23.4.1790
Dimensions 130 ft x 32 ft x 11 ft 9 pairs of oars
720 tons standard
Armament 1790 LD 2 x 24pdrs, 20 x 18pdrs
FC & QD 2 x 18pdrs, 14 x 6pdrs
250 men
Aleksandr class. Rowing frigate. Lost during the 2nd battle of Rochensalm on 28.6.1790. 4 survivors.

Sviataia Mariia 38 Kronshtadt
Constructors   D. Masal'skiy and I. Kutygin
Laid down 1.1790   *Launched* 23.4.1790
Dimensions 130 ft x 32 ft x 11 ft 9 pairs of oars
720 tons standard
Armament 1790 LD 2 x 24pdrs, 20 x 18pdrs
FC & QD 2 x 18pdrs, 14 x 6pdrs
250 men
Aleksandr class. Rowing frigate. Surrendered and then capsized during the 2nd battle of Rochensalm on 28.6.1790. Capt. Dennison, commander of the rowing frigate division, was mortally wounded. 70 survivors.

Sviatoi Nikolai 38 Kronshtadt
Constructors   D. Masal'skiy and I. Kutygin
Laid down 1.1790   *Launched* 23.4.1790
Dimensions 130 ft x 32 ft x 11 ft 9 pairs of oars
720 tons standard
Armament 1790 LD 2 x 24pdrs, 20 x 18pdrs
FC & QD 2 x 18pdrs, 14 x 6pdrs
250 men
Aleksandr class. Rowing frigate. Named to commemorate the capture of Ochakov on the saint day of St Nicholas in 1788. Heavily damaged and sunk during the 2nd battle of Rochensalm on 28.6.1790. Capt. Marshall refused to leave her and went down with his ship. 12 survivors.

Sviatoi Pavel 34/38 Kronshtadt
Constructors   D. Masal'skiy and I. Kutygin
Laid down 1.1790   *Launched* 23.4.1790
Dimensions 130 ft x 32 ft x 11 ft, 9 pairs of oars
720 tons standard
Armament 1790 LD 2 x 24pdrs, 20 x 18pdrs
FC & QD 2 x 18pdrs, 14 x 6pdrs
250 men
1791 LD 22 x 24pdrs
FC & QD 2 x 18pdrs, 10 x 12pdrs
Aleksandr class. Rowing frigate. Arrived at Rochensalm on 30.6.1790, two days after the disastrous battle. Became the flag to Vice-Adm. Nassau-Siegen. Cruised in the Baltic in 1791–5. Stationed in Kronshtadt Roads in 1801. Broken up in 1804.

Sviatoi Aleksandr 34 St Petersburg
Constructors   D. Masal'skiy
Laid down 24.1.1792   *Launched* 10.10.1792
Dimensions 130 ft x 32 ft x 11 ft, 9 pairs of oars
720 tons standard
Armament LD 22 x 24pdrs
FC & QD 2 x 18pdrs, 10 x 12pdrs
250 men
Aleksandr class. Rowing frigate. Cruised in the Baltic in 1793–97. Cruised to Stockholm with naval cadets in 1800. Stationed in Kronshtadt Roads in 1801. Broken up in 1804.

Sviatoi Pavel (38) of 1790 was one of a group of innovative rowing frigates laid down in great haste in 1790 and known collectively as the Aleksandr class. They were an attempt to provide a counter to Swedish rowing gunboats capable of manoeuvring in the kind of windless days that characterized the northern Baltic and exposed becalmed sailing warships to attack from quarters not covered by their broadside batteries. The sheer and profile here shows a ship that might be mistaken for a conventional frigate of the period, but with only 10 gunports on her broadside in contrast to the 13 to 14 of a normal sailing frigate of the same period.

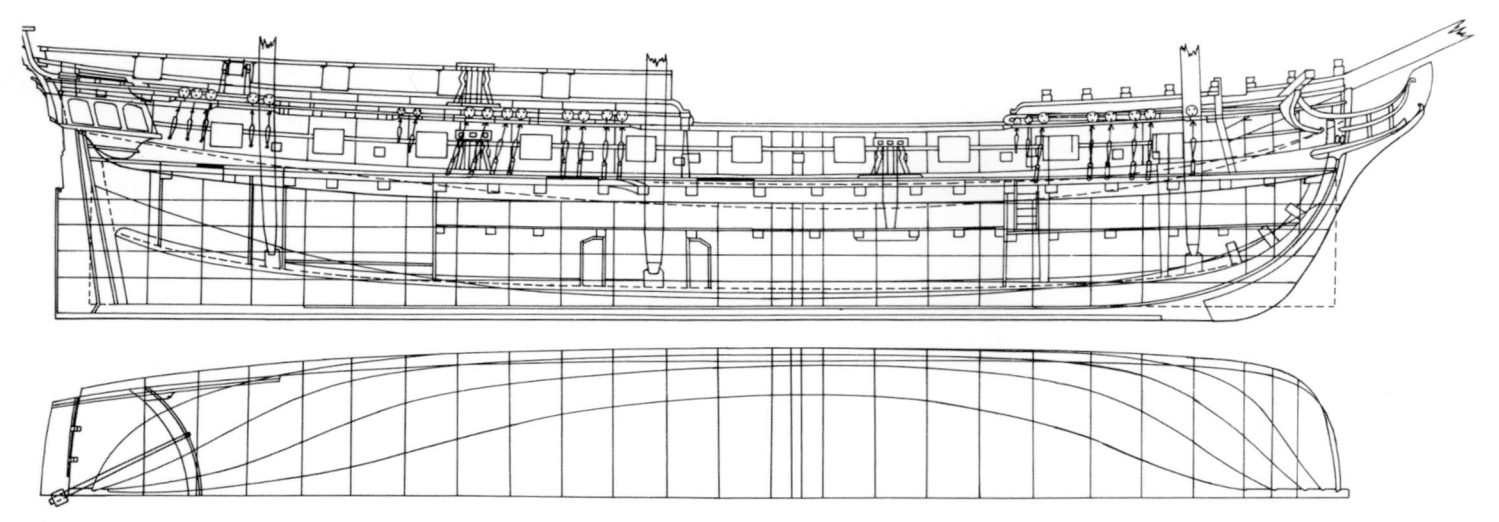

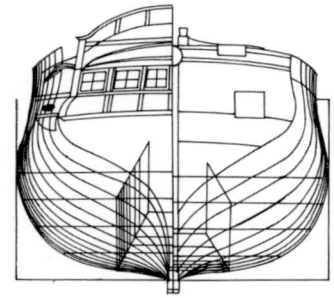

Sviataia Ekaterina 34 St Petersburg
Constructors   D. Masal'skiy
Laid down   22.1.1792   Launched   17.10.1792
Dimensions   130 ft x 32 ft x 11 ft, 9 pairs of oars
                720 tons standard
Armament   LD 22 x 24pdrs
                FC & QD 2 x 18pdrs, 10 x 12pdrs
                250 men

Aleksandr class. Rowing frigate. Cruised in the Baltic in 1793–4. Fire watch ship at Rochensalm galley base in 1795. Cruised in the Baltic in 1797–8. Broken up in 1804.

Sviataia Elisaveta 34 St Petersburg
Constructors   D. Masal'skiy
Laid down   28.1.1793   Launched   25.8.1794
Dimensions   130 ft x 32 ft x 11 ft, 9 pairs of oars
                720 tons standard
Armament   LD 22 x 24pdrs
                FC & QD 2 x 18pdrs, 10 x 12pdrs
                250 men

Aleksandr class. Rowing frigate. Cruised in the Baltic in 1795–7 and 1799–1801. Broken up in 1803.

Sviataia Mariia 34 St Petersburg
Constructors   D. Masal'skiy
Laid down   28.1.1793   Launched   25.8.1794
Dimensions   130 ft x 32 ft x 11 ft, 9 pairs of oars
                720 tons standard
Armament   LD 22 x 24pdrs
                FC & QD 2 x 18pdrs, 10 x 12pdrs
                250 men

Aleksandr class. Rowing frigate. Cruised in the Baltic in 1795–6. Driven ashore in a squall off Gogland on 17.7.1796. Broke up on 18.7.1796. No casualties.

Sviatoi Konstantin 34 St Petersburg
Constructors   D. Masal'skiy
Laid down   7.3.1795   Launched   9.10.1796
Dimensions   130 ft x 32 ft x 11 ft, 9 pairs of oars
                720 tons standard
Armament   LD 22 x 24pdrs
                FC & QD 2 x 18pdrs, 10 x 12pdrs
                250 men

Aleksandr class. Rowing frigate. Cruised in the Baltic in 1798. Departed for England as a troopship with Rear-Adm. P. Chichagov's squadron in 1799. Damaged and forced to return to Russia. After repairs, arrived off the Texel with troops for the joint Anglo-Russian invasion. Returned to Kronshtadt in 1800. Stationed in Kronshtadt Roads in 1801. As part of Adm. Thate's fleet in 1805, landed troops on the German coast. Storm damaged and repaired at Karlskrona. Returned to Kronshtadt in 1806. Broken up in 1808.

Sviatoi Nikolai 34 St Petersburg
Constructors   D. Masal'skiy
Laid down   7.3.1795   Launched   9.10.1796
Dimensions   130 ft x 32 ft x 11 ft, 9 pairs of oars
                720 tons standard
Armament   LD 22 x 24pdrs
                FC & QD 2 x 18pdrs, 10 x 12pdrs
                250 men

Aleksandr class. Rowing frigate. Cruised in the Baltic in 1798. Departed for England as a troopship with Rear-Adm. P. Chichagov's

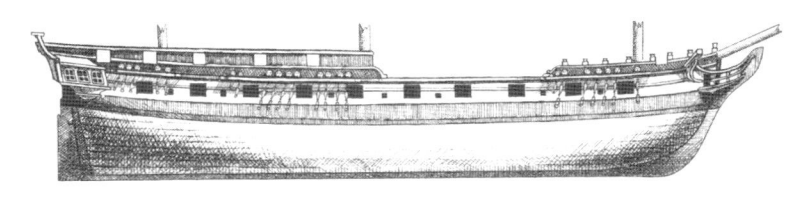

The rowing frigate Sviatoi Pavel *in side profile. Unlike contemporary Russian shebecks, these rowing frigates not only had sufficient draught to accompany sailing fleets into offshore waters when called upon but scantlings appropriate for protecting their 18- and later 24pdr batteries.*

squadron in 1799. Damaged and forced to return to Russia. After repairs, arrived off the Texel with troops for the invasion. Returned to Kronshtadt in 1800. Stationed in Kronshtadt Roads in 1801. As part of Adm. Thate's fleet in 1805, landed troops on the German coast. Cruised to Danzig in 1806. Training duties in Kronshtadt Roads in 1807. Broken up in 1809.

Bogoiavlenie Gospodne 34 St Petersburg
Constructors A. I. Melikhov and M. Sarychev
Laid down 7.3.1795 *Launched* 2.9.1798
Dimensions 130 ft x 32 ft x 11 ft, 9 pairs of oars
720 tons standard
Armament LD 2 x 24pdrs, 12 x 18pdrs
FC & QD 2 x 11pdrs, 14 x 6pdrs
136 men + 40 cadets
Aleksandr class. Rowing frigate. Cruised in the Baltic in 1800 with naval cadets. Stationed in Kronshtadt Roads in 1801. Fire watch ship at Rochensalm in 1804. As part of Adm. Thate's fleet in 1805, landed troops on the German coast. Operated with Adm. Khanykov's fleet in 1808 and then transferred to the rowing flotilla. Attacked by two Swedish 48-gun frigates off the Swedish coast in 6.1809 and successfully forced their retreat. Fire watch ship in Kronshtadt Roads in 1810. Hulked. Broken up in 1816.

Emmanuil 24/38 St Petersburg
Constructors A. I. Melikhov and I. P. Vasilyev
Laid down 31.12.1796 *Launched* 1.4.1800
Dimensions 130 ft x 32 ft x 11 ft, 9 pairs of oars
720 tons standard
Armament LD 22 x 24pdrs
FC & QD 2 x 18pdrs, 10 x 12pdrs
250 men
Aleksandr class. Rowing frigate. Cruised in the Baltic in 1800. Cruised with naval cadets in 1801–2. Reduced to 24 guns and transferred to the sailing navy in 1804. Cruised in the Baltic in 1805–7. Fire watch ship at Revel' in 1808–13. Broken up in 1817.

Vifleem 38 St Petersburg
Constructor
Laid down 31.12.1796 *Launched* unfinished
Dimensions 130 ft x 32 ft x 11 ft, 9 pairs of oars
720 tons standard
Armament LD 22 x 24pdrs
FC & QD 2 x 18pdrs, 10 x 12pdrs
250 men
Aleksandr class. Rowing frigate. Scrapped incomplete 1799.

Nazaret 38 St Petersburg
Constructor ?
Laid down 31.12.1796 *Launched* unfinished
Dimensions 130 ft x 32 ft x 11 ft, 9 pairs of oars
720 tons standard
Armament LD 22 x 24pdrs
FC & QD 2 x 18pdrs, 10 x 12pdrs
250 men
Aleksandr class. Rowing frigate. Scrapped incomplete 1799.

For the sake of completeness, mention is made here of three vessels, originally classed as 'secret ships' and found under that category in section II. After failing in their designed mission as warships disguised as merchantmen, these ships were reclassified in 1790–2 as rowing frigates and then converted into floating batteries in 1792.

Arkhipelago privateers taken into service (21 acquired 1762–1800)

During the Arkhipelago campaigns of 1770–5, numerous local privateers were bought (or captured) and used in the Russian fleet as 'frigates'. Veselago included them in his list as true (but small) frigates, but they would more reasonably have been classed as ship sloops in most instances. Due to the conditions of their acquisition and service, information about these ships is scanty, but they were primarily engaged as privateers operating against the Turks in the Aegean and the Adriatic. In the interests of clarity, it should be mentioned here that the Russian use of the term 'privateer' was broader in scope than that in use in Western navies and might more properly be defined as encompassing hired or purchased private ships attached to battle fleets for a variety of duties and under the operational control of the Russian navy. The Russian use of privateers in the Black Sea at this time was a reflection of their limited resources, both in terms

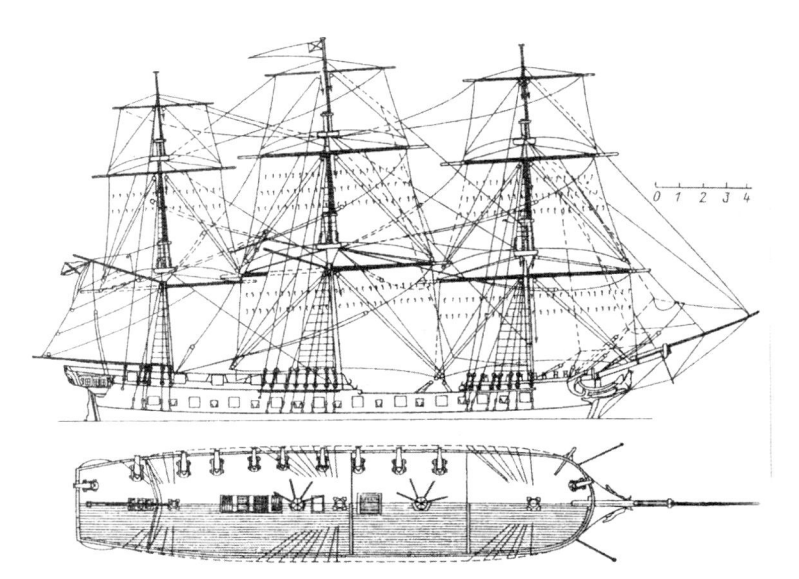

Although five of the eight original rowing frigates laid down in 1790 had been lost at the 2nd battle of Rochensalm, rowing frigates had proved their worth and ten duplicates were authorized. This is Bogoiavlenie Gospodne of 1798, showing the arrangement of her rigging and main armament, her internal layout, and her underwater lines. She proved her worth and the value of her 24pdr armament in 1808 by standing off two attacking Swedish frigates in 1808.

of available smaller ships and in terms of trained seamen and officers. Four were grounded or wrecked during the war, 8 were broken up or sold between 1772 and 1776, and 9 made their way to the Baltic post-war where they served in various capacities while a single unit succeeded in entering the Black Sea post-war and joined the Sea of Azov (later Black Sea) fleet.

Ungariia class (2 ships)
Ungariia 26 Port Taro
Constructor ?
Laid down ? *Launched* 1766 *Purchased* 1775
Dimensions 127 ft x 36 ft 11 in x 10 ft 11 in
Armament ?
Ungariia class Purchased at Livorno in 1775. Sister ship to *Bogemiia*. To Russia in company with *Bogemiia* in 9.1775, wintering at Portsmouth. Arrived at Kronshtadt in 6.1776 and participated in the Imperial Review. Cruised in the Baltic in 1781 and 1783. Broken up in 1796.

Bogemiia 26 Trieste
Constructor ?
Laid down   *Launched* 1768 *Purchased* 1775
Dimensions 127 ft x 36 ft 11 in x 10 ft 11 in
Armament ?
Ungariia class Purchased at Livorno in 1775. Sister ship to *Ungariia*. Wintered at Portsmouth in 1775. Arrived at Kronshtadt in company with *Ungariia* on 19.6.1776. Participated in the Imperial Review of 1776. Cruised in the Baltic in 1777–8. Carried cargo to Spain in 1781. Grounded en route in the Skagerrak and repaired at Vlissingen. Arrived at Cadiz on 24.1.1782. Departed Cadiz on 14.5.1782 and arrived at Kronshtadt on 30.7.1782. Fire watch ship in Kronshtadt Roads in 1783–89. Broken up in 1796.

Severnyi Oryol 40 ?
Constructor ?
Laid down ? *Launched* 1752 *Purchased* 1770
Dimensions 130 ft x 32 ft 4 in x ?
Armament ?
Purchased in London in 1770. Believed to have originally been a privateer. Crew provided on 20.8.1770 from her namesake *Severnyi Oryol* (66), then being sold for breaking up in England. Departed for the Arkhipelago for operations against Turkey in 1770–4. Assisted in refloating the grounded frigate *Arkhipelag* in the Bay of Mitilini on 5.11.1771. The similarly grounded frigate *Santorin* was blown ashore and captured by the Turks only to be set afire by gunfire from *Severnyi Oryol*. Arrived at Revel' on 9.1.1775. Escorted Russian merchant ships to the Dardanelles in 1776, but forced to turn back at Messina. Repaired at Livorno. Arrived at Kronshtadt on 14.5.1779. Converted to a store ship in 1780. Broken up in 1790.

Sviatoi Nikolai 26 ?
Constructor ?
Laid down ? *Launched* ? *Acquired* 1770
Dimensions ?
Armament ?
Greek privateer, voluntarily acquired with captain and crew by the Russian navy on 21.2.1770. Fought at the battle of Chios on 5.7.1770 and at Patras Bay on 28.10.1772 in company with *Ches'ma* (74), *Graf Orlov* (66) and *Slava* (16) against a Turkish squadron of 9 frigates and 16 xebecs. Attacked and fired the xebec flagship. Present at the capture of Beyrouth, Syria in 9.1773. Entered the Black Sea in 1775 and assigned to the Sea of Azov Flotilla. To Marseilles and back in 1781 and 1783. Escorted store ships to Ochakov in 1787. Fought at the battle of Ochakov on 17.6.1788 and forced the surrender of a grounded Turkish 64 which was incorporated into the Russian navy as *Leontii Muchenik*. Broken up after 1788.

Pobeda 16 ?
Constructor ?
Laid down ? *Launched* ? *Purchased* 1770
Dimensions ?
Armament ?
Purchased in the Arkhipelago in 1770. Operations against the Turks in 1770–4. Departed Auza on 21.5.1775 with Greek settlers for the Black Sea. Wrecked off Balakava in the Crimea with no casualties.

Slava 16 ?
Constructor ?
Laid down ? *Launched* ? *Purchased* 1770
Dimensions ?
Armament ?
Purchased in the Arkhipelago in 1770. Operations against the Turks in 1770–4. Fought at the battle of Patras on 28.10.1772, setting fire to a Turkish frigate and 2 xebecs. In 9.1773, participated in the capture of Beyrouth, Syria. Navigated to the Crimea in 1774–5 and returned to Auza. Sold at Livorno in 1776.

Paros 10 ?
Constructor ?
Laid down ? *Launched* ? *Purchased* 1770
Dimensions 84 ft x 22 ft 4 in x 10 ft 2 in
Armament ?
Purchased in the Arkhipelago in 1770. Operations against the Turks in 1770–4. Arrived at Revel' with Vice-Adm. Elmanov's squadron on 6.11.1775. Attended the Imperial Review in 1776. Fire watch ship at Kronshtadt in 1777–9 and 1781–2 and at Revel' in 1785–90. Broken up in 1790.

Fyodor ? ?
Constructor ?
Laid down ? *Launched* ? *Purchased* 1770
Dimensions ?
Armament ?
Purchased in the Arkhipelago in 1770. Grounded and lost off St Eustraty on 18.10.1771 taking in 9 ft of water. No casualties.

Grigorii ? ?
Constructor ?
Laid down ? *Launched* ? *Purchased* 1770
Dimensions 111 ft x 28 ft 5 in x 16 ft 8 in
Armament ?
Purchased in England in 1770 for service in the Arkhipelago. Operations against the Turks in 1771–4. Arrived at Kronshtadt on 11.7.1774. Carried troops from Pernov to Kronshtadt in 1775. Attempted entry into the Black Sea as an 8-gun merchant ship carrying iron, leather, wax and caviar with the rest of her armament hidden in sand ballast, a deceit also attempted unsuccessfully by frigates *Pavel* and *Natal'ia* in 1777. Passage to the Black Sea refused at Istanbul on 16.12.1778. Arrived at Kronshtadt on 14.5.1779. Arrived at Copenhagen on 21.9.1781 with cargo. Repaired at Copenhagen. Arrived at Cadiz on 18.5.1782. Returned to Revel' on 22.10.1782. Carried cargo between Kronshtadt and Revel' in 1784 and 1786. Broken up after 1786.

Andro ? ?
Constructor ?
Laid down ?   *Launched* ?   *Captured* 1771
Dimensions ?
Armament ?
Captured in the Arkhipelago and taken into naval service in 1771. Broken up at Auza in 1772.

Mikono ? ?
Constructor ?
Laid down ?   *Launched* ?   *Captured* 1771
Dimensions
Armament
Captured in the Arkhipelago and taken into naval service in 1771. Broken up at Auza in 1773.

Santorin ? ?
Constructor ?
Laid down ?   *Launched* ?   *Captured* 1771
Dimensions ?
Armament ?
Captured in the Arkhipelago and taken into naval service in 1771. Grounded off Mitilini Island on 3.11.1771 and taken by the Turks. 30 men were captured by the Turks, and the rest were rescued by the frigate *Arkhipelago*. Set afire by *Severnyi Oryol* to prevent salvage by the Turks on.4.11.1771.

Zeia ? ?
Constructor ?
Laid down ?   *Launched* ?   *Captured* 1771
Dimensions ?
Armament ?
Captured in the Arkhipelago and taken into naval service in 1771. Broken up in 1772 at Auza.

Milo ? ?
Constructor ?
Laid down ?   *Launched* ?   *Captured* 1770
Dimensions ?
Armament ?
Captured in the Arkhipelago and taken into naval service in 1770. Broken up in 1772 at Auza.

Delos ? ?
Constructor ?
Laid down ?   *Launched* ?   *Captured* 1770
Dimensions ?
Armament ?
Captured in the Arkhipelago and taken into naval service in 1770. Cruised in the Arkhipelago in 1772–4. Sold in 1775 at Auza.

Naktsiia 22 ?
Constructor ?
Laid down ?   *Launched* ?   *Captured* 1770
Dimensions ?
Armament ?
Captured in the Arkhipelago and taken into naval service in 1770. Cruised in the Arkhipelago in 1772–4. Sold in 1775 at Auza.

Minerva 32 ?
Constructor ?
Laid down ?   *Launched* ?   *Captured* 1771
Dimensions 86 ft x 26 ft 8 in x 10 ft 3 in
Armament ?
            162 men
Captured in the Arkhipelago and taken into naval service in 1771. Cruised in the Arkhipelago in 1771–4. Arrived at Kronshtadt on 30.7.1774. Sailed to Revel' and embarked naval cadets and marines en route to Kronshtadt. Grounded and sunk off Ensker Island with losses of 95 out of 164. The captain was considered to have abandoned the ship prematurely and was subsequently broken by courts martial.

Zapasnyi ? ?
Constructor ?
Laid down ?   *Launched* ?   *Purchased* 1772
Dimensions ?
Armament ?
Purchased in the Arkhipelago in 1772. Operations in the Arkhipelago against the Turks in 1772–4. Arrived at Kronshtadt on 19.8.1775. Transferred to Riga as a fire-watch ship in 1776–8. Employed as a cargo ship in 1779–80 and 1782. Broken up after 1782.

Pomoshchnyi 20 ?
Constructor ?
Laid down ?   *Launched* ?   *Purchased* 1772
Dimensions 68 ft x 22 ft x 11 ft
Armament ?
Purchased in the Arkhipelago in 1772. Fire watch ship at Auza in 1772–4. Arrived at Kronshtadt on 19.8.1775. Transferred to Riga as a fire watch ship in 1778–83. Broken up after 1783.

Sviatoi Pavel (renamed *Arkhipelag*) 22 ?
Constructor ?
Laid down ?   *Launched* ?   *Purchased* 1770
Dimensions 94 ft x 25 ft x 7 ft 11 in
Armament ?
Purchased at Livorno in 1770. Operations in the Arkhipelago against the Turks in 1770–4. Captured and burnt several Turkish vessels at Damietta in Egypt while under heavy fire from shore batteries on 21.10.1772. Captured a Turkish ship with Selim-Pasha and his staff (commander-in-chief of Turkish armies in Egypt) on board. Repaired at Livorno in 1774–6. Arrived at Istanbul on 28.1.1777 with Capt. Kozlyaninov's division of warships disguised as merchant ships unsuccessfully seeking entry into the Black Sea. Visited Port Mahon, Gibraltar and Tangiers in company with the frigate *Konstantin*. Arrived at Kronshtadt on 14.5.1779. Renamed *Arkhipelag* in 1779 and cruised in the Baltic off the Swedish coast. Broken up in 1782.

Konstantsiia 22 ?
Constructor ?
Laid down ?   *Launched* ?   *Purchased* 1772
Dimensions 89 ft 6 in x 23 ft 4 in x 12 ft
Armament ?
Purchased in the Arkhipelago in 1772. Operations in the Arkhipelago against the Turks in 1772–4. Repaired at Livorno in 1774–6. Arrived at Istanbul disguised as a merchant ship in Capt. Kozlyaninov's division on 20.1.1777 and refused entry into the Black Sea. Visited Port Mahon, Gibraltar and Tangiers. Arrived at Kronshtadt on 14.5.1779, after having been delayed by storms. Cruised in the Baltic in 1780–1. Fire watch ship at Revel' in 1784–5. Broken up in 1787.

Baltic corvettes (1 converted 1762–1800)

Lovkii 12 ?
Constructor ?
Laid down ?   *Launched* ?*Converted*   1797
Dimensions approx. 78 ft x 21 ft x 6 ft
               23.2 m x 6.3 m x 1.9 m (Chernyshev)
Armament ?
Corvette converted from *Lovkaia* (fem. form of *Lovkii*), a *kaik* (half-galley) in 1797. Attached to the rowing flotilla. Fire watch ship at galley ports Fridrikshamn (Kotka) and Rochensalm in 1798–1812. Broken up in 1812.

Baltic brigs (3 built, 1 purchased 1762–1800)

Purpose-built

During the first half of the eighteenth century, the Russians had favoured snow-rigged ships for coastal and cruising duties. Snows fell into disfavour after 1723, but a need continued to exist for this type of small warship and their role was reassumed by the similarly rigged brigs in the closing years of the century. A similar process of supersession may be observed in the British Royal Navy during the same period. It is unclear whether the Russians were following the British lead in this as in other areas, or whether the same design dynamics led them to a similar solution.

Kotka class (2 ships)
Kotka 8 ?
Constructor ?
Laid down 28.1.1793   *Launched* 1.11.1794
Dimensions 75 ft x 26 ft x 9 ft (Veselago)
Armament 8 x 6pdrs
Kotka class. Purpose-built brig. Cruised with the rowing flotilla in 1795–9. Fire watch ship on the border with Sweden in 1800–5. Broken up in 1808.

Kutsal-Mulim 8 ?
Constructor ?
Laid down 28.1.1793   *Launched* 1.11.1794
Dimensions 75 ft x 25 ft 2 in x 11 ft (Veselago)
Armament 8 x 6pdrs
Kotka class. Purpose-built brig. Named after the islands of the 1st battle of Rochensalm on 13–21.8.1789. Cruised in the Baltic in 1796. Fire watch ship at Riga in 1797–1800. Broken up in 1804.

Legkii 8 ?
Constructor ?
Laid down 3.9.1798   *Launched* 1799
Dimensions 60 ft 1 in x 15 ft x 4 ft 10 in (Veselago)
Armament 8 x 6pdrs
Purpose-built brig. Fire watch ship at Dinamunde in 1801–5. Cruised in the Baltic from 1804–7. Customs service ship 1710–1814. Broken up in 1815.

Purchased abroad
Neptun 18   Great Britain
               Constructor ?
Laid down ?   *Launched* ?
Purchased 2.1789
Dimensions 79 ft x 25 ft 4 in x 10 ft 9 in (Veselago)
Armament 18 x 18pdr carr.
Brig purchased at Revel' in 2.1789 for £4,000. Participated in action with the Swedish Flotilla in 1789. Fought at Revel' on 2.5.1790 and at Vyborg on 22.6.1790 where she captured 3 Swedish rowing vessels and set afire another. Cruised with the fleet in the Baltic in 1791 and 1797. Repaired in 1799–1800. Cruised to Copenhagen in 1800. Cruised with the fleet in the Baltic in 1801–4. Carried Alexander I and his retinue to Moon Island and back in 1804. Cruised with the fleet in the Baltic 1805–9. Broken up in 1819.

Baltic cutters (one- and two-masted) (15 built, 6 purchased 1762–1800)

Cutters first appeared in the Baltic Navy in the mid-1780s during the build up towards the Russo-Swedish War. Because of their small size, limited draft, and great handiness, cutters were ideally suited for operations with the rowing squadrons and for low-end duties with the sailing fleet. They were involved in all of the major galley actions of the 1788–90 war, and one particular cutter was involved in one of the most spectacular and daring operations undertaken by Russian warships during the age of sail – the capture of the Swedish heavy frigate *Venus*.

Purpose-built cutters
Vestnik 29   St Petersburg
Constructor D. Masal'skiy
Laid down 19.4.1782   *Launched* 20.10.1786
Dimensions 80 ft 4½ in x 26 ft 6½ in x 9 ft (Veselago)
Armament Small guns and carronades
Purpose-built cutter. Cruised in the Baltic in 1789. Fought at Revel' on 2.5.1790. Fought at Vyborg on 22.6.1790, capturing 4 Swedish flotilla vessels and burning another. Cruised in the Baltic in 1791–5. No further mention.

Volkhov 32   St Petersburg
Constructor M. Sarychev
Laid down 24.5.1787   *Launched* 8.5.1788
Dimensions 72 ft x 19 ft 10 in x 9 ft 6 in (Veselago)
Armament 20 x 3pdr falconets 12 x 24pdr carr.
Purpose-built cutter. Named after the Volkhov River. Cruised in the Baltic in 1788. In action with the Swedish rowing flotilla in 1789. Fought at Revel' on 2.5.1790 and at Vyborg on 22.6.1790. Cruised in the Baltic in 1791, 1794, and 1798. Broken up after 1800.

Neva 8   St Petersburg
Constructor Pospelov
Laid down 24.5.1787   *Launched* 8.5.1788
Dimensions 69 ft x 20 ft 6 in x 10 ft (Veselago)
Armament ?
               60 men
Purpose-built cutter. Named after the Neva River. Fought at Gogland on 6.7.1788. Fought at Öland on 15.7.1789. Escorted supply ships in 1790. Cruised to the North Sea in 1793. Cruised to Bornholm in 1798. Broken up after 1800.

Letuchii 28   St Petersburg
Constructor D. Masal'skiy
Laid down 3.11.1787   *Launched* 14.5.1788
Dimensions 78 ft x 29 ft 8 in x 11 ft 4 in (Veselago)
Armament Small guns and carronades
Purpose-built cutter. Fought at Gogland on 6.7.1788. In action with

the Swedish rowing flotilla in 1789. Fought at Revel' on 2.5.1790 and at Vyborg on 22.6.1790. Cruised in the Baltic in 1791–3. Broken up after 1794.

Nadyozhnyi 8 St Petersburg
Constructor V. D. Vlasov
Laid down 20.5.1787   *Launched* 24.5.1788
Dimensions 65 ft x 19 ft 6 in x 9 ft 11 in (Veselago)
Armament ?
Purpose-built cutter. Cruised in the Baltic in 1790–1. Fire watch ship in 1796. Stationed at Kronshtadt in 1802–5. Broken up in 1815.

Schastlivyi 8 Kronshtadt
Constructor Kapaev
Laid down 20.5.1787   *Launched* 24.5.1788
Dimensions 67 ft x 20 ft x 9 ft 5 in (Veselago)
Armament ?
           58 men
Purpose-built cutter. Fought at Gogland on 6.7.1788. In action with the Swedish rowing flotilla in 1789. Fought at Revel' on 2.5.1790 and at Vyborg on 22.6.1790. Stationed in Kronshtadt Roads in 1791–5. Broken up after 1795.

Lebed' class (3 ships)
Lebed' 38 St Petersburg
Constructor D. Masal'skiy
Laid down 1.12.1788   *Launched* 7.5.1789
Dimensions 78 ft (LK) x 58 ft 6 in (LGD) x 29 ft 8 in x 11 ft 4 in
           (Veselago)
Armament Carronades and falconets
Lebed' class. Purpose-built cutter. Fought at the 1st battle of Rochensalm on 13–21.8.1789. Fought at Revel' on 2.5.1790 and at Vyborg on 22.6.1790. Cruised in the Baltic in 1791. No further mention.

Baklan 38 St Petersburg
Constructor D. Masal'skiy
Laid down 1.12.1788   *Launched* 15.5.1789
Dimensions 78 ft (LK) x 58 ft 6 in (LGD) x 29 ft 8 in x 11 ft 4 in
           (Veselago)
Armament Carronades and falconets
Lebed' class. Purpose-built cutter. Fought at the 1st battle of Rochensalm on 13–21.8.1789. Fought at Krasnaia Gorka on 23–24.5.1790 and Vyborg on 22.6.1790. Fire watch ship at Kronshtadt in 1791. Cruised in the Baltic in 1792–4 and 1797–8. Broken up after 1798.

Gagara 38 St Petersburg
Constructor D. Masal'skiy
Laid down 1.12.1788   *Launched* 19.5.1789
Dimensions 78 ft (LK) x 58 ft 6 in (LGD) x 29 ft 8 in x 11 ft 4 in
           (Veselago)
Armament Carronades and falconets
Lebed' class. Purpose-built cutter. In action with the Swedish rowing flotilla in 1789. Fought at Krasnaia Gorka on 23–24.5.1790. Escorted the damaged ship of the line *Ioann Bogoslov* to Kronshtadt to Kronshtadt after the battle. Cruised in the Baltic in 1791–4 and 1798. No further mention.

Sokol class (3 ships)
Sokol 20 St Petersburg
Constructor D. Masal'skiy
Laid down 1.12.1788   *Launched* 10.5.1789
Dimensions 55 ft 2 in x 22 ft x 7 ft 4 in (Veselago)
Armament ?
Sokol class. Purpose-built cutter. Fought at the 1st battle of Rochensalm on 13–21.8.1789. Stationed in Kronshtadt Roads in 1790. Cruised in the Baltic in 1791–2. Fire watch ship off Windava. No further mention.

Krechet 20 St Petersburg
Constructor D. Masal'skiy
Laid down 1.12.1788   *Launched* 10.5.1789
Dimensions 55 ft 2 in x 21 ft 8 in (inside plank) x 7 ft 4 in (Veselago)
Armament ?
Sokol class. Purpose-built cutter. Fought at the 1st battle of Rochensalm on 13–21.8.1789. Stationed off Kronshtadt in 1790. No further mention.

Iastreb 20 St Petersburg
Constructor D. Masal'skiy
Laid down 1.12.1788   *Launched* 19.5.1789
Dimensions 55 ft 2 in x 21 ft 8 in (inside plank) x 7 ft 4 in (Veselago)
Armament ?
Sokol class. Purpose-built cutter. Fought at the 1st battle of Rochensalm on 13–21.8.1789. Stationed off Kronshtadt in 1790. Cruised off Gogland in 7.1790. Stationed off Petergof in 1791. Fire watch ship at Rochensalm in 1792–7. To Great Britain in 1798–9. Fire watch ship at Rochensalm in 1800. No further mention.

Kater no. 1 20 Arkhangel'sk, Solombala
Constructor M. D. Portnov
Laid down 19.2.1790   *Launched* 22.5.1790
Dimensions 90 ft (lgd) x 78 ft (LK) x 32 ft x 11 ft 9 in (Veselago)
           231 tons displacement
Armament ?
Three unnamed two-masted cutters were built for the defence of the North Dvina. Stationed in Arkhangel'sk Roads and cruised in the White Sea in 1790. Fire watch ship off the North Dvina mouth in 1801. No further mention.

Kater no. 2 20 Arkhangel'sk, Solombala
Constructor M. D. Portnov
Laid down 19.2.1790   *Launched* 22.5.1790
Dimensions 90 ft (lgd) x 78 ft (LK) x 32 ft x 11 ft 9 in (Veselago)
           231 tons displacement
Armament ?
Three unnamed two-masted cutters were built for the defence of the North Dvina. Stationed in Arkhangel'sk Roads and cruised in the White Sea in 1790. Later stationed at Arkhangel'sk. No further mention.

Kater no. 3 20 Arkhangel'sk, Solombala
Constructor M. D. Portnov
Laid down 19.2.1790   *Launched* 22.5.1790
Dimensions 90 ft (lgd) x 78 ft (LK) x 32 ft x 11 ft 9 in (Veselago)
           231 tons displacement
Armament ?
Three unnamed two-masted cutters were built for the defence of the North Dvina. Stationed in Arkhangel'sk Roads and cruised in the White Sea in 1790. Later stationed at Arkhangel'sk. No further mention.

Purchased abroad

Merkurii 22 Great Britain
Constructor ?
Laid down ? *Launched* ?
Purchased 1788
Dimensions approx. 96 ft x 30 ft x 13½ in
    29.4 m (lgd) x 9.2 m x 4.1 m (Chernyshev)
Armament 22 x 24pdr carr.
    110 men
Purchased two-masted cutter. Joined Vice-Adm. Fondezin's squadron at Copenhagen on 28.6.1788. Cruised off Copenhagen in 7–8.1788. Cruised in the Baltic in 4–5.1789 and captured 29 Swedish merchant ships. While under the command of Lieutenant Commander (later Adm.) Roman Crown, she captured the Swedish cutter *Snapupp* on 29.4.1789 off Bornholm and brought her into Copenhagen on 3.5.1789. Discovered Swedish frigate *Venus* in Christianfiord, Norway on 21.5.1789, closed while disguised as a merchantman and raked and captured her with losses of 4 killed and 6 wounded. Cruised in the Baltic and arrived at Revel' on 8.1789. Fought at Revel' on 2.5.1790 and, in company with ship of the line *Podrazhislav*, engaged and destroyed the grounded Swedish *Riksens Stander*. Fought at Vyborg on 22.6.1790. Cruised in the Baltic in 1791. Cruised to Holland and Stockholm in 1793. Cruised in the Baltic in 1794–1800 and 1803–4. Broken up after 1805.

Del'fin ? Great Britain
Constructor ?
Laid down ? *Launched* ?
Purchased 1788
Dimensions ?
Armament ?
Purchased cutter. Joined Vice-Adm. Fondezin's squadron at Copenhagen on 28.6.1788. Cruised off Copenhagen in 7–8.1788 and captured 4 Swedish merchant ships. Sent to Bornholm in 1789 and wrecked there on 28.7.1789.

Los' class (2 ships)
Los' ? Great Britain
Constructor ?
Laid down ? *Launched* ?
Purchased 1789
Dimensions 53 ft x 18 ft x 7 ft 7 in (Veselago)
Armament ?
Los' class. Purchased cutter. Purchased in Great Britain by Prince Potemkin in 1789. Captured by Sweden off Porkkala-udd.

Olen' ? Great Britain
Constructor ?
Laid down ? *Launched* ?
Purchased 1789
Dimensions 53 ft x 18 ft x 7 ft 7 in (Veselago)
Armament ?
Los' class. Purchased cutter. Purchased in Great Britain by Prince Potemkin in 1789. Fought at Revel' on 2.5.1790 and Vyborg on 22.6.1790. No further mention.

Severnyi Oryol ? Great Britain
Constructor ?
Laid down ? *Launched* ?
Purchased 1790
Dimensions ?
Armament ?
Purchased cutter. Purchased in Great Britain in 1790. To Sveaborg in.5.1790 for negotiations with Sweden. Cruised in the Gulf of Finland in 8.1790. Training service in 1791. Cruised in the Baltic in 1793–5. Broken up after 1796.

Dispach 18/20 Great Britain
Constructor ?
Laid down ? *Launched* 1795
Purchased 5.5.1796
Dimensions 96 ft x 30 ft 6 in x 12 ft 9 in (Veselago)
    365 tons displacement
Armament ? 130 men
Purchased cutter. Purchased on 5.5.1796 by Vice-Adm. Khanykov at Catherine II's order. Cruised with Vice-Adm. Khanykov's and Vice-Adm. Makarov's squadrons between Great Britain and Copenhagen in 1796–7. Departed Kronshtadt with Vice-Adm. Makarov's First Division in.5.1798 and arrived in Britain in 7.1798. Operated in North Sea waters in 1798–1800 with Vice-Adm. Makarov's squadron. Carried a courier from Russia to Great Britain in 1801. Cruised in the Baltic in 1802–3. Escorted transports to Germany in 1805. Wrecked off Rugen in a storm on 5.10.1805. No casualties.

Baltic schooners (2 purpose-built 1762–1800)

Legma 6 ?
Constructor ?
Laid down ? *Launched* 1790
Dimensions 61 ft 6 in x 15 ft x 4 ft 10 in (Veselago)
Armament ?
    14 oars
Purpose-built schooner. Named after the site of the battle of Rochensalm. Assigned to the rowing flotilla. Cruised in the Baltic 1971–1800. Broken up in 1801.

Unnamed 4 ?
Constructor ?
Laid down ? *Launched* 1791
Dimensions 52 ft x 10 ft 6 in x 3 ft 7 in (Veselago)
Armament ?
    12 oars
Purpose-built schooner. Assigned to the rowing flotilla. Cruised in the Baltic in 1792–1800. Broken up in 1801.

Baltic lugger (1 purchased abroad 1762–1800)

Velikii Kniaz' 12 Great Britain
Constructor ?
Laid down ? *Launched* ?
Purchased 1789
Dimensions ?
Armament ?
Lugger purchased in Great Britain in 1789. Arrived at Kronshtadt in 1790. Cruised in the Baltic in 1791–1803. Repaired in the winter of 1803/1804. Escorted the brig *Neptune* with Alexander I as passenger to the island of Moon in 1804. Cruised in 1805–7. Actions against Sweden as part of Adm. Khanykov's squadron in 1808. Broken up in 1814.

THE BALTIC FLEET 1762–1800

Baltic bomb vessels (7 purpose-built, 2 purchased 1762–1800)

In contrast to the inshore artillery support vessels found in section II, bomb vessels had the mobility and seaworthiness for offensive operations and were designed to accompany the main fleet at sea. Bomb vessels built during this period not only found active employment against Sweden in the 1788–90 war, they were actively employed against Turkey in the earlier conflict, with *Grom* playing a major role at Ches'ma.

Purpose-built

Donder class 2nd group (3 ships, see previous section for group 1)

Grom 10 St Petersburg
Constructor I. Davydov
Laid down 23.8.1762 Launched 19.8.1765
Dimensions 95 ft x 27 ft x 11 ft x 12 ft (draft) (Veselago)
Armament 6 cannon, 2 mortars, 2 howitzers
100 men
Donder class. Purpose-built bomb vessel. Active in the Arkhipelago in 1769–74. Fought at Ches'ma on 24–26.6.1770. Broken up at Auza due to deterioration.

Iupiter 10 Kronshtadt
Constructor V. A. Selyaninov
Laid down 27.1.1771 Launched 30.5.1771
Dimensions 95 ft x 27 ft x 11 ft x 12 ft (draft) (Veselago and Chernyshev)
Armament 6 cannon, 2 mortars, 2 howitzers
100 men
Donder class. Purpose-built bomb vessel In commission in 1776–7. Broken up in 1780.

Mars 10 St Kronshtadt
Constructor V. A. Selyaninov
Laid down 7.3.1771 Launched 21.6.1771
Dimensions 95 ft x 27 ft x 11 ft x 12 ft (draft) (Veselago and Chernyshev)
Armament 6 cannon, 2 mortars, 2 howitzers
100 men
Donder class. Purpose-built bomb vessel. In commission in 1773–8. At sea only at the end of her life in 1780. Broken up in 1780.

Perun class (2 ships)
Perun 14 Kronshtadt
Constructor A. S. Katasanov
Laid down 2.2.1779 Launched 6.7.1780
Dimensions 100 ft x 22 ft 8 in x 11 ft 8 in (Veselago)
Armament ?
Perun class. Purpose-built bomb vessel. Named after the Slavonic god of thunder. In commission in 1784–91. Fought at Rochensalm on 21.8.1789. Fought at Vyborg on 22.6.1790. Stationed at Kronshtadt harbour and roads in 1792–1801. Broken up in 1803.

Grom 14 St Petersburg
Constructors V. A. Selyaninov and G. Korchebnikov
Laid down 14.1.1779 Launched 11.5.1783
Dimensions 100 ft x 22 ft 8 in x 11 ft 8 in (Veselago)
Armament ?
Perun class. Purpose-built bomb vessel. In commission in 1785–91. Fought at Rochensalm on 21.8.1789. Fought at Vyborg on 22.6.1790. Stationed at Kronshtadt harbour and roads in 1792–1. Broken up in 1803.

Strashnyi 14 St Petersburg
Constructor S. Durakin
Laid down 3.12.1786 Launched 8.5.1788
Dimensions 95 ft x 27 ft x 11 ft x 10 ft (Veselago)
Armament ? 105 men
Purpose-built bomb vessel. In commission in 1785–90. Fought at Gogland on 6.7.1788. Fought at Öland on 15.7.1789. Fought at Revel' on 2.5.1790. Fought at Vyborg on 22.6.1790. Stationed in Kronshtadt Roads in 1791–4. Broken up after 1794.

Pobeditel' 18 St Petersburg
Constructor D. Masal'skiy
Laid down 3.11.1787 Launched 20.5.1788
Dimensions 100 ft x 29 ft 4 in x 13 ft 3½ in (Veselago)
Armament ?
130 men
Purpose-built bomb vessel. Fought at Gogland on 6.7.1788. Fought at Öland on 15.7.1789. Fought at Revel' on 2.5.1790. Fought at Vyborg on 22.6.1790 where she lost two masts. In commission at Kronshtadt in 1791–8. Broken up after 1798.

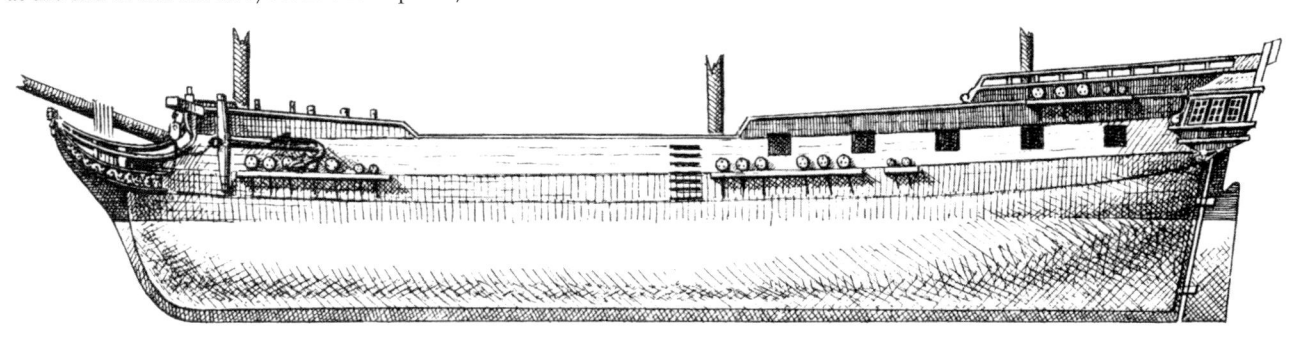

This drawing of the 1780 bomb-vessel Perun *clearly establishes the close connection between this specialized type of warship and the design of conventional ship sloops. Six aft-mounted gunports provide for some degree of defensive fire by conventional cannon against hostile warships and small craft, while the normal complement of two mortars and two howitzers intended for inshore work against enemy positions is safely and solidly mounted in forward firing positions amidships behind the cover of unbroken bulkheads forward. British bomb vessels were frequently operated as conventional ship sloops when not needed for their designed function, but the Russian navy's closer tie-in with amphibious operations precluded this type of multipurpose adaptability.*

Purchased abroad (2 purchased 1762–1800)

Molniia 16 Great Britain
Constructor ?
Laid down ?   *Launched* ?
Purchased 1771
Dimensions 91 ft 4 in (LGD) x 25 ft (inside plank) x 16 ft 10 in (Veselago)
Armament ?
Bomb vessel purchased in Great Britain. Active against Turkey in the Arkhipelago in 1771–4. Arrived at Revel' in 1775. Cruised in the Baltic in 1777. Converted into a transport in 1779. No further mention. (See also under Baltic converted transports)

Strashnyi 14 Great Britain
Constructor ?
Laid down ?   *Launched* ?
Purchased 1771
Dimensions 96 ft x 23 ft 6 in x 13 ft 6 in (Veselago)
Armament ?
Bomb vessel purchased in Great Britain. Active against Turkey in the Arkhipelago in 1771–4. Arrived at Kronshtadt in 1775. Transported Vice-Adm. Greig to Scotland in 1777. Cruised off Norway with Rear-Adm. Khmetevskiy's squadron in 1779. No further mention.

The Navy of Alexander I (1801–24)

Ships with 90–110 guns (5 built 1800–24)

The series production of First Rates in the 1780s had been inspired by the expansionist tendencies of Russia under Catherine II, motivated by the growing likelihood of war with Sweden, and formalized by the Establishment of 1782. With the authorization of the Establishment of 1798, Paul I approved the ongoing maintenance of a force level of 9 First Rates for the Baltic fleet. Only the 8 *Ches'ma*s were in service at this time, but the required ninth First Rate took form at the turn of the century with the construction of the massive 130-gun *Blagodat'*. Unfortunately by 1800 *Rostislav* and *Sviatoi Nikolai* were the only *Ches'ma*s found to be sea-worthy when the class was surveyed in preparation for possible hostilities with Great Britain. Both were earmarked for the campaign of 1801 while the others were scheduled for premature disposal. By 1801 even the *Rostislav* and *Nikolai* were beyond repair, and the entire class had been taken out of active service and relegated to various forms of block ship and harbour duty. The Russian Baltic fleet's proud centrepiece and its primary naval asset had been needlessly squandered by negligent maintenance practices. Of the First Rates begun by Catherine II and rounded out by Paul I, only the 130-gun *Blagodat'* was left to soldier on into the nineteenth century and the reign of Alexander.

Alexander I succeeded to the throne of Russia on his father Paul's assassination and proved to be no friend of naval expansion or even of prudent maintenance policies of the existing fleet. Plans for the construction of large numbers of expensive and prestigious First Rates were no longer in the offing under the new emperor, and only three First Rates were authorized and commissioned during the Napoleonic War period between 1800 and 1812. Although the new century saw the appearance of a new generation of independently minded Russian surveyors and constructors, all three First Rates drew heavily upon British design influences. Two additional First Rates, built along the lines of the Establishment of 1805, were authorized and completed post-war, bringing the total number of Baltic First Rates built during the reign of Alexander I to a modest five.

It does not appear that any lasting lessons with respect to timber seasoning and preventative maintenance had been learned by Alexander or his ministers as a result of the rapid and wasteful deterioration of the earlier *Ches'ma* class vessels. All of these new ships had relatively short service lives, with the newly completed *Rostislav* – final heir to Slade's *Victory* – being the only Napoleonic era First Rate to see extensive post-war service.

Emperor Alexander I is admiringly portrayed in military uniform in 1815 by the artist Gerard in Paris. Alexander is regarded with distaste by Russian naval historians as having presided over the deterioration of the fleet under the corrupt administration of the Marquis Traversay and for the persecution of a number of dedicated officers with exemplary records, most notably Dmitriy Seniavin.

Gavriil 100/110 St Petersburg
Constructors A. S. Katasonov and I. P. Amosov
Laid down 3.8.1800 *Launched* 30.10.1802
Dimensions 188 ft x 51 ft 9 in x 20 ft 6 in
Armament LD 24 x 36pdrs, 4 x 60 u (1 pood)
MD 26 x 24pdrs (short), 4 x 24u (½ pood)
UD 30 x 12pdrs
FC & QD 22 x 6pdrs (probable)

A slightly enlarged version of the *Ches'ma* class and half-sister to the Black Sea *Iagudiil*. Coppered in 1804. Transported troops to Pomerania in 1805. In Kronshtadt Roads for training duties in 1807. Operated in Adm. Khanykov's squadron in 1808. Khanykov encountered the Anglo-Swedish squadron on 13.8.1808 and was forced to retreat to Rogervik (Baltiyskiy). In Kronshtadt Roads for training duties in 1809. Rearmed en flute and used to transport troops from Sveaborg to Revel' in 1812. Determined to be in poor condition and reduced to harbour service at the end of 1812. Broken up in 1819.

Khrabryi 120 St Petersburg
Constructors Le Brune de St Catherine the Elder and Kurepanov
Laid down 18.7.1805 *Launched* 1.7.1808
Dimensions 206 ft 11 in x 51 ft 5 in x 23 ft 6 in (Veselago)
201.6 ft x 52.4 ft x 21.6 ft 4184.4 tons displacement (Fincham 1851)
Armament LD 32 x 36pdrs (short)
MD 34 x 24pdrs (short)
UD 34 x 18pdrs (short)
FC & QD 20 x 6/8pdrs or 24pdr carr. (probable)

Kurepanov studied for several years in England and returned to Russia with plans for the British *Caledonia*. Draughts of *Khrabryi* and *Caledonia* are nearly identical and it is clear that Kurepanov used the British design as his model. While Le Brune de St Catherine signed off on the draught of *Khrabryi*, Kurepanov was clearly the author.

Cruised on trials between Kronshtadt and Revel' on trials in 1808. Stationed in Kronshtadt Roads in 1809. In England with Adm. Thate's squadron in 1812–14. Repaired in 1817. Damaged and grounded in the Great Flood of 1824. Decommissioned in 1824. Broken up in 1829.

Rostislav 110 Kronshtadt
Constructor I. P. Amosov
Laid down 27.12.1811 *Launched* 31.7.1813
Dimensions 186 ft x 51 ft 4 in x 26 ft 6 in
Armament LD 28 x 36pdrs (short)
MD 30 x 24pdrs (short)
UD 30 x 18pdrs (short)
FC & QD 22 x 6pdrs/24pdr carr.

Ches'ma class. Built to the slightly modified and depened lines of the *Ches'ma* class. Cruised in the Gulf of Finland in 1814. 1816, 1818, and 1820. Severely damaged during the Great Flood of 7.11.1824. Broken up in 1827.

Leiptsig class (2 ships)
These two ships were the first Russian First Rates designed and pierced for 30 lower-deck guns as compared to the 28 guns of earlier ships. Their dimensions were close to those of the 130-gun *Blagodat'* and may have traced back to French antecedents. They saw almost no operational deployment, apparently being maintained for prestige and deterrence purposes in the manner of pre-*Ches'ma* class First Rates. Their largely untested design became the design basis for the Imperator *Aleksandr* class when construction of First Rates resumed after the Great Flood of 1824.

Leiptsig 110/118 St Petersburg
Constructor G. S. Isakov
Laid down 7.8.1814 *Launched* 20.9.1816
Dimensions 198 ft x 51 ft 8 in x 23 ft 6 in
Armament LD 30 x 36pdrs (short)
MD 32 x 24pdrs (short)
UD 32 x 18pdrs (short)
FC & QD 20 x 6pdrs, 4 x 24pdr carr.

Leiptsig class. First First Rate built under the Establishment of 1805. Cruised only in 1816, spending the rest of her career in harbour. Damaged and grounded in the Great Flood of 7.11.1824. Refloated and hulked in 12.1824. Broken up in 1832.

Tvyordyi 110/118 St Petersburg
Constructor I. V. Kurepanov
Laid down 17.8.1817 *Launched* 5.9.1819
Dimensions 198 ft x 51 ft 8 in x 23 ft 6 in
Armament LD 30 x 36pdrs (short)
MD 32 x 24pdrs (short)
UD 32 x 18pdrs (short)
FC & QD 20 x 6pdrs, 4 x 24pdr carr.

Leiptsig class. Never commissioned for service and never at sea. Badly damaged and grounded by the Great Flood on 7.11.1824. Said to have been broken up in 1828 at Kronshtadt, but actually resold to Great Britain for breaking up.

Ships with 80–88 guns (5 Built 1801–24)

With the completion of the last member of the *Sviatoi Pavel* class in 1770, the Russians abandoned further construction of the by-then-obsolescent three-decker 80. Construction of 80-gun ships resumed on a limited basis in the Baltic after 1800 with longer, more powerful, and more seaworthy two-decker 80s replacing the unwieldy and unsuccessful three-deckers of the previous era. The rebirth of the 80-gun Second Rate in Russia was inspired at least in part by the ongoing French construction of highly successful two-decker 80s. The adoption of two-decker 80-gun warships had been previously avoided by the British and other European nations, including Russia, because the greater length of these ships encouraged hull deformation after extended active service. This maintenance headache went a long way towards negating their obvious advantages in firepower and performance over both the weaker 74s and the equally powerful, but more unwieldy, three-decker 98s favoured as command ships by the British. Structural advances after 1800 made possible the introduction of longer two-decker ships better able to resist premature hogging and they proved to be ideal second rate command ships, offering savings in both economic and manpower terms.

In contrast to the British, who constructed only two purpose-built 80-gun two-deckers (*Caesar* and *Foudroyant*) in the 1790s, and who relied instead upon captured French 80s to meet their needs in this area until 1815, the Russians completed four new 80-gun ships in the Baltic between 1800 and 1808, following two similar 80-gun two-deckers completed for the Black Sea fleet during the 1790s. Given Alexander I's lack of enthusiasm for naval expenditure and the falling off of new First Rate construction in Russia after 1800, this burst of construction may have been the result of the targeted use of two-decker 80s as a cheaper command alternative to the larger and more expensive 100-gun ships of the earlier period. Considering the limited capabilities of Russia's likely adversaries during this period, this may not have been an entirely unrealistic policy for a largely landlocked navy with no deep water commitments or goals. After the completion of the initial four 80s, no further 80s were laid down during the Napoleonic War period. A fifth ship, *Emgeiten*, once again reflecting French design influences, was laid down in 1820 and would be the precursor of revived Russian series production of the type during the second quarter of the century under a new, more naval minded emperor, Nicholas I.

Rafail 80/82 St Petersburg
Constructor M. Sarychev
Laid down 3.8.1800 *Launched* 6.8.1802
Dimensions 182 ft x 49 ft 6 in x 21 ft
Armament LD 24 x 36pdrs, 4 x 60 u (1 pood)
    UD 26 x 24pdrs (short), 4 x 24u (½ pood)
    FC & QD 22 x 8pdrs (Morskoi Sbornik)
Transported troops to Pomerania in 1805. To the Mediterranean in 1806 with Commodore Ignatyev's squadron to reinforce Adm. Seniavin. Bombarded Tenedos as flag to Rear-Adm. Greig, expending 2,760 rounds in 1807. Fought in the Dardanelles battle on 10–11.5.1807 and the battle of Mount Athos on 19.6.1807 with the loss of Capt. Lukin. Arrived at Lisbon on 30.10.1807 after the signing of the Peace of Tilsit. Ceded to Great Britain in 1808, but abandoned at Lisbon due to poor condition.

Arkhangel Uriil class (2 ships)
Arkhangel Uriil 80/76 St Petersburg
Constructor M. Sarychev
Laid down 3.8.1800 *Launched* 16.8.1802
Dimensions 186 ft x 49 ft 6 in x 21 ft 4 in
Armament LD 24 x 36pdrs, 4 x 60 u (1 pood)
    UD 26 x 24pdrs, (short) 4 x 24u (½ pood)
    FC & QD 22 x 8pdrs (Morskoi Sbornik)
Arkhangel Uriil class. Coppered in 1804. Departed Kronshtadt for the Mediterranean in Vice-Adm. Seniavin's squadron on 10.9.1805. Conducted operations in the Adriatic and off Tenedos. Fought in the Dardanelles battle on 10–11.5.1807 and at Mount Athos on 19.6.1807. Pursued the damaged Turkish 84 *Besaret-Numah* and two frigates resulting in their being scuttled by burning. Storm damaged and sent to Trieste with Commodore Saltanov. Ceded to France in 10.1789.

Tvyordyi 84/90/74 St Petersburg
Constructors M. Sarychev and A. I. Melikhov
Laid down 16.8.1802 *Launched* 18.7.1805
Dimensions 186 ft x 49 ft 6 in x 21 ft 4 in
Armament LD 24 x 36pdrs, 4 x 60 u (1 pood)
    UD 26 x 24pdrs (short), 4 x 24u (½ pood)
    FC & QD 22 x 8pdrs (probable)
Arkhangel Uriil class. Some sources consider her a cut-down 90. To the Mediterranean with Commodore Ignatyev's squadron in 1806 to reinforce Vice-Adm. Seniavin's fleet. Made Seniavin's flagship on arrival. Landed troops at Tenedos in 1807. Took part in the Dardanelles battle on 10–11.5.1807 and at the battle of Mount Athos on 19.6.1807. Arrived in Lisbon on 30.10.1807 after the Peace of Tilsit. Escorted into Portsmouth along with other elements of Adm. Seniavin's squadron by Vice-Adm. Cotton's squadron on 26.9.1808. Impounded in Portsmouth until her sale to Great Britain in 1813.

Smelyi 88 St Petersburg, New Admiralty
Constructors Le Brune the Younger and A. I. Melikhov
Laid down ? *Launched* 15.7.1808
Dimensions 198 ft x 50ft 4 in x 19 ft 6 in
Armament LD 30 x 36pdrs (short)
    UD 32 x 34pdrs (short)
    FC & QD 26 x 8pdrs or 24pdr carr.
Designed primarily by the French constructor Le Brune and probably similar to contemporary Sane designs. She would serve as the model for the new generation of 80-gun ships constructed during the 1820s. Stationed in Kronshtadt Roads in 1809. To England with Adm. Thate's squadron in 1812–13. Cruised in the Baltic and transported troops from Lübeck to Kronshtadt in 1814. Decommissioned in 1814. Broken up in 1819.

Emgeiten (later *Kronshtadt*) 84 St Petersburg
Constructor G. S. Isakov
Laid down 20.11.1820 *Launched* 22.8.1822
Dimensions 196 ft x 51 ft x 24 ft 7 in
Armament LD 26 x 36pdrs (short), 4 x 60 u (1 pood)
    UD 32 x 24pdrs (short)
    FC & QD 22 x 12pdrs (probable)
Cruised to Rostock with soon-to-be Emperor Nikolai I as passenger in 1824. Damaged and grounded in the Great Flood on 7.11.1824. Refloated and repaired in 10.1828. Renamed *Kronshtadt* in 1829 to make the name available for a new *Emgeiten*. Cruised in the Baltic in 1829–32 and 1834–5. Sailed from Kronshtadt to Sveaborg for decommissioning and hulking in 7.1835.

Ships with 70–78 guns (32 built 1801–24)

A total of 32 74-gun line of battle ships were authorized and completed for the Baltic fleet during the first quarter of the nineteenth century. They were larger and more heavily armed than their late eighteenth century predecessors and fell sequentially into three groups of twenty three, two and seven ships. Construction of 74s continued in Russia after 1815 and into the 1840s, well past the time when the deep water navies of the Atlantic powers had moved on to the adoption of 80 and 90 gun two-deckers as their standard capital ship types. As had been the case previously with the 66-gun line of battleships, smaller capital ships continued to find useful and economic employment in the shallow waters of the Baltic, most especially in the absence of any serious challenges from the somnolent Scandinavian navies in the years after the defeat of Napoleon.

Selafail class (23 ships)
Twenty-three ships of the *Selafail* class were completed between 1802 and 1823, making this the second-largest class of 74-gun ships commissioned to that date in Russia, and only slightly less numerous than the 26 ships of the subsequent *Iezekiil* class. As was the case with other designs, the prototype, *Selafail*, was built at St Petersburg and the rest of the class were assigned to Arkhangel'sk. Their design is attributed to original work by A. S. Katasonov. As chief constructor in Arkhangel'sk A. M. Kurochkin is said to have made design alterations to Katasonov's design in the areas of hull strengthening and improved fastenings in order to facilitate operations in the rougher conditions prevailing in northern waters around Arkhangel'sk. This greater degree of deep-water seaworthiness may or may not have reflected Russian plans for expanding their naval horizons beyond the constricted waters of the landlocked Baltic.

Although construction of the first pair was initiated in 1800

THE BALTIC FLEET 1801–24

and 1801, the *Selafail*'s were the first 74-gun ships built and armed along the lines of the Establishment of 1805, although it is probable that the instability and dislocations of the struggle with Napoleonic France led to many of the earlier ships being put into service with whatever ordnance may have been available upon their commissioning. Short barrelled 24pdr and 36pdr guns replaced the heretofore standard 18pdr and 30pdr long guns of earlier Russian 74s for a considerable augmentation in weight of broadside, while the previously standard edinorogs were conspicuously absent. Although they proved to be as short-lived as other Russian warships of the period, the *Selafail*s were well regarded in service and are said to have been capable of 14 knots. The high quality of the original design is evidenced by their unbroken production run from 1802 to 1825, a span that encompasses the shorter production runs of the other two intended subsequent classes of 74s which were both introduced in 1810.

As was the case with so many other Russian sailing warships, the *Selafail*s were a paradoxical mix of high-quality design work and shoddy construction materials and inadequate maintenance practices. They were probably as well thought out by their designers as the products of contemporary British, French and Spanish shipyards and were quite capable of giving a good account of themselves in battle. Their problem was that they wore out too quickly, in most cases, more rapidly than either their crews or guns. Since they could be replaced quickly and cheaply by the shipyards at Arkhangel'sk, and since the Russians were fighting an uphill battle in terms of preventative maintenance because of the generally poor quality of the timber available for their construction, and finally because the low salinity and cold temperatures of the Baltic encouraged rapid deterioration of even adequately seasoned timber, the Russian policy, whether intentional or not, made a good deal of economic sense.

Fourteen of the 23 *Selafail*'s were commissioned before the end of the Napoleonic Wars. Members of the class were involved in operations with the British fleet in 1814 and in repatriation duties helping to transport victorious Russian troops from Cherbourg to Kronshtadt as the Napoleonic Wars wound down. Three class members were later involved in the sale of surplus Russian warships to Spain in 1818, where their material state caused a minor diplomatic contretemps between the two nations. The two final *Selafail*s, *Kniaz' Vladimar* and *Tsar' Konstantin*, took part in operations against Turkey in the 1828–30 conflict, although neither was present at Navarino.

Selafail 74 St Petersburg, New Admiralty
Constructor I. P. Amosov
Laid down 3.8.1800 *Launched* 22.8.1802
Dimensions 178 ft x 48 ft x 19 ft 3 in
Armament As built LD 26 x 30pdrs, 2 x 60 u (1 pood)
UD 26 x 18pdrs, 2 x 24u (½ pood)
FC & QD 18 x 8pdrs (Morsky Skorbnik)

Selafail class. Lead ship of a new class designed in compliance with the Establishment of 1805 (actually introduced in 1803) with increased length and with short-barrelled 24- and 36pdrs replacing the long standard 18- and 30pdrs – at least in theory. Coppered in dock. Departed Kronshtadt with Vice-Adm. Seniavin's squadron in 1805. Operated in the Mediterranean in 1806–7. Fought in the Dardanelles battle on 10–11.5.1807 and at Mount Athos on 19.6.1807, capturing the flagship of the Turkish second in command Adm. Sed-ul Bahr. Arrived at Lisbon on 30.10.1807. Escorted into Portsmouth by Vice-Adm. Cotton along with other elements of Adm. Seniavin's squadron on 26.9.1808. Impounded in Portsmouth until her sale to Great Britain in 1813 – minus her ordnance, which was returned to Russia.

Sil'nyi 74 Arkhangel'sk
Constructors G. Ignatyev and A. M. Kurochkin
Laid down 29.8.1801 *Launched* 28.5.1804
Dimensions 178 ft x 48 ft x 19 ft 3 in
Armament As built LD 26 x 30pdrs, 2 x 60 u (1 pood)
UD 26 x 18pdrs, 2 x 24u (½ pood)
FC & QD 18 x 8pdrs
1805 LD 28 x 36pdrs (short)
UD 30 x 24pdrs(short)
FC & QD 18 x 8

Selafail class. Sailed from Arkhangel'sk to Kronshtadt in 8.10.1804. Carried troops to Pomerania in Adm. Thate's squadron in 1805. To the Mediterranean with Commodore Ignatyev's squadron in 1806 to reinforce Vice-Adm. Seniavin's squadron. Landed troops at Tenedos in 1807. Took part in the Dardanelles battle on 10–11.5.1807, during which Commodore Ignatyev was killed. Fought at the battle of Mount Athos on 19.6.1807, during which she and *Rafail* engaged, damaged, and raked the Turkish *Mesudiye* (120). Arrived in Lisbon on 30.10.1807

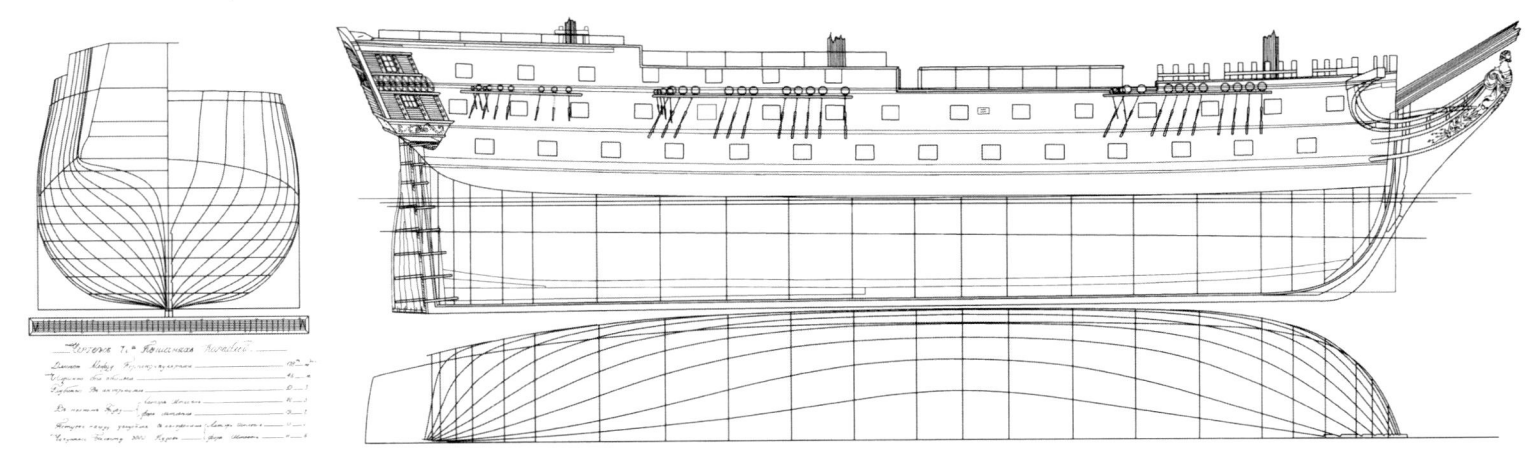

Drezden was a typical member of the Selafail *class completed in 1813. After a brief and routine career in the Baltic fleet at the end of the Napoleonic War, she was one of five 74s sold to Spain in 1817. Her lines above and below the waterline are shown to very good advantage in this sheer and may be regarded as typical for the* Selafail *class.*

after the Peace of Tilsit. Escorted into Portsmouth by Vice-Adm. Cotton along with other elements of Adm. Seniavin's squadron on 26.9.1808. Impounded in Portsmouth until her return to Kronshtadt with Rear-Adm. Korobka's squadron in 1813. Broken up in 1819.

Oryol 74 Arkhangel'sk
Constructor A. M. Kurochkin
Laid down 16.12.1805 *Launched* 23.5.1807
Dimensions 178 ft x 48 ft x 19 ft 3 in
Armament LD 28 x 36pdrs (short)
            UD 30 x 24pdrs (short)
            FC & QD 18 x 8pdrs
Selafail class. Sailed from Arkhangel'sk to Kronshtadt with Commodore Smirnov's squadron in 1807. Retreated with Adm. Khanykov's squadron in the face of the Anglo-Swedish squadron to Rogervik on 13.8.1808 and then to Kronshtadt on 30.9.1808. Stationed in the northern freeway of Kotlin in 1809. Carried troops from Sveaborg in 1812 and then with Adm. Thate's squadron to England. Returned to Russia in 1813. Cruised in the Baltic in 1814 and then transported troops from Lübeck to Kronshtadt in Vice-Adm. Crown's squadron. Repaired in 1815. Repatriated troops from France to Kronshtadt in Vice-Adm. Crown's squadron in 1817. Cruised in the Baltic in 1824. Decommissioned in 1824. Hulked in 1828. Broken up in 1833.

Severnaia Zvezda 74 Arkhangel'sk
Constructor A. M. Kurochkin
Laid down 16.12.1805 *Launched* 23.5.1807
Dimensions 178 ft x 48 ft x 19 ft 3 in
Armament LD 28 x 36pdrs (short)
            UD 30 x 24pdrs (short)
            FC & QD 18 x 8pdrs
Selafail class. Sailed from Arkhangel'sk to Kronshtadt in Commodore Smirnov's squadron in 1808. Retreated with Adm. Khanykov's squadron in the face of the Anglo-Swedish squadron to Rogervik on 13.8.1808 and then to Kronshtadt on 30.9.1808. Stationed in the northern freeway of Kotlin in 1809. Stationed in Kronshtadt Roads in 1810. Carried troops from Sveaborg to Revel' and naval cadets from Kronshtadt to Sveaborg in 1812. To England in Vice-Adm. Crown's squadron 1812–14. Repaired in 1815. Repatriated troops from France to Kronshtadt in Vice-Adm. Crown's squadron in 1817. Training duties in Kronshtadt Roads in 1818. Damaged and grounded in the Great Flood of 1824. Decommissioned in 1824. Broken up in 1827.

Borey 74 Arkhangel'sk
Constructor A. M. Kurochkin
Laid down 16.12.1805 *Launched* 23.5.1807
Dimensions 178 ft x 48 ft x 19 ft 3 in
Armament LD 28 x 36pdrs (short)
            UD 30 x 24pdrs (short)
            FC & QD 18 x 8pdrs
Selafail class. Sailed from Arkhangel'sk to Kronshtadt in Commodore Smirnov's squadron in 1807. Retreated with Adm. Khanykov's squadron in the face of the Anglo-Swedish squadron to Rogervik on 13.8.1808 and then to Kronshtadt on 30.9.1808. Stationed in the northern freeway of Kotlin in 1809. Stationed in Kronshtadt Roads in 1810. Carried troops from Sveaborg to Revel' and naval cadets from Kronshtadt to Sveaborg in 1812. Arrived at Sheerness in Vice-Adm. Crown's squadron on 29.11.1812. Returned to Russia in 1813. Repaired in 1817. Cruised in the Baltic in 1818–20. Damaged and grounded in the Great Flood of 1824. Decommissioned in 1824. Broken up in 1829.

Ne Tron' Menia 74 Arkhangel'sk
Constructor A. M. Kurochkin
Laid down 28.8.1807 *Launched* 9.5.1809
Dimensions 178 ft x 48 ft x 19 ft 3 in
Armament LD 28 x 36pdrs (short)
            UD 30 x 24pdrs (short)
            FC & QD 18 x 8pdrs
Selafail class. Left Arkhangel'sk with Vice-Adm. Crown's squadron on 11.8.1812. Severely damaged in a 4-day storm off the Shetlands in 9.1812 and forced to lay into Gothenburg for repairs. Arrived at Sveaborg on 9.10.1812. Departed at Sveaborg on 28.10.1812 for England in Vice-Adm. Crown's squadron. Arrived at Shearness on 29.11.1812. Departed Shearness for Cherbourg on 25.5.1814 and arrived there on 27.5.1814. Embarked Russian Guard troops for repatriation and arrived at Kronshtadt on 8.7.1814. Repatriated additional Russian troops from France to Kronshtadt in 1817. Decommissioned in 1817. Repaired in 1819–22. Hulked in 1823. Damaged and grounded in the Great Flood on 7.11.1824. Broken up in 1828.

Trekh Ierarkhov 74 Arkhangel'sk
Constructor A. M. Kurochkin
Laid down 28.8.1807 *Launched* 9.5.1809
Dimensions 178 ft x 48 ft x 19 ft 3 in
Armament LD 28 x 36pdrs (short)
            UD 30 x 24pdrs (short)
            FC & QD 18 x 8pdrs
Selafail class. Left Arkhangel'sk with Vice-Adm. Crown's squadron on 11.8.1812. Severely damaged in a 4-day storm off the Shetlands in 9.1812 and forced to lay into Gothenburg for repairs. Arrived at Sveaborg on 9.10.1812. Departed Sveaborg on 28.10.1812 for England in Vice-Adm. Crown's squadron. Arrived at Shearness on 29.11.1812. Departed Shearness for Cherbourg on 25.5.1814 and arrived there on 27.5.1814. Embarked Russian Guard troops for repatriation and arrived at Kronshtadt on 8.7.1814. Cruised in the Baltic in 1816. Repatriated additional Russian troops from France to Kronshtadt in 1817. Damaged and grounded in the Great Flood on 7.11.1824. Converted into a store ship in 1827.

Sviatoslav 74 Arkhangel'sk
Constructor A. M. Kurochkin
Laid down 2.8.1807 *Launched* 14.8.1809
Dimensions 178 ft x 48 ft x 19 ft 3 in
Armament LD 28 x 36pdrs (short)
            UD 30 x 24pdrs (short)
            FC & QD 18 x 8pdrs
Selafail class. Stationed in the mouth of the Severnaya Dvina River in 1810. Departed Arkhangel'sk with Vice-Adm. Crown's squadron on 11.8.1812. Involved in a violent storm off the Shetlands in 9.1812. Arrived at Sveaborg on 9.10.1812. Departed Sveaborg on 28.10.1812 and arrived at Sheerness on 29.11.1812. Departed Sheerness with Vice-Adm. Crown's squadron on 25.5.1814. Arrived at Cherbourg on 27.5.1814 and embarked Russian Guard troops for repatriation. Arrived at Kronshtadt on 8.7.1814. Cruised in the Baltic in 1816. Damaged and grounded in the Great Flood on 7.11.1824. Unsuccessful effort at repair in 1825. Broken up in 1828.

Nord-Adler 74 Arkhangel'sk
Constructor A. M. Kurochkin
Laid down 20.11.1809 *Launched* 9.5.1811
Dimensions 178 ft x 48 ft x 19 ft 3 in (Veselago)

2,897.2 tons displacement (Kuznetsov)
Armament LD 28 x 36pdrs (short)
　　　　　 UD 30 x 24pdrs (short)
　　　　　 FC & QD 18 x 8pdrs

Selafail class. Larch built. Left Arkhangel'sk as flag to Vice-Adm. Crown's squadron on 11.8.1812. Lost topmasts in a 4-day storm off the Shetlands in 9.1812. Arrived at Sveaborg on 9.10.1812 with 219 men down with scurvy. Departed Sveaborg on 28.10.1812 and arrived at Sheerness on 29.11.1812. Departed Sheerness with Vice-Adm. Crown's squadron on 25.5.1814. Embarked Russian Guards at Cherbourg for repatriation on 27.5.1814. Arrived at Kronshtadt on 8.7.1814. Cruised in the Baltic in 1817 and transported troops from Revel' to Sveaborg. Sent to Spain in 1817 and sold there in 1818.

Prints Gustav 74 Arkhangel'sk
Constructor A. M. Kurochkin
Laid down 20.11.1809 *Launched* 9.5.1811
Dimensions 178 ft x 48 ft x 19 ft 3 in
Armament LD 28 x 36pdrs (short)
　　　　　 UD 30 x 24pdrs (short)
　　　　　 FC & QD 18 x 8pdrs

Selafail class. Name commemorates the Swedish flagship captured at Gogland. Departed Arkhangel'sk with Vice-Adm. Crown's squadron on 11.8.1812. Severely damaged in a 4-day storm off the Shetlands. Arrived at Sveaborg on 9.10.1812 and unable to proceed to England due to storm damage. Transported troops in Vice-Adm. Crown's squadron from Lübeck to Kronshtadt in 8.1814. In 1817, still as part of Vice-Adm. Crown's squadron, transported troops from Calais to Kronshtadt. Cruised in the Baltic in 1818. Repaired in 1819. Cruised in the Baltic in 1820. Severely damaged and grounded in the Great Flood of 7.11.1824 and never repaired. Broken up in 1827.

Berlin 74 Arkhangel'sk
Constructor A. M. Kurochkin
Laid down 10.3.1810 *Launched* 19.7.1813
Dimensions 178 ft x 48 ft x 19 ft 3 in
Armament LD 28 x 36pdrs (short)
　　　　　 UD 30 x 24pdrs (short)
　　　　　 FC & QD 18 x 8pdrs

Selafail class. Sailed from Arkhangel'sk to Revel' with Rear-Adm. Moller's squadron in 8–10.1813. Cruised in the Baltic in 1814 and 1817–20. Decommissioned in 1824. Reduced to a stores hulk in 1827.

Gamburg 74 Arkhangel'sk
Constructor A. M. Kurochkin
Laid down 10.3.1810 *Launched* 19.7.1813
Dimensions 178 ft x 48 ft x 19 ft 3 in
Armament LD 28 x 36pdrs (short)
　　　　　 UD 30 x 24pdrs (short)
　　　　　 FC & QD 18 x 8pdrs

Selafail class. Sailed from Arkhangel'sk to Revel' with Rear-Adm. Moller's squadron in 8–10.1813. Cruised in the Baltic in 1814 and 1816. Transported troops from Calais with Adm. Crown's squadron in 1817. Cruised in the Baltic in 1817. Damaged and grounded in the Great Storm on 7.11.1824. Reduced to a stores hulk in 1827.

Drezden 74 Arkhangel'sk
Constructor A. M. Kurochkin
Laid down 10.3.1810 *Launched* 19.7.1813
Dimensions 178 ft x 48 ft x 19 ft 3 in (Veselago)
　　　　　　 2,700 tons displacement (Kuznetsov)
Armament LD 28 x 36pdrs (short)
　　　　　 UD 30 x 24pdrs (short)
　　　　　 FC & QD 18 x 8pdrs

Selafail class. Larch built. Sailed from Arkhangel'sk to Revel' with Rear-Adm. Moller's squadron in 8–10.1813. Cruised in the Baltic in 1814 and 1816. Transported Russian troops from Calais with Adm. Crown's squadron in 1817. Sent to Spain in 1817 and sold to Spain in 1818.

Liubek 74 Arkhangel'sk
Constructor A. M. Kurochkin
Laid down 10.3.1810 *Launched* 19.7.1813
Dimensions 178 ft x 48 ft x 19 ft 3 in (Veselago)
　　　　　　 3,093.25 tons displacement (Kuznetsov)
Armament LD 28 x 36pdrs (short)
　　　　　 UD 30 x 24pdrs (short)
　　　　　 FC & QD 18 x 8pdrs

Selafail class. Larch built. Sailed from Arkhangel'sk to Revel' with Rear-Adm. Moller's squadron in 8–10.1813. Cruised in the Baltic in 1814 and 1816. Carried Russian troops from Calais with Adm. Crown's squadron in 1817. Sent to Spain in 1817 and sold to Spain in 1818.

Katsbakh 74 Arkhangel'sk
Constructor A. M. Kurochkin
Laid down 30.1.1814 *Launched* 26.5.1816
Dimensions 178 ft x 48 ft x 19 ft 3 in
Armament LD 28 x 36pdrs (short)
　　　　　 UD 30 x 24pdrs (short)
　　　　　 FC & QD 18 x 8pdrs

Selafail class. Name commemorates a Russian victory in 1813. Sailed from Arkhangel'sk to Kronshtadt in 7–9.1816, her only time at sea. Damaged and grounded in the Great Flood of 7.11.1824. Hulked in 1828.

Arsis 74 Arkhangel'sk
Constructor A. M. Kurochkin
Laid down 30.1.1814 *Launched* 26.5.1816
Dimensions 178 ft x 48 ft x 19 ft 3 in
Armament LD 28 x 36pdrs (short)
　　　　　 UD 30 x 24pdrs (short)
　　　　　 FC & QD 18 x 8pdrs

Selafail class. Name commemorates a Russian victory in 1814. Sailed from Arkhangel'sk to Kronshtadt in Commodore Machakov's squadron in 7–9.1816. Cruised in the Baltic in 1821. Damaged and grounded in the Great Flood of 7.11.1824. Hulked as a store ship in 1825. Broken up in 1832.

Retvizan 74 Arkhangel'sk
Constructor A. M. Kurochkin
Laid down 12.7.1816 *Launched* 20.5.1818
Dimensions 178 ft x 48 ft x 19 ft 3 in
Armament LD 28 x 36pdrs (short)
　　　　　 UD 30 x 24pdrs (short)
　　　　　 FC & QD 18 x 8pdrs

Selafail class. Sailed from Arkhangel'sk to Kronshtadt. Cruised in the Baltic in 1822–4. Decommissioned in 1824. Hulked in 1829. Broken up in 1833.

Trekh Sviatitelei 74 Arkhangel'sk
Constructor A. M. Kurochkin
Laid down 8.2.1818 *Launched* 31.7.1819

Dimensions 178 ft x 48 ft x 19 ft 3 in
Armament LD 28 x 36pdrs (short)
UD 30 x 24pdrs (short)
FC & QD 18 x 8pdrs

Selafail class. Sailed from Arkhangel'sk to Kronshtadt in 1820. Cruised to Iceland in 1824 in Adm. Crown's squadron. Severely damaged and grounded in the Great Flood on 7.11.1824. Never refloated and broken up in place in 1828.

Sviatoi Andrei 74 Arkhangel'sk
Constructor A. M. Kurochkin
Laid down 1820 Launched 18.5.1821
Dimensions 178 ft x 48 ft x 19 ft 3 in
Armament LD 28 x 36pdrs (short)
UD 30 x 24pdrs (short)
FC & QD 18 x 8pdrs

Selafail class. Sailed from Arkhangel'sk to Kronshtadt in 1821. Cruised in the Atlantic in Adm. Crown's squadron to Iceland. Cruised in Adm. Crown's squadron to Dogger Bank in 1826. Escorted Rear-Adm. Geiden's squadron to Portsmouth in 1827, under the overall command of Adm. Seniavin. Returned to Kronshtadt on 13.9.1827. Decommissioned in 1828. Converted to a hulk and then a target in 1829. Employed as test bed for mines under K. A. Shilder in 1840. Sank after the explosion of three experimental mines in 1840.

Sysoi Velikii 74 Arkhangel'sk
Constructor A. M. Kurochkin
Laid down 1820 Launched 20.5.1822
Dimensions 178 ft x 48 ft x 19 ft 3 in
Armament LD 28 x 36pdrs (short)
UD 30 x 24pdrs (short)
FC & QD 18 x 8pdrs

Selafail class. The name commemorates the saint day on which the battle of Gogland was fought. Sailed from Arkhangel'sk to Kronshtadt in 1822. Cruised in the Baltic in 1825. Cruised to Dogger Bank with Adm. Crown's squadron in 1826. Escorted Rear-Adm. Geiden's squadron to Portsmouth in 1827, under the general command of Adm. Seniavin. Returned to Kronshtadt on 13.9.1827. Training duties in Kronshtadt Roads in 1828. Cruised in the Baltic in 1829–30. Decommissioned in 1830. Hulked in 1831. Broken up in 1837.

Prokhor 74 Arkhangel'sk
Constructor A. M. Kurochkin
Laid down 28.11.1821 Launched 23.5.1823
Dimensions 178 ft x 48 ft x 19 ft 3 in
Armament LD 28 x 36pdrs (short)
UD 30 x 24pdrs (short)
FC & QD 18 x 8pdrs

Selafail class. Sailed from Arkhangel'sk to Kronshtadt in 1823. Damaged and grounded in the Great Flood of 7.11.1824. Repaired and refloated on 27.9.1829. Cruised in the Baltic in 1831–5. Carried Imperial Guards from Kronshtadt to Danzig in the squadron of Vice-Adm. Rikord in 7.1835 and returned the Guards to Revel' before the end of the year. Cruised in the Baltic in 1836 and participated in the Imperial Review of Nikolai I. Cruised in the Baltic in 1838–40. Decommissioned in 1840. Broken up in 1846.

Kniaz' Vladimir 74 Arkhangel'sk
Constructor A. M. Kurochkin
Laid down 1822 Launched 27.5.1824
Dimensions 178 ft x 48 ft x 19 ft 3 in
Armament LD 28 x 36pdrs (short)
UD 30 x 24pdrs (short)
FC & QD 18 x 8pdrs

Selafail class. Coppered on completion. Sailed from Arkhangel'sk to Kronshtadt in 1824. On 13.7.1826 served as site for the sentencing and degradation of 13 naval officers who had participated in the Decembrist Uprising on 14.12.1825. Escorted Rear-Adm. Geiden's squadron to Portsmouth under the general command of Adm. Seniavin in 1827 and returned to Kronshtadt on 13.9.1827. Departed Kronshtadt with Rear-Adm. Rikord's squadron bound for the Mediterranean in 6.1828. Operated in the Mediterranean against Turkey until the autumn of 1830 at which time she returned to Kronshtadt. Decommissioned in 1830. Hulked in 1831.

Tsar' Konstantin 74 Arkhangel'sk
Constructor A. M. Kurochkin
Laid down 5.7.1824 Launched 21.5.1825
Dimensions 178 ft x 48 ft x 19 ft 3 in
Armament LD 28 x 36pdrs (short)
UD 30 x 24pdrs (short)
FC & QD 18 x 8pdrs

Selafail class. Sailed from Arkhangel'sk to Kronshtadt in 1825. To the Mediterranean under Rear-Adm. Bellingsgauzen in 1826–7. Escorted Rear-Adm. Geiden's squadron to Portsmouth in 1827. Returned to Russia on 13.9.1827. To the Mediterranean under Rear-Adm. Rikord's squadron and then under Rear-Adm. Lazarev in operations against Turkey in 1828–30. Captured the Turkish corvette L'vitsa (Lioness) 26 and brig Candia 14 off Crete on 28.1.1829. Returned to Kronshtadt and decommissioned on 12.5.1830. Broken up in 1831.

Pamiat' Evstafii class (2 ships)

The two ships in this group were laid down some eight years after the first vessels of the *Selafail* class and were almost 7 feet longer and slightly less beamy than the earlier class. In spite of their greater dimensions, armament was still in line with the Establishment of 1805. They were designed by I. V. Kurepanov, who had studied in Great Britain in 1793–1801 and who, in contrast to A. S. Katsanov and Kurochkin, was deeply influenced by British design philosophy. Although they had longer and more active service lives than most other Russian 74s, their design does not appear to have been particularly successful or well regarded, possibly because of their size and cost. Both the earlier *Selafail*s and the contemporaneous *Sviatitelei*s continued to be built in some numbers while only two of the even larger *Evstafii*s were completed.

Pamiat' Evstafii 74 St Petersburg
Constructors G. S. Isakov and I. V. Kurepanov
Laid down 15.1.1810 Launched 30.9.1810
Dimensions 184 ft 10 in x 47 ft 4 in x 23 ft 5 in
Armament LD 28 x 36pdrs (short)
UD 30 x 24pdrs (short)
FC & QD 18 x 8pdrs (1805 Establishment)

Pamiat' Evstafii class. The name commemorates the *Evstafii Plakida*, the Russian flagship lost at the battle of Chios. Departed Kronshtadt in 10.1812 as flag to Rear-Adm. Korobka. Arrived at Sheerness on 29.11.1812. Departed Sheerness for Cherbourg on 25.5.1814 with Vice-Adm. Crown's squadron. Arrived at Cherbourg on 27.5.1814 and embarked Russian Guard troops for repatriation. Arrived at Kronshtadt on 8.7.1814. Transported troops from Lübeck to Kronshtadt in 8.1814 as part of Vice-Adm. Crown's squadron. Cruised in the Baltic in 1818 and 1819. Repaired in 1824. Decommissioned. Broken up in 1828.

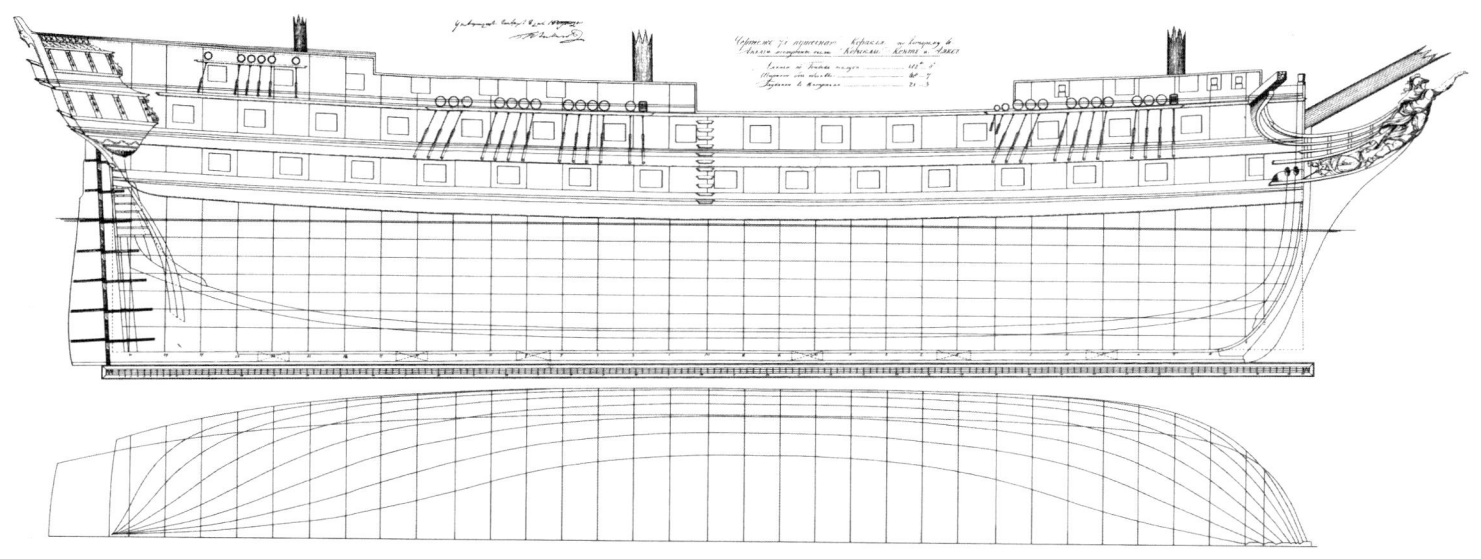

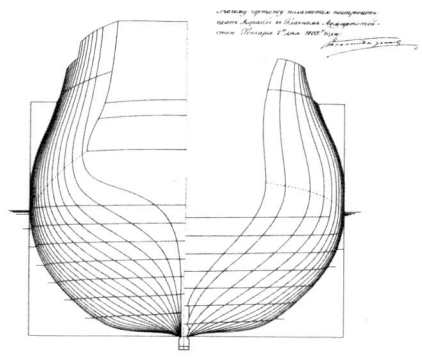

THE BALTIC FLEET 1801–24

The draught of HMS Kent *(74) completed in 1795 and based on the lines of the captured French* Invincible *was the model for* Trekh Sviatitelei *(74) of 1810, and her six sisters. Naval minister Traversay ordered* Trekh Sviatitelei's *completion in a record time of only eight months, necessitating the temporary suspension of three other 74s. After serving alongside British ships in North Sea waters during the closing years of the Napoleonic Wars, she was one of the ships sold to Spain in 1818. The poor condition of her hull when she arrived at Cadiz may have related not only to her hard use from 1812 to 1814 but also to her accelerated construction.*

Ches'ma 74 St Petersburg
Constructor I. V. Kurepanov
Laid down 15.1.1809 *Launched* 24.5.1811
Dimensions 184 ft 10 in x 47 ft 4 in x 23 ft 5 in
Armament LD 28 x 36pdrs (short)
UD 30 x 24pdrs (short)
FC & QD 18 x 8pdrs
Pamiat' Evstafii class. Stationed in Kronshtadt and cruised off Krasnaia Gorka in 5–9.1812. Left Kronshtadt in Adm. Thate's squadron on 15.10.1812 and arrived at Sheerness on 30.11.1812. Left the Downs with Adm. Thate's squadron on 24.6.1814 and arrived at Kronshtadt on 16.7.1814. As part of Vice-Adm. Crown's squadron in 8.1818, transported troops from Lübeck to Kronshtadt. Cruised in the Baltic in 1817 and 1821. Repaired in 1824. Decommissioned in 1824. Broken up in 1828.

Trekh Sviatitelei class (7 ships)
The ships of the *Trekh Sviatitelei* class appear to have been originally planned as replacements for the *Selafail*s. They are said to have been based on the design of the British *Kent* and *Ajax* large class 74s of 1798. Seven ships were laid down and completed between 1810 and 1817. In service, they were found to be less successful than the earlier and smaller *Selafail*s, which continued in production until 1825. They were, however, evaluated as being more efficient and economical ships than their other contemporaries, the two *Evstafii*s.

Trekh Sviatitelei 74 St Petersburg
Constructor I. V. Kurepanov
Laid down 15.1.1810 *Launched* 30.9.1810
Dimensions 182 ft 7 in x 48 ft 8 in x 22 ft 3½ in

3,093.25 tons displacement (Kuznetsov)
Armament LD 28 x 36pdrs (short)
UD 30 x 24pdrs (short)
FC & QD 18 x 8pdrs
Trekh Sviatitelei class. Pine built. Departed Kronshtadt with Rear-Adm. Korobka's squadron in 10.1812. Arrived at Sheerness on 29.11.1812. Left Sheerness in Vice-Adm. Crown's squadron for Cherbourg on 25.5.1814. Arrived at Cherbourg on 27.5.1814 and embarked Russian Guard troops for repatriation. Arrived at Kronshtadt on 8.7.1814. Transported troops from Lübeck to Kronshtadt in 8.1814 in Vice-Adm. Crown's squadron. Sent to Spain in 1817 where she was sold in 1818.

Sviatyk Zhen Mironosits 74 St Petersburg, New Admiralty
Constructor G. S. Isakov
Laid down 15.1.1809 *Launched* 24.5.1811
Dimensions 182 ft 7 in x 48 ft 8 in x 22 ft 3½ in
Armament LD 28 x 36pdrs (short)
UD 30 x 24pdrs (short)
FC & QD 18 x 8pdrs
Trekh Sviatitelei class. Stationed in Kronshtadt and cruised off Krasnaia Gorka in 5–9.1812. Left Kronshtadt in Adm. Thate's squadron on 15.10.1812 and arrived at Sheerness on 30.11.1812. Departed Sheerness with Vice-Adm. Crown's squadron on 25.5.1814. Embarked Russian Guards at Cherbourg on 27.5.1814 and arrived at Kronshtadt in 8.1814. While serving in Vice-Adm. Crown's squadron, transported troops from Calais to Kronshtadt in 1817 and from Lübeck to Kronshtadt in 8.1818. Repaired in 1819. Repaired in 1824. Decommissioned in 1824. Broken up in 1825.

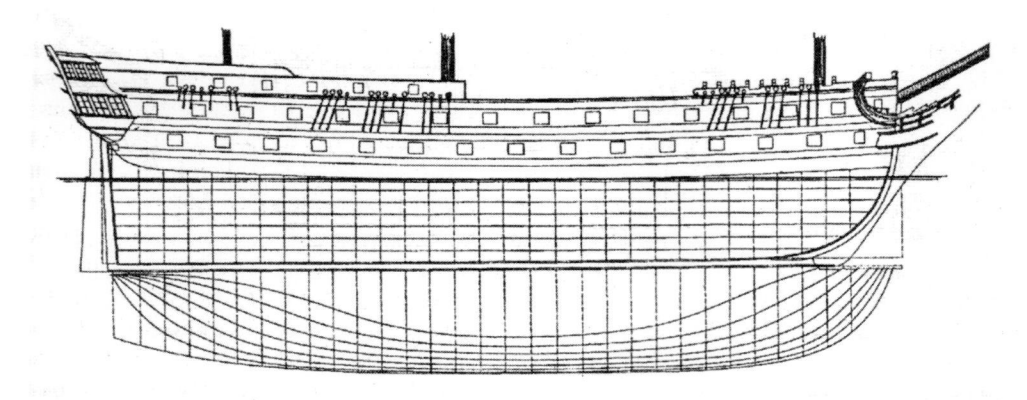

Neptunus (74) served with the Russian fleet operating in British waters against Napoleon from 1812 to 1814. Her lines, shown here, should have been familiar to her British allies because she was one of 7 Russian 74s modelled after the large class 74s *Kent* and *Ajax*. In 1818 she was also one of the Baltic 74s sold to Spain and attracted as much criticism as the others for her allegedly decrepit condition. This was a questionable claim for this ship at least. Even though she had seen hard service during the war, she was only six years old at the time of the sale, and had been constructed at St Petersburg out of Kazan oak rather than of pine as had been the case with her sister-ship *Trekh Sviatitelei*, also sold to the Spanish.

Iupiter 74 St Petersburg
Constructor G. S. Isakov
Laid down 28.1.1811   *Launched* 7.9.1812
Dimensions 182 ft 7 in x 48 ft 8 in x 22 ft 3½ in
Armament   LD 28 x 36pdrs (short)
             UD 30 x 24pdrs (short)
             FC & QD 18 x 8pdrs

Trekh Sviatitelei class. Left Kronshtadt for England in Rear-Adm. Korobka's squadron in 10.1812. Arrived at Sheerness on 29.11.1812. Departed Sheerness in Vice-Adm. Crown's squadron on 25.5.1814. Arrived at Cherbourg on 27.5.1814 and embarked Russian Guard troops for repatriation. Arrived at Kronshtadt on 8.7.1814. Transported troops in Vice-Adm. Crown's squadron from Lübeck to Kronshtadt in 8.1814. Escorted three of the Russian frigates being sold to Spain, and returned with their crews to Russia in 1818. Decommissioned in 1824. Grounded and irreparably damaged in the Great Flood of 7.11.1827. Broken up in 1828.

Neptunus 74 St Petersburg
Constructor I. S. Razumov
Laid down 22.12.1811   *Launched* 6.6.1812
Dimensions 182 ft 7 in x 48 ft 8 in x 22 ft 3½ in
              2,897.2 tons displacement (Kuznetsov)
Armament   LD 28 x 36pdrs (short)
             UD 30 x 24pdrs (short)
             FC & QD 18 x 8pdrs

Trekh Sviatitelei class. Oak built. Cruised in the Baltic in 1814. Transported troops from Lübeck to Kronshtadt with Vice-Adm. Crown's squadron in 8.1814. Sent to Spain in 1817 and sold to Spain in 1818.

Pyotr 74 St Petersburg
Constructor I. V. Kurepanov
Laid down 22.12.1811   *Launched* 7.8.1814
Dimensions 182 ft 7 in x 48 ft 8 in x 22 ft 3½ in
Armament   LD 28 x 36pdrs (short)
             UD 30 x 24pdrs (short)
             FC & QD 18 x 8pdrs

Trekh Sviatitelei class. Cruised in the Baltic in 1820–4. Severely damaged in the Great Flood of 7.11.1824. Broken up in 1828.

Finland 74 St Petersburg
Constructor B. F. Stoke
Laid down 5.12.1812   *Launched* 7.8.1814
Dimensions 182 ft 7 in x 48 ft 8 in x 22 ft 3½ in
Armament   LD 28 x 36pdrs (short)
             UD 30 x 24pdrs (short)
             FC & QD 18 x 8pdrs

Trekh Sviatitelei class. Cruised in the Baltic in 1821. Damaged and grounded in the Great Flood of 7.11.1824. Broken up in 1828.

Fershampenuaz 74 St Petersburg
Constructor I. S. Razumov
Laid down 16.9.1816   *Launched* 4.8.1817
Dimensions 182 ft 7 in x 48 ft 8 in x 22 ft 3½ in
              3,093.25 tons displacement
Armament   LD 28 x 36pdrs (short)
             UD 30 x 24pdrs (short)
             FC & QD 18 x 8pdrs

Trekh Sviatitelei class. Name commemorates a military victory in 1814 in the closing stages of the Napoleonic Wars. Cruised in the Baltic in 1822. To the Mediterranean in 6.1828 as Rear-Adm. Rikord's flag. Joined Vice-Adm. Geiden's squadron at Malta on 10.9.1828 to participate in the blockade of the Dardanelles. Returned to Kronshtadt in 1831. Destroyed by fire on 8.10.1831 in Kronshtadt Roads with a loss of 49 men. Arson suspected.

Ships with 60–68 guns (6 built 1801–24)

Provision had been made for a permanent Baltic Establishment of nine active and three reserve 66-gun ships in the General Establishment of 1803, and also for a new and heavier establishment of guns for 66-gun ships as specified under the 1805 Establishment of Guns; but it is evident that the 60-gun ship of the line had seen its day as a viable component of the Russian battle fleet by this time. Upon the completion of the last of the *Aziias* in 1797 and of *Arkhistratig Mikhail* and *Zachatie Sviatoi Anni*, the two derivative 66s patterned upon captured Swedish ships, further construction of ships in the 60–66 gun range was limited to a mixed bag of five ships falling into four separate groups all between 1804 and 1809, and to a final 66 of a very experimental nature in 1824. All of these ships were armed with short 36pdrs on the Swedish model and five of the six with short 24pdrs, but there was no evidence of close adherence to the specifications of the gunnery Establishment of 1805 beyond the choice of calibre. Nor is there any commonality at all in specified dimensions among the six ships, except for those of the two sister ships. The strategic and tactical underpinnings for this heterogeneous group of ships remains something of a mystery, but it is clear that none of the six owe much to the earlier, more traditional, 66-gun ships of the *Aziia* class. The draught for

THE BALTIC FLEET 1801–24

Pobedonosets was purchased from Great Britain and she stands in a class by herself as a sort of test bed for new developments in hull framing. It is reasonable to consider that the Russian designed 66s built after 1800 represented attempts to expand and improve still further upon the designs of the captured Swedish ships that had been used as the basis for *Arkhistratig Mikha* and *Zachatie Sviatoi Anni*.

Although they had no settled place in the Russian line of battle after 1800, all six of the 64/66 gun ships were actively and profitably employed during their lifetimes, with the sad exception of *Saratov* which was damaged in a storm in 1812 and sunk after striking an uncharted rock.

Moshchnyi 66 Arkhangel'sk
Constructor A. M. Kurochkin
Laid down 16.7.1804 *Launched* 17.7.1805
Dimensions 168 ft x (116 ft keel) x 45 ft 6 in x 18 ft 6 in
Armament LD 26/28 x 36pdrs (short)
UD 28 x 24pdrs (short)
FC & QD 14 x 8pdrs

Sailed from Arkhangel'sk to Kronshtadt in 1805. To the Mediterranean with Commodore Ignatyev's squadron to reinforce Vice-Adm. Seniavin's fleet in 1806. Landed troops at Tenedos in 1807. Took part in the Dardanelles battle on 10–11.5.1807 and fought at the battle of Mount Athos on 19.6.1807. In company with *Iaroslav*, she attacked and heavily damaged *Anka-I Bahri* (84) in the Turkish centre during which she received serious damage. Arrived in Lisbon on 30.10.1807 after the Peace of Tilsit. Escorted into Portsmouth by Vice-Adm. Cotton along with other elements of Adm. Seniavin's squadron on 26.9.1808. Impounded in Portsmouth until her return to Kronshtadt with the guns of those Russian ships sold for scrap as part of Rear-Adm. Korobka's squadron in 1813. Broken up in 1817.

Skoryi 60/62 St Petersburg
Constructors M. Sarychev and A. M. Kurochkin
Laid down 16.8.1802 *Launched* 18.7.1805
Dimensions 176 ft x 46 ft x 20 ft (Morskoi Sbornik)
Armament LD 30 x 36pdrs (short)
UD 32 x 36pdr carr. (Morskoi Sbornik)

An unusual design with an unusual uniform calibre armament. She should probably be considered as a two decked frigate rather than as a ship of the line in spite of her great size. *Krepkii* (54) of 1801 built in the Black Sea was apparently her sister ship on the basis of their identical dimensions and was classed as a frigate. To the Mediterranean with Commodore Ignatyev's squadron in 1806 to reinforce Vice-Adm. Seniavin's fleet. Landed troops at Imbros. Took part in the Dardanelles battle on 10–11.5.1807 and at the battle of Mount Athos on 19.6.1807 where she was damaged in an engagement with three Turkish Ships of the line and a frigate. Arrived in Lisbon on 26.9.1808 after the Peace of Tilsit. Escorted into Portsmouth by Vice-Adm. Cotton along with other elements of Adm. Seniavin's squadron on 26.9.1808. Impounded in Portsmouth until her sale to Great Britain in 1813.

Pobedonosets 64 Arkhangel'sk
Constructor A. M. Kurochikn
Laid down 28.8.1807 *Launched* 9.5.1809
Dimensions 163 ft x 44 ft 8 in x 17 ft 6 in
Armament LD 26 x 36pdrs (short)
UD 28 x 24pdrs (short)
FC & QD 10 x 8pdrs

Another rather unique Russian ship, built to plans obtained in Great Britain. Introduced the use of iron knees (gussets) and diagonal framing to Russian warships. Although her dimensions were only slightly greater than those of the final purpose-built British 64s of the late 1780s, their armament was unprecedented by British standards, with short 24- and 36pdrs replacing the 18- and 24pdr long guns that were standard for British 64s. This weight of armament could not have been born without the structural reinforcements mentioned above.

Left Arkhangel'sk in 1812 with Vice-Adm. Crown's squadron. Damaged in a storm off the Shetlands in 9.1812 and repaired at Gothenburg. Arrived at Sveaborg on 9.10.1812. Departed Sveaborg for England with Vice-Adm. Crown's squadron on 28.10.1812. Arrived at Shearness on 29.11.1812. Returned to Kronshtadt on 8.7.1814. Decommissioned in 1814. Transferred to Sveaborg and hulked in 1822.

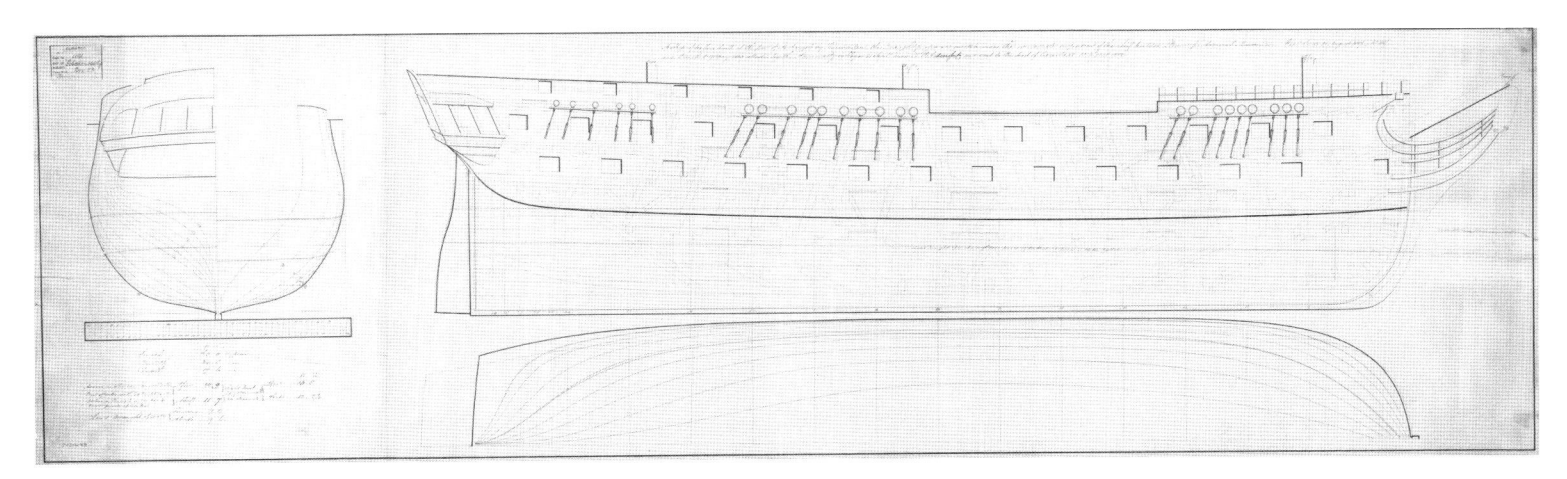

While a fair number of Russian designs were influenced by contemporary British designs, Pobedonosets *stands alone in having been specifically designed in Great Britain for construction in Russia. No record exists to our knowledge regarding the circumstances behind her design and construction; but she would appear to have combined construction techniques just coming into general use in Great Britain at the time, with the dimensions of a traditional 64 and the heavy armament allowed for by the Russian adoption of short-barrelled heavy guns on the Swedish pattern. Although she was never tested in combat,* Pobedonosets *served actively throughout the final stages of the Napoleonic War. She was decommissioned at the war's (first) ending in 1814, either as a result of her strenuous employment or because she had no real place in the postwar Russian battle fleet.*

Vsevolod class
Vsevolod 66 Arkhangel'sk
Constructor A. M. Kurochkin
Laid down 2.8.1807 *Launched* 10.5.1809
Dimensions 172 ft x 47 ft x 19 ft 3 in
Armament LD 26/28 x 36pdrs (short)
            UD 28 x 24pdrs (short)
            FC & QD 14 x 8pdrs

Vsevolod class. Left Arkhangel'sk with Vice-Adm. Crown's squadron on 11.8.1812. Severely damaged in 9.1812 in a 4-day storm off the Shetlands. Wintered in Fridrikhsvern in 1812–13. Arrived at Kronshtadt in 1813. Cruised in the Baltic in Vice-Adm. Sarychev's squadron in 1814. Decommissioned in 1814. Transferred to Sveaborg and hulked in 1820.

Saratov 66 Arkhangel'sk
Constructor A. M. Kurochkin
Laid down 2.8.1807 *Launched* 19.5.1809
Dimensions 172 ft x 47 ft x 19 ft 3 in
Armament LD 26/28 x 36pdrs (short)
            UD 28 x 24pdrs (short)
            FC & QD 14 x 8pdrs

Vsevolod class. Left Arkhangel'sk with Vice-Adm. Crown's squadron on 11.8.1812. Severely damaged in 9.1812 in a 4-day storm off the Shetlands. Repaired at Gothenburg. Arrived at Sveaborg on 9.10.1812. Departed Sveaborg en route to England on 27.10.1812 and struck an underwater rock off Grokhara (Harmaya) and sank with no losses on 30.10.1812.

Emmanuil 64 St Petersburg
Constructor V. F. Stoke
Laid down 24.2.1822 *Launched* 29.7.1824
Dimensions 172 ft x 46 ft x 19 ft
Armament LD 26 x 36pdrs (short)
            UD 28 x 24pdrs (short)
            FC & QD 14 x 8pdrs (1805 establishment)

Vsevolod class. No definite information is available about this experimental ship said to have been a member of the *Vsevolod* class. She is sometimes referred to as a two-decker heavy frigate. Known to have been the first Russian ship of composite construction with iron knees and copper lashings in the bows and with a rounded stern. Sailed from St Petersburg to Kronshtadt in 1825. Cruised to Dogger Bank under Adm. Crown. Escorted Rear-Adm. Geydon's squadron to Portsmouth under the general command of the reinstated Adm. Seniavin. Returned to Kronshtadt on 13.9.1827. Departed Kronshtadt for the Mediterranean in Rear-Adm. Rikord's squadron in 6.1828. Operated in the Mediterranean until the summer of 1829. Converted into a hospital ship in 1829 due to poor condition. Sold to the Greek government for 30,000 Spanish pesos.

Baltic frigates (47 purpose-built 1801–24)

24pdr heavy frigates (20 purpose-built 1801–24)

At the end of the eighteenth century, Russians were concerned with working out a standard design for frigates as the basis for future development. Ships of several classes were built all patterned to some degree on the captured Swedish *Venus*. These included the enlarged *Geroi* and *Venera*, the seven marginally successful *Amfitrida* class ships, the extremely successful *Speshnyi* class ships and the very similar *Nazaret* in the Black Sea. The *Speshnyi* class design proved the most successful design in service and became the standard for future Russian development with an impressive total of 34 ships being laid down and completed between 1801 and 1844.

These frigates were considered to be good sea-boats and rather fast sailors. In exercises, they were generally employed as advance scouts for Russian battle squadrons, taking up positions behind the formal line of battle in a supportive role once contact had been made with opposing battle fleets in a traditional frigate manner. Unlike their Swedish progenitors which had been intended to supplement the Swedish line of battle, the *Speshnyi*s were never intended for inclusion in the line, but were valued instead for their worth as cruising and scouting ships.

While the Russians took and held the lead with respect to the construction of heavy frigates to the exclusion of all other types after 1800, the other major powers did build limited numbers of heavy frigates during the Napoleonic War period. A comparison between the Russian frigates of the *Speshnyi* class and contemporaneous British, French, and American heavy frigates is of interest in this respect:

Russia: *Speshnyi* 44 1801
        159 ft 3 in x 41 ft 6 in x 12 ft 8 in
        28 x 24pdrs (short), 16 x 6pdrs, 6 x 24pdr carr.
Great Britain: *Endymion* 50 1797
        159 ft x 42 ft x 12 ft
        26 x 24pdrs (long), 2 x 9pdrs, 20 x 32pdr carr.
France: *Egyptienne* 50 1800
        169 ft 8 in x 43 ft 8 in x 15 ft 1 in
        (British measurements)
        30 x 24pdrs (long), 20 x 8pdrs
United States: *President* 44 1800
        173 ft 3 in x 44 ft 4 in x 13 ft 11 in
        30 x 24pdrs (long), 22 x 12pdrs

The dimensions of *Endymion*, *Egyptienne* and *President* were all taken in England after completion or capture and are fully comparable for that reason. The dimensions of *Speshnyi* may also be considered reliably comparable to the British *Endymion* and the two prizes because the Russians also applied British standards of measurement to their ships. The French and American heavy frigates were rather larger than the British and Russian 24pdr designs, but *Speshnyi* and *Endymion* were so similar in their basic dimensions that the Russian design gives the appearance of having been influenced to some degree by the slightly earlier British ship, which was herself patterned upon the lines of the captured French *La Pomone* of 1785. Russian sources maintain that the only foreign influence in *Speshnyi*'s design was that of af Chapman's highly regarded *Venus* and that any similarity in dimensions with *Endymion* is only fortuitous. This being the case, the convergence of the two designs must be considered simply as an interesting example of convergent evolution in response to similar design pressures.

The Russian ships differed from the heavy frigates of other nations' in their reliance upon short-barrelled guns of the Swedish type instead of the long guns standard in the deep water navies. These shorter and lighter guns allowed for less hull deformation in service, and also facilitated the use of smaller gun crews and higher rates of fire, while still offering a weight of broadside comparable to that of ships armed with heavier long guns. They were well adapted to conditions in the shallow and confined waters of the Baltic where weight of broadside was more important than long range fire. In comparing the armaments of these 4 ships, consideration should be given to the fact that the British and American artillery in pounds in were some 8 to 10 per cent lighter than French and Russian 'pounds' and that their '24pdr' cannon would actually have been the equivalents of 26pdrs – had the British and Americans possessed such guns.

After 1815, both the French and the American navies followed the Russian lead and adopted the heavy frigate as their basic type. The British, on the other hand, built only limited numbers of heavy frigates, relying instead on razeed 74s to counter French heavy frigates, and continued to build and operate very large numbers of the more traditional 18pdr *Leda* class, with 24 *Leda*s being completed prior to 1815 and a further 23 of a modified design being completed in the post-war years.

Geroi and *Venera*
Very little is known of the background of these two 24pdr ships. Although they were built separately at Arkhangel'sk and St Petersburg, their dimensions were similar and they may have constituted as a single class. It should be noted that they were marginally larger than the standard heavy Russian frigates of the *Speshnyi* and *Amfitrida* classes and apparently less successful in service in their original form as evidenced by the conversion of *Venera* into a 56-gun ship with two complete gun decks.

Geroi 48 Arkhangel'sk
Constructor ?
Laid down 30.6.1806   *Launched* 31.5.1807
Dimensions 162 ft 6 in x 42 ft x 13 ft 2 in
Armament   LD 30 x 24pdrs (short)
             FC & QD 18 x 6pdrs

Cruised in Adm. Khanykov's squadron in 1808. Grounded and sunk on 20.9.1808 at Rogervik while weighing anchor. No casualties, guns removed, captain court martialled and broken to a common seaman. Alexander I amended the sentence to reduction to the rank of midshipman echoing the restrained leniency shown on similar occasions by his illustrious predecessor Peter I.

Venera 48/56 St Petersburg
Constructor A. I. Melikhov
Laid down ?   *Launched* 15.7.1808
Dimensions 162 ft 6 in x 42 ft x 19 ft
Armament   1808 LD 30 x 24pdrs
             FC & QD 18 x 6pdrs
             1810 LD 28 x 24pdrs
             UD 28 x 24pdr carr.

Stationed as a guardship at Kronshtadt Roads in 1809, and participated in the defence of Kotlin. Converted to a 56-gun ship with two complete gun decks in 1810. Carried troops from Sveaborg to Revel' in 1812 and proceeded to England with Adm. Thate's squadron. Returned to Kronshtadt in 1813. Cruised in the Baltic in 1814. Broken up in 1819 per Veselago. Chernyshev erroneously states that she was broken up in 1829. She does not appear in the list of Russian warships for 1824.

Speshnyi class group 1 (11 ships)
Construction of the initial eleven ships of this successful class was spread over a period of 24 years and continued after 1825 in modified form with another 23 being completed by 1844. Three of the 11 were built during the first decade of the century, and a second triad in the closing years of the Napoleonic Wars. These three follow-on ships were cheaply built of larch and pine and were amongst the group of Russian frigates sold to Spain in 1818. The final five ships of the first group were laid down between 1818 and 1823 and may be regarded, at least in part as replacements for the ships sold to Spain. Three were damaged in the Great Flood of 1824, but all were salvaged and returned to service, an indication perhaps of their perceived worth at a time when many damaged ships were simply written off. Two fought at Navarino in 1827. All members of Group I were worn out and stricken by 1831, save only for the last, *Konstantin*, which was finally hulked in 1837 and broken up in 1848.

Speshnyi 44/50 Arkhangel'sk
Constructor G. Ignatyev
Laid down 10.3.1800   *Launched* 29.8.1801
Dimensions 159 ft 2.6 in x 41 ft 6 in x 12 ft 8 in
             1,950 tons displacement
Armament   LD 28 x 24pdrs (short frigate guns)

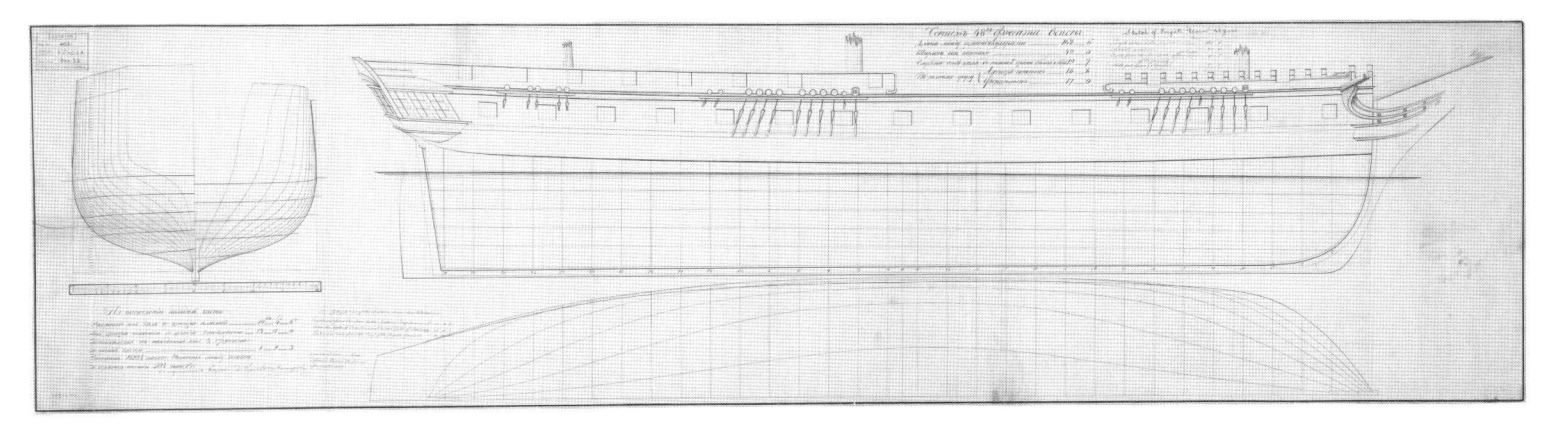

This draught of Venera *as completed in 1808 shows an apparently formidable design with an absence of sheer and an impressive line of 14 upper deck gunports plus a bridle port, bespeaking both power and speed. Although she had a reasonably long and active career of at least a decade, it would appear that she was not entirely successful as a frigate as evidenced by her reconstruction as a conventional, if unorthodox, two-decker with a uniform battery of 56–24pdrs. Her sister ship* Geroi *grounded and sank while getting underway in her first year, and this disaster may also have related to some type of defective design work. Little is known about their design origins, but the presence of this draught at the National Maritime Museum may be indicative of a British connection.*

FC & QD 16 x 6pdrs 6 x 24pdr carr.

Speshnyi class group 1. Sailed from Arkhangel'sk to Kronstadt in 7–9.1803. Cruised to Danzig and Lübeck in 1804–5. Departed from Kronstadt with the payroll for Vice-Adm. Seniavin's squadron in the Mediterranean on 21.7.1807 in company with the transport *Vilgelmina*. Arrived at Portsmouth on 11.8.1807 and taken into British custody on 20.11.1807 along with the *Vilgelmina*. The payroll consisting of 601,167 Spanish doubloons and 140,197 Dutch ducats was expropriated by the British due to the Russian withdrawal from the struggle with Napoleonic France.

Argus 44 Arkhangel'sk
Constructor ?
Laid down 30.6.1806   *Launched* 1.6.1807
Dimensions 159 ft 2¾ in x 41 ft 6 in x 12 ft 8 in
Armament LD 28 x 24pdrs (short)
            FC & QD 16 x 6pdrs

Speshnyi class group 1. Sailed from Arkhangel'sk to Kronstadt in 1807. Grounded on 22.10.1808 and wrecked on 25.10.1808 while en route from Sveaborg to Revel'. No casualties.

Bystryi 44 Arkhangel'sk
Constructor A. M. Kurochkin
Laid down 16.12.1805   *Launched* 1.6.1807
Dimensions 159 ft 2¾ in x 41 ft 6 in x 12 ft 8 in
Armament LD 28 x 24pdrs (short)
            FC & QD 16 x 6pdrs

Speshnyi class group 1. Sailed from Arkhangel'sk to Kronstadt in 1807. To Sveaborg as a guardship in 1808. While cruising to Gottland in 1809, attacked by HMS *Implacable* and *Melpona* and forced to retreat to Kronstadt. Fire watch ship in Kronstadt Roads in 1810–11. Carried troops to Revel' in 1812 and then deployed to England with Adm. Thate's squadron. Returned to Kronstadt in 1813. Cruised in the Baltic in 1814. Fire watch ship in Kronstadt Roads in 1820–5. Broken up in 1827.

Merkurii 44 St Petersburg, Okhta
Constructor V. F. Stoke
Laid down 14.3.1814   *Launched* 13.7.1815
Dimensions 159 ft 6 in x 41 ft 8 in x 12 ft 10 in (Veselago)
            1,950 tons displacement (Kuznetsov)
Armament LD 28 x 24pdrs (short)
            FC & QD 16 x 6pdrs   363 men (1817)

Speshnyi class group 1. Pine built. Carried the dowry of Grand Duchess Anna Pavlovna (future queen of Holland) to Holland and then proceeded to England in 1816. Returned to Kronstadt in Spring of 1817. To Cadiz for sale to Spain with Rear-Adm. Moller's squadron in Autumn of 1817. Crew of 363 returned by transports.

Patrikii 44 Arkhangel'sk
Constructor A. M. Kurochkin
Laid down 30.4.1814   *Launched* 21.6.1816
Dimensions 159 ft 6 in x 41 ft 8 in x 12 ft 10 in (Veselago)
            1,950 tons displacement (Kuznetsov)
Armament LD 28 x 24pdrs (short)
            FC & QD 16 x 6pdrs   362 men (1817)

Speshnyi class group 1. Larch and pine built. Arrived at Kronstadt from Arkhangel'sk in 9.1816. Cruised in the Baltic in 1817. To Cadiz for sale to Spain with Rear-Adm. Moller's squadron in Autumn of 1817. Crew of 362 returned by transports.

Legkii 44 St Petersburg
Constructor V. F. Stoke
Laid down 24.2.1815   *Launched* 16.8.1816
Dimensions 159 ft 6 in x 41 ft 8 in x 12 ft 10 in (Veselago)
            1,950 tons displacement (Kuznetsov)
Armament LD 28 x 24pdrs (short)
            FC & QD 16 x 6pdrs
            250 men (1818)

Speshnyi class group 1. To Cadiz for sale to Spain with Capt. Ratmanov's division in 1818. Crew of 250 returned by transports.

Patrikii 44 Arkhangel'sk
Constructor A. M. Kurochkin
Laid down 18.2.1818   *Launched* 31.7.1819
Dimensions 159 ft 2¾ in x 41 ft 6 in x 12 ft 8 in
Armament LD 28 x 24pdrs (short)
            FC & QD 16 x 6pdrs

Speshnyi class group 1. Launch attended by Alexander I. Sailed from Arkhangel'sk to Kronstadt in 1820. Cruised in the Baltic in 1823 and 1825. Cruised to Dogger Bank in 1826 with Adm. Crown's squadron. Broken up in 1827.

Merkurii 44 Arkhangel'sk
Constructor A. M. Kurochkin
Laid down 31.7.1819   *Launched* 31.5.1820

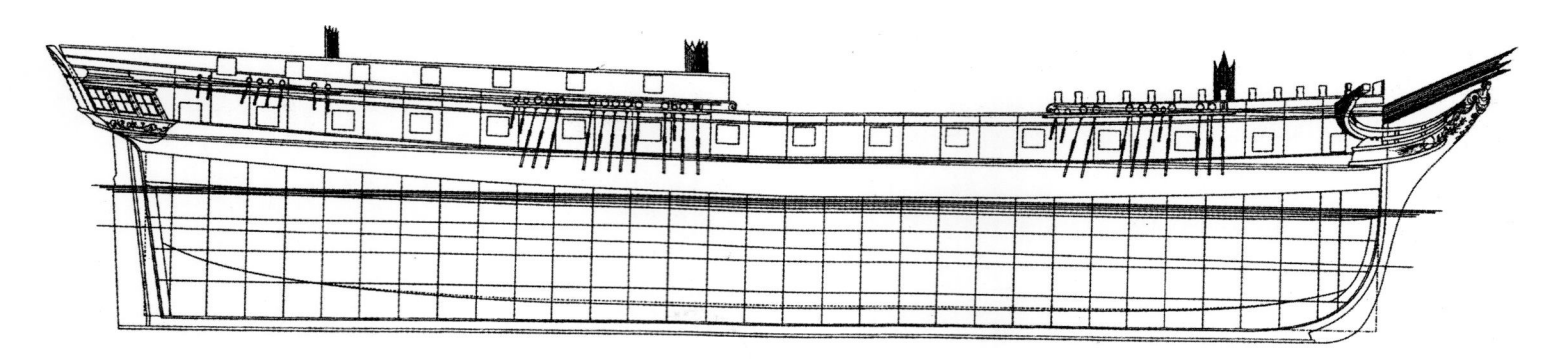

Speshnyi, 44, was completed at Arkhangel'sk in 1801 as the lead ship in what was almost certainly the largest and longest running class of frigates built anywhere during the age of sail – and one of the best. The presence of solid wooden barricades on the quarterdeck paralleled similar developments in the British navy at the time and was a reflection of the attempt to provide a degree of protection for both gun crews and officers exposed to the fire of carronades.

THE BALTIC FLEET 1801–24

The 44-gun Speshnyi *class frigate* Merkurii *1815 had a very short career in the Russian navy before being sold to Spain by a cash-starved Alexander I in 1818. A member of a highly regarded class of ships in the prime of her life, her allegedly poor condition on arrival at Cadiz created a diplomatic furore and much press controversy in Spain. Recent research indicates that the controversy may have been overblown and more the product of agitation by Spanish enemies of the monarchy than a reflection of her true condition. The truth of the matter may never be determined with certainty, but this painting of* Merkurii *does the* Speshnyi *class full justice. By A. K. Beggrov, 1879.*

Dimensions 159 ft 2¾ in x 41 ft 6 in x 12 ft 8 in
Armament LD 28 x 24pdrs (short)
            FC & QD 16 x 6pdrs

Speshnyi class group 1. Sailed from Arkhangel'sk to Kronshtadt in 1820. Cruised in the Baltic in 1823–4. Damaged and grounded in the Great Flood of 1824. Refloated in 7.1825. To Portsmouth and back to Kronshtadt with Adm. Seniavin's squadron in 1827. Cruised to Copenhagen in 1828. Broken up in 1830.

Provornyi 44/48 St Petersburg, Okhta
Constructor V. F. Stoke
Laid down 20.1.1820   *Launched* 21.10.1820

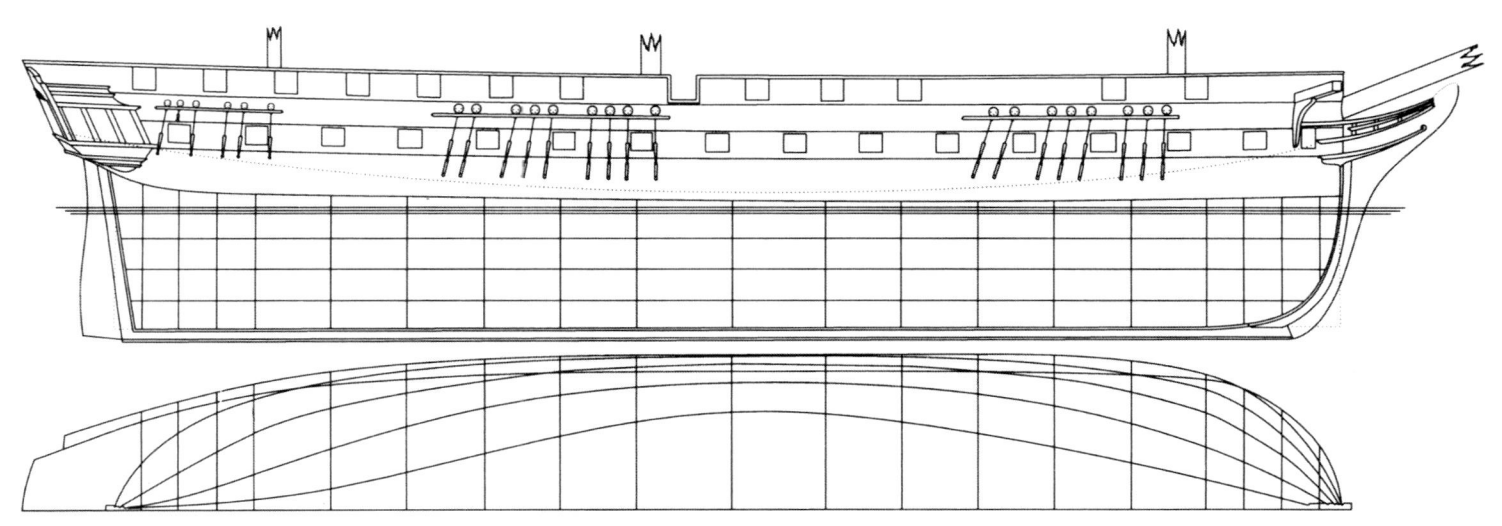

A comparison of the drawings of Merkurii *of 1815 with* Speshnyi *of 1800 reveals ships closely identical in proportions and basic lines, but visually dissimilar as a result of the newer ship's even more extensive use of solid barricades.*

Dimensions 159 ft 2¾ in x 41 ft 6 in x 12 ft 8 in
Armament Planned LD 28 x 24pdrs (short)
FC & QD 16 x 6pdrs
Actual 1827 LD 28 x 24pdrs (short)
FC & QD 2 x 8pdr (short), 18 x 6pdrs
(Sudostroenie 1974)

Speshnyi class group 1. Assigned an elite Guards crew in 1823–4. Cruised in the Atlantic in 1823. Cruised to Plymouth in 1824. Damaged by the Great Flood of 1824. Cruised to Dogger Bank in 1826. To Portsmouth with Adm. Seniavin's squadron in 1827 and to the Mediterranean with Rear-Adm. Geiden's squadron. Fought at Navarino on 20.10.1827 with casualties of 3 killed and 4 wounded. Returned to Kronshtadt in 1828. Broken up in 1831.

Vestovoi 44 Arkhangel'sk
Constructor A. M. Kurochkin
Laid down 1821 *Launched* 12.5.1822
Dimensions 159 ft 2¾ in x 41 ft 6 in x 12 ft 8 in
Armament LD 28 x 24pdrs (short)
FC & QD 16 x 6pdrs

Speshnyi class group 1. Sailed from Arkhangel'sk to Kronshtadt in 1822. Cruised to Iceland with Adm. Crown's squadron in 1824. Damaged during the Great Flood of 1824. Repaired in 1825. Cruised to Dogger Bank with Adm. Crown's squadron in 1826. Participated in the Imperial Review at Kronshtadt in 1827 and departed for the Mediterranean with Rear-Adm. Geiden's squadron. Grounded on 3.7.1827. Broken up by wave action on 6–7.7.1827 with no casualties.

Konstantin 44/46 Arkhangel'sk
Constructor A. M. Kurochkin
Laid down 18.7.1823 *Launched* 27.5.1824
Dimensions 159 ft 2¾ in x 41 ft 6 in x 12 ft 8 in
Armament Planned LD 28 x 24pdrs (short)
FC & QD 16/18 x 6pdrs
Actual 1827 LD 28 x 24pdrs (short)
FC & QD 18 x 8pdrs (short) 2 x 3pdrs
(Sudostroenie 1974)

Speshnyi class group 1. Sailed from Arkhangel'sk to Kronshtadt in 1826. To England with *Elena* carrying gold bullion in 1826. Fought at Navarino on 20.10.1827 without sustaining damage or casualties and providing a tow for HMS *Mosquito* after the battle. Cruised in the Arkhipelago in 1828. Blockaded the Dardanelles in 1829. Returned to Kronshtadt in 1830. Cruised in the Baltic in 1830. Fire watch ship at Kronshtadt Roads in 1832–5. Transferred to Sveaborg and hulked in 1837. Broken up in 1848.

Amfitrida class (7 ships)
These ships were designed as an improved *Venus* type. In service, they proved to be inferior to the *Speshnyi* class in both armament and sea keeping qualities. Five ships were laid down between 1808 and 1816, with the final pair being ordered in 1818 to replace two ships sold to Spain – the *Speshnyi* class *Legkii* and the *Amfitrida* class *Avtroil*. Only the name ship of the class saw actual combat at Copenhagen in 1813. Three were damaged beyond useful repair in the Great Flood of 1824 while a fourth, *Diana*, survived the flood to accompany Adm. Seniavin's squadron to England and back in 1827. She was the last of her class to go, being broken up in 1830.

Amfitrida 44 St Petersburg
Constructor I. V. Kurepanov
Laid down 11.10.1806 *Launched* 11.7.1808
Dimensions 151 ft x 38 ft 4 in x 18 ft 11 in
Armament LD 28 x 24pdrs (short)
FC & QD 16 x 6pdrs
350 men

Amfitrida class. At Kronshtadt Roads in 1809 as a guardship. To Toulon and back in 1810. Cruised in the Baltic in 1812, escorted merchant ships, convoyed Russian troops from Riga in company with British ships, and blockaded Danzig. Bombarded Danzig in 1813. Cruised in the Baltic in 1814 and 1819. Damaged during the Great Flood of 1824. Broken up in 1828.

Arkhipelag 44 St Petersburg
Constructors I. S. Razumov and I. V. Kurepanov
Laid down 28.1.1811 *Launched* 17.9.1811
Dimensions 151 ft 2 in x 38 ft 4 in x 18 ft 11 in
Armament LD 28 x 24pdrs (short)
FC & QD 16 x 6pdrs

Amfitidra class. To England with Rear-Adm. Korobka's squadron in 1812. Returned to Kronshtadt in 7.1814. Cruised to Rotterdam in 1815. Cruised in the Baltic in 1816. Damaged during the Great Flood of 1824. Broken up in 1828.

Avtroil 44 St Petersburg
Constructors I. S. Razumov and I. V. Kurepanov
Laid down 28.1.1811 *Launched* 17.9.1811
Dimensions 151 ft 2 in x 38 ft 4 in x 18 ft 11 in (Veselago)
1,342 tons displacement (bm?) (Kuznetsov)
Armament LD 28 x 24pdrs (short)
FC & QD 16 x 6pdrs

Amfitidra class. Pine built. Cruised to Copenhagen in 1812-13. Cruised in the Baltic in 1814 and 1816. Cruised to Cadiz with Rear-Adm. Moller's squadron and sold to Spain in 1817.

Argus 44 St Petersburg, Okhta
Constructor V. F. Stoke
Laid down 3.6.1812 *Launched* 26.8.1813
Dimensions 152 ft3 in x 38 ft 4 in x 18 ft 1 in
Armament LD 28 x 24pdrs (short)
FC & QD 16 x 6pdrs

Amfitidra class. Cruised to Rotterdam in 1815. Cruised in the Baltic in 1816. To France with Adm. Crown's squadron in 1817 to transport returning Russian troops to Kronshtadt. Heavily damaged during the Great Flood of 1824. Broken up in 1828.

Diana 44 Arkhangel'sk
Constructor A. M. Kurochkin
Laid down 12.7.1816 *Launched* 10.6.1818
Dimensions 151 ft 3 in x 38 ft 4 in x 18 ft 1 in
Armament LD 28 x 24pdrs (short)
FC & QD 16 x 6pdrs

Amfitidra class. Sailed from Arkhangel'sk to Kronshtadt in 1818. Cruised in the Baltic in 1821–3. Survived the Great Flood of 1824 after breaking away from her moorings. To England and back with Adm. Seniavin's squadron in 1827. Cruised in the Baltic in 1828–9. Broken up in 1830.

Avtroil 44 St Petersburg, Okhta
Constructor V. F. Stoke
Laid down 11.2.1818 *Launched* 1.7.1819
Dimensions 151 ft 3 in x 38 ft 4 in x 18 ft 1 in
Armament LD 28 x 24pdrs (short)
FC & QD 16 x 6pdrs

Amfitidra class. Replacement for the earlier *Avtroil* sold to Spain in 1817. Cruised in the Baltic in 1823. Converted to a floating magazine in 1827.

Legkii 44 St Petersburg, Okhta
Constructor V. F. Stoke
Laid down 3.12.1818 *Launched* 16.10.1819
Dimensions 151 ft 2 in x 38 ft 4 in x 18 ft 11 in
Armament LD 28 x 24pdrs (short)
  FC & QD 16 x 6pdrs

Amfitrida class. Cruised in the Baltic in 1822–3. Cruised to Iceland with Adm. Crown's squadron in 1824. Cruised in the Baltic in 1825–6. Reduced to a floating magazine in Kronshtadt in 1827.

Standard frigates (11 purpose-built 1801–24)

Medium-sized frigates of the sort that typified the standard eighteenth-century European frigate fell into disfavour in the Baltic fleet after 1800. Only 10 medium-sized ships entered service between 1803 and 1825 and preference was given to the construction of larger heavy frigates originally patterned on Swedish designs. These smaller frigates were initially armed with 24pdr short guns in compliance with the Establishment of 1805, but these heavier weapons were replaced by lighter and longer-ranged 12pdrs in those class members entering service after 1816. It may be that 24pdrs, even short guns of the Swedish type, overstressed the hulls of these ships in extended service. It is also conceivable that the lighter but longer ranged guns were chosen because of their greater suitability for employment outside of the narrow confines of the Baltic where combat tended to occur at shorter battle ranges. These were the last moderately sized frigates built for the Russians in the Baltic. In post-war service, they fulfilled much the same range of duties for the Russians as the generally similar *Leda* class fulfilled in the Royal Navy, that of undertaking routine cruising and patrol activities suited to their greater economy of operation, while larger, heavily armed frigates were reserved for operations with the main fleet.

Kildyuin 32 Arkhangel'sk?
Laid down 14.11.1796 *Launched* 19.5.1798
Converted 1803
Dimensions 135 ft x 35 ft x 14 ft 6 in
Armament LD 24 x 12pdrs
  FC & QD 8 x 6pdrs

Completed as a flute in 1798 and intended to function as an armed transport. Sailed as such from Arkhangel'sk to Kronshtadt in 1803. Converted into a frigate at Kronshtadt to accompany Vice-Adm. Seniavin's squadron to Corfu in 1803. Departed Kronshtadt for the Mediterranean in Vice-Adm. Seniavin's squadron on 10.9.1805. Operations in the Adriatic in 1806. Interred in the Tagus in 1807. Arrived at Portsmouth on 19.10.1808 in British custody. Sold in Great Britain in 1813. (See also under transports)

Legkii 38 Arkhangel'sk
Constructor G. Ignatyev
Laid down 18.10.1800 *Launched* 7.5.1803
Dimensions 145 ft (pp) x 141 ft 8 in (lgd) x 40 ft x 13 ft 6 in
Armament LD 26 x 24pdrs (short frigate guns)
  FC & QD 10 x 6pdrs 280 men

Sailed from Arkhangel'sk to Kronshtadt in 7–9.1803. Cruised in the Baltic in 1804 and visited by Alexander I. Landed troops on the German coast with Adm. Thate's squadron in 1805. Departed for the Mediterranean with Commodore Ignatyev's squadron. In 1806 Operated in the Mediterranean in 1806–7. Impounded in Trieste with Commodore Saltanov's squadron in 1808. Ceded to France in 1809.

Sveaborg 36 St Petersburg
Constructor I. V. Kurepanov
Laid down 9.1.1808 *Launched* 18.9.1809
Dimensions 150 ft x 38 ft 8 in x 16 ft 8 in
Armament LD 26 x 24pdrs (short)
  FC & QD 10 x 6pdrs
  250 men

Designed as a flagship. Cruised off Krasnaia Gorka in 1810. Transported troops from Sveaborg to Revel' in 1812, and then proceeded to England as Adm. Thate's flagship. Carried Russian Guards from Cherbourg to Kronshtadt under Vice-Adm. Crown in 1814. Cruised in the Gulf of Finland in 1818–20. Damaged in the Great Flood of 1824. Broken up in 1828.

Provornyi class (8 ships)

Although smaller than contemporary British *Leda* class 36-gun 18pdr frigates, the *Provornyi*s were more heavily armed in their original incarnation, having been designed around short-barrelled 24pdr main deck guns in compliance with the specifications of the Establishment of 1805. The first three ships of the class laid down in the last year of the Napoleonic Wars were completed with 24pdrs, but the five postwar units all completed with long barreled 12pdrs. A generally similar unit built for the Black Sea fleet, the ill-fated *Rafail*, also carried short-barrelled 24pdrs although this heavy armament did not prevent her capture by greatly superior Turkish forces in 1829.

The class led active and varied service lives. The first two were among the Russian frigates sold to Spain in 1818. Four were caught up in the Great Flood of 1824 and only two were later returned to active service, one as a transport. One ship, *Kreiser*, circumnavigated the globe between 1822 and 1825, a signal achievement for a Russian frigate. *Kastor* distinguished herself at Navarino in 1827, participating in the capture of a Turkish corvette. All were gone by 1831.

Provornyi 36 Arkhangel'sk
Constructor A. M. Kurochkin
Laid down 8.11.1815 *Launched* 26.5.1816
Dimensions 144 ft 4 in x 38 ft x 19 ft 8 in (Veselago)
  1,294 tons displacement (Kuznetsov)
Armament LD 26 x 24pdrs (short)
  FC & QD 10 x 6pdrs
  crew 220 men (1818)

Provornyi class (8 ships). Sailed from Arkhangel'sk to Kronshtadt in 1816. Cruised to Cadiz in 1817. Sold to Spain in 1818. Crew of 220 men returned aboard ship of the line *Iupiter*.

Pospeshnyi 36/44 St Petersburg
Constructor V. F. Stoke
Laid down 22.9.1815 *Launched* 16.8.1816
Dimensions 144 ft 4 in x 38 ft x 19 ft 8 in (Veselago)
  1,294 tons displacement (Kuznetsov)
Armament LD 28 x 24pdrs (short)
  FC & QD 16 x 6pdrs
  crew 225 men (1818)

Provornyi class (8 ships). To Cadiz in 1818 for sale to Spain. Crew of 225 returned by ship of the line *Iupiter*.

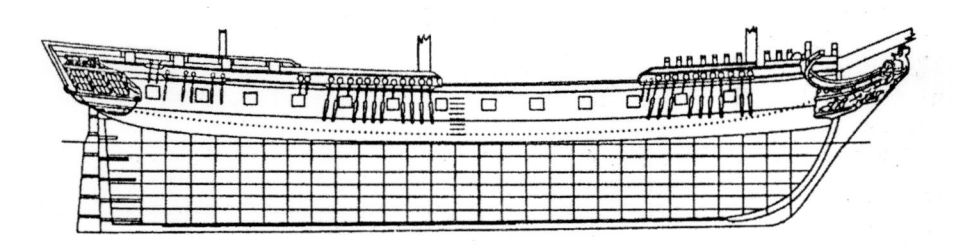

Although not related in any way to Great Britain's Leda *class, the 36-gun frigates of the* Provornyi *class occupied a similar niche in the Russian navy – that of a moderately sized post-war frigate capable of being built in quantity and serving as a low profile maid-of-all-work. This is* Kastor *of 1823, whose claim to fame was in fighting at Navarino and assisting in the capture of a Turkish corvette a year later.*

Gektor 36 St Petersburg, Okhta
Constructor V. F. Stoke
Laid down 7.10.1816   *Launched* 1.9.1817
Dimensions 144 ft 4 in x 38 ft x 19 ft 8 in
  1,294 tons displacement
Armament LD 26 x 24pdrs (short)
  FC & QD 10 x 6pdrs
Provornyi class (8 ships). Visited England France, and Prussia in 1819. Cruised in the Baltic in 1821–3. Damaged during the Great Flood of 1824. Broken up in 1828.

Kreiser 36 Arkhangel'sk
Constructor A. M. Kurochkin
Laid down 11.6.1820   *Launched* 18.5.1821
Dimensions 144 ft 4 in x 38 ft x 19 ft 8 in
  1,294 tons displacement
Armament LD 26 x 12pdrs
  FC & QD 10 x 6pdrs
Provornyi class (8 ships). Sailed from Arkhangel'sk to Kronshtadt in 1821. Departed Russia to circumnavigate the globe in company with the transport *Ladoga* in 1822. Travelled to Rio de Janeiro and arrived at Novo-Arkhangel'sk (Russian North America) on 3.9.1823 and visited San Francisco. Departed for Russia in 10.1824 and arrived at Kronshtadt on 5.8.1825. Cruised to Portsmouth with Adm. Seniavin's squadron in 1827 and returned to Kronshtadt. Cruised in the Baltic in 1828. Fire watch ship at Kronshtadt in 1829–31. Converted to a floating magazine in 1831.

Aleksandr Nevskii (*Vind-Khund*) 36 St Petersburg, Okhta
Constructor V. F. Stoke
Laid down ?   *Launched* 11.8.1821
Dimensions 144 ft 4 in x 38 ft x 19 ft 8 in
  1,294 tons displacement
Armament LD 26 x 12pdrs
  FC & QD 10 x 6pdrs
Provornyi class (8 ships). Cruised in the Baltic in 1824. Damaged and grounded in the Great Flood of 1824. In 1825, was refloated, repaired as a transport, and renamed *Vind-Khund*, retaining her full armament. Transported building materials from Kronshtadt to Arkhangel'sk and returned with cargo from Arkhangel'sk in 1826. Carried cargo to Sveaborg in 1828. Broken up in 1829. (See also under Baltic converted transports)

Kastor 34/36 St Petersburg, Okhta
Constructor V. F. Stoke
Laid down 24.2.1822   *Launched* 22.5.1823
Dimensions 144 ft 4 in x 38 ft x 19 ft 8 in
  1,294 tons displacement
Armament Designed LD 26 x 12pdrs
  FC & QD 10 x 6pdrs
  Actual 1827 LD 24 x 12pdrs
  FC & QD 19 6pdrs (Sudostroenie 1974)

Provornyi class (8 ships). Grounded during the Great Flood of 7.11.1824 and later refloated. Cruised to Dogger Bank in 1826. To the Mediterranean in 1827. Fought at Navarino on 20.10.1827. Captured a Turkish corvette on 24.4.1828 in company with *Iezekiil* (74). Repaired at Malta. Returned to Kronshtadt on 16.7.1829. Broken up in 1830.

Vind-Khund 36 Arkhangel'sk
Constructor Kurochkin
Laid down 1822   *Launched* 05.1823
Dimensions 144 ft 4 in x 38 ft x 19 ft 8 in
  1,294 tons displacement
Armament LD 26 x 12pdrs
  FC & QD 10 x 6pdrs
Provornyi class (8 ships). Sailed from Arkhangel'sk to Kronshtadt in 1823. Heavily damaged and grounded during the Great Flood of 1824. Stricken in 1826. Broken up in 1828.

Elena 36 Arkhangel'sk
Constructor A. M. Kurochkin
Laid down 5.7.1824   *Launched* 21.5.1825
Dimensions 144 ft 4 in x 38 ft x 19 ft 8 in
  1,294 tons displacement
Armament LD 26 x 12pdrs
  FC & QD 10 x 6pdrs, 3 x 3pdrs, 2 x 8pdr mortars
  (Sudostroenie 1974)
Provornyi class (8 ships). Sailed from Arkhangel'sk to Kronshtadt in 1825. To England carrying gold bullion in company with *Konstantin* (44) in the summer of 1826. Training cruise in the Mediterranean under the command of Commodore Bellinsgauzen in 1826–7. Fought at Navarino as signal repeater for the flagship *Azov* on 20.10.1827, suffering casualties of 5 wounded and setting a Turkish brig afire. In company with HMS *Warspite*, brought Count Kapodistria to serve as Greece's first president in 1829. Stationed in Greece in 1829. Returned to Kronshtadt in 1830. Converted into a transport retaining her full armament in 1831. Carried cargo in the Gulf of Finland in 1832–5. Hulked at Revel' in 1835. (See also under Baltic converted transports)

Small frigates/sloops (4 purpose-built 1801–24)
These ships of intermediate dimensions were variously rated as either small frigates or sloops. In compliance with the establishment of 1805, they are all believed to have to have normally carried 24pdr carronades.

Kastor class (2 ships)
Kastor 36 Lodeynoe Pole
Constructor G. S. Isakov
Laid down ?   *Launched* 1807
Dimensions 130 ft x 32 ft 8 in x 17 ft
Armament ?
  232 men
Kastor class. Sometimes classed as a sloop. Sailed to Kronshtadt in 1807. Cruised in the Baltic in 1808. Stationed as a guardship in

THE BALTIC FLEET 1801–24

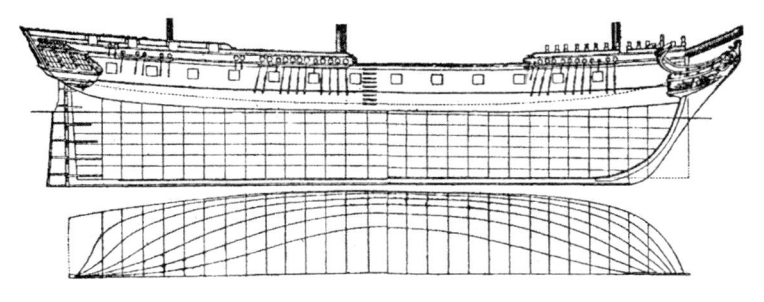

In the Royal Navy a 36-gun frigate was hardly a rarity in 1807; but not so with the Russian navy in either the Baltic or the Black Sea. This is Kastor (36) of 1807, built at Lodeynoe Pole for the Baltic fleet. She is a fine example of her type in a fleet given over in the main to much larger and heavier frigate designs. In some sources, she is classed as a sloop, an indication of then-current Russian thinking on the subject of appropriate frigate size and an indignity that would never have been conferred on a British frigate of similar size.

Kronshtadt Roads in 1809. Carried French ambassador Lauriston to Pilau and the Russian ambassador to England in 1812. Joined Vice-Adm. Crown's squadron at Gothenburg, and deployed to England in 1812. Returned to Kronshtadt in 1813. Broken up in 1817.

Poluks 36 Lodeynoe Pole
Constructor G. S. Isakov
Laid down ?   *Launched* 1807
Dimensions 130 ft x 32 ft 8 in x 17 ft
Armament ?
                232 men

Kastor class. Sometimes classed as a sloop. Sailed to Kronshtadt in 1807. Cruised in the Baltic, and joined Adm. Khanykov's squadron in 1808. Took the damaged *Vsevolod* (74) in tow. Stayed at Rogervik until 20.9.1808 and then returned to Kronshtadt. Cruised in the Gulf of Finland in 1809. Grounded off Urregrunt after striking an underwater rock on 25.10.1809. Refloated only to be driven against a second rock. 140 men including the captain were lost and 94 saved.

Poluks 32 St Petersburg
Constructor V. F. Stoke
Laid down 13.7.1811   *Launched* 4.6.1812
Dimensions 121 ft x 33 ft8 in x 10 ft
Armament ?

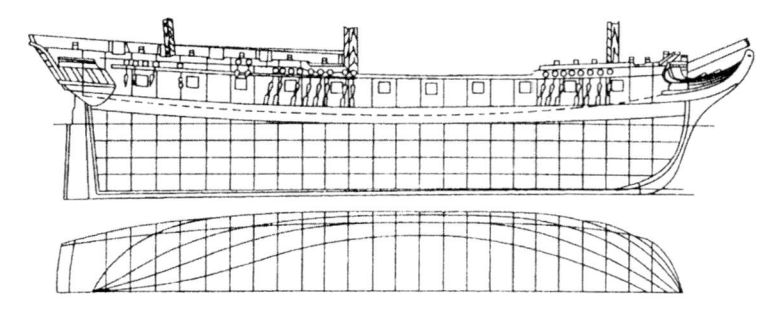

Poluks (32) built to replace the 36-gun Poluks of 1807 after she was wrecked in 1809. Built in 1812, the 32-gun Poluks was both smaller and more lightly armed. She joined the Russian battle fleet during its exile to Great Britain in 1812–14, and led an otherwise uneventful life until caught up in and destroyed by the Great Flood of 1824.

Sometimes rated as a sloop. Cruised in the Baltic in 1812. To England with the Russian squadron in 1813 and involved in blockading the French coast. Cruised in the North Sea in 1814 and returned to Kronshtadt. Carried the Russian ambassador to Copenhagen in 1817. Fire watch ship at Kronshtadt in 1818–20. Damaged in the Great Flood of 1824.

Pomona 24 Arkhangel'sk
Constructor A. M. Kurochkin
Laid down 12.7.1816   *Launched* 13.8.1817
Dimensions 106'8 in x 28 ft 9½ in x 13 ft 10 in
Armament 18 x 24pdrs (short), 6 x 6pdrs

Small frigate. Sailed from Arkhangel'sk to Kronshtadt in 1818. Cruised in the Baltic in 1820–2. Fire watch ship at Revel' in 1823–8. Broken up in 1829.

Small training frigates (6 purpose-built 1801–24)

The Russians differed from Western European navies, particularly Great Britain, in consistently designing and building small ship rigged vessels specifically programmed for training purposes. They were administratively attached to the Naval Cadet Corps and did not operate as combat ships during war time. The impulse for their development probably relates to Russia's lack of a large maritime population and tradition and consequent need for structured training of young officers.

Neva 24/28 St Petersburg
Constructors M. Sarychev and I. V. Kurepanov
Laid down 9.10.1800   *Launched* 18.7.1805
Dimensions 88 ft x 22 ft x 9 ft 8 in
                330 tons
Armament ?
                48 crewmen and 95 cadets

This ship was officially listed as a 'small' frigate. She was almost certainly a purpose-built training frigate. Cruised in the Gulf of Finland in 1805–11. Repaired in 1812. Cruised in the Gulf of Finland in 1813–20. Broken up in 1829.

Rossiia class (2 ships)

Rossiia (renamed *Petergof*) 20 St Petersburg
Constructor A. K. Kaverznev
Laid down 20.12.1813   *Launched* 23.6.1814
Dimensions 100 ft x 25 ft 11 in x 7 ft 10 in
Armament 14 x 6pdrs, 6 x ½pdr falconets

Rossiia class. Purpose-built training frigate. Cruised in the Baltic in 1816–17. Renamed *Petergof* in 1827 and used by Nikolai I as the royal yacht at the Imperial Review of ships leaving for the Mediterranean. Fire watch ship in the mouth of the Neva in 1828–30. Floating magazine at Okhta in 1831.

Neva 20 St Petersburg
Constructor V. F. Stoke
Laid down 30.11.1815   *Launched* 18.5.1816
Dimensions 100 ft x 25 ft 11 in x 7 ft 10 in
Armament 14 x 6pdrs 6 x ½pdr falconets

Rossiia class. Purpose-built training frigate. Cruised in the Gulf of Finland in 1816–26. Broken up in 1830.

Malyi class group 1 (3 ships)

Six training frigates were built to a common design. *Malyi* is Russian for small (i.e. small frigate). Three fall into this period and the final trio may be found in the next section.

Uraniia 24 St Petersburg, Okhta
Constructor ?
Laid down ?   *Launched* 1820
Dimensions 100 ft 10 in (pp) x 26 ft 9 in (inside plank) x 10 ft 2 in
Armament 18 x 24pdrs (short), 6 x 6pdrs
Malyi class (6 ships). Purpose-built training frigate. Cruised annually in the Gulf of Finland with naval cadets in 1821–33. Repaired in 1834. Cruised in the Baltic in 1835. Participated in the Imperial Review of 1836. Cruised in the Baltic in 1836–7. Broken up in 1838.

Pomoshchnyi 24 Arkhangel'sk
Constructor A. M. Kurochkin
Laid down 11.6.1819   *Launched* 18.5.1821
Dimensions 100 ft 10 in (pp) x 26 ft 9 in (inside plank) x 10 ft 2 in
Armament 18 x 24pdrs (short), 6 x 6pdrs
Malyi class (6 ships). Purpose-built training frigate. Sailed from Arkhangel'sk to Kronshtadt in 1821. Cruised in the Baltic in 1823–5. Grounded during the Great Flood of 1824. Cruised with Adm. Crown's squadron to Dogger Bank in 1826. Fire watch ship at Kronshtadt in 1827–8. Grounded and wrecked off Odensholm on 22.5.1829.

Rossiia 24 St Petersburg, Okhta
Constructor V. F. Stoke
Laid down 24.2.1824   *Launched* 2.5.1825
Dimensions 100 ft 10 in (pp) x 26 ft 10 in x 9 ft 2 in
Armament 18 x 24pdrs (short), 6 x 6pdrs
Malyi class (6 ships). Purpose-built training frigate. Annual cruises in the Gulf of Finland with naval cadets in 1826–34. Repaired in 1834. Broken up in 1838.

Rowing frigates (6 purpose-built 1801–24)

When hostilities again broke out with Sweden in 1808, a new group of rowing frigates was completed. This was done in the expectation of a repeat of the kind of inshore warfare that had characterized the 1788–90 conflict. As it was, the type had clearly outlived its time and little active use was made of the completed vessels, although two did participate in the bombardment of Danzig. For whatever reason, a sixth class member was laid down in 1821 and had a brief career training naval cadets.

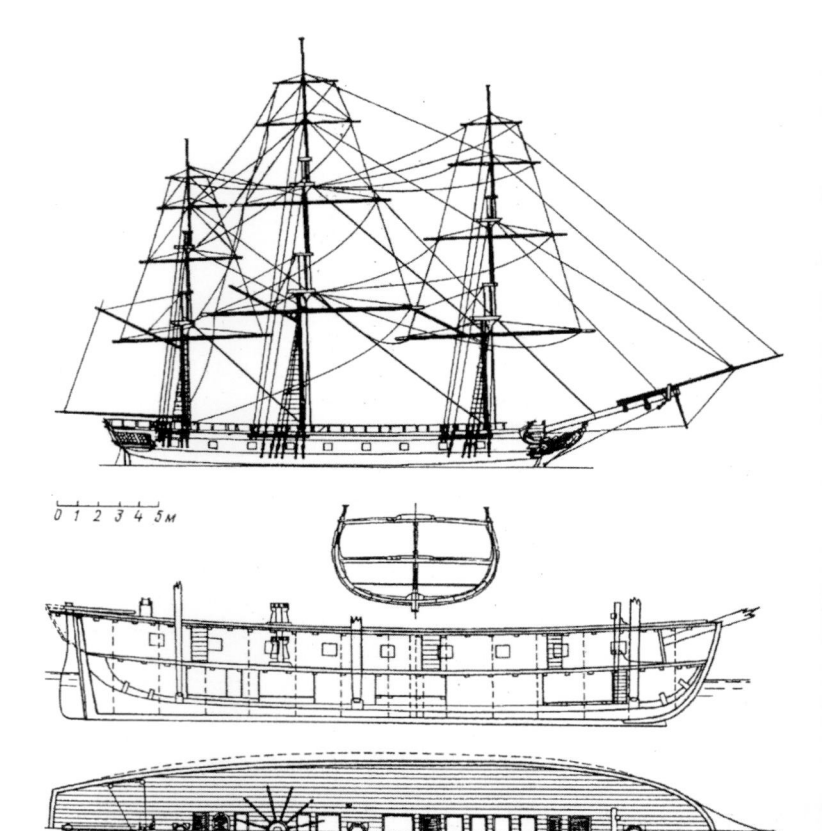

Elegant and graceful in its simplicity, these drawings displaying the rigging and internal layout of the training ship Uraniia *of 1820 should be compared to the builder's model*

Bodryi class (6 ships)

This class was larger and more heavily armed than the preceeding *Aleksandr* class, having been patterned after the captured Swedish *Hjalmar* and *Stybjorn*. *Bodryi* and *Torneo* took part in the bombardment of Danzig in 1812–13, but the others led uneventful lives.

The training frigate Uraniia *(24) of 1820, on display at St Petersburg. These graceful and beautiful little ships were a uniquely Russian concept, intended solely for the training of cadets and never for actual combat.* Uraniia *was the work of Russia's most prolific constructor, V. F. Stoke. During the long course of his career, he built a total of 540 vessels, all at the Okhta Yard.*

Bodryi 32 St Petersburg
Constructor A. I. Melikhov
Laid down 1808   *Launched* 7.1808
Dimensions 144 ft x 35 ft 9 in x 8 ft 6 in
Armament LD 24 x 36pdrs
            FC & QD 2 x 12pdrs, 6 smaller
Bodryi class (6 ships). Rowing frigate. Stationed in Kronshtadt Roads in 1809–10. Transferred to Rochensalm in 1812. Transferred to Sveaborg and participated in the bombardment of Danzig in 1813. Disabled by the Great Flood of 7.11.1824. Broken up in 1829.

Neva 32 St Petersburg
Constructor A. I. Melikhov
Laid down 1808   *Launched* 7.1808
Dimensions 144 ft x 35 ft 9 in x 8 ft 6 in
Armament LD 24 x 36pdrs
            FC & QD 2 x 12pdrs, 6 smaller
Bodryi class (6 ships). Rowing frigate. Stationed in Kronshtadt Roads in 1809. Stationed off Petergof in 1810. Stationed in Kronshtadt Roads and transferred to Rochensalm in 1812. Returned to Kronshtadt in 1813. Fire watch ship in Kronshtadt Roads in 1815–17. Broken up in 1829.

Sveaborg 32 St Petersburg
Constructor A. I. Melikhov
Laid down 1808   *Launched* 7.1808
Dimensions 144 ft x 35 ft 9 in x 8 ft 6 in
Armament LD 24 x 36pdrs
            FC & QD 2 x 12pdrs, 6 smaller
Bodryi class (6 ships). Rowing frigate. Stationed in Kronshtadt Roads in 1809–10. To Sveaborg and back to Kronshtadt in 1812. Broken up in 1822.

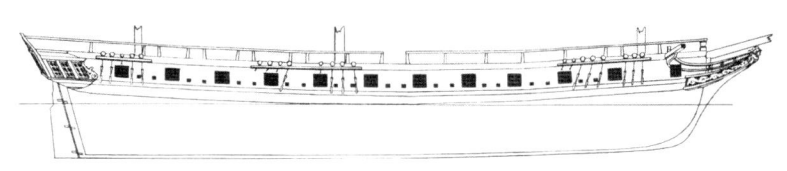

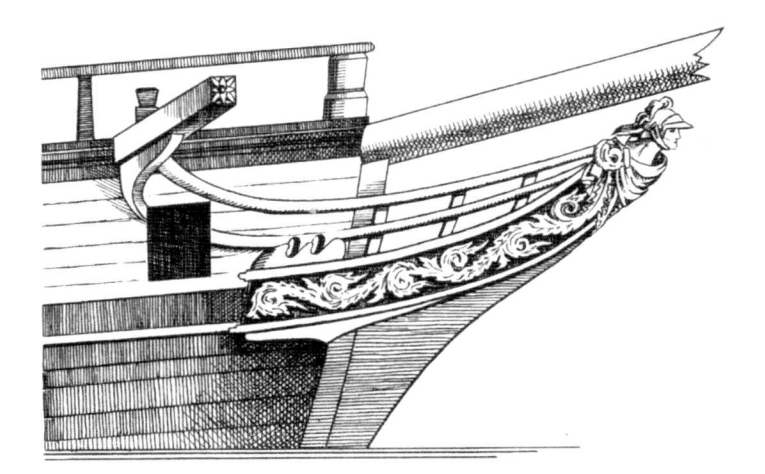

Petergof 32 St Petersburg
Constructor A. I. Melikhov
Laid down 1808   *Launched* 7.1808
Dimensions 144 ft x 35 ft 9 in x 8 ft 6 in
Armament LD 24 x 36pdrs
            FC & QD 2 12pdrs, 6 smaller
Bodryi class (6 ships). Rowing frigate. Stationed in Kronshtadt Roads in 1809–12. Transferred to Rochensalm in 1812. Returned to Kronshtadt in 1813. Broken up in 1822.

Torneo 32 St Petersburg
Constructor I. V. Kurepanov
Laid down 9.1.1808   *Launched* 13.9.1808
Dimensions 144 ft x 35 ft 9 in x 8 ft 6 in
Armament LD 24 x 36pdrs
            FC & QD 2 12pdrs, 6 smaller
Bodryi class (6 ships). Rowing frigate. Stationed in Kronshtadt Roads in 1810. To Riga and the bombardment of Danzig in 1812–13 as flag to Rear-Adm. von Moller. To Sveaborg in 1814. Transferred to Kronshtadt in 1815. Fire watch ship at Revel' in 1817–21. Transferred to Kronshtadt in 1821. Broken up in 1824.

Mirnyi 32 St Petersburg
Constructor I. V. Kurepanov
Laid down 28.8.1821   *Launched* 12.7.1823
Dimensions 144 ft x 35 ft 9 in x 8 ft 6 in
Armament LD 24 x 36pdrs
            FC & QD 2 x 12pdrs, 6 smaller
Bodryi class (6 ships). Rowing frigate. Cruised in the Baltic in 1826. Cruised in the Baltic with naval cadets in 1829. Fire watch ship in the mouth of the Neva in 1831–4. Broken up after 1834

Baltic sloops (16 purpose-built/3 converted 1801–24)

In the Russian navy corvettes and sloops were distinctly different types. Corvettes (the name was derived from the French) were purpose-built warships, actually small frigates, with frigate rig, very fast, and employed as scouts, avisos and for cruising operations.

Although the name 'sloop' was taken from the English, Russian sloops differed from British sloops in design and employment. As was the case with corvettes, they were used as needed as scouts, avisos and patrol vessels; but they had smaller length-to-breadth ratios than corvettes, more spacious holds and were more frequently employed as armed store ships for transporting supplies than as combat vessels.

Russian sloops were best suited for long-range voyages, hydrographic surveys, circumnavigations, etc.

Sloops were not popular in the Black Sea fleet as they could not pass through the Turkish-controlled Bosporus and Dardanelles and so could not be used for long voyages in the manner customary for the Baltic sloops. They were similarly excluded from the Caspian flotilla.

Employed as needed in combat roles during the Napoleonic Wars, the sloop designation came to be entirely reserved after 1815 for self-contained, ship-rigged vessels specifically intended for survey, exploration, and circumnavigation work. Sixteen purpose-built and three purchased sloops were employed by the Baltic fleet in the first quarter of the nineteenth century.

A side profile and detail of the bow of Torneo *(32) of 1808, one of the final six rowing frigates built by Russia and inspired by two captured Swedish ships. Larger and more heavily armed than their 1790 predecessors, they were known as Gemams from the Swedish hemmema, a special type of Swedish inshore warship designed by Frederik af Chapman.*

Purpose-built

Shpitsbergen 32 Arkhangel'sk, Solombala
Constructor M. Sarychev
Laid down 16.7.1804   *Launched* 17.6.1805
Dimensions 110 ft x 30 ft x 14 ft (Veselago)
Armament ?

Purpose-built sloop of considerable size. Sailed from Arkhangel'sk to Kronshtadt in 1805. To the Mediterranean with Commodore Ignatyev's squadron in 1806. Joined Vice-Adm. Seniavin's squadron in 1807. Departed Corfu for Russia with Vice-Adm. Seniavin's squadron on 19.9.1807 after the signing of the Peace of Tilsit. Damaged and forced to put at Vigo and then Portello. Sold at Vigo for 10,000 Spanish pesos on 5.7.1812.

Kola class (2 ships)

Kola 26 Arkhangel'sk, Solombala
Constructor ?
Laid down 16.9.1805   *Launched* 23.6.1806
Dimensions ?
Armament ?

Kola class. Purpose-built sloop. Sailed from Arkhangel'sk to Kronshtadt in 1807. Transferred to Sveaborg as a fire watch ship in 1808–10. Cruised in the Baltic in 1810–12. Transported naval personnel to Sveaborg in 1812. Returned to Kronshtadt in 1813. Transported equipment for newly completed warships to Arkhangel'sk in 1814. Returned to Kronshtadt in 1815. Cruised in the Baltic in 1816–19. Broken up after 1820.

Solombal 26 Arkhangel'sk, Solombala
Constructor ?
Laid down 16.9.1805   *Launched* 23.6.1806
Dimensions ?
Armament ?

Kola class. Purpose-built sloop. Sailed from Arkhangel'sk to Kronshtadt in 1807. Stationed in Kronshtadt Roads in 1808. Transferred to Sveaborg as a fire watch ship in 1809–10. Carried cargo to Sveaborg in 1812. Transferred to Kronshtadt in 1813. Cruised in the Baltic in 1814–15. Cruised to Danzig in 1816. Cruised in the Baltic in 1817–19. Broken up in 1822.

Piram class (3 ships)

Piram 18 Lodeynoe Pole
Constructor V. F. Budantsev
Laid down ?   *Launched* 23.6.1806
Dimensions approx. 103 ft x 30 ft x 10 ft
31.3 m x 9.1 m x 3.1 m (Chernyshev)
Armament ?

Piram class. Purpose-built sloop. Sailed from Arkhangel'sk to Kronshtadt in 1806. Transferred to Arkhangel'sk in 1807. Cruised in the White Sea in 1808–9. Fire watch ship at Arkhangel'sk in 1812–15. Broken up at Arkhangel'sk in 1826.

Tiz'ba 18 Lodeynoe Pole
Constructor V. F. Budantsev
Laid down ?   *Launched* 1806
Dimensions 102 ft 6 in x 30 ft x 10 ft 3 in (Veselago)
Armament ?

Piram class. Purpose-built sloop. Sailed from Arkhangel'sk to Kronshtadt in 1806. Cruised off Sveaborg in 1808. Stationed in Kronshtadt Roads with the defence division and then transferred to the rowing flotilla at Abo in 1809. Fire watch ship at Sveaborg in 1810–16. Broken up at Sveaborg in 1820.

Edinorog 18 Lodeynoe Pole
Constructor V. F. Budantsev
Laid down ?   *Launched* 1806
Dimensions approx. 103 ft x 30 ft x 10 ft
31.3 m x 9.1 m x 3.1 m (Chernyshev)
Armament ?

Piram class. Purpose-built sloop. Sailed from Arkhangel'sk to Kronshtadt in 1806. Cruised in the Baltic in 1808. Transferred to the rowing flotilla at Abo in 1809. Escorted merchant vessels in 1810. Carried cargo in 1811. Grounded and destroyed by fire on 6.9.1812 while en route to assist in the siege of Danzig.

Lizeta 16 Lodeynoe Pole
Constructor V. F. Budantsev
Laid down ?   *Launched* 1806
Dimensions 92 ft 10 in x 27 ft 11 in x 9 ft 9 in (Veselago)
Armament ?

Purpose-built sloop. Sailed from Arkhangel'sk to Kronshtadt in 1806. Cruised in the Baltic in 1807. Cruised with Adm. Khnaykov's squadron in 1808. Cruised in the Baltic in 1809. Training duties at Kronshtadt and transferred to Sveaborg in 1710. Cruised between Riga and Revel' in 1812. Participated in the bombardment of Danzig in 1813. Broken up in 1815.

Volkhov 16 Lodeynoe Pole
Constructor V. F. Budantsev
Laid down ?   *Launched* 1806
Dimensions 92 ft 6 in x 21 ft x 9 ft (Veselago)
Armament ?

Purpose-built sloop. Sailed from Arkhangel'sk to Kronshtadt in 1806. Cruised in the Baltic in 1807. Cruised with Adm. Khnaykov's squadron in 1808. Stationed in Kronshtadt Roads to protect Kotlin in 1809 and then transferred to the rowing flotilla at Abo. Carried cargo in 1811. Operated off Danzig in 1812. Blockaded Danzig in 1813. Broken up in 1815.

Svir' 16 Lodeynoe Pole
Constructor V. F. Budantsev
Laid down ?   *Launched* 1806
Dimensions 88 ft x 25 ft x 12 ft (Veselago)
Armament ?

Sailed from Arkhangel'sk to Kronshtadt in 1806. Cruised in the Baltic in 1807. Cruised in the Baltic and transferred to Sveaborg in 1808. Transferred to the rowing flotilla at Abo in 1809. Transferred to Kronshtadt in 1810. Carried cargo in 1811. Evacuated 238,000 Roubles in copper coins from Riga to Kronshtadt during the approach of Napoleon's Great Army in 1812. Bombarded Danzig in 1813. Fire watch ship at Riga in 1814–17. Hydrographic survey work in 1820–4. Grounded and wrecked off Nerva Island on 6.10.1824. Crew saved.

Kamchatka class (3 ships)

Three ships built for long range exploration were laid down and completed after the Napoleonic Wars. All were built at Okhta and designed by V. F. Stoke. They were highly regarded for their excellent sea keeping qualities.

Kamchatka 28 St Petersburg, Okhta
Constructor V. F. Stoke
Laid down 17.10.1816   *Launched* 17.5.1817
Dimensions 130 ft x 32 ft 8 in x 17 ft (Veselago)
1,000 tons displacement
Armament 16 cannon, 12 carronades

Kamchatka class. Purpose-built sloop. On 26.8.1817, departed Kronshtadt for the Far East via Rio de Janeiro and Callao. Arrived at Novo Arkhangel'sk, Alaska on 28.7.1818. On 19.8.1818, departed Novo Arkhangel'sk for Russia via Guam, Manila, and St Helena. Arrived at Kronshtadt on 5.9.1819. Employed as a transport from 1822 and as a cargo ship in 1822–4. Grounded and damaged in the Great Flood of 7.11.1824. Fire watch ship at Kronshtadt in 1828.

Vostok 28 St Petersburg, Okhta
Constructor V. F. Stoke
Laid down 31.12.1817 *Launched* 4.7.1818
Dimensions approx. 130 ft x 33 ft x 14 ft
    39.7 m x 10 m x 5.2 m x 4.4 m (Chernyshev)
    1,000 tons displacement
Armament 16 cannon, 12 carronades
Kamchatka class. Purpose-built sloop. Departed Kronshtadt in company with the sloop *Mirnyi* on 3.7.1819 bound for the Antarctic by way of Rio de Janeiro. Surveyed the Southern Sandwich Islands, Tuamoto, the Fijis and numerous smaller islands, becoming the first ship on record to sight the Antarctic mainland. Returned to Kronshtadt on 24.7.1821. Grounded and damaged during the Great Flood of 7.11.1824. Broken up in 1828.

Otkrytie 18/28 St Petersburg, Okhta
Constructor V. F. Stoke
Laid down 1817 *Launched* 1.5.1818
Dimensions approx. 130 ft x 33 ft x 14 ft
    39.7 m x 10 m x 5.2 m x 4.4 m (Chernyshev)
    1,000 tons displacement
Armament 16 cannon, 12 carronades
Kamchatka class. Purpose-built sloop. In company with the sloop *Blagonamerennyi*, left Kronshtadt on 3.7.1817 seeking a northern passage from the Pacific to the Atlantic. Arrived at Kamchatka in 6.1820. Achieved the northernmost penetration of the Arctic to date (71° 6') until turned back by massive ice floes. Proceeded south to St Lawrence Island, Novo Arkhangel'sk and San Francisco. Attempted a second time to find a northern passage, reaching 70° 40' and forced to return to Kronshtadt via Rio de Janeiro on 1.8.1822. Fire watch ship at Sveaborg in 1823–6. Cruised in the Baltic in 1827. Broken up after 1828.

Ladoga ? Lodeynoe Pole
Constructor Y. A. Kolodkin

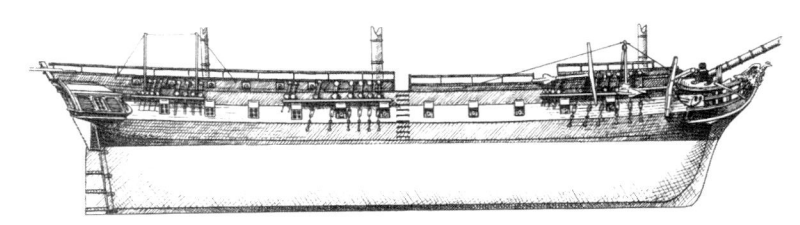

A drawing of the purpose-built Baltic sloop Vostok *of 1818. Comparing this depiction to those of the Black Sea corvettes* Menelai *and* Andromakha *should make clear the differences between Russian sloops and corvettes, with the high-sided* Vostok *having been designed for carrying capacity and seaworthiness, while the corvettes were given more limited freeboard emphasizing speed at the expense of range and robustness.* Vostok *and her consort* Mirnyi *achieved fame by completing a two year circumnavigation between 1819 and 1821 and making the first recorded sighting of the Antarctic mainland.*

Laid down 8.2.1819 *Launched* 8.6.1820
Dimensions ?
Armament ?
Purpose-built sloop. Sailed to St Petersburg in 1821. Departed Kronshtadt on 17.8.1822 in company with the frigate *Kreiser* for the Far East. Visited Tahiti, Petropavlovsk, Novo Arkhangel'sk and San Francisco. Departed San Francisco in company with the sloop *Apollon* on 12.1.1824. Arrived at Kronshtadt on 13.10.1824. Damaged during the Great Flood of 7.11.1824. Broken up in 1828.

Apollon ? St Petersburg, Okhta
Constructor V. F. Stoke
Laid down 21.12.1820 *Launched* 7.5.1821
Dimensions ?
Armament ?
Purpose-built sloop. Departed for the Far East on 28.9.1821. in company with the brig *Aiaks*, which was grounded in the North Sea off Holland. Passed through the Indian Ocean to Petropavlovsk and Novo Arkhangel'sk to winter in San Francisco in 1822–3. Cruised along the Pacific coast of North America in 1823 and returned to Russia with the sloop *Ladoga*. Damaged by the Great Flood of 7.11.1824. Broken up in 1828.

Predpriiatie 24 St Petersburg, Okhta
Constructor A. A. Popov
Laid down 22.12.1822 *Launched* 7.5.1823
Dimensions approx. 130 ft x 36 ft x x16 ft
    39.6 m x 11 m x 5 m (Chernyshev)
Armament ? 120 men
Purpose-built sloop, intended specifically for circumnavigation. The first Russian ship to be built in a covered building slip. Departed Kronshtadt for the Far East on 28.7.1823 with a consignment of scientists on board. Visited Samoa, Petropavlovsk, and Novo Arkhangel'sk and returned via the Indian Ocean to Kronshtadt on 10.7.1826. Carried cargo to Arkhangel'sk in 1828. Returned to Kronshtadt in 1829. Employed as a transport after 1830. Broken up in 1832.

Smirnyi 24 St Petersburg, Okhta
Constructor ?
Laid down 1823 *Launched* 14.5.1824
Dimensions ?
Armament ?
Purpose-built sloop. Departed Kronshtadt on 27.9.1824 for global circumnavigation. Damaged in the North Sea, wintered in Norway, and returned to Kronshtadt on 17.5.1825. Carried cargo to Arkhangel'sk in 1825. Returned to Kronshtadt in 1826. Carried cargo to Arkhangel'sk in 1829. Departed Arkhangel'sk for Kronshtadt in 1830. Wrecked and grounded in the Kattegat on.4.8.1830.13 men lost. Broken up in place.

Converted

Diana 16/22 Lodeynoe Pole
Constructor V. F. Budantsev
Laid down ? *Launched* 1806
Dimensions approx. 91 ft x 25 ft x 12 ft x 14 ft
    27.7 m x 7.6 m x 3.7 m x 4.2 m (Chernyshev)
    300 tons displacement
Armament LD 14 x 6pdrs
    FC & QD 4 x 8pdr carr., 4 x 3pdr falconets
    60 men

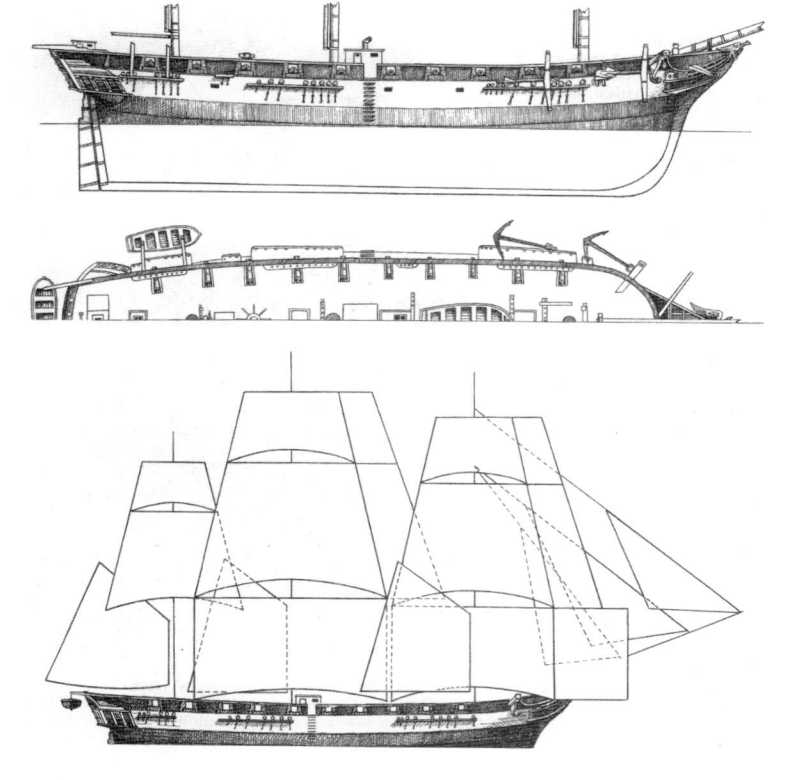

Three different perspectives of the sloop Mirnyi *of 1818. Completed as the transport* Ladoga, *she was modified to accompany* Vostok *on her famous circumnavigation of the globe. Her origin as a transport is apparent in the improvised mounting of her entire main battery on the exposed open decks in contrast to the below decks arrangement in the more orthodox* Vostok.

Storeship/transport converted to sloop. Sailed to St Petersburg in 1806. Departed Kronshtadt for the Far East on 25.7.1807. War having been declared, she was detained by the British at Simonstown on 20.4.1808 and partly dismantled. Escaped to sea on 16.5.1809 by cutting her cables and taking advantage of strong winds. Reached Petropavlovsk on 25.9.1809. To Russian North America in 6–7.1810. Surveyed the Kuriil's in 5–6.1811. Detained by the Japanese at Kunashir island on 11.6.1811, with Capt. Golovnin and 7 seamen being taken into custody. *Diana*, under command of Lt Capt. Rikord escaped to Okhotsk and captured several Japanese vessels in 1811–13. Capt. Golovnin and seamen returned to Petropavlovsk on 5.10.1813. *Diana* grounded and converted into a magazine due to poor material state.

Mirnyi class (2 ships)
Mirnyi 20 Lodeynoe Pole
Constructor Y. A. Kolodkin
Laid down 14.10.1816   *Launched* 18.6.1818
Dimensions approx. 120 ft x 30 ft x 15 ft
   36.6 m x 9.2 m x 4.6 m (Chernyshev)
Armament ?
   72 men
Mirnyi class. Completed as a transport *Ladoga*. Converted into a sloop for circumnavigation and renamed *Mirnyy* on 22.4.1819. Departed for the Antarctic in company with the sloop *Vostok* on 3.7.1819. Reached the continent of Antarctica on 16.1.1820. Returned to Kronshtadt on 24.7.1821. Cruised to Rostok in 1822–4. Carried cargo in 1826–8. Fire watch ship at Sveaborg in 1825. Damaged by storm in 10.1828. Broken up in 1830.

Blagonamerennyi 20 ?
Constructor Y. A. Kolodkin
Laid down 14.10.1816   *Launched* 3.8.1818
Dimensions approx. 120 ft x 30 ft x 16 ft
   36.5 m x 9.1 m x 5 m (Chernyshev)
   530 tons displacement
Armament ?
   83 men
Mirnyi class. Completed as the transport *Svir'*. Converted into a sloop for circumnavigation and renamed *Blagonamerennyi* on 22.4.1819. Accompanied the sloop *Otkrytie* seeking a Northern passage between the Pacific and Atlantic on 3.7.1819. Surveyed the Alaskan coasts and visited Novo Arkhangel'sk and San Francisco. Proceeded north, reaching 70° 13' before turning back. Returned to Kronshtadt on 1.8.1822. Damaged by the Great Flood of 7.11.1824. Broken up in 1828.

Baltic corvettes (4 purpose-built, 4 purchased 1801–24)

As noted above, corvettes were effectively small frigates with finer lines than sloops with similar dimension, and they were intended for use with battle fleets as scouts and avisos. Although they were more widely employed in the Black Sea and Caspian squadrons than in northern waters, four purpose-built and four purchased corvettes were acquired for the Baltic fleet during the first quarter of the nineteenth century.

Purpose-built (4 purpose-built 1801–24)
Flora class (3 ships)
Flora 22 St Petersburg
Constructor G. S. Isakov
Laid down 1805   *Launched* 9.7.1806
Dimensions 106 ft 8 in x 28 ft 9½ in x 13 ft 10 in (Veselago)
Armament 22 x 18pdr carr.
Flora class. Purpose-built corvette. To the Mediterranean in 1806 with Ignatyev's squadron. Dismasted and wrecked off the Albanian coast on 26–28.1.1807. 28 sailors lost.

Mel'pomena 22 St Petersburg
Constructor G. S. Isakov
Laid down 1805   *Launched* 19.7.1806
Dimensions 106 ft 8 in x 28 ft 9½ in x 13 ft 10 in (Veselago)
Armament 22 x 18pdr carr.
Flora class. Purpose-built corvette. 6–7.1807 brought the Russian army payroll of 1 million silver thalers to Pilau. Operated with Adm. Khanykov's squadron in the Baltic in 1808. Escorted merchant ships in the Baltic in 1809. Training duty in the Baltic in 1810–11. To Great Britain with Rear-Adm. Korobka's squadron in 1812. Returned to Russia in 1813. Cruised in the Baltic in 1814–16. Broken up in 1823.

Pomona 22 St Petersburg
Constructor G. S. Isakov
Laid down 1805   *Launched* 19.7.1806
Dimensions 106 ft 8 in x 28 ft 9½ in x 13 ft 10 in (Veselago)
Armament 22 x 18pdr carr.
Flora class. Purpose-built corvette. Cruised in the Baltic in 1807. Operated with Adm. Khanykov's squadron in the Baltic in 1808. Cruised in the Baltic in 1809–10. Fire watch ship in 1811. Escorted

merchants in the Baltic in 1812. Blockaded Danzig in 1813. Cruised in the Baltic in 1814–20. Broken up in 1823.

Gremiashchii 24 St Petersburg, Okhta
Constructor A. A. Popov
Laid down 11.8.1821   *Launched* 30.6.1827
Dimensions ?
Armament carronades
Purpose-built corvette. Damaged during the Great Flood of 7.11.1824. Refloated on 14.12.1824 and repaired at Kronshtadt 10.1826–5.1827. To the Mediterranean in 1827. Fought at Navarino on 8.10.1827. Returned to Kronshtadt in 1829. Broken up in 1830.

Purchased abroad

Al'tsinoe 18 ?
Constructor ?
Laid down ?   *Launched* ? *Purchased* 1805
Dimensions ?
Armament ?
Corvette purchased at Monte-Negro and employed as a store-ship in Vice-Adm. Seniavin's squadron. Sold to France at Corfu in 1809.

Verona 22 ?
Constructor ?
Laid down ?   *Launched* ? *Purchased* 1805
Dimensions ?
Armament ?
Corvette purchased at Monte-Negro and employed as a store-ship in Vice-Adm. Seniavin's squadron. Sold to France at Corfu in 1809.

Derzkii 28 ?
Constructor ?
Laid down ?   *Launched* ? *Purchased* 1806
Dimensions ?
Armament ?
Corvette purchased at Monte-Negro in 1806. Actively employed in operations in Vice-Adm. Seniavin's squadron in 1806–9. Sold to France at Corfu in 1809.

Sharlota 16 ?
Constructor ?
Laid down ?   *Launched* ? *Purchased* 1808
Dimensions 86 ft 6 in x 26 ft x 11 ft (Veselago)
Armament carronades
Corvette purchased in France. Operated under the command of then Commander, future Adm., Geiden, with cutter *Opyt* in 1808. Avoided British patrols and escaped from Hangö to join Adm. Khanykov's fleet. Assigned to the rowing flotilla. Cruised in the Baltic in 1809–11. Cruised to Danzig in 1812–13. Broken up in 1817.

Polar exploration was a perilous and difficult undertaking in the days of sail. Here we see the sloop Blagonamerennyi *in serious difficulty in the ice of the Chukcha sea in 1821. She would survive this ordeal by ice and successfully complete her circumnavigation of the globe in the following year, only to fall prey to ice in another form, the tidal wave generated by the Great Flood of 1824. By I. P. Pshenichnyy, 1989.*

Baltic brigs (15 purpose-built/6 purchased 1801–24)

Fifteen purpose-built and six purchased brigs were acquired for the Baltic fleet during this period. They were rather smaller than contemporary Russian corvettes and ship sloops and armed with carronades as was customary for similar ships in the Western navies. Brigs were widely employed in routine patrol, escort, and survey duties. Their popularity would grow during the second quarter of the century with the decline in popularity of corvettes and ship sloops.

Purpose-built
Sobol' class (2 ships)
Sobol' 14 Lodeynoe Pole
Constructor V. F. Budantsev
Laid down ? *Launched* 1806
Dimensions ?
Armament ?
Sobol' class. Purpose-built brig. Sailed to Riga in 1807. Fire watch ship at Riga 1807–11. Participated in the defence of Riga in 1812. Participated in the bombardment of Danzig in 1813. Transferred to Kronshtadt in 1814. Converted into a prison hulk in 1816.

Iastreb 14 Lodeynoe Pole
Constructor V. F. Budantsev
Laid down ? *Launched* 1806
Dimensions ?
Armament ?
Sobol' class. Purpose-built brig. Fire watch ship at Riga in 1807–14. Broken up at Riga in 1815.

Gonets class (2 ships)
Gonets 20
Constructor A. I. Melikhov
Laid down ? *Launched* 7.7.1808
Dimensions 97 ft 4 in x 30 ft 2 in x 12 ft 8 in (Veselago)
Armament ?
Gonets class. Purpose-built brig. Guardship in Kotlin and escort for transports from Kotlin to Abo in.5.1809. Cruised in the Baltic in 1810–11. Carried troops from Sveaborg to Revel' in Adm. Thate's squadron in 1812 and then deployed to Great Britain with Vice-Adm. Crown's squadron. Returned to Kronshtadt on 16.7.1814. Broken up in 1819.

Merkurii 20 St Petersburg
Constructor A. I. Melikhov
Laid down ? *Launched* 7.7.1808
Dimensions 97 ft 4 in x 30 ft 2 in x 12 ft 8 in (Veselago)
Armament ?
Gonets class. Purpose-built brig. Escorted gun boats to Finland in 1809. Cruised in the Baltic in 1810–11. Escorted 19 transports from Libava to Riga in 1812 and participated in the blockade of Danzig. Cruised in the Baltic in 1813–14. Repaired in 1815. Cruised in the Baltic in 1816. To France in 1817 with Vice-Adm. Crown's squadron. Cruised in the Baltic in 1818–20. Broken up in 1830.

Feniks class (3 ships)
Feniks 20/22 Kronshtadt
Constructor A. V. Zenkov
Laid down 6.10.1809 *Launched* 12.7.1811
Dimensions 98 ft 10 in x 30 ft 8 in x 12 ft 6 in x 13½ ft (Veselago)
470 tons displacement
Armament 20 x 24pdr carr.
85 men
Feniks class. Purpose-built brig. Cruised off Danzig in 1812. Cruised in the Baltic in 1813–19. Broken up in 1825.

Olimp 20 St Petersburg, Okhta
Constructor V. F. Stoke
Laid down 20.11.1816 *Launched* 15.6.1817
Dimensions 98 ft 10 in x 30 ft 8 in x 12 ft 6 in x 13½ ft (Veselago)
470 tons displacement
Armament 20 x 24pdr carr.
85 men
Feniks class. Purpose-built brig. Cruised in the Baltic in 1817–18 and 1820–3. Grounded in the Great Flood of 7.11.1824. Cruised in the Baltic in 1825–6. Broken up in 1827.

Gonets 20 St Petersburg
Constructor A. I. Melikhov
Laid down 20.3.1817 *Launched* 27.7.1818
Dimensions 98 ft 10 in x 30 ft 8 in x 12 ft 6 in x 13½ ft (Veselago)
470 tons displacement
Armament 20 x 24pdr carr.
85 men
Feniks class. Purpose-built brig. Cruised in the Baltic in 1821. Fire watch ship at Rochensalm in 1823–4. Cruised in the Baltic in 1825–6. Broken up in 1828.

Akhilles 16 Sveaborg
Constructor A.V. Zenkov
Laid down 1818 *Launched* 31.8.1819
Dimensions 89 ft x 20 ft x 11 ft 5 in (Veselago)
Armament 12 x 18pdrs, 2 x 12pdr u
Purpose-built brig. Cruised in the Baltic in 1820–4. Cruised to Copenhagen, Portsmouth and Palermo in 1827. Joined Rear-Adm. Geiden's squadron at Malta on 6.12.1827. Operated in the Arkhipelago in 1828–33 against Turkey and then against Greek insurgents. Arrived at Sevastopol' and reassigned to the Black Sea fleet in 1833. Cruised in the Black Sea in 1834. Cruised in the Arkhipelago in 1835–7. Cruised in the Black Sea in 1838, and 1840. Fire watch ship at Odessa in 1841, 1854, and 1856–7. Broken up after 1857.

Aiaks class (4 ships)
Aiaks 16 St Petersburg, Okhta
Constructor V. F. Stoke
Laid down 13.12.1819 *Launched* 5.5.1820
Dimensions ?
Armament ?
Aiaks class (4 ships). Purpose-built brig. Cruised in the Baltic in 1820. Sailed for Kamchatka in 1821 in company with the sloop *Apollon* to prevent British and American poaching. Grounded in the North Sea off Holland on 25.11.1821 and unable to continue her deployment. Repaired in Holland in 1822 and returned to Kronshtadt. Hydrographic survey ship in 1824. Damaged in the Great Flood of 7.11.1824. Broken up in 1827.

Ida 16 St Petersburg, Okhta
Constructor V. F. Stoke
Laid down 13.12.1819 *Launched* 5.5.1820
Dimensions ?
Armament ?
Aiaks class (4 ships). Purpose-built brig. Cruised in the Baltic in

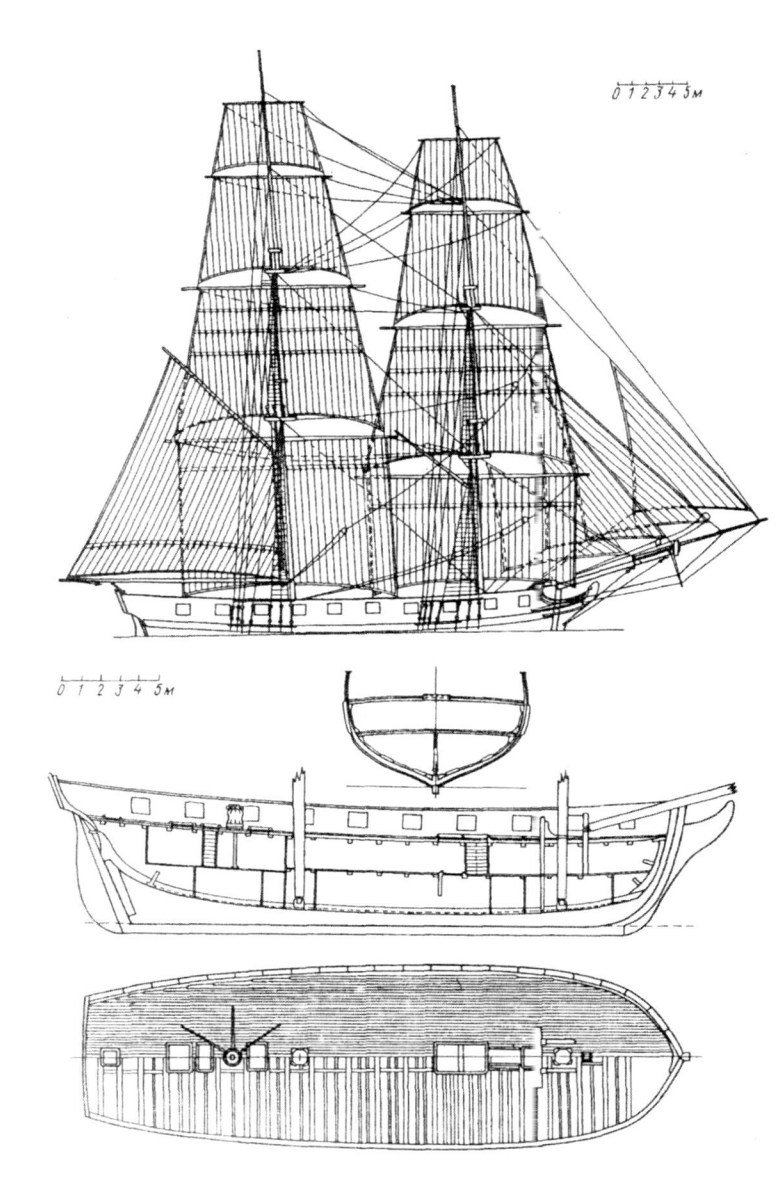

The brig Feniks *(20) as completed for the Baltic fleet in 1811 showing the great spread of sails carried by these small ships and the basic, cramped nature of the below decks layout.*

1820–4. Damaged in the Great Flood of 7.11.1824. Broken up in 1827.

Sviatoi Lavrentii 16 St Petersburg, Okhta
Constructor V. F. Stoke
Laid down 21.1.1820   *Launched* 5.10.1820
Dimensions ?
Armament ?
Aiaks class (4 ships). Purpose-built brig. Cruisec in the Baltic in 1822–5. Fire watch ship at Riga in 1826–30. Expended as a target for shore batteries off Revel' in 1832.

Okhtenka 16 St Petersburg, Okhta
Constructor V. F. Stoke
Laid down 28.10.1820   *Launched* 28.10.1821
Dimensions ?
Armament ?
Aiaks class (4 ships). Purpose-built brig. Cruised in the Baltic in 1822–7. Fire watch ship at Revel' in 1828. Wrecked and sunk during a snowstorm at Revel' on 5.10.1828. 16 men saved, 41 perished.

Novaia Zemlia 6/16 Arkhangel'sk, Solombala
Constructor A. M. Kurochkin
Laid down 4.12.1817   *Launched* 10.7.1819
Dimensions ?   200 tons displacement
Armament 6 x 3pdrs (Arctic exploration)
Purpose-built brig, specifically designed for Arctic exploration. Departed Arkhangel'sk for Novaia Zemlia Island in 1819, but driven back to Arkhangel'sk by ice floes and by scurvy amongst the crew. Fire watch ship at Arkhangel'sk in 1820. Departed Arkhangel'sk on 14.7.1821 and reached Novaia Zemlia on 31.7.1821 and completed hydrographic surveys. Returned to Arkhangel'sk on 11.9.1821. Cruised to the northern coastline of the Kola peninsula and to Novaia Zemlia in 1822. Surveyed the Murman coastline to Norway in 1823, until damage from grounding forced her to return to Arkhangel'sk. Cruised to the north of the Kara Sea until forced back by ice floes in 1824. Fire watch ship at the mouth of the Severnaya Dvina River in 1826–37. Cruised several times during this period and considered a member of the White Sea flotilla. Broken up in 1841.

Riga 14 St Petersburg
Constructor K. A. Glazyrin
Laid down 1820   *Launched* 7.5.1821
Dimensions ?
Armament ?
Purpose-built brig. Fire watch ship at Riga in 1821–4. Cruised as a survey ship in 1828–9. Broken up in 1830.

Revel' 16 St Petersburg, Okhta
Constructor V. F. Stoke
Laid down 1823   *Launched* 13.9.1824
Dimensions 80 ft x 28 ft 4 in x 11 ft 5 in (Veselago)
Armament ?
Purpose-built brig. Cruised in the Baltic in 1825–6. To the Mediterranean in 1827 in a group consisting of 3 brigs, including *Okhta* and *Userdie*. Joined Rear-Adm. Geiden's squadron at Malta on 6.12.1827. In the company of HMS *Warspite*, carried the Greek President Kapodistriya to Greece in 1828. Returned to Kronshtadt in 1828. Involved in hydrographic survey work in 1829–30. Participated in the blockade of Poland in 1831. Involved in hydrographic survey work in 1832–8. Broken up in 1839.

Purchased abroad

Feniks 18 Great Britain
Constructor ?
Laid down ?   *Launched* ?*Purchased*   1805
Dimensions 70 ft x 20 ft x 9 ft (Veselago)
Armament carronades
Brig purchased in Great Britain in 1805. Joined Vice-Adm. Seniavin's squadron in Portsmouth for operations in the Mediterranean in 1806–8. To Trieste with Commodore Saltanov's squadron in 1808. Sold to France in 1809.

Argus 12 Great Britain
Constructor ?
Laid down ?   *Launched* ?*Purchased*   1805
Dimensions 76 ft x 19 ft x 10 ft (Veselago)
Armament carronades
Brig purchased in Great Britain in 1805. Joined Vice-Adm. Seniavin's

squadron in Portsmouth in 1805 for operations in the Mediterranean in 1806–7. Abandoned at Corfu in 1807.

Letun 12 ?
Constructor ?
Laid down ?   *Launched* ?   *Purchased* 1805
Dimensions ?
Armament ?
Brig purchased at Malta in 1805. Operated in the Mediterranean in 1806–8 with Vice-Adm. Seniavin's squadron. To Trieste with Commodore Saltanov's squadron in 1808. Sold to France in 1809.

Bogoiavlensk 16 ?
Constructor ?
Laid down ?   *Launched* ?   *Purchased* 1806
Dimensions ?
Armament ?
Brig purchased in the Mediterranean in 1806. Left as a guardship for Tenedos Island in 6.1807. In combination with shore batteries, engaged a Turkish squadron of ten ships of the line and five frigates on 15.6.1807, damaging a Turkish frigate and receiving serious damage in return with casualties of 3 killed and 6 wounded. Repulsed a second attack on 17.6.1807, sinking two Turkish gunboats. Abandoned at Corfu in 1807 and sold to France.

Oryol 16 ?
Constructor ?
Laid down ?   *Launched* ?*Purchased* 1806
Dimensions ?
Armament ?
Brig purchased in the Mediterranean in 1806. Stationed at Corfu in 1806–9. Sold to France at Corfu in 1809.

Pozharskii 14 ?   *Constructor* ?
Laid down ?   *Launched* ?   *Purchased* 1824
Dimensions ?
Armament ?
Brig purchased in 1824. Cruised in the Baltic with naval cadets 1824–9. Broken up in 1830.

Baltic cutters (one- and two-masted) (27 purpose-built 1801–24)

Twenty-seven one- and two-masted cutters were built for the Baltic fleet during this period. Most remained in Baltic waters throughout their service lives, but *Strela* was deployed to the Mediterranean with Adm. Ignatyev's squadron.

***Vestnik* class** (2 ships)
Vestnik 20 St Petersburg, New Admiralty
Constructor A. I. Melikhov
Laid down ?   *Launched* 1800
Dimensions ?
Armament ?
Vestnik class. Purpose-built cutter. Cruised in the Baltic in 1800–3. Acted as escort for the brig *Neptun* carrying Alexander I to Moon Island in 1804. Fire watch ship at Riga in 1804–6. Broken up in 1810.

Gonets 20 St Petersburg
Constructor A. I. Melikhov
Laid down ?   *Launched* 1800
Dimensions ?
Armament ?
Vestnik class. Purpose-built cutter. Fire watch ship at Kronshtadt Roads in 1801. Cruised in the Baltic in 1802–7. Escorted gun boats to Vyborg in 1808. Broken up after 1810.

***Begun* class** (2 ships)
Begun 8 Kronshtadt
Constructor V. D. Vlasov
Laid down ?   *Launched* 1804
Dimensions approx. 55 ft x 18 ft x 7 ft 6 in
16.8 m x 5.5 m x 2.3 m (Chernyshev)
Armament ?
Begun class. Purpose-built cutter. Cruised to Rostock and Copenhagen in 1805–6. Cruised off Finland in 1807–14. Broken up in 1815.

Sokol 8 Kronshtadt
Constructor V. D. Vlasov
Laid down ?   *Launched* 1804
Dimensions 55 ft x 18 ft x 7 ft 7 in (Veselago)
Armament ?
Begun class. Purpose-built cutter. Cruised in the Gulf of Finland in 1805–10. Fire watch ship off the Aland Islands in 1812–21. No further mention.

Strela 20 Kronshtadt
Constructor V. D. Vlasov
Laid down ?   *Launched* 1804
Dimensions ?
Armament ?
Purpose-built cutter. Cruised in the Baltic in 1805. To the Mediterranean in 1806 with Commodore Ignatyev's squadron. Operations in the Mediterranean in 1806–7. Arrived at Trieste with Commodore Saltanov's squadron. To Venice in 1.1808. Sold to France at Venice on 27.9.1809.

Solombal 20 Arkhangel'sk, Solombala
Constructor A. M. Kurochkin
Laid down 16.7.1804   *Launched* 1.7.1805
Dimensions 99 ft (LGD) 91 ft (LK) x 30 ft x 12 ft 1 in (Veselago)
Armament ?
Purpose-built cutter. White Sea flotilla. Cruised in the White Sea in 1805–6. Stationed in Arkhangel'sk Roads in 1807–8 against the threat of British incursions. Cruised in the White Sea in 1809–21. Broken up in 1825.

***Zhemchug* class** (2 ships)
Zhemchug 8 St Petersburg
Constructor A. I. Melikhov
Laid down 1805   *Launched* 19.7.1806
Dimensions 60 ft x 20 ft 10 in x 10 ft (Veselago)
Armament ?
Zhemchug class. Purpose-built cutter. Cruised in the Baltic in 1807–8 with Adm. Khanykov's squadron. Transferred to Revel' in 1809. Escorted transports to Finland in 1812–13. Broken up in 1815.

Topaz 8 St Petersburg
Constructor A. I. Melikhov
Laid down 1805   *Launched* 19.7.1806
Dimensions 60 ft x 20 ft 10 in x 10 ft (Veselago)
Armament ?

THE BALTIC FLEET 1801–24

Zhemchug class. Purpose-built cutter. Cruised in the Baltic in 1808 with Adm. Khanykov's squadron. Dispatch vessel to Sveaborg, Riga, and Stockholm in 1812. Participated in the blockade of Danzig in 1813. Broken up in 1815.

Opyt 14 St Petersburg
Constructor I. V. Kurepanov
Laid down 1805 *Launched* 9.10.1806
Dimensions 65 ft 10 in x 21 ft 10 in x 9 ft 4 in (Veselago)
Armament 14 12pdr carr.
   53 men

Purpose-built cutter. Cruised in the Baltic in 1807. Arrived at Sveaborg in 1808. Intercepted on 11.6.1808 by HMS *Salsette* (44) and forced to surrender after a four-hour fight with casualties of 2 killed and 11 wounded. HMS *Salcette* fired two full broadsides into the cutter during the action. After the surrender, the British captain returned the Russian commander's sword and landed the survivors near Libawa.

Navigator 8 ?
Constructor ?
Laid down ? *Launched* 1806
Dimensions ?
Armament ?

Purpose-built cutter. Cruised in the Gulf of Finland as inspector and supplier of lighthouses 1807–17. Carried the German envoy to Pillau and escorted troopships from Revel' to Finland in 1812. Broken up at Revel' in 1819.

***Drozd* class** (10 ships)
Drozd 14 Lodeynoe Pole
Constructors G. S. Isakov and A. P. Antip'ev
Laid down ? *Launched* 1808
Dimensions ?
Armament ?

Drozd class. Purpose-built one-masted cutter. Operated off Kotlin in defence of Kronshtadt and escorted transports to Abo in 1809. Cruised in the Baltic in 1810–11. Stationed at Kronshtadt from 1812. Broken up at Kronshtadt in 1825.

Leshch 14 Lodeynoe Pole
Constructors G. S. Isakov and A. P. Antip'ev
Laid down ? *Launched* 1808
Dimensions ?
Armament ?

Drozd class. Purpose-built one-masted cutter. Stationed at Kronshtadt 1809–14. Floating lighthouse off the London Ground (site of the wreck of *London* (54) in 1719) in 1815–19. Broken up in 1825.

Los' 14 Lodeynoe Pole
Constructors G. S. Isakov and A. P. Antip'ev

The heroic action of the cutter Opyt *in conflict with HMS* Salsette *on 11 June 1808 has received little attention among British naval historians. A small incident in Royal Navy history, it has always been seen by Russians as a great symbolic moment, not for its strategic importance, but as an example of stubborn heroism against heavy odds. In this 1889 painting by L. D. Blinov, the* Opyt *is seen as a battered but defiant wreck in the foreground with the Russian flag still flying, while her British opponent stands off almost untouched save only for the numerous holes in her sails.* Salsette *appears to be still firing slowly and deliberately at her smaller opponent, but the moment of surrender can hardly be far off.*

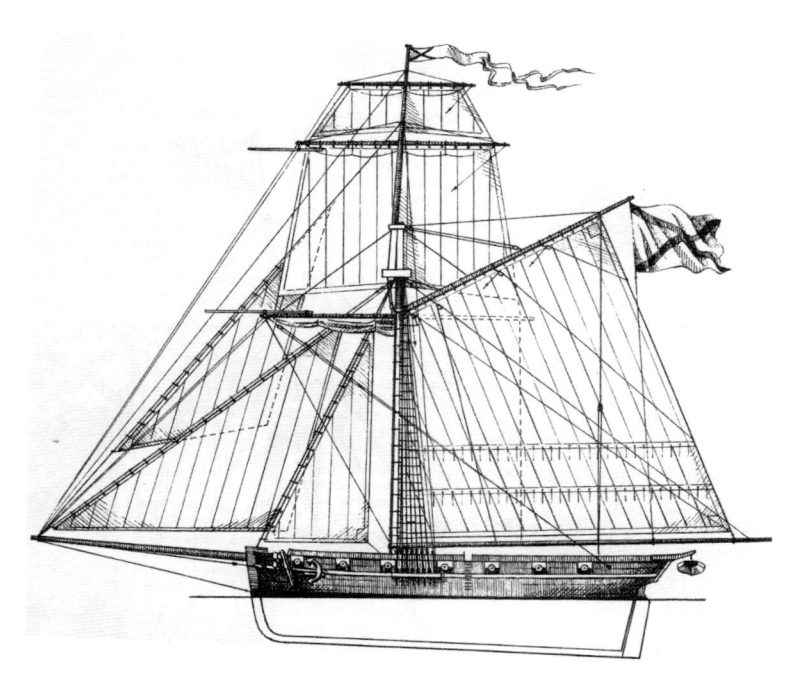

A drawing of the Baltic cutter Drozd *of 1808 showing her rig in detail and giving a clear idea of the simplicity of the type. Cutters were built or acquired in numbers after 1800. As was the case in Britain and elsewhere, they proved ideally suited for coastguard activities and the escort of merchant ships.*

Laid down ?   *Launched* 1808
Dimensions ?
Armament ?
Drozd class. Purpose-built one-masted cutter. Cruised in the Baltic in 1812–13. Stationed at Revel' from 1815. Broken up at Revel' in 1819.

Muravei 14 Lodeynoe Pole
Constructors   G. S. Isakov and A. P. Antip'ev
Laid down ?   *Launched* 1808
Dimensions ?
Armament ?
Drozd class. Purpose-built one-masted cutter. Cruised in the Baltic in 1809 and 1811–13. Broken up in 1825.

Olen' 14 Lodeynoe Pole
Constructors   G. S. Isakov and A. P. Antip'ev
Laid down ?   *Launched* 1808
Dimensions ?
Armament ?
Drozd class. Purpose-built one-masted cutter. Stationed at Sveaborg in 1809–10. Stationed at Kronshtadt from 1812. Broken up at Kronshtadt in 1825.

Sverchok 14 Lodeynoe Pole
Constructors   G. S. Isakov and A. P. Antip'ev
Laid down ?   *Launched* 1808
Dimensions ?
Armament ?
Drozd class. Purpose-built one-masted cutter. Sailed from Kronshtadt to Riga in 1813. Broken up at Kronshtadt in 1825.

Shchyoglenok 14 Lodeynoe Pole
Constructors   G. S. Isakov and A. P. Antip'ev
Laid down ?   *Launched* 1808
Dimensions ?
Armament ?
Drozd class. Purpose-built one-masted cutter. Stationed at Kronshtadt in 1812. Broken up in 1825.

Iastreb 14 Lodeynoe Pole
Constructors   G. S. Isakov and A. P. Antip'ev
Laid down ?   *Launched* 1808
Dimensions ?
Armament ?
Drozd class. Purpose-built one-masted cutter. Stationed off Kotlin in defence of Kronshtadt and escorted transports to Abo in 1809. Cruised in the Baltic in 1811–14 and in 1817. Fire watch ship at Rochensalm in 1816 and 1818–19. Broken up in 1820.

No. 89 Lodeynoe Pole
Constructors   G. S. Isakov and A. P. Antip'ev
Laid down ?   *Launched* 1808
Dimensions ?
Armament ?
Drozd class. Purpose-built one-masted cutter. Stationed at Kronshtadt in 1812. Broken up at Kronshtadt in 1825.

No. 90 Lodeynoe Pole (renamed *Kiumen'*)
Constructors   G. S. Isakov and A. P. Antip'ev
Laid down ?   *Launched* 1808
Dimensions ?
Armament ?
Drozd class. Purpose-built one-masted cutter. Renamed *Kiumen'* in 1812 after the river separating Russia and Sweden. Cruised off Rochensalm in 1812–14. Sailed from Kronshtadt to Riga as a fire watch ship in 1815–22. Broken up in 1825 at Riga.

Vestnik class (6 ships)
Vestnik 12 St Petersburg, Okhta
Constructor V. F. Stoke
Laid down 21.11.1811   *Launched* 3.7.1813
Dimensions 70 ft x 25 ft 2 in x 10 ft 9 in (Veselago)
Armament ?
Vestnik class. Purpose-built cutter. Blockaded Danzig in 1813. Cruised in the Baltic in 1814–18. Fire watch ship at Revel' in 1819–22. Broken up at Revel' in 1823.

Khameleon 12 St Petersburg, Okhta
Constructor V. F. Stoke
Laid down 24.2.1814   *Launched* 7.8.1814
Dimensions 70 ft x 25 ft 2 in x 10 ft 9 in (Veselago)
Armament ?
Vestnik class. Purpose-built cutter. Cruised in the Baltic in 1815–18. Fire watch ship at Riga in 1819–22. Broken up at Kronshtadt in 1823.

Ianus 12 St Petersburg, Okhta
Constructor V. F. Stoke
Laid down 24.2.1814   *Launched* 7.8.1814
Dimensions 70 ft x 25 ft 2 in x 10 ft 9 in (Veselago)
Armament ?
Vestnik class. Purpose-built cutter. Cruised in the Baltic in 1815–21. Damaged during the Great Flood of 7.11.1824. Broken up in 1827.

Eol 12 St Petersburg, Okhta

Constructor V. F. Stoke
Laid down 28.6.1817   *Launched* 17.9.1817
Dimensions approx. 70 ft x 25 ft x 11 ft
21.3 m x 7.6 m x 3.3 m (Chernyshev)
Armament ?
Vestnik class. Purpose-built cutter. Cruised in the Baltic in 1817–25. Damaged in the Great Flood of 7.11.1824. Broken up in 1829.

Zefir 12 St Petersburg, Okhta
Constructor V. F. Stoke
Laid down 1817   *Launched* 1817
Dimensions approx. 70 ft x 25 ft x 11 ft
21.3 m x 7.6 m x 3.3 m (Chernyshev)
Armament ?
Vestnik class. Purpose-built cutter. Cruised in the Baltic in 1818–19 and 1821. Fire watch ship at Riga in 1822–5. Broken up in 1827.

Pegas 12 St Petersburg, Okhta
Constructor V. F. Stoke
Laid down 29.11.1817   *Launched* 17.8.1818
Dimensions approx. 70 ft x 25 ft x 11 ft
21.3 m x 7.6 m x 3.3 m (Chernyshev)
Armament ?
Vestnik class. Purpose-built cutter. Survey work in the Gulf of Finland in 1819–24. Floating lighthouse off London Ground in 1825–6. Broken up in 1830.

Kolym 12 St Petersburg, Okhta
Constructor V. F. Stoke
Laid down 29.1.1819   *Launched* 1.6.1819
Dimensions 91 ft x 25 ft x 9 ft 8 in (Veselago)
Armament ?
Purpose-built cutter. Engaged in cruising and fire watch duties at Abo and off Fliseberg in 1820–8. Broken up in 1830.

Baltic schooners (2 purpose-built 1801–24)

Representing a type that would become more popular – and larger – after 1825, schooners were rarely built or employed by the Russians during the early years of the century. Lacking the maritime fishing and commercial interests of more developed western nations, the Russians had little need for large numbers of coastal patrol craft to inhibit smuggling, as was the case with Great Britain, and only began to develop the type as their investment in exploration, survey work, and expansion increased after 1825.

Raduga 14 St Petersburg, Okhta
Constructor V. F. Stoke
Laid down 5.1.1818   *Launched* 1.7.1818
Dimensions ?
Armament ?
Purpose-built schooner. Hydrographic survey work in the Gulf of Finland in 1820–7. Broken up in 1828.

Opyt 8 St Petersburg, Okhta
Constructor V. F. Stoke
Laid down 1818   *Launched* 1819
Dimensions ?
Armament ?
Purpose-built schooner. Cruised with naval cadets in 1820 and 1829. Broken up in 1830.

Baltic luggers (3 purpose-built/1 converted 1801–24)

Purpose-built

Ganimed class (2 ships)
Ganimed 14 St Petersburg
Constructor A. I. Melikhov
Laid down 1807   *Launched* 7.7.1808
Dimensions 70 ft x 20 ft 11 in x 10 ft 4 in (Veselago)
Armament ?
Ganimed class. Purpose-built lugger. Cruised in the Baltic in 1809–10. Grounded in 10.1810, but refloated by the brig *Merkurii*. Cruised in the Baltic in 1811–12. Blockaded Danzig in 1813. Cruised in the Baltic in 1814–16. Broken up in 1819.

Iashcheritsa 14 St Petersburg
Constructor A. I. Melikhov
Laid down 1807   *Launched* 7.7.1808
Dimensions 70 ft x 20 ft 11 in x 10 ft 4 in (Veselago)
Armament ?
Ganimed class. Purpose-built lugger. Cruised in the Baltic in 1809–11. Carried troops in 1812. Cruised to Karlskrona in 1813. Cruised in the Baltic in 1814–16. Broken up in 1819.

Tserber 14 St Petersburg, Okhta
Constructor V. F. Stoke
Laid down 11.3.1813   *Launched* 7.4.1814
Dimensions 70 ft x 20 ft 11 in x 10 ft 4 in (Veselago)
Armament ?
Purpose-built lugger. Cruised in the Baltic in 1814–20. Broken up in 1828.

Converted

Strela 16 St Petersburg, Okhta
Constructor V. F. Stoke
Laid down 14.2.1810   *Launched* 13.7.1811
Dimensions 81'6 in x 22 ft 8 in x 8 ft (Veselago)
Armament ?
Schooner converted into a lugger while building. Cruised in the Baltic in 1812–18. Fire watch ship at Sveaborg in 1819–23. Broken up at Sveaborg in 1824.

Baltic bomb vessels (1801–24) (2 purpose-built 1801–24)

Perun 20/24 St Petersburg
Constructor I. V. Kurepanov
Laid down 9.1.1808   *Launched* 1.7.1808
Dimensions 119 ft 11 in x 32 ft x 15 ft (Veselago)
Armament 14 x 24pdr carr., 2 x 5 pood mortars, 2 x 3 pood howitzers, 2 x 8pdr mortars
Purpose-built bomb vessel. In commission in 1809–13. Stationed at Kronshtadt in 1814–22. Broken up in 1822.

Molniia 18/20 St Petersburg
Constructor I. V. Kurepanov
Laid down 9.1.1808   *Launched* 1.7.1808
Dimensions 95 ft x 26 ft 8 in x 11 ft 11 in (Veselago)
Armament 14 x 24pdr carr., 2 x 5 pood mortars, 2 x 3 pood howitzers, 2 x 8pdr mortars
Purpose-built bomb vessel. Brig rigged. Cruised in the Baltic in 1809–14. Fire watch ship at Sveaborg in 1815–24. No further mention.

The Navy of Nicholas I and the Creation of the Steam Navy (1825–60)

Two formative events in the history of the Russian Baltic Navy occurred nearly simultaneously, the Great Flood of 1824 and the succession of Nicholas I to the throne in 1825 upon the death of his brother Alexander I.

In marked contrast to his older brother, who had had very low regard for naval matters and who begrudged every rouble spent on warships, dockyards, and seamen, Nicholas was favourably inclined towards all forms of military spending and national expansion, at least in his early years as emperor. Upon taking the throne, he initiated a series of investigations into the disaster of the previous year that had served to highlight the poor material state of Russian warships as well as the endemic laxity and negligence on the part of the naval authorities responsible for maintaining naval readiness under the Navy Minister, the Marquis de Traversay. As a result of these investigations, extensive reforms were initiated within the navy including the reinstatement of Adm. Seniavin, heroic veteran of the Napoleonic Wars, and the promotion and rapid rise of Adm. Lazarev whose energy and leadership did much to guide and inspire Russian naval developments in the 1830s and 1840s.

During the flood, which had resulted from strong westerly winds raising water levels by as much as 11 ft 6 in on 7 November, 22 out of 28 line of battle ships, 15 of 19 frigates, and 5 of 6 brigs were grounded among the shoals and shallows at Kronshtadt The harbours, both naval and merchant, were effectively destroyed with very great loss of life. Between 1825 and 1829, 20 of the surviving line of battle ships were surveyed as being beyond salvage and were broken up along with 4 frigates. Four of the remaining line of battle ships were hulked, leaving the formerly powerful Baltic fleet in a shambles.

This was unquestionably the greatest natural disaster in Russian naval history; but, in one regard, it was a blessing in disguise. clearing away deadwood in the form of obsolescent and poorly maintained warships and making possible needed reforms and the planned reconstruction of the Baltic fleet into a more balanced and effective force. Unfortunately, as Adm. Lazarev was quick to point out in 1830, many of the new ships were thrown together with unseemly haste, reverting to the use of unseasoned timber and to the shoddy building practices of previous years. Lazarev may have exaggerated the situation somewhat to drive home his point, but there was a good deal of validity to the his charge and his energy and determination did much to redress the situation in later years.

Possibly the most significant and telling of the reforms resulting from the accession of Nicholas I and the resulting inquiries into the poorly maintained state of the navy was the institution of a system of mandatory repair and maintenance for all warships. The efficacy of these reforms may be most clearly illustrated by comparing the average lifespan of 74-gun ships of the *Selafail* class built during the neglectful years of the Traversay regime with that of the structurally similar *Iezekiil* class which were just beginning to enter service in the early years of Nicholas's reign. The *Selafail* class ships had an average lifespan of 16.87 years (excluding those ships lost to combat, weather, or their sale to Spain in 1818.). This figure should not be taken to reflect the active service lifespan of the *Selafail* class members, but rather of the longer period between their launching and breaking up. This period stands in marked contrast, not only to the greatly improved 21.44-year lifespan of the *Iezekiil'* class members, but also to the 18.47 years of the earlier class of 74s, the *Iaroslavs*, built under Catherine II. The greater attention paid during Nicholas I's reign to the basics of naval power, adequate infrastructure and logistical backup, was reflective of a coming of age for the Russian Navy, but one that went largely unnoticed by Great Britain and the other European naval powers.

Seen from the narrow perspective of Russian naval growth and development, Nicholas I was one of the great figures in Russian history. Inheriting a navy that was in serious decay, he revitalized it and made it into the world's second most powerful (if still geographically restricted) fleets by the 1830s, eclipsing that of France in size and possibly in operating efficiency. The last decade of Nicholas's life saw the fleet that he had created overwhelmed by the pace of technological change and by the coalition of two great European powers, nervous about the southern extension of Russian power. He died in 1855 and the Russian sailing navy effectively died with him.

THE BALTIC FLEET 1825–60

Imperial review of Baltic fleet in 1848 as painted by A. P. Bogolyubov in 1850. Ships of the line are in the right-hand column and frigates to the left. The emperor and his party are reviewing the fleet from the deck of a paddle steamer emitting clouds of smoke, all apparently unaware that they are aboard the very type of vessel that would, in just a few more years, render this impressive display obsolete.

The Great Flood of 1824 was an unparalleled catastrophe even by Russian standards. The collapse of a huge ice dam on the Neva just above St Petersburg is believed to have caused at least 10,000 deaths in the city. The tidal wave generated by the bursting ice dam reached the naval base at Kronshtadt and destroyed most of the Baltic fleet lying at anchor in preparation for the winter freeze. This contemporary drawing shows the scale of the devastation, which resulted in the loss of eleven line ships and a host of smaller craft. All of the ships in the drawing have had their masts and rigging removed, not an indication of their being held in ordinary, but the normal procedure in the ice-bound northern Baltic. Artist unknown.

A dramatic scene from a lithograph by K. P. Beggrov displaying several liners under construction with the stern of one of the three Imperator Aleksandr class 110s well advanced and dominating the scene. In the foreground, a group of workers is dragging a heavy piece of wood while a group of officers is engaged in conversation.

Ships with 90–135 guns (4 purpose-built 1825–60)

Four First Rates were laid down and completed in the Baltic during Nicholas I's reign. These ships were much more actively employed than the First Rates of Alexander I's reign had been, cruising frequently during their lifetimes, and with two being given what amounted to mid-life refits in the late 1840s. The final Baltic First Rate, the *Rossiia*, saw action during the Baltic phase of the Crimean War, being involved in the defence of Sveaborg in 1855 where she was heavily damaged.

Imperator Aleksandr class (3 ships)

These three ships were hurriedly laid down in the aftermath of the Great Flood and were developments of the earlier *Leiptsig* class with nearly identical dimensions. There is some evidence that the design of all 5 of these Russian 110-gun ships were based in part on draughts of the French 110s of the 1780s obtained by Paul I in his role as General Adm. of the Russian navy prior to ascending the throne. This choice of a prototype was probably an unfortunate one. Neither of the earlier ships had been adequately tested in service. *Leiptsig* could only lay claim to a single brief deployment in 1816 before her effective retirement, while *Tvyordyi* spent her entire career in harbour as a symbol of Russian naval supremacy without a single period of active service.

If Adm. Lazarev is to be relied upon, all three of the *Aleksandr*'s were hastily built and poorly constructed. Lazarev's critique, in a private letter to a friend 1830, is scathing: 'Three 100-gunners built by Ignatyev are no good at all, and the money spent for them has literally been thrown into the water. They steer badly, do not answer the helm due to excessive fullness at their stern part, and in spite of their having enormous ballast, they, nevertheless, roll greatly.' Lazarev may have been overstating his criticisms of the *Aleksandr*'s in order to drive home his point. They undoubtedly benefited from the periodic inspection and maintenance programme implemented in the wake of the Great Flood, and all three ships had long and active service lives. This would appear to belie or at least mitigate his charges about their allegedly shoddy construction.

Imperator Aleksandr 110/118 St Petersburg
Constructor G. S. Isakov
Laid down 26.5.1826 Launched 13.10.1827
Dimensions 198 ft (pp) x 51 ft 8 in (inside plank) x 21 ft 3 in (Veselago)
  198 ft x 51 ft 8 in x 23.6 in (Zapiski)
  197.16 ft x 53.08 ft x 21.33 ft, 4244.6 tons displacement (Fincham 1851)
Armament LD 26 x 36pdrs (short), 4 x 60 u (1 pood)
  MD 32 x 24pdrs (short)
  UD 32 12pdrs (long)
  FC & QD 24 x 24pdr carr. (1830 'Establishment')

Imperator Aleksandr class. Cruised in the Baltic in 1829–30, 1833–4 and 1836. Repaired in 1837–9. Cruised in the Baltic with naval cadets in 1839–40, 1842–3 and 1846. To Denmark during the Schleswig-Holstein Crisis as flag to Vice-Adm. Lazarev, brother of the more prominent Black Sea commander in chief, in 1848–50. Decommissioned in 1850. Broken up in 1854.

Imperator Pyotr I 110/118 St Petersburg
Constructor G. S. Isakov
Laid down 5.12.1827 Launched 2.5.1829
Dimensions 198 ft (pp) x 51 ft (inside plank) x 23 ft 6 in
  4,413 tons displacement (Pamyatnaya)
Armament 1829 LD 26 x 36pdrs (short), 4 x 60 u (1 pood)
  MD 32 x 24pdrs (short)
  UD 32 x 12pdrs (long)
  FC & QD 24 x 24pdr carr.
  940 men (1830 'Establishment')
  1854 LD 26 x 36pdrs (short), 4 x 9.65 in shell guns (2 pood)
  MD 28 x 24pdrs (short), 4 x 60 u (1 pood)
  UD 32 x 24pdr gunnades
  FC & QD 14 x 24pdr carr. (Pamyatnaya)
  1855 LD 26 x 36pdrs (short), 4 x 9.65 in shell guns (2 pood)
  MD 28 x 24pdrs (short), 4 x 60 u (1 pood)
  UD 2 x 24pdrs (long), 30 x 24pdr gunnades
  FC & QD 6 x 24pdrs (short), 12 x 24pdr carr. (Pamyatnaya)
  1857 LD 26 x 36pdrs (short), 4 x 9.65 in shell guns (2 pood)
  MD 2 x 24pdrs (long), 26 x 24pdrs (short), 4 x 60 u (1 pood)
  UD 2 x 24pdrs (short), 30 x 24pdr gunnades
  FC & QD 18 x 24pdrs (short), 2 x 24pdr gunnades
  12 x 24pdr carr. (Pamyatnaya)

Imperator Aleksandr class. Cruised in the Baltic in 1830, 1832–3, 1836,

THE BALTIC FLEET 1825–60

A painting of Imperator Aleksandr I *(110) of 1827 completed in 1840 by F. Perro. The straight and unbroken sheer line and relative absence of tumblehome clearly identify her as a post-Napoleonic design. She is most likely at rest at Kronshtadt and windless conditions and the glassy surface of the surrounding waters speaks volumes about the differences between service in the Baltic and the North Atlantic.*

1838–9, and 1841–2. Repaired in 1849–50. Commissioned in 1854 as flag to commander in chief Adm. Rikord. Stationed in Kronshtadt Roads in 1855. Harbour service in 1856. Stricken on 5.1.1863.

Sviatoi Georgii Pobedonosets 110/118 St Petersburg
Constructor G. S. Isakov
Laid down 15.12.1828   *Launched* 15.10.1829
Dimensions 198 ft x 51 ft 8 in x 21 ft (Veselago)
198 ft x (181 ft 1 in keel) x 51 ft 8 in (inside plank)
x 23 ft x 23 ft 6 in (Zapiski)
Armament 1829   LD 26 x 36pdrs (short), 4 x 60 u (1 pood)
MD 32 x 24pdrs (short)

UD 32 x 12pdrs (long)
FC & QD 24 x 24pdr carr. (as built)
940 men (1830 'Establishment')
1854   LD 26 x 36pdrs (short), 4 x 9.65 in shell guns
(2 pood)
MD 28 x 24pdrs (short), 4 x 60 u (1 pood)
UD 32 x 24pdr gunnades
FC & QD 2 x 24pdrs (short), 14 x 24pdr carr.
(Pamyatnaya)
1855   LD 2 x 36pdrs (long), 24 x 36pdrs (short),
4 x 9.65 in shell guns (2 pood)
MD 2 x 24pdrs (long), 26 x 24pdrs (short),

The launching of a great warship was as much a pageant in the nineteenth century as it is today. This is Rossiia *(120) entering the waters of the Neva in 1839. Not only is the pier filled with gathered dignitaries and the river with small boats, but the line of battle ships in the background also all have their yards manned with sailors in honour of the occasion. Of note is the covered brick building slip, an indication of the progress made under Nicholas I over the early days when ships were built in the open and exposed to all the ravages of Russian weather.* Rossiia *was herself of particular interest, having been completed with an experimental uniform armament of 60pdr cannon – long, short and gunnades – an innovation that had been introduced earlier in the Black Sea for 84s and frigates by Admiral Lazarev, but never applied to ships of this size armed with massive 60pdrs.*

```
                4 x 60 u (1 pood)
            UD 2 x 24pdrs (long), 30 x 24pdr gunnades
            FC & QD 4 x 24pdrs (long), 2 x 24pdrs (short),
            12 x 24pdr carr. (Pamyatnaya)
     1856  LD 26 x 36pdrs (long), 4 x 9.65 in shell guns
                (2 pood)
            MD 2 x 24pdrs (long), 26 x 24pdrs (short), 4 x 60 u
                (1 pood)
            UD 2 x 24pdrs (long), 30 x 24pdr gunnades
            FC & QD 2 x 24pdrs (long), 2 x 24pdrs (short),
            14 x 24pdr carr, (Pamyatnaya)
```

Imperator Aleksandr class. Cruised in the Baltic in 1830, 1834–8, 1840, 1843 and 1845. Repaired in 1847–8. To Denmark during the Schleswig-Holstein Crisis in 1849–50. Cruised in the Baltic in 1852–3. Commissioned in Kronshtadt Roads in 1854–5. Decommissioned in 1855. Broken up in 1858.

Rossiia 120/128 St Petersburg, New Admiralty
Constructor A. A. Popov
Laid down 11.2.1836   *Launched* 5.7.1839
Dimensions 208 ft x 55 ft 8 in x 25 ft 1 in (Veselago)
  4,904 tons displacement (Pamyatnaya)
  208 ft x (195 ft keel) x 55 ft 4 in x 24 ft 11 in (Zapiski)
Armament 1839 LD 32 x 60pdrs (long), 4 x 9.65 in shell guns
                (2 pood)
            MD 32 x 60pdrs (short)
            UD 34 x 60pdr gunnades
            FC & QD 4 x 60pdr gunnades, 2 x 96pdr carr.,
            22 x 60pdr carr.
            1,015 men
     1854 LD 30 x 60pdrs (long), 4 x 9.65 in shell guns
                (2 pood)
            MD 28 x 60pdrs (short), 4 x 8.75 in shell guns
                (1½ pood)
            UD 34 x 36pdr gunnades
            FC & QD 4 x 36pdr gunnades 16 x 36pdr carr.
            (Pamyatnaya)
     1855 LD 30 x 60pdrs (long), 4 x 9.65 in shell guns
                (2 pood)
            MD 10 x 60pdrs (short), 20 x 36pdrs (short)
            UD 34 x 36pdr gunnades
            FC & QD 4 x 36pdr gunnades, 16 x 36pdr carr.
            (Pamyatnaya)

An experimental design with a uniform battery of 60pdrs (officially rated as 48pdrs). Trials in 1840. Cruised in the Baltic in 1841 and 1843. To Denmark in 1845. Cruised in the Baltic in 1847. To Denmark during the Schleswig-Holstein Crisis to provide support against the threat of Prussian invasion in 1850. Cruised in the Baltic in 1851–53. Stationed at Sveaborg in 1854–5. Participated in the defence of Sveaborg on 28.7.1855 taking casualties of 11 killed and 89 wounded and 85 shot holes. Decommissioned in 1856. Receiving ship at Sveaborg in 1857. Broken up in 1860.

Ships with 80–88 guns (12 purpose-built 1825–60)

In the 1820s the French émigré naval architect Le Brune worked out the basic design for the Russian 84-gun ships that would become the standard Russian second rates in the closing years of the age of sail. They were based in large part on the lines of the celebrated French designer Jacque-Noel Sane's highly successful 80-gun ships of the Napoleonic War period; but with reduced draught for Baltic conditions and with reputedly very high

The Russian fleet avoided contact with the overwhelmingly powerful Anglo-French forces in the Baltic phase of the Crimean War. Most of the battle fleet was gathered in passive defence of Kronshtadt and St Petersburg, but the 120-gun Rossiia *found herself at Sveaborg in 1855 where she was used to defend the fortress and harbour as a stationary floating battery. She is seen here, with masts and spars removed and cables linking her to both sides of the main channel, exchanging fire with the attacking allied gunboats. As befitted her status as a First Rate, she absorbed heavy punishment without sinking and survived the war, only to be decommissioned in 1856. By A. A. Tron 2002.*

speeds in service. The design work was done by Le Brune, but the actual construction work was supervised by I. V. Kurepanov, A. A. Popov, and A. K. Kaverznev between 1822 and 1840.

In contrast to the contemporary 74s of the *Iezekiil'* class which were all built at Arkhangel'sk of larch and were subject to rapid deterioration, the 84s were all built in the New Admiralty Yards at St Petersburg of seasoned Kazan' oak and had significantly longer service lives as a consequence, lasting up to the 1860s in most cases. They were held in the highest regard in the Russian Navy at large, and by Adm. Lazarev in particular, who preferred them to the allegedly fragile and unwieldy 110-gun first rates. The Russian 84s differed from both the larger First Rates and the smaller 74s in being armed with long 24- and 36pdrs in contrast to the standard Swedish pattern short guns, although some appear to have reverted to short guns in the 1850s.

Given their great success and long service lives, it seems extremely likely that they were completed with a level of structural reinforcements and diagonal bracing that allowed them to avoid problems with hull deformation of the sort that had bedeviled captured Sane designed 80-gun ships in British service during the Napoleonic Wars.

In service, the Russian 84 occupied a secondary command and control position between the first rates and the more numerous 74-gun line of battle ships of the *Iezekiil* class. *Gangut*, the first of the post-war 84s, was significantly larger than the seven ships of the *Imperatritsa Aleksandra* class which followed her four years later. She greatly distinguished herself at Navarino in 1827. The seven *Aleksandra*s all avoided serious combat, but led active and useful lives. One of the group, *Vola*, was converted into a screw ship between 1854 and 1857. An additional 84-gun ship, *Lefort*, entered service in 1835. She is incorrectly classed with the *Aleksandra*s by Chernyshev, but was actually a distinct design. Very much a prestige ship, she was completely rebuilt in 1850–1, only to be lost with all hands in a squall in 1857. Three final 84s, the *Krasnoi* class, laid down between 1845 and 1851 were of improved design used experimentally as test beds for various types of ordnance. The final unit, *Oryol*, was converted to a screw ship while building, bringing the total of post-war 84-gun ships built for Baltic service to twelve.

Gangut 84 St Petersburg
Constructor I. V. Kurepanov
Laid down 8.8.1822   *Launched* 19.9.1825
Dimensions 196 ft x 51 ft x 23 ft 7 in (as built)
   212 ft x 53 ft 8 in (outside plank) x 23 ft 8 in x 22 ft 3 in
   3,814 tons displacement as rebuilt to steam
Armament 1825 LD 26 x 36pdrs (short) 6 x 60 u (1 pood)
   UD 32 x 24pdrs (short)
   FC & QD 2 x 24pdrs (short), 26 x 24pdr carr.
   (Sudostroenie 1974)
   1848 LD 24 x 36pdrs (long), 2 x 9.65 in shell guns
   (2 pood), 4 x 60 u (1 pood)
   UD 32 x 24pdrs (long)
   FC & QD 2 x 24pdrs (short), 26 x 24pdr carr.
   1856 (as steamship) LD 28 x 60pdr shell guns
   4 x 30pdrs (long)
   UD 4 x 30pdrs (long), 28 x 30pdrs (short)
   FC & QD 4 x 30pdrs (short), 16 x 30pdr gunnades

Departed Kronshtadt for the Mediterranean on 10.6.1827 in Rear-Adm. Geiden's squadron under the overall command of the recently reinstated Adm. Seniavin. Fought at Navarino on 8.10.1827 during which she destroyed two Turkish frigates, a fireship and a shore battery at a cost of 14 killed, 37 wounded, and 51 hits received. Departed for the Baltic for repairs after offloading ammunition except for 2 rounds per gun. Arrived at Kronshtadt in 8.1828 where she was fully repaired. Cruised in the Baltic in 1829–30 and 1832–3. Underwent long repair in 1834–7. Cruised in the Baltic in 1838–42 and 1845–6. Repaired in 1848. To Denmark during the Schleswig-Holstein Crisis to provide security against Prussia in 1848–50. Rebuilt as a screw frigate with four boilers between 2.6.1854 and 24.10.1856. Trials completed in 10.1857. Cruised in the Baltic in 1858. To the Mediterranean with Rear-Adm. Nordman's squadron in 1859–60. Gunnery training ship in 1862–3. Stricken in 1871. (See under Steam and Sail section for further details.)

***Imperatritsa Aleksandra* class** (7 ships)
Imperatritsa Aleksandra 84/96 St Petersburg, New Admiralty
Constructor A. A. Popov
Laid down 8.5.1826   *Launched* 19.10.1827

Dimensions 196 ft x 50 ft x 23 ft 7 in (Veselago)
3,586 tons displacement (Pamyatnaya)
191 ft x 50 ft x 22 ft 11 in (Zapiski)
Armament 1827 LD 28 x 36pdrs (long), 4 x 60 u (1 pood)
UD 32 x 24pdrs (long)
FC & QD 6 x 12pdrs, 26 x 24pdr carr.
779 men (1830 'Establishment')
1840 LD 26 x 36pdrs, 6 x 9.65 in shell guns
 (2 pood)
UD 28 x 24pdrs (long), 4 x 60 u (1 pood)
FC & QD 6 x 24pdr gunnades 14 x 24pdr carr.
1854 LD 26 x 36pdrs (long) 6 x 9.65 in shell guns
 (2 pood)
UD 28 x 24pdrs (long) 4 x 60 u (1 pood)
FC & QD 4 x 24pdrs (short), 16 x 24pdr carr.
 (Pamyatnaya)
1855 LD 26 x 36pdrs (long), 6 x 9.65 in shell guns
 (2 pood)
UD 26 x 24pdrs (long), 6 x 60 u (1 pood)
FC & QD 1 x 36pdr pivot gun (bored up 24pdr),
 2 x 24pdrs (long), 6 x 24pdrs (short), 12 x 24pdr
 gunnades (Pamyatnaya)
1856 LD 2 x 9.65 in shell guns (2 pood)
FC & QD 1 x 36pdr pivot (bored up 24pdr)
 12 x 24pdr gunnades (as transport) (Pamyatnaya)
1857 LD 4 x 36pdrs (long), 22 x 36pdrs (short) 6 x 9.65
 in shell guns (2 pood)
UD 4 x 24pdrs (long), 28 x 24pdrs (short)
FC & QD 4 x 24pdrs (short), 16 x 24pdr gunnades
 (Pamyatnaya)

Imperatritsa Aleksandra class. Named after the wife of Nicholas I. Training service in Kronshtadt Roads in 1828. Cruised in the Baltic in 1829–30. Blockaded Kurlandia during the Polish mutiny of 1831. Cruised in the Baltic in 1833. Carried Guard troops to Danzig and returned them to Kronshtadt in 1835. Cruised in the Baltic and participated in the Imperial Review of 1836. Repaired in 1837–9. Cruised in the Baltic in 1839–42, and 1846–7. Repaired in 1849–51. Stationed in Kronshtadt harbour for the defence of Kronshtadt on 16.6.1854. Cruised with Vice-Adm. Zamytskiy's squadron to Krasnaia Gorka in 7.1854. Stationed at Kronshtadt in 1855. Transported troops from Sveaborg and Revel' to Kronshtadt in 1856–7. Broken up on 5.1.1863.

Emgeiten 84/94 St Petersburg, New Admiralty
Constructor A. A. Popov
Laid down 25.11.1827 *Launched* 29.9.1828
Dimensions 196 ft x 50 ft x 23 ft 7 in
Armament 1828 LD 28 x 36pdrs (long), 4 x 60 u (1 pood)
UD 32 x 24pdrs (long)
FC & QD 6 x 12pdrs, 26 x 24pdr carr.
779 men (1830 'Establishment')
1840 LD 26 x 36pdrs, 6 x 9.65 in shell guns (2 pood)
UD 28 x 24pdrs (long), 4 x 60 u (1 pood)
FC & QD 6 x 24pdr gunnades, 14 x 24pdr carr.
1854 LD 30 x 36pdrs (short) 2 x 9.65 in shell guns
 (2 pood)
UD 28 x 24pdrs (long), 4 x 60 u (1 pood)
FC & QD 4 x 24pdrs (long), 16 x 24pdr carr.
 (Pamyatnaya)
1856 LD 26 x 36pdrs (short), 2 x 9.65 in shell guns
 (2 pood)
UD 28 x 24pdr gunnades
FC & QD 1 x 36pdr pivot gun (bored up 24pdrs),
 14 x 24pdrs (short) (Pamyatnaya)
1857 LD 26 x 36pdrs (short), 2 x 9.65 in shell guns
 (2 pood)
UD 28 x 24pdrs (short)
FC & QD 14 x 24pdrs (short) (Pamyatnaya)

Imperatritsa Aleksandra class. Cruised in the Baltic in 1829–30, 1833, 1834, 1836–7 and 1839–40. Repaired in 1841–5. To Denmark in 1848–9 to deter invasion by Prussia. Cruised in the Baltic in 1853. Cruised to Krasnaia Gorka in 10–15.7.1854 and 21–26.8.1854. Harbour service in Kronshtadt Roads in 1855. Broken up in 1858.

Poltava 84/90 St Petersburg, New Admiralty
Constructor A. A. Popov
Laid down 5.12.1828 *Launched* 12.10.1829
Dimensions 191 ft x 50 ft x 23 ft (Veselago)
3,586 tons displacement (Pamyatnaya)
191 ft 10 in x (180 ft2 in keel) x 50 ft (inside plank)
x 23 ft 7 in x 22 ft 11 in (Zapiski)
Armament 1827 LD 28 x 36pdrs (long), 4 x 60 u (1 pood)
UD 32 x 24pdrs (long)
FC & QD 6 x 12pdrs 26 x 24pdr carr.
779 men (1830 'Establishment')
1840 LD 26 x 36pdrs, 6 x 9.65 in shell guns (2 pood)
UD 28 x 24pdrs (long), 4 x 60 u (1 pood)
FC & QD 6 x 24pdr gunnades, 14 x 24pdr carr.
1854 LD 28 x 36pdrs (short), 4 x 9.65 in shell guns
 (2 pood)
UD 30 x 24pdrs (short), 2 x 60 u (1 pood)
FC & QD 4 x 24pdrs (short), 16 x 24pdr carr.
 (Pamyatnaya)
1855 LD 4 x 36pdrs (long), 22 x 36pdrs (short),
 6 x 9.65 in shell guns (2 pood)
UD 4 x 24pdrs (long), 24 x 24pdrs (short),
 2 x 60 u (1 pood)
FC & QD 10 x 24pdrs (short) 10 x 24pdr carr.
 (Pamyatnaya)
1856 LD 4 x 36pdrs (long), 22 x 36pdrs (short),
 6 x 9.65 in shell guns (2 pood)
UD 4 x 24pdrs (long), 24 x 24pdrs (short),
 2 x 60 u (1 pood)
FC & QD 16 x 24pdr carr. (Pamyatnaya)
1857 LD 4 x 36pdrs (long), 24 x 36pdrs (short),
 4 x 9.65 in shell guns (2 pood)
UD 4 x 24pdrs (long), 28 x 24pdrs (short)
FC & QD 4 x 24pdrs (short), 16 x 24pdr carr.
 (Pamyatnaya)

Imperatritsa Aleksandra class. Cruised in the Baltic in 1830–2, 1834 and 1836–9. Repaired in 1846–8. To Denmark with Rear-Adm. Balk's 2nd Division in 1849–50. Cruised in the Baltic in 1851 and 1853. Sailed from Sveaborg to Kronshtadt in 11.1854. In commission at Kronshtadt in 1855. Carried troops from Sveaborg to Kronshtadt in 1856. Stricken in 21.3.1860 and broken up.

Ne Tron' Menia 84/92 St Petersburg, New Admiralty
Constructor A. A. Popov
Laid down 7.11.1830 *Launched* 1.5.1832
Dimensions 196 ft x 50 ft x 23 ft 8 in (Veselago)
3,586 tons displacement (Pamyatnaya)
191 ft 4 in x (179 ft 3 in keel) x 50 ft7 in x ? (Zapiski)

Armament 1832 LD 28 x 36pdrs (long), 4 x 60 u (1 pood)
UD 32 x 36pdrs (short)
FC & QD 4 x 18pdrs (long), 24 x 36pdr carr.
4 18pdr carr. (experimental)
1854 LD 26 x 36pdrs (short), 6 x 9.65 in shell guns
(2 pood)
UD 28 x 24pdrs (short), 4 x 60 u (1 pood)
FC & QD 4 x 24pdrs (short), 16 x 24pdr carr.
(Pamyatnaya)
1855 LD 26 x 36pdrs (short), 6 x 9.65 in shell guns
(2 pood)
UD 26 x 24pdrs (short), 6 x 60 u (1 pood)
FC & QD 1 x 36pdr (bored up 24pdr), 4 x 24pdrs
(short) 16 x 24pdr carr. (Pamyatnaya)
1856 LD 26 x 36pdrs (short), 6 x 9.65 in shell guns
(2 pood)
UD 26 x 24pdrs (short), 4 x 60 u (1 pood)
FC & QD 1 x 36pdr (bored up 24pdr), 4 x 24pdrs
(short) 16 x 24pdr carr. (Pamyatnaya)
1857 LD 4 x 36pdrs (long), 22 x 36pdrs (short), 6 x 9.65
in shell guns (2 pood)
UD 4 x 24pdrs (long), 28 x 24pdrs (short)
FC & QD 4 x 24pdrs (short), 16 x 24pdr carr.
(Pamyatnaya)

Imperatritsa Aleksandra class. Original uniform calibre armament was experimental and too heavy to be maintained in service. Cruised in the Baltic in 1832–3. Carried a corp of Guard troops from Kronshtadt to Danzig and back to Sveaborg in 1835. Cruised in the Baltic in 1836–9 and 1841–2. Repaired in 1849–50. Cruised in the Baltic in 1853. Stationed in Kronshtadt Roads in 1854–5. Carried cargo in the Baltic in 1856–7. Decommissioned in 1857. Stricken in 11.9.1863.

Vladimir 84/92 St Petersburg, New Admiralty
Constructor A. K. Kaverznev
Laid down 28.6.1832   *Launched* 10.8.1833
Dimensions 196 ft x 50 ft x 23 ft 7 in (Veselago)
3,586 tons displacement (Pamyatnaya)
191 ft 4 in x (179 ft 3 in keel) x 50 ft x ? (Zapiski)
Armament 1827 LD 28 x 36pdrs (long), 4 x 60 u (1 pood)
UD 32 x 24pdrs (long)
FC & QD 6 x 12pdrs, 26 x 24pdr carr.
779 men (1830 'Establishment')
1840 LD 26 x 36pdrs, 6 x 9.65 in shell guns, (2 pood)
UD 28 x 24pdrs (long), 4 x 60 u (1 pood)
FC & QD 6 x 24pdr gunnades, 14 x 24pdr carr.
1854 LD 26 x 36pdrs (long), 6 x 9.65 in shell guns
(2 pood)
UD 28 x 24pdrs (long), 4 x 60 u (1 pood)
FC & QD 4 x 24pdrs (short) 16 x 24pdr carr.
(Pamyatnaya)
1855 LD 26 x 36pdrs (long), 6 x 9.65 in shell guns
(2 pood)
UD 28 x 24pdrs (long), 4 x 60 u (1 pood)
FC & QD 1 x 36pdr (bored up 24pdr),
10 x 24pdrs (short), 10 x 24pdr carr. (Pamyatnaya)
1856 LD 2 x 36pdrs (long), 6 x 9.65 in shell guns
(2 pood)
UD 4 x 60 u (1 pood)
FC & QD 1 x 36pdr (bored up 24pdr) 10 x 24pdrs
(short) 10 x 24pdr carr.(Pamyatnaya)
1857 LD 26 x 36pdrs (long), 6 x 9.65 in shell guns
(2 pood)
UD 4 x 24pdrs (long), 28 x 24pdrs (short)
FC & QD 4 x 24pdrs (short), 16 x 24pdr carr.
(Pamyatnaya)

Imperatritsa Aleksandra class. Cruised in the Baltic in 1834–5. Transported Guard troops to Danzig in 1835. Participated in the Imperial Review in 1836. Cruised in the Baltic in 1838–9 and 1841–3. Cruised in the North Sea in Vice-Adm. Plater's squadron in 1844. Repaired in 1846. Cruised in the North Sea in 1847. To Denmark during the Schleswig-Holstein Crisis to provide support against the Prussians in 1848. Repaired in 1850–1. Cruised in the Baltic in 1853. Stationed in Sveaborg in 1854. Transferred to Kronshtadt in 11.1854. Stationed at Kronshtadt in 1855. Carried cargo with reduced armament in the Baltic in 1856–7. Decommissioned in 1857. Converted to a sheer hulk in 1860.

Vola 84/92 St Petersburg, New Admiralty
Constructor A. K. Kaverznev
Laid down 23.10.1835   *Launched* 30.7.1837
Dimensions 196 ft x 50 ft x 23 ft 7 in (Veselago)
191 ft 4 in x (173 ft 2 in keel) x 50 ft x ? (Zapiski)
215 ft x 53 ft 8 in (outside plank) x 23 ft 8 in x 22 ft 3 in
3,814 tons displacement (as screw ship)
Armament 1837   LD 28 x 36pdrs (long) 4 x 60 u (1 pood)
UD 32 x 24pdrs (long)
FC & QD 6 x 12pdrs 26 x 24pdr carr.
779 men (1830 'Establishment')
1840 LD 26 x 36pdrs, 6 x 9.65 in shell guns (2 pood)
UD 28 x 24pdrs (long), 4 x 60 u (1 pood)
FC & QD 6 x 24pdr gunnades, 14 x 24pdr carr
1857 (as a screw ship) LD 26 x 60pdr shell guns,
4 x 30pdrs (long)
UD 28 x 30pdrs (short), 4 x 30pdrs (long)
FC & QD 4 x 30pdrs (short), 16 x 30pdr
howitzers

Imperatritsa Aleksandra class. The name Vola commemorates a Warsaw suburb taken by the Russian army during the suppression of the Polish Mutiny of 1831. Cruised in the Baltic in 1839–43 and 1846–7. To Denmark during the Schleswig-Holstein Crisis to provide support against the Prussians. Converted to a screw ship from 4.6.1854 to 26.10.1856. Hull elongated to accommodate machinery and four boilers. Trials in 1857. Cruised in the Baltic in 1857–61. Stricken on 26.8.1871. (See Steam and Sail section for further details.)

Andrei 80/84 St Petersburg, New Admiralty
Constructor A. K. Kaverznev
Laid down 15.11.1840   *Launched* 19.8.1844
Dimensions 196 ft x 50 ft x 23 ft 7 in (Veselago)
3,500 tons displacement (Pamyatnaya)
Armament 1844 LD 26 x 36pdrs (long), 6 x 9.65 in shell guns
(2 pood)
UD 28 x 24pdrs (long), 4 x 60 u (1 pood)
FC & QD 6 x 24pdr gunnades, 14 x 24pdr carr.
(1842 Establishment)
1854 LD 26 x 36pdrs (long), 6 x 9.65 in shell guns
(2 pood)
UD 28 x 24pdrs (long), 4 x 60 u (1 pood)
FC & QD 6 x 24pdrs (short), 14 x 24pdr carr.
(Pamyatnaya)
1855 LD 26 x 36pdrs (long), 6 x 9.65 in shell guns
(2 pood)

UD 28 x 24pdrs (long), 4 x 60 u (1 pood)
FC & QD 1 x 36pdr pivot (short), 6 x 24pdrs
(short) 14 x 24pdr carr. (Pamyatnaya)

Imperatritsa Aleksandra class. Cruised in the Baltic in 1846–7. To Denmark during the Schleswig-Holstein Crisis to provide support against the threat of Prussian invasion in 1848–50. Cruised in the Baltic in 1851 and 1853. Stationed at Sveaborg in 1854–5. Participated in defending Sveaborg from allied naval assault on 28.7.1855. Decommissioned in 1856. Receiving ship at Helsingfors in 1857. Stricken on 28.10.1861.

Lefort 84/94 St Petersburg, New Admiralty
Constructor   Y. A. Kolodkin
Laid down   18.11.1833   Launched   28.7.1835
Dimensions   196 ft x 50 ft x 23 ft 7 in (16 ft 2½ in) (Veselago)
3,588 tons displacement/3,768 tons (1857) (Pamyatnaya)
200 ft 2 in x (180 ft keel) x 50 ft x ? (Zapiski)
Armament   1835 LD 28 x 36pdrs (long), 4 x 60 u (1 pood)
UD 32 x 24pdrs (long)
FC & QD 6 x 12pdrs, 26 x 24pdr carr.
779 men (1830 'Establishment')
1840 LD 26 x 36pdrs, 6 x 9.65 in shell guns (2 pood)
UD 28 x 24pdrs (long), 4 x 60 u (1 pood)
FC & QD 6 x 24pdr gunnades, 14 x 24pdr carr.
1853 LD 24 x 36pdrs (long), 8 x 9.65 in shell guns
(2 pood)
UD 28 x 36pdrs (short), 4 x 60 u (1 pood)
FC & QD 4 x 36pdr gunnades, 16 x 36pdr carr.
1854 LD 24 x 36pdrs (long), 8 x 9.65 in shell guns
(2 pood)
UD 28 x 36pdrs (short), 4 x 60 u (1 pood)
FC & QD 4 x 36pdrs (bored up 24pdrs),
16 x 36pdr carr. (Pamyatnaya)
1855 LD 24 x 36pdrs (long) 8 x 9.65 in shell guns
(2 pood)
UD 28 x 36pdrs (short), 4 x 60 u (1 pood)
FC & QD 1 x 68pdr (pivot), 16 x 36pdr carr.
4 x 24pdrs (long) (Pamyatnaya)
1856 LD 26 x 36pdrs (long), 4 x 9.65 in shell guns
(2 pood)
UD 22 x 36pdrs (short), 2 x 60 u (1 pood)
FC & QD 1 x 68pdr (pivot), 4 x 36pdr carr.
(Pamyatnaya)
1857 LD 15 x 36pdrs (long), 11 x 36pdrs (?), 6 x 9.65 in
shell guns (2 pood)
UD 4 x 36pdrs (bored up 24pdrs), 32 x 36pdrs
(short) 6 x 36pdr carr. (Pamyatnaya)

Incorrectly listed as an *Imperatrista Aleksandra* class member by Chernyshev. Lefort was a close friend of Peter I and served as the first Russian admiral. Cruised in the Baltic 1836–8, 1840–1, and 1843 Cruised in the North Sea in 1844. Cruised in the Baltic in 1846. Cruised in the North Sea in 1847. To Denmark during the Schleswig-Holstein Crisis to provide support against the threat of Prussian invasion in 1848. Repaired and rearmed in 1850–1, after which she was considered the strongest 2-decker in the Baltic fleet. Cruised in the Baltic in 1853. Stationed in Kronshtadt Roads with an elite crew of Imperial Guards in 1854–5. Carried troops and cargo in the Baltic in 1856–7. Capsized in a squall off on 10.9.1857 with the loss of the entire crew of 756 men and 81 women and children (family members).

Krasnoi 84 St Petersburg, New Admiralty
Constructor   Pipin
Laid down   28.4.1845   Launched   12.8.1847
Dimensions   196 ft x (179 ft 6 in keel/201 ft 2 in upper deck) x 48 ft
x 19 ft 3 in
3,669 tons displacement (Pamyatnaya)
Armament   1854 LD 26 x 30pdrs (long), 6 x 9.65 in shell guns
(2 pood)
UD 28 x 30pdr gunnades, 4 x 60 u (1 pood)
FC & QD 4 x 30pdr gunnades, 14 x 30pdr carr.
(Pamyatnaya)
1855 LD 26 x 30pdr gunnades, 6 x 9.65 in shell guns
(2 pood)
UD 26 x 30pdr gunnades, 6 x 60 u (1 pood)
FC & QD 1 x 36pdr pivot guns (short), 6 x 30pdr
gunnades, 12 x 30pdr carr. (Pamyatnaya)

Name commemorates two battles in 1812. Experimentally rearmed as above at the suggestion of Ilyi Nauki Morskoy Artilleri. To Denmark during the Schleswig-Holstein Crisis to provide support against the threat of Prussian invasion in 1848–9. Cruised in the Baltic in 1851–2. Stationed in Kronshtadt Roads in 1854–5. Operated with Adm. Rikord's squadron off Krasnaia Gorka in 8.1854. Carried cargo in the Baltic in 1856–7. Decommissioned in 1857. Stricken on 5.1.1863.

Prokhor class (2 ships)

Prokhor 84 St Petersburg, New Admiralty
Constructor   M. N. Grinvald
Laid down   15.1.1848   Launched   11.4.1851
Dimensions   196 ft x 51 ft 6 in (outside plank) x 23 ft 6 in (Veselago)
3,526 tons displacement (Pamyatnaya)
Armament   1854 LD 26 x 36pdrs (long), 6 x 9.65 in shell guns
(2 pood)
UD 28 x 36pdr gunnades, 4 x 60 u (1 pood)
FC & QD 4 x 36pdr gunnades, 16 x 36pdr carr.
(Pamyatnaya)
1855 LD 26 x 36pdrs (long), 6 x 9.65 in shell guns
(2 pood)
UD 30 x 36pdrs (bored up 24pdrs), 4 x 60 u
(1 pood)
FC & QD 1 x 36pdr (short) pivot, 2 x 36pdrs
(bored up 24pdrs), 16 x 36pdr carr. (Pamyatnaya)
1856 LD 2 x 36pdrs (long), 12 x 36pdrs (bored up
24pdrs), 1 x 36pdr pivot (bored up 24pdr)
2 x 9.65 in shell guns (2 pood), 4 x 60 u (1 pood)
(Pamyatnaya)
1857 LD 26 x 36pdrs (long), 6 x 9.65 in shell guns
(2 pood)
UD 4 x 36pdrs (long), 28 x 36pdrs (bored up
24pdrs)
FC & QD 4 x 36pdrs (bored up 24pdrs),
16 x 36pdr   carr. (Pamyatnaya)
1858 LD 1 x 68pdr shell gun, 10 x 60pdrs, 18 x 36pdrs
(long), 3 x 9.65 in shell guns (2 pood)
UD 4 x 36pdrs (long), 14 x 36pdrs (bored up
24pdrs), 14 x 30pdrs (short)
FC & QD 1 x 60pdr pivot gun, 12 x 36pdrs (bored up
24pdrs) 4 x 30pdr gunnades, 4 x 36pdr carr.
(Pamyatnaya)

Prokhor class. Similar to *Krasnoi*, but of greater width, depth of hold and draught, *Prokhor* was considered to be the most successful Russian 84. Cruised in the Baltic in 1851 and 1853. Stationed in Sveaborg in

1854 and towed to Kronshtadt in 11.1854. Stationed in Kronshtadt Roads in 1855. Cruised in the Baltic in 1856–7. Gunnery training ship at Revel' in 1858–61. Used as a test bed for rockets being developed by General Konstantinov in 1860. Stricken on 11.9.1863.

Oryol 84 St Petersburg, New Admiralty
Constructor Panin
Laid down 14.6.1851 *Launched* 12.8.1854
Dimensions 196 ft x 51 ft 6 in (outside plank) x 23 ft 6 in
   3,526 tons displacement (as designed)
   206 ft 8 in x 51 ft 6 in (outside plank) x 23 ft 7 in
   3,713 tons displacement (as a screw ship)
Armament 1855 LD 28 x 68pdrs (shell guns), 4 x 24pdrs (long)
   UD 4 x 24pdrs (long), 24 x 24pdrs (short)
   FC & QD 2 x 68pdr (pivot), 4 x 24pdr (short),
   16 x 24pdr carr.

Prokhor class (as authorized). Screw ship. Laid down as a sailing ship of the *Prokhor* class. Ordered completed as a screw ship in July 1852. Lengthened and converted to steam while building. Cruised in the Baltic in 1856 and 1859–60. Stricken on 7.12.1863. (See under Steam and Sail section for additional details.)

Ships with 70–78 guns (31 purpose-built 1825–60)

Iezekiil' class (25 ships)

The traditional standard line of battle ship of the Napoleonic War period had been the 74-gun two-decker. In the years after the war, these ships were effectively replaced by larger and more powerful 80- and 90-gun ships in the British, French, and American navies. The Russians, in contrast, continued to rely on significant numbers of smaller 74-gun ships of the *Iezekiil'* class as their basic battleship type in the Baltic, supplemented by smaller numbers of 84-gun ships of the *Aleksandr* and related classes. Russian attention in the second quarter of the nineteenth century continued to focus upon shallow Baltic conditions and upon the more limited potential threat of Swedish and Danish naval revival than upon the unlikely possibility of conflict with the Atlantic-based fleets of the other great European powers. Both of the lesser Baltic powers had very small numbers of 74- and 84-gun ships in service during this period and the active strength of the Russian Baltic fleet 74s would have easily sufficed by themselves to dominate the fleets of either Denmark or Sweden or both together had the need arisen.

The 25 74s of the *Iezekiil'* class were straightforward developments of the successful and popular *Selafail* class with similar dimensions and with an increase in displacement of 300 tons bringing the nominal displacement of the new class to 3,000 tons.

Russian technological sophistication continued to advance during the long production run of the new frigates from 1825 to 1849. This was reflected in reforms made to expedite the speed and ease of production during the building process, and in the application of new technologies in the fitting out and equipage of the finished frigates. From 1832 on, the length of construction was reduced to an average of two years from the normal range of one to seven years for the *Selafails*. Suitable sections of ships' hull were now cut at the point of harvesting in forests, using prepared moulds in order to save time in the shipyards. The speed of transportation of cut timber to the shipyards was greatly improved by the use of cargo vessels or by roads in place of the traditional method of slow rafting down local rivers. This change also eliminated the problem of premature dry rot as a result of fresh water contamination of the floating logs. Diagonal bracing on the Sepping's pattern was introduced in 1837 providing for greater structural strength and durability. Scuppers were made of copper, powder rooms covered with lead, bread storage spaces with zinc-coated iron, water barrels replaced by iron cisterns, anchor cables replaced by iron chains, lightning rods installed on the masts, and four iron wood stoves per ship supplied for the drying out lower deck spaces. Of very great significance in terms of improving performance under sail and extending lifespans by improving the protection provided to the underwater hull surfaces, was the introduction of felt impregnated with tar in place of less durable paper as the interface between copper plating and wooden hulls. The labour-intensive and expensive use of gilded decorations gave way to simple standardized bow-figures of double-headed eagles.

These and similar innovations and the greater attention being paid to preventive maintenance throughout the Baltic fleet after the Great Flood resulted in the *Iezekiil'* class members having average lifespans that were on the order of 20 per cent longer than those of the *Selafails*.

The use of edinorogs had been officially abandoned in the Russian navy with the implementation of the Establishment of 1805. The decision was made in 1826 to reintroduce this uniquely Russian ordnance throughout the fleet. The *Iezekiil'* class members were accordingly armed with four edinorogs firing either 63-pound solid shot or 44-pound bombs in place of four of the main deck 36pdrs, giving them a reduced main deck battery of only 24 conventional cannon in contrast to the 28 carried by the earlier ships, but having the advantage of adding to the adaptability and offensive capability of the ships. This armament was augmented after 1842 in most active ships of this and other classes with four 2-pood (126-pound) 9.65-inch shell guns replacing the 1-pood (63-pound) edinorogs originally mounted, and with an additional two 1-pood edinorogs substituting for two of the short upper deck 24pdr guns. It should be noted that mixed batteries of 16 to 18 8pdrs and 4 to 6 24pdr carronades were the norm for the upper decks with an additional 6 6pdrs being frequently mounted on the roundhouse.

Although they were not as long-lived as the more solidly constructed and prestigious 84-gun *Aleksandras*, the *Iezekiil'* class members had long and useful careers in a variety of incarnations. Three served with distinction at Navarino in 1827 and nine were still sufficiently viable a quarter of a century later to be put into service as floating batteries during the Crimean War. Three were cut down to frigates or corvettes in the 1850s in a move that is distantly reminiscent of the British reconstruction of Napoleonic era 74s in the 1820s into razees to counter the large 30pdr French frigates that were entering service. Sadly, the potential value of these three innovative reconstructions was negated by their relegation to blockship duty in defence of Kronshtadt in 1855.

Iezekiil' 74/80 Arkhangel'sk
Constructor A. M. Kurochkin
Laid down 29.9.1825 (or 20.10.1825) *Launched* 26.5.1826
Dimensions 178 ft x 48 ft (inside plank) x 19 ft 3 in
   3,000 tons displacement -official
   176.7 ft x 49.33 ft x 19.4 ft
   2,918.7 tons displacement (Fincham 1851)
Armament LD 24 x 36pdrs (short), 4 x 60 u (1 pood)

A model of the second Iezekiil' *class ship completed, the heroic* Azov *(74) on exhibition at the Naval Museum at St Petersburg. Her imposing warrior figurehead and the expensive gilding on her bow can be made out here, recreated by the modeller with loving attention to detail. She was the final ship completed by the prominent constructor A. M. Kurochkin, but short-lived, with only five years passing between her launch in 1826 and breaking up in 1831.*

UD 30 x 24pdrs (short)
FC & QD 22 x 24pdr carr. (Sudostroenie 1974)

Iezekiil' class. Sailed from Arkhangel'sk to Kronshtadt in 8–9.1826. Left Kronshtadt for the Mediterranean in Rear-Adm. Geiden's squadron under the supreme command of Adm. Seniavin on 10.6.1827. Fought at Navarino on 8.10.1827 destroying a fireship and shore battery with losses of 13 killed and 21 wounded. Cruised in the Mediterranean in 1828–30. Captured the Turkish corvette *Eastern Star* (renamed *Navarino* in Russian service) on 21.4.1828. Blockaded the Dardanelles in 1829. Repaired at Malta in 1829–30. Returned to Kronshtadt on 12.5.1830. Cruised in the Baltic in 7–10.1830. Repaired in 1831–2. Cruised in the Baltic in 1832–4. Cruised in the Baltic and attended the Imperial Review in 1836. Cruised in the Baltic in 1838–9. Decommissioned in 1841. Transferred to Sveaborg and hulked in 1842. Broken up in 1849.

Azov 74/80 Arkhangel'sk
Constructor A. M. Kurochkin
Laid down 29.9.1825 (or 20.10.1825) *Launched* 26.5.1826
Dimensions 178 ft x 48 ft (inside plank) x 19 ft 3 in
3,000 tons displacement (official)
Armament LD 24 x 36pdrs (short), 4 x 60 u (1 pood)
UD 30 x 24pdrs (short)
FC & QD 22 x 24pdr carr. (Sudostroenie 1974)

Iezekiil' class. Sailed from Arkhangel'sk to Kronshtadt in 8–9.1826. Left Kronshtadt for the Mediterranean in Rear-Adm. Geiden's squadron under the supreme command of the recently reinstated Adm. Seniavin on 10.6.1827. Fought at Navarino on 8.10.1827 destroying three frigates and a corvette and forcing the Turkish flagship *Muharrem-bey* (80) to beach herself and then burning her. Casualties suffered at Navarino included 24 killed, 67 wounded and 153 shot holes. Cruised in the Mediterranean in 1828-30 and participated in the blockade of the Dardanelles in 1829. Returned to Kronshtadt on 12.5.1830. Cruised in the Baltic in 7–10.1830. Decommissioned in 1830. Broken up in 1831.

Aleksandr Nevskii 74/80 St Petersburg, Okhta
Constructor V. F. Stoke
Laid down 24.9.1825 *Launched* 7.10.1826
Dimensions 178 ft x 48 ft x 19 ft 4 in
Armament 1826 LD 24 x 36pdrs (short), 4 x 60 u (1 pood)
UD 30 x 24pdrs (short)
FC & QD 16 x 8pdrs, 6 x 6pdrs (Sudostroenie 1974)
1832 LD 30 x 36pdrs (short)
FC & QD 32 x 36pdr carr. (as a razee) (Sudostroenie 1974)

Iezekiil' class. *Aleksandr Nevskii* was one of a small number of Russian ships of the line completed with round sterns on the pattern introduced in the British Royal Navy by Seppings. Another known example of Russian ships with round sterns was the *Tri Sviatitelia* (120) of 1838. Resistance to the structurally sound approach of Seppings was apparently at least as strong in the Russian Navy as in the British and round sterns never became standard.

Departed Kronshtadt for the Mediterranean as part of Rear-Adm. Geiden' squadron under the supreme command of the recently reinstated Adm. Seniavin on 10.6.1827. Fought at Navarino on 8.10.1827 and destroyed two frigates with casualties of 5 killed, 7 wounded, and 17 shot holes. At La Valetta on 27.12.1827 sailors mutinied due to the extreme brutality of some officers. Court martial tribunal dismissed several officers including the executive officer and sentenced 16 crewmen to penal servitude. Cruised in the Mediterranean in 1828–30, participating in the blockade of the

A painting of the battle at Navarino in 1827 seen from the Russian perspective by I. K. Ayvazovskiy. In the centre is Rear Admiral Geiden's 74-gun flagship Azov *engaging a Turkish frigate.* Azov *was the most heavily damaged allied warship in the battle, single-handedly engaging five Turkish warships at one point. She acquitted herself heroically, sinking three frigates and a corvette and forcing the grounding of the Turkish 84-gun flagship.*

Dardanelles in 1829. Returned to Kronshtact on 10.9.1831. Razeed and converted to a frigate in 1832. Conducted trials in 10.1834. Transported troops to Danzig and back to Kronshtadt in 1835. Participated in the Imperial Review in 1836. Cruised in the Baltic in 1837–9 and 1841–2. Cruised in the Baltic with naval cadets in 1844. Decommissioned in 1844. Hulked in 1846. Broken up in 1847.

Velikii Kniaz' Mikhail 74/86 St Petersburg, Okhta
Constructor V. F. Stoke
Laid down 15.11.1826 *Launched* 15.10.1327
Dimensions 178 ft x 48 ft (inside plank) x 19 ft 3 in (Veselago)
 2,378 tons displacement (Pamyatnaya)
 180 ft x 48 ft x 22 ft 4 in (Zapiski)
Armament 1830 LD 24 x 36pdrs (short), 4 x 60 u (1 pood)
 UD 30 x 24pdrs (short)
 FC & QD. 20 x 24pdr carr., 4 18pdr carr.,
 6 x 12pdr carr. (Pamyatnaya)
 1840 LD 24 x 36pdrs (short), 4 x 60 u (1 pood)
 UD 30 x 24pdrs (short)
 FC & QD 16 x 8pdrs, 6 x 24pdr carr. or
 20 x 24pdr carr.
 699 men (1830 'Establishment')
 1854 LD 24 x 36pdrs (short), 4 x 9.65 in shell guns
 (2 pood)
 UD 26 x 24pdrs (short), 4 x 60 u (1 pood)
 FC & QD 4 x 24pdrs (short), 12 x 24pdr carr.
 (Pamyatnaya)
 1855 LD 24 x 36pdrs (short), 4 x 9.65 in shell guns
 (2 pood), 1 x 60 u (1 pood)
 UD 26 x 24pdrs (short) 4 x 60 u (1 pood)
 FC & QD 1 x 36pdr (bored up 24pdr), 16 x 24pdr
 carr. (Pamyatnaya)

1856 LD 24 x 36pdrs (short), 4 x 9.65 in shell guns
    (2 pood)
UD 26 x 24pdrs (short), 4 x 60 u (1 pood)
FC & QD 1 x 36pdrs (bored up 24pdrs),
    16 x 24pdr carr. (Pamyatnaya)
1856 LD 24 x 36pdrs (short), 4 x 9.65 in shell guns
    (2 pood)
UD 26 x 24pdrs (short), 4 x 60 u (1 pood)
FC & QD 16 x 24pdr carr. (Pamyatnaya)

Iezekiil' class. Named after the younger brother of Nicholas I. To the Mediterranean in 1828–30. Returned to Kronshtadt on 12.5.1830. Cruised in the Baltic in 1830–1 and 1833–4. Repaired in 1834–5. Cruised in the Baltic in 1839–43. Repaired in 1850–2. Commissioned and stationed in Kronshtadt Roads in 1854–5. Sheer hulk in 1860. Stricken in 11.9.1863.

Katsbakh 74/80 Arkhangel'sk
Constructor V. A. Ershov
Laid down 5.9.1827   *Launched* 25.5.1828
Dimensions 178 ft x 48 ft (inside plank) x 19 ft 3 in
    3,000 tons displacement
Armament 1840 LD 24 x 36pdrs (short) 4 x 60 u (1 pood)
    UD 30 x 24pdrs (short)
    FC & QD 16 x 8pdrs, 6 x 24pdr carr. or
    20 x 24pdr carr.
    699 men (1830 'Establishment')
    1855 LD 28 x 36pdrs (short)
    UD 30 x 24pdrs (short)
    FC & QD 22 x 44pdr carr., 4 12pdrs
    (Pamyatnaya)

Iezekiil' class. Name commemorates a Russian victory in 1813. Sailed from Arkhangel'sk to Kronshtadt in 1828. Cruised in the Baltic in 1829–30. Carried troops to Libavia in 1831 during the Polish Mutiny. Cruised in the Baltic in 1833–4, and 1836–7. Repaired in 1837–42. Cruised in the Baltic in 1843. Cruised in the North Sea with Vice-Adm. Plater's squadron in 1844. Cruised in the Baltic in 1845. Cruised to Dogger Bank in 1847. Cruised to Denmark during the Schleswig-Holstein Crisis to protect Denmark from the threat of Prussian invasion in 1848–50. Cruised in the Baltic in 1851–53. Employed with two other 74s and three heavy frigates as a floating battery off Kotlin in 5–10.1854. While serving as a floating battery, fitted with an unprecedented main battery of 24 1-pood edinorogs. Broken up in 1857.

Kul'm 74/90 Arkhangel'sk
Constructor V. A. Ershov
Laid down 5.9.1827   *Launched* 25.5.1828
Dimensions 178 ft x 48 ft (inside plank) x 19 ft 3 in
    3,000 tons displacement
Armament 1840 LD 24 x 36pdrs (short), 4 x 60 u (1 pood)
    UD 30 x 24pdrs (short)
    FC & QD 16 x 8pdrs, 6 x 24pdr carr. or
    20 x 24pdr carr.
    699 men (1830 'Establishment')
    1855 LD 28 x 36pdrs (short)
    UD 28 x 24pdrs (short) 4 x 60 u (1 pood)
    FC & QD 20 x 24pdr carr., 4 12pdrs
    (Pamyatnaya)
    1856 LD 4 x 36pdrs (short), 24 x 60 u (1 pood)
    UD 4 x 24pdrs (long), 26 x 24pdrs (short)
    FC & QD 20 x 24pdr carr., 4 12pdrs
    (Pamyatnaya)

Iezekiil' class. Sailed from Arkhangel'sk to Kronshtadt in 1828. Cruised in the Baltic in 1829–30. Transported the Grand Duchess Elena Pavlona to Plymouth in 1831. Carried heavy artillery to Danzig in 1832. Cruised in the Baltic in 1833–4 and 1837. Repaired in 1839–42. Cruised in the Baltic in 1843 and 1846–7. To Denmark during the Schleswig-Holstein Crisis to protect against the threat of Prussian invasion in 1848–50. Employed with two other 74s and three heavy frigates as a floating battery off Kotlin in 5–10.1854. While serving as a floating battery, fitted with an unprecedented main battery of 24 1-pood edinorogs. Broken up in 1857.

Arsis 74/80 St Petersburg
Constructor V. F. Stoke
Laid down 30.11.1827   *Launched* 29.9.1828
Dimensions 179 ft x 47 ft 10 in x 19 ft 3 in
Armament 1840 LD 24 x 36pdrs (short), 4 x 60 u (1 pood)
    UD 30 x 24pdrs (short)
    FC & QD 16 x 8pdrs, 6 x 24pdr carr. or
    20 x 24pdr carr.
    699 men (1830 'Establishment')
    1854 LD 26 x 36pdrs (short), 4 x 9.65 in shell guns
    (2 pood)
    UD 22 x 24pdrs (short), 4 x 60 u (1 pood)
    FC & QD 6 x 12pdrs, 12 x 24pdr carr.
    (Pamyatnaya)

Iezekiil' class. Name commemorates a Russian victory in 1814. Cruised in the Baltic in 1829–31 and 1833. Grounded in 1833 and repaired in Abo in 1834. Cruised in the Baltic in 1835–7. Repaired in 1837–42. Cruised in the Baltic in 1843. Cruised in the North Sea in 1844 and 1847. Cruised to Denmark during the Schleswig-Holstein Crisis in 1848–50 to protect against the threat of Prussian invasion. Cruised in the Baltic in 1851–53. Floating battery in Sveaborg in 1854. Broken up in 1857.

Narva 74/80 Arkhangel'sk
Constructor V. A. Ershov
Laid down 24.8.1828   *Launched* 21.5.1829
Dimensions 178 ft x 48 ft (inside plank) x 19 ft 3 in (Veselago)
    3,000 tons displacement
    178 ft x 48 ft (inside plank) x ? x 14 ft 10½ in (Zapiski)
Armament 1840 LD 24 x 36pdrs (short) 4 x 60 u (1 pood)
    UD 30 x 24pdrs (short)
    FC & QD 16 x 8pdrs, 6 x 24pdr carr. or
    20 x 24pdr carr.
    699 men (1830 'Establishment')

Iezekiil' class. Sailed from Arkhangel'sk to Kronshtadt in 1829. Cruised in the Baltic in 1830–2, 1834–8 and 1840. Decommissioned in 1844. Hulked at Sveaborg in 1844.

Lesnoe 74/80 Arkhangel'sk
Constructor V. A. Ershov
Laid down 24.8.1828   *Launched* 21.5.1829
Dimensions 178 ft x 48 ft (inside plank) x 19 ft 3 in (Veselago)
    3,000 tons displacement
    178 ft x 48 ft (inside plank) x 19 ft 3 in x 20 ft 9 in (Zapiski)
Armament 1840 LD 24 x 36pdrs (short), 4 x 60 u (1 pood)
    UD 30 x 24pdrs (short)
    FC & QD 16 x 8pdrs, 6 x 24pdr carr. or
    20 x 24pdr carr.
    699 men (1830 'Establishment')

Iezekiil' class. Name commemorates one of Peter I's major land battle victories over the Swedes in 1708. Sailed from Arkhangel'sk to

Kronshtadt in 1829. Cruised in the Baltic in 1830–2 and 1834–8. Decommissioned in 1838. Converted into a store hulk at Kronshtadt in 1842.

Brien 74/80 St Petersburg, Okhta
Constructor V. F. Stoke
Laid down 29.11.1828   *Launched* 10.9.1829
Dimensions 178 ft x 48 ft (inside plank) x 19 ft 3 in (Veselago)
2,980 tons displacement (Pamyatnaya)
180 ft x (164 ft 4 in keel) x 48 ft (inside plank) x 23 ft 1 in x 22 ft 4 in (Zapiski)
Armament 1840 LD 24 x 36pdrs (short) 4 x 60 u (1 pood)
UD 30 x 24pdrs (short)
FC & QD 16 x 8pdrs, 6 x 24pdr carr. or 20 x 24pdr carr.
699 men (1830 'Establishment')
1854 LD 24 x 36pdrs (short), 4 x 9.65 in shell guns (2 pood)
UD 28 x 36pdrs (bored up 24pdrs) 2 x 60 u (1 pood)
FC & QD 2 x 36pdrs (bored up 24pdrs), 14 x 36pdr carr. (Pamyatnaya)
1855 LD 4 x 36pdrs (long), 20 x 36pdrs (short), 4 x 9.65 in shell guns (2 pood)
UD 24 x 36pdrs (bored up 24pdrs), 4 x 60 u (1 pood)
FC & QD 1 x 36pdr pivot (short), 6 x 36pdrs (bored up 24pdrs), 12 x 36pdr carr. (Pamyatnaya)
1856 LD 4 x 36pdrs (long), 20 x 36pdrs (short), 4 x 9.65 in shell guns (2 pood); UD 28 x 36pdrs (bored up 24pdrs) 2 x 60 u (1 pood)
FC & QD 1 x 36pdr pivot (short) 14 x 36pdr carr. (Pamyatnaya)

Iezekiil' class. Cruised in the Baltic in 1830–2, 1834–6, 1839–40 and 1842–3. Repaired in 1845–9. To Denmark during the Schleswig-Holstein Crisis with the 3rd Division of Rear-Adm. E. Epanchin in 1848–50. Cruised in the Baltic in 1851–53. Sailed from Sveaborg to Kronshtadt in 11.1854. Harbour service in 1855. Stricken on 21.3.1860 and broken up.

Krasnoi 74/80 Arkhangel'sk
Constructor V. A. Ershov
Laid down 16.8.1829   *Launched* 23.5.1830
Dimensions 178 ft x 48 ft (inside plank) x 19 ft 3 in (Veselago)
3,000 tons displacement
178 ft x 48 ft (inside plank) x 19 ft 3 in x 20 ft 9 in
Armament 1830 LD 24 x 36pdrs (short) 4 x 60 u (1 pood)
UD 30 x 24pdrs (short)
FC & QD 16 x 8pdrs (long) 6 x 24pdr carr.
699 men (1830 'Establishment')
1840 LD 24 x 36pdrs (short) 4 x 60 u (1 pood)
UD 30 x 24pdrs (short)
FC & QD 16 x 8pdrs 6 x 24pdr carr. or 20 x 24pdr carr.
699 men

Iezekiil' class. Name commemorates two battles in 1812. Sailed from Arkhangel'sk to Kronshtadt in 1830. Cruised in the Baltic in 1831–2, 1834–8, 1840–1 and 1843. Decommissioned in 1843. Hulked at Sveaborg in 1844.

Borodino 74/80 Arkhangel'sk
Constructor V. A. Ershov
Laid down 16.8.1829   *Launched* 23.5.1830
Dimensions 178 ft x 48 ft (inside plank) x 19 ft 3 in (Veselago)
3,000 tons displacement
178 ft x 48 ft (inside plank) x 19 ft 3 in x 20 ft 9 in (Zapiski)
Armament 1830 LD 24 x 36pdrs (short) 4 x 60 u (1 pood)
UD 30 x 24pdrs (short)
FC & QD 16 x 8pdrs 6 x 24pdr carr. or 20 x 24pdr carr.
699 men (1830 'Establishment')

Iezekiil' class. Sailed from Arkhangel'sk to Kronshtadt in 1830. Cruised in the Baltic in 1831–2, 1834–8 and 1843. Decommissioned in 1845. Hulked at Kronshtadt in 1847.

Berezino 74/80 St Petersburg, Okhta
Constructor V. F. Stoke
Laid down 21.11.1829   *Launched* 25.8.1830
Dimensions 178 ft x 48 ft 10 x 19 ft (Veselago)
178 ft x (164 ft 4 in keel) x 48 ft x 23 ft 1 in x 22 ft 4 in (Zapiski)
Armament 1830 LD 24 x 36pdrs (short), 4 x 60 u (1 pood)
UD 30 x 24pdrs (short)
FC & QD 16 x 8pdrs, 6 x 24pdr carr. or 20 x 24pdr carr.
699 men (1830 'Establishment')
1854 LD 24 x 30pdrs (long), 4 x 9.65 in shell guns (2 pood)
UD 30 x 30pdr gunnades
FC & QD 2 x 30pdr gunnades 16 x 30pdr (long carr.) (Pamyatnaya)
1855 LD 24 x 30pdrs (long), 4 x 9.65 in shell guns (2 pood)
UD 2 x 30pdrs (long), 28 x 30pdr gunnades
FC & QD 1 x 30pdr pivot gun
4 x 30pdr gunnades, 14 x 30pdr carr. (Pamyatnaya)

Iezekiil' class. Name commemorates the rout of the Grand Armee in 1812. Experimentally rearmed as above at the suggestion of Ilyi Nauki Morskoy Artilleri Carried heavy artillery to Danzig in 1832. Cruised in the Baltic in 1834. Carried Guard troops to Danzig in 1835. Cruised in the Baltic in 1836–8, 1840–1 and 1844. Repaired in 1844–7. To Denmark during the Schleswig-Holstein Crisis in 1848–9. Operated off Krasnaia Gorka with Vice-Adm. Zamytskiy in 7.1854. Stationed in Kronshtadt Roads in 1854–5. Decommissioned in 1855. Towed to Sveaborg for breaking up in 1856. Broken up in 1860.

Smolensk 74/80 St Petersburg, New Admiralty
Constructor A. A. Popov
Laid down 21.11.1829   *Launched* 25.8.1830
Dimensions 178 ft x 48 ft (inside plank) x 19 ft 3 in (Veselago)
2,978 tons displacement (Pamyatnaya)
178 ft x (164 ft 5 in keel) x 48 ft (inside plank) x 22 ft 10 in x 22 ft 5 in (Zapiski)
177.12 ft x 49.6 ft x 20 ft
2,876.7 tons displacement (Fincham 1851)
Armament 1830 LD 24 x 36pdrs (short), 4 x 60 u (1 pood)
UD 30 x 24pdrs (short)
FC & QD 16 x 8pdrs, 6 x 24pdr carr. or 20 x 24pdr carr.
699 men (1830 'Establishment')
1854 LD 26 x 36pdrs (short), 2 x 9.65 in shell guns (2 pood)
UD 26 x 24pdrs (short), 4 x 60 u (1 pood) (Pamyatnaya)
FC & QD 4 x 24pdrs (short), 14 x 24pdr carr.
1855 LD 26 x 36pdrs (short), 2 x 9.65 in shell guns (2 pood) (Pamyatnaya)
UD 26 x 24pdrs (short), 4 x 60 u (1 pood)

FC & QD 6 x 24pdrs (short), 12 x 24pdr carr.,
1 x 36pdr pivot gun (bored up 24pdr)
1856 LD 28 x 36pdrs (short) (as corvette)

Iezekiil' class. Name commemorates the heroic defence of Smolensk in 1812. Cruised in the Baltic in 1831–3. Carried troops to Danzig in 1835. Cruised in the Baltic in 1836, and 1838–9. Repaired in 1841–4. Cruised in the Baltic in 1845. To Denmark during the Schleswig-Holstein Crisis as deterrence against invasion by Prussia in 1848. Cruised in the North Sea in 1852. Operated off Krasnaia Gorka with Vice-Adm. Zamytskiy in 7.1854. Stationed in Kronshtadt Roads in 1854–5. Cut down to a 28 gun corvette and hulked in 1856.

Pamiat' Azova 74/86 Arkhangel'sk
Constructor V. A. Ershov
Laid down 29.9.1830 *Launched* 21.5.1831
Dimensions 178 ft x 48 ft (inside plank) x 19 ft 3 in
3,000 tons displacement (Veselago)
178 ft x (165 ft keel) x 48 ft (inside plank) x 28 ft 8 in x 20 ft 9 in (Zapiski)
Armament 1831 LD 24 x 36pdrs (short), 4 x 60 u (1 pood)
UD 30 x 24pdrs (short)
FC & QD 16 x 8pdrs, 6 x 24pdr carr. or
20 x 24pdr carr.
699 men (1830 'Establishment')

Iezekiil' class. Sailed from Arkhangel'sk to Kronshtadt in 1832. Cruised in the Baltic in 1833–4, 1836–7, 1839–40, 1842–3 and 1845. Decommissioned in 1847. Hulked at Kronshtadt in 1848. Broken up in 1854.

Oryol 74/80 Arkhangel'sk
Constructor V. A. Ershov
Laid down 31.8.1831 *Launched* 21.5.1833
Dimensions 178 ft x 48 ft (inside plank) x 19 ft 3 in
3,000 tons displacement
Armament 1840 LD 24 x 36pdrs (short), 4 x 60 u (1 pood)
UD 30 x 24pdrs (short)
FC & QD 16 x 8pdrs, 6 x 24pdr carr. or
20 x 24pdr carr.
699 men (1830 'Establishment')

Iezekiil' class. Sailed from Arkhangel'sk to Kronshtadt in 1833. Cruised in the Baltic in 1834, 1836, 1839 and 1841–2. Decommissioned in 1846. Transferred to Sveaborg in 1848 and broken up.

Ostrolenka 74/80 Arkhangel'sk
Constructor V. A. Ershov
Laid down 21.12.1832 *Launched* 21.5.1834
Dimensions 178 ft x 48 ft (inside plank) x 19 ft 3 in
3,000 tons displacement (Veselago)
178 ft x (165 ft 4 in lk) x 48 ft x 20 ft 9 in (Zapiski)
Armament 1840 LD 24 x 36pdrs (short), 4 x 60 u (1 pood)
UD 30 x 24pdrs (short)
FC & QD 16 x 8pdrs, 6 x 24pdr carr. or
20 x 24pdr carr.
699 men (1830 'Establishment')

Iezekiil' class. Name commemorates the 1831 defeat of the Polish Mutiny. Sailed from Arkhangel'sk to Kronshtadt in 7–9.1834. Transported Guard troops to Danzig in 1835. Cruised in the Baltic in 1835–42 and 1844–6. Decommissioned in 1846. Hulked at Sveaborg in 1848.

Leiptsig 74/80 Arkhangel'sk
Constructor V. A. Ershov
Laid down 22.9.1834 *Launched* 20.4.1836
Dimensions 178 ft x 48 ft (inside plank) x 19 ft 3 in
3,000 tons displacement (Veselago)
185 ft 4 in x 165 ft 4 in x 48 ft x ? (Zapiski)
Armament 1840 LD 24 x 36pdrs (short) 4 x 60 u (1 pood)
UD 30 x 24pdrs (short)
FC & QD 16 x 8pdrs, 6 x 24pdr carr. or
20 x 24pdr carr.
699 men (1830 'Establishment')

Iezekiil' class. Sailed from Arkhangel'sk to Kronshtadt in 1836. Cruised in the Baltic in 1837–8 and 1840–3. Cruised in the North Sea in 1844. Cruised in the Baltic in 1845. Cruised in the North Sea in 1847. To Denmark during the Schleswig-Holstein Crisis to provide support against the threat of Prussian invasion in 1848–9. Decommissioned in 1849. Hulked at Sveaborg in 1850.

Retvizan 74/80 Arkhangel'sk
Constructor V. A. Ershov
Laid down 21.5.1837 *Launched* 21.5.1839
Dimensions 178 ft x 48 ft (outside plank) x 19 ft 3 in
3,000 tons displacement (Veselago)
185 ft 4 in x (165 ft 4 in keel) x 48 ft x ? (Zapiski)
Armament 1840 LD 24 x 36pdrs (short), 4 x 60 u (1 pood)
UD 30 x 24pdrs (short)
FC & QD 16 x 8pdrs, 6 x 24pdr carr. or
20 x 24pdr carr.
699 men (1830 'Establishment')

Iezekiil' class. Sailed from Arkhangel'sk to Kronshtadt in 1839. Cruised in the Baltic in 1840–1 and 1843. Cruised in the North Sea in 1844. Cruised in the Baltic in 1845–6. Cruised in the North Sea in 1847. To Denmark during the Schleswig-Holstein Crisis to provide support against the threat of Prussian invasion in 1848 and 1850. Decommissioned in 1851. Hulked at Sveaborg in 1852.

Finland 74/80 Arkhangel'sk
Constructor V. A. Ershov
Laid down 12.6.1839 *Launched* 21.5.1840
Dimensions 178 ft x 48 ft (inside plank) x 19 ft 3 in
3,000 tons displacement (Veselago)
185 ft 4 in x (165 ft 4 in keel) x 48 ft x? (Zapiski)
Armament 1840 LD 24 x 36pdrs (short) 4 x 60 u (1 pood)
UD 30 x 24pdrs (short)
FC & QD 16 x 8pdrs, 6 x 24pdr carr. or
20 x 24pdr carr.
699 men (1830 'Establishment')
1855 LD 28 x 36pdrs (short), 4 x 60 u (1 pood)
UD 26 x 24pdrs (short)
FC & QD 22 x 24pdr carr. (Pamyatnaya)
1856 LD 4 x 36pdrs (short), 24 x 60 u (1 pood)
UD 4 x 24pdrs (long), 26 x 24pdrs (short)
FC & QD 4 x 24pdrs (long), 18 x 24pdr carr. (Pamyatnaya)

Iezekiil' class. Sailed from Arkhangel'sk to Kronshtadt in 7–8.1840. Cruised in the Baltic in 1841–2. Cruised in the North Sea in 1844. Cruised in the Baltic in 1845–7. To Denmark during the Schleswig-Holstein Crisis to provide support against the threat of Prussian invasion in 1848–9. Cruised in the Baltic in 1853. Decommissioned in 1853. Employed with two other 74s and three heavy frigates as a floating battery off Kotlin in 5–10.1854. While serving as a floating battery, fitted with an unprecedented main battery of 24 1-pood edinorogs. Broken up in 1857.

The coastline of Norway is littered with the wrecks of countless sailing warships lost while making the perilous journey from their birthplace in Arkhangel'sk to join the Baltic fleet at Revel' or Kronshtadt. Even as late as 1842 the maiden voyage was filled with danger from summer storms and uncharted rocks, and size was no guarantee of safe passage. Pictured here in a contemporary painting is the wreck of the brand new Ingermanland *(74) off the Skagerrak in Norway while on her maiden voyage. Out of 838 aboard, only 509 were saved by local Norwegians, long resigned to pulling exhausted Russian sailors from their icy waters. Of the 389 who perished in the disaster there were 21 women and 7 children accompanying their husbands and fathers, who were, of course, officers and not seamen. Nicholas I shared the public outrage over the incident and ordered an inquiry to determine why preference had been given to saving officers over common seamen in violation of tradition and regulations. By K. V. Krugovikhin, 1843.*

Ingermanland 74/80 Arkhangel'sk
Constructor V. A. Ershov
Laid down 30.8.1840 Launched 24.5.1842
Dimensions 178 ft x 48 ft (inside plank) x 19 ft 3 in
3,000 tons displacement
Armament 1842 LD 24 x 36pdrs (short), 2 x 60 u (1 pood)
UD 30 x 24pdrs (short)
FC & QD 16 x 8pdrs, 6 x 24pdr carr. or
20 x 24pdr carr.
699 men (1830 'Establishment')

Iezekiil' class. Departed Arkhangel'sk on 24.7.1842. Grounded and wrecked in a storm off the Skagerrak on 30.8.1842 with 329 men lost and 509 saved.

Ingermanland (ex-*Iezekiil'*) 74/80 Arkhangel'sk
Constructor F. T. Zagulyaev
Laid down 1.9.1842 Launched 2.5.1844
Dimensions 178 ft x 48 ft (inside plank) x 19 ft 3 in (Veselago)
2,800 tons displacement (Pamyatnaya)
Armament 1844 LD 24 x 36pdrs (short), 2 x 60 u (1 pood)
UD 30 x 24pdrs (short)
FC & QD 16 x 8pdrs, 6 x 24pdr carr. or
20 x 24pdr carr.
699 men (1830 'Establishment')
1854 LD 24 x 36pdrs (short), 4 x 9.65 in shell guns
(2 pood)
UD 28 x 24pdrs (short), 2 x 60 u (1 pood)
FC & QD 16 x 24pdr carr. (Pamyatnaya)
1855 LD 2-36pdrs (long), 22 x 36pdrs (short), 4 x 9.65 in
shell guns (2 pood)
UD 4 x 24pdrs (long), 26 x 24pdrs (short), 2 x 60 u
(1 pood)
FC & QD 1 x 36pdr pivot gun (bored up 24pdr),
4 x 24pdrs (short) 14 x 24pdr carr. (Pamyatnaya)
1856 LD 20 x 30pdrs (long), 8 x 9.65 in shell guns
(2 pood)
UD 4 x 30pdrs (long), 20 x 30pdr gunnades,
6 x 60 u (1 pood)
FC & QD 1 x 30pdr pivot gun, 4 x 30pdr
gunnades, 12 x 30pdr carr.   (Pamyatnaya)

Iezekiil' class. Laid down as *Iezekiil'*, and renamed to commemorate the loss of *Ingermanland* in 1842. Sailed from Arkhangel'sk to Kronshtadt in 6–7.1844. To the Mediterranean with the squadron of Vice-Adm. Litke and Adm. General Grand Duke Konstantin (younger son of Nicholas I) in 1845–6. To Denmark during the Schleswig-Holstein Crisis to provide support against the threat of Prussian

Although the two nations had been looking with suspicion upon each other's intentions towards the decaying Ottoman Empire for some time, they were still outwardly cordial when Nicholas I paid his visit to Great Britain in 1844. The 74 receiving the salute of a British three-decker with all yards manned would be the newly completed Ingermanland, *with Emperor Nicholas I aboard, built to replace the ship of the same name lost just two years previously. The screw steamer to the right of the picture may or may not be intended by the artist as symbolic of the coming demise of such great ships. The identity of the First Rate is unknown. Painting by N. M. Condy the younger, 1846.*

invasion in 1849–50. Cruised in the Baltic in 1852–3. Stationed in Kronshtadt Roads in 1854–5. Decommissioned in 1857. Stricken on 21.3.1860.

Narva (ex-*Sviatoslav*) 74/80 Arkhangel'sk
Constructor F. T. Zagulyaev
Laid down 1.9.1844   *Launched* 7.5.1846
Dimensions 178 ft x 48 ft (inside plank) x 19 ft 3 in (Veselago)
   3,371 tons displacement (Pamyatnaya)
Armament 1846 LD 24 x 36pdrs (short) 4 x 60 u (1 pood)
   UD 30 x 24pdrs (short)
   FC & QD 16 x 8pdrs, 6 x 24pdr carr. or
   20 x 24pdr carr.
   699 men (1830 'Establishment')
   1854 LD 24 x 36pdrs (short) 4 x 9.65 in shell guns
   (2 pood)
   UD 28 x 24pdrs (short) 2 x 8.75 in shell guns
   (1½ pood)
   FC & QD 16 x 24pdr carr. (Pamyatnaya)
   1855 LD 20 x 36pdrs (short), 4 x 9.65 in shell guns
   (2 pood), 4 x 60 u (1 pood)
   UD 26 x 24pdrs (short), 2 x 60 u (1 pood)
   FC & QD 1 x 36pdr pivot gun (short), 16 x 24pdr
   carr. (Pamyatnaya)
   1856 LD 20 x 30pdrs (long) 8 x 9.65 in shell guns
   (2 pood)
   FC & QD 4 x 30pdrs (long), 20 x 30pdr gunnades,
   6 x 60 u (1 pood) (as frigate) (Pamyatnaya)
   1857 LD 20 x 36pdrs (long), 8 x 9.65 in shell guns
   (2 pood)
   FC & QD 4 x 36pdrs (long), 20 x 36pdrs (short),
   6 x 60 u (1 pood). (as frigate) (Pamyatnaya)

Iezekiil' class. Laid down as *Sviatoslav*, completed as *Narva*. Sailed from Arkhangel'sk to Kronshtadt in 1846. To Denmark during the Schleswig-Holstein Crisis to provide support against the threat of Prussian invasion in 1848–9. Cruised in the Baltic in 1850–2. Stationed in Kronshtadt Roads in 1854. To Krasnaia Gorka with Vice-Adm. Zamytskiy's squadron in 7.1854. Converted into a 58-gun frigate in 1855 (see also *Sysoi Velikii*, *Vilagosh* and *Borodino* below). Harbour service in 1856. Stricken on 11.9.1863.

Pamiat' Azova 74 Arkhangel'sk
Constructor F. T. Zagulyaev
Laid down 27.8.1847 (or 29.9.1847)   *Launched* 29.4.1848
Dimensions 178 ft x 48 ft (inside plank) x 19 ft 3 in (Veselago)
   3,370 tons displacement (Pamyatnaya)
Armament 1847 LD 24 x 36pdrs (short) 4 x 60 u (1 pood)
   UD 30 x 24pdrs (short)
   FC & QD 16 x 8pdrs, 6 x 24pdr carr. or
   20 x 24pdr carr.
   699 men (1830 'Establishment')
   1854 LD 24 x 36pdrs (short), 4 x 9.65 in shell guns
   (2 pood)
   UD 28 x 24pdrs (short), 2 x 60 u (1 pood)
   FC & QD 16 x 24pdr carr. (Pamyatnaya)
   1855 LD 20 x 36pdrs (short), 4 x 9.65 in shell guns
   (2 pood) 4 x 60 u (1 pood)
   UD 26 x 24pdrs (short), 4 x 60 u (1 pood)

FC & QD 1 x 36pdr pivot gun (bored up 24pdr),
16 x 24pdr carr. (Pamyatnaya)
1856 LD 20 x 36pdrs (long), 8 x 9.65 in shell guns
(2 pood)
UD 4 x 36pdrs (long), 20 x 36pdrs (short),
6 x 60 u (1 pood)
FC & QD 3 x 36pdrs (long), 13 x 36pdrs (short)
1 x 36pdr pivot gun (bored up 24pdr)
(Pamyatnaya)
1857 LD 24 x 36pdrs (short), 4 x 9.65 in shell guns
(2 pood)
UD 30 x 24pdrs (short)
FC & QD 16 x 24pdr carr. (Pamyatnaya)

Iezekiil' class. Sailed from Arkhangel'sk to Kronshtadt in 1848. To Denmark during the Schleswig-Holstein Crisis to provide support against the threat of Prussian invasion in 1849–50. Cruised in the Baltic in 1851–53. Stationed in Kronshtadt Roads in 1854-5. Carried cargo between Kronshtadt and Revel' in 1856–7. Decommissioned in 1857. Stricken on 5.1.1863.

Sysoi Velikii 74 Arkhangel'sk
Constructor F. T. Zagulyaev
Laid down 8.5.1848   *Launched* 10.5.1849
Dimensions 178 ft x 48 ft (inside plank) x 19 ft 3 in (Veselago)
2,934 tons displacement (Pamyatnaya)
Armament 1849 LD 24 x 36pdrs (short), 4 x 60 u (1 pood)
UD 30 x 24pdrs (short)
FC & QD 16 x 8pdrs, 6 x 24pdr carr. or
20 x 24pdr carr.
699 men (1830 'Establishment')
1854 LD 24 x 36pdrs (short), 4 x 9.65 in shell guns
(2 pood)
UD 28 x 24pdrs (short), 2 x 60 u (1 pood)
FC & QD 16 x 24pdr carr. (Pamyatnaya)
1855 LD 20 x 36pdrs (short), 4 x 9.65 in shell guns
(2 pood) 4 x 60 u (1 pood)
UD 26 x 24pdrs (short), 4 x 60 u (1 pood)
FC & QD 16 x 24pdr carr., 1 x 36pdr pivot gun
(bored up 24pdr) (Pamyatnaya)
1856 LD 20 x 30pdrs (long), 8 x 9.65 in shell guns
(2 pood)
UD 4 x 30 pdrs (long), 20 x 30pdr gunnades,
6 x 60 u (1 pood) (as frigate) (Pamyatnaya)
1857 LD 20 x 36pdrs (long), 8 x 9.65 in shell guns
(2 pood)
UD 4 x 36pdrs (long), 20 x 36pdrs (short), 6 x 60 u
(1 pood) (as frigate) (Pamyatnaya)

Iezekiil' class. The name commemorates the saint day on which the battle of Gogland was fought. Sailed from Arkhangel'sk to Kronshtadt in 7–8.1849. To Denmark during the Schleswig-Holstein Crisis to provide support against the threat of Prussian invasion in 1850. Cruised in the Baltic in 1852–3. Stationed in Kronshtadt Roads in 1854. Converted into a 58 gun frigate in 1855 (see also *Narva*, *Vilagosh* and *Borodino*). Harbour service in 1857–63. Stricken on 11.9.1863.

Fershampenuaz class (3 ships)

Fershampenuaz 74 82 St Petersburg, Okhta
Constructor I. A. Amosov
Laid down 6.10.1832   *Launched* 16.9.1833
Dimensions 188 ft x 50 ft x 19 ft 3 in
3,283 tons displacement (Pamyatnaya)
188 ft x (173 ft 4 in keel) x 50 ft x ? (Zapiski)
Armament 1840 LD 24 x 36pdrs (short), 4 x 60 u (1 pood)
UD 30 x 24pdrs (short)
FC & QD 16 x 8pdrs, 6 x 24pdr carr. or
20 x 24pdr carr.
699 men (1830 'Establishment')
1854 LD 24 x 36pdrs (long), 4 x 9.65 in shell guns
(2 pood)
UD 26 x 24pdrs (long), 4 x 60 u (1 pood)
FC & QD 4 x 24pdrs (short), 14 x 24pdr carr.
(Pamyatnaya)
1855 LD 24 x 30 pdrs (long), 4 x 9.65 in shell guns
(2 pood)
UD 26 x 24pdrs (long), 4 x 60 u (1 pood)
FC & QD 1 x 36pdr pivot gun (short), 18 x 24pdr
carr. (Pamyatnaya)
1856 LD 24 x 30pdr gunnades, 4 x 9.65 in shell guns
(2 pood)
FC & QD 1 x 36pdr pivot gun (short), 14 x 24pdr
carr. 8 x 60 u (1 pood) (Pamyatnaya)
1857 LD 24 x 30pdr gunnades, 4 x 9.65 in shell guns
(2 pood)
FC & QD 14 x 24pdr carr., 8 x 60 u (1 pood)
(Pamyatnaya)

Fershampenuaz class. Name commemorates a victory in 1814. Completed with a round stern. Cruised in the Baltic in 1834. Transported Guard troops from Kronshtadt to Danzig and back to Sveaborg in 1835. Cruised in the Baltic in 1836, 1838–42, and 1845–6. Repaired in 1848–9. To Denmark during the Schleswig-Holstein Crisis to provide support against the threat of Prussian invasion in 1850. Cruised in the Baltic in 1851–52. Operated off Krasnaia Gorka with Vice-Adm. Zamytskiy's squadron in 7.1854. Stationed in Kronshtadt Roads in 1854–5. Decommissioned in 1855 and reduced to a blockship. Stricken on 21.3.1860 and broken up.

Tsar' Konstantin 74 St Petersburg, Okhta
Constructor I. A. Amosov
Laid down 16.12.1835   *Launched* 24.8.1837
Dimensions 188 ft x 50 ft x 19 ft 3 in (Veselago)
188 ft x (173'4 in keel) x 50 ft x ? (Zapiski)
214 ft x 51 ft 6 in (inside plank) x 23 ft (as screw ship)
Armament 1840 LD 24 x 36pdrs (short), 4 x 60 u (1 pood)
UD 30 x 24pdrs (short)
FC & QD 16 x 8pdrs, 6 x 24pdr carr. or
20 x 24pdr carr.
699 men (1830 'Establishment')
1854 LD 26 x 68pdr shell guns, 2 x 30pdrs (long)
UD 4 x 30pdrs (long), 20 x 24pdrs (short) 4 x 60 u
(1 pood)
FC & QD 2 x 30pdrs (short), 1 x 36pdr gunnades,
14 x 30pdr (long carr.), 1 x 9.65 in shell guns (2 pood)

Fershampenuaz class. Cruised in the Baltic in 1839–47. To Denmark during the Schleswig-Holstein Crisis to provide support against the threat of Prussian invasion in 1849–50. Repaired, elongated, and converted to a screw ship in 1852–4. Transported troops from Sveaborg to Kronshtadt in 1856. Cruised in the Baltic in 1857–60. Stricken on 8.2.1864. (See in Steam and Sail section for further details.)

Vyborg 74 St Petersburg, Okhta
Constructor I. A. Amosov
Laid down 23.6.1839   *Launched* 30.7.1841

Dimensions   188 ft x 50 ft (inside plank) x 19 ft 3 in
                3,505 tons displacement (Veselago)
                192 ft 2 in x (173'4 in keel) x 50 ft x ? (Zapiski)
Armament   1840 LD 24 x 36pdrs (short), 4 x 60 u (1 pood)
                UD 30 x 24pdrs (short)
                FC & QD 16 x 8pdrs, 6 x 24pdr carr. or
                20 x 24pdr carr.
                699 men (1830 'Establishment')
              1854 LD 24 x 68pdr shell guns, 4 x 30pdrs (long)
                UD 4 x 30pdrs (long), 24 x 30pdrs (short)
                FC & QD 1 x 68pdr shell gun, 2 x 30pdrs (short)
                16 x 30pdr (carr.)

Fershampenuaz class. Cruised in the Baltic in 1843. Cruised in the North Sea in 1844. Cruised in the Baltic in 1845 and 1847. To Denmark during the Schleswig-Holstein Crisis to provide support against the threat of Prussian invasion in 1848–50. Cruised in the Baltic in 1851. Converted to a screw ship from 23.10.1852 to 21.5.1854. Transported troops from Sveaborg to Kronshtadt in 1854. Cruised to the Mediterranean with Rear-Adm. Beren's squadron in 1856–7. Cruised in the Baltic in 1858–60. Stricken on 7.12.1863. (See Steam and Sail section for further details.)

Iezekiil' 74/80 Arkhangel'sk
Constructor F. T. Zagulyaev
Laid down 1.9.1846   *Launched* 20.5.1847
Dimensions   178 ft x (165 ft 4 in keel) x 48 ft (inside plank) x
                19 ft 3 in (Veselago)
                2,807 tons displacement (Pamyatnaya)
Armament   1847 LD 24 x 36pdrs (short), 4 x 60 u (1 pood)
                UD 30 x 24pdrs (short)
                FC & QD 16 x 8pdrs, 6 x 24pdr carr. or
                20 x 24pdr carr.
                699 men (1830 'Establishment')
              1854 LD 24 x 36pdrs (short), 4 x 9.65 in shell guns
                (2 pood)
                UD 28 x 24pdrs (short), 2 x 60 u (1 pood)
                FC & QD 16 x 24pdr carr. (Pamyatnaya)

A one-off design. Sailed from Arkhangel'sk to Kronshtadt in 1847. To Denmark during the Schleswig-Holstein Crisis to provide support against the threat of Prussian invasion in 1848 and 1850. Cruised in the Baltic in 1851–53. Stationed at Sveaborg in 1854–5. Repulsed allied attack with gunboats and mortar vessels on Sveaborg on 28–29.7.1855. Towed from Sveaborg to Kronshtadt in 1855. Decommissioned in 1857. Hulked in 1860. Stricken on 5.1.1863.

Borodino class (2 ships)

Borodino 74 Arkhangel'sk
Constructor F. T. Zagulyaev
Laid down 20.8.1849   *Launched* 11.5.1850
Dimensions   183 ft x 48 ft 10 in x 19 ft 3 in
Armament   1850 LD 24 x 36pdrs (short), 4 x 60 u (1 pood)
                UD 30 x 24pdrs (short)
                FC & QD 16 x 8pdrs, 6 x 24pdr carr. or
                20 x 24pdr carr.
                699 men (1830 'Establishment')
              1854 LD 24 x 36pdrs (short), 4 x 9.65 in shell guns
                (2 pood)
                UD 28 x 24pdrs (short), 2 x 60 u (1 pood)
                FC & QD 4 x 24pdrs (short), 12 x 24pdr carr.
                (Pamyatnaya)
              1855 LD 20 x 36pdrs (short), 4 x 9.65 in shell guns
                (2 pood), 4 x 60 u (1 pood)
                UD 26 x 24pdrs (short), 4 x 60 u (1 pood)
                FC & QD 1 x 36pdr pivot gun (short), 16 x 24pdr
                carr. (Pamyatnaya)
              1856 LD 20 x 36pdrs (short), 4 x 9.65 in shell guns
                (2 pood), 4 x 60 u (1 pood)
                UD 4 x 24pdrs (long), 22 x 24pdrs (short)
                8 x 60 u (1 pood) (as frigate) (Pamyatnaya)
              1857 LD 20 x 36pdrs (short), 4 x 9.65 in shell guns
                (2 pood), 4 x 60 u (1 pood)
                UD 14 x 36pdrs (short) (as frigate) (Pamyatnaya)

Borodino class. Sailed from Arkhangel'sk to Kronshtadt in 7–9.1850. Cruised in the Baltic in 1852. Stationed in Kronshtadt Roads in 1854. Operated off Krasnaia Gorka with Adm. Rikord's squadron in 8.1854. Converted into a 3,050 ton, 58 gun frigate in 1855 (see also *Narva*, *Vilagosh* and *Sysoi Velikii*). Stationed in Kronshtadt Roads in 1856–7. Harbour service in 1858–63. Stricken on 11.9.1863.

Vilagosh 74 Arkhangel'sk
Constructor F. T. Zagulyaev
Laid down 11.6.1850   *Launched* 3.5.1851
Dimensions   183 ft x 48 ft 10 in x 19 ft 3 in (Veselago)
                3,578 tons displacement (Pamyatnaya)
Armament   1851 LD 24 x 36pdrs (short), 4 x 60 u (1 pood)
                UD 30 x 24pdrs (short)
                FC & QD 16 x 8pdrs, 6 x 24pdr carr. or
                20 x 24pdr carr.
                699 men (1830 'Establishment')
              1854 LD 24 x 36pdrs (short), 4 x 9.65 in shell guns
                (2 pood)
                UD 28 x 24pdrs (short), 2 x 60 u (1 pood)
                FC & QD 4 x 24pdrs (short), 12 x 24pdr carr.
                (Pamyatnaya)
              1855 LD 20 x 36pdrs (short), 4 x 9.65 in shell guns
                (2 pood), 4 x 60 u (1 pood)
                UD 26 x 24pdrs (short), 4 x 60 u (1 pood)
                FC & QD 16 x 24pdr carr. 1 x 36pdr (pivot)
                (Pamyatnaya)
              1856 LD 20 x 36pdrs (long), 8 x 9.65 in shell guns
                (2 pood)
                UD 4 x 36pdrs (long), 20 x 36pdrs (short), 6 x 60 u
                (1 pood) (as frigate)
              1856 LD 4 x 36pdrs (long), 20 x 36pdrs (short)
                4 x 9.65 in shell guns (2 pood)
                UD 30 x 24pdrs (short) (as frigate) (Pamyatnaya)

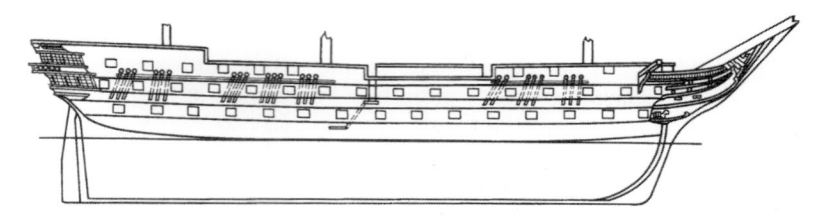

Bearing the name of one of the key battles of the Napoleonic Wars, Borodino (74) was commissioned at Arkhangel'sk in 1850, second to the end of the long line of Russian 74s. Borodino was cut down and transformed into a 58-gun rasée frigate in 1858 in a manner distantly reminiscent of similar British conversions of Napoleonic War 74s in the 1820s. Converted into a harbour hulk after the Crimean War, she lived to see the end of sail in Russia in the early 1860s.

1857 LD 24 x 36pdrs (short), 4 x 9.65 in shell guns
     (2 pood)
UD 18 x 24pdrs (short) (as frigate) (Pamyatnaya)

Borodino class. The name *Vilagosh* commemorates the surrender of Hungarian insurgents to Russian troops assisting Austria in 1849. Sailed from Arkhangel'sk to Kronstadt in 1851. Cruised in the Baltic in 1852–3. Stationed in Kronstadt Roads in 1854. Converted into a 58-gun frigate in 1855 with a reduced displacement of 3,005 tons. (see *Narva*, *Sysoi Velikii* and *Borodino*). Stationed in Kronstadt Roads in 1856–7. Harbour service in 1858–63. Stricken on 11.9.1863.

Baltic sailing frigates (31 purpose-built 1825–60)

24pdr heavy frigates (25 purpose-built 1825–60)
Speshnyi class group 2 (23 ships)

The decision to continue building *Speshnyi* class ships in quantity as the standard heavy frigate design for the Baltic fleet in the second quarter of the nineteenth century was testimony to the quality of the original design. Twenty three additional *Speshnyi*s were laid down between 1827 and 1844. Their only apparent departure from the original design lay in their heavier armament, with an additional two to six short-barrelled 24pdrs carried on the main gun deck and with the 18 6pdr long guns superseded by 22 to 24 24pdr carronades in the upper works. Some of the possible armament variations were as follows:

       LD 30 x 24pdrs (short)
       FC & QD 24 x 24pdr carr.
       LD 30 x 24pdrs (short)
       FC & QD 4 x 24pdr gunnades, 22 x 24pdr carr.
       LD 30 x 24pdrs (short)
       FC & QD 2 x 24pdr (short), 22 x 24pdr carr.
       LD 25 x 24pdrs (short), 2 x 60 u (1 pood)
       FC & QD 18 x 24pdr carr. (Est. 1842)

With the exception of the much larger *Pallada* and *Diana*, of 1832 and 1852 respectively, both modelled upon HMS *President* and thus indirectly upon the Humphrey frigates of the United States Navy, the *Speshnyi* class frigates were the only frigates in service in the Baltic during Nicholas I's reign.

The *Speshnyi*s were among the most active major warships in the Russian navy, being extensively employed in routine cruising, training, and hydrographic work. *Aurora* demonstrated the soundness of her construction by being reassigned to the distant and inhospitable Kamchatka Peninsula when she was eighteen years old in 1853 and by successfully participating in the defence of Petropavlovsk against a combined Anglo-French squadron in 1854. *Kniaginia Lovich* and *Anna* were assigned to the Mediterranean and took advantage of the temporary opening of the straits in the 1830s to join Adm. Lazarev's command and the Black Sea fleet where they were involved in operations against the guerillas in the Caucasus.

With a total of 34 ships built over a period of 44 years, the *Speshnyi* class ranks not only as one of the most successful Russian frigate designs, but as one of the most successful frigate classes built during the nineteenth century for any navy.

Mariia 44/54 Arkhangel'sk
Constructor V. A. Ershov
Laid down 15.7.1826 Launched 21.5.1827
Dimensions 159 ft 2¾ in (pp) x 41 ft 6 in (inside plank) x 12 ft 8 in
Armament LD 30 x 24pdrs (short)
         FC & QD 24 x 24pdr carr.
         405 men

Speshnyi class group 2. Armament upgraded with 24pdr carronades in place of 6pdrs. Sailed from Arkhangel'sk to Kronstadt in 7–8.1827. Operated in the Mediterranean with Rear-Adm. Rikord's squadron in 1828–30. Returned to Kronstadt with Rear-Adm. Lazarev's squadron in 1830. Cruised in the Baltic in 1831. Repaired in 1832. Cruised in the Baltic in 1834–5. Participated in the Imperial Review of 1836. Cruised in the Baltic in 1836–7, 1839, and 1842–3. Converted into a floating magazine at Kronstadt in 1847.

Ol'ga 44/54 Arkhangel'sk
Constructor V. A. Ershov
Laid down 15.7.1826 Launched 21.5.1827
Dimensions 159 ft 2¾ in (pp) x 41 ft 6 in (inside plank) x 12 ft 8 in
Armament LD 30 x 24pdrs (short)
         FC & QD 24 x 24pdr carr. (probable)
         405 men

Speshnyi class group 2. Sailed from Arkhangel'sk to Kronstadt in 7–8.1827. Operated in the Mediterranean with Rear-Adm. Rikord's squadron in 1828–30. Returned to Kronstadt with Rear-Adm. Lazarev's squadron in 1830. Cruised in the Baltic in 1830. Escorted transports to Danzig in 1831. Repaired in 1832. Cruised in the Baltic in 1834. Participated in the Imperial Review of 1836. Cruised in the Baltic in 1836–40 and 1842–3. Fire watch ship at Kronstadt Roads in 1844. Broken up in 1849.

Aleksandra 44/54 Arkhangel'sk
Constructor V. A. Ershov
Laid down 15.7.1826 Launched 21.5.1827
Dimensions 159 ft 2¾ in (pp) x 41 ft 6 in (inside plank) x 12 ft 8 in
Armament LD 30 x 24pdrs (short)
         FC & QD 24 x 24pdr carr (probable)
         405 men

Speshnyi class group 2. Sailed from Arkhangel'sk to Kronstadt in 7–8.1827. Operated in the Mediterranean with Rear-Adm. Rikord's squadron in 1828–30. Returned to Kronstadt with Rear-Adm. Lazarev's squadron in 1830. Cruised in the Baltic in 1830, 1832–4 and 1836–40. Broken up in 1845. Salvageable timber from her dismantling used to build the schooner *Opyt*.

Kniaginia Lovich 44/54 St Petersburg
Constructor V. F. Stoke
Laid down 1.12.1827 Launched 26.5.1828
Dimensions 159 ft 2¾ in (pp) x 41 ft 6 in (inside plank) x 12 ft 8 in
Armament LD 30 x 24pdrs (short)
         FC & QD 24 x 24pdr carr (probable)
         405 men

Speshnyi class group 2. Named after the Polish wife of Grand Duke Konstantin, Viceroy to Poland. Operated in the Mediterranean against Turkey and in support of the Greek War of Independence in 1828–33. Arrived at Istanbul in 1833, joined Vice-Adm. Lazarev's squadron, and transferred to Sevastopol' and the Black Sea fleet. Fire watch ship at Sevastopol' in 1834–5. Transferred to Nikolaev and hulked in 1837.

Elisaveta 44/63 St Petersburg
Constructor K. A. Glazyrin
Laid down 15.1.1828 Launched 18.8.1828
Dimensions 159 ft 2¾ in (pp) x 41 ft 6 in (inside plank) x 12 ft 8 in

Armament LD 30 x 24pdrs (short)
FC & QD 24 x 24pdr carr. (probable)
405 men

Speshnyi class group 2. Operated in the Mediterranean transporting arms and ammunition in support of the Greek War of Independence in 1829–31. Returned to Kronshtadt in 1831. Cruised in the Baltic in 1832. Cruised to Danzig in 1835. Cruised in the Baltic in 1836. Converted into a floating magazine at Kronshtadt in 1838.

Ekaterina 44/56 St Petersburg, New Admiralty
Constructor Y. A. Kolodkin
Laid down 5.12.1827   *Launched* 10.9.1828
Dimensions 159 ft 2¾ in (pp) x 41 ft 6 in (inside plank) x 12 ft 8 in
Armament LD 30 x 24pdrs (short)
FC & QD 24 x 24pdr carr (probable)
405 men

Speshnyi class group 2. Cruised in the Baltic in 1829. Cruised to Lübeck in 1830. Blockaded Poland in 1831. Cruised in the Baltic in 1832–4. Repaired in 1837. Cruised in the Baltic in 1840–1 and 1843. Cruised in the North Sea in 1844. Cruised in the Baltic in 1847–8. Broken up in 1854.

Anna 44/54 St Petersburg, Okhta
Constructor V. F. Stoke
Laid down 29.9.1828   *Launched* 19.5.1829
Dimensions 159 ft 2¾ in (pp) x 41 ft 6 in (inside plank) x 12 ft 8 in
(Veselago)
159 ft 2¾ in x (149 ft 10 in keel) x 41 ft 6 in (inside plank) x 21 ft 5 in x 18 ft 10 in (Zapiski)
Armament LD 30 x 24pdrs (short)
FC & QD 24 x 24pdr carr. (probable)
405 men

Speshnyi class group 2. Cruised in the Baltic in 1829. Cruised to Iceland in 1830. To the Mediterranean to provide support for the Greek War of Independence in 1831–3. Joined Vice-Adm. Lazarev's squadron at Istanbul and went to Sevastopol' as a member of the Black Sea fleet in 1833. Cruised in the Black Sea in 1834. Landed troops against the Caucasus guerillas in 1836–7. Broken up in 1838.

Prints Oranskii (renamed *Korol'Niderlandskii*) 44/54 St Petersburg
Constructor K. A. Glazyrin
Laid down 18.10.1828   *Launched* 13.7.1829
Dimensions 159 ft 2¾ in (pp) x 41 ft 6 in (inside plank) x 12 ft 8 in
(Veselago)
159 ft 2¾ in x (150 ft3 in keel) x 41 ft 6 in (inside plank) x 21 ft 5 in x 18 ft 6 in (Zapiski)
Armament LD 30 x 24pdrs (short)
FC & QD 24 x 24pdr carr (probable)
405 men
1855 LD 30 x 24pdrs (short)
UD 24 x 24pdr carr. (Pamyatnaya)

Speshnyi class group 2. Named to commemorate the marriage of Nikolai I's sister to the Prince of Orange. Cruised in the Baltic in 1829. Cruised to Iceland in 1830. Cruised in the Baltic in 1831–2 and 1834–7. Repaired in 1839. Cruised in the Baltic in 1839–41. Renamed *Korol'Niderlandskii* on the Prince of Orange's accession to the throne in 1841. Cruised in the Baltic in 1843, and 1846–7. Fire watch ship in Kronshtadt Roads in 1850–3. Employed with three 74s and two other heavy frigates as a floating battery off Kotlin in 5–10.1854. Broken up in 1858.

Neva 44/54 St Petersburg, New Admiralty
Constructor Y. A. Kolodkin
Laid down 18.10.1828   *Launched* 7.8.1829
Dimensions 159 ft 2¾ in (pp) x 41 ft 6 in (inside plank) x 12 ft 8 in
(Veselago)
159 ft 2¾ in x (150 ft3 in keel) x 41 ft 6 in (inside plank) x 21 ft x 18 ft 6 in (Zapiski)
Armament LD 30 x 24pdrs (short)
FC & QD 24 x 24pdr carr. (probable)
405 men

Speshnyi class group 2. Cruised in the Gulf of Finland in 1830–3. Cruised in the Gulf of Finland with naval cadets in 1836. Cruised in the Gulf of Finland in 1837. Converted into a floating magazine in 1837.

Venera (ex-*Skoryi*) 44/62 Arkhangel'sk
Constructor V. A. Ershov
Laid down 14.8.1828   *Launched* 19.9.1829
Dimensions 159 ft 2¾ in (pp) x 41 ft 6 in (inside plank) x 12 ft 8 in
(Veselago)
159 ft 2¾ in x 41 ft 6 in (inside plank) x 19 ft 3 in x 18 ft 9 in (Zapiski)
Armament LD 30 x 24pdrs (short)
FC & QD 24 x 24pdr carr. (probable)
405 men

Speshnyi class group 2. Laid down as *Skoryi*. Sailed from Arkhangel'sk to Kronshtadt in 1830. Cruised in the Baltic in 1831–2. Cruised in the Baltic with naval cadets in 1833. Cruised in the Baltic in 1834–5. Cruised in the Baltic with naval cadets in 1836. Repaired in 1838. Cruised in the Baltic in 1840 and 1843–4. Fire watch ship at Kronshtadt in 1847. Broken up in 1852.

Bellona 44/54 St Petersburg
Constructor V. F. Stoke
Laid down 21.11.1829   *Launched* 16.5.1830
Dimensions 159 ft 2¾ in (pp) x 41 ft 6 in (inside plank) x 12 ft 8 in
(Veselago)
167 ft 2¾ in x (149 ft 9 in keel) x 41 ft 6 in (inside plank) x 20 ft 9 in x 18 ft 10 in (Zapiski)
Armament LD 30 x 24pdrs (short)
FC & QD 24 x 24pdr carr. (probable)
405 men

Speshnyi class group 2. Cruised in the Baltic in 1834. Hydrographic survey in the Baltic in 1835. Cruised in the Baltic with naval cadets in 1836. Converted into a floating magazine in 1837.

Iunona 44/54 St Petersburg
Constructor K. A. Glazyrin
Laid down 12.10.1829   *Launched* 13.6.1830
Dimensions 159 ft 2¾ in (pp) x 41 ft 6 in (inside plank) x 12 ft 8 in
(Veselago)
159 ft 2'¾ in x (149 ft 3¾ in keel) x 41 ft 6 in (inside plank) x 12 ft 8 in x18 ft 6 in (Zapiski)
Armament LD 30 x 24pdrs (short)
FC & QD 24 x 24pdr carr (probable)
405 men

Speshnyi class group 2. Cruised in the Baltic in 1831–2, 1834–5 and 1837–8. Converted into a floating magazine in 1845.

Pomona 44/54 St Petersburg
Constructor K. A. Glazyrin
Laid down 12.10.1829   *Launched* 24.6.1830

Dimensions 159 ft 2¾ in (pp) x 41 ft 6 in (inside plank) x 12 ft 8 in
 (Veselago)
 159 ft 2¾ in x (149 ft 8¾ in keel) x 41 ft 6 in (inside
 plank) x 12 ft 8 in x 18 ft 6 in (Zapiski)
Armament LD 30 x 24pdrs (short)
 FC & QD 24 x 24pdr carr. (probable)
 405 men
 159 ft 2¾ in x (149 ft 3 in keel) x 41 ft 6 in x ? (Zapiski)

Speshnyi class group 2. Cruised in the Baltic in 1831–5. Fire watch ship in 1836. Cruised in the Baltic in 1837–8. Broken up in 1848.

Tserera 44/54 St Petersburg New Admiralty
Constructor Y. A. Koledkin
Laid down 12.10.1829   Launched 7.7.1830
Dimensions 159 ft 2¾ in (pp) x 41 ft 6 in (inside plank) x 12 ft 8 in
 (Veselago)
 159 ft 2¾ in x (149 ft 11¾ in keel) x 41 ft 6 in (inside
 plank) x 14 ft 9 in x 18 ft 6 in (Zapiski)
Armament LD 30 x 24pdrs (short)
 FC & QD 24 x 24pdr carr (probable).
 405 men
 1855 LD 2 x 24pdrs (long), 28 x 24pdr (short)
 FC & QD 4 x 24pdrs (short), 16 x 24pdr carr.
 (Pamyatnaya)

Speshnyi class group 2. Blockaded the Polish coastline in 1831. Transported heavy ordnance to Danzig in 1832. Cruised in the Baltic in 1832–3. Transported Guards to Danzig in 1835. Towed to Revel' for repair in 1836. Fire watch ship at Kronshtadt in 1837–40. Repaired in 1844. Cruised in the Baltic in 1846–7. Cruised To Denmark during the Schleswig-Holstein Crisis in 1848–50. Cruised in the Baltic in 1851–3. Employed with three 74s and two other heavy frigates as a floating battery off Kotlin in 5–10 1854. Broken up in 1859.

Kastor 44/54 Arkhangel'sk
Constructor V. A. Ershov
Laid down 27.9.1830   Launched 21.5.1831
Dimensions 159 ft 2¾ in (pp) x 41 ft 6 in (inside plank) x 12 ft 8 in
 (Veselago)
 1,974 tons displacement (Pamyatnaya)
 159 ft 2¾ in x (152 ft 6 in keel) x 41 ft 6 in (inside plank)
 x 21 ft x 18 ft 6 in (Zapiski)
Armament 1831 LD 30 x 24pdrs (short)
 FC & QD 24 x 24pdr carr (probable)
 405 men
 1856 LD 22 x 24pdrs (long) 4 x 9.65 in shell guns
 (2 pood)
 FC & QD 18 x 24pdrs (short) (Pamyatnaya)
 1857 LD 4 x 68 i- shell guns, 22 x 24pdrs (long)
 FC & QD 4 x 24pdrs (long), 14 x 24pdrs (short)
 (Pamyatnaya)
 1860 LD 4 x 68 i- shell guns 22 x 24pdrs (long)
 FC & QD 18 x 24pdr gunnades (Pamyatnaya)

Speshnyi class group 2. Sailed from Arkhangel'sk to Kronshtadt in 1832. Carried the Imperial Family to Holland in 1833. Accompanied the Prince and Princess of Prussia to Memel in 1834. Hydrographic survey in 1835. Cruised to Lübeck in 1837. Cruised to Lübeck and Copenhagen in 1838. Cruised in the Baltic with naval cadets in 1840. Fire watch ship at Kronshtadt in 1841–3. Harbour ship at Kronshtadt in 1844. Surplus ship at Kronshtadt in 1847. Repaired and placed in reserve in 1849. Repaired again in 1854. Floating battery at Kronshtadt in 1855. Cruised with Rear-Adm. Beren's squadron to Alger in 1856–7. Cruised in the Baltic with naval cadets in 1861–3. Stricken on 7.12.1863. Sold in 1865.

Amfitrida 44/52 Arkhangel'sk
Constructor V. A. Ershov
Laid down 31.8.1831   Launched 17.5.1832
Dimensions 159 ft 2¾ in (pp) x 41 ft 6 in (inside plank) x 12 ft 8 in
 (Veselago)
 159 ft 2¾ in x (152 ft 6 in keel) x 41 ft 6 in x ? (Zapiski)
Armament 1832 LD 30 x 24pdrs (short)
 FC & QD 24 x 24pdr carr (probable)
 405 men
 1855 LD 22 x 24pdrs (long), 2 x 8.75 in shell guns
 (1½ pood), 2 x 60 u (1 pood)
 FC & QD 8 x 24pdrs (short), 6 x 24pdr gunnades,
 4 x 8pdrs (long) (Pamyatnaya)
 1856 LD 22 x 24pdrs (long), 2 x 8.75 in shell guns
 (1½ pood), 2 x 60 u (1 pood)
 FC & QD 8 x 24pdrs (short), 6 x 24pdr gunnades
 4 x 18pdrs (long) (Pamyatnaya)
 1857 LD 18 x 24pdrs (long), 4 x 36pdrs (long),
 2 x 8.75 in shell guns (1½ pood), 2 x 60 u (1 pood)
 FC & QD 6 x 24prs (short), 6 x 24pdr gunnades
 2 x 24pdr gunnades (short), 4 x 18pdrs (long)
 (Pamyatnaya)

Speshnyi class group 2. Sailed from Arkhangel'sk to Kronstadt in 1832. Cruised in the Baltic in 1833–4. Cruised in the Baltic with naval cadets in 1837. Cruised in the Baltic in 1838–9 and 1841–2. Repaired in 1849. Guardship in Kronshtadt Roads in 1854–5. Troop transport in 1856. Scuttled at the Kronshtadt freeway in 1859.

Prozerpina 44/56 St Petersburg
Constructors K. A. Glazyrin and I. A. Amoksov
Laid down 10.10.1831   Launched 31.8.1832
Dimensions 159 ft 2¾ in (pp) x 41 ft 6 in (inside plank) x 12 ft 8 in
Armament LD 30 x 24pdrs (short)
 FC & QD 24 x 24pdr carr (probable)
 405 men

Speshnyi class group 2. Cruised in the Baltic in 1833, 1836–9, 1841 and 1844–7. Fire watch ship at Kronshtadt in 1849. Broken up in 1855.

Diana 44/56 St Petersburg
Constructor K. A. Glazyrin
Laid down 3.12.1832   Launched 24.8.1833
Dimensions 159 ft 2¾ in (pp) x 41 ft 6 in (inside plank) x 12 ft 8 in
 (Veselago)
 159 ft 2¾ in x (150 ft 6¾ in keel) x 41 ft 6 in x ? (Zapiski)
Armament LD 30 x 24pdrs (short)
 FC & QD 24 x 24pdr carr (probable)
 405 men

Speshnyi class group 2. Cruised in the Baltic in 1834–7, 1839–41, 1843–7, and 1849. Converted into a floating magazine in 1850. Broken up in 1854.

Avrora 44/56 St Petersburg, Okhta
Constructor I. A. Amosov
Laid down 23.11.1833   Launched 27.7.1835
Dimensions 159 ft 2¾ in (pp) x 41 ft 6 in (inside plank)/42 ft 1 in
 (outside plank) x 12 ft 8 in (Veselago)
 165 ft 2¾ in x (150 ft 6¾ in keel) x 41 ft 6 in x ? (Zapiski)
Armament 1835 LD 30 x 24pdrs (short)

The Speshnyi *class frigate* Diana *cruising in the Baltic in 1847. A picture of perfect grace and elegance requiring no further comment. By A.P. Bogolyubov, 1860.*

```
         FC & QD 4 x 24pdrs (short) 22 x 24pdr carr.
         405 men
1854     LD 24 x 24pdrs (long) 2 x 60 u (1 pood)
         FC & QD 18 x 24pdr carr. (Pamyatnaya)
```

Speshnyi class group 2. Constructed mainly of larch, with small amounts of pine and oak. Cruised in the Baltic in 1836–43. Transported 5 tons of gold to England in 1844, the year of Nikolai I's visit. Cruised in the Baltic in 1845. Cruised To Denmark during the Schleswig-Holstein Crisis in 1849. Repaired in 1851. Cruised in the Baltic in 1852. Departed for the Pacific in 1853 and forced by storm damage into Portsmouth for repairs. Arrived at Kamchatka on 19.6.1854 after a difficult passage with 8 deaths and 35 seriously ill. Took part in the defence of Petropavlovsk against an Anglo-French attack on 20–24.8.1854, landing half of her guns to create a shore battery, and suffering serious damage. Arrived at the mouth of the Amur in 6.1855. Left for the Baltic in 10.1856 and completed global circumnavigation; arriving at Kronshtadt in 6.1857 after encountering several severe storms and rolling as much as 40°. Stricken on 8.7.1861 and sold for breaking up.

Mel'pomena 44/52 Arkhangel'sk
Constructor V. A. Ershov
Laid down 2.9.1834   *Launched* 29.4.1836
Dimensions 159 ft 2¾ in (pp) x 41 ft 6 in (inside plank) x 12 ft 8 in (Veselago)
165 ft 3½ in x (151 ft 8 in keel) x 31 ft 6 in x ? (Zapiski)
Armament LD 30 x 24pdrs (short)
FC & QD 24 x 24pdr carr (probable)
405 men

Speshnyi class group 2. Sailed from Arkhangel'sk to Kronshtadt in 1836. Cruised in the Baltic in 1837–8. Transported artillery being presented to Prussia by Nikolai I to Stettin in 1839. Cruised in the Baltic in 1840–3. Cruised to the North Sea in 1844. Cruised in the Baltic in 1846. Cruised to the North Sea in 1847. Fire watch ship at Sveaborg in 1848–9. Mentioned in 1850, but missing from the fleet inventory in 1852.

Tsesarevna (ex-*Bellona*) 44/58 St Petersburg
Constructor M.N. Grinvald
Laid down 24.3.1838   *Launched* 30.4.1841
Dimensions 159 ft 2¾ in (pp) x 41 ft 6 in (inside plank) x 12 ft 8 in (Veselago)
165 ft 3 in x (150 ft6 in keel) x 41 ft 6 in x ? (Zapiski)
Armament 1841 LD 30 x 24pdrs (short)
FC & QD 24 x 24pdr carr (probable)
405 men
1855 LD 12 x 24pdrs (long), 18 x 24pdrs (short)
FC & QD 4 x 24pdrs (short), 18 x 24pdr carr. (Pamyatnaya)

Speshnyi class group 2. *Laid down* as Bellona. Cruised in the Baltic in 1842–3 and 1846–7. Cruised To Denmark during the Schleswig-Holstein Crisis in 1848. Cruised in the Baltic in 1852–3. Employed with three 74s and two other heavy frigates as a floating battery off Kotlin in 5–10.1854. Broken up in 1858.

Tsesarevich 44/52 St Petersburg
Constructor M. N. Grinvald
Laid down 24.3.1838   *Launched* 30.4.1841
Dimensions 159 ft 2¾ in (pp) x 41 ft 6 in (inside plank) x 12 ft 8 in (Veselago)
165 ft 3 in x (150 ft6 in keel) x 41 ft 6 in x ? (Zapiski)
Armament 1841 LD 30 x 24pdrs (short)
FC & QD 24 x 24pdr carr (probable)
405 men

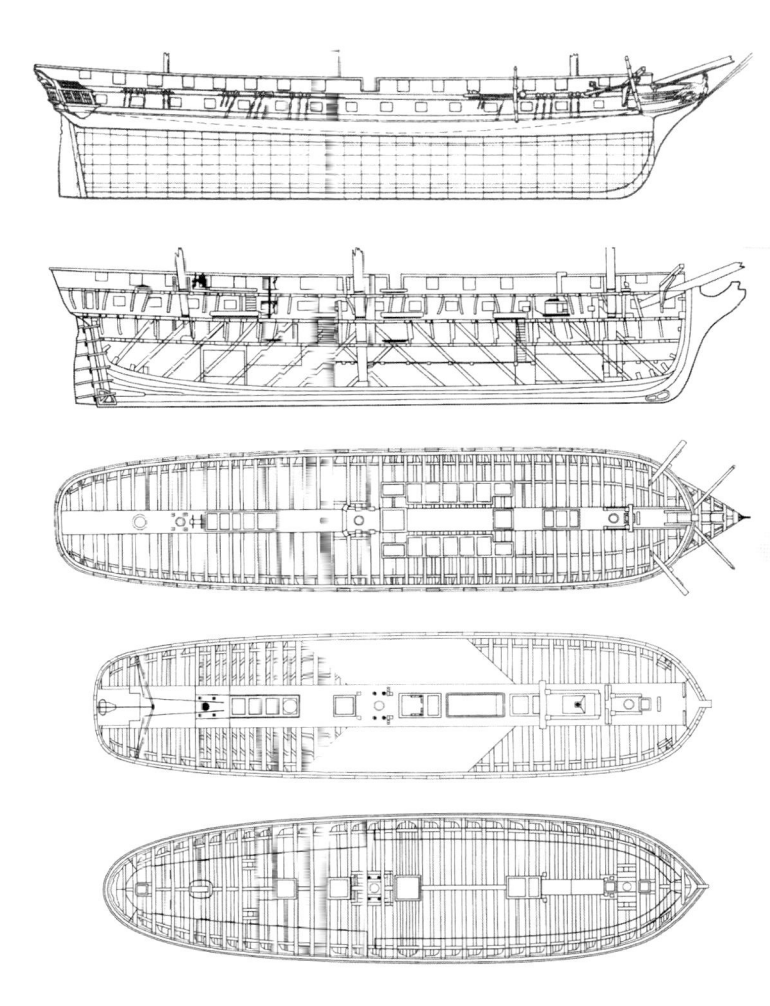

A cutaway diagram showing the internal layout of the Speshnyi *class frigate* Avrora *completed in 1835 a full third of a century after the launching of her prototype. A comparison of the two ships shows similarities and some significant differences.* Avrora *has continuous protective barricades running from bow to stern topside and apparently was completed with diagonal trusses, hardly a surprising improvement for this period. The two ships are reported as having had identical dimensions, but the later frigate has traded in all of her upper deck 6pdr long guns for 24pdr carronades.*

```
1854 LD  30 x 24pdrs (long)
     FC & QD 4 x 24pdrs (short) 18 x 24pdr carr.
            (Pamyatnaya)
```

Speshnyi class group 2. Laid down as Elisaveta. Cruised in the Baltic in 1844 and 1847. Cruised To Denmark during the Schleswig-Holstein Crisis in 1848–50. Cruised in the Baltic in 1851 and 1853. Assigned to the 3rd Division in defence of Sveaborg in 1854. In action with the Anglo-French fleet during the bombardment of Sveaborg on 28.7.1855. Converted into a floating magazine at Helsingfors in 1858.

Konstantin 44/48/58 Arkhangel'sk
Constructor F. T. Zagulyaev
Laid down 1.9.1842   *Launched* 2.5.1844
Dimensions 159 ft 2½ in (pp) x 41 ft 6 in (inside plank) x 12 ft 8 in
Armament 1844 LD 26 x 24pdrs (short), 2 x 60 u (1 pood) (1842 establishment)

```
1854 LD  24 x 24pdrs (short) 4 x 24pdrs (long) 2 x 60 u
         (1 pood)
     FC & QD 4 x 24pdrs (short) 14 x 24pdr carr.
            (Pamyatnaya)
```

Speshnyi class group 2. Cruised in the Baltic in 1844–7. Cruised To Denmark during the Schleswig-Holstein Crisis in 1848 and 1850. Cruised in the Baltic in 1852–3. Stationed at Kronshtadt Roads in defence of Kronshtadt in 1854–5. Fire watch service at Kronshtadt in 1856. Broken up in 1860.

Pallada **class** (2 ships)
Pallada 52 St Petersburg, Okhta
Constructor V. F. Stoke
Laid down 2.11.1831   *Launched* 1.9.1832
Dimensions 173 ft (pp) x 43 ft 6 in (inside plank) x ? (Veselago)
            2,090 tons displacement (Pamyatnaya)
            177 ft x (158 ft keel) x 44 ft x ? (Zapiski)
Armament 1832 LD 30 x 24pdrs (long)
            FC & QD 22 x 24pdrs (gunnades chambered)
          1855 LD 26 x 24pdrs (long)
            FC & QD 18 x 24pdr carr. (Pamyatnaya)

Pallada class. Built to the amended plan of HMS *President* (52) and said to be capable of 12 knots. Cruised in the Baltic in 1833 under Capt. Nakhimov whose timely action saved the squadron he was with from going onto the rocks. Escorted the Prince and Princess of Prussia to Germany in 1834. Hydrographic survey work in the Baltic in 1835. Cruised in the Baltic in 1836. Transported gold to London in 1837. Training cruise in the Baltic in 1838. Cruised in the Baltic in 1841–4. Repaired in 1846. Cruised to Portsmouth in 1847. Cruised in the Baltic in 1848. Cruised to Madeira and Lisbon in 1849–50. Cruised in the Baltic in 1851. Departed for Japan with the Russian Ambassador in 1852. Arrived at Nagasaki on 10.8.1853. Visited China in 1854 and entered Imperial Harbour at the mouth of the Amur where she was forced to shelter due to the war. Wintered at Imperatorslaya Gavan' where she was heavily damaged by ice, found to be irreparable, and scuttled on 31.1.1856.

Diana 54 Arkhangel'sk
Constructor F. T. Zagulyaev
Laid down 21.5.1851   *Launched* 19.5.1852
Dimensions 180 ft 1 in (lgd) x 173 ft 3 in (pp) x 44 ft 6 in (outside plank) x 14 ft 1 in (Veselago)
            2,051 tons displacement (Pamyatnaya)
Armament 1853 LD 30 x 24pdrs (long)
            FC & QD 22 x 24pdrs (gunnades chambered)
              (Pamyatnaya)
          1855 LD 32 x 24pdrs (long), 2 x 60 u (1 pood)
            FC & QD 18 x 24pdrs (gunnades chambered)
              (Pamyatnaya)

Pallada class. The last Russian sailing frigate and nominal sister to *Pallada*. Sailed from Arkhangel'sk to Kronshtadt in 6–7.1852. Cruised in the Baltic in 1853. Left for the Far East in 10.1853. Arrived at Simoda Japan with the Russian envoy on 21.11.1854. Sunk in Japan during an earthquake on 7.1.1855. Her crew constructed a schooner from her salvageable timbers and reached the Amur.

Small training frigates (6 purpose-built 1825–60)
Malyi **class group 2** (3 ships)
A continuation of a six ship purpose-built class of small training frigates. The first trio had been begun in 1820 and may be found in the previous section.

A painting by E. Voishvillo from 1995 of the Baltic fleet's most prestigious frigate, Pallada *(52), with every conceivable piece of canvas in use giving meaning to the phrase 'under full sail'.* Pallada *was said to have been capable of 12 knots, and this comports nicely with the reported speeds of the Humphrey's frigates that very distantly inspired her design. While a respectable speed for a frigate of this size, 12 knots was not a remarkable speed. Nevertheless, she makes a brave showing in this picture.*

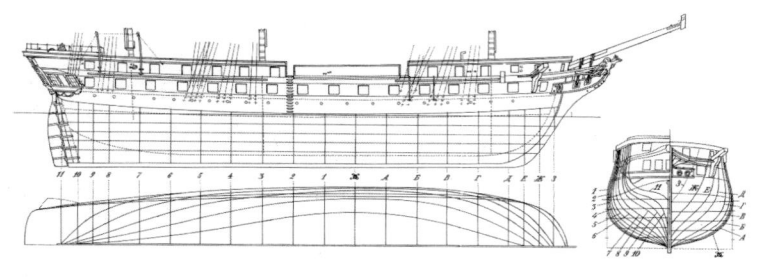

Old Ironsides in Russian dress? The one-off Russian heavy frigate Pallada *(52) was completed at Okhta in 1832 and based on the lines of HMS* President, *which in turn duplicated those of the captured USS* President, *sister to the famous USS* Constitution. *The briefest comparison between this plan and those of the Humphrey frigates will confirm the relationship, as will a glance at the dimensions of the two ships. Alone during the closing years of sail in the Baltic among a sea of smaller* Speshnyi *class heavy frigates,* Pallada *was the prestige frigate of the Baltic fleet. She was long-lived and well maintained, and visited Japan and China in the early 1850s. Storm damage and the Crimean war doomed her and she was scuttled in Eastern waters in 1856.*

Nadezhda 24 St Petersburg, Okhta
Constructor V. F. Stoke
Laid down 1.12.1827 *Launched* 19.9.1828
Dimensions 100 ft 10 in (pp) x26 ft 10 in (inside plank) x 7 ft 1 in
Armament ?
Malyi class (6 ships). Purpose-built training frigate. Cruised in the Baltic with naval cadets in 1829–35. Repaired in 1836. Cruised in the Baltic with naval cadets in 1837–44. Broken up in 1845.

Otvazhnost' 12/24 Arkhangel'sk
Constructor I. A. Amosov
Laid down 10.7.1834 *Launched* 13.10.1834
Dimensions 100 ft 10 in (pp) x26 ft 10 in (inside plank) x 7 ft 1 in
Armament ?
Malyi class (6 ships). Purpose-built training frigate. Cruised in the Baltic with naval cadets in 1835–44. Repaired in 1846. Cruised in the Baltic with naval cadets in 1847–53. Receiving ship in 1854–8. Broken up after 1858.

Postoianstvo 12/24 St Petersburg
Constructor Shoumburg
Laid down 12.5.1834 *Launched* 23.10.1834
Dimensions 100 ft 10 in (pp) x26 ft 10 in (inside plank) x 7 ft 1 in
 (Veselago)
 107 ft x (95 ft 8 in keel) x 26 ft 10 in x ? (Zapiski)
Armament ?
Malyi class (6 ships). Purpose-built training frigate. Cruised in the Baltic with naval cadets in 1835–44. Repaired in 1845. Cruised in the Baltic with naval cadets in 1846–53. Receiving ship in 1854–8. Broken up after 1858.

Vernost' class (3 ships)
This trio of ships represents the final group of training frigates completed for the Russian Navy.

Vernost' 24 St Petersburg, Okhta
Constructor I. A. Amosov
Laid down 30.12.1833   *Launched* 23.6.1834
Dimensions 115 ft (pp) x 30 ft 10 in (inside plank) x 5 ft 9½ in
500 tons displacement
Armament ?
130 men + 75 cadets
Vernost' class. Purpose-built training frigate. At the Neva in 1834. Cruised in the Baltic with naval cadets in 1835–44. Repaired in 1846. Cruised in the Baltic with naval cadets in 1847–53. Receiving ship in 1854–8. Broken up after 1858.

Uspekh 24 St Petersburg, Okhta
Constructor I. A. Amosov
Laid down 25.8.1838   *Launched* 24.8.1839
Dimensions 115 ft (pp) x 30 ft 10 in (inside plank) x 6 ft 9½ in
120 ft x (129 ft 6 in keel) x ? ?
Armament ?
Vernost' class. Purpose-built training frigate. Cruised in the Baltic with naval cadets in 1840–52. Broken up in 1855.

Nadezhda 24 St Petersburg, Okhta
Constructor I. A. Amosov
Laid down 8.7.1844   *Launched* 12.5.1845
Dimensions 115 ft (pp) x 33 ft (inside plank) x 12 ft 8½ in
Armament ?
Vernost' class. Purpose-built training frigate. Cruised in the Baltic with naval cadets in 1845–52. Broken up in 1855.

Baltic sloops (2 purpose-built 1825–60)

Moller class (2 ships)
Moller 16 St Petersburg, Okhta
Constructor V. F. Stoke
Laid down 23.9.1825   *Launched* 14.5.1826
Dimensions 90 ft x 29 ft 5 in (inside plank) x 9 ft 4 in (Veselago)
Armament ?
Moller class. Purpose-built sloop. Named after the navy minister serving from 1821–36 who oversaw the rehabilitation of the Russian fleet after years of neglect under Alexander I. Departed Kronshtadt for global circumnavigation with the sloop *Seniavin* on 20.8.1826. Arrived at Petropavlovsk on 13.7.1827 and proceeded to Novo Arkhangel'sk. Arrived at Honolulu on 5.12.1827 and returned to Petropavlovsk. Surveyed the Aleutians from 4–8.1828 and returned to Petropavlovsk. Departed Petropavlovsk with *Seniavin* on 30.10.1828 and returned to Kronshtadt via the Cape of Good Hope on 23.8.1829, two days ahead of *Seniavin*. Surveyed the Gulf of Finland from 1830–34. Transferred to Revel' as a blockship in 1835.

Seniavin 16 St Petersburg, Okhta
Constructor V. F. Stoke
Laid down 23.9.1825   *Launched* 14.5.1826
Dimensions 90 ft x 29 ft 5 in (inside plank) x 9 ft 4 in (Veselago)
Armament ?
Moller class. Purpose-built sloop bearing one of the Russian navy's most illustrious names. Departed Kronshtadt with sister ship *Moller* on 20.8.1826. Surveyed the Bering Sea, the Central Pacific and visited Guam from 15.6.1828 to 25.8.1828 when she returned to Petropavlovsk. Returned to Kronshtadt with Moller via the Cape of Good Hope and arrived on 25.8.1829, two days behind her sistership. Fire

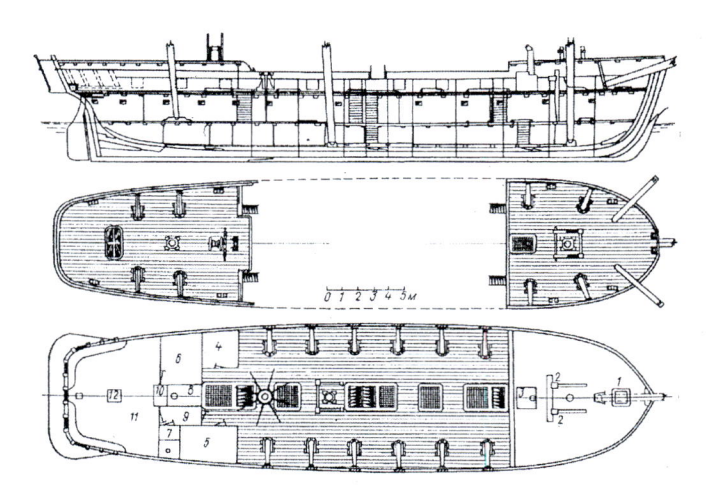

This is a detailed portrayal of the internal layout of the last ship in the long line of Russian training frigates, Nadezhda of the Vernost' class as completed in 1845. Very much larger and more elaborately laid out than previous training frigates, she lacks the graceful elegance of the earlier Malyi class flush-decked ships.

watch ship at Revel' in 1830–2. Carried cargo in the Baltic in 1833–4. Stationary fire watch ship at Kronshtadt in 1835. Broken up in 1844.

Baltic corvettes (1 purchased 1825–60)

Purchased abroad
Kniaz' Varshavskii 22/30 Philadelphia
Constructor ?
Laid down ?   *Launched* ? *Purchased* 1830
Dimensions 165 ft x 43 ft 1½ in x 20 ft 6 in (Veselago)
2,031.2 tons displacement (Pamyatnaya)
Armament 1830 30 x 24pdrs (short) (Pamyatnaya)
1855 30 x 24pdrs (long) (Pamyatnaya)
This ship was rated as a corvette in spite of being large enough to have been considered a frigate. Originally ordered for Mexico. Purchased at Philadelphia for 146,000 roubles. Named after field marshal Paskevich who broke the Polish mutiny of 1831 and took Warsaw, actions that led to his being created a prince (*kniaz'*). Cruised in the Baltic in 1832–53. Assigned to the defence division for the protection of Kronshtadt in 1854–5. Participated in the Imperial Review of 1856. Fire watch ship at Kronshtadt in 1857–8. Stricken in 11.9.1863.

Baltic brigs (1825–60) (22 purpose-built 1825–60)

Of the 22 brigs built during the reign of Nicholas I two were built for service with the White Sea flotilla and the remaining 20 fell within two uniform groups, the *Okhta* class and the *Diomid* class, all save three having been built in the Baltic. The two classes largely carried names taken from Greek mythology, were similar in dimensions and armament, and overlapped in their periods of production. It is unclear what design or structural differences may have differentiated them, but the final three *Okhta*s were unique in having been built at Arkhangel'sk in the early 1830s at a time when production in the Baltic had shifted to the *Diomid* class. What is clear is that the basic design was deemed satisfactory and that design uniformity was very much the order of the day in the navy of Nicholas I.

Lapominka 16 Arkhangel'sk, Solombala
Constructor A. M. Kurochkin
Laid down 5.7.1824   *Launched* 7.8.1825
Dimensions ?
Armament ?
Purpose-built brig. White Sea flotilla. Surveyed the White Sea coastline in 1826–33. Fire watch ship at Mud'yug Island in 1834–44. Broken up in 1848 at Arkhangel'sk.

Okhta class (11 ships)

Six of the *Okhta*s served in the Mediterranean in the Russo-Turkish War of 1828–30 and four made their way into the Black Sea fleet with the postwar conversion of Turkey from hereditary enemy to temporary ally. Two of ships that stayed in Baltic waters were wrecked, one in 1831 and one in 1847. The longest serving member of the class, *Filoktet*, was still active in 1860.

Okhta 20 St Petersburg, Okhta
Constructor V. F. Stoke
Laid down 13.11.1826   *Launched* 30.4.1827
Dimensions 98 ft 10 in (pp) x 30 ft 8 in (inside plank) x 15 ft 1 in (Veselago)
Armament 20 x 24pdr carr.
167 men
Okhta class. Purpose-built brig. Departed for the Mediterranean on 10.7.1827 in company with two other brigs, *Revel'* and *Userdie*. Joined Rear-Adm. Geiden's squadron at Malta on 30.11.1827. Operated in the Mediterranean against the Turks in 1828–30. Returned to the Baltic in 1830. Transferred to Memel in 1831. Fire watch ship at Sveaborg in 1832–4. Repaired in 1835. Training and survey cruises in 1837–44. Broken up in 1847.

Userdie 20 St Petersburg, Okhta
Constructor V. F. Stoke
Laid down 15.11.1826   *Launched* 30.4.1827
Dimensions 98 ft 10 in (pp) x 30 ft 8 in (inside plank) x 15 ft 1 in (Veselago)
Armament 20 x 24pdr carr.
167 men
Okhta class. Purpose-built brig. Departed for the Mediterranean on 10.7.1827 in company with two other brigs, *Revel'* and *Okhta*. Joined Rear-Adm. Geiden's squadron at Malta on 30.11.1827. Operated in the Mediterranean against the Turks in 1828–30. Returned to the Baltic in 1830. Cruised in the Baltic in 1830–3. Repaired in 1834. Cruised in the Baltic in 1835–6, 1838–9 and 1841–4. Broken up in 1845.

Telemak 20 St Petersburg, Okhta
Constructor V. F. Stoke
Laid down 1.12.1827   *Launched* 12.5.1828
Dimensions 98 ft 10 in (pp) x 30 ft 8 in (inside plank) x 12 ft 8 in (Veselago)
Armament 20 x 24pdr carr.
167 men
Okhta class. Purpose-built brig. To the Mediterranean with Rear-Adm. Rikord's squadron in 1828. Operated against the Turks and Greek insurrectionists in 1828–33. Joined Vice-Adm. Lazarev's squadron in the Bosporus and transferred to the Black Sea fleet in 1833. Cruised in the Black Sea in 1834. Repaired in 1836. Cruised in the Arkhipelago in 1837–8. Cruised off the Caucasus in 1839–42. Fire watch ship at Odessa in 1843–4. Fire watch ship at Sevastopol' in 1845–52. Broken up in 1852.

Uliss 20 St Petersburg, Okhta
Constructor V. F. Stoke
Laid down 1.12.1827   *Launched* 12.5.1828
Dimensions 98 ft 10 in (pp) x 30 ft 8 in (inside plank) x 15 ft 1 in (Veselago)
Armament 20 x 24pdr carr.
167 men
Okhta class. Purpose-built brig. To the Mediterranean with Rear-Adm. Rikord's squadron in 1828. Operated against the Turks and then the Greek insurrectionists in 1828–33. Joined Vice-Adm. Lazarev's squadron in the Bosporus and transferred to the Black Sea fleet in 1833. Carried the Russian consul to Alexandria in 1833. Fire watch ship at Sevastopol' in 1834 and 1837–41. Fire watch ship at Sukhum in 1837–41. Converted into a floating magazine in 1841.

Feniks 20 Kronshtadt
Constructor A.V. Zenkov
Laid down 10.2.1828   *Launched* 16.8.1828
Dimensions 98 ft 10 in (pp) x 30 ft 8 in (inside plank) x 15 ft 1 in (Veselago)
Armament 20 x 24pdr carr.
167 men
Okhta class. Purpose-built brig. Cruised in the Baltic in 1828–31. Wrecked off Dagerort on 24.9.1831. No casualties.

Gektor 20 St Petersburg, Okhta
Constructor V. F. Stoke
Laid down 29.11.1828   *Launched* 11.5.1829
Dimensions approx. 99 ft x 32 ft x 13 ft
30.2 m (pp) x 9.7 m x 3.9 m (Chernyshev)
98 ft 10 in x (86 ft keel) x 30 ft 6 in x 15 ft 6 in x 16 ft 5 in (Zapiski)
Armament 20 x 24pdr carr.
167 men
Okhta class. Purpose-built brig. Cruised in the Baltic in 1829–34. Fire watch ship at Sveaborg in 1835–6. Broken up in 1844.

Aiaks 20 St Petersburg, Okhta
Constructor V. F. Stoke
Laid down 29.11.1828   *Launched* 18.5.1829
Dimensions approx. 99 ft x 32 ft x 13 ft
30.2 m (pp) x 9.7 m x 3.9 m (Chernyshev)
98 ft 10 in x (86' keel) x 30 ft 6 in (inside plank) x 15 ft 1 in x 15 ft 6 in (Zapiski)
Armament 20 x 24pdr carr.
167 men
Okhta class. Purpose-built brig. Cruised to Brest in 1829–30. To the Arkhipelago in 1831 with Capt. Selivanov's division to join Rear-Adm. Rikord's squadron operating off Greece. Formally transferred to the Black Sea fleet in 1833. Arrived at Sevastopol' in 1834. Cruised off the Caucasus in 1835–7. Converted into a floating magazine in 1838.

Paris 20 St Petersburg, Okhta
Constructor V. F. Stoke
Laid down 29.9.1828   *Launched* 18.5.1829
Dimensions approx. 99 ft x 32 ft x 13 ft
30.2 m (pp) x 9.7 m x 3.9 m (Chernyshev)
98 ft 9 in x (86 ft keel) x 30 ft 8 in (inside plank) x 15 ft 1 in x 15 ft 6 in (Zapiski)
Armament 20 x 24pdr carr.
167 men

Okhta class. Purpose-built brig. Cruised in the Baltic in 1829–30. To the Arkhipelago in 1831 with Capt. Selivanov's division to join Rear-Adm. Rikord's squadron operating off Greece. Formally transferred to the Black Sea fleet in 1833. Arrived off Sevastopol' in 1834. Cruised off the Caucasus in 1835–6. Converted into a transport in 1837. Broken up in 1842.

Priam 20 Arkhangel'sk, Solombala
Constructor G. Ivanov
Laid down 30.12.1833   *Launched* 21.5.1834
Dimensions 98 ft 10 in (pp) x 30 ft 8 in (inside plank) x 12 ft 10 in
            (Veselago)
Armament 20 x 24pdr carr. 167 men
Okhta class. Purpose-built brig. Sailed from Arkhangel'sk to Kronshtadt in 7–9.1834. Cruised in the Baltic in 1835–9. Fire watch ship at Sveaborg in 8.1839. Cruised in the Baltic in 1840–1 and 1843. Fire watch ship at Revel' in 1847. Cruised in the Baltic in 1849–50. Broken up in 1857.

Filoktet 20 Arkhangel'sk, Solombala
Constructor Mordvinov
Laid down 30.12.1833   *Launched* 21.5.1834
Dimensions 98 ft 10 in (pp) x 30 ft 8 in (inside plank?) x 12 ft 8 in
            (Veselago)
Armament 1855 20 x 24pdr carr.
            167 men
            1857 4 x 12pdr (long), 16 x 24pdr carr.
Okhta class. Purpose-built brig. Sailed from Arkhangel'sk to Kronshtadt in 7–9.1834. Cruised in the Baltic in 1835–6. Participated in the Imperial Review of 1836. Cruised in the Baltic in 1837–49. Repaired in 1853–4. Participated in the Imperial Review of 1856. Cruised in the Mediterranean with Rear-Adm. Beren's squadron in 1856–8. Rearmed in 1856–7 with 'elongated carronades' bored up from smaller guns and firing 60-pood shells in place of the 44-pood shells normally carried. Survey work in the Baltic in 1859–60. Fire watch ship at Kronshtadt in 1861–2. Hulked in 1863.

Nestor 20 Arkhangel'sk, Solombala
Constructor F. T. Zagulyaev
Laid down 22.9.1834   *Launched* 21.5.1835
Dimensions 98 ft 10 in (pp) x 30 ft 8 in (inside plank) x 12 ft 8 in
            (Veselago)
Armament 20 x 24pdr carr.
            167 men
Okhta class. Purpose-built brig. Sailed from Arkhangel'sk to Kronshtadt in 1836. Cruised in the Baltic and involved in survey work in 1837–47. Wrecked off Stensher Island on 7.6.1847. No casualties.

Diomid class (9 ships)
In contrast to their adventurous near-sisters in the *Okhta* class, the *Diomids* all remained in the Baltic and led relatively uneventful lives, save only for *Aiaks* which was engaged in combat and scuttled in the defence of Sveaborg during the Crimean War.

Diomid 20 St Petersburg, Okhta
Constructor V. F. Stoke
Laid down 30.12.1830   *Launched* 8.8.1831
Dimensions approx. 100 ft x 30 ft x 13 ft x 13 ft
            30.5 m (pp) x 9.1 m (inside plank) x 3.9 m x 4 m
            (Chernyshev)
            440 tons displacement
            102 ft x (87 ft 4 in keel) x 30 ft (inside plank) x 14 ft 2 in
            x 14 ft 7 in (Zapiski)
Armament 20 x 24pdr carr.
Diomid class. Purpose-built brig. Cruised in the Baltic in 1832–5 and 1837–42. Repaired in 1843. Cruised in the Baltic in 1844 and 1845–7. Cruising and survey work in 1849–52. Broken up in 1858.

Patrokl 20 St Petersburg
Constructor K. A. Glazyrin
Laid down 28.12.1830   *Launched* 14.8.1831
Dimensions approx. 100 ft x 30 ft x 13 ft x 13 ft
            30.5 m (pp) x 9.1 m (inside plank) x 3.9 m x 4 m
            (Chernyshev)
            440 tons displacement
            99 ft 2 in x (86 ft 6 in keel) x 30 ft (inside plank) x 9 ft
            x 17 ft 7 in (Zapiski)
Armament 20 x 24pdr carr.
Diomid class. Purpose-built brig. Cruising and survey work in 1832–43. Fire watch ship in 1845. Broken up in 1845.

Kazarskii 20 St Petersburg, New Admiralty
Constructor I. I. Lemuan
Laid down 9.12.1833   *Launched* 25.8.1834
Dimensions 100 ft (pp) x 30 ft 8 in (inside plank) x 12 ft 8 in
            x 13 ft (Veselago)
            440 tons displacement
Armament 20 x 24pdr carr.
Diomid class. Purpose-built brig. Named after the captain of the heroic brig *Merkurii* in action against vastly superior Turkish forces in 1829. Cruised in the Baltic in 1835–8 and 1840–5. Fire watch ship at Revel' in 1847–8. Cruised in the Baltic in 1850–3. Broken up in 1854.

Agamemnon 20 St Petersburg, Okhta
Constructor K. I. Shvabbe
Laid down 9.12.1833   *Launched* 29.8.1834
Dimensions 100 ft (pp) x 30 ft 8 in (inside plank) x 12 ft 8 in x 13 ft
            (Veselago)
            440 tons displacement
Armament 20 x 24pdr carr.
            1855 18 x 24pdr carr.
            1856 5 x 24pdrs (long), 9 x 24pdr carr.
            1857 5 x 24pdrs (long), 2 x 8pdrs (long), 8 x 24pdr carr.
Diomid class. Purpose-built brig. Cruised in the Baltic in 1835–7. Fire watch ship at Odensholm in 1838. Cruised in the Baltic in 1839–41. Fire watch ship at Sveaborg in 1842. Cruised in the Baltic in 1843–8. Repaired in 1849–50. To Denmark during the Schleswig-Holstein Crisis with Vice-Adm. Epanchin's division in 1850. Cruising and survey work in 1851–2. Harbour service at Kronshtadt in 1853–61. Stricken on 16.1.1862.

Antenor 20 St Petersburg
Constructor A. S. Mikhelson
Laid down 31.1.1835   *Launched* 26.9.1835
Dimensions 100 ft (pp) x 30 ft (inside plank) x 12 ft 9 in x 13 ft
            (Veselago)
            440 tons displacement
Armament 20 x 24pdr carr.
            1855 18 x 24pdr carr.
            1856 5 x 24pdrs (long), 8 x 24pdr carr.
            1857 16 x 24pdr carr.
Diomid class. Purpose-built brig. Cruising and survey work in

1836–45. Fire watch ship at Sveaborg and Revel' in 1846–9. Repaired in 1850–1. Cruising and survey work in 1852–3. Participated in the defence of the northern approaches to Kronshtadt in 1855. Stationed at Kronshtadt in 1858–60. Stricken on 8.4.1861 and sold for breaking up.

Palinur 20 St Petersburg, New Admiralty
Constructor A. I. Pipin
Laid down 31.1.1835 *Launched* 26.9.1835
Dimensions 100 ft (pp) x 30 ft 8 in (inside plank) x 12 ft 9 in x 13 ft (Veselago)
440 tons displacement
Armament 20 x 24pdr carr.
1855 16 x 24pdr carr.
1857 2 x 8pdr (long), 14 x 24pdr carr.
Diomid class. Purpose-built brig. Cruised in the Baltic in 1836–43. Cruised in the North Sea in 1844. Cruised in the Baltic in 1845. Repaired in 1849–50. Cruised in the Baltic in 1851–3. Harbour service in 1854–63. Stricken on 11.9.1863.

Paris 20 St Petersburg, Okhta
Constructor I. A. Amosov
Laid down 30.7.1842 *Launched* 21.7.1843
Dimensions 100 ft (pp) x 30 ft 8 in (inside plank) x 12 ft 9 in x 13 ft (Veselago)
440 tons displacement
Armament 20 x 24pdr carr.
1855 18 x 24pdr carr.
1856 5 x 24pdrs (long), 9 18pdr carr.
Diomid class. Purpose-built brigs. Cruised in the Baltic in 1844–6. Fire watch ship at Sveaborg in 1847. Cruised in the Baltic in 1848. To Denmark during the Schleswig-Holstein Crisis with Vice-Adm. Epanchin's squadron in 1849–50. Guardship in the northern approaches to Kronshtadt in 1855. Sold for breaking up in 1860.

Ulis 20 St Petersburg
Constructor A. I. Popov
Laid down 26.5.1842 *Launched* 22.7.1843
Dimensions 100 ft (pp) x 30 ft 8 in (inside plank) x 12 ft 4 in x 13 ft (Veselago)
440 tons displacement
Armament 20 x 24pdr carr.
1855 16 x 24pdr carr.
Diomid class. Purpose-built brigs. Cruised in the Baltic in 1844–7. To Denmark during the Schleswig-Holstein Crisis with Vice-Adm. Lazarev's division in 1848–9. Cruised in the Baltic in 1850. Fire watch ship at Sveaborg in 1851–52. Cruised in the Baltic in 1853. Harbour service at Kronshtadt in 1854–9. Sold for breaking up in 1860.

Aiaks 20 St Petersburg
Constructor A. I. Pipin
Laid down 26.5.1842 *Launched* 22.7.1843
Dimensions 100 ft (pp) x 30 ft 8 in (inside plank) x 12 ft 4 in x 13 ft (Veselago)
440 tons displacement
Armament 20 x 24pdr carr.
Diomid class. Purpose-built brigs. Cruised in the Baltic in 1844–7. To Denmark in the Schleswig-Holstein Crisis with Vice Epanchin's division in 1848–9. Cruising and survey work in 1850–3. Participated in the defence of Sveaborg in Vice-Adm. Shikhmanov's squadron in 1854–5. Scuttled at Sveaborg on 15.6.1855 to block entry by the Anglo-French fleet.

Novaia Zemlia 16 Arkhangel'sk, Solombala
Constructor Rikhter
Laid down 7.4.1845 *Launched* 17.6.1845
Dimensions 85 ft (pp) x 26 ft (inside plank) x 5 ft 6½ in (Veselago)
Armament ?
Purpose-built brig. White Sea flotilla. Rather clearly built to replace *Lapominka*, which was 20 years old by 1845. Cruised in the White Sea and provided fire watch coverage at Arkhangel'sk and Mud'ug Island 1845–62. Stricken in.4.8.1862.

Baltic schooners (22 Purpose-built 1825–60)

Schooners came of age in Russia during the reign of Nicholas I. They were particularly well suited to the kind of coastal survey work being undertaken in the White Sea flotilla and 7 of the 22 served there.

No. 1 class (2 ships)
Schooner no. 1 8 Arkhangel'sk, Solombala
Constructor V. A. Ershov
Laid down 9.3.1826 *Launched* 5.7.1826
Dimensions 49 ft(pp) x16 ft 6 in (inside plank) x 6 ft 9 in (Veselago)
Armament ?
No. 1 class. Purpose-built schooner. Deployed with the White Sea flotilla. Survey work in the White Sea in 1827–32. Work selecting lighthouses in 1836–41. Repaired in 1841. Broken up in 1845.

Schooner no. 2 8 Arkhangel'sk, Solombala
Constructor V. A. Ershov
Laid down 24.8.1826 *Launched* 31.5.1827
Dimensions 49 ft(pp) x16 ft 6 in (inside plank) x 6 ft 9 in (Veselago)
Armament ?
No. 1 class. Purpose-built schooner. Deployed with the White Sea flotilla. Survey work in the White Sea in 1827–32. Fire watch ship at Lapominka 1833–8. Surveyed the Laplandia coast in 1840. Broken up in 1844.

Raduga 14 Kronshtadt
Constructor A. V. Zenkov
Laid down 20.3.1828 *Launched* 16.8.1828
Dimensions 84 ft(pp) x22 ft 6 in (inside plank) x10 ft 9 (Veselago)
Armament ?
Purpose-built schooner. Cruised in the Baltic in 1829–35. Fire watch ship off Kronshtadt in 1836–41. Broken up in 1842.

Sneg 14 Sveaborg
Constructor F.A. Bersenev
Laid down 8.12.1828 *Launched* 30.6.1829
Dimensions 80 ft (pp) x22 ft (inside plank) x9 ft (Veselago)
Armament ?
Purpose-built schooner. Sailed from Sveaborg to Kronshtadt in 1829. Cruised in the Baltic in 1830–43. Repaired in 1844. Fire watch ship at Sveaborg in 1845. Hydrographic survey work in the Gulf of Finland in 1846–79. Stationed at Riga in 1852. No further mention.

Vikhr' class (4 ships)
Vikhr' 14 Lodeynoe Pole
Constructor N.I. Federov
Laid down 19.5.1829 *Launched* 3.9.1829
Dimensions approx. 80 ft (pp) x 22 ft x 9 ft
24.4 m (pp) x 6.7 m x 2.7 m (Chernyshev)

80 ft x 22 ft x 8 ft 10 in (Zapiski)
Armament ? 50 men
Vikhr' class (4 ships). Purpose-built schooner. Dimensions are identical to those of *Sneg*, built at Sveaborg at the same time. Sailed from Lodeynoe Pole to St Petersburg in 1829. Cruising and survey work in the Baltic in 1830–5. Stationed at Kronshtadt in 1837–40. Broken up in 1843.

Gonets 14 Lodeynoe Pole
Constructor N. I. Federov
Laid down 19.5.1829 *Launched* 3.9.1829
Dimensions approx. 80 ft (pp) x 22 ft x 9 ft
    24.4 m (pp) x 6.7 m x 2.7 m) (Chernyshev)
    80 ft x 22 ft x 8 ft 10 in (Zapiski)
Armament ?
    50 men
Vikhr' class (4 ships). Purpose-built schooner. Sailed from Lodeynoe Pole to St Petersburg in 1829. Cruised in the Baltic in 1831–3. Fire watch ship at Revel' in 1834. Cruised in the Baltic in 1835. Stationed at Riga in 1836–41. Broken up in 1842.

Molniia 14 Lodeynoe Pole
Constructor N.I. Federov
Laid down 19.5.1829 *Launched* 3.9.1829
Dimensions approx. 80 ft (pp) x 22 ft x 9 ft
    24.4 m (pp) x 6.7 m x 2.7 m (Chernyshev)
    80 ft x 22 ft x 8 ft 10 in (Zapiski)
Armament ?
    50 men
Vikhr' class (4 ships). Purpose-built schooner. Sailed from Lodeynoe Pole to St Petersburg in 1829. Cruising and survey work in the Baltic in 1831–4. Fire watch ship at Riga in 1835. Cruising and survey work in the Baltic in 1836. Broken up in 1844.

Strela (Arrow) 14 Lodeynoe Pole
Constructor N. I. Federov
Laid down 19.5.1829 *Launched* 3.9.1829
Dimensions approx. 80 ft (pp) x 22 ft x 9 ft
    24.4 m (pp) x 6.7 m x 2.7 m) (Chernyshev)
    80 ft x 22 ft x 8 ft 10 in (Zapiski)
Armament ?
    50 men
Vikhr' class (4 ships). Purpose-built schooner. Sailed from Lodeynoe Pole to St Petersburg in 1829. Cruised in the Baltic in 1830–1. Separated from her division off Dagerort on 20.8.1831 and lost without a trace.

Grad 10/16 St Petersburg, Okhta
Constructor V. F. Stoke
Laid down 30.12.1830 *Launched* 8.8.1831
Dimensions approx. 100 ft (pp) x 25 ft x 10 ft
    30.5 m (pp) x 7.6 m x 3 m) (Chernyshev)
    100 ft x (78 ft 7 in keel) x 25 ft (inside plank) x 11 ft 4 in
    x 16 ft (Zapiski)
Armament ?
Purpose-built schooner. Cruised in the Baltic in 1831–40. Repaired in 1840. Cruised in the Baltic in 1841. Fire watch ship at Riga in 1842–8. Cruised in the Baltic in 1851–3. Guardship at Kronshtadt in 1854–5. Present at the Imperial Review in 1856. Sold in 1861. Stricken on 16.1.1862.

Krotov ? Arkhangel'sk, Solombala
Constructor ?
Laid down ? *Launched* 1834
Dimensions approx. 35 ft x ? x? (10.7 m x ? x (Chernyshev)
Armament ?
Purpose-built schooner. Named after polar explorer Lt Krotov who perished with his ship in 1833. Deployed in the White Sea flotilla. To Novaia Zemlia in 1834–7. Broken up in 1843.

Unnamed 2 St Petersburg
Constructor F. A. Bersenev
Laid down 27.11.1833 *Launched* 19.8.1834
Dimensions approx. 41 ft x 10 ft x 3½' (12.5m x 3.1m x 1.1m) (Chernyshev)
Armament ?
Purpose-built schooner. Attached to the rowing flotilla. No further data.

Dozhd' 16 St Petersburg, Okhta
Constructor K. I. Shvabbe
Laid down 9.12.1833 *Launched* 15.9.1834
Dimensions 98 ft 6 in (pp) x 25 ft 6 in (inside plank) x 11½ ft
    (Veselago)
Armament ?
Purpose-built schooner. Cruising and survey work the Baltic in 1834–44. Repaired in 1848. Cruising and survey work in the Baltic in 1849–53. Fire watch ship at Sveaborg in 1854–5. Participated in the defence of Sveaborg in 1855. Stationed at Kronshtadt in 1856–62. Stricken on 5.1.1863.

Meteor 16 Arkhangel'sk
Constructor A. I. Melikov
Laid down 6.11.1835 *Launched* 6.5.1836
Dimensions 100 ft (pp) x25 ft (inside plank) x'10 in (Veselago)
Armament ?
Purpose-built schooner. Sailed from Arkhangel'sk to Kronshtadt in 1837. Cruised in the Baltic in 1838–46. Repaired in 1850. Cruised in the Baltic in 1851–53. Stationed at Kronshtadt in 1854–6. Stricken on 5.1.1863.

***Novaia Zemlia* class** (2 ships)
Novaia Zemlia 2 Arkhangel'sk
Constructor V. A. Ershov
Laid down 9.2.1838 *Launched* 21.5.1838
Dimensions 39 ft(pp) x11 ft (inside plank) x 3 ft 9 in (Veselago)
Armament ?
Novaia Zemlia class. Purpose-built schooner. Deployed in the White Sea flotilla. Participated in expeditions to the Kara and White seas in 1838–9 with *Shpitsbergen*. Wrecked on 3.9.1839. No casualties.

Shpitsbergen 2 Arkhangel'sk
Constructor V. A. Ershov
Laid down 9.2.1838 *Launched* 21.5.1838
Dimensions 38 ft x 11 ft (inside plank) x 3 ft 9 in (Veselago)
Armament ?
Novaia Zemlia class. Purpose-built schooner. Deployed in the White Sea flotilla. Participated in expeditions to the Kara and White seas in 1838–9 with *Novaia Zemlia*. Fire watch ship at Arkhangel'sk in 1840–5. Cruised in the Baltic in 1846–8. Broken up after 1850.

Poliarnaia Zvezda 6 Arkhangel'sk (?)
Constructor F. T. Zagulyaev
Laid down 1.9.1843   *Launched* 10.5.1844
Dimensions 76 ft 9 in x 20 ft 3 in (inside plank) x 8 ft 2 in (Veselago)
Armament ?
Purpose-built schooner. Deployed in the White Sea flotilla in 1844–58. Broken up in 1859.

Raduga 16 Arkhangel'sk
Constructor F. T. Zagulyaev
Laid down 1.9.1844   *Launched* 17.6.1845
Dimensions 100 ft (pp) x 25 ft 6 in x 4 ft 10 in (Veselago)
Armament ?
Purpose-built schooner. Deployed in the White Sea in 1845. Deployed in the Baltic from 1846–53. Stationed at Kronshtadt from 1854–63. Stricken on 5.1.1863.

Opyt ? Kronshtadt
Constructor Petrov
Laid down 26.6.1847   *Launched* 8.10.1847
Dimensions 67 ft (pp) x 19 ft 5 in (inside plank) x 8 ft (Veselago)
Armament ?
Purpose-built two-masted schooner, also rated as a yacht. Built from timber taken from the frigate *Aleksandr*a which was broken up in 1845. Employed as a fast yacht for the commander-in-chief of Kronshtadt from 1848–58. To Denmark during the Schleswig-Holstein Crisis in 1850. Stricken on 5.1.1863.

Aleksandra ? Arkhangel'sk
Constructor Rikhter
Laid down 26.5.1847   *Launched* 8.5.1848
Dimensions 70 ft (pp) x 19 ft 5 in (inside plank) x 2 ft 4¼ in (Veselago)
Armament ?
Purpose-built schooner, also rated as a yacht. Built to an experimental new system designed by S. A. Burachek. Sailed from Arkhangel'sk to Kronshtadt in 1848. Commissioned from 1849–59. Broken up in 1860.

Strela 16 St Petersburg
Constructor Dementyev
Laid down 18.12.1843   *Launched* 12.6.1848
Dimensions 100 ft (pp) x 25 ft 6 in (inside plank) x 12 ft 9 in (Veselago)
Armament ?
Purpose-built schooner. Commissioned in 1848–58. To Denmark during the Schleswig-Holstein Crisis in 1850. Harbour service in 1860. Stricken on 16.1.1862.

Vikhr' 10 Kronshtadt
Constructor Tirnshtein
Laid down 31.8.1851   *Launched* 6.10.1852
Dimensions 105 ft pp x 24 ft (inside plank) x 11 ft (Veselago)
Armament ?
Purpose-built schooner. Commissioned in 1853–60. Harbour service in 1861. Stricken on 11.9.1863.

Zadornaia ? Arkhangel'sk
Constructor F.T. Zagulyaev
Laid down ?   *Launched* 9.9.1856
Dimensions 99 ft x 24 ft 7 in (inside plank) x 10 ft 6 in (Veselago)
Armament ?
Purpose-built schooner. Deployed in the White Sea flotilla. Commissioned in 1856–63. Stricken on 16.10.1863.

Baltic luggers (4 purpose-built/1 converted 1825–60)

Purpose-built

Petergof 12 St Petersburg, Okhta
Constructor V. F. Stoke
Laid down 7.3.1829   *Launched* 1.11.1829
Dimensions approx. 66 ft (pp) x 20 ft (inside plank) x 7½ ft (20.1 m (pp) x 6.1 m (inside plank) x 2.3 m) (Chernyshev)
66 ft x 20 ft x 10 ft 7 in
Armament 1855 2 x 6pdrs 10 x 4pdrs
Purpose-built lugger. Named after a famous palace famed for its parks and fountains on the outskirts of St Petersburg. Cruised in the Baltic in 1830–5. Repaired in 1836. Cruised in the Baltic in 1837–53 and 1856. Sold for breaking up in 1861. Stricken on 14.10.1861.

Oranienbaum 12 St Petersburg, Okhta
Constructor V. F. Stoke
Laid down 22.4.1829   *Launched* 9.11.1829
Dimensions approx. 65 ft (pp) x 22 ft x 12 ft (19.8m (pp) x 6.7m x 3.6m) (Chernyshev)
65 ft x 21 ft 1½ in x 11 ft 10 in x 8 ft 5 in (Zapiski)
Armament ?
Purpose-built lugger. Named after a palace on the outskirts of St Petersburg. Cruised in the Baltic in 1830–6. Repaired in 1837. Cruised in the Baltic in 1838–44 and 1846–7. Broken up in 1848.

Strel'na 12/14 ?
Constructor ?
Laid down ?   *Launched* 28.8.1831
Dimensions 80 ft (pp) x 20 ft 6 in (inside plank) x 9 ft 4 in (Veselago)
Armament 1855 14 x 18pdr carr.
Purpose-built lugger. Named after a palace on the outskirts of St Petersburg. Cruised in the Baltic in 1832–9. Fire watch ship at Revel' in 1840–1. Cruised in the Baltic in 1842. Fire watch ship at Revel' in 1843–6. Repaired in 1848. Cruised in the Baltic in 1848–9. Fire watch ship at Revel' in 1850–1. Cruised in the Baltic in 1852–3. Guardship in Revel' Roads in 1854–5. Fire watch ship at Revel' in 1856. Fire watch ship at Riga in 1857–8. Broken up after 1858.

Oranienbaum 12 St Petersburg, Okhta
Constructor I. A. Amosov
Laid down 26.10.1848   *Launched* 14.6.1849
Dimensions 65 ft (pp) x 21 ft (inside plank) x 11 ft 6 in (Veselago)
Armament 1855 2 x 6pdrs 10 x 4pdrs
Purpose-built lugger. Cruised in the Baltic in 1851–53. Stationed at Kronshtadt in 1854–7. Sold for breaking up in 1861. Stricken on 14.10.1861.

Converted

Narova 4 ?
Constructor ?
Laid down ?   *Launched* 31.7.1830   *Converted* 1833
Dimensions 60 ft 6 in (pp) x 21 ft 6 in (inside plank) x ? (Veselago)
Armament ?
Lugger converted from a trebaka of the same name. Named after the Narva River. Cruised in the Baltic in 1833–4 with naval cadets. Cruised in the Baltic in 1835. Survey work in the Gulf of Finland in 1838.

Cruised in the Baltic in 1840. Used as a floating lighthouse in 1843–4. Broken up in 1845.

Baltic one-masted tenders (4 purpose-built 1825–60)

Lebed' 12 St Petersburg, Okhta
Constructor V. F. Stoke
Laid down 31.12.1830   *Launched* 30.6.1831
Dimensions approx. 71 ft (pp) x 24 ft (inside plank) x 10 ft (21.6m
　　　　　　(pp) x 7.3 m (inside plank) x 3.1 m) (Chernyshev)
　　　　　　68 ft 10 in x 59 ft 6 in keel) x 24 ft (inside plank)
　　　　　　x 12 ft 1 in x 14 ft 1 in (Zapiski)
Armament ?
Purpose-built one-masted tender. Cruised in the Baltic in 1832–6. Fire watch ship at Revel' in 1837. Cruised in the Baltic in 1838–40. Cruised off Kronshtadt in 1841–2. Repaired in 1843. Cruised in the Baltic in 1844–9 and 1851–52. Fire watch ship at Revel' in 1853. Broken up in 1857.

Snapop 12 St Petersburg, Okhta
Constructor I. A. Amosov
Laid down 24.3.1836   *Launched* 14.10.1837
Dimensions 67 ft (pp) x 24 ft (inside plank) x 9 ft 3 in (Veselago)
Armament ?
Purpose-built one-masted tender. Cruised in the Baltic in 1837–51. Repaired in 1852. Stationed at Kronshtadt in 1854–5. Cruised in the Baltic in 1856. Stationed at Kronshtadt in 1857–61. Stricken on 16.1.1862 and sold for breaking up.

Uchenik ? St Petersburg
Constructor Dementyev
Laid down 27.6.1838   *Launched* 30.4.1841
Dimensions 44 ft 2 in (pp) x 16 ft 3 in (inside plank) x 2 ft 1 in
　　　　　　50 tons displacement (Veselago)
Armament ?
Purpose-built one-masted tender. Cruised with naval cadets in 1841–9. Fire watch ship at Sveaborg in 1850–1. No further mention.

Kopchik ? St Petersburg
Constructor Dementyev
Laid down 9.7.1849   *Launched* 21.6.1851
Dimensions 70 ft 8 in (pp) x 24 ft (inside plank) x 10 ft 6 in
　　　　　　(Veselago)
Armament ?
Purpose-built one-masted tender. Cruised in the Baltic in 1852. Fire watch ship at Revel' in 1853. Stationed at Revel' in 1854–5. Cruised in the Baltic in 1856. Stationed at Kronshtadt in 1856. Fire watch ship off Kronshtadt in 1858–63. Harbour service at Kronshtadt in 1863.

Baltic Prizes

Captured ships were normally rearmed with the Russian guns, but those captured during the 1788–90 war retained their Swedish guns for some time thanks to the abundant amount of the captured Swedish ammunition.

Where known, data relating to the ship as originally constructed is included along with the Russian data. Please note that Swedish dimensions are recorded in Swedish feet with one Swedish foot being equal to 0.9741 British feet.

Captured line of battle ships

Vakhmeister 44/52/56 Riga, Sweden
Constructor Francis Shelton Sr
Laid down ?   *Launched* 1681   *Captured* 24.5.1719
Dimensions 120 ft x 36 ft 2 in x 12 ft 2 in (English measure)
　　　　　　120 ft 7½ in x 31 ft 9 in x 11 ft 11½ in (Apraksin)
　　　　　　130 ft x 30 ft x 15 ft, 775 tons (Swedish measure)
Armament LD 4 x 18pdrs, 14 x 12pdrs (Swedish)
　　　　　　UD 20 x 6pdrs
　　　　　　FC & QD 6 x 4pdrs, 2 x 3pdrs, 4 x 1pdrs
　　　　　　1719 LD 18 x 12pdrs
　　　　　　UD 20 x 6pdrs
　　　　　　FC & QD 14 x 6pdrs (as rearmed, conjecture)
Swedish ship of the line *Wachtmeister* captured with *Karlskrona Vapen* and *Vestenshliup* by Naum Seniavin on 22.5.1719 off Osel. Sailed from Revel' to Kronshtadt in 9.1719. Fire watch ship at Kronshtadt in 1721–7. Broken up after 1728.

Rodos 60 Turkey
Constructor ?
Laid down ?   *Launched* ?   *Captured* 24–26.6.1770
Dimensions ?
Armament ?
Turkish ship of the line captured at Chesma on 24–26.6.1770. Abandoned by her crew and towed to Russia in very poor condition. Departed Auza on 22.10.1770 for repairs at Port Mahon. Heavily damaged in a storm on 31.10.1770. Grounded deliberately off Mezata Island to prevent sinking. Destroyed by fire on 7.11.1770 with 23 seamen lost.

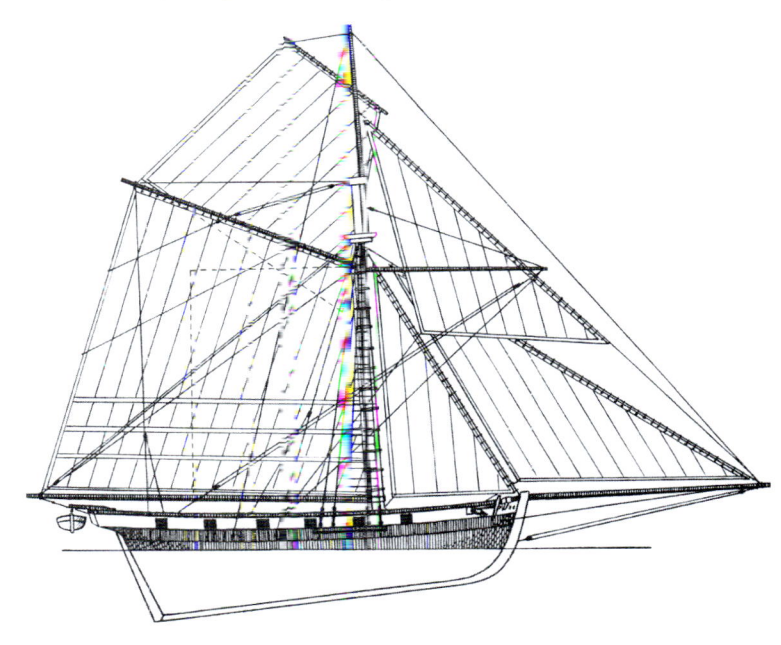

Tenders were considered as seagoing warships and not as auxiliaries in the Russian navy. This is Lebed' *of 1831 and shows her rig and simplicity of design. She is rated as carrying 12 cannon, but it is clear that these must have been the smallest weapons available, possibly 3pdrs, and useful only against small boats and as anti-personnel weapons.*

The battle of Osel 1719 as seen by A. P. Bogolyubov. The unfortunate Swedish Wachtmeister *is in the centre of the action, under attack by several of the Russian line of battle ships acting in concert, while her frigate and brigantine consorts are being similarly dealt with in the background. The Russian line of battle ships involved were all 50-gun warships and rather small by the standards of the Atlantic navies of the day.* Wachtmeister *would be captured and taken into the Russian navy as* Vakhmekeister, *only to be broken up in 1728.*

Finland 52/56 Stockholm, Sweden
Constructor G. C. Falk
Laid down 1721 *Launched* 28.6.1735 *Captured* 22.6.1790
Dimensions 151 ft x 39 ft x 17¼ ft x 17 ft, 1.380 tons (Swedish measure)
145 ft x 38 ft 6 in (inside plank) x 15 ft 6 in (Russian measure)
Armament LD 22 x 24pdrs
UD 20/22 x 12pdrs
FC & QD 10/14 x 6pdrs (Swedish armament)

Swedish ship of the line captured at Vyborg on 22.6.1790. Harbour service in 1791. Broken up after 1794.

Emgeiten 62 Karlskrona, Sweden
Constructor Charles Shelyon
Laid down 12.1727 *Launched* 10.1732 *Captured* 22.6.1790
Dimensions 166 ft x 44 ft x 20 ft x 20 ft, 2,000 tons (Swedish measure)
160 ft x 46 ft (inside plank) x 18 ft 6 in (Russian measure)
Armament LD 26 x 24pdrs
UD 26 x 18pdrs
FC & QD 16/8 x 6pdrs (as built)
LD 24 x 36pdrs (short)
UD 28 x 24pdrs (short)
FC & QD 10 x 6pdrs, 8 x 3pdr falconets (Veselago)

Swedish ship of the line *Enigheten* captured at Vyborg on 22.6.1790. Rebuilt in Sweden in 1768–9. Cruised in the Baltic in 1791. Cruised to Denmark and the North Sea in 1793. Cruised in the Baltic in 1794–9. Cruised to England with troops in Rear-Adm. Chichagov's squadron in 1799–1800. Cruised to Copenhagen in 1804. Transported troops to Prussia in 1805. Retreated with Adm. Khanykov's squadron in the face of the Anglo-Swedish squadron to Rogervik on 13.8.1808 and then to Kronshtadt on 30.9.1808. Guardship in Kronshtadt Roads in 1809–11. Hulked in 1812. Broken up in 1816.

Prints Karl 64 Karlskrona, Sweden
Constructor Gilbert Shelton
Laid down 18.8.1755 *Launched* 6.11.1758 *Captured* 2.5.1790
Dimensions 160 ft x 42 ft x 20 ft x 21 ft 6 in (Swedish measure)
Armament Captured LD 24 x 24pdrs
UD 24 x 12pdrs
FC & QD 16 x 8pdrs (Veselago)
Rearmed LD 24 x 24pdrs
UD 24 x 12pdrs
FC & QD 16 x 8pdrs, 6 x 36pdr carr. (all guns were Swedish)

Swedish ship of the line *Prins Karl* captured at Revel' on 2.5.1790. Fought at Vyborg on 22.6.1790. Cruised in the Baltic in 1791, 1794–5, and 1797. Cruised to Bornholm and Lübeck in 1798. Cruised in the Baltic in 1799 and 1800. Cruised to Copenhagen in 1804. Participated in the landing of troops in Prussia in 1805 and reduced to harbour service. Guardship in Kronshtadt Roads in 1808–10 and 1812. Broken up after 1813.

Prints Gustav 70/74 Karlskrona
Constructor Gilbert Shelton
Laid down 2.8.1756 *Launched* 6.4.1758 *Captured* 6.7.1788
Dimensions 171 ft x 44 ft 6 in x 22 ft 3 in x 23 ft (Swedish measure)
Armament Designed LD 26 x 24pdrs
UD 26 x 18pdrs
FC & QD 20 x 6pdrs
590/620 men
Captured LD 26 x 26pdrs

The capture of an enemy ship of the line was always a moment of great significance and the surrender of the 62-gun Prints Karl *to the 100-gun* Rostislav *at the battle at Revel in 1790 was no exception. Seen in the centre left of this painting by A. P. Bogolyubov, the disparity in size of the two ships is readily apparent as is the severe disadvantage faced by the attacking Swedish line as their ships fought heeled over by the moderate winds, while the Russian ships waited at anchor with sails furled and steady as rocks. This work dates from the 1860s and is one of very many excellent paintings by A. P. Bogolyubov, a highly regarded naval officer turned artist and a favourite of the imperial family. The Admiralty at St Petersburg is now home to a collection of his work once the property of the emperor and displayed in the Summer Palace.*

    UD 26 x 19pdrs
    FC & QD 18 x 6pdrs (French?) (Veselago)
  Rearmed LD 26 x 24pdrs
    UD 26 x 12pdrs
    FC & QD 18 x 6pdrs
    774 men

Swedish ship of the line *Prins Gustav* captured at Gogland on 6.7.1788. Previously rebuilt by Sweden in 1784–5. Fought at Oland on 15.7.1789. fought at Krasnaia Gorka on 23–24.5.1790 with 1 killed and 2 wounded. Fought at Vyborg on 22.6.1790. Training duties at Kronshtadt Roads in 1791–2 and 1794–5. Cruised in the Baltic in 1797. To Bornholm with Adm Kruz's squadron in 1798. Departed Revel' for England as flag to Rear-Adm. Kartsov's 3rd Division on 20.8.1798. Developed a severe leak during a violent storm off Skagen on 19.9.1798. Leak repaired but the sheath planks in the bow opened on 30.10.1798, dooming the ship. Abandoned and sunk on 4.11.1798. Crew saved by *Iziaslav* 66.

Sofiia Magdelina 74 Karlskrona, Sweden
Constructor Gilbert Sheton
Laid down 21.7.1759 *Launched* 22.7.1774 *Captured* 22.6.1790
Dimensions 171 ft x 44 ft 6 in x 22 ft 3 in x 23 ft, 2,400 tons (Swedish measure)
Armament LD 26 x 24pdrs
    UD 26 x 18pdrs
    FC & QD 16/20 x 6pdrs (Swedish)
    590/670 men (Swedish)
    651 men in Russian service

Swedish ship of the line *Drottning Sofia Magdalena* captured at Vyborg in 1790. Cruised in the Baltic in 1791 and 1793–4. Stationed in Revel' Roads in 1795–6. Cruised in the Baltic in 1797. Left for England on 20.8.1798 with Rear-Adm. Kartsov's 3rd Division. Delayed in transit by a severe storm off Skagen, Norway. Operated in the North Sea in 1798–1800. Cruised in the Baltic in 1801. Broken up after 1805.

Kronprins Gustaf-Adol'f 64 Karlskrona, Sweden
Constructor F. Chapman
Laid down 18.7.1782 *Launched* 6.11.1782 *Captured* 26.7.1788
Dimensions 167 ft x 45 ft 9 in x 19 ft 6 in (Swedish measure)
Armament LD 26 x 24pdrs
    UD 28 x 18pdrs
    FC & QD 8 x 6pdrs
    Swedish peacetime 570 men (Swedish)
    LD 26 x 36pdrs
    UD 26 x 24pdrs
    FC & QD 8 x 6pdrs (Swedish wartime)
    553 men (Russian)

Swedish ship of the line *Kronprins Gustav Adolf* captured by Rear-Adm. Kozlyaninov's squadron on 26.7.1788 while grounded off Sveaborg. Burnt in place two days after capture.

Retvizan 62 Karlskrona, Sweden
Constructor F. Chapman
Laid down 19.7.1783 *Launched* 2.9.1783 *Captured* 22.6.1790

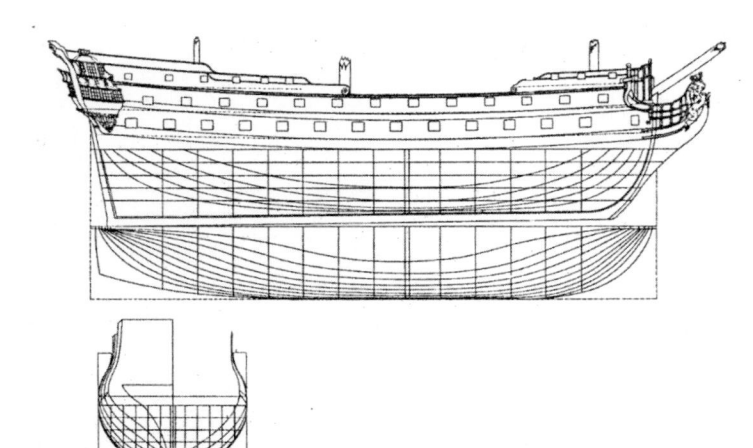

When captured and taken into Russian service, Swedish ships were always highly regarded for their qualities of design and solid construction; Prints Gustav *(74) of 1758 depicted here was no exception. After being captured at Gogland in 1788, she fought against her country of origin at Öland, Styrsudden and Vyborg. After the war's end, she remained in Russian service until her 40-year old timbers gave way in a storm in 1798 while on the way to England to join the fight against France.*

Dimensions 167 ft x 45 ft 9 in x 19 ft 6 in (Swedish measure)
  163 ft x 46 ft 8 in x 18 ft 3 in (Russian measure)
Armament LD 26 x 24pdrs
  UD 28 x 18pdrs
  FC & QD 8 x 6pdrs (Swedish peacetime)
  LD 26 x 36pdrs
  UD 26 x 24pdrs
  FC & QD 8 x 6pdrs (Swedish wartime)
  LD 24 x 36pdrs (short)
  UD 28 x 24pdrs (short)
  FC & QD 10 x 6pdrs, 8 x 3pdr falconets
  632 men (Veselago)

Swedish ship of the line *Rättvisan* captured at Vyborg on 22.6.1790. Cruised in the Baltic in 1791. Stationed at Revel' Roads in 1792–4. To England in 1795–6 with Rear-Adm. Khanykov's squadron. Cruised in the Baltic in 1797. Docked and surveyed in 1797 to obtain draughts for duplication of her design and lines. Departed Kronshtadt in.5.1798 with Vice-Adm. Markarov's First Division and arrived in Britain in 7.1798. Operated under the overall command of British Vice-Adm. Duncan in North Sea waters in 1798–1800. Repaired in 1803–4. To the Mediterranean with Commodore Greig's squadron in 1804. Engaged in operations under Vice-Adm. Seniavin's squadron. Present at the surrender of Tenedos. Fought at the battle of the Dardanelles on 10–11.5.1807. Fought at Mount Athos on 19.6.1807. At Lisbon in 1807–8. To Portsmouth for internment in 1808. Sold in England in 1813. Guns returned to Russia.

Washington 72 Dutch/Amsterdam
Constructor R. Dorman
Laid down 1795 *Launched* 28.2.1796
Captured 20.8.1799
Dimensions 168 ft 5 in x (1358 ft 1 in LK) x 46 ft 2 in x 18 ft 5½ in, 1,565 ^{20}/94 bm
Armament LD 28 x 32pdrs
  UD 28 x 18pdrs
  FC & QD 4 x 18pdrs, 14 x 32pdr carr.

Dutch ship of the line allocated to Russia after the Dutch surrender at the Texel on 20.8.1799. Ceded to the British at Sheerness at the orders of Paul I.

Beskermer 50/56 Dutch/Enkhuizen
Constructor ?
Laid down ? *Launched* 1784
Captured 20.8.1799
Dimensions 154½ ft x 43 ft x 20 ft (Dutch measure)
  145 ft 11 in x (118 ft 7 in LK) x 40 ft 10 in x 16 ft 4 in 1,051 ^{6}/94 bm (British measure)
Armament LD 24 x 18pdrs
  UD 24 x 32pdr carr.
  FC & QD 8 x 32pdr carr.

Dutch ship of the line allocated to Russia after the Dutch surrender at the Texel on 20.8.1799. Ceded to the British at Sheerness at the orders of Paul I.

Captured frigates

Karlskronvapen 34 Karlshamn, Sweden
Constructor ?
Laid down 1703 *Launched* ? *Captured* 24.5.1719
Dimensions 89 ft 4 in x 23 ft 6 in x 8 ft 9 in (Russian measurement)
  94 ft x 24 ft x 10 ft, 290 tons (Swedish measurement)
Armament 18 x 6pdrs, 8 3pdrs, 2 x 16pdr howitzers

Swedish frigate *Karlskronavapen* (28) captured with *Wachtmeister* and *Vestenshliup* on 24.5.1719 off Osel. Sailed to Kronshtadt in 9.1719. Fire watch ship at Kronshtadt in 1719–23. Sailed to Revel' in 1724. Fire watch ship at Revel' in 1725–8. Repaired in 1729. Fire watch ship at Revel' in 1730–3. Sailed to Kronshtadt in 10.1733. Sailed to St Petersburg and broken up there in 1737.

Storfeniks 32/34 Karlskrona, Sweden
Constructor Charles Shelton
Laid down ? *Launched* 26.10.1708 *Captured* 27.7.1720
Dimensions 106 ft 3 in/110 ft x 28 ft 4 in/29 ft 7 in x 11 ft 2 in/13 ft (Russian measurement)
  110 ft x 27 ft 6 in/27 ft x 12 ft/11 ft, 425 tonnes (Swedish measurement)
Armament 1720 2 x 12pdrs, 20 x 8pdrs, 12 x 3pdrs

Swedish frigate *Stora Fenix* (34) captured off Grengam on 27.7.1720. Sailed from Revel' to Kronshtadt in 8.1720. Cruised in the Gulf of Finland in 1721–4 and 1726–7. Fire watch ship at Kronshtadt in 1728–33. Expedition to Danzig in 1734 with Adm. Gordon's squadron. Fire watch ship at Kronshtadt in 1735. Stationed in Kronshtadt Roads in 1736. Broken up after 1738.

Venker 30 France
Constructor ?
Laid down ? *Launched* ? *Captured* 27.7.1720
Dimensions 119 ft/109 ft x 32 ft/30 ft x 14 ft 4 in/17 ft (Russian measurement)
  109 ft 6 in x 30 ft x ? (Swedish measurement)
Armament 1720 24 x 6pdrs, 6 x 3pdrs

Swedish frigate *Venker*, captured off Grengam on 27.7.1720. Former French privateer *Le Vainqueur* hired by Sweden in 1720. Sailed to Kronshtadt in 8.1720. To St Petersburg as a memorial. Broken up at St Petersburg after 1838.

THE BALTIC FLEET 1825–60

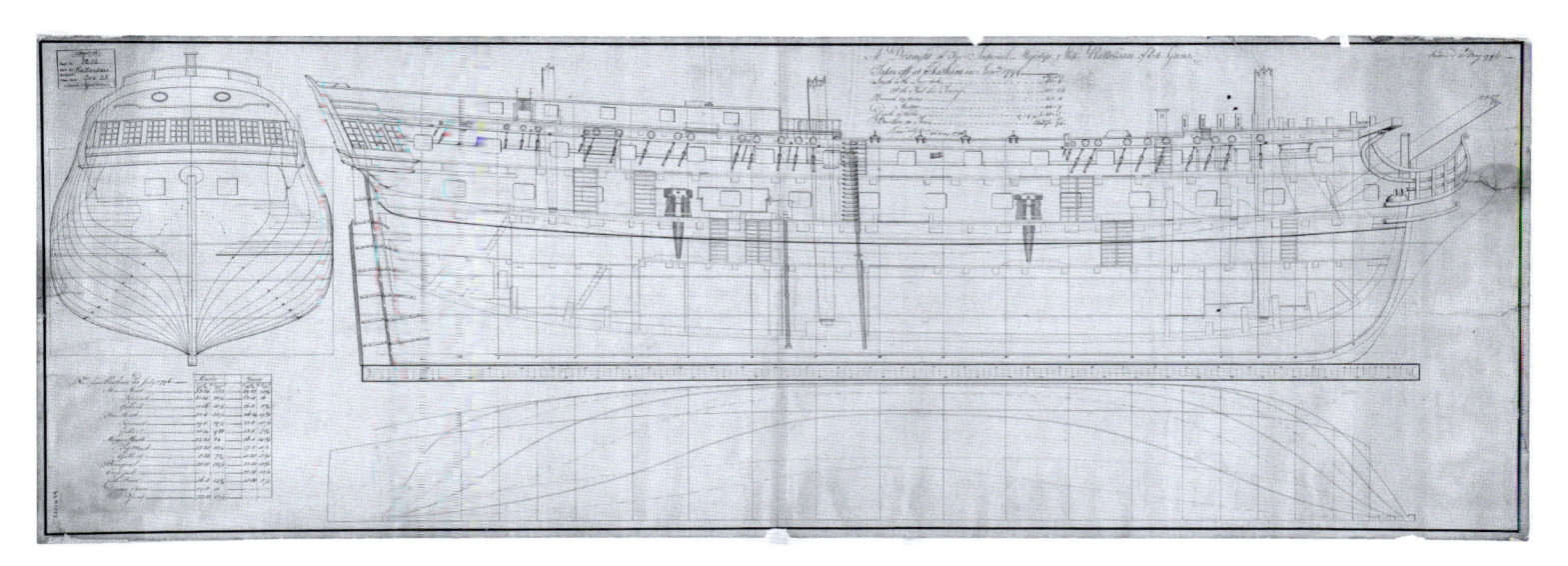

Seven Swedish ships of the line were captured by Russia during the 1788-90 war and five were taken into Russian service, including this product of Fredrik af Chapman's genius. Retvizan had a long, active, and successful career in Russian service until she found herself a hostage to changing alliances in 1808 after the Russian victory at Mount Athos. Escorted to Portsmouth by Royal Navy ships along with the majority of Vice-Adm. Seniavin's unfortunate Mediterranean squadron, she ended her days in British internment until she was sold to her captors for scrap in 1813. It may, in fact, have been during her British internment that her lines were taken for this draught. An excellent design and as well thought out as the smaller Venus, Retvizan had the misfortune of being too small for her era. A small number of Russian 60-gun ships were built in imitation of her design during the first decade of the new century, but the future belonged to 74-gun ships in the Baltic and even larger 84-gun ships in the Black Sea.

Kisken 22/32 Sweden
Constructor ?
Laid down ?   *Launched* 1715
Captured 27.7.1720
Dimensions 72 ft/76 ft x 22 ft/20 ft 2 in x 9 ft 6 in (Russian measurement)
76 ft x 20 ft x 9 ft 6 in, 250 tons (Swedish measurement)
Armament 1720 6 x 8pdrs, 12 x 4pdrs, 12 3pdrs
Swedish frigate *Kisken* captured off Grengam on 27.7.1720. Sailed to Kronshtadt in 8.1720. Cruised in the Baltic in 1721 and 1724. Repaired in 1727. Fire watch ship at Revel' in 1728-30. Fire watch ship at Kronshtadt in 1734–5. Broken up after 1738.

Dansk-Ern 18/24 Denmark
Constructor ?
Laid down ?   *Launched* 1694   *Captured* 27.7.1720
Dimensions 99 ft 3 in/109 ft x 25 ft 7 in/22 ft 2 in x 14 ft/13 ft (Russian measurement)
109 ft x 25 ft x 13 ft (Swedish measurement)
90 ft x 21 ft x 11.3 ft (Danish measurement)
Armament 4 x 6pdrs, 14 x 4pdrs
Swedish frigate *Danska Orn* captured off Grengam on 27.7.1720. Originally the Danish *Ornen* (1694), captured by Sweden in 1715. Technically this ship was a sloop although rated a frigate. Sailed to Kronshtadt in 8.1720. Cruised in the Baltic in 1721 and 1724. Sailed to St Petersburg for preservation in 1728. Broken up at St Petersburg after 1737.

Brilliant 30 France
Constructor ?
Laid down ?   *Launched* ?
Captured 13.6.1734
Dimensions ?
Armament 1736 16 x 4pdrs

French privateer captured at Danzig on 13.6.1734 and rated a frigate. Damaged by ice while in transit to St Petersburg and forced to winter at Biork-e zund. Carried cargo between Baltic ports in 1735. Fire watch ship at Kronshtadt in 1736–40. Cruised in the Baltic as a training ship in 1741–3. Cruised in the Baltic in 1745. Broken up after 1746.

Ul'riksdal' 24 Skeppsholmen
Constructor Daniel Friese
Laid down ?   *Launched* 1738
Captured 24.10.1742
Dimensions 330 tons (Swedish measurement)
Armament 20 x 6pdrs 4 x 3pdrs (Swedish)
Swedish flat-bottomed frigate *Ulriksdal* captured after drifting to Revel' and surrendering on 24.10.1742 with an extremely sick crew. Arrived at Helsingfors to escort prams to Revel' on 1.6.1743. Fire watch ship at Revel' in 1743–5. Transferred to Kronshtadt in 1746. Fire watch ship at Kronshtadt in 1747–73 (*sic*). Broken up after 1773.

Tino ? Turkey
Constructor ?
Laid down ?   *Launched* ?   *Captured* 1770
Dimensions ?
Armament ?
Turkish ship captured in the Arkhipelago in 1770 and rated a frigate. Operations against the Turks in the Arkhipelago in 1771–4. Sailed from Auza to Kerch in the Black Sea in 1775. No further mention.

Arkhipelag 30 Turkey
Constructor ?
Laid down ?   *Launched* ?   *Captured* 1770
Dimensions ?
Armament ?
Turkish ship captured in the Arkhipelago in 1770 and converted into a frigate. Operations against the Turks in the Arkhipelago. Grounded off

The capture of the Swedish heavy frigate Venus *by the much smaller* Merkurii *in 1789 was quite naturally a favourite subject for Russian artists. A. P. Bogolyubov was no exception, and painted the brief and one-sided battle on at least two occasions.* Merkurii *is shown here, oars out in the prevailing calm, manoeuvring off the battered quarter of the larger and completely unprepared frigate, which would soon be forced to surrender. Taken into Russian service,* Venus *would have a long, varied and entirely honourable career before being sold to Naples in 1807.*

Mitilini on 5.11.1771 and freed by *Severnyi Oryol*. Arrived at Kerch in the Black Sea as a merchant ship with Albanian settlers on 18.5.1775. Cruised in the Black Sea in 1776–8. Transferred to Kherson in 1779. Carried the Russian ambassador to Istanbul in 1781. Converted into a merchant ship in 1781. No further mention.

Venus 44/50 Karlskrona
Constructor F. Chapman
Laid down 31.3.1783 *Launched* 19.7.1783 *Captured* 21.5.1789
Dimensions 156 ft x 40 ft x 17 ft 6 in (Swedish measurement)
  151 ft 6 in x 38 ft 10 in x 15 ft 9 in (Russian measurement)
Armament Captured 26/30 x 24pdrs, 14 x 6pdrs (Veselago)
Swedish heavy frigate captured on 21.5.1789 by Russian cutter *Merkurii*. Attached to Vice-Adm. Kozlyaninov's squadron at Copenhagen in 1789. Fought at Revel' on 2.5.1790 with 1 killed and 2 wounded and 737 rounds fired. Fought at Vyborg on 22.6.1790, capturing 2 Swedish galleys. On 3.5.1790, assisted by *Iziaslav* (66), she captured the Swedish *Rättvisan* (64). Cruised in the Baltic in 1791, 1793–4, 1795–7 and 1798. To England in 1799–00. Cruised in the Baltic with naval cadets in 1801. Repaired in 1804. To the Mediterranean as flag to Commodore Greig (Adm. Greig's son) in 1804. Involved in the capture of Tenedos in 1807. Engaged in the pursuit of Turkish squadron on 9.5.1807, leading the Russian attack and engaging a Turkish line of battle ship. Dispatched by Adm. Seniavin on 9.11.1807 in search of Commodore Baratynskiy's division. Damaged, repaired at Palermo, blockaded by the British, and placed in Neapolitan custody to avoid bloodshed. Crew evacuated to Trieste.

Captured Swedish rowing frigates

Olifant 18 Sweden
Constructor ?
Laid down ? *Launched* 1713
Captured 27.7.1714
Dimensions 116 ft x 28 ft x 8 ft 6 in
  380 tons displacement
  103 ft (LGD) x 26 ft 8 in (inside plank) x 7 ft 6 in
  x 8 ft 6 in (stern) x 7 ft 6 in (bow)
Armament 14 x 12pdrs, 4 x 3pdrs (Veselago)
  16 x 12pdrs, 8 x 3pdr (Swedish armament)
Swedish frigate *Elefanten* captured at Gangut on 27.7.1714. Described by Veselago as a rowing frigate, but lacked oars in Swedish service and was almost equipped like a pram with 6 stern guns, including 2 x 12pdrs. Preserved as a memorial. Broken up in 1737.

Avtroil 24 Djurgard, Stockholm
Constructor H. Sohlberg
Laid down ? *Launched* 1767
Captured 13.8.1789
Dimensions 115 ft 6 in x 30 ft 10 in x 7 ft 6 in, 7 pairs of oars
Armament 24 x 12pdrs
  210 men
Rowing frigate. Former Swedish *Af Trolle*, captured at the 1st battle of Rochensalm on 13.8.1789 and renamed Avtroil. In Russian service, she repulsed the attack of the blockaded Swedish rowing flotilla under Capt. Sir Sidney Smith at Tranzund on 5.6.1790. Fought as flag to Vice-Adm. Kozlyaninov at the 2nd battle of Rochensalm on 28.6.1790. Cruised in the Baltic in 1791–3 and 1795–8. Transported the Russian dowry for the Duke of Mecklenburg in 1799. Cruised in the Baltic

THE BALTIC FLEET 1825–60

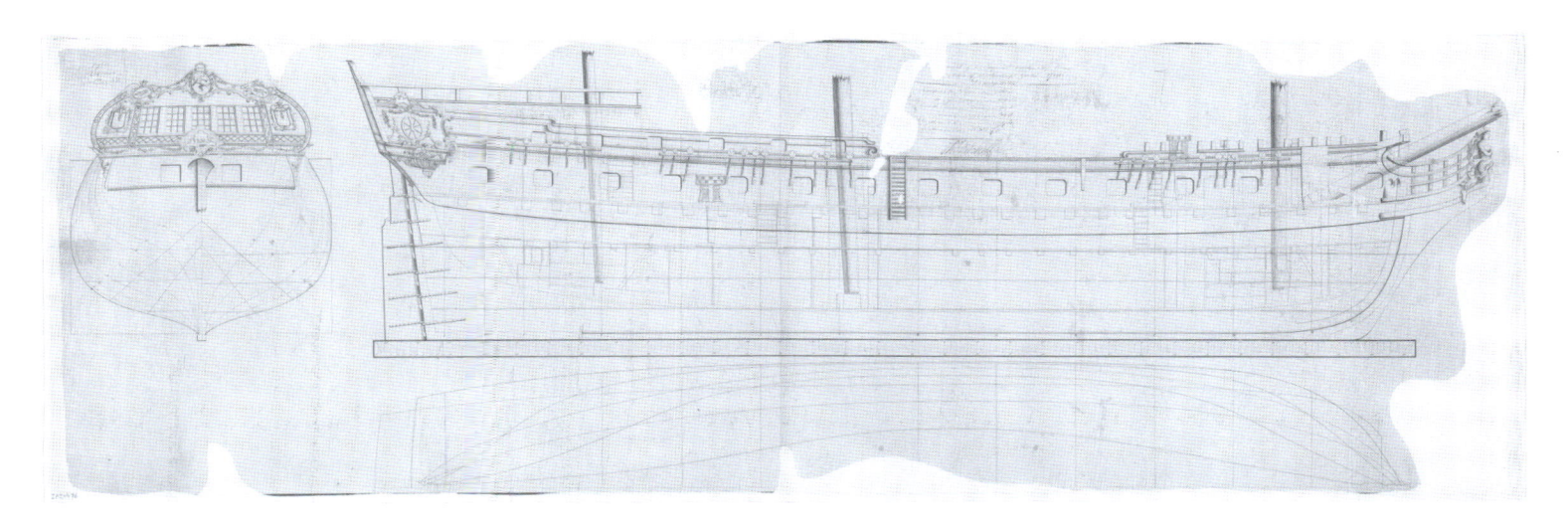

Venus, 44, seen here in a somewhat ragged but still readable draught in possession of the National Maritime Museum, was a member of Frederik af Chapman's ten-strong Bellona *class of heavy frigates laid down and completed on the eve of the 1788 Russo-Swedish War. These ships, in conjunction with the generally similar, but larger, ten* Gustavisan *class 62-gun ships of the line were the Swedish shipbuilder's attempt to redress the quantitative imbalance between the larger Russian Baltic fleet and the smaller Swedish fleet by creating a homogeneous fleet capable of being upgunned in wartime, with 24pdrs replacing 18pdrs for the frigates and with 36pdrs replacing 24pdrs for the battle ships.* Venus *and her sisters were not only capable of carrying a then extraordinary armament for frigates, they were built to withstand fire from opposing ships of the line. In the event, Chapman's plan proved unworkable, but the Russians were greatly impressed by the strength and durability of his creations and the design of the captured* Venus *became the basis for future Baltic heavy frigate development.*

with naval cadets in 1800. Stationed in Kronshtadt Roads in 1801. Repaired in 1801–4. To the Mediterranean with marines in 1804 with Commodore Greig (jr)'s division. Operated in the Mediterranean in 1805–8. With Commodore Saltanov's division at Trieste and Venice in 1808. Ceded to France in 1809.

Gel'gomar 26/32 Västervik
Constructor Frederik af Chapman
Laid down ? *Launched* 18.5.1790
Captured 21.4.1808
Dimensions 146 ft x 36 ft x 10 ft, 10 pairs of oars (Swedish measurement)
143 ft x 35 ft 1 in x 8 ft 11 in, 10 pairs of oars (Russian measurement)
Armament 24 x 36pdrs, 2 x 12pdrs, 6 guns/carronades added on upper deck in Russian service

Rowing frigate (also classed as a hemmema). Swedish *Hjalmar*, captured at Sveaborg on 21.4.1808 and renamed *Gel'gomar*. Fought at Junferzund on 7.8.1808 and recaptured the Stor-Biorn from the Swedes. Operated off Finland in 1809. Broken up in 1828.

Stor-Biorn 26/32 Djurgäden, Stockholm
Constructor Frederik af Chapman
Laid down ? *Launched* ? *Captured* 21.4.1808
Dimensions 146 ft x 36 ft x 10 ft, 10 pairs of oars (Swedish measurement)
143 ft x 35 ft 1 in x 8 ft 11 in, 10 pairs of oars (Russian measurement)
Armament 24 x 36pdrs, 2 x 12pdrs, 6 guns/carronades added on upper deck in Russian service

Rowing frigate (also classed as a hemmema). Swedish *Styrbjorn*, captured at Sveaborg on 21.4.1808 and renamed *Stor-Biorn*. Fought heroically at Jungferzund on 7.8.1808 where she was captured and taken in tow by the Swedes after the captain and most officers had been killed in action. Successfully retaken by *Gel'gomar* immediately after being taken. Operated off Finland in 1809. Receiving ship in 1817.

Captured snows

Astril'd 8 Karlskrona
Constructor ?
Laid down ? *Launched* 1699 *Captured* 7.5.1703

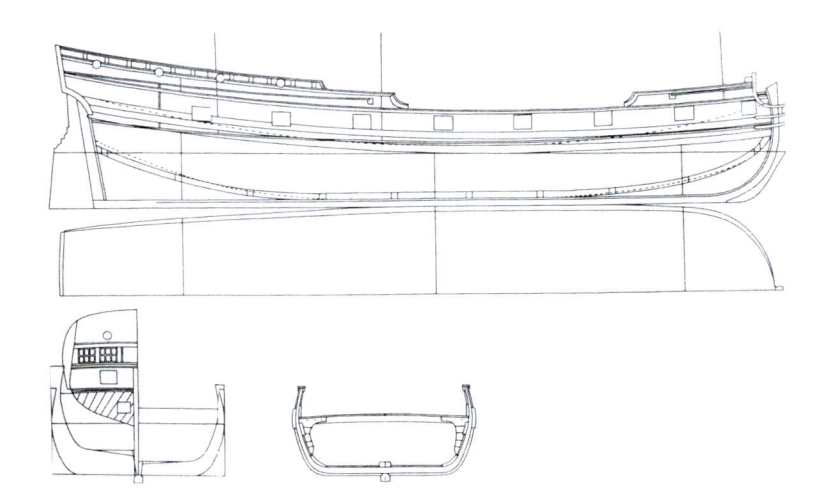

A profile and end-on drawing of Olifanten, *the somewhat problematic Swedish prize of 1714. Veselago describes her as a 'rowing frigate', but others argue that she lacked oars and was in fact built more closely along the lines of what would later be considered a pram, with reinforced decks and the capacity for firing 6 guns from the stern*

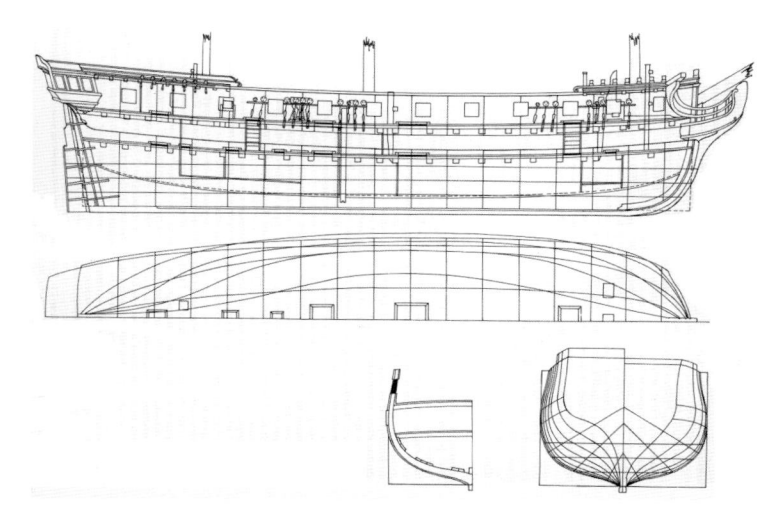

This sheer and profile of the Swedish frigate af Trolle, *built in 1766 and captured at the 1st battle of Rochensalm in 1789, makes for an interesting comparison with* Sviatoi Pavel *built in 1790. The Russian ship may be considered loosely as a 'reply' to the Swedish design and was predictably larger, longer, and more heavily armed than her Swedish inspiration. As was almost inevitable with captured Swedish prizes,* af Trolle, *renamed* Avtroil *in Russian service, was solidly constructed and had a long career in her new owner's navy and ending her service in the ill-fated Mediterranean squadron from 1804 to 1808.*

Dimensions ?
Armament ?
Swedish snow captured at the mouth of the Neva by soldiers under the direct command of Peter I on 7.5.1703. Preserved as a memorial in 1725. Broken up in 1737.

Rak (*Krevet*) 14 Sweden
Constructor ?
Laid down ?   *Launched* ?   *Captured* 20.8.1712
Dimensions 86 ft x 16 ft x 5 ft 3 in
Armament 14 cannons plus 13 swivels
58 men
Swedish snow captured on 20.8.1712 by Russian galleys. Cruised in the Baltic in 1713. Preserved as a memorial until 1737. Broken up after 1737.

Poluks 24 Sweden
Constructor ?
Laid down ?   *Launched* ?   *Captured* 31.7.1717
Dimensions ?
Armament ?   60 men
Swedish snow captured off the Aland Islands by Russian cruisers on 31.7.1717. Cruised in the Baltic in 1718–21. Repaired in 1727. Preserved until 1737. Broken up after 1737.

Evva-Katerina 10/14 Sweden
Constructor ?
Laid down ?   *Launched* ?   *Captured* 5.9.1718
Dimensions ?
Armament ?
Swedish snow captured by frigate *Landsdou* on 5.9.1718. Towed to Revel' for repair. No further mention.

Evva-Elenora ? Sweden
Constructor ?
Laid down ?   *Launched* ?   *Captured* 1719 (?)
Dimensions ?
Armament ?
Swedish snow. Cruised in the Baltic in 1719–21. Preserved on shore in 1727–37. Broken up after 1737.

Vestenshliup (ex-*Bernhardus*) 12 Sweden
Constructor ?
Laid down ?   *Launched* ?   *Captured* 24.5.1719
Dimensions ?
Armament ?   60 men
Swedish snow *Bernhardus* captured with *Wachtmeister* and *Karlskrona Vapen* off Osel on 24.5.1719 by Naum Seniavin. Cruised in the Baltic in 1721–3. Fire watch ship at Biork-e zund (Beryozovye Islands) in 1725–34. Cruised in the Baltic in 1741–4. Fire watch ship at Kronshtadt in 1745–6. Brought to St Petersburg for preservation in 1747.

Kruis (*Kreiser*) 8 Sweden
Constructor ?
Laid down ?   *Launched* ?   *Captured* 1718(?)
Dimensions ?
Armament ?
Swedish snow. Cruised in the Baltic in 1718–19. No further details.

Falk 8 Sweden
Constructor ?
Laid down ?   *Launched* ?   *Captured* 1720 (?)
Dimensions 60 ft x 17 ft 4 in x 7 ft 10
Armament ?
Swedish snow. Employed as a packet boat in 1721–3. No further information.

Eingorn 8 Sweden
Constructor ?
Laid down ?   *Launched* ?   *Captured* 1720 (?)
Dimensions ?
Armament ?   60 men
Swedish snow. Cruised in the Baltic in 1721. Fire watch ship at Revel' in 1722. No further information.

Captured corvettes

Navarin (ex-*Nessabih Sabah*) 20 Egypt
Constructor ?
Laid down ?   *Launched* ?   *Captured* 21.4.1828
Dimensions 128 ft (pp) x 32 ft (inside plank) x 10 ft (Veselago)
Armament 4 x 12pdrs, 16 x 18pdr carr.
160 men
Egyptian corvette *Nessabih Sabah* captured off Modon by the frigate *Kastor* and ship of the line *Iezekiil'* on 21.4.1828. Operated against Turkey in the Arkhipelago in 1828–30. To Kronshtadt in 1830. Cruised in the Baltic in 1831–49. Cruised to Denmark during the Schleswig-Holstein Crisis in 1850. Cruised in the Baltic in 1851–52. Departed for the Far East in 1853. Forced into Portsmouth for repairs to storm damage sustained during a North Sea storm in 11.1853. Forced back to Portsmouth for repairs to storm damage sustained in the North Sea for a second time in 12.1853. Damaged yet a third time by storm damage, this time in the North Atlantic, and forced to returned Vlissingen. Condemned and sold in 1854 for 36,161 guilders.

THE BALTIC FLEET 1825–60

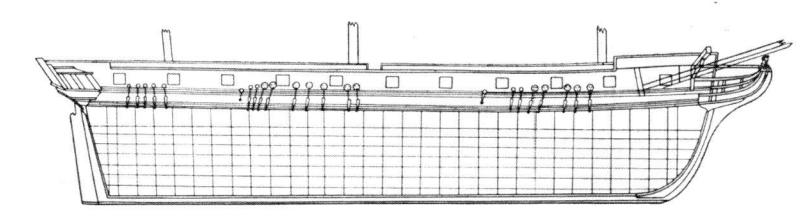

A starboard profile of the Egyptian corvette Nessabih Sarah *captured in 1828 and renamed* Navarin *to commemorate the allied victory at Navarino. Built in Venice of high quality Adriatic oak, this excellent ship was highly regarded by her captors and served in the Baltic fleet until 1854.*

L'vitsa 26 Turkey
Constructor ?
Laid down ?   Launched ?   Captured 28.1.1829
Dimensions 125 ft (pp) x 34 ft 11 in (inside plank) x 10 ft 10 in (Veselago)
Armament ?
Turkish corvette *L'vitsa* captured off Candia, Crete on 28.1.1829 by ship of the line *Tsar' Konstantin*. Repaired at Toulon in 1829. Joined Rear-Adm. Rikord's squadron off Paros for transit to Kronshtadt. To Plymouth in 1831. Cruised in the Baltic in 1832–48. Broken up after 1854.

Captured brigs

Falk 20 Sweden
Constructor ?
Laid down ?   Launched ?   Captured 2.8.1808
Dimensions 81 ft x 22 ft x 7 ft 2 in (Veselago)
Armament ?
Brig captured from Sweden on 2.8.1808 by Adm. Khanykov's squadron. Cruised in the Baltic in 1809–10, 1812–14 and 1816–18. Grounded and wrecked off Styrsudden on 20.10.1818. 2 men killed.

Kommerstraks 14 Sweden
Constructor ?
Laid down ?   Launched ?   Captured 21.4.1808
Dimensions 91 ft 3 in x 33 ft x 10 ft (Veselago)
Armament ?
Brig captured from Sweden at the capitulation of Sveaborg on 21.4.1808. Operations against the Swedish flotilla in 1808–9. Cruised in the Baltic in 1810–17. Fire watch ship at Kronshtadt in 1818–27. Hydrographic survey work in 1828–30. Cruised off Poland in 1831. Hydrographic survey work in 1832–43. Repaired in 1851 and employed as a pilot vessel. No further mention.

Kandiia 14 Egypt
Constructor ?
Laid down ?   Launched ?   Captured 28.1.1829
Dimensions 100 ft x 22 ft 4 in x 13 ft 2 in (Veselago)
Armament ?
Brig captured from Egypt on 28.1.1829 by ship of the line *Tsar' Konstantin*. In poor condition and employed as a floating magazine. Sold at Poros in 1830.

Captured cutters

Snapop (ex-*Snapupp*) 12 Sweden
Constructor ?
Laid down ?   Launched ?   Captured 29.4.1789
Dimensions ?
Armament ?
Captured Swedish cutter *Snapupp*. Taken on 29.4.1789 by Russian cutter *Merkurii*. Cruised in the Baltic in 1789–1807. Escorted transports to Finland in 1808–9. Brought French Embassy personnel to Pillau in 1812. No further mention.

Atis 18 Sweden
Constructor ?
Laid down ?   Launched ?   Captured 1808
Dimensions 48 ft 3 in x 16 ft 6 in x 5 ft 6 in (Veselago)
Armament ?
Captured Swedish cutter. Captured in 1808. Cruised in the Baltic 1808 and involved in actions with the Swedish flotilla. Cruised in the Baltic in 1809–10. Fire watch ship at Sveaborg in 1811–18. Survey work off Finland in 1819–23. Fire watch ship off Hangö. Wrecked off Hangö on 10.10.1823. No casualties.

The Sea of Azov Fleet 1696–1711

The available information on the Azov fleet is scarce and limited. The primary source for information about the warships built along the Don for the fleet is S. I. Elagin (1824–68), the editor of the *Materialy dlya Istorii Russkogo Flota. Period Azovskiy'* (1864) Due to the paucity of information available even to Elagin, the Sea of Azov fleet remains something of a conundrum. During its brief lifetime of approximately 15 years between 1696 and 1711, no fewer than 79 sailing warships were authorized and laid down along with large numbers of rowing brigantines and galleys, with 65 ships actually launched. The breakdown according to rated armament is as follows:

Rating	Launched	Cancelled	Active Service
80	1	4	0
70–78	3	2	0
60–68	9	0	2
50–58	10	0	4
40–48	12	9	2
30–38	15	1	8
20–28	0	1	0
Snows	6	0	4
Bombs	5	2	1
Oared Frigates	2	0	2
Total	65	17	26

The actual situation is murkier because the figures given for rated armament are open to considerable debate and interpretation due to the inclusion of 4pdrs and smaller guns in the totals and to discrepancies in the available data. Eleven ships were completed and able to transit to the mouth of the Don, only to be found unfit for active service on reaching Azov. This leaves a total of 54 ships known to have been accepted for service, but only 26 of these have left any definite record of service at sea between 1700 and 1710 or of action against the Turks in 1711. When the Azov fleet was mobilized in 1711, only *Bozhye Predvidenie* (58), *Lastka* (50), *Uniya* (30), *Merkurius* (28), 2 galleys, 3 snows, 2 brigantines, 1 tartan and 4 gunboats were able to assemble at Taganrog for service under Vice-Adm. Kruys. The other ships may or may not have seen active service prior to the surrender of all surviving vessels to the Turks in 1711, but the historical record is unclear.

This should not be seen as a criticism of the Russian accomplishment in putting together the elements of a sea going battle fleet in primitive conditions and in shipyards entirely unsuited for the construction of deep draft seagoing ships. The real birth of a Black Sea fleet in 1783 would have to await more favorable conditions and the establishment of shipyards up to the task of building large warships.

Sea of Azov ships were always assigned both Russian and Dutch names as a reflection of the Dutch influence prior to Peter I's decision not to renew the contracts of Dutch shipwrights in 1700. Where the Dutch names and English translations are jointly displayed, the first name given is the transliterated Russian name, the Dutch name follows in parentheses, and the third name, also in parentheses, is the English translation of the Russian name where appropriate. Many of the ships carrying significant armaments were not ship rigged as one might expect considering the number of guns reportedly carried. To clarify matters, they are herein described by their rig or type, when this is known, with 'ship of the line' standing for ship rigged warships irrespective of their relative size and power. A clear distinction was made between these three-masted square riggers and two other types of lesser vessels. 'Barbary ships' were a type unique to the Russian navy although they may have been commonly used in the Turkish and other Islamic navies of the period. They are described below and stand immediately below ships of the line in the hierarchy although they frequently carried broadsides as heavy as those of the smaller ships of the line. Whether they would have been expected to also stand in line of battle is unclear. 'Bark rigged' ships were apparently either two-masted ships with square rigs or three-masted lateen rigged ships, both types being equipped with oars. The rated number of guns ascribed to Sea of Azov ships is so clearly unrelated to gun calibre or weight of broadside as to make reliance on numbers alone essentially meaningless. Our usual approach of in by the numbers in classification of what would be described in Great Britain as First to Sixth Rate ships is accordingly being set aside here in the interests of clarity and in order to make some orderly sense out of the construction programme instituted at this largely experimental and formative stage. Ships of the line appear to have had either 12pdrs or 16pdrs as their main armament while Barbary ships generally carried only 12pdrs. Bark rigged ships were much more lightly armed and generally carried two 6pdr chase guns and 4pdrs on the broadside.

The reader will also notice significant discrepancies between recorded low/high gun ratings and the actual armaments reported as being carried. There is no easy resolution to this and the decision was made to 'class' the various ships by their highest reported rating, not because it is necessarily realistic but because any classification system presents irresoluble problems.

Sea of Azov line of battle ships (34 laid down/17 completed)

Of the 34 ships ordered and laid down, only 17 were launched and of this total only 6 of these appear to have seen any active duty with the remainder trapped upriver on the Don due to persistently low water levels. Main armament appears to have ranged from 12pdrs to 18pdrs in the active ships, although guns as large as 36pdrs seem to have been projected for the 80-gun ships laid down but not completed. The number of guns carried appears to have varied from 36 to 70 for those ships completed and armed. Dimensions ranged from as little as 105 ft for the 36-gun ship to 160 ft for the single 80-gun ship to be launched. Breadth ranged from 28 ft to 42 ft but exceeded 31 ft for all of the ships except for the 36-gun diminutive. As a result of his disillusionment with Dutch shipbuilding during his tour of European capitals, all ship of the line construction begun after 1700 was confined to state-run shipyards under the immediate control of Peter I himself and his close assistants Joseph Nye and Richard Cozens.

Staryi Oryol (*Out Adler*) 80/82 Voronezh
Constructor Peter I and F. M. Sklyaev
Laid down 1702 *Launched* 1709
Dimensions 160 ft x 42 ft x 10 ft 6 in
Armament ?   500 men
Ship of the line. Transited to Tavrov. Repaired at Tavrov for war in 1710, but not relaunched due to low water levels. Broken up in 1727 at Tavrov.

Samson 70 Voronezh
Constructor P. Bas
Laid down 1697 *Launched* 1704
Dimensions 136 ft x 34 ft 8½ in x 8 ft 7 in
Armament ?
          430 men
Ship of the line. Transited to Tavrov on completion. Broken up at Tavrov in 1710.

Stary Dub class (2 ships)
Staryi Dub (*Out Eketbom*) 70 Voronezh
Constructor R. Kosentz (Richard Cozens)
Laid down 29.9.1701 *Launched* 1705
Dimensions 151 ft 6 in x 40 ft x 10 ft 6 in
Armament ?   450 men
Starry Dub class. Ship of the line. Transited to Tavrov on completion. Repaired for war at Tavrov in 1710, but never relaunched due to low water levels. Broken up in 1727 at Tavrov.

Spiashchii Lev (*Shlay Leu*) 70 Voronezh
Constructor R. Kosentz (Richard Cozens)
Laid down 12.9.1701 *Launched* 1709
Dimensions 151 ft 6 in x 40 ft x 10 ft 6 in
Armament ?
          450 men
Starry Dub class. Ship of the line. Transited to Tavrov. Repaired at Tavrov for war in 1710, but never relaunched due to low water levels. Broken up in 1727 at Tavrov.

Sviatoi Georgii (*Sant Ioriy*) 66 ?
Constructor ?
Laid down 10.1697 *Launched* 1701
Dimensions 135 ft x 37 ft x ?
Armament ?   430 men
Ship of the line. Transited to the mouth of the Don in 1702. Transferred to Azov in 1703. In service at sea in 1706. Under repair at Azov 1709–11. Abandoned to Turkey in 1711.

Del'fin class (2 ships)
Del'fin 62/64 Voronezh
Constructor R. Semesen
Laid down 11.1697 *Launched* 28.5.1703
Dimensions 123 ft 1½ in x 35 ft 6 in x 9 ft 1 in
Armament ?
          330 men
Del'fin class. Ship of the line. Transformed into a 48-gun ship with 18pdrs on the lower deck in 1710. Stationed at the mouth of the Don in 1710. Transferred from Azov to Cherassk in 1711. In active service until 1714. Broken up in 1716.

Vinkel'gak (*Winkelhaak*) 62 Voronezh
Constructor M. Beter
Laid down 11.1697 *Launched* 22.5.1703
Dimensions 123 ft 10 in x 35 ft 6 in x 9 ft 1 in
Armament ?
          330 men
Del'fin class. Ship of the line. Transformed into a 48-gun ship with 18pdrs on the lower deck in 1710. Stationed at the mouth of the Don in 1710. Transferred from Azov to Cherassk in 1711. In active service until 1714. Broken up in 1716.

Voronezh 62 Voronezh
Constructor V. Gerens
Laid down 11.1697 *Launched* 1703
Dimensions 122 ft 10½ in x 34 ft x 9½ ft x 9 ft
Armament ?
          327 men
Ship of the line. Broken up at Tavrov in 1710.

Aist (*Oifar*) 64 ?
Constructor Y. Kol
Laid down 11.1697 *Launched* 4.1706
Dimensions 123 ft 5½ in x 35'8 in x 9 ft
Armament ?   327 men
Ship of the line. Transited to the mouth of the Don in 1706. Repaired for war at Tavrov in 1710, but never relaunched due to low water levels. Broken up in 1727 at Tavrov.

Shpaga class (2 ships)
Shpaga (*Degen*) 60 Voronezh
Constructor O. Nye (Joseph Noy)
Laid down 1700 *Launched* 1709
Dimensions 134 ft x 34 ft4 in x 10 ft 1½ in
Armament 12pdrs
          267 men
Shpaga class. Ship of the line. Transited to Azov in 1709. Found unfit for service in 1711 and sold. Destroyed by fire in 1711.

Sulitsa (*Lants*) 60 Voronezh
Constructor O. Nye (Joseph Noy)
Laid down 1700 *Launched* 1709
Dimensions 134 ft4 in x 34 ft4 in x 10 ft 1½ in
Armament 12pdrs 267 men
Shpaga class. Ship of the line. Repaired at Tavrov in 1710. Broken up in 1727.

Skorpion class (2 ships)
Skorpion 60/62 Voronezh
Constructor O. Nye (Joseph Noy)
Laid down 1.1704 *Launched* 1709
Dimensions ?
Armament 18pdrs 350 men
Skorpion class. Ship of the line. Transited to Tavrov. Repaired at Tavrov for war in 1710. Unable to relaunch in 1711 due to low water levels. Broken up in 1727 at Tavrov.

Goto Predestinatsiya *(58) of 1701 as portrayed by Adriaan Schonebeck seen in action against Turkish warships in 1711. Peter I's personal flagship, and the most powerful unit in the Sea of Azov fleet,* Goto Predestinatsiya *would have been classified as a Third Rate in the Royal Navy. Nevertheless, she makes a fine display with battle flags flying and her design and construction was a major accomplishment for Russian shipbuilding.*

Tsvet Voiny 60/62 Voronezh
Constructor O. Nye (Joseph Noy)
Laid down 1.1704 *Launched* 1709
Dimensions ?
Armament 18pdrs
350 men
Skorpion class. Ship of the line. Transited to Tavrov. Repaired at Tavrov for war in 1710. Unable to relaunch in 1711 due to low water levels. Broken up in 1727 at Tavrov.

Goto Predestinatsiia (*Bozh'e Predvidenie*) 58 Voronezh
Constructors Peter I and F. M. Sklyaev
Laid down 19.11.1698 *Launched* 24.4.1700
Dimensions 118 ft x 31 ft x 9 ft 9 in
Armament 26 x 16pdrs, 24 x 8pdrs, 8 x 3pdrs
253 men
Ship of the line. The pride of the Azov fleet. Based on a British design modified and improved by Peter I who personally supervised all aspects of her construction. Constructed entirely by Russian workers on all levels. Transited to the mouth of the Don in.4.1702. Transferred to Azov in 6.1710. In action against Turkey in 6.1711. Sold to Turkey in 1711.

Cherepakha (*Shkhelpot*) 56/58 Voronezh
Constructor O. Nye (Joseph Noy)
Laid down 11.1698 *Launched* 24.4.1700
Dimensions 123 ft x 35 ft 6 in x 10 ft 3 in
Armament 26 x 16pdrs, 24 x 8pdrs, 8 x 3pdrs
253 men (probable armament/16 pdrs on lower deck)
Ship of the line. Transited to the mouth of the Don in 1702. Repaired at Tavrov in 1710. Unable to proceed to Azov in 1711 due to low water levels. Broken up at Tavrov in 1727.

Lastka (*Shval*) 50 Voronezh
Constructor Peter I and F.M. Sklyaev
Laid down 8.3.1703 *Launched* 4.1709
Dimensions 118 ft x 32 ft 7 in x 10 ft 10 in
Armament 18 x 12pdrs, 20 x 4pdrs, 7 x 3pdrs, 8 x 2pdrs
230 men
Ship of the line. Transited to Taganrog in June–August of 1709. Operated against the Turks in 1711. Sold to Turkey in 10.1711. The name translates as nightingale, the colloquial name for an old type of weapon.

Razzhyonnoe Zhelezo (*Git eyzer*) 36 Voronezh
Constructor V. Gerens
Laid down 1697 *Launched* 1701
Dimensions 105 ft x 28 ft x ?
Armament 18 x 12pdrs, 4 x 6pdrs, 12 x 3pdr swivels
135 men
Ship of the line. The rationale for this ship is unclear but she was classified as a line ship based solely on her three-masted square rig. Transited to Azov and Taganrog in April or May of 1702. In service at sea in 1702, 1703, 1706, 1707 and 1709. Broken up in 1710.

17 ships laid down but never completed

Uncompleted Sea of Azov ships of the line fall into two groups. The first includes two 70-gun ships laid down in 1698 and well advanced but never completed due to the refusal of the Venetian shipwrights to continue work upon learning that Peter I had decided not to renew their contracts upon the completion of work in progress. The second and larger group consists of 15 ships laid down between 1707 and the loss of Azov in 1711. All of these ships were being built under the direct supervision of Peter's most skilled shipwrights, Noy and Cozens, 13 at Tavrov and 2 at the newly established and very short lived shipyard at Sereda.The ships begun between 1707 and 1710 were well under way by the war's end, but the final 4 assigned to Joseph Nye were just begun in the spring of 1711 and can hardly have been far along when they were abandoned on their slips.

These ships collectively represented a significant commitment of labour and capital, especially at a time when Russia was heavily engaged in the Baltic with Sweden. This by itself should silence some Western historians who question the seriousness of Peter I's commitment to expansion southward against Turkey.

2 ships unnamed 70 Voronezh
Constructor Y. Fafsto
Laid down 10.1698 *Never launched*
Dimensions 136 ft 10 in x 30 ft 3 in x 11 ft 5½ in
Armament ?
Ship of the line. Venetian design. Completed in 1700 but never launched. Broken up on the slip in 1700.

4 ships unnamed 80 Tavrov
Constructors R. Kosentz (Richard Cozens) and O. Nye (Joseph Noy)
Laid down 1707 *Unfinished*
Dimensions ?
Armament 36pdrs, 18pdrs, 8pdrs
Ship of the line. These ships had progressed to launch stage, but low

water levels prevented this when renewed war with Turkey led to the urgent dispatch of Adm. Apraksin to Tavorov to attempt to facilitate their evacuation down river. Broken up incomplete in 1727.

3 ships unnamed 48 Tavrov
Constructor R. Kosentz (Richard Cozens) and O. Nye (Joseph Noy)
Laid down 10.1709 *Unfinished*
Dimensions 120 ft x 35 ft x 10 ft
Armament 18pdrs
Ship of the line. Construction ceased upon the departure of Richard Cozens and Joseph Noy to St Petersburg in 1711 Broken up incomplete in 1727.

4 ships unnamed 48 Tavrov
Constructor R. Kosentz (Richard Cozens) and O. Nye (Joseph Noy)
Laid down 10.1710 *Unfinished*
Dimensions ?
Armament 18pdrs
Ship of the line. Construction ceased upon the departure of Richard Cozens and Joseph Noy to St Petersburg in 1711. Broken up in 1727.

2 ships unnamed 48 Tavrov
Constructor O. Nye (Joseph Noy)
Laid down Spring 1711 *Unfinished*
Dimensions ?
Armament ?
Ship of the line. Construction ceased upon the departure of Joseph Noy to St Petersburg in 1711. Very little work can have been done prior to their being abandoned on slip.

2 ships unnamed ? Sereda
Constructor O. Nye (Joseph Noy)
Laid down Spring 1711 *Unfinished*
Dimensions ?
Armament ?
Ship of the line. Construction ceased upon the departure of Joseph Noy to St Petersburg in 1711. Very little work can have been done prior to their being abandoned on slip.

Sea of Azov Barbary ships (15 laid down/14 completed 1696–1711)

Barbary ships (*barbaskii korabl'*) were the largest and most ambitious ships left in the hands of the private companies. They apparently drew their inspiration from ships in use by Islamic nations and differed from the larger three-masted line of battle ships being built in state run shipyards by having a lateen rigged mizzen. Armament appears to have been standardized (at least in theory) around 18 lower deck 12pdrs and 6 short 12pdrs on the open decks with 6pdr chase guns and 3pdrs for close in defence against personnel. Lengths ranged from 104–124 ft and breadth was generally in the range of 31–33 ft although the longest ships, the four *Skorpion*s, were the narrowest at 24 ft. Of the 15 ships authorized, only 14 were launched. Of the 14 completed vessels, only two were found fit for service and the remainder were rejected due to shoddy construction.

Skorpion class (4 ships)
These four two-decked ships are grouped together as a class on the basis of their common shipyards, dates of construction, similar dimensions, and armament.

Skorpion (*Scorpion*) 40/52 Panshin
Constructor ?
Laid down ? *Launched* 1699
Dimensions 124 ft x 23 ft x ?
Armament 18 x 12pdrs, 6 x 12pdrs (short-barrelled), 4 x 6pdrs, 12 x 3pdrs, 236 men in 1699
Skorpion class (4 ships) Barbary ship. Transited from Panshin to Azov in.5.1699. Flagship of Adm. Golovin on the cruise to Kerch in 1699. Based at Azov from 1700. Broken up before 1709.

Flag 40/52 Panshin
Constructor I. Thomas
Laid down ? *Launched* 1699
Dimensions 124 ft x 24 ft x ?
Armament 18 x 12pdrs, 6 x 12pdrs (short-barrelled), 4 x 6pdrs, 12 x 3pdrs
Skorpion class (4 ships) Barbary ship.Transited from Panshin to Azov in.5.1699 and found unfit for service. Burnt to the waterline and broken up in 1709.

Zvezda/Zolotaia Zvezda (*Starn/Degoudestarn*) 40/52 Panshin
Constructor I. Thomas
Laid down ? *Launched* 1699
Dimensions 124 ft x 24 ft x ?
Armament 18 x 12pdrs, 6 x 12pdrs (short-barrelled) 4 x 6pdrs, 12 x 3pdrs 230 men
Skorpion class (4 ships) Barbary ship. Transited from Panshin to Azov in.5.1699 and found unfit for service. Broken up at Azov in 1709.

Krepost' (*Zamok, Kastel, Stargeyt, Sitadel*) 46/52 Panshin
Constructor ?
Laid down ? *Launched* 5.1699
Dimensions 124 ft x 24 ft x 13 ft 1½ in
Armament 18 x 12pdrs, 6 x 12pdrs (short-barrelled), 4 x 6pdrs, 12 x 3pdrs 110 men in 1699
Skorpion class (4 ships) Barbary ship. *Zamok* may have been a separate ship. Participated in the cruise to Kerch in 1699. Carried the Russian ambassador to Istanbul in 1699. Returned to Azov in 1700. Repaired in 1704. Turned into a floating memorial at Azov in 1709. Determined to be rotten in 1711 and abandoned at Azov.

Dumkrakht 44 Stupino
Constructors Y. Teodorov and Y. Kornilisen
Laid down 1697 *Launched* 1699
Dimensions 106 ft x 32 ft x 9 ft 6 in
Armament 18 x 12pdrs, 6 x 12pdrs (short-barrelled), 4 x 6pdrs, 12 x 3pdrs
Barbary ship. Transferred to Voronezh after 1704. Condemned on arrival due to shoddy construction and broken up at Voronezh in 1710.

Strus 44 Stupino
Constructors I. Fafsto and Y. Kornilisen
Laid down 1697 *Launched* 1699
Dimensions 105 ft 2 in x 32 ft 8 in x 13 ft
Armament 18 x 12pdrs, 6 x 12pdrs (short-barrelled), 4 x 6pdrs, 12 x 3pdrs
Barbary ship. Transited to the mouth of the Don after 1704. Condemned on arrival due to shoddy construction and broken up in 1710.

Kamen' (*Stein*) 44 Stupino
Constructors Y. Teodorov and Y. Kornilisen

Laid down 1697   *Launched* 1699
Dimensions   105 ft 6 in x 32 ft 8 in x 11 ft 7 in
Armament   18 x 12pdrs, 6 x 12pdrs (short-barrelled), 4 x 6pdrs,
12 x 3pdrs
Barbary ship. Transited to the mouth of the Don after 1704. Condemned on arrival due to shoddy construction and broken up in 1710.

Slon (*Olifant*) 44 Stupino
Constructors E. Dobomiy and Y. Kornilisen
Laid down 1697   *Launched* 1699
Dimensions   106 ft x 33 ft x 9 ft
Armament   18 x 12pdrs, 6 x 12pdrs (short-barrelled), 4 x 6pdrs,
12 x 3pdrs 200 men
Barbary ship. Transited to the mouth of the Don after 1704. Found unfit for service in.5.1710. Abandoned at Azov in 1711.

Rys' (*Luks*) 44 Stupino
Constructors E. Deboniy and Y. Terpliy
Laid down 1697   *Launched* 1699
Dimensions   105 ft x 32 ft 9 in x ?
Armament   18 x 12pdrs, 6 x 12pdrs (short-barrelled), 4 x 6pdrs,
12 x 3pdrs
Barbary ship. Condemned on arrival at Stupino due to shoddy construction and broken up after 1709.

Zhuravl' Steregushchii (*Kroan Opvakht*) 44 Stupino
Constructor I. Fafsto and Y. Kornilisen
Laid down 1697   *Launched* 1699
Dimensions   104 ft 6 in x 33 ft2 in x 13 ft
Armament   18 x 12pdrs, 6 x 12pdrs (short-barrelled), 4 x 6pdrs,
12 x 3pdrs
Barbary ship. Condemned on arrival at Stupino due to shoddy construction and broken up after 1709.

Sokol (*Falk*) 44 Stupino
Constructors I. Detoniko and Y. Terpliy
Laid down 1697   *Launched* 1699
Dimensions   107 ft x 32 ft x 13 ft
Armament   18 x 12pdrs, 4 x 6pdrs, 12 x 3pdr swivels, 200 men
Barbary ship. Condemned on arrival at Stupino due to shoddy construction and broken up after 1709.

Sobaka (*Treigun*) 44 Stupino
Constructors I. Detoniko and Y. Kornilisen
Laid down 1697   *Launched* 1699
Dimensions   104 ft 6 in x 32 ft x 14 ft
Armament   18 x 12pdrs, 4 x 6pdrs, 12 x 3pdr swivels
Barbary ship. Condemned on arrival at Stupino due to shoddy construction and broken up after 1709.

Arfa 36 Stupino
Constructors A. Mosilin and Y. Terpliy
Laid down 1697   *Launched* 1699
Dimensions   105 ft 6 in x 31 ft 8 in x 12 ft 8 in
Armament   18 x 12pdrs, 4 x 6pdrs, 12 x 3pdr swivels
150 men
Barbary ship (?) Condemned on arrival at Stupino due to shoddy construction and broken up after 1709.

Granat-Apol' 36 Stupino
Constructors   A. Mosilin and Y. Terpliy
Laid down 1697   *Launched* 1699
Dimensions   106 ft x 31 ft 10 in x 13 ft 6 in
Armament   18 x 12pdrs 4 x 6pdrs 12 x 3pdr swivels
150
Barbary ship (?) Condemned on arrival at Stupino due to shoddy construction and broken up after 1709.

Unnamed 36 Voronezh
Constructor A. Mosilin
Laid down 10.1698 *Never launched*
Dimensions   105 ft 9 in x 31 ft x 11 ft
Armament   ?
Barbary ship (?) Italian design. Completed in 1700 but never launched. Broken up on slip in 1700.

Sea of Azov bark rigged ships (19 completed 1696–1711)

The Russian term for bark was *barkalon*, taken from the Italian *barca longa*, and originally applied to small one-masted, lateen rigged vessels serving in the Mediterranean. In the Sea of Azov fleet, the term came to be generically and erroneously applied to rather larger two- or three-masted vessels, square rigged on the fore and main masts, but with a lateen on the mizzen. They were the most successful members of the newly built fleet and at least 8 of the 19 saw active service. As was the case with the Barbary ships, armament was standardized (in theory at least) at two 6pdr chase guns and 18 4pdr broadside cannon supported by variable numbers of 2- and 3pdr anti-personnel guns on the open decks. Barks ranged from 114–26 ft in length and 24–28 ft in breadth and were longer and narrower than the more powerful Barbary ships.

Gerkules 48/50/52 Chertovitskaya
Constructor P. Goor
Laid down 10.1697   *Launched* 5.1699
Dimensions   122 ft x 26 ft 10 in x 9 ft 5 in
Armament   2 x 6pdrs, 18 x 4pdrs, 6 x 3pdrs, 12 x 2pdrs
230 men
Bark rigged. Transited from Voronezh to the mouth of the Don in.4.1702. Repaired at Azov in 1710–11. Ceded to Turkey in 1711.

Vinogradnaia Vetv' (*Veinshtok*) 56/58 Chizhevka
Constructor D. Albes
Laid down 16.10.1697   *Launched* 4.1702
Dimensions   119 ft x 28 ft x 9 ft 4 in
Armament   2 x 6pdrs, 18 x 4pdrs, 6 x 3pdrs, 12 x 2pdr swivels
230 men
18 x 12pdrs, 4 x 6pdrs, 12 x 3pdr swivels (also reported)
Bark rigged. Transited to the mouth of the Don in 1702. Broken up in 1710 at Tavrov.

Miach (*Bal*) 54/50 Chizhevka
Constructor A. Meyer
Laid down 16.10.1697   *Launched* 4.1702
Dimensions   121 ft x 27 ft x 8 ft 10 in
Armament   2 x 6pdrs, 18 x 4pdrs, 6 x 3pdrs, 12 x 2pdr swivels
215 men
18 x 12pdrs, 4 x 6pdrs, 12 x 3pdr swivels (also reported)
Bark rigged. Transited to the mouth of the Don in.4.1702. Broken up in 1710.

Kolokol (*Klok*) 42/46 Voronezh
Constructor K. Kok
Laid down 9.1697   *Launched* 12.1697
Dimensions 125 ft x 27 ft x 10 ft 2 in
Armament 2 x 6pdrs, 18 x 4pdrs, 6 x 3pdrs, 12 x 2pdr swivels
            180 men
Bark rigged. Completed transit from Voronezh to the mouth of the Don in.4.1702. Broken up in 1710.

Iozh (*Igel*) 40 Khoper
Constructor D. Feykes
Laid down 6.1697   *Launched* 1700
Dimensions 126 ft x 26 ft 5½ in x ?
Armament 2 x 6pdrs, 18 x 4pdrs, 6 x 3pdrs, 12 x 2pdr swivels
            150 men
Bark rigged. Transited to Taganrog in 1704. In service at sea in 1704, 1707, 1709, and 1710. Broken up at Taganrog in 1710.

Liliia 34/36 Voronezh
Constructor P. Nekor
Laid down 6.1697   *Launched* 5.1699
Dimensions 115 ft 4 in x 25 ft 9 in x 12 ft 2 in
Armament 2 x 6pdrs, 18 x 4pdrs, 6 x 3pdrs, 12 x 2pdr swivels
            135 men
Bark rigged. Completed transit from Voronezh to the mouth of the Don in.4.1702. Broken up in 1710.

Stul 36 Voronezh
Constructor K. Bokar and Intelous
Laid down 6.1697   *Launched* 5.1699
Dimensions 115 ft 4 in x 24 ft 4 in x 9 ft 5 in
Armament 2 x 6pdrs, 18 x 4pdrs, 6 x 3pdrs, 12 x 2pdr swivels
            135 men
Bark rigged. Completed transit from Voronezh to the mouth of the Don in.4.1702. Broken up in 1710.

Unnamed 38 Voronezh
Constructor A. Naning and Y. Yansen
Laid down 7.1698   *Launched* 5.1699
Dimensions 115 ft 6 in x 24 ft 8 in x 9 ft 4 in
Armament 2 x 6pdrs, 18 x 4pdrs, 6 x 3pdrs, 12 x 2pdr swivels
Bark rigged. Transited from Voronezh to the mouth of the Don in.5.1703. Broken up in 1710.

***Bezboiazn'* class** (3 ships)
These three ships are grouped together as a class on the basis of their common shipyards, dates of construction, similar dimensions, and armament.
Bezboiazn' (*Sunderban, Sonderfres, Onberfrest*) 36 Khoper (Anderson)
Constructor Y. Borvut
Laid down ?   *Launched* Spring 1699
Dimensions 115 ft x 24 ft 5 in x ?
Armament 2 x 6pdrs, 18 x 4pdrs, 6 x 3pdrs, 10 x 2pdr swivels
            120 men
Bezboiazn' class Bark rigged. Arrived at Azov in.5.1699. Took part in cruise to Kerch in 1699. In service at sea in 1700 and 1703. Broken up in 1710.

Blagoe Nachalo (*Gut-anfangen, Gut-begin, Desegel-begin*) 32/36
Khoper (per Anderson)
Constructor Y. Borvut
Laid down ?   *Launched* 1699 (?)
Dimensions 115 ft x 24 ft 5½ in x ?
Armament 2 x 6pdrs, 18 x 4pdrs, 6 x 3pdrs 10 x 2pdr swivels
            115 men (1699)
Bezboiazn' class Bark rigged. Arrived at Azov in 1699. Took part in the cruise to Kerch in 1699 as Vice Adm. Cruy's flagship. Transferred to Kerch as a cargo ship in 1704. Sent to Taganrog for repair in 1704. Broken up in 1710.

Soedinenie (*Uniya, Enihkeit*) 30 Khoper
Constructor Y. Borvut
Laid down ?   *Launched* 1699 (?)
Dimensions 115 ft x 24 ft 5½ ft x ?
Armament 2 x 6pdrs, 18 x 4pdrs, 6 x 3pdrs, 10 x 2pdr swivels,
            110 men
Bezboiazn' class Bark rigged. Arrived at Azov in 5.1699. Took part in the cruise to Kerch in 1699. Transferred to Taganrog in 1703. Voyage to Istanbul planned for 1704. In service at sea in 1707. In action against Turkey in 1711. Set afire at the abandonment of Taganrog in 1711.

***Sila* class** (4 ships)
These four ships are grouped together as a class on the basis of their common shipyards, dates of construction, similar dimensions, and armament.
Sila (*Starkt*) 32/34/36 Voronezh
Constructor Dutch constructors
Laid down ?   *Launched* 1699 (?)
Dimensions 125 ft x 26 ft 5½ in x ?
Armament 2 x 6pdrs, 18 x 4pdrs, 6 x 3pdrs, 10 x 2pdr swivels
            135 men
Sila class (4 ships). Bark rigged. Participated in the cruise to Kerch in 1699. Transferred to Taganrog in 1703. Broken up in 1710.

Otvoryonnye Vrata (*Opon-de-Port*) 32/34/36 Voronezh
Constructor Dutch constructors
Laid down ?   *Launched* 1699 (?)
Dimensions 125 ft x 26 ft 5½ in x ?
Armament 2 x 6pdrs, 18 x 4pdrs, 6 x 3pdrs, 10 x 2pdr swivels,
            135 men
Sila class (4 ships). Bark rigged. Participated in the cruise to Kerch in 1699. Transferred to Taganrog in 1703. Broken up in 1710.

Tsvet Voiny (*Orlah-blum*) 32/34/36 Voronezh
Constructor Dutch constructors
Laid down ?   *Launched* 1699 (?)
Dimensions 125 ft x 26 ft 5½ in x ?
Armament 2 x 6pdrs, 18 x 4pdrs, 6 x 3pdrs, 10 x 2pdr swivels,
            135 men
Sila class (4 ships). Bark rigged. Participated in the cruise to Kerch in 1699. Transferred to Taganrog in 1703. Repaired in 1704. Broken up in 1710.

Merkurii (*Merkurius*) 22/28/36 Voronezh
Laid down ?   *Launched* 1699 (?)
Dimensions 125 ft x 26 ft x ?
Armament 2 x 6pdrs, 18 x 4pdrs, 6 x 3pdrs, 10 x 2pdr swivels
            135 men
Sila class (4 ships). Bark rigged. Participated in the cruise to Kerch in 1699. Grounded and sunk in 1699. Raised and repaired at Azov in 1700. In service at sea in 1710. In action against Turkey in 1711. In serviceable condition at Cherkassk until 1714. Broken up in 1716.

Lev (*Lev s sableiu*) 36/44 Voronezh
Constructor K. Kok
Laid down 11.1697   *Launched* 5.1699
Dimensions 116 ft 4 in x 26 ft 2 in x 9 ft 6 in
Armament 2 x 6pdrs, 18 x 4pdrs, 6 x 3pdrs, 12 x 2pdr swivels,
            180 men
Bark rigged. Transited from Voronezh to the mouth of the Don in 4.1702. Broken up after 1710.

Edinorog 36/44 Voronezh
Constructor Y. Kornilisen
Laid down 11.1697   *Launched* 5.1699
Dimensions 117 ft x 26 ft 4 in x 9 ft 6 in
Armament 2 x 6pdrs, 18 x 4pdrs, 6 x 3pdrs, 12 x 2pdr swivels,
            180 men
Bark rigged. Transited from Voronezh to the mouth of the Don in 6.1702. Broken up after 1710.

Baraban (*Trumel*) 26/36 Voronezh
Constructor S. Sereysen and L. Chapman
Laid down 6.1697   *Launched* 5.1699
Dimensions 114 ft 6 in x 24 ft 8 in x 8 ft 8 in
Armament 2 x 6pdrs, 18 x 4pdrs, 6 x 3pdrs, 12 x 2pdr swivels
            135 men
Bark rigged. Completed transit from Voronezh to the mouth of the Don in.4.1702. Broken up in 1710.

Tri Riumki (*Dri Ryumor*) 26/36 Voronezh
Constructor S. Peterson and Y. Edrek
Laid down 6.1697   *Launched* 5.1699
Dimensions 114 ft x 24 ft 2 in x 8 ft 8 in
Armament 2 x 6pdrs, 18 x 4pdrs, 6 x 3pdrs, 12 x 2pdr swivels
            135 men
Bark rigged. Completed transit from Voronezh to the mouth of the Don in.4.1702. Broken up in 1710.

Sea of Azov snows (6 Completed 1696–1711)

Unnamed 16/18 Ramon'skaya
Constructor I. Fedotov
Laid down 1.4.1700   *Launched* ?
Dimensions 65 ft x 12 ft 6 in x 6 ft 4 in
Armament ?
Unnamed snow, referred to simply as 'shnau'. Stationed at the mouth of the Don on 28.2.1704.

Taimalar 14 Ramon'skaya
Constructor I. Fedotov
Laid down 15.9.1702   *Launched* ?
Dimensions 60 ft x 16 ft x 6 ft 6 in
Armament ?   41 men
Snow. Transited to Taganrog on 5.1711 and joined the squadron of Vice-Adm. Kruys. Engaged against the Turks in 7.1711. Retreated to Cherkassk when Azov was ceded to Turkey. Broken up after 1716.

Degas class (2 ships)
Degas 14 Tavrov
Constructor I. Nemtsov
Laid down 1710   *Launched* 1710
Dimensions ?
Armament ?   82 men
Degas class. Snow. Transited to Taganrog from Azov in.5.1711 and joined Vice-Adm. Kruy's squadron. Engaged against the Turks in 7.1711. Final fate is unknown.

Falk 14 Tavrov
Constructor I. Nemtsov
Laid down 1710   *Launched* 1710
Dimensions ?
Armament ?   82 men
Degas class. Snow. Transited to Taganrog from Azov in.5.1711 and joined Vice-Adm. Kruy's squadron. Engaged against the Turks in 7.1711. Final fate is unknown.

Lizet class (2 ships)
Lizet 14 Voronezh
Constructor S. Robinson and I. Nemtsov
Laid down 1710   *Launched* 6.1711
Dimensions ?
Armament ?
Lizet class. Three-masted snow. Name is he diminutive for Elizabeth, for Peter I's daughter. For a similar three-masted design carrying the same name, see *Lizet* in the Baltic fleet. Prepared for transfer to the Baltic in 9.1711. Transfer prohibited by Turkey. Sold to Turkey in 1712.

Munker (*Mon Coeur*) 14 Voronezh
Constructor S. Robinson and I. Nemtsov
Laid down 1710   *Launched* 6.1711
Dimensions ?
Armament ?
Lizet class. Three-masted snow. Prepared for transfer to the Baltic in 9.1711. Transfer prohibited by Turkey. Sold to Turkey in 1712.

Sea of Azov floating battery (1 laid down 1697–1711)

Unnamed 24 Tavrov
Constructor R. Kosentz (Richard Cozens) and O. Nye (Joseph Noy)
Laid down 29.10.1709   *Unfinished*
Dimensions ?
Armament 24 x 24pdrs (on open deck)
This ship is sometimes described as a ship of the line but, based on her armament, was apparently intended as a floating battery. Broken up incomplete in 1727.

Sea of Azov bomb vessels (7 laid down/5 completed 1696–1711)

Grom (*Donder*) 14 Chizhovskaya
Constructor A. Meyer
Laid down 9.1697   *Launched* 5.1699
Dimensions approx. 88 ft x 28 ft x 10 ft (26.9 m x 8.5 m x 3.1 m)
              (Chernyshev)
Armament 10 x 24pdrs, 2 x 6pdrs, 2 mortars
Purpose-built bomb vessel. Brought to the mouth of the Don in 3.1710. Rebuilt by Y. Kornilisen in 1710. On blocks at Tavarov in 1710. No further mention.

Molniia (*Bliksem*) 14 Chizhovskaya
Constructor A. Meyer
Laid down 9.1697   *Launched* 5.1699
Dimensions approx. 86 ft x 28 ft x 10 ft (27.3 m x 8.5 m x 3.1 m)
              (Chernyshev)

Armament 10 x 24pdrs, 2 x 6pdrs, 2 mortars
Purpose-built bomb vessel. Brought to the mouth of the Don in 3.1710. Grounded and rebuilt by Y. Kornilisen in 1710. Broken up in 1710.

Gromovaia Strela (*Donderpeyl*) 14 Chizhovskaya
Constructor A. Meyer
Laid down 9.1697 *Launched* 5.1699
Dimensions approx. 83 ft x 28 ft x 10 ft (25.4 m x 8.5 m x 3.1 m) (Chernyshev)
Armament 10 x 4pdrs, 2 x 6pdrs, 2 mortars
Purpose-built bomb vessel. Brought to the mouth of the Don in 3.1710. Rebuilt by D. Feykes. Broken up after 1709.

Mirotvorets (*Vredemaker*) 14 Chizhovskaya
Constructor A. Meyer
Laid down 1697 *Launched* 1699
Dimensions approx. 99 ft x 29 ft x ? (30.1 m x 8.8 m x ? m) (Chernyshev)
Armament 10 x 24pdrs, 2 x 6pdrs, 2 mortars
Purpose-built bomb vessel. Sailed to Azov in 30.2–24.5.1699. Prevented from joining the squadron by grounding at the mouth of the Don. Returned to Azov on 25.11.1699. Broken up after 1699.

Bomba (*Bomb*) 24 Voronezh
Constructors Y. Moro and Y. Venturini
Laid down 6.1697 *Launched* ?
Dimensions approx. 92 ft x 29 ft x 12 ft (28.3 m x 8.8 m x 3.6 m) (Chernyshev)
Armament 18 x 12pdrs, 4 x 6pdrs, 12 swivels, 2 mortars
Bomb vessel. Brought to the mouth of the Don in 3.1703. On blocks at Tavrov in 1710. No further mention.

Agnets (*Lamgotes*) 24 ?
Constructors Y. Moro and Y. Venturini
Laid down 6.1697 *Launched* ?
Dimensions approx. 87 ft x 28 ft x 10 ft 6 in (26.5 m x 8.5 m x 3.2 m) (Chernyshev)
Armament 18 x 12pdrs, 4 x 6pdrs, 12 swivels, 2 mortars
Bomb vessel. *Agnets* means 'lamb', meant to be a bit of humour on Peter I's part. Brought to the mouth of the Don in 3.1703. On blocks at Tavrov in 1710. No further mention.

Strakh (*Sshkrek*) 14 Voronezh
Constructor Y. Moro
Laid down 1698 *Launched* ?
Dimensions approx. 90 ft x 28 ft x 11 ft (27.4 m x 8.5 m x 3.4 m) (Chernyshev)
Armament 12 cannon, 2 mortars
Purpose-built bomb vessel. Brought to the mouth of the Don in 3.1703. On blocks at Tavrov in 1710. No further mention.

Sea of Azov oared frigates (2 Purpose-built 1696–1711)

Apostol Pyotr (*Sviatoi Peter*) 36 Voronezh
Constructor A. Meyer
Laid down 3.1696 *Launched* 26.4.1696
Dimensions 113 ft x 25 ft x ? Displacement 700 tons
Armament ?
125 men
Oared frigate. *Apostol Pyotr* and *Sviatoi Pavel* were the first major warships completed for the Sea of Azov fleet. 15 pairs of oars. In

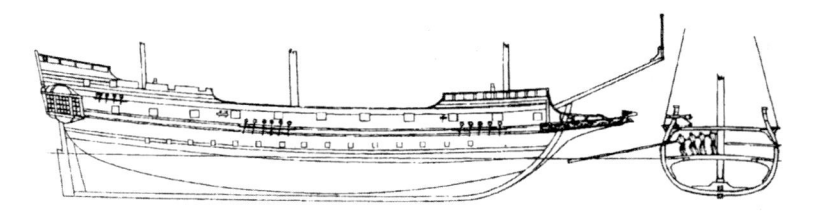

Sviatoi /Apostol Pavel. Described as a 34-gun ship, the drawing only shows her pierced for 20 on the gundeck, with positions for 6 or 8 smaller guns on the quarterdeck and the accuracy of this drawing may be in question.

service at sea in 1696 and 1699. Found unfit for service in 1710. Abandoned at Azov in 1711.

Sviatoi Pavel (*Apostol Pavel*) 34 Voronezh
Constructor A. Meyer
Laid down 3.1696 *Launched* 28.4.1696
Dimensions 98 ft x 30 ft x ?
Armament ?
Oared frigate. 15 pairs of oars. Not ready for active service in 1696. Deployed to Azov in 1698. Found unfit for service in 1710. Abandoned at Azov in 1711.

Miscellaneous Azov construction

Five more ships were laid down in 1697 and launched in May, 1699, all unnamed. In 1701 all of them were converted to store ships with 6 guns. In 1703, they were transferred to the mouth of the Don, and all five were broken up in 1710. Their particulars:
No. 1 115 ft 9 in x 24 ft 9 in x 8 ft 10 Voronezh; builder Y. Yansen, rebuilt by Y. Terpliy
No. 2 115 ft x 24 ft 7 in x 9 ft 5 in Voronezh; builder Y. Kornilisen, rebuilt by L. Chapman
No. 3 115 ft x 24 ft 6 in x 9 ft 2 in Voronezh; builder P. Goor, rebuilt by Intedous
No. 4 116 ft 8 in x 25 ft x 9 ft 8 in Voronezh; builder P. Goor, rebuilt be D. Feykes
No. 5 115 ft 4 in x 24 ft 8 in x 9 ft 10 Voronezh; builder Y. Martisen, rebuilt by Y. Terpliy (not in Veselago's list)

One more private ship called **Vesy** (*Libra*) was laid down 1697; completed 5.1699 as 6-gun store ship (116 ft x 25 ft x 9 ft 3 in, builders D. Feykes, Y. Terpliy); said to be rigged as a bark transferred from Voronezh to the Mouth of the Don in 4.1702; broken up 1710 (not in Veselago's list)

Velikii Galeas, a copy of the Venetian *Bucentaure*, was laid down in 1699 and launched in 1711; 161 ft x 31 ft, a luxury ship to be used during parades, etc. She remained on the beach at Tavrov until 1727 and was then broken up. The cost of her ornamentation was equal to the cost building of 6 ships.

In 1723, Peter I laid down nine large prams of 44 guns in Tavrov and six small prams with 8 x 8pdrs in anticipation of the coming war with Turkey. They remained uncompleted on slips until war with Turkey began. All were finally launched in 1735 and they took an active part in bombardment and taking of Azov in 1736. (See section II for further details.)

The Black Sea Fleet

The Navy of Catherine and Paul 1770–1800

Early square rigged vessels (10 purpose-built 1762–1800)

The first 10 ships of the newly reconstituted Sea of Azov flotilla – which was formally renamed the Black Sea fleet in 1783 – were small flat-bottomed vessels designed in 1768 for the shallow sea of Azov. They were built in old shipyards created on the Don by Peter I for the Sea of Azov fleet.

Khotin 16 Novopavlovsk
Constructor S. I. Afanasyev
Laid down 9.1.1769 *Launched* 1.3.1770
Dimensions 128 ft x 19 ft x 9 ft
Armament 16 x 12pdrs
           175 men
           1784 15 x 12pdrs, 10 x 6pdrs, 4 x 3pdr swivels, 4 x 18u
Three-masted ship named for a Turkish fortress taken in 1769. Transited to Taganrog upon completion in 9.1770. Flagship of Vice-Adm. A. I. Seniavin. Cruised in the Sea of Azov and Black Sea in 1771. Repaired in 1772. In service in the Black Sea 1773–5, 1777. Repaired at Taganrog in 1778–9. Cruised in the Black Sea in 1782–3. Fireguard ship at Sevastopol' in 1785. Floating battery at Sevastopol' in 1787.

Azov class (7 ships)
Azov 16 Novopavlovsk
Constructor S. I. Afanasyev
Laid down 1769 *Launched* 14.3.1770
Dimensions 103 ft x 28 ft x 8½ ft x 9 ft
Armament 1784 12 x 10pdrs, 4 x 3pdr swivels, 2 x 60 u (1 pood),
           2 x 3-pood mortars (11 in)
           128 men
Azov class. Two-masted ship. Cruised at sea 1771–3. In combat with the Turks in 1773. Cruised in the Black Sea in 1774–5, 1777, 1779–80 and 1783. Broken up after 1784.

Taganrog 16 Novopavlovsk
Constructor S. I. Afanasyev
Laid down 1769 *Launched* 14.3.1770
Dimensions 103 ft x 28 ft x 8½ ft x 9 ft
Armament ?
Azov class. Two-masted ship. Cruised at sea in 1771–3. In combat with four larger Turkish ships (three 52s and one 36) at Balaklava in 1773, repulsing their attack and pursuing her attackers. Three crewmen killed and 28 wounded. Cruised in the Black Sea in 1774–5, 1777–8 and 1779. Repaired in 1779. Driven ashore by ice from Taganrog in 12.1781 with 39 men drowned and 28 frozen. Raised and repaired in 1782. In service at sea in 1782, cruising to the Crimea. Crushed by ice in the Sea of Azov in 25.11.1782 without casualties.

Modon 16 Ikoretskaya
Constructor S. I. Afanasyev
Laid down 1769 *Launched* 19.3.1770
Dimensions 103 ft x 28 ft x 8½ ft x 9 ft
Armament ?
Azov class. Two-masted ship. Cruised at sea 1771–3. In action with the Turks in 1773. Cruised in the Black Sea in 1774–8. Repaired in 1779. Storm damaged in 1782. Assigned as a fire watch ship off the straits of Kerch in 1783.

Moreia 16 Novopavlovsk
Constructor S. I. Afanasyev
Laid down 1769 *Launched* 26.3.1770
Dimensions 103 ft x 28 ft x 8½ ft x 9 ft
Armament ?
Azov class. Two-masted ship. Cruised at sea in 1771–3. Repaired at Balaklava in 1773. Broken up after 1774.

Novopavlovsk 16 Ikoretskaya
Constructor S. I. Afanasyev
Laid down 1769 *Launched* 18.3.1770
Dimensions 103 ft x 28 ft x 8½ ft x 9 ft
Armament ?
Azov class. Two-masted ship. Cruised at sea in 1771–4. Repaired at Balaklava in 1774. Broken up after 1774.

Koron 16 Novopavlovsk
Constructor S. I. Afanasyev
Laid down 1769 *Launched* 20.4.1770
Dimensions 103 ft x 28 ft x 8½ ft x 9 ft
Armament ?
Azov class. Two-masted ship named after a Turkish fortress in Morea blockaded in 1770. Cruised at sea 1771–3. In action with the Turks off Balaklava in 1773 with 1 killed and 2 wounded. Cruised at sea in 1774–8. Repaired in 1779. Driven aground by ice in 12.1781. Raised and repaired in 1782. Cruised in 1782. Crushed by ice in the Sea of Azov on 23.11.1782, crew saved.

Zhurzha 16 Novopavlovsk
Constructor S. I. Afanasyev
Laid down 1769 *Launched* 24.4.1770
Dimensions 103 ft x 28 ft x 8½ ft x 9 ft
Armament ?
Azov class. Two-masted ship named after the Romanian town where the 1772 armistice with Turkey was signed. Cruised in 1771–4 and 1777–8. Repaired in 1779. In service in the Black Sea in 1782. Assigned as a fire watch ship in the Straits of Kerch in 1783–4. Broken up after 1784.

Bukharest 12 Ikoretskaya
Constructor S. I. Afanasyev
Laid down 1769 *Launched* 26.4.1770
Dimensions 86 ft x 24.5 ft x 8 ft
Armament ?
Two-masted ship. Completed as a store ship. Cruised in 1771–8. Harbour service in 1780.

Iassy 12 Ikoretskaya
Constructor S. I. Afanasyev
Laid down 1769 *Launched* 26.1.1770
Dimensions 86 ft x 24.5 ft x 8 ft
Armament 12 x 6pdrs 2-3pood mortars (11 in)
Two-masted ship, designed as a transport and completed as a mortar vessel. Cruised in 1771–5. Converted to a transport and store ship from 1778–9. Lost in 1785. (See also under transports)

Ships with 110 guns (2 purpose-built 1762–1800)

The performance of the Turkish Navy in the Russo-Turkish War of 1787–91 revealed serious shortcomings with respect to command, training and discipline; but their ships were the product of French designers and were reputed to be of excellent quality. Two First Rate Turkish three-deckers, *Selimiye* and *Mesudiye*, built along French lines were commissioned in the closing years of the eighteenth century, events undoubtedly noted by Adm. Ushakov during his stopover at Istanbul in 1798. Their completion made mandatory a more ambitious Russian response beyond that of the earlier two-decker 80s, *Josef II* and *Sviatoi Pavel*. (*Ratnyi* was begun in 1801 and should properly be in the next section. She is placed here because, in our opinion, she belongs more logically to this earlier era.)

Iagudiil 110 Kherson
Constructor M. K. Surovtsov
Laid down 6.12.1799 *Launched* 17.11.1800
Dimensions 188 ft 6 in x 53 ft 9 in x 20 ft 6 in
2,500 tons bm (Veselago)
188 ft x 51 ft 9 in x 22 ft 4 in (Golovachev)
Armament LD 24 x 36pdrs 4 x 60 u (1 pood)
MD 26 x 24pdrs 4 x 24u
UD 30 12pdrs
FC & QD 20 x 6pdrs
LD 30 x 36pdrs (short) MD 32 x 24pdrs
UD 32 x 18pdrs
FC & QD 20 x 6pdrs 4 x 24pdr carr. (probable rearmament

Slightly enlarged Black Sea version of the *Ches'ma* class with 28 gun ports on the lower deck. Converted into a 110-gun ship while building, although retaining her original dimensions. Her half-sister *Gavriil* may be found in the Baltic fleet. Sailed from Kherson to Sevastopol' in 1801. Cruised in the Black Sea in 1802. Coppered in 1804. Landed troops successfully at Anapa and bombarded Trabizon but failed to capture the city in 1807. At Sevastopol' in 1809. Involved in the unsuccessful pursuit of the Turkish squadron in 1810. Part of Vice-Adm. Gall's squadron in 1811. Surveyed and found to be in poor condition in 1812. Decommissioned in 1812. Broken up after 1812.

Ratnyi 110 Kherson
Constructor Potapov
Laid down 9.3.1801 *Launched* 22.11.1802
Dimensions 190 ft x 51 ft 10 in x 22 ft (Veselago)
190 ft x 52 ft x 23 ft 6 in (Golovachev)
Armament LD 30 x 36pdrs (short) MD 32 x 24pdrs
UD 32 x 18pdrs
FC & QD 20 x 6pdrs 4 x 24pdr carr.

Coppered in 1804. Sailed from Kherson to Sevastopol' in 1807. Flagship of Rear-Adm. Pustoshkin in 1807 in operations against Anapa and Trabizon. In Sevastopol' in 1808. Cruised off Varna in 1809. Participated in the pursuit of the Turkish squadron in 1810, and again bombarded Trabizon. Cruised off Varna in 1811 and transported troops from Sevastopol' to Odessa. Decommissioned in 1812. Ordered to be broken up in 1825. Broken up in 1826.

Ships with 80–84 guns (2 purpose-built 1762–1800)

Although 80-gun, two-deckers replaced 74s as the mainstay of the Black Sea fleet after 1825, only two 80s were built during this earlier period. They were intended to act as flagships and strong points in the line of battle, and served as such until replaced as flag ships by the new three-deckers at the turn of the century.

Josif II (renamed *Rozhdestvo Khristovo*) 80 Kherson
Constructor S. I. Afanasyev
Laid down 8.1786 *Launched* 15.6.1787
Dimensions 180 ft x 49 ft 6 in x 20 ft 3 in
Armament 1788 LD 30 x 36pdrs
UD 30 x 18pdrs
FC & QD 20 x 8pdrs (Admiralty Order)
1789 LD 30 x 36pdrs
UD 30 x 18pdrs
FC & QD 20 x 12pdrs or 24u (½ pood)
(Golovachev)
1791 LD 28 x 36pdrs (iron) 2 x 60 u (1 pood/brass)
UD 20 x 18pdrs (iron), 4 x 18pdrs (brass) 4 x 24u
(½ pood)
FC & QD 15 x 12pdrs, 3 x 18u (Golovachev)

Upon her completion in 1787, *Josif II* represented a major augmentation to the size and power of the Black Sea battle line. She joined a fleet made up of only five 60–66-gun ships armed with 30pdrs and measuring 156–160 ft in length, in contrast with the new flagship's lower deck 36pdr main battery (imported from England) and her 180 ft length. *Josif II* may be looked upon as a rather smaller Black Sea analogue to the larger *Ches'ma* class ships then under construction for the Baltic fleet. Her role was that of providing a strong point for the small but growing Black Sea battle line and also offering sufficient size and presence to fulfil flagship duties in peace and war.

Great Britain would not undertake the construction of two-decker 80-gun ships until 1793 with the construction of the *Caesar* and the *Foudroyant* five years later. It seems probable that *Josif*'s construction and basic characteristics were either arrived at independently or that it owed its inspiration to the highly regarded French two-decker 80s of the period which were built in quantity from the 1750s through 1815 and of which the *Deux Freres* 1784 was a typical example for this period.

193 ft x 50 ft x,
LD 30 x 36pdrs
UD 32 x 24pdrs
FC & QD 20 x 8pdrs

The French ship was significantly larger than *Josif II* and carried a heavier upper deck battery. On the plus side, the shorter length of the Russian ship would have reduced the known tendency of the longer French ships to suffer from hogging under strenuous service conditions. Diagonal framing and the use of iron reinforcing knees and braces were developments of the next century, and the Russian 80s may have avoided the problems experienced by the French with hull deformation either fortuitously or by deliberate design with their shorter hulls.

Josif II sailed from Kherson to the Dnieper estuary in 1787, where she joined the squadron of Rear-Adm. John Paul Jones in actions against the Turks. Collided with *Ioann Bogoslov* (46) in 10.1789, forcing the smaller ship to return to Sevastopol' for repairs. Cruised as the flag of Rear-Adm. Voynovich in 1789. On 15.3.1790 renamed *Rozhdestvo Khristovo*. Fought as the flagship of Rear Vice-Adm. Ushakov at Kerch and at Tendra in 1790, where she captured the 80-gun Turkish *Kapudaniye*. Armed in reserve in 1792–3. Cruised in the Black Sea in 1794. Decommissioned in 1794. Broken up in 1800.

Sviatoi Pavel 84/90 Nikolaev
Constructor S. I. Afanasyev and Sokolov
Laid down 20.11.1791 *Launched* 9.8.1794
Dimensions 180 ft x 50 ft x 20 ft 6 in
Armament 1794 LD 24 x 36pdrs 6 x 60 u (1 pood)
UD 26 x 24pdrs 6 x 60 u (1 pood bombs)
FC & QD 24 x 18pdrs, RH 4 x 12u (¼ pood)
(Sudostroenie 1984)
1798 LD 24 x 36pdrs 6 x 60 u (1 pood) (brass)
UD 26 x 24pdrs 4 x 60 u (1 pood) (brass)
FC & QD 22 x 6pdrs (iron) (Ushakov and Sudostroenie)
1,030 men

The largest and most powerful Black Sea warship of the eighteenth century and the prestige ship of the newly formed fleet until the completion of the three-decker 110-gun *Iagudiil* in 1800. *Sviatoi Pavel* was completed too late to participate in the Russo-Turkish War; but she was nearly identical in her dimensions to *Josif II* and was clearly her half-sister. Her completion was greatly delayed due to bureaucratic delays and inadequate funding. The newer ship was completed with 24pdr upper deck guns in place of her near-sister's upper deck 18pdrs and with 18pdr forecastle and quarterdeck guns in place of her 8pdrs. The 18pdrs were apparently too heavy for the open decks and they were replaced by 6pdrs by 1798. Both the 36pdrs and the 24pdrs were brass weapons, an indication of the status of *Sviatoi Pavel* had as Black Sea flagship and also an indication of the high regard for brass cannon, even at this comparatively late date.

Sailed from Nikolaev to Sevastopol' in 1795. Cruised in the Black Sea in 1797 and 1798. Acted as Vice-Adm. Ushakov's flagship in the Mediterranean campaign in 1798–1800 and involved in the capture of Corfu, the Ionic islands, Messina, Palermo, and Naples. Repaired 1801–4. Sailed for Corfu on 2.11.1804 with 1,095 soldiers bound for Corfu. Severely damaged by storm off the Bosporus and forced into Buyuk-dere for repairs. Returned to Sevastopol' in 12.1805.

Decommissioned in 1805. Assigned as a floating battery and fire watch ship in 1806. Broken up in 1810.

Ships with 74 guns (7 purpose-built 1762–1800)

74-gun ships of the line had been introduced into the Baltic fleet in 1772, and the type was well established in the Russian Navy by the time that it was similarly introduced into the expanding Black Sea fleet in 1794 to supplement and then supplant the five remaining 66-gun ships that had previously formed the core of the fleet. The 7 ships of the *Sviatoi Pyotr* class were intermediate in size between the 66s and the larger 80/84 gun flagships, being 8 ft shorter than the 80/84s and armed with 30pdrs in lieu of the larger ships' 36pdrs. They generally paralleled Baltic 74s in size and capability, although they were slightly larger than their nearest Baltic contemporaries, the *Iaroslav*s. Their designer, A. S. Katasanov added one significant innovation to their design by connecting the forecastle and quarterdeck and beginning the process of closing off the waist of the Black Sea ships with a continuous deck in a manner that foreshadowed the spar-decked frigates of the 1800s. The class formed the core of Adm. Ushakov's forces during the Mediterranean campaign and they were hard pressed and worn out by the demands of their service and by the lack of suitable maintenance facilities in both the Mediterranean and in the Black Sea. *Tolakaya Bogoroditsa* was wrecked in 1804, and the remaining six ships were withdrawn from service between 1805 and 1810.

Sviatoi Pyotr class (7 ships)
Sviatoi Pyotr 74 Kherson
Constructor A. S. Katasanov
Laid down 3.2.1794 *Launched* 5.11.1794
Dimensions 172 ft x 47 ft x 19 ft
Armament Projected LD 26 x 30pdrs 2 x 60 u (1 pood)
UD 26 x 18pdrs 2 x 24u (½ pood)
FC & QD 18 x 8pdrs
1798 LD 24 x 30pdrs 4 x 60 u (1 pood)
UD 24 x 18pdrs 4 x 24u (½ pood)
FC & QD 18 x 8pdrs (Ushakov)

Sviatoi Pyotr class. The 30pdrs were manufactured in England. Sailed from Kherson to Sevastopol' in 1796. Cruised in the Black Sea in 1796–98. Assigned in 1798 to the Mediterranean campaign as Vice-Adm.

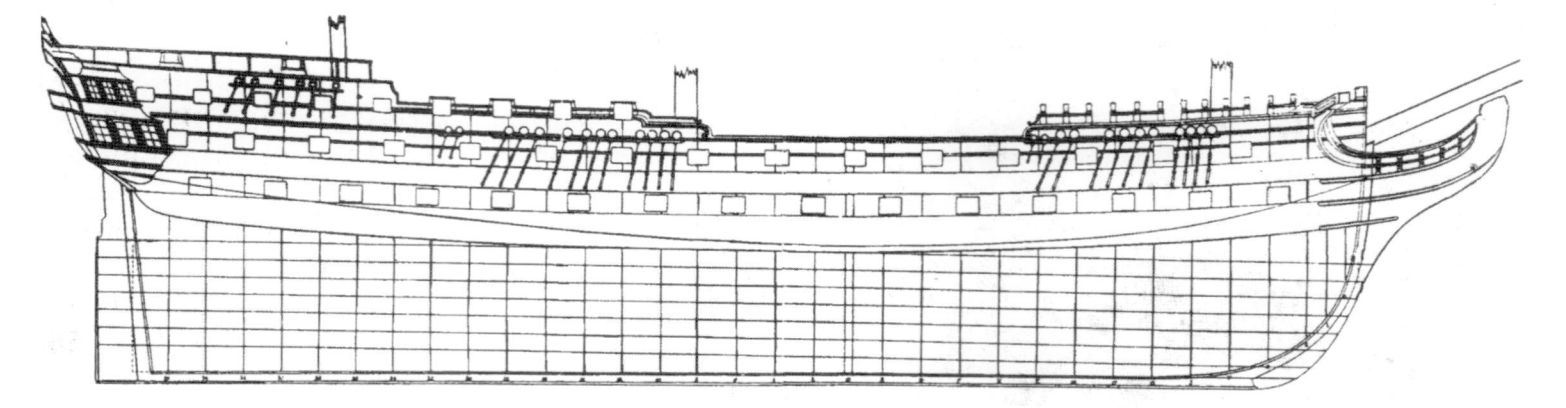

Sviatoi Pavel (90) was completed at Nikolaev in 1794. Her 36pdr armament made her the most powerful two-decker built for the Russian navy during the eighteenth century in either the Black Sea or the Baltic, Armed with all brass cannon as a mark of her status as a prestige ship, she served as the flagship of the Black Sea fleet and flew Vice Admiral Ushakov's flag during the Mediterranean campaign of 1798–1800.

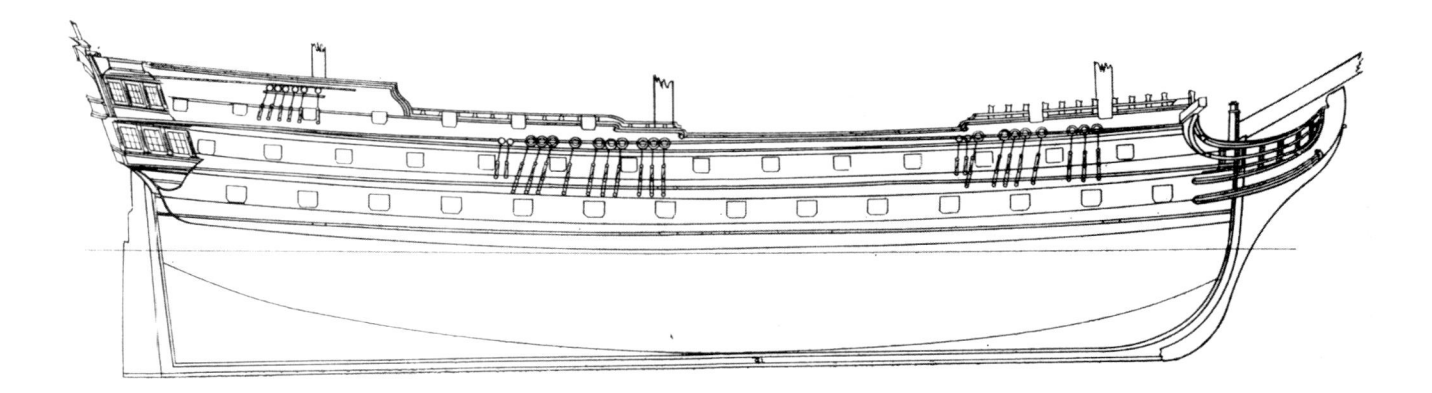

Sviatoi Pyotr, completed at Kherson in 1794, had the distinction of being the first 74 built in the Black Sea and the lead ship of a class of 7. She was also an example of Russian innovative design, being completed with a continuous upper deck although the waist was still open. Although completed too late to see combat against Turkey, she had the distinction of acting as Vice-Admiral Ushakov's flagship during the Ionian campaign in 1798–1800.

Ushakov's flagship and involved in the capture of Corfu, the Ionic Islands, Messina, Palermo, and Naples. Repaired in 1801 at Nikolaev. Decommissioned in 1802. Assigned as a harbour storeship in 1803. Broken up in 1805.

Zakharii i Elisavet 74 Kherson
Constructor A. S. Katasanov
Laid down 18.3.1794 *Launched* 1.8.1795
Dimensions 172 ft x 47 ft x 19 ft
Armament Projected LD 26 x 36pdrs 2 x 60 u (1 pood)
          UD 26 x 18pdrs 2 x 24u (½ pood)
          FC & QD 18 x 8pdrs
1798   LD 24 x 36pdrs 4 x 60 u (1 pood)
          UD 24 x 18pdrs 4 x 24u (½ pood)
          FC & QD 18 x 8pdrs (Ushakov)

Sviatoi Pyotr class. The 36pdrs were manufactured in England. Sailed from Kherson to Sevastopol' in 1796. Cruised in the Black Sea in 1796–8. Took part in Vice-Adm. Ushakov's Mediterranean campaign in 1798–1800. Repaired at Nikolaev in 1801. Decommissioned in 1802. Assigned as a harbour storeship in 1803. Broken up in 1805.

Simion i Anna 74 Kherson
Constructor A. S. Katasanov
Laid down 15.11.1795 *Launched* 19.7.1797
Dimensions 176 ft x 47 ft x 19 ft
Armament Projected LD 26 x 30pdrs 2 x 60 u (1 pood)
          UD 26 x 18pdrs 2 x 24u (½ pood)
          FC & QD 18 x 8pdrs
          1798 LD 24 x 30pdrs 4 x 60 u (1 pood)
          UD 24 x 18pdrs 4 x 24u (½ pood)
          FC & QD 18 x 8pdrs

Sviatoi Pyotr class. Sailed from Kherson to Sevastopol' in 1798. Took part in Vice-Adm. Ushakov's Mediterranean campaign in 1798–1800 as part of the 2nd squadron under Rear-Adm. Pustoshkin, joining Ushakov's squadron on 30.12.1798. Participated in the siege of Corfu, the bombardment of Ancona, and the blockade of Genoa. Transported 376 soldiers to Corfu in 1804 prior to returning to Sevastopol'. Reduced to a shear hulk in 1805. Broken up in 1809.

Mikhail/Sviatoi Mikhail 74 Kherson
Constructor A. S. Katasanov
Laid down 31.10.1796 *Launched* 20.6.1798
Dimensions 176 ft x 47 ft x 19 ft
Armament Projected LD 26 x 30pdrs 2 x 60 u (1 pood)
          UD 26 x 18pdrs 2 x 24u (½ pood)
          FC & QD 18 x 8pdrs
1798   LD 24 x 30pdrs 4 x 60 u (1 pood)
          UD 24 x 18pdrs 4 x 24u (½ pood)
          FC & QD 18 x 8pdrs

Sviatoi Pyotr class. Sailed from Kherson to Sevastopol' in 1798. Took part in Vice-Adm. Ushakov's Mediterranean campaign in 1798–1800 as part of the 2nd squadron under Rear-Adm. Pustoshkin, joining Ushakov's squadron on 30.12.1798. Participated in the siege of Corfu, the bombardment of Ancona, and the blockade of Genoa. Decommissioned and converted into a troopship in 1804. Carried troops from Sevastopol' to Poti in 1804. Carried troops from Sevastopol' to Corfu in 1805. Landed troops at Castelnovo in 1806. Converted to a hospital ship at Corfu in 1807, transferring her masts and rigging to the Turkish prize *Sed-ul Bahr*. Found unfit for service at Corfu in 12.1807 and sold to France in 1808 for 5000 thalers.

Tol'skaya Bogoroditsa 74 Kherson
Constructor Tarusov
Laid down 9.3.1798 *Launched* 7.8.1799
Dimensions 176 ft x 47 ft x 19 ft
Armament Projected LD 26 x 30pdrs 2 x 60 u (1 pood)
          UD 26 x 18pdrs 2 x 24u (½ pood)
          FC & QD 18 x 8pdrs
1798   LD 24 x 30pdrs 4 x 60 u (1 pood)
          UD 24 x 18pdrs 4 x 24u (½ pood)
          FC & QD 18 x 8pdrs (*Materialy*) XVI

Sviatoi Pyotr class. Sailed from Kherson to Sevastopol' in 1800. Cruised in the Black Sea in 1802. Wrecked at the mouth of the Khopi River on 8.12.1804 while transporting troops from Sevastopol' to the Caucasus with 164 perishing and 99 saved.

Mariia Magdalina vtoraia 74 Kherson
Constructor Potapov
Laid down 9.3.1798 *Launched* 7.8.1799
Dimensions 176 ft x 47 ft x 19 ft
Armament Projected LD 26 x 30pdrs 2 x 60 u (1 pood)
          UD 26 x 18pdrs 2 x 24u (½ pood)
          FC & QD 18 x 8pdrs
          1798 LD 24 x 30pdrs 4 x 60 u (1 pood)

UD 24 x 18pdrs 4 x 24u (½ pood)
FC & QD 18 x 8pdrs (*Materialy*) XVI

Sviatoi Pyotr class. Named *Mariia Magdalina vtoraia* to distinguish her from her Black Sea contemporary, *Mariia Magdalina pervaia* (66) launched in 1789 and not stricken until 1803. Sailed from Kherson to Sevastopol' in 1800. Cruised in the Black Sea in 1802. Carried troops to Corfu and returned to Sevastopol' in 1804 and again in 1805. Returned to Sevastopol' in 1806 at the direction of Vice-Adm. Seniavin. Decommissioned in 1806. Assigned as a fire watch ship 1807–10. Broken up after 1810.

Sviataia Paraskeva 74 Kherson
Constructor M. K. Surovtsov
Laid down 4.11.1798   *Launched* 6.11.1799
Dimensions 176 ft x 47 ft x 19 ft
Armament   Projected LD 26 x 30pdrs 2 x 60 u (1 pood)
             UD 26 x 18pdrs 2 x 24u (½ pood)
             FC & QD 18 x 8pdrs
1798   LD 24 x 30pdrs 4 x 60 u (1 pood)
             UD 24 x 18pdrs 4 x 24u (½ pood)
             FC & QD 18 x 8pdrs (*Materialy*) XVI

Sviatoi Pyotr class. Sailed from Kherson to Sevastopol' in 1800. Cruised in the Black Sea in 1802. Coppered in 1804. Transported two battalions of 1,125 soldiers to Corfu in 1804. At the disposal of the King of Naples 1804–5 transporting troops and similar duties. Carried the King of Sardinia from Naples to Caglari in 2–3.1806, bombarded Kotor and blockaded Ragusa. Subsequent to the signing of the Peace of Tilsit in 1807 moved first to Venice, back to Corfu and finally to Trieste on 28.12.1807. Decommissioned in 1809. Ceded to France on 27.9.1809.

Isidor 74
Transferred from the Baltic fleet in 1801. Reduced to a sheer hulk in 1809. (See under Baltic fleet.)

Ships with 60–66 guns (10 laid down/9 completed 1762–1800)

Although Russian 66-gun capital ships were approaching obsolescence in the Baltic by 1780, moderately sized ships of this type were well suited for the young and expanding naval force in the Black Sea acquiring basic naval operating skills as well as providing the opportunity for the newly opened Kherson shipyard to acquire experience in constructing warships of this size. Within the short space of ten years, the new shipyard would graduate from 66s to 74s and finally to 110s, a not inconsiderable achievement.

Sviataia Ekaterina 60 Kherson
Constructor V. A. Selyaninov
Laid down 26.5.1779   *Launched* broken up incomplete
Dimensions 155 ft x 41 ft 4 in x 15 ft 1 in
Armament (Est. 1723)

The first major warship ordered for the Black Sea Navy was laid down as a 60-gun frigate and then reordered as a 50-gun ship in 1784 by Prince Potemkin. Broken up incomplete 10.3.1785 due to dry rot in both her framing and her building slip.

Slava Ekateriny class (5 ships)

The first class of line of battle ships constructed for the Black Sea fleet was designed by A. S. Kasatonov, a future Surveyor, and their construction was supervised by Ivan Afanasyev. Their dimensions and armament were apparently identical to that of the Baltic fleet's *Aziia* class 66s, one of which, the *Sviatoi Pobedonosets* of 1780, has also been credited to A. S. Kasatonov, although there is some uncertainty in this regard (see below). The degree of design similarity between the Baltic and Black Sea fleets' 66s must remain a matter for conjecture at present, but it seems likely that the *Ekateriny*s were very probably straightforward duplicates of the successful and well-tried 66s of the Baltic fleet.

Two of the 5 *Ekateriny*s were lost before having the opportunity to prove their worth in battle. *Aleksandr* was wrecked in 1786. *Mariia Magdalina* grounded accidentally and was captured by the Turks in the second month of the Russo-Turkish War of 1787–92. These two major losses bear witness to the problems attendant to working up a new born fleet with inexperienced crews and officers. The other 3 ships all distinguished themselves in combat, taking part in all of the major battles of the war. The first two ships to complete, *Sviatoi Ekateriny* and *Sviatoi Pavel* were broken up in 1794 after 10 years of service, The last of the *Ekateriny*s, *Sviatoi Vladimir*, was in better condition and not put out of commission until 1798 by colliding with *Aleksandr Nevskii*, a frigate, while part of Adm. Ushakov's Mediterranean Squadron.

Slava Ekateriny (renamed *Preobrazhenie Gospodne*) 66 Kherson
Constructor S. I. Afanasyev
Laid down 26.5.1779   *Launched* 16.9.1783

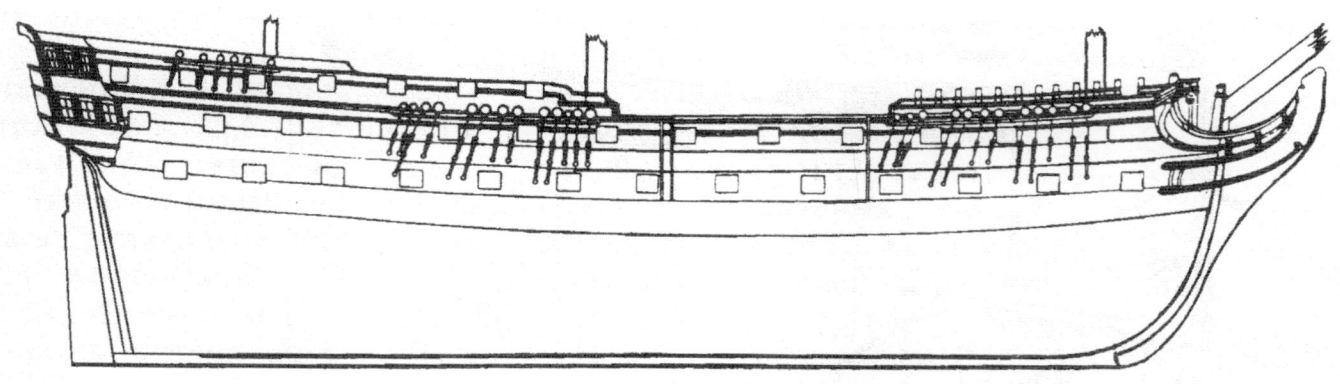

Slava Ekateriny (66) *was launched in 1783 as the first capital ship completed for the newly formed Black Sea fleet. She was closely modelled on the 66-gun ships of the* Slava Rossii *and* Aziia *classes that had been the standard line of battle ship in the Baltic fleet for half a century until they were gradually replaced by more powerful 74-gun ships after 1770. The lead ship in a class of 5,* Slava Ekateriny *fought with distinction in all of the major battles of the Russo-Turkish War in 1787–92.*

Dimensions 160 ft x 44 ft 4 in x 19 ft or 155 ft x 44 ft 2 in x 16 ft
(design uncertain) (Veselago)
155 ft x 41 ft 6 in x 19 ft (Golovachev)
Armament 1788 LD 26 x 30pdrs
UD 26 x 12pdrs
FC & QD 16 x 6pdrs (Admiralty Order)
1790 (beginning) LD 26 x 30pdrs
UD 26 x 12pdrs
FC & QD 16 x 6pdrs (Golovachev)
1790 (as re-armed) LD 24 x 24pdrs 2 x 60 u (1 pood)
UD 26 x 12pdrs 2 x 24u (½ pood)
FC & QD 14 x 6pdrs (Golovachev)

Slava Ekateriny class. Renamed *Preobrazhenie Gospodne* on 3.3.1788. Sailed from Kherson to Kinburn in 6–7.1784. Cruised in the Black Sea in 1785–86. Visited by Catherine II at Sevastopol' in 1787. Cruised in the Black Sea in 1787, losing all masts during a 5-day storm. Flag of Rear-Adm. Voinovich at the battle of Fidonisi in 7.3.1788 and caught up in two violent storms. Cruised in the Black Sea in 1789. Fought in the straits of Kerch and Tendra in 1790 and provided cover for the transfer of the rowing flotilla from the Dnieper to the Danube. Fought at Kaliakra on 31.7.1791. Decommissioned in 1791. Broken up before 1794.

Sviatoi Pavel 66 Kherson
Constructor S. I. Afanasyev
Laid down 9.7.1780 *Launched* 12.10.1784
Dimensions 160 ft x 44 ft 4 in x 19 ft (Veselago)
155 ft x 41 ft 6 in x 19 ft (Golovachev)
Armament 1784 LD 13 x 30pdrs 11 x 24pdrs 2 x 60 u (1pood)
UD 24 x 12pdrs 2 x 24u (½ pood)
FC & QD 16 x 6pdrs 2 x 18u (Golovachev)
1788 LD 26 x 30pdrs
UD 26 x 12pdrs
FC & QD 16 x 6pdrs (Admiralty Order)
1790 LD 26 x 30pdrs
UD 26 x 12pdrs
FC & QD 16 x 6pdrs (Golovachev)

Slava Ekateriny class. Sailed from Kherson to Sevastopol' in 1785. Cruised in the Black Sea in 1786 and 1787. Lost main and mizzen masts during a 5-day storm while cruising in 1787. Fought at Fidonisi under Commodore Ushakov in command of the vanguard on 7.3.1788 and caught up in two violent storms. Cruised in the Black Sea in 1789. Fought in the straits of Kerch and Tendra in 1790 and provided cover for the transfer of the rowing flotilla from the Dnieper to the Danube. Fought at Kaliakriva on 31.7.1791. Decommissioned in 1791. Broken up after 1794.

Mariia Magdalina 66 Kherson
Constructor S. I. Afanasyev
Laid down 28.6.1781 *Launched* 16.5.1785
Dimensions 155 ft x 42 ft 6 in x 19 ft (Veselago)
156 ft x 42 ft x 18 ft (Golovachev)
Armament 1785 LD 26 x 30pdrs
UD 26 x 12pdrs
FC & QD 16 x 6pdrs
1789 LD 26 x 30pdrs 2 x 60 u (1 pood)
UD 26 x 12pdrs 2 x 24u (½ pood)
FC & QD 12 x 8pdrs (Golovachev)

Slava Ekateriny class (5 ships). The 30 pdrs were manufactured in England. Sailed from Kherson to Sevastopol' in 1785. Cruised in the Black Sea in 1786. Took part in the Imperial Review at Sevastopol' in 1787. Severely damaged in a violent storm 8.9 to 13.9.1787; losing all masts, bowsprit, and rudder and tiller. Drifted to the Bosporus and grounded, surrendering to the Turks 13.9.1787. Commanding officer Capt. Tisdale was dismissed by Adm. Ushakov for failing to blow up the ship rather than surrendering to the Turks.

Aleksandr 66 Kherson
Constructor S. I. Afanasyev
Laid down 28.6.1781 *Launched* 11.4.1786
Dimensions 160 ft x 44 ft 4 in x 19 ft
Armament 1788 LD 26 x 30pdrs
UD 26 x 12pdrs
FC & QD 16 x 6pdrs

Slava Ekateriny class. Grounded and wrecked on 24.9.1786 while passing from Kherson to Sevastopol'.

Vladimir/Sviatoi Vladimir/Kniaz' Vladimir 66 Kherson
Constructor S. I. Afanasyev
Laid down 9.7.1780 *Launched* 15.5.1787
Dimensions 155 ft x 42 ft 6 in x 19 ft (Veselago)
155 ft x 41 ft 6 in x 19 ft (Golovachev)
Armament 1788 LD 26 x 30pdrs
UD 26 x 12pdrs
FC & QD 16 x 6pdrs (Admiralty Order)
1790 LD 26 x 30pdrs
UD 26 x 12pdrs
FC & QD 16 x 6pdrs (Golovachev)
1798 LD 24 x 30pdrs 2 x 60 u (1 pood)
UD 24 x 12pdrs 2 x 24u (½ pood)
FC & QD 18 x 8pdrs (Ushakov)

Slava Ekateriny class. Fought at Kinburn in 1787. Fought as John Paul Jones' flagship against the Turkish squadron off Ochakov in 1788. Sailed to Sevastopol' in the spring of 1789. Fought at Kerch and Tendra in 1790. Fought at Kaliakra in 1791. Cruised in the Black Sea in 1794, 1796, and 1797. In 1798, while part of Vice-Adm. Ushakov's squadron, collided with the frigate *Aleksandr Nevskii* and was forced to return to Sevastopol' for repairs. Decommissioned in 1800. Broken up after 1804.

Mariia Magdalina pervaia 66 Kherson
Constructor S. I. Afanasyev
Laid down 13.6.1786 *Launched* 12.4.1789
Dimensions 155 ft x 42 ft 6 in x 18 ft 6 in (Veselago)
156 ft x 42 ft x 18 ft (Golovachev)
Armament 1788 LD 28 x 30pdrs
UD 28 x 18pdrs
FC & QD ? (Admiralty Order) (as projected)
1789 LD 28 x 30pdrs
UD 24 x 18pdrs, 4 x 60 u (1 pood)
FC & QD 10 x 24u (½ pood)
1790 LD 26 x 30pdrs
UD 28 x 18pdrs
FC & QD 12 x 24u (½ pood) (Golovachev)
1790 LD 26 x 30pdrs
UD 26 x 12pdrs
FC & QD 16 x 6pdrs (Golovachev)
1798 LD 26 x 30pdrs, 2 x 60 u (1 pood)
UD 26 x 12pdrs, 2 x 24u (½ pood)
FC & QD 12 x 8pdrs (Ushakov)

Named in memory of *Mariia Magdalina* (66), lost in 1787. The 30pdrs were manufactured in England. Sailed to Sevastopol' in 1789. Cruised in the Black Sea in 1789. In 1791, fought at the straits of Kerch and Tendra where she captured the *Mulk-i Bahri* (66). Fought at Kaliakra in 1791. Cruised in the Black Sea in 1794, 1796, and 1797. Renamed *Mariia Magdalina pervaia* in 1799 to distinguish her from *Mariia Magdalina vtorya* (74) upon that ship's commissioning. Took part in Vice-Adm. Ushakov's Mediterranean Campaign and the capture of Corfu, Palermo, Naples, and Messina in 1798–1800. Decommissioned in 1800. Harbour service in 1801–2. Broken up in 1803.

Bogoiavlenie Gospodne 66 Kherson
Constructor S. I. Afanasyev
Laid down 15.3 1789   *Launched* 22.3.1791
Dimensions 162 ft x 45 ft x 19 ft 3 in (Veselago)
           156 ft x 42 ft x 18 in (Golovachev)
Armament 1790 (projected) LD 28 x 30pdrs
           UD 24 x 18pdrs, 4 x 60 u (1 pood)
           FC & QD 10 x 24u
         1790 (beginning) LD 26 x 30pdrs
           UD 28 x 18pdrs
           FC & QD 12 x 24u (½ pood) (Golovachev)
         1790 (as re-armed) LD 26 x 36pdrs
           UD 26 x 18pdrs
           FC & QD 14 x 12pdrs, 6 x 18u (Golovachev)
         1790 (as re-armed) and 1798 LD 26 x 36pdrs
           UD 26 x 18pdrs
           FC & QD 14 x 6pdrs 6 x 18u (Golovachev and Ushakov)

The 36pdrs were manufactured in England. Sailed from Kherson to Sevastopol' in 1791. Cruised in the Black Sea in 1794, 1796 and 1797. Took part in Vice-Adm. Ushakov's Mediterranean Campaign in 1798–1800 during which she captured a French 18-gun chebek and, at Corfu, the ex-British *Leander* (50) and the French *La Brune* (50). Decommissioned in 1801. Broken up in 1804.

Sviataia Troitsa (ex-*Soshestvie Avyatogo Dukha*) 66 Kherson
Constructor S. I. Afanasyev
Laid down 30.9.1790   *Launched* 6.5.1791
Dimensions 160 ft x 44 ft 6 in x 19 ft
Armament 1790 LD 26 x 36pdrs
           UD 26 x 18pdrs
           FC & QD 14 x 12pdrs, 6 x 18u (Golovachev)
         1798 LD 26 x 30pdrs
           UD 26 x 18pdrs
           FC & QD 14 12pdrs, 6 x 18u (Ushakov)

Originally *Soshestvie Sviatogo Dukha*, renamed before launch exchanging names with a frigate building at the same time. The 30pdrs were manufactured in England. Sailed from Kherson to Sevastopol' in 1791. Cruised in the Black Sea in 1794, 1796 and 1797. Took part in Vice-Adm. Ushakov's Mediterranean Campaign in 1798–00. Carried troops from Odessa to Corfu and returned to Sevastopol' in 1804. Condemned in 1805. Broken up after 1806.

Varakhail 66/68 Kherson
Constructor Potapov
Laid down 6.11.1798   *Launched* 12.10.1800
Dimensions 168 ft x 45 ft 6 in x 18 ft
           1,800 tons bm 2,100 tons displacement (Veselago)
           168 ft x 45 ft 6 in x 19 ft 4 in (Golovachev)
Armament LD 22 x 30pdrs, 4 x 60 u (1 pood)
           UD 24 x 18pdrs, 4 x 24u (½ pood)
           QD&FC 14 x 8pdrs (probable)

Sailed from Kherson to Sevastopol' in 1801. Transported a regiment to Corfu in 1804. Operations off Anapa and Trabizon in 1807. Bombardment and capture of Anapa in 1809. Bombardment and capture of Sukhum-kale in 1810 and bombardment of Trabizon in 1810. Assigned to Vice-Adm. Gall's squadron in 1811. Returned to Sevastopol' in poor condition in 1812. Training ship in 1812. Broken up after 1813.

Aziia 66 ?
Transferred from the Baltic fleet in 1801. (See under Baltic fleet.)

Pobeda 66 ?
Transferred from the Baltic fleet in 1801. (See under Baltic fleet.)

Black Sea frigates (39 purpose-built/13 converted 1762–1800)

Battle frigates/heavy frigates (15 purpose-built 1762–1800)

In 1788 Prince Potemkin ordered that large 50-gun frigates armed with 24pdrs recently completed for the Black Sea be rated as ships of the line or 'frigates of the line' ('battle frigates'). They may have been patterned after the Swedish heavy frigates of the *Bellona* class designed by Frederik af Chapman and launched between 1782 and 1785, although their completion with long 24pdrs in contrast to the short 24pdrs of the Swedish ships calls this into some question and they may have been an entirely original design. They were re-rated as heavy frigates in 1793. More than half of these ships were ultimately completed with bored-up 30- and 36pdrs and their lower deck firepower was far beyond that of other European and American heavy frigates.

Sviatoi Georgii Pobedonosets 50 Kherson
Constructor S. I. Afanasyev
Laid down 28.12.1783   *Launched* 16.6.1785
Dimensions 153 ft x 42 ft x 14 ft
           150 ft x 40 ft x 15 ft V. F. Golovachev
Armament 1788 LD 28 x 24pdrs
           UD 24 x 6pdrs (Admiralty Order)
         1790 LD 28 x 24pdrs
           UD 24 x 12pdrs (Golovachev)
         1790 LD 26 x 24pdrs, 2 x 60 u (1 pood)
           UD 20 x 6pdrs, 2 x 18u (Golovachev)

Arrived at Sevastopol' in 10.1785. Cruised in the Black Sea in 1787 and lost masts in a storm. Fought at Fidonisi in 1788. Participated in three wartime cruises in 1789. Fought at Kerch and Tendra in 1790 and at Kaliakra in 1791. Found unseaworthy in 1797. Broken up after 1801.

Apostol Andrei (*Andrei Pervozvannyy/Sviatoi Andrei*) 50 Kherson
Constructor S. I. Afanasyev
Laid down 1.3.1785   *Launched* 13.4.1786
Dimensions 154 ft x 42 ft 6 in x 15 ft (Veselago)
           150 ft x 40 ft x 15 ft (Golovachev)
Armament 1788 LD 28 x 24pdrs
           UD 24 x 6pdrs (Admiralty Order)
         1790 LD 28 x 24pdrs
           UD 24 x 12pdrs (Golovachev)
         1790 LD 26 x 24pdrs 2 x 60 u (1 pood)
           UD 20 x 18pdrs 2 x 6pdrs (Golovachev)

Sailed to Sevastopol' in 1786. Cruised in the Black Sea in 1787 and lost masts in a storm. Fought at Fidonisi in 1788. Participated in three wartime cruises in 1789. Fought at Kerch and Tendra in 1790 and at Kaliakra in 1791. Found unseaworthy in 1797. Reduced to a shear hulk in 1800–2

Aleksandr Nevskii (*Sviatoi Aleksandr*) 48/50/52 Kherson
Constructor S. I. Afanasyev
Laid down 1786   *Launched* 15.5.1787
Dimensions 154 ft x 42 ft 6 in x 15 ft (Veselago)
150 ft x 40 ft x 15 ft (Golovachev)
Armament 1788 LD 28 x 24pdrs
UD 24 x 6pdrs (Admiralty Order)
1789 LD 24 x 24pdrs, 4 x 60 u (1 pood)
UD 24 x 12pdrs
1790 LD 28 x 24pdrs
UD 24 x 12pdrs (Golovachev)
1790 LD 22 x 24pdrs, 4 x 60 u (1 pood)
UD 2 x 18pdrs, 14 12pdrs, 4 x 18u (Golovachev)
1798 LD 24 x 24pdrs, 4 x 60 u (1 pood)
UD 18 x 6pdrs (Ushakov)

Assigned as the flagship of Rear-Adm. Mordvinov's Liman Squadron covering the mouth of the Don against the Turks in 1787. Fought at Ochakov on 17.6.1788. Cruised with Rear-Adm. Voinovich's Sevastopol' Squadron in 1789. In 1790, operated as part of Vice-Adm. Ushakov's Squadron in the bombardment of Sinop and Anapa and the battles of Kerch and Tendra. In 11.1790, provided cover for the passage of the Liman flotilla to the Danube. Fought at Kaliakra in 1791. Cruised in the Black Sea in 1794 and 1796. Determined to be in poor condition in 1797. In.5.1798, she lost her mizzen-mast in collision with the *Vladimir* (66) and returned to Sevastopol' for repairs. On 14.11.1799, she carried troops to Corfu as part of Rear-Adm. S. Pustoshkin's Division and returned to Nikolaev. Last listed in 1801. (See *Aleksandr Nevskii* (74), commissioned in the Baltic from 1786–1801 for a rare instance of two Russian warships with the same names being commissioned during the same time period) (See also under converted Baltic transports as *Aleksandr*.)

Pyotr Apostol class (6 ships)

These six ships stand alone among Black Sea heavy frigates of the period in having been built to a common design and in completing with bored-up 30- and 36pdrs. The entire class was built at the Rogozhskaya shipyard and they were the only major warships built at that yard. Four fought against Turkey in the 1788–91 war, and the last two joined Adm. Ushakov's squadron in the Mediterranean in 1798. Two were lost in a storm in 1798, one to fire while on the way to the breakers, and three were broken up in their eleventh years.

Pyotr Apostol 46 Rogozhskaya
Constructor I. V. Dolzhnikov
Laid down 23.12.1783, *Launched* 10.8.1788
Dimensions 143 ft x 43 ft x 13 ft (Veselago)
148 ft x 38 ft 6 in x 14 ft 3 in (Golovachev)
Armament 1788 LD 24 x 36pdrs (bored up)
UD 22 x 12pdrs (Admiralty Order)
1790 LD 24 x 30pdrs (bored up)
UD 22 x 12pdrs (Golovachev)

Pyotr Apostol class. Sailed to Taganrog and then Sevastopol' in 1789. Cruised in the Black Sea in 1789. Fought at Kerch and Tendra in 1790 and at Kaliakra in 1791. Found unseaworthy in 1795. Broken up after 1799.

Ioann Bogoslov 46 Rogozhskaya
Constructor I. V. Dolzhnikov
Laid down 23.12.1787, *Launched* 10.8.1788
Dimensions 143 ft x 43 ft x 13 ft (Veselago)
148 ft s 38 ft 6 in x 14 ft 3 in (Golovachev)
Armament 1788 LD 24 x 36pdrs (bored up)
UD 22 x 12pdrs (Admiralty Order)
1790 LD 24 x 30pdrs (bored up)
UD 22 x 12pdrs (Golovachev)
1790 LD 24 x 30pdrs (bored up)
UD 19 12pdrs, 3 x 18u (Golovachev)
1790 LD 24 x 36pdrs (bored up)
UD 22 x 12pdrs

Pyotr Apostol class. Sailed to Taganrog and then Sevastopol' in 1789. In 10.1789, collided with the flagship *Josif II* (80) in strong winds, losing both anchors and returned to Sevastopol' for repairs. Fought at Kerch and Tendra in 1790 and at Kaliakriva in 1791. Reduced to a training ship in 1792–3. Transferred to Nikolaev for breaking up in 1794. Accidentally destroyed by fire with the loss of 12 sailors on 11.11.1794.

Tsar' Konstantin 46 Rogozhskaya
Constructor M. Ivanov and A. S. Katasanov
Laid down 20.7.1788 *Launched* 27.6.1789
Dimensions 143 ft x 43 ft x 13 ft (Veselago)
148 ft x 38 ft 6 in x 14 ft 3 in (Golovachev)
Armament 1788 LD 24 x 36pdrs (bored up)
UD 22 x 12pdrs (Admiralty Order)
1790 LD 24 x 30pdrs (bored up)
UD 22 x 12pdrs (Golovachev)

Pyotr Apostol class. Arrived at Sevastopol' in 10.1790. Cruised in the Black Sea in 11.1790 as cover for the Liman flotilla's passage to the Danube. Fought at Kaliakra in 1791. Cruised in the Black Sea in 1794. Employed as a cargo carrier in 1796. Forced to winter at Istanbul in 1796–7 due to storms. While serving as Rear-Adm. Ovtsyn's flagship, she was wrecked off the Danube on 14.10.1798 with 399 men lost, in the same storm that claimed *Fyodor Stratilat* (46).

Fyodor Stratilat 46 Rogozhskaya
Constructor M. Ivanov and A. S. Katasanov
Laid down 1788 *Launched* 9.4.1790
Dimensions 143 ft x 43 ft x 13 ft (Veselago)
148 ft x 38 ft 6 in x 14 ft 3 in (Golovachev)
Armament 1788 LD 24 x 36pdrs (bored up)
UD 22 x 12pdrs (Admiralty Order)
1790 LD 24 x 30pdrs (bored up)
UD 22 x 12pdrs (Golovachev)

Pyotr Apostol class. Arrived at Sevastopol' in 10.1790. Cruised in the Black Sea in 11.1790 as cover for the Liman flotilla's passage to the Danube. Fought at Kaliakra in 1791. Cruised in the Black Sea in 1794 and 1797. On 13.10.1798, she was wrecked off the Danube with the loss of all 269 men. in the same storm that claimed *Tsar' Konstantin* (46).

Soshestvie Sviatogo Dukha (ex-*Sviataia Troitsa*) 46 Rogozhskaya
Constructor M. Ivanov
Laid down 20.11.1789 *Launched* 4.4.1791
Dimensions 143 ft x 43 ft x 13 ft (Veselago)
148 ft x 38 ft 6 in x 14 ft 3 in (Golovachev)
Armament 1790 LD 24 x 30pdrs (bored up)
UD 22 x 12pdrs
1790 LD 24 x 24pdrs
UD 20 x 12pdrs (Golovachev)

Pyotr Apostol class. Originally *Sviataia Troitsa*, renamed before launch exchanging names with a ship of the line building at the same time. Sailed to Taganrog in 1791. Cruised in the Black Sea in 1794. Participated in Vice-Adm. Ushakov's Mediterranean campaign from

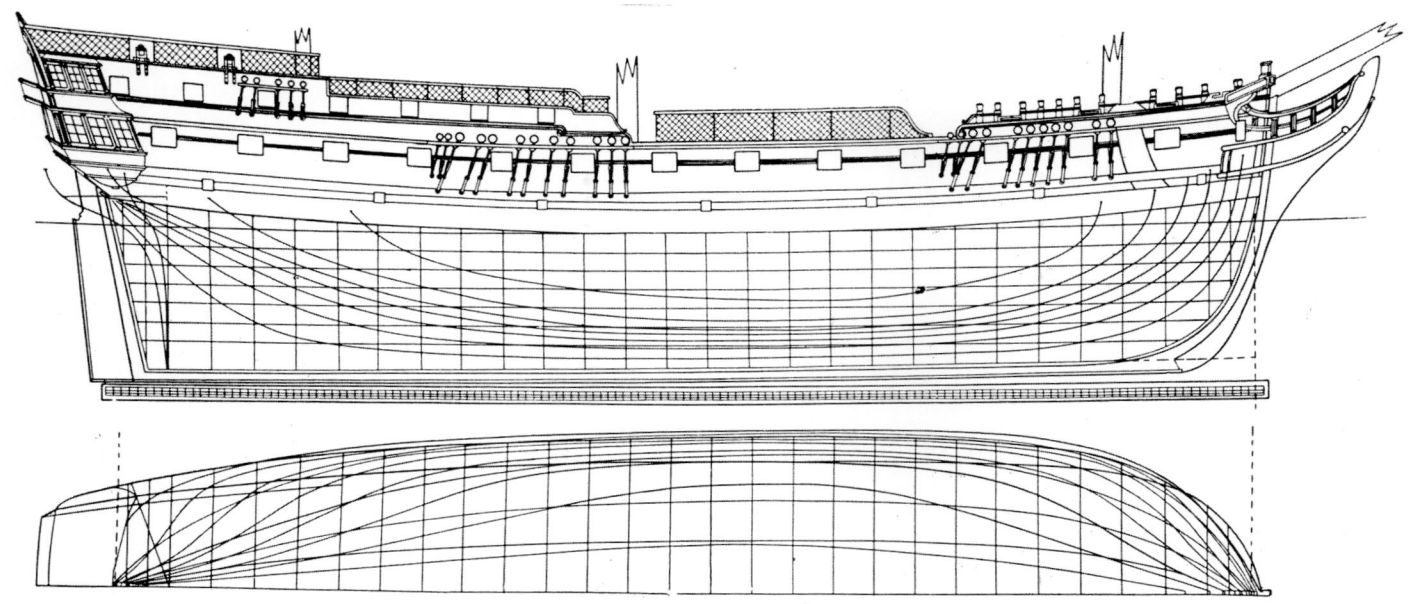

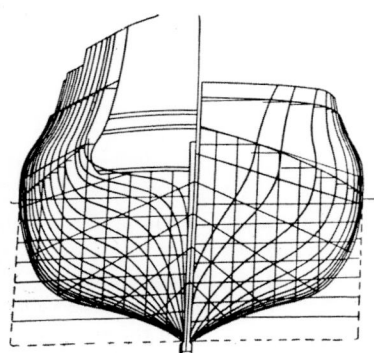

The frigate Sviatoi Nikolai *(46) as completed in 1790 for the Black Sea fleet. She was the first warship built in the newly constructed shipyard at Nikolaev and was a typical early representative of the heavy frigate design that came to be the norm for Russian frigates in both the Black Sea and the Baltic over the next half century.* Sviatoi Nikolai *fought with distinction and served under Vice-Admiral Ushakov in the Mediterranean campaign of 1798–1800.*

1798–1800. Left at Corfu at 1800 due to her poor condition and visited Brindisi. Wintered at Istanbul in 1801–2. Returned to Sevastopol' on 25.4.1802 and broken up.

Kazanskaya Bogoroditsa 46 Rogozhskaya
Constructor M. Ivanov
Laid down 16.10.1789   Launched 10.7.1791
Dimensions 143 ft x 43 ft x 13 ft
Armament   1790 LD 22 x 30pdrs (bored up) 4 x 24u (½ pood)
           UD 16 x 8pdrs, 4 x 18u (Golovachev)

Pyotr Apostol class. Unable to pass down the Don due to low water in 1791. Transported by 'camel' to Taganrog and then to Sevastopol' in 1792. Training ship in 1793. Cruised in the Black Sea in 1794. Training ship in 1795. Cruised in the Black Sea in 1796. Training ship in 1797. Participated in Vice-Adm. Ushakov's Mediterranean Campaign from 1798–1800. Detached as part of Capt. Sorokin's detachment with the frigate *Sviatoi Mikhail* and two Turkish frigates to cooperate with Adm. Nelson. Participated in the British blockade of Alexandria under Sydney Smith. Escorted 10 gun-boats to Aboukir in 10.1798. Took part in the capture of Ancona in 11.1799. Left at Corfu in 1799 due to poor condition and visited Brindisi. Wintered at Istanbul in 1801–2. Returned to Sevastopol' on 25.4.1802 where she was broken up.

Voznesenie Gospodne (*Navarkhiia*) 40/46 Kherson
Constructor S. I. Afanasyev
Laid down 16.11.1789   Launched 23.4.1790
Dimensions 142 ft x 42 ft 6 in x 14 ft 6 in (Veselago)
           150 ft x 40 ft x 15 ft (Golovachev)
Armament   1790 LD 28 x 24pdrs
           UD 24 x 12pdrs (Golovachev)
           1790 LD 20 x 24pdrs, 4 x 60 u (1 pood)
           UD 12 x 18pdrs, 8 x 4pdrs (Golovachev)
           1798 LD 20 x 24pdrs, 4 x 60 u (1 pood)
           UD 12 x 18pdrs, 4 x 12pdrs   (Ushakov)

Design prepared by S. I. Afanasyev at Prince Potemkin's order, and not A. S. Katasanov as asserted incorrectly by Chernyshev. Katasanov did not supersede Afanasyev until 1792 and the design of Voznesenie Gospodne was prepared by Afanasyev at the direct order of Prince Potemkin. All guns were brass. Cruised in the Black Sea in 11.1790 as cover for the Liman flotilla's passage to the Danube. Fought at Kaliakra in 1791. Cruised from 1794–8. Part of Vice-Adm. Ushakov's Squadron in the Mediterranean campaign of 1798–1800. Wintered in Corfu in 1800–1 due to poor material condition. Wintered again at Istanbul in 1801–2. Returned to Sevastopol' on 4.25.1802 and broken up.

Sviatoi Nikolai 46/50 Nikolaev
Constructors A. P. Sokolov and I. V. Dolzhnikov
Laid down 6.1.1790   Launched 25.8.1790
Dimensions 150 x 42 ft 6 in x 15 ft (Veselago)
           150 ft x 40 ft x 15 ft
           1,840 tons displacement (Golovachev)
Armament   1790 LD 28 x 24pdrs
           UD 24 x 12pdrs (Golovachev)
           1790 LD 22 x 24pdrs, 4 x 60 u (1 pood)

THE BLACK SEA FLEET 1770–1800

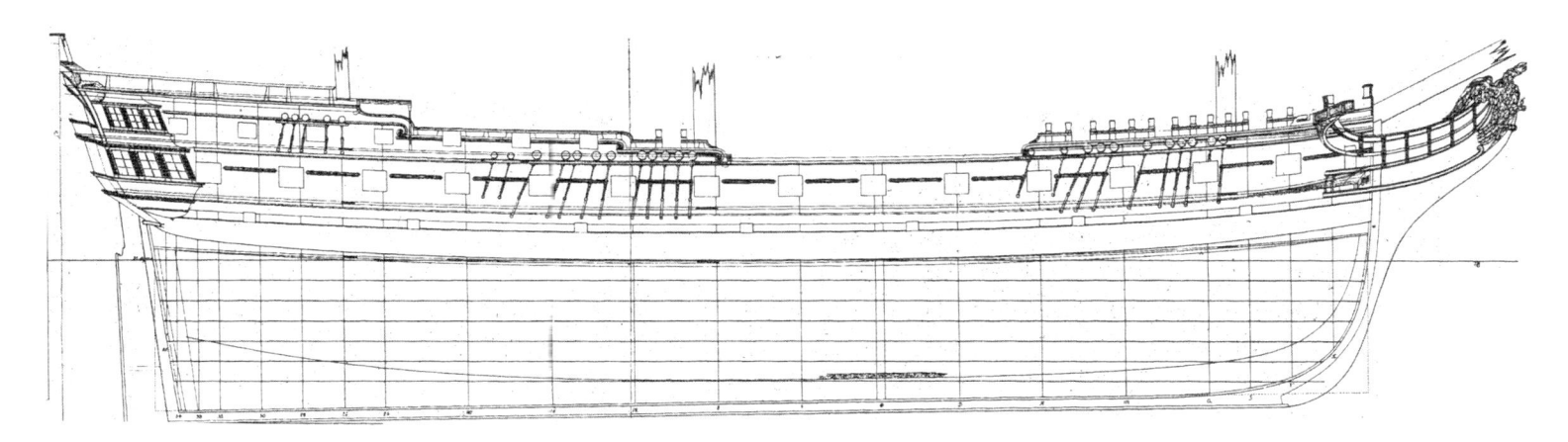

Grigorii Velikiia Armenii (50) was completed in 1791 at Nikolaev. Her size and armament made her the most powerful of the growing number of heavy frigates entering service in the Black Sea in the early 1790s. Had she been completed as designed with 62 guns, she might well have been regarded as a ship of the line rather than as a frigate. Grigorii Velikiia Armenii helped set the pattern for later generations of Black Sea heavy frigates, but lacked a continuous upper gun deck and bore no direct relationship to the heavy Swedish frigates designed slightly earlier.

UD 20 x 18pdrs, 4 x 7pdrs (Golovachev)
1798 LD 22 x 24pdrs, 4 x 60 u (1 pood)
UD 20 x 18pdrs (Ushakov)

Named to commemorate the capture of Ochakov on the saint day of St Nicholas. Arrived at Sevastopol' on 29.11.1790. Fought at Kaliakra in 1791. Cruised from 1794–7. Part of Vice-Adm. Ushakov's Squadron in the Mediterranean campaign of 1798–1800. Stationed at Naples until 1802 at the request of the Neapolitan government. By 1802, her hull was rotten and she was sold at Naples for 11,460 ducats on 26.7.1802 after her guns and crew had been sent to Russia via the frigate *Mikhail*.

Grigorii Velikiia Armenii 50 Nikolaev
Constructor A. P. Solokov
Laid down 30.9.1790   *Launched* 12.6.1791
Dimensions 158 ft x 44 ft 6 in x 18 ft 6 in
Armament 1798 LD 28 x 30pdrs (long/brass)
UD 22 x 18pdrs (brass) (Ushakov)

The most powerful Russian frigate of the eighteenth century. Unlike the captured Swedish 44-gun frigates, this ship did not have a complete second gun deck. All guns were brass to enable the installation of heavier ordnance. Sailed to Sevastopol' in 1791. Cruised in the Black Sea in 1794–8. Participated in Vice-Adm. Ushakov's Mediterranean Campaign from 1798–1800. Stationed at Naples at the request of the Neapolitan government until 1802. Wintered at Istanbul in 1802–3. Returned to Nikolaev on 23.7.1803. Transported troops to Corfu in 1804 and remained as a hospital ship. Sold at Corfu in 1809.

Sviatoi Mikhail 50 Kherson
Constructor A. S. Katasanov
Laid down 6.11.1795   *Launched* 31.10.1796
Dimensions 159 ft x 42 ft x 15 ft 9 in
Armament 1798 LD 24 x 24pdrs, 2 x 60 u (1 pood)
UD 18 x 12pdrs, 4 x 18u (Ushakov)

Sailed to Sevastopol' in 1797. Cruised in the Black Sea in 1798. Participated in Vice-Adm. Ushakov's Mediterranean Campaign from 1798–1800. Stationed in Naples at the request of the Neapolitan government from 1800 through 6.1802. Transported guns from the deteriorated frigate *Sviatoi Nikolai* to Corfu in 6.1802. Wintered at Corfu in 1802 due to storms. Arrived at Sevastopol' in 1803. Carried troops to Corfu in 1804. Cruised in the Mediterranean in 1805. Joined Vice-Adm. Seniavin's Squadron in 1806. Arrived at Venice in 9.1807 in poor condition and sailed to Trieste in 12.1807 as part of Commodore Saltanov's division. Blockaded by the British at Trieste for one month in 1809. Ceded to France on 20.10.1809.

Nazaret 44 Kherson
Constructor M. K. Surovtsov
Laid down 6.11.1799   *Launched* 12.10.1800
Dimensions 159 ft 2¾ in x 42 ft x 12 ft 5 in (Veselago)
159 ft 3 in x 41 ft 6 in x 18 ft (Golovachev)
Armament LD 28 x 24pdrs (short frigate guns)
FC & QD 16 x 6pdrs 6 x 24pdr carr (probable)

Nazaret was patterned after the captured Swedish heavy frigate *Venus*. In a reversal of pattern, she preceded the name ship for the enormously successful Baltic *Speshnyi* class into service by 10 months. The two ships were virtually identical in armament and dimensions and the Baltic *Speshnyi* class, which came to number 34 ships after 1800, might well have been named the *Nazaret* class. Although the Black Sea fleet was to complete twenty heavy frigates in the coming century, none would again be based on the design of the captured *Venus*. Just why a design so suitable for the Baltic was not regarded favourably in the Black Sea is something of a mystery.

Sailed to Sevastopol' in 1801. Relieved *Sviatoi Mikhail* at Corfu in 1802. Returned to Sevastopol' in the autumn of 1804. Transported troops to Corfu in 1805 and returned to Sevastopol' in 1806. Participated in the bombardment of Trabizon in 1807 and the capture of Anapa in 1809. Lost contact with her division on 4.10.1809 and engaged and successfully fled from two Turkish ships of the line. Her captain was court-martialled and broken for alleged cowardice. Participated in the capture of Sukhum and the bombardment of Trabizon in 1810. Cruised in the Black Sea in 1811. Condemned in 1812. Broken up after 1813.

Krepkii 54 Kherson
Constructor V. I. Potaov
Laid down 13.1.1801   *Launched* 10.11.1801
Dimensions 176 ft x 46 ft x 20 ft (Morskoi Sbornik)
176 ft x 46 ft x 19 ft (Golovachev)
Armament LD 30 x 36pdrs (short)
UD 32 x 36pdr carr. (conjecture)

Although she was nominally completed as a frigate, *Krepkii* was a sister ship to the Baltic fleet line of battle ship *Skoryi* (62) and was clearly of a transitional type. Sailed to Sevastopol' in 1801 Cruised in the Black Sea in 1802. Transported troops to Corfu, in 1804, returning to Sevastopol' in 1806. In 1807, cruised to Sinop and participated in the bombardment and conquest of Anapa. Cruised off Trabizon for the rest of the year. Participated in the pursuit of a Turkish squadron off Varna on 17.8.1810. Bombarded Trabizon in 1810. Cruised in the Black Sea in 1811. Condemned and hulked in 1812.

Early frigate types (16 purpose-built, 3 converted 1762–1800)
Sixteen numbered but originally unnamed shallow draught ships, falling generally into the frigate category with two unusual exceptions, were completed between 1771 and 1783 in the very early years of the Black Sea fleet. They were all shallow draft flat-bottomed ships, not well suited to Black Sea conditions and the products of the small Novokhoperskaya and Gnilotonskaya shipyards set up on tributaries of the Don River. Five were built to plans submitted by Adm. A. N. Seniavin and two by Adm. Knowles, while the remainder were presumably designed by I. I. Afanasyev. With the exception of Adm. Knowle's pair, the purpose-built ships were completed as conventionally armed 12pdr frigates and were not dissimilar in overall dimensions to contemporary British 12pdr frigates. For example, the *Vos'moi* class which began entering service in 1778 had dimensions of 128 ft x 34 ft 6 in x 11 ft 9 in and was armed with 24 x 12 pdrs and 4 x 18pdr edinorogs on the main deck. This compares quite closely with the British *Amazon* class of the same year with dimensions of 126 ft x 35 ft x 12 ft 2 in and a main deck armament of 26 x 12pdrs. Their Baltic contemporaries were the 12pdr frigates of the *Pavel* class with dimensions of 130 ft x 32 ft x 14 ft, but only carrying 20 x 12pdrs on the main gun deck. The *Pavel*s were almost certainly more primitive 'frigates' lacking the hallmark of 'true' late eighteenth century frigates, an unarmed lower deck with reduced overhead clearance, and these early Black Sea frigates may in fact have been the first 'true' Russian frigates, preceeding the larger 18pdr *Briachislav*s by some 15 years.

After the battle of Fidonisi demonstrated a need on 3.7.1788 for greater Russian firepower, seven were converted into either 'newly invented frigates' mounting 18pdrs or floating batteries with bored-up 30pdrs in an attempt to turn them into more useful vessels with sufficient firepower to enable them to deal with more heavily armed Turkish ships. These 16 numbered ships were followed by two pinks that were similarly converted into 'newly invented frigates' and one more shallow draft 12pdr frigate that was converted into a bomb vessel. All of these early ships were gone by the early 1790s, after the successful resolution of the Russo-Turkish War.

Pervyi **class** (2 ships)
These two shallow draught ships were built according to plans submitted by Adm. A. N. Seniavin and were fairly close in dimensions to their British contemporaries in the *Active* and *Amazon* classes, being 4 ft longer and 1 ft beamier. Seniavin reportedly wanted to arm them with brass 8- and 18pdrs, but they were completed with 6- and 12pdr iron guns due to a lack of availability of brass.
Pervyi (First) 32 Novokhoperskaya
Constructor I. I. Afanasyev
Laid down 20.9.1770 Launched 12.4.1771
Dimensions 130 ft x 36 ft x 11 ft 6 in
Armament LD 22 x 12pdrs
 FC & QD 10 x 6pdrs + falconets

Pervyi class. Sailed to Taganrog for completion and commissioning in 8.1771. Exchanged fire with Turkish ships in 1774 as part of Rear-Adm. Chichagov's squadron. Suffered severe storm damage in 30.11.1775 and wrecked with 55 men lost and 97 saved.

Vtoroi (Second) 32 Novokhoperskaya
Constructor I. I. Afanasyev
Laid down 20.9.1770 Launched 13.4.1771
Dimensions 130 ft x 36 ft x 11 ft 6 in
Armament LD 22 x 12pdrs
 FC & QD 10 x 6pdrs + falconets
Pervyi class. Sailed to Taganrog for completion and commissioning in 8.1771. Exchanged fire with Turkish ships in 1774 as part of Rear-Adm. Chichagov's squadron. Arrived at Kherson in 1779. Broken up there in 1783.

Tretii **class** (2 ships)
Two unusual ships were built according to plans submitted by Adm. Knowles. Veselago and Chernyshev are in disagreement about their primary armament, with Veselago specifying conventional 18pdrs and Chernyshev equipping them with an unprecedented armament of 18pdr edinorogs. The secondary armament of 28 x 3pdr falconets, which were little more than anti-personnel weapons, does point to a rather unconventional approach to armament on Adm. Knowles' part, making the choice of edinorogs at least conceivable, especially given the fact that the utility and tactical effectiveness of the new weapon would have been something of a cipher at the time. Their length might have given them something of the status of heavy frigates, but their narrow beam and comparatively lightweight armament relegates them to a unique place among the other numbered shallow draught 'frigates'.
Tretii (Third) 58 Novokhoperskaya
Constructor O. Matveev
Laid down 1.5.1772 Launched 28.4.1773
Dimensions 150 ft x 30 ft 8 in x 9 ft 9 in
Armament LD 30 x 18u
 FC & QD 28 x 3pdr falconets
Tretii class. Trapped in the Autumn of 1773 on the Don until Spring of 1774, when she sailed to Taganrog. Cruised in the Sea of Azov in 1777–8. Suffered a magazine explosion at Kerch on 23.3.1779, caught fire and exploded with a loss of 20 killed.

Chetvertyi (Fourth) 58 Novokhoperskaya
Constructor O. Matveev
Laid down 23.5.1772 Launched 29.4.1773
Dimensions 150 ft x 30 ft 8 in x 9 ft 9 in
Armament LD 30 x 18u
 FC & QD 28 3pdr falconets
Tretii class. Sailed to Taganrog in 1773. Cruised in the Sea of Azov in 1774–7. Exchanged fire with Turkish ships in 1774 as part of Rear-Adm. Chichagov's squadron. Repaired in 1778. Last mentioned in 1785 and believed to have been broken up.

Piatyi **class** (3 ships)
Three shallow draught 12pdr frigates laid down in 1774 were also designed by Adm. A. N. Seniavin and constructed by I. I. Afanasyev. They were approximately 10 ft shorter and 5 ft narrower than contemporary British 12pdr frigates which carried an additional four 12pdrs on larger dimensions. As was the case with the *Pervyi* class, it appears that Seniavin wished to

arm these ships with 18- and 8pdr brass guns in place of the 12- and 6pdr cannon with which they were completed. The first two were broken up in 1785, but *Sed'moi*, the last of the trio survived to fight at Ochakov and was chosen for conversion into a 'newly converted frigate'.

Piatyi (5th) 42 Novokhoperskaya
Constructor I. I. Afanasyev
Laid down 14.1.1774 *Launched* 26.4.1774
Dimensions 114 ft x 30 ft x 11 ft
Armament LD 22 x 12pdrs
    FC & QD 10 x 6pdrs + falconets

Piatyi class. Sailed from the Don to Taganrog in.4.1774. Cruised in 1777–8. Repaired in 1779. Broken up in 1785.

Shestoi (6th) 42 Novokhoperskaya
Constructor I. I. Afanasyev
Laid down 16.1.1774 *Launched* 3.5.1774
Dimensions 114 ft x 30 ft x 11 ft
Armament LD 22 x 12pdrs
    FC & QD 10 x 6pdrs + falconets

Piatyi class. Sailed to Taganrog in 1776. Cruised in 1777–9. Broken up in 1785.

Sed'moi (7th) (renamed *Kherson* and *Vasilii Velikii*) 42 Novokhoperskaya
Constructor I. I. Afanasyev
Laid down 18.1.1774 *Launched* 2.4.1777
Dimensions 114 ft x 30 ft x 11 ft
Armament LD 22 x 12pdrs
    FC & QD 10 x 6pdrs + falconets
    LD 24 x 12pdrs
    FC & QD 12 x 6pdrs 4 x 3pdr falconets
    1788 14 x 30pdrs (probably bored up)

Piatyi class. Sailed from the Don to Taganrog in 1777. Adm. A. N. Seniavin had wanted to rearm her with brass 18- and 8pdrs in place of the heavier iron 12- and 6pdrs, but this could not be done because of the expense. Cruised in 1777–9. Repaired at Kherson in 1783 and renamed *Kherson* as the first of the numbered frigates to be given a ship's name. Arrived at Sevastopol' in 1784. Cruised in the Black Sea in 1785 and 1787. Renamed *Vasilii Velikii* in 1788. Fought at Ochakov on 17.6.1788 as part of Rear-Adm. John Paul Jones's squadron. Converted in 1788 into one of the first flat-bottomed 'newly invented frigates', rearmed with 14 30pdrs, presumably bored-up weapons. Frozen at the mouth of the Dnieper on 21.11.1788 and grounded off Kinburn. Her crew was saved and her guns subsequently salvaged. Determined unfit for further service in 1790.

Vos'moi class (9 ships)

Nine ships, all built to common dimensions and, originally at least, a common armament of 12pdrs. They represent the first Black Sea design approaching the size and power of contemporary British 12pdr frigates to be placed in series production in the Black Sea fleet. All started out with numbers in place of names, as had been the custom with earlier Black Sea 'frigates'; but all were reassigned proper ship names in 1783, with five of the nine being renamed a second time in 1788. One ship, *Krym*, was lost before the Russo-Turkish War of 1788 and three others were broken up. The remaining five all fought with distinction in the war and four were selected for conversion into 'newly invented frigates' in 1788 after the battle of Fidonisi demonstrated the need for heavier firepower on the part of available Russian Black Sea warships.

Vos'moi (8th) (renamed *Ostorozhnyi*) 44 Novokhoperskaya
Constructor S. I. Afanasyev
Laid down 22.1.1774 *Launched* 25.4.1778
Dimensions 128 ft x 34 ft 6 in x 11 ft 9 in
Armament LD 24 x 12pdrs, 4 x 18u
    FC & QD 12 x 6pdrs, 4 x 3pdr falconets, 2 x 8pdr mortars (Veselago)

Vos'moi class. Sailed to Taganrog in 1779. Cruised from 1780–3. Renamed *Ostorozhnyi* on 18.5.1783. Cruised in the Black Sea in 1785. Found unfit for service in 1786 and laid up at Sevastopol. Reduced to a floating battery at Sevastopol' in 8.1787. Broken up after 1790.

Deviatyi (9th) (renamed *Pospeshnyi*) 44 Novokhoperskaya
Constructor S. I. Afanasyev
Laid down 13.9.1778 *Launched* 15.4.1779
Dimensions 128 ft x 34 ft 6 in x 11 ft 9 in
Armament LD 24 x 12pdrs, 4 x 18u
    FC & QD 12 x 6pdrs 4 x 3pdr falconets 2 x 8pdr mortars (Veselago)

Vos'moi class. Sailed to Taganrog in 1782. Sailed to Kerch and then to Sevastopol' in 1783. Renamed *Pospeshnyi* (Hurrying) on 18.5.1783. Cruised in the Black Sea in 1785. Found unfit for service in 1786. Reduced to a floating battery at Sevastopol' in 8.1787. Broken up after 1790.

Desiatyi (10th) (renamed *Krym*) 44 Novokhoperskaya
Constructor S. I. Afanasyev
Laid down 29.9.1778 *Launched* 14.4.1779
Dimensions 128 ft x 34 ft 6 in x 11 ft 9 in
Armament LD 24 x 12pdrs
    FC & QD 12 x 6pdrs, 4 x 3pdr falconets
    LD 24 x 12pdrs, 4 x 18 u
    FC & QD 12 x 6pdrs, 4 x 3pdr falconets, 2 x 8pdr mortars (Veselago)

Vos'moi class. Sailed to Taganrog in 1782. Cruised off the Crimea in 1782–3. Renamed Krym (Crimea) on 18.5.1783. Lost without trace in a 5-day storm on 9.9.1787.

Odinnadtsatyi (11th) (renamed *Khrabryi*) 44 Gnilotonskaya
Constructor O. Matveev
Laid down 18.1.1778 *Launched* 19.4.1779
Dimensions 128 ft x 34 ft 6 in x 11 ft 9 in
Armament LD 24 x 12pdrs
    FC & QD 12 x 6pdrs, 4 x 3pdr falconets
    LD 24 x 12pdrs, 4 x 18 u
    FC & QD 12 x 6pdrs, 4 x 3pdr falconets, 2 x 8pdr mortars (Veselago)

Vos'moi class. Cruised off the Crimea in 1782–3. Renamed *Khrabryi* on 18.5.1783. Found unfit for service on 9.1787 and had her masts removed. Broken up after 1788.

Dvenadtsatyi (12th) (renamed *Strela* and *Ioann Voinstvennik*) 40/44 Gnilotonskaya
Constructors O. Matveev and Yukharin
Laid down 24.7.1778 *Launched* 26.8.1782
Dimensions 128 ft x 34 ft 6 in x 11 ft 9 in (Veselago)
    121 ft x 34 ft 6 in x 13 ft (Golovachev)
Armament 1782 LD 24 x 12pdrs
    FC & QD 12 x 6pdrs, 4 x 3pdr falconets
    1782 LD 24 x 12pdrs, 4 x 18 u
    FC & QD 12 x 6pdrs, 4 x 3pdr falconets, 2 x 8pdr mortars (Veselago)

1788 LD 20 x 18pdrs
FC & QD 10 x 6pdrs (Admiralty Order)
1790 LD 20 x 18pdrs
FC & QD 10 x 8pdrs (Golovachev)
1790 FC & QD 6 x 6pdrs (as a transport)

Vos'moi class. Sailed from the Don to Taganrog. Renamed *Strela* on 18.5.1783. Cruised off the Crimea in 1783 and 1785. While cruising in 1787, received severe storm damage losing her masts and steering gear. Renamed *Ioann Voinstvennik* in 1788. Fought at Fidonisi on 3.7.1788. Converted into a 'newly invented frigate' in 1788. Cruised in the Black Sea in 1789. Fought at Kerch on 8.7.1790 and at Tendra on 28.8.1790. Sent to Kherson in very poor condition in 1791. Broken up after 1792.

Trinadtsatyi (13th) (renamed *Pobeda* and *Matvei Evangelist*) 42 Gnilotonskaya
Constructors O. Matveev and Yukharin
Laid down 24.7.1778 *Launched* 1782
Dimensions 128 ft x 34 ft6 in x 11 ft 9 in; 121 ft x 34 ft6 in x 13 ft (Golovachev)
Armament 1782 LD 24 x 12pdrs
FC & QD 12 x 6pdrs, 4 x 3pdr falconets
1782 LD 24 x 12pdrs, 4 x 18 u
FC & QD 12 x 6pdrs, 4 x 3pdr falconets, 2 x 8pdr mortars (Veselago)
1788 LD 20 x 18pdrs
FC & QD 10 x 6pdrs (Admiralty Order)
1790 LD 20 x 18pdrs
FC & QD 10 x 8pdrs (Golovachev)

Vos'moi class. Sailed to Taganrog in 1782. Sailed to Sevastopol' in 1783. Renamed *Pobeda* on 5.18.1783. Cruised in the Black Sea in 1784. Lost her main mast during a storm in 1787. Renamed *Matvei Evangelist* in 1788. Fought at Fidonisi in 1788. Converted into a flat-bottomed 'newly invented frigate' in 1788. Made three cruises in 1789. Left at Sevastopol' in 1790 due to poor condition. Broken up after 1791.

Chetyrnadtsatyi (14th) (renamed *Perun* and *Amvrosii Mediolanskii*) 40/44 Gnilotonskaya
Constructors O. Matveev and Yukharin
Laid down 26.2.1779 *Launched* 4.4.1783
Dimensions 128 ft x 34 ft6 in x 11 ft 9 in
121 ft x 34 ft x 13 ft (Golovachev)
Armament 1782 LD 24 x 12pdrs
FC & QD 12 x 6pdrs, 4 x 3pdr falconets
1782 LD 24 x 12pdrs, 4 x 18u
FC & QD 12 x 6pdrs, 4 x 3pdr falconets, 2 x 8pdr mortars (Veselago)
1790 LD 20 x 18pdrs
FC & QD 10 x 6pdrs (Admiralty Order)
1790 LD 20 x 18pdrs
FC & QD 10 x 8pdrs (Golovachev)

Vos'moi class. Sailed to Taganrog in.5.1783 and then to Sevastopol. Renamed *Perun* on 18.5.1783. Cruised in the Black Sea in 1787, losing her masts in a storm. Renamed *Amvrosii Mediolanskii* in 1788. Fought at Fidonisi in 1788. Fought at Kerch and Tendra in 1790. Found unseaworthy and converted into a floating magazine in 1791.

Piatnadtsatyi (15th) (renamed *Legkii* and *Kiriil Belozerskiyy*) 40/44 Gnilotonskaya
Constructors O. Matveev and Yukharin
Laid down ? *Launched* 1783
Dimensions 128 ft x 34 ft6 in x 11 ft 9 in
121 ft x 34 ft x 13 ft (Golovachev)
Armament 1782 LD 24 x 12pdrs
FC & QD 12 x 6pdrs, 4 x 3pdr falconets
1782 LD 24 x 12pdrs, 4 x 18 u
FC & QD 12 x 6pdrs, 4 x 3pdr falconets, 2 x 8pdr mortars(Veselago)
1788 LD 20 x 18pdrs
FC & QD 10 x 6pdrs (Admiralty Order)
1790 LD 20 x 18pdrs
FC & QD 10 x 8pdrs (Golovachev)

Vos'moi class. Sailed to Taganrog and then to Kerch and Sevastopol' in 1783. Renamed *Legkii* in 1783. Cruised in the Black Sea in 1783 and 1785 without incident. Damaged by storm during the 1787 cruise. Renamed *Kiriil Belozerskiy* in 1788. Fought at Fidonisi in 1788. Converted to a flat-bottomed 'newly invented frigate' in 1788. Participated in three wartime cruises in 1789. Fought at Kerch and Tendra in 1790. Found unfit for sea service and reduced to a sheer hulk in 1791.

Shestnadtsatyi (16th) (renamed *Skoryi* and *Fedot Muchenik*) 40/44 Gnilotonskaya
Constructors O. Matveev and Yukharin
Laid down ? *Launched* 4.5.1783
Dimensions 128 ft x 34 ft6 in x 11 ft 9 in (Veselago)
114 ft x 31 ft x 11 ft (Golovachev)
Armament 1782 LD 24 x 12pdrs
FC & QD 12 x 6pdrs, 4 x 3pdr falconets
1782 LD 24 x 12pdrs
FC & QD 10 x 6pdrs, 2 4pdrs 4 x 3pdrs (Veselago)
1788 LD 20 x 30pdrs
1789 LD 16 x 18pdrs 4 x 18u
FC & QD 10 x 6pdrs
1790 LD 16 x 36pdrs (bored up), 10 x 24pdrs (bored up) (Golovachev)

Vos'moi class. Sailed to Taganrog and then Sevastopol' in 1783. Renamed *Skoryi* in 1783. Cruised in the Black Sea in 1785. Attacked on 21.8.1787 by 11 Turkish galleys prior to a formal declaration of war. Returned fire for 3 hours, sinking 1 galley and driving the others off after expending 580 rounds and taking casualties of 3 killed and 1 wounded. Renamed *Fedot Muchenik* in 1788. Fought at Ochakov on 17.6.1788. Missed the battle of Fidonisi as a result of being assigned to the Liman squadron off Ochakov throughout the entire year. Converted into a flat-bottomed 'newly invented frigate' in 1788. Grounded on 3.1789. Repaired in 9.1790. Escorted the captured Turkish *Mulk-I-Bahr* to Ochakovi. Converted to a transport and last mentioned in 1800.

Vestnik (renamed *Arkhangel Gavriil*) 30/32 Kherson
Constructor ?
Laid down ? *Launched* ? *Purchased* 1783 *Converted* 1788
Dimensions 100 ft x 28 ft 6 in x 9 ft 6 in
Armament 1784 LD 20 x 12pdrs
UD 10 x 4pdrs (*Materialy*)
1788 4 x 18pdr carr., 2 x 5-pood 13 in mortars, 2 x 3-pood 11 in howitzers (Chernyshev)

A nominal frigate, originally built as a merchant ship, purchased in 1783 and armed as a frigate although officially referred to as a 'cruising vessel'. Converted into a bomb vessel. In 1788. Carried troops from Sevastopol' to Taganrog for the newly completed frigates. Renamed *Arkhangel Gavriil* on 19.7.1788. Broken up after 1790. (Golovachev in *History of Sevastopol* mentions that *Vestnik* (32) participated in the battle of Fidonisi in 1788 as a cruiser; the exact list of all Russian ships in that battle is not known) (See also under Black Sea bomb vessels.)

Sviatoi Antonii 30 Gnilotonskaya
Constructor ?
Laid down ?   *Launched* 1784   *Converted* 1788
Dimensions 130 ft x 32 ft 6 in x 12 ft
    125 ft x 34 ft x 13 ft 6 in (Golovachev)
Armament 1788 22 x 30pdrs (bored up)
    1790 18 x 30pdrs (bored up), 12 x 24pdrs (bored up)
    (Golovachev)
Pink no. 1 converted into a flat-bottomed 'newly invented frigate' in 1788. Stationed at Sevastopol' in 1788–90. Found unseaworthy and moved to Liman at the mouth of the Don for repairs. Destroyed by fire during repair in 1791. (See also under Black Sea pinks.)

Sviatoi Feodosii 30 Gnilotonskaya
Constructor ?
Laid down ?   *Launched* 1784   *Converted* 1788
Dimensions 130 ft x 32 ft 6 in x 12 ft
    125 ft x 34 ft x 13 ft 6 in (Golovachev)
Armament 1788 22 x 30pdrs (bored up)
    1790 18 x 30pdrs (bored up), 12 x 24pdrs (bored up)
    (Golovachev)
Pink no. 2 converted into a flat-bottomed 'newly invented frigate' in 1788. Stationed at Sevastopol' in 1788. Found unseaworthy in 1790. Last mentioned in 1791. (See also under Black Sea pinks.)

18pdr frigates (6 purpose-built 1762–1800)

These ships, all launched after 1784 were 10–15 ft shorter than standard European 18pdr frigate types and carried proportionally fewer main battery guns – 20 main deck guns in contrast to 26–28. They were in no way comparable to their Baltic contemporaries in the *Brachislav* class and give the appearance of having been little more than slightly enlarged versions of the *Vos'moi* class, with fewer, but heavier main armament guns. As was the case with their 12pdr predecessors, they do not appear to have been able to escape the Black Sea proclivity for over-gunning anything larger than a rowing boat, with five of the six having their 18pdrs replaced in 1790 by bored-out 24- and 30pdrs in a manner similar to that adopted by the 'newly invented frigates' of 1788.

Taganrog (renamed *Sviatoi Ieronim*) 30/34 Gnilotonskaya
Constructor ?
Laid down 1784   *Launched* 7.3.1785
Dimensions 128 ft x 34 ft6 in x 11 ft 1 in
Armament 1788 LD 20 x 18pdrs
    UD 10 x 6pdrs   (Admiralty Order)
    1789 LD 16 x 30pdrs (bored up)
    UD 12 x 24pdrs (bored up)
    1790 LD 18 x 12pdrs
    UD 12 x 8pdrs 4 x 18u (Golovachev)
Completed as a shallow draft frigate and converted into a bomb vessel in 1788 according to Veselago. Renamed *Sviatoi Ieronim* in 1788. Fought at Fidonisi in 1788. Participated in three wartime cruises in 1789. Cruised to Kerch, Tendra and Kaliakra in 1790–1. Fire watch ship at Sevastopol' 1792–4. Broken up after 1795.

Kinburn class (3 ships)

Kinburn (renamed *Pokrov Bogoroditsy*) 28/40 Gnilotonskaya
Constructor ?
Laid down ?   *Launched* 1786
Dimensions 130 ft x 34 ft6 in x 11 ft 9 in (Veselago)
    125 ft x 34 ft x 13 ft 6 in (Golovachev)
Armament 1788 LD 20 x 18pdrs
    UD 10 x 6pdrs (Admiralty Order)
    1790 LD 16 x 30pdrs (bored up)
    UD 12 x 24pdrs (bored up) (Golovachev)
Kinburn class. Sailed to Sevastopol' in 1787. Renamed *Pokrov Bogoroditsy* in 1788. Fought at Fidonisi in 1788. Participated in three wartime cruises in 1789. Fought at Kerch and Tendra in 1790. Found unseaworthy in 1791 and converted into a hulk.

Berislav (renamed *Luka Evangelist*) 28/40 Gnilotonskaya
Constructor ?
Laid down ?   *Launched* 1786
Dimensions 130 ft x 34 ft6 in x 11 ft 9 in
    125 ft x 34 ft x 13 ft 6 in (Golovachev)
Armament 1788 LD 20 x 18pdrs
    UD 10 x 6pdrs (Admiralty Order)
    1790 LD 16 x 30pdrs (bored up)
    UD 12 x 24pdrs (bored up) (Golovachev)
Kinburn class. Named after a captured Turkish fortress. Sailed to Sevastopol' in 1787. Renamed *Luka Evangelist* in 1788. Fought at Fidonisi in 1788. Participated in three wartime cruises in 1789. Determined to be in poor condition in 1790 and broken up in 12.1790.

Fanagoriia (renamed *Prepodobnyi Nestor*) 28/40 Gnilotonskaya
Constructor ?
Laid down ?   *Launched* 1786
Dimensions 130 ft x 34 ft6 in x 11 ft 9 in
    121 ft x 34 ft x 11 ft (Golovachev)
Armament 1788 LD 20 x 18pdrs
    FC & QD 10 x 6pdrs (Admiralty Order)
    1790 LD 16 x 30pdrs (bored up)
    FC & QD 12 x 24pdrs (bored up) (Golovachev)
    1790 LD 24 x 12pdrs
    FC & QD 2 x 8pdrs 10 x 6pdrs 4 x 18u (Golovachev)
Kinburn class. Sailed to Sevastopol' in 1787. Renamed *Prepodobnyi Nestor* in 1788. Fought at Fidonisi in 1788. Participated in three wartime cruises in 1789. Fought at Kerch and Tendra in 1790 and at Kaliakra in 1791. Broken up after 1795.

Ioann Zlatoust 32/36 Taganrog
Constructor Fursov
Laid down ?   *Launched* 16.7.1791
Dimensions 130 ft x 36 ft x 14 ft
    121 ft x 34 ft x 11 ft (Golovachev)
Armament 1790 LD 20 x 18pdrs
    UD 12 x 24u (½ pood) (planned armament)
    1790 LD 16 x 30pdrs (bored up)
    FC & QD 12 x 24pdrs (bored up)
Sailed to Sevastopol' in 1792. Cruised in the Black Sea in 1793–4, and 1798. Participated in Vice-Adm. Ushakov's Mediterranean campaign from 1798–1800. Returned to Sevastopol' in 6.1800. Cruised in the Black Sea in 1801–3. Transported troops to Corfu in 1804, while armed *en flute*. Returned to the Black Sea in 1804 and cruised off the Caucasus in 1804–6. In 1807, as part of Rear-Adm. S. Pustoshkin's squadron, participated in the taking of Anapa and the bombardment of Trabizon. Operated off Anapa in 1809. Bombarded Trabizon a second time in 1810. Cruised in the Black Sea in 1811–12. Served as fire watch ship at Sevastopol' in 1813–15. No further mention.

Schastlivyi 36 Kherson
Constructor A. S. Katasanov

Laid down 21.1.1793 *Launched* 18.9.1793
Dimensions 124 ft x 34 ft 6 in x 14 ft
Armament ?

Sailed to Sevastopol' in 1794. Cruised in the Black Sea in 1795–7. Participated in Vice-Adm. Ushakov's Mediterranean campaign from 1798–9. Returned to Nikolaev with transports in 1799. Deployed to Zante and back in 1800. Involved in hydrographic survey work in 1801. Training ship with naval cadets in 1804. Broken up after 1805.

Small frigates (2 purpose-built, 10 purchased or converted 1762–1800)

These ships were a hotchpotch of unrelated types, many of them converted merchantmen and they would probably all have been rated as ship sloops in Great Britain. Not all dimensions are known, but it appears that the upper limit was 100 ft in length. Three were completed with massive 30pdr batteries, but these appear to have been quickly replaced in service by 18pdrs. Even when armed with 12- and 18pdr guns, the Russian 'small frigates' of this period were heavily over gunned in comparison with similarly sized British ship sloops with 6pdr main batteries. The Black Sea small frigates of this period were a mixed bag of unrelated designs and most ended up as either 'newly invented frigates' or bomb vessels. While serving nominally as frigates, they were frequently employed as transports and cargo carriers.

Pochtal'on (renamed *Nikita Muchenik*) 20/24 Olonetskaya
Constructor I. I. Afanasyev
Laid down 27.9.1765 *Launched* 27.5.1766
Dimensions 95 ft x 25 ft x 9 ft 6 in (95 ft x 27 ft x 8 ft 6 in
 (as modified) (Veselago)
Armament 1784 LD 18 x 12pdrs 2 x 60 u (1 pood)
 FC & QD 8 x 4pdrs 4 x 3pdr falconets (Veselago)
 1790 2 x 18pdrs 18 x 12pdrs (Golovachev)

Originally built in 1766 for the Baltic fleet as a packet boat. Transferred from the Arkhipelago to the Black Sea in 1775 and reclassified as a small frigate. Cruised in the Black Sea in 1776–8. Fire watch ship at Kerch in 1780. Repaired in 1783 and sailed from Taganrog to Sevastopol'. Transported crews to Taganrog for 'newly built frigates'. Converted into a 'newly invented floating battery' in 1788 and renamed *Nikita Muchenik*. Found unfit for further service as a cruiser and relegated to fire watch service at Sevastopol' from 1788–91. Broken up after 1791. (See also under Black Sea fleet Bombs and Baltic fleet packet boats.)

Grigorii Bogoslov (ex-*Boristen*) 14/18 Kherson
Constructor M. L. Faleev
Laid down ? *Launched* 1781
Dimensions 112 ft x 30 ft 6 in x 13 ft (Veselago)
 96 ft x 35 ft x 12 ft (Golovachev)
Armament 1788 14 x 30pdrs
 1789 14 x 18pdrs 4 x 12u
 1790 14 x 24pdrs (bored up), 4 x 12u (¼ pood)
 (Golovachev)

Completed as a merchant ship *Boristen* (named after the ancient Greek name for the Dnieper). Converted into a flat-bottomed 'newly invented frigate' in 1788 by M. L. Faleev. Fought at Ochakov on 17.6.1788 as part of the Liman flotilla. Broken up after 1791. (See also under Sea of Azov cargo vessels.)

Grigorii Velikiia Armenii (ex-*Pchela*) 24/26 Kherson
Constructor M. L. Faleev
Laid down 14.1.1781 *Launched* 30.9.1782 *Converted* 1788

Dimensions 91 ft 6 in x 24 ft 6 in x 11 ft 6 in (Veselago)
 93 ft x 25 ft x 12 ft 6 in (Golovachev)
Armament 1788 10 x 30pdrs
 1789 6 x 18pdrs (brass), 4 x 60 u (1 pood), 2 x 18u 4 x 12 u
 1790 12 x 18pdrs, 4 12pdrs (edinorogs?) (Golovachev)
 1790 12 x 6pdrs, 4 x 3pdrs (Golovachev)

Merchant ship *Pchela* built in 1782 and converted into a flat-bottomed 'newly invented frigate' in 1788 by M. L. Faleev who, as head of logistics, was normally involved with the construction of small craft. Assigned to the Liman squadron in the mouth of the Don. Fought at Ochakov on 17.6.1788. Transferred to Sevastopol' in 1790. Assigned as a fire watch ship in 1791 and later converted into a transport. Last listed in 1806. (May be the *Grigorii* (24) listed by Anderson at Corfu in 1806.) (See also under Sea of Azov cargo vessels.)

Ioann Zlatoust (ex-*Taganrog*) 10/16 ?
Constructor M. L. Faleev
Laid down ? *Launched* 1785 *Converted* 1788
Dimensions 93 ft x 25 ft x 12 ft 6 in (Golovachev)
Armament 1788 10 x 30pdrs
 1789 (planned rearmament) 12 x 18pdrs, 4 12pdrs
 (Golovachev)
 1790 12 x 18pdrs, 4 12pdrs (Golovachev)

Merchant ship *Taganrog* converted into a flat-bottomed 'newly invented frigate' in 1788 by M. L. Faleev. Fought at Ochakov on 17.6.1788 as part of the Liman flotilla. Damaged by ice in the Dnieper and sunk in 1788. (See also under Black Sea transports.)

Filipp 24 ?
Constructor ?
Laid down ? *Launched* 1788 *Converted* 1792?
Dimensions ?
Armament LD 18 x 12pdrs
 FC & QD 6 x 6pdrs (Golovachev)

Originally a small frigate converted from a galiot *Tsaplia*. Converted into a bomb-vessel, probably in 1792. (See also under Black Sea galiots.)

Iona 24 ?
Constructor ?
Laid down ? *Launched* 1788 *Converted* 1792?
Dimensions ?
Armament LD 18 x 12pdrs
 FC & QD 6 x 6pdrs (Golovachev)

Originally a small frigate converted from a galiot *Te'ermol*. Converted into a bomb-vessel, probably in 1792. (See also under Black Sea Galiots where she is listed as *Termernik*.)

Sviatoi Sergei Chudotvorets 20 Khoper
Constructor ?
Laid down ? *Launched* ? *Converted* 1788
Dimensions ?
Armament 1790 LD 20 x 30pdrs

Kater (Cutter) no. 1 converted into a 'newly invented frigate' in 1788. Sailed to Taganrog in 1789 and to Sevastopol' in 1791. Cruised in the Black Sea in 1795. Converted to a store ship in 1797. Fire watch service in the Sevastopol' Roads in 1798–1802. Broken up after 1802.

Sviatoi Nikolai Chudotvorets 20 Khoper
Constructor ?
Laid down ? *Launched* ? *Converted* 1788
Dimensions ?

Armament 1790 LD 20 x 30pdrs (probable)
Kater (Cutter) no. 2 converted to a 'newly invented frigate' in 1788.

Sviatoi Nikolai Belomorskiy 20 ?
Constructor ?
Laid down ?   *Launched* ? *Purchased* 1792
Dimensions 87 ft x 24 ft x 9 ft 6 in
Armament ?
Purchased in the Mediterranean and assigned to the Black Sea fleet in 1792. Cruised in the Black Sea in 1797–8. Carried 100 tons of supplies to Corfu in 1797 and returned to Sevastopol. Visited Corfu in 1801. Wintered in Istanbul in 1801–2. Brought home the guns of the frigate *Navarkhiia*. Cruised in the Black Sea in 1802. Transported troops and supplies to Corfu in 1804 and returned to Sevastopol. Fire watch ship at Nikolaev in 1806. Cargo service between Black Sea ports in 1807–8. Broken up after 1808.

Sviatoi Matvei 16 ?
Constructor ?
Laid down ?   *Launched* ?   Purchased   1792
Dimensions 87 ft x 23 ft in x 10 ft 6 in
Armament ?
Purchased in the Mediterranean and assigned to the Black Sea fleet in 1792. Transported cargo between Black Sea ports in 1794–7. Broken up in 1804.

Pospeshnyi 32 Taganrog
Constructor I. Dolzhnikov
Laid down 6.10.1791   *Launched* 26.7.1793
Dimensions 100 ft x 30 ft x 14 ft
Armament ?
Sailed to Sevastopol' in 1794. Cruised in the Black Sea in 1797. Transported 100 tons of supplies to Corfu for Vice-Adm. Ushakov's squadron and returned with sick and injured in 1798. Transported supplies to Zante (near Corfu) in 1800. Wrecked off the Bosporus on 9.10.1800 with loss of captain and 12 crew members.

Legkii 26 Nikolaev
Constructor A.P. Sokolov
Laid down 23.11.1790 *Launched* 2.10.1793
Dimensions 100 ft x 30 ft x 14 ft
Armament ?
Fire watch duty off Ochakov in 1794–9. Transported supplies to Vice-Adm. Ushakov's squadron at Istanbul in 11.1800. Broken up in 1804.

Black Sea schooners (8 purpose-built 1762–1800)

Schooners were the smallest purpose-built warships in the Black Sea fleet. During this period, they were not much in demand, with only 4 being built in the 1770s, 2 in the 1780s and 2 in the 1790s.

Pobedoslav-Dunaiskii class (4 ships)
Pobedoslav-Dunaiskii 12 Danube River
Constructor M. I. Ryabinin
Laid down 26.5.1772, *Launched* 2.12.1772
Dimensions 90 ft x 25 ft 4 in x 11 ft 4 in (Veselago)
Armament 1772 12 x 12pdrs
           1784 18 x 6pdrs
Pobedoslav-Dunaiskii class (4 ships). Purpose-built schooner built to the plan of Adm. Knowles. Assigned to the Danube flotilla in 1772. Cruised in 1772–4. Transferred to the Azov fleet in 1775. Cruised in 1775–9. Repaired at Taganrog in 1780. Cruised in 1782–3. Reassigned to the Black Sea fleet in 1783. Fire watch ship at Kozlov 1784–8. Fought at the battle of Fidonisi in 7.3.1788. No further mention.

Vecheslav 12 Danube River
Constructor M. I. Ryabinin
Laid down 26.5.1772 *Launched* 5.3.1773
Dimensions 90 ft x 25 ft 3 in x 11 ft 4 (Veselago)
Armament 1772 12 x 12pdrs
           1784 18 x 6pdrs
Pobedoslav-Dunaiskii class (4 ships). Purpose-built schooner built to the plan of Adm. Knowles. Assigned to the Danube flotilla in 1772. Cruised in 1773–4. Transferred to the Azov fleet in 1775. Cruised in 1775–9. Repaired at Taganrog in 1780. Cruised in 1782–6. Reassigned to the Black Sea fleet in 1783. Fire watch ship at Sevastopol' in 1787. No further data.

Izmail 12 Danube River
Constructor M.I. Ryabinin
Laid down 6.6.1772, *Launched* 14.3.1773
Dimensions 90 ft x 25 ft 3 in x 11 ft 4 in (Veselago)
Armament 1772 12 x 12pdrs
           1784 18 x 6pdrs
Pobedoslav-Dunaiskii class (4 ships). Purpose-built schooner built to the plan of Adm. Knowles. Named after a Turkish fortress taken in 1770. Assigned to the Danube flotilla in 1772. Cruised in 1773–4. Transferred to the Azov fleet in 1775. Fire watch ship at the mouth of the Dnieper in 1775. Cruised in 1776–80. Repaired at Taganrog in 1781. Cruised in 1782. Reassigned to the Black Sea fleet in 1783. Fire watch ship at Feodosii in 1783–5. Carried the Russian envoy to Istanbul in 1787 and captured by the Turks upon the declaration of war.

Brailov 12 Danube River
Constructor M.I. Ryabinin
Laid down 6.6.1772 *Launched* 14.4.1773
Dimensions 90 ft x 25 ft 3 in x 11 ft 4 in (Veselago)
Armament 1772 12 x 12pdrs
           1784 18 x 6pdrs
Pobedoslav-Dunaiskii class (4 ships). Purpose-built schooner built to the plan of Adm. Knowles. Named after a Turkish fortress taken in 1770. Assigned to the Danube flotilla in 1772. Cruised in 1773–4. Transferred to the Azov fleet in 1775. Wrecked in a winter storm on 30.1.1775 without casualties.

Kur'er class (2 ships)
Kur'er 16 Gnilotonskaya
Constructor ?
Laid down ?   *Launched* 1783
Dimensions ?
Armament 12 x 3pdrs, 4-falconets
Kur'er class. Purpose-built schooner. Stationed at Sevastopol' 1784–6. Fire watch ship at Kozlov in 1787. No further mention.

Sokol 16 Gnilotonskaya
Constructor ?
Laid down ?   *Launched* 1783
Dimensions ?
Armament 12 x 3pdrs, 4 falconets
Kur'er class. Purpose-built schooner. Cruised in 1783. Fire watch ship at Kerch in 1786. At Sevastopol' in 1790. No further mention.

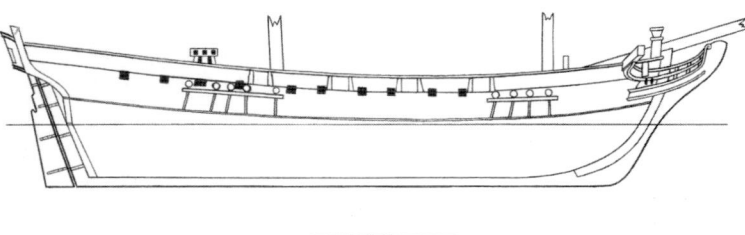

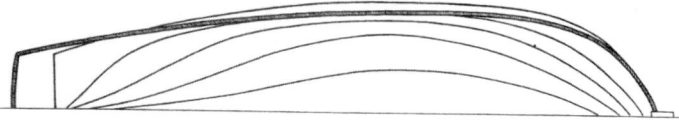

Schooners were of limited value in the Black Sea environment. Many of those built received only hull numbers in place of names. This is a draught of schooner no. 1, completed in 1795 and originally employed with the rowing flotilla. In spite of her modest size and armament, she was transferred to Corfu as part of Vice-Admiral Ushakov's Ionian squadron in 1798 where she was probably of considerable use for inshore work in the Adriatic.

Schooner no. 1 8 Sevastopol'
Constructor ?
Laid down 1794   *Launched* 18.8.1795
Dimensions 78 ft x 24 ft x 9 ft 9 in (Veselago)
Armament ?
Numbered schooner built for the rowing flotilla. Cruised in the Black Sea in 1797. Transferred to Corfu as part of Vice-Adm. Ushakov's squadron in 1798.

Schooner no. 2 8 Sevastopol'
Constructor ?
Laid down 1794   *Launched* 19.11.1795
Dimensions 78 ft x 24 ft x 9 ft 9 in (Veselago)
Armament ?
Numbered schooner built for the rowing flotilla. Cruised in the Black Sea in 1798–1800. Fire watch ship at Odessa 1801–2.

Black Sea fleet bomb vessels (3 purpose-built, 13 converted, 1 purchased 1762–1800)

Purpose-built
Given the amphibious nature of the Russo-Turkish War of 1787–91, Russia's acquisition of 17 purpose-built, converted, and purchased bomb vessels comes as no surprise. Most mounted a pair of mortars and a pair of howitzers for inshore work, very modest firepower by later standards.

Sviatoi Nikon 18/22 Khoper
Constructor Kotsov
Laid down 1788   *Launched* 1789
Dimensions 111 ft x 40 ft 6 in x 17 ft (Veselago)
Armament 1790 2 x 12pdrs, 6 x 8pdrs, 4 x 24u (½ pood), 6 x 12u
            (¼ pood) (Golovachev)
Purpose-built bomb vessel. Sailed to Taganrog in 1790. Arrived at Sevastopol' in 6.1791 after the end of hostilities. Disarmed and used as a transport. (See also under Black Sea converted transports.)

Sergii Radonezhskii 18/22 Khoper
Constructor Kotsov
Laid down 1788   *Launched* 1789
Dimensions approx. 115 ft x 43 ft x 11 ft (35.1 m x 13.1 m x 3.4 m)
            (Chernyshev)
Armament 1790 2 x 12pdrs 6 x 8pdrs 4 x 24 u (½ pood) 6 x 12 u
            (¼ pood) (Golovachev)
Purpose-built bomb vessel. Sailed to Taganrog in 1790. Arrived at Sevastopol' in 6.1791 after the end of hostilities. Disarmed and used as a transport.

Novopavlovsk 15 Novopavlovsk
Constructor S. I. Afanasyev
Laid down 1788   *Launched* 1789
Dimensions 66 ft x 18 ft 6 in x 8 ft 3 in (Veselago)
Armament ?
Purpose-built bomb vessel. Sailed to Taganrog in 1789. Cruised in the Sea of Azov in 1796–1803. Fire watch duties at Kerch and Taganrog. Broken up in 1804.

Converted from other classes
Pervyi (*First*) 10 Ikoretskaya
Constructor S. I. Afanasyev
Laid down 7.9.1769   *Launched* 19.3.1770
Dimensions approx. 60 ft x 17 x 6 ft (18.3 m x 5.2 m x 1.8 m)
            (Chernyshev)
Armament 8 x 3pdrs, 1 x 2-pood mortar, 1 x 1-pood howitzer
            60 men
'Newly invented bomb vessel'. Arrived at Taganrog in 1770. Operated with Vice-Adm. A. N. Seniavin's squadron in 1771. Foundered in the Sea of Azov on 29.5.1771 with loss of the captain and 32 crew members.

Vtoroi (*Second*) 10 Ikoretskaya
Constructor S. I. Afanasyev
Laid down 7.9.1769   *Launched* 26.5.1770
Dimensions approx. 60 ft x 17 ft x 6 ft (18.3 m x 5.2 m x 1.8 m)
            (Chernyshev)
Armament 8 x 3pdrs, 1 x 2-pood mortar, 1 x 1-pood howitzer
            60 men
'Newly invented bomb vessel'. Arrived at Taganrog in 1770. Operated with Vice-Adm. A.N. Seniavin's squadron in the Sea of Azov and the Black Sea in 1771–4. Fire watch ship at Taganrog and Kerch in 1775–8. No further mention.

Iassy 14 Ikoretskaya
Constructor ?
Laid down ?   *Launched* 26.5.1770
Dimensions 86 ft x 24 ft 6 in x 8 ft (Veselago)
Armament 12 x 6pdrs, 2 x 3 pood mortars
            60 men
Bomb vessel converted from a transport. Arrived at Taganrog in 1771. Cruised in 1771–5. Converted back into a transport in 1778–9. Lost in 1785.

Bomb no. 1 8 Kiev
Constructor ?
Laid down ?   *Launched* ? *Converted* 1787
Dimensions 75 ft x 19 ft x 4 ft 6 in (Veselago)
Armament ?
            113 men
Bomb vessel converted from a transport built for Catherine II. In action with the Turks at Liman and Ochakov in 1788.

Bomb no. 2 7 Kiev
Constructor ?
Laid down ?   *Launched* ?   *Converted* 1787
Dimensions 70 ft x 19 ft x 4 ft 6 in (Veselago)
Armament ?
        98 men
Bomb vessel converted from a transport built for Catherine II. In action with the Turks at Liman and Ochakov in 1788.

Nikita Muchenik (ex-*Pochtal'on*) 8 ?
Constructor ?
Laid down 27.9.1765   *Launched* 27.5.1766   *Converted* 1788
Dimensions approx. 95 ft x 27 ft x 8½ ft (28.9 m x 3.2 m x 2.6 m) (Chernyshev)
Armament 4 x 18pdrs, 2 mortars, 2 howitzers (as converted)
'Newly invented floating battery', converted from frigate *Pochtal'on* in 1788. Fire watch ship at Sevastopol' in 1788–91. Broken up after 1791. (See also under Black Sea fleet small frigates and Baltic fleet packet boats.)

Arkhangel Gavriil (ex-*Vestnik*) 8 Kherson
Constructor ?
Laid down ?   *Launched* 1781   *Converted* 1788
Dimensions 100 ft x 28 ft 6 in x 9 ft 6 in (Veselago)
Armament 4 x 18pdrs, 2 mortars, 2 howitzers
Bomb vessel converted from frigate *Vestnik* in 1788 (renamed 19.7.1788). Stationed at Sevastopol' in 1788–91. Broken up after 1791. (See also under Black Sea early frigates.)

Spiridon Trimifiiskii 6 ?
Constructor ?
Laid down ?   *Launched* ?   *Converted* 1788
Dimensions 70 ft x 19 ft x 9 ft (Veselago)
Armament 4 x 18pdrs, 2 x 3 pood howitzers
Bomb vessel converted from boat *Bityug* in 1788. Stationed at Dnieper Liman in 1788–91. Broken up after 1791.

Rozhdestvo Bogoroditsy 4/8 ?
Constructor ?
Laid down ?   *Launched* ?   *Converted* 1788
Dimensions 84 ft x 24 ft x 9 ft (Veselago)
Armament 4 cannons, 2 mortars, 2 howitzers
Bomb vessel converted from a transport in 1788. Took part in the battle of Tendra in 1790 and in the battle of Kaliakra in 1791. Stationed at Sevastopol' in 1792–7. Converted back into a transport in 1797. (See also under Black Sea converted transports.)

Sviatoi Pyotr class (4 ships)
Sviatoi Pyotr 8 Glubokaya Pristan
Constructor ?
Laid down 1778   *Launched* 1779   *Converted* 1788
Dimensions 80 ft x 24 ft x 11 ft (Veselago)
Armament 4 x 18pdrs, 2 mortars, 2 howitzers
Sviatoi Pyotr class. Bomb vessel converted from the galiot *Taruntul* in 1788 and intended for the actions at Liman, but completed after the fact. (See under Black Sea galiots.)

Aleksei 8 Glubokaya Pristan
Constructor ?
Laid down 2.1773   *Launched* 1774   *Converted* 1788
Dimensions 80 ft x 24 ft x 11 ft (Veselago)
Armament 4 x 18pdrs, 2 mortars, 2 howitzers
Sviatoi Pyotr class. Bomb vessel converted from the galiot *Verbliud* in 1788 and intended for the actions at Liman, but completed after the fact. (See under Black Sea galiots.)

Iona 8 Glubokaya Pristan
Constructor ?
Laid down 1782   *Launched* 1783   *Converted* 1788
Dimensions 80 ft x 24 ft x 11 ft (Veselago)
Armament 4 x 18pdrs, 2 mortars, 2 howitzers
Sviatoi Pyotr class. Bomb vessel converted from the galiot *Temerik* in 1788 and intended for the actions at Liman, but completed after the fact. (See under Black Sea galiots.)

Filipp 8 Glubokaya Pristan
Constructor ?
Laid down 1778   *Launched* 1779   *Converted* 1788
Dimensions 80 ft x 24 ft x 11 ft (Veselago)
Armament 4 x 18pdrs, 2 mortars, 2 howitzers
Sviatoi Pyotr class. Bomb vessel converted from the galiot *Tsalplya* in 1788 and intended for the actions at Liman, but completed after the fact. (See under Black Sea galiots.)

Purchased abroad
Konstantin 4/8 Marseille
Constructor ?
Laid down ?   *Launched* 1777   *Purchased* 1788
Dimensions 84 ft x 24 ft x 9 ft (Veselago)
Armament 4 cannons, 2 mortars, 2 howitzers
Transport purchased from France and converted into a bomb vessel in 1788. In action with the Turks in 1789–90. Assigned to the Danube Flotilla in 1790. Hit and destroyed by a Turkish bomb while bombarding Izmail on 10.12.1790. All hands lost.

Purchased cruising vessels (38 purchased 1762–1800)

The Black Sea fleet in its early years was a top-heavy organization with a respectable number of line of battle ships and heavy frigates, and inadequate support in the form of scouting and logistical support vessels. A large and heterogeneous collection of smaller ship types was purchased during the Russo-Turkish War of 1787–91 for lower end functions ranging from scouting and raiding to more mundane cargo and transport work. Their employment was not disimilar to the use of Greek privateers in the Arkhipelago campaign in the previous Russo-Turkish War from 1768–74. They were largely acquired from Black Sea or Arkhipelago Greek owners and took an active part in the war with Turkey in 1787–91, frequently in combat roles. Many of them retained their original Greek names. Most had brig or brigantine rigs. During the war, *Lifartun* founderd and *Konductor* was lost to accidental explosion. Most were discarded at the war's end but some were retained. *Printsessa Elena* was wrecked in 1797 and *Berezan'* in 1798 while, the longest surviving vessel was *Panagiia Apotumengano*, which was in service at least until 1813.

Abel'tazh 14/18 ?
Constructor ?
Laid down ?   *Launched* ?   *Purchased* 1787
Dimensions 80 ft x 24 ft 6 in x 9 ft 3 in (Veselago)
Armament ?
        52 men

Purchased brigantine. Active in the Black Sea against the Turks in 1788–91. Converted into a transport 1793–1800.

Aleksandr 16 ?
Constructor ?
Laid down ? *Launched* ? *Purchased* 1787
Dimensions 60 ft x 23 ft x 10 ft (Veselago)
Armament ?
Purchased vessel. Active in the Black Sea against the Turks in 1788–90. No further mention.

Berezan' 6/14 ?
Constructor ?
Laid down ? *Launched* ? *Purchased* 1787
Dimensions 78 ft x 23 ft x 10 ft (Veselago)
Armament ?
             39/40 men
Purchased vessel. Active in the Black Sea against the Turks in 1788–91. Cruised in the Black Sea in 1793–8. Wrecked at the entrance to Sevastopol' in 1798. No casualties.

Bogoroditsa Pskovskaya ? ?
Constructor ?
Laid down ? *Launched* ? *Purchased* 1787
Dimensions ?
Armament ?
Purchased vessel. Employed as a cargo ship between Kherson and Taganrog and Sevastopol. Fate is indeterminate.

Donai 12 ?
Constructor ?
Laid down ? *Launched* ? *Purchased* 1787
Dimensions 71 ft 6 in x 23 ft 2 in x 8 ft 10 in (Veselago)
Armament ?
Purchased vessel. Active in the Black Sea against the Turks in 1788–91. No further mention.

Karl Konstantin 10 ?
Constructor ?
Laid down ? *Launched* ? *Purchased* 1787
Dimensions ?
Armament ?
             42/43 men
Purchased vessel. Active in the Black Sea against the Turks in 1788–91. No further mention.

Keko Tavro 12 ?
Constructor ?
Laid down ? *Launched* ? *Purchased* 1787
Dimensions ?
Armament ?
             42 men
Purchased vessel. Active in the Black Sea against the Turks in 1788–91. No further mention.

Konductor ? ?
Constructor ?
Laid down ? *Launched* ? *Purchased* 1787
Dimensions ?
Armament ?
Purchased vessel. Active in the Black Sea against the Turks in 1788–90.

Accidentally blown up at Sevastopol' on 16.2.1790.

Panagiia Apotogrilli ? ?
Constructor ?
Laid down ? *Launched* ? *Purchased* 1787
Dimensions 59 ft 6 in x 22 ft 3 in x 8 ft 10 in (Veselago)
Armament ?
Purchased vessel. Sailed from Taganrog to Kerch in 1787. Active in the Black Sea against the Turks in 1788–91. No further mention.

Panagiia Apotokofory ? ?
Constructor ?
Laid down ? *Launched* ? *Purchased* 1787
Dimensions ?
Armament ?
Purchased vessel. Sailed from Taganrog to Kerch and then Sevastopol. Active in the Black Sea against the Turks in 1788–90.

Panagiia Apotumengano 14/16 ?
Constructor ?
Laid down ? *Launched* ? *Purchased* 1787
Dimensions ?
Armament ?   53/55/76 men
Purchased brig. Sailed from Taganrog to Kerch and then Sevastopol. Active in the Black Sea against the Turks in 1788–91. Cruised in 1792–8 in the Black Sea. In the Mediterranean in 1798–1800 in Adm. Ushakov's squadron. Carried cargo in the Black Sea in 1801–6. Active in the campaigns against the Turks in 1809–12. Sailed from Sevastopol' to Glubokaya Pristan in 1813. No further mention.

Panagiia Turleni 10 ?
Constructor ?
Laid down ? *Launched* ? *Purchased* 1787
Dimensions 68 ft x 21 ft x 9 ft (Veselago)
Armament ?   42 men
Purchased vessel. Sailed from Taganrog to Kerch and then Sevastopol. Active in the Black Sea against the Turks in 1788–91. Cruised in Black Sea in 1792–7 in the Black Sea. Fire watch ship at Odessa in 1798. No further mention.

Panagiia Kaligati 8 ?
Constructor ?
Laid down ? *Launched* ? *Purchased* 1787
Dimensions ?
Armament ?
Purchased vessel. Sailed from Taganrog to Kerch and then Sevastopol. Active in the Black Sea against the Turks in 1788–91. No further mention.

Panagiia Popandi ? ?
Constructor ?
Laid down ? *Launched* ? *Purchased* 1787
Dimensions 63' x 30 ft x 9 ft (Veselago)
Armament ?   50 men
Purchased vessel. Sailed from Taganrog to Kerch and then Sevastopol. Active in the Black Sea against the Turks in 1788–91. No further mention.

Prints Aleksandr 12/14 ?
Constructor ?
Laid down ? *Launched* ? *Purchased* 1787
Dimensions 75 ft x 28 ft x 12½ ft (Veselago)
Armament ?   40/50 men

Purchased vessel. Active in the Black Sea against the Turks in 1788–91. Cruised in the Black Sea as a cargo vessel in 1792–7. Broken up at Taganrog in 1804.

Printsessa Elena 16/20 ?
Constructor ?
Laid down ?   *Launched* ?   *Purchased* 1787
Dimensions 74 ft 6 in x 27 ft 6 in x 10 ft 2 in (Veselago)
Armament ?   53 men
Purchased vessel. Active in the Black Sea against the Turks in 1788–91. Cruised in the Black Sea as a cargo vessel in 1793–7. Lost in a storm at Odessa Roads without casualties in 1797.

Aleksandr 16 ?
Constructor ?
Laid down ?   *Launched* ?   *Purchased* 1787
Dimensions approx. 74½ ft x 22 ft x 7½ ft (22.7 m x 6.8 m x 2.3 m) (Chernyshev)
Armament ?   44 men
Purchased brigantine. Active in the Black Sea against the Turks in 1788–91. Converted to cargo ship. No further mention.

Sviatoi Nikolai I ? ?
Constructor ?
Laid down ?   *Launched* ?   *Purchased* 1787
Dimensions 55 ft 6 in x 23 ft x 8 ft (Veselago)
Armament ?
Purchased vessel. Named to commemorate the capture of Ochakov on the Saint Day of St Nicholas in 1788. Sailed from Taganrog to Kerch and Sevastopol. Converted to cargo ship. Broken up in 1804.

Sviatoi Nikolai II ? ?
Constructor ?
Laid down ?   *Launched* ?   *Purchased* 1787
Dimensions 71 ft 6 in x 22 ft 6 in x 8 ft 10 in (Veselago)
Armament ?
Purchased vessel. Named to commemorate the capture of Ochakov on the saint day of St Nicholas in 1788. Sailed from Taganrog to Kerch and Sevastopol. Converted to cargo ship. No further mention.

Sviatoi Nikolai III 16 ?
Constructor ?
Laid down ?   *Launched* ?   *Purchased* 1787
Dimensions ?
Armament ?
   43 men
Purchased vessel. Named to commemorate the capture of Ochakov on the Saint Day of St Nicholas in 1788. Sailed from Taganrog to Kerch and Sevastopol. Active in the Black Sea against the Turks in 1788–91. Cruised in the Black Sea in 1792–8 as a cargo ship.

Paraskeva ? ?
Constructor ?
Laid down ?   *Launched* ?   *Purchased* 1787
Dimensions ?
Armament ?
Purchased vessel. Sailed from Taganrog to Kerch and Sevastopol. Active in the Black Sea against the Turks in 1788–91. No further mention.

Sviataia Tat'iana ? ?
Constructor ?
Laid down ?   *Launched* ?   *Purchased* 1787
Dimensions ?
Armament ?
Purchased vessel. Sailed from Taganrog to Kerch and Sevastopol. Active in the Black Sea against the Turks in 1788–91. No further mention.

Feniks 12 ?
Constructor ?
Laid down ?   *Launched* ?   *Purchased* 1787
Dimensions 80 ft x 24 ft x 9 ft 6 in (Veselago)
Armament ?
   52 men
Purchased brig. Sailed from Taganrog to Kerch and Sevastopol. Active in the Black Sea against the Turks in 1788–91. Cruised in the Black Sea in 1794–1802. Broken up in 1803.

Sviatoi Andrei 4/16 ?
Constructor ?
Laid down ?   *Launched* ?   *Purchased* 1788
Dimensions 75 ft x 22 ft 6 in x 7 ft 6 in (Veselago)
Armament ?
Purchased brigantine. Sailed from Taganrog to Kerch and Sevastopol. Active in the Black Sea against the Turks in 1788–91. Cruised in the Black Sea in 1792–8. Broken up in 1804.

Georgii Pobedonosets ? ?
Constructor ?
Laid down ?   *Launched* ?   *Purchased* 1788
Dimensions ?
Armament ?
Purchased vessel. Active in the Black Sea against the Turks in 1788–91. No further mention.

Krasnolsely 14 ?
Constructor ?
Laid down ?   *Launched* ?   *Purchased* 1788
Dimensions 70 ft x 21 ft 6 in x 8 ft 6 in (Veselago)
Armament ?
   40/92 men
Purchased brigantine. Active in the Black Sea against the Turks in 1788–91. Cruised in the Black Sea in 1794. Operated in the Mediterranean in 1798–1800 with Ushakov's squadron. Broken up in 1804.

Mogileti 4/6 ?
Constructor ?
Laid down ?   *Launched* ?   *Purchased* 1788
Dimensions approx. 71 ft x 22 ft x 12 ft (21.7 m x 6.7 m x 3.7 m) (Chernyshev)
Armament ?
   44/48 men
Purchased vessel. Active in the Black Sea against the Turks in 1788–91. Cruised in the Black Sea in 1794. Operated in the Mediterranean in 1798–1800 with Ushakov's squadron. Cruised in the Black Sea in 1801–5. No further mention.

Nadezhda Blagopoluchiia ? ?
Constructor ?
Laid down ?   *Launched* ?   *Purchased* 1788
Dimensions ?

Armament ?

Purchased vessel. Active in the Black Sea against the Turks in 1790–1. No further mention.

Sviatoi Spiridon 18 ?
Constructor ?
Laid down ? *Launched* ? *Purchased* 1788
Dimensions ?
Armament ?

Purchased vessel. Active in the Black Sea against the Turks in 1790–1. Fire watch ship at Nikolaev in 1793. No further mention.

Slava Georgiia Pobedonostsa 8 ?
Constructor ?
Laid down ? *Launched* ? *Purchased* 1789
Dimensions ?
Armament ?
   42 men

Purchased brigantine. Active in the Black Sea against the Turks in 1790–1. No further mention.

Graf Severnyi 12 ?
Constructor ?
Laid down ? *Launched* ? *Purchased* 1789
Dimensions ?
Armament ?

Purchased vessel. Active in the Black Sea against the Turks in 1791. Cruised in the Black Sea in 1792–3. No further mention.

Dmitrii Solunskii ? ?
Constructor ?
Laid down ? *Launched* ? *Purchased* 1789
Dimensions 70 ft x 25 ft x 9 ft 7 in (Veselago)
Armament ?

Purchased vessel. Active in the Black Sea against the Turks in 1790–1. No further mention.

Kliment Papa 18 ?
Constructor ?
Laid down ? *Launched* ? *Purchased* 1789
Dimensions ?
Armament ?
   60 men

Purchased brigantine. Active in the Black Sea against the Turks in 1790–1. No further mention.

Lifartun (*Le Fortune*) ? ?
Constructor ?
Laid down ? *Launched* ? *Purchased* 1789
Dimensions approx. 64 ft x 20 ft x 8½ ft (19.5 m x 6 m x 2.6 m) (Chernyshev)
Armament ?

Purchased vessel. Rated as a poleacre. Active in the Black Sea against the Turks in 1790–1. Foundered due to excessive dry rot on 8.5.1791.

Sviatoi Vasilii 18 ?
Constructor ?
Laid down ? *Launched* ? *Purchased* 1789
Dimensions 70 ft x 20 ft x 10½ ft (Veselago)
Armament LD 14 x 24pdrs
   FC & QD 4 12pdrs

Purchased vessel. Active in the Black Sea against the Turks in 1790–1. Carried cargo in 1792–3. No further mention.

Panagiya Turlyeni 12 ?
Constructor ?
Laid down ? *Launched* ? *Purchased* c. 1789
Dimensions ?
Armament ?
   47 men

Purchased vessel. Active in the Black Sea against the Turks in 1790–1. No further mention.

Taganrogskaya 14 ?
Constructor ?
Laid down ? *Launched* ? *Purchased* c. 1789
Dimensions ?
Armament ?

Purchased vessel. Active in the Black Sea against the Turks in 1790–1. No further mention.

Sviataia Elena 28 ?
Constructor ?
Laid down ? *Launched* ? *Purchased* 1792
Dimensions 88 ft x 26 ft x 8 ft (Veselago)
Armament ?

Purchased vessel. Carried cargo in the Black Sea in 1795–1805. Escorted gun boats in 1806. Employed as a fire ship in Rear-Adm. Pustoshlin's squadron in 1807. Broken up after 1810.

The Navy of Alexander I (1801–24)

The ships built during the reign of Alexander I were governed, in theory at least, by the joint provisions of the Establishment of Ships of 1803 and the Establishment of Guns of 1805. Absent from the ships built under the new establishments were the edinorogs of the previous period. New to the fleet were the short-barrelled heavy guns developed from Swedish weapons captured in the 1788–91 war. Of interest in the 1803 Establishment of Ships relating to the Black Sea is the provision for the continued construction of 64-gun ships of the line – an obsolete type by this time and one that was to be abandoned in practice after 1800 in favour of a comparable number of 74-gun ships. Of equal interest is the provision for a five to two ratio of capital ships to cruiser types and the provision for equal numbers of heavy and standard frigates.

Ships of 110 guns (4 purpose-built 1801–24)

Four First Rates were built for the Black Sea fleet between 1806 and 1821. The same number of First Rates were built for the larger Baltic fleet during this period. This inordinate emphasis on construction of the largest type of capital ships in what had been the secondary area of Russian naval concern may have reflected a shifting of Russian focus from the Baltic to the Black Sea; or it may have been a simply fortuitous development unrelated to foreign policy concerns. All four ships were patterned after the very similar *Ratnyi* of 1802 and do not appear to have owed anything at all to contemporary Baltic developments of the *Ches'ma* class design. Their opposite numbers in the British

Royal Navy were the *Hibernia* and the *Caledonia* class ships and the Russian 110-gun ships carried a comparable, but slightly heavier (Russian 36pdrs to British 32pdrs) main armament on hulls that were 11–15 ft shorter and 1 ft narrower. The ability of Russian First Rates to mount fire power comparable to that carried on significantly larger British first rates was a reflection of the different operating environments of the two navies.

Poltava class (3 ships)
Poltava 110 Kherson
Constructor M. K. Surovtsov
Laid down 20.10.1806   Launched 20.6.1808
Dimensions 190 ft x 52 ft x 21 ft 6 in (Veselago)
          190 ft x 52 ft x 23 ft 6 in (Golovachev)
Armament LD 30 x 36pdrs (short)
          MD 32 x 24pdrs
          UD 32 x 18pdrs
          FC & QD 20 x 6pdrs, 4 x 24pdr carr.

Poltava class. Sailed from Kherson to Sevastopol' in 1809. In 1810, as part of Rear-Adm. Sarychev's squadron, unsuccessfully pursued the Turkish squadron off Varna and bombarded Trabizon. In 1811, as part of Vice-Adm. Gall's squadron, cruised off Varna. Decommissioned at Sevastopol' in 1812. Hulked in 1825. Broken up in 1832.

Dvenadtsat' Apostolov 110 Kherson
Constructor M. K. Surovtsov
Laid down 12.11.1808   Launched 31.5.1811
Dimensions 190 ft x 52 ft x 21 ft 6 in (Veselago)
          190 ft x 52 ft x 23 ft 6 in (Golovachev)
Armament LD 30 x 36pdrs (short) MD 32 x 24pdrs
          UD 32 x 18pdrs
          FC & QD 20 x 6pdrs, 4 x 24pdr carr.

Poltava class. Sailed from Kherson to Sevastopol' in 1811. At Sevastopol' in 1812. Cruised in the Black Sea in 1813. Decommissioned in 1813. Hulked in 1825. Broken up in 1832.

Parizh 110 Kherson
Constructor M. K. Surovtsov
Laid down 8.9.1812   Launched 22.11.1814
Dimensions 190 ft x 52 ft x 22 ft 3 in
Armament LD 30 x 36pdrs (short) MD 32 x 24pdrs
          UD 32 x 18pdrs
          FC & QD 20 x 6pdrs, 4 x 24pdr carr.

Poltava class. Name commemorates the allied entry into Paris in 1814. Sailed from Kherson to Sevastopol' in 1815. Cruised in the Black Sea from 1817–20. Decommissioned in 1822. Hulked in 1827. Broken up in 1830.

Imperator Frants 110 Kherson
Constructor Melikhov
Laid down 8.5.1818   Launched 25.6.1821
Dimensions 190 ft x 52 ft 10 in x 22 ft
Armament LD 30 x 36pdrs (short)
          MD 32 x 24pdrs
          UD 32 x 18pdrs
          FC & QD 20 x 6pdrs, 4 x 24pdr carr.

Similar to the *Poltava* class, but with an additional 10 in beam. Named after the Emperor of Austria for reasons related to the formation of the Holy Alliance between Russia, Austria and Prussia. Cruised in the Black Sea in 1822, 1823 and 1825. Successfully bombarded Varna in 1828, but prevented from bombarding Anapa because of her enormous draught. Cruised off the Bosporus in 1829, but returned to Sizopol after transferring part of her crew to frigates *Flora* and *Shtandart*. Transported 1458 troops from Sevastopol' to Sizopol' and returned to Sevastopol' with sick and wounded. Cruised in the Black Sea in 1830. Decommissioned in 1830. Broken up in 1832

Ships of 74–80 guns (17 purpose-built 1801–24)

Seventeen 74-gun ships were built during this period, 12 to the same general pattern, and the last 5 to a variety of different designs. In compliance with the Gun Establishment of 1805, they were all armed with 24- and 36pdrs in place of the 18- and 30pdrs of earlier and smaller eighteenth-century 74s. They were far more actively employed during their service lives than their largely inactive First Rate contemporaries, taking part in two different Russo-Turkish conflicts and engaging in a variety of anti-ship, shore bombardment and troop transport activities.

Pravyi 74/76 Kherson
Constructor M. K. Surovtsov
Laid down 14.7.1801   Launched 10.7.1804
Dimensions 178 ft x 48 ft x 20 ft (Veselago)
          178 ft x 48 ft x 20 ft 8 in (Golovachev)
Armament LD 28 x 36pdrs (short)
          UD 30 x 24pdrs (short)
          FC & QD 18 x 8pdrs or 24pdr carr.

The first Black Sea ship to be coppered while building. This 74 duplicated the armament and dimensions of the Baltic *Selafail* class and the likelihood that she was a direct copy seems inescapable. She was also armed with short 24- and 36pdrs according to the Establishment of 1805 and had a significantly greater weight of broadside than earlier Black Sea 74s with their 18- and 30pdr long guns.

Sailed from Kherson to Sevastopol' in 1803. Cruised to Sinop, Anapa and Trabzon in 1807. Cruised off Varna in 1809. Cruised in the Black Sea and pursued the Turkish squadron off Varna in 1810. Cruised as part of Vice-Adm. Gall's squadron off Varna in 1811. At Sevastopol' in 1812. Cruised in the Black Sea in 1813. Decommissioned in 1813. Hulked in 1825. Broken up in 1830.

Anapa class (11 ships)
The 11 frigates of the *Anapa* class were the largest single group of warships purpose-built for the Black Sea fleet during the age of sail. They appear to have been an expansion of the *Pravyi* (and hence the *Selafail* class) design with an extra 2 ft in length worked in and with 5 in less beam. The first four were actively involved in the Russo-Turkish War of 1806–12 while the last class member, *Skoryi*, was heavily involved in shore bombardment during the Russo-Turkish War of 1828–9, during the course of which she received and survived substantial damage from Turkish shore batteries. None were lost to combat or accident. The *Anapa*s had average lifespans between launch and final disposal of 18 years. This represents a small improvement over that of their Baltic contemporaries, the *Selafail*s, with lifespans of 16.87 years and this may reflect less demanding operational deployment of the *Anapa*s.

Anapa 74 Kherson
Constructor M. K. Surovtsov
Laid down 5.2.1806   Launched 30.7.1807
Dimensions 180 ft x 47 ft 7 in x 22 ft 3 in (Veselago)
          180 ft x 47 ft 6 in x 22 ft (Golovachev)

Armament LD 28 x 36pdrs (short)
UD 30 x 24 (short)
FC & QD 18 x 8pdrs or 24pdr carr.

Anapa class. Sailed from Kherson to Sevastopol' in 1808. Cruised off Varna in 1809. Participated in the pursuit of the Turkish squadron off Varna in 1810. Participated in the capture of the Turkish frigate *Magubey-Subhan* (40) and the corvette *Shahin-Girey* (20) in 1811. At Sevastopol' in 1812. Cruised in the Black Sea in 1816. Decommissioned in 1816. Hulked in 1825. Broken up 1837.

Mariia 74 Kherson
Constructor M. K. Surovtsov
Laid down 28.2.1807   *Launched* 12.11.1808
Dimensions 180 ft x 47 ft 7 in x 21 ft 6 in (Veselago)
180 ft x 47 ft 6 in x 22 ft (Golovachev)
Armament LD 28 x 36pdrs (short)
UD 30 x 24 pdrs (short)
FC & QD 18 x 8pdrs or 24pdr carr.

Anapa class. Sailed from Kherson to Sevastopol' in 1809. Cruised off Varna in 1809. Participated in the pursuit of the Turkish squadron off Varna in 1810. Participated in the capture of the Turkish frigate *Magubey-Subhan* (40) and the corvette *Shahin-Girey* (20) in 1811. Transported troops from Sevastopol' to Odessa in 1812. Decommissioned in 1812. Hulked in 1825.

Aziia 74 Kherson
Constructor M. K. Surovtsov
Laid down 28.7.1807   *Launched* 5.8.1810
Dimensions 180 ft x 47 ft 7 in x 21 ft 6 in (Veselago)
180 ft x 47 ft 6 in x 22 ft (Golovachev)
Armament LD 28 x 36pdrs (short)
UD 30 x 24pdrs (short)
FC & QD 18 x 8pdrs or 24pdr carr.

Anapa class. Sailed from Kherson to Odessa in 1810. Cruised off Varna in Vice-Adm. Gall's squadron in 1811. Transported troops from Sevastopol' to Odessa in 1812. Cruised in the Black Sea in 1814. Decommissioned in 1814. Hulked in 1825. Broken up in 1830.

Dmitrii Donskoi 74 Kherson
Constructor M. K. Surovtsov
Laid down 28.2.1807   *Launched* 6.11.1810.
Dimensions 180 ft x 47 ft 7 in x 21 ft 6 in
180 ft x 47 ft 6 in x 22 ft (Golovachev)
Armament LD 28 x 36pdrs (short)
UD 30 x 24pdrs (short)
FC & QD 18 x 8pdrs or 24pdr carr.

Anapa class. Sailed from Kherson to Odessa in 1810. Participated in the pursuit of the Turkish squadron off Varna in 1810. Cruised off Varna in Vice-Adm. Gall's squadron in 1811. At Sevastopol' in 1812. Cruised in the Black Sea in 1813, 1814, and 1818 during an Imperial visit by Alexander I. Decommissioned in 1818. Hulked in 1825.

Lesnoe 74 Kherson
Constructor Kuznetsov
Laid down 6.11.1809   *Launched* 6.7.1811
Dimensions 180 ft x 47 ft 7 in x 21 ft 6 in
180 ft x 47 ft 6 in x 22 ft (Golovachev)
Armament LD 28 x 36pdrs (short)
UD 30 x 24pdrs (short)
FC & QD 18 x 8pdrs or 24pdr carr.

Anapa class. Name commemorates one of Peter I's major land battle victories over the Swedes in 1708. Sailed from Kherson to Sevastopol' in 1811. At Sevastopol' in 1812. Cruised in the Black Sea in 1813, 1814, 1816, and 1821. Decommissioned in 1821. Hulked in 1825.

Maksim Ispovednik 74 Kherson
Constructor M. K. Surovtsov
Laid down 4.2.1810   *Launched* 9.6.1812
Dimensions 180 ft x 47 ft 7 in x 21 ft 6 in
180 ft x 47 ft 6 in x 22 ft (Golovachev)
Armament LD 28 x 36pdrs (short)
UD 30 x 24pdrs (short)
FC & QD 18 x 8pdrs (long)

Anapa class. Name commemorates the date of the 1789 victory of Rochensalm. Sailed from Kherson to Sevastopol' in 1812. Cruised in the Black Sea in 1814, and 1818–22. Decommissioned in 1822. Hulked in 1826. Determined unfit in 1827. Broken up 1832.

Brien 74 Nikolaev
Constructor Kuznetsov
Laid down 24.12.1811   *Launched* 1.11.1813
Dimensions 180 ft x 47 ft 7 in x 21 ft 6 in
Armament LD 28 x 36pdrs (short)
UD 30 x 24pdrs (short)
FC & QD 18 x 8pdrs or 24pdr carr.

Anapa class. Sailed from Kherson to Sevastopol' in 1814. Cruised in the Black Sea in 1815–20. Decommissioned in 1820. Hulked in 1826. Broken up 1830.

Kul'm 74 Kherson
Constructor Tarusov
Laid down 23.11.1810   *Launched* 4.11.1813
Dimensions 180 ft x 47 ft 7 in x 21 ft 6 in
Armament LD 28 x 36pdrs (short)
UD 30 x 24pdrs (short)
FC & QD 18 x 8pdrs or 24pdr carr.

Anapa class. Sailed from Kherson to Sevastopol' in 1814. Cruised in the Black Sea in 1816 and 1818. Decommissioned in 1818. Hulked in 1826. Broken up 1830.

Krasnoi 74 Kherson
Constructor M. K. Surovtsov
Laid down 13.7.1813   *Launched* 16.5.1816
Dimensions 180 ft x 47 ft 7 in x 22 ft 6 in
Armament LD 28 x 36pdrs (short)
UD 30 x 24pdrs (short)
FC & QD 18 x 8pdrs or 24pdr carr.

Anapa class. Name commemorates two battles in 1812. Sailed from Kherson to Sevastopol. Cruised in the Black Sea in 1817–18 and 1821–2. Decommissioned in 1826. Hulked in 1827. Broken up 1830.

Nikolai 74/81 Kherson
Constructor Kuznetsov
Laid down 25.11.1811   *Launched* 16.6.1816
Dimensions 180 ft x 47 ft 7 in x 21 ft 6 in
Armament LD 28 x 36pdrs (short)
UD 30 x 24 (short)
FC & QD 18 x 8pdrs or 24pdr carr.

Anapa class. Sailed from Nikolaev to Sevastopol' in 1816. Cruised in the Black Sea from 1817–24. Decommissioned in 1826. Hulked at Nikolaev in 1827. Broken up 1830.

Skoryi 74/81 Kherson
Constructor M. K. Surovtsov
Laid down 16.5.1816   Launched 8.5.1818
Dimensions 180 ft x 47 ft 7 in x 21 ft 6 in
Armament   LD 28 x 36pdrs (short)
            UD 30 x 24pdrs (short)
            FC & QD 18 x 8pdrs or 24pdr carr.

Anapa class. Cruised in the Black Sea in 1822, 1823, and 1826. In 1828 bombarded Anapa and was hit 9 times in the hull and received severe damage to the rigging. Bombarded Varna the same year, taking 6 casualties, and being hulled 8 times in addition to receiving 25 hits aloft. Transported 400 wounded and sick from Anapa to Sevastopol' and again from Varna to Sevastopol. Decommissioned in 1829. Converted to a hospital ship in 1829 with the removal of 42 guns and transported sick and wounded from Sizopol' to Sevastopol. Broken up after 1830.

Nord-Adler 74/91 Nikolaev
Constructor Melikhov
Laid down 21.5.1817   Launched 24.5.1820
Dimensions 178 ft x 48 ft 2 in x 19 ft 6 in
Armament   LD 28 x 36pdrs (short)
            UD 30 x 24pdrs (short)
            FC & QD 18 x 8pdrs or 24pdr carr.

Sailed from Nikolaev to Sevastopol' in 1820. Cruised in the Black Sea from 1822–7. Bombarded Anapa in 1828 with no casualties. Bombarded Varna the same year with 2 killed and 2 wounded, 15 hits to the hull and 47 hits aloft. Transported 209 sick to Odessa. In 1829 at Penderaklia participated in the destruction of a Turkish ship of the line and 16 smaller ships and helped capture the fortress at Inada. Cruised in the Black Sea in 1830. Decommissioned in 1830. Broken up in 1839.

Pimen 74/95 Kherson
Constructor A.K. Kaverznev
Laid down 26.5.1822   Launched 2.9.1823
Dimensions 179 ft 8 in x 48 ft 6 in x 21 ft 5 in
Armament   LD 28 x 36pdrs (short)
            UD 30 x 24pdrs (short)
            FC & QD 18 x 8pdrs or 24pdr carr.
            (1805 Establishment)
         1833 LD 28 x 30pdrs (long)
            UD 30 x 24pdrs (short)
            FC & QD 18 x 8pdrs or 24pdr carr. (Veselago)

Sailed from Kherson to Sevastopol' in 1823. Cruised in the Black Sea from 1824–7. Participated in the bombardment of Anapa and Varna in 1828. In 1829, participated in the bombardment and conquest of Sizopol' and the fortress Midia. Transported troops from Rumelia to Russia in 1833. Exchanged her short 36pdrs for long 30pdrs in 1833–4, possibly to reduce hull stress. In the Bosporus expedition in 1833. Cruised in the Black Sea in 1834 and 1837. Decommissioned in 1838. Hulked in 1839. Broken up in 1840.

Parmen 74/89 Nikolaev
Constructor I. S. Razumov
Laid down 27.4.1822   Launched 18.10.1823
Dimensions 170 ft x 47 ft 7 in x 20 ft 3 in
Armament   LD 28–30pdrs (long)
            UD 30 18pdrs
            FC & QD 16 x 8pdrs (Veselago)

Broke with the normal pattern for Black Sea 74s by completing with 30pdr long guns. Sailed from Nikolaev to Kherson in 1824. Cruised in the Black Sea in 1825. Participated in the bombardment of Anapa and Varna in 1828, where she was severely damaged and suffered casualties of 2 killed and 7 wounded with 20 holes in her hull and 45 hits aloft. Repulsed the land attack of Turkish troops at the captured fortress of Sizopol' the same year. Participated in the destruction of a Turkish ship of the line and 16 smaller ships at Penderaklia in 1829. Transported troops from Rumelia to Russia in 1830. Involved in the Bosporus expedition in 1833. Decommissioned in 1834. Hulked in 1835. Broken up in 1842.

Panteleimon 80 Nikolaev
Constructor I. S. Razumov
Laid down 17.10.1823   Launched 8.11.1824
Dimensions 180 ft 4 in x 48 ft 8 in x 20 ft 9 in
Armament   LD 28 x 36pdrs (short)
            UD 30 x 24pdrs (short)
            FC & QD 18 x 8pdrs or 24pdr carr.

Sviatoi Panteleimon is the saint day on which the battle of Gangut was won. Nominally an 80-gun ship, but a 74 in dimensions and armament without any obvious characteristics warranting the higher status and included here for that reason. Sailed from Nikolaev to Kherson in 1825. In 1828, as part of Vice-Adm. Greig's squadron, participated in the bombardment of Anapa, where she received 15 shot holes and 37 hits aloft in the sails and rigging, and of Varna and Sizopol'. Operated off the Bosporus in 1829. Transported troops from Rumelia to Russia in 1830. Participated in the Bosporus expedition of 1833. Cruised in the Black Sea in 1834. Decommissioned in 1837. Hulked in 1838. Broken up in 1840.

Ioann Zlatoust 74/83 Kherson
Constructor A. K. Kaverznev
Laid down 30.1.1824   Launched 7.9.1825
Dimensions 176 ft x 48 ft x 19 ft 6 in
Armament   LD 28 x 36pdrs (short)
            MD 30 x 24pdrs (short)
            FC & QD 18 x 8pdrs (long)
            (smaller guns for boats 6 x 8pdr carr., 6 x 3pdr falconets,
            3 x 8pdr mortars)

In the strictest sense, this ship belongs to the next period (Nicholas I) by virtue of having been launched nine months into 1825, the first year of his reign. She is placed here at the tail-end of the age of Alexander I because of her status as the last Black Sea 74-gun ship.

Sailed from Nikolaev to Kherson in 1826. Participated in the bombardment of Anapa and Varna in 1828. Participated in the destruction of a Turkish ship of the line and 16 smaller vessels at Penderaklia in 1829. Bombarded Midia the same year, receiving 18 hull hits and 35 hits to rigging from shore batteries. Transported troops from Rumelia to Russia in 1830. Participated in the Bosporus expedition of 1833. Cruised in the Black Sea in 1837. Assisted in the fortification of the Caucasus line in 1838–40 by carrying troops and logistic elements. Broken up in 1840. Hulked in 1841.

Frigates

Heavy frigates (5 purpose-built 1801–24)

Five heavy frigates were built for the Black Sea fleet between 1809 and 1824. All were individual designs with no common thread beyond their status as 24pdr heavy frigates. The great flowering of even heavier 44- and 60-gun frigates in the Black Sea fleet would come in 1825 after the accession of Nicholas I. *Minerva* was worn out by 1825, but the other 4 were all involved in the Russo-Turkish War of 1828–9 and 3 of them sustained heavy damage from Turkish counter-battery fire during the bombardment of Anapa.

Minerva 44 Nikolaev
Constructor D. V. Kuznetsov
Laid down 16.12.1809   *Launched* 29.10.1811
Dimensions 147 ft 6 in x 40 ft x 19 ft Golovachev
Armament   LD 28 x 24pdrs
             FC & QD 16 x 8pdrs, 2 x 3pdrs, 2 x 8pdr carr., 2 x 8pdr mortars

Reported dimensions are identical to those of the 36-gun *Liliia* which was laid down in 1805 at Kherson with M. I. Surovtsov as constructor. It is not clear whether the two ships represented a common design. Cruised as a cadet training ship in 1812. Cruised off Abhasia from 1813–16. Carried the Russian ambassador to Istanbul in 1816. Cruised 1817–22. Relegated to harbour service in 1825 and hulked.

Evstafii 44/48 Kherson
Constructor M. I. Surovtsov
Laid down 16.5.1815   *Launched* 7.10.1817
Dimensions 153 ft x 42 ft x 13 ft 1 in
Armament   LD 28 x 24pdrs (short)
             FC & QD 16 x 8pdrs and/or 24pdr carr. (1805 Establishment)

Cruised in the Black Sea 1819–22. Cruised off Abhasia in 1826–7. In 1828 she took 13 hits in the hull while participating in the bombardment of Anapa and the sinking of 3 Turkish warships. After the engagement, she escorted 12 Turkish prizes, transported supplies to Varna, and transported sick and injured back to Sevastopol. In 1829, participated in the landing of troops at Sizpool and the capture of the city prior to returning to Bosporus. Found unseaworthy in 1831, but listed until 1837.

Flora 44/48 Nikolaev
Constructor A. I. Melikhov
Laid down 18.2.1816   *Launched* 7.5.1818
Dimensions 159 ft x 42 ft x 19 ft 8 in
Armament   LD 28 x 24pdrs (short)
             FC & QD 16 x 8pdrs and/or 24pdr carr. (1805 Establishment)

Sailed to Sevastopol' in 1818. Cruised in the Black Sea in 1819–23 and 1826–7. In 1828, she participated in the bombardment of Anapa, receiving 11 hits to the hull and 29 in the upper works. Twice transported Nikolai I to Varna and back to Odessa. In 1829, participated in the landing and conquest of Agatopol' and the bombardment of Inada. Transported troops in 1830. Stationed at Nikolaev in 1832 and listed there until 1837.

Pospeshnyi 44/52 Nikolaev
Constructor A. I. Melikhov
Laid down 10.2.1820   *Launched* 2.11.1821
Dimensions 156 ft 9 in x 41 ft 6 in x 19 ft 3 in
Armament   LD 28 x 24pdrs (short)
             FC & QD 20/24 x 6pdrs and/or 24pdr carr.

Sailed to Sevastopol' in 1822. Cruised in the Black Sea in 1823–4 and 1826–7. In 1828, participated in the bombardment of Anapa, receiving 34 hits in the hull. Transported supplies and PoWs. Operated off Turkish Bulgaria in 1829. Fire watch duty at Sevastopol' in 1830. Broken up in 1839.

Shtandart 44/60 Kherson
Constructor A. K. Kaverznev
Laid down 26.5.1822   *Launched* 31.5.1824
Dimensions 160 ft x 40 ft x 20 ft
Armament   1824 LD 28 x 24pdrs (short)
                  FC & QD 16 x 8pdrs, 2 x 3pdrs, 2 x 8pdr carr., 2 x 8pdr mortars
             1835 LD 28 x 18pdrs (long)
                  FC & QD 16 x 8pdrs, 2 x 3pdrs, 2 x 8pdr carr., 2 x 8pdr mortars

Sailed to Sevastopol' in 1824. Cruised in the Black Sea in 1825. Involved in major operations against Anapa, Sujuk-kale, Varna, Agatopol', and Messemvriia during the war with Turkey from 1828–9. Forced to flee a superior Turkish squadron off the Bosporus on 14.5.1829. Transported troops in 1830. Carried the Russian envoy to Alexandria for talks with the Egyptian pasha Muhammed Ali in 1832. In 1833, returned from Alexandria to the Bosporus where she was attached to Rear-Adm. Lazarev's Squadron. Repaired in 1835. Short 24pdrs replaced by long 18pdrs taken from *Varshava* (121) at Adm. Lazarev's order. Cruised in the Caucasus in 1837–9 assisting in the fortification of the coastline. Converted into a floating magazine in 1841.

Standard frigates (5 purpose-built 1801–24)

The Gun Establishment of 1805 mandated short-barrelled 24pdrs for standard as well as heavy frigates and it is probable that all five of the 32–36-gun frigates built specifically for the Black Sea fleet were so armed. With heavy short-range main armament batteries, they would not have been well suited for ocean deployment against the more lightly armed, but longer-ranged 18pdr frigates that frequented the Mediterranean and the Atlantic, but they were well suited for Black Sea conditions. *Voin* and *Liliia* were involved in the kind of shore bombardment activities against Turkish positions during the Russo-Turkish War of 1806–12 that seemed almost the raison d'etre for Black Sea frigates. The pair also involved themselves in true frigate-like activity in 1810 by becoming involved in the 6 hour pursuit of a fleeing Turkish squadron. *Vezul* was wrecked in 1812, a fate that was becoming a much rarer fate for Russian ships than had been the norm in the previous century.

Pospeshnyi 36
Transferred from the Baltic fleet in 1801. See Baltic fleet for details.

Voin class (2 ships)
Voin 32 Kherson
Constructor M. I. Surovtsov
Laid down 5.6.1803   *Launched* 26.10.1804
Dimensions 135 ft x 35 ft x 15 ft 5 in (Veselago)
             135 ft x 35 ft x 15 ft 8 in (Golovachev)
Armament   ?

Voin class. Cruised in the Black Sea in 1805–6. Operated off the Danube in 1807, participating in the conquest of Anapa and the bombardment of Trabizon. Operated off the Danube in 1809 and participated in the bombardment of Sujuk-kale. Participated in the conquest of Sukhum-kale in 1810. Participated in the 6-hour pursuit of a Turkish squadron on 17.8.1810. Cruised to Varna in 1811 and served as a troop transport. Fire watch duty at Sevastopol' in 1815–21. Not afterwards mentioned.

Afrika 32 Kherson
Constructor M. I. Surovtsov
Laid down 26.10.1809   *Launched* 3.6.1811

Dimensions 135 ft x 35 ft x 15 ft 5 in (Veselago)
135 ft x 35 ft x 15 ft 8 in (Golovachev)
Armament ?
Voin class Cruised in the Black Sea in 1814. Served to transport troops and ammunition in 1815–16. Cruised 1816–19. Fire watch duty at Sevastopol' from 1821–7. Not afterwards mentioned.

Liliia 36 Kherson
Constructor M. I. Surovtsov
Laid down 28.6.1805 *Launched* 30.10.1806
Dimensions 147 ft 6 in x 40 ft2 in x 14 ft 3 in (Veselago)
147 ft 6 in x 40 ft x 19 ft (Golovachev)
Armament LD 26 x 24pdrs (short)
FC & QD 10 x 6pdrs and/or 24pdr carr. (1805 establishment)
Reported dimensions parallel those of *Minerva* (44). Sailed to Sevastopol' in the summer of 1807. Operated off the Danube in 1808. Participated in the conquest of Anapa and operated off Varna in 1809. Participated in the pursuit of the Turkish squadron on 17.8.1810, bombarded Trabizon, and carried supplies to Sukhum in 1810. Cruised off Varna in 1811–12. Transported troops to the Danube for the army formed by Adm. Chichagov (son of a more famous father) in his unsuccessful attempt to intercept the retreating army of Napoleon in 1812. Cruised in the Black Sea in 1815–19 and in 1821. Not afterwards mentioned. (see *Minerva* (44) of 1807).

Vezul **class** (2 ships)
Vezul 32 Kherson
Constructor M. I. Surovtsov
Laid down 9.3.1812 *Launched* 1.11.1813
Dimensions 121 ft 3 in x 33 ft 6 in x 12 ft 6 in
Armament ?
Vezul class. Sailed to Sevastopol' in 8.1814. Cruised in the Black Sea in 1816–17. Drifted ashore and wrecked on the Cape of Khersones with loss of two sailors on 2.10.1817.

Speshnyi 32 Kherson
Constructor M. I. Surovtsov
Laid down 9.3.1812 *Launched* 15.11.1813
Dimensions 121 ft 3 in x 33 ft 6 in x 12 ft 6 in
Armament ?
Vezul class. Sailed to Sevastopol' in 8.1814. Transported troops in 1815. Cruised in the Black Sea in 1816–17, 1820–2 and 1825. Fire watch duty at Odessa 1826–7 and at Sevastopol' 1828–9. Broken up in 1830.

Corvettes (3 purpose-built/3 purchased 1801–24)

Purpose-built
Six corvettes were built or converted for the Black Sea fleet during this period. They appear to have taken over many of the functions of frigates and were armed with 24pdr carronades, much in the manner of British sloops of the same period. From the operational summaries, it appears that they were more actively employed than the larger ships in the Black Sea. *Krym* of 1810 was wrecked in 1825 after a 15-year career. The 3 purchased corvettes were all assigned to Adm. Seniavin's Mediterranean squadron and the trio were among the Russian ships in sold in to the French in 1809.

Abo 12 Nikolaev
Constructor D. V. Kuznetsov
Laid down 18.11.1808 *Launched* 4.5.1809
Dimensions ?
Armament ?
Purpose-built corvette. Cruised in the Black Sea in 1810 and participated in the bombardment of Trabizon. Cruised 1811–15. Fire watch ship at Odessa and Feodosii. Reduced to harbour service in 1826.

Krym 18 Sevastopol'
Constructor A. I. Melikhov
Laid down 15.12.1808 *Launched* 13.1.1810
Dimensions approx. 91 ft x ? x ? (27.7 m x ? x ?) (Chernyshev)
Armament 18 x 24pdr carr.
130 men
Purpose-built corvette. Cruised in the Black Sea in 1810–24. Grounded and wrecked during a storm on 1.1.1825 with a loss of 49 sailors.

Iason 24 Sevastopol'
Constructor A. I. Melikhov
Laid down 1.5.1814 *Launched* 12.12.1815
Dimensions 119 ft (LGD) x 32 ft x 15 ft (Veselago)
Armament 24pdr carr.
Purpose-built corvette. Cruised 1817–30. Broken up in 1831.

Converted from other classes
Pavel 18 ?
Constructor ?
Laid down ? *Launched* ? *Purchased* 1804
Dimensions ?
Armament ?
Corvette converted from a privateer at Kherson in 1804. Cruised in 1805. To Corfu in 1806 and joined Vice-Adm. Seniavin's squadron. Sold to France at Corfu in 1809.

Diomid 24 ?
Constructor V. I. Potapov
Laid down 30.1.1804 *Launched* 29.10.1804 *Converted* 1805
Dimensions 140 ft x 40 ft x 16 ft (Veselago)
Armament 24pdr carr.
Corvette converted from transport *Diomed* in 1805. To Corfu in 1806, joining Vice-Adm. Seniavin's squadron. Sold to France at Trieste on 27.9.1809. (See also under transports.)

Kherson 24 ?
Constructor M. K. Surovtsev
Laid down 10.7.1804 *Launched* 28.6.1805 *Converted* 1805
Dimensions 120 ft x 34 ft x 12 ft (Veselago)
Armament 24pdr carr.
Corvette converted from transport *Kherson* in 1805. To Corfu in 1806, joining Vice-Adm. Seniavin's squadron. Sold to France at Trieste on 27.9.1809. (See also under transports.)

Black Sea sloop (1 purpose-built 1801–24)

Diana 18/34 Sevastopol
Constructor I. Y. Osminin
Laid down 4.9.1821 *Launched* 24.9.1823
Dimensions 108 ft x 26 ft 2 in x 8 ft 3 in (Veselago)
Armament ?
Purpose-built sloop, a type rarely found in the Black Sea fleet. Her unusual armament of 34 guns implies very low-calibre guns, possibly primarily anti-personnel weapons. Training cruises in 1824–5. Cruised

off the Bosporus in 1828–9 capturing 4 Turkish ships. Landed troops at Gagry (Abhasia). Cruised in the Black Sea in 1830–8. Reduced to a magazine in 1839.

Black Sea brigs (5 purpose-built, 3 converted, 4 purchased 1801–24)

Twelve brigs were acquired between 1803 and 1824 for the kind of low-end activities typical of brigs everywhere. Five were purpose-built and the others were a mix of purchased and converted ships. As a group, the brigs were smaller than Black Sea corvettes and their armament appears to have consisted in the main of 18- and 24pdr carronades on the broadside and 6pdr chase guns on the forecastle. *Merkurii* (18/20) may have become the most famous Russian sailing ship of the nineteenth century as a result of her successful and astonishing 4-hour running battle with two Turkish line of battle ships in 1829.

Purpose-built

Iason 12 Kherson
Constructor ?
Laid down ? Launched 1805
Dimensions ?
Armament 12 x 18pdr carr.
Purpose-built brig. Cruised to Corfu and back in 1806. Wrecked in transit to Odessa on 17.3.1807. Crew and cargo saved.

Mingreliia 16/18 Sevastopol'
Constructor A. I. Melikhov
Laid down 22.6.1811 Launched 15.7.1813
Dimensions 88 ft 3 in x 28 ft x 13 ft 2 in (Veselago)
Armament ?
Purpose-built brig. Trials in 1814. Cruised in the Black Sea in 1814–27. Escorted 5 gun boats to Varna in 1828 and employed there as a fire watch ship. Engaged in operations off the Bosporus and Turkish coastlines in 1829, capturing several prizes and transporting troops. Served as a fire watch ship at Odessa in 1830–3. Stationed at Nikolaev in 1832. Carried the Russian ambassador to Istanbul in 1833. Stationed at Nikolaev 1834–5. Broken up in 1842.

Merkurii 18/20 Sevastopol'
Constructor I. Y. Osminin
Laid down 28.1.1819 Launched 7.5.1820
Dimensions 96 ft 8 in x 30 ft 10 in x 13 ft/13 ft (Veselago)
445 tons displacement
Armament 2 x 6pdrs 16/18 x 24pdr carr.
Purpose-built brig. Possibly the most heroic Russian warship during the Age of Sail. Cruised in the Black Sea in 1820–7. Engaged in operations against the Turks in 1828–9. On 14.5.1829 while in company with frigate *Shtandart* and brig *Orfei*, she was intercepted by a Turkish squadron of 6 ships of the line and supporting frigates. *Shtandart* and *Orfei* escaped, but *Merkurii* fought off the Turkish *Selimiye* (128) and *Rivale* (74) in a 4-hour action during which she received 22 hits to her hull, 16 in her standing rigging, 148 in her running rigging with casualties of 4 killed and 8 wounded. Awarded the Georgian Cross for her heroism. Repaired in 1829 and returned to active cruising. Cruised off the Caucasus in 1830–1. Repaired a second time in 1837–8. Cruised in the Black Sea in 1839–53. Stationed at Nikolaev in 1854–6. Broken up after 1857.

Ganimed 18/22 Nikolaev
Constructor A. I. Melikhov

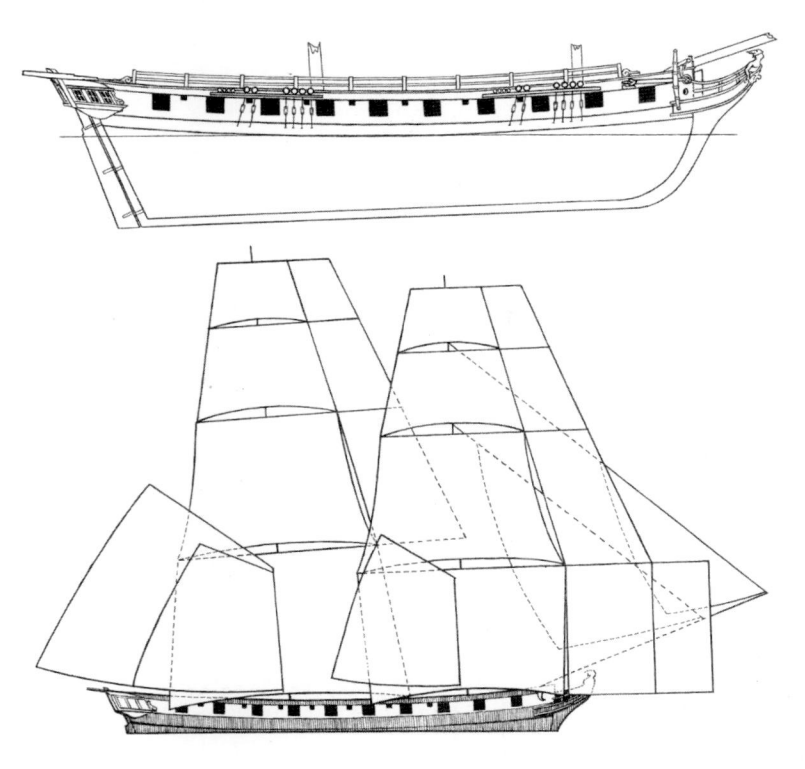

Two drawings showing the rig and the basic appearance of the flush-decked brig Merkurii *of 1820. Of interest as a depiction of a typical post-Napoleonic brig, and of particular interest as the star performer in one of the most striking mismatches in Russian naval history when this tiny David exchanged fire with two Turkish Goliaths in the guise of the 128-gun* Selimiye *and the 74-gun* Rivale *in 1829.* Merkurii *escaped with heavy casualties and hull damage after a four-hour ordeal, a tribute both to Russian shiphandling and Turkish incompetence.*

Laid down 13.12.1819 Launched 24.5.1820
Dimensions 99 ft x 30 ft x 12 ft 9 in (Veselago)
Armament ?
Purpose-built brig. Cruised in the Black Sea in 1820–7. Engaged in operations against Turkey in 1828–9, during which she captured and set afire several Turkish ships. Cruised in the Black Sea in 1830–1 and bombarded Caucasus mountaineers. Broken up in 1836.

Orfei 18/24 Nikolaev
Constructor A. I. Melikhov
Laid down 21.9.1820 Launched 3.3.1821
Dimensions 100 ft x 30 ft x 12 ft 9 in (Veselago)
Armament ?
Purpose-built brig. Cruised in the Black Sea in 1821–7. Engaged in operations against Turkey 1828–9, capturing and burning several Turkish ships. Cruised in the Black Sea in 1830–1 and bombarded Caucasus mountaineers. Fire watch duties at Sevastopol' in 1832–4. Broken up in 1836.

Converted from other classes

Tsar' Konstantin ? ?
Constructor ?
Laid down ? Launched ? Converted 1806
Dimensions ?
Armament ?
Brig converted from a transport of the same name. Cruised in the

The brig Merkurii *in action against two Turkish ships of the line on 14 May 1829. The 74-gun* Rivale *is engaged with the brig while the 128-gun* Selimye *has been temporarily left behind although she is apparently trying to bring some of her guns to bear. This portrayal is one of many inspired by the remarkable engagement and does a fairly good job of showing the tactics of the tiny Russian ship, which is using its speed to attempt to stay off of its opponents' quarters and avoid facing their full broadsides. That the engagement took place at all was the result of extremely light wind conditions that made escape difficult for the* Merkurii. *Light winds do not seem to be a problem here and the artist may be portraying the brig at its moment of escape. By M. S. Tkachenko, 1907.*

Black Sea in 1806–11. Wrecked on 9.1.1812. (See also under Black Sea purchased transports.)

Aleksei ? ?
Constructor ?
Laid down ?   Launched ?   Converted 1807
Dimensions approx. 80 ft x 22 ft x 11 ft (24.4 m x 7.6 m x 3.5 m)
          (Chernyshev)
Armament ?
Brig converted from a rowing brigantine of the same name in 1807. Cruised in the Black Sea in 1808–14. Fire watch ship at Odessa from 1815–17 and at Ochakov from 1819–26. Not afterwards mentioned. (See also under Black Sea rowing brigantines.)

Lavrentii ? Kherson
Constructor M.I. Surovtsev
Laid down 5.2.1806   Launched 30.9.1807   Converted 1807
Dimensions approx. 75 ft x 20 ft x 9 ft (22.6 m x 6.2 m x 2.9 m)
          (Chernyshev)
Armament ?
Brig converted from transport *Lanson* (sail and oar vessel). Cruised in the Black Sea in 1807–10. Fire watch ship at Feodosii from 1812–14 and at Taganrog from 1817–24. Broken up after 1825.

Purchased (4 purchased 1804–24)
Aleksandr 12/16 Kherson
Constructor ?
Laid down ?   Launched ?   Purchased 1804
Dimensions ?
Armament 12 x 4pdrs (R. C. Anderson)
          75 men
Brig purchased from private owners while under construction as a transport. Sailed to Corfu in 1805. Operated as part of Vice-Adm. Seniavin's squadron in 1806–8. On 17.12.1806, she was attacked by a French tartane and 3 gunboats armed with 18- and 12pdrs. Boarding attempts were repulsed and two of the gunboats (including the *Napoleon*) were sunk. The French lost 217 men in the engagement and the *Alexandr* suffered only 4 killed and 7 wounded. The symbolism of a Russian brig named *Aleksandr* sinking a French gunboat named *Napoleon* was not lost upon the Russians. Arrived at Venice on 20.1.1808, where she was sold to France in 10.1809.

Naval engagements between the Russians and the French were a rarity. This engagement off the Dalmatians on 17 December 1806 between the Aleksandr, *a purchased brig carrying only 4pdrs, and a French tartane and three gunboats, all armed with 12pdrs and 18pdrs should have gone easily to the French. In a three-hour night engagement, the* Aleksandr *sank two of the gunboats and drove the others off. The painting here does justice to what must have been a fierce and bloody engagement. By A. A. Blinkov, 1957.*

Elisaveta 16 Kherson
Constructor ?
Laid down ?   *Launched* ?   *Purchased* 1804
Dimensions ?
Armament ?   75 men
Brig purchased from private owners while under construction as a transport. Cruised in the Black Sea in 1804–13 and engaged in numerous operations against the Turks. Not mentioned after 1813.

Diana 16 Kherson
Constructor ?
Laid down ?   *Launched* ?   *Purchased* 1804
Dimensions ?
Armament ?   75 men
Brig purchased from private owners while under construction as a transport. Carried supplies to Corfu in 1805. At Istanbul in 1806. Engaged in operations against Turkey in 1807–8. Wrecked on 5.9.1808.

Nikolai 20 20 ?
Constructor ?
Laid down ?   *Launched* ?   *Purchased* 1822
Dimensions approx. 83 ft x 28 ft x 11 ft (25.3 m x 8.4 m x 3.4 m) (Chernyshev)
Armament ?
Brig purchased from private owners. Cruised in the Black Sea in 1822–7 doing occasional survey work. Fire watch ship in the Kerch Straits in 1831. Not afterwards mentioned.

Black Sea schooners (1 purpose-built, 1 purchased 1801–24)

Purpose-built

Sevastopol' 14 Sevastopol'
Constructor Tarusov
Laid down 12.12.1815   *Launched* ?
Dimensions ?
Armament ?
Purpose-built schooner. Cruised in the Black Sea in 1819–24. Fire watch ship at Sukhum in 1825–6 at Sukhum. Cruised in 1827–30. Fire watch ship at Sevastopol' in 1833. Broken up after 1833.

Purchased

Gonets 14 ?
Constructor ?
Laid down ?   *Launched* ?   *Purchased* 1820
Dimensions ?
Armament ?
Purchased schooner. Cruised from 1821–31. Broken up after 1831.

Black Sea cutter (1 purpose-built 1801–24)

Sokol (Falcon) 12/15 Sevastopol'
Constructor I. Y. Osminin
Laid down 19.11.1820   *Launched* 7.8.1821
Dimensions 53 ft 10 in x 22 ft 4 in x 9 ft 11 in (Veselago)
Armament ?
Purpose-built cutter. Cruised from 1821–9, capturing a Turkish ship carrying 200 soldiers in 1828. Repaired in 1834. Fire watch ship at Sukhum and Evpatoria from 1835–41. Broken up in 1846.

Black Sea lugger (1 purpose-built 1801–24)

Strela 15 Sevastopol'
Constructor I. Y. Osminin
Laid down 24.2.1822   *Launched* 22.9.1822
Dimensions 60 ft 3 in x 16 ft 8 in x 6 ft 5 in (Veselago)
Armament ?
Lugger. Cruised in the Black Sea in 1823–8. Grounded off Anapa on 5.10.1828. Salvaged and repaired. Fire watch ship at Evpatoria in 1831–4. Stationed in the Kerch straits in 1835–6. Transferred to the Quarantine Administration.

Black Sea single-masted tenders (2 purpose-built 1801–24)

Andrei 8 Nikolaev
Constructor A. I. Melikhov
Laid down 27.4.1817   *Launched* 9.10.1817
Dimensions 33 ft x 13 ft 8 in x 6 ft 8 in (Veselago)
Armament ?
Single-masted tender. Fire watch ship at Kherson 1825–6. Broken up in 1828.

Dionisii 8 Sevastopol'
Constructor Tarusov
Laid down 27.6.1816   *Launched* 11.10.1817
Dimensions 36 ft x 18 ft x 11 ft 3 in (Veselago)
Armament ?
Single-masted tender. Cruised 1818–26. Fire watch ship at Feodosii 1831–7. Broken up in 1846.

Black Sea bomb vessels (1 purpose-built, 2 converted 1801–24)

Purpose-built

Liman ? Kherson
Constructor Toroshilov
Laid down 15.12.1805   *Launched* 14.6.1806
Dimensions approx. 108 ft x 30 ft x 15 ft
              32.9 m x 9.1 m x 4.6 m (Chernyshev)
Armament ?
Purpose-built bomb vessel. Sailed to Sevastopol' in 1806. Cruised in the Black Sea in 1807–9. Converted to a transport in 1809. (See also under Black Sea converted transports.)

Converted from other classes

Mikhail ? ?
Constructor ?
Laid down ?   *Launched* ?   *Converted* 1806
Dimensions ?
Armament ?
Bomb vessel converted from a transport in 1806. Cruised in the Black Sea in 1807–10. No other information.

Evlampii ? ?
Constructor ?
Laid down ?   *Launched* ?   *Converted* 1807
Dimensions 88 ft 6 in x 27 ft 7 in x 10 ft 10 in (Veselago)
Armament ?
Bomb vessel converted from a transport purchased in 1807. Cruised in the Black Sea in 1808–13. Converted back into a transport in 1814. (See also under Black Sea converted transports.)

The Navy of Nicholas I and the Creation of the Steam Navy (1825–60)

Ships of 110–135 guns (6 purpose-built 1825–60)

Between 1826 and 1858, 8 First Rates were completed for the Black Sea fleet in comparison with only 5 for the larger Baltic fleet. Although the final 2 ships were designed as steam screw ships, completed after the Crimean War, and transferred to the Baltic in order to comply with the Treaty of Paris; this was a marked reversal of the balance of power that had traditionally prevailed between the two regional fleets, as was the greater size and firepower of the Black Sea ships. The bulk of the Black Sea naval construction came after 1830 and was in clear reaction to Egyptian and Turkish building programmes.

The 6 ships commissioned before the Crimean War led eventful lives. *Parizh* was actively engaged in the Russo-Turkish War of 1828–9 and 3 of the later ships fought at Sinop in 1853. Their great size made them ideal troop transports during the struggles with Caucasus insurgents and also during the early phases of the Crimean War.

Derbent (renamed *Parizh*) 110/112 Nikolaev
Constructor I. S. Razumov
Laid down 17.10.1823   *Launched* 23.9.1826
Dimensions 193 ft x 52 ft 2 in x 21 ft 10 in
Armament   LD 30 x 36pdrs (short)
             MD 32 x 24pdrs
             UD 32 x 18pdrs
             FC & QD 20 x 6pdrs 4 x 24pdr carr.
Originally named *Derbent*, renamed *Parizh* in 2.1827. Flagship of Vice-Adm. Greig in 1828–9 for operations in the Black Sea at Anapa, Kovarna, Varna and Sizopol'. Carried troops from Russia to Rumelia in 1830. Flag of Rear-Adm. Stozhevskiy in the Bosporus expedition in 1833. Decommissioned in 1835. Hulked in 1836. Broken up in 1845.

The Black Sea fleet in review in 1850 as imagined in 1886 by I. P. Ayvazovskiy. The ships are in line ahead with perfect intervals and heeling slightly to port. In the lower right may be seen Emperor Nicholas I admiring his navy with Admiral M. P. Lazarev and lesser officers in respectful attendance. Unbeknownst to the participants, this moment of glory and pageant will very shortly be followed by the Crimean War and the ending of Russian naval aspirations in the Black Sea for a generation.

The three-decker Parizh *(110) off Varna in 1828. The Russian flagship, seen in the left of the painting, is not apparently directly involved in the assault on the Turkish fortress in the distance, with the white smoke of naval and land based artillery being overwhelmed by the plume of dirty brown smoke rising from the burning city. Such amphibious operations were a well-practised activity on the part of the Black fleet by this time. As flagship to the operation and possibly with consideration being given to her large draught, close in bombardment of the Turkish positions would have generally been left to lesser craft. By K. V. Krugovikhin, 1843.*

THE BLACK SEA FLEET 1825–60

A fragment from a painting by A. P. Bogolyubov from 1846 entitled Sevastopol' Roads *showing the 120-gun* Tri Sviatitelia *entering the roadstead and receiving the salute of a smaller compatriot.* Tri Sviatitelia *was one of a small number of Russian ships to receive the Seppings-style round stern introduced in to the Royal Navy after 1815. Russian officers, like their British counterparts, were not enamoured of the new design, even though it provided greater resistance against the horrors of raking fire, and both services soon reverted to more traditional 'flat' sterns.*

Varshava 120/121 Nikolaev
Constructor Osminin
Laid down 30.3.1832 *Launched* 6.11.1833
Dimensions 206 ft 7 in x 54 ft 9 in x 22 ft 8 in/24 ft 8 in
3,333 tons bm, 5,000 tons displacement (Veselago)
205.89 ft x 55.64 ft x 22.26 ft
4,857.1 tons displacement (Fincham 1851)
206 ft 7 in x (198 ft 8 in keel) x 54 ft 9 in x 22 ft 6 in x 23 ft 8 in /25 ft 8 in (draught fore/aft) (O Sudakh)
Armament LD 16 x 36pdrs (long), 10 x 36pdrs (short), 4 x 60 u (1 pood)
MD 34 x 24pdrs (short)
UD 32 x 18pdrs (long) (later replaced by 32 x 24pdr gunnades)

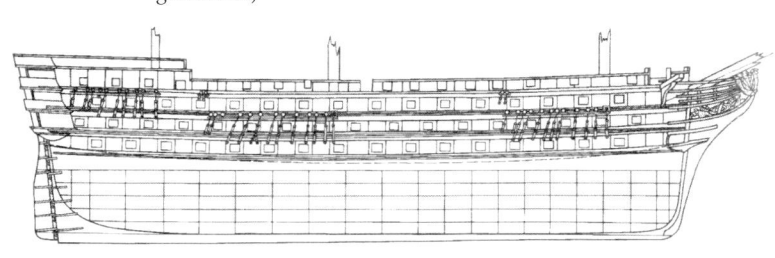

Varshava, the first 120-gunned ship in the Black Sea fleet. This profile reveals her deep draft, without showing her underwater lines in detail, but is of value in showing off her massive appearance and her status as an apparent four-decker, with an unbroken line of 34 weather deck gunports servicing only 26 cannon.

FC & QD 10 x 12pdrs, 6 x 36pdr carr., 1 x 24pdr carr., 6 x 18pdr carr., 2 x 8pdr carr. (Veselago)

Trials under Vice-Adm. Lazarev in 1834. Found to be seriously overgunned, with the upper deck long 18pdrs being replaced by lighter 24pdr gunnades as compensation. Cruised from 1837–42. Assisted in the transportation of 4th Division from Sevastopol' to Odessa in 1843. Repaired in 1843–4. Cruised in the Black Sea in 1845, 1846, and 1848. Scheduled for repair in 1850, but found to be badly deteriorated and broken up that year to the great dissatisfaction of Nicholas I.

Tri Sviatitelia 120/130 Nikolaev
Constructor Vorobyov
Laid down 29.12.1835 *Launched* 28.8.1838
Dimensions 208 ft x 56 ft 8 in x 25 ft 3 in (Veselago)
3,130 tons bm, 4,700 tons displacement (Pamyatnaya)
210 ft 6 in x (199 ft 4 in keel) x 56 ft 8 in x 27 ft x 24 ft 6 in /26 ft (draught fore/aft) (O Sudakh)
Armament LD 28 x 36pdrs (long), 4 x 60 u (1 pood)
MD 34 x 36pdrs (short)
UD 34 x 36pdr gunnades
FC & QD 24 x 24pdr gunnades, 2 x 24pdr carr., 6 x 18pdr carr.
RH 2 x 12pdr carr., 2 x 8pdr carr.
1854 LD 28 x 36pdrs (long), 4 x 60 u (1 pood)
MD 34 x 36pdrs (short)
UD 34 x 36pdr gunnades
FC & QD 24 x 24pdr gunnades
RH 6 x 18pdr gunnades (Pamyatnaya)

An impressive model of Dvenadtsat' Apostolov *(120) of 1841 on display at the Central Naval Museum at St Petersburg. With a main armament of 68pdr shell guns, she was one of the last and most powerfully armed sailing three-deckers built in Russia. In spite of her great firepower, she was never given the opportunity to challenge the numerically superior Anglo-French forces during the Crimean war. Her guns were instead landed and employed against the allies during the siege of Sevastopol. The disarmed liner was first converted into a hospital ship and then scuttled to block the harbour entrance in 1855.*

Along with the earlier and smaller *Aleksandr Nevskii* (74) of 1826, *Tri Sviatitelia* was one of a very small number of Russian ships of the line known to have been completed with round Sepping sterns. Sailed from Nikolaev to Sevastopol' in 1839. Cruised in the Black Sea in 1840–2. Assisted in the transportation of 13th Division from Sevastopol' to Odessa in 1843. Cruised in the Black Sea in 1844–5, 1847, and 1849. Scheduled for decommissioning after the completion of the *Velikii Kniaz' Konstantin* in 1852, but retained and repaired in 1851–2 as a result of her excellent condition. Displacement after refit was 4913 tons. Carried 1369 troops from Sevastopol' to Sukhum-kale in 10.1853. Joined Vice-Adm. Nakhimov's squadron on 16.11.1853 and fought in the battle of Sinop on 18.11.1853. During the battle she fired 1923 rounds, was hit 48 times, and suffered casualties of 8 killed and 18 wounded. Based at Sevastopol' from 4.1854 and scuttled there on 11.9.1854.

Dvenadtsat' Apostolov class (3 ships)

Dvenadtsat' Apostolov 120/130 Nikolaev
Constructor Chernyavskiy
Laid down 4.10.1838 *Launched* 15.7.1841
Dimensions 208 ft 9 in x 59 ft 2 in x 25 ft 3 in (Veselago)
 3,190 tons bm, 4,790 tons displacement (Pamyatnaya)
 211 ft 2 in x (193 ft 9 in keel) x 57 ft 10 in x 27 ft 6 in x 24 ft 6 in / 25 ft 9 in (draught fore/aft) (O Sudakh)
 211 ft 2 in (pp) x 208 ft 9 in (deck) x 59 ft 6 in x ? (Grebenshchikova)
Armament LD 28 x 68pdr shell guns 4 x 36pdrs (long)
 MD 34 x 36pdrs (short)
 UD 34 x 36pdr gunnades
 FC & QD 24 x 24pdr gunnades, 1 x 24pdr carr., 2 x 12pdr carr. 2 x 8pdr carr
 1853 LD 28 x 68pdr shell guns, 4 x 36pdrs (long)
 MD 34 x 36pdrs (short)
 UD 34 x 36pdr gunnades
 FC & QD 24 x 24pdr gunnades (Pamyatnaya)

Dvenadtsat' Apostolov class. Sailed from Nikolaev to Sevastopol' 1842. Cruised in the Black Sea in 1842. Assisted in the transportation of 13th Division from Sevastopol' to Odessa and back in 1843. Cruised in the Black Sea in 1843–7 and 1849–50. Repaired in 1851–52. Transported 1466 troops from Sevastopol' to Sukhum-kale in 10.1853. Returned to Sevastopol' road in.4.1854. All guns had been landed by 12.1854 and only 80 sailors were still aboard. Converted into a temporary hospital 18.12.1854. Scuttled on 13.2.1855.

Parizh 120/130 Nikolaev
Constructor Chernyavskiy
Laid down 18.6.1847 *Launched* 23.10.1849
Dimensions 209 ft x 57 ft 10 in x 25 ft 3 in (Veselago)
 3,190 tons bm, 4,790 tons displacement (Pamyatnaya)
 211 ft 2 in (pp) x 208 ft 9 in (deck) x 59 ft 6 in x ? (Grebenshchikova)
Armament LD 28 x 68pdr shell guns, 4 x 36pdrs (long)
 MD 34 x 36pdrs (short)
 UD 34 x 36pdrs (short)
 FC & QD 24 x 24pdr gunnades, 2 x 24pdr carr., 2 x 12pdr carr., 2 x 12pdr carr., 2 x 8pdr carr.
 1853 LD 28 x 68pdr shell guns, 4 x 36pdrs (long)
 MD 34 x 36pdrs (short)
 UD 34 x 36pdr gunnades
 FC & QD 24 x 24pdr gunnades (Pamyatnaya)

Dvenadtsat' Apostolov class. Name commemorates the entry of Russian troops into Paris in 1815. Sailed from Nikolaev to Sevastopol' in 1850. Cruised in the Black Sea in 1851–53. Transported 1483 troops from Sevastopol' to Sukhum-kale in 10.1853. Joined Vice-Adm. Nakhimov's squadron as the flag of Rear-Adm. Novosilskiy on 16.11.1853. Fought at Sinop on 18.11.1853 where she fired 3952 rounds, took 16 hits and suffered casualties of 1 killed and 16 wounded. Stationed at Sevastopol' Roads in 4.1854. Reduced to 82 guns and 214 sailors by 1855. Scuttled at Sevastopol' on 28.8.1855. Wreckage blown up in 1857–9 and metal salvaged.

Velikii Kniaz' Konstantin 120/130 Nikolaev
Constructor I. S. Dmitriev
Laid down 7.5.1850 *Launched* 29.9.1852
Dimensions 209 ft x 59 ft 6 in x 25 ft 3 in (Veselago)
 3,190 tons bm, 4,790 tons displacement (Pamyatnaya)
 211 ft 2 in (pp)/208 ft 9 in (deck) x 59 ft 6 in x ? (Grebenshchikova)
Armament LD 32 x 68pdr shell guns
 MD 34 x 36pdrs (short)
 UD 34 x 36pdr gunnades
 FC & QD 24 x 24pdr gunnades, 2 x 24pdr carr., 2 x 12pdr carr. 2 x 8pdr carr.
 1853 LD 28 x 68pdr shell guns 4 x 36pdrs (long)
 MD 34 x 36pdrs (short)
 UD 34 x 36pdr gunnades
 FC & QD 26 x 24pdr gunnades (Pamyatnaya)

Dvenadtsat' Apostolov class. Named after the elder brother of Nicholas I who abdicated in favour of Nicholas on the death of Alexander I. Sailed from Nikolaev to Sevastopol' 7.1853. Transported 1437 troops from Sevastopol' to Sukhum-kale in 10.1853. On 16.11.53, she joined Vice-Adm. Nakhimov's squadron. Fought at Sinop on 18.11.1853 where she fired 2,466 rounds, received 30 hits, and had casualties of 8 killed and 26 wounded. Stationed in the Sevastopol' Roads 12.1853. By 1855, she had been reduced to 90 guns and 337 sailors. Scuttled at Sevastopol' on 28.8.1855.

The formidable 120-gun Parizh *of 1849 in heavy weather with a paddle steamer running effortlessly against the wind in the background.* Parizh *was heavily engaged at Sinop in 1853 and scuttled at Sevastopol' two years later. The artist Evald painted the scene in 1854 on the eve of the Crimean War.*

Ships of 84 guns (19 purpose-built 1825–60)

Nineteen 84-gun ships were completed in the Black Sea between 1827 and 1849. As was the case with the First Rates, this number significantly surpasses the total number of Baltic 84s completed during a considerably longer period – with only 13 Baltic 84s having been laid down between 1825 and 1857 (including two that were ultimately completed as steam ships). The overall balance of naval power still lay with the northern fleet which also added 31 74-gun ships during the same period in contrast to none for the Black Sea fleet. The coastline and harbours of the Baltic were shallower than those of the Black Sea, and this gave shallow draft 74s an operational advantage over the larger 84s that encouraged their continued use in northern waters at a time when other European navies were abandoning the type. These conditions did not exist in the Black Sea where the construction of 74s was discontinued after 1825 at the urging, among others, of Adm. Lazarev. Russia in the late 1820s was becoming increasingly concerned over the power vacuum being created by the decline of the Ottoman Empire and the growing potential for conflict with Egypt, France, and Great Britain in the region. Both France and Great Britain were moving decisively away from 74-gun capital ships in the post-Napoleonic era and Egypt was also building up a potentially dangerous fleet of larger line of battle ships with French assistance. The combined action of the navies of Russia, France and Great Britain at Navarino only served to highlight the rivalries developing between the Great Powers and prudence dictated the construction of the most capable capital ships practicable; 84-gun line of battle ships were the logical choice.

All of the 84s had active service lives, being involved in patrol and interdiction activities and frequently finding themselves employed as troop transports – the apparent doom of all Black Sea capital ships. Most of the 84s avoided combat, but 3 of the later ships – *Rostislav, Imperatritsa Mariia* and *Ches'ma* – were present at Sinop in 1853. A year later, in 1854, *Iagudiil* was heavily engaged by allied shore batteries at Sevastopol' before being scuttled in 1855.

Imperatritsa Mariia class (3 ships)
Imperatritsa Mariia 84/96 Nikolaev
Constructor I. S. Razumov
Laid down 23.9.1826 *Launched* 17.10.1827
Dimensions 196 ft x 51 ft x 29 ft (Veselago)
 196 ft x 51.8 ft x 20.63 ft
 3,575.5 tons displacement (Fincham 1951)
 195 ft 6 in x (186 ft 3 in keel) x 51 ft 4 in x 22 ft 6 in
 (O Sudakh)
Armament LD 28 x 36pdrs (long), 4 x 60 u (1 pood)
 UD 32 x 24pdrs
 FC & QD 6 x 12pdrs, 26 x 24pdr carr.

Imperatritsa Mariia class. Carried 920 troops to Varna, bombarded Varna and transported Emperor Nikolai I to Sevastopol in 1828. Cruised off the Bosporus, Sizopol', Akhiollo, Inada, and Mikdiya in 1829. Transported troops from Rumelia to Russia in 1830. Participated in the Bosporus expedition in 1833. Repaired in 1834. Cruised in the Black Sea from 1834–40, carrying the 13th Division from Odessa to Sevastopol' in 1837. Decommissioned in 1842. Hulked in 1843.

The Imperatritsa Mariia *(84) caught up in 1828 in one of the all-too-common storms common to the northern half of the Black Sea. She was to survive the storm, which is just as well since this painting may well be meant to represent her voyage that year transporting Emperor Nikolai I to Sevastopol'. By K. V. Krugovikhin, 1843.*

Ches'ma 84/91 Nikolaev
Constructor A. K. Kaverznev
Laid down 2.12.1826   *Launched* 24.6.1828
Dimensions 196 ft x 51 ft 7 in x 22 ft 6 in (Veselago)
  195 ft 6 in x (186 ft 3 in keel) x 50 ft 9 in x 22 ft 2 in (O Sudakh)
Armament LD 28 x 36pdrs (long) 4 x 60 u (1 pood)
  UD 32 x 24pdrs
  FC & QD 6 x 12pdrs, 26 x 24pdr carr.

Imperatritsa Mariia class. Sailed from Nikolaev to Sevastopol' in 1828. Cruised off Sizopol' and the Bosporus in 1829. Transported troops from Rumelia to Russia in 1830. Participated in the Bosporus expedition in 1833. Repaired in 1833–4. Cruised in the Black Sea in 1834–5 and 1837–8. In 1840 landed troops in the Caucasus against rebels. Decommissioned in 1840. Hulked after 1841.

Anapa 84/108 Nikolaev
Constructor M. K. Surovtsov
Laid down 22.7.1828   *Launched* 7.9.1829
Dimensions 196 ft x 51 ft 7 in x 22 ft 6 in (Veselago)
  195 ft 6 in x (187 ft 3 in keel) x 50 ft 9 in x 22 ft 2 in (O Sudakh)
Armament LD 28 x 36pdrs (long), 4 x 60 u (1 pood)
  UD 32 x 24pdrs
  FC & QD 6 x 12pdrs, 26 x 24pdr carr.

Imperatritsa Mariia class. Anapa was the Turkish fortress taken by Adm. Greig in 1828. Sailed from Nikolaev to Sevastopol' in 1830. Participated in the Bosporus expedition in 1833. Cruised in the Black Sea in 1831–2, 1834–5, 1837–8 and 1841–4. Decommissioned in 1844. Reduced to harbour service in 1845. Broken up in 1850.

Pamyat' Evstafii 84/108 Nikolaev
Constructor I. Y. Osminin
Laid down 11.5.1829   *Launched* 24.8.1830
Dimensions 196 ft 6 in x 51 ft 4 in x 22 ft 4 in (Veselago)
  196 ft 6 in x (192 ft 8 in keel) x 51 ft 4 in x 22 ft 4 in (O Sudakh)
Armament LD 28 x 36pdr (long), 4 x 60 u (1 pood)
  UD 32 x 24pdrs
  FC & QD 6 x 12pdrs, 26 x 24pdr carr.

The name commemorates the *Evstafii*, the Russian flagship lost at the battle of Chios. Sailed from Nikolaev to Sevastopol' in 1831. Flagship of Rear-Adm. Lazarev during the Bosporus expedition of 1833. Cruised in the Black Sea during 1834 and 1835. Repaired in 1836. Cruised in the Black Sea in 1837. Landed troops for the fortification of the Caucasus coastline in 1838–40. Cruised in the Black Sea in 1841. Decommissioned in 1844. Reduced to harbour service in 1845. Broken up in 1850.

Adrianopol' 84/108 Nikolaev
Constructor A. K. Kaverznev
Laid down 27.8.1827(1829?)   *Launched* 11.11.1830
Dimensions 191 ft 10 in x 51 ft 8 in x 21 ft (Veselago)
  192 ft x (189 ft 2 in keel) x 51 ft 4 in x 23 ft 6 in (O Sudakh)
Armament LD 28 x 36pdrs (long) 4 x 60 u (1 pood)
  UD 32 x 24pdrs
  FC & QD 6 x 12pdrs 26 x 24pdr carr.

Named after the Turkish city captured in 1829 and the site of the peace treaty ending the war. Sailed from Nikolaev to Sevastopol' in 1831. Flagship of Rear-Adm. Kumani during the Bosporus expedition of

THE BLACK SEA FLEET 1825–60

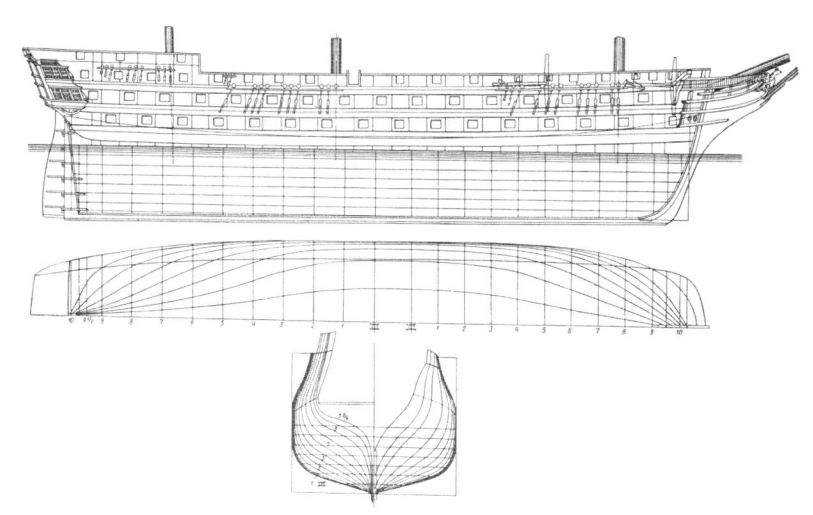

The growing threat presented by Turkish and Egyptian construction programmes led to the abandonment of the 74 as the standard line ship and its replacement in the Black Sea by the more capable 84. Silistriia, seen here, was completed in 1835 and became the model for future ships of this type. She had an active career operating against the Caucasus coastline throughout the 1840s. Worn out by the time of the Crimean War, she became a floating battery during the siege of Sevastopol' and suffered the final indignity of being scuttled to block the harbour entrance in 1854.

1833. Cruised in the Black Sea in 1834, 1835 and 1837. Repaired in 1836. Landed troops for the fortification of the Caucasus coastline in 1838–40. Transported troops to Sukhum-kale in 1841. Cruised in the Black Sea in 1841–3. Decommissioned in 1844. Reduced to harbour service in 1845. Broken up in 1850. Listed to 1855.

Imperatritsa Ekaterina II 84/96 Nikolaev
Constructor M. K. Surovtsov
Laid down 27.8.1827 (1829?)   Launched 31.7.1831
Dimensions 191 ft 10 in x 51 ft x 23 ft (Veselago)
 191.93 ft x 52.21 ft x 21.18 ft
 3,516.6 tons displacement (Fincham)
 194 ft 2 in x (183 ft 7 in keel) x 51 ft 4 in x 23 ft 9 in (O Sudakh)
Armament LD 28 x 36pdrs (long), 4 x 60 u (1 pood)
 UD 32 x 24pdrs
 FC & QD 6 x 12pdrs 26 x 24pdr carr.

Sailed from Nikolaev to Sevastopol' in 1832. Part of Rear-Adm. Lazarev's squadron during the Bosporus expedition of 1833. Cruised in the Black Sea in 1834, 1835, and 1837. Assisted in the transportation of 13th Division from Odessa to Sevastopol' in 1837. Landed troops for the fortification of the Caucasus coastline in 1838–40. Transported troops to Gelendzhik in 1841. Cruised from 1842–4. Decommissioned in 1844. Reduced to harbour service in 1845. Hulked in 1847.

Silistriia 84/88 Nikolaev
Constructor A. S. Akimovi (Apostoli?)
Laid down 24.12.1833   Launched 11.11.1835
Dimensions 191 ft 10 in x 52 ft2 in x 24 ft 11½ in x 23 ft
 2,350 tons bm, 3,540 tons displacement (Lazarev)
 193 ft 5 in x (183 ft keel) x 51 ft 4 in x 25 ft x 22 ft 2 in/ 24 ft (draught fore/aft) (O Sudakh)
Armament LD 26 x 36pdrs (long) 4 x 60 u (1 pood)
 UD 32 x 24pdrs (long)
 FC & QD 22 x 24pdr (gunnades) (Lazarev)

Named after a Turkish fortress captured in 1829. Served as a prototype for subsequent 84-gun ships, although later vessels were slightly larger. Sailed from Nikolaev to Sevastopol' in 1836. Cruised in the Black Sea in 1837. Landed troops for the fortification of the Caucasus coastline in 1838–40. Cruised in the Black Sea in 1841–3. Patrolled the Caucasus coastline in 1844. Cruised in the Black Sea in 1845. Patrolled the Caucasus coastline in 1846. Cruised in the Black Sea in 1847. Patrolled the Caucasus coastline in 1848 and 1852. Decommissioned in 1852 and reduced to harbour service at Sevastopol. Reduced to a floating battery in the Sevastopol' roads from 1853–4. Scuttled at the entrance of the Sevastopol' harbour on 11.9.54.

Sultan Makhmud class (8 ships)
Eight ships completed between 1836 and 1845, arguably falling into two subclasses based on differences of 1 ft in length and 1 ft 6 in in breadth recorded by Lazarev, but not by Chernyshev. They introduced uniform batteries to Black Sea ships of the line, an innovation promoted by Adm. Lazarev. Two were condemned and broken up in 1854. The other six were all scuttled during the Crimean War.

It was a long-standing Russian custom to honour allies by naming line of battle ships after their rulers. Sultan Makhmud *(84) of 1836 was the product of the short-lived alliance between Russia and Turkey against Egypt during the 1830s. This painting of the liner at sea shows just a hint of her unique figurehead, a turbaned and mustachioed Turkish sultan – a most unlikley decoration for a Russian warship. Not apparent here is the round stern, also a rarity for Russian warships.* Sultan Mahmud *was the lead ship in a group of eight 84-gun ships built to answer similar Egyptian building programmes, and the Black Sea replacement for the 74.*

Sultan Makhmud 84/86 Nikolaev
Constructor V. Apostoli
Laid down 1.2.1835 *Launched* 31.10.1836
Dimensions 196 ft x 53 ft 6 in x 26 ft 7/23 ft 8 in
2,500 tons bm, 3790 tons displacement (Lazarev)
197 ft 6 in x (184 ft 4 in keel) x 52 ft (inside plank)
x 25 ft 6 in x 23 ft/24 ft 3 in (draught fore/aft) (O Sudakh)
Armament LD 28 x 36pdrs (long), 4 x 60 u (1 pood)
UD 32 x 36pdrs (short)
FC & QD 6 x 18pdrs (long) 16 x 36pdr carr. (Lazarev)

Sultan Makhmud class (8 ships). Built with round stern to improve hull strength. Distinguished by a bow carving of a Turkish sultan with turban and mustaches. Sailed from Nikolaev to Sevastopol' in 1837. Landed troops for the fortification of the Caucasus coastline in 1838–40. Cruised in the Black Sea in 1840–2. Assisted in the transportation of 13th Division from Odessa to Sevastopol' in 1843. Cruised in the Black Sea in 1844–5, 1847 and 1849. Decommissioned in 1850. Hulked after 1852. Determined to be beyond repair in 1854 and broken up.

Trekh Ierarkhov 84/90 Nikolaev
Constructor S. I. Chernyavskiy
Laid down 19.11.1836 *Launched* 28.8.1838
Dimensions 196 ft x 53 ft 6 in x 26 ft 7 in /23 ft 8 in
2,500 tons bm, 3,790 tons displacement (Lazarev)
197 ft 4 in x (184 ft keel) x 52 ft x 26 ft 4 in x 23 ft/
24 ft 3 in (draught fore/aft) (O Sudakh)
Armament LD 26 x 36pdrs (long), 4 x 60 u (1 pood)
UD 32 x 36pdrs (short)
FC & QD 6 x 18pdrs, 20 x 36pdr carr., 2 x 24pdr carr.
1 x 12pdr carr., 2 x 8pdr carr. (Lazarev)
1853 LD 26 x 36pdrs (long), 4 x 60 u (1 pood)
UD 32 x 36pdrs (short)
FC & QD 6 x 18pdrs (gunnades), 20 x 36pdr carr.
(Pamyatnaya)

Sultan Makhmud class (8 ships). Sailed from Nikolaev to Sevastopol' in 1839. Landed troops for the fortification of the Caucasus coastline in 1840–1. Cruised in the Black Sea in 1842. Assisted in the transportation of 13th Division from Sevastopol' to Odessa and back in 1843. Cruised in the Black Sea in 1844–5. Again assisted in the transportation of 13th Division from Sevastopol' to Odessa and back in 1847. Cruised in the Black Sea in 1849. Repaired in 1852. Plans for conversion to screw propulsion rejected due to poor material state and lack of funds. Broken up in 1854.

Arkhangel Gavriil 84/86 Nikolaev
Constructor A. S. Akimov
Laid down 28.8.1838 *Launched* 19.11.1839
Dimensions 197 ft 4 in x 52 ft x 26 ft 7 in /23 ft 8 in (Veselago)
2,500 tons bm, 3,790 tons displacement (Pamyatnaya)
197 ft 4 in x (184 ft keel) x 52 ft x 26 ft 4 in x 23 ft/
24 ft 3 in (draught fore/aft) (O Sudakh)
Armament LD 26 x 36pdrs (long), 4 x 60 u (1 pood)
UD 32 x 36pdrs (short)
FC & QD 8 x 18pdrs (long), 14 x 36pdr carr., 1 x 24pdr carr., 2 x 12pdr carr., 2 x 8pdr carr.
1853 LD 26 x 36pdrs (long) 4 x 60 u (1 pood)
UD 32 x 36pdrs (short)
FC & QD 8 x 18pdrs (long), 14 x 36pdr carr.
(Pamyatnaya)
1854 LD 26 x 36pdrs (long), 4 x 60 u (1 pood)
UD 32 x 36pdrs (short)
FC & QD 20 x 36pdr carr., 8 x 18pdr gunnades
RH 6 x 18pdr (short) (Pamyatnaya)

Sultan Makhmud class (8 ships). Sailed from Nikolaev to Sevastopol' in 1840. Landed troops for the fortification of the Caucasus coastline in 1840–1. Cruised in the Black Sea in 1842. Assisted in the transportation of 13th Division from Sevastopol' to Odessa and back in 1843. Cruised in the Black Sea in 1844–5. Again assisted in the transportation of 13th Division from Sevastopol' to Odessa and back in 1847. Cruised in the Black Sea in 1849 and 1852. Received superficial repairs in 12.1853. Scuttled on 11.9.1854 at Silistrilia.

Selafail 84/96 Nikolaev
Constructor V. Apostoli
Laid down 28.8.1838 *Launched* 10.7.1840
Dimensions 197 ft 4 in x 52 ft x 26 ft 7 in /23 ft 8 in (Veselago)
2,500 tons bm, 3,790 tons displacement (Pamyatnaya)
197 ft 4 in x (184 ft keel) x 52 ft x 26 ft 4 in x 23 ft/
24 ft 3 in (draught fore/aft) (O Sudakh)
Armament LD 26 x 36pdrs (long) 4 x 60 u (1 pood)
UD 32 x 36pdrs (short)
FC & QD 8 x 18pdrs (long), 10 x 36pdr carr.,
2 x 24pdr, carr. 2 x 12pdr carr., 2 x 8pdr carr.
1853 LD 26 x 36pdrs (long) 4 x 60 u (1 pood)
UD 32 x 36pdrs (short)
FC & QD 8 x 18pdrs (long), 10 x 36pdr carr.
(Pamyatnaya)
1854 LD 26 x 36pdrs (long), 4 x 60 u (1 pood)
UD 32 x 36pdrs (short)
FC & QD 20 x 36pdr carr., 8 x 18pdr (gunnades)
RH 6 X 18pdr (short) (Pamyatnaya)

Sultan Makhmud class (8 ships). Sailed from Nikolaev to Sevastopol' in 1841. Cruised in the Black Sea in 1842. Assisted in the transportation of 13th Division from Sevastopol' to Odessa and back in 1843. Cruised in the Black Sea in 1844–5, 1847, 1849 and 1852. Assisted in the transportation of 13th Division from Odessa to Sevastopol' in 1853. Prevented from joining Vice-Adm. Nakhimov's squadron in 11.53 due to a leak. Based in Sevastopol' roads in 1854 and scuttled on 11.9.1854.

Uriil 84/96 Nikolaev
Constructor A. S. Akimov
Laid down 28.8.1838 *Launched* 31.10.1840
Dimensions 197 ft 4 in x 52 ft x 26 ft 7 in/23 ft 8 in (Veselago)
2,500 tons bm, 3,790 tons displacement (Pamyatnaya)
197 ft 4 in x (184 ft keel) x 52 ft x 26 ft 4 in x 23 ft/
24 ft 3 in (draught fore/aft) (O Sudakh)
Armament LD 26 x 36pdrs (long), 4 x 60 u (1 pood)
UD 32 x 36pdrs (short)
FC & QD 8 x 18pdrs (long), 10 x 36pdr carr., 2 x 24pdr carr. 1 x 12pdr carr., 2 x 8pdr carr.
1853 LD 26 x 36pdrs (long), 4 x 60 u (1 pood)
UD 32 x 36pdrs (short)
FC & QD 8 x 18pdrs (long), 10 x 36pdr carr.
(Pamyatnaya)
1854 LD 26 x 36pdrs (long), 4 x 60 u (1 pood)
UD 32 x 36pdrs (short)
FC & QD 20 x 36pdr carr., 8 x 18pdr gunnades
RH 6 x 18pdr (short) (Pamyatnaya)

Sultan Makhmud class (8 ships). Sailed from Nikolaev to Sevastopol' in 1841. Cruised in the Black Sea in 1842, 1844–5, 1847, 1849 and 1852.

Assisted in the transportation of 13th Division from Odessa to Sevastopol' in 1853. Prevented from joining Vice-Adm. Nakhimov's squadron in 11.53 due to leaks acquired during heavy weather. Based at Sevastopol' and docked with crews being distributed among the shore batteries. Scuttled at Sevastopol' on 11.9.1854.

Varna 84/96 Nikolaev
Constructor I. D. Vorobyov
Laid down 4.10.1838   Launched 26.7.1842
Dimensions 196 ft x 53 ft 6 in x 26 ft 7 in /23 ft 8 in (Veselago)
 2,500 tons bm, 3,790 tons displacement (Pamyatnaya)
 197 ft 4 in x (184 ft keel) x 52 ft x 26 ft 4 in x 23 ft/
 24 ft 3 in (draught fore/aft) (O Sudakh)
Armament LD 26 x 36pdrs (long), 4 x 60 u (1 pood)
 UD 32 x 36pdrs (short)
 FC & QD 20 x 24pdr gunnades, 2 x 24pdr carr.,
 6 x 18pdr carr., 2 x 12pdr carr., 2 x 8pdr carr.
 1853 LD 26 x 36pdrs (long), 4 x 60 u (1 pood)
 UD 32 x 36pdrs (short)
 FC & QD 20 x 24pdr gunnades
 1854 LD 26 x 36pdrs (long), 4 x 60 u (1 pood)
 UD 32 x 36pdrs (short)
 FC & QD 20 x 24pdr gunnades
 RH 6 x 18pdrs (short)
Sultan Makhmud class. Named for the Turkish fortress in Bulgaria taken by the Russians 29.9.1828. Sailed from Nikolaev to Sevastopol' in 1843. Assisted in the transportation of 13th Division from Sevastopol' to Odessa and back in 1843. Cruised in the Black Sea in 1844–5, 1847–9 and 1852. Transported 910 troops from Sevastopol' to Sukhum-kale in 10.53. Repaired 1853–4. Based in the Sevastopol' Roads in 1854. Scuttled at the entrance to Sevastopol' on 11.9.1854.

Iagudiil 84/96 Nikolaev
Constructor I. S. Dmitriev
Laid down 21.9.1839   Launched 17.9.1843
Dimensions 197 ft 4 in x 52 ft x 26 ft 7 in /23 ft 8 in (Veselago)
 2,500 tons bm, 3,790 tons displacement (Pamyatnaya)
 197 ft 4 in x (184 ft keel) x 52 ft x 25 ft 6 in x 23 ft/
 24 ft 3 in (draught fore/aft) (O Sudakh)
Armament LD 26 x 36pdrs (long), 4 x 60 u (1 pood)
 UD 32 x 36pdrs (short)
 FC & QD 20 x 24pdr gunnades, 2 x 24pdr carr.
 7 x 18pdr carr. 2 x 12pdr carr. 2 x 8pdr carr.
 1853 LD 26 x 36pdrs (long) 4 x 60 u (1 pood)
 UD 32 x 36pdrs (short)
 FC & QD 20 x 24pdr gunnades
 1854 LD 26 x 36pdrs (long) 4 x 60 u (1 pood)
 UD 32 x 36pdrs (short)
 FC & QD 20 x 24pdr gunnades
 RH 6 x 18pdrs (short)
Sultan Makhmud class. Sailed from Nikolaev to Sevastopol' in 1844. Cruised in the Black Sea in 1845, 1847, 1849, and 1851–53. Transported 947 troops from Sevastopol' to Sukhum-kale in 10.1853. Prevented from joining Vice-Adm. Nakhimov's squadron due to leaks. Heavily engaged with enemy shore batteries throughout 10.1854. Scuttled and set afire upon the retreat of Russian troops from Sevastopol' on 28.8.1855. Wreckage blown up in 1857.

Sviatoslav 84/94 Nikolaev
Constructor I. S. Dmitriev
Laid down 16.5.1843   Launched 7.11.1845
Dimensions 197 ft 4 in x 52 ft x 26 ft 7 in /23 ft 8 (Veselago)
 2,500 tons bm, 3,790 tons displacement (Pamyatnaya)
Armament LD 4 x 68pdr shell guns, 28 x 36pdrs (long)
 UD 32 x 36pdrs (short)
 FC & QD 20 x 24pdr gunnades, 2 x 24pdr carr.
 8 x 18pdr carr. 1 x 12pdr carr. 3 x 8pdr carr.
 1853 LD 4 x 68pdr shell guns (short), 28 x 36pdrs (long)
 UD 32 x 36pdrs (short)
 FC & QD 20 x 24pdr gunnades (Pamyatnaya)
 1854 LD 4 x 68pdr shell guns, 28 x 36pdrs (long)
 UD 32 x 36pdrs (short)
 FC & QD 20 x 24pdr gunnades
 RH 6 x 18pdr carr. (Pamyatnaya)
Sultan Makhmud class. Sailed from Nikolaev to Sevastopol' in 1846. Cruised in the Black Sea in 1847, 1849, and 1852–3. Transported 935 troops from Sevastopol' to Sukhum-kale in 10.1853. While part of Vice-Adm. Nakhimov's squadron in 11.1853, severely storm damaged and forced to return to Sevastopol. Stationed in the Sevastopol' roads in 1854, during which time her crew built a 17-gun shore battery. Converted to a hospital ship on 18.12.1854. Scuttled on 13.2.1855 at Sevastopol.

Rostislav 84/90 Nikolaev
Constructor I. S. Dmitriev
Laid down 16.5.1843   Launched 1.11.1844
Dimensions 196 ft x 55 ft x 26 ft 7 in /23 ft 8 in (Veselago)
 2,590 tons bm, 3,890 tons displacement (Pamyatnaya)
Armament LD 8 x 68pdr shell guns, 24 x 36pdrs (long)
 UD 34 x 36pdrs (short)
 FC & QD 20 x 24pdr gunnades, 2 x 24pdr carr.
 6 x 18pdr carr., 1 x 12pdr carr.
 1853 4 x 68pdr shell guns, 28 x 36pdrs (long)
 UD 4 x 68pdr shell guns, 28 x 36pdrs (short)
 FC & QD 20 x 24pdr gunnades (Pamyatnaya)
 1854 4 x 68pdr shell guns, 28 x 36pdrs (long)
 UD 4 x 68pdr shell guns, 28 x 36pdrs (short)
 FC & QD 20 x 24pdr gunnades, 6 x 18pdrs
 (roundhouse) (Pamyatnaya)
Broad beamed to carry 68pdrs on LD. Sailed from Nikolaev to Sevastopol' in 1846. Cruised in the Black Sea in 1847, 1849, and 1852–3. Transported 943 troops from Sevastopol' to Sukhum-kale in 10.1853. Fought at Sinop on 18.11.1853, firing 3960 rounds and receiving 25 hits with casualties of 3 killed and 105 wounded. Repaired in 1854 and stationed in the Sevastopol' Roads. Scuttled at Sevastopol' on 13.2.1855.

Khrabryi class
Khrabryi 84/86 Nikolaev
Constructor S. I. Chernyavskiy
Laid down 15.6.1841   Launched 25.6.1847
Dimensions 200 ft x 56 ft 3 in x 24 ft (Veselago)
 2,770 tons bm, 4,160 tons displacement (Pamyatnaya)
Armament LD 28 x 68pdr shell guns, 4 x 36pdrs (long)
 UD 32 x 36pdrs (short)
 FC & QD 24 x 24pdr gunnades, 2 x 24pdr carr.,
 6 x 18pdr carr. 2 x 12pdr carr., 2 x 8pdr carr.
 1853 LD 28 x 68pdr shell guns, 4 x 36pdrs (long)
 UD 32 x 36pdrs (short)
 FC & QD 24 x 24pdr gunnades (Pamyatnaya)
Khrabryi class. Sailed from Nikolaev to Sevastopol' in 1848. Cruised in the Black Sea in 1849 and 1852–3. Transported 955 troops from Sevastopol' to Sukhum-kale in 10.1853. While part of Vice-Adm.

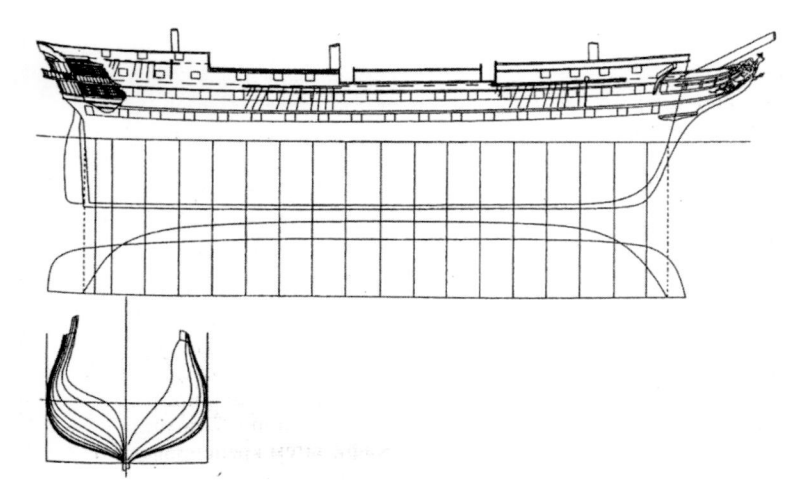

Imperatritsa Mariya (84) as built in 1853. She was the last Russian sailing line of battle ship completed, and took part in the battle of Sinop as Vice-Admiral Nakhimov's flag. Her young age and excellent qualities as a warship did not keep her from being scuttled at Sevastopol' along with her older sisters in 1855.

Nakhimov's squadron in 11.1853, severely storm damaged and forced to return to Sevastopol. Repaired and returned to service in 11.1853, too late for the battle of Sinop. Stationed in Sevastopol' Roads in 1854. Reduced to 59 guns and 248 crew members by 1.1855. Scuttled at Sevastopol' on 28.8.1855.

Imperatritsa Mariia 84/90 Nikolaev
Constructor I. S. Dmitriev
Laid down 23.4.1849 *Launched* 9.5.1853
Dimensions 200 ft x 56 ft 8 in x 24 ft (Veselago)
 2,770 tons bm, 4,160 tons displacement (Pamyatnaya)
Armament LD 8 x 68pdr shell guns, 24 x 36pdr long guns
 UD 34 x 36pdr short guns
 FC & QD 20 x 24pdr gunnades, 2 x 24pdr carr.,
 2 x 12pdr carr., 2 x 8pdr carr.
 1853 4 x 68pdr shell guns, 28 x 36pdrs (long)
 UD 4 x 68pdr shell guns, 28 x 36pdrs (short)
 FC & QD 20 x 24pdr gunnades (Pamyatnaya)

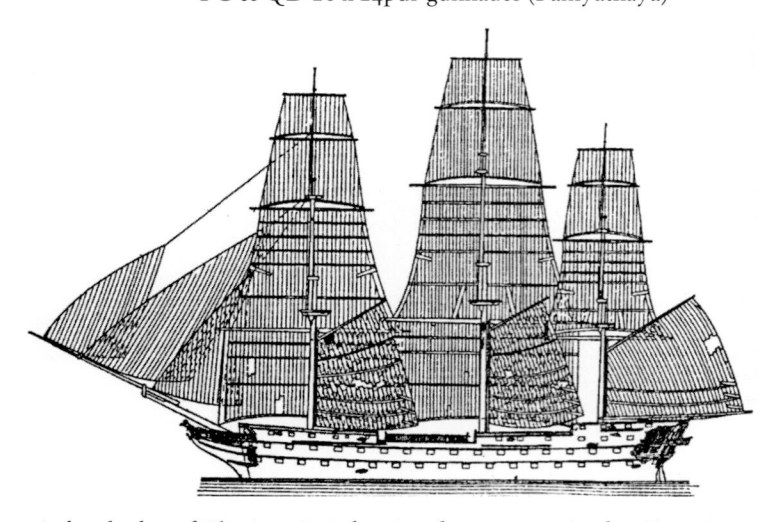

A sketch plan of Ches'ma (84) showing damage sustained at Sinop in 1853.

Khrabryi class. Sailed from Nikolaev to Sevastopol' in 1853. Transported 939 troops from Sevastopol' to Sukhum-kale in 10.1853. Fought at Sinop as the flagship of Vice-Adm. Nakhimov on 18.11.1853 where she fired 2128 rounds, took 60 hits, and suffered casualties of 16 killed and 39 wounded. Repaired and stationed in the Sevastopol' Roads in 1854. Scuttled at Sevastopol' on 28.8.1855.

Ches'ma 84/92 Nikolaev
Constructor I. S. Dmitriev
Laid down 26.7.1842 *Launched* 23.10.1849
Dimensions 196 ft x 57 ft x 23 ft 8 in (Veselago)
 4,030 tons displacement (Pamyatnaya)
Armament LD 4 x 68pdr shell guns (short), 28 x 36pdrs (long)
 UD 32 x 36pdrs (short)
 FC & QD 8 x 18pdrs (long), 10 x 36pdr carr.,
 2 x 24pdr carr., 2 x 18pdr carr., 2 x 8pdr carr.
 1853 LD 4 x 68pdr shell guns (short), 28 x 36pdrs (long)
 UD 32 x 36pdrs (short)
 FC & QD 10 x 36pdr carr.
 RH 8 x 18pdr gunnades (Pamyatnaya)
 1854 LD 4 x 68pdr shell guns, 28 x 36pdrs (long)
 UD 32 x 36pdrs (short)
 FC & QD 20 x 24pdr gunnades
 RH 6 x 18pdr carr. (Pamyatnaya)

Sailed from Nikolaev to Sevastopol' in 1850. Cruised in the Black Sea in 1851–53. Transported 935 troops from Sevastopol' to Sukhum-kale in 10.1853. Fought at Sinop on 18.11.1853 where she fired 1539 rounds, received 20 hits, and had casualties of 4 wounded. Stationed in the Sevastopol' Roads in 1854. Employed her guns to repel the storming of Sevastopol' on 12.2.1855. Scuttled at Sevastopol' on 28.8.1855.

Black Sea frigates (16 Purpose-built 1825–60)

60-gun heavy frigates (12 Purpose-built 1825–60)

The Russian predilection for building large and heavily armed frigates reached its apex in the Black Sea fleet during this period with the construction of twelve very large and powerful 60-gun frigates of between 170 ft and 179 ft in length over the twenty year period between 1828 and 1847. These ships were significantly larger and more powerful than the contemporary Baltic heavy frigates of the *Speshnyi* class, and they were sometimes considered as ships of the line. They were approached and in some cases exceeded by similar developments taking place in France, the United States, and, to a more limited degree, Great Britain. Comparative statistics for the frigates built during this period are of interest:

Russia *Tenedos* class (60)
 170 ft x 42 ft x 17 ft
 30 x 24pdrs (long), 4 x 24pdrs (short), 28 x 24pdr carr.
France *Surveillante* class (60)
 178 ft x 46 ft x 20 ft
 30 x 30pdrs, 28 x 30pdr carr., 2 x 18 pdrs
United States *Potomac* class (52)
 177 ft x 46 ft x 20 ft
 4 x 8 in, 28 x 32pdrs, 20 x 42pdr carr.
Great Britain *Southampton* class (52)
 172 ft x 43 ft x 14 ft
 36 x 24pdrs, 16 x4 2pdr carr.

All four of the Great Power large frigate classes had generally similar overall dimensions, but the French and American frigates had significantly heavier armaments and were both longer and broader-beamed than Russian ships. Great Britain broke company with the her Atlantic rivals by building comparatively few of these larger frigate types during the 1820s and 1830s, relying primarily on the combination of razeed 74s completed before 1815 and large numbers of 18pr *Leda* class ships to counter French and American heavy frigates.

The Russian designers were undoubtedly aware of and influenced by design developments amongst the Atlantic powers; however the construction of large numbers of 60-gun frigates was most directly related to similar developments in the Ottoman and Egyptian navies. Both nations were in the process of building large numbers of 50- and 60-gun frigates during the 1820s and 1830s – 9 for Egypt and 13 for Turkey – and Russia had, perforce, to follow suit.

With the exception of the last 60-gun frigate built, the *Kulvechi*, which pursued and exchanged heavy fire with the Turkish frigate *Taif* at the battle of Sinop in 1853, the Russian super-heavy frigates were untested against their opposite numbers during their lifetimes, being much engaged instead in providing gunfire support against the Caucasus rebels in the 1830s and 1840s and in the unglamorous role of acting as troop transports in support of the long running battle against ethnic groups resistant to Russian expansion into territories seized from the Turks.

Tenedos class (6 ships)
Tenedos 60 Nikolaev
Constructor A. K. Kaverznev
Laid down 14.8.1827   *Launched* 4.11.1828
Dimensions 170 ft x 42 ft x 17 ft (Veselago)
170 ft 10 in x (160 ft 10 in keel) x 42 ft 5 in x 19 ft 4 in (O Sudakh)
Armament UD 30 x 24pdrs (long)
FC & QD 4 x 24pdrs (short), 28 x 24pdr carr.
Tenedos class. Named to commemorate the capture of the Greek isle Tenedos taken in 1807. Transported 588 troops offloaded from a foundering troop transport on 11.7.1829 to Messemvriia where she joined the Russian squadron operating against the Turks and made three cruises to the Bosporus. Transported Russian troops from Rumelia to Russia in 1830. Bombarded Caucasus mountaineers off Gelendzhik and landed troops there in 1831. Participated in the Bosporus expedition of 1833 as part of Vice-Adm. Lazarev's squadron. Cruised in the Black Sea in 1834–5. Repaired in 1837. Landed troops for the fortification of the Caucasus coastline in 1838. Bombarded the forts at Adler and Sochi in the campaign against the Caucasus mountaineers in 1841. Hulked in 1842.

Erivan 60 Nikolaev
Constructor A. K. Kaverznev
Laid down 15.3.1828   *Launched* 30.5.1829
Dimensions 170 ft x 42 ft x 17 ft (Veselago)
170 ft 10 in x (166 ft 6 in keel) x 42 ft 5 in x 19 ft 3 in (O Sudakh)
Armament UD 30 x 24pdrs (long)
FC & QD 4 x 24pdrs (short), 28 x 24pdr carr
Tenedos class. Named after the city captured during the war with Persia 1826–8. Joined the Russian fleet operating off Messemvriia in 10.29. Transported troops in 1830. Bombarded Caucasus mountaineers off Gelendzhik and landed troops there in 1831. Participated in the Bosporus expedition of 1833 as part of Vice-Adm. Lazarev's squadron. Cruised in the Black Sea in 1834–6. Hulked in 1837.

Arkhipelag 60 Nikolaev
Constructor A. K. Kaverznev
Laid down 21.1.1828   *Launched* 30.7.1829
Dimensions 170 ft x 42 ft x 17 ft (Veselago)
170 ft 10 in x (160 ft 6 in keel) x 43 ft 10 in x 19 ft 4 in (O Sudakh)
Armament UD 30 x 24pdrs (long)
FC & QD 4 x 24pdrs (short), 28 x 24pdr carr
Tenedos class. Carried troops in 1830. Cruised in the Black Sea in 1831–2. Participated in the Bosporus expedition of 1833. Cruised in the Black Sea in 1834–6. Bombarded positions of Caucasus mountaineers off Sukhum-kale in 1837 and helped establish fort St Spirit. Hulked in 1838.

Varna 60 Nikolaev (private yard)
Constructor M. K. Surovtsov
Laid down ?.?.1829   *Launched* 16.8.1830
Dimensions 170 ft x 43 x 17 ft (Veselago)
170 ft 10 in x (160 ft 10 in keel) x 42 ft 5 in x 19 ft 11 in (O Sudakh)
Armament UD 30 x 24pdrs (long)
FC & QD 4 x 24pdrs (short), 28 x 24pdr carr
Tenedos class Named for the Turkish fortress in Bulgaria taken by the Russians 29.9.1828. Sailed to Sevastopol' in 1843. Participated in the Bosporus expedition of 1833. Cruised in the Black Sea in 1834–7. Participated in the Abhasian expedition of 1838. Drifted ashore during a storm off Sochi on 31.5.1838 and wrecked with a loss of 17 men.

Enos 60 Nikolaev (private yard)
Constructor M.I. Surovtsov
Laid down ?   *Launched* 10.10.1831
Dimensions 170 ft x 43 ft x 17 ft (Veselago)
170 ft 10 in x (164 ft 3 in keel) x 43 ft x 19 ft 10 in (O Sudakh)
Armament UD 30 x 24pdrs (long)
FC & QD 4 x 24pdrs (short), 28 x 24pdr carr
Tenedos class. Named for the point on the coast of the Aegean Sea where Russian troops met the Mediterranean squadron of Rear-Adm. V. A. Geiden on 26.8.1829. Sailed to Sevastopol' in 1832. Cruised in the Black Sea in 1833–43 along the Caucasus, participating in the creation of the line of coastal fortifications. Hulked in 1845.

Burgas 60 Nikolaev (private yard)
Constructor M.I. Surovtsov
Laid down 11.11.1831   *Launched* 7.11.1832
Dimensions 170 ft x 43 ft x 17 ft (Veselago)
170 ft 10 in x (166 ft 3 in keel) x 43 ft x 23 ft 9 in (O Sudakh)
Armament UD 30 x 24pdrs (long)
FC & QD 4 x 24pdrs (short), 28 x 24pdr carr
Tenedos class. Named for the Turkish fortress taken 12.7.1829. Sailed to Sevastopol' in 1833. Cruised along the Caucasus in 1834–9 and in 1841, participating in the creation of the line of coastal fortifications. Hulked in 1842.

Agatopol' 60 Nikolaev
Constructor I. D. Vorobyev
Laid down 6.9.1833   *Launched* 11.11.1834

Dimensions 171 ft x 44 ft 7 in x 19 ft 4 in (Veselago)
174 ft 5 in x (159 ft 9 in keel) x 44 ft 4 in x 23 ft 6 in
x 18 ft 6 in /20 ft 3 in (draught fore/aft) (O Sudakh)
Armament UD 30 x 24pdrs (long)
FC & QD 4 x 24pdrs (short), 28 x 24pdr carr
Named for the Turkish fortress taken 24.7.29 by Russian naval forces. Carried troops in 1827. Cruised 1837–42 and 1844–8, participating in the creation of the line of coastal fortifications. Broken up in 1853.

Messemvriia 60 Nikolaev
Constructor S. I. Chernyavskiy
Laid down 4.10.1838 *Launched* 31.10.1840
Dimensions 179 ft x 46 ft 6 in x 24 ft 7 in x 22 ft (Veselago)
179 ft 6 in x (157 ft 8 in keel) x 46 ft 6 in x 24 ft 6 in
x 21 ft 3 in /22 ft 4 in (draught fore/aft) (O Sudakh)
Armament UD 30 x 24pdrs (long)
FC & QD 4 x 24pdrs (short), 28 x 24pdr carr
1853 UD 30 x 24pdrs (long)
FC & QD 24 x 24pdr gunnades (Pamyatnaya)
Named for the Turkish fortress taken 10.7.1829. Sailed to Sevastopol' in 1841. Cruised in the Black Sea in 1842–8 and 1850. Repaired 1852–3. Cruised in the Black Sea in 1853 bombarding Poti. Converted into a hospital ship 12.1854. Scuttled on 13.2.1855 in Sevastopol' harbour.

Sizopol' 60/54 Sevastopol'
Constructor A. P. Prokofyev
Laid down 22.10.1838 *Launched* 4.3.1843
Dimensions 174 ft x 44 ft 4 in x 24 ft x 20 ft (Veselago)
174 ft 4 in x (162 ft 2 in keel) x 43 ft 8 in x 23 ft 11 in
x 19 ft 5 in /20 ft 5 in (draught fore/aft) (O Sudakh)
Armament UD 30 x 24pdrs (long)
FC & QD 4 x 24pdrs (short), 28 x 24pdr carr
1853 UD 30 x 24pdr (long)
FC & QD 24 x 24pdr gunnades (Pamyatnaya)
Named for the Turkish fortress taken 18.2.1829. Cruised in the Black Sea in 1842–50. Repaired in 1851. Cruised in the Black Sea in 1825–53. Carried troops and bombarded Poti in 10.1853. Scuttled 11.9.1854 at the entrance to the Sevastopol' harbour.

Midiia 60/54 Nikolaev
Constructor V. Apostoli
Laid down 10.7.1840 *Launched* 17.9.1843
Dimensions 175 ft x 45 ft 6 in x 23 ft x 20 ft 8 in (Veselago)
172 ft 3 in x (164 ft keel) x 45 ft x 22 ft 9 in x 19 ft 6 in/
21 ft 6 in (draught fore/aft) (O Sudakh)
Armament UD 30 x 24pdrs (long)
FC & QD 4 x 24pdrs (short), 28 x 24pdr carr
1853 UD 30 x 24pdr (long)
FC & QD 24 x 24pdr gunnades (Pamyatnaya)
Named for the Turkish fortress taken 17.8.1829. Sailed to Sevastopol' 1844. Cruised 1845–9 and 1851–3. Converted into a hospital 12.1854. Scuttled on 16.2.1855.

Kovarna 60/54 Sevastopol'
Constructor A. P. Prokofyev
Laid down 4.3.1841 *Launched* 11.9.1845
Dimensions 174 ft x 48 ft 9 in x ? (Veselago)
2,130 tons displacement (Pamyatnaya)
Armament UD 30 x 24pdrs (long)
FC & QD 4 x 24pdrs (short), 28 x 24pdr carr
1853 UD 30 x 24pdrs (long)
FC & QD 22 x 24pdr gunnades
Named for the port on the Bulgarian coast where the Russian army was landed for the siege of Varna. Cruised in the Black Sea in 1847–9 and 1851–3. Destroyed by fire on 26.8.1855 in harbour during the bombardment of Sevastopol.

Kulevchi 60/52 Nikolaev
Constructor A. S. Akimov
Laid down 18.3.1844 *Launched* 21.9.1847
Dimensions 174 ft x 48 ft 9 in x ? (Veselago)
2,130 tons displacement (Pamyatnaya)
Armament UD 30 x 24pdrs (long)
FC & QD 4 x 24pdrs (short), 28 x 24pdr carr
1853 UD 30 x 24pdrs (long)
FC & QD 22 x 24pdr gunnades (Pamyatnaya)
Name celebrates the victory of the Russian army on 30.5.1829. Cruised in the Black Sea in 1848–53. Fought in the battle of Sinop 18.11.1853; pursued the Turkish frigate Taif and fired 260 rounds at her. Scuttled on 27.8.1855 prior to the retreat of the Russians from Sevastopol.

44-gun heavy frigates (3 purpose-built 1825–60)

Forty-four gun frigates were relative lightweights in the top heavy Black Sea fleet of the 1830s and 1840s. Two *Speshnyis* found their way from the Baltic into the Black Sea in 1833 and they may have inspired the construction of an additional three Black Sea 44s between 1835 and 1843. As was the frequent case with smaller warships – if these ships may be called smaller warships – they were actively employed during their service lives and two became heavily engaged with Turkish frigates during the opening phases of the Crimean War.

Kniaginia Lovich 44 ?
Transferred from the Baltic in 7.1833. Fire watch vessel at Sevastopol' in 1834–5. Hulked in 1837.

Anna 44 ?
Transferred from the Baltic in 7.1833. Cruised in the Black Sea in 1834 and 1836–7, landing troops to quell a mutiny in the Caucasus. Broken up in 1838.

Brailov 44 Sevastopol'
Constructor S. I. Chernyavskiy
Laid down 14.2.1835 *Launched* 6.10.1836
Dimensions 159 ft 2 in x 45 ft 5 in x 18 ft 9 in (Veselago)
160 ft x (150 ft keel) x 41'4 in x 21 ft 4 in x 18 ft 3 in/
19 ft 3 in (draught fore/aft) (O Sudakh)
Armament ?
Named for the Turkish fortress taken 7.6.1828. Participated in the creation of the line of fortresses in the Caucasus, cruising in 1838–41, 1843–6 and 1848–50. Broken up in 1851.

Flora 44 Nikolaev
Constructor A. S. Akimov
Laid down 24.11.1837 *Launched* 21.9.1839
Dimensions 166 ft 6 in x 45 ft 5 in x 19 ft 8 in (Veselago)
1,787 tons displacement (Pamyatnaya)
164 ft 2 in x (146 ft keel) x 44 ft 1 in x 22 ft 10 in
x 19 ft 6 in/19.6 in (draught fore/aft) (O Sudakh)
Armament 1853 UD 26 x 24pdrs (short), 2 x 60 u (1 pood)
FC & QD 18 x 24pdr gunnades (Pamyatnaya)
Cruised in the Black Sea in 1841, 1843, 1846–9 and 1851–3. Attacked

A fight that Turkey should have won. This is the 44-gun sailing frigate Flora *in action on 9 November 1853 against three Turkish paddle frigates. The paddle frigates were individually smaller than* Flora, *but they carried heavier guns and had the advantages of numbers and the mobility conferred by steam. By A. P. Bogolyubov, 1860.*

9.11.1853 off Pitsunda by three Turkish paddle frigates (mounting 62 guns in all including a number of 10 in shell guns) under the command of the Turkish Rear-Adm. Mushaver Pasha (Adolphus Slade). In an action lasting 7 hours (due to the very calm conditions) *Flora* fired 437 rounds and was only hit twice, suffering no personnel losses. The Turkish frigates were damaged, the flagship *Taif* having to be towed away. Scuttled on 11.9.1854 at the entrance to the Sevastopol' harbour.

Kagul 44 Nikolaev
Constructor Apostoli
Laid down 31.10.1840   *Launched* 17.9.1843
Dimensions 160 ft 6 in x 45 ft 5 in x 19 ft 8 in (Veselago)
164 ft 2 in x (146 ft keel) x 44 ft 1 in x 22 ft 10 in x 19 ft 6 in /19 ft 6 in (draught fore/aft) (O Sudakh)
Armament 1853 UD 26 x 24pdrs (long)
FC & QD 18 x 24pdr gunnades (Pamyatnaya)
Sailed to Sevastopol' 1844. Cruised in the Black Sea in 1846 and 1848–53. On 7.11.1853 was intercepted by five Turkish frigates but escaped. Fought in the battle of Sinop 18.11.1853, and joined the pursuit of the fleeing steam frigate *Taif*. Converted into a hospital 12.1854. Scuttled on 13.2.1855 in Sevastopol' harbour.

36-gun frigate (1 purpose-built 1825–60)
Rafail 36/44 Sevastopol'
Constructor I. Y. Osminin
Laid down 20.4.1825   *Launched* 8.5.1828
Dimensions 137 ft(pp) x 38 ft 6 in (outside plank) x 13 ft 4 in (Veselago)
139 ft 6 in /137 ft (pp) x (125 ft keel) x 37 ft 8 in (inside plank)/38 ft 8 in (outside plank) x 18 ft 4 in (O Sudakh)
Armament LD 26 x 24pdr short guns
FC & QD 10 x 8pdrs, 8 x 36pdr carr. (Sudostroenie 1974)
A small frigate by Black Sea standards, *Rafail* was destined to be the unfortunate star in one of the most remarkable incidents in Russian naval history, suffering imperial censure and disgrace in circumstances that would have gone unremarked elsewhere, even in the demanding and unforgiving world of the British Royal Navy. Her early career was fairly routine for a Black Sea frigate. She bombarded Varna and Inada in 1828, escorted transports supplying troops to Bulgaria, and transported Turkish PoWs. In 1829 she bombarded Sizopol' and other fortified strong points. On 11.5.29, while becalmed, she was forced to surrender to a Turkish squadron consisting of no fewer than 6 ships of the line, 2 frigates, 5 corvettes and 2 brigs. The captain and all officers were subsequently court-martialled and disgraced for yielding to overwhelming force without putting up a fight. Nicholas I was so outraged by what he considered to be flagrant cowardice that he forbade the disgraced captain from ever having children and further staining the honour of Russia.

Black Sea corvettes (10 purpose-built 1825–60)

Ten corvettes were built for the Black Sea fleet during the reign of Nicholas I. They were all purpose-built and not purchased from foreign vessels up for sale as had been the practice before 1825. As indicated elsewhere, Russian corvettes were a type distinct from the Russian sloops frequenting northern waters, which were more capacious, more adapted to transporting troops and cargoes, and were frequently used on long range cruises of exploration and global circumnavigation. One Black Sea corvette, *Menelai* was able to break out of the confined Black Sea environment by transporting the Imperial family to Sicily and joining the Baltic fleet very briefly before being transferred to the Pacific where she exchanged fire with a British squadron off the Kamchatka peninsula in 1855 before returning to Kronshtadt in 1857.

Sizopol' **class** (3 ships)
Sizopol' 24 Nikolaev
Constructor I. Y. Osminin
Laid down 30.7.1829 Launched 6.9.1830
Dimensions approx. 133 ft x 35 ft x 19 ft x 15 ft
40.5 m x 10.7 m x 5.7 m x 4.6 m (Chernyshev)
133 ft x (121 ft 6 in keel) x 35 ft 2 in x 15 ft 9 in (O Sudakh)
Armament 24 x 24pdr carr.
190 men
Sizopol' class. Purpose-built corvette. Cruised in the Black Sea in 1832. Cruised and participated in the Bosporus expedition in 1833. Cruised in the Black Sea in the Arkhipelago in 1835–6. Cruised in the Black Sea in 1837–8. Reduced to a store ship in 1838. Broken up in 1845.

Penderakliia 24 Nikolaev
Constructor I. Y. Osminin
Laid down 6.3.1830 Launched 6.9.1831
Dimensions approx. 133 ft x 35 ft x 19 ft x 15 ft
40.5 m x 10.7 m x 5.7 m x 4.6 m (Chernyshev)
133 ft x (121 ft 6 in keel) x 35 ft 2 in x 15 ft 9 in (O Sudakh)
Armament 24 x 24pdr carr.
190 men
Sizopol' class. Purpose-built corvette. Cruised in the Black Sea in 1832. Cruised and participated in the Bosporus expedition in 1833. Cruised in the Black Sea in 1834–5. Visited Istanbul and Athens in 1837. Reduced to a store ship in 1838. Broken up in 1844.

Messemvriia 24 Sevastopol'
Constructor A. P. Prokovyev
Laid down 3.5.1831 Launched 24.4.1832
Dimensions approx. 133 ft x 35 ft x 19 ft x 15 ft
40.5 m x 10.7 m x 5.7 m x 4.6 m (Chernyshev)
133 ft x (122 ft 8 in keel) x 35 ft 2 in x 35 ft 2 in x 18 ft 8 in x 14 ft 5 in /15 ft 8 in (draught fore/aft) (O Sudakh)
Armament 24 x 24pdr carr.
190 men
Sizopol' class. Purpose-built corvette. Cruised in the Black Sea in 1831–5 and 1838. Stranded and wrecked by a storm on 31.5.1838 with a loss of 13 sailors.

Ifigeniia 22 Nikolaev
Constructor V. Apostoli
Laid down 6.9.1833 Launched 30.5.1834
Dimensions approx. 121 ft x 33 ft x 19 ft x 13 ft
36.8 m x 10 m x 5.7 m x 4 m) (Chernyshev)
120 ft 9 in x (110 ft 1 in keel) x 32 ft 8 in x 18 ft 7 in x 14 ft 5 in/15 ft 10 in (draught fore/aft) (O Sudakh)
Armament 22 x 24pdr carr.
180 men
Purpose-built corvette. Cruised to Greece in 1835. Cruised in the Black Sea in 1836–7. Cruised to Livorno in 1838. Cruised 1839–47. Reduced to harbour service in 1848.

Orest 18 Nikolaev
Constructor A. S. Akimov
Laid down 29.12.1835, Launched 31.10.1836
Dimensions approx. 113 ft x 30 ft x 17 ft x 13 ft
34.6 m x 9.3 m x 5.1 m x 4.1 m) (Chernyshev)
113 ft 6 in x (101 ft 9 in keel) x 30 ft x 16 ft 8 in x 13 ft 3 in/14 in (draught fore/aft) (O Sudakh)
Armament 18 x 8pdrs (other sources say carronades)
Purpose-built corvette. Cruised in the Black Sea in 1837–53. In Sevastopol' roads in 1854. Scuttled there on 9.1854.

Pilad **class** (2 ships)
Pilad 20 Nikolaev
Constructor I. V. Mashkin
Laid down 4.10.1838 Launched 23.6.1840
Dimensions 129 ft 1 in x (115 ft 9 in keel) x 35 ft 3 in x 19 ft 7 in x 16 ft/16 ft 8 in (draught fore/aft) (O Sudakh)
Armament 20 x 24pdr gunnades
Pilad class. Purpose-built corvette. Cruised to Greece in 1841–2. Cruised 1843–9. Cruised to Greece in 1850–1. Bombarded Poti on 7.11.1853 after its capture by the Turks. Scuttled at Sevastopol' on 14.12.1854.

Menelai (renamed *Olivutsa*) 20 Sevastopol'
Constructor A. P. Prokofyev
Laid down 10.5.1839 Launched 2.11.1841
Dimensions 1840 129 ft 1 in x (115 ft 9 in) x 35 ft3 in x 19 ft 7 in x 16 ft/16 ft 8 in (draught fore/aft) (O Sudakh)
1850 125 ft x 35 ft 9 in x 19 ft 9 in 2978.5 tons displacement (after reconstruction)
Armament 1840 20 x 24pdr carr.
1850 18 x 24pdrs (short)

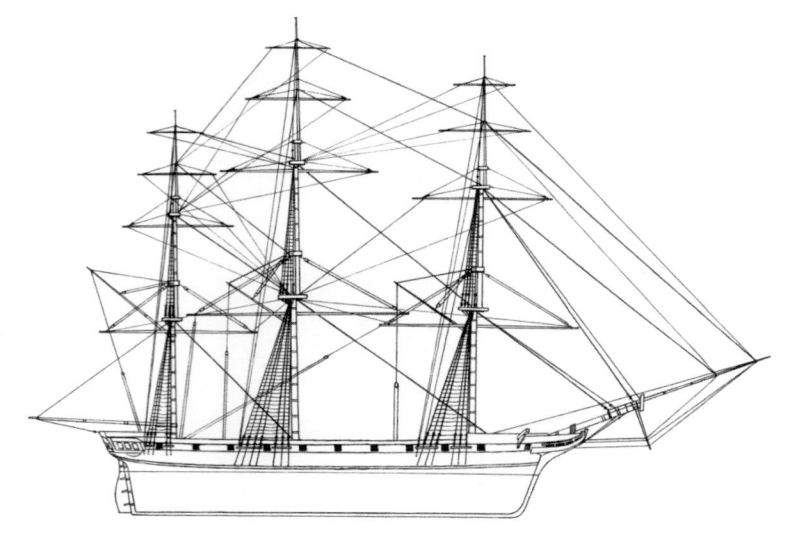

This profile of the 20-gun corvette Menelai *intended to show the rigging, but giving an overall impression of the speed, elegance and simplicity of the type. She transported Emperor Nikolai and his family to Olivutsa in Sicily in 1844–5 and Nikolai was so pleased with both the ship and the Sicilian resort that he had her renamed* Olivutsa *in commemoration of the stay.*

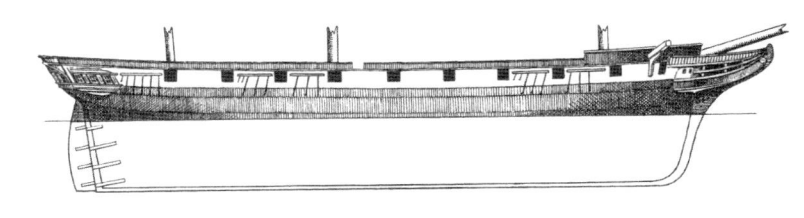

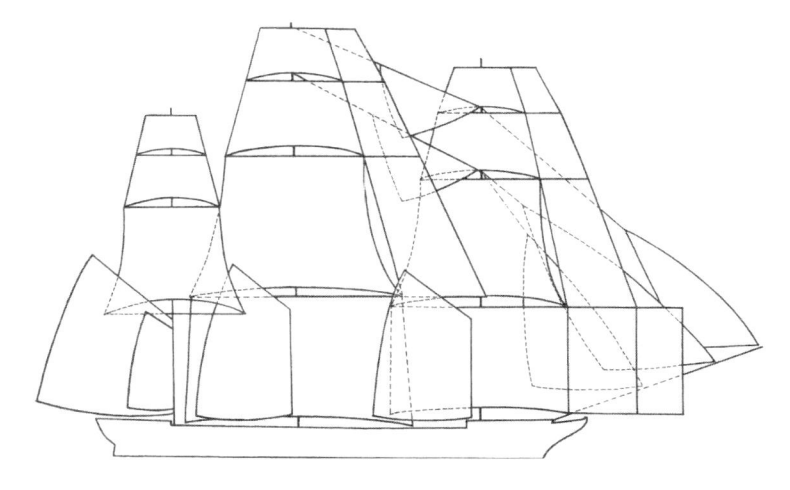

A two-fold depiction of the Black Sea corvette Andromakha *completed in 1841. The top drawing shows her general appearance minus masts and rigging, while the lower shows her sail plan. Generally similar to the earlier and larger* Menelai, Andromakha *spent most of her career in the Black Sea, venturing no further than Palermo in 1845.*

    1855 18 x 24pdrs (short) (Pamyatnaya)
    1858 18 x 24pdr gunnades (Pamyatnaya)
Pilad class. Purpose-built corvette. Cruised in the Black Sea in 1842–3. Cruised with the Imperial family to Olivutsa, Sicily in 1844–5. Renamed *Olivutsa* in 1844. Arrived at Kronshtadt and joined the Baltic fleet in 1846. Cruised in the Baltic in 1847–9. Received a large repair in 1850 and transferred to the Pacific. Arrived at Petropavlovsk on 29.5.1851. Served as a cargo ship in 1851–2. Arrived at Honolulu on 24.4.1853 and joined Vice-Adm. Putyatin's squadron, Arrived at Nagasaki on 10.8.1853 and departed for Manila on 24.1.1854. Reached Manila on 17.2.1854 and returned to Kamchatka on 26.5.1854. Served as a fire watch ship in 1854. On 8.5.1855, as part of Rear-Adm. Zavoyko's squadron, exchanged fire with the British squadron under Commodore Elliot. Returned to Kronshtadt on 16.9.1857. Found surplus to fleet requirements in 1858. Stricken on 11.9.63.

Andromakha class (2 ships)
Andromakha 18 Nikolaev
Constructor I. V. Mashkov
Laid down 19.6.1840 *Launched* 20.7.1841
Dimensions 123 ft x (113 ft 7 in keel) x 36 ft 6 in x 19 ft 11 in
    x 14 ft 11 in /15 ft 11 in (draught fore/aft) (O Sudakh)
Armament 4 x 12pdrs, 14 x 24pdr gunnades
    190 men
Andromakha class. Purpose-built corvette. Cruised to Greece in 1842–3. Cruised in 1844. Cruised to Palermo in 1845. Cruised 1846–52. Transported 250 soldiers and participated in the bombardment of Poti in 1853. Scuttled at Sevastopol' on 27.8.1855.

Kalipso 18 Nikolaev
Constructor I. V. Mashkov
Laid down 20.6.1841 *Launched* 9.9.1845
Dimensions 120 ft 9 in x 37 ft 6 in x 19 ft x 15 ft (draught) (Veselago)
Armament 18 x 24pdr gunnades
    190 men
Andromakha class. Purpose-built corvette. Cruised in the Black Sea in 1846–8. Cruised to Greece in 1849–50. Cruised in the Black Sea in 1851–3. Scuttled at Sevastopol' on 27.8.1855.

Ariadna 20 Sevastopol'
Constructor Rozhnov
Laid down 28.1.1847, *Launched* 26.8.1851
Dimensions 125 ft x 35 ft x ? (Veselago)
Armament 2 x 24pdrs 18 x 24pdr gunnades
Purpose-built corvette. Left for Greece in 7.1852. Trapped by the outbreak of the Crimean War and sold at Trieste in 1854.

Black Sea brigs (15 purpose-built 1825–60)

Fifteen brigs were built between 1826 and 1847. They were smaller than Black Sea corvettes and more lightly armed, with 18pdr carronades in contrast to the larger vessels' 24pdr gunnades and carronades. They appear to have been much more intensively employed in inshore patrol activities in both the Greek Arkhipelago and the Caucasus coastline than the larger corvettes. Two were wrecked and lost in heavy weather, an indication of the often severe conditions prevailing in the Black Sea and the aggressive employment of Russian small craft. Seven were scuttled in 1855 at the siege of Sevastopol' and *Ptolomei* was sunk by allied gunfire.

Pegas 22 ?
Constructor ?
Laid down ?.?.1825 *Launched* 16.5.1826
Dimensions 98 ft (pp) x 31 ft (inside plank) x 14 ft 10 (Veselago)
Armament ?
    142 men
Purpose-built brig. Cruised in the Black Sea in 1826–7. Engaged in operations against Turkey in 1828–9, bombarding Akhiollo receiving 13 hull hits and suffering casualities of 4 dead and 12 wounded. Cruised off the Caucasus in 1830–31. Participated in the Bosporus expedition of 1833. Cruised in the Black Sea in 1834–6. Reduced to a floating magazine in 1838.

Kastor class (2 ships)
Kastor 18 Nikolaev
Constructor A. K. Kaverznev
Laid down 21.2.1829 *Launched* 25.10.1829
Dimensions 96 ft x 30 ft x 13 ft (Veselago)
Armament ?
Kastor class. Purpose-built brig. Cruised in the Black Sea in 1830–8. Reduced to a floating magazine in 1839.

Poluks 18 Nikolaev
Constructor A. K. Kaverznev
Laid down 21.2.1829 *Launched* 9.11.1829
Dimensions 96 ft x 30 ft x 13 ft (Veselago)
Armament ?
Kastor class. Purpose-built brig. Cruised in the Black Sea in 1830–8. Reduced to a floating magazine in 1839.

Femistokl 18 Nikolaev
Constructor A. S. Akimov
Laid down 21.10.1832 *Launched* 6.9.1833
Dimensions approx. 97 ft x 31 ft (inside plank) x 15 ft x 13 ft
29.7 m x 9.4 m (inside plank) x 4.7 m x 4.2 m (Chernyshev)
97 ft 6 in x (83 ft 9 in keel) x 30 ft 10 in x 15 ft 6 in
x 11 ft 6 in/16 ft 10 in (draught fore/aft) (O Sudakh)
Armament 2 x 8pdrs, 14 x 18pdr carr.
Purpose-built brig. Sailed to Sevastopol' and then Athens in 7.1834. Returned to Sevastopol' in 8.1835. Cruised with cadets in 1836. Cruised to Greece in 1837. Cruised off the Caucasus in 1838. Wrecked off Tuapse on 31.5.1838 with a loss of two sailors.

Argonavt 12 ?
Constructor A. P. Prokhorov
Laid down ? *Launched* 3.9.1838
Dimensions 90 ft x 26 ft (inside plank) x 11 ft (Veselago)
90 ft 4 in x (75 ft keel) x 26 ft x 13 ft 4 in x 11 ft 4 in/
12 ft 4 in (draught fore/aft) (O Sudakh)
Armament 2 x 6pdrs, 10 x 18pdr carr.
Purpose-built brig. Cruised off the Caucasus from 1839–53. Stationed in the Sevastopol' roads in 8.1853. Scuttled on 27.8.1855 at Sevastopol.

Endimion class (2 ships)
Endimion 12 Nikolaev
Constructor S. I. Chernyavskiy
Laid down 24.11.1837 *Launched* 16.6.1839
Dimensions approx. 91 ft x 29 ft (inside plank) x 14 ft x 12 ft
27.8 m x 8.8 m (inside plank) x 4.4 m x 3.6 m (Chernyshev)
91 ft x (84 ft 9 in keel) x 28 ft 8 in x 14 ft 5 in
x 10 ft/13 ft 9 in (draught fore/aft) (O Sudakh)
Armament 2 x 6pdrs, 10 x 18pdr carr.
Endimion class. Purpose-built brig. Cruised to the Arkhipelago in 1839 and returned to Sevastopol' in 1841. Cruised off the Caucasus in 1842–53. Stationed at Sevastopol'1854–5. Scuttled at Sevastopol' on 27.8.1855.

Neark 12 Nikolaev
Constructor Kirillov
Laid down 5.9.1839 *Launched* 13.11.1840
Dimensions approx. 91 ft x 29 ft (inside plank) x 14 ft x 12 ft
27.8 m x 8.8 m (inside plank) x 4.4 m x 3.6 m (Chernyshev)
91 ft 2 in x (82 ft 9 in keel) x 28 ft 8 in x 14 ft 5 in
x 10 ft/13 ft 9 in (draught fore/aft) (O Sudakh)
Armament 2 x 6pdrs, 10 x 18pdr carr.
Endimion class. Purpose-built brig. Cruised in the Black Sea in 1841–2. Stationed at Istanbul 1843–4. Cruised in the Black Sea in 1845–9. Stationed at Istanbul in 1850. Cruised in the Black Sea in 1851–2. Fire watch ship at Sevastopol' in 1853. At Sevastopol' 1853–5. Scuttled on 27.8.1855 at Sevastopol.

Palamed class (3 ships)
Palamed 18 Nikolaev
Constructor Kirillov
Laid down 4.10.1837 *Launched* 5.9.1839
Dimensions approx. 101 ft x 32 ft x 16 ft x 14 ft
30.9 m x 9.8 m x 5 m x 4.2 m) (Chernyshev)
101 ft 3 in x (93 ft 7 in keel) x 32 ft x 16 ft 6 in
x 12 ft 8 in/15 ft (draught fore/aft) (O Sudakh)
Armament 2 x 8pdrs, 16 x 24pdr carr.
Palamed class. Purpose-built brig. Cruised in the Black Sea in 1840–1. Stationed in the Arkhipelago in 1842–3. Cruised in the Black Sea in 1844–8. Wrecked off Novorossiysk on 13.1.1848 during heavy weather with 5 sailors lost and many others severely frostbitten.

Ptolomei 18 Nikolaev
Constructor G. V. Afamasyev
Laid down 26.7.1842 *Launched* 9.9.1845
Dimensions approx. 101 ft x 32 ft x 16 ft x 14 ft
30.9 m x 9.8 m x 5 m x 4.2 m) (Chernyshev)
101 ft 3 in x (93 ft 7 in keel) x 32 ft x 16 ft 6 in x 15 ft
(max draught)
Armament 2 x 6pdrs, 16 x 24pdr carr.
Palamed class. Purpose-built brig. Cruised in the Black Sea in 1847 and 1849. Stationed in the Arkhipelago in 1850–1. Cruised in the Black Sea in 1852–3. Damaged and sunk by allied gunfire at Sevastopol' in 1855.

Tezei 18 Nikolaev
Constructor G. V. Afanasyev
Laid down 26.7.1844 *Launched* 9.9.1845
Dimensions approx. 101 ft x 32 ft x 16 ft x 14 ft
30.9 m x 9.8 m x 5 m x 4.2 m) (Chernyshev)
101 ft 3 in x (93 ft 7 in keel) x 32 ft x 16 ft 6 in x 15 ft
(max draught)
Armament 2 x 6pdrs 16 x 24pdr carr.
Palamed class. Purpose-built brig. Cruised in the Black Sea in 1846–53. Stationed at Sevastopol' in 1853–5. Scuttled at Sevastopol' on 27.8.1855.

Femistokl class (3 ships)
Femistokl 16 Nikolaev
Constructor G. V. Afanasyev
Laid down 4.10.1838 *Launched* 17.11.1839
Dimensions approx. 105 ft x 33 ft x 16 ft x 13 ft
32.1 m x 10.2 m x 5 m x 4.1 m (Chernyshev)
105 ft 4 in x (95 ft 4 in keel) x 32 ft 8 in x 16 ft 5 in
x 12 ft 9 in/14 ft 11 in (draught fore/aft) (O Sudakh)
Armament 2 x 8pdrs, 14 x 18pdr carr
Femistokl class. Purpose-built brig. Cruised in the Black Sea in 1840–1. Stationed at Istanbul in 1842–3. Cruised in the Black Sea in 1844–6. Stationed in the Arkhipelago in 1847. Stationed at Sevastopol' in 1854–55 and scuttled there. Raised and broken up in 1857.

Persei 16 Nikolaev
Constructor G. V. Afanasyev
Laid down 16.6.1839 *Launched* 23.6.1841
Dimensions approx. 105 ft x 33 ft x 16 ft x 13 ft
32.1 m x 10.2 m x5 m x 4.1 m (Chernyshev)
105 ft 4 in x (95 ft 4 in keel) x 32 ft 8 in x 16 ft 5 in
x 12 ft 9 in /14 ft 11 in (draught fore/aft) (O Sudakh)
Armament 2 x 8pdrs 14 x 18pdr carr.
Femistokl class. Purpose-built brig. Cruised in the Black Sea in 1841–3. Stationed in the Arkhipelago in 1843–4. Cruised in the Black Sea in 1846–8. Stationed in the Arkhipelago in 1851–4. Sold at Zara in 1854.

Enei 16 Nikolaev
Constructor G. V. Afanasyev
Laid down 23.6.1840 *Launched* 26.7.1842
Dimensions approx. 105 ft x 33 ft x 16 ft x 13 ft
32.1 m x 10.2 m x 5 m x 4.1 m) (Chernyshev)
105 ft 4 in x (95 ft 4 in keel) x 32 ft 8 in x 16 ft 5 in
x 12 ft 9 in /14 ft 11 in (draught fore/aft) (O Sudakh)

Armament 2 x 8pdrs, 14 x 18pdr carr.
Femistokl class. Purpose-built brig. Cruised in the Black Sea in 1843. Stationed in the Arkhipelago in 1844–9 and again in 1850–1. Visited at Trieste on 22.3.1853 by Emperor Franz Josef. Cruised in the Black Sea in 1853. Stationed in Sevastopol' roads in 1854 and scuttled there on 27.8.1855.

Orfei 16 Sevastopol'
Constructor Delyabel
Laid down 8.12.1842   *Launched* 11.9.1845
Dimensions ?
Armament 4 x 6pdrs, 12 x 18pdr carr.
Purpose-built brig. Cruised in the Arkhipelago in 1847–8. Cruised in the Black Sea in 1849–51. To the Arkhipelago in 1852 where she was trapped at the outbreak of war and sold at Trieste.

Iason 12 Sevastopol'
Constructor Red'kin
Laid down 28.1.1847   *Launched* 20.10.1850
Dimensions 104 ft x 30 ft 6 in x ? (Veselago)
Armament ?
Purpose-built brig. Stationed in the Arkhipelago in 1851–52. Cruised off the Bosporus in 1853. Stationed in Sevastopol' roads in 1854. Scuttled at Sevastopol' in 27.8.1855.

Black Sea schooners (13 purpose-built, 1 purchased 1825–60)

Russian responsibilities in both the Greek Arkhipelago and the Caucasus after 1830 created a demand for nimble small craft that was most effectively met by brigs and schooners. Thirteen purpose-built schooners were built between 1830 and 1852 and a single small schooner purchased in 1856. The larger 99 ft schooners approached brigs with regard to length and armament, but were from 5–7 ft less in beam. Of the purpose-built vessels, *Vestnik* was wrecked in service, while four were scuttled and two sunk by allied gunfire during the Crimean War.

Purpose-built

Kur'er II class (2 ships)
Kur'er 12 Nikolaev
Constructor G. Ivanov
Laid down 12.5.1830   *Launched* 19.5.1831
Dimensions 75 ft x 21 ft x ? (Veselago)
Armament ?
Kur'er II class. Purpose-built schooner. Cruised in the Black Sea in 1831–4. Repaired in 1835. Cruised in the Black Sea in 1836–8. Broken up in 1852.

Vestnik 12 Nikolaev
Constructor G. Ivanov
Laid down 1.6.1830   *Launched* 1.6.1831
Dimensions 75 ft x 21 ft x ? (Veselago)
Armament ?
Kur'er II class. Purpose-built schooner. Cruised in the Black Sea in 1831–6. Broken up in 1837.

Vestovoi 14 Nikolaev
Constructor G. Ivanov
Laid down 12.9.1833   *Launched* 4.6.1835
Dimensions approx. 91 ft x 25 ft x 14 ft
     27.7 m x 7.6 m x 4.3 m (Chernyshev)
     88 ft x (70 ft 10 in keel) x 25 ft x 14 ft 1 in x 10 ft 8 in/
     12 ft 10 in (draught fore/aft) (O Sudakh)
Armament ?
Purpose-built schooner. Cruised in the Black Sea in 1836–7. Stationed in Greece in 1838–9. Cruised in the Black Sea in 1840–2. Fire watch ship in 1843–50 at various ports. Broken up after 1850.

Gonets class (5 ships)
Gonets 16 Nikolaev or Sevastopol'
Constructor V. Karachurin
Laid down 1.9.1833   *Launched* 12.5.1835
Dimensions approx. 99 ft x 26 ft x 13 ft
     30.3 m x 7.8 m x 4 m (Chernyshev)
     99 ft 3 in x (87 ft 5 in keel) x 25 ft 6 in x 13 ft 1 in
     x 9 ft 6 in/14 ft 3 in (draught fore/aft) (O Sudakh)
Armament 2 x 3pdrs, 14 x 18pdr carr.
Gonets class. Purpose-built schooner. Stationed in Greece in 1835–6. Cruised in the Black Sea in 1837–47. Fire watch ship at Kerch in 1851–3 and at Sevastopol' in 1854–5. Scuttled at Sevastopol' in 1855.

Lastochka 16 Nikolaev or Sevastopol'
Constructor S. I. Chernyshev
Laid down 10.2.1837   *Launched* 12.6.1838
Dimensions approx. 99 ft x 26 ft x 13 ft
     30.3 m x 7.8 m x 4 m (Chernyshev)
     99 ft 3 in x (87 ft 5 in keel) x 25 ft 6 in x 13 ft 1 in
     x 9 ft 6 in/14 ft 3 in (draught fore/aft) (O Sudakh)
Armament 2 x 3pdrs, 1 x 36pdr gunnades, 14 x 18pdr carr.
Gonets class. Purpose-built schooner. Cruised in the Black Sea in 1838–40. Stationed in Greece in 1841–2. Cruised in the Black Sea in 1844–53. Scuttled at Sevastopol' in 1854.

Smelaia 16 Nikolaev or Sevastopol'
Constructor A. P. Prokofyev
Laid down 22.10.1838   *Launched* 10.5.1839
Dimensions approx. 99 ft x 26 ft x 13 ft
     30.3 m x 7.8 m x 4 m (Chernyshev)
     99 ft 3 in x (87 ft 5 in keel) x 25 ft 6 in x 13 ft 1 in
     x 9 ft 6 in/14 ft 3 in (draught fore/aft) (O Sudakh)
Armament 2 x 3pdrs, 14 x 18pdr carr., 1 x swivel
Gonets class. Purpose-built schooner. Cruised in the Black Sea in 1840–3, 1845, and 1847–53. Sunk by gunfire at Sevastopol' in 1855.

Drotik 16 Nikolaev or Sevastopol'
Constructor A. Veinberger
Laid down 24.11.1837   *Launched* 16.6.1839
Dimensions approx. 99 ft x 26 ft x 13 ft
     30.3 m x 7.8 m x 4 m (Chernyshev)
     99 ft 3 in x (87 ft 5 in keel) x 25 ft 6 in x 13 ft 1 in
     x 9 ft 6 in/14 ft 3 in (draught fore/aft) (O Sudakh)
Armament 2 x 3pdrs, 14 x 18pdr carr.
Gonets class. Purpose-built schooner. Cruised in the Black Sea in 1839–51 and 1853. Scuttled in 1855. Raised after 1856 and broken up.

Zabiiaka 16 Nikolaev or Sevastopol'
Constructor G. F. Afanasyev
Laid down 4.10.1838   *Launched* 24.8.1839
Dimensions approx. 99 ft x 26 ft x 13 ft
     30.3 m x 7.8 m x 4 m (Chernyshev)
     99 ft 3 in x (87 ft 5 in keel) x 25 ft 6 in x 13 ft 1 in
     x 9 ft 56 in/14 ft 3 in (draught fore/aft) (O Sudakh)

Armament 2 x 3pdrs, 14 x 18pdr carr.
Gonets class. Purpose-built schooner. Cruised in the Black Sea in 1840–53. Scuttled in 1855. Raised and broken up after 1856.

Vestnik 12 Nikolaev
Constructor ?
Laid down 13.11.1840 *Launched* 27.9.1841
Dimensions approx. 94 ft x 24 ft x 10 ft
 28.7 m x 7.4 m x 3.1 m (Chernyshev)
 94 ft x (85 ft 8 in keel) x 24 ft 2 in x 10 ft x 9 ft 7 in/
 11 ft 1 in (draught fore/aft) (O Sudakh)
Armament ?
Purpose-built schooner. Cruised doing hydrographic survey work, training, and fire watch duty in 1842–7. Wrecked in 22.12.1847 with no casualties.

Alupka 2 Nikolaev
Constructor I. S. Dimitriev
Laid down 31.10.1840 *Launched* 20.6.1842
Dimensions 71 ft x (60 ft keel) x 21 ft 3 in x 12 ft 6 in x 9 ft /9 ft
 (draught fore/aft) (O Sudakh)
Armament ?
Purpose-built schooner. Named for a town in the Crimea.

Skuchnaia 10/14 Nikolaev
Constructor G. V. Afanasyev
Laid down 18.3.1844 *Launched* 9.9.1845
Dimensions 76 ft 5 in x 21 ft 4 in x ? (Veselago)
Armament 10 x 3pdr swivels
Purpose-built schooner. Fire watch ship from 1846–59. Reduced to a floating magazine at Kerch.

Unylaya 8 Nikolaev
Constructor G. V. Afanasyev
Laid down 18.3.1844 *Launched* 9.9.1845
Dimensions 72 ft 3 in x 20 ft x ? (Veselago)
Armament 8 x 3pdr swivels
Purpose-built schooner. Fire watch ship from 1846–55. Sunk by naval gunfire at Taganrog.

Opyt 7/16 Nikolaev
Constructor I. S. Dmitriev
Laid down 23.10.1849 *Launched* 29.9.1852
Dimensions 99 ft x 25.6 ft x ? (Veselago)
 310 tons displacement
Armament 4 x 18pdr gunnades, 2 x 3pdrs, 1 x 60 u (1 pood)
Purpose-built schooner. Cruised in the Black Sea in 1854–6. Sold in 1867 and stricken on 8.11.68.

Purchased
Aiu-Dakh 8 ?
Constructor ?
Laid down ? *Launched* ? *Purchased* 1856
Dimensions approx. 94 ft x 22 ft x 9 ft
 28.6 m x 6.7 m x 2.7 m (Chernyshev)
 175 tons displacement
Armament ?
Schooner purchased from Prince Kochubey. Named after a cape in the Crimea. Cruised in 1857–64. Sold in 1867 and stricken on 30.11.68

Black Sea cutters (3 purpose-built 1825–60)

Only three cutters were built for the Black Sea fleet in the mid-1820s. They appear to have been superseded by the slightly larger schooners.

Zhavoronok 12/15 Sevastopol'
Constructor I. Y. Osminin
Laid down 20.4.1825 *Launched* 28.10.1825
Dimensions 49 ft 11 in (pp) x 20 ft (inside plank) x 10 ft (Veselago)
Armament ?
Purpose-built cutter. Cruised from 1826–9. Fire watch ship at Varna in 9.1829. Cruised from 1831–5. Fire watch ship at the Kerch Straits from 1836–43. Broken up in 1844.

Lastochka class (2 ships)
Lastochka 12/18 Nikolaev
Constructor I. S. Razumov
Laid down 28.7.1825 *Launched* 26.7.1826
Dimensions 49 ft 9 in x 22 ft x 8 ft (Veselago)
Armament ?
Lastochka class. Purpose-built cutter. Cruised in the Black Sea in 1826–33. Broken up in 1835.

Slolvei 12/16 Nikolaev
Constructor I. S. Razumov
Laid down 28.7.1825 *Launched* 26.7.1826
Dimensions approx. 51 ft x 22 ft x 8 ft
 15.7 m x 6.7 m x 2.4 m) (Chernyshev)
Armament ?
Lastochka class. Purpose-built cutter. Cruised in the Black Sea in 1826–30. At Istanbul in 1833. Cruised in the Black Sea in 1834–8. Reduced to a floating magazine in 1841.

Black Sea luggers (4 purpose-built 1825–60)

Glubokii 10/12 Kherson
Constructor A. K. Kaverznev
Laid down 24.7.1826 *Launched* 27.7.1827
Dimensions 65 ft x 19 ft 6 in x 9 ft 2 in (Veselago)
Armament ?
 40 men
Lugger. Sailed to Sevastopol' in 1827. Engaged in operations against the Turks in 1828–9. Cruised 1830–2. At Istanbul in 1833. Cruised 1834–40. Fire watch ship at Berdyansk in 1841 and at Kerch in 1842. Broken up in 1843.

Shirokii 10/12 Kherson
Constructor A. K. Kaverznev
Laid down 24.7.1826 *Launched* 27.7.1827
Dimensions 65 ft x 21 ft 9 in x 8 ft 8 in (Veselago)
Armament 10 x 8pdr carr., 2 x 3 u
Lugger. Sailed to Sevastopol' in 1827. Engaged in operations against the Turks in 1828–9. Cruised in the Black Sea in 1830. Operated in the Arkhipelago in 1831–2. Stationed at Istanbul in 1833. Cruised 1834–8. Broken up in 1839.

Gelendzhik class (2 ships)
Gelendzhik 12 Nikolaev
Constructor I. Y. Osminin
Laid down 31.1.1831 *Launched* 8.10.1831

Dimensions 77 ft x 17 ft x ? (Veselago)
Armament ?
Gelendzhik class. Lugger. Cruised in the Black Sea in 1832–4. Fire watch ship at Feodosii in 1835. Cruised in the Black Sea in 1836–9. Began sinking on 22.11.1839 at Norovossiysk due to icing on deck. Drifted ashore and wrecked with no casualties.

Poti 12 Nikolaev
Constructor I. Y. Osminin
Laid down 31.1.1831 *Launched* 8.10.1831
Dimensions 77 ft x 17 ft x ? (Veselago)
Armament ?
Gelendzhik class. Lugger. Cruised in the Black Sea in 1833. Fire watch ship at Kerch in 1834. Cruised in the Black Sea in 1835. Fire watch ship at Feodosii 1836–40. Converted to a store ship in 1841. Broken up in 1847.

Black Sea single-masted tenders (10 purpose-built 1825–60)

Bystryi 12 Sevastopol'
Constructor S. I. Chernyavxkiy
Laid down 9.8.1832 *Launched* 25.5.1833
Dimensions approx. 54 ft x 22 ft x 11 ft
  16.4 m x 6.8 m x 3.4 m (Chernyshev)
  49 ft 5 in x (42 ft 3 in keel) x 18 ft 4 in x 10 ft 3 in
  x 9 ft/7 in 6 in (draught fore/aft) (O Sudakh)
Armament ?
One-masted tender. Cruised 1834–40. Store ship in 1841. Fire watch ship at Ochakov 1841–51. No further mention.

Skoryi 6 Sevastopol'
Constructor S. I. Chernyavskiy
Laid down 9.8.1832 *Launched* 28.5.1833
Dimensions approx. 49 ft 6 in (LGD) x 19 ft x 10 ft
  15.1 m (LGD) x 5.7 m x 3.1 m (Chernyshev)
  49 ft 5 in x (42 ft 3 in keel) x 12 ft 4 in x 10 ft 3 in
  x 7 ft 6 in /9 ft (draught fore/aft) (O Sudakh)
Armament ?
One-masted tender. Cruised 1834–8. Drifted ashore and wrecked during a storm off Tuapse on 31.5.1833. No casualties.

Luch 12 ?
Constructor G. Ivanov
Laid down 12.9.1834 *Launched* 4.6.1835
Dimensions approx. 71 ft x 24 ft x12 ft x 10 ft
  21.6 m x 7.2 m x 3.7 m x 3 m (Chernyshev)
  70 ft 2 in x (57 ft 6 in keel) x 23 ft 7 in x 12 ft 2 in
  x 8 ft/12 ft 5 in (draught fore/aft) (O Sudakh)
Armament ?
One-masted tender. Cruised in the Black Sea in 1836. At Istanbul in 1837. Sunk by a storm on 31.5.1838 off the Tuapse River and subsequently raised and repaired. Cruised 1838–41. Fire watch ship at Feodosii in 1842. Cruised in the Black Sea in 1843. Fire watch ship at Kerch in 1844. Cruised in the Black Sea in 1845–9. Fire watch ship at Kerch 1850–3. Broken up in 1855.

Speshnyi 10 Nikolaev
Constructor G. V. Afanasyev
Laid down 12.9.1834 *Launched* 4.6.1835
Dimensions approx. 64 ft x 22 ft x 10 ft 6 in x 10 ft
  19.4 m x 6.7 m x 3.2 m x 3m (Chernyshev)
  61 ft 4 in x (51 ft 9 in keel) x 21 ft 9 in x 16 ft 6 in
  x 7 ft 1 in/13 ft 1 in (draught fore/aft) (O Sudakh)
Armament ?
One-masted tender. Cruised 1835–50. Repaired at Sevastopol' in 1850. Cruised in the Black Sea in 1851. Reduced to harbour service at Sevastopol' in 12.1851, Scuttled at Sevastopol' in 1855.

Legkii 10/12 Nikolaev
Constructor G. V. Afanasyev
Laid down 12.9.1834 *Launched* 6.7.1835
Dimensions approx. 38 ft x 24 ft x 12 ft x 11 ft
  20.6 m x 7.4 m x 3.7 m x 3.3 m (Chernyshev)
  67.5 ft x (51 ft 9 in keel) x 21 ft 9 in x 10 ft 6 in x 7 ft 1 in/
  13 ft 1 in (draught fore/aft) (O Sudakh)
Armament 2 x 3pdrs, 10 x 12pdr carr.
One-masted tender. Cruised in the Black Sea in 1836. Stationed in Greece in 1837–8. Cruised in the Black Sea in 1839–42. Fire watch ship at Evpatoria in 1843–53. Fire watch ship at Sevastopol' in 1854–5. Scuttled at Sevastopol' in 1855. Raised and broken up in 1857.

Struia 12 Nikolaev
Constructor G. Ivanov
Laid down 12.9.1834 *Launched* 13.7.1835
Dimensions approx. 70 ft x 24 ft x 13 ft x 10 ft 6 in
  21.4 m x 7.3 m x 3.9 m x 3.2 m (Chernyshev)
  70 ft 2 in x (59 ft 5 in keel) x 24 ft x 12 ft 9 in x 7 ft 11 in/
  14 ft 6 in (draught fore/aft) (O Sudakh)
Armament 2 x 3pdrs, 10 x 12pdr carr.
One-masted tender. Cruised in the Black Sea in 1836–9. Stationed at Greece in 1840–1. Fire watch ship at Evpatoria in 1842. Cruised in the Black Sea in 1844–8. Sunk with all hands during a blizzard at Novorossiysk on 14.1.1848. Raised and repaired on 4.8.1848. Served as a fire watch ship at Berdyansk in 1850–3. Repaired in 1853. Sunk in 1855 at Enikale.

Nyrok 10 Sevastopol'
Constructor A. P. Prokofyev
Laid down 22.10.1838 *Launched* 3.7.1839
Dimensions approx. 64 ft x 22 ft x 10 ft 6 in x 10 ft
  19.5 m x 6.7 m x 3.2 m x 3 m (Chernyshev)
  61 ft 4 in x (52 ft keel) x 21 ft 7 in x 10 ft 6 in x 7 ft 3 in/
  13 ft 1 in (draught fore/aft) (O Sudakh)
Armament 2 x 3pdrs, 8 x 8pdr carr.
One-masted tender. Cruised 1841–50. Fire watch ship at Feodosii and Enikale in 1851–55. Scuttled to avoid capture by allied forces at Enikale in.5.1855.

Pospeshnyi **class** (2 ships)
Pospeshnyi 10/12 Nikolaev
Constructor A. S. Akimov
Laid down 18.3.1844 *Launched* 9.9.1845
Dimensions 63 ft 6 in x 21 ft 7 in x ? (Veselago)
Armament 2 x 3pdrs, 4 x 12pdr carr.
Pospeshnyi class. One-masted tender. Engaged in survey work in 1846–50. Operated off the Caucasus in 1852–3. Stationed at Sevastopol' in 1854–5. Scuttled at Sevastopol' on 27.8.1855.

Provornyi 10/12 Nikolaev
Constructor A. S. Akimov
Laid down 18.3.1844 *Launched* 9.9.1845
Dimensions 63 ft 9 in x 21 ft 2 x ? (Veselago)

Armament 2 x 3pdrs, 8 x 12pdr carr.
Pospeshnyi class. One-masted tender. Engaged in survey work in 1846. Cruised in the Black Sea in 1847. Operated in Greece in 1848–9. Cruised off the Caucasus in 1850–2. Stationed at Kerch in 1853–4. Scuttled at Sevastopol' in 1855.

Skoryi 12 Nikolaev
Constructor A. S. Akimov
Laid down 18.3.1844 *Launched* 9.9.1845
Dimensions 69 ft 3 in x 24 ft x ? (Veselago)
Armament 2 x 3pdrs, 10 x 12pdr carr.
36 men
One-masted tender. Engaged in survey work in 1848–53. Stationed at Sevastopol' in 1854–5. Sunk by gunfire at Sevastopol' in 1855. Raised and repaired in 1856. Cruised in the Black Sea in 1856. Broken up after 1858.

Black Sea fleet bomb vessels (1 purpose-built, 4 converted 1825–60)

There was no great demand for bomb vessels of the traditional sort during Nicholas' reign. Four transports were converted to bomb vessels on an ad hoc basis during the Russo-Turkish War of 1828–9. These and a single purpose-built bomb completed in 1840 met Black Sea requirements in this area to the end of sail.

Purpose-built

Perun 16 Nikolaev
Constructor G. V. Afanasyev
Laid down 16.6.1840 *Launched* 26.7.1842
Dimensions 109 ft 9 in x 29 ft x 16 ft x 13 ft (Veselago)
 108 ft 2 in x (95 ft 6 in keel) x 29 ft x 16 ft 6 in x 12 ft 10 in/14 ft (draught fore/aft) (O Sudakh)
Armament 16 x 6pdrs (as a transport?)
Purpose-built bomb vessel. In service as a bomb vessel 1843–55. Converted to a transport in 1856–7. Stricken in 1859.

Converted from other classes

Opyt 10 ?
Constructor ?
Laid down ? *Launched* ? *Converted* 14.4.1825
Dimensions approx. 72 ft x 22 ft x 19 ft (22 m x 6.7 m x 5.8 m) (Chernyshev)
 168 tons displacement
Armament ?
Bomb vessel converted from a transport of the same name. Cruised in the Black Sea in 1828–30 and in action with the Turks in 1828–9. Converted back into a transport in 1831. (See also under Black Sea transports.)

Uspekh 8 ?
Constructor ?
Laid down ? *Launched* ? *Converted* 6.19.1826
Dimensions 74 ft x 22 ft 6 in x 18 ft (Veselago)
Armament ?
Bomb vessel converted from a transport of the same name. In action with the Turks in 1828–9. Disarmed and converted back into a transport in 1830. (See also under Black Sea transports.)

Podobnyi class (2 ships)
Podobnyi 7/12 Kherson
Constructor A. K. Kaverznev
Laid down ? *Launched* 1826 *Converted* 1827
Dimensions 75 ft x 23 ft x 11 ft 3 in (Veselago)
Armament 9 x 3pdrs, 2 x 24u (½ pood), 1 x 3 pood mortar
80 men
Podobnyi class. Bomb vessel converted from a transport of the same name. In action with the Turks in 1828–9. Fire watch ship at Burgas in 1829. Disarmed and converted back into a transport in 1830. (See under Black Sea transports.)

Sopernik 11/12 ?
Constructor A. K. Kaverznev
Laid down ? *Launched* 1826 *Converted* 21.5.1826
Dimensions 75 ft x 23 ft x 11 ft 3 in (Veselago)
Armament 9 x 3pdrs, 2 x 24 u (½ pood), 1 x 3 pood mortar
80 men
Podobnyi class. Bomb vessel converted from a transport of the same name. In action with the Turks in 1828–9. Fire watch ship at Messemvriia in 1829. Disarmed and converted back into a transport in 1830. (See under Black Sea transports.)

Black Sea fleet Prizes 1770–1860

Captured ships of the line

Leontii Muchenik 62/66 ?
Constructor ?
Laid down ? *Launched* ?
Captured 1788
Dimensions 141 ft x 44 ft 5 in x 16 ft 6 in (Veselago)
 144 ft x 41 ft 6 in x 18 ft (Golovachev)
Armament 1788 LD 24 x 24pdrs
 UD 24 x 12pdrs
 FC & QD 16 x 6pdrs (Admiralty Order)
 1789 LD 22 x 24pdrs (Turkish brass), 4 x 60 u (1 pood)
 UD 26 x 12pdrs
 FC & QD 2 x 20pdr carr., 8 x 12pdr howitzers
 1790 LD 26 x 24pdrs
 UD 26 x 12pdrs
 FC & QD 14 x 6pdrs (Golovachev)
 1790 LD 4 x 30pdrs, 4 x 24pdrs, 20 x 18pdrs, 2 x 60 u (1 pood)
 UD 22 x 6pdrs
 FC & QD 4 x 4½pdrs, 2 x 24u (½ pood) (Golovachev)
Turkish ship of the line captured on 18.6.1788 at the battle of Ochakov by rowing vessels. On 21.6.1788 she arrived at Kinburn for repair and rearmament. Stationed at the mouth of the Dnieper until 9.1789. Arrived at Sevastopol' on 9.9.1789. On 10.11.1790 as part of Rear-Adm. Ushakov's squadron, provided the passage of the rowing flotilla from the Dnieper to the Danube. Fought at Kaliakra on 31.7.1791 where she had the distinction of being the slowest ship in the Russian fleet. This was an interesting accomplishment given the consistently demostrated ability of Turkish warships to outrun their Russian counterparts when either avoiding contact with Russian warships or fleeing from defeat in battle. Broken up after 1791.

Ioann Predtecha (ex-Turkish *Mulk-i Bahri*) 66 ?
Constructor ?
Laid down ? *Launched* ? *Captured* 1790

Dimensions 156 ft 4 in x 53 ft 6 in x 18 ft 10 in (165 ft x 55 ft x 27 ft - other reports)
Armament 1790 LD 4 x 66pdrs 22 x 24pdrs MD 26 x 15pdrs
　　　　　　　　FC & QD 14 x 8½pdrs -Turkish
　　　　　　1791 LD 28 x 24pdrs MD 28 x 18pdrs
　　　　　　　　FC & QD 22 x 8pdrs 4 x 12u (¼ pood) (Golovachev)
Turkish ship of the line captured at Tendra on 29.8.1790 and renamed *Ioann Predtecha*. Repaired at Kherson and then transferred to Sevastopol' on 29.11.1790. Fought at Kaliakriva on 29.11.1790 as part of the vanguard division. Reduced to a floating battery in 1800.

Sedel'-Bakhr 42 ?
Constructor ?
Laid down ?　*Launched* ?　*Captured* 1807.
Dimensions ?
Armament LD 22pdrs
　　　　　　UD 12pdrs
Turkish flagship captured at the battle of Mount Athos in 1807 and repaired at Corfu. Arrived at Trieste as part of Commodore Saltanov's squadron. Ceded to Austria on 20.10.1809.

Captured frigates

Arkhipelag 30 ?
Constructor ?
Laid down ?　*Launched* ?　*Captured* 1770
Dimensions ?
Armament ?
Turkish prize transferred from the Arkhipelago to the Black Sea in 1775. Grounded and lost on 15.10.1782. Lost on 20.10.1782 without casualties.

Tino ? ?
Constructor ?
Laid down ?　*Launched* ?　*Captured* 1770
Dimensions ?
Armament ?
Turkish prize captured in 1770 in the Arkhipelago and transferred to the Black Sea. Last mentioned at Kerch in 1775.

Sviatoi Mark (ex-*Markopleya*) 36 ?
Constructor ?
Laid down ?　*Launched* ?　*Captured* 1.7.1788
Dimensions 148 ft 4/153 ft in x 32 ft x 10 ft 6 in
Armament 1789 LD 10 x 18pdrs
　　　　　　　　UD 8 x 60 u (1 pood) (as a galleas)
　　　　　　1790 LD 22 x 12pdrs (bored up) (projected)
　　　　　　1790 LD 22 x 12pdrs, 2 x 60 u (1 pood) (1 pood)
　　　　　　　　UD 12 x 4pdrs (Golovachev)
Large 5-gun Turkish galley captured on 1.7.1788 at the mouth of the Don. Initially rearmed as a galleas, but converted to a frigate in 1790. Known formally as *Sviatoi Mark* and informally as *Makropleia*, which means 'large galley' in Greek. Served with the Liman flotilla at the mouth of the Don in 1790 and transferred to Vice-Adm. Ushakov's squadron. Escorted the Liman flotilla to the Danube in 11.1790. Fought at Kaliakra in 1791. Broken up after 1800.

Le Briun (ex-French *Brune*) 32 Toulon Dockyard
Constructor J. M. B. Coulomb
Laid down 8.1780 (N.S.)　*Launched* 15.1.1781 (N.S.)　*Captured* 1799
Dimensions 139 ft x (106 ft keel) x 30 ft 6 in x 15 ft 6 in (French measure)
Armament 1799 20/22 x 8pdrs, 6 x 6pdrs (as captured)
French frigate captured by Russia at Corfu in 1799 and handed over to Turkey.

Magubei-Subkhan 40 ?
Constructor ?
Laid down ?　*Launched* ?　*Captured* 24.7.1811
Dimensions ?
Armament ?
Turkish prize, captured on 24.7.1811. Cruised in the Black Sea in 1811–13. Transported troops in 1815. Cruised off Abhasia in 1817–18. Broken up after 1818.

Captured corvettes

Shagin-Girei ? ?
Constructor ?
Laid down ?　*Launched* ?　*Captured* 24.7.1811
Dimensions ?
Armament ?
Turkish corvette captured off Penderakliia on 24.7.1811. Cruised as a training ship and cargo ship 1811–19. Fire watch ship at Odessa 1819–24. Reduced to harbour service in 1825.

Ol'ga (ex-*Messemvriia*) (renamed *Arkhiolo*) 24 Akhiollo
Constructor ?
Laid down ?　*Launched* 9.1829　*Captured* 11.7.1829
Dimensions 127.95 ft x 35.1 ft x 7.39 ft (39 m x 10.7 m x 5.3 m)
Armament ?
Turkish corvette *Messemvriia* captured on the stocks and completed as Ol'ga. Sailed to Sevastopol' on 1829. Cruised in the Black Sea in 1830–2. Renamed *Arkhiolo* and converted into a transport in 1833. (See also under converted Black Sea transports.)

Captured brigs

Sviatoi Aleksandr 8 ?
Constructor ?
Laid down ?　*Launched* ?　*Captured* 2.3.1799
Dimensions ?
Armament ?
　　　　　　80 men
French brig taken on 2.3.1799 off Brindizi with despatches for Napoleon by frigate *Schastlivyi*. Operated in the Mediterranean in 1799–1801. Arrived at Sevastopol' on 1801. Cruised in the Black Sea in 1803–4. After colliding with the wrecked ship of the line *Tol'skaya Bogoroditsa* on 12.8.1804, she drifted ashore and was also wrecked with a loss of her captain and 6 sailors.

Bonasorte 16 ?
Constructor ?
Laid down ?　*Launched* ?　*Captured* 1799
Dimensions ?
Armament ?
French brig taken on 11.3.1799 off Ancona by Russian gunboats. Sailed to Sevastopol' in 1800. Cruised in the Black Sea in 1802. To Istanbul in 1803. To Corfu in 1804. Operated with Vice-Adm. Seniavin's Mediterranean squadron in 1805–7. Determined unfit for service in 1807 and abandoned at Corfu.

A drawing of the French polyakra Ekspedition *captured at Corfu by Ushakov's Ionian squadron in 1799. Described as a schooner in some sources, her rig is unusual to say the least. However bizarre her appearance may have been to unaccustomed eyes, she met with approval in Russian hands and had a long and varied career in the Adriatic, the Mediterranean, and finally in the Black Sea where she ended her days as a quarantine ship at Sevastopol'.*

Captured polyakra

Ekspedition 16 ?
Constructor ?
Laid down ? Launched ? Captured 1799
Dimensions ?
Armament ?

French polyakra captured at Corfu on 1.3.1799 by Ushakov's squadron. Operated in the Mediterranean with Ushakov's squadron in 1799–1800. To Sevastopol' in 1800. Surveyed the Black Sea coast in 1801. To Istanbul in 1803. Transported Russian army officers to Corfu in 1804. Escorted Austrian cargo ships to Messina in 1805. Operated with Vice-Adm. Seniavin's squadron in the Adriatic and then transferred to Nikolaev in 1806. Operated with Rear-Adm. S. Pustoshkin's squadron in 1807. Operated in the Black Sea in 1807–9. Escorted merchant ships to the Caucasus in 1810–12. Cruised off the Crimean in 1813 and repaired at Sevastopol'. Cruised off the Caucasus from 1815–20. Assigned as a quarantine ship in 1821. No further information.

The Caspian Flotilla

Caspian flotilla two-masted hoeker

This unique warship does not properly belong here, having been completed long before the formal creation of the Imperial Russian Navy in 1696. She was built as part of an aborted project to expand trade contacts with Persia and is included because of her historical significance and because she has been long recognized as the first Russian warship built according to modern European standards.

Oryol 22 Dedinovo
Constructor K. Bukoven
Laid down 14.11.1667 *Launched* 5.1668
Dimensions approx. 80 ft x 21 ft x 5 ft (24.5 m x 6.5 m x 1.5 m)
(Chernyshev) 150 tons displacement
Armament Designed 18 x 6pdrs, 4 x 3pdrs
Actual 5 x 6pdrs, 1 x 5pdr, 2 x 4pdrs, 11 x 3pdrs, 3 x 2pdrs
60 men

The first Russian sailing warship. Designed by a Dutchman and hoeker rigged with three masts. Completed along with two smaller unnamed and unarmed sloops and a yacht. Built for trade with Persia. Departed Dedinovo on 7.5.1669 and arrived at Nizhniy, Novgorod on 8.6.1669 where she was armed. Departed Niznhiy on 21.6.1669 and arrived at Astrakhan' on 13.8.1669. Unsuccessfully attempted to enter the Caspian several times in 8–9.1669 but failed due to poor quality sails. Successfully entered the Caspian in 9.1669. Captured by insurgents in 1670 during the Great Peasant War of Stepan Razin and partially burnt. Never repaired and left to rot in place.

Caspian flotilla small frigates (5 purpose-built)

Three warships were authorized as part of Catherine II's naval expansion programme, just two years after the formal establishment of the Caspian flotilla in 1783. They were ambitiously rated as frigates. It seems likely that the trio was intended to replace the three over-gunned and cramped ship sloops, nos 1–3, completed in 1779 and 1780. The final two in frigates in in the class, nos 1 and 2, were probably begun as replacements for the first trio, in company with the similarly armed rowing frigate *Tsaritsyn*. In the absence of any sort of Persian response, these modest vessels were de facto capital ships, able to project Russian naval power at will throughout the Caspian.

A painting of the Oryol (22) of 1668 in harbour that probably relies heavily upon the imagination of the artist. Nonetheless, it does a good job of showing the enormously exaggerated sheer, the limited rigging, and the ornate sterns of this period of decorative extravagance. By V. M. Golitsyn 1940.

***Kavkaz* class** (5 ships)
Kavkaz 20 Kazan'
Constructor F. D. Ignatyev and Protopopov
Laid down 1783 *Launched* 1784
Dimensions 100 ft x 26 ft x 8 ft
Armament 14 x 6pdrs, 6 x ½pdr falconets
Kavkaz class. Sailed to Astrakhan' in 1784. Cruised in the Caspian in 1784–95. Bombarded Baku in 1791. Broken up in 1791.

Astrakhan' 20 Kazan'
Constructor F. D. Ignatyev and Protopopov
Laid down 25.9.1783 *Launched* 2.5.1784
Dimensions 100 ft x 26 ft x 8 ft
Armament 14 x 6pdrs, 6 x ½pdr falconets
Kavkaz class. Sailed to Astrakhan' in 1784. Cruised in the Caspian Sea in 1784–95. Repaired in 1790–1. Bombarded Baku in 1791. Broken up in 1798.

Kizliar 20 Kazan'
Constructor Protopopov
Laid down 20.6.1785 *Launched* 8.5.1785
Dimensions 100 ft x 26 ft x 8 ft
Armament 14 x 6pdrs, 6 x ½pdr falconets
Kavkaz class. Arrived at Astrakhan' on 12.7.1785. Cruised in the Caspian in 1785–90. No further mention.

Frigate no. 1 20 Kazan'
Constructor A. G. Stepanov and V. D. Vlasov
Laid down 23.12.1796 *Launched* 24.4.1798
Dimensions 100 ft x 26 ft x 8 ft
Armament 1798 14 x 6pdrs, 6 x ½pdr falconets
         1799 2 x 12pdrs, 12 x 6pdrs
Kavkaz class. Arrived at Astrakhan' in 1798. Cruised in the Caspian in 1799–1802. Bombarded Baku to free captured Russian merchants in 1799. Bombarded Enzeli and Baku during the War with Persia. Cruised off Baku and Persia in 1806–9. Broken up in 1810.

Frigate no. 2 20 Kazan'
Constructor A. G. Stepanov and V. D. Vlasov
Laid down 23.12.1796 *Launched* 24.4.1798
Dimensions 100 ft x 26 ft x 8 ft
Armament 1798 14 x 6pdrs, 6 x ½pdr falconets
         1799 2 12pdrs, 12 x 6pdrs
Kavkaz class. Arrived at Astrakhan' in 1798. Cruised in the Caspian to Persia in 1799–1802. Cruised off Baku and Persia in 1803–5. Broken up in 1809.

Caspian flotilla rowing frigate (1 purpose-built)

This interesting ship stands alone as a Caspian diminutive of the much larger rowing frigates so successfully employed in the Baltic during the Russo-Swedish War of 1788–90.

Tsaritsyn 12 Kazan'
Constructor V. D. Vlasov
Laid down 8.7.1794 *Launched* 18.5.1795
Dimensions 89 ft 3 in x 30 ft 10 in x 7 ft 6 in (27.4 m x 8.7 m x 1.7 m)
Armament 12 x 6pdrs
Sailed from Kazan' to Astrakhan' in 1795. Cruised in 1796–8. Broken up in 1808.

Caspian flotilla corvettes (4 purpose-built)

This class of corvettes was brought into service as the last of the *Kavkaz* class in small frigates in were being retired and were clearly intended as their replacements. Their armament is not known, but they were significantly larger than their 'frigate' predecessors and were probably armed with 24pdr carronades and 6pdr chase guns.

***Ariadna* class** (4 ships)
Ariadna 16 Kazan
Laid down ? *Launched* 21.5.1808
Dimensions 110 ft x 30 ft x 12 ft 6 in (Veselago)
Armament ?
Ariadna class. Corvette built at Kazan' on the Volga for the Caspian flotilla. Active from 1808–19.

Kazan' (no. 1) 16 Kazan
Laid down ? *Launched* 11.6.1807
Dimensions 110 ft x 30 ft x 12 ft 6 in (Veselago)
Armament ?
Ariadna class. Corvette built at Kazan' on the Volga for the Caspian flotilla. Active from 1807–18.

Kazan' (no. 2) 16 Kazan
Laid down ? *Launched* 11.3.1816
Dimensions 110 ft x 30 ft x 12. ft 6 in (Veselago)
Armament ?
Ariadna class. Corvette built at Kazan' on the Volga for the Caspian flotilla. Active from 1816–27.

Gerkules 16 Kazan
Laid down ? *Launched* 14.5.1820 (Veselago)
Dimensions approx. 110 ft x 31 ft x 12½ ft (33.6 m x 9.5 m x 3.8 m) (Chernyshev)
Armament ?
Ariadna class. Corvette built at Kazan' on the Volga for the Caspian flotilla. Active from 1820–31.

Caspian flotilla ship sloops (3 purpose-built)

The first evidence of renewed Russian interest in the Caspian, this trio of ship sloops was completed prior to the formal creation of a Caspian flotilla. They were too small to effectively operate their batteries of 6pdrs and were replaced by the three *Kavkaz* class 'frigates' mentioned previously.

Ship Sloop no. 1 20 Kazan'
Constructor ?
Laid down 1778 *Launched* 1779
Dimensions 48 ft x 26 ft x 8 ft
Armament 20 x 6pdrs
Unsuccessful design. Cramped and with gun ports having inadequate waterline clearance. Sailed to Astrakhan' in 1779. Cruised in the Caspian in 1781–3 and either 1786 or 1789. Broken up at Astrakhan'.

Ship Sloop no. 2 20 Kazan'
Constructor ?
Laid down 1778 *Launched* 1779
Dimensions 48 ft x 26 ft x 8 ft
Armament 20 x 6pdrs

Unsuccessful design. Cramped and with gun ports having inadequate waterline clearance. Sailed to Astrakhan' in 1779. Cruised in the Caspian in 1781–3 and either 1786 or 1787. Broken up at Astrakhan'.

Ship Sloop no. 3 20 Kazan'
Constructor ?
Laid down 1779   *Launched* 1780
Dimensions 48 ft x 26 ft x 8 ft
Armament 20 x 6pdrs
Unsuccessful design. Cramped and with gun ports with inadequate waterline clearance. Sailed to Astrakhan' in 1780. Cruised in the Caspian in 1781–4 and 1787. Broken up at Astrakhan'

Caspian flotilla brigs (19 purpose-built)

As was the case in the Baltic and Black Sea fleets, two-masted brigs gradually replaced three-masted ship sloops in the Caspian in the years following the Napoleonic Wars. Nineteen were commissioned between 1806 and 1839, with nine authorized during the Persian War of 1828–30. Detailed information on the later ships is hard to come by, but it would appear that they were probably armed with 24pdr carronades, as were similar vessels in the Black Sea and Baltic. One ship capsized in a squall but reentered service after being righted. A second was wrecked. The others led generally uneventful lives transporting cargo and troops as needed and establishing the Russian presence in the area.

Volga class (4 ships)
Volga 8 Kazan'
Constructor G. I. Koshkin
Laid down ?   *Launched* 15.5.1806
Dimensions 75 ft x 21 ft 6 in x 9 ft (Veselago)
Armament 8 x 24pdr carr.
Volga class. Purpose-built brig. Fire watch service at Astrakhan' and occasional cruises in the Caspian from 1806–17.

Raduga (Rainbow) 8 Kazan'
Constructor G. I. Koshkin
Laid down ?   *Launched* 15.5.1806 (1816?)
Dimensions 75 ft x 21 ft 6 in x 9 ft (Veselago)
Armament 8 x 24pdr carr.
Volga class. Purpose-built brig. Fire watch service at Astrakhan' and occasional cruises in the Caspian from 1806–20.

Zmeia 8 Kazan'
Constructor G. I. Koshkin
Laid down ?   *Launched* 21.5.1808
Dimensions 75 ft x 21 ft 6 in x 9 ft (Veselago)
Armament 8 x 24pdr carr.
Volga class. Purpose-built brig. Fire watch service at Astrakhan' and occasional cruises in the Caspian from 1808–17.

Iashcheritsa 8 Kazan'
Constructor G. I. Koshkin
Laid down ?   *Launched* 21.5.1808
Dimensions 75 ft x 21 ft 6 in x 10 ft 1 in (Veselago)
Armament 8 x 24pdr carr.
Volga class. Purpose-built brig. Fire watch service at Astrakhan' and occasional cruises in the Caspian from 1808–19.

Baku 12 Kazan'
Constructor A. P. Antip'ev
Laid down 28.10.1820   *Launched* 15.5.1821
Dimensions ?
Armament ?
Purpose-built brig. Arrived at Astrakhan' in 1821. Cruised in 1822–5. Landed troops against Persia at Astrabad in 1827. Cruised in 1830. Broken up in 1832.

Astrakhan' 12 Astrakhan'
Constructor ?
Laid down 1823   *Launched* 13.9.1824
Dimensions ?
Armament ?
Purpose-built brig. Cruised in 1824–5. Engaged in operations against Persia and Turkey in 1826–9. Cruised in 1830–2. Broken up in 1833.

Erivan class (4 ships)
These four brigs were purpose-built for the Russo-Persian War of 1826–8. They were named after Persian fortresses captured by Russian troops in 1827.

Erivan 12 Astrakhan'
Constructor S. O. Burachek
Laid down ?   *Launched* 16.4.1827
Dimensions 83 ft 6 in (pp) x 23 ft (inside plank) x 11 ft (Veselago)
Armament ?
Erivan class. Purpose-built brig. In service 1827–37. Carried supplies for the Russian army 1827–9 and thereafter employed cruising the Caspian and as a fire watch ship.

Sardar-abad 12 Astrakhan'
Constructor S. O. Burachek
Laid down ?   *Launched* 27.5.1827
Dimensions 83 ft 6 in (pp) x 23 ft (inside plank) x 11 ft (Veselago)
Armament ?
Erivan class. Purpose-built brig. In service 1827–36. Carried supplies for the Russian army 1827–9 and thereafter employed cruising the Caspian and as a fire watch ship.

Tavriz 12 Astrakhan'
Constructor S. O. Burachek
Laid down ?   *Launched* 27.5.1827
Dimensions 83 ft 6 in (pp) x 23 ft (inside plank) x 10 ft 10 in (Veselago)
Armament ?
Erivan class. Purpose-built brig. In service 1827–36. Carried supplies for the Russian army 1827–9 and thereafter employed cruising the Caspian and as a fire watch ship.

Abbas-Abad 12 Astrakhan'
Constructor S. O. Burachek
Laid down ?   *Launched* 16.8.1827
Dimensions 83 ft 6 in (pp) x 23 ft (inside plank) x 10 ft 10 in (Veselago)
Armament ?
Erivan class. Purpose-built brig. In service 1827–37. Carried supplies for the Russian army 1827–9 and thereafter employed cruising the Caspian and as a fire watch ship.

Dzhevan-Bulak 8 Astrakhan'
Constructor S.O. Burachek
Laid down ?   *Launched* 13.6.1828

Dimensions 68 ft 2 in x 22 ft x 10 ft 10 in (Veselago)
Armament ?
Purpose-built brig named to commemorate a victory over the Persian army in 1827. Carried 1828–32. Acted as a fire watch ship in 1833–40. Reduced to a floating magazine in 1841.

Turkmenchai 8
Constructor S. O. Burachek
Laid down ?   *Launched* 13.6.1828
Dimensions 67 ft 4 in x 21 ft x 11 ft (Veselago)
Armament ?
Purpose-built brig named after the site where the peace treaty with Persia was signed. Carried cargo 1828–34. Acted as a fire watch ship at Astrakhan' in 1835–6. Broken up in 1837.

Miana 8   Astrakhan'
Constructor S. O. Burachek
Laid down ?   *Launched* 24.9.1828
Dimensions 73 ft 6 in x 21 ft x 9 ft (Veselago)
Armament ?
Purpose-built brig named after a Persian fort taken by the Russians in 1828. Carried cargo 1828–35. Acted as a fire watch ship in 1836–7. Reduced to a floating magazine in 1838.

Ardebil' 8   Astrakhan'
Constructor S. O. Burachek
Laid down ?   *Launched* 27.4.1828
Dimensions 71 ft 2 in x 21 ft x 9 ft 6 in (Veselago)
Armament ?
Purpose-built brig named after a Persian fort taken by the Russians in 1828. Carried cargo for the army until capsized by a squall on 23.6.1829 with five members of the captain's family being lost. Raised and repaired and cruised from 1830–6. Broken up in 1837.

Kamchatka ?   ?
Constructor ?
Laid down 25.6.1828   *Launched* 25.6.1829
Dimensions ?
Armament ?
Purpose-built brig. Cruised in 1830–41. Wrecked 20.9.1841.

Baku 14   Astrakhan'
Constructor S. G. Bebikhov
Laid down 6.10.1834   *Launched* 15.5.1835
Dimensions 82 ft x 25 ft x 10 ft 1 in (Veselago)
Armament ?
Purpose-built brig. Cruised from 1836–44. In 1839 she carried presents from Emperor Nicholas I to the Persian Shah. Fire watch ship at Astrakhan' from 1846–50. No further mention.

Mangishlak class (2 ships)
Mangishlak 8   Astrakhan'
Constructor S. G. Bebikhov
Laid down 23.3.1836   *Launched* 14.4.1837
Dimensions 76 ft x 24 ft 3 in x 10 ft 10 in (Veselago)
Armament ?
Mangishlak class. Purpose-built brig. Cruised in 1837–43. Repaired in 1845. Cruised in 1848–56. Hulked at Astrabad in 1857.

Ardon 8   Astrakhan'
Constructor S. N. Neverov
Laid down 21.7.1837   *Launched* 16.4.1838
Dimensions 77 ft x (71 ft 6 in keel) x 24 ft 3 in x 10 ft 10 in (Veselago)
Armament ?
Mangishlak class. Purpose-built brig, named after the Ardon River. Cruised in 1838–44. Repaired in 1845. Cruised in 1846–57. Hulked in 1858.

Araks 12   Astrakhan'
Constructor S. N. Neverov
Laid down 11.8.1838   *Launched* 31.8.1839
Dimensions 84 ft x (72 ft keel) x 25 ft x 11 ft 6 in (Veselago)
Armament ?
Purpose-built brig named after the Arax River. Cruised off Persia in 1839–44. Repaired at Astrakhan' in 1846. No further mention.

Caspian flotilla schooners (6 purpose-built)

In a progression duplicating the replacement of ship sloops by smaller, handier brigs after 1820, fore-and-aft-rigged schooners replaced the larger and clumsier square rigged brigs in their turn after 1840. Six were purpose built between 1843 and 1859 and all outlasted the passing of the age of sail for the Russian Navy in the Black Sea and the Baltic.

Opyt 4   Abo, Finland
Constructor ?
Laid down 6.1843   *Launched* 7.10.1843
Dimensions 67 ft (pp) x 22 ft 7 in (inside plank) x 9 ft (Veselago)
Armament 1 x 8pdr, 3 falconets
Two-masted purpose-built schooner. Sailed from Abo to the Caspian Sea by rivers. Commissioned from 1846–59. Hulked after 1858.

Zmeia class (4 ships)
Zmeia 4   Abo, Finland
Constructor Yurgenson
Laid down 1847   *Launched* 1847
Dimensions 66 ft (pp) x 21 ft x 6 ft (Veselago)
          134 tons displacement
Armament ?
Zmeia class. Purpose-built schooner. Sailed to Astrakhan' in 1848. Commissioned from 1849–61. Broken up in 1861.

Tarantul 4   Abo, Finland
Constructor Yurgenson
Laid down 1847   *Launched* 1847
Dimensions 67 ft (pp) x 21 ft x 6 ft (Veselago)   134 tons displacement
Armament ?
Zmeia class. Purpose-built schooner. Sailed to Astrakhan' in 1848. Commissioned from 1849–53. Repaired in 1854. Commissioned from 1855–61. Broken up in 1861.

Komar 4   Abo, Finland
Constructor Yurgenson
Laid down 1849   *Launched* 1849
Dimensions approx. 66 ft x 21 ft x 6 ft (20.1 m x 6.4 m x 1.8 m) (Chernyshev)
          134 tons displacement
Armament ?
Zmeia class. Purpose-built schooner. Sailed to Astrakhan' in 1850. Commissioned from 1850–74. Broken up in 1875.

Mukha 4 Abo, Finland
Constructor Yurgenson
Laid down 1849   *Launched* 1849
Dimensions 67 ft (pp) x 21 ft x 6 ft (Veselago)
             134 tons displacement
Armament ?
Zmeia class. Purpose-built schooner. Sailed to Astrakhan' in 1850. Commissioned from 1851–70. Broken up in 1872.

Lomonosov ? Astrakhan'
Constructor Gagarin
Laid down 15.11.1858   *Launched* 26.5.1859
Dimensions 67 ft pp x 20 ft 5 in (inside plank) x ? (Veselago)
Armament ?
Purpose-built schooner. Named after a famed Russian scientist. Stricken on 7.12.1863. No further data.

Caspian flotilla luggers (4 purpose-built)

Scchyogol class (4 ships)
Scchyogol 8 Kazan'
Constructor G.I. Koshkin
Laid down 15.5.1806   *Launched* 11.5.1807
Dimensions 60 ft x 18 ft x 9 ft 9 in (Veselago)
Armament ?
Scchyogol class. Purpose-built lugger. Sailed to Astrakhan' in 1807. Cruised in 1808–13, supporting army operations in the war with Persia. Bombarded Lenkoran in 1813. Broken up in 1813 at Astrakhan'.

Gornostai I 8 Kazan'
Constructor G.I. Koshkin
Laid down 15.5.1806   *Launched* 11.5.1807
Dimensions 60 ft x 18 ft x 9 ft 9 in (Veselago)
Armament ?
Scchyogol class. Purpose-built lugger. Sailed to Astrakhan' in 1807. Cruised in 1808–13, supporting army operations in the war with Persia. Cruised in 1814–20. Broken up in 1822 at Astrakhan'.

Belka 8 Kazan'
Constructor G. I. Koshkin
Laid down 17.8.1807   *Launched* 21.5.1808
Dimensions 60 ft x 18 ft x 9 ft 9 in (Veselago)
Armament ?
Scchyogol class. Purpose-built lugger. Sailed to Astrakhan' in 1807. Cruised in 1808–13, supporting army operations in the war with Persia. Bombarded Lenkoran in 1813. Cruised in 1814–16. Broken up in 1817 at Astrakhan'.

Gornostai II 8 Kazan'
Constructor G. I. Koshkin
Laid down 17.8.1807   *Launched* 21.5.1808
Dimensions 60 ft x 18 ft x 9 ft 9 in (Veselago)
Armament ?
Scchyogol class. Purpose-built lugger. Sailed to Astrakhan' in 1807. Cruised in 1808–13, supporting army operations in the war with Persia. Broken up in 1819 at Astrakhan'.

Caspian flotilla one-masted tenders (2 purpose-built)

Muravei 6 Kazan
Constructor ?
Laid down 22.11.1820   *Launched* 16.5.1821
Dimensions 65 ft x 22 ft 6 in x 10 ft 10½ in (Veselago)
Armament ?
Purpose-built one-masted tender. Sailed to Astrakhan'. Cruised in 1822–8. Fire watch ship in 1828–35.

Cherepakha 8 Astrakhan'
Constructor D.I. Alexeev
Laid down 3.1.1833   *Launched* 20.5.1833
Dimensions 53 ft x 19 ft x 7 ft (Veselago)
Armament ?
Purpose-built one-masted tender. Cruised in 1833–40. Repaired in 1841. Cruised and served as a fire watch ship at Baku in 1842–3. Broken up in 1854.

Caspian flotilla bomb vessels (7 purpose-built)

Naval operations in the Caspian were largely concerned with amphibious operations relating to the transportation of troops and the provision of fire support against forts and other fixed positions. The first of seven Caspian bomb vessels was laid down prior to the formal creation of the Caspian Flotilla in 1783 and the last was not broken up until 1831 upon the successful completion of the last significant Russo-Persian war in 1828–30.

Unnamed 14 Kazan'
Constructor ?
Laid down 1779   *Launched* 1780
Dimensions 95 ft x 27 ft x 11 ft (Veselago)
Armament 10 x 6pdrs, 2 x 2 pood mortars, 2 x 1 pood howitzers
Purpose-built bomb vessel. Sailed to Astrakhan' in 1780. In commission in 1781–85. Broken up in 1785 due to premature timber dry rot resulting from the use of unseasoned timber.

Mozdok 10 Kazan'
Constructor M. Protopopov
Laid down 20.7.1784   *Launched* 8.5.1785
Dimensions ?
Armament ?
Purpose-built bomb vessel. Arrived at Astrakhan'. In commission in 1786–93. Broken up in 1794.

Kizliar class (2 ships)
Kizliar 10/18 Kazan'
Constructor V. D. Vlasov
Laid down 7.5.1793   *Launched* 5.5.1794
Dimensions 95 ft x 27 ft x 11 ft (Veselago)
Armament 2 x 6pdrs, 4 falconets, 2 x 3-pood mortars, 2 x 1-pood howitzers
Kizliar class. Purpose-built bomb vessel. Sailed to Astrakhan' in 1795. Cruised in 1796–1801. Bombarded Baku in 1799 to resolve a dispute between a Russian merchant and the local prince. Broken up in 1804.

Mozdok 10 Kazan'
Constructor V. D. Vlasov
Laid down 8.7.1794   *Launched* 8.5.1795

Dimensions approx. 95 ft x 27 ft x 11 ft (28.9 m x 8.2 m x 3.4 m) (Chernyshev)
Armament 2 x 6pdrs, 4 falconets, 2 x 3-pood mortars, 2 x 1-pood howitzers

Kizliar class. Purpose-built bomb vessel. Sailed to Astrakhan' in 1795. Cruised in 1796–1804. Broken up in 1805.

Grom 14 Astrakhan'
Constructor Lukmanov
Laid down 19.12.1804   *Launched* 04.7.1805
Dimensions ?
Armament 1 x 12pdr, 10 x 6pdrs, 2 x 3-pood mortars, 1 x 1-pood howitzer

Purpose-built bomb vessel. Cruised in 1806–13. Bombarded Lenorkan fortress in 1812–13 prior to its conquest. Broken up in 1814.

Vulkan class (2 ships)
Vulkan 14 Kazan'
Constructor E. I. Koshkin
Laid down 15.5.1806   *Launched* 11.5.1807
Dimensions 95 ft x 28 ft x 11 ft (Veselago)
Armament 1 12pdr, 10 x 6pdrs, 2 x 3-pood mortars, 1 x 1-pood mortar

Vulkan class Purpose-built bomb vessel. Sailed to Astrakhan' in 1807. Cruised in 1808–15. Shear hulk in 1816.

Vulkan 14 Kazan'
Constructor A. P. Antipyev
Laid down 11.3.1816   *Launched* 1817
Dimensions 95 ft x 28 ft x 11 ft (Veselago)
Armament ?

Vulkan class Purpose-built bomb vessel. Assigned the same name as her predecessor of the same class. Sailed to Astrakhan' in 1817. Cruised in 1818–23. Broken up in 1831.

Aral Sea flotilla schooners

No permanent naval presence was called for in the Aral Sea and the only naval vessels of any size to be constructed in the age of sail were these two schooners intended only for survey work.

Nikolai 2 Orenburg
Constructor Mertvago
Laid down ?   *Launched* 1847
Dimensions 38 ft (pp) x 11 ft 8 in x 5 ft 5 in (Veselago)
Armament ?

Purpose-built schooner. Designed for survey work in the Aral Sea. Survey work in 1848–9. Stricken on 12.6.1870.

Konstantin 2 ?
Constructor A. I. Butakov
Laid down ?   *Launched* 1848
Dimensions 47 ft (pp) x 16 ft x 6 ft 1 in (Veselago)
Armament ?

Purpose-built schooner. Designed for survey work in the Aral Sea. Survey work in 1848–9. Stricken on 21.7.1863.

Sea of Okhotsk Ships

As a frontier region at the extreme limit of the Russian empire, the Sea of Okhotsk only operated modest vessels intended to maintain lines of communication and conduct local and extended survey work. These ships were all built locally and do not truly qualify as warships. They were definitely seagoing vessels, but only four of them were known to carry cannon of any sort. Their attrition rate in service was not just severe, it was total. Out of 14 vessels of all types laid down and completed between 1739 and 1862 (past the formal end of this book), 13 were wrecked and the 14th was destroyed by Anglo-French forces during the Crimean War.

Far Eastern sloops (3 Purpose-built)

Bol'sheretsk ? ?
Constructor ?
Laid down ?   *Launched* 5.1739
Dimensions approx. 50 ft x 10½ ft x 5 in (15.2 m x 3.2 m x 1.4 m)
(Chernyshev)
Armament ?   18 oars
Purpose-built sloop. Birch built by sailors under Capt. Shpanberg. To Japan in 5–8.1739. Cruised in the Sea of Okhotsk in 1740–4. Stranded and lost in 1744. Crew saved.

Sviataia Mariia ? Okhotsk
Constructor Bubnov
Laid down ?   *Launched* ?
Dimensions ?
Armament ?
Purpose-built sloop. Wrecked near the mouth of the Kamchatka River in 1786.

Sviataia Ekaterina ? ?
Constructor ?
Laid down ?   *Launched* ?
Dimensions ?
Armament ?
Purpose-built sloop. Wrecked off the south-western coast of Kamchatka in 9.1774.

Okhotsk flotilla brigs (6 purpose-built)

Mikhail ? Okotskaya
Constructor ?
Laid down 1819   *Launched* 11.6.1820
Dimensions ?
Armament ?
Purpose-built brig. Carried cargo between ports in the Sea of Okhotsk in 1820–3. Wrecked near the Cape of Amvon in 1823.

Elisaveta 4 Okhotsk
Constructor ?
Laid down 1820   *Launched* 2.7.1821
Dimensions ?
Armament ?
Purpose-built brig. Carried cargo between ports in the Sea of Okhotsk in 1822–5. Wrecked on the coast of Avachinskaya Bay on 8.10.1835.

Ekaterina 2 Okhotsk
Constructor I. S. Chernogubov
Laid down ?   *Launched* 2.7.1823
Dimensions ?
Armament ?
Purpose-built brig. Carried cargo between ports in the Sea of Okhotsk in 1823–38. Drifted ashore, grounded and repaired in 1823. Carried cargo between ports in the Sea of Okhotsk in 1823–38. Grounded and wrecked off Simushir Island on 30.9.1838. All hands were lost. Wreckage not discovered for two years.

Aleksandr 4 ?
Constructor I. S. Chernogubov
Laid down 1.3.1824   *Launched* 25.6.1825
Dimensions ?
Armament ?
Purpose-built brig. Cruised in the Sea of Okhotsk in 1825–7. Drifted ashore, grounded and wrecked on 28.9.1827. Crew and cargo were saved.

Nikolai 4 Okhotsk
Constructor I. S. Chernogubov
Laid down 25.6.1826   *Launched* 25.6.1827
Dimensions 74 ft 4 in (pp) x 23 ft 2 in (inside plank) x 13 ft 3 in
(Veselago)
Armament ?
Purpose-built brig. Carried cargo between ports in the Sea of Okhotsk in 1827–42. Wrecked on 27.8.1842.

Kuril 4 Okhotsk
Constructor I. S. Chernogubov
Laid down 26.11.1839   *Launched* 28.7.1842
Dimensions 73 ft 6 in (pp) x 23 ft 1 in (inside plank) x 12 ft 4 in
(Veselago)
Armament ?   42 men
Purpose-built brig. Carried cargo between ports in the Sea of Okhotsk in 1842–8. Repaired in 1849. Left Okhotsk on 5.7.1850 and lost without a trace.

Okhotsk flotilla cutters (2 purpose-built)

Chernyi Oryol Kamchatka, Nizhnekamchatsk
Constructor R. R. Gall
Laid down 1790   *Launched* 31.5.1791
Dimensions ?
Armament ?
Purpose-built cutter. Built for the expedition of I. I. Billings and G. A. Sarychev. Met the *Slava Rossii* on 2.9.1891 at Unalashka island.

Returned to Petropavlovsk in 1792 and then to Okhotsk. Cruised in the Sea of Okhotsk from 1793–1806. Drifted ashore and grounded during a storm in 1806 and later salvaged. Reduced to harbour service at Okhotsk in 1808.

Sviatoi Zotik Okhotsk ? ?
Constructor I. Popov
Laid down 22.3.1806 *Launched* 8.7.1806
Dimensions ?
Armament ?
Purpose-built cutter. Cruised in the Sea of Okhotsk in 1807–11. On 28.8.1812, in company with the sloop *Diana*, arrived at Kunashir where Capt. Golovin and 7 sailors were being held in Japanese captivity. Wrecked in transit to Petropavlovsk on 11.9.1812, crew survived.

Okhotsk flotilla schooners (2 purpose-built)

Nikolai ? ?
Constructor ?
Laid down ? *Launched* 1822
Dimensions ?
Armament ?
Purpose-built schooner. Cruised in the Sea of Okhotsk in 1823–7. Wrecked on 18.8.1827.

Anadyr' ? Kamchatka
Constructor ?
Laid down ? *Launched* 23.6.1853
Dimensions ?
Armament ?
Purpose-built schooner. Commissioned in 1853–4. Set afire by Anglo-French ships in the Sea of Okhotsk on 27.8.1854.

Okhotsk flotilla one-masted tenders (1 purpose-built)

Kamchadal ? ?
Constructor ?
Laid down ? *Launched* 1849
Dimensions ?
Armament ? 13 men
Purpose-built one-masted tender. Cruised in the Sea of Okhotsk in 1850–58. Lost in 10.1858. No further information.

Siberian flotilla schooners (3 purpose-built)

These three schooners have the distinction of having been built at the very end of the age of sail and for service in one of the most inhospitable environments on the planet. *Purga* has the dubious honour of being the only Russian sailing ship built in the United States.

Pervyi ? Nikolaevsk
Constructor Chikurov
Laid down 1858 *Launched* 14.8.1859
Dimensions 87 ft 9 in x 24 ft 8 in x ? (Veselago)
Armament ?Purpose-built schooner. Commissioned in 1860–3. Wrecked off Japan on 26.10.1863. Stricken on 17.8.1864.

Vtoraia/Farvater ? Nikolaevsk
Constructor ?
Laid down ? *Launched* 1862
Dimensions approx. 57 ft x 16 ft x 6 ft (17.5 m x 5 m x 1.7 m)
  60 tons displacement (Chernyshev)
Armament ?
Purpose-built schooner. Renamed *Farvater* after completion. Commissioned in 1862–74. Stricken in 1891.

Purga 4 USA
Constructor ?
Laid down ? *Launched* ? *Purchased* 1857
Dimensions 79 ft 8 in (pp) x 21 ft 7 in x 8½ ft (Veselago)
  394 tons displacement
Armament ?
Purchased schooner. Commissioned in 1858–69. Wrecked off the Kuriils on 10.8.1869.

Section II
The Inshore Navy

Russian Rowing Warships and Amphibious Support Ships

During the age of sail, the Russian Navy was effectively divided into two distinctive elements, separated structurally, administratively and operationally. The seagoing sailing navy has already been covered in Section I and the inshore amphibious forces are presented here. Because of the very different nature of the waterborne vessels that constituted this force, the organization and presentation of basic data will vary to some degree from that of the first section. On the one hand, there is not so much data available for many of these smaller and more numerous craft or as much operational information for the careers of individual vessels, many of which are identified only by numbers and not names – when they were identified at all. On the other, the lines of development for the various types of vessels and the geographical scale of deployment are so very different here as to preclude the relevance of much of the organizational structure applied previously to the sailing fleet. The great majority of these vessels were constructed during the first two periods of our coverage (1696–1761 and 1762–1800) because amphibious warfare became a lesser concern with the resolution of the struggle for domination over the Turkish and Swedish navies. During the successive reigns of Alexander I and Nicholas I, Russian resources were able to be more fully directed towards meeting the needs of the seagoing navy and the preoccupation with shallow-water rowing vessels was greatly reduced, although not entirely abandoned, after the final brief struggle with Sweden in 1808.

In the most general sense, the inshore fleet may be divided into two large groups: highly mobile oared vessels designed for active combat against similar foreign vessels, and relatively stationary vessels intended to provide gunfire support against land installations in support of the Russian army.

It should be mentioned that the operations of the inshore flotillas were very largely independent from those of the seagoing navy on a tactical level, even though the operations of seagoing and inshore fleets were closely linked on a strategic level. Put simply, rowing vessels did not engage sailing warships in anything but extraordinary circumstances, a situation that was enforced by the fact that seagoing ships could not easily intrude into the shallow waters frequented by rowing vessels, and that rowing vessels, for their part, did poorly in open waters and lacked the firepower or durability to exchange fire with sailing ships. The most highly evolved use of inshore and amphibious vessels was in the Baltic, with its very extensive network of shallow-water coastal areas in and around the Gulf of Finland, and with an opponent, Sweden, that developed the largest and most sophisticated fleet of shallow draught rowing vessels of all kinds found in Europe after 1720. In contrast, the Black Sea environment as a whole was not as conducive to the extensive employment of inshore rowing craft as the Baltic, because the steeper coastal drop-offs in the Black Sea provided seagoing warships with the freedom to operate in and around harbours and other potential landing sites in a manner denied them in the Baltic. There were, however, two exceptions to this generalization, the early campaigns in the Sea of Azov and the later campaign in the Liman area, both of which involved extensive use of the smaller classes of rowing vessels on both sides.

One final caveat is in order. The galleys, shebecks and similar vessels employed by Russia and her opponents in the eighteenth century were not primitive warships or straightforward relics of the galley wars in the Mediterranean in the previous centuries. Although these warship types had fallen into general disfavour in the Mediterranean after 1700, they continued to be developed, most particularly in the Baltic, until the close of the century and were as technologically advanced in their own way as contemporary seagoing vessels.

Shebecks (Jabeques) (8 purpose-built)

Russian shebecks were three-masted vessels patterned after Swedish turunmaas (turumas). They carried up to 40 oars, with 3 oarsmen per oar. Shorter and beamier than comparable galleys, they were armed with main deck broadsides on a par with those of contemporary light frigates, as well as with extensive open deck batteries of 3pdrs for close-in action against personnel. Shebecks do not seem to have found much favour in the Russian Navy and their only operational use was in the Baltic during the 1788–90 war with Sweden. Total production was limited to 8 shebecks and 10 half-shebecks laid down at Galley Yard in St Petersburg in 1788 and completed in 1789. An additional 3 large and 1 small galleys were taken from Sweden during the Russo-Swedish War; while Russian squadrons operating in the Mediterranean under Ushakov and Seniavin captured 3 large and 1 small French shebecks between 1699 and 1807. Four shebecks were lost in the 2nd battle of Rochensalm and the four survivors were later refitted as floating batteries.

Letuchaia St Petersburg, Admiralty
Constructor D. Masalskiy
Laid down 8.5.1788, *Launched* 1.9.1788
Dimensions approx. 120 ft x 28 ft x 8.2 ft (36.6m x 8.5m x 2.5m)
Armament 4 x 18pdrs, 20 x 12pdrs, 22 x 3pdrs, 40 oars, 230 men
Heavily damaged at the 1st battle of Rochensalm with 83 shot holes and 7 guns disabled. After the battle of Vyborg, she escorted the Swedish prize *Finland* to Kronshtadt. Converted to a floating battery and renamed *Pobezhdayushchaya* in 1792. Final fate is unknown.

4 shebecks built at Galley Yard by D. Masalskiy. They were over-gunned as completed and refitted with reduced armaments in the winter of 1789–90. All were laid down on 1.12.1788 and lost during 2nd battle of Rochensalm.
Dimensions approx. 120 ft x 34 ft x 11 ft 6 in (36.6 m x 10.4 m x 3.5 m)
Armament 20 x 24pdrs, 10 x 6pdrs (as built)
    2 x 24pdrs, 18 x 12pdrs, 8 x 6pdrs (as rearmed)
Minerva
Launched 4.5.1789. Lost on 28.6.1790, with only 21 crewmen saved.
Bellona
Launched 7.5.1789. Lost on 28.6.1790, with only 9 crewmen saved.

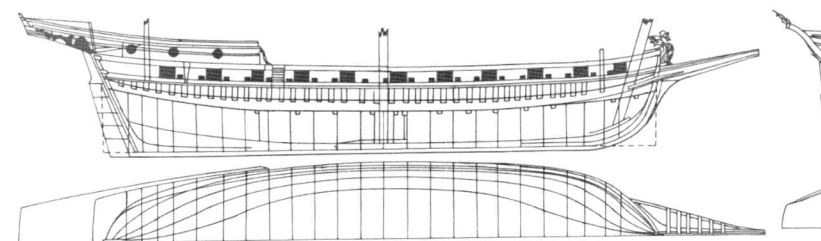

SHEBECKS

Minerva *was the lead ship of a class of four shebecks built in haste upon the outbreak of war with Sweden. All four were lost at the 2nd battle of Rochensalm, demonstrating the unsuitability of this Mediterranean type for the kind of combat that typified the shallows of the northern Baltic. Their original armament of 24pdrs was too heavy for such a lightly built type and was quickly replaced by a mixed armament of two 24pdrs and eighteen 12pdrs.*

Diana
Launched   16.5.1789. Lost on 28.6.1790, with only 19 crewmen saved.
Prozerpina
Launched   16.5.1789. Lost 28.6.1790 (burnt to avoid capture), with only 11 crewmen being rescued.

3 shebecks built at Galley Yard by D. Masalskiy.
Dimensions approx. 120 ft x 30 ft x 8.2 ft (36.6 m x 9.2 m x 2.5 m)
Armament   4 x 18pdrs, 20 x 12pdrs, 22 x 3pdrs, 40 oars, 230 men
Skoraia
Laid down   24.10.1788   Launched 4.5.1789
Rebuilt as floating battery *Krepkaia* in 1792. Final fate is unknown
Legkaia
Laid down   24.10.1788   Launched 4.5.1789
Rebuilt as floating battery *Khrabraia* in 1792. Final fate is unknown.
Bystraia
Laid down   1.12.1788   Launched 4.5.1789
Rebuilt as floating battery *Svirepaia* in 1792. Final fate is unknown.

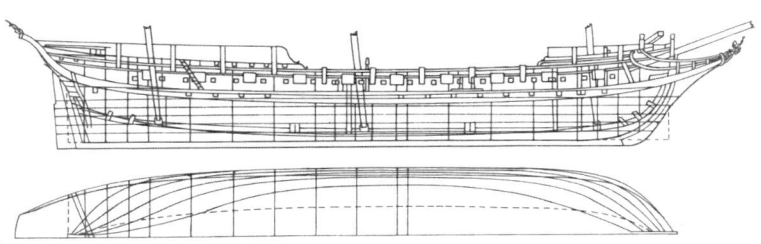

Skoraya *was one of three shebecks designed in 1789 by the same builder, D. Masalskiy, and was built concurrently with the larger* Minerva *class, as was the one-off* Letuchaya. *Although these ships were as long as the* Minervas, *they were 4 feet narrower and more lightly armed as originally designed. All three were rebuilt as floating batteries after the Russo-Swedish war drew to a close, a commentary on Russian disenchantment with long, large, speedy rowing vessels.*

Baltic shebeck prizes

Sellan Vere
Dimensions approx. 120 ft x 30 ft x 8.9 ft (36.6 m x 9.2 m x 2.7 m)
            (incorrect Russian measurement)
            120 ft x 30 ft x 10 ft 6 in, 490 tons (corrected Swedish measurement)
Armament   24 x 12pdrs, 10 x 3pdrs, 16 swivels (as designed)
            2 x 24pdrs, 24 x 12pdrs, 22 x 3pdrs, 3 masts, 38 oars
            240 men (Russian service)
Ex-Swedish turunmaa *Sällan Varre*, incorrectly cited in Russian sources as sister-ship to *Bjorn Ernsida*. Designed by Frederik af Chapman, launched in 1764 as *Tor*, renamed *Sällan Varre* in 1770 and captured at the 1st battle of Rochensalm on 13.8.1789. Recaptured by Sweden on 4.5.1790.

Björn Ernsida
Dimensions approx. 120 ft x 30 ft x 8.9 ft (36.6 m x 9.2 m x 2.7 m)
            (Russian measurement)

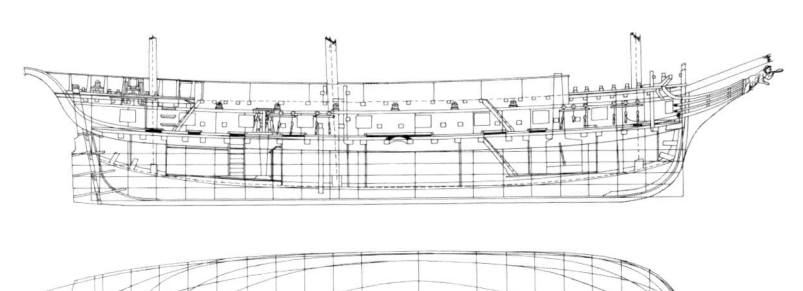

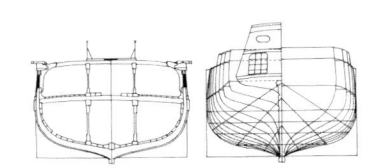

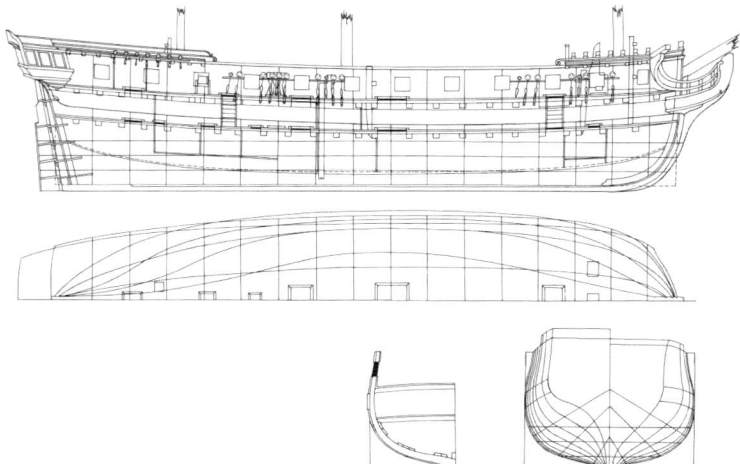

A detailed drawing of the Swedish Oden *captured at the 1st battle of Rochensalm in 1789. Classified by her new owners as a 'gemam' or hemmema, she was actually a turuma within the Swedish classification system. Built in 1764 and rebuilt in 1784,* Oden *probably holds the record for changing hands, having been recaptured by her Swedish builders at the 2nd battle of Rochensalm in 1790, and finally recaptured yet a second time by Russia in 1808.*

The Swedish turuma Rogvald, *completed in 1774 and captured at the 1st battle of Rochensalm in 1789 along with* Oden. *At 126 feet in length, she was larger and more powerfully armed than the 110-foot* Oden. *Both shebecks were exceptionally long-lived by Russian standards, and this was a direct outgrowth of Sweden's more careful construction and maintenance standards, born in turn of her smaller size and more limited financial and shipbuilding resources.*

126 ft x 31 ft x 11 ft, 550 tons (Swedish measure)
Armament 2 x 18pdrs, 24 x 12pdrs, 22 x 3pdrs (as designed)
2 x 24pdrs, 24 x 12pdrs, 22 x 3pdrs, 3 masts, 38 oars, 240 men (Russian service)

Ex-Swedish 3-masted turunmaa *Björn Ernsida*. Designed by Frederik af Chapman, launched in 1774 and captured at the 1st battle of Rochensalm on 13.8.1789. Sunk in 1808 to block the entrance to Kronshtadt.

Rogvald
Dimensions approx. 120 ft x 30 ft x 8.9 ft (36.6 m x 9.2 m x 2.7 m)
(Russian measure)
126 ft x 31 ft x 11 ft, 550 tons (Swedish measure)
Armament 2 x 18pdrs, 24 x 12pdrs, 22 x 3pdrs (as designed)
2 x 24pdrs, 24 x 12pdrs, 22 x 3-pdrs, 3 masts, 38 oars, 240 men (Russian service)

Swedish *Ragvald*, sister-ship to *Björn Ernsida*. Designed by Frederik af Chapman, launched in 1774 and captured at the 1st battle of Rochensalm on 13.8.1789. Last mentioned in 1791.

Oden (1764, rebuilt 1784)
Dimensions approx. 107 ft x 27 ft x 8 ft 9 in (32.7 m x 8.16 m x 2.7 m)
(Swedish measure)
110 ft 2 in x ? x ? (Russian measure)
Armament 18 x 12pdrs, 4 x 4pdrs, 16 x 3pdrs, 28 oars

Swedish hemmemmaa. Designed by Frederik af Chapman, launched in 1764 and rebuilt in 1784. Captured at the 1st battle of Rochensalm on 13.8.1789. Recaptured by Sweden at the 2nd battle of Rochensalm on 28.6.1790. Recaptured by Russia in 1808.

Makarii
Armament 18 guns, 100 men

French shebeck captured by the ship of the line *Bogoiavlenie Gospodne* of Adm. Ushakov's squadron in 1799. Driven ashore near the Bosphorus on 9.10.1800 and lost.

Zabiiaka
Armament 2 x 8pdrs, 12 x 4pdrs

French shebeck *Henry*, captured 22.6.1806 off Spolatro by frigate *Avtroil*. Sold to the French at Corfu after 27.9.1809.

Azard
Armament 14 guns, 60 men

French shebeck captured by Seniavin's squadron on 17.2.1807 off Castelnuovo. Sold to the French at Corfu after 27.9.1807.

Baltic half-shebecks (10 purpose-built)

10 half-shebecks built at Galley Yard and Lodeynoe Pole.
Dimensions approx. 76 ft x 19 ft x 7.9 ft (23.2 m x 5.8 m x 2.4 m)
Armament 8 x 8pdrs, 8 x 6pdrs (as built)
3 x 18pdrs, 6 x 8pdrs, 32 oars, 120 men (as rearmed 1790)

Bars
Lost at the 2nd battle of Rochensalm on 28.6.1790. 2 crewmen saved.
Volk
Last mentioned 1790.
Drakon
Last mentioned 1790.
Kit
Lost at the 2nd battle of Rochensalm on 28.6.1790. 5 crewmen men saved.

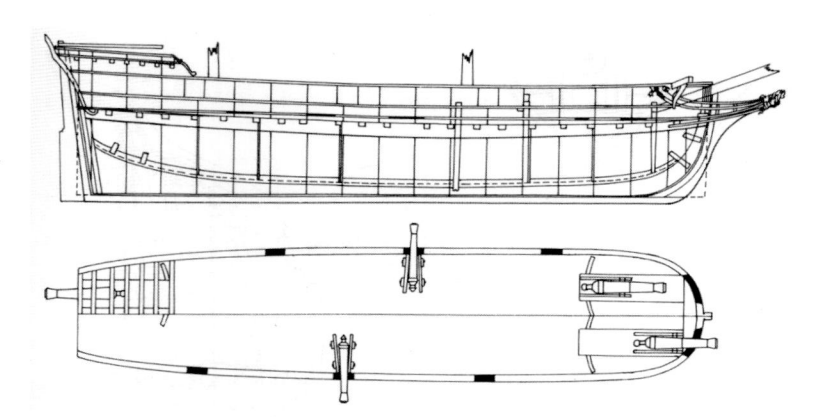

A typical half-shebek, one of ten built during the Russo-Swedish war. These vessels were not well-suited for war in the Baltic and eight of the ten fell prey to Swedish gunboats at the 2nd battle of Rochensalm.

Lev
Lost at the 2nd battle of Rochensalm on 28.6.1790. 38 crewmen saved.
Medved'
Lost at the 2nd battle of Rochensalm on 28.6.1790. 22 crewmen saved.
Oryol
Lost at the 2nd battle of Rochensalm on 28.6.1790. 19 crewmen saved.
Rys'
Lost at the 2nd battle of Rochensalm on 28.6.1790.
Slon
Blown up in action on 21.6.1790.
Tigr
Lost at the 2nd battle of Rochensalm on 28.6.1790. 16 crew men saved.
Laid down 1788 *Launched* 1789

Half-shebeck prize

Uzhasnaia
French *Tremenda*, captured off Spolatro 22.6.1806 by frigate Venus. Never commissioned and sold back to France at Corfu after 27.9.1809.

War Galleys

Russian galleys were originally divided into three classes: galleys, half-galleys (kaiks) and skampaveas (from Italian *scampare*, to escape). The scampaveas were of so-called 'Greek' (or Turkish) design and resulted from F. M. Sklyaevs expansion of an idea of Peter I's for a smaller, more agile version of the standard Venetian galley design suitable for use in Baltic waters. With Peter I's naval reforms in 1720–1, all three types were collectively referred to simply as 'galleys'. Unlike sailing warships which were rated in terms of the numbers of guns carried, galleys were always described in terms of the number of banks of oars. Early galleys generally had between 14 and 20 banks of oars, but were most commonly of 15 banks. They were usually named after birds and fish.

Greek (or Turkish) style galleys were very handy for shallow-water use in the numerous small islands in the Baltic, but had poor seagoing capabilities. Therefore, from the 1720s 'French'- and 'Venetian'-style galleys were introduced, with reinforced hulls and with oar banks at an angle of 81–82 degrees. In 1721 galleys were formally subdivided into 16-, 20-, 22- and 25-bank classes.

After the death of Peter I, Prince Aleksandr Menshikov, who was the *de facto* ruler of Russia from 1725 until his deposition in

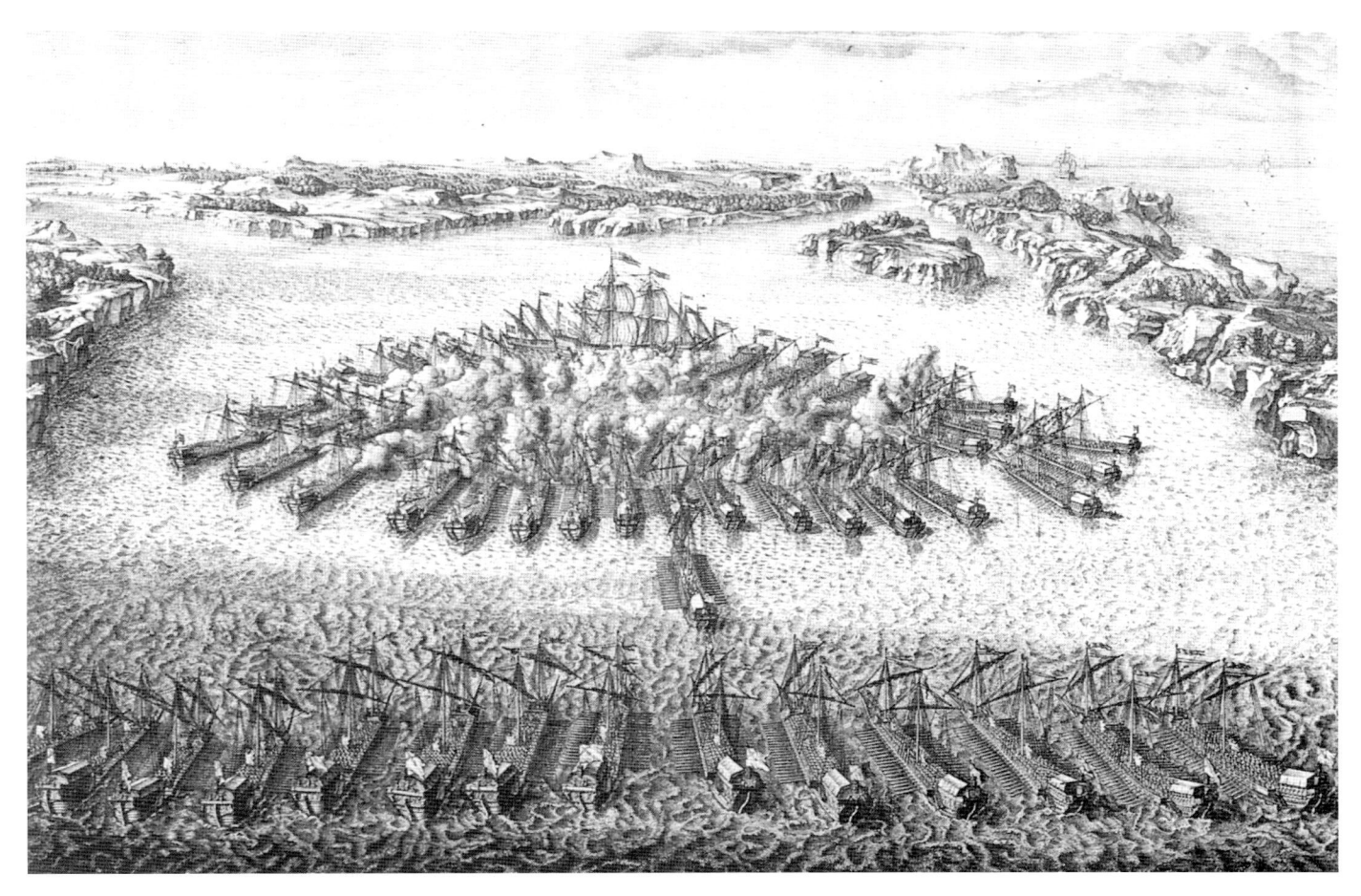

Given the right circumstances, galleys could be devastatingly effective in the kind of shallow-water environment provided by the northern Baltic, especially on windless days. This depiction of the battle of Hango (Gangut) in 1714 by M. Bokouis shows Russian galleys closing on the doomed Swedish squadron in parade ground order. Once contact was made, this military precision would collapse into the chaos shown in the Kamenev depiction shown on page 330.

1727, was of the opinion that sailing ships were superfluous and that galleys would suffice for Russian naval requirements. Between 1727 and 1730, approximately 130 galleys of all types were built. His successors, prior to *their* fall from grace under Empress Anna, were the Princes Dolgorukov (father and two sons). Although the Dolgorukovs paid no attention whatsoever to naval requirements during their ascendancy, some limited construction of galleys continued over the next several decades under both Ann and Elizabeth.

Large-scale construction was again undertaken in the Baltic under Catherine II in preparation for renewed hostilities with Sweden. This was done in spite of the fact that Sweden had abandoned the construction (but not the deployment of) of galleys after 1749 in favour of large-scale construction of other types of oared vessels, trading the speed of the galley for the manoeuvrability of beamier oared vessels, particularly gunboats. Russia followed the Swedish lead and abandoned the construction of galleys in 1796. This decision may well have resulted from their lack of success in the 1788–90 war against smaller and more numerous Swedish gunboats, which were capable of turning more rapidly than galleys in confined waters, presenting a smaller target area, and bringing their guns to bear more quickly.

During the reigns of Catherine II and Paul I, three major disasters occurred affecting significant portions of the Baltic galley fleet. The first was a major fire at the Galley Port on 11.7.1771 which involved the loss of 25 galleys, built or building. The second was the disastrous defeat suffered at the 2nd battle of Rochensalm on 28.6.1790, with 20 ships lost or captured by the Swedes in part due to the incompetence of the Russian commander and in part to the lack of manoeuvrability of the Russian galleys. The third was an even more disastrous peacetime fire at the main Galley Port on 25.5.1796 with 45 galleys and large numbers of other oared vessels destroyed.

Sea of Azov galleys

Galleys destined for service in the Sea of Azov fleet came from two sources: those built near Moscow and then transferred to the Sea of Azov, and those built on the Don by the notorious *kumpanstva* or private companies.

Galleys built at Preobrazhenskoe for the Azov expedition of 1696

22 galleys were built at the Preobrazhenskoe settlement near Moscow (now a Moscow district) for the Azov expedition of 1696. As was the case with many early seagoing warships during this period, the prototype galley was ordered in Holland and delivered to Moscow

This portion of a contemporary engraving commemorating the taking of Azov in 1696 by Adriaan Schonebeck was completed in 1699 and gives a good picture of the first generation of galleys completed for the Russian navy. Schonebeck was invited to Russia by Peter I during his European tour, and spent seven years instructing Russian artists in the art of engraving. The first Russian capital ship, Sviatoi Pavel *is also shown here firing on Turkish fortifications.*

unassembled in 11.1695. This vessel had been originally intended at the time of its having been ordered in 1694 as a prototype for a fleet of galleys to operate in the Caspian against Persia. Peter I's goals changed in a very short period from war with Persia to war with Turkey and the failure of the 1695 assault on Azov led him to divert his planned galley fleet from the Caspian to the Sea of Azov. Russian builders in the Moscow area included O. Shcheka and Ya. Ivanoov, while imported Dutch contractors included I. Vilimsen, P. Klar and Y. Yansen. In 2.1696, the completed galleys were transferred to Voronezh in disassembled state, where they were completed and launched towards the Sea of Azov from April onward. These two-masted vessels came in various sizes. Most were armed with three 5pdr guns. Because they had been built in great haste and of unseasoned timber, all 22 were unfit for further service by 1699. They were all broken up after 1701.

With the exception of Peter I's flagship *Principium*, these galleys were named after their commanders in a manner not dissimilar to Turkish practice. The oarsmen at this early period were soldiers transferred from two guard regiments.

Principium
    3 guns, 17 banks for rowers (i.e. 34 oars), flagship of Peter I
Admiral Lefort
    3 guns, 14 banks, 2 masts
Dimensions approx. 125 ft x 30 ft x 5.9 ft (38.1 m x 9.2 m x 1.8 m)

Armament 3 mortars, 133men
Built by an order of Russia in Holland in 1694. In 1695 brought (disassembled) on a merchant ship to Arkhangelsk, then via Vologda on 20 special rollers to Moscow. Used as a prototype for first Russian-built galleys. In 2.1696 brought to Voronezh, reassembled and launched.
Vice-Admiral Y. S. Lima
    4 guns, 14 banks
Captain A. Veyde
    3 guns, 14 banks
Captain A. A. Grott
    3 guns, 14 banks
Captain B. Pristav
    3 guns, 14 banks
Captain F. Hotunskiy
    3 guns, 14 banks
Captain D. Inglis
    3 guns, 16 banks
Captain V. Turlavil
    3 guns, 16 banks
Captain V. Ushakov
    3 guns, 18 banks
Shoutbenakht B. E. de Lozier
    3 guns, 15 banks

(Shout-bej-nacht was the Dutch equivalent of Rear-Admiral and the term remained in Russian use until 1732.)

Captain A. Bykovskiy
  4 guns, 14 banks
Captain Y. V. Bruce
  4 guns, 15 banks
Captain P. Cunningham
  4 guns, 16 banks
Captain Prince I. Y. Trubetskoy
  5 guns, 17 banks
Captain F. Bulart
  3 guns, 17 banks
Captain A. Gasenius
  2 guns, 17 banks
Captain Khotunskiy
  4 guns, 18 banks
Captain Oleshev
  3 guns, 18 banks
Captain Prince N. I. Repnin
  3 guns, 18 banks
Captain R. Bruce
  4 guns, 18 banks
Captain Shmidt
  6 guns, 19 banks

Galleys built by kumpanstva

It was decided at the same time to build 18 galleys privately, with specified dimensions of 125 ft length and 24 ft breadth and 14 banks of oars. Having been built by different builders, their completed lengths varied considerably and ranged from 137 ft to 174 ft.

Veter
Laid down 1697 *Launched* 1699
8.1711 transferred to Cherkassk. BU after 1716.

Zaiachii Beg
Laid down 1697 *Launched* 1699
Participated in the voyage to Kerch in 1699. Found unfit in 1710 and abandoned at Azov in 1711.

Zolotoi Oryol
Laid down 1697 *Launched* 1699
Found unfit in 1710 and abandoned at Azov in 1711.

Perinaia Tiagota
Laid down 1697 *Launched* 1699
Participated in the voyage to Kerch in 1699. Found unfit in 1710 and abandoned at Azov in 1711.

Unnamed
Constructor Y. Moro
Laid down 1697 *Launched* before 1707
Dimensions approx. 174 ft x 20 ft x 6.9 ft (53.1 m x 6.4 m x 2.1 m)
BU after 1709.

Unnamed
Constructor Y. Moro
Laid down 1697
Dimensions approx. 141 ft x 21.6 ft x 9.8 ft (43 m x 6.6 m x 2 m)
Never launched. BU on the slip after 1709.

Unnamed
Constructor K. Duyts
Laid down 1697
Dimensions approx. 138 ft x 20 ft x 6.6 ft (42.1 m x 6 m x 2 m)
BU on the slip after 1709.

Unnamed
Constructor K. Duyts
Laid down 1697
Dimensions approx. 139 ft x 20 ft x 6.2 ft (42.4 m x 6.1 m x 1.9 m)
BU on the slip after 1709.

Unnamed
Constructor I. Vilimsen
Laid down 1697
Dimensions approx. 138 ft x 20 ft x 6.6 ft (42.1 m x 6.2 m x 2 m)
BU on the slip after 1709.

Although details are lacking, a further 2 were laid down in 1697 and the final 7 in 1698. Begun variously by private contractors I. Vilimsen, Klas, Y. Y. Taneman, Borutsiy, Piccolo and K. Duyts, all were broken up incomplete after 1709. Dimensions varied from 136 ft to 150 ft length, 5.8 19 ft to 21 ft 4 in breadth and 5.9 ft to 6.6 ft draught.

Galleys built after the dissolution of the Sea of Azov fleet

In April 1723, Peter I signed an order for the construction of 8 18-bank and 7 16-bank galleys at Tavrov in preparation for an anticipated future war with Turkey. In 1724 a new treaty was signed in Istanbul and all ships under construction at Tavrov were suspended, but retained for resumption at a future date. In 1734 Russia began preparations for a renewal of hostilities with Turkey and on 27.6.1735 Empress Anna ordered the resumption of work for completion of these vessels and the construction of new galleys.

22-bank galleys (3 purpose-built)
3 22-bank galleys built at Tavrov in 1736, *Kavaler Sviatoi Andrei, Korona, Sviataia Anna*. BU after 1739.

20-bank galleys (18 purpose-built)
13 20-bank galleys were built at Tavrov in 1736, *Amur, Apollo, Diana, Elena, Gektor, Kavaler Sviatoi Aleksandr, Minerva, Monplezir, Moris, Paris, Plato, Venus, Zolotoe Iabloko*. BU after 1739.

5 20-bank galleys built at Bryansk for the Dnieper River flotilla,
Laid down 1737 *Launched* 1738 BU after 1739.

18-bank galleys (8 purpose-built)
8 18-bank galleys laid down at Tavrov and suspended, *Dobraia, Zabavnaia, Zadornaia, Laskovaia, Priyatelnaya, Terpelivaia, Uchtivaia, Chestnaia*
Laid down 1723 *Launched* 5.1734
Construction was initially suspended in 10.1724. Priyatelnaya served as flagship to Vice-Admiral Bredal in 1736. BU after 1739.

16-bank galleys (36 purpose-built)
7 16-bank galleys laid down at Tavrov and suspended until 1734, *Vedraia, Prevoskhoditel'naia, Razumnaia, Siiatel'naia, Sklonnaia, Ubornaia, Khval'naia*
Laid down 1723 *Launched* 5.1734 BU after 1739.

4 16-bank galleys built at Tavrov, *Palyulos, Telemakus, Uliss, Yanos*
Laid down 1735 *Launched* 1736 BU after 1739.

5 16-bank unnamed galleys built at Bryansk on the Desna River.
Laid down 1737 *Launched* 1738 BU after 1739.

20 16-bank galleys built near the fortress of Svyata Anna on the Don, near the town of Cherkassk, *Bystraia, Del'fin, Kit, Lev, Minerva,*

Russian galleys in action at the climactic moment in the battle of Hango (Gangut) in 1714 as depicted by L. L. Kamenev in 1857. In the centre, surrounded by Russian galleys, is Admiral Ehrensköld's flagship Elefant *shortly before her surrender. Peter I is said to have been present at the final attack. He was so greatly impressed by Ehrensköld's heroism that he personally greeted him as a hero after the battle.*

Molniia, Nadezhda, Nepobedimaia, Oryol, Pobeda, Salamandra, Svirepaia, Sokol, Strakh, Upovanie, Venera, Vydra, Iupiter, Zmeia, Zvezda
Laid down 1738 *Launched* 1739
BU after 1739.

The Caspian flotilla (15 purpose-built)

15 scampaveas built at Kazan yard by M. Cherkasov
Laid down 12.1715 *Launched* 1716
BU at Astrakhan' in 1722.

Baltic fleet galleys

Galleys built under Peter I
Between 1712 and 1800, Baltic galleys were built at Galley Yard (called Galernyy Dvor, Galley Court Yard, before 1721), located on the Neva at St Petersburg. The New Admiralty Shipyard was established on the site in 1800 and devoted exclusively thereafter to the construction of large seagoing warships.

Galleys (69 purpose-built)
7 two-masted 16-bank galleys were built at Okhta.
Sviatoi Pyotr, Zolotoy Oryol, Fyodor Stratilat, Aleksandr Makedonskiy, Nadezhda, Liubov', Vera
Laid down 1703 (Vera 1704) *Launched* 1704–5

Dimensions approx. 115–128.5 ft x 16–22 ft x 3.6 ft (35–39.2 m x 4.9–6.7 m x 1.1 m)
Armament 19 guns (inc. swivels)
Constructor Y. A. Rusinov, M. Leontyev, S. Meles and Lutersen
All seven were BU in 1710–11.

Natal'ia Olonetskaya
Constructor N. Mutts
Laid down 1708 *Launched* ?
Dimensions approx. 176 ft x 25 ft x 8.5 ft (53.7 m x 7.6 m x 2.6 m)
Armament 1 x 24pdr, 2 x 12pdrs, 12 x 3pdrs
21-bank galley. Served as flagship to General-Adm. F. M. Apraksin at Gangut in 1714.

20 galleys built at Galley Yard.
Known names: ***Anstiza, Del'fin, Kolomar, Kolumba, Laust, Raza, Svoilo, Sepa, Skobra, Folpo, Shubra***
Laid down 1716 *Launched* 1717

8 galleys built at Galley Yard.
Bagulya, Golub', Zuy, Karneika, Langvila, Oryol, Treska, Feniks
Launched 1719

20 galleys built at Galley Yard.
Known names: ***Viktoriia, Gasbora, Konstantsiya, Postoianstvo, Semga, Shchegol'***
Launched 1720

WAR GALLEYS

One of the great moments for Russian galleys in the century of warfare between Russia and Sweden came at the battle of Grengamn (1720) in the closing phases of the Great Northern War. The Swedes, virtually becalmed and trapped in a narrow channel, lost four sailing frigates to the determined attack of Russian galleys. This painting by F. Perrot in 1841 shows what appears to be a 20-bank galley, possibly a flagship, approaching the melee with oars rising in perfect unison.

11 22-bank galleys were built in 1721 at Galley Yard and armed with 7 guns: **Volga, Ladoga, Melkovodnaia, Onega, Okhta, Tosna** BU 1729. **Visla, Izhora, Pronia, Slavianka, Sokol** final fate unknown.

2 16-bank galleys built in 1721, **Zhar** and **Ziablitsa**
Launched 1721
Armament 2 guns

Scampaveas (146 purpose-built)

13 scampaveas built at Olonetskayaby Y. Kol.
Laid down 10.1703 *Launched* 1.1704
Dimensions approx. 72 ft x 57 ft x 10 ft x 2.6 ft (22 m (deck) x 17.4 m (keel) x 3.1 m x 0.8 m)

10 scampaveas built at Kronverk by M. Leontyev
Laid down 1706 *Launched* 1707.

13 scampaveas built at Vyborg by Y. A. Rusinov
Laid down 1710 *Launched* 1711
Armament 1 x 6pdr, 2 x 3pdrs, 4 falconets.

50 scampaveas built at Galley Yard by Y. A. Rusinov
Known names include: **Anshtura, Bardun, Brongo, Gavun, Gorishcha, Gota, Karp, Krabby, Lomi, Moklets, Parta, Poust, Ritsa, Rumba, Zherekh**
Laid down 10.1712 *Launched* 4–5.1713

30 scampaveas built at Galley Yard by Y. A. Rusinov
Laid down 9.1713 *Launched* 4.1714

30 scampaveas built at Galley Yard by N. Muts
Laid down 6.11.1713 *Launched* 4.1714.

The following 70 galley names are mentioned in documents in 1714. It is not known what specific classes are represented:
Aist, Anchous, Baba, Bagulya, Baraban, Belaia, Chaika, Cherepakha, Chekhonya, Datulya, Dantan, Del'fin, Drozd, Ersh, Fivra, Filin, Forel', Gagara, Gabora, Gogol', Grach, Grendulina, Grenok, Gus, Kanona, Karakatitsa, Karas', Karostel', Krasnoperaia, Kopchik, Krokodil, Kulik, Laks, Lastka, Lebed', Leshch, Musels, Mushula, Navaga, Netopyr', Parasim, Pitsa, Plamida, Potatuy, Rak, Riabchik, Sazan, Sal'pa, Sarga, Sviatoi Nikolai, Seld, Semga, Sig, Skvorets, Soika, Som, Soroka, Straus, Sudak, Tonina, Treska, Tsaplia, Uringe, Utka, Val'fish, Vasfish, Voron, Iaz', Yastre, Zhuravl'

Galley construction after Peter I's death

25-bank galleys (44 laid down/36 completed)

These were the largest galleys built in Russia, with 3 masts and 6 oarsmen per oar. 25-bank galleys were built only in the Baltic. They represented the last galleys built for Russia when 13 were authorized to replace the losses sustained in the 1796 fire.

2 25-bank galleys built at St Petersburg with 'Venetian rigging'.

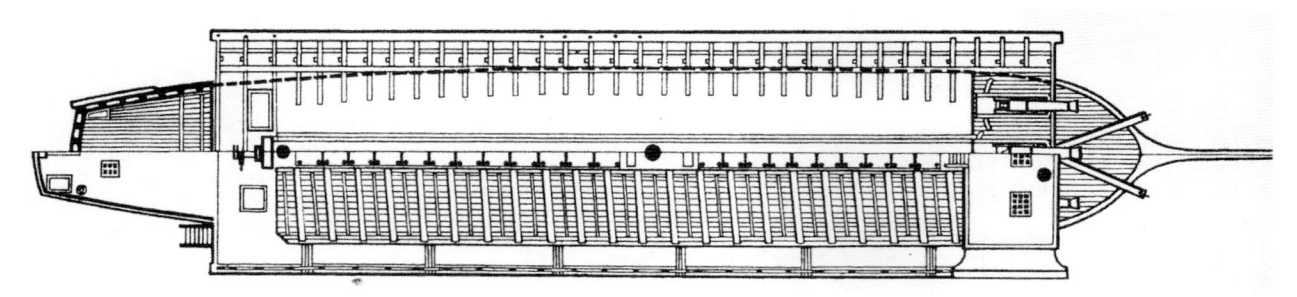

An overhead view of the upper and lower decks of the 25-banked galley Dvina *of 1721 showing the complexity, elaboration and congestion of the rowing arrangements of an eighteenth-century galley at its highest point of development.*

Dvina, Neva
Laid down: 16.5.1721
Dimensions approx. 159 ft x 31.5 ft x ? (48.5 m x 9.6 m (with oars' posts) x ?)
Armament 1 x 24pdr, 2 x 12pdrs, 12 x 3pdrs

14 25-bank galleys laid down at Galley Yard. 7 were completed and 7 destroyed on their slips on 11.7.1771. The lead ship, *Nadezhda*, was built by A. I. Alatcheninov and the others by Borisov.

Nadezhda
Laid down: 6.11.1764   Launched 19.7.1765
Driven ashore by a storm in May, 1770 and later BU.

Unnamed numbers 1–7
Laid down: 12.12.1766
All destroyed on slips by fire on 11.7.1771 at the Galley Port.

Legkaia, Slavnaia, Spesivaia, Strashnaya, Schastlivaia
Laid down 12.12.1766   Launched 1769
Destroyed by the fire at the Galley Port on 25.5.1796.

Khitraia
Laid down: 12.12.1766   Launched 1769.
Present at the 1st battle of Rochensalm in 1789. Flagship to Prince Nassau-Siegen at the 2nd battle of Rochensalm on 28.6.1790 where she was captured by Sweden.
Dimensions approx. 147 ft x 21 ft x 6.9 ft (44.8 m x 6.4 m x 2.1 m)
Armament 1 x 24pdr, 4 x 12pdrs, 12 x 3pdrs
362 men (inc. 300 oarsmen)

1 25-bank double-decked galley built by Shepin.
Svirepaia
Laid down: 12.12.1766   Launched 1769
Dimensions approx. 160 ft x 23 ft x 8.9 ft (48.8 m x 7 m x 2.7 m)
BU 1781.

14 25-bank galleys built at Galley Yard by Borisov, I. Grigoryev and G. Korchebnikov.
Dimensions approx. 147 ft x 21 ft x 6.9 ft (44.8 m x 6.4 m x 2.1 m)
Armament 1 x 24pdr, 4 x 12pdrs, 2 x 8pdrs, 12 x 3 x pdrs (1788)
362 men (incl. 300 oarsmen)

Unnamed
Laid down 4.4.1771
Lost in the Galley Port fire while still on the slip on 11.7.1771.

Antiparos
Laid down 3.12.1771   Launched 1772
Lost in the Galley Port fire on 25.5.1796.

Drug, Umnaia
Laid down 30.9.1771   Launched 1772
Lost in the Galley Port fire on 25.5.1796.

Bodaia, Bystraia, Volga, Dvina, Zlaia, Kostyl'
Laid down 4.7.177   Launched 1773
Lost in the Galley Port fire on 25.5.1796.

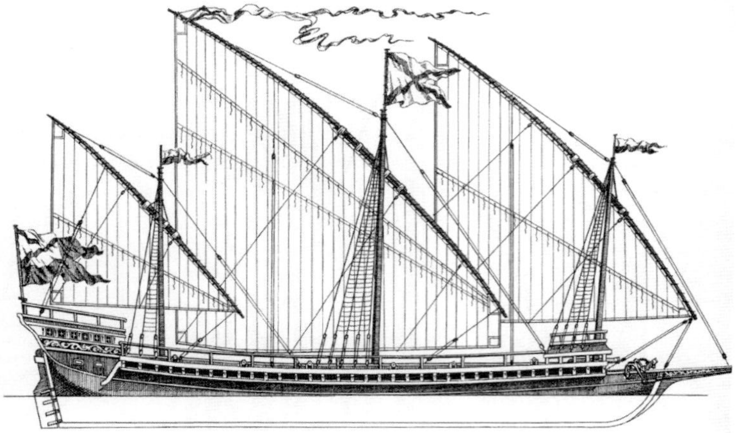

The 25-bank galley Nadezhda *of 1765. These large and impressive ships were the capital ships of the galley fleet and carried an impressive forward firing armament of a single 24pdr flanked by four 12pdrs. By this time, Sweden had stopped building galleys of any size and had turned her energies to the construction of large quantities of smaller, more manoeuvrable, oar-driven gunboats. The Russo-Swedish War of 1788 and the Russian defeat at the 2nd battle of Rochensalm would mark the demise of the galley as a serious combatant in northern waters.*

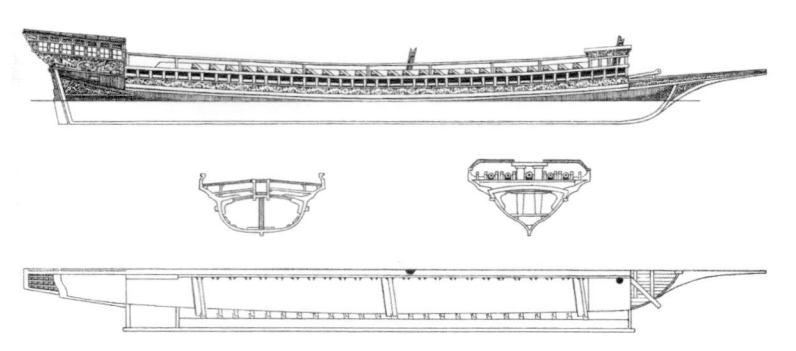

A side view and internal cross-sections of the 25-bank galley Nadezhda *of 1765. Besides showing the grace and elegance of the galley type, this frontal cross-section shows the concentrated end-on firepower of the ships and makes one ponder the human congestion when all 5 cannon were being served together in combat.*

Dnieper
Laid down 12.10.1772 *Launched* 1773
Damaged by accidental explosion in 1789. BU 1790.
Don, Neva
Laid down 12.10.1772 *Launched* 1773
Lost in the Galley Port fire on 25.5.1796.
Sviyaga
Laid down 1775 *Launched* 1776
Lost in the Galley Port fire on 25.5.1796.

3 25-bank galleys built at Galernyy Ostrovok by Pospelov.
Dimensions approx. 139 ft x 22 ft x 7.9 ft (42.4 m x 6.7 m x 2.4 m)
Armament 16 guns
Bodaya, Bystraia
Launched 1796 BU 1818
Kostyl'
Launched 1796 BU 1829

10 25-bank galleys built at Galernyy Ostrovok Yard by Pospelov.
Dimensions approx. 127 ft x 21 ft x 7.5 ft (38.7 m x 6.4 m x 2.3 m)
Armament 16 guns
Sommers
Launched 1796 BU 1819
Vulf, Zlaia, Slavnaia, Strashnaia, Schastlivaia, Torsar, Umnaia
Launched 1796 BU 1828
Vil'manstrand, Neva
Launched 1796 BU 1829

23/24-bank galleys (7 purpose-built)
7 galleys with 23–24 banks were built at Galley Yard by I. S. Kuchkovskiy. *Gus'* had 24 banks of oars and the others 23 banks.
Blagaia
Launched 1727 BU 1746
Svetlaia, Slavnaia
Launched 1727 Final fate is unknown.
Letuchaia, Pospeshnaia
Launched 1750 BU 1759
Spesivaia
Launched 1750 BU 1760
Gus'
Launched 1728 Final fate is unknown.

22-bank galleys (82 purpose-built)
22-bank galleys were often named after rivers and lakes as well as the usual birds and fish. They were two-masted, medium-size galleys, somewhat larger than the 20-banked galleys that formed the mainstay of the rowing flotillas. 22-banked galleys carried 5 oarsmen per oar and were generally armed with 1 x 18pdr, 2 x 12pdrs and 10–12 x 3pdrs.

3 22-bank galleys built in 1729 at Galley Yard by F. Dipontiy (De Pontis?).
Volga
BU 1754
Viktoriia, Slavianka
Final fate is unknown.

5 22-bank galleys built in 9.1732 at Galley Yard by Dipontiy.
Ziablitsa, Snigir
BU 1748
Zhavoronok
BU 1750
Karas'
BU 1753
Beluga
BU 1754

7 22-bank galleys built in 1738-1739 at Galley Yard by I. Nemtsov and I. A. Tolbukhin.
Drakon, Val'fish, Dnieper, Osetr, Sterliad', Straus
Launched 1738 BU 1753
Il'men'
Launched 1739 BU 1752

6 22-bank galleys built in 1739 at Galley Yard.
Don, Narova
Wrecked 1743
Shchuka
BU 1751
Volkhov
BU 1752
Leshch, Oka
BU 1753

14 22-bank galleys built at Galley Yard in 1749 and 1753 by A. I. Alatcheninov and I. S. Kuchkovskiy.
Nadezhnaia
Launched 1749 Wrecked 1753
Bodraia, Natal'ia Dvina, Sviatoi Nikolai, Medved'
Launched 1749 BU 1759
Gus, Ladoga, Don
Launched 1749 BU 1762
Krokodil
Launched 1749 Final fate is unknown.
Il'men'
Launched 1753 BU 1753
Voron
Launched 1753 BU 1760
Smelaia
Launched 1753 Accidentally destroyed by fire on 11.7.1771 at the Galley Port.

29 22-bank galleys built by A. I. Alatcheninov, I. S. Kuchkovskiy, Borisov, I. Grigoryev and Ozerov at Galley Yard.
Dimensions approx. 140 ft x 20 ft x 6.5 ft (42.7 m x 6.1 m x 2 m)
Armament 1 x 18 or 24pdrs, 4 x 12pdrs, 10 x 3pdrs
274 men inc. 220 oarsmen
Veselaia
Launched 1753 Wrecked off Finland on 13.9.1789
Numbers 1–6
Launched 1755 *Laid down* and launched by A. I. Alatcheninov. Destroyed by fire at the Galley Port on 11.7.1771. There is a possibility that these ships were identical with the six 20-bank galleys of the Galka Type recorded as lost in the same fire.
Neposhchada
Launched 1755 BU 1778
Peterburg
Launched 1755 Flagship of Major-General Count de Litta, a Maltese knight in Russian service, in 1789. Captured by Sweden on 28.6.1790 at the 2nd battle of Rochensalm.
Lemnos
Launched 1772 Destroyed by fire at the Galley Port on 25.5.1796.
Vil'manstrand

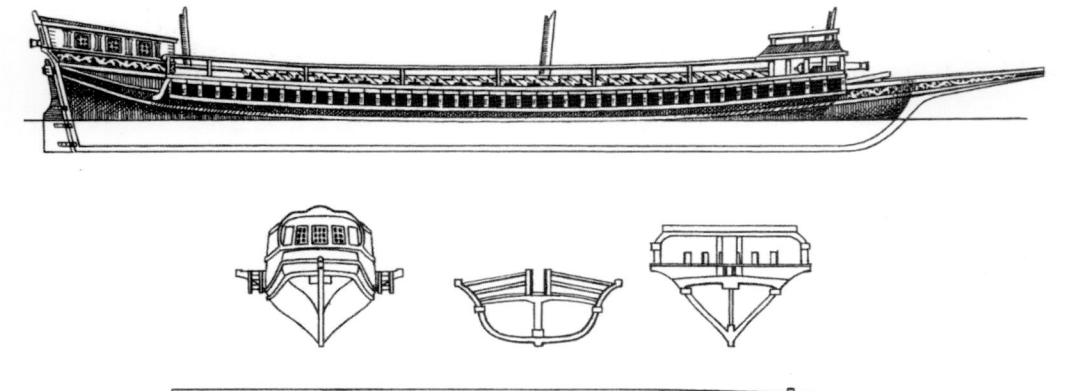

The 22-bank galley Veselaia. *A comparison between this galley and the 20-bank* Sviataia Anna *of 1711 will show the degree of growth and elaboration of galley design that took place in the forty year interval. The overhead shows the potential for repositioning the three heavier guns in response to the demands of combat.*

Launched 1773 Destroyed by fire at the Galley Port on 25.5.1796.
Moskva
Launched 1773 Destroyed by fire at the Galley Port on 25.5.1796.
Narva
Launched 1773 Lost at the 2nd battle of Rochensalm on 28.6.1790.
Oka
Launched 1773 Rebuilt on the Swedish model in 1789. Wrecked off Finland on 13.9.1789.
Pernov, Selo Sarskoe
Launched 1773 All three rebuilt on the Swedish model in 1789. Destroyed by fire at the Galley Port on 25.5.1796
Pustel'ga
Launched 1773 All three rebuilt on the Swedish model in 1789. Captured by Sweden 28.6.1790 at the 2nd battle of Rochensalm.
Krasnaia Gorka
Launched 1774 Destroyed by fire at the Galley Port on 25.5.1796.
Petergof
Launched 1774 Destroyed by fire at the Galley Port on 25.5.1796
Nerva, Peni, Seskar
Launched 1774 Peni and Seskar were rebuilt in 1789 on the Swedish model. All three were lost at the 2nd battle of Rochensalm battle 28.6.1790
Sommers, Torsar
Launched 1774 Both were destroyed by fire at the Galley Port on 25.5.1796
Tiuters
Launched 1774 Destroyed by fire at the Galley Port on 25.5.1796
Mologa
Launched 1775 Rebuilt on the Swedish model in 1789. Destroyed by fire at the Galley Port on 25.5.1796.
Tikhvin
Launched 1775 Destroyed by fire at the Galley Port on 25.5.1796
Chagodoshcha
Launched 1775 Destroyed by fire at the Galley Port on 25.5.1796
Sheksna
Launched 1775 Destroyed by fire at the Galley Port on 25.5.1796

Rossiia Galley Yard
Constructor A. I. Alatcheninov
Laid down 1748 Launched 1762
Dimensions approx. 140 ft x 20 ft x 6.5 ft (42.7 m x 6.1 m x 2 m)
Armament 35 guns.
This highly gilded galley was laid down for the Empress Elizabeth in 1748, but since she showed no interest in it, the galley remained on the slip until 1762 when she was completed for Catherine II. Destroyed by the fire at the Galley Port on 25.5.1796.

10 22-bank galleys built by I. Grigoryev, G. Korchebnikov, Borisov, Okonishnikov and Katasanov at the Galley Yard.
Dimensions approx. 140 ft x 17 ft x 6.5 ft (42.7 m x 5.2 m x 2 m)
Armament 1 x 18pdr, 4 x 12pdrs, 10 x 3pdrs
274 men (inc. 220 oarsmen)
Vulf, Zhavoronok, Zhuravl', Kronverk
Launched 1776 Rebuilt on the Swedish model in 1789. Destroyed by fire at the Galley Port on 25.5.1796
Kulik, Oryol, Ustyuzhna
Launched 1776 Captured by Sweden at the 2nd battle of Rochensalm on 28.6.1790
Lastochka, Malaya Neva
Launched 1776 Destroyed by fire at the Galley Port on 25.5.1796
Tsyvilsk
Launched 1776 Rebuilt on the Swedish model in 1789. Lost in action 13.8.1789 at the 1st battle of Rochensalm.

Smelaia Built in by Okonishnikov.
Launched 1786
Dimensions approx. 140 ft x 23 ft x 9.2 ft (42.7 m x 7 m x 2.8 m)
Armament 1 x 18pdr, 4 x 12pdrs, 10 x 3pdrs
274 men (220 incl. oarsmen)
Patterned after Swedish galleys. Destroyed by fire at the Galley Port on 25.5.1796

Khrabraia Galley Yard
Constructor A. S. Katasanov
Laid down 1786 Launched 1786
Dimensions approx. 134 ft x 22 ft x 7.2 ft (40.9 m x 6.8 m x 2.2 m)
Armament 1 x 18pdr, 4 x 12pdrs, 10 x 3pdrs
274 men (incl. 220 oarsmen)

WAR GALLEYS

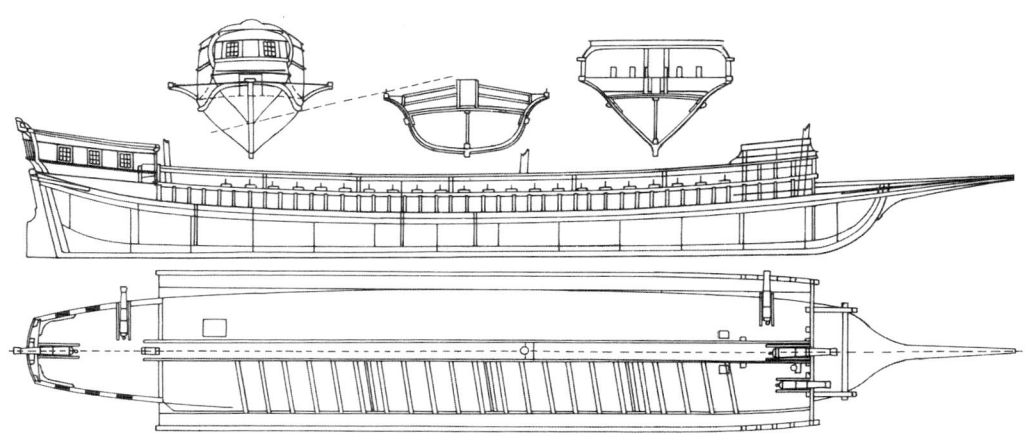

As a result of early wartime experience, 13 Russian 22-bank galleys were rebuilt in 1789 in the more robust style of their Swedish opponents. An additional 22-bank galley, Smelaia, had already anticipated the rebuilds by being designed and completed 'in the Swedish style' in 1786. This drawing represents the resulting design. The rebuilds did not prevent the type's obsolescence after the 1788 war.

Destroyed by fire at the Galley Port on 25.5.1796
5 three-masted and one four-masted (khrabraia) 22-bank galleys built at Galernyy Ostrovok in 1796 by Pospelov.
Dimensions approx. 127 ft x 21 ft x 7.5 ft (38.7 m x 6.4 m x 2.3 m)
Armament 4–16 guns
Don
BU 1828
Moskva
BU 1829
Petergof, Smelaia
BU 1816
Khrabraia
BU 1830
Sheksna
BU 1818

20-bank galleys (102 laid down/96 completed)
20- and 22-bank galleys were the mainstays of the galley flotilla. They were generally armed with 1 x 18pdr, 2 x 8pdrs and 10 x 3pdrs and had 5 rowers per oar.

32 20-bank galleys were built at Galley Yard between 1726 and 1728, all armed with 13 guns.
Del'fin
BU in 1754
Merkurii
BU in 1745
Pelikan
BU in 1744
Bystraia, Veselaia, Dobraia
BU in 1736
Gnevnaia, Troitskaia
BU in 1744
Legkaia, Smelaia
BU in 1738
Ostraia, Skoraia, Khitraia
BU in 1746
Anchous, Bochan, Visla, Dvin, Zuy, Parasim, Piglatsiia, Repolov, Semga, Shchegol'
BU in 1746
Golub'
Wrecked in 1743
Kopchik
BU in 1739
Lavalaktii
BU in 1749
Soika
BU in 1738

24 20-bank galleys built at Galley Yard in 1740-9 by I. Nemtsov, A. I. Alatcheninov and I. S. Kuchkovskiy.
Dimensions approx. 122 ft x 21 ft x 5.6 ft (37.2 m x 6.3 m x 1.7 m)
Oryol
Launched 1740 BU in 1752.
Udalaia
Launched 1742 BU in 1750.
Promyshlennaia
Launched 1742 BU in 1754.
Dobychnaya
Launched 1742 BU in 1756.
Zhar
Launched 1742 BU in 1762.
Kopchik, Soika
Launched 1742 Final fate is unknown.
Voronaia, Solovaia, Golub', Mushula
Launched 1743 Final fate is unknown.
Sviatoi Nikolai
Launched 1743 Wrecked in 1743.
Sudak
Launched 1743 BU in 1756.
Sokol
Launched 1743 BU in 1759.
Blagaia
Launched 1743 BU in 1760.
Pelikan, Slavnaia, Fivra, Utka
Launched 1747 BU in 1760.
Merkurii
Launched 1747 BU in 1762.
Khitraia
Launched 1747 Final fate is unknown.
Svetlaia
Launched 1748 BU in 1763.
Veselaia
Launched 1749 BU in 1760.
Skoraia
Launched 1749 BU in 1762.

10 20-bank galleys built in 1749–50 at Galley Yard by A. I.

Alatcheninov and I.S. Kuchkovskiy.
Schastlivaia
Wrecked in 1757.
Neva, Figura
BU in 1759.
Bystraia, Kit, Ognevaia
BU in 1761.
Vernaia, Udalaia
BU in 1762.
Slolvei, Soroka
Final fates are unknown.

4 20-bank galleys built at Galley Yard by A. I. Alatcheninov and I. S. Kuchkovskiy
Dimensions approx. 133 ft x 19 ft x 5.9 ft (40.6 m x 5.8 m x 1.8 m)
Armament 1 x 18pdr, 4 x 8pdrs, 10 x 3pdrs
250 men (inc. 200 oarsmen)
Bezdelka
Launched 1754 Surrendered to Sweden on 28.6.1790 at the 2nd battle of Rochensalm.
Sokol
Launched 1754 Destroyed by the fire at the Galley Port on 25.5.1796.
Kagul
Launched 1755 Destroyed by the fire at the Galley Port on 25.5.1796.
Kiliia
Launched 1755 Destroyed by the fire at the Galley Port on 25.5.1796.

31 20-bank galleys known collectively as the Galka Type were laid down at Galley Yard by I. Grigoryev, Borisov, Kirillov, G. Korchebnikov and A. I. Ozerov.
Dimensions approx. 133 ft x 19 ft x 6.2 ft (40.6 m x 5.8 m x 1.9 m)
Armament 14–15 guns
6 unnamed galleys
Launched 1771 Laid down by I. Grigoryev and Borisov on 10.1.1771. Destroyed on slips during a fire at the Galley Port on 11.7.1771. There is a possibility that these vessels are identical to the six 22-bank galleys lost in the same fire.
Soroka, Vorona
Launched 1771 Captured by Sweden on 28.6.1790 at the 2nd battle of Rochensalm.
Auza, Paros
Launched 1771 BU in 1791.
Galka, Mogilev, Orsha, Polotsk, Fokshany, Snigir
Launched 1771 Destroyed by the fire at the Galley Port on 25.5.1796.
Tver'
Launched 1773 Captured by Sweden on 28.6.1790 at the 2nd battle of Rochensalm.
Ustritsa
Launched 1773 BU in 1791.
Rak, Sterliad'
Launched 1773 BU in 1792.
Isakcha, Zhurzha
Launched 1774 Destroyed by the fire at the Galley Port on 25.5.1796.
Buinaia, Zarez, Izmail, Larga, Lebed', Osetr, Finliandia
Launched 1773 Destroyed by fire at the 2nd battle of Rochensalm on 28.6.1790.
Perepelka, Sestrebek
Launched 1775 Destroyed by the fire at the Galley Port on 25.5.1796.

Pernov Galley Port
Constructor ?
Dimensions approx. 127 ft x 21 ft x 7.5 ft (38.7 m x 6.4 m x 2.3 m)
Armament 4 guns
Three-masted galley launched in 1796 and permanently stationed at Galley Port.

16-bank galleys (107 purpose-built)
Smaller 16-bank galleys were built in great numbers from the 1720s through the 1750s. They were two-masted ships, with 4 rowers per oar, and were generally armed with 1 x 12pdr, 2 x 8pdrs and 8–10 falconets.

After the death of Peter I, 41 16-bank galleys were built at Galley Yard between 1726 and 1734.
Lyurik, Popugai, Iastreb
1726
Pitsa
1726 BU in 1746.
Bagul, Gasbora, Izhora, Konstantsiya, Langvila, Laruzet, Oryol, Pronia, Saiga, Soroka, Treska
1728 BU in 1739
Zhar, Karneika, Sokol, Feniks, Fivra, Shchuka
1728 BU in 1738.
Beluga, Drakon, Lisitsa, Osetr, Rak, Sterliad', Turukhtan Kolpitsa, Cherepakha, Chechetka
1729 by F. Depontiy. BU in 1738.
Krokodil, Pustel'ga
1729 by F. Depontiy. Both were wrecked in 1743 at Biork-e Zund.
Leshch
1729 by F. Depontiy. BU in 1739.
Neva
1730 by F. Depontiy and A. I. Adtcheninov. BU in 1750.
Ladoga
1730 by F. Depontiy. Driven ashore by storm in 1747 and later BU.
Onega
1730 by F. Depontiy. BU in 1748.
Okhta
1730 by F. Depontiy. Final fate is unknown.
Tosna
1730 by F. Depontiy. Wrecked in 1742.
Kometa
1733 by F. Depontiy. BU in 1754.
Planeta
1733 by A.I. Alatcheninov. Final fate is unknown.
Forel'
1734 by I. Nemtsov. Final fate is unknown.

22 16-bank galleys were built at Galley Yard between 1739 and 1741.
Dimensions approx. 100 ft x 17 ft x 4.3 ft (30.5 m x 5.3 m x 1.3 m)
Bodraia
1739 by I. Nemtsov BU 1754
Bystraia
1739 by K. I. Ostretsov BU 1750
Vernaia
1739 by K. I. Ostretsov BU 1748
Veselaia
1739 by K. I. Ostretsov Wrecked in the Baltic in 1743.
Izhora
1739 by I. Nemtsov BU 1748
Legkaia
1739 by K.I. Ostretsov BU 1752
Nadezhnaia
1739 by K.I. Ostretsov BU 1758

Nepobedimaia
1739 by I. Nemtsov BU 1755
Smelaia
1739 by I. Nemtsov BU 1754
Schastlivaia
1739 by I. Nemtsov Blown up in 1742.
Butsefal
1740 by I. Nemtsov Wrecked in 1742.
Edinorog
1740 by I. A. Alatcheninov BU 1752
Elen
1740 by I. A. Alatcheninov Final fate is unknown.
Lofer
1741 by I. A. Alatcheninov BU 1753
Morskaia loshad'
1740 by I. Nemtsov BU 1758
Pegas
1740 by I. A. Alatcheninov BU 1752
Serna
1740 by I. A. Alatcheninov BU 1751
Karneika
1741 by I. A. Alatcheninov BU 1762
Konstantsiya
1741 by I. Nemtsov BU 1753
Letuchaia
1741 by I. Nemtsov BU 1753
Saiga
1741 by I. Nemtsov Final fate is unknown.
Feniks
1741 by I. A. Alatcheninov BU 1754

10 16-bank galleys were built at Galley Yard in 1743.
Bagulya, Gasbora
1743 by I. Nemtsov Final fate is unknown.
Vil'manstrand, Fridrikhsgam
8.1743 by Alatcheninov BU 1750
Kyumen-Reka
8.1743 by Alatcheninov BU 1759
(The above three galleys were named after two towns and a river, all ceded to Russia by the Abo Treaty of 1743)
Neyshlot
8.1743 by Alatcheninov BU 1753
Pronia, Turukhtan Kolpitsa
1743 by I. S. Kuchkovskiy Final fate is unknown.
Treska
1743 by I. S. Kuchkovskiy BU 1753
Cherepakha
1743 by I. S. Kuchkovskiy BU 1754

24 16-bank galleys built at Galley Yard between 1748 and 1755.
Anchous, Nadezhda
1748–9 by I. S. Kuchkovskiy BU 1759
Beluga
1748–9 by Alatcheninov BU 1760
Bochan
1748–9 by I. S. Kuchkovskiy BU 1759
Butsefal, Lebed', Ostraia
1748–9 by Alatcheninov BU 1759
Golub', Dobraia
1748–9 by I. S. Kuchkovskiy Final fate is unknown.
Zuy
1748–9 by Alatcheninov BU 1759
Lisitsa
1748–9 by Alatcheninov BU 1761
Morskaia loshad'
1748–9 by Alatcheninov BU 1759
Narova
1748–9 by I. S. Kuchkovskiy BU 1760
Bars, Iastreb
1749–50 by Alatcheninov BU 1762
Izhora
1749–50 by I. S. Kuchkovskiy BU 1760
Pavlin, Slon
1749–50 by Alatcheninov BU 1762
Tosna
1749–50 by I. S. Kuchkovskiy BU 1759
Fridrikhsgam
1749–50 by I. S. Kuchkovskiy BU 1759
Edinorog
1751–3 by I. S. Kuchkovskiy BU 1762
Nepobedimaia
1752–4 by Alatcheninov BU 1767
Cherepakha
1753–5 by Alatcheninov BU 1770
Chechetka
1753–5 by Alatcheninov BU 1778

10 16-bank galleys built at Galley Yard between 1756 and 1762.
Dimensions approx. 126 ft x 18 ft x 5.9 ft (38.4 m x 5.5 m x 1.8 m)
Bodraia, Kometa
1756 by Alatcheninov BU 1762
Karneika
1756 Final fate is unknown.
Lyufer, Mir
1756–7 BU 1762
Snigir
1756–7 BU 1762
Sokol
1756–7 Final fate is unknown.
Dobychnaya, Udalaia
9.8.1762 by A. I. Ozerov and Borisov with 11 guns. Last mentioned in 1781.
Chesma
1762 by A. I. Alatcheninov and Borisov with 11 guns. Destroyed by the fire at the Galley Port on 25.5.1796. The name was given this galley after 1770 to commemorate the famous battle. The previous name is unknown.

Small galleys (20 purpose-built)

A small number of galleys with fewer than 15 banks were built. These were frequently intended primarily as transports for royalty and had little combat value.

Dnieper flotilla

7 small galleys built at Bryansk. Three were flat-bottomed for shallow-water operation. None were able to pass the Dnieper rapids and took no part in the Russo-Turkish War of 1735–9.
Laid down 1726–7 *Launched* 1737 BU after 1739.
Ekaterina   6-bank galley built by A. I. Alatcheninov and launched in 1756. Used at Oranienbaum by Grand Duke Pavel (later Emperor).

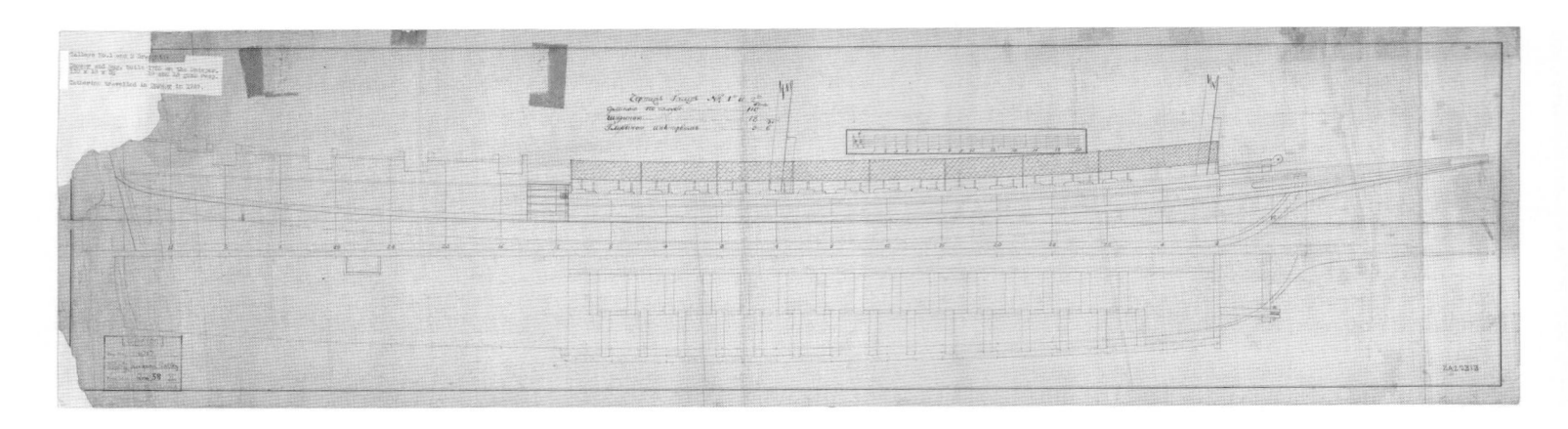

This draught depicts one of the four small galleys built specifically for the use of Catherine II and her entourage during their travels on the Volga. Although provision seems to have been made for the mounting of a small number of cannon, this ship is clearly not intended for any sort of combat, being more in the nature of a luxury yacht than a warship.

4 galleys built at Tver' Yard (north of Moscow) by Shchepin for Catherine II for her travels on the Volga.
Tver'
Laid down 1767   Launched 3.04.1767
12-bank galley used by Catherine II during her cruise on the Volga 2.5–5.6.1767.
Bug, Kazan, Iaroslavl'
Laid down 3.4.1767 10-bank galleys used for travel by Catherine II.

2 12-banked galleys launched in 1785. In 1787, they were employed by Catherine II during her navigation down the Dnieper. Formally assigned to the Black Sea fleet in 1787 and active participants in the Russo-Turkish War from 1787–92.

Bug
Launched 1785
Used by Prince Potemkin and ladies of the court during Catherine II's voyage down the Dnieper from Kiev to Kherson. Participated in the Russo-Turkish War of 1787–92.

5 10-banked galleys, all launched in 1785 and used to provide transport for Catherine II's trip down the Dnieper prior to the Russo-Turkish War.

Desna
Used for dining by Catherine II and her entourage. Later famous for her heroic solo fight with Turkish fleet in the Liman under Sub-lieutenant Lombard on 15–19.9.1787.

Iput', Seim, Snov, Sozha
All actively employed in 1787–92.

Black Sea fleet galleys (scampaveas) (9 purpose-built)

These 9 small vessels were referred to as scampaveas and are the only galleys built for the Black Sea fleet. All were active during the Russo-Turkish War of 1787–92.

4 scampaveas built at Bendery.
Launched 1790
Dimensions approx. 34 ft x 6.2 ft x 1.6 ft (10.4 m x 1.9 m x 0.5 m)
Armament 2 guns

1 scampavea built at the mouth of the Danube by I. Dolzhnikov.
Launched 1790
Dimensions approx. 68 ft x 10.5 ft x 5.6 ft (20.7 m x 3.2 m x 1.7 m)
Armament 4 guns

4 scampaveas (nos 1–4) built at Kriulyany by Nefedyev
Launched 1790
Dimensions approx. 68 ft x 10.5 ft x 5.6 ft (20.7 m x 3.2 m x 1.7 m)
Armament 2 guns

Galley prizes

Valfisk, Gaddan, Gripen, Laksen, Trana, Orn
Swedish galleys captured at the battle of Gangut on 27.7.1714. Kept as a memorial until 1742, by which time they were completely decayed and BU.

Makropleia
Dimensions approx. 148 ft x 32 ft x 10 ft 6 in (45.2 m x 9.8 m x 3.2 m)
Armament 5 guns
Turkish galley taken in the Liman on 1.7.1788. Rebuilt in 1790 as the frigate *Sviatoi Mark*.

Tsederkreits
Dimensions 130 ft x 21 ft x 7 ft, 190 tons (Swedish measure)
 approx. 127 ft x 19 ft x 5.9 ft (38.7 m x 5.9 m x 1.8 m) (Russian measure)
Armament 1 x 24pdr, 2 x 6pdrs, 23 x 3pdrs (Swedish service)
 15 guns (Russian service)
Swedish *Cedercreutz*, 20-bank galley, built in 1749. Captured on 13.8.1789 at the 1st battle of Rochensalm.

Dallarna
Dimensions 130 ft x 20 ft 3 in x 7 ft 9 in, 205 tons (Swedish measure)
Armament 1 x 24pdr, 2 x 6pdrs, 23 x 3pdrs
Swedish Dalarna, 20-bank galley, built in 1749. Taken 22.6.1790 at Biork-e zund.

Nordosten-Norden (Osten-Norden)
Dimensions 140 ft x 31 ft x 8 ft 6 in (Swedish measure)
Armament 1 x 24pdr, 2 x 6pdrs, 19 x 3pdrs (Swedish service)

9 guns (Russian service)

Swedish *Nordstjarneorden*, 22-bank galley, designed by J. Acrell and built at Skeppsholmen in 1749. Taken 22.6.1790 at Biork-e zund). Destroyed by the fire at the Galley Port on 25.5.1796.

Oster-Gotland
Dimensions 130 ft x 21 ft x 7 ft, 190 tons (Swedish measure)
Armament 1 x 24pdr, 2 x 6pdrs, 23 x 3pdrs (Swedish service)
29 guns (Russian service)

Swedish *Östergötland*, 20-bank galley designed by J. Acrell and built at Norrköping's in 1749. Taken 22.6.1790 at Biork-e zund. Destroyed by the fire at the Galley Port on 25.5.1796.

Palmsherna
Dimensions 130 ft x 21 ft x 7 ft (Swedish measure)
Armament 1 x 24pdr, 2 x 6pdrs, 19 x 3pdrs (Swedish service)

Swedish *Palmstierna*, 20-bank galley, designed by J. Acrell and built at Djurgarden in 1749. Taken 22.6.1790 at Biork-e zund. Destroyed by the fire at the Galley Port on 25.5.1796.

Etkeblas
Dimensions 140 ft x 21 ft x 8 ft 6 in, 250 tons (Swedish measure)
Armament 1 x 24pdr, 2 x 6pdrs, 25 x 3pdrs (Swedish service)
28 guns (Russian service)

Swedish *Etkeblas*, 22-bank galley, designed by J. Acrell and built at Skeppsholmen in 1749. Taken 22.6.1790 at Biork-e zund. Destroyed by the fire at the Galley Port on 25.5.1796.

Horse galleys

These specialized galleys were invented during the Great Northern war 1700–21 and used for the transportation of cavalry horses in line with the amphibious commitments of Russian naval forces. They should arguably be assigned to Section III as they are amphibious support vessels rather than combat units. Nevertheless, they are being included here because they represent the only galleys falling into this unique category. As it was difficult for cavalry to move by land along Finnish coastal areas, horse galleys facilitated the landing of both infantry and cavalry. These galleys could carry from 16 to 40 horses. Some were given equine names.

Baltic fleet (45 purpose-built)

11 horse galleys built at Abo yard.
Vorona, Kopchik, Laruzet, Mushula, Parasim, Pitsa, Pustel'ga, Repolov, Soika, Sudak, Utka
Launched 1720
Shchuka
Launched 1721 21-bank horse galley with 4 guns.
Chechetka, Turukhtan Kolpitsa
Launched 1721 16-bank horse galleys with 2 guns.
Lebed'
Launched 1726 22-bank horse galley.

10 20-bank horse galleys built at Galley Yard.
Armament 2 x 12pdrs, 10 x 3pdrs
Bodraia, Letuchaia, Nadezhda
Launched 1727 BU 1738
Voronaia, Mushula, Pegaia, Solovaia, Sudak, Utka
Launched 1728 BU 1738

Letuchaia
Launched 1728 Final fate is unknown.
Rak Galley Port
Constructor I. A. Tolbukhin
Launched 1739
Dimensions approx. 99 ft x 17 ft x 4.3 ft (30.1 m x 5.3 m x 1.3 m)
Armament 2 x 8pdrs, 8 x 3pdrs
16-bank horse galley. BU 1762.
Mir
Launched 1743 16-bank horse galley, built by A. I. Alatcheninov, and similar to *Rak*. BU 1759
Finlyadia
Launched 12.7.1743 16-bank horse galley, built at Abo by A. I. Alatcheninov, and similar to Rak. BU 1759

7 16-bank, 16 horse galleys built at St Petersburg, Admiralty by A. I. Alatcheninov.
Dimensions approx. 126 ft x 18 ft x 5.9 ft (38.4 m x 5.5 m x 1.8 m)
Armament 2 x 8pdrs, 8 x 3pdrs
Elen, Planeta, Smelaia, Turukhtan Kolpitsa
Laid down 1753 *Launched* 1756
Destroyed on slip during fire at the Galley Port on 11.7.1771.
Lifliandiia, Treska
Laid down 1753 *Launched* 1756
Rebuilt on the Swedish model in 1789.
Cherepakha
Laid down 1753 *Launched* 1756
Destroyed by the fire at the Galley Port on 25.5.1796.

7 22-banked, 24-horse galleys built at St Petersburg, Admiralty by Borisov.
Dimensions approx. 140 ft x 20 ft x 6.6 ft (42.7 m x 6.1 m x 2 m)
Armament 1 x 24pdr, 3 x 12pdrs, 12 x 3pdrs
252 men (incl. 220 oarsmen)
Vyborg, Koron, Modon, Riga
Laid down 20.11.1772 *Launched* 1773
Vyborg was rebuilt on the Swedish model in 1789. All were destroyed by the fire at the Galley Port on 25.5.1796.
Dinamind, Izhora
Laid down 20.11.1772 *Launched* 1773
Rebuilt on the Swedish model in 1789.
Fridrikhsgam
Laid down 24.10.1772
Destroyed by the fire at the Galley Port on 25.5.1796.

3 16-horse galleys built at St Petersburg, Admiralty by G. Korchebnikov.
Laid down 1775 *Launched* 1776
Dimensions approx. 126 ft x 18 ft x 5.9 ft (38.4 m x 5.5 m x 1.8 m)
Armament 3 x 8pdrs, 8 x 3pdrs
Biork, Iniia, Chernyy Drozd
Destroyed by the fire at the Galley Port on 25.5.1796.

Dnieper flotilla (25 purpose-built)

25 16-bank horse-galleys built at Bryansk Yard.
Laid down 1737 *Launched* 1738 BU after 1739.

Kayks, kaiks, or half-galleys

Kayk is a Turkish word meaning 'boat'. These vessels were also referred to as 'half-galleys'. They were equipped with 12 banks of oars and armed with one or more cannon and several falconets. After 1788–90 they were replaced by gunboats.

Baltic fleet kayks (117 purpose-built)

3 20-bank half-galleys built at Vyborg by Y. A. Rusinov.
Sviataia Anna, Sviatoi Aleksandr, Sviatoi Fyodor
Laid down 1710 *Launched* 1711
Armament 1 x 12pdr, 2 x 6pdrs
            250 men

1 large half-galley built at Galley Yard by Y. A. Rusinov.
Laid down 15.10.1713 *Launched* 5.1714

7 large half-galleys built at Galley Yard by Y. A. Rusinov.
Laid down 10.1714 *Launched* 4.1715

26 small half-galleys built at Galley Yard.
Laid down 10.1714 *Launched* 5.1715
Known names include ***Kambala, Kit, Okun'*** and ***Shchuka***, all mentioned in 1715.

3 large half-galleys built at Galley Yard.
Laid down 11.10.1715 *Launched* 5.1716.

14 small half-galleys built at Galley Yard.
Laid down 11.10.1715 *Launched* 4–5. 1716.

Names of 23 half-galleys mentioned in 1716 as being stationed in St Petersburg. Classes are uncertain.
Anguzhiguli, Bavulo, Bachan, Dunzhelo, Ekht, Kaban, Kaporotsul, Khornus, Kolpitsa, Lobra, Losos, Lokh, Minulo, Morzh, Neva, Osetr, Piskar', Rayna, Sevriuga, Shereshpyor, Slovei, Sterliad', Vyrezub

No. 1 Galley Yard, St Petersburg
Constructor F. Dipontiy
Launched 1723
Dimensions approx. 68 ft x 11 ft x 3.6 ft (20.6 m x 3.4 m x 1.1 m)
Armament 1 x 3pdr, 24 oars
Final fate is unknown. Veselago describes this vessel as 'old-fashioned' but without comment. This may mean that it was built according to pre-Western construction standards.

30 kayks laid down in 1726 and launched in 1727 at Galley Yard by F. Dipontiy. Named after birds. BU 1740.
Vorobei, Voron, Golubitsa, Gorlitsa, Grach, Drozd, Diatel, Zhavoronok, Karneika, Karostel', Konoplianka, Kopets, Kochet, Kulik, Kuropatka, Lastovitsa, Lastochka, Perepelka, Remes, Ryabets, Sinitsa, Skvorets, Snigir, Sova, Slovei, Strizh, Turukhtan Kolpitsa, Cheglik, Chizh, Shchegol'.

6 kayks laid down 20.8.1727 and launched in 1728. BU 1740.
Ziablitsa, Kagarka, Klest, Malinovka, Chaika and ***Cherenok.***

No. 1 Galley Yard, St Petersburg
Launched 1764
Dimensions approx. 66 ft x 11 ft x 4.2 ft (20.1 m x 3.3 m x 1.3 m)
Armament 17 guns, 22 oars
Destroyed by fire at the Galley Port on 11.7.1771.

23 kayks built at Galley Yard in 1767–6.
Dimensions approx. 70 ft x 14 ft x 5.2 ft (21.4 m x 4.3 m x 1.6 m)
Armament 1 x 18pdr, 1 x 12pdr, 1 x 3pdr, 6 falconets, 22 oars
            60 men (inc. 44 oarsmen).
Beglaia
Launched 1767 Foundered at the Neva river.
Dobraia, Doezzhaia, Osmotritel'naia
Launched 1767 BU 1792
Skoraia
Launched 1767 BU 1791
Tsapkaia
Launched 1767 BU 1801
Nos 2, 3, and 4
Launched 1767 Destroyed by fire at the Galley Port on 11.7.1771.
Nos 5 and 6
Launched 1767 BU 1789
Buinaia
Launched 1773 BU 1792
Krasnaia
Launched 1773 Lost without trace 1790
Nezhnaia
Launched 1773 BU 1801
Perekhvat, Prigozhaia, Svetlaia, Iasnaia
Launched 1773 Lost during the 2nd battle of Rochensalm on 28.6.1790.
Veselaia, Zalet, Prilezhnaia, Prolet
Launched 1776 Lost during the 2nd battle of Rochensalm on 28.6.1790.

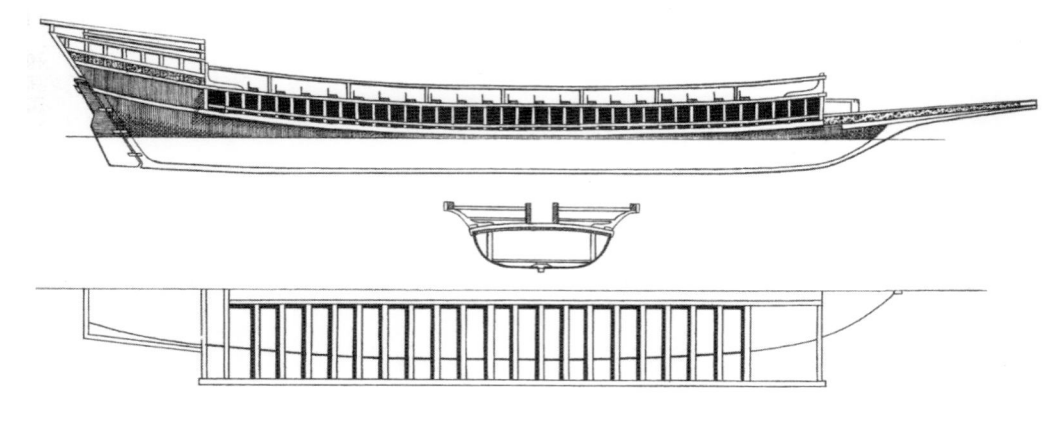

Sviataia Anna *of 1711 was built in the Baltic and classified variously as a kayk (Turkish term) or as a half-galley. Given her apparent size and complement, this designation is hard to explain. After 1720, she would have been designated simply as a 20-bank galley.*

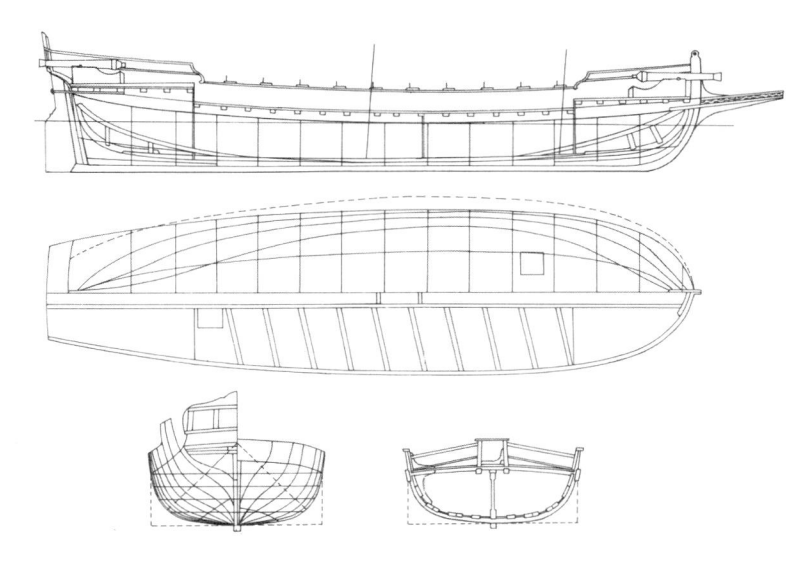

A 10-bank Russian half-galley laid down in 1788, believed to represent either the Zlobnaya, lost at the 2nd battle of Rochensalm, or Lovkaya, converted into a corvette in 1789.

Nepokin'
Launched 1776 BU 1791
Zlobnaia
Launched 1789
Dimensions approx. 75 ft x 19 ft x 3.3 ft (22.9 m x 5.9 m x 1 m)
Armament 12 guns, 20 oars
Lost during the 2nd battle of Rochensalm on 28.6.1790.

Lovkaia
Launched 1789
Dimensions approx. 76 ft x 21 ft x 6.2 ft (23.2 m x 6.3 m x 1.9 m)
Armament 12 guns, 20 oars
1797 transformed into the corvette *Lovkii* (the name was also changed from feminine to masculine with same meaning, 'adroit'; Russian ship names were assigned gender according to the type of vessel: galleys were feminine and sailing vessels masculine), was attached to rowing flotilla, 1798–1812; fire watch at Fridrikhshamn and Rochensalm; BU here in 1812.

Sea of Azov fleet kayks (80 purpose-built)

30 kayks built at Tavrov yard.
Laid down 1723 *Launched* 1734
Work suspended in 1724 to comply with treaty requirements. Resumed in 1734 and launched in the same year. Transferred to Azov in 1736. Participated in the blockade of Azov in 1736. BU after 1739.

50 kayks built at Tavrov yard by A. I. Alatcheninov:
Laid down 1738 *Launched* 1738
Dimensions approx. 66 ft x 10.5 ft x 3 ft (20 m x 3.2 m x 0.9 m)
Armament 1 gun, 24 oars
BU after 1739.

Caspian flotilla kayks (50 purpose-built)

50 kayks built at Kazan yard (10 in 1744, 24 in 1745, 16 in 1748).
Dimensions approx. 66 ft x 10.5 ft x 3 ft (20 m x 3.2 m x 0.9 m)
Armament 1 gun, 24 oars
BU after 1751.

Baltic secret vessels (3 purpose-built)

These unusual ships were intended to mimic merchant ships and act as decoys. Their design was modelled on that of the Swedish udenmaas. They were originally lateen-rigged with 3 masts, but from autumn 1789 were re-rigged as square riggers with 44 oars. As completed they had a superstructure of 6 ft 6 in height and with 20 ft width between the fore- and mizzen-masts. The covered deck concealed 8–12pdrs on each broadside. The gun ports were covered with shields and, in the vertical position, these shields created the impression of a continuous unbroken side giving them the appearance of unarmed merchant vessels or transports. In action, these shields were dropped outwards in much the manner of the Q ships of the First and Second World Wars. Other guns were mounted at bow and stern. Their design, while imaginative, was not successful. In winter 1789–90, they were rebuilt as conventional rowing frigates; and then in 1792 as floating batteries. From 1792 they were given new names with feminine genders replacing the earlier masculine names in order to correspond with the feminine gender of the Russian word for battery.

3 vessels built at St Petersburg, Admiralty in 1788.
Dimensions approx. 118 ft x 28 ft x 8.9 ft (36 m x 8.5 m x 2.7 m)
Armament 22 x 12pdrs, 5 x 3pdrs, 17 falconets on swivels
   236 men
Ostorozhnoe renamed *Nepristupnaia* in 1792
Nastupatel'noe renamed *Porazhaiushchaia* in 1792
Okhranitel'noe renamed *Oboronitel'naia* in 1792
All were destroyed in the disastrous fire on 25.5.1796 at Galley Port together with 4 floating batteries converted from shebecks and 45 galleys.

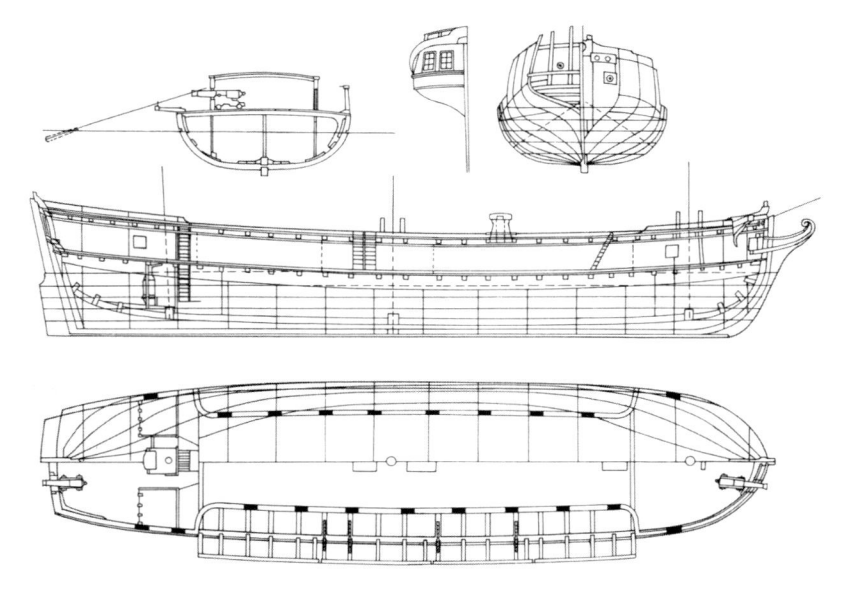

Okhranitelnoe, Nastupatelnoe and Ostorozhnoe (27) of 1788. These three Russian 'secret vessels' were the Q ships of their day. This detailed perspective clearly shows how the 12pdr battery was mounted behind drop-down bulkheads that would have been looked upon approvingly by the captain of the German Atlantis *and other similar ships in the Second World War.*

Rowing brigantines

During the Great Northern War 1700–21 in the Baltic and in the Sea of Azov fleet, rowing brigantines (small galleys) were built, patterned after Venetian models and called 'Italian' brigantines. They had 1 or 2 masts, square sails forward and lateen sails on the mizzen, and 16–32 oars. In 1704 Peter I designed a new type of rowing brigantine that came to be known as 'Russian' brigantines. These had 2 masts, the foremast with square sails, and the mizzen or main mast with lateen sails, giving them something of the appearance of hermaphrodite brigs. The oars carried by these ships were more substantial than the sweeps sometimes carried by similarly sized British sloops, brigs and similar smaller craft. Early rowing brigantines were generally armed with 10 small guns with 70-man crews. Rowing brigantines were built in large numbers in both the Baltic and Sea of Azov fleets during the reign of Peter I. In the second half of the eighteenth century, they continued to be popular in the Black Sea and the Sea of Okhotsk, but were almost entirely absent from the Baltic.

Baltic fleet (147 purpose-built)

A total of 81 'Italian' rowing brigantines in three groups were laid down and completed in 1703–4, very probably in response to the Swedish crisis. All were built to the same dimensions.

13 Italian rowing brigantines, built at Olonetskaya by Ya. Kol.
Laid down 1703 *Launched* 1704
Dimensions approx. 67.5 ft x 9.8 ft x ? (20.6 m x 3 m x ? m)

44 Italian rowing brigantines, built at Luzhskaya at the mouth of the Luga by Kh. Andreev.
Laid down 1703 *Launched* 1704
Dimensions approx. 67.5 ft x 9.8 ft x ? (20.6 m x 3 m x ? m)

24 Italian rowing brigantines, built at Olonetskaya by Ya. Kol.
Laid down 1703 *Launched* 1704.
Dimensions approx. 67.5 ft x 9.8 ft x ? (20.6 m x 3 m x ? m)

Two further groups of 10 'Russian' rowing brigantines apiece were laid down in 1704 and 1707. Peter I supervised the first group at Galley Yard and his recently imported English constructor Richard Brown supervised the second ten at Olonetskaya. As was the case with the 'Italian' rowing brigantines, they followed similar specifications, but they were both shorter and beamier than the first type.

10 rowing brigantines designed by Peter I and built at Galley Yard.
Laid down 1704 *Launched* 11.1704
Dimensions approx. 52 ft x 14 ft x ? (15.9 m x 4.3 m x ? m)

10 rowing brigantines built at Olonetskaya by R. Brown.
Laid down 1707 *Launched* 1708
Dimensions approx. 52 ft x 14 ft x ? (15.9 m x 4.3 m x ? m)

20 rowing brigantines built at Izhora by Osip Nay (Joseph Nye).
Laid down 1712 *Launched* 1713
Dimensions approx. 60 ft x 15 ft x ? (18.3 m x 4.6 m x ? m)

20 rowing brigantines built in 1712–13 at Luzhskaya by Y. A. Rusinov.

2 rowing brigantines built at St Petersburg.
Laid down 1714 *Launched* 1715
Unnamed St Petersburg
Constructor I. V. Yames
Laid down 19.12.1766 *Launched* 7.1767
Struck by lightning and burnt 11.7.1771

2 rowing brigantines built at Olonetskaya by I. I. Afanasyev:
Laid down 1771 *Launched* 1772
Dimensions approx. 70 ft x 15 ft x 5.2 ft (21.4 m x 4.6 m x 1.6 m)
Armament 18 x 3pdrs
24 oars, 91 men (incl. 72 oarsmen)
No. 1
BU 1790.
No. 2
Renamed *Slavolyubivaya* BU 1791.

Vakhmeister Galley Yard, St Petersburg
Constructor M. D. Portnov
Laid down 1773 *Launched* 1773
Dimensions approx. 100 ft x 22 ft x 7.5 ft (30.5 m x 6.7 m x 2.3 m)
Armament 6 x 12pdrs, 10 falconets
125 men (incl. 90 oarsmen)
Designed by Rear-Adm. Madzini. Repaired 1781. BU 1792.

Sea of Azov fleet rowing brigantines (62 purpose-built)

60 Italian rowing brigantines were built at Voronezh in 1697–8 by N. Likhudyev and Ya. Moro.

2 rowing brigantines of 'Russian' type, built at Voronezh.
Launched 1708 BU after 1716.

Dnieper flotilla (20 purpose-built)

20 rowing brigantines were built at Bryansk. All were laid down in 1737 and launched in 1738.

Black Sea fleet rowing brigantines (26 purpose-built)

Pavel Smelyanskaya
Constructor Belyaev
Launched 1788
Dimensions approx. 83 ft x 23 ft x 9.5 ft (25.2 m x 6.9 m x 2.9 m)
Armament 6 guns
Last mentioned in 1804.

Pyotr Smelyanskaya
Constructor Belyaev
Launched 1788
Dimensions approx. 81 ft x 22 ft x 8.5 ft (24.7 m x 6.9 m x 2.6 m)
Armament 6 guns
BU 1804.

Iosif Dnieper
Constructor Belyaev
Launched 1788
Dimensions approx. 70 ft x 22 ft x 3.3 ft (21.4 m x 6.7 m x 3.1 m)
Armament 8 guns
Last mentioned 1806.

Nikolai Dnieper
Constructor Belyaev
Launched 1788
Dimensions approx. 70 ft x 22 ft x 3.3 ft (21.4 m x 6.7 m x 3.1 m)
Armament 8 guns
Last mentioned 1802.

Prokofii Dnieper
Constructor Belyaev
Launched 1788
Dimensions approx. 69 ft c.20 ft x 7.9 ft (21 m x 6.1 m x 2.4 m)
Armament 8 guns
Last mentioned 1795.

Foma Dnieper
Constructor Belyaev
Launched 1788
Dimensions approx. 69 ft x 21 ft x 7.9 ft (21 m x 6.4 m x 2.4 m)
Armament ? guns
Wrecked off the Crimea 30.3.1812.

3 rowing brigantines built at Sekerinskaya yard by Belyaev.
Dimensions approx. 69 ft x 19 ft x 6.9 ft (21 m x 5.9 m x 2.1 m)
Armament 8 guns
No. 1
Launched 1789 Wrecked off the Crimea 2.11.1799.
No. 2
Launched 1790 Last mentioned 1796
No. 3
Launched 1790 Last mentioned 1798

Blagoveshchenie Kherson
Constructor Konstantinopulo
Laid down 1789 *Launched* 25.3.1790
Dimensions approx. 90 ft x 28 ft x 8.5 ft (27.5 m x 8.5 m x 2.6 m)
Armament 12 x 6pdrs
Built by a Greek shipwright. Last mentioned 1800.

Dmitriy Kremenchug
Constructor Toroshilov
Launched 1790
Dimensions approx. 64 ft x 22 ft x 11 ft (19.5 m x 6.7 m x 3.4 m)
Armament 6 guns
BU after 1805.

Mokkey Kremenchug
Constructor Toroshilov
Launched 1790
Dimensions approx. 79 ft x 24 ft x 10 ft (24.1 m x 7.3 m x 3.1 m)
Armament 10 guns
To Corfu and back with supplies in 1804–5. Last mentioned 1805.

Nikodim Kremenchug
Constructor Toroshilov
Launched 1790
Dimensions approx. 69 ft x 20 ft x 11.5 ft (21 m x 6.2 m x 3.5 m)
Armament 6 guns
BU 1804.

Taganrogskaia Taganrogskaia
Constructor Fursov
Laid down 1789 *Launched* 1790
Dimensions approx. 69 ft x 19 ft x 6.9 ft (21 m x 5.9 m x 2.1 m)
Armament 8 guns
Last mentioned 1803.

2 rowing brigantines built at Taganrogskaia yard in 1791 by I. Ivanov.
Dimensions approx. 80 ft x 25 ft x 11.5 ft (24.4 m x 7.6 m x 3.5 m)
Armament 8 guns

Aleksei
Converted into a brig in 1807. Last mentioned 1826. (See also under Black Sea fleet brigs.)

Lev
BU 1800.

Illarion Dnieper
Constructor Nefedyev
Laid down 1791 *Launched* 8.4.1792
Dimensions approx. 87 ft x 21 ft x 8.9 ft (26.5 m x 6.4 m x 2.7 m)
Armament 10 guns
Last mentioned 1805.

Desna, Dnestr
Both launched at Nikolaev in 1807. Last mentioned 1814.

Arkhangel Mikhail
Built around 1807. Wrecked 9.8.1811.

Volga
Launched in 1812 at Kherson. Last mentioned 1825.

Kleopatra
Launched in 1812 at Kherson. Last mentioned 1821.

Kiliia
Launched in 1813 at Nikolaev. Wrecked 13.10.1818 off Midiia.

Mariia Magdalina
Launched in 1814 at Kherson. Last mentioned in 1819.

Elisaveta Sevastopol
Constructor I. Ya. Osminin,
Laid down 23.9.1823 *Launched* 19.7.1824
Dimensions approx. 79 ft x 25 ft x 11 ft (24 m x 7.6 m x 3.4 m)
Armament 6–14 guns
Hulked in 1840.

Nartsiss Sevastopol
Constructor I. Ya. Osminin,
Laid down 24.10.1826 *Launched* 15.12.1829
Dimensions approx. 79 ft x 25 ft x 11 ft (24 m x 7.7 m x 3.4 m)
Armament 10 guns
Hulked in 1841.

Caspian flotilla rowing brigantines (6 purpose-built)

3 rowing brigantines built at Kazan in 1715.
Unnamed Kazan   *Constructor* ?
Laid down 12.1716   *Launched* 4.1717
Dimensions approx. 53 ft 15 ft x 4.9 ft (16.1 m x 4.7 m x 1.5 m)

Two rowing brigantines built at Kazan Admiralty.

Pobeda, Slava
Laid down 1793 *Launched* 1794
Last mentioned in 1800.

Okhotsk flotilla rowing brigantines (12 purpose-built)

Arkhangel Mikhail Okhotsk
Constructors M. Rugachev and A.I. Kuzmin
Laid down 1715 *Launched* 1737
Dimensions approx. 60 ft x 18 ft x 7.5 ft (18.3 m x 5.5 m x 2.3 m)
            63 men
Participated in the expedition of Captain M. P. Shpanberg, in search of the mythical 'Land of Juan de Gama', allegedly to the East of Kamchatka in 1738–42 and visited Japan. Wrecked 1753 in the Sea of Okhotsk.

Sviataia Elisaveta
Built at Okhotsk by Zakharov in 1760. Wrecked 20.10.1767 off Kamchatka with the loss of 15 crewmen.

Sviataia Elisaveta
Built 1762–6 for the expedition to the Pacific. Wrecked 25.10.1766 at the beginning of the expedition.

Sviatoi Pavel
Launched 1775. Employed for cargo transportation in 1775–88. BU 1789.

Natal'ia
Launched 1775 at Okhotsk by A. I. Kuzmin. Wrecked 1780 during earthquake on the island of Urup in the Kuriils.

Nadezhda Blagopoluchiia
Launched 1779 at Okhotsk. Lost with all hands in 1782 off the Kuriils.

Sviataia Ekaterina
Built 1789 at Okhotsk by A. I. Kuzmin. Grounded and lost on 30.10.1809.

Obnovlenie Khrama Rossii
Launched at Nizhnekamchatsk in Kamchatka on 15.7.1789. Wrecked 1796.

Konstantin i Elena Okhotsk
Constructor A. I. Kuzmin
Laid down 29.10.1790 *Launched* 21.5.1796
Dimensions approx. 58 ft x ? x 1 ft (17.7 m (LK) x ? x 0.3 m)
Hulked in 1805.

Sviatoi Feodosii Totemskii
Constructor B. I. Vashutkin and Popov
Laid down 1801 *Launched* 1801 at Okhotsk
Wrecked off the Kuriils with the loss of 7 crewmen on 5.9.1811.

Sviatoi Ioann
Laid down 1807 *Launched* 1807 at Okhotsk
Stuck in ice on 2.6.1819 and grounded off Kamchatka. Total loss.

Dionisii
Constructor Vasilyev
Laid down 1808 at Okhotsk *Launched* 1810
BU 1832.

Baltic purchased rowing brigantines (1 purchased)

Sviatoi Pyotr
Purchased in 1787 and assigned to the Mediterranean with Greigs squadron. In 1788 she was assigned as an aviso in Greigs squadron. Not afterwards mentioned.

Black Sea purchased rowing brigantines (11 purpose-built)

Novokuplennaia
Purchased as a new ship at Kherson. Last mentioned in 1799 off Ancona as part of Ushakovs fleet

Bug, Ingulets, Tiligul
All purchased in 1805. Final fates are unknown.

Kuban'
Purchased in 1805. Last mentioned in 1814.

Ingul
Purchased in 1805. Last mentioned in 1810.

Nikolai
Purchased in 1806. Last mentioned in 1824.

Mikhail
Purchased in 1807. Last mentioned 1824.

Sukhum
Purchased in 1812. Grounded and lost in heavy weather at the mouth of the Danube on 23.9.1821.

Il Fortunato
Dimensions approx. 74 ft x 25.5 ft x 8.2 ft (22.6 m x 7.8 m x 2.5 m)
Completed in 1817. Purchased in 1821. Last mentioned 1833.

Trekh Sviatitelei
Built in 1818. Purchased in 1821. Repaired in 1822
Dimensions approx. 78 ft x 27 ft x 8.9 ft (23.8 m x 8.2 m x 2.7 m)
Grounded to prevent sinking in a storm off Balaban Island. Later BU.

Prize rowing brigantines

Arkhip
Turkish vessel, captured at Ochakov 1788
Dimensions approx. 72 ft x 18 ft x 9.2 ft (22 m x 5.6 m x 2.8 m)
Armament 6 guns
Turkish prize, captured at Ochakov in 1788. Last mentioned in 1804.

Timofei
Turkish prize, captured at Ochakov 1788. Last mentioned in 1803.

Black Sea fleet lansons

Lansons were rowing warships with 1 or 2 masts, used as troop transports for coastal and river operations and found only in the Black Sea. Their design traces back to Turkish prizes captured during the 1787–92 war. Usual armament consisted of 4–8 small

BLACK SEA FLEET LANSONS

guns and 1–2 small mortars. With a single short-lived exception built in 1807, lansons were only built or acquired during the Russo-Turkish War period.

Purpose-built lansons (11 purpose-built)

3 lansons were built at the Dniestr by Nefedyev.
Launched 1790
Dimensions approx. 72 ft x 17 ft x 6.5 ft (22 m x 5.2 m x 2 m)
Armament 6 guns inc. a single 1-pood mortar.
Miron
Last mentioned 1795.
Moisei
Last mentioned 1797.
Samuil
Last mentioned 1798.

7 lansons built by Toroshilov at Kremenchug:
Launched 1790
Dimensions approx. 72 ft x 17 ft x 6.2 ft (22 m x 5.2 m x 1.9 m)
Antip
Last mentioned 1798.
Dionisii
Last mentioned 1806.
Erofei
Last mentioned 1802.
Nikon
Last mentioned 1804.
Rodion
Final fate is unknown.
Feofan
Last mentioned 1798.
Fyodor
Last mentioned 1802.

Lavrentii Kherson
Constructor M. I. Surovtsev,
Laid down 5.2.1806 *Launched* 30.9.1807
Dimensions approx. 74 ft x 20 ft x 9.5 ft (22.6 m x 6.2 m x 2.9 m)
Converted into a brig in 1807. Broken up after 1805. (See under brigs.)

Turkish prize lansons

8 lansons captured off Ochakov in 1788.
Gerasim
Dimensions approx. 70 ft x 17 ft x 4.9 ft (21.4 m x 5.1 m x 1.5 m)
Armament 6 guns
Last mentioned in 1797.
Dem'ian
Dimensions approx. 60 ft x 14 ft x 3.6 ft (18.3 m x 4.3 m x 1.1 m)
Final fate is unknown.
Evdokim
Dimensions approx. 54 ft x 11 ft x 3.9 ft (16.5 m x 3.4 m x 1.2 m)
Last mentioned in 1794.
Zakharii
Dimensions approx. 80 ft x 14 ft x 3.9 ft (24.4 m x 4.3 m x 1.2m)
Last mentioned in 1796.
Iasson
Dimensions approx. 60 ft x 12 ft x 3.9 ft (18.3 m x 3.7 m x 1.2 m)
Armament 5 guns
Final fate is unknown.

Iustin
Dimensions approx. 60 ft x 14 ft 1 in x 3.9 ft (18.3 m x 4.3 m x 1.2 m)
Last mentioned in 1796.
Manuil
Dimensions approx. 60 ft x 15 ft x 3.9 ft (18.3 m x 4.6 m x 1.2 m)
Final fate is unknown.
Simion
Last mentioned in 1795.
Tit
Dimensions approx. 70 ft x 22 ft x 10.2 ft (21.4 m 6.7 m x 3.1 m)
Captured off Akkerman on 26.9.1789. Last mentioned in 1797.

12 lansons captured off Izmail in 1790.
Amos
Dimensions approx. 61 ft x 13 ft x 4.3 ft (18.6 m x 4.1 m x 1.3 m)
Armament 5 guns
Last mentioned in 1804.
Andronik
Dimensions approx. 52 ft x 13 ft x 3.9 ft (15.7 m x 3.9 m x 1.2 m)
Last mentioned in 1798.
Dorofei
Dimensions approx. 60 ft x 13 ft x 3.9 ft (18.3 m x 4. m x 1.2 m)
Last mentioned in 1794.
Irina
Dimensions approx. 52 ft x 12 ft x 3 ft (15.8 m x 3.7 m x 0.9 m)
Last mentioned in 1797.
Isidor
Dimensions approx. 52 ft x 12 ft x 3.3 ft (15.7 m x 3.7 m x 1 m)
Last mentioned in 1799.
Lavrentii
Dimensions approx. 57 ft x 14 ft x 4.6 ft (17.5 m x 4.3 m x 1.4 m)
Armament 3 guns
Last mentioned in 1797.
Leontii
Dimensions approx. 60 ft x 14 ft x 3.9 ft (18.3 m x 4.3 m x 1.2 m)
Armament 5 guns
Last mentioned in 1798.
Mavra
Dimensions approx. 61 ft x 14 ft x 3.9 ft (18.6 m x 4.3 m x 1.2 m)
Armament 5 guns
BU 1804.
Mark
Dimensions approx. 52 ft x 12 ft x 3.6 ft (15.8 m x 3.7 m x 1.1 m)
Last mentioned in 1797.
Savva
Dimensions approx. 60 ft x 14 ft x 3.6 ft (18.3 m x 4.4 m x 1.1 m)
Final fate is unknown.
Trofim
Dimensions approx. 61 ft x 14 ft x 4.3 ft (18.5 m x 4.4 m x 1.3 m)
Armament 5 guns
Last mentioned in 1798.
Iakov
Dimensions approx. 60 ft x 18 ft x 3.9 ft (18.3 m x 5.6 m x 1.2 m)
Armament 5 guns
Last mentioned in 1813.

9 lansons of unknown origin

No. 1
First mentioned in 1789. Lost 11.12.1790 in a flotilla commanded by de Ribas, a Spaniard on Russian service in a storm off Izmail.

Nos 11 and *14*
First mentioned in 1790. Lost 11.12.1790 in a flotilla commanded by de Ribas, a Spaniard on Russian service in a storm off Izmail.
Irinarkh, Kipriian
Mentioned as damaged and sunk by ice in 11.1796 at the mouth of the Dnieper.
Mariia
Mentioned in 1794–6. Damaged and sunk by ice in 11.1796 at the mouth of the Dnieper.
Mikhail
Mentioned in 1793–7
Patrikii
Mentioned in 1796–7.
Sviatoi Andrei
Mentioned as wrecked 5.4.1792 off the mouth of the Danube.

Galets (or golets)

Galets were small two-masted vessels, generally similar to brigs and also called schooner-brigs. All had oars and could manoeuvre freely, making them useful for work in narrow passages and among the numerous small islands and banks of the Baltic. Many galets saw service in the sailing navy as well as the rowing flotillas. They proved useful for survey work and, in later years, as *de facto* yachts for high ranking naval staff. 26 were built in the Baltic between 1790 and 1821. Only a single example was built for service in the Black Sea in 1811.

Baltic fleet galets (26 purpose-built)

2 galets built at Gorodskaya City Yard in St Petersburg by A. I. Melikhov.
Launched   1790
Dimensions approx. 60 ft x 15 ft x 6.2 ft (18.3 m x 4.7 m x 1.9 m)
Armament   4 guns
             48 men
Gus
Employed almost yearly in the rowing flotillas for training and hydrographic works. BU 1811
Chepura
Employed almost yearly in the rowing flotillas for training and hydrographic works. BU 1812

2 galets built in 1794 at Gorodskaya City Yard by A. I. Melikhov.
Launched   1794
Dimensions approx. 55 ft x 17 ft x 6.2 ft (16.8 m x 5.2 m x 1.9 m)
Armament   4 guns
Utka
BU 1806
Chaika
BU 1806

Tserera Admiralty, St Petersburg
Constructor M. Sarychev
Laid down   13.7.1801   *Launched* 27.5.1802
Dimensions approx. 71 ft x 19 ft x 6.8 ft (21.7 m x 5.8 m x 2.1 m)
Armament   10 guns
Transferred to the sailing navy in 1812–13. Used for transportation by courtiers. BU 1814.

Pallada Admiralty, St Petersburg
Constructor J. J. Le Brune
Laid down   13.7.1801   *Launched* 1.7.1802
Dimensions approx. 73 ft x 21 ft x 8.9 ft (22.3 m x 6.3 m x 2.7 m)
Armament   14 guns
Transferred to the sailing navy in 1812–13. Used for transportation by courtiers. BU 1814.

Aglaia Rochensalm
Laid down   1804   *Launched* 1.9.1806
Captured by Sweden in 1808.

Olen' Admiralty, St Petersburg
Constructor G. S. Isakov
Laid down   1809   *Launched* 18.6.1809
Dimensions approx. 66 ft x 18 ft x 7.9 ft (20.2 m x 5.5 m x 2.4 m)
Armament   14 guns.
Employed in hydrographic work 1828–31. BU 1833.

Pchela Admiralty, St Petersburg
Constructor G. S. Isakov
Laid down   1809   *Launched* 18.6.1809
Dimensions approx. 66 ft x 19 ft x 7.9 ft (20.1 m x 5.8 m x 2.4 m)
Armament   14 guns
BU 1822.

10 galets built at Lodeynoe Pole.
Laid down   1809   *Launched* 1809
Dimensions approx. 57 ft x 18 ft x 6.2 ft (17.5 m x 5.4 m x 1.9 m)
No. 1
Always in the sailing navy with the exception of the 1812 and 1813 campaigns. Last mentioned 1826.
Nos 2, 3 and *5*
Always in the sailing navy with the exception of the 1812 and 1813 campaigns. BU 1830.
No. 3
Always in the sailing navy with the exception of the 1812 and 1813 campaigns. BU 1830.
No. 4
Always in the sailing navy with the exception of the 1812 and 1813 campaigns. BU 1828
No. 5
Always in the sailing navy with the exception of the 1812 and 1813 campaigns. BU 1830.
No. 6
Always in sailing navy with exception of the 1812 to 1816 campaigns. BU 1830
No. 7
BU 1819.
No. 8
Always in the sailing navy with the exception of the 1812 to 1815 campaigns. BU 1830.
No. 9
Always in the sailing navy with the exception of the 1812 and 1813 campaigns. Used by Emperor Alexander I for a trip from St Petersburg to Kronshtadt in 1810. BU 1830.
No. 10
Always in the sailing navy with the exception of the 1812 and 1813 campaigns. Last mentioned in 1814.

Kyumen Admiralty, St Petersburg
Constructor G. S. Isakov

GALETS – DUBBEL-SHLYUPKAS

The 14-gun galet Torneo *of 1810 was a very different ship from her Baltic contemporary, the 32-gun* Torneo *of 1808. As is evident from the drawing, galets were closely related to brigs, the difference being their heavy reliance (not apparent from the drawing) on oars to facilitate manoeuvring among the shoals and shallows of the Baltic. This particular galet had the dubious distinction of becoming the personal yacht of the notorious naval minister Traversay in 1820 towards the end of his career and the ship's life.*

Laid down 10.3.1810   Launched 19.7.1810
Dimensions approx. 73 ft x 21 ft x 8.9 ft (22.4 m x 6.3 m x 2.7 m)
Armament 14 guns
BU 1828.

Torneo Admiralty, St Petersburg
Constructor G. S. Isakov
Laid down 10.3.1810   Launched 19.7.1810
Dimensions approx. 73 ft x 23 ft x 11.2 ft (22.4 m x 6.9 m x 3.4 m)
Armament 14 guns
Usually attached to the sailing navy. In 1820 assigned to naval minister Marquis Traversay for sailing in the Gulf of Finland. BU 1825.

2 galets built at Rochensalm by Korolev.
Dimensions approx. 66 ft x 19 ft x 10.1 ft (20.1 m x 5.9 m x 3.1 m)
Armament 8 guns
Ekho
Laid down 14.9.1807   Launched 26.5.1811
Assigned to the rowing flotilla under Rear-Adm. von Moller in 1812. Left Riga together with a British squadron under Rear-Adm. T. Marten for the blockade of Danzig on 10.8.1812. Assigned to Capt. I. S. Tulubyev's flotilla in 1813 and again to the blockade of Danzig with Capt. Geydens flotilla. BU 1823.
Aglaia
Laid down 14.9.1807   Launched 26.5.1811
Assigned to the rowing flotilla under Rear-Adm. von Moller in 1812. Left Riga together with a British squadron under Rear-Adm. T. Marten for the blockade of Danzig on 10.8.1812. Assigned to Capt. I. S. Tulubyevs flotilla in 1813 and again to the blockade of Danzig with Capt. Geyden's flotilla. BU 1825.

Volkhov Okhta
Constructor V. F. Stoke
Laid down 6.3.1815   Launched 13.7.1815

Dimensions approx. 73 ft x 30 ft x 8.9 ft (22.4 m x 9.1 m x 2.7 m)
Armament 14 guns
Stationed permanently in the Volkhov River, near the estate of Alexander's all-powerful minister Count Arakcheev at Gruzino. BU 1834 at Gruzino.

Fakel Okhta
Constructor V. F. Stoke
Laid down 19.12.1817   Launched 17.8.1818
Dimensions approx. 61 ft x 18 ft x 9.8 ft (18.9 m x 5.6 m x 3 m)
Armament 3 guns
Employed for hydrographic work in the Gulf of Finland and the Gulf of Riga from 1819–27.

Torneo Okhta
Constructor V. F. Stoke
Laid down 1820   Launched 7.5.1821
Armament 14 guns
Used as a yacht by the Chief of Naval Staff, Vice-Adm. von Moller from 1822–5. Used by Nicolas I in 1827 to accompany Adm. Seniavin as far as Krasnaia Gorka, with the Russian squadron bound for the Mediterranean and the battle of Navarino. Training ship in 1839–45. Last mentioned in 1845.

Black Sea fleet galet

Mukha
Built around 1806. Assigned to the sailing squadron in 1807. Last mentioned in 1811

Dubbel-shlyupkas ('double-boats')

The precise translation for *dubbel-shlyupka* is 'enlarged usual boat'. These were originally enlarged ships' long boats used for operations in rivers, estuaries and coastal areas, as well as for cutting out operations. Later, they became bigger, with deck lengths of up to 23 m (75 ft), with 8–12 guns, including swivels and a few of larger calibre, giving them the characteristics of the

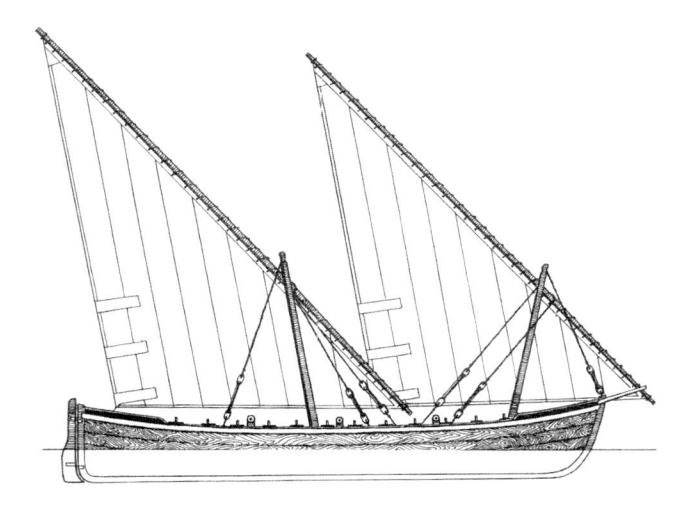

The long-boat origins of dubbel-shlyupkas are clear from this drawing of one built built at Byansk yard in 1737 for the conquest of Azov. Over 400 were built for the campaign and this is a typical example with open decks, 2 lateen masts, 6 small cannon and a crew of 40.

purpose built gunboats by which they were gradually replaced in the 1790s. Their greatest use by far was with the Dnieper flotilla in the 1737 war with Turkey. Over 400 were built for this campaign, a reflection of the pressing need to provide a cheap and easily built shallow water counter to the Turkish navy in the absence of any sort of established seagoing naval force.

Siberia (2 purpose-built)

2 dubbel-shlyupkas built specially for Great Northern expedition.
Tobol
Dimensions approx. 70 ft x 15 ft x 6.9 ft (21.4 m x 4.6 m x 2.1 m)
Built in 1733 at Toblsk on the Tobol River, which is itself a branch of the Ob', one of the major rivers in Siberia. Explored the Ob' and Enisey rivers in 1737–8 and twice went out into the Arctic Sea, last mentioned 1738.

Iakutsk
Dimensions approx. 70 ft x 18 ft x 6.6 ft (21.4 m x 5.5 m x 2 m)
Built in 1735 at Iakutsk with two masts and a crew of 56 men. Explored the Lena River in 1735–40, and twice went out into the Arctic Sea. Sailed along the Taimir peninsula and became trapped in heavy ice. Severely damaged 13.8.1740, abandoned, and carried away to the sea 30.8.1740.

Okhotsk flotilla (1 purpose-built)

Nadezhda
Constructor M. Rugachev and A. I. Kuzmin
Laid down 1735 *Launched* 1737
Dimensions approx. 70 ft x 18 ft x 4.9 ft (21.4 m x 5.5 m x 1.5 m)
3-masted with triangular schooner-type sails, 44 men. Took part in the Shpanbergs expedition (1738-1742) and paid two visits to Hokkaido and Honshu, Japan. Wrecked off the Kuriils in 1753.

Dnieper flotilla (408 purpose-built)

400 dubbel-shlyupkas built at Bryansk.
Laid down 1736 *Launched* 1737
Dimensions approx. 60 ft x ? x ? (18.3 m x ? m x ? m)
Armament 6 x 2pdr falconets
          40 men
The first 16 arrived at Azov in 1737. Some 50 were employed as troopships in 1738. BU after 1739.

6 dubbel-shlyupkas built at Novo-Zaporozhskaya yard.
Launched 1738
Dimensions approx. 56–60 ft x 20 ft x 5.9–7.5 ft (17.1–18.3 m x 6.1 m x 1.8–2.3 m)
Armament 8–10 guns
BU after 1739.

2 bombardment dubbel-shlyupkas built at the Dnieper in 1738.
Dimensions approx. 56 ft x 20 ft x 5.9 ft (17.1 m x 6.1 m x 1.8 m)
Armament 6 guns
BU after 1739.

Sea of Azov fleet (1 purpose-built)

Unnamed Tavrov
Laid down 1737 *Launched* 1738
Dimensions approx. 74 ft x 17 ft x 5.6 ft (22.5 m x 5.2 m x 1.7 m)
Operated with Vice-Adm. Bredals flotilla. BU after 1739.

Baltic fleet (19 purpose-built)

3 dubbel-shlyupkas built at Galley Yard, St Petersburg.
Dimensions approx. 70 ft x 14 ft x 5.2 ft (21.4 m x 4.3 m x 1.6 m)
Armament 8 guns
          20 oars
No. 1
Constructor A.I. Alatcheninov
Laid down 1764 *Launched* 1764
Destroyed by fire on 11.7.1771 at the Galley Port.
No. 2
Constructor Shchepin
Laid down 1767 *Launched* 1764
Destroyed by fire on 11.7.1771 at the Galley Port.
No. 3
Constructor Shchepin
Laid down 1767 *Launched*1768
Destroyed by fire on 11.7.1771 at the Galley Port.

Unnamed Galley Yard, St Petersburg
Constructor Borisov
Laid down 1771 *Launched* 1771
Dimensions approx. 70 ft x 13 ft x 4.9 ft (21.4 m x 4 m x 1.5 m)
Armament 1 x 12pdr, 1 x 8pdr, 6 falconets
Destroyed by fire on 11.7.1771 at the Galley Port.

13 dubbel-shlyupkas built at Olonetsk built by Shchepin, A. I. Ozerov and I. I. Afanasyev.
Dimensions approx. 70 ft x 14 ft x 4.9 ft (21.4 m x 4.3 m x 1.5 m)
Armament 1 x 12pdr, 1 x 8pdr, 6 falconets
          20 oars, 56 men (inc. 40 oarsmen)
All were laid down 1772. The first 10 were launched in 1773 and the last 3 in 1776. It would appear that nos 10–13 were renumbered 1–4 after the first 4 were lost at the 2nd battle of Rochensalm.
No. 1
Lost at the 2nd battle of Rochensalm on 28.6.1790.
No. 2
Lost at the 2nd battle of Rochensalm on 28.6.1790.
No. 3
Lost at the 2nd battle of Rochensalm on 28.6.1790.
No. 4
Lost at the 2nd battle of Rochensalm on 28.6.1790.
Nos 5, 6, 7, 8, 9
BU 1792.
Nos 1 (2nd) and *3* (2nd)
BU 1800.
No. 2 (2nd) , *4* (2nd)
BU 1792.

Unnamed
Launched 1789
Dimensions approx. 75 ft x 19 ft x 6.2 ft (22.9 m x 5.7 m x 1.9 m)
Armament 12 guns
          22 oars
Lost at the 2nd battle of Rochensalm on 28.6.1790.

No. 4 Galley Yard, St Petersburg
Launched 1789

A dramatic and possibly over-romanticized painting of Captain Reingold Saken's heroic last moments prior to his having his crew abandon ship and then deliberately blowing it up along with those of several of his Turkish foes. Whatever its historical accuracy, the painting by M. Grachev is of considerable value for its realistic portrait of Saken's dubbel-shlyupka and the lateen-rigged warships of the Turks.

Dimensions approx. 75 ft x 19 ft x 6.2 ft (22.9 m x 5.7 m x 1.9 m)
Armament 12 guns
22 oars.
BU 1802.

Black Sea fleet (25 purpose-built)

7 dubbel-shlyupkas built at Kherson.
Laid down 1787 *Launched* 1788
Dimensions approx. 72 ft x 17 ft x 5.6 ft (22 m x 5.2 m x 1.7 m)
Armament 2 x 30pdrs (or 1-pood edinorogs), 1 x 12pdr, 4 x 4pdrs,
4 falconets
42 oars, 60–70 men.

No. 1 Last mentioned in 1793.
No. 2 On 26.5.1788, under the command of Captain von der Osten-Saken, she was surrounded by 13 Turkish galleys at the mouth of the Bug and deliberately blown up, taking all of the Turkish ships with her.
No. 3 Last mentioned in 1789.
No. 4 Last mentioned in 1793.
No. 5 Last mentioned in 1793.
No. 6 Last mentioned in 1794.
No. 7 Apparently renumbered as no. 2 after the loss of Sakens boat. Last mentioned in 1793.

6 dubbel-shlyupkas laid down at Novokhoperskaya in 1787 and launched in 1788. Final fates not known.

12 dubbel-shlyupkas were laid down in 1787 at the yard at the Moshna settlement and launched in 1788. They were unable to pass the Dnieper rapids and remained at Kremenchug.

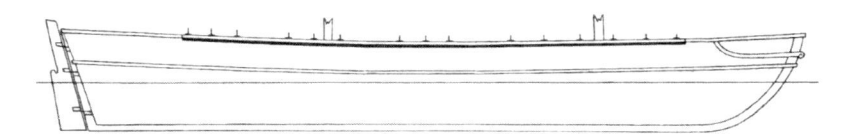

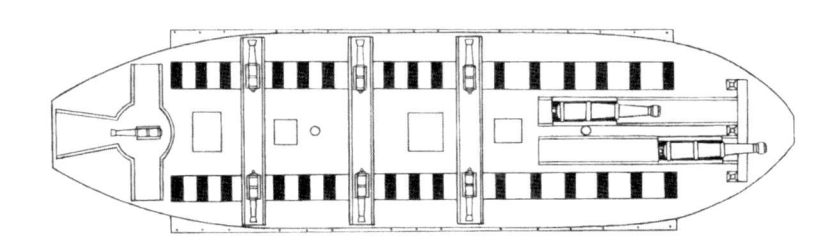

A side view and overhead of Captain Saken's famous dubbel-shlyupka no. 2 in 1788. A comparison of this boat with the drawing of a typical dubbel-shlyupka of the 1737 campaign against Azov shows considerable elaboration of a once basic design. A comparison of this drawing with the painting of Captain Saken's last fight above is also of interest.

Gunboats

Gunboats (*kanonerskie lodki*, cannon boats) were introduced in the Russian navy in 1788 and built in enormous quantities by both Russia and Sweden to the end of sail. They replaced the generally similar dubbel-shlyupkas and could be quickly and easily built and put into action upon the onset of hostilities and just as quickly disposed of after fighting had ended. Gunboats were open decked and lacked any sort of berthing facilities. By Jan Glete's definition, they distinguished themselves from ships' boats carrying small cannon on an ad hoc basis by being armed with at least one cannon that was equal in calibre to that found in the lower decks of the smallest line of battle ships. For Glete, this meant an 18pdr in the eighteenth century and a 24pdr in the nineteenth century. The gunboat brought about the demise of the larger galley in Russia as a result of its having demonstrated greater manoeuvrability in the narrow and congested waters of the northern Baltic archipelagos during the 1788–90 war. Most gunboats had between 7 and 15 banks of oars and carried from one to three large guns. In 1853–6 steam gunboats were also introduced and they may be found in Section III.

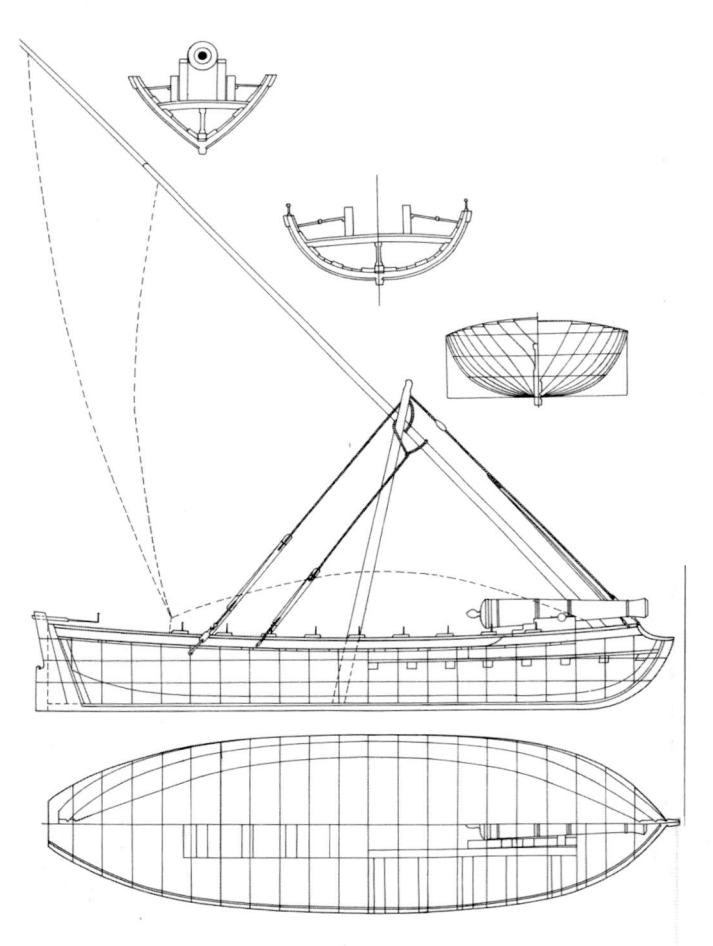

Baltic fleet gunboats (773 purpose-built)

21 2-masted gunboats built at Volkhov, St Petersburg, with the exception of the lead boat which was built at Galley Yard, by M. Sarychev.
Laid down 1788 *Launched* 1788
Dimensions approx. 68 ft x 15 x 4.9 ft x (20.7 m x 4.6 m x 1.5 m)
Armament 1 x 18pdr, 1 x 12pdr, 6 x 3pdr
30 oars, 70 men (incl. 60 oarsmen)
4 boats lost without trace in 1790. 17 BU 1799.

11 gunboats built in 1788 at Volkhov, St Petersburg, with the exception of the lead boat which was built at Galley Yard by M. Sarychev.
Dimensions approx. 63 ft x 15 x 4.9 ft (19.2 m x 4.6 m x 1.5 m)
Armament 1 x 24pdr
20 oars, 50 men (inc. 40 oarsmen).
2 boats lost in 1790, 9 BU 1806.

11 1-masted gunboats built in 1788 at Volkhov, St Petersburg, with the exception of lead boat which was built at Galley Yard by M. Sarychev.
Dimensions approx. 45 ft x 14 ft x 4.6 ft (13.8 m x 4.3 m x 1.4 m)
Armament 1 x 16pdr
18 oars, 44 men
7 boats were transferred to Vil'manstrand by land to be employed at Lake Sayma in Finland. 4 BU 1800.

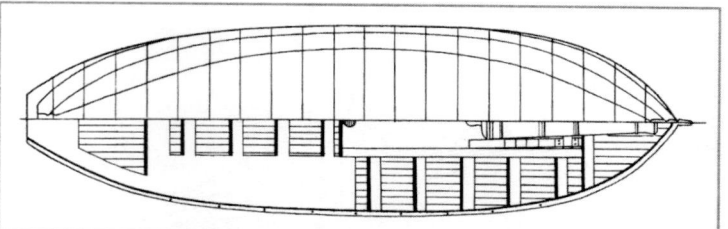

A standard gunboat of 1788 showing the lateen rig and great simplicity of the basic design; 18-oared gunboats of this type carried a single 16pdr gun, while their slightly larger sisters carried 24pdrs. The Russians came into the Russo-Swedish War in 1788 heavily dependent upon traditional galleys in contrast to their Swedish opponents who had turned to smaller more manoeuvrable gunboats after 1748. Massive construction programmes by the Russians on the outbreak of war in 1788 quickly redressed the balance.

GUNBOATS

10 gunboats built at Revel' in 1789.
Dimensions approx. 60 ft x 15 ft x 3.9 ft (18.3 x 4.6 x 1.2 m)
Armament 2 guns
Final fates are unknown.

9 gunboats built at Vil'manstrand in 1789.
Dimensions approx. 52.5 ft x 13 ft x 4.9 ft (16 m x 4 m x 1.5 m)
Armament 2 guns
Employed at Lake Sayma in Finland. Final fates are unknown.

40 boats built at Fridrikhshamn in 1790.
Dimensions approx. 62 ft x 14 ft x 4.9 ft (18.9 m x 4.3 m x 1.5 m)
Armament 2 guns
           28 oars
7 burnt on 25.5.1796 at the Galley Port fire. 8 BU 1805. 4 BU 1800. 12 converted to transport craft. 9 not known.

15 boats built at Vil'manstrand in 1790.
Dimensions approx. 46 ft x 8.9 ft x 4.9 ft (14 m x 2.7 m x 1.5 m)
Armament 2 guns
Employed at the Lake Sayma in Finland. Final fates are not known.

70 boats built at Galley Yard in 1790.
Dimensions approx. 62 ft x 14 ft x 5.2 ft (19.1 m x 4.3 m x 1.6 m)
Armament 2 guns
           28 oars
2 burnt on 25.5.1796 at the Galley Port fire. 20 BU 1804. 8 BU 1801, 5 BU 1802. 6 BU 1803. 18 BU 1805. 11 are indeterminate.

20 boats built at Riga in 1791.
Dimensions approx. 62 ft x 15 ft x 5.2 ft (18.9 m x 4.6 m x 1.6 m)
Armament 1 gun
Final fates are not known.

10 boats built at Gorodskaya in 1796 at St Petersburg.
Dimensions approx. 61 ft x 15 ft x 5.2 ft (18.9 m x 4.6 m x 1.6 m)
Armament 2 guns
           28 oars
All BU by 1810.

1 boat built by I. Spiridonov at Rochensalm in 1797.
Dimensions approx. 58 ft x 14 ft x 5.2 ft (17.7 m x 4.2 m x 1.6 m)
Armament 2 guns
BU by 1810.

1 boat built by A.S. Katasanov in 1799 at Galley Yard.
Dimensions approx. 64 ft x 17 ft x 8.5 ft (19.5 m x 5.2 m x 2.6 m)
Armament 2 guns
           20 oars
Final fate: Wrecked in 1805 while en route from St Petersburg to Kronshtadt.

10 boats built at Rochensalm in 1801:
Armament 2 guns
All BU 1820.

30 boats built at Galley Yard by A. K. Kaverznev in 1804–6
Dimensions 19 boats: approx. 66 ft x 15 ft x 5.9 ft (20.2 m x 4.5 m x 1.8 m)
7 boats: approx. 61 ft x 13 ft x 4.2 ft (18.7 m x 4 m x 1.3 m)
4 boats: approx. 62 ft x 13 ft x 4.6 ft (18.8 m x 4 m x 1.4 m)

Armament 2 guns
1 BU 1818. 7 BU 1820. 11 BI 1822. 11 BU 1824.

54 boats built in 1807 at Lodeynoe Pole by A. P. Antipyev and A. K. Kaverznev.
Dimensions approx. 66 ft x 15 ft x 5.9 ft (20.2 m x 4.5 m x 1.8 m)
Armament 2 guns
2 captured by the British in 1809, 1 wrecked off Krasnaia Gorka in 1810. 2 BU 1817. 2 BU 1818. 10 BU 1820. 8 BU 1826 5 BU 1827. 24 not known.

13 boats built in 1808 at Lodeynoe Pole by A.P. Antipyev and A. K. Kaverznev.
Dimensions approx. 67 ft x 15 ft x 5.9 ft (20.3 m x 4.6 m x 1.8 m)
Armament 2 guns
4 BU 1820. 9 BU 1822.

42 boats built in 1808 at Lodeynoe Pole by G. S. Isakov, A. P. Antipyev and A. K. Kaverznev.
Dimensions approx. 66 ft x 15 ft x 5.9 ft (20.2 m x 4.5 m x 1.8 m)
Armament 2 guns
12 sold in 1812. 6 BU 1818. 4 BU 1821. 1 BU 1822. 7 BU 1823. 8 BU 1826. 4 BU 1827.

6 boats built in 1808 at Kupio, Finland by A. K. Kaverznev.
Dimensions approx. 53 ft x 15 ft x 4.3 ft (16.2 m x 4.5 m x 1.3 m)
Armament 2 guns
Handed over to local authorities in Kupio in 1810.

4 boats built in 1808 at Vil'manstrand.
Armament 2 guns
Sold at Uleaborg in 1810.

6 boats built in 1808 at Riga by A. K. Kaverznev.
Armament 2 guns
2 BU 1821. 4 repaired 1817 and BU 1843.

32 boats built in 1809 at Lodeynoe Pole by A. K. Kaverznev.
Dimensions approx. 81 ft s 17 ft x 6.2 ft (24.8 m x 5.3 m x 1.9 m)
Armament 2 guns
4 boats handed over to local authorities at Uleaborg in 1811. 7 BU 1821. 11 BU 1824. 10 BU 1825.

20 boats built at Iakobshtadt in 1809.
Dimensions approx. 67 ft x 15 ft x 5.6 ft x (20.3 m x 4.6 m x 1.7 m)
Armament 2 guns
10 handed over to local authorities at Kuopio in 1810. 3 handed over to local authorities at Uleaborg in 1811. 4 wrecked at sea in 1812. 3 more wrecked off Nargen and Wulf, also in 1812.

10 boats built in 1809 at Gamle-Karlebu in 1809.
Dimensions approx. 67 ft x 15 ft x 6.2 ft (20.3 m x 4.6 m x 1.9 m)
Armament 2 guns
Handed over to local authorities at Uleaborg in 1811.

8 boats built in 1809 at Lodeynoe Pole by A. K. Kaverznev.
Dimensions approx. 81 ft x 17 ft x 5.9 ft (24.8 m x 5.3 m x 1.8 m)
Armament 2 guns
7 BU 1821. 1 repaired 1827 and relegated to harbour service in 1846.

15 boats built in 1809 at Vaza town.

Dimensions approx. 66 ft x 16 ft x 4.3 ft (20.2 m x 4.8 m x 1.3 m)
Armament 2 guns
BU 1821.

2 boats built in 1809 at Galley Yard by J. J. Le Brune.
Dimensions approx. 76 ft x 17 ft x 4.6 ft x (23.1 m x 5.3 m x 1.4 m)
All BU 1822.

60 boats built at Galley Yard by G. S. Isakov and I. S. Razumov in 1812.
Dimensions approx. 81 ft x 17 ft x 6.2 ft x (24.8 m x 5.3 m x 1.9 m)
Armament 3 guns
4 wrecked in 1812. 6 wrecked in 1813. 2 sunk by shore batteries off Danzig in 1813. 25 BU 1820. 14 BU 1821. 3 BU 1843. 16 not known.

16 boats built at Okhta, St Petersburg by V. F. Stoke in 1821:
Armament 2 guns
5 BU 1822. 2 BU 1835. 2 BU 1847. 4 to harbour service 1832. 2 to harbour service in 1833. 1 not known.

1 boat built at Okhta, St Petersburg in 1822 and relegated to harbour service in 1832.

1 boat rated as a bomb built at Okhta, St Petersburg in 1823 by V. F. Stoke.
Armament 2 guns
BU 1833.

7 boats built in 1824 at Okhta, St Petersburg.
Armament 2 guns
1 boat repaired in 1833. 5 repaired in 1834. 1 BU 1835. 2 BU 1846. 1 to harbour service 1839. 3 not known.

6 boats built at Okhta, St Petersburg in 1824.
Armament 2 guns
1 boat repaired in 1833, 3 repaired in 1839. 1 BU 1835. 2 BU1842. 1 BU 1843. 2 not known.

20 boats built at Lodeynoe Pole by I. V. Kurepanov in 1826.
Dimensions approx. 66 ft x 15 ft x 5.9 ft (20.2 m x 4.6 m x 1.8 m)
Armament 2 guns
4 BU 1835. 2 BU 1839. 14 not known.

1 boat built at Kronshtadt in 1828.
Dimensions approx. 65 ft x 16 ft (inside plank) x 5.9 ft (19.7 m x 5 m (inside plank) x 1.8 m)
Armament 2 guns
Final fate is unknown.

20 boats built in 1829–30 at Lodeynoe Pole by N. I. Fyodrov.
Dimensions approx. 66 ft x 15 ft x 5.9 ft (20.2 m x 4.6 m x 1.8 m)
Armament 2 guns
Final fates are not known.

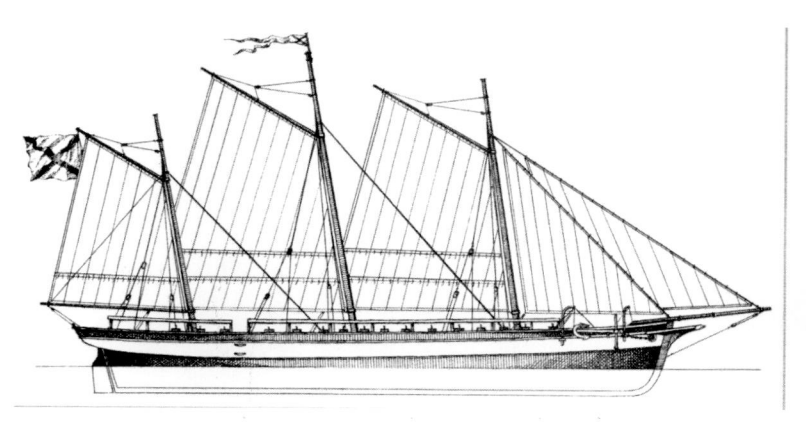

A gunboat of 1846 showing remarkable progress from the simple prototypes that first appeared in 1788.

6 boats built at 'Novaya Gollandiya' in 1831–2 by K. A. Glazyrin and Marchevskiy.
Dimensions approx. 65 ft x 15 ft (inside plank) x 5.9 ft (19.7 m x 4.5 m (inside plank) x 1.8 m)
Armament 2 guns
Final fates are not known.

1 boat built at New Admiralty, St Petersburg by I. A. Amosov in 1834.
Dimensions approx. 74 ft x 17 ft x 6.9 ft (22.6m x 5.3m x 2.1m)
Armament 3 guns
Final fate is unknown.

9 boats built at New Admiralty, St Petersburg in 1835.
Armament 2 guns
Final fates are unknown.

2 boats built at Abo in 1844.
Armament 2 guns
Final fates are unknown.

1 boat built at Kronshtadt in 1845.
Armament 2 guns
Final fate is unknown.

17 boats built at New Admiralty, St Petersburg
Launched 16 1848, 1 1849
Armament 2 guns
Final fates are unknown.

1 boat built at 'Galernyy Ostrovok' by I. I. Lemuan after design of Rear-Adm. I. I. von Shantz.
Laid down 1854 *Launched* 20.5.1854
Dimensions approx. 73.5 ft x 15 ft (inside plank) x 4.9 ft (22.4 m x 4.6 m (inside plank) x 1.5 m)
Armament 2 guns
Final fate is unknown.

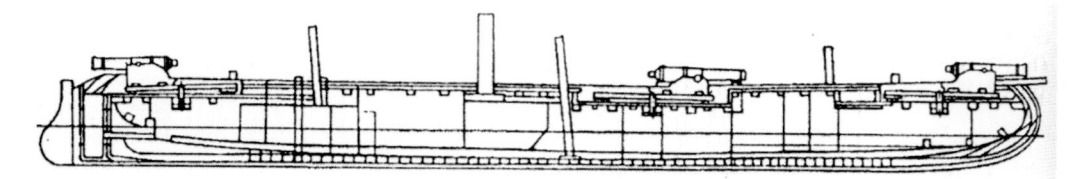

This one-off design for a gunboat reduced to its essential elements was designed by Adm. von Shantz and constructed by I. I. Lemuan in 1854 under the threat of allied incursions into the Gulf of Finland.

77 boats built at St Petersburg.
Launched 1854
Armament 2 guns
Final fates are not known.

16 boats built at Riga.
Launched 1854
Armament 2 guns
Final fates are not known.

40 boats built at Finnish yard.
Launched 1854
Armament 2 guns
Final fates are not known.

White Sea flotilla gunboats (12 purpose-built)

Six boats built at Bykovskaya.
Laid down 4.3.1790   *Launched* 19.5.1790
Dimensions approx. 60 ft x 15 ft x 3 ft (18.3 m x 4.6 m x 0.9 m)
Armament 2 guns
All BU 1801.

6 boats built in 1801 at Solombala. 2 boats were converted to transport craft. 4 were BU 1814.

Black Sea fleet gunboats (140 purpose-built)

53 boats built at Kherson in 1793–5.
Dimensions approx. 60 ft x 15 ft x 7.2 ft (18.3 m x 4.6 m x 2.2 m)
Armament 3 guns
Last mentioned in 1809 at the siege of Silistriya.

15 boats built at Kherson in 1815 by M. I. Surovtsev.
Dimensions approx. 60 ft x15 ft x5.6 ft (18.3 m x 4.6 m x 1.7 m)
Armament 1 gun
Final fates are not known.

30 boats built in 1819–28 at Nikolaev and Kherson after the design of Adm. A. S. Greig by A. I. Melikhov, I. S. Razumov and A. K. Kaverznev.
Dimensions approx. 75 ft x 17 ft x 5.2 ft (22.9 m x 5.2 m x 1.6 m)
Armament 3 x 24pdrs
Derzkaia, Buian, Strela, Giena, Krokodil, Korshun
BU 1832.
Zabiiaka, Barsuk
BU 1837.
Groza, Shumnaia, Zmeia, Skorpion, Krot, Vikhr', Shchuka, Iashcheritsa, Pchela, Osa, Khorek, Uzh, Iozh
BU 1831.
Zlaia
Sunk in the Danube 1839.
Stazh
BU 1839.
Iastreb
Sunk 1829.
Azartnaya, Krikun, Serditaia, Tarantul
BU 1833.
Gromkaia
Last mentioned 1829
Bespokoinaia

15 boats built at Nikolaev Admiralty.
Dimensions approx. 80 ft x 17 ft x 4.9 ft x 4.9 ft (draught) (24.5 m x 5.3 m x 1.8 m x 1.5 m (draught)
Armament 3 guns
5 were built in 1841 by G. V. Afanasyev and V. Apostoli and BU 1852.
10 were built in 1850–1 by S. I. Chernyavskiy and sold for BU 1859.

17 boats built at Nikolaev Admiralty by S. I. Chernyavskiy.
Dimensions approx. 80 ft x 17 ft x ? (24.4 m x 5.3 m x ?)
Armament 3 guns
10 boats launched 1846. 7 boats launched 1852. BU 1859.

10 boats built at Nikolaev by Aleksandrov in 1854.
Dimensions approx. 80 ft x 18 ft x ? (24.4 m x 5.5 m x ?)
Armament 3 guns
Final fates: Handed over to the Kherson authorities in 1868.

Black Sea gunboat prizes

Two Turkish gunboats taken 1.7.1788 in the Liman by the flotilla of Prince Nassau-Siegen. Final disposition is not known.

Baltic Sea gunboat prizes

3 Swedish gunboats taken at the 1st battle of Rochensalm on 13.8.1789.
Armed with 2 guns.
One of them burnt 1796 at the Galley Port fire on 25.5.1796.

3 2-masted Swedish gunboats taken 22.6.1790 at Biork-e zund by Prince Nassau-Siegen.
Dimensions approx. 62 ft x 14 ft x 4.9 ft (18.9 m x 4.3 m x 1.5 m)
Armament 2 guns
          28 oars
Final dispositions are not known.

25 ex-Swedish boats taken in 1808 at the capitulation of Sveaborg. No information is available on their fate.

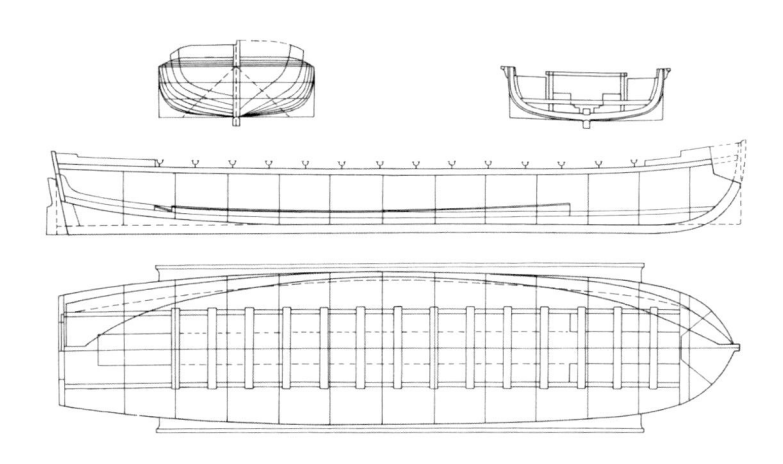

A detailed drawing of a Swedish gunboat captured in 1790. It makes clear the simple and basic design of the Swedish boats that so easily out-manoeuvred the larger, faster, but less handy, Russian galleys at the 2nd battle of Rochensalm. Later gunboats built in Russia and elsewhere would be more elaborately designed, but this boat would have contented itself with a single bow-mounted cannon – not shown here.

Yawls

Yawls were small craft, smaller than gunboats but more handy and better suited for operations in shallow waters, among reefs, banks and grounds. They generally mounted a single gun, although some in the Black Sea carried two, 1 or 2 masts and from 8 to 16 oars. The first yawls were modelled on Swedish prizes which were built according to plans developed by Frederik af Chapman in 1788 and captured at the battle of Vyborg 22.6.1790. From 1790 through the end of sail, yawls and gunboats formed the backbone of the inshore squadrons.

Baltic fleet yawls (97 purpose-built)

20 yawls built at Riga in 1791 by S. Durakin.
Dimensions approx. 25 ft x 8.5 ft x 3 ft (7.8 m x 2.6 m x 0.9 m)
Armament 1 x 24pdr
          8 oars
8 BU 1809, 8 BU 1810, 4 BU 1814.

2 yawls launched in 1796.
Dimensions approx. 48.5 ft x 12 ft x 4.9 ft (14.8 m x 3.6 m x 1.5 m)
Armament 1 gun
BU by 1810.

30 yawls built at Galley Yard in 1799.
Dimensions approx. 48.5 ft x 12 ft x 4.9 ft x 3.9 ft (draught) (14.8 m x 3.6 m x 1.5 m x 1.2 m (draught))

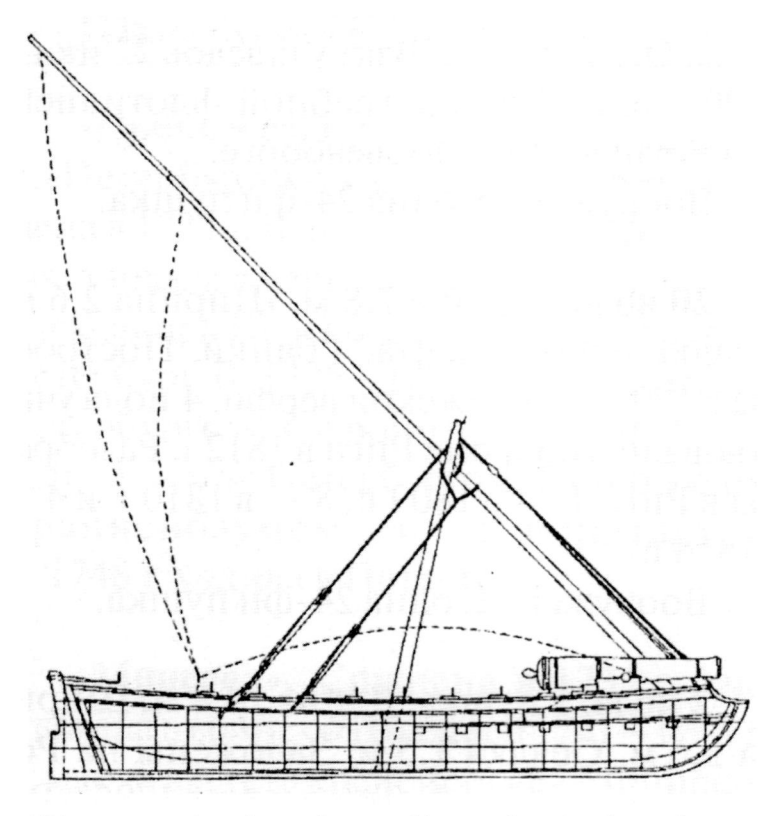

This representation of a yawl captured in 1790 from Sweden at the battle of Vyborg became the model for 20 similar boats and a moderate degree of further construction continuing up to 1833. The original design for the type came from the redoubtable Frederik af Chapman.

Armament 1 x 30pdr
          16 oars
21 BU 1820. 9 were repaired 1820. The final fate of the repaired boats is not known.

30 yawls built at Galley Yard in 1801 by M. Sarychev.
Dimensions approx. 46 ft x 11 ft x 3.9 ft (14 m x 3.4 m x 1.2 m)
Armament 1 gun
11 BU 1815. 2 BU 1816. 1 BU 1817. 3 BU 1819. 9 BU 1822. 4 BU 1824.

4 yawls built at Rochensalm, 2 in 1807 and 2 in 1808.
1 BU 1817. 1 BU 1820. 2 BU 1821.

Moika and *Fontanka* built in 1830 at 'Novaya Gollandiya'.
Dimensions approx. 52 ft x 13 ft x 6.9 ft (15.9 m (pp) x 4 m (inside plank) x 2.1 m)
Armament 1 x 24pdr, 4 x 3pdrs
These two boats were named after branches of the Neva. Repaired 1839. Final fate is not known.

Kanonerskii built in 1833 at New Admiralty by A. K. Kaverznev.
Dimensions approx. 52 ft x 11 ft x ? (15.9 m (pp) x 3.4 m (inside plank) x ?)
Final fate is not known.

8 yawls built at Nikolaev Admiralty in 1833 by S. I. Chernyavskiy and I. Y. Osminin.
Dimensions approx. 51 ft x 12.5 ft x 6.9 ft x 6.2 ft (15.5 m x 3.8 m x 2.1 m x 1.9 m (draught))
BU 1838.

White Sea flotilla yawls (30 purpose-built)

30 yawls built at Solombala in 1801.
2 BU 1805. 4 captured by the British in 1808. 2 BU 1812. 4 BU 1813. 12 BU 1814. 3 BU 1815. 1 BU 1816. Fate of the final two boats is not known.

Black Sea flotilla yawls (41 purpose-built)

All yawls built before 1830 were employed in 1828–9 on the Danube.

17 yawls built at Nikolaev Admiralty by I. S. Razumov, 1 in 1822, 1 in 1823, 15 in 1824.
Dimensions approx. 35 ft x 12 ft x 4.9 ft (10.7 m x 3.7 m x 1.5 m)
Armament 1 x 18pdr
BU 1832–6.

5 yawls built at Nikolaev Admiralty in 1829 by A. K. Kaverznev.
Final fates are not known.

5 yawls built at Kherson yard in 1829 by Serkov.
Final fates are not known.

8 yawls built at Nikolaev Admiralty in 1829 by A. K. Kaverznev.
Dimensions approx. 52 ft x 13 ft x 4.9 ft (15.9 m x 4 m x 1.5 m)
Armament 1 x 24pdr carr., 1 x 18pdr carr., 5 x 3pdr falconets
Mark-Antonii
Built   1829   BU 1839
Kleopatra
Built   1829   BU 1840

Orfei
Built   1829 Final fate is not known.
Evridika
Built   1829 BU 1840
Agamemnon and *Uliss*
Built   1829 BU 1840
Klitemnestra and *Penelopa*
Built   1829 Final fates are not known.

6 yawls transferred in 1830 from 'land authorities' (i.e. of not naval origin).
Dimensions approx. 40 ft x 11 ft x 3 ft (12.2 m x 3.4 m x 0.9 m)
Arnaut, *Pobeda*
BU 1839.
Nadezhda, *Sofiia*
BU 1838.
Boelesht, *Rokhovo*
Final fates are not known.

Caspian flotilla yawls (8 purpose-built)

8 yawls built at Kazan Admiralty in 1823. Final fates are not known.

Severnye (northern) vessels

These were small craft, used variously as troopships and tugs.

Baltic fleet (11 purpose-built)

11 16-oar, single-masted craft built at Gorodskaya Yard in St Petersburg.
Dimensions approx. 34 ft x 9.8 ft x 3.9 ft (10.4 m x 3 m x 1.2 m)
Armament 16 x 1pdr falconets
            17 men
No. 1
Launched 1777 BU 1792
No. 1 (second *No. 1*)
Launched 1780 BU 1803
No. 2
Launched 1780 BU 1801
No. 3
Launched 1780 Renamed *Serditoe* in 1788. BU after 1807.
No. 4
Launched 1780 Renamed *Burnoe* in 1788. BU 1801.
No. 5
Launched 1780 Renamed *Nepristupnoe* in 1788. BU 1801.
Nos 6, 7, 9, and *10*
Launched 1780 BU 1801
No. 8
Launched 1788 Final fate is unknown.

Caspian flotilla gardecotes

Small craft used exclusively on the Volga and its branches for protecting navigation and fishery. Administratively assigned to the Caspian Flotilla. In 1829 they were transferred to the Ministry of Communications. Gardecotes had lateen sails and one or two masts. All 18 gardecotes were built at Kazan.

Nos 1–9
Laid down 1797 *Launched* 1798

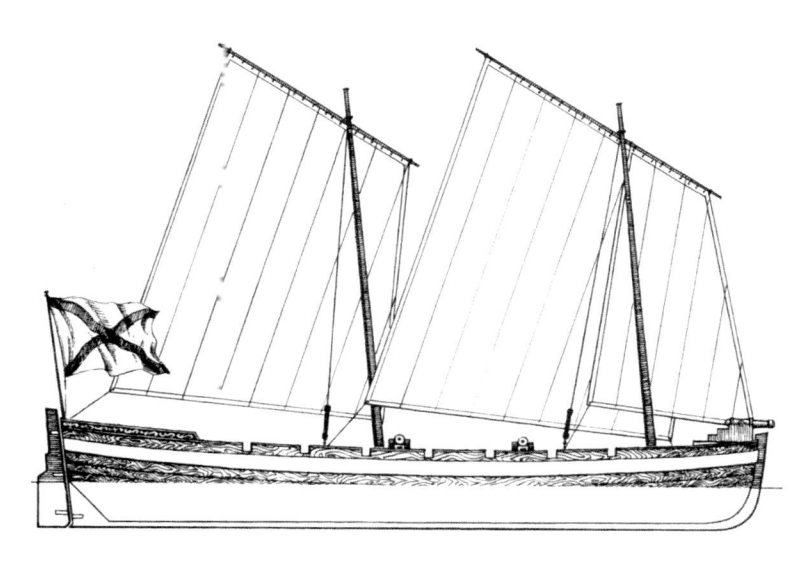

Taking their name from the French, gardecotes were built in limited numbers and served as patrol boats exclusively along the Volga. This boat is from the early 1800s and shows a lightly armed open vessel with two lateen rigged masts, a cannon mounted on the bow and a broadside of falconets suitable for anti-personnel use.

Dimensions approx. 34 ft x 9 ft x 3.9 ft (10.3 m x 2.8 m x 1.2 m (height of board))
Armament 1 gun several falconets
            14 oars
Listed till 1826–7. No. 7 was used by Alexander I for his trip from Stavropol to Samara.
Nos 10–12
Laid down 1804 *Launched* 1805
Dimensions approx. 34 ft x 9 ft x 3.9 ft (10.3 m x 2.8 m x 1.2 m (height of board))
Armament 1 gun, several falconets
            14 oars
Listed till 1826–9
Nos 13–18
Laid down 1823 *Launched* 1823
Dimensions approx. 32 ft x 10 ft x ? (9.8 m x 3 m x ? m
            12 oars)
Listed till 1826–9

Prams

Prams were shallow-draught quadrangular boxes with a single mast. They were used as stationary units for close inshore bombardment and for the defence of sea ports. They also served as strong points in galley battles, operating either on the flanks or at the centre of the line. Prams had to be towed at sea by galleys operating in pairs, with their single mast serving only for maintaining course and assisting in turns. Because of their unhandy construction, it was not unheard of for prams to drift ashore and beach themselves when anchored or even when under tow. In line with their intended roles, they were massively constructed to resist enemy gunfire. As a result of their rugged construction, they were highly resistant to fire and could not be readily set afire, even when they were being scuttled to avoid capture, as at Fridrikshamn on 4.5.1790. Prams were built in relatively small numbers in both the Baltic and the Black Sea, and successfully employed in most of the major conflicts. They began to be replaced by more handy, if less heavily armed and stoutly constructed, floating batteries towards the end of the eighteenthth century and were gone by the end of Paul I's reign.

Sea of Azov fleet prams (15 purpose-built)

In 1723, Peter I undertook the construction of 15 prams at Tavrov (near Voronezh) for the anticipated renewal of war with Turkey. As was the case with galleys and other craft laid down at the same time, the construction of these vessels was suspended, but not abandoned, in 1724, when a revised treaty was signed with Turkey. In 1735, with a renewal of war with Turkey imminent, work was resumed on the suspended vessels and all 15 were launched the same year. They were extensively and successfully employed for the bombardment of Azov in 1736 under the command of Vice-Admiral Bredal. By 1737 they were rotten and unserviceable and were broken up in 1738.

9 large prams were laid down at Tavrov in 1723, suspended in 1724, and finally launched in 1735. All 15, including the 6 small prams laid down concurrently, had to be beached in 1737 to avoid their sinking at their moorings. They were broken up in 1738.

Blizko Ne Podkhodi
Bombarded Azov on 10.6.1736, firing 766 rounds and having 1 wounded casualty. Bombarded Azov again on 7–18.6.1736 firing 1365 rounds with 3 wounded.

Grom i Molniia
Bombarded Azov on 14.6.1736, firing 720 rounds with casualties of 5 killed and 19 wounded.

Dikii Byk
Bombarded Azov on 9.6.1736, firing 422 rounds and having 1 wounded. Bombarded Azov again on 12-16.6.1736, firing 800 rounds, with 1 killed and 1 wounded. Bombarded Azov again on 17–18.6.1736, firing 745 rounds, with 2 killed and 3 wounded.

The Russian navy probably had more experience in the design, construction and deployment of inshore fire support craft of all types, sizes and varieties than any other sailing navy. This is the small 8-gun pram Blokha, *laid down in 1723 in preparation for Peter I's planned renewal of hostilities with the Ottoman Empire, but not launched until 1735 when war actually broke out. She and her seven sisters helped block the approaches to Azov in 1736 and were quickly disposed of after the successful resolution of the war had rendered them superfluous.*

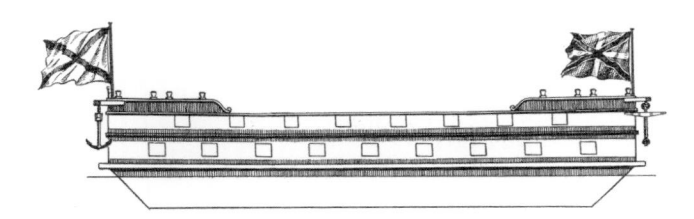

The pram Gektor *(Pram no. 1) seen here is one of five similar vessels suspended in construction between the end of the Russo-Turkish War of 1737–9 and the resumption of hostilities in 1768. As is evident from the drawing, prams were blockish and slab-sided, lacking in the most basic refinements for manoeuvring under their own power. They were, however, solidly built and nearly impervious to the artillery of the time.*

Neboiazlivyi
Bombarded Azov on 12–13.6.1736, firing 722 rounds, with 6 killed and 17 wounded.
Razgenevannyi
Bombarded Azov on 1–2.6.1736, firing 741 rounds, with 6 wounded.
Severnyi Medved'
Bombarded Azov on 1–2.6.1736, firing 778 rounds, with 2 wounded.
Serdityi
Bombarded Azov 2.6.1736.
Spiashchii Lev
Bombarded Azov 14.6.1736, firing 885 rounds, with 6 killed and 17 wounded.
Strashnyi
Bombarded Azov on 1–2.6.1736, firing 661 rounds, with 1 killed.

6 small 8-gun prams were laid down at Tavrov in 1723, suspended in 1724, and launched in 1735. In 1736 they were used to block the approaches to Azov. All were broken up in 1738.
Blokha, Klop, Komar, Ovod, Sverchok, Tarakan.
Dimensions approx. 69 ft x 19 ft x 3.3 ft (21 m x 5.8 m x 1 m)

5 prams were laid down at Ikoretskaia in 1738 to replace those built between 1723 and 1735. Their construction was suspended until they were completed by S. I. Afanasiev for the coming war with Turkey. All had been originally assigned numbers, but they were given proper names on commissioning.

Pram no. 1 (*Gektor*), **Pram no. 2** (*Parizh*), **Pram no. 3** (*Lefeb*), **Pram no. 4** (*Elen'*), **Pram no. 5** (*Troil*)
Laid down 1738 Launched 1769
Stationed in the Don in 1770–1. Broken up after 1771.

Dnieper flotilla prams (3 purpose-built)

3 small prams were built at Bryansk yard for the Dnieper flotilla. They were laid down and suspended in 1726 and finally launched in 6.1737. By 1738 they had only reached the Samara River, where further progress was prevented by shallow water rapids. BU after 1739.
Dimensions approx. 60 ft x 20 ft x ? (18.3 m x 6.1 m x ? m)

2 large 44-gun prams were built at Bryansk for the Dnieper flotilla. All were launched in 1737, but were unable to negotiate the Dnieper and returned to Kiev as floating batteries. BU after 1739.

Baltic prams (19 purpose-built)

2 prams were built at St Petersburg in 1706 and formally designated as prams *nos 1* and *2*. Although they were known at the time as *Arcke de Verbondes* and *Arkanne*, these names were never officially assigned.

Arcke des Verbondes (*no. 1*) St Petersburg, Admiralty
Constructor V. Gerens
Launched 29.4.1706
Dimensions approx. 80 ft x 26 ft x 5.9 ft (24.4 m x 7.9 m x 1.8 m)
Armament 18 x 12 and 18pdrs
BU 1710.

Arkanne (*no. 2*) St Petersburg, Admiralty (?)
Constructor V. Gerens
Launched 27.5.1706
Dimensions approx. 80 ft x 26 ft x 5.9 ft (24.4 m x 7.9 m x 1.8 m)
Armament 18 x 12 and 18pdrs
BU 1710.

Buivol (*Boul*) St Petersburg, Admiralty
Constructor V. Graf
Laid down 28.1.1710 *Launched* 1710
BU 1719 at Revel'.

Byk (*Oss*) St Petersburg, Admiralty
Constructor V. Graf
Laid down 28.1.1710 *Launched* 1710
Armament 18 guns
BU 1721 at Revel'.

3 prams built at St Petersburg, Admiralty by F. M. Sklyaev.
Dimensions approx. 110 ft x 35 ft x 10.1 ft (33.6 m x 10.7 m x 3.1 m)
Armament 18 guns
          70 men.

Dikii Byk (*Auroks, Wilde Boul*)
Launched 1.1713 BU after 1719

Dumkrat
Launched 1713 Final fate is unknown.

Medved' (*Ber*)
Launched 1713 BU after 1719

Olifant St Petersburg, Admiralty (?)
Constructor F. M. Sklyaev
Laid down 20.1.1717 *Launched* 7.5.1718
Dimensions approx. 116 ft x 35 ft x 2.9 ft (35.4 m x 10.7 m x 9 m)
Armament 40 guns
          130 men
Name taken from Swedish prize captured at Gangut in 1714. BU 1724.

2 prams built at Olonetsk by V. Fogel.
Medved', Dikii Byk
Launched 1727 BU circa 1739

2 prams built at St Petersburg, Admiralty by D. Sutherland.
Dimensions approx. 115 ft x 34 ft x 9.5 ft (35.2 m x 10.4 m x 2.9 m)
Armament 24 x 12 and 24pdr guns
Olifant
Laid down 27.6.1739 *Launched* 20.6.1740
On 20.5.1743 participated in the galley battle off Korpo Island and received 20 hits in the hull, with 3 killed and 7 wounded. BU after 1750 at Kronshtadt.

Dikii Byk
Laid down 27.6.1739 *Launched* 20.6.1740
On 20.5.1743 participated in the galley battle off Korpo Island and received 39 hits in the hull, 3 killed and 2 wounded. BU 1755 at Kronshtadt.

5 36-gun prams.
Dimensions approx. 115 ft x 36 ft x 9.8 ft (35.2 m x 10.9 m x 3 m)
Armament 18 x 36pdrs, 18 x 18pdrs

Olifant (from 1759 *Buivol*)
Laid down in St Petersburg, Admiralty by D. Sutherland, in 1751 and launched on 23.9.1752. Bombarded Memel in 1757. Grounded on 10.1757. Repaired in 1759–60. Broken up at Kronshtadt in 1765.

Dikii Byk
Laid down at Olonetskayayard by P. G. Kachalov in 1753 and launched in 1754. Bombarded Memel in 1757. Broken up at Kronshtadt in 1767.

Olifant
Laid down at St Petersburg, Admiralty by Selyaninov on 27.11.1757 and launched on 26.6.1758. Refitted in 1768 as a salvage ship for capsized and sunken ships.

Olifant
Laid down at Serdobol' Yard by Klimov and Skuvarov on 27.2.1774. Broken up at Kronshtadt in 1785.

Serdobol'
Laid down at Serdobol' Yard by Klimov and Skuvarov on 27.2.1774. Broken up at Kronshtadt in 1785.

2 38-gun prams:
Dimensions approx. 120 ft x 35 ft x 9.5 ft (36.6 m x 10.7 m x 2.9 m)
Armament 18 x 30pdrs, 20 x 12pdrs

Gremiashchii
Laid down at Galley Yard in St Petersburg by S. Durakin on 9.12.1785 and launched on 16.10.1786. Broken up at Kronshtadt before 1805.

Lev
Laid down at Lodeynoe Pole by Rogachev on 5.9.1788 and launched on 5.5.1789. Broken up before 1805.

Baltic half-prams (6 purpose-built)

Leopard Olonetskaya
Constructor M. Protopopov
Laid down 30.12.1772 *Launched* 13.5.1773
Dimensions approx. 100 ft x 30 ft x 5.9 ft (30.5 m x 9.2 m x 1.8 m)
Armament 16 guns
BU 1780.

Bars St Petersburg, Admiralty
Constructor ?
Laid down 24.10.1788 *Launched* 11.5.1789
Dimensions approx. 100'x 30 ft x 7.2 ft (30.5 m x 9.2 m x 2.2 m)
Armament 18 x 24pdrs, 9 x 6pdrs, 7 x 3pdrs
Sustained heavy damage at Fridrikshamn on 4.5.1790. Unsuccessfully set on fire by her crew and captured by Sweden.

Leopard St Petersburg, Admiralty
Constructor?
Laid down 24.10.1788 *Launched* 15.5.1789
Dimensions approx. 108 ft x 33 ft x 6.9 ft (32.9m x 10.1m x 2.1m)

Armament 18 x 24pdrs, 9 x 6pdrs, 7 x 3pdrs
Sustained heavy damage at Fridrikshamn on 4.5.1790. Unsuccessfully set on fire by her crew and captured by Sweden.

3 half-prams.
Dimensions approx. 110 ft x 33 ft x 7.9 ft (33.6 m x 10.1 m x 2.4 m)
Armament 18 x 18pdrs, 10 x 6pdrs, 14 x 3pdrs
Lev, Tigr St Petersburg, Admiralty
Constructor A. I. Melikhov
Laid down 5.12.1790 *Launched* 16.9.1791 Hulked in 1804.
Olonets
Laid down 3.4.1791 *Launched* 29.7.1791 BU 1803.

Floating batteries

Floating batteries were developed in the 1790s to supplement and replace the larger and more heavily armed prams. As was the case with prams, they were shallow-draught vessels; but, in contrast, they were tapered fore and aft, without the squared off blunt ends of the earlier vessels. They still lacked the capacity to manoeuvre at sea without the assistance of galleys, although they were much easier to handle under sail or anchored on station. Early floating batteries had a single mast, but later vessels had a square mast forward and two lateen rigged masts amidships and aft, giving them some capacity for independent movement. The first floating batteries were limited to broadside batteries of 36pdrs, but later ships had guns on pivots, and sometimes carried 2–4 mortars in addition to their regular batteries.

Baltic floating batteries (60 purpose-built)

3 floating batteries laid down and launched at Kronshtadt by Kutygin in 1790.
Dimensions approx. 106 ft x 31 ft x 7.5 ft (32.3 m x 9.5 m x 2.3 m)
Armament 8 x 36pdrs
    128 men
No. 1 Lost at the 2nd battle of Rochensalm on 28.6.1790. 12 crewmen saved.
No. 2 Lost at the 2nd battle of Rochensalm on 28.6.1790. 11 crewmen saved.
No. 3 Renamed *Nepobedimaia*. Destroyed in the disastrous fire at the Galley Port on 25.5.1796.

~

4 floating batteries *Laid down* in 1790 at the Galley Port and launched in 1791.
Dimensions approx. 70 ft x 25 ft x 6.6 ft (21.4 m x 7.6 m x 2 m)
Armament 4 guns
    83 men

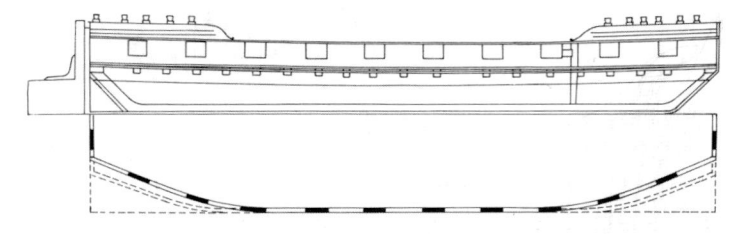

A floating battery of 1789. Although far from elegant in their lines, their smaller size and tapered ends made these gunships easier to handle in transit and while anchored in action against shore batteries and fortresses than the earlier prams.

Bars
BU 1798
Krokodil
BU 1798
Lev
1798
Tigr
BU 1798

~

12 floating batteries built at St Petersburg, Lodeynoe Pole and Riga by S. Durakin, Pospelov and D. Masalskiy. All were laid down and launched in 1791.
Dimensions approx. 96 ft x 28 ft x 6.5 ft (29.3 m x 8.4 m x 2 m)
Armament 7 guns, 2 howitzers
    109 men
Vitebsk, Dvina, Mogilev, Riga, Volga, Svir', Strela
Last mentioned 1798.
Vuoksa, Dnieper, Don, Molniia, Neva
BU 1800

~

2 bombardment batteries laid down and launched at Galley Yard in 1791 by D. Masalskiy.
Dimensions approx. 96 ft x 28 ft x 6.5 ft (29.3 m x 8.4 m x 2 m)
Armament 4 mortars and howitzers
Grom, Strashnaya
BU 1800.

~

Nepobedimaia St Petersburg, Admiralty
Constructor Gorodskaya
Laid down 1796 *Launched* 1797
Dimensions approx. 96 ft x 28 ft x 6.5 ft (29.3 m x 8.4 m x 2 m)
Armament 7 guns
Destroyed by fire and explosion on 28.1.1797 without casualties. Wreck BU 1800.

~

6 bombardment batteries built at Lodeynoe Pole by Pospelov. All laid down and launched in 1798.
Dimensions approx. 88 ft x 30 ft x 7.2 ft (26.8 m x 9.2 m x 2.2 m)
Armament 2 guns
No. 1 BU 1808
No. 2 BU 1814
No. 3 BU 1807
No. 4 BU 1807
No. 5 BU 1807
No. 6 BU 1807

~

23 floating batteries built at Lodeynoe Pole by Pospelov. All laid down and launched in 1798.
Dimensions approx. 96 ft x 28 ft x 6.5 ft (29.3 m x 8.4 m x 2 m)
Armament 7 guns
No. 1 BU 1811.
Nos 2, 3, 4, 5, 17, 19, 20 and *23* BU 1814.
No. 6 BU 1808.
No. 7 BU 1806.
No. 8 BU 1804.
Nos 9, 11, 14, 15, 16, 18 BU 1813.
No. 10 BU 1803.
No. 12 BU 1815.
No. 13 BU 1802.
Nos 21 and *22* BU 1819.

~

Drakon St Petersburg, Admiralty
Constructor A. I. Melikhov
Laid down ?   *Launched* 1807
Dimensions approx. 79 ft x 24, x 6.5 ft (24 m x 7.3 m x 2 m)
Armament 7 guns
BU 1819.

Edinorog St Petersburg, Admiralty
Constructor A. I. Melikhov
Laid down ?   *Launched* 1807
Dimensions approx. 88 ft x 27 ft x7.5 ft (26.8 m x 8.2 m x 2.3 m)
Armament 7 guns
BU 1819.

4 3-masted floating batteries built at St Petersburg, Admiralty by I. V. Kurepanov (first pair) and Pamfilov (second pair):
Dimensions approx. 96 ft x 27.5 ft x 69 ft (29.3 m x 8.4 m x 2.1 m)
Armament 7 guns
No. 1
Laid down 9.1.1808   *Launched* 18.6.1808 BU 1821.
No. 2
Laid down 9.1.1808   *Launched* 18.6.1808 BU 1822.
Nos 3 and *4*
Laid down 25.1.1808   *Launched* 3.7.1809 BU 1822

2 floating batteries built at Lodeynoe Pole by I. V. Kurepanov
Armament 7 guns
Nos 12 and *13*
Laid down 28.8.182   *Launched* 7.1822 Final fate is unknown.

Gremiashchaia St Petersburg, Admiralty
Constructor A. Kh. Shaumburg
Laid down: 30.4.1834   *Launched* 7.10.1834
Dimensions 87 ft (pp) x 27 ft (inside plank) x 7.2 ft (26.6 m (pp) x 8.2 m (inside plank) x 2.2 m)
Armament 7 guns
Last mentioned 1845.

Black Sea floating batteries (1 purpose-built)

Unnamed Kherson
Constructor M. I. Surovtsev
Laid down 10.7.1804   *Launched* 14.7.1806
Dimensions approx. 150 ft x 30 ft x 9.5 ft (45.8 m x 9.2 m x 2.9 m)
Armament 7 guns
Last mentioned 1809.

White Sea floating batteries (4 purpose-built)

4 14-gun floating batteries were built at Solombala, intended for the defence of Arkhangelsk against the British. All laid down 4.1.1808 and launched 29.4.1808

Floating batteries converted from other ships

Converted Baltic floating batteries (7 converted)
4 ex-shebecks converted in 1792. Destroyed in the catastrophic fire in the Galley Port on 25.5.1796.
Pobezhdaiushchaia (ex-*Letuchaia*)
Krepkaia (ex-*Skoraia*)
Khrabraia (ex-*Legkaia*)
Svirepaia (ex-*Bystraia*)

3 ex-secret ships converted in 1792. Destroyed in the catastrophic fire in the Galley Port on 25.5.1796:
Nepristupnaia (ex-*Ostorozhnoe*)
Porazhaiushchaia (ex-*Nastupatel'noe*)
Oboronitel'naia (ex-*Okhranitel'noe*)

Converted Black Sea floating batteries (1 converted)
1 converted from a store-ship in 1787. Grounded and lost off Ochakov on 4.10.1787.

Converted Dnieper floating batteries (6 converted)
6 floating batteries converted in 1788 from store ships used by Catherine II during her prewar navigation of the Dnieper river.
Nos 1–6
All were converted a second time to transports in 1790.

Bomb Cutters

Bomb cutters were oar-powered bomb vessels armed variously with 2 x 3-pood howitzers or 2 x 2-pood edinorogs, 4 x 12pdr or 4 x 6pdr cannon, and with falconets for close-in defence. They were sometimes armed with mortars instead of howitzers or edinorogs.

Baltic Bomb cutters (8 purpose-built)

4 unnamed 22-oar vessels built at Galley Yard by Pospelov in 1788.
Dimensions approx. 57 ft x 21 ft x 6.5 ft (17.3 m x 6.3 m x 2 m)
Armament 2 x 3-pood howitzers, 4 light edinorogs, 10 falconets
76 men (inc. 44 soldiers-oarsmen)
The first three were lost during the 2nd battle of Rochensalm on 28.6.1790. (the number of rescued crewmen were respectively 27, 21 and 2). No. 4 was renamed *Gekla* in 1791. Last mentioned in 1791.

4 2-masted 20-oar vessels built at St Petersburg, Admiralty by A. M. Kurochkin.
Dimensions approx. 69 ft x 25 ft x 7.5 ft (20.9 m x 7.6 m x 2.3 m)
Armament 6 guns
Gremiashchii
Laid down 24.1.1792   *Launched* 17.6.1792
Last mentioned 1803.
Nepobedimyi
Laid down 24.1.1792   *Launched* 27.6.1793
Last mentioned 1801.
Etna
Laid down 28.1.1793   *Launched* 26.10.1794
BU after 1802.
Sopka
Laid down 28.1.1793   *Launched* 26.10.1794
BU after 1805.

Black Sea bomb cutters (10 purpose-built)

No. 7 (renamed *Ksenofont*) Kremenchug
Constructor Toroshilov
Laid down 1788   *Launched* 1788
Dimensions approx. 55 ft x 18 ft x 5.9 ft (16.8m x 5.5m x 1.8)
Armament one 5-pood mortar, 4 x 6pdrs

In 1790, employed in the bombardment of Izmail on the Danube. Last mentioned 1795.

No. 8 (renamed *Kir*) Kremenchug
Constructor Toroshilov.
Laid down 1788   *Launched* 1788
Dimensions approx. 60 ft x 17 ft x 7.2 ft (18.3 m x 5.3 m x 2.2 m)
Armament 6 guns.
In 1790, employed in the bombardment of Izmail on the Danube. Last mentioned 1795.

Aleksandr Kherson
Constructor S. I. Afanasyev.
Laid down 1788   *Launched* 1788
Dimensions 56 ft x 19 ft x 6.5 ft (17.1 m x 5.8 m x 2 m)
Armament 6 guns
Last mentioned 1798.

Andrei Kherson
Constructor S. I. Afanasyev
Laid down 1788   *Launched* 1788
Dimensions approx. 42 ft x 17 ft x 5.2 (12.8 m x 5.3 m x 1.6 m)
Armament 6 guns
Final fate is unknown.

Grigorii Kherson
Constructor S. I. Afanasyev
Laid down 1788   *Launched* 1788
Dimensions approx. 78 ft x 20 ft x 4.9 ft (23.8 m x 6.1 m x 1.5 m)
Armament 6 guns
Last mentioned 1794.

Kirill Kherson
Constructor S. I. Afanasyev
Laid down 1788   *Launched* 1788
Dimensions approx. 56 ft x 21 ft x 6.9 ft (17.1 m x 6.4 m x 2.1 m)
Armament 6 guns
Last mentioned 1798.

Nikifor Kherson
Constructor S. I. Afanasyev
Laid down 1788   *Launched* 1788
Dimensions approx. 56 ft x 18 ft x 7.5 ft (17.1 m x 5.6 m x 2.3 m)
Armament 6 guns
Last mentioned 1794.

Stepan (or *Stefaniy*) Kherson
Constructor S. I. Afanasyev
Laid down 1788   *Launched* 1788
Dimensions approx. 60 ft x 17 ft x 7.2 ft (18.3 m x 5.3 m x 2.2 m)
Armament 6 guns
Last mentioned 1797.

Khristofor Kherson
Constructor S. I. Afanasyev
Laid down 1788   *Launched* 1788
Dimensions approx. 45 ft x 17 ft x 5.9 ft (13.7 m x 5.2 m x 1.8 m)
Armament 6 guns
BU 1804.

Grom Galats
Constructor ?
Laid down 1791   *Launched* 1791
Dimensions approx. 56 ft x 17 ft x 7.9 ft (17.1 m x 5.2 m x 2.4 m)
Armament one 5-pood mortar, 4 x 6pdrs
Last mentioned 1798.

Section III
Russian Naval Auxiliaries

Russian Naval Auxiliaries

Owing to its enormous geographical extent and wide range of littoral and climatic conditions, the Russian navy operated a very wide range of fleet auxiliaries. Square and lateen (fore-and-aft) rigged vessels were fairly evenly distributed in all theatres from Okhotsk to the Black Sea, and the variety of names assigned to the various types reflected both their northern European and Mediterranean origins. A few categories, such as the pinks and galiots, could be found in both northern and southern fleets and flotillas; but a much greater diversity of types could be found in the Baltic and its ancillaries than in the Black Sea and Sea of Azov. Most ship types had fairly short periods of production and employment with the fleet, but galiots and buers both surpassed the century mark, lasting well into the nineteenth century. Excluding the nearly 4,000 strugs from consideration for obvious reasons, the total number of all known auxiliaries found in the various regional navies during the period from 1696–1860 was 1195. This figure included 920 purpose-built vessels, 101 ships purchased from foreign and domestic sources, 87 prizes turned to logistical uses and a variety of other acquisitions also numbering 87.

Various approaches for organizing and classifying Russian naval auxiliaries suggest themselves – geographical distribution, styles of rigging, number built, average dimensions – but the approach taken here has been simply to list the various types in the chronological order of appearance, without regard to numbers, distribution, or classification. The inevitable exception to this sequential approach may be found in the miscellaneous listing at the end of the section, which includes a number of types produced in insignificant numbers, some highly specialized designs, and the catch-all category of 'cargo ships'.

Strugs (approx. 3,888 purpose-built)

Strugs were flat-bottomed square rigged open decked sailing and rowing vessels with antecedents tracing back to the 6th century. Traditionally, they had been used by Eastern Slavic peoples on rivers and lakes for the transportation of cargo and people. By the seventeenth century, they were of 60–150 feet in length and 12–30 feet in width with 20–24 oars. They were often covered with wooden roofs and with cabins for high officials and could carry from 2 to 4 light cannon and 60–80 men.

Strugs were used on a large scale by Peter I during the Azov expeditions of 1695–6. For the initial assault on Azov in 1695, they were used to transport 30,000 Russian troops with their equipment the entire length of the Don from Voronezh to the Sea of Azov – a journey of 540 miles. 1,260 and 1,300 units were said to have been built in each year. An additional 600 were built for the siege of the fortress of Narva in 1704.

Based on a very strict interpretation of the parameters of this work, those strugs completed prior to the formal creation of the Russian Imperial Navy in 1696 should be excluded, since some were completed in preparation for the siege of Azov as early as 1694. For the sake of complete coverage and because it is impossible to separate out the earlier strugs from those built in 1696 and later, we are waiving our own time constraints as we did with *Oryol* of 1668 in the Caspian and *Sviatoe Prochestvo* of 1694 in the Baltic.

Sea of Azov fleet strugs (3105 purpose-built)

27 were built at Preobrazhenskaya in 1695.

712 were built at Voronezh in 1694–6.

967 were built at Kozlovskaya in 1694–6.

744 were built at Sokolskaya in 1694–8.

565 were built at Dobroyskaya in 1694–8.

30 were built at Pyatiizbenskaya in 1695–6.

30 were built at Rinanovskaya in 1695–6.

30 were built at Savitskaya in 1695–6.

Baltic fleet strugs (approx. 783 purpose-built)

182 were built a Novgorod in 1702–3.
Employed in the siege of Noteburg ('Nut Castle', in Russian *Oreshek*, hard nut).

About 600 were built at Luga in 1701–3 for the siege of Narva in 1704.

Moskvoretskii
Dimensions   approx. 138 ft x 22 ft x ? (42 m x 6.6 m x ?)
                 18 oars

The name means literally 'Of Moscow River' to reflect the fact that it was built in 1722 on the Moscow River. Built specially for the use of Peter I and his family. Used by them in 1722 for a trip along the Moscow, Oka and Volga rivers to Astrakhan'. Preserved for some time at Astrakhan'. Final fate is not known.

Galiots (72 purpose-built, 14 purchased and 21 prizes)

Galiot derives from the French galiote and refers to a class of small, handy, square-rigged cargo vessels with two, and very occasionally three, masts. They were used for the transportation of cargo and, very occasionally, troops, hydrographic work, expeditions of exploration, and as avisos. Galiots continued in service with the Russian fleet until the 1820s.

Baltic fleet galiots (26 purpose-built)

3 galiots built at Olonets.
Dimensions   approx. 57 ft x 15 ft x 5 ft (17.3 m x 4.6 m x 1.5 m)

Armament 6 x 3pdrs

Kur'er
Constructors V. Gerens and Y. Kol
Laid down 5.1703 *Launched* 22.7.1703.
Last mentioned in 1710.

Sol
Constructor Y. Kol
Laid down 21.5.1703 *Launched* 8.8.1703
Mentioned only in 1703.

Pocht-galiot
Constructor Y. Kol
Laid down 5.1703 *Launched* 15.8.1703
Last mentioned in 1707.

Kars-Maker St Petersburg
Laid down ? *Launched* 1723
The private galiot of Peter I until his death. To Kiel in 1727. To Danzig in 1733, where she was captured by the French in 5.1734. Recaptured on 18.6.1734. Wrecked off Revel' on 10.9.1734.

Gogland Novoladozhskaya
Laid down ? *Launched* 1720
From 1730–3 Carried cargo between Baltic ports. Visited Kiel in 1731. In 5.1734 she was captured by the French off Danzig. Recaptured on 18.6.1734. Carried cargo and inspected lighthouses from 1734–8. Wrecked en route to Stockholm on 5.10.1743.

Elenora Novoladozhskaya
Laid down ? *Launched* 1730
From 1730–3 Carried cargo between Baltic ports. To Copenhagen in 1732. Last mentioned in 1737 as bound for France.

Aleksandra Novoladozhskaya
Laid down ? *Launched* 1731
From 1731–4 Carried cargo between Baltic ports. To Danzig in 1734.

Vologda Bykovskaya
Laid down 1734 *Launched* 24.5.1734
Remained at Arkhangel'sk. Last mentioned there in 1741.

Olonets Novoladozhskaya
Laid down 1740 *Launched* 8.1741
From 1742–4 Carried cargo between Baltic ports. Wrecked en route to Stockholm on 23.9.1744.

Rak
Laid down ? *Launched* 1750
From 1751–6 Carried cargo between Baltic ports. Carried naval supplies to Pomerania in 1757–9 in support of the siege of Memel. Stationed in the Baltic from 1764–6. Stricken in 1770.

Cherepakha
Laid down ? *Launched* 1750
Stationed in the Baltic 1754-56. Aviso for the Russian squadron 1758–0. Post vessel to Lubeck in 1760. To Kolberg and Pillau in 1761–2.

Kronshlot
Laid down ? *Launched* 1766
Stationed in the Baltic 1766–76. To Copenhagen with Adm. Spiridov's squadron in 1769.

Kronshtadt
Laid down ? *Launched* 1766
Stationed in the Baltic 1766–84. To Copenhagen with Adm. Spiridov's squadron in 1769. Wrecked on 17.8.1784.

Strel'na
Laid down ? *Launched* 1766
Stationed in the Baltic 1766–73. Wrecked on 14.9.1773.

Tsitadel'
Laid down ? *Launched* 1766
Stationed in the Baltic 1766–88.

Fyodor Gorodskaya
Laid down ? *Launched* 1790
Carried cargo between Baltic ports from 1791–4. Wrecked on 10.10.1794.

Perfilii Gorodskaya
Laid down ? *Launched* 1790
Carried cargo between Baltic ports from 1791–6. Stranded due to leaks on 11.11.1796.

7 galiots were built at the Kazan Admiralty in 1797 and transferred to the Baltic where they were assigned to the rowing flotilla. BU 1806–12 at St Petersburg, Kronshtadt, Sveaborg and Abo.

Sviatoi Iakov Galley Yard, St Petersburg
Laid down 1798 *Launched* 1799
Carried cargo between Baltic ports from 1800–6. Wrecked on 31.7.1806.

Aleksandr Galley Yard, St Petersburg
Laid down 1798 *Launched* 1799
Carried cargo between Baltic Ports 1800–10. Foundered in 1810.

Purchased Baltic galiots (14 purchased)

Yunge-Piter
Purchased in 1719. Carried supplies for the Baltic squadron in 1719–20. Hydrographic work from 1720–3.

Tonein
Purchased in 1720. Participated in the transfer of Princess Ann and her husband, the Duke of Holstein, to Kiel in 7–9.1727. Returned in company with ships under the command of Adm. Bredal with the body of the Princess from Kiel to Kronshtadt. Transported horses from Kiel in 1731. Carried cargo in the Baltic from 1732–3. To Stockholm in 1737. BU after 1739.

Nikolai Purchased 1803
Dimensions approx. 61 ft x 23 ft x 11 ft (18.6 m x 7 m x 3.4 m)
Carried cargo in the Baltic. BU 1805.

Sviatoi Nikolei Purchased 1805
Dimensions approx. 86 ft x 26 ft x 11 ft (26.2 m x 7.9 m x 3.4 m)
Wrecked off Revel' on 28.9.1806.

Vasilii
Purchased in 1806. Carried cargo in the Baltic 1806–10. BU 1811 at Revel'.

Grigorii
Purchased in 1806. Carried cargo in the Baltic 1806–10. BU 1811 at Revel'.

Kuz'ma
Purchased in 1806. Carried cargo in the Baltic 1806–10. BU 1811 at Revel'.

Mikhail
Purchased in 1806. Carried cargo in the Baltic 1806–10. BU 1811 at Revel'.

Nikolai, Iakov, Ioann
All three purchased in 1806. Carried cargo in the Baltic from 1806–10. BU 1811 at Revel'.

Anna
Purchased in 1814. Carried cargo in the Baltic. BU at Sveaborg in 1821.

Ioann
Purchased in 1814. Grounded and wrecked in a storm on 19.9.1814.

Filipp
Purchased in 1814. Carried cargo in the Baltic 1814–20. BU at Rochensalm in 1822.

Baltic galiot prizes (16 prizes)

Aleksandr, Prorok Daniil
Swedish prizes, captured at Narva on 9.8.1704. Participated in the expedition to Vyborg on 5.1710.

Mozas, Santa Anna, Sviatoi Pyotr, Yungfrau Mariia
Swedish prizes, captured at Narva on 9.8.1704. Participated in the expeditions to Vyborg on 5.1710 and 5.1712.

Elenora
Swedish prize captured by A. Reys off Pomerania in 1712. Last mentioned as having arrived at Revel' in 1712.

Elizabet-Ekaterina
Dutch smuggler, captured in 7.1719.

Anna-Mariia
Swedish prize captured in 1743. Numerous trips to Stockholm, Danzig, Konigsberg, Kolberg, and Pillau from 1746–62.

Merkurius
Swedish prize captured in 1743 at Danzig. Foundered *en route* to Kronshtadt on 21.8.1743.

Yunge-Tobias
Prussian prize, captured in 1757 by frigate *Arkhangel Mikhail* off Drako Island. Fire watch duty at Revel' from 1758–61 combined with cargo service in the Baltic from 1758–71. Wrecked on 28.10.1771 off Hogland.

No. 1, No. 2
Prussian prizes, taken in 1760 at Kolberg. Carried cargo in the Baltic. Final fate is indeterminate.

No. 3
Prussian prize, taken in 1760 at Kolberg. Carried cargo in the Baltic 1764–8 Grounded 4.9.1768 at Odensholm. Cargo was recovered and the galiot was later BU.

No. 4
Prussian prize taken in 1760 at Kolberg. Fire watch duties at Revel' 1762–3.

Sviatoi Ioann
Swedish prize taken 22.6.1790 in the Bay of Vyborg. Carried cargo in the Baltic 1790–1806. Driven ashore in bad weather on 27.9.1806.

Sea of Azov fleet galiots (11 purpose-built)

Eleven vessels were built at Voronezh and launched in 1699. They left Voronezh for Azov in 1699. Flat-bottomed with a single mast and 17–23 banks of oars, they were very similar to the galleys of the period.

Black Sea fleet galiots (10 purpose-built)

4 galiots were built at the Don and Khoper rivers (2 at Novopavlovskaya and 2 at Novokhoperskaya). Prior to 1783, they were formally assigned to the Azov Flotilla.
Dimensions   approx. 80 ft x 22 ft x 11.5 ft (24.4 m x 6.7 m x 3.5 m)
Armament   6 guns
Buivol
Laid down   2.1773   Launched 1774
To Istanbul from 1775–6. To Black Sea ports from 1777–83.
Verbliud
Laid down   2.1773   Launched 1774
Carried cargo from 1774–87. Converted into bomb vessel *Aleksei* in 1788. (See under Black Sea bomb vessels.)
Osel
Laid down   2.1773   Launched 1774
Carried cargo from 1775–86.
Slon
Laid down   2.1773   Launched 1774
Carried cargo from 1774–87. Wrecked on 18.10.1787.

~

6 galiots were built on the Don and Khoper rivers (2 at Novopavlovskaya and 2 at Novokhoperskaya and 2 at Gnilotonskaya).
Dimensions   approx. 80 ft x 23 ft x 11 ft (24.4 m x 7.3 m x 3.4 m)
Drofa
Laid down   1778   Launched 1779
Carried cargo from 1779–86.
Lebed'
Laid down   1778   Launched 1779
Carried cargo from 1779–86. Wrecked off Akkerman on 16.12.1786.
Tarantul
Laid down   1778   Launched 1779
Carried cargo from 1779–87. Converted into the bomb vessel *Sviatoi Pyotr* at the end of 1788. (See under Black Sea bomb vessels.)
Tsaplia
Laid down   1778   Launched 1779
Carried cargo from 1779–87. Converted into the bomb vessel *Filipp* at the end of 1788. (See under Black Sea bomb vessels.)
Donets
Laid down   1782   Launched 1783
Carried cargo from 1783–5. Wrecked off Ialta on 22.2.1785.

Temernik
Laid down 1782 *Launched* 1783
Carried cargo from 1783–7. Converted into the bomb vessel *Iona* at the end of 1788. (See under Black Sea bomb vessels where she is listed as *Te'ermol.*)

Caspian flotilla galiots (12 purpose-built)

Twelve galiots built at the Kazan Admiralty.
Laid down 1796 *Launched* 1797
No. 1
Carried cargo from 1798–1808. Landed troops at Enzeli and Baku in 1805. Engaged in hydrographic work off Astrakhan' in 1809.
No. 2
Carried cargo from 1798–1804. Stationed at Astrakhan' from 1805–8.
No. 3
Carried cargo from 1798–1802. Landed troops at Enzeli in 1805.
No. 4
Carried cargo from 1798–1801. At Baku in 1804. Cruised off the Persian coast in 1805–6.
No. 5
Carried cargo from 1798–1802. At Astrakhan' in 1803–4. Landed troops at Enzeli on 22.6.1805. Wrecked off Enzeli on 24.6.1805.
No. 6
Carried cargo from 1797–1802. Final fate is indeterminate.
No. 7
Carried cargo from 1798-1802. Operated off Persia and Baku in 1803–4. Landed troops at Enzeli in 1805. Wrecked at Lenkoran in 9.1806.
No. 8
Carried cargo from 1798–1802. Operated off Persia from 1803–10.
No. 9
Carried cargo from 1798–1802. Operated off Persia from 1803–5.
No. 10
Carried cargo from 1798–1802. Landed troops at Enzeli in 1805.
No. 11
Carried cargo from 1798–1802. Final fate is indeterminate.
No. 12
Carried cargo from 1798–1806. Operated off Persia from 1804–6.

Danube flotilla galiot prizes (5 prizes)

Peremierenosets
Turkish prize, captured in 1771 on the Danube. Operated from Izmail in the Sea of Azov and the Black Sea from 1772–4.

No. 2
Turkish prize, captured in 1771 on the Danube. Stationed at the mouth of the Danube from 1772–4.

No. 3
Turkish prize, captured in 1771 on the Danube. Stationed at the mouth of the Danube from 1772–3.

No. 4
Turkish prize, captured in 1771 on the Danube. Operated from Izmail in the Sea of Azov and the Black Sea from 1772–4.

No. 5
Turkish prize, captured on the Danube in 1771 and renamed *Danube* in 1775. Assigned to the Azov Flotilla in 1775 and to the Black Sea fleet in 1783. Operated from Izmail in the Sea of Azov and the Black Sea from 1772–84.

No. 6
Dimensions approx. 35 ft x 15 ft x 6 ft (10.7 m x 4.6 m x 1.9 m)
Turkish prize. Captured in 1771 on the Danube. Operated from Izmail in the Sea of Azov and the Black Sea from 1772–4. Foundered off Ochakov due to leaks on 12.11.1774.

Okhotsk flotilla galiots (13 purpose-built)

Okhotsk Okhotsk
Constructor M. Rogachev
Laid down ? *Launched* 1739
Wrecked on 24.10.1748.

Zakharii Okhotsk
Constructor Zakharov
Laid down ? *Launched* 9.1755
Wrecked on 25.10.1766.

Sviatoi Pavel Okhotsk
Constructor Zakharov
Laid down 1757 *Launched* 9.07.1758
Operated in the Sea of Okhotsk and Pacific in 1758–67. Wrecked off Harimkotan Island in the Kuriils on 8.1.1767 while on an expedition to Alaska with *Sviatoi Ekaterina* (see below). 30 men lost out of 43.

Sviataia Ekaterina Okhotsk
Constructor Zakharov
Laid down ? *Launched* 1761
Carried cargo in 1761–3. Participated in company with *Sviatoi Pavel* (see above) on an ill-fated expedition under naval officers P. K. Krenitsyn and M. D. Levasov to locate the mouth of the Lena River in Siberia and to survey the northwestern coastline of North America. Wintered in 1769 at Unimak, Alaska with the loss of 60 men. Returned to Okhotsk in 1770. Carried cargo in 1771–87. BU 1788.

2 galiots built by Bubnov at Okhotsk.
Sviatoi Pavel
Laid down ? *Launched* 5.7.1768
Grounded and lost on 3.9.1774.
Sviatoi Pyotr
Laid down ? *Launched* 1768
No information on career or fate.

Sviatoi Konstantin
Laid down ? *Launched* 1769
Wrecked 1786.

Sviatoi Georgii Okhotsk
Constructor A. I. Kuzmin
Laid down ? *Launched* 1776
Carried cargo from 1776–80. Stricken in 1780.

Vozobnovlennyi Okhotsk Okhotsk
Constructor A. I. Kuzmin,
Laid down 1785 *Launched* 29.5.1787
Carried cargo from 1787–9. Wrecked in 1789.

Sviataia Nadezhda Okhotsk
Constructor   A. I. Kuzmin,
Laid down   29.10.1790   *Launched* 21.5.1791
Dimensions   approx. 58 ft x 10 ft x ? (17.7 m (lk) x 3.1 m x ? m)
Carried cargo from 1791–2. Wrecked in 1792.

Nadezhda Okhotsk
Laid down   ?   *Launched* ?
Wrecked in 1800.

Sviatoi Nikolai Okhotsk
Constructor   A. I. Kuzmin
Laid down   1798   *Launched* 1799
Carried cargo from 1799–1806. Grounded on 12.10.1806, but manned until 1808.

Okhotsk Okhotsk
Constructors   B. I. Vashutkin and Popov
Laid down   ?   *Launched* 16.6.1805
Carried cargo from 1805–6. Grounded off of Shumshu Island in the Kuriils on 30.10.1806

Shmaks (102 purpose-built and 1 purchased)

Shmaks were two-masted, lateen-rigged, cargo vessels and store ships found in the Baltic and the Caspian during the first half of the eighteenth century.

Caspian flotilla shmaks (86 purpose-built)

All Caspian flotilla shmaks launched in 1702 and 1703 were intended for service in the Baltic, but failed to negotiate the Volga.
4 shmaks built at Kazan.
Laid down   ?   *Launched* 1702
Dimensions   approx. 74 ft x 19 ft x ? (22.6 m (lk) x 5.8 m x ?)

~

7 shmaks built at Kazan.
Laid down   ?   *Launched* 1702
Dimensions   approx. 64 ft x 18 ft x ? (19.5 m (lk) x 5.5 m x ?)

~

4 shmaks built at Kazan.
Laid down   1701   *Launched* 1702
Dimensions   approx. 56 ft x 16 ft x ? (17.2 m (lk) x 5 m x ?)

~

20 shmaks built at Kazan yard.
Laid down   1701   *Launched* 1702
Dimensions   approx. 91 ft x 97 ft x 22 ft x 24 ft (27.8 m x 29.5 m (lk) x 6.9 m x 7.3 m)

~

39 shmaks built at Uslonskaya on the Volga.
Laid down   1702   *Launched* 1703
Dimensions   approx. 92.5 ft x 93.5 ft x ? x ? (28.2 m x 28.5 m (lk) x ? x ?)
13 of this group were sent to St Petersburg by inland waterways: **Gorod Kazan', Oryol, Polumesiats, Severnaia Zvezda**, and **Solntse** in 1705; and **Blagoveshchenskiy, Voinsliy, Georgievskii, Edinorog, Iozh, Natal'ia, Samson, Sviatoi Pyotra** in 1708. They all failed to pass the shallows of the Volkhov and Msta rivers and were BU after 1710.

~

The following shmaks were purpose-built for service in the Caspian.
7 shmaks built at Kazan by F. P. Palchikov.
Laid down   1734   *Launched* 1735

Dimensions   approx. 77 ft x 22 ft x 10 ft (23.5 m x 6.6 m x 3.1 m)

~

5 shmaks built at the Kazan Admiralty.
Laid down   1741   *Launched* 1741
Dimensions   approx. 77 ft x 22 ft x 10 ft (23.5 m x 6.6 m x 3.1 m)
Known names include **Baklan, Gus, Lebed'** and **Chepura**. The last two were crushed by ice on 3.1743.

Baltic fleet shmaks (16 purpose-built)

Koren-Shkhern
Constructor   S. Meles
Laid down   1703   *Launched* 1.8.1703.
Took part in the expeditions to Vyborg on 5.1710 and 5.1712.

Gut-Drager
Constructor   V. Shlengraf
Laid down   1703   *Launched* 15.8.1703
Took part in the expedition to Vyborg on 5.1710.

Last-Drager
Constructor   S. Meles
Laid down   ?   *Launched* 1704
Took part in the expedition to Vyborg on 5.1710. Carried supplies for the Russian squadron at Copenhagen from 7–10.1716.

6 shmaks built at Syaskaya.
Dimensions   approx. 70 ft x 20 ft x 8 ft (21.4 m x 6.1 m x 2.4 m)
   15 men
Onega Syaskaya
Constructor   V. Litkin
Laid down   5.1703   *Launched* 1704
Took part in the expeditions to Vyborg on 5.1710.
Syas Syaskaya
Constructor   ?
Laid down   5.1703   *Launched* 1704
Took part in the expeditions to Vyborg on 5.1710
No. 1 Syaskaya
Constructor   V. Litkin
Laid down   1703   *Launched* 1705
No. 2 Syaskaya
Constructor   Kh. Andreev
Laid down   1703   *Launched* 1705
No. 3 Syaskaya
Constructor   V. Litkin
Laid down   1703   *Launched* 1705
No. 4 Syaskaya
Constructor   V. Litkin
Laid down   1703   *Launched* 1705

~

Chernyy Byk
Laid down   ?   *Launched* 1725
Carried cargo in the Baltic from 1726–33. To Kiel with Vice-Adm. Sinyavin's squadron escorting Princess Anna and the Duke of Holstein to Germany in 7–8.1727. Carried supplies to the Russian squadron off Danzig in 1734.

De Bir-Drager Olonetskaya
Constructor   V. Fogel
Laid down   ?   *Launched* 5.1726
Carried cargo in the Baltic from 1726–33. To Kiel with Vice-Adm.

Seniavin's squadron escorting Princess Anna and the Duke of Holstein to Germany in 7–8.1727. Carried supplies to the Russian squadron off Danzig in 1734.

Vein-Drager Olonetskaya
Constructor   V. Fogel
Laid down   ?   Launched 5.1726
Carried cargo in the Baltic from 1726–31. Grounded off Revel' in 10.1731 and successfully refloated.

Beber Novoladozhskaya
Laid down   1731   Launched 1732
Carried cargo in the Baltic from 1732–47.

Nerva Olonetskaya
Laid down   14.11.1732   Launched 1734.
Carried cargo in the Baltic from 1735–41. Wrecked in 1741.

Shlissel'burg Novoladozhskaya
Laid down   ?   Launched 1741
Carried cargo in the Baltic from 1742–4. Set out spar buoys from 1745–6.

Ladoga Novoladozhskaya
Laid down   ?   Launched 1741

Purchased shmak (1 purchased)

Degop
Purchased in 1719. Carried cargo and laid out spar buoys in the Baltic from 1722–45. Wrecked off Virgin Island on 21.8.1745.

Buers (118 purpose-built)

Buer derives from the Dutch *boyer*. Buers were inshore cargo carriers with lateen sails and one or two masts. They were most popular in the early eighteenth century, but continued to be built in limited numbers into the nineteenth century.

Baltic fleet buers (22 purpose-built)

4 buers built at Olonets.
Dimensions   approx. 80 ft x 24 ft x 9 ft (24.4 m x 7.3 m x 2.7 m)
15 men

Gel'd-Sak or *Sak-Drager*
Constructor   S. Meles
Laid down   24.3.1703   Launched 1.8.1703
Carried cargo from 1704–18. Participated in the expedition to Vyborg in 5.1712. Grounded and salvaged in 8.1713.

Sout-Drager
Laid down   24.3.1703   Launched 8.8.1703
Carried cargo from 1704–18. Participated in the expedition to Vyborg in 5.1712.

Bir-Drager
Constructor   V. Shlengraf
Laid down   24.3.1703   Launched 22.8.1703
Carried cargo in 1704. Converted into a bomb vessel in 1705. (See under Baltic bomb vessels.)

Vein-Drager
Constructor   V. Gerens
Laid down   24.3.1703   Launched 22.8.1703
Carried cargo in 1704. Converted into a bomb vessel in 1705. (See under Baltic bomb vessels.)

~

2 buers built at Syaskaya.
Lyustikh Syaskaya
Constructor   V. Litkin
Laid down   ?   Launched 1704
Carried cargo from 1704–15. Served with the main fleet at Copenhagen in 1716. Lost without trace on the return voyage.

Ik-Gebe-Gevest Syaskaya
Constructor   V. Litkin
Laid down   ?   Launched 1704
Carried cargo from 1704–10.

~

5 large buers: *Nos 1–5* BU in 1779.
5 small buers: *Nos 6–10* BU 1785.

~

4 buers.
No. 1 BU 1807.
No. 2 BU 1811.
No. 3 and *No. 4* Both wrecked in 1806.

~

Dutch buer No. 1
Dimensions   approx. 30 ft x 9.5 ft x 3.6 ft (9.2 m x 2.9 m x 1.1 m)
Presented by the King of the Netherlands in 1816. Part of the Elite Guard and used by members of the Imperial family for navigation in the Neva. Repaired in 1833 and 1870. BU after 1890.

Dutch buer No. 2 Admiralty, St Petersburg
Constructor   I. V. Kurepanov
Laid down   ?   Launched 1819
Dimensions   approx. 30 ft x 9.5 ft x 3.6 ft (9.2 m x 2.9 m x 1.1 m)
Apparently a duplicate of Dutch buer No. 1. Part of the Elite Guard and used by members of the Imperial family for navigation in the Neva. Repaired in 1859.

Caspian flotilla buers (96 purpose-built)

96 buers were built at Kazan by K. Y. Truin and V. Shipilov: Laid down in 1712 and launched in 1713. In 1713, 15 passed successfully from Kazan to St Petersburg by interior water ways. Employed in the Baltic for cargo service.

Fleyts (26 purpose-built)

Fleyt derives from the French *flute* and the Dutch *fluyt*, seventeenth-century cargo vessels developed for use in northern European waters. Russian fleyts were two- or three-masted square rigged vessels armed with from 4 to 8 guns. They were used to transport cargo, stores, ammunition, and artillery in the Baltic and Caspian during the first half of the eighteenth century.

Baltic fleet fleyts (19 purpose-built)

Vel'kom Olonetskaya
Constructor   P. Kornilisen
Laid down   24.3.1703   Launched 15.8.1703.
Dimensions   approx. 74 ft x 22 ft x 8.5 ft (22.6 m x 6.8 m x 2.6 m)
Armament   2 x 18pdrs, 6 x 3pdrs
2 masts, 27 men
Two-masted fleyt. Passed to St Petersburg via the Svir' river in 1704.

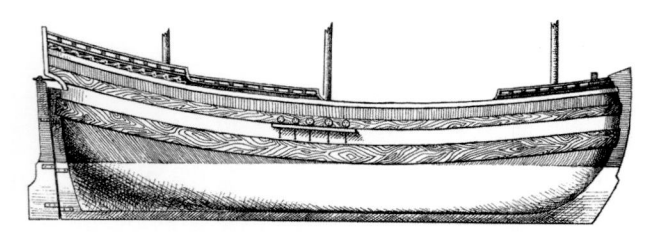

Fleyts were Russian developments of the flutes developed by the Dutch in the seventeenth century. They were basic and unpretentious square rigged cargo ships and Dubki of 1728 is representative of the type. By the second half of the eighteenth century fleyts were replaced by more advanced transports in Russia and throughout the Baltic.

Carried cargo in the Baltic from 1704–13. Participated in the expedition to Vyborg in 5.1710. Grounded in Biork-e zund in 8.1713.

Patriarkh Syaskaya
Constructor V. Vouterson
Laid down 1703 *Launched* 1704
Dimensions approx. 74 ft x 22 ft x 8.5 ft (22.6 m x 6.8 m x 2.6 m)
29 men
Two-masted fleyt. Carried cargo in the Baltic from 1704–14. Participated in the expedition to Vyborg in 5.1710.

5 fleyts built at Olonetskaya yard by V. Fogel.
Dimensions approx. 90 ft x 24 ft x 11 ft x (27.5 m x 7.3 m x 3.4 m)
Dagerort *Launched* 1725
Carried cargo in the Baltic from 1726–33. Converted into an 80-patient hospital ship for the Russian squadron off Danzig in the autumn of 1734. Wrecked that year in a storm off Borgo Island.

Dubki
Launched 1725
Carried cargo in the Baltic in 1726 and from 1728–30. To Kiel in 1727 as part of Vice-Adm. Sinyavin's squadron escorting Princess Anna and the Duke of Holstein to Germany.

Ekateringof
Launched 1725
Carried cargo in the Baltic in 1726 and from 1728–33. To Kiel in 1727 as part of Vice-Adm. Sinyavin's squadron escorting Princess Anna and the Duke of Holstein to Germany. Transported siege artillery to Pillau in 1734 during the siege of Danzig.

Kil'
Launched 1725
Carried cargo in 1726, 1728, 1730 and 1732. To Kiel in 1727 as part of Vice-Adm. Sinyavin's squadron escorting Princess Anna and the Duke of Holstein to Germany. In 1729 she departed for Kilduin in the White Sea with Captain Kalmykov's squadron, but was forced to return due to leaks. Operated at Kiel with the Russian squadron in 1731.

Ezel'
Launched 1725
Carried cargo in the Baltic in 1726–8, 1730, 1732, 1733 and 1735. In 1729 she departed for Kilduin in the White Sea with Captain Kalmykov's squadron, but was forced to return due to leaks. Transported siege artillery to Pillau in 1734 during the siege of Danzig.

~

Golshtiniia
Launched about 1730
Carried cargo in the Baltic in 1730. Operated at Kiel with the Russian squadron in 1731. Grounded off Revel' and BU in spring of 1732.

Ekaterina
Launched about 1730
Carried cargo in the Baltic in 1730–3 and 1735. Transported siege artillery to Pillau in 1734. Left Kronshtadt for Arkhangel'sk in 1736 and forced back by leaks. Repaired and departed again for Arkhangel'sk where she arrived in 1737 after wintering at Kola. Departed for Kronshtadt on 27.6.1738 in company with other ships. Wrecked off Hango on 5.9.1738.

Lavrentii
Launched about 1730
Mentioned as carrying cargo in the Baltic in 1730. No further information.

Petergof
Launched about 1732
Carried cargo in the Baltic in 1732 and 1739. Plans to send her to Arkhangel'sk in 1734 abandoned because of hostility with France over the Danzig situation. Proceeded to Arkhangel'sk in 1735 and returned to Kronshtadt in 1736. Crushed by waves at Kronshtadt on 3.10.1741.

Lavensar Olonetsaya
Laid down 14.11.1732 *Launched* 1734
Carried cargo in the Baltic from 1735-39. Grounded and wrecked (ironically) off Lavensari Island on 20.9.1739.

Nargin Olonetskaya
Laid down 14.11.1732 *Launched* 1734
Carried cargo in the Baltic from 1735–6. Transferred to Arkhangel'sk in 1737. Forced to ground and crushed by a squall on 25.6.1743.

Arkhangel Mikhail Bykovskaya
Laid down 15.9.1734 *Launched* 30.4.1735
Departed Arkhangel'sk for Kronshtadt in convoy with other ships in 7.1736. Wintered in Norway and arrived at Kronshtadt in 1737. Returned to Arkhangel'sk with naval cadets and remained there. Driven to ground by a squall on 15.6.1743. Repaired and BU at Arkhangel'sk after 1749.

Ezel' Bykovskaya
Laid down 13.9.1735 *Launched* 6.5.1736
Departed Arkhangel'sk in convoy and arrived at Kronshtadt in 1737. Carried cargo in the Baltic in 1739.

Dagerort Bykovskaya
Laid down 15.12.1735 *Launched* 8.5.1736
Departed Arkhangel'sk for Kronshtadt in convoy with other ships in 7.1736. Transferred to Revel' in 1738 and then permanently returned to Arkhangel'sk. Grounded, damaged, and sunk in the Gulf of Kola in 9.1742.

Krasnaia Gorka Olonetskaya
Laid down ? *Launched* 6.1748
No other information.

Sommers Olonetskaya
Laid down ? *Launched* 6.1748
No other information.

Novopostroennyi Bykovskaya
Laid down 12.1.1755 *Launched* 31.7.1756

Passed from Arkhangel'sk to Kronshtadt in 6–9.1757, stopping at Copenhagen to pick up a tiger for Catherine II. Returned to Arkhangel'sk in 1758. Damaged in 1759 off Kilduin. Arrived at Revel' in 1761. To Kolberg and Pillau in 1762 to return Russian troops home.

Purchased Baltic fleyts (3 purchased)

Sviatoi Ioann
Purchased for 1,200 roubles in 1732. Carried cargo in the Baltic in 1732 and 1735, Transported artillery to Pillau for the siege of Danzig in 1734.

Seskar
Purchased   1732
Dimensions   approx. 120 ft x 27 ft x 12 ft (36.6 m x 8.1 m x 3.7 m)
Carried cargo in the Baltic in 1733 and 1735. Transported artillery to Pillau for the siege of Danzig in 1734. Wrecked off Narva in 9.1735.

Sommers
Purchased   1732
Dimensions   approx. 120 ft x 27 ft x 12 ft (36.6 m x 8.1 m x 3.7 m)
Carried cargo in the Baltic in 1733 and 1735. Transported artillery to Pillau for the siege of Danzig in 1734. Departed for Arkhangel'sk in 1736 and forced to return to Kronshtadt due to leaks. Repaired, departed a second time, wintered in the Gulf of Kola, and arrived at Arkhangel'sk in 1737. Returned to the Baltic in 1738. Carried supplies to the Russian squadron operating against Sweden in 1742. Captured by Sweden on 18.7.1742.

Caspian flotilla fleyts (7 purpose-built)
5 fleyts built at Kazan.
Laid down   1703   Launched 1705
Dimensions   approx. 97 ft x 25 ft x 8.5 ft (29.6 m x 7.6 m x 2.6 m)
              33 men
Carried cargo in the Caspian and on the Volga. BU after 1719.

~

2 fleyts built at Kazan.
Laid down   1712   Launched 1713
BU after 1719.

Pilot boats (Lots-bots) (23 purpose-built, 2 converted and 2 confiscated)

Pilot vessels were used for hydrographic works (surveying coastlines, setting out buoys, etc), and for bringing supplies to lighthouses. They were variously rigged as galiots, brigs, schooners, cutters and ships.

Baltic fleet pilot boats (16 purpose-built, 2 converted and 2 confiscated)

Lots-Galiot Okhta
Constructor   I. Tatishchev
Laid down   29.8.1703   Launched 18.5.1704
              10 men
Carried out hydrographic work off the mouth of the Neva and around Kotlin Island. Participated in the expedition to Vyborg in 5.1712.

2 vessels built at Okhta yard by V. Solovyev.
Pervyi/(Pilot)
Laid down   1725   Launched 7.1726
Renamed *Lotsman* prior to 23.6.1730. Operated in the Gulf of Finland from 1726–42, supplying light houses and setting out buoys in the spring and removing them in autumn. Captured by the French in 5.1734, brought to Danzig, and returned to Russia after Danzig's capitulation. Repaired at Galley Yard, St Petersburg in 1735. Accompanied the galley fleet to Hango in 4.1743. Postal duties between Kronshtadt and Danzig from 1744–6. Resumed hydrographic duties in the Gulf of Finland from 1747–54. Also involved in seeking out breeding grounds for oysters in 1753–4.

Vtoroi/Shturman
Laid down   9.1726   Launched 6.1727
Renamed *Shturman* prior to 23.6.1730. Operated in the Gulf of Finland from 1727–42, supplying light houses and setting out buoys in the spring and removing them in the autumn. Captured by the French in 5.1734, brought to Danzig, and returned to Russia after Danzig's capitulation. Repaired at Galley Yard, St Petersburg in 1735. Operated with Adm. Golovin's squadron on 9.5.1743. Resumed hydrographic duties in 1744–5. Postal duties between Kronshtadt and Lubeck in 1746. Hydrographic duties in 1747. Postal duties in 1749. Hydrographic duties in 1750. Postal duties between Kronshtadt and Revel' in 1754.

~

Tonein Galley Yard, St Petersburg
Laid down   1739   Launched 1740
Hydrographic duties off Moon Island in 1740. Laid out buoys in the Gulf of Finland in 1742. Operated with the Russian squadron during the war with Sweden in 1743. To Lubeck in 1745. Laid out buoys in the Gulf of Finland in 1745. Trapped by ice in the Gulf of Finland on 30.10.1745, grounded, and damaged. 520 men were involved in salvaging her and returning her to Kronshtadt. Laid out buoys in the Gulf of Finland in 1746. To Danzig in 1747. Laid buoys near Kronshtadt in 1748–9 and off Revel' from 1756–8. Supplied troops at Danzig in 1759. Supplied the Russian squadron off Kolberg in 1760. Laid buoys off Revel' in 1761 and 1765–6. Driven ashore in a storm and wrecked in 11.1768.

Lotsman Olonetskaya
Launched 4.1755
Hydrographic duties from 1755–9. Operated with the Russian squadron off Kolberg in 1760. Laid buoys from 1761–4. Fire watch duties at Kronshtadt in 1765.

Shturman Olonetskaya
Launched 4.1755
Postal duties between Kronshtadt and Danzig in 1756. Fire watch duties at Revel' in 1757. Stationed at Kronshtadt in 1759. Supplied ammunition to the Russian squadron off Kolberg in 1760. Laid buoys from 1761–3.

Lots-galiot no. 1 Galley Yard, St Petersburg
Launched 11.5.1772
Hydrographic duties in the Gulf of Finland from 1777–9.

Lots-bot no. 3 Olonetskaya
Laid down   1772   Launched 1773
Hydrographic duties in the Gulf of Finland from 1773–82. Sent to assist a grounded British ship on 11.11.1782, but driven on to the rocks of Nargen Island and wrecked.

Lots-bot no. 1
Built around 1812. Hydrographic duties in the Gulf of Finland from

1811. Carried supplies to Sveaborg in 1812. Hydrographic duties in the Gulf of Finland in 1813–14. Conducted tests with magnetic compasses off Yusari Island from 1815–17.

Lots-bot no. 2
Built around 1811. Hydrographic duties in the Gulf of Finland in. Brought supplies to Sveaborg in 1812. Hydrographic duties in the Gulf of Finland from 1813–17. Fire watch duties off Utte Island from 1818–22.

Lots-bot no. 3
Built around 1811. Hydrographic duties in the Gulf of Finland from 1811-18. Fire watch duties off Hango from 1819–22. Stationed at Sveaborg in 1823.

Lots-bot no. 8
Built around 1815. Hydrographic duties in the Gulf of Finland in 1815. Fire watch duties at Rochensalm in 1816–17.

Vindava Okhta
Constructor   V. F. Stoke
Laid down   2.11.1831   Launched 1.9.1832
Dimensions   approx. 82 ft x 22 ft x 14.8 ft (25 m (pp) x 6.7 m (inside plank) x 4.5 m)
Armament   6 guns
Rigged as a brig. Laid buoys and supplied light houses in the Gulfs of Finland and Riga from 1833–41. BU at Kronshtadt in 1843.

3 ships built at Kronshtadt and St Petersburg.
Dimensions   approx. 100 ft x 29.5 ft x 8.9 ft (30.5 m (pp) x 9 m (inside plank) x 2.7 m)
Armament   14 guns
Triton Kronshtadt
Constructor   Semenov
Laid down   22.2.1835   Launched 3.5.1835
Laid buoys, supplied light houses, and trained naval cadets from 1836–44. BU in 1849.
Neptun Okhta
Constructor   I. A. Amosov
Laid down   28.11.1844   Launched 11.8.1845
Hydrographic duties and supply of light houses in the Gulf of Finland from 1849–58. Sold for BU 1860.
Sirena Okhta
Constructor   I. A. Amosov
Laid down   28.11.1844   Launched 21.8.1845
Hydrographic duties and supply of light houses in the Gulf of Finland from 1849–58. Sold for BU 1860.

~

Yunge-Eduard
Confiscated 1812. Laid buoys in the Gulfs of Finland and Riga in 1813–14.

Filadel'fiia
Dimensions   approx. 87 ft x 24 ft x 11.2 ft (26.4 m x 7.3 m x 3.4 m)
Converted in 1818 from the transport *Filadel'fiia Pekst*. Laid buoys in the Gulf of Finland and carried supplies from Kronshtadt to other ports from 1818–24. BU 1826. (See also under transports.)

Allert
Dimensions   approx. 73 ft x ? x 11.5 ft (22.3 m x ? x 3.5 m)
Armament   6 guns
Confiscated 1820. Rigged as a brig. Hydrographic duties and supply of light houses in the Gulf of Finland from 1821–33. Hulked in 1834.

Kommerstraks
Dimensions   approx. 91 ft x 33 ft x 9.9 ft (27.8 m x 10.1 m x 3 m)
Converted to a pilot boat in 1851 from the brig of the same name. Hydrographic duties off Revel' from 1853–7.

Black Sea fleet pilot boats (7 purpose-built)

Alupka Nikolaev
Constructor   I. S. Dmitriev
Laid down   31.10.1840   Launched 20.6.1842
Dimensions   approx. 71 ft x 22 ft x 12.5 ft x 8.9 ft) 21.7 m x 6.6 m x 3.8 m x 2.7 m)
Armament   2 guns
Schooner rigged. Hydrographic duties in the Black Sea from 1842–50. Repaired at Nikolaev in 1851. Hydrographic duties in the Black Sea in 1852–3. Driven in a storm to the Bosphorus in 12.1853 and captured by the Turks.

4 ships built at Nikolaev by G. V. Afanasyev.
Dimensions   approx. 79 ft x 22 ft x 11.2 ft (24.2 m x 6.7 m 3.4 m)
Armament   6–10 guns
Astroliabiia
Laid down   20.06.1840   Launched 6.11.1843
Hydrographic duties in the Black Sea from 1844–53. Stationed at Kerch in 1854–5 and scuttled upon the approach of the Anglo-French squadron.
Kvadrant
Laid down   18.3.1844   Launched 9.9.1845
Hydrographic duties in the Black Sea from 1846–53. Stationed at Nikolaev in 1854–5. Hydrographic duties in the Black Sea from 1856–8. Sold for BU in 1859.
Menzula
Laid down   18.3.1844   Launched 9.9.1845
Hydrographic duties in the Black Sea from 1846–53. Stationed at Nikolaev in 1854–5. Hydrographic duties in the Black Sea from 1856–8. Sold for BU in 1859.
Sekstan
Laid down   18.3.1844   Launched 9.9.1845
Hydrographic duties in the Black Sea from 1846–53. Stationed at Kerch in 1853 at the outbreak of the Crimean War and later transferred to Taganrog. Destroyed by gunfire by Anglo-French ships on 22.5.1855.

~

2 ships built of iron and rigged as tenders.
Dimensions   84 ft x 20 ft x 4.6 ft (25.6 m x 6.1 m x 1.4 m)
Bug Nikolaev
Constructor   M. M. Okunev
Laid down   1849   Launched 1850
In the Black Sea fleet from 1861. Hydrographic duties in the Black Sea from 1862–9. Hulked at Nikolaev in 1880.
Berezan' Nikolaev
Constructor   M. M. Okunev
Laid down   1852   Launched 1853
In the Black Sea fleet from 1861. Hydrographic duties in the Black Sea from 1862–72. Fire watch duties at Ochakov in 1873–4. Hydrographic duties in the Black Sea from 1875–9. Hulked at Nikolaev in 1880.

Packet boats (29 purpose-built and 1 purchased)

Packet boats were small, light two-masted ships used as avisos, for postal and passenger service, hydrographic and scientific work, and for naval operations as needed. They usually had from 12 to 16 light guns. Packet boats were built in quantity in the Baltic throughout the eighteenth century, but they never found favour in the Black Sea.

Baltic fleet packet boats (23 purpose-built and 1 purchased)

Unnamed Olonetskaya
Constructors   L. Vereshchagin and F. P. Palchikov
Laid down   1.8.1703   *Launched* 20.6.1704
Dimensions   approx. 55 ft x 15 ft x 7.5 ft (16.8 m x 4.7 m x 2.3 m)
                10 men
Unnamed vessel, usually simply referred to as 'packet-boat' or 'post-boat'. Accompanied the main fleet to Kotlin every year from1705–10.

Pocht-Wagen Olonetskaya
Constructor   V. Fogel
Laid down   1725   *Launched* 1726
Between 1728–33 made two to three trips annually from Kronshtadt to Danzig, Lubeck and Memel. Accompanied Adm. Gordon's squadron to Danzig and cruised in the Baltic in 1734. Transferred to Danzig in 1735. BU sat Kronshtadt after 10.1735.

Pocht-Gorn Olonetskaya
Constructor   V. Fogel
Laid down   1725   *Launched* 1726
Carried post between Kronshtadt, Danzig and Lubeck in 1727–8. BU at Kronshtadt in 1732.

Fligel'-de-Fam Olonetskaya
Constructor   V. Fogel
Laid down   1725   *Launched* 1726
Carried post between Kronshtadt and Lubeck in 1727–8.

5 ships built at Olonetskaya yard by V. Fogel.
Kur'er
Laid down   1726   *Launched* 22.9.1727
Made two to three trips annually from Kronshtadt to Danzig and Lubeck from 1729–32, Accompanied Adm. Gordon's squadron off Danzig in 1734. Made two to three trips annually from Kronshtadt to Danzig and Lubeck from 1735–41 and in 1744–5. Operated with the main fleet in 1746. Made two to three trips annually from Kronshtadt to Danzig and Lubeck in 1747 and 1749–50. Damaged by leaks in 1750. BU at Kronshtadt in 1755.
Lastka
Laid down   1726   *Launched* 22.9.1727
Transported cavalry horses purchased in Germany from Kiel to Kronshtadt in 1731.
Fortuna
Laid down   1726   *Launched* 22.9.1727
Transported cavalry horses purchased in Germany from Kiel to Kronshtadt in 1731
Merkurii
Laid down   1726   *Launched* 22.9.1727
To Lubeck in 1731.Grounded on 22.5.1732 and declared a total loss. Later BU.
Pochtal'on
Laid down   1726   *Launched* 22.9.1727
Two annual trips to Danzig and Lubeck from 1729–33. Repaired at St Petersburg in 1734. Two annual trips to Danzig and Lubeck from 1735–6. Repaired at St Petersburg in 1734. BU after 1737.

Merkurius Galley Yard, St Petersburg
Constructor   V. Solovyev
Laid down   7.1737   *Launched* 9.1732
Carried post between Kronshtadt, Danzig, and Lubeck in 1733. Operated with Adm. Gordon's squadron off Danzig in 1734. Carried post between Kronshtadt, Danzig, and Lubeck from 1735–9 and in 1741. Operated with the galley squadron during the Russo-Swedish War in 1742 and then with Rear-Adm. Kalmykov's squadron. On 5.3.1743 captured the Swedish galiot *Mercurius* off Danzig in what surely stands as an almost unique instance of ships with nearly identical names engaging in one-to-one combat. Captured the Swedish yacht *Yung-Frau Katerina* on 22.3.1743. *Mercurius* lost in a storm on 21.8.1743 while being escorted to Revel' in company with *Yung-Frau Katerina*. Reached Revel' with the surviving prize on 22.9.1743. Carried post between Kronshtadt, Danzig, and Lubeck from1744–54. BU after 1755.

Novyi Kur'er Galley Yard, St Petersburg
Constructor   V. Solovyev
Laid down   1732   *Launched* 5.1733
Carried post between Kronshtadt, Danzig, and Lubeck in 1733, 1735 and 1736–40. On 11.7.1740, ordered to stop for inspection by a Swedish 12-gun snow. Refused Swedish orders and cleared for action. Swedish vessel gave way. Grounded and lost on rocks off Kokshar Island on 27.9.1740.

Novyi Pochtal'on Galley Yard, St Petersburg
Laid down   1735   *Launched* 1736 (?)
Carried post between Kronshtadt, Danzig and Lubeck from 1736–41. Assigned to the galley flotilla in 1742 and then to Rear-Adm. Kalmykov's squadron. Assigned to Adm. Golovin's squadron in 1743 and took part in the action with the Swedish fleet on 6.6.1743. Carried post between Kronshtadt, Danzig, and Lubeck from 1744–6 and in 1749.

3 ships built at St Petersburg Admiralty.
Dimensions   approx. 90 ft x 24 ft x 11.2 ft (27.5 m x 7.4 m x 3.4 m)
Armament   12 guns
Sokol
Constructor   D. Sutherland
Laid down   7.7.1749   *Launched* 25.5.1750
Carried post between Kronshtadt, Danzig, and Lubeck from 1750–6. Transported supplies to the Russian main fleet in 1757. Carried post between Kronshtadt, Danzig, and Lubeck from 1758–61 and in 1764. Operated with Adm. S. I. Mordvinov's training squadron under Catherine II's inspection in 1765. Carried post between Kronshtadt, Danzig, and Lubeck 1766–7. Brought Rear-Adm. Chichagov to his assignment as commander of the Revel' Squadron in 1770. Returned to Kronshtadt in 1771. BU after 8.1771.
Lebed'
Constructor   D. Sutherland
Laid down   7.7.1749   *Launched*; 31.5.1750
Carried post between Kronshtadt, Danzig, and Lubeck from 1751–6 and from 1758–61. To Kiel in 1762. Repaired in 1763–4. Operated with Adm. S. I. Mordvinov's training squadron with Catherine II observing in 1765. Transported German colonists from Lubeck to Kronshtadt in

1766. Fire watch duties at Revel' from 1767–75.
Merkurius
Constructor   Khvadriev
Laid down   28.10.1754   Launched 10.5.1755
Carried cargo to Lubeck in 1755. Carried post between Kronshtadt, Danzig, and Lubeck from 1756–8. Transported supplies to Russian squadrons off Kolberg in 1759–60. Carried post between Kronshtadt, Danzig, and Lubeck in 1761 and 1764. Operated with Adm. S. I. Mordvinov's training squadron under Catherine II's inspection in 1765. Carried post between Kronshtadt, Danzig, and Lubeck in 1769. Wintered in Danzig due to leaks in 1769–70. Assigned to the training squadrons in 1766–7 and 1770.

~

6 ships built at St Petersburg and Lodeynoe Pole.
Dimensions   approx. 90 ft x 25 ft x 11.2 ft (27.5 m x 7.7 m x 3.4 m)
Armament   16 guns
              60 men
Kur'er Galley Yard, St Petersburg
Constructor   I. I. Ilyin
Laid down   15.8.1756   Launched 29.4.1757
Carried post between Kronshtadt, Danzig, and Lubeck in 1757. Hydrographic work measuring depths between Bornholm and Stralsund in 1758. Transported supplies to Pillau and operated with the Russian squadron in 1759. Grounded and lost off Danzig while transporting the sick on 11.9.1759.
Kur'er Galley Yard, St Petersburg
Constructor   Lodygin
Laid down   13.11.1760   Launched 8.5.1761
Carried post to Lubeck in 1761. Operated as a troopship off Kolberg in 1762. Carried post to Lubeck in 1764. Operated with Adm. S. I. Mordvinov's training squadron under Catherine II's inspection in 1765. Assigned to the training squadron in 1766–7. Fire watch duties at Kronshtadt in 1768. Brought the Polish ambassador to Narva in 1769. Assigned to the training squadron in 1773. Stationed at Revel' from 1774–9. BU 1780.
Pochtal'on (Nikita Muchenik) Olonetskaya
Constructor   I. I. Afanasyev
Laid down   27.9.1765   Launched 27.5.1766
Dimensions   95 ft x 25 ft x 9 ft 6 in
Carried post to Kiel and Lubeck in 1767–8. To the Mediterranean with Adm. Spiridov's squadron in 1769 and participated in operations against the Turks. Arrived at Kerch in 1775 and assigned to the Azov Flotilla. Reclassified as a small frigate in 1775. Cruised in the Black Sea in 1776–8. Fire watch ship at Kerch in 1780. Repaired in 1783 and sailed from Taganrog to Sevastopol'. Transported crews to Taganrog for 'newly built frigates'. Converted into a 'newly invented floating battery' in 1788 and renamed *Nikita Muchenik*. Found unfit for further service as a cruiser and relegated to fire watch service at Sevastopol' from 1788-91. Broken up after 1791. (See also under Black Sea small frigates and Black Sea bomb vessels.)
Letuchii Olonetskaya
Constructor   I. I. Afanasyev
Laid down   7.10.1765   Launched 10.7.1766
Carried post to Kiel and Lubeck in 1768. To the Mediterranean with Spiridov's squadron in 1769 and participated in operations against the Turks. Wrecked during a storm off Vitulo Island on 17.3.1770.
Sokol Olonetskaya
Constructor   I. I. Afanasyev
Laid down   26.10.1771   Launched 18.8.1772
Escorted the future bride of Russian Emperor Paul I from Lubeck in 1773. Fire watch duties at Kronshtadt in 1776. Assigned to the training squadron in 1777. Transferred from Kronshtadt to Revel' in 1779. Assigned fire watch duties at Revel' until 1782. BU 1784.
Bystryi Olonetskaya
Constructor   I. I. Afanasyev
Laid down   28.9.1771   Launched 2.9.1772
Escorted the future bride of Russian Emperor Paul I from Lubeck in 1773. Assigned fire watch duties at Kronshtadt in 1776. Assigned to the training squadron in 1777–8. Brought Voltaire's library, which had been purchased by Catherine II, from Lubeck to Kronshtadt.

~

Pospeshnyi
Armed with 10 carronades. Believed to have been purchased around 1787 for Adm. Greig's Mediterranean squadron. Operated with Greig's squadron in 1788. Carried news of the approach of the Swedish battle fleet to Kronshtadt on 7.7.1788. Operated with the main fleet off Sveaborg throughout the remainder of 1788. Stationed at Revel' in 1789 and cruised with Vice-Adm. Kruz's squadron in the Gulf of Finland. Reassigned to the galley flotilla and participated in the 1st battle of Rochensalm. Severely damaged and captured by the Swedes in sinking condition. Beached by the Swedes and recaptured by the Russians.

Caspian fleet packet boats (2 purpose-built)

2 ships built at Astrakhan' and armed with 10 x 3pdrs.
Sokol
Laid down   ?   Launched 1794.
Made annual cruises from Astrakhan' to Persia from 1794–9.
Letuchii
Laid down   ?   Launched 1795
Made annual cruises from Astrakhan' to Persia from 1794–9. BU at Astrakhan' in 1801.

Okhotsk flotilla packet boats (3 purpose-built)

2 ships built at Okhotsk yard by M. Rugachev and A. I. Kuzmin.
Dimensions   approx. 80 ft x 22 ft x 9.5 ft (24.4 m x 6.7 m x 2.9 m)
              200 tons
Armament   14 guns
             75 men
Sviatoi Pyotr
Laid down   ?   Launched 29.6.1740
Participated in the 2nd Kamchatka Expedition. On 8.9.1740 left Okhotsk under the command of Commodore Bering in company with *Sviatoi Pavel*. Wintered in 1740–1 at a harbour given the name Petropavlovskaya, combining the names of the two ships. Departed for the Pacific on 4.6.1741 in search of the legendary 'Land of Juan de Gama'. Became separated from *Sviatoi Pavel* in a storm on 20.6.1741. Off Kayak Island in North America on 20.7.1741. The scientist Steller, a member of the Russian Academy of Science, landed and discovered a new species of seal, which came to be referred to as 'Steller's Cow'. Navigated to the southern Aleutians and discovered a number of islands, including Atka and Kyska. By November, food supplies were exhausted and 12 crew members had died of scurvy. On 5.11.1741, anchored off an island, since named Bering after its discoverer. On 12.11.1741, the ship was wrecked by a storm. During the winter, 19 more crewmen died of scurvy, including Bering himself on 5.12.1741. The survivors of the winter constructed a new ship from the remnants of the old, rechristened it *Sviatoi Pyotr*, and returned to Kamchatka.
Sviatoi Pavel
Laid down   ?   Launched 2.7.1740

Departed Okhotsk on 8.9.1740 in company with *Sviatoi Pyotr*. After separating from *Sviatoi Pyotr* on 20.6.1740, surveyed 250 miles of North American coastline. On the return to Kamchatka, discovered Unmak, Adah, Agattu and Attu in the Aleutian chain. Returned successfully to Okhotsk on 10.10.1741 after suffering casualties of 9 men dead of disease and scurvy and 15 lost overboard at Jakobi Island. Set sail on a second expedition on 23.5.1742, but driven back to Okhotsk by fogs and illness.

~

Sviatoi Ioann Krestitel' Okhotsk
Constructor A. I. Kuzmin
Laid down ? *Launched* 1741
Dimensions approx. 69 ft x 18 ft x 6.2 ft (21 m x 5.5 m x 1.9 m)
Sailed to Honshu, Japan in 1742 under Captain Shpanberg. Driven back to the Kuriils and ultimately to Okhotsk by leaks. Wrecked en route to Kamchatka on 2.10.1753.

Sea of Azov fleet packet boats (1 purpose-built)

Unnamed
Built on the Voronezh River around 1709. Arrived at Azov on 1.7.1709 and remained there until the dissolution of the Sea of Azov fleet in 1711.

Shkuts (shkouts) (113 purpose-built)

The designation shkut derives from the Dutch *schoot*. Shkuts were flat-bottomed sailing and rowing cargo vessels with 1 or 2 lateen rigged masts. They were employed for off shore and littoral navigation as well as for inshore work on rivers and lakes. The type was only found in the Baltic and the Caspian. No shkuts were Laid down after 1717.

Baltic fleet shkuts (107 purpose-built)

2 shkuts built at Shlissel'burg with F. M. Sklyaev as constructor.
Laid down ? *Launched* 1704
No other data available.

~

5 shkuts built at Selitskiy Ryadok.
Dimensions approx. 54 ft x 16 ft x 5.6 ft (16.5 m x 4.9 m x 1.7 m)
Laid down ? *Launched* 1704
No other data available.

~

100 shkuts built at Novoladozhskaya.
70 *Laid down* 1716 *Launched* 1717
30 *Laid down* 1717 *Launched* 1718
No other data available.

Caspian flotilla shkuts (6 purpose-built)

Aleksandr Nevskii Kazan
Laid down ? *Launched* 1716
Dimensions approx. 75 ft x 20 ft x 8.5 ft (22.9 m x 6 m x 2.6 m)

Kamel Kazan
Laid down ? *Launched* 1716
Dimensions 72 ft x 20 ft x 8.5 ft (21.9 m x 6.1 m x 2.6 m)

3 shkuts, built at Kazan in 1716, were BU at Astrakhan' in 1722–4. A fourth was wrecked in 1724.

Of all the Russian warships to carry the name of Sviatoi Pavel, *the packet-boat built at Okhotsk in 1740 has to have been the humblest. Her pretentious name, and that of her sister,* Sviatoi Pyotr, *can be explained by their great distance from the Russian centres of power in the Baltic and Black Sea where such names graced only line of battle ships. As this profile shows, the two ships had the general look of small, simply rigged brigs, albeit amply armed for their size. Both saints accompanied Commodore Bering in his famous and ill-fated expedition to the Aleutian chain in 1741. Only* Sviatoi Pavel *returned.*

Pinks (29 purpose-built and 2 purchased)

Pink derived from the French *pinque*. Russian pinks were 3-masted, square rigged, seagoing store ships, sufficiently well armed to provide supplies for the fleet without requiring escort. Between 1715 and 1784, a total of 29 purpose-built pinks were completed in the Baltic, the Black Sea and the Caspian, with an additional 2 purchased pinks acquired, 1 for the Mediterranean in 1769 and 1 for service with the Armed Neutrality Patrols. The last 2 built were converted into 'flat-bottomed frigates' in 1788. 6 were wrecked in service; but 1 of these was salvaged, repaired, and returned to duty. 2 were captured by Sweden.

Baltic fleet pinks (25 purpose-built)

Prints Aleksandr Admiralty, St Petersburg
Constructor R. Brown
Laid down 29.6.1715 *Launched* 9.9.1716
Dimensions approx. 83 ft x 22 ft x 8.5 ft (25.2 m x 6.8 m x 2.6 m)
Armament 18–24 guns
182 men
Named after Prince Aleksandr Menshikov, a favourite of Peter I, and *de facto* ruler of Russia in 1725–7. Menshikov was held responsible for her upkeep (see also *Shlissel'burg* (64)) and paid for the elaborate wood carvings on her exterior, particularly her stern galleries. Cruised 1717–20 with the squadron in the Baltic and employed primarily as a warship. Captured the Swedish snow *Pollux* on 31.7.1717 and took 6 Swedish ships including 2 in 1720 armed with Russian trophy guns taken at Narva in 1700. BU after 1727.

5 pinks built at Solombala and named after islands near Arkhangel'sk.

Kola Solombala
Laid down 13.9.1741 *Launched* 13.5.1742
Dimensions approx. 120 ft x 27 ft x 12.1 ft (36.6 m x 8.2 m x 3.7 m)
Armament 12 guns

7–10.1746 transferred to Kronshtadt. From 1747–60 she was almost yearly at sea transferring cargos between Baltic ports. Made four voyages to Arkhangel'sk and returned back to Kronshtadt in 1749–57. Stopped off Skagen on 12.6.1757 by a British frigate and inspected and released. Last trip in 1760. No further mention.

Novaia Dvinka Solombala
Laid down 13.9.1741 *Launched* 13.5.1742
Dimensions approx. 120 ft x 27 ft x 12.1 ft (36.6 m x 8.2 m x 3.7 m)
Armament 12 guns

Left for the Baltic on 12.7.1746. Wrecked in transit on 16.9.1746 off Gotland. All hands saved.

Kildyuin Solombala
Laid down 12.10.1742 *Launched* 1.5.1743
Dimensions approx. 120 ft x 27 ft x 12.1 ft (36.6 m x 8.2 m x 3.7 m)
Armament 12 guns

Arrived in the Baltic in 1745. Made 5 voyages from Kronshtadt to Arkhangel'sk in 1747–56 with materials etc for ships building there and four successful returns. On her fifth return, forced to return to Arkhangel'sk by storm off Nordkap on 13.7.1756. No further mention.

Lapomink Solombala
Laid down 13.10.1742 *Launched* 1.5.1743
Dimensions approx. 120 ft x 27 ft x 12.1 ft (36.6 m x 8.2 m x 3.7 m)
Armament 12 guns

While leaving Arkhangel'sk on 6.1744, was sunk by a squall in shallow water with no serious damage. Raised and repaired. 1745 arrived in the Baltic. 1746–68 numerous trips with cargos. 1747 removed cargo from the wrecked pink *Novaia Dvinka*;. 1749 to Arkhangel'sk. Returned to Kronshtadt 1750. Repaired at Kronshtadt 1758–9. 7.11.1763 damaged by ice in Kronshtadt Roads and sunk. Raised and repaired. BU 1769.

Povrakul Solombala
Laid down 29.9.1742 *Launched* 14.6.1743
Dimensions approx. 120 ft x 27 ft x 12.1 ft (36.6 m x 8.2 m x 3.7 m)
Armament 12 guns

1744 arrived in the Baltic. 1745–6 trips in the Baltic. Wrecked 11.1746 in the Bay of Rogervik.

~

2 pinks built at Solombala.

Novaia Dvinka Solombala
Laid down 19.6.1748 *Launched* 9.5.1749
Dimensions approx. 120 ft x 28 ft x 12.5 ft (36.6 m x 8.5 m x 3.8 m)
Armament 22 guns

6–9.1749 went to Revel'. 1750 to Arkhangel'sk with materials for building ships. 1751 returned to Kronshtadt. En route to Arkhangel'sk in 1752, forced to winter at Stavanger due to leaks. Reached Arkhangel'sk in 1753. Returned to Kronshtadt in 1754. Round trip to Arkhangel'sk in 1755–6. Transported guns, etc., to Riga and Pillau from 1757–9. Repaired at Kronshtadt 1761–2. Transported cargo in the Baltic 1762-69. BU 1771.

Povrakul Solombala
Laid down 7.7.1748 *Launched* 10.5.1749
Dimensions approx. 120 ft x 28 ft x 12.5 ft (36.6 m x 8.5 m x 3.8 m)
Armament 22 guns

1749 went to Revel'. Transported cargo in the Baltic 1750–60, with two round trips to Arkhangel'sk. Final trip to Arkhangel'sk in 1760. BU 1773 at Arkhangel'sk.

~

2 pinks built at Solombala. These and the following class were named after towns and settlements near Arkhangel'sk and in northern Russia.

Vologda Solombala
Laid down 7.7.1748 *Launched* 10.5.1749
Dimensions approx. 114 ft x 28 ft x 12.8 ft (34.8 m x 8.5 m x 3.9 m)
Armament 22 guns

1751 to Kronshtadt. 1752–72 numerous trips with cargos, always in the Baltic. BU 1774.

Kargopol' Solombala
Laid down 18.9.1749 *Launched* 18.4.1750
Dimensions approx. 114 ft x 28 ft x 12.8 ft (34.8 m x 8.5 m x 3.9 m)
Armament 22 guns

1752 to Kronshtadt. 1753–72 numerous trips with cargos, always in the Baltic. BU 1774.

~

2 pinks built at Solombala.

Ustyug Solombala
Laid down 20.10.1748 *Launched* 10.07.1749
Dimensions approx. 100 ft x 27 ft x 13.8 ft (30.5 m x 8.2 m x 4.2 m)
Armament 12 guns

Always based at Arkhangel'sk. Sailed in the White Sea. BU 1770.

Kholmogory Solombala
Laid down 18.9.1749 *Launched* 17.5.1750
Dimensions approx. 100 ft x 27 ft x 13.8 ft (30.5 m x 8.2 m x 4.2 m)
Armament 12 guns

1757 to Kronshtadt. 1758–9 to Arkhangel'sk and back. 1760–5 usual cargo missions in the Baltic. BU 1769.

~

9 pinks built at Solombala.

Verbliud Solombala
Laid down 17.10.1757 *Launched* 3.6.1758
Dimensions approx. 130 ft x 31.5 ft x 12.5 ft (39.7 m x 9.6 m x 3.8 m)
Armament 22 guns
  160–70 men

1759 to Kronshtadt. Mentioned only as having carried cargo in 1759–60

Slon Solombala
Constructor I. V. Yames
Laid down 24.10.1757 *Launched* 3.6.1758
Dimensions approx. 130 ft x 31.5 ft x 12.5 ft (39.7 m x 9.6 m x 3.8 m)
Armament 22 guns
  160–70 men

1758 to Revel'. 1759–73 cargo missions. 1761–2 to White Sea and back to Baltic. 1763 to Arkhangel'sk for the 'secret expedition' of Brigadier Chichagov to Spitzbergen. Damaged by ice there but returned to Arkhangel'sk;. 1765 to Kronshtadt. 1766 73 trips in the Baltic. BU 1774.

Lev Solombala
Constructor I. V. Yames
Laid down 25.9.1758 *Launched* 1.5.1759
Dimensions approx. 130 ft x 31.5 ft x 12.5 ft (39.7 m x 9.6 m x 3.8 m)
Armament 22 guns
  160–70 men

1759 to Revel'. 1759–71 cargo missions;. 3 trips to Arkhangel'sk. 1771 left at Arkhangel'sk due to age and condition.

Edinorog Solombala
Constructor I. V. Yames
Laid down 25.9.1758 *Launched* 25.05.1759
Dimensions approx. 130 ft x 31.5 ft x 12.5 ft (39.7 m x 9.6 m x 3.8 m)
Armament 22 guns
  160–70 men

1759 to Revel'. 1760 departed for Arkhangel'sk, but wrecked 31.10 off Norway. 10 men saved.

Lapomink Solombala
Constructor   V. A. Selyaninov
Laid down   1761   Launched; 1762
Dimensions   approx. 130 ft x 31.5 ft x 12.5 ft (39.7 m x 9.6 m x 3.8 m)
Armament   22 guns
              160–70 men

1762 to Kronshtadt. Returned to Arkhangel'sk in 1763 for the 'secret expedition' of Chichagov, to Spitzbergen in 1765–6. 1767 returned to Kronshtadt. 1769 was with Adm. Spiridov's squadron bound for the Mediterranean. Wrecked on 16.9.1769 due to an inoperative lighthouse but succeeded in warning the other squadron members about the danger.

Gogland Solombala
Constructor   I. V. Yames
Laid down   22.7.1763   Launched 30.4.1765
Dimensions   approx. 130 ft x 31.5 ft x 12.5 ft (39.7 m x 9.6 m x 3.8 m)
Armament   22 guns
              160–70 men

1765–6 transited to Kronshtadt, wintering at Bergen. 1767–71 two trips to Arkhangel'sk. Remained there after 1771. BU 1780.

Nargin Solombala
Constructor   V. A. Selyaninov
Laid down   22.7.1763   Launched 30.4.1765
Dimensions   approx. 130 ft x 31.5 ft x 12.5 ft (39.7 m x 9.6 m x 3.8 m)
Armament   22 guns
              160–70 men

1765 to Kronshtadt. 1766–70 three round trips to Arkhangel'sk. Fourth and final trip to Arkhangel'sk in 1772. BU 1780.

Venera Solombala
Constructors V. A. Selyaninov and A. Davydov
Laid down   12.10.1766   Launched 13.5.1768
Dimensions   approx. 130 ft x 31.5 ft x 12.5 ft (39.7 m x 9.6 m x 3.8 m)
Armament   22 guns
              160–70 men

1768 to Kronshtadt. 1769 accompanied Adm. Spiridov's squadron with *Saturn* and *Solombal* to the Mediterranean. Returned to Kronshtadt 10.1775. 1776–85 cargo trips in the Baltic. BU 1787.

Saturn Solombala
Constructors V. A. Selyaninov and A. Davydov
Laid down   12.10.1766   Launched 13.5.1768
Dimensions   approx. 130 ft x 31.5 ft x 12.5 ft (39.7 m x 9.6 m x 3.8 m)
Armament   22 guns
              160–70 men

1768 to Kronshtadt; 1769 accompanied Adm. Spiridov's squadron with *Venera* and *Solombal* to the Mediterranean. Returned to Kronshtadt 10.1775. 1776–85 cargo trips in the Baltic. Not mentioned after 1785.

Solombal Solombala
Constructor   I. V. Yames
Laid down   1.8.1761   Launched 12.5.1762
Dimensions   approx. 120 ft x 31 ft x 12.5 ft (36.6 m x 9.5 m x 3.8 m)
Armament   22 guns
              146 men

1762–3 transited to Kronshtadt, wintering at Danzig. 1765–6 round trip to Arkhangel'sk. 1769 accompanied Adm. Spiridov's squadron with *Venera* and *Saturn* to the Mediterranean. 1775 unable to return to the Baltic due to poor condition. Sold at Port-Mahon.

3 pinks built at Solombala.

Evstafii Solombala
Constructor   A. Maltsov
Laid down   12.8.1772   Launched 29.9.1773
Dimensions   approx. 130 ft x 31 ft x 12.5 ft (39.7 m x 9.5 m x 3.8 m)
Armament   38 guns

1774–5 transited to Kronshtadt, wintering at Danzig. 1775–8 cargo trips in the Baltic. 1779 to Arkhangel'sk. 9.9.1780 on return to Kronshtadt, wrecked off Shetland Islands (Groskery Island). Out of 180 men, only 5 were saved.

Kola Solombala
Constructor   Prugovin
Laid down   1773   Launched 1774
Dimensions   approx. 130 ft x 31 ft x 12.5 ft (39.7 m x 9.5 m x 3.8 m)
Armament   38 guns

1775 passed to Kronshtadt. 1775–8 cargo trips in the Baltic. 1779 to Arkhangel'sk. 1780–1 back to Kronshtadt, wintering at Copenhagen. 1781–5 continued transporting cargo in the Baltic. BU 1787.

Solombal Solombala
Constructor   D. Masalskiy
Laid down   26.9.1781   Launched 21.5.1782
Dimensions   approx. 109 ft x 30 ft x 10.1 ft (33.3 m (lgd) x 9.2 m x 3.1 m)
Armament   22 guns

Given the nearly identical dimensions of the purchased pink *Kildyuin*, (see below) the possibility exists that this ship was a deliberate copy. 1782 to Kronshtadt. 1783–7 two round trips to Arkhangel'sk. On 5.8.1788 in company with *Kildyuin* (see below) and unaware of the declaration of war, was intercepted by Swedish frigates in the Kattegat, but managed to escape to Copenhagen. Attached to the main fleet in 1789–90. Captured by Sweden on 28.6.1790 during the 2nd battle of Rochensalm.

Purchased Baltic pinks (2 purchased)

Sviatoi Pavel
Purchased in 1769 for the Mediterranean expedition. Accompanied Elphinstone's squadron to the Mediterranean in 1769. Arrived at Leghorn on 22.9.1772 and burnt there same year.

Kildyuin
Dimensions   approx. 109 ft x 30 ft x 12.1 ft (33.3 m x 9.2 m x 3.7 m), 456 tons burthen

Purchased from a merchant named Kale, probably British, in 1779. 1779–80 to Kronshtadt, wintering in Copenhagen. Participated in 1780 in the 'Armed Neutrality' as part of Rear-Adm. S. P. Khmetevskiy's squadron. 1781–7 four round trips to Arkhangel'sk and back to Kronshtadt. 6.6.1788 departed Kronshtadt with 100 guns for new ships under construction at Arkhangel'sk, in company with *Solombal* (see above) as part of Vice-Adm. von Desin's squadron. Separated from the main squadron on 3.8.1788 and captured by Swedish frigates in the Kattegat on 5.8.1788.

Black Sea fleet pinks (2 purpose-built)

2 pinks built at Gnilotonskaya.
Laid down   1783   Launched 1784
Dimensions   approx. 130 ft x 32.5 ft x 12.1 ft (39.7 m x 9.9 m x 3.7 m)
Nos 1 and 2

1784 88 cargo trips in the Black Sea. 1788 transformed into shallow draught, 'newly invented' frigates in 1788 and renamed *Antonii* and *Feodosii* (see frigates).

Caspian flotilla pinks (2 purpose-built)

Samson
Built around 1747, mentioned as operating in the Caspian in 1747–9. 1749 sailed to Persia. No further information.
Unnamed Astrakhan'
Constructor   S. N. Neverov
Laid down   11.4.1838   Launched 3.4.1839
Two-masted 4-gunned pink. 1839–43 cargo trips in the Caspian. 1845 fire-guard duty. Not afterwards mentioned.

Gukors (24 purpose-built, 11 purchased and 3 prizes)

The designation gukor derives from the Dutch *hoeker*. These were small, two-masted, square rigged vessels with broad bows and round sterns. The main mast was mounted amidships and the mizzen was two thirds its height and mounted towards the stern. Gukors had very long bowsprits, equipped with retractable jib-booms and were fast and handy, with excellent seagoing qualities. Displacement reached a maximum of 350 tons and they carried as many as 16 guns. As a result of their excellent sailing qualities, gukors were widely employed, not only as cargo vessels, but as avisos and watch/guard ships. Although none were found in the Sea of Azov or the Black Sea, gukors were popular in the Caspian and in all of the northern areas. They continued to be built or acquired in moderate numbers into the early nineteenth century.

Baltic fleet gukors (8 purpose-built)

2 gukors built at St Petersburg Admiralty by I. Nemtsov.
Dimensions   approx. 65 ft x 17 ft x 7.9 ft (19.9 m x 5.2 m x 2.4 m)
Armament   12–14 guns
    60 men

Vater-Falk
Laid down   1718   Launched 15.11.1719
Participated in cruising operations in the Baltic and cargo transfer in 1720–1.

Pervyi Kaper
Laid down   6.4.1718   Launched 6.9.1719
Participated in cruising operations in the Baltic in 1720–1 and cargo transfer from 1722–4. BU after 1727.

~

2 gukors
Gut-Drager, Cherepakha
Launched 1725. No other data available.

~

Dvina Bykovskaya
Laid down   23.12.1734   Launched 8.9.1735
Dimensions   approx. 80 ft x 24 ft x 10.5 ft (24.4 m x 7.3 m x 3.2 m)
Stationed at Arkhangel'sk from 1736–9. Carried cargo from Arkhangel'sk to Kola in 1738 and 1745. At Kola in 6–7.1741.

Sviatoi Savvatii Bykovskaya
Laid down   25.10.1753   Launched 20.6.1754
Stationed at Arkhangel'sk. BU there in 1772.

Sviatoi Andrei Bykovskaya
Laid down   10.10.1757   Launched 26.5.1759
Stationed at Arkhangel'sk.

Onega Bykovskaya
Laid down   10.10.1757   Launched 26.5.1759
Stayed at Arkhangel'sk port. Repaired in 1784.

Purchased Baltic gukors (11 purchased)

Lasorser
Armament   6 guns
    60 men
Purchased in France in 1716. Escorted merchantmen to Revel' and cargo to Danzig in 1716, wintering at Lubeck. Carried cargo in 1718. Escorted 18 prizes from Revel' to St Petersburg in 1719. Cruised in the Gulf of Finland from 1719–21. Stationed at Kronshtadt from 1722–9. BU 1729.

Novyi Kronshlot
Dimensions   99 ft 6½ in x 28 ft x 11 ft 6 in (30.3 m x 8.5 m x 3.5 m)
Armament   12–16 x 6pdrs
    120 men
Purchased in Holland in 1717. Transferred from Copenhagen to Revel' under hired French 'masters' in 8.1717. Cruised with the battle fleet in 1719–20. Employed as a flagship by Peter I and returned prisoners of war to Sweden in 1722. Planned voyage to Spain cancelled in 1723. Round trip to La Rochelle and Bordeaux as a merchantman in 1724. Returned to Russia in 1725. To Kiel in 1727. Carried cargo in the Baltic in 1728. Carried cargo to Holland in 1729. Transported 14 horses from Kiel in 1731. To Arkhangel'sk in 1735 and repaired at Solombala from 1736–7. Returned to Kronshtadt in 1737. Departed for Arkhangel'sk in 1739 with ammunition, but forced to winter at Revel' due to leaks. Arrived at Arkhangel'sk in 1740. Visited Kola in 1741. Departed Arkhangel'sk for the Baltic with Vice-Adm. Bredal's squadron on 19.7.1742. Separated from the squadron during a storm on 11.8.1742 and forced to winter at Christiansand in Norway. Arrived at Kronshtadt in 1743. Visited Stockholm in 1744. To Danzig and Lubeck in 1745. Carried cargo in the Baltic in 1746. BU after 1746.

Deson
Purchased in Holland in 1720. Carried cargo in the Baltic. Wrecked in the Gulf of Finland in 1727. 5 men saved.

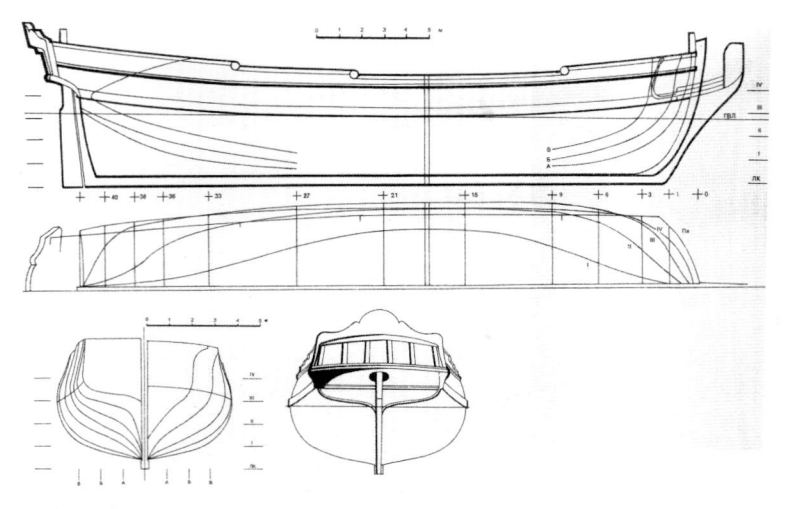

The gukor Novyy Kronshlot *purchased in Holland in 1717 as seen from several perspectives. A typical and unpretentious representative of a basic and unspectacular type.*

Belaia Gora
Purchased at Arkhangel'sk in 1772. Stationed there until 1775. Departed for the Baltic in 1775. Wintered at Karlsham (near Copenhagen) and arrived at Kronshtadt in 1776. Carried cargo in the Baltic in 1776, 1777 and 1782. Fire guard ship at Revel' in 1779. Set up sparbuoys off Revel' in 1781.

Sviatoi Andrei
Purchased in 1794. Carried cargo in the Gulf of Finland. BU 1806 at Kronshtadt.

Korneliia
Dimensions   approx. 72 ft x 22 ft x 11.5 ft (22 m x 6.7 m x 3.5 m)
Purchased in 1802. Carried cargo in the Baltic from 1802–12. Wrecked by a squall at Revel' on 30.12.1812.

Aleksandr
Dimensions   approx. 72.5 ft x 25 ft x 11 ft (22.1 m x 7.6 m x 3.4 m)
Purchased in 1802. Carried cargo in the Baltic from 1802–4. Converted into a harbour store ship in 1805.

Grigorii
Dimensions   approx. 82 ft x 24 ft x 11 ft (25 m x 7.3 m x 3.4 m)
Purchased in 1802. Carried cargo in the Baltic from 1802–9. BU 1814 at Abo.

Efim
Dimensions   approx. 80 ft x 25 ft x 12 ft (24.4 m x 7.6 m x 3.7 m)
Purchased in 1802. Carried cargo in the Baltic from 1802–8. Foundered in 1808 at Kronshtadt.

Nikolai
Dimensions   approx. 68 ft x 22 ft x 11 ft (20.7 m x 6.7 m x 3.4 m)
Built in 1800. Purchased in 1802. Carried cargo in the Baltic from 1802–7. BU 1815 at Kronshtadt.

Pyotr
Dimensions   approx. 70 ft x 24 ft x 11 ft (21.4 m x 7.3 m x 3.4 m)
Purchased in 1802. Hydrographic work in the Baltic from 1802–1810. BU at Kronshtadt 1815.

Baltic gukor prizes (3 prizes)

Unnamed
12-gun gukor captured by the frigate *Landsdou* in 10.1716.

Unnamed
14-gun gukor captured at Danzig by Adm. Gordon's squadron in 1734. Usually referred to as a 'French gukor'. Carried cargo between Riga and Kronshtadt in 1734–35. Fire watch ship at Biork-e zund from 1736–8 and at Kronshtadt from 1739–46. Carried food supplies to Stockholm for Russian troops on 9.1743. BU after 1746.

Anna-Mariia
Swedish prize captured in the Gulf of Vyborg by Adm. Chichagov's squadron on 22.6.1790. Carried food supplies for the fleet in 1790. Carried cargo in the Baltic from 1791–1803. BU 1804.

Caspian flotilla gukors (14 purpose-built)

Baku
Launched at Kazan in 1719. No other data available.

Printsessa Anna Astrakhan'
Laid down   ?   *Launched* 1722
Dimensions   approx. 54 ft x 15 ft x 5.9 ft (16.6 m x 4.7 m x 1.8 m)
Participated in the Persian expedition of 1722–4.

8 gukors built at Kazan by V. Fogel and V. Solovyev.
Laid down   1726   *Launched* 1727
Dimensions   approx. 70 ft x 22 ft x 11 ft (21.4 m x 6.7 m x 3.4 m)
Gunaki, Demozin, Kumik, Mugan, Urtemizh, Erpelei and two others

Aleksandr   Kazan
Laid down   ?   *Launched* 1740
Dimensions   approx. 88 ft x 23 ft x 13.4 (26.8 m x 7 m x 4.1 m)
Employed in the Caspian.

Ioann Kazan
Laid down   ?   *Launched* 1740
Dimensions   approx. 70 ft x 23 ft x 11 ft (21.4 m x 6.9 m x 3.4 m)
Employed in the Caspian. Wrecked in 1750 on a Zenzili bank (Zezilii is a Persian port in the southern Caspian, now Enzili).

Mariia Kazan
Laid down   ?   *Launched* 1740
Dimensions   approx. 70 ft x 23 ft x 11 ft (21.4 m x 6.9 m x 3.4 m)
No other data available.

Selafail Kazan
Laid down   ?   *Launched* 1740
Dimensions   approx. 70 ft x 22 ft x 11 ft (21.4 m x 6.7 m x 3.4 m)
Wrecked in 1750.

Okhotsk flotilla gukors (2 purpose-built)

Sviatoi Pyotr
Laid down   ?   *Launched* 8.1742
Dimensions   approx. 35 ft x 12 ft x 5.2 ft (10.7 m x 3.7 m x 1.6 m)
Built on Bering Island by S. Starodubtsev from the remains of the wrecked packet boat *Sviatoi Pyotr*. Carried cargo in the sea of Okhotsk. Sailed as part of a squadron under Lieutenant V. A. Khmetevskiy from Okhotsk to Kamchatka in 10.1753. Grounded on Kamchatka in a storm on 12.10.1753 but salvaged. Wrecked off Kamchatka in 1755.

Sviatoi Pavel Okhotskaya
Constructor   Moshchnitskiy
Laid down   23.12.1762   *Launched* 23.8.1766
                55 men
Constructed for the expedition of P. K. Krenitsyn and M. D. Levashov. Did survey work in the Aleutians and along the Alaskan coastline from 1766–70. Returned to Okhotsk in 1770. Cruised in the Sea of Okhotsk from 1774–86. BU at Okhotsk in 1786.

Purchased White Sea flotilla gukors (6 purchased)

Sviatoi Andrei Stratilat
Purchased in 1734. Stationed at Arkhangel'sk.

Lubianka
Purchased at Arkhangel'sk in 1772. Stationed at Arkhangel'sk and repaired there in 1781.

Sviatoi Zosima
Purchased at Arkhangel'sk in 1772. Stationed there.

Sviatoi Pavel
Purchased at Arkhangel'sk in 1772 and stationed there from 1772–4. Ordered to transfer to the Baltic in 1775. Two attempts at making the transit failed – allegedly due to leaks. The commanding officer was dismissed and degraded to seaman ranks for 6 months as punishment. Stationed at Arkhangel'sk from 1776–88. Repaired in 1784. Ordered to transport guns and anchors for the new ship of the line *Severniy Oryol* in 1788. Sunk due to a leak in a depth of 16 ft.

Sviatoi Pyotr
Purchased at Arkhangel'sk in 1772 and stationed there from 1772–4. Ordered to the Baltic in 1775, but returned due to a leak. Repaired, sailed again, and wintered at Copenhagen. Arrived at Kronshtadt in 1776 and permanently transferred to the Baltic fleet.

Sovatiy
Purchased at Arkhangel'sk in 1772 and stationed there. Repaired there in 1781.

Gekbots (155 purpose-built)

The Russian classification of gekbot derived from the German *heckboot*. In Russian service, gekbots were three-masted, square rigged vessels used for the transfer of both cargo and troops. Their use was limited to the Caspian Sea, where they were introduced specifically for the Persian expedition of the 1720s. Because sailing ships operating in the Baltic during summer months were frequently becalmed for long periods, large-scale troop movements were normally accomplished by large numbers of open-deck rowing vessels in the Baltic prior to the introduction of purpose-built transports in the 1770s. Although inefficient and uncomfortable, this practice ensured the timely arrival of troops at their destination and avoided the real possibility of starvation at sea for becalmed and overloaded sailing transports. This was not the case in the livelier Caspian, and the Russians were able to utilize troop transports of the more traditional sort. While gekbots were usually unarmed, those participating in at the siege of Baku had temporarily installed guns, howitzers and mortars to remedy the absence of more traditional warship types. Although produced in large numbers from 1723, the construction of gekbots was discontinued after 1746 as the threat of hostilities with Persia wound down.

Caspian flotilla gekbots (155 purpose-built)

41 gekbots built 1723 at Kazan and Nizniy Novgorod.
Dimensions   approx. 100 ft x 27 ft x ? (30.5 m x 8.2 m x ?)

~

26 gekbots built at Kazan 1723.

~

15 gekbots built in 1723. All participated in the Persian expedition.
Laid down   12.1722   Launched 11.5.1723
Astrakhan', Vulkan, Gilyan, Gerkaniya, Dagestan, Kazan' (wrecked in 1726), **Kaspiiskii Neptun, Ryashch, Sviataia Anna, Sviataia Ekaterina,**

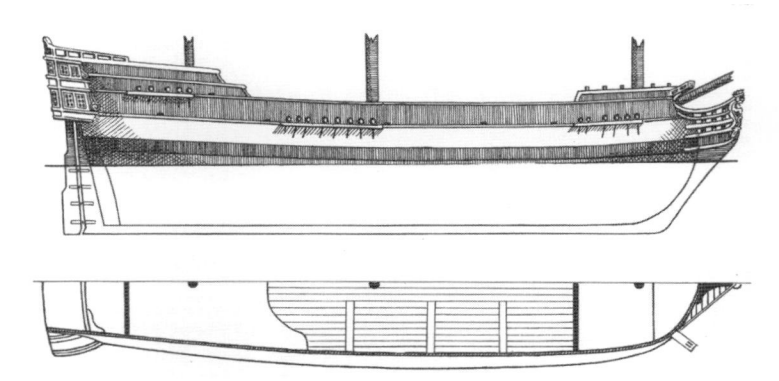

Gekbots, like fleyts, were Russian adaptations of a variety of square rigged cargo carrier long in use by the trading nations of the North Sea and the Baltic. They were found only in Russian service in the Caspian Sea where they were produced in very large numbers to supply transportation for Peter I's campaign in 1723 and to act as ad hoc warships in the absence of any Persian naval opposition. Astrakhan', shown here in profile and overhead views, was named after Russia's northern seaport in the Caspian at the base of the Volga. Her non-military nature is advertised clearly by the absence of gunports or swivel guns topside.

Sviataia Elisaveta (wrecked in 1730 off Zenzili), **Sviataia Natal'ia, Sviatoi Nikolai, Sviatoi Pavel, Sviatoi Pyotr** (wrecked in 1725)

~

15 gekbots built at Nizhnyi Novogorod. All participated in the Persian expedition.
Laid down   1722   Launched 1723
Agrakhan', Aleksandr Magnus, Apsheron, Ararat, Astrabad (lost without trace in 1731 in the Caspian), **Zinanoy, Kavkaz, Moskva, Nizhnyi Novogorod, Sagozan, Saratov, Simbirsk, Tmutarakan, Shakhdan, Tsaritsyn** (1726 survey of Caspian coast)

~

5 gekbots built in 1725, including **Zenzili** (wrecked in 1726 in Gilyan).

~

8 gekbots launched in 1726 at Kazan' and 80–85 ft (24.4–25.9 m) long:
Aleksandr Magnus, Girkaniia, Dagestan, Moskva, Sankt-Peterburg (wrecked in 1729 off Zenzili), **Sviatoi Pyotr, Shakhdag,** one other.

~

6 gekbots built in 1727 and launched in 1727.
Apsheron, Vulkan, Zenzili, Kavkaz, Kazan', Sviatoi Diodor.

~

8 gekbots launched in 1729 at Kazan'.
Dimensions   approx. 81 ft x 24 ft x 11 ft (24.8 m x 7.4 m x 3.4 m)
Astrakhan', Astrabad, Kaspiiskii Neptun, Pyotr II, Sviataia Anna, Sviataia Ekaterina, Sviatoi Nikolai, Sviatoi Pavel.

~

5 gekbots built at Kazan' in 1729.
Dimensions   approx. 85 ft x 24 ft x 12 ft (25.9 m x 7.3 m x 3.7 m)
Astrakhan', Zinait, Saratov, Simbirsk (driven ashore by storm 21.12.1733 off Dagestan), **Tsaritsyn.**

~

5 gekbots launched in 1731 at Kazan'.
Dimensions   approx. 86 ft x 22 ft x 11.5 ft (26.2 m x 6.7 m x 3.5 m)
Kronshtadt, Narva, Revel', Riga, St Petersburg.

~

5 gekbots built at Kazan' in 1735.
Kiev, Seskar, Ezel', two others

~

5 gekbots built at Kazan' in 1741.
Azov, Moskva, Sankt-Peterburg, Iaroslavl', one other

7 gekbots built at Kazan' in 1745.
Dimensions approx. 83 ft x 24 ft x 12 ft (25.3 m x 7.3 m x 3.7 m)
Varakhail, Devora, Selafail, Tovi, Uriil, Iagudiil, one other

Also, the following four gekbots were mentioned as being at Astrakhan' in 1745–6.
Ekaterina, Elizaveta, Lev, Feolog.

Kraers (8 purpose-built)

The term kraer derives from the Dutch *kraaier*, a type of three-masted flat-bottomed cargo ships employed primarily in the North Sea during the sixteenth to nineteenth centuries by Holland and Sweden. The type found limited use in Russia in northern waters during the second half of the eighteenth century.

4 kraers built at Olonetskaya yard by Mikhailov.
Dimensions approx. 100 ft x 27 ft x 10.2 ft (30.5 m x 8.2 m x 3.1 m)
170 last capacity (The Russian 'last' was the equivalent of 120 36 pound poods)
No. 1
Laid down 22.10.1762 Launched 9.5.1763
BU 1774.
No. 2
Laid down 22.9.1762 Launched 22.5.1763
BU 1773.
No. 3
Laid down 27.9.1762 Launched 14.6.1763
BU 1772.
No. 4
Laid down 27.9.1762 Launched 24.6.1763
BU 1772.

4 kraers built at Olonetskaya yard by I. I. Afanasyev: *Dimensions* approx. 80 ft x 27 ft x 9.5 ft (24.4 m x 8.2n m x 2.9 m)
Rak
Laid down 29.11.1772 Launched 16.5.1773
BU 1768.
Cherepakha
Laid down 29.11.1772 Launched 29.5.1773
Repaired 1782, BU 1789.
Laima
Laid down 1773 Launched 5.1774
Repaired 1781.
Don
Laid down 1775 Launched 26.5.1776
BU 1788.

Transports (328 ships, all types)

Purpose-built transports were first introduced in the Sea of Azov Flotilla in 1771 during the early stages of its rebirth as a significant naval organization under Prince Potemkin. By the beginning of the nineteenth century, square rigged ships designed and built as transports had replaced all previous types of cargo vessels in this and other roles in all Russian naval commands. Besides transporting cargo and troops as required,

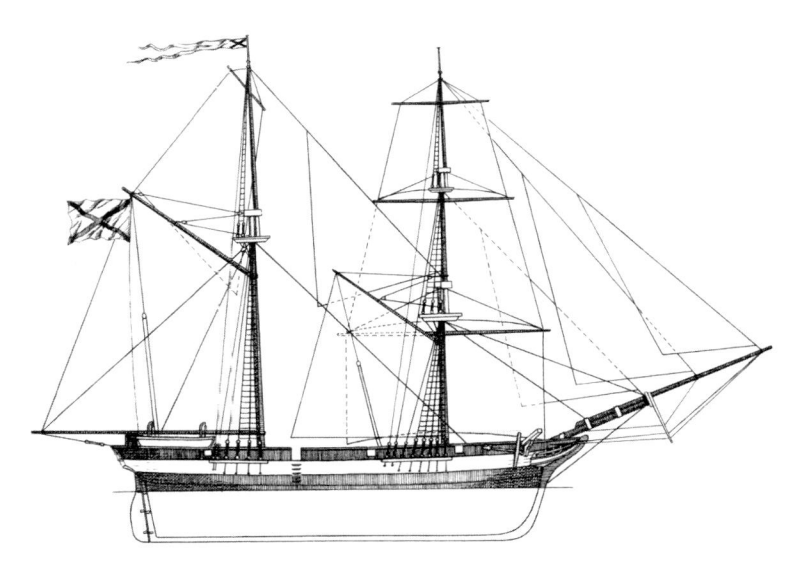

The descendant of the fleyts and gekbots of the early eighteenth century, the transport Baikal, *named after a lake in Siberia and completed in 1848 for service in the Sea of Okhotsk, served essentially the same function as her predecessors in spite of great improvements in design and construction. Given her intended service in an unsettled part of the world, it comes as no surprise to see her sides pierced for and carrying 6 cannon of unknown calibre.*

transports were used as quasi-warships for routine cruising and patrol, hydrographic survey, scientific expeditions, and fire-watch service. They were variously armed with from 2–30 guns. Three-masted ships were classed as transports, and sometimes described as store ships. Two-masted vessels were described as transport brigs. Size varied considerably, with lengths ranging from 40 ft–150 ft for extreme examples, but with a range of 54 ft–135 ft being more representative. During wartime, those ships with the strongest hulls were frequently converted into bomb vessels or floating batteries, reverting to their designed roles as transports at the end of hostilities. Transports were also converted into corvettes and assigned combat roles on two occasions (*Diomid* and *Kherson*). In yet another instance, a large transport (*Kildyuin*) was reclassified and profitably employed as a frigate. One final example of a transport converted to military uses is provided by the conversion of *Taganrog* into a 16-gun 'flat-bottomed frigate'.

A total of 136 transports were purpose-built between 1771 and the end of sail. The numerical breakdown was somewhat unexpected, with the Black Sea fleet leading the way with 59 ships, followed by the Baltic with 42, the Caspian with 22, the White Sea with 6, the Sea of Okhotsk with 4 and landlocked Lake Baikal in Siberia with 3. An even more pronounced disparity between the numbers in the Black Sea and the Baltic existed with regards to purchased and converted transports, with 43 in the Black Sea against only 24 in the Baltic. Two factors accounted for the Black Sea fleet's lead over the larger Baltic fleet in the number of transports built and employed. The first had to do with the geographical and meteorological advantages that the Black Sea, with its deep harbours and steep coastal drop-offs, offered to large sailing vessels for the operation of large square rigged sailing ships in coastal waters as contrasted with the Baltic, with its shallow inshore conditions. The Baltic was also plagued by unreliable wind conditions and frequent extended calms that made the use of small open-oared vessels a more reliable proposition for the movement of troops than large and unwieldy transports – death from lack of water was a real possibility in becalmed ships overloaded with troops. Of possibly greater importance in explaining the numerical edge the Black Sea had over the Baltic in naval transports were the enormous demands for logistical and manpower support created by the long running hostility to Russian dominance in the newly conquered Caucasus during the 1830s and later. Given the rough terrain and absence of roads along the coast, the deployment and support of large numbers of troops could only be accomplished by the Black Sea fleet operating significant numbers of both warships and transports. The Caspian offered similar challenges on a lesser, but still significant, level. Both areas contrasted with the Baltic in the continuing demand for naval logistical support after 1815.

A complete summary of all transport vessels known to have served in the Russian Navy in all theatres from 1770 to the end of sail in 1860 is as follows:

Purpose-built	136
Converted	20
Purchased	48
Confiscated	25
Prizes	61
Unknown origin	38
Total	328

Azov flotilla transports (7 purpose-built)

2 two-masted transport brigs built at Ikoretskaya by S. I. Afanasyev.
Laid down   9.1769   *Launched* 26.5.1770
Dimensions   approx. 86 ft x 24 ft x 7.9 ft (26.2 m x 7.3 m x 2.4 m)
Armament   12 x 6pdrs
               57 men

Bukharest
Cruised in sea of Azov from 1770–8. Harbour service after 1780.

Iassy
Mortars installed for temporary service as a bomb vessel in 1770. Cruised as a bomb from 1771–5. Repaired and converted into a transport from 1778–9. Foundered during a storm on 24.5.1785. (See also under Bomb vessels.)

~

5 transports launched at Novokhoperskaya in 1771.

Akhtapom
Cruised in the Sea of Azov from 1774–9. Crushed by ice and foundered off the mouth of the Mius River on 11.11.1779.

Kambala
Reassigned to the Black Sea fleet in 1783. Cruised in the Sea of Azov and Black Sea from 1774–87.

Rak
Cruised in the Sea of Azov from 1774–7. Driven ashore in a storm and lost on 5.8.1777.

Tarantul
Cruised in the Sea of Azov from 1774–5. Damaged in a storm on 5.12.1775. Later BU.

Cherepakha
Reassigned to the Black Sea fleet in 1783. Cruised in the Sea of Azov and Black Sea from 1774–87.

Baltic fleet transports (42 purpose-built)

2 transports built at Olonetskaya.
Launched   1785
               450 tons burthen
               110 men

Kolpitsa
To Arkhangel'sk with guns and ammunition for new ships in 1785. Returned to Kronshtadt in 1786. Permanently transferred to Arkhangel'sk from 1787–1806.

Turukhtan Kolpitsa
To Arkhangel'sk with guns and ammunition for new ships in 1785. Returned to Kronshtadt in 1786. Scheduled for circumnavigation in 1787, but this was cancelled due to war with Sweden in 1788. Assigned to Greig's squadron in 1788. Participated at Hogland from behind the line. Cruised in the Baltic 1788–91 with intermittent employment as a hospital ship. Permanently transferred to Arkhangel'sk in 1792. BU after 1800.

~

3 transports built at Arkhangel'sk.
Dimensions   approx. 135 ft x 128 ft x 35 ft x 14.4 ft
               (41.2 m x 39 m (lk) x 10.7 m (inside plank) x 4.4 m)
               600 tons burthen
Armament   26–32 guns
               170 men

Kholmogory Bykovskaya
Laid down   1785   *Launched* 18.5.1786
Passed to Kronshtadt 7–8.1786. Intended for circumnavigation in 1787, but this was cancelled due to the war with Sweden in 1788. Assigned to Greig's Mediterranean squadron as a hospital ship. Operated with the main fleet during the Russo-Swedish War in 1788–90. Permanently transferred to Arkhangel'sk in 1792. Last mentioned in 1795.

Boets Bykovskaya
Laid down   21.11.1787   *Launched* 20.5.1788
Passed to Kronshtadt in 1792. Carried cargo in the Gulf of Finland from 1793–1801.

Naian Bykovskaya
Laid down   21.11.1787   *Launched* 20.5.1788
Fire watch ship at Arkhangel'sk from 1788–90. Remained there till BU 1804.

~

Kniaz' Mikhail
Laid down   ?   *Launched* 1792
Dimensions approx. 72 ft x 23 ft x 12.5 ft (22 m x 7 m x 3.8 m)
Carried cargo in the Baltic from 1792–1800. BU 1804.

Sviatoi Nikolai Solombala
Laid down   25.10.1791   *Launched* 13.6.1792
Surveyed the coast of the White Sea from 1792–8. Wrecked while crossing shallows of the Severnaya Dvina River on 23.9.1798.

Kildyuin Solombala
Laid down   14.11.1796   *Launched* 19.5.1798
Dimensions   approx. 135 ft x 35 ft x 14.4 ft (41.2 m x 10.7 m x 4.4 m)
Cruised in the White Sea from 1798-1801. Transferred to Kronshtadt in 1803. Cruised in the Baltic in 1804. Converted into a frigate in 1805 and assigned to Seniavin's Mediterranean squadron. (See also under frigates.)

6 transports built at Lodeynoe Pole.
Dimensions   approx. 82 ft x 25 ft x 9.2 ft (24.9 m x 7.6 m x 2.8 m)
Atlas
Launched   1806

Carried cargo in the Baltic from 1807–12. Hydrographic surveys in Finland in 1814–15. BU 1815.
Beber
Launched   1806
Transferred supplies to Rochensalm during the Russo-Swedish War from 1808–9. Cruised in the Baltic from 1810–12. At the siege of Danzig in 1813. Cruised in the Baltic in 1814–15. BU 1817.
Vol
Launched   1806
Stationed at Kronshtadt Roads in 1807. Active in the Gulf of Botnicus in 1812. At the siege of Danzig in 1813. Cruised in the Baltic in 1814–15. BU 1817.
Domkrat
Launched   1806
Stationed in the Baltic in 1807. Carried supplies to Rochensalm during the Russo-Swedish War in 1808–9. Wrecked off the coast of Finland 7.11.1809.
Kit
Launched   1806
Stationed at Kronshtadt Roads in 1808. Carried cargo in the Baltic from 1810–12. At the siege of Riga in 1813. Wrecked off Danzig on 13.8.1813.
Navaga
Launched   1806
Stationed at Kronshtadt in 1807. Operated with the rowing flotilla against Sweden in 1808–9. BU 1810.

Vetryanitsa Lodeynoe Pole
Launched 1806
Operated in the Baltic in 1807. Burnt by the Swedes in 1808.

Ladushka
Launched 1806
Dimensions   approx. 73 ft x 25 ft x 9.5 ft (22.3 m x 7.5 m x 2.9 m)
Carried cargo in the Baltic from 1806–13. BU 1815.

Chaika
Launched 1806
Dimensions   approx. 72 ft x 26 ft x 7.9 ft (22 m x 7.9 m x 2.4 m)
Carried cargo in the Baltic from 1806–12. Fire watch duties at Rochensalm from 1813–15. BU 1816.

Polifem Okhta
Constructor   V. F. Stoke
Laid down   1.2.1815   *Launched* 12.8.1815
To Goteborg in 1816. To Arkhangel'sk and back to Kronshtadt in 1817. Carried cargo in the Gulf of Finland from 1818–23. Grounded and repaired in 1819.

Ural Solombala
Constructor   A. M. Kurochkin
Laid down   14.1.1814   *Launched* 26.5.1816
Armament   30 guns
Passed from Arkhangel'sk to Kronshtadt in 1816. Round trips from Kronshtadt to Arkhangel'sk with stores for ship construction in 1817–18, 1819–20 and 1823–4. Grounded during the Great Flood of 7.11.1824 and later BU.

Mezen' Solombala
Laid down   10.7.1818   *Launched* 19.6.1819
Armament   30 guns.

Named after the Mezen' River, which flows into the White Sea. Passed from Arkhangel'sk to Kronshtadt in 1819. Round trips from Kronshtadt to Arkhangel'sk in 1820–1, 1822–3 and 1824–5. Grounded and wrecked en route to Revel' on 27.8.1826.

3 transports built at St Petersburg by Pomorskiy and K. A. Gazyrin.
Laid down   12.1821
Dimensions   approx. 54 ft x 18 ft x 8.2 ft (16.5 m x 5.4 m x 2.5 m)
                17 men
Nevka
Launched   27.6.1822
Named after the Neva River which enters the Baltic at St Petersburg. Carried cargo in the Baltic in 1823 and 1827. Fire watch duties at Sveaborg in 1824–5. Grounded and lost en route to Sveaborg on 23.10.1828 due to pilot error.
Priazhka
Launched   14.7.1822
Named after a branch of the Neva. Carried cargo in the Baltic from 1822–8. Fire watch duties at Kronshtadt from 1829–33. Used as a floating lighthouse at St Petersburg from 1834–5.
Fontanka
Launched   11.8.1822
Named after a branch of the Neva. Carried cargo in the Baltic from 1823–9. Fire watch duties at Sveaborg in 1830–1. Carried cargo in the Baltic in 1832. Fire watch duties at Kronshtadt in 1834–5.

Krotkii Okhta
Constructor   V. F. Stoke
Laid down   28.8.1824   *Launched* 2.5.1825
Dimensions   approx. 90 ft x 27 ft x 12.8 ft (27.5 m x 8.3 m x 3.9 m)
Armament   16 guns
                50 men
Designed and built specifically for delivering cargo to Kamchatka. Departed for Kronshtadt on 23.8.1825 and arrived at Petropavlovsk on 12.6.1826. Returned to Kronshtadt on 14.9.1827. Sailed for Petropavlovsk a second time on 10.9.1828 and arrived there on 10.7.1829, discovering the Marshalls en route. Arrived at Novoarkhangel'sk on 26.10.1829 (Russian North America). Returned to Kronshtadt on 16.9.1830. Carried cargo in the Gulf of Finland in 1831–2. BU after 1833.

Dvina Solombala
Constructor   V. A. Ershov
Laid down   24.8.1828   *Launched* 21.5.1829
Dimensions   approx. 130 ft x 33 ft x ? (39.7m (pp) x 10.1m
                (inside plank) x ?)
Armament   8 guns
Passed from Arkhangel'sk to Kronshtadt in 1829. Returned to Arkhangel'sk with supplies for building ships in 1830. Returned to Kronshtadt in 1832. Carried cargo in the Gulf of Finland from 1833–8 and 1840–2. Hulked in 1845.

Libava New Admiralty, St Petersburg
Constructor   I. A. Amosov
Laid down   14.11.1831   *Launched*   31.8.1832
Dimensions   approx. 89 ft x 23 ft x 12.1 ft (27.2m (pp) x 7m
                (inside plank) x 3.7 m)
Armament   4 guns
Carried cargo in the Baltic in 1833. Laid buoys in 1834. Wrecked off Moon-zund on 5.5.1834.

6 transports built at Solombala by F. T. Zagulyaev.

Dimensions   approx. 128 ft x 30 ft x 14.8 ft (39.1m (pp) x 9 m x 4.5 m)
480 tons burthen

Armament   4–12 guns

Gapsal

Laid down   21.9.1833   *Launched* 21.5.1834

Passed to Revel' from Arkhangel'sk in 1834. Carried cargo in the Baltic from 1835–49. BU after 1850.

Svir'

Laid down   18.11.1837   *Launched* 21.5.1839

Passed from Arkhangel'sk to Kronshtadt in 1839. Carried cargo from 1840–53. Stationed at Kronshtadt from 1854–6. BU 1857.

Msta

Laid down   23.8.1839   *Launched* 21.5.1840

Passed from Arkhangel'sk in 1840. Carried cargo in the Baltic from 1841–7. Struck a rock and sank off Biork-e zund on 13.9.1847.

Tver'

Laid down   23.8.1839   *Launched* 6.5.1841

Passed from Arkhangel'sk to Kronshtadt in 1841. Carried cargo in the Baltic from 1842–6 and from 1848–52. Wrecked during storm off Revel' on 2.10.1852.

Volga

Laid down   30.8.1840   *Launched* 21.5.1842

Passed from Arkhangel'sk to Kronshtadt in 1842. Carried cargo in the Baltic in 1843. To Stockholm in 1844. Carried cargo in the Baltic from 1845–53. During the Crimean War, she carried supplies to Sveaborg and Abo in 1854–5 by passing extremely close to the shore to avoid discovery by British and French warships. While so engaged, she grounded off Kursalo Island on 18.5.1855. Cargo was offloaded and the ship was blown up.

Tvertsa

Laid down   30.8.1840   *Launched* 24.5.1842

Passed from Arkhangel'sk to Kronshtadt in 1842. Carried cargo in the Baltic from 1843–53. Stationed at Sveaborg with the main fleet in 1854-55. Scuttled in 7.1855 to block passage into Sveaborg.

~

3 transports built at Solombala yard.

Dimensions   approx. 107 ft x 28 ft x17.4 ft (32.6m (pp) x 8.6 (inside plank) x 5.3 m)
300 tons burthen

Armament   4 guns

Volkhov

Constructor   F. T. Zagulyaev

Laid down   22.9.1834   *Launched* 21.5.1835

Passed from Arkhangel'sk to Kronshtadt in 1836. Carried cargo in the Baltic from 1837–43. Hydrographic work in the Gulf of Riga from 1844–6 and in 1849. Carried cargo in the Baltic from 1851–3. BU 1857.

Pechora

Constructor   Koshkarev

Laid down   6.11.1835   *Launched* 6.5.1836

Passed from Arkhangel'sk to Kronshtadt in 1836. Carried cargo in the Baltic from 1837–42. Hydrographic work in the Gulf of Riga in 1843–4. Carried cargo in the Baltic from 1845–8. Hydrographic work in the Gulf of Riga in 1849. Carried cargo in the Baltic from 1850–3. BU 1858.

Pinega

Constructor   Koshkarev

Laid down   21.5.1837   *Launched* 21.5.1839

Passed from Arkhangel'sk to Kronshtadt in 1839. Carried cargo in the Baltic from 1840–52. Hydrographic work in 1853. BU 1857.

~

2 transports built at St Petersburg.

Dimensions   approx. 78 ft x 24 ft x 9.8 ft (23.9m (pp) x 7.2m (inside plank) x 3 m)

Armament   4 guns

Oka Admiralty, St Petersburg

Constructor   A. I. Pipin

Laid down   9.2.1835   *Launched* 1836

Carried cargo in the Baltic from 1840–5. Laid marker buoys in the Gulfs of Riga and Finland in 1847. BU after 1853.

Mologa New Admiralty, St Petersburg

Constructor   N. I. Fyodrov

Laid down   13.12.1835   *Launched* 5.10.1835

Carried cargo in the Baltic in 1836, 1838–40 and 1842–3. Repaired in 1851. Carried cargo in the Baltic in 1853. Stationed at Revel' from 1853–6. Hydrographic works from 1857–61.

~

Abo Abo

Laid down   24.5.1839   *Launched* 27.4.1840

Dimensions   approx. 128 ft x 34 ft x 14.1 ft (39m (pp) x 10.3 (inside plank) x 4.3 m)
665 tons burthen

Armament   10 guns

Departed Kronshtadt for Kamchatka on 5.9.1840. Arrived at Petropavlovsk on 21.9.1841, losing 5 men during transit. Departed Petropavlovsk on 24.11.1841. Arrived at Kronshtadt on 13.10.1842. Carried gifts to Swinemunde from Nikolai to the King of Prussia in 1843. Carried cargo in the Baltic in 1844–5. To Naples in 1846. Accompanied the Russian squadron to Denmark in 1848 to counter the threat of Prussian invasion. Carried supplies to Vyborg and Sveaborg in 1854–5, hugging the coastline to avoid capture. BU before 1861.

Aland Gelsingfors (private shipyard)

Laid down   ?   *Launched* 1851

Dimensions   approx. 87 ft x 25 ft x 8.9 ft (26.4m (pp) x 7.5 m x 2.7 m)
150 tons burthen

Operated with the Finnish rowing flotilla from 1852–6. Carried cargo in the Baltic from 1856–62. Stricken on 5.1.1863.

Dvina Okhta

Constructor   Shatten

Laid down   23.6.1851   *Launched* 5.6.1852

Dimensions   approx. 128 ft x 35 ft x 15.7 ft (39m (pp) x 10.6 m x 4.8 m)
655 tons burthen

Armament   10 x 18pdrs
65 men

Departed Kronshtadt for Kamchatka on 20.9.1852. Arrived at Petropavlovsk on 27.8.1853, completing a journey of 6,000 nautical miles in 54 days and discovering 16 new islands in the Marshalls while en route. Employed as a troopship in 5.1854 and transferred 5 of her guns to a shore battery. Participated in the successful defence of Petropavlovsk against a combined Anglo-French squadron on 24.8.1854. Transported 270 passengers and baggage to De Castries Bay on 6.4.1855. Exchanged fire with enemy ships on 8.5.1855. Arrived at Nikolaevsk on 18.7.1855. Departed for the Baltic on 20.8.1856, arriving at Kronshtadt on 15.9.1857. Carried cargo in the Baltic from 1858–60. Stricken on 26.8.1871.

Neman Okhta

Constructor   I. A. Amosov

Laid down   13.9.1852   *Launched* 2.6.1853

Dimensions   approx. 109 ft x 29 ft x 20 ft (33.2m (pp) x 8.7m (inside plank) x 6.1 m)
322 tons burthen

Departed Kronshtadt for Kamchatka on 22.8.1853. Wrecked en route in the Kattegat on 23.9.1853.

Gapsal Solombala
Constructor   F. T. Zagulyaev
Laid down   10.10.1852   *Launched* 13.6.1854
Dimensions   approx. 128 ft x 35 ft x 14.1 ft (39m (pp) x 10.6 m x 4.3 m)
  655 tons burthen
  93 men
Stationed at Arkhangel'sk from 1854–6. Departed for Kronshtadt on 6.8.1857. Grounded, damaged, and forced to return for repairs. Passed from Arkhangel'sk in 6–8.1858. Carried cargo in the Baltic in 1859. BU before 1861.

Caspian flotilla transports (22 purpose-built)

2 transports launched in 1788 at the Kazan' Admiralty.
Volga
Carried cargo from 1789–92. Surveyed coastlines from 1793–4. Carried cargo from 1795–7. Fire watch duties in 1798.
Ural
In action against mutineers off Baku in 1791. Fire watch duties at Baku in 1793. Carried cargo from 1794–7.

~

9 transports built to common dimensions.
Dimensions   approx. 68 ft x 20 ft x 9.8 ft (20.7 m x 6.1 m x 3 m)
Armament   4 guns
Osetr (I) Astrakhan'
Laid down   21.10.1805   *Launched* 22.9.1806
Transported stores and food to Russian troops at war with Persia from 1806–13. BU after 1814.
Luna Kazan'
Laid down   ?   *Launched* 11.5.1807
Transported stores and food to Russian troops at war with Persia from 1807–13. Cruised in the Caspian from 1814–17. BU 1817.
Mukha Kazan'
Constructor   A. P. Antipov
Laid down   7.11.1807   *Launched* 21.5.1808
Transported stores and food to Russian troops at war with Persia from 1809–13. Cruised in the Caspian from 1814–20. BU 1823.
Pchela Kazan'
Constructor   A. P. Antipov
Laid down   7.8.1807   *Launched* 21.5.1808
Transported stores and food to Russian troops at war with Persia from 1809–13. Cruised in the Caspian from 1814–20. Fire watch duties from 1821–8. BU 1830.
Baku Kazan'
Constructor   E. I. Koshkin
Laid down   29.5.1810   *Launched* 25.5.1811
Transported stores and food to Russian troops at war with Persia from 1812–13. Cruised in the Caspian from 1814–17.
Volga Kazan'
Constructor   E. I. Koshkin
Laid down   29.5.1810   *Launched* 25.5.1811
Stationed at Astrakhan' in 1812. Cruised in the Caspian from 1813–17.
Osetr (II)   Kazan'
Constructor   A. P. Antipev
Laid down   11.3.1816   *Launched* 13.5.1817
Cruised in the Caspian from 1817–20. Fire watch duties from 1821–3. BU 1828.

Kura Kazan'
Constructor   A. P. Antipev
Laid down   11.6.1818   *Launched* 1819
Took part in the survey of the southeastern Caspian under N. N. Muravyev-Karskiy and the survey of the mouth of the Volga in 1820–1. Cruised off the Persian coast in 1822–3 and 1825–7. BU 1828.
Volga Kazan'
Constructor   A. P. Antipev
Laid down   1822   *Launched* 3.5.1823
Cruised off the Persian coast in 1824. Carried supplies to Russian troops during the war with Persian in 1826–8. Carried supplies to Russian troops at the mouth of the Kura in 1828–9 during the subsequent war with Turkey. BU 1833.

~

2 transports built at Astrakhan ft by A. P. Utlov and S. O. Burachek.
Dimensions   approx. 66 ft x 21 ft x 6.9 ft (20.1 m x 6.4 m x 2.1 m)
Armament   4 guns
Yaik
Laid down   1823   *Launched* 18.10.1823
Cruised off the Persian coast in 1824–5. Transported supplies to Russian troops during the war with Persia from 1826–8. Employed as a troopship in the 1828–9 in the war with Turkey. Reverted to carrying cargo in 1831. BU 1832.
Pyotr
Laid down   1824   *Launched* 5.11.1825
Named in honour of the commander of Astrakhan', Pyotr G. Orlovskiy. Foundered in the Volga in 1826, but salvaged. Cruised off the Persian coast from 1826–8. Employed as a troopship in the 1828–9 war with Turkey. Cruised off the Persian coast in 1830. BU 1837.

~

2 transports built at Astrakhan' by S. O. Burachek.
Dimensions   approx. 78 ft x 23 ft x 10 ft (23.9 m x 6.9 m x 3.1 m)
Armament   6 guns
Don
Laid down   7.1.1829   *Launched* 10.9.1829
Carried cargo in the Caspian from 1830–4. Fishery guard duties from 1836–41. Fire watch duties in 1842. BU 1843.
Donets
Laid down   7.1.1829   *Launched* 2.11.1829
To Persia in 1830. Driven ashore and wrecked in a storm on 24.10.1830.

~

Emba Astrakhan' Admiralty
Constructor   D. I. Alekseev
Laid down   20.8.1831   *Launched* 14.5.1832
Dimensions   approx. 70 ft x 13 ft x 10.5 ft (21.4 m x 3.9 m x 3.2 m)
Armament   2 guns
Carried cargo in the Caspian from 1832–8. Cruised off the Persian coast in 1840–1. Repaired in 1842. Fire watch duties at Baku in 1843. Carried cargo in 1844. Cruised off the Persian coast in 1845–6. BU 1847.

Ural Astrakhan' Admiralty
Constructor   D. I. Alekseev
Laid down   24.2.1834   *Launched* 6.6.1834
Dimensions   approx. 69 ft x 21 ft x 7.5 ft (20.9 m x 6.3 m x 2.3 m)
Carried cargo in the Caspian from 1834–42. Fire watch duties in 1843. BU 1844.

Terek Astrakhan' Admiralty
Constructor   S. G. Bebikhov
Laid down   26.7.1834   *Launched* 15.5.1835

Dimensions   approx. 80 ft x 26 ft x 11.5 ft (24.4 m x 7.8 m x 3.5 m)
Armament   8 guns
Carried cargo in the Caspian in 1835. Fire watch duties in 1836–7. Carried cargo from 1838–46. Flagship of the Caspian Flotilla in 1843. BU 1846.

2 transports built at Astrakhan' Admiralty by S. G. Bebikhov.
Dimensions   approx. 70 ft x 21 ft x 7.5 ft (21.4 m x 6.4 m x 2.3 m)
Armament   2 guns
Kura
Laid down   26.8.1836   *Launched* 14.4.1837
Carried cargo in the Caspian in 1837–8 and from 1843–6. Damaged by ice and wrecked in a storm on 15.11.1846.
Kuma
Laid down   26.8.1836   *Launched* 25.5.1837
Carried cargo in the Caspian in 1838 and from 1843–7. BU 1848.

~

Derbent Astrakhan' Admiralty
Constructor   S. N. Neverov
Laid down   30.9.1839   *Launched* 5.5.1842
Dimensions   approx. 82 ft x 26 ft x 11.8 ft (25 m x 7.9 m x 3.6 m)
Armament   12 guns
Carried cargo in the Caspian from 1842–4. Cruised off the Persian coast in 1845–6. Fire watch duties in 1848–9. Hulked in 1849.

Kura Kamsko-Botkinskiy Plant
Constructor   Johnson
Laid down   1851   *Launched* 1852
Dimensions   approx. 150 ft x 23 ft x ? (45.8 m x 7 m x ?)
Armament   7 guns
Carried cargo in the Caspian from 1853–9. Stricken on 20.11.1876.

Black Sea fleet transports (59 purpose-built)

Grigorii Nikolaev
Laid down   1797   *Launched* 1798
Carried bombs and solid shot for the Russian squadron in 1799. Returned to Sevastopol' in 1800. Carried cargo to Corfu in 1801, 1802 and 1804. Arrived at Corfu and assigned to Captain Sorokin's squadron in 1805. Operated with Seniavin's squadron in 1806. At Messina and Naples in 1806. Sold in 1809.

2 transports built at Kherson.
Dimensions   approx. 140 ft x 40 ft x 16 ft (42.7 m x 12.2 m x 4.9 m)
Diomid
Constructor   V. I. Potapov
Laid down   30.1.1804   *Launched* 29.10.1804
Transported troops to Corfu in 1805 and returned to Sevastopol'. Converted into a corvette in 1806. (See under Black Sea corvettes.)
Rion
Constructor   M. I. Surovtsov
Laid down   26.10.1809   *Launched* 1.12.1810
Carried cargo in the Black Sea from 1811–22. BU after 1823.

~

Kherson Kherson
Constructor   M. I. Surovtsov
Laid down   10.7.1804   *Launched* 28.7.1805
Dimensions   approx. 120 ft x 34 ft x 12.1 ft (36.6 m x 10.4 m x 3.7 m)
Carried cargo in the Black Sea in 1805. Converted into a corvette at the end of 1805. (See under Black Sea corvettes.)

Dunay Nikolaev Admiralty
Constructor   D. V. Kuznetsov
Laid down   23.2.1810   *Launched* 28.9.1810
Carried cargo in the Black Sea from 1811–22. BU 1824.

Prut Nikolaev Admiralty
Constructor   D. V. Kuznetsov
Laid down   16.12.1812   *Launched* 24.5.1813
Carried cargo in the Black Sea from 1814–20. Wrecked off the Crimea on 28.10.1820.

Lev
Laid down   ?   *Launched* 1816
Carried cargo in the Black Sea from 1817–26.

Mariia Nikolaev Admiralty
Constructor   A. I. Melikhov
Laid down   16.2.1818   *Launched* 4.5.1819
Dimensions   approx. 133 ft x 35 ft x 14.4 ft (41.5 m x 10.7 m x 4.4 m)
Armament   6 guns
Took part annually in Black Sea fleet manoeuvres from 1819–27. Transported supplies to the fleet during the war with Turkey and evacuated the sick to Sevastopol' in 1828–9. Cruised in the Black Sea in 1830–1. Sold for BU in 1837.

Utka
Laid down   28.1.1819   *Launched* 29.7.1819
Dimensions   approx. 54 ft x 17 ft x 9.8 ft (16.5 m x 5.1 m x 3 m)
Armament   2 guns
Cruised in the Black Sea from 1820–4. Wrecked in the mouth of the Danube in 1824.

3 small transports built at Kherson by M. I. Surovtsov.
Dimensions   approx. 45 ft x 16 ft x 5.9 ft (13.7 m x 4.9 m x 1.8 m)
Kit
Laid down   20.3.1819   *Launched* 13.8.1819
Cruised in the Black Sea from 1819–27 and with the Danube Flotilla in 1828–9. BU 1838.
Kambala
Laid down   20.3.1819   *Launched* 14.2.1820
Cruised in the Black Sea from 1820–7 and with the Danube Flotilla in 1828–9. Foundered in 1831.
Cherepakha
Laid down   20.3.1819   *Launched* 9.4.1820
Cruised in the Black Sea from 1820–7 and with the Danube Flotilla in 1828–9.

~

Ingul Nikolaev Admiralty
Constructor   A. I. Melikhov
Laid down   1.6.1819   *Launched* 1.7.1820
Dimensions   approx. 138 ft x 35 ft x 14 ft (42.2 m x 10.7 m x 4.3 m)
Cruised in the Black Sea from 1819–27. Carried supplies to Adm. Greig's squadron in and returned with sick to Sevastopol' in 1828–9. Cruised in the Black Sea in 1830. Harbour service at Sevastopol' in 1831–2. BU 1838.

Lebed' Sevastopol' Admiralty
Constructor   I. Y. Osminin
Laid down   18.11.1820   *Launched* 7.8.1821
Dimensions   approx. 57 ft x 17 ft x 9.5 ft (17.4 m x 5.1 m x 2.9 m)
Armament   6 guns

Carried cargo in the Black Sea from 1821–7. Transported supplies to Sizopol during the war with Persia in 1828–9. Carried cargo in the Black Sea in 1830 and from 1832–40. Fire watch duties at the mouth of the Danube in 1842. BU 1844.

Primer
Laid down ? *Launched* 20.6.1824
Dimensions approx. 76 ft x 22 ft x 10 ft (23.2 m x 6.7 m x 3.1 m) 168 tons burthen
Armament 4 guns
Carried cargo in the Black Sea in 1825–6. To the Archipelago in 1827. Operated with Vice-Adm. L. P. Geyden's squadron in 1828–9 during the war with Turkey. Returned to Sevastopol' in 1830. Carried cargo in the Black Sea and the Sea of Azov from 1830–6. BU 1839.

Nadezhda Spasskoe Admiralty
Laid down ? *Launched* 1825
Driven ashore and wrecked on 21.3.1826 while departing Sevastopol'.

Chaika Nikolaev Admiralty
Constructor I.S. Razomov
Laid down 8.11.1824 *Launched* 28.7.1825
Dimensions approx. 49 ft x 16 ft x 11.2 ft (15 m x 5 m x 3.4 m)
Armament 6 guns.
Carried cargo in the Black Sea from 1825–7. Transported supplies to the Russian squadron off Varna in 1828. Carried cargo from 1829–32. Participated in the Bosphorus operations of the Black Sea fleet in 1833. Carried cargo from 1834–6. Wrecked off the Crimea on 30.6.1836.

Zmeia (Snake) Nikolaev Admiralty
Constructor I.S. Razomov
Laid down ? *Launched* 29.7.1825
500 tons burthen
Carried cargo in the Black Sea from 1826–7. Made numerous trips carrying supplies to the Russian squadron at Anapa and returning to Sevastopol' with sick and wounded and Turkish PoWs in 1828. Foundered during a storm on 26.10.1828.

3 transports built at Kherson by A. K. Kaverxnev.
Dimensions approx. 75 ft x 23 ft x 11.2 ft (22.9 m x 7 m x 3.4 m)
Armament 10 guns
Revnitel'
Laid down 9.1.1825 *Launched* 11.8.1825
Fire watch duties at Sukhum-kale in 1825–6. Grounded during a storm on 11.3.1827, but salvaged and repaired. Transported supplies and troops to Varna in 1828–9 during the Russo-Turkish War and returned to Sevastopol' with sick and wounded. Cruised off the coasts of Abhasia from 1830–6. Carried cargo in the Black Sea in 1838. Storage hulk in 1840.
Sopernik
Laid down 9.1.1825 *Launched* 21.5.1826.
Modified with heavy artillery in 1827 and used as a bomb vessel until 1830. Reverted to transport status and cruised in squadron off the Caucasus coast from 1831–8. Harbour storage hulk in 1840. (See also under Black Sea bomb vessels.)
Podobnyi
Laid down 9.1.1825 *Launched* 4.6.1826
Modified with heavy artillery in 1827 and used as a bomb vessel until 1830. Reverted to transport status and cruised in squadron off the Caucasus in 1830–2. Carried troops as part of the Bosphorus Expedition in 1833. Cruised in squadron off the Caucasus in 1834–5.

Grounded and wrecked in a storm off Sukhum on 17.12.1835. (See also under Black Sea bomb vessels.)

Opyt Nikolaev Admiralty
Constructor I.S. Razumov
Laid down 8.11.1824 *Launched* 14.8.1825
Dimensions approx. 72 ft x 22 ft x 19 ft (22 m x 6.7 m x 5.8 m) 168 tons burthen
Armament 10 guns
Completed as a bomb vessel in 1825. Cruised in the Black Sea in 1828–30 and in action with the Turks in 1828–9. Heavy guns removed 1831 and reclassified as a transport. Carried cargo in the Black Sea from 1831–40. BU 1842. (See also under Black Sea bomb vessels.)

Nyrok Spasskoe Admiralty
Laid down 23.7.1825 *Launched* 19.6.1826
Dimensions approx. 49 ft x 16 ft x 11.2 ft (15 m x 4.9 m x 3.4 m)
Armament 6 guns
Carried cargo in the Black Sea in 1826–7. Brought supplies to Adm. Greig's squadron in 1828. Carried cargo in the Black Sea in 1829–33. Harbour hulk in 1838.

Uspekh Nikolaev Admiralty
Constructor I.S. Razumov
Laid down 25.7.1825 *Launched* 19.6.1826
Dimensions approx. 74 ft x 20 ft x 18 ft (22.6 m x 6. m x 5.5 m)
Armament 8 guns
Converted while building into a bomb vessel in 1825. In action with the Turks in 1828–9. Converted back to a transport with the removal of the heavy guns in 1830. Employed as a transport from 1830–2. Participated in the 1833 Bosphorus Expedition as a troop ship. BU 1842. (See also under Black Sea bomb vessels.)

2 transports at Kherson by A. K. Kaverxnev.
Dimensions approx. 74 ft x 18 ft x 8.9 ft (22.6 m x 5.5 m x 2.7 m)
Armament 4 guns
Renni
Laid down 18.3.1826 *Launched* 24.7.1826
Named after a town on the Danube. Employed with the Danube Flotilla from 1826–42. BU 1843.
Repida
Laid down 18.3.1826 *Launched* 7.8.1826
Named after a branch of the Danube. Employed with the Danube River Flotilla from 1826–42. BU 1843.

2 transports built at Nikolaev Admiralty.
Dimensions approx. 103 ft x 28 ft x 18 ft (31.4 m x 8.5 m x 5.5 m) 355 tons burthen
Armament 10–22 guns
Ingulets
Laid down 23.3.1826 *Launched* 18.11.1826
Carried cargo in the Black Sea from 1827–8. Carried supplies for the Black Sea fleet during the Russo-Turkish War of 1828–9 and returned to Sevastopol' with sick and wounded. Carried cargo in 1830–1. To Istanbul in 1832. Took part in the Bosphorus Expedition of 1833. Cruised off the Caucasus in 1834–5. Wrecked off the Caucasus on 14.7.1835.
Bug
Laid down 28.1.1826 *Launched* ?
Carried supplies for the Black Sea fleet and served as a troopship during the Russo-Turkish War of 1828–9. Landed troops off the

Abhasian coast in 1830–3. Took part in the Bosphorus Expedition of 1833. Cruised off the Caucasus in 1837. Harbour hulk in 1838.

~

Kit Spasskoe Admiralty
Laid down 28.1.1825 *Launched* 26.11.1826
Dimensions approx. ? x 32 ft x 18 ft (? x 9.8 m x 5.5 m)
587 tons burthen
Armament 4 guns
120 men

Trip to the Danube in 1827. Carried supplies to Adm. Greig's squadron during the Russo-Turkish War of 1828–9. Carried cargo in the Black Sea from 1830–2. Took part in the Bosphorus Expedition of 1833. Carried cargo in the Black Sea from 1834–9. Harbour hulk in 1840.

Redut-Kale Nikolaev Admiralty
Constructor M. I. Surovtsov
Laid down 1826 *Launched* 23.3.1827
Dimensions approx. 92 ft x 27 ft x 8.9 ft (28.1 m x 8.2 m x 2.7 m)
290 tons burthen
Armament 6 guns
82 men

Carried cargo in the Black Sea in 1827. Carried supplies to Adm. Greig's squadron during the Russo-Turkish War of 1828–9. Carried cargo in the Black Sea from 1830–2. Took part in the Bosphorus Expedition of 1833. Cruised off the Abhasian in 1834–5. BU 1837.

Gagan Nikolaev Admiralty
Laid down 1826 *Launched* 11.6.1827
Dimensions approx. 49 ft x 14 ft x 8.9 ft (15 m x 4.3 m x 2.7 m)
Armament 4 guns

Carried supplies to Adm. Greig's squadron during the Russo-Turkish War of 1828–9. Carried cargo in the Black Sea from 1829–40. BU 1840.

Sukhum-Kale Nikolaev Admiralty
Constructor I. S. Razumov
Laid down ? *Launched* 17.6.1827
Dimensions approx. 92 ft x ? x 15 ft (28.1 m x ? x 4.6 m)
Armament 6 guns

To the Archipelago in 1827 with Vice-Adm. Geyden's squadron. Operated in the Archipelago during the Russo-Turkish War of 1828–9, participating in the capture of the Turkish corvette *Navarin* in 1828. Returned to Nikolaev in 1830. Operated off the Caucasus landing troops from 1831–3. Driven ashore and wrecked in a storm on 13.3.1833.

Slon
Laid down 27.7.1831 *Launched* 19.11.1832
Dimensions approx. 131 ft x 30 ft x 13.1 ft (40 m x 9.2 m x 4 m)
500 tons burthen
Armament 12 guns

Carried cargo in the Black Sea from 1833–7. Operated off the Caucasus in 1838–9. Carried cargo in the Black Sea from 1840–8. BU after 1848.

Chapman
Laid down 27.7.1831 *Launched* 19.11.1832
Dimensions approx. 128 ft x 30 ft x 15.4 ft (39.1 m x 9.2 m x 4.7 m)
500 tons burthen
Armament 5–15 guns.

Named in honour of the famous Swedish designer Fredrik af Chapman. Carried cargo in the Black Sea from 1834–5. Operated with a squadron off the Caucasus from 1837–40, landing troops in 1837–8. Carried cargo in the Black Sea from 1841–5.

Berezan' Nikolaev Admiralty
Constructor V. Karachurin
Laid down 29.12.1835 *Launched* 5.9.1837
Dimensions approx. 139 ft x 35 ft x 25.5 ft (42.4 m x 10.6 m x 8.7 m)
715 tons burthen
Armament 6 guns

Named after a Black Sea island in the Dnieper estuary. Carried cargo and troops in the Black Sea from 1838–49. Repaired at Sevastopol' in 1851. Carried troops to Anakriya as part of Vice-Adm. Nakhimov's squadron in 1853. Burnt by enemy fire at Sevastopol' in 1855.

Ingul Nikolaev Admiralty
Constructor G. V. Afanasyev
Laid down 19.10.1836 *Launched* 5.9.1837
Dimensions approx. 80 ft x 22 ft x 11.5 ft (24.4 m x 6.6 m x 3.5 m)
160 tons burthen
Armament 2 guns

Carried cargo in the Black Sea from 1840–53. Converted into a fire ship at Sevastopol' in 1853. Scuttled in shallow water off Sevastopol' in 9.1854 to avoid being set afire by enemy shelling.

Kuban' Nikolaev Admiralty
Constructor G. Ivanov
Laid down 19.11.1836 *Launched* 5.9.1837
Dimensions approx. 107 ft x 29 ft x 20.3 ft (32.5 m x 8.9 m x 6.2 m)
350 tons burthen
Armament 4 guns

Named after a river in the Caucasus. Carried cargo in the Black Sea in 1838. Carried supplies to the Caucasus defensive line in 1843–9. Carried cargo in the Black Sea from 1850–3. Scuttled in shallow water off Sevastopol' in 9.1854 to avoid being set afire by enemy shelling.

Dnepr Nikolaev Admiralty
Constructor A. P. Profoyev
Laid down 6.10.1836 *Launched* 26.5.1838
Dimensions approx. 136 ft x 35 ft x 23 ft (41.6 m x 10.7 m x 7 m)
550 tons burthen
Armament 4 guns

Carried cargo in the Black Sea in 1838. Operated off the Caucasus in 1839–40. Landed troops in the Caucasus in 1840. Carried cargo in the Black Sea from 1841–7. Operated off the Caucasus from 1848–53. Carried from her moorings by a severe storm, but saved from disaster by dropping additional anchors in 1848. Carried troops to Anakriya in 1853 as part of Vice-Adm. Nakhimov's squadron. Transferred to Nikolaev in 1854. Hulked in 1855.

Kinburn Nikolaev Admiralty
Constructor G. V. Afanasyev
Laid down 19.11.1837 *Launched* 10.9.1838
Dimensions approx. 69 ft x 19 ft x 13 ft (21.1 m x 5.9 m x 4 m)
176 tons burthen
Armament 2 guns

Carried cargo in the Black Sea from 1841–8. Repaired in 1843–4. Carried cargo in the Black Sea in 1852–3. Converted into a fire ship in 1854. Scuttled in shallow water off Sevastopol' in 9.1854 to avoid being set afire by enemy shelling.

Socha Nikolaev Admiralty
Constructor I. V. Mashkin
Laid down 4.10.1838 *Launched* 22.11.1839

Dimensions approx. 110 ft x 29 ft x 12.1 ft (33.6 m x 8.8 m x 3.7 m)
350 tons burthen
Armament 4 guns
Carried cargo in the Black Sea from 1839–45. Repaired in 1852–3. Carried cargo in the Black Sea from 1847–52. BU 1854.

Ialta Sevastopol' Admiralty
Constructor A. P. Profyev
Laid down 3.7.1839 *Launched* 11.12.1840
Dimensions approx. 82 ft x 22 ft x 13.8 ft (25 m x 6.7 m x 4.2 m)
Armament 8 guns
Carried cargo in the Black Sea from 1841–53. Scuttled at Sevastopol' in 1855.

Gagra Nikolaev Admiralty
Constructor I. V. Mashkin
Laid down 22.11.1839 *Launched* 20.8.1841
Dimensions approx. 118 ft x 30 ft x 21 ft (36.1 m x 9.2 m x 6.4 m)
450 tons burthen
Armament 10 guns
Carried cargo in the Black Sea from 1841–53. Carried troops to Anakriya in 1853 as part of Vice-Adm. Nakhimov's squadron. Scuttled at Sevastopol' in 1855.

2 transports built at Sevastopol'.
Dimensions approx. 95 ft x 25 ft x 17 ft (28.9 m x 7.5 m x 5.2 m)
250 tons burthen
Armament 2 guns 40 men

Sukhum-Kale
Constructor A. P. Prokofyev
Laid down 11.12.1840 *Launched* 27.1.1842
Carried cargo in the Black Sea from 1842–53. Repaired in 1854. Scuttled at Sevastopol' in 1855.

Bug
Constructor Delabel
Laid down 27.1.1842 *Launched* 8.12.1842
Carried cargo in the Black Sea from 1841–53. Carried troops to Anakriya in 1853 as part of Vice-Adm. Nakhimov's squadron. Scuttled at Sevastopol' in 1855.

~

2 transports of identical dimensions:
Dimensions approx. 132 ft x 34 ft x 23 ft (40.2 m x 10.4 m x 7 m)
650 tons burthen
Armament 4 guns

Rion Nikolaev Admiralty
Constructor I. V. Mashkin
Laid down 20.8.1840 *Launched* 17.9.1843
Carried cargo in the Black Sea from 1844–53. Carried troops to Anakriya in 1853 as part of Vice-Adm. Nakhimov's squadron. Carried cargo in the Black Sea from 1856–7. Armed at Nikolaev as a floating battery in 1854–5. Sold for BU in 1858.

Dunay Sevastopol' Admiralty
Constructor Delabel
Laid down 1841 *Launched* 5.10.1847
Carried cargo, cruised off the Caucasus, and landed troops from 1849–53. Carried troops to Anakriya in 1853 as part of Vice-Adm. Nakhimov's squadron. Scuttled at Sevastopol' in 1855 and salvaged in 1856. Carried cargo in the Black Sea in 1857-58 and from 1862–6. Stricken on 8.11.1868.

~

2 transports built at Nikolaev Admiralty by G. A. Okunev.

Dimensions approx. 104 ft x 29 ft x ? (31.8 m x 8.8 m x ?)
350 tons burthen
Armament 4 guns

Prut
Laid down 8.6.1846 *Launched* 23.10.1849
Carried cargo in the Black Sea from 1851–4. Carried troops to Anakriya in 1853 as part of Vice-Adm. Nakhimov's squadron. Scuttled at Sevastopol' in 1855.

Kiliia
Laid down 8.6.1846 *Launched* 23.10.1849
Carried cargo and landed troops in the Black Sea from 1851–3. Carried troops to Anakriya in 1853 as part of Vice-Adm. Nakhimov's squadron. Carried cargo from 1856–66. Sold for BU in 1867 and stricken on 8.11.1868.

~

Aragva Nikolaev Admiralty
Constructor G. A. Okunev
Laid down 12.4.1847 *Launched* 23.10.1849
Dimensions approx. 94 ft x 24 ft x ? (28.7 m x 7.3 m x ?)
250 tons burthen
Armament 2 guns
Carried cargo in the Black Sea from 1851–3. Fire watch duties at Enikale in 1854–5. Scuttled at Enikale to avoid capture on 12.5.1855.

Rymnik Nikolaev Admiralty
Constructor S. I. Chernyavskiy
Laid down 12.4.1847 *Launched* 23.10.1849
Dimensions approx. 60 ft x 18 ft x ? (18.3 m x 5.5 m x ?)
90 tons burthen
Armament 2 guns
Carried cargo in the Black Sea from 1850–2. Declared surplus to the Establishment in 1853. Sold for BU in 1859.

Akkerman Sevastopol' Admiralty
Constructor Delabel
Laid down 6.10.1846 *Launched* 12.11.1849
Dimensions approx. 92 ft x 24 ft x? (28.2 m x 7.3 m x ?)
250 tons burthen
Armament 2 guns
Carried cargo in the Black Sea from 1851–3. Stationed at Kerch and then Taganrog in 1855. Destroyed at Taganrog by gunfire from Anglo-French warships on 22.5.1855.

4 transports at Nikolaev Admiralty.
Dimensions approx. 100 ft x 27 ft x ? (30.5 m x 8.2 m x ?)
250 tons burthen
Armament 2 guns

Renni
Constructor G. A. Okunev
Laid down 2.6.1849 *Launched* 11.10.1850
Carried cargo in the Black Sea from 1851–53. Stationed at Sevastopol' in 1854–5 and scuttled there. Salvaged and repaired in 1856. Carried cargo in the Black Sea from 1857–67. Stricken 21.9.1868.

Portitsa
Constructor A. S. Akimov
Laid down 2.6.1849 *Launched* 2.8.1849
Carried cargo in the Black Sea from 1852–3 and 1856–8. Fire watch duties at Enikale from 1859–67. Stricken on 16.11.1868.

Liman
Constructor Chernyavskiy
Laid down 2.6.1849 *Launched* 25.11.1849

Carried cargo in the Black Sea from 1851–3. Sunk by gunfire at Sevastopol' in 1855.

Kishinev
Constructor   I. S. Dmitriev
Laid down   2.6.1849   *Launched* 22.9.1851
Carried cargo in the Black Sea in 1852–3. Scuttled at Sevastopol' in 1855.

~

3 transports built at Nikolaev Admiralty.
Dimensions   approx. 130 ft x 34 ft x ? (39.6 m x 10.4 m x ?)
               650 tons burthen
Armament   4 guns

Balaklava
Constructor   A. S. Akimov
Laid down   21.9.1849   *Launched* 20.10.1851
Carried cargo in the Black Sea from 1852–4. Carried troops to Anakriya in 1853 as part of Vice-Adm. Nakhimov's squadron to Anakriya. Carried cargo in the Black Sea from 1856–8. Stationed at Nikolaev as a floating battery in 1854–5. Harbour service in 1860. Stricken on 11.11.1861.

Dnestr
Constructor   S. I. Chernyavskiy
Laid down   8.6.1846   *Launched* 19.11.1851
Carried cargo and landed troops in the Black Sea in 1852–3. Carried troops to Anakriya in 1853 as part of Vice-Adm. Nakhimov's squadron. At Nikolaev as a floating battery in 1854–5. Carried cargo and landed troops in the Black Sea from 1856–66. Sold for BU in 1867.

Feodosiia
Constructor   I. V. Mashkin
Laid down   20.10.1851   *Launched* 4.10.1853
Armament   14 guns
Fire watch duties at Nikolaev from 1853–5. Employed as a troopship in 1856. Carried cargo in the Black Sea from 1857–62. Stricken on 8.11.1868.

Okhotsk flotilla transports (4 purpose-built)

Boris i Gleb   Okhotskaya
Constructor   B.I. Vashutkin
Laid down   7.1.1808   *Launched* 26.5.1808
Dimensions   approx. 39 ft x 13 ft x 6.9 ft (11.9 m x 4.1 m x 2.1 m)
Cruised in the Sea of Okhotsk from 1808–12. To Japan in 1813–14. Cruised in the Sea of Okhotsk from 1815–29. BU 1830.

Okhotsk   Okhotsk
Constructor   I. V. Vonlyarlyarskiy
Laid down   2.4.1832   *Launched* 16.6.1836
Dimensions   approx. 74 ft x 23 ft x 15 ft (22.7 m x 7 m x 4.6 m)
Carried cargo in the Sea of Okhotsk from 1836–46. Hydrographic work from 1847–8. Driven ashore in a storm in 1850. Used as storehouse until burnt in 1855 when the Anglo-French squadron appeared.

Gizhiga   Okhotsk
Constructor   Shteyngerter
Laid down   25.6.1843   *Launched* 4.7.1844
Dimensions   approx. 73 ft x 23 ft x 12.1 ft (22.4 m x 7 m x 3.7 m)
Carried cargo in the Sea of Okhotsk in 1844–5. Driven ashore and wrecked on 27.9.1845.

Baikal   Gelsingfors (private yard)
Laid down   9.1847   *Launched* 5.7.1848
Dimensions   approx. 94 ft x 25 ft x 16.7 ft (28.7 m x 7.5 m x 5.1 m)
               250 tons burthen
               30 men
Privately built, two-masted, transport-brig. Departed Kronshtadt with cargo on 21.8.1848. Arrived at Petropavlovsk on 12.5.1849. Discovered a passage between Sakhalin Island and the continent on 27.6.1849. Took part in the transfer of the Okhotsk flotilla base from Okhotsk to Petropavlovsk from 1850–2. Cruised in the Sea of Okhotsk from 1853–7. Stationed at the mouth of the Amur from 1858–9. BU before 1861.

White Sea flotilla transports (6 purpose-built)

2 transports built at Solombala by V. A. Ershov.
Dimensions   approx. 75 ft x 26 ft x 12.1 ft (22.9 m x 7.9 m x 3.7 m)

Kola
Laid down   3.3.1831   *Launched* 12.6.1831
Based at Arkhangel'sk. BU 1851.

Onega
Laid down   16.2.1833   *Launched* 21.9.1833
Supplied lighthouses in the White Sea from 1834–44. Fire watch duties at Arkhangel'sk from 1845–50.

~

2 transports built at Solombala by V. A. Ershov.
Dimensions   approx. 96 ft x 29 ft x 13.4 ft (29.3 m x 8.7 m x 4.1 m)

Solombala
Laid down   15.10.1831   *Launched* 11.5.1832
Based at Arkhangel'sk. BU 1851.

Mezen'
Laid down   16.2.1833   *Launched* 21.9.1833
Named after a river flowing into the White Sea. Fire watch duties at Arkhangel'sk from 1834–46. BU after 1853.

Solovetsk   Solombala
Constructor   Rikhter
Laid down   26.1.1849   *Launched* 20.8.1849
Dimensions   approx. 104 ft x 31 ft x 14.1 ft (31.6m (pp) x 9.5m (inside plank) x 4.3 m)
               552 tons burthen
Based at Arkhangel'sk from 1850–9. Cruised in the White Sea.

Kem'   Solombala
Constructor   Vikhman
Laid down   7.5.1846   *Launched*; 3.9.1846
Dimensions   approx. 80 ft x 26 ft x 11.5 ft (24.4 m x 7.9 m x 3.5 m)
               267 tons burthen
Cruised in the White Sea from 1847–56. Stricken 4.8.1862.

Lake Baikal transports (3 purpose-built)

Ermak   Irkutsk
Constructor   Vasilyev
Laid down   28.8.1825   *Launched* 7.6.1827   *Dimensions*
approx. 60 ft x 19 ft x 5.9 ft (18.3 m x 5.7 m x 1.8 m)
Named after the Russian Cossack leader of the sixteenth century who made the first conquests in Siberia. Employed on Lake Baikal for coastline survey and coastguard duties against local outlaws. BU 1839.

Irkutsk   Irkutsk
Constructor   Vasilyev
Laid down   21.4.1833   *Launched* 16.9.1834
Dimensions   approx. 63 ft x 20 ft x 6.9 ft (19.2 m x 6.2 m x 2.1 m)

16 men
Cruised in Lake Baikal from 1833–8. Driven ashore and wrecked in a storm on 18.9.1838.

Irtysh Irkutsk
Constructor Vishnevskiy
Laid down 21.2.1837   *Launched* 16.9.1838
Dimensions approx. 64 ft x 21 ft x 6.9 ft (19.4 m x 6.3 m x 2.1 m)
Cruised in Lake Baikal from 1839–44, carrying cargo, passengers, and mail. Sold 1844.

Transports converted from other types (20 converted)

Baltic fleet converted transports (3 converted)
Molniia
Dimensions 91 ft 4 in (LGD) x 25 ft (inside plank) x 16 ft 10 in (listed in Veselago as a bomb vessel)
Former bomb vessel purchased in Great Britain in 1771 and converted into a transport in 1779. Departed for Arkhangel'sk in 4.1781 with cargo for building ships. Fired on in error on 26.5.1781 by a British privateer and returned fire. The British captain subsequently boarded the *Molniia* and apologized for his errors. After making repairs, arrived at Arkhangel'sk on 19.7.1781. Upon leaving Arkhangel'sk to return to the Baltic, she was forced to return in August due to leaks, finally reaching Arkhangel'sk in September. Returned to Kronshtadt in 1782. Carried cargo in the Baltic from 1783–7. Wrecked off Moon-zund in 1787. (See also under Baltic bomb vessels.)

Vind-Khund
Laid down ?   *Launched* 11.8.1821 (as frigate)
Dimensions 144 ft 4 in x 38 ft x 19 ft 8 in
Armament 36–38 guns
Converted in 1826 from the *Provornyi* class frigate *Aleksandr Nevskii*, retaining her original armament. Carried building materials to Arkhangel'sk in 1826 and returned to Kronshtadt in 1827. Carried cargo to Sveaborg in 1828. BU 1829. (See also under Baltic frigates.)

Elena
Laid down 5.7.1824   *Launched* 21.5.1825 (as a frigate)
Dimensions 144 ft 4 in x 38 ft x 19 ft 8 in
Armament 36–38 guns
Converted in 1831 from the *Provornyi* class frigate of the same name, retaining the original armament. Carried cargo in the Gulf of Finland from 1832–5. Hulked at Revel' in 1835. (See also under Baltic frigates.)

Black Sea fleet converted transports (17 converted)
Ten ships converted in 1790 to transports from rowing vessels, both floating batteries and galleys.

No. 1
1795–99 Laid out buoys.
No. 2
1792–1800 Carried cargo in the Black Sea.
No. 3
1792–1800 Carried cargo in the Black Sea.
No. 4
1791–1800 Carried cargo in the Black Sea. BU 1804.
No. 5
1791–6 Cruised with the fleet.
No. 6
1792–6 Carried cargo in the Black Sea.
No. 7
Wrecked on 11.4.1793.

No. 8
1793–8 Carried cargo in the Black Sea.
No. 9
1793–6 Carried cargo in the Black Sea. Attached to the port of Sevastopol' from 1799–1804. BU 1804.
No. 10
1793–7 Carried cargo in the Black Sea.

~

Nikon
Laid down 1788   *Launched* 1789 (as a bomb vessel)
Dimensions approx. 108 ft x 40 ft x 17 ft (33.2 m x 12.3 m x 5.2 m)
    111 ft x 40 ft 6 in x 17 ft (listed in Veselago as a bomb vessel)
Converted into a transport in 1791 from the bomb vessel of the same name. Carried cargo in the Black Sea from 1792–1802. (See also under Black Sea bomb vessels.)

Sergii
Dimensions approx. 115 ft x 43 ft x 11 ft (35.1 m x 13.1 m x 3.4 m)
Converted into a transport in 1791, from the bomb vessel of the same name. Carried cargo in the Black Sea from 1792–8. (See also under Black Sea bomb vessels.)

Rozhdestvo Bogoroditsy
Dimensions 84 ft x 24 ft x 9'
Converted into a transport in 1797, from the bomb vessel of the same name (which is said itself to have been originally converted into a bomb vessel from a transport in 1788). Surveyed the Black Sea coast from 1797–8. Carried cargo in the Black Sea from 1799–1803. Stationed in the Mediterranean in 1804. Carried supplies to Corfu. Returned to the Black Sea in 1805. Converted into a fire ship in 1806. (See also under Black Sea bomb vessels.)

Aleksandr
Laid down 1786   *Launched* 15.5.1787 (as frigate *Aleksandr Nevskii*)
Dimensions approx. 154 ft x 43 ft x 15 ft (47 m x 13 m x 4.6 m)
Converted into a two-masted transport brig in 1800 (1799?) from the three-masted frigate *Aleksandr Nevskii*. Arrived at the Archipelago in 1800 with supplies for Adm. Ushakov's squadron. Separated from the squadron. Returned to the Black Sea and again sailed to Zante in Ionia. Returned to Sevastopol'. (See also *Aleksandr Nevskii* under Black Sea frigates.)

Liman Kherson
Laid down 15.12.1805   *Launched* 14.6.1806 (as a bomb vessel)
Dimensions approx. 108 ft x 30 ft x 15 ft (32.9 m x 9.1 m x 4.6 m)
Converted into a transport in 1809 from the bomb vessel of the same name. Carried cargo in the Black Sea from 1809–18. (See also under Black Sea bomb vessels.)

Evlampii
Dimensions 88 ft 6 in x 27 ft 7 in x 10 ft 10 in (Veselago)
Converted into a transport in 1814 from the bomb vessel of the same name (said to have been itself converted into a bomb vessel from a transport purchased in 1807). Carried cargo in the Black Sea from 1814–20. BU after 1820. (See also under Black Sea bomb vessels.)

Akhiollo
Launched 9.1829
Dimensions approx. 128 ft x 35 ft x 18 ft (39 m x 10.7 m x 5.5 m)

Converted into a transport in 1833 and renamed *Arkhiollo*. Originally the Turkish prize corvette *Ol'ga (Messemvriia)* captured on the stocks and completed for Russia. Stationed at Nikolaev in 1834–5. Cruised and landed troops off the Caucasus from 1836–41. Carried cargo in the Black Sea from 1842–7. (See also under Black Sea prizes.)

Transports purchased from private owners (31 purchased)

Baltic fleet purchased transports (14 purchased)
Kasatka
Purchased in 1783. Carried cargo in the Baltic from 1783–7. Converted into a fire ship in 1788.

Lebedka
Purchased in 1783. Carried cargo in the Baltic from 1783–7. Converted into a fire ship in 1788.

Lovets
Dimensions   approx. 122 ft x 32 ft x 14.1 ft (37.2 m x 9.8 m x 4.3 m)
Armament   30 guns
Purchased in 1784 at Arkhangel'sk. Employed in the defence of Arkhangel'sk from 1788–90. Fire watch duties at Arkhangel'sk from 1793–5. Damaged by ice and foundered on 11.10.1795.

Kulik
Dimensions   approx. 104 ft x 27 ft x 14 ft (31.7 m x 8.2 m x 4.3 m)
Purchased in 1785. Renamed *Voz'mi* on 23.8.1788. Carried cargo in the Baltic in 1786. Transferred to Arkhangel'sk in 1787. Last mentioned in 1788.

Solovki
Dimensions   approx. 116 ft x 32 ft x 14.1 ft (35.5 m x 9.8 m x4.3 m)
                530 tons burthen
                150 men
Purchased in 1786 from a local merchant at Arkhangel'sk, Passed to Kronshtadt in 1786. Earmarked for global circumnavigation with Mulovskiy's expedition in 1787. Included in Adm. Greig's squadron instead, because of the war with Turkey. Passed to Copenhagen in 1788 in company with three *Chesma* class 1st Rates under Vice-Adm. Fondezin von Desin. Returned to Revel' in 1790, Transferred to Arkhangel'sk in 1792. Fire watch duties at Arkhangel'sk from 1793–1801. BU at Arkhangel'sk in 1804.

Sokol
                450 tons burthen
                110 men
Purchased in 1787. Earmarked for global circumnavigation with Mulovskiy's expedition. Included in Adm. Greig's squadron instead, because of the war with Turkey. Took part in the battle of Hogland on 7.7.1788 from behind the line. Carried supplies and ammunition to Greig's squadron throughout the remainder of 1788.

Udaloi
Purchased in 1787. Earmarked for global circumnavigation with Mulovskiy's expedition in 1787. Included in Adm. Greig's squadron instead, because of the war with Turkey. Passed to Copenhagen in 1788 in company with three *Chesma* class First Rates under Vice-Adm. Fondezin von Desin. In 1790 left Copenhagen for Kronshtadt, but developed a leak and returned to Denmark. Wintered at Karlshamn. Returned to Kronshtadt in 1791. Carried cargo in the Baltic from 1791–4.

Smelyi
Purchased in 1787. Earmarked for global circumnavigation with Mulovskiy's expedition, but remained in the Baltic because of war with Turkey. Carried supplies and ammunition to the Russian squadron from 1788–90.

Khvat
Purchased in 1787. Earmarked for global circumnavigation with Mulovskiy's expedition in 1787. Included in Adm. Greig's squadron instead, because of the war with Turkey. Passed to Copenhagen in 1788 in company with three *Chesma* class First Rates under Vice-Adm. Fondezin von Desin. Returned to Revel' in 1790, and took part in the battle of Revel' from behind the line. Struck a rock and sank on 24.5.1790 while leaving harbour.

Elena
Purchased at Libava in 1810, and sold there in 1811.

Vesna
Purchased in 1815. Passed from Arkhangel'sk to Kronshtadt in 1821. Carried cargo in the Baltic in 1822–3. During the Great Flood on 7.11.1824, she was driven ashore at Kronshtadt and damaged. BU in 1827.

Leto
Purchased in 1815. Passed from Arkhangel'sk to Kronshtadt in 1821. Carried cargo in the Baltic in 1822–3. During the Great Flood on 7.11.1824, she was driven ashore at Kronshtadt and damaged. BU in 1827.

Graf Khvostov
Purchased in 1820. Carried cargo in the Baltic from 1821–3. Burnt at Revel' in 1837.

Amerika
Dimensions   131 ft x 30 ft x 14.1 ft (40m (pp) x 9.2m (inside plank) x 4.3 m)
                700 tons burthen
Armament   12 guns
                115 men
Purchased in 1830. Departed Kronshtadt for the Far East on 26.8.1831 with 400 tons of cargo. Arrived at Petropavlovsk on 26.8.1832. Departed Petropavlovsk on 20.11.1832 and reached Kronshtadt on 13.9.1833. Departed Kronshtadt on 13.9.1835. Returned to Kronshtadt on 15.7.1836, In autumn of 1836, sailed to Stockholm. Carried cargo in the Baltic from 1837–51. During the Crimean War in 1854–5, she transported supplies to Sveaborg and Rochensalm. Driven on to Gottland and wrecked on 15.10.1856, while en route to Revel'.

Black Sea fleet purchased transports (17 purchased)
Tsar' Konstantin
Purchased in 1796. Carried cargo in the Black Sea from 1796–8. Arrived at Corfu as part of Captain S. Pustoshkin's squadron in 1799. Returned to Odessa in 1800. Carried cargo in the Black Sea in 1803–4. Carried troops and supplies to Corfu in 1805 and returned to Sevastopol'. Converted into a brig in 1806. (See also under Black Sea brigs.)

Dnepr
Purchased in 1804 and passed to Corfu. Cruised between Corfu and

Istanbul. Assigned to Vice-Adm. Seniavin's squadron at Castelnov in 1806. Passed from Corfu to Trieste in 1807. To Venice in 1808 with Commodore Saltanov's squadron. Remained at Venice until her sale to the French in 9.1809.

Sviatoi Nikolai
Purchased in 1816. Fire watch duties at Sevastopol' in 1817. Carried cargo in the Black Sea in 1818–19. Driven to Istanbul by a storm in 9.1818. Wintered in Istanbul. Driven ashore and wrecked by a squall off Sevastopol' on 28.2.1819.

Pantikopey
Purchased in 1815. Carried cargo in the Black Sea from 1818–27.

Kherson
Dimensions   approx. 102 ft x 30 ft x 10.9 ft (31.1 m x 9.1 m x 3.4 m)
Purchased in 1818. Carried cargo in the Black Sea from 1818–27. Foundered off Kherson in a squall on 7.5.1819, but was salvaged and repaired.

Gagara
Purchased in 1819. Fire watch duties at Sevastopol' and Evpatoria from 1820–30. Grounded and wrecked during a storm off the Crimea on 12.12.1830.

Georgii
Purchased in 1819. Carried cargo in the Black Sea from 1819–27. BU 1830.

Verbliud
Dimensions   approx. 92 ft x 26 ft x 8.5 ft (28.1 m x 7.9 m x 2.6 m)
Purchased in 1820. Carried cargo during the war with Turkey from 1820–7 and in 1830–1. Operated off Izmail in 1828. At the siege of Silistriya in 1829. BU 1838.

Arkhistratig Mikhail
Dimensions   approx. 74 ft x 24 ft x 8.5 ft (22.6 m x 7.3 m x 2.6 m)
Purchased in 1821. Fire watch duties in the Strait of Kerch in 1822. Attached to the Danube Flotilla as a hospital ship in 1828–9.

Baklan
Purchased in 1821. Carried cargo in the Black Sea from 1821–3.

3 transports purchased in 1821.
Dimensions   approx. 61 ft x 21 ft x 7.5 ft (18.6 m x 6.4 m x 2.3 m)
Elizaveta
Carried cargo in the Black Sea from 1822–7. Assigned to the Danube Flotilla in 1828–9. Sold in 1832.
Pavel
Carried cargo in the Black Sea from 1822–7. Assigned to the Danube Flotilla in 1828–9.
Pyotr
Carried cargo in the Black Sea from 1822–7. Assigned to the Danube Flotilla in 1828–9.

Nikolai
Purchased in 1821. Carried cargo in the Black Sea from 1821–5. Fire watch duties in the Strait of Kerch in 1826–7. Carried cargo in the Black Sea from 1830–9. Grounded and wrecked at the mouth of the Danube on 11.10.1839.

Pelageia
Dimensions: approx. 63 ft x 21 ft x 7.9 ft (19.1 m x 6.4 m x 2.4 m)
Armament   4 guns
Purchased in 1829. No record of her service.

2 transports purchased 1832.
Dimensions   approx. 100 ft x 30 ft x 12.1 ft (30.5 m x 9.2 m x 3.7 m)
Armament   4 guns
Andromeda
Carried cargo in the Black Sea from 1832–41.
Persei
Carried cargo in the Black Sea from 1832–40. Cruised off the Caucasus in 1837–8.

Transports purchased abroad (17 purchased)

Baltic fleet transports purchased abroad (7 purchased)
Sharlotta
Dimensions   approx. 90 ft x 25 ft x 11.8 ft (27.5 m x 7.5 m x 3.6 m)
Purchased in England in 1802, with armament included for 22500 rubles. Carried cargo in the Baltic from 1802–8. 4 mortars were installed in 1809 and she was used for the defence of Kronshtadt roadstead through 1810. Carried cargo in the Baltic from 1811–13. BU 1816.

2 transports built in England, purchased in 1803 with armament included for 5,000 rubles apiece.
Dimensions   approx. 63 ft x 20 ft x 11.2 ft (19.2 m x 6.1 m x 3.4 m)
Aleksandr
Carried cargo in the Baltic from 1803–5. Fire watch duties in the northern approaches to Kronshtadt in 1806–7. BU after 1807.
Ioann
Carried cargo in the Baltic from 1803–6. BU 1806 at Kronshtadt.

Vilgelmina
Dimensions   approx. 102 ft x 28 ft x 6.9 ft (31.1 m x 8.5 m x 2.1 m)
Purchased in 1807. Left Kronshtadt to join Vice-Adm. Seniavin's squadron in company with the frigate *Speshnyi* on 21.07.1807. Left behind by *Speshnyi* due to slow speed, arriving at Yarmouth on 8.11.1807 and at Portsmouth on 2.11.1807 where she rejoined *Speshnyi*. Both ships were taken into British custody on 20.11.1807 (along with Seniavin's payroll) as a result of Russia's withdrawal from the war with Napoleon.

Iogan-Sharlotta
Dimensions   approx. 127 ft x 31.5 ft x 13.1 ft (38.7 m x 9.6 m x 4 m)
Purchased in 1807. Carried cargo and troops from 1808–20. At Sheerness with the Russian Baltic squadron temporarily evacuated to avoid the Napoleonic invasion in 1812–13. BU 1825 at Kronshtadt.

Fortuna
Dimensions   approx. 87 ft x 24 ft x 8.9 ft (26.5 m x 7.3 m x 2.7 m)
Constructed in 1807. Purchased in Sweden. Stationed at Arkhangel'sk from 1816–27. BU at Arkhangel'sk in 1828.

Gilyak   Hamburg
Laid down   1.5.1861   *Launched* 20.10.1861
Dimensions   approx. 129 ft x 30 ft x 15 ft (39.3 m x 9.2 m x 4.6 m)
              397 tons burthen
Armament   6 x 12pdr carr.
Departed Kukshafen on 1.12.1862. Arrived at Nikolaevsk in the Sea of

Okhotsk on 12.9.1862. Returned to Kronshtadt via Manila and Singapore on 3.8.1863. Departed for the Far East on 26.7.1864 and arrived at Nikolaevsk on 13.6.1865. Returned to Kronshtadt on 7.8.1866. Rerated as a corvette and employed as a training ship from 1867–84. Harbour service in 1885, Stricken on 23.6.1887.

Black Sea fleet transports purchased abroad (9 purchased)

Kodos
Dimensions   approx. 80 ft x 22 ft x ? (24.5 m x 6.6 m x ?)
               212 tons burthen
Armament   4 guns
Purchased in England in 1838. Carried supplies to the fortified Caucasian coastal line from 1839.53. Participated in the evacuation of this line in 1853 during the Crimean War. Stationed at Kerch in 1854–5 and scuttled there during the attack of the Anglo-French fleet.

Adler
Armament   2 guns
Purchased in England in 1839. Cruised off the Caucasus from 1839–47. Wrecked in a storm on 17.2.1847.

Lava
Dimensions   approx. 96 ft x 22 ft x ? (29.3 m x 6.7 m x ? m)
               280 tons burthen
Armament   4 guns
Purchased in England in 1839. Carried supplies to the fortified Caucasian line from 1840–53. Scuttled at Sevastopol' in 1855.

Mamay
Dimensions   approx. 90 ft x 25 ft x ? (27.4 m x 7.7 m x ?)
               262 tons burthen
Armament   4 guns
Purchased in England in 1839. Carried supplies to the fortified Caucasus line from 1840–53. Scuttled at Kerch upon the arrival of the Anglo-French fleet on 12.5.1855.

Subashi
Dimensions   approx. 89 ft x 24 ft x ? (27.1 m x 7.3 m x ?)
               304 tons burthen
Armament   4 guns
Purchased in England in 1839. Carried cargo to the Caucasus and cruised off the coastline from 1839–52. Scuttled at Kerch upon the arrival of the Anglo-French fleet on 12.5.1855.

Abin
289 tons burthen
Armament   4 guns
Purchased in England in 1843. Carried supplies to the fortified Caucasus line from 1845–8. Wrecked in 1848.

Bzyb'
346 tons burthen
Armament   4 guns
Purchased in England in 1843. Carried supplies to the fortified Caucasus line from 1843–53. Scuttled at Kerch upon the arrival of the Anglo-French fleet on 12.5.1855.

Gostogai
346 tons burthen
Armament   4 guns
Purchased in England in 1843. Carried supplies to the fortified Caucasus line from 1843–53. Scuttled at Kerch upon the arrival of the Anglo-French fleet on 12.5.1855.

Dob
Dimensions   approx. 94 ft x ? x ? (28.7 m x ? x ?)
               350 tons burthen
Armament   4 guns
Purchased in England in 1843. Carried supplies to the fortified Caucasus line from 1843–53. Scuttled at Kerch upon the arrival of the Anglo-French fleet on 12.5.1855.

Okhotsk flotilla transports purchased abroad (1 purchased)

Irtysh
Dimensions   approx. 90 ft x 23 ft x ? (27.4 m x 7.1 m x ?)
               310 tons burthen
               63 men
Purchased in England in 1843. Departed Kronshtadt for Okhotsk with 290 tons of cargo on 14.10.1843 Arrived at Manila on 4.9.1844, Arrived at Petropavlovsk on 15.5.1845 after cutting her way through the ice. Arrived at Okhotsk on 1.7.1845. Carried cargo in the Sea of Okhotsk from 1847–58. Fire watch duty in the Bay of Olga from 1859–62. BU after 1862.

Transports confiscated, requisitioned and commandeered (25 vessels)

Baltic fleet confiscated, requisitioned and commandeered transports (14 vessels)

Alfius
Dimensions   approx. 76 ft x 23 ft x 11.8 ft (23.3 m x 7 m x 3.6 m)
Confiscated from her American owner in 1810. Carried cargo in the Baltic in 1811. Supplied the rowing flotilla under Rear-Adm. von Moller and Captain Geyden at the siege of Danzig in 1812–13. Carried cargo in the Baltic from 1814–24. BU 1828.

Kaledoniia
Confiscated in 1811. Carried cargo in the Baltic from 1813–15. To Arkhangel'sk and back in 1816–17. Carried cargo in the Baltic in 1818–19. Conducted hydrographic surveys from 1820–24. BU 1828.

Abikhail
Dimensions   approx. 77 ft x 24 ft x 15.4 ft (23.5 m x 7.3 m x 4.7 m)
Confiscated in 1812. Sailed to Danzig in 1813 and wrecked while in transit to Memel

Ketti
Confiscated 1812. Stationed at Arkhangel'sk and assigned fire watch duties in the mouth of the Northern Dvina from 1817–22. Conducted hydrographic survey in the White Sea in 1823–4. Reverted to fire watch duties from 1825–30. BU 1832.

Montetsello
Dimensions   approx. 110 ft x 26 ft x ? (33.6 m x 7.8 m x ?)
Confiscated in 1812. Participated at the siege of Danzig in 1812 with the rowing flotilla of Rear-Adm. von Moller and the sailing squadron of Rear-Adm. Martin. Wrecked off the island of Osel in 1814.

Unter Nemung
Dimensions   approx. 80 ft x 21 ft x 8.9 ft (24.4 m x 6.4 m x 2.7 m)
Confiscated in 1812. Carried cargo in the Baltic in 1813.

Returned to owners in 1814.

Filadel'fiia Pekst
Dimensions approx. 86 ft x 24 ft x 11.2 ft (26.4 m x 7.3 m x 3.4 m)
Confiscated in 1812. Participated in the siege of Danzig in 1812 with the rowing flotilla of Rear-Adm. von Moller and the sailing squadron of Rear-Adm. Martin. To Arkhangel'sk in 1814. Returned to Revel' in 1815. Accompanied the frigate *Merkurii* to Holland in 1816 with the dowry of Grand Duchas Anna Pavlovna (sister of Aleksandr and Nicholas and future Queen of the Netherlands). Returned to Kronshtadt in 1817. Carried cargo in the Baltic in 1817–18. Converted to a pilot boat in 1818. (See also under pilot boats.)

Fortuna
Dimensions approx. 62 ft x 19 ft x 12.1 ft (19 m x 5.8 m x 3.7 m)
Confiscated in 1812. Blockship in the Western Dvina in 1812–13. BU at Riga in 1814.

Frau Zhanetta
Dimensions approx. 66 ft x 17 ft x 6.9 ft (20.1 m x 5.2 m x 2.1 m)
Confiscated in 1812. BU at Riga.

Frau Margarita
Dimensions approx. 71 ft x 17 ft x 7.9 ft (21.7 m x 5.2 m x 2.4 m)
Confiscated in 1812. Stationed at Sveaborg from 1812–14. Carried cargo in the Baltic from 1815–18.

Ianus
Dimensions approx. 63 ft x 22 ft x 8.5 ft (19.2 m x 6.6 m x 2.6 m)
Confiscated in 1812. Carried cargo in the Baltic in 1813. BU at Revel' in 1814.

Meri
Confiscated in 1820. Carried cargo in the Baltic from 1821–4. Grounded and damaged at Kronshtadt during the Great flood of 7.11.1824. BU 1827.

Dora
Armament 6 guns
Confiscated in 1822. Carried cargo in the Baltic from 1823–7. BU at Revel' in 1828.

Der-Yung-Ioann
Confiscated in 1825. Cruised in the Gulf of Riga from 1825–7. Wrecked 5.10.1827 due to pilot error.

Black Sea fleet confiscated, requisitioned and commandeered transports (5 vessels)

Aleksandr
Dimensions approx.97 ft x 28 ft x 13.4 ft (29.7 m x 8.4 m x 4.1 m)
             325 tons burthen
Armament   8–18 guns
             82 men
Transferred from the transport flotilla in 1826. Carried cargo in the Black Sea in 1826–7. Transported supplies and troops to the Russian armies at Varna and Sizopol in 1828–9. Carried cargo in the Black Sea in 1830. Operated off the Caucasus landing troops in 1831–2. Carried supplies to the squadron operating in the Bosphorus in 1833. Carried cargo in the Black Sea from 1834–7. Harbour service at Nikolaev in 1838–9. BU at Nikolaev in 1840.

Dmitriy
Transferred from the transport flotilla in 1826. Carried cargo in the Black Sea from 1818-27.

Lanzheron
Dimensions approx. 89 ft x 25 ft x ? (27.1 m x 7.7 m x ?)
             247 tons burthen
Armament   4–8 guns
             70 men
Transferred from the transport flotilla in 1826. Carried cargo in the Black Sea from 1818–27. Operated off the Caucasus in 1828. Operated as a troopship in 1829. Carried cargo in the Black Sea from 1830–2. Took part in the Bosphorus expedition in 1833. Carried cargo in the Black sea in 1834–5. Operated off the Caucasus in 1837–8. Wrecked during a storm off Tuapse on 31.8.1838.

Emmanuil
Transferred from the transport flotilla in 1826. Cruised off the Caucasus in 1830.

Tsemes
Dimensions approx.96 ft x ? x ? (29.4 m x ? x ?)
             286 tons burthen
Armament   4 guns
Transferred from the War Ministry Land Administration in 1840. Carried cargo in the Black Sea from 1840–7. Carried supplies to the fortified Caucasus defence line in 1848–52. Scuttled at Kertch upon the arrival of the Anglo-French fleet on 12.5.1855. scuttled at Kerch (at arrival of Anglo-French fleet).

Caspian flotilla confiscated, requisitioned and commandeered transports (6 vessels)

No. 1
Confiscated in 1827. Carried supplies to the Russian army in the Caucasus in 1828–9. Carried cargo in the Black Sea from 1830–31.

No. 2
Confiscated in 1827. Carried supplies to the Russian army in the Caucasus in 1828–9. Carried cargo in the Black Sea in 1830.

No. 3
Confiscated in 1827. Carried supplies to the Russian army in the Caucasus in 1828–9. Carried cargo in the Black Sea from 1830–1

No. 4
Confiscated in 1827. Carried supplies to the Russian army in the Caucasus in 1828–9. Carried cargo in the Black Sea 1830.

No. 5
Confiscated in 1827. Carried supplies to the Russian army in the Caucasus in 1828–9.

No. 6
Confiscated in 1827. Carried supplies to the Russian army in the Caucasus in 1828–9.

Prize transports (61 ships)

Baltic fleet prize transports (43 ships)
A total of 33 Swedish ships suitable for use as transports were

captured during the Russo-Swedish War of 1788–90. They were extensively employed in the Baltic and in the North Sea in support of Russian operations in the war with France in the 1790s, filling a logistical void for the Russian Baltic fleet in one of its major deployments outside of the Baltic. 16 were deployed to service Vice-Adm. Khanykov's squadron at Sheerness in 1796. A further 2 found their way to the Texel in 1799 as troopships with Rear-Adm. Chichagov's squadron. A single Hamburg ship was captured in 1799 and the final batch of 9 prize transports was captured in 1808 during the final conflict with Sweden.

Al'bertin
Swedish prize captured in 1788. Carried freight in the Baltic from 1792–7. BU 1808 at St Petersburg.

Al'ians
Swedish prize captured in 1788. Stationed at Revel' in 1789. 1790 brought supplies to the Russian squadron during the Russo-Swedish War. Carried freight in the Baltic from 1792–5. Carried supplies to Vice-Adm. Khanykov's squadron at Sheerness in 1796. Carried freight in the Baltic in 1797–8. Grounded and wrecked on 12.9.1799.

Britta-Margarita
Dimensions   approx. 80 ft x 22 ft x 23.9 ft (24.4 m x 6.7 m x 7.3 m)
Swedish prize captured in 1788. Carried cargo in the Baltic in 1792–3 and 1795. Carried supplies to Vice-Adm. Khanykov's squadron at Sheerness in 1796. Carried cargo in the Baltic from 1798–1802. Wrecked on 14.7.1802 off Torsari on the coast of Finland.

Hofnung (1st)
Dimensions   approx. 65 ft x 22 ft x 12.1 ft (19.8 m x 6.7 m x 3.7 m)
Swedish prize taken in 1788. Carried cargo in the Baltic from 1793–5. Carried supplies to Vice-Adm. Khanykov's squadron at Sheerness in 1796. Carried cargo in the Baltic from 1797–1808. BU at Kronshtadt in 1808.

Gribsvald
Dimensions   approx. 90 ft x 27.5 ft x 11.5 ft (27.5 m x 8.4 m x 3.5 m)
Swedish prize taken in 1788. Participated at the 1st battle of Rochensalm on 13.8.1789 and transported Swedish PoWs to Kronshtadt after the battle. Carried supplies to the Kronshtadt squadron in 1789–90 during the Russo-Swedish War. Carried cargo in the Baltic from 1791-95. Carried supplies to Vice-Adm. Khanykov's squadron at Sheerness in 1796. Carried cargo in the Baltic from 1798–1803 Wrecked off Vindava on 9.10.1803.

Dibel-Shley-Yung
Swedish prize taken in 1788. Carried supplies to the Russian squadron in 1789–90 during the Russo-Swedish War. Carried cargo in the Baltic from 1791–5. Wrecked off Hogland on 6.9.1795.

Elizaveta
Swedish prize taken in 1788. Passed from Copenhagen to Kronshtadt in 1788. Cruised in the Baltic in 1794.

Iogan
Swedish prize taken in 1788. Carried cargo in the Baltic from 1794–8 and in 1802. Fire watch duties at the Tolbukhin light-house in 1804. Carried cargo in the Baltic in 1805–6. BU at St Petersburg in 1811.

Karolina
Dimensions   approx. 86 ft x 24 ft x 12.1 ft (26.2 m x 7.4 m x 3.7 m)
Swedish prize taken in 1788. Carried cargo in the Baltic from 1791–1806. BU in 1815 at Kronshtadt.

Karolina-Frederika
Dimensions   approx. 76 ft x 21 ft x 11.2 ft (23.2 m x 6.3 m x 3.4 m)
Swedish prize taken in 1788. Employed as a pilot vessel. Hydrographic work in gulf of Finland from 1791–1802. BU at Kronshtadt in 1804.

Kron-Prints
Dimensions   approx. 80 ft x 23 ft x 11.2 ft (24.4 m x 7 m x 3.4 m)
Swedish prize taken in 1788. Carried cargo in the Baltic from 1793–5. Carried supplies to Vice-Adm. Khanykov's squadron at Sheerness in 1796. Carried cargo in the Baltic in 1797 and from 1800–5.

Minerva
50-man Swedish prize taken in 1788. Carried supplies to the Russian squadron in 1789 and took part in the battle of Oland. Carried cargo in the Baltic from 1791–5. Carried supplies to Vice-Adm. Khanykov's squadron at Sheerness in 1796. Carried cargo in the Baltic in 1797–8. Transported 123 soldiers to Rear-Adm. Chichagov's squadron in the Texel in 1799 and then remained in England with Vice-Adm. Makarov's squadron. Returned to Kronshtadt in 1800. Cruised with the fleet at Copenhagen in 1801. Carried cargo in the Baltic in 1802–3. Wintered at Copenhagen in 1805. Grounded and abandoned on the way back to Kronshtadt on 4.5.1806.

Observatorium
Swedish prize taken in 1788. Carried cargo in the Baltic from 1792–5. Carried supplies to Vice-Adm. Khanykov's squadron at Sheerness in 1796. Carried cargo in the Baltic from 1797–1803. Struck a rock and sank in 1800. Salvaged and repaired. Fire watch duties along the border with Sweden off Svartholm from 1805–7.

Prints Karl
Dimensions   approx. 70 ft x 18 ft x 9.5 ft (21.4 m x 5.6 m x 2.9 m)
Swedish prize taken in 1788. Carried cargo in the Baltic from 1791–6.

Tsvey Bruders No. 1
Dimensions   approx. 61 ft x 21 ft x 11.8 ft (18.6 m x 6.4 m x 3.6 m)
Swedish prize taken in 1788. Carried cargo in the Baltic from 1791–5. Carried supplies to Vice-Adm. Khanykov's squadron at Sheerness in 1796. Carried cargo in the Baltic from 1797–1804. BU at Kronshtadt in 1807.

Sharlotta-Karolina
Dimensions   approx. 74 ft x 24 ft x 12.5 ft (22.6 m x 7.3 m x 3.8 m)
Swedish prize taken in 1788. To Revel' in 1788. Carried cargo in the Baltic in 1793–4. Carried supplies to Vice-Adm. Khanykov's squadron at Sheerness in 1796. Carried cargo in the Baltic in 1797, 1800 and from 1804–8. Employed as a troopship in 1812–13. BU at Kronshtadt in 1814.

Emmanuil
Dimensions   approx. 65 ft x 20 ft x 11.5 ft (19.8 m x 6.1 m x 3.5 m)
Swedish prize taken in 1788. Carried cargo in the Baltic from 1792–8.

Eynikhkeyt
Dimensions   approx. 67 ft x 19 ft x 8.9 ft (20.4 m x 5.8 m x 2.7 m)

Swedish prize taken in 1788. Carried cargo in the Baltic and assigned fire watch duties at Kronshtadt from 1791–1800.

Iunga Peters
Swedish prize taken in 1788. Carried cargo in the Baltic from 1794–1803. Driven ashore and wrecked by a storm off Narva on 30.9.1803.

Anna-Margarita
Swedish prize taken in 1789. Carried cargo in the Baltic from 1790–2. To Stockholm in 1793 with the Russian ambassador, escorted by the cutter *Merkurii*. Wintered in Stockholm and returned to Kronshtadt in 1794 Carried cargo in the Baltic in 1795. Carried supplies to Vice-Adm. Khanykov's squadron at Sheerness in 1796. Transferred to Rochensalm in 1801. BU at Rochensalm in 1808.

Ekaterina-Magdalina
Dimensions approx. 84 ft x 25 ft x 9.9 ft (25.6 m x 7.5 m x 3 m)
Swedish prize taken in 1789. Carried cargo in the Baltic in 1790 and 1793–4. Destroyed 18 armed Polish ships off Polangen in 1794. At Revel' in 1795. Carried supplies to Vice-Adm. Khanykov's squadron at Sheerness in 1796. At Kronshtadt roads in 1797. Carried cargo in the Baltic from 1798–1803. Driven ashore and wrecked in a storm off Revel' roads on 29.9.1803.

Neptun
Dimensions approx. 97 ft x 27 ft x 13 ft (29.6 m x 8.2 m x 4 m)
Swedish Prize taken in 1789. Carried supplies to Vice-Adm. Khanykov's squadron at Sheerness in 1796. To the Texel as a troopship in Rear-Adm. P. V. Chichagov's squadron in 1799. Returned to Russia in 1800. Carried cargo in the Baltic in 1801–2. Hydrographic work in 1803. BU at Kronshtadt in 1807.

Anna-Suzana
Dimensions approx. 72 ft x 23 ft x 14.1 ft (22 m x 7 m x 4.3 m)
Swedish prize taken in 1790. Carried cargo in the Baltic from 1793–5. Carried supplies to Vice-Adm. Khanykov's squadron at Sheerness in 1796. Carried cargo in the Baltic from 1797–1802. BU at Kronshtadt in 1804.

Iogan-Frau-Mariia
Dimensions approx. 60 ft x 17 ft x 9.9 ft (18.3 m x 5.2 m x 3 m)
Swedish prize taken in 1790. Carried cargo in the Baltic from 1792–1803. BU at Rochensalm in 1804.

Konkordiia
Swedish prize taken in 1790. Carried cargo in the Baltic from 1794–7. Damaged and sunk at the mouth of the Neva in 1797. Subsequently salvaged and repaired. Fire watch duties in the main channel of the Neva in 1814–15.

Nordshtern
Swedish prize taken in 1790. Carried cargo in the Baltic from 1792–5. Carried supplies to Vice-Adm. Khanykov's squadron at Sheerness in 1796. Carried cargo in the Baltic from 1797–1800.

Tsvey Bruder No. 2
Swedish prize taken in 1790. Carried cargo in the Baltic from 1791–8. Fire watch duties in the northern channel of the Neva in 1799. Carried cargo in the Baltic in 1800. Wrecked at Urengrund off the coast of Finland on 26.9.1800.

Ailla-Margarita
Swedish prize taken in 1788–90. Carried cargo in the Baltic. Rescued the crew of the wrecked *Impressa* in 1794. Grounded and lost off Surikari Island off Rochensalm in the autumn of 1794.

Hofnung (2nd)
Swedish prize taken in 1788-90. Carried cargo in the Baltic from 1793–7. Wrecked in a squall off Rochensalm on 6.11.1797.

Degog
Swedish prize taken in 1788–90. Carried cargo in the Baltic from 1791–6.

Impressa
Swedish prize taken in 1788–90. Carried cargo in the Baltic from 1792–4. Driven ashore and lost in a storm off the Finnish coast on 1.7.1794.

Liberta
Swedish prize taken in 1788–90. Carried cargo in the Baltic in 1794–5. Carried supplies to Vice-Adm. Khanykov's squadron at Sheerness in 1796. Carried cargo in the Baltic from 1797–1804

Margarita
Swedish prize taken in 1788–90. Carried cargo in the Baltic from 1791–4. Driven ashore in a storm to Seskar Island on 3.9.1794 and then driven and wrecked on Cape Styrsudden.

Lang Dreyd
Hamburg ship taken as a prize by Rear-Adm. Borisov's squadron in 7.1799. Carried cargo in the Baltic in 1800.

Genrietta
Dimensions approx. 106 ft x 29 ft x 8.5 ft (32.3 m x 8.8 m x 2.6 m)
Swedish prize taken in 1808. Carried cargo in the Baltic in 1808–9. Wrecked off Sveaborg on 28.10.1809.

Elena-Margarita
Swedish prize taken in 1808. Sold at Uleaborg in 1810.

Kristina-Uliana
Dimensions approx. 110 ft x 28 ft x 10.1 ft (33.6 m x 8.4 m x 3.1 m)
Swedish prize taken in 1808. Carried cargo in the Baltic from 1808–10. Grounded on a bank and lost on 9.5.1810.

Mit Byurger
Swedish prize taken in 1808. Supplied Russian warships in 1813–14. Carried cargo in the Baltic from 1815–18.

Frau Korneliia
Dimensions approx. 88 ft x 25 ft x 14.1 ft (26.8 m x 7.6 m x 4.3 m)
Swedish prize taken in 1808. Carried cargo in the Baltic from 1808–11. Assigned to the rowing flotilla at the siege of Danzig in 1812–13. Grounded and lost off Gottland on 3.10.1813.

Chapman
Dimensions approx. 117 ft x 28 ft x 7.9 ft (35.7 m x 8.5 m x 2.4 m)
Swedish prize taken in 1808. Carried cargo in the Baltic from 1808–11. Driven ashore and wrecked in a squall off Rodsher Island on 22.10.1811.

Gustav-Adol'f
Swedish prize taken in 1808. Hospital ship at Sveaborg from 1809–21. Permanently transferred to Kronshtadt in 1821. BU at Kronshtadt in 1828.

Frigant
Dimensions   approx. 60 ft x 19 ft x 7.9 ft (18.3 m x 5.7 m x 2.4 m)
Swedish prize taken on 2.8.1808 by Adm. Khanykov's squadron. Carried cargo in the Baltic in 1811 and from 1816–20. Stationed on Londonskaya ground as a lighthouse from 1820–4. BU 1825. (This ground – or bank – is the resting place of *London* (54), a ship purchased in England and lost in 1719 off Kotlin. See under Baltic sailing fleet.)

Einikkheit
Dimensions   approx. 60 ft x 19 ft x 7.9 ft (18.3 m x 5.8 m x 2.4 m)
Swedish prize taken in 2.8.1808 by Adm. Khanykov's squadron. Stationed at Sveaborg from 1809–12. Carried cargo in the Baltic from 1813–14. Grounded and wrecked of Bolshoy Island on 15.6.1814.

Black Sea fleet prize transports (18 ships)
17 Turkish ships were captured in the Russo-Turkish War of 1828–30, and a final Turkish smuggler was swept up in 1838. Only 5 of these ships appear to have been assigned names in place of numbers in Russian service, and they appear to have been of limited value to their captors – in marked contrast to the Swedish ships listed above.

Vulan
Turkish prize taken in 1828. Carried cargo in the Baltic from 1829–39. Fire watch duties at Feodosiia from 1840–2. BU 1844.

Mikhail
Turkish prize taken in 1828. BU in 1834.

Chambers
Turkish prize taken in 1828 and BU in 1834.

Nikolai
Dimensions   approx. 80 ft x 21 ft x ? (24.4 m x 6.4 m x ?)
Armament   2 guns
Turkish prize taken in 5.1828. Assigned to the Danube flotilla in 1828–9. Accidentally blown up off Izmail on 1.12.1829.

No. 1
Turkish prize taken in the Russo-Turkish War of 1828–9. Carried cargo in the Black Sea from 1829–34. Caught fire and scuttled at Izmail on 25.3.1834.

No. 2
Turkish prize taken in the Russo-Turkish War of 1828–9. Carried cargo in the Black Sea from 1829–31. Driven ashore and lost at the Sulin Danube's mouth on 30.7.1831.

No. 3
Turkish prize taken on 4.5.1829 by the brig *Orfei* (see under Black Sea brigs). Assigned to the rowing flotilla and lost without trace during a storm on 6.10.1829.

No. 4
Turkish prize taken in the Russo-Turkish War of 1828–9. Carried cargo transfer in the Black Sea. No further mention.

No. 6
Turkish prize taken in the Russo-Turkish War of 1828–9. Carried cargo in the Black Sea in 1829–30. Grounded in a storm at Odessa on 13.9.1830 at Odessa and lost the following day.

No. 8
Turkish prize taken in the Russo-Turkish War of 1828–9. Fire watch duties at Sevastopol' (?)

No. 9
Turkish prize taken in the Russo-Turkish War of 1828–9. Departed Sevastopol' with troops for Sizopol on 8.7.1829. A major leak developed on 11.7.1829, the crew and troops were offloaded to the frigate *Tenedos* (see under Black Sea frigates) and the ship foundered.

No. 11
Turkish prize taken in the Russo-Turkish War of 1828–9. No further information.

No. 12
Turkish prize taken in the Russo-Turkish War of 1828–9. No further information.

No. 13
Turkish prize taken in the Russo-Turkish War of 1828–9. No further information.

No. 14
Turkish prize taken in the Russo-Turkish War of 1828–9. Carried cargo in the Black Sea in 1829–30. Wrecked off the mouth of the Danube in 1830.

No. 15
Turkish prize taken in the Russo-Turkish War of 1828–9. No further information.

No. 17
Turkish prize taken in the Russo-Turkish War of 1828–9. No further information.

Sudzhuk-Kale
Dimensions   approx. 69 ft x 15 ft x ? (21.1 m x 4.5 m x ?)
Armament   4 guns
Turkish prize taken smuggling in 1837 off the Caucasus. Carried cargo in the Black Sea from 1837–50. Repaired at Sevastopol' in 1850. Fire watch duties at Ochakov in 1853. Stricken in 1858.

Transports of uncertain origin (38 ships)

Baltic fleet transports of unknown origin (28 ships)
No information is available on the origin of these ships, most of which were unnamed. Nevertheless, a good deal of information is available on their service careers which extended from 1786–1824 and they appear to have been very actively employed.

Konstantin
Arrived at Narva for a cargo consignment on 20.9.1806. Diverted to assist the grounded galiot *Sviatoi Nikolai*. Driven ashore and wrecked in a squall on 25.9.1806 after successfully freeing the galiot.

No. 1
Carried cargo in the Baltic from 1786–7 and from 1791–9. Driven ashore and wrecked by a squall on 26.11.1799.

No. 2
Carried cargo in the Baltic in 1792.

No. 1
Fire watch duties at Rochensalm from 1804–6. Carried cargo in the Baltic from 1807–11.

No. 2
Carried cargo in the Baltic in 1806. Carried supplies to the Russian army during the conflict with Sweden in 1808. Operated with the rowing flotilla off the Aland Islands in 1809. Carried cargo in the Baltic from 1811–14.

No. 3
Carried cargo in the Baltic in 1804–5. Grounded and lost off Narva roads while attempting to enter the Narova River on 8.10.1805.

No. 3
Carried cargo in the Baltic from 1811–16.

No. 4
Carried cargo in the Baltic in 1811–12. Participated in the blockade of Danzig in 1813 and wintered at Konigsberg. Carried cargo in the Baltic in 1814.

No. 9
Assigned to the rowing flotilla during the conflict with Sweden in 1809. Carried cargo in the Baltic in 1810–11.

No. 11
Assigned to the rowing flotilla during the conflict with Sweden in 1809. Laid out buoys in 1810–11. Participated in the blockade of Danzig in 1812 with the British squadron under Rear-Adm. T. Marten. Supplied the rowing flotilla in 1813–14. Laid out buoys in 1815–17.

No. 12
Carried cargo in the Baltic in 1810–11. Participated in the blockade of Danzig in 1812 with the British squadron under Rear Adm. T. Marten. Removed cargo and crew from the wrecked sloop *Edinorog* (see under Baltic sloops), which had been grounded and destroyed by fire on 6.9.1812 while en route to assist in the siege of Danzig. Returned to Kronshtadt to Riga in 1813.

No. 13
Carried cargo in the Baltic in 1809.

No. 15
Carried cargo in the Baltic in 1812.

No. 18
Carried cargo in the Baltic from 1813–17.

No. 20
Transported supplies to Sveaborg in 1809. Carried cargo in the Baltic in 1810–11. Participated in the blockade of Danzig in 1812 with the British squadron under Rear-Adm. T. Marten. Carried supplies and escorted 5 transports transporting munitions from Sveaborg to Danzig in 1813. Wintered in Konigsberg. Stationed at Sveaborg in 1814. Carried cargo in the Baltic in 1815–19.

No. 21
Carried cargo in the Baltic in 1811. Evacuated foreigners from St Petersburg to Pillau upon Napoleon's invasion of Russia in 1812. Participated in the blockade of Danzig in 1813. Stationed at Sveaborg in 1814. Carried cargo in the Baltic in 1815–16.

No. 22
Cruised in the Gulf of Finland in 1807. Carried supplies to Rochensalm and Sveaborg during the conflict with Sweden in 1808–9. Wrecked on 6.10.1809.

No. 23
Operated with the rowing flotilla off the Aland Islands in 1809. Carried cargo in the Baltic in 1810–11. Participated in the blockade of Danzig in 1812 with the British squadron under Rear-Adm. T. Marten. Transported munitions to the Russian squadron blockading Danzig in 1813. Carried cargo in the Baltic from 1814–16. BU at Kronshtadt in 1819.

No. 24
Carried cargo in the Baltic from 1811–17.

No. 25
Carried cargo in the Baltic in 1811.

No. 26
Carried cargo in the Baltic in 1812.

No. 48
Cruised in the Gulf of Finland in 1807. Transported supplies to Rochensalm and Sveaborg during the conflict with Sweden in 1808–9. Wrecked in a storm off Somers Island on 6.10.1809.

No. 49
Carried cargo to Sveaborg, Abo, and Stockholm in 1810–11. Carried cargo between Riga and the Aland Islands from 1812–14. Carried cargo in the Baltic from 1815–21.

No. 50
Participated in the blockade of Danzig in 1812 with the British squadron under Rear-Adm. T. Marten. Transported supplies from Riga to Danzig in 1813 and wintered at Konigsberg. Stationed at Sveaborg in 1814. Carried cargo in the Baltic from 1815. BU at Kronshtadt in 1819.

No. 51
Carried cargo in the Baltic in 1811. Transported supplies to the rowing flotilla in 1813–14. Carried cargo in the Baltic from 1814–18. To Danzig in 1816. BU at Kronshtadt in 1819.

No. 52
Transported supplies to Rochensalm in 1809 during the conflict with Sweden. Carried cargo in the Baltic in 1811. Transported troops from Sveaborg to Riga in 1812. Developed a severe leak on 8.10.1812. Grounded to prevent sinking. Declared a total loss.

Tseres
To Abo in 1813. Carried cargo in the Baltic from 1814–16. Driven

ashore and wrecked in a storm on 4.10.1816.
Farvater
Carried cargo between Kronshtadt and Sveaborg from 1816–24.

Black Sea fleet transports of unknown origin (10 ships)
As little is known about the origins of these ships as about the Baltic transports of unknown origin. As was the case with the Baltic ships, they served from 1786–1824. Unlike the northern ships, all had assigned names, even though almost nothing is known about their service lives.

Aleksandr
Carried cargo in the Black Sea from 1786–7. Sunk in action at Ochakov on 17.6.1788, while part of Rear-Adm. John Paul Jones's squadron.

Desna
Carried cargo in the Black Sea from 1786–7. Probable participant in the war with Turkey from 1787–92.

Dubrovka
Carried cargo in the Black Sea from 1786–7. Probable participant in the war with Turkey from 1787–92.

Mezha
Carried cargo in the Black Sea from 1786–7. Probable participant in the war with Turkey from 1787–92.

Revna
Carried cargo in the Black Sea from 1786–7. Probable participant in the war with Turkey from 1787–92.

Dnepr
Carried cargo in the Black Sea from 1786–7. Damaged by ice and sunk on 30.11.1788, while stationed at the mouth of the Dnieper.

Krichev
Carried cargo in the Black Sea from 1786–7. Damaged by ice and sunk on 30.11.1788, while stationed at the mouth of the Dnieper.

Taganrog
Carried cargo in the Black Sea from 1786–7. Converted into a 10–16 gun flat-bottomed 'newly invented frigate' in 1788 by M. L. Faleev. Fought at Ochakov on 17.6.1788 as part of the Liman flotilla. Damaged by ice in the Dnieper and sunk in 1788. (See also under Black Sea frigates.)

Vasilii
Carried cargo in the Black Sea from 1818–24.

Nikolai
First mentioned as having capsized in a squall on 4.6.1819 and having been subsequently salvaged. Carried cargo in the Black Sea and the Sea of Azov from 1820–4.

Flashkouts (plashkouts) (32 purpose-built)

Derived from the Dutch *Plaatschuit*. These were flat-bottomed vessels used for unloading large ships and transferring cargos across shallow waters in coastal waters and ports. Flashkouts in Russian service were confined to the Sea of Azov and the Black Sea fleets.

Sea of Azov fleet flashkouts (7 purpose-built)

7 ships built at Taganrog yard, around 1775 and attached to the port of Taganrog.

Black Sea fleet flashkouts (25 purpose-built)

2 ships built around 1785 at Kherson and attached to the port.
No. 1, No. 2

～

4 ships built around 1785 at Taganrog and attached to the port.
Karakatitsa, Kit, Morzh, Paltus

～

2 ships built at Kherson by M. I. Surovtsev.
Zhuk
Laid down 18.1.1822 Launched 24.3.1822
BU 1830.
Rak Laid down 18.1.1822 Launched 31.3.1822
BU 1837.

～

2 ships built at Nikolaev Admiralty.
Dimensions approx. 100 ft x 27 ft x 5.9 ft (30.5 m x 8.2 m x 1.8 m)
Ulitka
Laid down 7.1823 Launched 25.9.1823
BU 1842.
Zhaba
Laid down 7.1823 Launched 17.10.1823
BU 1837.

～

2 ships built at Kherson
Dimensions approx. 170 ft x 28 ft x 11.2 ft (51.9 m x 8.4 m x 3.4 m)
Buivol
Laid down 15.4.1825 Launched 13.9.1825
Final fate is unknown.
Slon
Laid down 15.4.1825 Launched 6.10.1825
Sank at Odessa in 1835.

4 ships built at Kherson by Serkov.
Dimensions approx. 95 ft x 30 ft x 8.5 ft (29 m x 9.2 m x 2.6 m)
Loshak
Laid down 1.2.1827 Launched 2.1827
BU 1842.
Verbliud
Laid down 1.2.1827 Launched 27.8.1827
BU 1840.
Nosorog
Laid down 1.2.1827 Launched 13.10.1827
BU 1840.
Dromader
Laid down 1.2.1827 Launched 3.4.1828
BU 1840.

～

Dub Nikolaev Admiralty
Constructor I. Y. Osminin
Laid down 18.12.1833 Launched 14.7.1834
Dimensions approx. 62 ft x 22 ft x 8.9 ft x 7.2 ft (18.9 m x 6.6 m (inside plank) x 2.7 m x 2.2 m)

2 ships built at Nikolaev Admiralty by I. S. Dmitriev.
Dimensions approx. 71 ft x 23 ft x 9.5 ft x 6.9 ft (21.6 m x 6.9 m

(inside plank) x 2.9 m x 2.1 m
No. 1
Laid down   10.9.1839   *Launched* 23.6.1840
Attached to the port of Novorossiysk.
No. 2 Nikolaev Admiralty
Constructor   I.S. Dmitriev
Laid down   10.9.1839   *Launched* 9.7.1840
Attached to the port of Novorossiysk.

~

3 ships built at Nikolaev Admiralty by Pchelnikov.
Dimensions   approx. 85 ft x 24 ft x 9.8 ft x 5.9 ft (25.9 m x 7.3 m
          (inside plank) x 3 m x 1.8 m)
No. 3
Laid down   10.9.1839   *Launched* 14.10.1840
No. 4
Laid down   10.9.1839   *Launched* 2.11.1840
No. 7
Laid down   10.9.1839   *Launched* 1.11.1841

~

2 ships built at Nikolaev Admiralty by Pchelnikov.
Dimensions   approx. 104 ft x 28 ft x 10.2 ft x 6.9 ft (31.6 m x 8.5 m
          (inside plank) x 3.1 m x 2.1 m)
No.5
Laid down   10.9.1839   *Launched* 3.10.1841
No.6
Laid down   10.9.1839   *Launched* 21.08.1841

~

No. 8 Nikolaev Admiralty
Constructor   Pchelnikov
Laid down   10.9.1839   *Launched* 26.11.1841
Dimensions   approx. 62 ft x 23 ft x 10.2 ft x 6.7 ft (18.8 m x 7 m
          (inside plank) x 3.1 m x 2 m)

Gabars (4 purpose-built)

The term gabar derives from the French *gabare*. Gabars were three-masted cargo ships used primarily in the Mediterranean by the French. Only four were built for the Black Sea fleet.

3 gabars built at Kichkasskaya.
Dimensions   approx. 123 ft x 34 ft x 16.4 ft (37.4 m x 10.5 m x 5 m)
Valerian
Launched   1790
Carried cargo between Black Sea ports from 1791–8. Carried powder to the Ionian squadron and secret orders for Adm. Ushakov from Sevastopol' to Naples in 1799. Returned to Sevastopol' in 1800. Cruised in the Black Sea from 1801–7.
Iosif
Launched   1790
Carried cargo between Black Sea and Sea of Azov ports from 1791–1802. Sailed to Spain in 1803 and 1804. Quarantined at Sevastopol' roads with 5 sick horses and 80 sheep from Spain. Driven ashore and wrecked by a sudden squall on 11.10.1804.
Kichkasy
Launched   1790
Carried cargo between Black Sea and Sea of Azov ports from 1791–8. Carried supplies to Adm. Ushakov's Ionian squadron in 1799. Left Nikolaev with supplies for Ushakov's squadron in 10.1800. Driven ashore and wrecked in a storm 12 miles off Sambul.
Platon
Launched   1790

Dimensions   approx. 110 ft x 31 ft x 15 ft (33.6 m x 9.5 m x 4.6 m)
Operated in the Black Sea in 1797. Visited Istanbul in 1798. Carried supplies to Adm. Ushakov's Ionian squadron in 1799 and returned to Sevastopol'. Visited Istanbul in 1802. Cruised in the Black Sea in 1800–1. Visited Istanbul in 1802. Cruised in the Black Sea from 1803–5.

Cargo yachts (11 purchased)

Cargo yachts were small lateen-rigged transport vessels found only in the Baltic. The majority were purchased in 1812. They were used for transporting supplies to squadrons and for supplying the ports of Rochensalm and Revel', ports then under construction.

Ekaterina
Dimensions   approx. 63 ft x 23 ft x 10.2 ft (19.2 m x 7 m x 3.1 m)
Built in 1800. Purchased in 1802. Carried cargo in the Baltic from 1802–6. Destroyed by fire during naval exercises.

Avdot'ia
Purchased in 1812. Brought supplies to the rowing flotilla from 1812–14. Carried cargo in the Baltic from 1814–16. BU at Rochensalm in 1816.

Anna
Purchased in 1812. Brought supplies to the rowing flotilla from 1812–14. Carried cargo in the Baltic from 1814–19. BU at Rochensalm in 1819.

Dmitriy
Purchased in 1812. Brought supplies to the rowing flotilla from 1812–14. Carried cargo in the Baltic from 1814–19. BU at Abo in 1816.

Evdokiia
Purchased in 1812. Brought supplies to the rowing flotilla from 1812–14. Carried cargo in the Baltic from 1814–19. BU at Abo in 1819.

Nadezhda
Purchased in 1812. Brought supplies to the rowing flotilla from 1812–14. Carried cargo in the Baltic from 1814–24. Grounded and wrecked on 23.9.1824.

Nikolai
Purchased in 1812. Brought supplies to the rowing flotilla from 1812–14. Driven ashore and wrecked by a squall off Pillau on 27.4.1814.

Fyodor
Purchased in 1812. Brought supplies to the rowing flotilla from 1812–14. Carried cargo in the Baltic from 1814–17. BU at Sveaborg in 1817.

Blagodat'
Purchased in 1814. Cargo transfer in the Baltic in 1814. Grounded and lost during a squall on 19.9.1814.

Nikolai
Purchased in 1814. Carried cargo in the Baltic. BU at Rochensalm in 1822.

Feodosiia
Purchased in 1814. Carried cargo in the Baltic in 1814. Sank during a storm off Hogland on 20.9.1814.

Baltic fleet passenger boats (12 purpose-built)

Passenger boats were small vessels for carrying passengers and cargo found only in the Baltic. They were yacht rigged, with one or two masts.

2 ships built at Galley Yard, St Petersburg by Lukin.
Dimensions   approx. 45 ft x 15 ft x 7.9 ft (13.7 m x 4.6 m x 2.4 m)
Del'fin, Sankt-Peterburg
Both launched in 1803 and BU in 1819 at Kronshtadt.

~

2 ships built at Kronshtadt.
Begun, Sokol
Laid down in 1803 and undocked on 1.8.1804. BU before 1812.

~

Belka   Admiralty, St Petersburg
Constructor   A. I. Melikhov
Dimensions   approx. 45 ft x 15 ft x 8.2 ft (13.7 m x 4.6 m x 2.5 m)
Believed to have been completed in the first decade of the nineteenth century. No other data is available.

Kuropatka   Admiralty, St Petersburg
Constructor   A. I. Melikhov
Dimensions   approx. 46 ft x 15 ft x 7.2 ft (14 m x 4.6 m x 2.2 m)
Believed to have been completed in the first decade of the nineteenth century. No other data is available.

2 ships built at Admiralty, St Petersburg by V. Berkov.
Del'fin
Laid down   1818   Launched 1819
BU 1830.
Sankt-Peterburg
Laid down   1818   Launched 1819
BU 1832.

~

Lidiia   Okhta
Constructor   V. F. Stoke
Laid down   1824   Launched 1825
BU 1836.

Struia
Laid down   ?   Launched 1834
Operated as a training ship with naval cadets in 1834–5, 1839, and 1842. Stationed as a floating light house in 1843. Assigned fire watch duties in the northern approaches to Kronshtadt in 1844.

2 ships built at Okhta by I. A. Amosov
Dimensions   approx. 51.5 ft x 16 ft x 7.5 ft (15.7m (pp) x 4.9m (inside plank) x 2.3 m)
Pavlin
Laid down   16.11.1835   Launched 20.8.1836
Repaired in 1842. Refitted as a yacht in 1845.
Pelikan
Laid down   16.11.1835   Launched 17.10.1836
BU 1853.

Miscellaneous auxiliaries

The following types include ships that were either highly specialized in function, or produced in insignificant numbers. As is the case with more established auxiliary categories, these vessels are presented in order of their introduction to the Russian navy.

Tartans (2 purpose-built and 1 purchased)

Tartan derives from the Italian *tartana* and refers to a type of small one- or two-masted vessels with lateen sails. Tartans were employed in a variety of naval, cargo and fishery roles as needed. The 3 vessels found in the Baltic and Sea of Azov fleets were all unnamed.

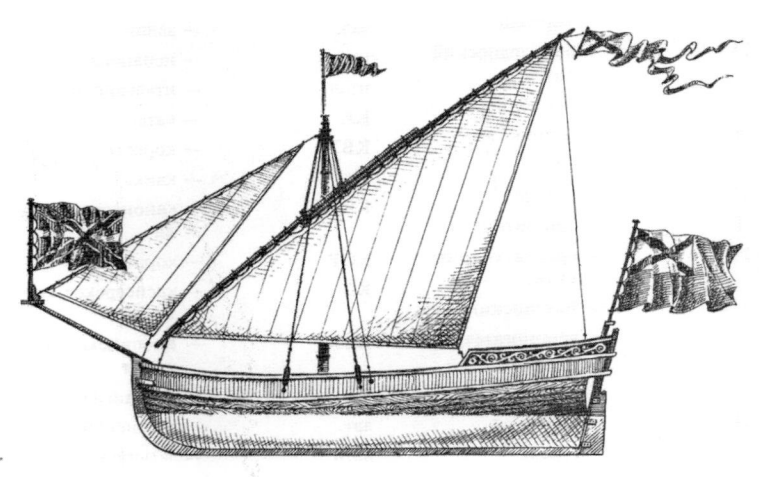

A profile of one of the 3 tartans constructed in the first decade of the eighteenth century, this one for the Sea of Azov. Her lateen sails betray her Mediterranean origins.

Baltic fleet tartans (2 purpose-built)
Unnamed   Selitskiy Ryadok
Constructor   V. Graf
Laid down   ?   Launched 1705
Dimensions   approx. 65 ft x 17 ft x ? (19.8 m x 5.2 m x ?)
Two-masted tartan used as an aviso. Participated in the expedition to Vyborg in 5.1712.

Unnamed   Selitskiy Ryadok
Constructor   V. Graf
Laid down   1704   Launched 1705
21-masted tartan used as an aviso. Participated in the expedition to Vyborg in 5.1712.

Sea of Azov fleet tartan (1 purchased)
Unnamed
Purchased in 1709. Arrived at Azov in 5.1709. Cruised in the Sea of Azov with Vice-Adm. Kruys' squadron in 1711. Transferred to Cherkassk upon the dissolution of the Sea of Azov fleet.

White Sea flotilla kochs (2 purpose-built)

Kochs were vessels designed by Russian polar explorers with strongly reinforced hulls and rudders to operate in heavy ice. 2

kochs were built at Arkhangel'sk and launched in 1734 for the Great Northern Expedition.

Ob'
The Ob' is a major Siberian river. Participated in the Great Northern Expedition led by Malygin and Muravyev. Departed Arkhangel'sk on 10.7.1734 in company with *Ekspeditsion* and headed towards its namesake river and surveyed Vaygach Island. Entered Kara Sea in the vicinity of Yamal peninsula on 29.7.1734. Wintered at the mouth of the Pechora River. Sailed in Kara Sea in the summer of 1735 and wintered at the Pechora in 1735-36. Returned to Arkhangel'sk.

Ekspeditsion
Participated in the Great Northern Expedition with the *Ob'*. Damaged by ice in 1736 and abandoned. Crew transferred to Ob'.

Cargo vessels (10 purpose-built, 1 purchased and 1 prize)

The designation 'cargo vessel' is a descriptive term and does not relate to any particular type of vessel or system of rigging. Very little definite information is available for most of these ships, with the exception of the two Sea of Azov ships that had the distinction of having been converted into 'newly invented flat-bottomed frigates'.

Baltic fleet cargo vessels (6 purpose-built)

Gogland
Built about 1747. Cruised in the Baltic in 1748. Carried cargo between Kronshtadt and Lubeck from 1749–53. Carried Hungarian wines for the Empress Elizabeth from 1754–6. To Memel in 1757. Wrecked at Memel on 6.10.1757.

2 vessels built at Irkutsk by K. I. Ostretsov and N. Popov:
Dimensions approx. 50 ft x ? x ? (15.3 m x ? x ? m)
Boris i Gleb
Laid down 27.6.1763 *Launched* 24.7.1765
Carried cargo and passengers across Lake Baikal. Driven ashore and burnt in a storm in 1772.
Svyatogo Kuzmy Svyatogradtsa
Laid down 7.9.1764 *Launched* 12.10.1765
Carried cargo and passengers across Lake Baikal. Final fate is not known.

~

Verbliud
Built at Arkhangel'sk about1783. Transferred to Kronshtadt in 1783. Fire watch duties at Riga in 1784. Carried cargo in the Baltic from 1785–7. Carried supplies from Kronshtadt to Vyborg and Rochensalm during the Russo-Swedish War from 1788–90.

~

Buivol
Built about1784. Carried cargo in the Baltic from 1784–7. Transported supplies to Greig's squadron off Seskar in 7.1788. Cruised with Vice-Adm. Kruz's squadron between Revel' and Porkkala-Udd in 1789. built around 1784.

Slon
Built about1786. Carried cargo in the Baltic in 1786–7. Transported cannons from Kronshtadt to Revel' in 7.1788. Transported the crew of *Rodislav* (66), grounded and wrecked on 15.10.1789, to Kronshtadt on 16.10.1789.

White Sea flotilla cargo vessel (1 purpose-built)
Sviatoi Ioann Solombala
Laid down 11.8.1787 *Launched* 6.5.1788
Permanently stationed at Arkhangel'sk.

Sea of Okhotsk flotilla cargo vessel (1 purpose-built)
Ioann Bogoslov Solombala
Constructor Kuzmin
Laid down ? *Launched* 1790
Transferred on completion to the Sea of Okhotsk Flotilla. Carried cargo from 1790–1807. Driven ashore and wrecked by a storm at Kamchatka on 30.9.1807.

Sea of Azov flotilla cargo vessels (2 purpose-built and 1 purchased)
Volik
Dimensions approx. 55 ft x 16 ft x 6.6 ft (16.8 m x 4.9 m x 2 m)
Armament 10 guns
3-masted vessel purchased in 1775. Sailed to Istanbul and carried cargo in the Black Sea in 1776. Carried cargo in the Black Sea from 1777–81. Sailed to Istanbul in 1782. Relegated to fire watch duties at Taganrog in 11.1782, where she was driven ashore in a winter storm and crushed by ice.

Boristen Kherson
Constructor S. I. Afanasyev
Laid down ? *Launched* 28.10.1781
Dimensions 112 ft x 30 ft 6 in x 13 ft (Veselago)
96 ft x 35 ft x 12 ft (Golochev)
Named after the ancient Greek name for the Dnieper. Assigned to the Sea of Azov Flotilla on completion and reassigned to the Black Sea fleet in 5.1783. Carried cargo in the Black Sea from 1782–7. Converted into a flat-bottomed 'newly invented frigate' in 1788 by M. L. Faleev and renamed *Grigorii Bogoslov*. Fought at Ochakov with the Liman Flotilla on 17.6.1788. Broken up after 1791. The discrepancy between Veselago's dimensions and Golochev's may relate to those pertaining before and after her conversion. (See also under Black Sea frigates.)

Pchela Kherson
Laid down 14.1.1781 *Launched* 30.9.1782
Dimensions 91 ft 6 in x 24 ft 6 in x 11 ft 6 in (Veselago)
93 ft x 25 ft x 12 ft 6 in (Golovachev)
Assigned to the Sea of Azov Flotilla on completion and reassigned to the Black Sea fleet in 5.1783. Carried cargo in the Black Sea from 1782–7. Converted into a flat-bottomed 'newly invented frigate' in 1788 by M. L. Faleev who, as head of logistics, was more normally involved with the construction of small craft. Renamed *Grigorii Velikiia Armenii* and assigned to the Liman Squadron in the mouth of the Don. Fought at Ochakov on 17.6.1788. Transferred to Sevastopol' in 1790. Assigned as a fire watch ship in 1791 and later converted into a transport. Last listed in 1806. (May be the *Grigorii 24* listed by R. C. Anderson at Corfu in 1806.) (See also under Black Sea fleet frigates.)

Black Sea fleet cargo ship (1 prize)
Chechersk

Refitted into a cargo ship from a Turkish shebeck captured in 1787. Fire watch duties at Sevastopol' from 1787–9. Attached to the rowing flotilla under de Ribas on the Dnieper Liman in 1790. Accompanied Ushakov's squadron on 7.1791.

White Sea flotilla fire watch ships (2 purpose-built)

Fire watch ships were generally ships built for other purposes and assigned to fire watch service when no longer needed for active service with the fleet. These two ships stand alone in having been purpose-built for the duty.

Prepodobnyy Zosim Solombala
Laid down   19.10.1749   *Launched* 20.5.1750
Fire watch duties at Arkhangel'sk.

Poliarnaia Zvezda Solombala
Laid down   21.7.1765   *Launched* 13.5.1766
Fire watch duties at Arkhangel'sk from 1765–6.

Expeditionary vessels (7 purpose-built)

The systematic exploration and development of the arctic waters extending across Siberia and the Alaskan peninsula was a high priority in the second half of the eighteenth century. Although these small vessels were not built for naval purposes, they were operated by the navy and are included here.

White Sea flotilla expeditionary vessels (3 purpose-built)

3 brigantine rigged vessels were built at Arkhangel'sk for expedition of V. Y. Chichagov in 1765. They were named after their commanders. As was the case with the earlier kochs built in 1734, they were specially designed to deal with severe weather and ice in northern waters. The trio was especially strongly constructed, the stem and sternpost being covered with lead sheets and iron stripes, the ribs enlarged, and the planking applied in two layers. They were also girdled and the contours were rounded like modern icebreakers in order that dangerously thick ice floes would exert vertical rather than lateral pressure on the hull, lifting the entire ship out of the water without crushing the hull if necessary.

Chichagov   Arkhangel'sk
Laid down   ?   *Launched* 1.8.1764
Sailed from Arkhangel'sk to Kola in Autumn of 1764. Wintered in Kola in 1764–5. Put to sea in 5.1765 'to find the Northern way to Kamchatka'. Encountered impenetrable ice off Spitzbergen and returned to Arkhangel'sk. Put to sea again in 1766 with the same objective – and with the same result. Sailed to Kronstadt in 1767. Included in Elphinstone's Second Archipelago Squadron in 1769. Lost contact with the squadron and wrecked on Porkla-udd Reef in Finland.

Babaev   Arkhangel'sk
Laid down   ?   *Launched* 1.8.1764
Dimensions   approx. 82 ft x ? x ? (25 m x ? x ?)
Armament   10 guns
             51 men
Sailed from Arkhangel'sk to Kola in Autumn of 1764. Wintered in Kola in 1764–5. Accompanied Chichagov on both unsuccessful attempts to find a northern route Kamchatka. Assigned fire watch duties at Arkhangel'sk in 1768. Cruised between Kola and Arkhangel'sk in 1769.

Panov   Arkhangel'sk
Laid down   ?   *Launched* 1764
Dimensions   approx. 82 ft x ? x ? (25 m x ?x ?)
Armament   10 guns
             51 men
Sailed from Arkhangel'sk to Kola in Autumn of 1764. Wintered in Kola in 1764–5. Accompanied Chichagov on both unsuccessful attempts to find a northern route Kamchatka. Cruised between Kola and Arkhangel'sk in 1769.

Okhotsk expeditionary vessels (4 purpose-built)

Pallas   Verkhnekolymsk
Constructor   Bakov
Laid down   ?   *Launched* 18.5.1787
Dimensions   approx. 45 ft x 15 ft x 5.6 ft (13.7 m x 4.6 m x 2 m)
Built at Verkhnekolymsk on the Iasashna River for the planned expedition of I. I. Billings and G. A. Sarychev. Named after the naturalist P. S. Pallas (1741–1811), planner of the expedition and member of the Russian Academy of Sciences. Left the Kolyma River in company with *Iasashna*, heading for the North Polar ocean on 24.06.1787, but forced back by heavy ice. Not subsequently employed.

Iasashna
Laid down   ?   *Launched* 19.5.1787
Dimensions   approx. 28 ft x ? x ? (8.6 m x ? x ?)
Built at Verkhnekolymsk on the Iasashna River for the planned expedition of I. I. Billings and G. A. Sarychev. Named after the naturalist P. S. Pallas (1741–1811), planner of the expedition and member of the Russian Academy of Sciences. Left the Kolyma River in company with *Pallas* heading for the North Polar ocean on 24.06.1787, but forced back by heavy ice. Not subsequently employed.

Slava Rossii   Okhotsk
Constructors   G. A. Sarychev and R. R. Gull
Laid down   ?   *Launched* 10.6.1789
Dimensions   approx. 81 ft x 24 ft x 9.5, (24.6 m x 7.2 m x 2.9 m)
Participated in an expedition organized under I. I. Billings and G. A. Sarychev departing Okhotsk for Kamchatka on 19.9.1789. Arrived at Petropavlovsk-Kamchatskiy after surveying the Sea of Okhotsk on 5.10.1789 and wintered there. Departed for North America in 1790. Entered Prince William Bay on 19.7.1790 and returned to Kamchatka. Entered the   Bering Straits in 1791 and wintered at Unalashka. Returned to Petropavlovsk in 1792 and hulked. Sank in the harbour at Petropavlovsk in 1801.

Dobroe Namerenie   Okhotsk
Constructor   G. A. Sarychev and R. R. Gull
Laid down   ?   *Launched* 8.7.1789
Entered the roadway at the port of Okhotsk in 8.1789. Driven ashore in a sudden squall and wrecked.

Black Sea fleet signal repeater ship (Repetichnoe) (1 purchased)

Polotsk
Dimensions approx. 76 ft x 25 ft x 11.2 ft (23.2 m x 7.6 m x 3.4 m)
Armament   14-6pdrs   120 men
Purchased as a repeater ship in 1788. Participated in the battle of Fidonisi on 7.3.1788. Accompanied other vessels bombarding Sinop, destroying the defending shore battery, and capturing 11 Turkish transports fully loaded with cargo. Cruised to the mouth of the Danube with Rear-Adm. Ushakov's squadron in 1789. Participated in the battles of Kerch, Tendra, and Kaliakriya in 1790-91. Cruised

annually with the Black Sea fleet from 1792-98. Left to join Adm. Ushakov's squadron in the Mediterranean in 1799 and lost without a trace. Believed to have been wrecked off the mouth of the Danube.

Black Sea fleet 'seagoing ships' (5 purpose-built)

'Seagoing ships' is a vaguely descriptive term applied to a very small group of vessels built in the Black Sea for the Russo-Turkish War of 1787–92. Little is known about these ships and they appear to have accomplished little in service, hardly surprising in view of the apparent inability of 4 of the 5 built to cross over the shallows of the Dnieper estuary into the Black Sea.

4 ships built at Sekerinskaya and launched in 1789.
Dimensions   approx. 76 ft x 23 ft x 8.9 ft (23.2 m x 6.9 m x 2.7 m)
Armament   10 guns
Nepristupnyi, Sil'nyi, Smelyi, Khrabryi.
It would appear that these ships were unable to cross over the shallows of the Dnieper. They were broken up at the war's end.

Ipogrif
Dimensions   approx. 70 ft x 19 ft x 8.9 ft (21.4 m x 5.9 m x 2.7 m)
Launched on the Dnieper in 1790. Operated with the rowing flotilla under de Ribas at the mouth of the Danube in 1790-91. Active with the rowing flotilla until 1795.

Black Sea kirlangichs (3 purpose-built and 1 purchased)

Kirlangich means 'swallow' in Turkish. Russian kirlangichs were built only in the Black Sea, where they served as light avisos.

3 ships launched at Shklovskaya in 1790 and broken up in 1800.
Andrei, Grigorii, Kir
Dimensions   approx. 72 ft x 25 ft x 12.5 ft (22 m x 7.5 m x 3.8 m)

Akhill
Dimensions   approx. 78 ft x 24 ft x 10.8 ft (23.8 m x 7.3 m x 3.3 m)
Armament   10 guns   75 men
Purchased in 1792. Sailed annually with the training squadron. Dispatched by Vice-Adm. Ushakov to Kozlovskiy Roads on 16.7.1798. Capsized in a squall on her return with only a single survivor.

Baltic fleet hospital ship (1 prize ship)

As was the case with fire watch ships, hospital ships were generally drawn from warships past their active service lives or from transports. The following ship stands alone in having been designed to care for the sick and wounded.
Merkurii
Swedish prize captured at the 1st battle of Rochensalm on 17.8.1798. Attached to Vice-Adm. Kozlyaninov's rowing squadron at the battle of Vyborg where she received sick and wounded. Assigned to the rowing flotillas in 1793. Sailed to Memel in 1794. Accompanied Vice-Adm. Khanykov's squadron to England in 1795 and returned to Kronshtadt with sick seamen. Assigned to the rowing flotillas from 1798–1803.

Black Sea fleet akats (2 purpose-built)

The Russian akat was invented by Prince Potemkin The name derives from the ancient Greek *akation*, a term for a small vessel or boat. Akats were three-masted ship-rigged vessels, equipped with oars. They were employed in service as avisos and scouts. Only two akats were actually completed for the Black Sea fleet. The planned production of a series of such vessels was abandoned after the death of Prince Potemkin.
Dimensions   approx. 95 ft x 26 ft x 11.2 ft x 10.2 ft (29 m x 7.9 m x 3.4 m x 3.1 m)
Armament   2 x 3-pood howitzers, 10 x ½-pood edinorogs, 6 x ¼-pood edinorogs
100 men

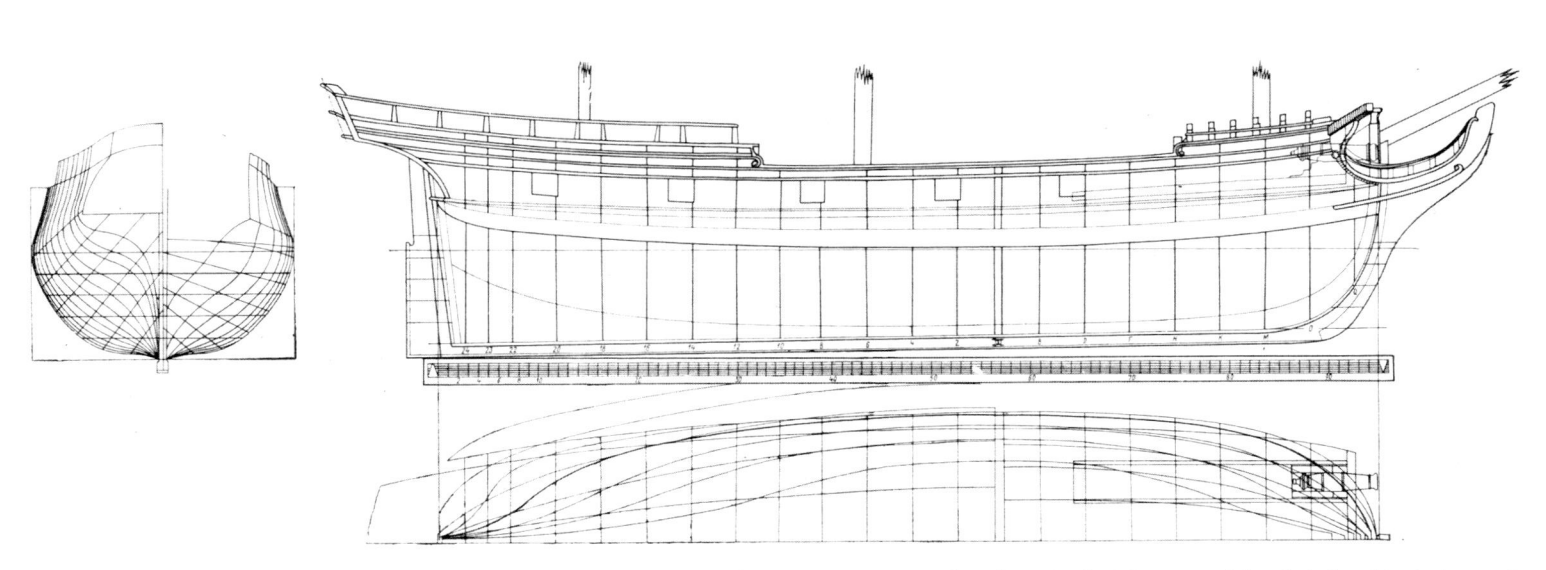

Besides being one of Catherine II's most favoured lovers, Prince Potemkin was an enormously talented administrator with a flair for ship design and technology. This sheer and profile of the Irina *of 1791 was one of only two akats completed before Potemkin's death resulted in the abandonment of the artificially conceived type. Armed as they were with 2 howitzers and 16 small edinorogs, their anticipated role would appear to have been inshore warfare against small rowing vessels. In spite of the lack of favour Potemkin's design attracted, both* Irina *and her unnamed sister proved successful in service in a variety of small ship roles.*

Irina Nikolaev Admiralty
Constructor   S. I. Afanasyev
Laid down   11.1790   *Launched* 14.8.1791
The name was chosen to commemorate the peace with Turkey concluded 31.7.1791 in Galats. Cruised in the Black Sea in 1792. Operated with the training squadron in 1794 and 1798. Departed Sevastopol' with Vice-Adm. Ushakov's Mediterranean Squadron on 12.8.1798. Forced to return for repairs because of a leak. Rejoined the Russian squadron at the Bosphorus, but again returned to Sevastopol' with Ushakov's report to Paul I. Rejoined Ushakov's squadron off Corfu with supplies on 22.1.1798. Participated in the attack on Corfu on 18.2.1799. Transported French PoWs to Toulon. Returned to Sevastopol' in 8.1799. Cruised annually in the Black Sea from 1800–4. Relegated to fire watch duties at Sevastopol' in 1805.

No. 2 Nikolaev Admiralty
Constructor   S. I. Afanasyev
Laid down   11.1790   *Launched* 30.9.1791
Cruised in the Black Sea in 1792 and 1794. Fire watch duties at Sevastopol' from 1795–8. Departed Sevastopol' for a cruise with Rear-Adm. Ovtsyn's squadron. Encountered a severe storm on 11.10.1798 and driven to the Bosphorus. Returned to Sevastopol' on 25.10.1798. Cruised annually in the Black Sea from 1799–1804.

Section IV
The Russian Steam Navy to 1862

The Russian Steam Navy

In 1815 the Russian navy emerged from the Napoleonic War as one the world's truly first-class fleets and retained this position throughout the rest of the period covered by this book. It took an early interest in steam power with its first steamer, *Elisabeta* (later *Skoryi*), being built in 1817 by the Izhora Works at St Petersburg and engined locally by Baird of St Petersburg also. Further small steamers of domestic construction followed during the period of experimentation in the 1820s. By the end of the decade the British navy had laid down *Dee*, a substantial vessel of some 700 tons builder's measurement and 200 nominal horsepower, and the French navy had launched the slightly smaller *Sphinx* of 160 nominal horsepower (nhp). The *Sphinx*, which proved its value in the Algerian campaign in 1830 in support of the French landing and as a dispatch vessel, was followed by a series of similar craft. *Dee* was not launched till 1832 but before this four still larger ships (over 800 tons and 220 nhp) were laid down for the British navy. Developments in Russia mirrored this progress with the first Russian ocean-going steam warship, the 200 nhp *Gerkules*, launched in 1831 at the Okhta Admiralty in St Petersburg and engined by the Izhora Works. A yet more powerful steamer, the 240 nhp *Bogatyr'*, was launched at the Main Admiralty in St Petersburg in 1836. The Izhora Works again provided the machinery. At 1,342 tons displacement, with a length of 186 ft and breadth of 33 ft, *Bogatyr'* surpassed its contemporaries in the British and French navies until the British *Gorgon* of 1,610 tons was launched in 1837. As completed, *Bogatyr'* mounted a useful armament of 28 x 24pdr guns giving a broadside weight of 336 pounds. It was classified as a steam frigate throughout its career (*Gerkules* was so classified from 1847).

Russian naval authorities were by now becoming convinced that these steam warships could replace sailing vessels in the Baltic for cruising and scouting duties and only four more sailing frigates were built for the Baltic fleet. Although steamers were dependant on specialised facilities for fuel, maintenance and repair in a way that sailing ships were not, the primary operational area for Russian steam warships was the Baltic Sea and they would thus never be far from the infrastructure they required. The next large Baltic steamer was *Kamchatka*, built and engined at New York in 1840, followed by *Otvazhnyi*, *Khrabryi*, *Smelyi*, *Grozyashchiy* and *Gremyashchiy* built at St Petersburg and *Riurik* and *Olaf* built in Finland. These vessels were engined variously with local and with foreign machinery.

The first steamer in the Black Sea was *Vesuvy* built in 1820 at Nikolaev with engines by Baird transported from St Petersburg. The Black Sea area, however, offered far fewer industrial resources than the Baltic to support the introduction of steam. An initial group of paddle frigates comprising *Krym*, *Odessa*, *Khersones*, *Bessarabiia* and *Gromonosets* was built at Northfleet on the Thames in 1842 and 1843 followed by the larger *Vladimir* built in London. All were powered by British machinery.

Between 1846 and 1848 the screw frigate *Arkimed* was built and engined at St Petersburg. Its early loss in 1850 slowed the creation of a Russian screw fleet which was only just beginning when the Crimean War erupted. There were no operational screw warships in service and only the screw frigate *Polkan*, newly launched at Arkhangel'sk, was at Kronshtadt completing. On the stocks at St Petersburg were the screw 84-gun ship *Oryol* and frigate *Mariia* (later *Askol'd*) while the 74-gun ships *Konstantin* and *Vyborg* were converting to steam at Kronshtadt. The screw frigate *Il'ia Muromets* was on the stocks at Arkhangel'sk. All were to have had British machinery. On the stocks at Nikolaev were a pair of 120-gun screw steamers, *Bosfor* (later *Sinop*) and *Tsesarevich*, to be fitted with British machinery also. Building at Northfleet for the Black Sea fleet were the screw frigates *Voin* and *Vityaz'*. It was planned to convert the sailing 120-gun *Tri Sviatitelia* and 84-gun *Trekh Ierakhov* to steam. There were in addition the 10 Baltic and 6 Black Sea paddle frigates but the British and French navies were able to send more numerous and powerful steam fleets into both the Baltic and Black Seas, with sailing vessels in these theatres increasingly replaced by steamers as the war progressed. In March 1854 *Voin* and *Vityaz'* were seized by the British and completed for the British navy. Machinery still on order from British firms was, of course, not delivered. All this placed the Russian navy at an enormous disadvantage and meant that, after the victory of Sinop, it saw relatively little action. It also meant that Russia was thrown back on its own resources and machinery of Russian manufacture was substituted for the unavailable original in *Oryol*, *Mariia* and *Il'ia Muromets*.

During the war the conversion of two more ships of the line for the Baltic fleet, *Gangut* and *Vola*, was begun and another two, *Retvizan* and *Imperator Nikolai I*, were laid down at St Petersburg as was the frigate *Gromoboy* at Helsingfors. But only *Vyborg* and *Polkan* had entered service before the war ended. The iron postal service paddle steamer *Vladimir* was refitted as a frigate in 1854. New construction in the Baltic concentrated instead on 75 screw gunboats for coastal defence. Vessels of 60–80 nhp, 170 to 178 tons displacement and three 68pdr shell guns each, they were all built and engined between 1854 and 1856. During the same period 14 screw corvettes of the *Boyarin* class were built and engined at St Petersburg and 6 screw clippers of the *Razboynik* class were built at Arkhangel'sk to be engined at St Petersburg. In the Black Sea the screw corvette *Voin* was laid down at Nikolaev together with the paddle frigate *Tigr* which was to use engines salvaged from the British paddle frigate *Tiger* destroyed at Odessa in April 1854. The former was completed after the war as a transport to comply with the demilitarisation of the Black Sea stipulated in the Treaty of Paris and the latter as an imperial yacht. No Black Sea sailing vessels had been converted to screw and the ships of the line *Sinop* and *Tsesarevich* were transferred to the Baltic eventually receiving new British machinery in 1860. The war had been fought primarily on land until the fall of Sevastopol but it was the huge steam fleet the allies were preparing for the 1856 Baltic campaign and the threat it posed to Kronshtadt and ultimately St

Petersburg that brought the war to an end. The war demonstrated that sailing fleets were obsolete while Russian industry and shipyards had risen to the immense challenge of supplying the coastal defence steam flotilla that became the highest Russian shipbuilding priority.

Following the war the Russian government sought to build a screw 90-gun ship, *Imperatritsa Mariia*, in New York but as no American builder had experience with such vessels the order was altered to a 70-gun screw frigate, *General Admiral*, comparable in size to the huge USS *Niagara* but with a far more numerous battery of lighter guns. No further ships of the line were begun and the emphasis shifted to creating a force of cruisers, large and small, for warfare against commerce. *General Admiral* was followed by an order for *Svetlana*, a smaller screw frigate, in France. Subsequently laid down were the frigates *Osliabia*, *Dmitrii Donskoi*, *Aleksandr Nevskii* and *Petropavlovsk* at St Petersburg, *Oleg* and *Sevastopol* at Kronshtadt and *Peresvet* at Arkhangel'sk. *Sevastopol* and *Petropavlovsk* were, like *General Admiral*, among the largest such vessels ever designed. Their size ensured they were very suitable for conversion into broadside ironclads when the need arose soon after they were commenced. The wartime corvettes were succeeded by the larger *Baian* built in France, *Kalevala*, *Varyag* and *Vityaz'* built in Finland and *Bogatyr'* and *Askol'd* built at St Petersburg. The wartime clippers were succeeded by *Abrek* and *Vsadnik* built in Finland, *Gaidamak* at Northfleet and *Almaz*, *Zhemchug*, *Izumrud* and *Iakhont* at St Petersburg. Within the terms of the Treaty of Paris, the corvettes *Sokol*, *Iastreb*, *Krechet*, *L'vista* and *Pamiat' Merkuriia* were built at Nikolaev. Foreign machinery was still purchased in some cases for domestically constructed hulls but Russia was largely self-sufficient in this regard after the war. Finally, several of the paddle frigates were rebuilt and *Solombala*, a new vessel constructed at Arkhangel'sk, reused the engines of the old *Bogatyr'*.

By the early 1860s Russia possessed a large force of cruising vessels. With this force the Russian Navy could potentially inflict far greater damage on the British or French than had been possible during the Crimean War. In 1863, when conflict with both over Poland appeared possible, a fleet from the Baltic sailed to New York while the Asiatic squadron cruised to San Francisco to be ready to act against enemy commerce should hostilities begin. Considering the havoc wrought by *Alabama* and other Confederate raiders on United States shipping, the former allies would have faced substantial risks in again going to war with Russia.

A point of clarification is in order with respect to the ships included in this section. A small number of vessels begun after 1860 are included for the sake of completeness. These vessels were all design sisters or near sisters of ships begun prior to 1861, or in the case of *Riurik* of 1869 a rebuild of an earlier ship.

Horsepower units defined

Nominal horsepower (nhp): An estimation by formula of the power of an engine based on its geometry. The formula was developed because measuring the real power of an engine was initially very difficult. For the earliest steam engines it was reasonably accurate but as engine design became more sophisticated and piston speeds increased the power generated began to exceed the nominal power. By the 1840s and 1850s the indicated horsepower of an engine (see below) could be three or four times its nominal power.

Indicated horsepower (ihp): The power theoretically generated by an engine. An instrument called an 'indicator' was developed in the early nineteenth century which could draw a graph of steam pressure against piston speed in a working cylinder. From the graph the power available in the steam could be calculated and the power output of the engine determined. This is a theoretical figure, however, as it does not take account of the inevitable losses due to friction within the engine itself.

Steam and Sail Warships: Baltic fleet

Steam screw ships of the line

Three-deckers

Tsesarevich 135 Nikolaev
Constructor I. S. Dmitriev
Laid down 3.8.1853 *Launched* 29.10.1857
Dimensions 241 ft 6 in (pp) x 60 ft (outside plank) x ? x 24 ft 5 in/
  25 ft 9 in (draught fore/aft)
  3,821 tons bm, 5,563 tons displacement
Armament 1862 LD 34 x 60pdr shell guns, 4 x 36pdr (long)
  MD 4 x 36pdrs (long), 32 x 36pdrs (short)
  UD 4 x 36pdrs (long), 34 x 36pdr gunnades
  FC & QD 1 x 60pdr (5 ton pivot), 4 x 36pdrs (short),
  13 x 36pdr howitzers
Machinery 800 nhp (Maudslay, London) = 11 kts

Purpose-built steam screw ship. The delivery of her original machinery from Great Britain was prevented by the outbreak of war. Completed without machinery for passage to the Baltic 12.10.1858 as per the provisions of the Treaty of Paris. Built of unseasoned oak. Sailed from Sevastopol to Kronshtadt in 1858–9. Repairs to stop leakage during voyage completed at Malta 8.4.59. Completed as a screw ship in 1860 with the installation of machinery and 6 boilers. Cruised in 1861. Stricken on 26.1.74.

Sinop (ex-*Bosfor*) 135 Nikolaev
Constructor A. S. Akimov
Laid down 29.10.1852 *Launched* 26.9.1858
Dimensions 242 ft 2 in (pp) x 59 ft 6 in (outside plank) x ? x 24 ft 2 in/
  25 ft 10 in (draught fore/aft)
  3,823 tons bm, 5,585 tons displacement
Armament 1862 LD 34 x 60pdr shell guns, 4 x 36pdr (long)
  MD 4 x 36pdrs (long), 32 x 36pdrs (short)
  UD 4 x 36pdrs (long), 34 x 36pdr gunnades
  FC & QD 1 x 60pdr (5 ton pivot), 4 x 36pdrs (short),
  18 x 36pdr howitzers
Machinery 800 nhp (Maudslay, London) = 11 kts

Purpose-built steam screw ship. Built of unseasoned oak. Laid down as *Bosfor*, renamed *Sinop* on 30.3.1856. The delivery of her original machinery from Great Britain for her completion was prevented by the outbreak of war. Completed without machinery for transit to the Baltic in compliance with the Treaty of Paris on 31.8.1858. Sailed from Sevastopol to Kronshtadt in 1858–9. Repairs to stop leakage completed at Toulon on 9.3.1859. Attended the Imperial review. Completed as a screw ship in 1860 with the installation of machinery and 6 boilers. Stricken on 26.1.1874.

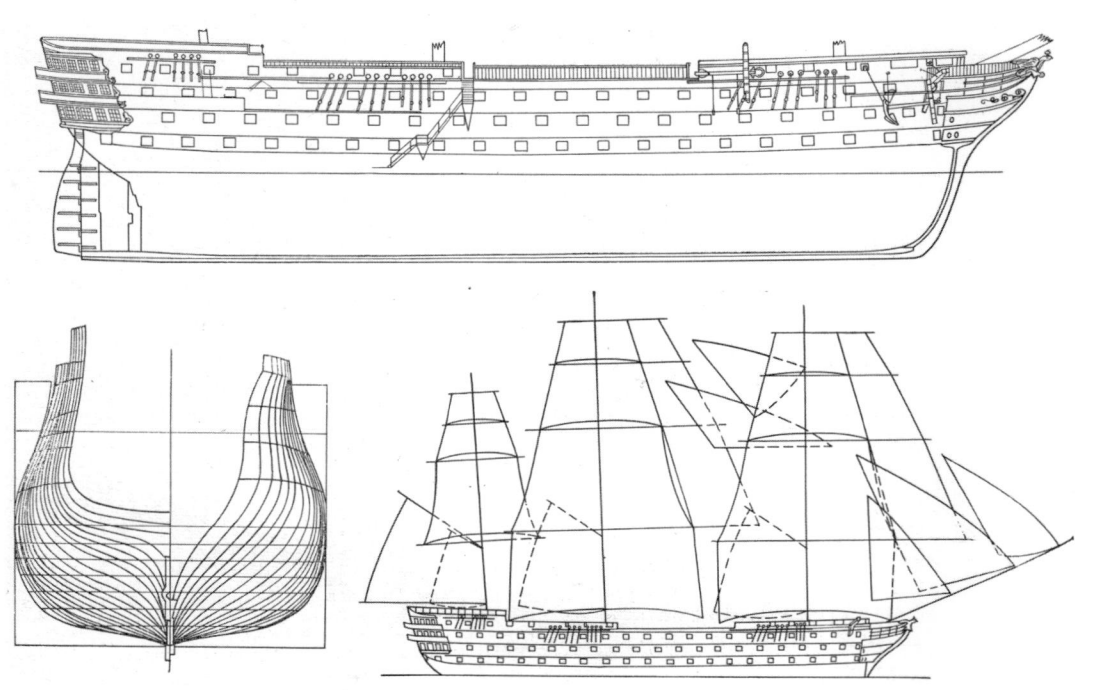

The purpose-built screw ship Sinop *(135) has the unusual distinction of having been begun at Nikolaev on the eve of the Crimean War, launched there without her engines at the conclusion of the war, transferred to Kronshtadt as a sailing ship, and then finally completed there at very long last with the installation of her long delayed engines as one of Russia's last wooden battleships in 1860. This draught gives a clear impression of her enormous size, but shows her as completed without either her funnel or machinery.* Sinop *shows a complete absence of any degree of sheer, but even at the very end of sail, wooden ships of this size still required a considerable amount of tumblehome as the cross-sectional drawing makes clear.*

Imperator Nikolai I (ex-*Imperator Aleksandr I*) 111 St Petersburg, New Admiralty
Constructors S. I. Chernyavskiy and K. G. Mikhailov
Laid down 26.6.1855   *Launched* 18.5.1860
Dimensions 233 ft 6 in (pp) x 58 ft 3½ in (outside plank) x ? x 25 ft 2 in/26 ft (draught fore/aft)
3,469 tons bm, 5,426 tons displacement
Armament 1862 LD 10 x 60pdr shell guns, 22 x 36pdrs (long)
MD 4 x 60pdr shell guns, 4 x 36pdrs (long), 26 x 36pdrs (short)
UD 4 x 36pdrs (long), 30 x 36pdr gunnades
FC & QD 1 x 60pdr (5 ton pivot), 6 x 60pdr shell guns, 2 x 36pdrs (long)
Machinery 600 nhp (Humphreys & Tennant, London) = 11 kts

Purpose-built steam screw ship. Design based on that of HMS *Duke of Wellington*. Originally named *Imperator Aleksandr I* on 8.10.1854 and renamed on 28.2.1855. Rated as 124 guns until armament revised in November 1857. Built without a poop for improved stability. Undocked on 1.6.1861 after installation of machinery and boilers. Trials in 1861. Conversion into a wooden-hulled ironclad planned 1862–3 but not carried out. Gunnery training ship in 1862–6. Transported troops in 1863–4. Stricken on 26.1.1874.

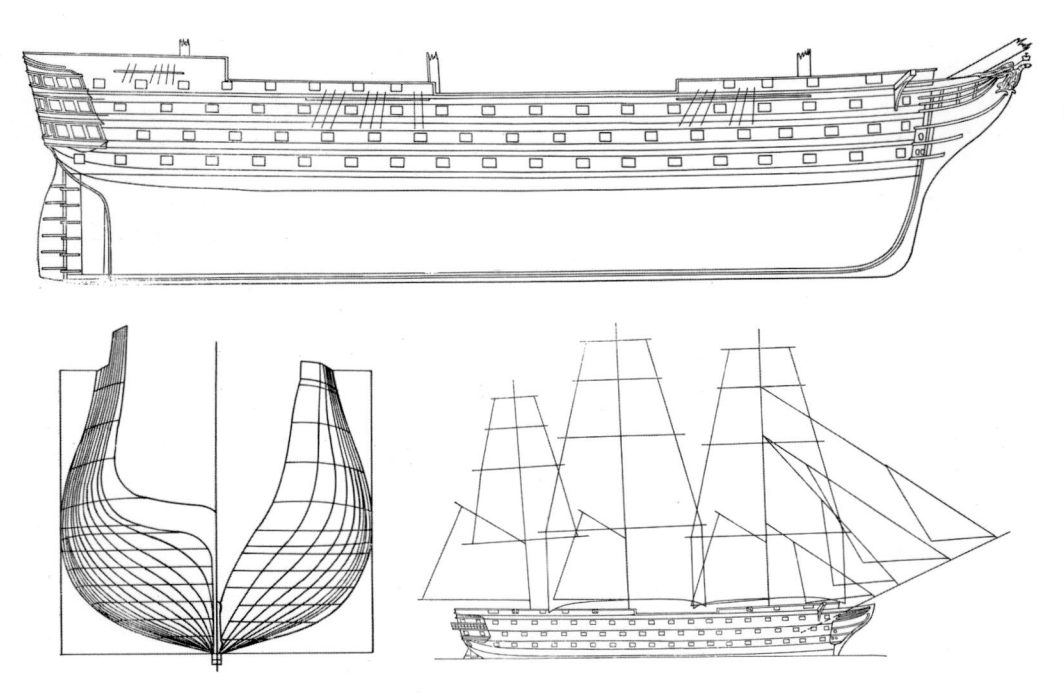

Nikolai I (111) was laid down at St Petersburg as the Crimean War was winding down and makes for an interesting comparison with the two earlier but slightly larger Black Sea First Rates Sinop *and* Tsesarevich *that joined her in the Baltic in 1860. Her design is said to have been based on that of the British* Duke of Wellington, *and represents a very late example of the British influence that had characterized Russian ship design before 1800, but which had vanished as Russian naval architecture matured and moved in increasingly independent directions.*

The launching of the last screw ship of the line, Imperator Nikolai I *in 1860 as seen in a contemporary painting. In contrast to the great display involved in the launching of the First Rate* Rossiia *in 1839 seen earlier, the atmosphere here is almost muted, with only a few casual onlookers gathered in small boats. In place of sailing line of battle ships firing salutes, the background here is made up of steamers seeming almost to ignore the proceedings. There is not a sail in sight. Artist unknown.*

2-deckers

Gangut 84/90 St Petersburg
Constructor I. V. Kurepanov
Laid down 8.8.1822 *Launched* 19.9.1825
Dimensions 196 ft (pp) x 51 ft (inside plank) x 23 ft 7 in (as built)
212 ft (pp) x 53 ft 8 in (outside plank) x 23 ft 8 in
x 21 ft 7 in/23 ft 1 in (draught fore/aft)
2,659 tons bm, 3,814 tons displacement (as steamer)
Armament 1825 LD 24 x 36pdrs (short), 6 x 60pdr u (1 pood)
UD 32 x 24pdrs (short)
FC & QD 2 x 24pdrs (short), 26 x 24pdr carr.
1848 LD 2 x 9.65-in shell guns, 24 x 36pdrs (long),
4 x 60pdr u (1 pood)
UD 32 x 24pdrs (long), FC & QD 2 x 24pdrs (short),
26 x 24pdr carr.
1856 LD 28 x 60pdr shell guns 4 x 30pdrs (long)
UD 4 x 30pdrs (long), 28 x 30pdrs (short)
FC & QD 4 x 30pdrs (short), 16 x 30pdr gunnades
Machinery 500 nhp (Nobel, St Petersburg) = 9 kts
Converted steam screw ship. Departed Kronshtadt for the Mediterranean on 10.6.1827 in Rear-Adm. Geiden's squadron under the command of Adm. Seniavin. Fought at Navarino on 8.10.1827 during which she destroyed two Turkish frigates and a fireship at a cost of 14 killed, 37 wounded, and 51 hits received. Departed for the Baltic for repairs after offloading ammunition. Arrived at Kronshtadt in 8.1828 where she was fully repaired. Cruised in the Baltic in 1829–30 and 1832–3. Underwent long repair in 1834–7. Cruised in the Baltic in 1838–42 and 1845–6. Repaired and refitted in 1848. To Denmark to provide security against Prussia in 1848–50. Rebuilt as a screw steamer with four boilers between 2.6.1854 and 24.9.1856. Trials completed in 10.1857. Cruised in the Baltic in 1858. To the Mediterranean with Rear-Adm. Nordman's squadron in 1859–60. Gunnery training ship in 1862–3. Stricken on 26.8.1871. (See also under Baltic sailing warships.)

Vola 84/92 St Petersburg, New Admiralty
Constructor A. K. Kaverznev
Laid down 23.10.1835 *Launched* 30.7.1837
Dimensions 196 ft (pp) x 51 ft (inside plank) x 23 ft 7 in (as built)
212 ft (pp) x 53 ft 8 in (outside plank) x 23 ft 8 in
x 21 ft 7 in/23 ft 1 in (draught fore/aft)
2,659 tons bm, 3,814 tons displacement (as steamer)
Armament 1837 LD 28 x 36pdrs (long), 4 x 60pdr u (1 pood)
UD 32 x 24pdrs (long)
FC & QD 6 x 12pdrs, 26 x 24pdr carr.
1840 LD 6 x 9.65-in shell guns, 26 x 36pdrs (long)
UD 28 x 24pdrs (long), 4 x 60pdr u (1 pood)
FC & QD 6 x 24pdr gunnades, 14 x 24pdr carr.
1857 LD 26 x 60pdr shell guns, 4 x 30pdrs (long)

UD 4 x 30pdrs (long) 28 x 30pdrs (short)
FC & QD 4 x 30pdrs (short), 16 x 30pdr howitzers
Machinery 500 nhp (Nobel, St Petersburg) = 9 kts

Converted steam screw ship. Cruised in the Baltic in 1839–43 and 1846–7. To Denmark to provide support against the Prussians. Rebuilt as a screw steamer from 1.6.1854 to 26.10.1856. Hull elongated to accommodate machinery and four boilers. Trials in 1857. Cruised in the Baltic in 1857–61. Stricken on 26.8.1871. (See also under Baltic sailing warships.)

Oryol 84 St Petersburg, New Admiralty
Constructor Panin
Laid down 14.6.1851 *Launched* 12.8.1854
Dimensions 202 ft 8 in (pp) x 51 ft 6 in (outside plank) x 23 ft 7 in x 20 ft 9 in/23 ft 6 in (draught fore/aft)
2,386 tons bm, 3,713 tons displacement
Armament 1854 LD 28 x 68pdr shell guns, 4 x 24pdrs (long)
UD 4 x 24pdrs (long), 24 x 24pdrs (short), 4 x 60pdr u (1 pood)
FC & QD 2 x 68pdrs (pivot), 4 x 24pdrs (short), 16 x 24pdr carr.
Machinery 450 nhp (Baird, St Petersburg) = 9½ kts

Converted steam screw ship. Lengthened and converted while building. Laid down as *Prokhor* class but reordered as a steamer in July 1852. Cruised in the Baltic in 1856 and 1859–60. Stricken on 7.12.1863. (See also under Baltic sailing warships.)

Retvizan 81 St Petersburg, New Admiralty
Constructor Gezekhus
Laid down 17.9.1854 *Launched* 17.9.1855
Dimensions 215 ft 10 in (pp) x 52 ft 8 in (outside plank) x ? x 21 ft 7 in/23 ft 1 in (draught fore/aft)
2,641 tons bm, 3,823 tons displacement
Armament 1855 LD 4 x 9.65-in shell guns, 24 x 68pdr shell guns, 4 x 36pdrs (long)
UD 4 x 36pdrs (long), 20 x 36pdr gunnades, 8 x 60pdr u (1 pood)
FC & QD 1 x 68pdr (5 ton pivot), 2 x 36pdrs (long pivots), 6 x 36pdrs (short) 8 x 36pdr gunnades
1857 LD 28 x 60pdr shell guns, 4 x 30pdrs (long)
UD 4 x 30pdrs (long), 28 x 30pdrs (short)
FC & QD 1 x 60pdr (5 ton pivot), 2 x 30pdrs (long), 14 x 30pdrs (short)
1858 FC & QD rearmed with 1 x 60pdr (5 ton pivot), 2 x 30pdrs (short), 10 x 30pdr howitzers
1862 LD 28 x 60pdr shell guns, 4 x 36pdrs (long)
UD 4 x 36pdrs (long), 28 x 36pdrs (short)
FC & QD 1 x 60pdr (5 ton pivot), 2 x 36pdrs (short), 10 x 36pdr howitzers
1867 LD 16 x 60pdr shell guns, UD 16 x 36pdrs (short)
Machinery 500 nhp (Nobel, St Petersburg) = 9½ kts

Purpose-built steam screw ship. Considered the best of the two-decker screw ships of the line. Trials in 1857. To the Mediterranean in 1858–9. Cruised in the Baltic in 1860–2. Engines removed in 1863. Gunnery training and target ship in 1874. Stricken on 22.11.1880.

Konstantin 74 Okhta
Constructor I. A. Amosov
Laid down 16.12.1835 *Launched* 24.8.1837
Dimensions 188 ft (pp) x 50 ft (inside plank) x 19 ft 3 in (as built)
215 ft (pp) x 51 ft 6 in (inside plank) x ? x 21 ft 6 in/23 ft (draught fore/aft)
2,631 tons bm, 3,697 tons displacement (as steamer)
Armament 1837 LD 24 x 36pdrs (short), 4 x 60pdr u (1 pood)
UD 30 x 24pdrs (short)
FC & QD 16 x 8pdrs, 6 x 24pdr carr. or 20 x 24pdr carr.
1854 LD 26 x 68pdr shell guns, 2 x 30pdrs (long)
UD 4 x 30pdrs (long), 20 x 24pdrs (short), 4 x 60pdr u (1 pood)
FC & QD 1 x 9.65-in shell gun, 1 x 36pdr gunnade, 2 x 30pdrs (short), 14 x 30pdr carr.
Machinery 450 nhp (Humphreys & Tennant, London) = 10½ kts

Converted steam screw ship. *Fershampenuaz* class. Cruised in the Baltic in 1839–47. To Denmark to provide support against Prussia in 1849–50. Repaired, lengthened, and converted to a screw ship in 1852–4. Transported troops from Sveaborg to Kronshtadt in 1856. Cruised in the Baltic in 1857–60. Stricken on 8.2.1864. (See also under Baltic sailing warships.)

Vyborg 74 Okhta
Constructor I. A. Amosov
Laid down 23.6.1839 *Launched* 30.7.1841
Dimensions 188 ft (pp) x 50 ft (inside plank) x 19 ft 3 in (as built)
215 ft (pp) x 50 ft (inside plank) x ? x 21 ft 6 in/23 ft (draught fore/aft)
2,496 tons bm, 3,505 tons displacement (as steamer)
Armament 1840 LD 24 x 36pdrs (short), 4 x 60pdr u (1 pood)
UD 30 x 24pdrs (short)
FC & QD 16 x 8pdrs, 6 x 24pdr carr. or 20 x 24pdr carr.
1854 LD 24 x 68pdr shell guns, 4 x 30pdrs (long)
UD 4 x 30pdrs (long), 24 x 30pdrs (short)
FC & QD 1 x 68pdr shell gun, 2 x 30pdrs (short), 16 x 30pdr carr.
Machinery 450 nhp (Robert Napier, Glasgow) = 7½ kts

Converted steam screw ship. *Fershampenuaz* Class. Cruised in the Baltic in 1843. Cruised in the North Sea in 1844. Cruised in the Baltic in 1845 and 1847. To Denmark to provide support against Prussia in 1848–50. Cruised in the Baltic in 1851. Converted to a screw ship from 23.10.1852 to 21.5.1854. Transported troops from Sveaborg to Kronshtadt in 1854. Cruised to the Mediterranean with Rear-Adm. Berens' squadron in 1856–7. Cruised in the Baltic in 1858–60. Stricken on 7.12.1863. (See also under Baltic sailing warships.)

Steam screw frigates

Arkhimed 48 Okhta
Constructor I. A. Amosov
Laid down 23.11.1846 *Launched* 20.7.1848
Dimensions 179 ft (pp) x 43 ft 8 in (inside plank) x 14 ft 9 in x 19 ft 4 in/20 ft 9 in (draught fore/aft)
2,400 tons displacement
Armament Projected LD 4 x 8.75-in shell guns, 26 x 36pdrs (long)
UD 6 x 9.65-in shell guns, 4 x 36pdrs (long), 14 x 36pdrs (short)
1850 LD 6 x 8.75-in shell guns, 14 x 24pdrs (short)
UD 1 x 9.65-in shell gun, 4 x 8.75-in shell guns, 2 x 60pdr u (1 pood)
Machinery 300 nhp (Baird, St Petersburg) = 6¾ kts

The first Russian steam screw frigate. Design based on that of the sailing frigate *Pallada*. Trials in 9.1848. Wrecked off Bornholm on 6.10.1850.

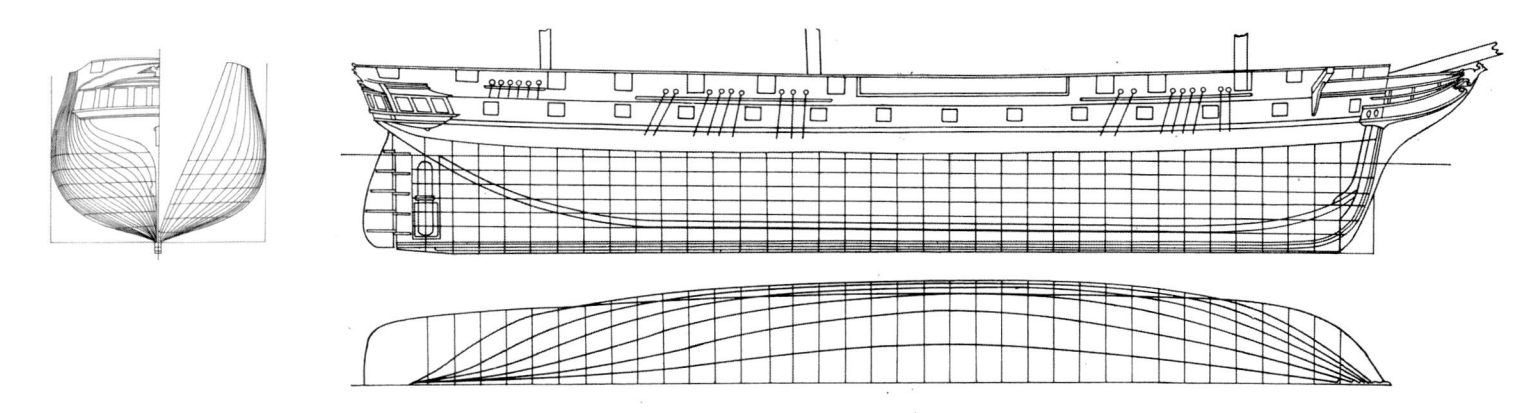

Polkan *(44) of 1853 was the most modern steam frigate available to the Baltic fleet in 1854, entering service just in time to participate in the Crimean War as a reconnaissance vessel, a task for which she was greatly overqualified. The profiles here invite comparison with* Pallada *(and hence the USS* Constitution*) which is said to have been the model for her design, with the length amidships having been increased by some 25 feet to allow for the installation of machinery.*

Polkan 44/45 Arkhangel'sk
Constructor   I. G. Karpovskiy
Laid down   9.9.1851   *Launched* 21.5.1853
Dimensions   199 ft 6 in (pp) x 44 ft 6 in (outside plank) x ? x 19 ft 4 in/
                21 ft (draught fore/aft)
                1,793 tons bm, 2,316 tons displacement
Armament   LD 4 x 68pdr shell guns, 24 x 36pdrs (long)
                UD 1 x 9.65-in shell gun, 2 x 68pdr shell guns,
                14 x 36pdr (long)
Machinery   360 nhp (John Penn, London) = 8½ kts

Steam screw frigate. A further design based on the *Pallada*. Sailed from Arkhangel'sk to Kronshtadt in the autumn of 1853. Commissioned in 1854. Participated in the Crimean War in 1853–6 in reconnaissance. Decommissioned on 9.1.1862. Stricken and scuttled on 11.9.1863.

Askol'd (ex-*Mariia*) 46 St Petersburg, New Admiralty
Constructor   K. F. Shatten
Laid down   18.9.1852   *Launched*   6.7.1854
Dimensions   206 ft 6 in (pp) x 48 ft 6 in (outside plank) x ? x 20 ft /
                21 ft (draught fore/aft)
                2,126 tons bm, 2,834 tons displacement
Armament   LD 24 x 68pdr shell guns, 4 x 36pdrs (long)
                UD 4 x 36pdrs (long), 16 x 36pdrs (bored up 24pdrs)
Machinery   360 nhp (Galvanoplastic Works, St Petersburg)

Steam screw frigate. Launched as *Mariia*, renamed on 30.8.1856 and commissioned in 1857. Assigned to the Pacific. Stricken on 15.7.1861, disarmed and broken up.

Il'ia Muromets class
Il'ia Muromets 53 Arkhangel'sk
Constructor   F. T. Zagulyaev
Laid down   21.12.1853   *Launched*   25.5.1856
Dimensions   212 ft (pp) x 50 ft (outside plank) x 16 ft 9 in x 21 ft /
                22 ft (draught fore/aft)
                2,337 tons bm, 3,199 tons displacement
Armament   LD 10 x 60pdr shell guns, 4 x 30pdrs (long),
                16 x 30pdrs (short)
                UD 1 x 60pdr (5 ton), 20 x 30pdr gunnades (chambered)
Machinery   360 nhp (Carr & MacPherson, St Petersburg) = 7½ kts

Muromets class (2 ships). Steam screw frigate. Design based on that of HMS *Imperieuse*. Commissioned on 25.5.1857. Sailed from Arkhangel'sk to Kronshtadt in 1857. Stricken and scuttled on 11.9.1863.

Gromoboy 53 Helsingfors (private yard)
Constructors I. A. Shestakov and A. A. Ivashchenko (later A. K. Rikhter)
Laid down   3.4.1855   *Launched*   8.6.1857
Dimensions   212 ft (pp) x 50 ft (outside plank) x 16 ft 9 in x 21 ft /
                22 ft (draught fore/aft)
                2,337 tons bm, 3,199 tons displacement
Armament   LD 10 x 60pdr shell guns, 4 x 30pdrs (long),
                16 x 30pdrs (short)
                UD 1 x 60pdr (5 ton), 2 x 30pdrs (long),
                20 x 30pdr howitzers
Machinery   360 nhp/700 ihp (Galvanoplastic Works, St Petersburg)
                = 7½ kts *Range* 1,200 nm

Muromets class (2 ships). Steam screw frigate. Design based on that of HMS *Imperieuse*. Construction delayed due to the bombardment of Sveaborg on 28–29.6.1855. Commissioned in the autumn of 1857. To the Mediterranean in 1858. Stricken and sold for breaking up on 9.6.1872.

Svetlana 40 L'Arman Fréres, Bordeaux
Constructor   ?
Laid down   1857   *Launched*   3.5.1858
Dimensions   229 ft 7 in (pp) x 47 ft 10 in (outside plank) x 14 ft 5 in
                x 18 ft 6 in/21 ft 6 in (draught fore/aft)
                2,458 tons bm, 3,187 tons displacement
Armament   Projected LD 28 x 60pdr shell guns, 4 x 30pdrs (long)
                UD 5 x 60pdrs (5 ton) 23 x 30pdrs (short)
                1859 LD 20 x 60pdr shell guns, 4 x 36pdrs (long)
                UD 2 x 60pdrs (5 ton), 14 x 60pdr shell guns
                1866 LD 24 x 60pdr shell guns, 4 x 30pdrs (long)
                UD 2 x 60pdrs (5 ton), 10 x 30pdrs (short)
                1868 LD 16 x 60pdr shell guns UD 2 x 60pdrs (5 ton),
                12 x 30pdrs (short)
                1870 LD 6 x 8-in rifled
                UD 4 x 8-in rifled, 1 x 6-in rifled
                1873 LD 6 x 8-in rifled
                UD 2 x -in rifled, 4 x 6-in rifled
                1875 LD 6 x 8-in rifled, 2 x 6-in rifled
                UD 4 x 6-in rifled
Machinery   450 nhp/1,113 ihp = 10½ kts 2,000 nm range

Steam screw frigate. Arrived at Kronshtadt on 3.5.1859. Deployed initially to the Far East. Repaired and rearmed in 1870. Stricken and sold for breaking up on 15.2.1892.

Russia began the slow process of rebuilding its fleet immediately upon the resolution of the Crimean War. This beautiful painting of 1878 by A. K. Beggrov shows the screw frigate Svetlana, *completed in 1858 in Bordeaux, France – Russia's recent enemy.* Svetlana *deployed to the Far East on completion, and this painting may represent her at sea in Pacific waters. For grace and beauty under sail, the last generation of screw steam frigates gave away very little to the sailing frigates of an earlier era.*

General Admiral 70 William Webb, New York
Constructor   ?
Laid down   9.9.1857   Launched 9.9.1858
Dimensions   305 ft (pp) x 54 ft 8 in (outside plank) x ? x 22 ft 1 in/
             23 ft 6 in (draught fore/aft)
             4,386 tons bm, 5,669 tons displacement
Armament   Projected LD 36 x 60pdr shell guns
             UD 3 x 60pdr (5 ton) 34 x 36pdrs (long)
             1859 LD 36 x 60pdr shell guns, 4 x 36pdrs (long)
             UD 2 x 10.75-in shell guns, 24 x 60pdr shell guns,
             2 x 36pdrs (long)
             1862 LD 36 x 60pdr shell guns, 4 x 36pdrs (long)
             UD 2 x 10.75-in shell guns, 22 x 60pdr shell guns
             1866 LD 38 x 60pdr shell guns, 2 x 36pdrs (long)
             UD 2 x 10.75-in shell guns, 20 x 60pdr shell guns,
             2 x 36pdrs (long)
Machinery   800 nhp/2,000 ihp = 12¼ kts 5,000 nm range

Purpose-built steam screw frigate. Originally to have been named *Imperatritsa Mariia*, renamed on 23.5.1857. Commissioned at the end of 1858. Arrived at Kronshtadt from New York in 1859. Stricken on 14.6.1869. Broken up in 1870.

In the 1850s, the American shipbuilding industry attracted the attention of Russian naval specialists and a Russian naval mission was sent to the United States in 1853 to gain familiarity with American developments. In 1857, in the aftermath of the Crimean War, Russia wished to contract abroad for the construction of an advanced 91-gun screw ship of the line. As political reasons in the aftermath of the war made it impossible to place an order in either Great Britain or France, the USA was chosen instead. Since United States shipyards did not have experience with the construction of screw ships of the line, but were already building powerful steam frigates, it was decided to contract for a large frigate instead of a line of battle ship.

General Admiral was a true frigate of enormous dimensions, but with only one closed gun deck. She was built of live white oak and American pine. In service, she proved to be an excellent sailer reaching 14 knots under sail. In 1859 she created a sensation, covering the distance from New York to Cherbourg in only 12 days. This ship was twice sent to the Mediterranean and stationed there in 1860–3 and 1866–7. Her machinery and boilers were found to be in poor condition in 1866. It was intended to repair her after returning from her second Mediterranean cruise; however, the inspection carried out in 1868 revealed such extensive decay in her hull that repairs were decided against as their cost would have been excessive. Since her value was negligible in the era of armoured ships, she was stricken in June 1869 and broken up in the next year with all other surviving Russian wooden ships of the line and frigates following soon after. The only exception was the frigate *Svetlana*, which was repaired and rearmed in 1870 for use as a training ship.

Oleg 57 Kronshtadt
Constructor A. Kh. Shaunburg
Laid down 29.1.1858 *Launched* 4.6.1860
Dimensions 253 ft (pp) x 53 ft (outside plank) x ? x 21 ft 9 in/
 23 ft 3 in (draught fore/aft)
 3,372 tons bm, 4,408 tons displacement
Armament LD 26 x 60pdr shell guns 4 x 36pdrs (long)
 UD 3 x 60pdrs (5 ton), 2 x 36pdrs (long), 22 x 36pdrs (short)
Machinery 800 nhp/2,500 ihp (Maudslay, London) = 10½ kts
Range 2,000 nm

Steam screw frigate. Commissioned in the autumn of 1860. Deployed initially to the Mediterranean. Took part in hydrographical surveys in the Baltic. Rammed and sunk accidentally by the armoured ship *Kreml* on 3.8.1869. 16 killed.

Peresvet 51 Arkhangel'sk
Constructors F. T. Zagulyaev and Bolshakov
Laid down 19.7.1858 *Launched* 9.6.1860
Dimensions 251 ft (pp) x 50 ft (outside plank) x 15 ft 9 in x 20 ft 4 in/
 22 ft 4 in (draught fore/aft)
 2,921 tons bm, 3,837 tons displacement
Armament Completed LD 10 x 60pdr shell guns, 4 x 36pdrs (long),
 18 x 36pdrs (short)
 UD 1 x 60pdr (5 ton), 2 x 36pdrs (long), 16 x 36pdrs gunnades (chambered)
 1866 LD 24 x 60pdr shell guns, 4 x 36pdrs (long)
 UD 1 x 60pdr (5 ton), 12 x 60pdr shell guns,
 2 x 36pdr (long)
Machinery 450 nhp/1,741 ihp (Carr & MacPherson, St Petersburg) = 10 kts

Steam screw frigate. Commissioned in the summer of 1861. Sailed from Arkhangel'sk to Kronshtadt in 10.1862. Transferred to the United States with other frigates in 1863–4 to act as a deterrent against British and French intervention in the American Civil War and in response to Anglo-French interference in the Polish insurrection of 1863. Stricken on 19.10.1874 and sold for breaking up.

Osliabia 45 Okhta
Constructor L. G. Shvede
Laid down 3.3.1857 *Launched* 8.10.1860
Dimensions 230 ft (pp) x 46 ft 6 in (outside plank) x ? 18 ft 6 in/
 20 ft 6 in (draught fore/aft)
 2,280 tons bm, 2,958 tons (as designed)/
 2,976 tons displacement
Armament Projected LD 10 x 60pdr shell guns, 4 x 36pdrs (long),
 16 x 36pdrs (short)
 UD 1 x 60pdr (5 ton), 2 x 36pdrs (long), 20 x 36pdr gunnades (chambered)
 1861 LD 28 x 60pdr shell guns
 UD 1 x 60pdr (5 ton), 6 x 60 pdr shell guns
Machinery 360 nhp/890 ihp (Carr & MacPherson, St Petersburg) = 9.73 kts
Range 1,100 nm

Steam screw frigate. Commissioned in the summer of 1861. Deployed initially to the Mediterranean. Sailed to the United States with other Russian frigates in 1863–4 Stricken on 19.10.1874 and sold for breaking up.

Dmitrii Donskoi 51 Galernyy Ostrovok
Constructor Tirenshtein
Laid down 20.10.1858 *Launched* 9.9.1861
Dimensions 272 ft (pp) x 51 ft (outside plank) x 18 ft x 21 ft 9 in
 (mean draught on trial)
 3,316 tons bm, 4,562 tons (as designed)/
 4,425.3 tons displacement
Armament LD 18 x 60pdrs (5 ton), 12 x 60pdr shell guns
 UD 4 x 60pdrs (5 ton), 16 x 60pdr shell guns
Machinery 800 nhp/2,625 ihp (Baird, St Petersburg)
 = 12.65 kts
Range 1,500 nm

Steam screw frigate. Commissioned 10.1862 and deployed to the Mediterranean. Stricken on 1.4.1872 and sold for breaking up.

Aleksandr Nevskii 51 Okhta
Constructors G. M. Dmitriev and Svistovskiy
Laid down 19.12.1859 *Launched* 16.6.1862.
Dimensions 272 ft (pp) x 51 ft (outside plank) x 18 x 22 ft 7 in
 (mean draught on trial)
 3,316 tons bm, 4,562 tons (as designed)/
 4,572.8 tons displacement
Armament LD 18 x 60pdrs (5 ton), 12 x 60pdr shell guns
 UD 4 x 60pdrs (5 ton), 16 x 60pdr shell guns
Machinery 800 nhp/2,556 ihp (Izhora Works, St Petersburg)
 = 11.77 kts *Range* 1,500 nm

Steam screw frigate. Commissioned in 7.1863. Sailed to the United States with other Russian frigates in 1863–4. Wrecked off of the Skagerrak on 13.9.1868.

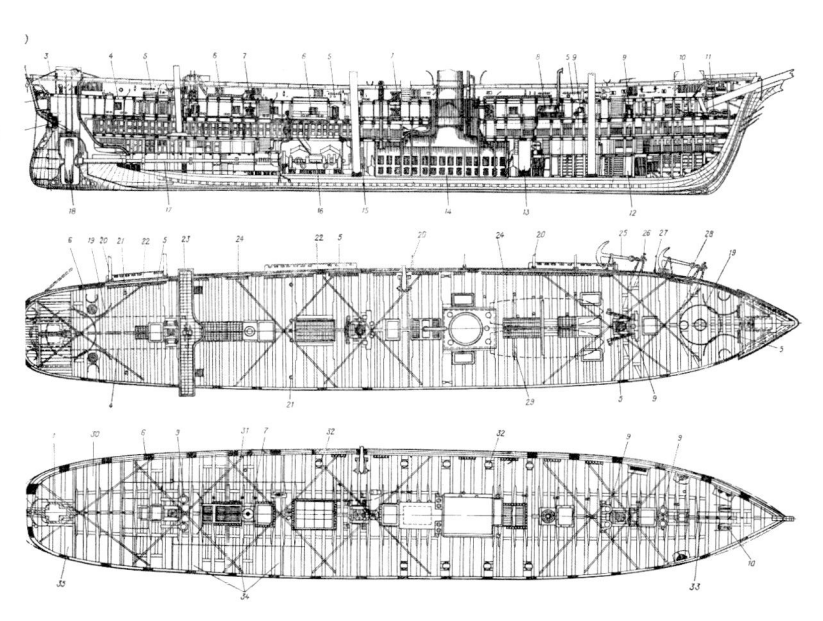

This detailed profile of the interior arrangements of the Russian steam frigate Aleksandr Nevskii *shows the large demands on internal space made by the machinery of the time. Included in this work because she and her sisters were authorized prior to 1860, she clearly anticipates the coming age of steam and iron warships.*

The only photograph of a warship contained in this work, this portrait of Aleksandr Nevskii *should be compared to the internal profile of the same ship. While her ties to the age of sail are shown by her ship rig and the long unbroken line of her broadside guns, her links to the coming era are equally evident in her midships funnel, her straight unbroken sheer line and the absence of quarter galleries. As a little-known footnote to the American Civil War it should be recorded that this ship accompanied a squadron of similar Russian steam frigates to New York city in the middle years of the conflict, where their presence in the harbour in 1863–4 helped cool British and French appetite for war with the Northern states in support of the Confederacy and the cotton lobby.*

Sevastopol 58 Kronshtadt
Constructor A. Kh. Shaunburg
Laid down 7.9.1860   *Launched* 12.8.1864
Dimensions 300 ft (pp) x 50 ft 4 in (outside plank) x 19 ft 3 in
  x 22 ft 2 in/24 ft (draught fore/aft)
  3,590 tons bm, 5,274 tons displacement (as designed)
  300 ft (pp) x 52 ft 1 in (outside armour) x ? x 24 ft/
  25 ft (draught fore/aft)
  3,869 tons bm, 6,135 tons displacement (as ironclad)
Armament Projected LD 34 x 60pdr shell guns, 4 x 36pdrs (long)
  UD 2 x 60pdrs (5 ton) 18 x 60pdr shell guns
  1865 LD 28 x 60pdrs (5 ton)
  UD 4 x 60pdrs (5 ton)
  1868 LD 2 x 8-in rifled, 26 x 60pdrs (5 ton)
  UD 1 x 8-in rifled 1 x 60pdr (5 ton)
  (11 of the 60pdrs replaced in 1870 by 7 x 8 in rifles)
  1877 LD 14 x 8-in rifled
  UD 2 x 8-in rifled 1 x 6-in rifled 10 x 3.4-in rifled
Armour 3–4½ in   *Backing* 6–10 in (as ironclad)
Machinery 800 nhp/3088 ihp (Izhora Works, St Petersburg)
  = 13.95 kts 400 tons coal (as ironclad)

Steam screw frigate reordered as an ironclad on 26.7.1862 while building. Commissioned on 8.7.1865. Training ship 23.3.1880. Decommissioned on 15.6.1885. Sold for breaking up in 5.1897.

Petropavlovsk 58 St Petersburg, New Admiralty
Constructor A. A. Ivashchenko
Laid down 12.1.1861   *Launched* 15.8.1865
Dimensions 300 ft (pp) x 50 ft 4 in (outside plank) x 19 ft 3 in
  x 22 ft 2 in/24 ft (draught fore/aft)
  3,590 tons bm, 5,274 tons displacement (as designed)
  298 ft (pp) x 55 ft 8 in (outside armour) x 25 ft x 22 ft 8 in/
  24 ft 6 in (draught fore/aft)
  4,289 tons bm, 6,040 tons displacement (as ironclad)
Armament Projected LD 34 x 60pdr shell guns, 4 x 36pdrs (long)
  UD 2 x 60pdrs (5 ton) 18 x 60pdr shell guns
  1868 LD 20 x 8-in rifled
  UD 2 x 60pdrs (5 ton) (another 2 x 60pdrs later added)
  1877 LD 20 x 8-in rifled
  UD 1 x 8-in rifled, 1 x 6-in rifled, 10 x 3.4-in rifled
Armour 3–4½ in   *Backing* 5–10 in (as ironclad)
Machinery 800 nhp/2,805 ihp (Baird, St Petersburg)
  = 11.80 kts 375 tons coal (as ironclad)

Steam screw frigate reordered as an ironclad on 29.10.1861 while building. Commissioned on 1.8.1867. Flagship of the Baltic fleet in the 1860s and 1870s. Decommissioned on 15.6.1885. Stricken on 4.1.1892 and sold for breaking up.

STEAM AND SAIL WARSHIPS: BALTIC FLEET

When completed in 1836, the paddle frigate Bogatyr' *was a tribute to progressive thinking in Russian naval circles, beating the British* Cyclops *into the water by three years. In her original incarnation, only her armament was traditional, taking the form of 28 entirely conventional 24pdrs. She would be extensively rearmed later and survive to fight in the Crimean War alongside the line of battle ship* Rossii *in the defence of Sveaborg. By N. K. Artseulov.*

Steam paddle frigates

Bogatyr' 28 St Petersburg
Constructor M. N. Grinvald
Laid down 26.10.1835 Launched 8.8.1836
Dimensions 186 ft (pp) x 32 ft (inside plank) x 22 ft 7 in
            1342 tons displacement
Armament Completed 28 x 24pdrs
          1848 1 x 10-in shell gun, 4 x 30pdrs
          1855 2 x 9.65-in shell guns, 6 x 30pdrs
Machinery 240 nhp (Izhora Works, St Petersburg)
          = 8 kts Range 2,000 nm

Steam paddle frigate. Repaired and refitted in 1848. Active in the Crimean War in 1853–6. Fought in the defence of Sveaborg in 7.1855. Stricken on 2.8.1857 and sold for breaking up.

Kamchatka 14/20 William Brown, New York
Constructor ?
Laid down 24.4.1840 Launched 4.11.1840
Dimensions 210 ft (pp) x 36 ft (inside plank) x 24 ft 6 in x 17 ft 8 in/
            17 ft 8 in (draught fore/aft) 2124 tons displacement
Armament 2 x 9.65-in shell guns 12/16 x 24pdrs (long) 2 x 60pdr u
          (1 pood)
Machinery 540 nhp (Dunham, New York) = 10 kts

Steam paddle frigate. First steam ship built for export in the USA. Completed in 9.1841. Operated off of Denmark in 1848 in support of the Danes against Prussia. Active in the Crimean War in 1853–6 in reconnaissance and as a transport. Repaired and refitted in 1857. Stricken on 28.5.1866. Broken up in 1867.

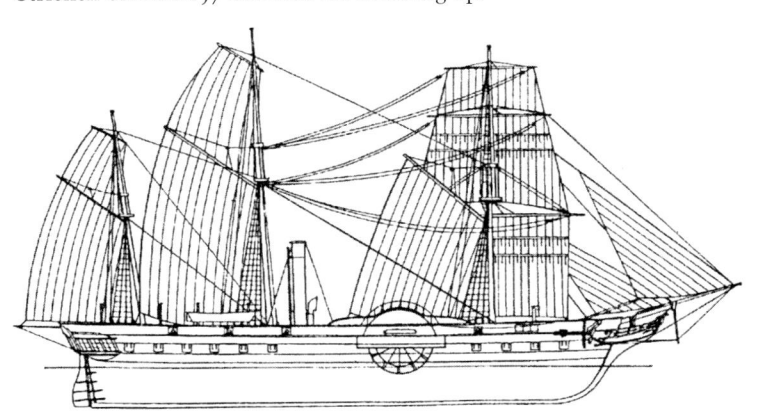

A profile of the paddle frigate Bogatyr' *in 1836 showing her rig and underwater proportions.*

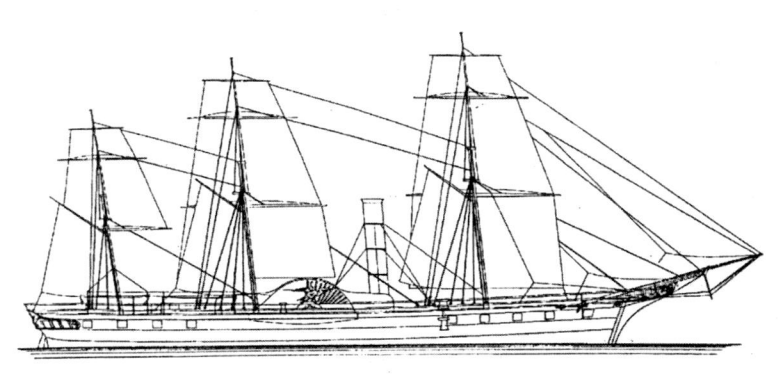

The American-built paddle frigate Kamchatka, *in profile and showing her rig.*

Russia's second steam powered frigate, Kamchatka, was completed in the United States in 1840. She was larger, faster, and more powerfully armed than the earlier Bogatyr'. Her purchase abroad was an unsettling sign of Russian technological lag at the time, but 12 of the 13 follow-on paddle frigates would be the products of Russian shipyards and indigenous expertise. By N. K. Artseulov.

Otvazhnyi class
Otvazhnyi 4/10 Okhta
Constructor I. A. Amosov
Laid down 30.11.1842 Launched 11.9.1843
Dimensions 185 ft (pp) x 32 ft 8 in (inside plank) x 21 ft 1 in
  1,450 tons displacement
Armament 2 x 9.65-in shell guns, 6 x 24pdrs (long), 2 x 24pdrs (short)
Machinery 300 nhp = 8½ kts

Otvazhnyi class (2 ships). Steam paddle frigate. Active in the Crimean War in 1853–6 in reconnaissance and as a transport. Stricken on 8.4.1861 and sold for breaking up.

Khrabryi 4/10 St Petersburg, New Admiralty
Constructor S. A. Burachek
Laid down 30.1.1843 Launched 16.7.1844
Dimensions 185 ft (pp) x 32 ft 8 in (inside plank) x 21 ft 1 in
  1450 tons displacement
Armament 1854 2 x 9.65-in shell guns, 4 x 24pdrs (long), 4 x 24pdrs (short)

Although unable to compete with the pace of industrial change in the 1840s against the more developed economic powers, the Russian Navy did what it could to keep up. This is the paddle frigate Khrabryy of 1844, built in the Baltic and employed extensively in reconnaissance and as a transport during the Crimean War. She is seen here in a contemporary drawing by N. K. Artseulov.

STEAM AND SAIL WARSHIPS: BALTIC FLEET

Smelyi in 1844. As was the case with other paddle steamers, she found useful employment in the Baltic during the Crimean War acting as a transport and as a scout. By N. K. Artseulov.

Machinery   300 nhp (Izhora Works, St Petersburg) = 8½ kts
Otvazhnyi class (2 ships). Steam paddle frigate. Active in the Crimean War in 1853–6 in reconnaissance and as a transport. Stricken in 1856, disarmed at Kronshtadt and broken up.

Gerkules 10 Okhta
Constructor   V. F. Stoke
Laid down   31.12.1830   *Launched* 8.8.1831
Dimensions   192 ft (pp) x 32 ft (inside plank) x 17 ft
               823 tons bm
Armament   4 x 24pdrs (long), 6 x 6pdrs
Machinery   200 nhp (Izhora Works, St Petersburg) = 8 kts
Paddle steamer. Undocked after repair on 4.10.1843. Rerated as a steam frigate in 1847. Disarmed and stricken in 1854.

Smelyi 14/21 St Petersburg
Constructor   Pipin
Laid down   28.10.1843   *Launched* 5.8.1844
Dimensions   198 ft (pp) x 33 ft 11 in (inside plank) x 22 ft 6 in
               1504 tons displacement
Armament   1854 3 x 9.65-in shell guns, 14 x 36pdrs (bored up
               24pdrs), 2 x 60pdr u (1 pood)
               1855 3 x 9.65-in shell guns, 14 x 24pdrs (long), 4 x 60pdr
               u (1 pood)
Machinery   400 nhp (Izhora Works, St Petersburg) = 9½ kts
Steam paddle frigate. Active in the Crimean War in 1853–6 in reconnaissance and as a transport. Stricken on 21.5.1860 and sold for breaking up.

Groziashshii 4/8 Okhta
Constructor   I. A. Amosov
Laid down   27.10.1843   *Launched* 9.8.1844
Dimensions   190 ft (pp) x 35 ft (inside plank) x 21 ft 2 in x 13 ft /
               13 ft 6 in (draught fore/aft)
               1,103 tons bm, 1,500 tons displacement

Armament   1854 2 x 9.65-in shell guns, 4 x 24pdrs (short), 2 x 60pdr u
               (1 pood)
               1855 2 x 9.65-in shell guns 4 x 30pdrs (short) 2 x 60pdr u
               (1 pood)
Machinery   400 nhp (Maudslay, London) = 9 kts
Steam paddle frigate. Active in the Crimean War in 1853–6 in reconnaissance and as a transport. Disarmed on 23.6.1862. Hulked in 1863. Stricken on 13.8.1866 and sold for breaking up.

Vladimir 2/5 Burry & Co., Liverpool
Constructor   ?
Laid down   ?   *Launched* 1845
Dimensions   179 ft 3 in (pp) x 29 ft x ? x 13 ft 6 in/13 ft 6 in (draught
               fore/aft)
               758 tons bm
Armament   1 x 9.65-in shell gun, 4 x 24pdrs gunnades (chambered)
Machinery   350 nhp = 10½ kts
Iron steam paddle frigate acquired from the Russian postal service in 1854 and returned to the postal service in 1856 only to be reacquired immediately. Attached to the armoured squadron as a floating workshop in 1867. Disarmed on 13.1.1891. Expended as a target for torpedoes.

Gremiashchi 4/11 Okhta
Constructor   I. A. Amosov
Laid down   15.9.1849   *Launched* 18.6.1851
Dimensions   190 ft (pp) x 36 ft (outside plank) x ? x 13 ft /13 ft 6 in
               (draught fore/aft)
               1,126 tons bm, 1,501 tons displacement
Armament   3 x 9.65-in shell guns, 8 x 30pdrs (short)
Machinery   400 nhp (Izhora Works, St Petersburg) = 9 kts
Steam paddle frigate. Active in the Crimean War in 1853–6 in reconnaissance and as a transport. Grounded on 17.9.1862 while assisting the stranded US steamer *Emperor* in the Gulf of Finland and sank 23.9.1862.

During the Crimean War, the Russian navy was happy to augment its limited stock of steamers from any possible source. This is Vladimir *of 1845, acquired from the Russian postal service, and classed as a paddle steamer. Her one unique feature almost excluded her from this book – she had an iron hull in a world of wooden hulled ships. She was employed postwar as a floating workshop and her iron hull saved her from being expended as a target for torpedoes until 1891. By N. K. Artseulov.*

Riurik 4/6 Gamla Warfsbolaget, Abo
Constructor ?
Laid down 1850 *Launched* 31.10.1851
Dimensions 185 ft (pp) x 33 ft 10 in (outside plank) x ? x 13 ft 9¼ in/
  13 ft 9¼ in (draught fore/aft)
  983 tons bm, 1,507 tons displacement
Armament 2 x 9.65-in shell guns, 2 x 60pdr u (1 pood), 2 x 24pdr u
  (½ pood)
Machinery 400 nhp (Cowie & Erikson, Abo) = 10 kts
Steam paddle frigate. Commissioned on 18.4.1854. Active in the Crimean War in 1853–6 in reconnaissance and as a transport. Fire watch ship at Kronshtadt in 1862. Stricken on 5.12.1870 and sold for breaking up.

Olaf 14/24 Helsingfors (private yard)
Constructor Fomin
Laid down 26.05.1851 *Launched* 24.09.1852
Dimensions 198 ft (pp) x 36 ft 2 in (outside plank) x ? x 15 ft 4 in/
  15 ft 4 in (draught fore/aft)
  1,203 tons bm, 1,796 tons displacement
Armament Completed 4 x 9.65-in shell guns, 16 x 24pdrs,
  4 x 60pdr u (1 pood)
  Later 2 x 6-in rifled, 6 x 4.1-in rifled, 2 x 3.5-in rifled
Machinery 400 nhp (Robert Napier, Glasgow) = 11 kts
Steam paddle frigate. Commissioned in 1853. Active in the Crimean War in 1853–6 in reconnaissance and as a transport. Heavily damaged by fire on 11.8.1875 but subsequently repaired. Decommissioned and disarmed on 2.12.1890. Stricken on 15.2.1892.

Khrabryi 8 Okhta
Constructor I. G. Karpovskiy
Laid down 3.3.1857 *Launched* 3.9.1858
Dimensions 185 ft (pp) x 33 ft 2 in (outside plank) x ? x 14 ft 11 in/
  15 ft 2 in (draught fore/aft)
  975 tons bm, 1,450 tons displacement
Armament 2 x 60pdrs (5 ton), 4 x 24pdrs (long), 4 x 24pdr gunnades
Machinery 300 nhp (from *Khrabryi* of 1852) = 9 kts
Steam paddle frigate. Commissioned in 1859. Decommissioned and laid up on 10.1.1881. Sold for breaking up.

Smelyi 8 Okhta
Constructor I. G. Karpovskiy
Laid down 10.9.1857 *Launched* 5.10.1858
Dimensions 199 ft 10 in (pp) x 36 ft 2 in (outside plank) x ? x 15 ft 4 in/
  15 ft 4 in (draught fore/aft)
  1,173 tons bm, 1,784 tons displacement
Armament 3 x 60pdrs (5 ton), 2 x 60pdr shell guns, 14 x 24pdrs (long)
Machinery 400 nhp (from *Smelyi* of 1844) = 9 kts
Steam paddle frigate. Commissioned in 1859. Stricken and hulked on 8.12.1879. Sold for breaking up in 1901–2.

Solombala 4/8 Arkhangel'sk
Constructors F. T. Zagulyaev and Kalsert
Laid down 5.3.1858 *Launched* 13.7.1859
Dimensions 190 ft (pp) x 33 ft 2 in (outside plank) x ? x 12 ft 5 in/12 ft
  5 in (draught fore/aft)
  1,004 tons bm, 1,180 tons displacement
Armament Completed 4 x 24pdrs (long)
  Later 2 x 6-in rifled, 2 x 4.2-in rifled, 2 x 3.5-in rifled
Machinery 240 nhp (from *Bogatyr'* of 1836)
Steam paddle frigate. Commissioned in 6.1862. Departed Arkhangel'sk for Kronshtadt on 27.6.1862. Stricken on 1.2.1875 and sold for breaking up.

Riurik 6 Abo (private yard)
Constructor ?
Laid down 1869 *Launched* 21.10.1870
Dimensions 183 ft 9 in x 33 ft 10 in (outside plank) x ? x 15 ft 6 in/
  15 ft 11 in (draught fore/aft)
  983 tons bm, 1,507 tons (as designed)/1,662 tons
  displacement
Armament 2 x 6-in rifled, 4 x 3.4-in rifled
Machinery 300 nhp/739 ihp (from *Riurik* of 1851) = 10 kts
Steam paddle frigate. Decommissioned and disarmed on 4.10.1885. Stricken on 22.1.1891 and sold for breaking up.

Steam screw corvettes

Boyarin class

Boyarin 11 Okhta
Constructor A. A. Ivashchenko
Laid down 9.10.1855 *Launched* 21.5.1856
Dimensions 163 ft 4 in (pp) x 31 ft 11 in (outside plank) x ? x 12 ft 4½ in/14 ft (draught fore/aft)
762 tons bm, 885 tons displacement
Armament 1 x 36pdr (long), 10 x 36pdr gunnades
Machinery 200 nhp/400 ihp (Galvanoplastic Works, St Petersburg) = 9½ kts
Range 800 nm

Boyarin class (14 ships). Steam screw corvette. Commissioned in the summer of 1857. Assigned to the Pacific. Repaired and refitted in 1865. New machinery of 160 nhp by Kronshtadt Dockyard installed in 1868. Reclassified as a sail training vessel on 1.1.1880. Disarmed and relegated to harbour service on 24.11.1891. Stricken on 31.7.1893. Sold for breaking up in 1901–2.

Volk 11 Okhta
Constructor I. G. Karpovskiy
Laid down 9.10.1855 *Launched* 21.5.1856
Dimensions 163 ft 4 in (pp) x 31 ft 11 in (outside plank) x ? x 12 ft 4½ in/14 ft (draught fore/aft)
762 tons bm, 885 tons displacement
Armament 1 x 36pdr (long), 10 x 36pdr gunnades
Machinery 200 nhp/400 ihp (Baird, St Petersburg) = 9½ kts
Range 800 nm

Boyarin class (14 ships). Steam screw corvette. Commissioned in the summer of 1857. Arrived in the Black Sea in the autumn of 1857 and assigned to the Black Sea fleet. Stricken on 25.1.1869.

Zubr 11 Okhta
Constructor I. G. Karpovskiy
Laid down 9.10.1855 *Launched* 1.6.1856
Dimensions 163 ft 4 in (pp) x 31 ft 11 in (outside plank) x ? x 12 ft 4½ in/14 ft (draught fore/aft)
762 tons bm, 885 tons displacement
Armament 1 x 36pdr (long), 10 x 36pdr gunnades
Machinery 200 nhp/400 ihp (Baird, St Petersburg) = 9½ kts
Range 800 nm

Boyarin class (14 ships). Steam screw corvette. Commissioned in the summer of 1857. Arrived in the Black Sea in 1857 and assigned to the Black Sea fleet. Stricken on 25.1.1869.

Vepr' 11 Okhta
Constructor I. G. Karpovskiy
Laid down 9.10.1855 *Launched* 10.6.1856
Dimensions 163 ft 4 in (pp) x 31 ft 11 in (outside plank) x ? x 12 ft 4½ in/14 ft (draught fore/aft)
762 tons bm, 885 tons displacement
Armament 1 x 36pdr (long) 10 x 36pdr gunnades
Machinery 200 nhp/400 ihp (Nobel, St Petersburg) = 9½ kts
Range 800 nm

Boyarin class (14 ships). Steam screw corvette. Commissioned in the summer of 1857. Arrived in the Black Sea in the autumn of 1857 and assigned to the Black Sea fleet. Stricken on 25.1.1869.

Novik 11 Okhta
Constructor A. A. Ivashchenko
Laid down 9.10.1855 *Launched* 10.6.1856
Dimensions 163 ft 4 in (pp) x 31 ft 11 in (outside plank) x ? x 12 ft 4½ in/14 ft (draught fore/aft)
762 tons bm, 885 tons displacement
Armament 1 x 36pdr (long), 10 x 36pdr gunnades
Machinery 200 nhp/400 ihp (Galvanoplastic Works, St Petersburg) = 9½ kts
Range 800 nm

Boyarin class (14 ships). Steam screw corvette. Commissioned in the summer of 1857. Assigned to the Pacific. Repaired and refitted in 1860. Grounded and lost off of De los Reyes (USA) on 14.9.1863.

Rys' 11/12 Okhta
Constructor I. G. Karpovskiy
Laid down 9.10.1855 *Launched* 21.5.1856
Dimensions 163 ft 4 in (pp) x 31 ft 11 in (outside plank) x ? x 12 ft 4½ in/14 ft (draught fore/aft)
762 tons bm, 885 tons displacement
Armament 2 x 68pdr shell guns, 8 x 36pdrs (long), 2 x 36pdr gunnades
Machinery 200 nhp/400 ihp (Baird, St Petersburg) = 9½ kts
Range 800 nm

Boyarin class (14 ships). Steam screw corvette. Commissioned in the summer of 1857. Arrived in the Black Sea in the autumn of 1857. Stricken on 21.5.1886.

Voevoda 11 Okhta
Constructor A. A. Ivashchenko
Laid down 9.10.1855 *Launched* 17.6.1856
Dimensions 163 ft 4 in (pp) x 31 ft 11 in (outside plank) x ? x 12 ft 4½ in/14 ft (draught fore/aft)
762 tons bm, 885 tons displacement
Armament 1 x 36pdr (long), 10 x 36pdr gunnades
Machinery 200 nhp/400 ihp (Galvanoplastic Works, St Petersburg) = 9½ kts
Range 800 nm

Boyarin class (14 ships). Steam screw corvette. Commissioned in the summer of 1857. Assigned to the Far East. Repaired, refitted and new machinery of 160 nhp by Kronshtadt Dockyard installed in 1865. Disarmed on 16.2.1885. Stricken on 23.7.1887.

Buivol 11 Okhta
Constructor I. G. Karpovskiy
Laid down 9.10.1855 *Launched* 1.7.1856
Dimensions 163 ft 4 in (pp) x 31 ft 11 in (outside plank) x ? x 12 ft 4½ in/14 ft (draught fore/aft)
762 tons bm, 885 tons displacement
Armament Completed 1 x 36pdr (long), 10 x 36pdr gunnades
1863 2 x 68pdr shell guns, 1 x 36pdr (long), 4 x 36pdr gunnades 4 x 36pdr carr.
Machinery 200 nhp/400 ihp (Nobel, St Petersburg) = 9½ kts
Range 800 nm

Boyarin class (14 ships). Steam screw corvette. Commissioned in the autumn of 1857 in the Black Sea fleet. Training ship in 1863. Stricken on 25.1.1869.

Medved' 11 Okhta
Constructor I. G. Karpovskiy
Laid down 9.10.1855 *Launched* 17.6.1856
Dimensions 163 ft 4 in (pp) x 31 ft 11 in (outside plank) x ? x 12 ft 4½ in/14 ft (draught fore/aft)

                762 tons bm, 885 tons displacement
Armament   1 x 36pdr (long), 10 x 36pdr gunnades
Machinery   200 nhp/400 ihp (Nobel, St Petersburg) = 9½ kts
Range   800 nm

Boyarin class (14 ships). Steam screw corvette. Commissioned in the summer of 1857. Assigned to the Baltic. Disarmed and reduced to harbour service in 1862.

Posadnik 11 Okhta
Constructor   A. A. Ivashchenko
Laid down   9.10.1855   *Launched* 1.7.1856
Dimensions   163 ft 4 in (pp) x 31 ft 11 in (outside plank) x ?
                x 12 ft 4½ in/14 ft (draught fore/aft)
                762 tons bm, 885 tons displacement
Armament   1 x 36pdr (long), 10 x 36pdr gunnades
Machinery   200 nhp/400 ihp (Galvanoplastic Works, St Petersburg) = 9½ kts *Range* 800 nm

Boyarin class (14 ships). Steam screw corvette. Commissioned in the summer of 1857. Assigned to the Far East. Decommissioned and relegated to harbour service on 3.3.1869. Stricken on 6.3.1871.

Udav 11 Okhta
Constructor   I. G. Karpovskiy
Laid down   9.10.1855   *Launched* 6.7.1856
Dimensions   163 ft 4 in (pp) x 31 ft 11 in (outside plank) x ?
                x 12 ft 4½ in/14 ft (draught fore/aft)
                762 tons bm, 885 tons displacement
Armament   1 x 36pdr (long) 10 x 36pdr gunnades
Machinery   200 nhp/400 ihp (Baird, St Petersburg) = 9½ kts
Range   800 nm

Boyarin class (14 ships). Steam screw corvette. Commissioned in the summer of 1857. Arrived in the Black Sea in autumn of 1857 and assigned to the Black Sea fleet. Stricken on 25.1.1869.

Griden' 11 Okhta
Constructor   A. A. Ivashchenko
Laid down   9.10.1855   *Launched* 7.7.1856
Dimensions   163 ft 4 in (pp) x 31 ft 11 in (outside plank) x ?
                x 12 ft 4½ in/14 ft (draught fore/aft)
                762 tons bm, 885 tons displacement
Armament   1 x 36pdr (long) 10 x 36pdr gunnades
Machinery   200 nhp/400 ihp (Galvanoplastic Works, St Petersburg) = 9½ kts
Range   800 nm

Boyarin class (14 ships). Steam screw corvette. Commissioned in the summer of 1857. Assigned to the Baltic. Repaired, refitted and new machinery of 160 nhp by Kronshstadt Dockyard installed in 1864. Transferred to the Far East. Stricken on 27.5.1883.

Vol 11 Okhta
Constructor   I. G. Karpovskiy
Laid down   9.10.1855   *Launched* 18.7.1856
Dimensions   163 ft 4 in (pp) x 31 ft 11 in (outside plank) x ?
                x 12 ft 4½ in/14 ft (draught fore/aft)
                762 tons bm, 885 tons displacement
Armament   1 x 36pdr (long) 10 x 24pdr gunnades
Machinery   200 nhp/400 ihp (Nobel, St Petersburg) = 9½ kts
Range   800 nm

Boyarin class (14 ships). Steam screw corvette. Commissioned in the summer of 1857. Assigned to the Baltic. Decommissioned, disarmed and relegated to harbour service on 13.8.1866. Stricken in 1889.

Rynda 11 Okhta
Constructor   A. A. Ivashchenko
Laid down   9.10.1855   *Launched* 21.7.1856
Dimensions   163 ft 4 in (pp) x 31 ft 11 in (outside plank) x ?
                x 12 ft 4½ in/14 ft (draught fore/aft)
                762 tons bm, 885 tons displacement
Armament   1 x 36pdr (long), 10 x 36pdr gunnades
Machinery   200 nhp/400 ihp (Galvanoplastic Works, St Petersburg)
                = 9½ kts
Range   800 nm

Boyarin class (14 ships). Steam screw corvette. Commissioned in the summer of 1857. Assigned to the Baltic. Assigned to the Pacific in 1863–4. Stricken on 25.3.1871.

Baian 16 Coll & Co., Bordeaux
Constructor   ?
Laid down   1.10.1856   *Launched* 11.7.1857
Dimensions   216 ft 5½ in (pp) x 36 ft (outside plank) x ? x 18 ft 6¾ in/
                18 ft 2½ in (draught fore/aft)
                1,479 tons bm, 1,969 tons (as designed)/1,997 tons
                displacement
Armament Completed   16 x 12pdr (long)
                1861 16 x 60pdr shell guns
                1870 4 x 6-in rifled 4 x 4.2-in rifled
                1880 4 x 6-in rifled 4 x 4.2-in rifled 1 3.4-in rifled
Machinery   300 nhp (Schneider & Co., Creusot) = 10 kts

Steam screw corvette. Commissioned in 8.1857. Arrived at Kronshtadt on 28.10.1857. Assigned to the Baltic. Repaired and refitted in 1873. Assigned to the Far East. Training ship on 1.2.1892. Disarmed and hulked on 10.1.1899. Sold for breaking up in 1901–2.

Kalevala 11/15 Gamla Warfsbolaget, Abo
Constructor   ?
Laid down   10.7.1856   *Launched* 15.6.1858
Dimensions   166 ft (pp) x 38 ft 8 in (outside plank) x ? x 14 ft /
                15 ft 6 in (draught fore/aft)
                1,062 tons bm, 1,290 tons (as designed)/1,392 tons
displacement
Armament   1 x 60pdr (5 ton), 10 x 36pdrs (short)
Machinery   250 nhp (Cowie & Erikson, Abo) = 10½ kts

Steam screw corvette. Commissioned in 1859. To the Pacific in 1863–4. Stricken on 23.12.1872.

Bogatyr' 17 St Petersburg, New Admiralty Constructor Korshikov
Laid down   15.4.1859   *Launched* 6.9.1860
Dimensions   220 ft (pp) x 39 ft 4 in (outside plank) x ? x 17 ft 3 in/
                19 ft 3 in (draught fore/aft)
                1,586 tons bm, 2,155 tons displacement
Armament Completed   1 x 60pdr (5 ton) 16 x 60pdr shell guns
                1871 8 x 6-in rifled, 4 x 3.4 inrifled
Machinery   360 nhp/1,440 ihp (Baird, St Petersburg) = 10½ kts

Steam screw corvette. Commissioned in 1861. Assigned to the Baltic. To the Pacific in 1863–4. Repaired and refitted in 1870. Decommissioned on 14.2.1887. Disarmed as blockship *Number 4* on 12.3.1888. Receiving ship. Sold for breaking up in 1901–2.

Varyag 17 Sandorf, Uleaborg
Constructor   ?
Laid down   6.12.1860   *Launched* 1.6.1862
Dimensions   225 ft (pp) x 39 ft 8 in (outside plank) x ? x 17 ft 3 in/
                19 ft 3 in (draught fore/aft)

STEAM AND SAIL WARSHIPS: BALTIC FLEET

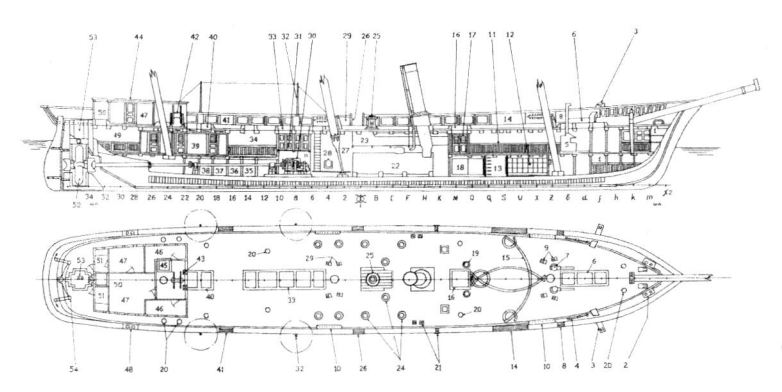

Overhead and cutaway views of the screw clipper Dzhigit, *one of 6 built in 1856 for service in the Pacific. The significant investment in tonnage and internal space needed to bring a 615-ton ship carrying a single 60pdr and two 24pdrs into action under steam power is striking when compared to the generous return in firepower offered by a 600-ton, 150 foot, 36-gun frigate of 50 years earlier.*

	1,609 tons bm, 2,156 tons displacement
Armament	Completed 1 x 60pdr (5 ton) 16 x 60pdr shell guns
	1871 5 x 6-in rifled, 4 x 3.4-in rifled
	1880 1 x 6-in rifled, 10 x 4.2-in rifled, 2 x 3.4-in rifled
Machinery	360 nhp (from *Polkan* of 1853) = 11 kts
Range	2,300 nm

Steam screw corvette. Commissioned at the end of 1862. Assigned to the Baltic. Cruised in the Atlantic in 1863–4. Repaired and refitted in 1876. Decommissioned on 16.2.1885. Stricken and sold for breaking up on 21.6.1886.

Vityaz' (later *Skobelev*) 17 Reposaari Shipbuilding Co., Bjorneborg
Constructor ?
Laid down 23.8.1861 Launched 24.7.1862
Dimensions 225 ft (pp) x 39 ft 8 in (outside plank) x ? x 17 ft 3 in/
 19 ft 3 in (draught fore/aft)
 1,609 tons bm, 2,156 tons displacement
Armament Completed 1 x 60pdr (5 ton) 16 x 60pdr shell guns
 1870 5 x 6-in rifled 4 x 4.2-in rifled
 1880 8 x 6-in rifled 4 x 4.2-in rifled
 1890 4 x 6-in rifled 4 x 4.2-in rifled 3 x 3.4-in rifled
Machinery 360 nhp/1618 ihp (Cockerill, Seraing) = 12 kts

Steam screw corvette. Commissioned in 1863. Assigned to the Baltic. Cruised in the Atlantic in 1863–4. Repaired and refitted in 1874. Repaired and refitted in 1881. Renamed *Skobelev* on 27.6.1882. Decommissioned on 1.2.1892 and reduced to a training ship. Disarmed on 26.11.1894. Stricken on 31.1.1895.

Askol'd 17 Okhta
Constructor ?
Laid down 6.10.1862 Launched 15.10.1863
Dimensions 225 ft (pp) x 39 ft 8 in (outside plank) x ? x 17 ft 3 in/
 19 ft 3 in (draught fore/aft)
 1,609 tons bm, 2,156 tons displacement
Armament Completed 1 x 60pdr (5 ton), 16 x 60pdr shell guns
 1870 5 x 6-in rifled, 4 x 3.4-in rifled
 1876 8 x 6-in rifled, 4 x 4.2-in rifled (1 x 3.4-in rifle later added)
Machinery 360 nhp (from *Askol'd* of 1854) = 11.48 kts

Steam screw corvette. Commissioned on 12.6.1864. Assigned to the Baltic in 1864 and later to the Pacific. Repaired and refitted in 1871–2. Decommissioned and disarmed on 5.5.1891. Stricken and hulked on 31.7.1893. Sold in 1901.

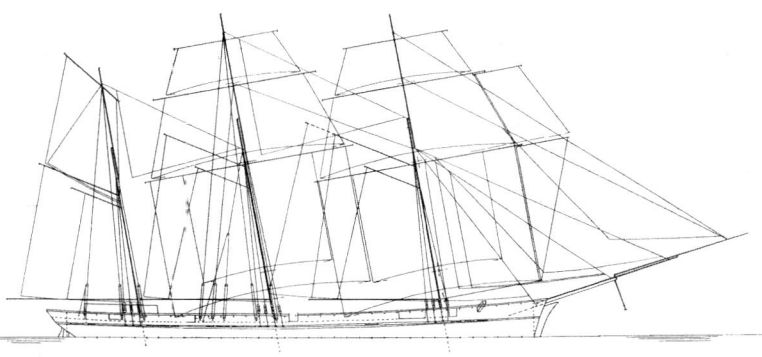

Spar and sail plan of Dzhigit.

Steam screw clippers

Razboynik class
Razboynik 3 Arkhangel'sk
Constructor Vasilevskiy
Laid down 5.1.1855 Launched 30.5.1856
Dimensions 152 ft (pp) x 27 ft 10 in (outside plank) x ? x 10 ft 11 in/
 12 ft 11 in (draught fore/aft)
 548 tons bm, 615 tons displacement
Armament 1 x 60pdr (5 ton), 2 x 24pdrs
Machinery 150 nhp (Izhora Works, St Petersburg) = 9 kts
Range 700 nm

Razboynik class (6 ships). Steam screw clipper. Commissioned on 26.7.1856. Assigned to the Pacific. Decommissioned on 16.7.1866. Stricken on 3.1.1867 and sold for breaking up.

Strelok 3 Arkhangel'sk
Constructor Mitrofanov
Laid down 5.1.1855 Launched 20.6.1856
Dimensions 152 ft (pp) x 27 ft 10 in (outside plank) x ? x 10 ft 11 in/
 12 ft 11 in (draught fore/aft)
 548 tons bm, 615 tons displacement
Armament 1 x 60pdr (5 ton), 2 x 24pdrs
Machinery 150 nhp (Izhora Works, St Petersburg) = 9 kts
Range 700 nm

Razboynik class (6 ships). Steam screw clipper. Commissioned on 26.7.1856. Assigned to the Pacific. Decommissioned on 16.7.1866. Stricken on 4.11.1878. Sold for breaking up.

Dzhigit 3 Arkhangel'sk
Constructor Mitrofanov
Laid down 5.1.1855 Launched 23.6.1856
Dimensions 152 ft (pp) x 27 ft 10 in (outside plank) x ? x 10 ft 11 in/
 12 ft 11 in (draught fore/aft)
 548 tons bm, 615 tons displacement
Armament 1 x 60pdr (5 ton), 2 x 24pdrs
Machinery 150 nhp (Izhora Works, St Petersburg) = 9 kts
Range 700 nm

Razboynik class (6 ships). Steam screw clipper. Commissioned on 26.7.1856. Assigned to the Pacific. Decommissioned on 16.7.1866. Expended as a gunnery target on 2.7.1869. Stricken on 21.8.1869.

Early steam ships spent most of their time at sea under sail to save fuel and engine wear, as this beautiful painting of the steam clipper Strelok *under full sail in the Pacific shows clearly. As was the case with her sisters, she commissioned after the end of the Crimean War. As was also the case with most of her sisters, she spent her life in the Pacific at a time when Russia was beginning to expand her activities and interests in Kamchatka and surrounding territories.*

Plastun 3 Arkhangel'sk
Constructor ?
Laid down 5.1.1855 *Launched* 23.6.1856
Dimensions 152 ft (pp) x 27 ft 10 in (outside plank) x ? x 10 ft 11 in/
12 ft 11 in (draught fore/aft)
548 tons bm, 615 tons displacement
Armament 1 x 60pdr (5 ton), 2 x 24pdrs
Machinery 150 nhp (Izhora Works, St Petersburg) = 9 kts
Range 700 nm
Razboynik class (6 ships). Steam screw clipper. Commissioned on 26.7.1856. Exploded on 18.8.1860 during a mutiny off of Gottland. Stricken on 3.9.1860.

Naezdnik 3 Arkhangel'sk
Constructor Mitrofanov
Laid down 5.1.1855 *Launched* 14.7.1856
Dimensions 152 ft (pp) x 27 ft 10 in (outside plank) x ? x 10 ft 11 in/
12 ft 11 in (draught fore/aft)
548 tons bm, 615 tons displacement
Armament 1 x 60pdr (5 ton) 2 x 24pdrs
Machinery 150 nhp (Izhora Works, St Petersburg) = 9 kts
Range 700 nm
Razboynik class (6 ships). Steam screw clipper. Commissioned on 12.9.1856. Assigned to the Pacific. Decommissioned on 2.7.1869 and expended as a target. Stricken on 21.8.1869.

Oprichnik 3 Arkhangel'sk
Constructor Vasilevskiy
Laid down 5.1.1855 *Launched* 14.7.1856
Dimensions 152 ft (pp) x 27 ft 10 in (outside plank) x ? x 10 ft 11 in/
12 ft 11 in (draught fore/aft)
548 tons bm, 615 tons displacement
Armament 1 x 60pdr (5 ton), 2 x 24pdrs
Machinery 150 nhp (Izhora Works, St Petersburg) = 9 kts
Range 700 nm
Razboynik class (6 ships). Steam screw clipper. Commissioned on 12.9.1856. Lost with all hands during a hurricane in the Indian Ocean on 26.12.1861.

Abrek class

Abrek 5 Reposaari Shipbuilding Co., Bjorneborg
Constructor ?
Laid down 22.6.1859 *Launched* 1.7.1860
Dimensions 200 ft (pp) x 31 ft 1 in (outside plank) x ? x 12 ft 2 in/
13 ft 2 in (draught fore/aft)
895 tons bm, 1,069 tons displacement
Armament Completed 3 x 60pdrs (5 ton), 2 x 4.2-in rifled
1871 3 x 6-in rifled, 4 x 3.4-in rifled
Machinery 300 nhp (Humphreys & Tennant, London) = 12½ kts
Abrek class (2 ships). Steam screw clipper. Commissioned in 1861. Assigned to the Pacific in 1863–4. Repaired, refitted and new machinery of 300 nhp/1109 ihp by Kronshtadt Dockyard installed in 1870. Transferred to the Siberian Flotilla on 12.6.1877. Decommissioned on 21.1.1889. Stricken and hulked at Vladivostok on 3.5.1892. Depot ship for submarines in 1905. Sold for breaking up on 2.9.1906.

Vsadnik 5 Reposaari Shipbuilding Co., Bjorneborg
Constructor ?
Laid down 22.6.1859 *Launched* 1.7.1860
Dimensions 200 ft (pp) x 31 ft 1 in (outside plank) x ? x 12 ft 2 in/
13 ft 2 in (draught fore/aft)
895 tons bm, 1,069 tons displacement
Armament Completed 3 x 60pdrs (5 ton), 2 x 4.2-in rifled
1871 3 x 6-in rifled, 2 x 4.2-in rifled
Machinery 300 nhp = 12½ kts
Abrek class (2 ships). Steam screw clipper. Original machinery by the Pori Mechanical Workshop Co. replaced before completion. Commissioned on 28.9.1862. Grounded off of Bornholm in the Baltic in 1864, but later repaired. Assigned to the Pacific. Decommissioned on 22.8.1880. Stricken on 7.11.1881 and sold for breaking up.

Gaidamak 7 W. & H. Pitcher, Northfleet
Constructor ?
Laid down 1859 *Launched* 1.4.1860
Dimensions 213 ft 5 in (pp) x 31 ft 4 in (outside plank) x ? x 10 ft 6 in/
10 ft 6 in (draught fore/aft)
1,001 tons bm, 1,094 tons displacement
Armament Completed 3 x 60pdr (5 ton), 4 x 3.4-in rifled
1871 3 x 6-in rifled 1 x 12pdr (12pdr later replaced by
4 x 3.4-in rifled)
Machinery 250 nhp (Maudslay, London) = 11 kts

Steam screw clipper. Commissioned in the summer of 1860. Assigned to the Baltic fleet. Driven ashore off of Sakhalin on 28.8.1861, and subsequently refloated and repaired. To the Siberian Flotilla from 12.5.1862–13.7.1863. Assigned to the Pacific in 1863–4. Stricken on 11.10.1886 and sold for breaking up.

Almaz class

Almaz 7 Galernyy Ostrovok
Constructor Tirenshtein
Laid down 31.12.1860 *Launched* 5.10.1861
Dimensions 250 ft (pp) x 30 ft 9 in (outside plank) x 19 ft 3 in
 x 13 ft 2 in/15 ft 6 in (draught fore/aft)
 1,154 tons bm, 1,585 tons displacement
Armament 3 x 6-in rifled 2 x 4.2-in rifled, 2 x 3.4-in rifled
Machinery 350 nhp/1453 ihp (Humphreys & Tennant, London)
 = 12½ kts

Almaz class (4 ships). Steam screw clipper. Commissioned on 14.8.1862. Assigned to the Baltic fleet. Assigned to the Atlantic in 1863–4. Decommissioned on 8.12.1879. Stricken on 7.11.1881 and sold for breaking up.

Zhemchug 7 Galernyy Ostrovok
Constructor Tirenshtein
Laid down 31.12.1860 *Launched* 5.10.1861
Dimensions 250 ft (pp) x 30 ft 9 in (outside plank) x 19 ft 3 in
 x 13 ft 2 in/15 ft 6 in (draught fore/aft)
 1,154 tons bm, 1,585 tons displacement
Armament 3 x 6-in rifled, 2 x 4.2-in rifled, 2 x 3.4-in rifled
Machinery 350 nhp/1438 ihp (Humphreys & Tennant, London)
 = 12½ kts

Almaz class (4 ships). Steam screw clipper. Commissioned on 20.8.1862. Assigned to the Baltic fleet. Cruised in the Barents and Kara Seas. Decommissioned on 12.2.1886 and relegated to harbour service. Stricken on 15.2.1892 and sold for breaking up.

Izumrud 7 St Petersburg, New Admiralty
Constructor A. A. Ivashchenko
Laid down 14.6.1861 *Launched* 1.9.1862
Dimensions 250 ft (pp) x 30 ft 9 in (outside plank) x 19 ft 3 in
 x 13 ft 2 in/15 ft 6 in (draught fore/aft)
 1,154 tons bm, 1,585 tons displacement
Armament 3 x 6-in rifled, 2 x 4.2-in rifled, 2 x 3.4-in rifled
Machinery 350 nhp/1254 ihp (Cockerill, Seraing) = 13 kts

Almaz class (4 ships). Steam screw clipper. Commissioned in 8.1863. Assigned to the Baltic fleet. Cruised in the Indian Ocean off New Guinea. Stricken on 11.10.1886 and sold for breaking up.

Iakhont 7 Okhta
Constructor Svistovskiy
Laid down 5.10.1860 or 2.8.1861 *Launched* 6.10.1862
Dimensions 250 ft (pp) x 30 ft 9 in (outside plank) x 19 ft 3 in
 x 13 ft 2 in/15 ft 6 in (draught fore/aft)
 1,154 tons bm, 1,585 tons displacement
Armament 3 x 6-in rifled, 2 x 4.2-in rifled, 2 x 3.4-in rifled
Machinery 350 nhp/1200 ihp (Cockerill, Seraing) = 12 kts

Almaz class (4 ships). Steam screw clipper. Commissioned in 8.1863. Assigned to the Baltic fleet. Participated in the opening ceremonies for the Suez canal on 5.11.1869. Decommissioned on 10.3.1879. Stricken on 7.11.1881 and sold for breaking up.

Steam and Sail Warships: Black Sea Fleet

Steam screw ships of the line

Three-deckers

The screw ships *Bosfor* (later renamed *Sinop*) and *Tsesarevich*, then rated as 120 guns, were building for the Black Sea fleet at Nikolaev when the Crimean War broke out. Their machinery, on order in England, was not delivered and their launch was delayed until after the war had ended. As a result of the peace treaty of 1856, which allowed Russia and Turkey to maintain only minimal naval forces in the Black Sea, they were transferred to the Baltic when launched and their machinery finally fitted in 1860. See under Baltic fleet for details.

Steam paddle frigates

Krym class

Krym 4/6 W. & H. Pitcher, Northfleet
Constructor ?
Laid down 1842 *Launched* 27.8.1842
Dimensions 175 ft x 31 ft 10 in x 20 ft x 14 ft 8 in (max. draught)
 824 tons bm, 1,305 tons displacement
Armament 1843 UD 2 x 10-in shell guns, 4 x 24pdr gunnades
 1853 UD 1 x 10-in shell gun, 1 x 56pdr, 10 x 24pdr
 gunnades
Machinery 260 nhp/600 ihp = 11 kts

Krym class (5 ships). Steam paddle frigate. Commissioned in 2.1843. Arrived at Odessa in 3.1843. Took part in the Crimean War 1853–6, arriving late at the battle of Sinop 18.11.1853. Scuttled 30.8.1855. Raised 8.12.1859 by a US company but beyond repair and remains broken up.

Odessa 4/6 W. & H. Pitcher, Northfleet
Constructor ?
Laid down 1842 *Launched* 7.10.1842
Dimensions 175 ft x 31 ft 10 in x 20 ft x 14 ft 8 in (max. draught)
 824 tons bm, 1,305 tons displacement
Armament 1843 UD 2 x 10-in shell guns, 4 x 24pdr gunnades
 1853 UD 1 x 10-in shell gun, 1 x 56pdr, 10 x 24pdr
 gunnades
Machinery 260 nhp/600 ihp = 11 kts

Krym class (5 ships). Steam paddle frigate. Arrived at Odessa in 3.1843. Took part in the Crimean War 1853–6, arriving late at the battle of Sinop 18.11.1853. Scuttled 30.8.1855. Raised 30.3.1860 by a US company but beyond repair and remains broken up.

Khersones 4/6 W. & H. Pitcher, Northfleet
Constructor ?
Laid down 1842 *Launched* 4.2.1843
Dimensions 175 ft x 31 ft 10 in x 20 ft x 14 ft 8 in (max. draught) 824 tons bm, 1,305 tons displacement
Armament 1843;UD 2 x 10-in shell guns, 4 x 24pdr gunnades
 1853 UD 1 x 10-in shell gun, 1 x 56pdr, 10 x 24pdr
 gunnades
Machinery 260 nhp/600 ihp = 11 kts

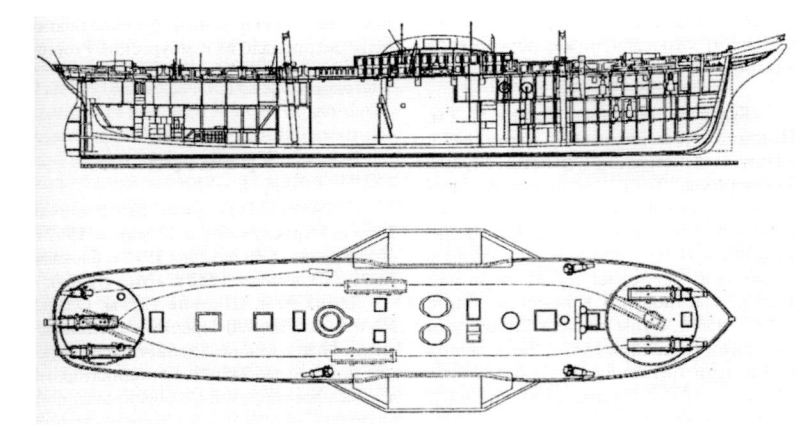

Overhead and side cutaway of the paddle frigate Gromonosets *completed in 1843. Of interest are the arrangements for moving the 10-inch shell guns and the 36pdr gunnades from bow to stern as needed and the internal arrangement of what would one day be called the machinery spaces.*

Krym class (5 ships). Steam paddle frigate. Commissioned in 4.1843. Arrived at Odessa 11.5.1843. Took part in operations during the Crimean War 1853–6, arriving late at the battle of Sinop 18.11.1853. Ran aground on 30.8.1855 in Sevastopol harbour and left by her crew during the retreat of the Russian troops. Refloated after the war 19.7.1856 and repaired at Nikolaev. Employed as a cargo and passenger steamer until wrecked 4.12.1861. Later salvaged and hulked.

Bessarabiia 6 W. & H. Pitcher, Northfleet
Constructor   ?
Laid down   1842   Launched 18.3.1843
Dimensions   175 ft x 31 ft 10 in x 20 ft x 14 ft 8 in (max. draught)
    824 tons bm, 1,305 tons displacement
Armament   1843 UD 2 x 10-in shell guns, 4 x 36pdr gunnades
    1853 UD 1 x 10-in shell gun, 1 x 56pdr, 4 x 24pdr gunnades, 2 x 8pdrs
Machinery   260 nhp/600 ihp = 11 kts

Krym class (5 ships). Steam paddle frigate. Commissioned in 5.1843. Arrived at Odessa 30.6.1843. Took part in the Crimean War 1853–6, capturing the Turkish armed steamer *Medar Tidzharet* on 4.11.1853. Scuttled in Sevastopol harbour on 30.8.1855 during the retreat of the Russian troops. Raised 17.2.1860 by a US company but beyond repair and remains broken up.

Gromonosets 6 W. & H. Pitcher, Northfleet
Constructor   ?
Laid down   1842   Launched 17.4.1843
Dimensions   175 ft x 31 ft 10 in x 20 ft x 14 ft 8 in (max. draught)
    824 tons bm, 1,305 tons displacement
Armament   1843 UD 2 x 10-in shell guns, 4 x 36pdr gunnades
    1853 UD 1 x 10-in shell gun, 1 x 56pdr, 4 x 24pdr gunnades, 2 x 8pdrs
Machinery   260 nhp/600 ihp = 11 kts

Krym class (5 ships). Steam paddle frigate. Arrived at Odessa in 1843. Took part in the Crimean War 1853–6. Scuttled on 30.8.1855. Raised 8.3.1860 by a US company but remains broken up.

Vladimir 9 Ditchburn & Mare, Blackwall
Constructor   ?
Laid down   1847   Launched 10.3.1848
Dimensions   200 ft (pp) x 35 ft 11 in (outside plank) x ? x 14 ft 4 in/ 14 ft 8 in (draught fore/aft)
    1,731 tons displacement
Armament   1848 UD 2 x 9.65-in shell guns, 4 x 24pdrs, 2 x 18pdrs, 1 x 8pdr
    1853 UD 2 x 10-in shell guns, 3 x 68pdr shell guns, 4 x 24pdr gunnades, 2 x 18 pdrs
Machinery   400 nhp/1,200 ihp (Rennie, London) = 11 kts
Range   2,000 nm

Steam paddle frigate. Commissioned in the autumn of 1848. Took part in the Crimean War 1853–6, capturing the Egyptian armed steamer *Pervaz-i Bahri* on 5.11.1853. Scuttled on 30.8.1855. Armament recovered by divers 24.6–10.7.1856. Raised 8.6.1860 by a U.S. company and taken to Nikolaev in the summer of 1861 for repairs but found to be too damaged and laid up. Eventually broken up some years later.

Tigr 4 Nikolaev
Constructor   I. S. Dmitriev
Laid down   1855   Launched 9.10.1858
Dimensions   206 ft (pp) x 36 ft 6 in (outside plank) x ? x 15 ft 3 in/ 15 ft 9 in (draught fore/aft)
    1,278 tons bm, 1,975 tons displacement
Armament   UD 4 saluting guns
Machinery   400 nhp (John Penn, London)

Steam paddle frigate. Built to take machinery salvaged from HMS *Tiger* which ran aground and was destroyed at Odessa on 30.4.1854. Completed as an Imperial yacht to comply with the peace treaty of 1856 which allowed Russia and Turkey to maintain only minimal naval forces in the Black Sea. Stricken on 26.8.1872.

Captured paddle steamers

Two enemy paddle steamers were added to the Black Sea fleet at the beginning of the Crimean War. The Turkish *Medar Tidzharet* of 4 guns and 200 nhp was captured by *Bessarabyia* on 4.11.1853. Renamed *Turok*. Scuttled on 30.8.1855 but raised on 4.7.1858 and returned to service as an auxiliary. Length 135 ft (pp), breadth 25 ft, displacement 425.8 tons. Originally built by Money Wigram, Blackwall, in 1846–7. Finally stricken on 19.1.1891. The Egyptian *Pervaz-i Bahri* of 10 guns and 200 nhp was captured by *Vladimir* on 5.11.1853. Renamed *Kornilov*. Scuttled on 30.8.1855. Originally built by Alexandria Dockyard in 1844–5.

Steam screw corvettes

The screw steamers *Voin* and *Vityaz'* of 250 nhp and 20 guns each were building for the Black Sea fleet by Pitcher at Northfleet, England, when war with Russia broke out. They were seized by the British government on 24.3.1854 (5.4.1854 NS). Renamed *Tartar* and *Cossack* respectively, they were launched soon after.

The screw steamers *Volk*, *Zubr*, *Vepr'*, *Rys*, *Buivol* and *Udav* were constructed in St Petersburg but assigned to the Black Sea fleet arriving in 1857. See Baltic fleet list for details.

Sokol class

Sokol 9 Nikolaev
Constructor   Akimov
Laid down   1857   Launched 30.8.1859
Dimensions   164 ft (pp) x 32 ft 4 in (outside plank) x ? x 14 ft / 14 ft 4 in (draught fore/aft)
    1,016 tons displacement

Armament Completed 1 x 60pdr (5 ton), 10 x 36pdr gunnades
1873 2 x 6-in rifled, 5 x 4.2-in rifled, 2 x 2.9-in rifled
Machinery 220 nhp (Maudslay, London) = 8 kts
Screw steamer. *Sokol* class (3 ships). Commissioned in 1860. Black Sea in 1860. Transferred to the Baltic fleet in 1861–3. Decommissioned on 27.10.1886. Stricken on 31.7.1893.

Iastreb 9 Nikolaev
Constructor Akimov
Laid down 1857 *Launched* 19.6.1860
Dimensions 164 ft (pp) x 32 ft 4 in (outside plank) x ? x 14 ft / 14 ft 4 in (draught fore/aft)
1,016 tons displacement
Armament Completed 9 x 36pdr (long)
Machinery 220 nhp (Maudslay, London) = 8 kts
Screw steamer. *Sokol* class (3 ships). Commissioned in the summer of 1860. Decommissioned and disarmed at Nikolaev 19.12.1870 but recommissioned 20.3.1871. Stricken on 27.3.1876, disarmed and sold for breaking up.

Krechet 9 Nikolaev
Constructor Akimov
Laid down 1857 *Launched* 7.8.1860
Dimensions 164 ft (pp) x 32 ft 3 in (outside plank) x ? x 12 ft 7 in/ 14 ft 8 in (draught fore/aft)
979 tons displacement
Armament Completed 9 x 36pdr (long)
Machinery 220 nhp (Maudslay, London) = 8 kts
Screw steamer. *Sokol* class (3 ships). Commissioned late 1860. To the Baltic in 1861–3. Stricken on 21.7.1871, disarmed and later broken up.

Voin 4/6 Nikolaev
Constructor Aleksandrov
Laid down 14.8.1854 *Launched* 1857
Dimensions 195 ft (pp) x 38 ft 8 in (outside plank) x ? x 16 ft 6 in/ 17 ft 6 in (draught fore/aft)
1,821 tons displacement
Armament Completed 2 x 60pdrs, 2 x 36pdrs
1871 1 x 8-in rifled pivot, 5 x 6-in rifled
Machinery 205 nhp (Maltzov, St Petersburg)
Screw steamer. Laid down as a corvette, but completed as a transport to comply with the terms of the 1856 peace treaty. Commissioned in 1857. Converted to a corvette and reclassified on 1.10.1871. Decommissioned on 27.10.1886. Stricken on 19.1.1891.

L'vitsa 9 Nikolaev
Constructor ?
Laid down 18.10.1863 *Launched* 1.6.1865
Dimensions 163 ft 4 in (pp) x 32 ft (outside plank) x 15 ft 9 in
774 tons bm, 885 tons displacement
Armament Completed 1 x 36pdr (long), 8 x 36pdr gunnades
1873 2 x 6-in rifled, 6 x 4.2-in rifled
Machinery 160 nhp/411 ihp (Carr & MacPherson, St Petersburg) = 8½ kts
Screw steamer. Commissioned in 1866. Decommissioned on 8.12.1879. Stricken on 31.7.1893 and hulked. Sold in about 1905.

Pamiat' Merkuriia 9 Nikolaev
Constructor ?
Laid down 18.12.1863 *Launched* 30.8.1865
Dimensions 163 ft 4 in (pp) x 32 ft (outside plank) x 15 ft 9 in
774 tons bm, 885 tons displacement
Armament Completed 1 x 36pdr (long) 8 x 36pdr gunnades
1873 2 x 6-in rifled, 6 x 4.2-in rifled
Machinery 160 nhp/382 ihp (Carr & MacPherson, St Petersburg) = 7½ kts
Screw steamer. Commissioned in 1866. Decommissioned and disarmed on 8.12.1879. Stricken on 9.4.1883 and hulked as a prison ship. Sold in about 1905.

Steam and Sail Gunboats: all fleets

Sterliad' 3 Gamla Warfsbolaget, Abo
Constructor ?
Laid down 22.7.1854 *Launched* 13.9.1854
Dimensions 110 ft (pp) x 19 ft 6 in (outside plank) x ? x 6 ft/ 7 ft (draught fore/aft)
178.5 tons displacement
Armament 3 x 68pdr shell guns
Machinery 58 rhp = 6 kts
Screw steamer. Commissioned on 30 September 1854. Disarmed on 3 March 1869. Stricken on 26 August 1871.

Molniia class
Dimensions 108 ft (pp) x 20 ft 9½ in (outside plank) x 7 ft /7 ft (draught fore/aft)
170 tons displacement (Group 1)
111 ft (pp) x 21 ft 3 in (outside plank) x 7 ft /7 ft (draught fore/aft)
176 tons displacement (Group 2)
125 ft (pp) x 22 ft 8 in (outside plank) x 4 ft /4 ft (draught fore/aft)
178 tons displacement (Group 3)
Armament 3 x 68pdr shell guns (one of the 68pdrs later replaced by a long 36pdr or long 30pdr)
Machinery 60–80 nhp (various St Petersburg builders) = 7–9 kts

Molniia Galernyy Ostrovok *Laid down* 4.2.1855 *Launched* 6.3.1855
Stricken on 13.12.1879.
Turman Galernyy Ostrovok *Laid down* 4.2.1855 *Launched* 2.4.1855
Stricken on 30.7.1876.
Zabiiaka Galernyy Ostrovok *Laid down* 4.2.1855 *Launched* 14.4.1855
Stricken on 17.7.1878.
Burun Galernyy Ostrovok *Laid down* 4.2.1855 *Launched* 14.4.1855
Stricken on 26.8.1871.
Tucha Galernyy Ostrovok *Laid down* 4.2.1855 *Launched* 14.4.1855
Stricken on 26.8.1871.
Likhach Galernyy Ostrovok *Laid down* 4.2.1855 *Launched* 22.4.1855
Stricken on 27.5.1882.
Khvat Okhta *Laid down* 4.2.1855 *Launched* 23.4.1855
Stricken on 5.1.1885.
Vikhr' Galernyy Ostrovok *Laid down* 4.2.1855 *Launched* 25.4.1855
Stricken on 5.11.1866.
Dozhd' Galernyy Ostrovok *Laid down* 4.2.1855 *Launched* 25.4.1855
Stricken on 19.12.1870.
Postrel Okhta *Laid down* 4.2.1855 *Launched* 28.4.1855
Stricken on 11.11.1867.

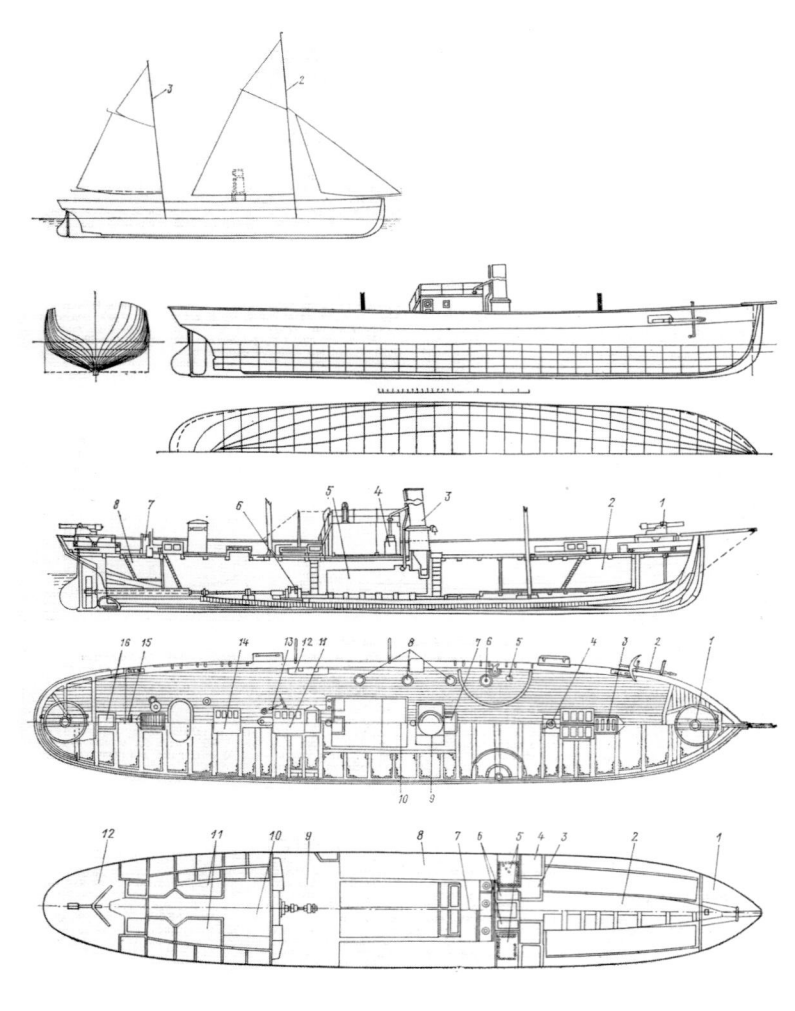

The threat to Kronshtadt and St Petersburg by the expected arrival of the Anglo-French fleet generated a massive construction program of steam screw gunboats similar, in concept at least, to the earlier rowing gunboats used in the wars with Sweden over a half century earlier. This is a highly detailed series of drawings of Shchit, *a typical member of the 74-boat Molniia class, showing both her internal arrangements and her underwater lines. These craft would likely have been of little practical use against the allied fleet, but their design and rapid construction is a tribute to Russian ingenuity under stress.*

Sneg Galernyy Ostrovok Laid down 4.2.1855 Launched 30.4.1855
Stricken on 18.5.1874.
Grad Galernyy Ostrovok Laid down 4.2.1855 Launched 30.4.1855
Stricken on 30.9.1872.
Zarnitsa Galernyy Ostrovok Laid down 4.2.1855 Launched 2.5.1855
Stricken on 19.12.1870.
Poryv Okhta Laid down 4.2.1855 Launched 2.5.1855
Stricken on 26.8.1871.
Grom Galernyy Ostrovok Laid down 4.2.1855 Launched 2.5.1855
Stricken on 4.3.1882.
Buian Okhta Laid down 4.2.1855 Launched 2.5.1855
Stricken on 4.11.1878.
Zyb' Galernyy Ostrovok Laid down 4.2.1855 Launched 5.5.1855
Stricken on 4.11.1878.
Volna Galernyy Ostrovok Laid down 4.2.1855 Launched 7.5.1855
Stricken on 25.9.1871.
Sorvanets Okhta Laid down 4.2.1855 Launched 8.5.1855
Stricken on 26.8.1871.
Balagur Okhta Laid down 4.2.1855 Launched 10.5.1855
Stricken on 23.6.1867.
Shchegol' Okhta Laid down 4.2.1855 Launched 10.5.1855
Stricken on 19.12.1870.
Gogol' Okhta Laid down 4.2.1855 Launched 11.5.1855
Stricken on 25.9.1871.
Burya Galernyy Ostrovok Laid down 4.2.1855 Launched 11.5.1855
Sunk as a target on 13.8.1873.
Tolcheia Galernyy Ostrovok Laid down 4.2.1855 Launched 14.5.1855
Stricken on 13.1.1879.
Shkval Galernyy Ostrovok Laid down 4.2.1855 Launched 18.5.1855
Stricken on 12.9.1869.
Komar Kronshtadt Laid down 11.12.1854 Launched 28.5.1855
Stricken on 5.11.1866.
Iorsh Kronshtadt Laid down 11.12.1854 Launched 31.5.1855
Stricken on 5.11.1866.
Kopchik Okhta Laid down 1.5.1855 Launched 1.6.1855
Stricken on 4.3.1882.
Shmel' Kronshtadt Laid down 11.12.1854 Launched 1.6.1855
Stricken on 26.8.1871.
Shchuka Kronshtadt Laid down 11.12.1854 Launched 2.6.1855
Stricken on 25.9.2871.
Korshun Okhta Laid down 1.5.1855 Launched 5.6.1855
Stricken on 1.2.1886.
Pchela Kronshtadt Laid down 11.12.1854 Launched 6.6.1855
Stricken on 25.9.1871
Osa Kronshtadt Laid down 11.12.1854 Launched 7.6.1855
Stricken on 11.11.1867.
Rusalka Okhta Laid down 1.5.1855 Launched 8.6.1855
Stricken on 24.12.1877.
Ved'ma Okhta Laid down 1.5.1855 Launched 11.6.1855
Stricken on 18.5.1874.
Povesa Okhta Laid down 1.5.1855 Launched 14.6.1855
Stricken on 26.8.1871.
Prokaznik Okhta Laid down 1.5.1855 Launched 15.6.1855
Stricken on 18.5.1874.
Osetr St Petersburg, New Admiralty Laid down 18.7.1855
  Launched 12.9.1855
Stricken on 4.11.1878.
Shalun Okhta Laid down 4.2.1855 Launched 14.9.1855
Wrecked on 4.6.1868 in the Bjorkesund Strait.
Domovoi Galernyy Ostrovok Laid down 8.1855 Launched 3.4.1856
Stricken on 12.9.1869.
Inei Galernyy Ostrovok Laid down 8.1855 Launched 3.4.1856
Stricken on 11.11.1867.
Priboi Galernyy Ostrovok Laid down 8.1855 Launched 7.4.1856
Stricken on 18.5.1874.
Moroz Galernyy Ostrovok Laid down 8.1855 Launched 11.4.1856
Stricken on 12.9.1869.
Plamya Galernyy Ostrovok Laid down 8.1855 Launched 21.4.1856
Stricken on 8.4.1867.
Legkii Galernyy Ostrovok Laid down 8.1855 Launched 25.4.1856
Stricken on 12.9.1869.
Priliv Galernyy Ostrovok Laid down 8.1855 Launched 28.4.1856
Sunk as a target on 13.8.1873.
Otliv Galernyy Ostrovok Laid down 8.1855 Launched 28.4.1856
Stricken on 3.3.1891.

Gul Galernyy Ostrovok *Laid down* 8.1855 *Launched* 2.5.1856 Sunk as a target on 13.8.1873.
Dym Galernyy Ostrovok *Laid down* 8.1855 *Launched* 6.5.1856 Stricken on 26.8.1871.
Marevo Galernyy Ostrovok *Laid down* 8.1855 *Launched* 8.5.1856 Stricken on 18.5.1874.
Roza Galernyy Ostrovok *Laid down* 8.1855 *Launched* 10.5.1856 Stricken on 4.11.1878.
Baba-Yaga Galernyy Ostrovok *Laid down* 8.1855 *Launched* 11.5.1856 Stricken on 12.6.1869.
Oboroten' Galernyy Ostrovok *Laid down* 8.1855 *Launched* 12.5.1856 Stricken on 26.8.1871.
Zvon Galernyy Ostrovok *Laid down* 8.1855 *Launched* 17.5.1856 Stricken on 11.11.1867.
Mech Galernyy Ostrovok *Laid down* 8.1855 *Launched* 11.6.1856 Foundered on 4.10.1871 off Cape Stirsudden.
Pantsir' Galernyy Ostrovok *Laid down* 30.12.1855 *Launched* 13.6.1856 Stricken on 28.8.1871.
Shchit Galernyy Ostrovok *Laid down* 9.2.1856 *Launched* 16.6.1856 Stricken on 31.7.1893.
Sekira Galernyy Ostrovok *Laid down* 16.1.1856 *Launched* 16.6.1856 Transferred to the Caspian Sea in 1862. Stricken on 22.3.1869.
Zarevo Galernyy Ostrovok *Laid down* 8.1855 *Launched* 18.6.1856 Stricken on 1.5.1871.
Treska Galernyy Ostrovok *Laid down* 8.1855 *Launched* 19.6.1856 Stricken on 23.3.1874.
Metel' Galernyy Ostrovok *Laid down* 2.1856 *Launched* 22.6.1856 Stricken on 1.5.1871.
Vystrel Galernyy Ostrovok *Laid down* 2.1856 *Launched* 22.6.1856 Stricken on 4.11.1878.
Vzryv Galernyy Ostrovok *Laid down* 8.1855 *Launched* 23.6.1856 Stricken on 11.11.1867.
Kol'chuga Galernyy Ostrovok *Laid down* 2.1856 *Launched* 23.6.1856 Stricken on 19.12.1870.
Chayka Galernyy Ostrovok *Laid down* 8.1855 *Launched* 26.6.1856 Stricken on 26.8.2871.
Kartech' Galernyy Ostrovok *Laid down* 2.1856 *Launched* 26.6.1856 Stricken on 3.3.1891.
Bronya Galernyy Ostrovok *Laid down* 2.1856 *Launched* 28.6.1856 Stricken on 11.11.1867.
Kop'e Galernyy Ostrovok *Laid down* 2.1856 *Launched* 30.6.1856 Stricken on 8.4.1867.
Iadro Galernyy Ostrovok *Laid down* 2.1856 *Launched* 30.6.1856 Stricken on 10.5.1875.
Shlem Galernyy Ostrovok *Laid down* 2.1856 *Launched* 2.7.1856 Stricken on 8.4.1867.
Vyiuga Galernyy Ostrovok *Laid down* 2.1856 *Launched* 4.7.1856 Stricken on 12.9.1869.
Pishchal' Galernyy Ostrovok *Laid down* 2.1856 *Launched* 5.7.1856 Transferred to the Caspian Sea in 1862. Stricken on 22.3.1869.
Kolchan Galernyy Ostrovok *Laid down* 2.1856 *Launched* 6.7.1856 Stricken on 13.10.1862.
Luk Galernyy Ostrovok *Laid down* 2.1856 *Launched* 7.7.1856 Stricken on 5.11.1866.

Screw steamers. Group 1 comprised 39 vessels laid down to July 1855 and Group 2 the remainder except the light draught *Serkira*, *Kop'e*, *Shlem*, *Pishchal'*, *Kolchan* and *Luk* which formed Group 3. Machinery supplied by Baird, the Aleksandrovskiy Works, Galvanoplastic Works, Izhora Works, Kronshtadt Dockyard, Nobel and Thomson.

Tyulen' 1 Augustin Normand, Le Havre
Constructor ?
Laid down 15.12.1859 *Launched* 1.7.1860
Dimensions 119 ft 9 in (pp) x 19 ft (outside plank) x ? x 4 ft 9 in/ 5 ft 3 in (draught fore/aft)
  215 tons displacement
Armament 1 x 60pdr (5 ton) pivot, 2 x 3.4 in rifles (60pdr replaced by a long 30pdr in 1867)
Machinery 40 nhp (Maudslay) = 9 kts
Screw steamer. Commissioned into the Baltic fleet in August 1860. Transferred to the Caspian Sea in 1862. Rebuilt at Baku in 1877. Stricken in 1892.

Morzh class

Morzh 2 Augustin Normand, Le Havre
Constructor ?
Laid down 27.12.1859 *Launched* 19.6.1860
Dimensions 148 ft 9 in (pp) x 22 ft 11 in (outside plank) x ? x 7 ft 8 in/ 8 ft 4 in (draught fore/aft)
  377 tons bm, 456.7 tons displacement
Armament 1861 2 x 60pdr (5 ton) pivot 4 x 3.4-in rifled
  1880 1 x 6-in rifled, 6 x 3.4-in rifled
Machinery 80 nhp/292 ihp (Maudslay) = 9.82 kts
Morzh class (3 ships). Screw steamer. Commissioned for the Pacific on 4 January 1861. Arrived at St Olga Bay near Vladivostok on 25 April. Stricken 3 May 1892.

Sobol' 2 Reposaari Shipbuilding Co., Bjorneborg
Constructor ?
Laid down 20.8.1862 *Launched* 27.4.1863
Dimensions 148 ft 9 in (pp) x 22 ft 11 in (outside plank) x ? x 7 ft 8 in/ 8 ft 4 in (draught fore/aft)
  377 tons bm, 456.7 tons displacement
Armament 1862 2 x 60pdr (5 ton) pivot, 4 x 3.4-in rifled
  1880 2 x 6-in rifled, 4 x 3.4-in rifled
Machinery 80 nhp (Kronshtadt Dockyard) = 9 kts
Morzh class (3 ships). Screw steamer. Original machinery by the Pori Mechanical Workshop Co replaced in 1864. Commissioned for the Pacific on 3 August 1865. Arrived at Vladivostok on 8 June 1866. Stricken 3 May 1892.

Gornostai 2 Reposaari Shipbuilding Co., Bjorneborg
Constructor ?
Laid down 20.8.1862 *Launched* 27.4.1863
Dimensions 148 ft 9 in (pp) x 22 ft 11 in (outside plank) x ? x 7 ft 8 in/ 8 ft 4 in (draught fore/aft)
  377 tons bm, 456.7 tons displacement
Armament 1861 2 x 60pdr (5 ton), pivot 4 x 3.4-in rifled
  1880 2 x 6-in rifled, 4 x 3.4-in rifled
Machinery 80 nhp (Kronshtadt Dockyard) = 9 kts
Morzh class (3 ships). Screw steamer. Original machinery by the Pori Mechanical Workshop Co. replaced in 1864. Commissioned on 3 August 1865 but did not leave for the Pacific until 12 August 1866. Arrived at Nikolaev-on-Amur on 5 August 1867. Stricken 19 December 1893.

Postscript: the Russian Navy 1861

By 1861 Russia had created a battle fleet of 9 screw ships of the line, a cruising force of 47 screw frigates, clippers and corvettes supplemented by 9 mostly older paddle frigates, and for coastal defence a flotilla of 79 screw gunboats; in all 144 steam warships built, building and to be built. The sailing fleet then comprised 10 ships of the line, 5 frigates, 3 corvettes and 3 brigs. Later that year in October the Russian Admiralty ordered the conversion of the recently commenced frigate Petropavlovsk into an ironclad. The order to convert *Sevastopol'* followed in July 1862. The 1861 edition of the official guide to the Russian Navy, *Pamyatnaya Knizhka Morskogo Vedomstva*, therefore detailed the unarmoured steam fleet shortly before the decision to construct ironclads was reached. The following material is taken directly from that edition and thus forms a suitable end point to this book. Also detailed in *Pamyatnaya Knizhka* were a wide variety of auxiliary steamers which have been omitted below. The remaining sailing ships were briefly listed as well.

The following data appears exactly as it does in *Pamyatnaya Knizhka* apart from the correction of a couple of typographical errors and the addition of a leading '1' to each year (the original truncates years to, for example, '861'). The columns are 'Name' (self-explanatory), 'Guns' (rated armament), 'H.P.' (nhp), 'Tonnage Disp.' (tonnage displacement at load draught), 'Tonnage B.M.' (tonnage bm), 'Length' (on the load waterline), 'Breadth' (outside plank), 'Draught Aft' (in load condition), 'Draught Fore' (in load condition), 'Launched' (the year of launch or last major repair/rebuilding) and 'Machinery' (the year machinery completed). Where no data appears in a cell none appears in the original, meaning it was unavailable. The launch year for all ships on the stocks is blank as is the year of machinery completion for most such vessels. For no apparent reason dates for the new gunboat *Tyulen'* are missing and so have been added below. Data on sailing ships comprises 'Name', 'Guns' and 'Launched' as in *Pamyatnaya Knizhka*. Notes on warships recently struck from the list of the fleet (lost in one case) have been added from other references.

The source tables in *Pamyatnaya Knizhka* provide information on the builders of hull and machinery (and these will be found in the main text above) as well as cost, but armament details are given separately as are details of the ships in commission, their commanders, etc. There are, however, a few anomalies in the data. For example, the breadth of the *Boyarin* class corvettes is given as 31 ft 1 in but in other sources as 31 ft 11 ins (or 9.73 m). The latter figure is as measured 'outside plank' which suggests the former is actually 'inside plank'. Readers will thus notice an occasional discrepancy between the data below and that in the main text. The data in the main text is considered the more reliable in these cases. For most steamers in the main text length is defined as that between perpendiculars (which is as Veselago defines it) but is usually identical to the load waterline length quoted in *Pamyatnaya Knizhka*. It should also be noted that 75 gunboats built for the Baltic during the Crimean War are not listed individually in the ships' data table of *Pamyatnaya Knizhka* and therefore appear below as a group just as they do in the original. Only two gunboats are in fact named, *Tyulen'* (Baltic fleet) and *Morzh* (Siberian Flotilla), while another two unnamed vessels appear as proposed for the Siberian Flotilla. (This pair was eventually built to the same design as *Morzh* and named *Sobol'* and *Gornostai*.)

Among the auxiliaries were several ships that had been built or begun as warships but converted to ancillary roles to comply with the Treaty of Paris signed in 1856 at the end of the Crimean War. The treaty included severe limitations on the number and size of warships that Turkey and Russia could maintain in the Black Sea. These ships were the former paddle frigates *Vladimir* and *Tigr* and former screw corvette *Voin*. Data on these is to be found in the main text.

Later editions of *Pamyatnaya Knizhka Morskogo Vedomstva* continued to include ships' data into the early years of the twentieth century. Thereafter such information was published in classified form. As a reference, however, it is not well known outside Russia. The following extract thus provides readers with a useful sample of the sort of material it contained.

Russian Navy 1861 steam warships

Name	Guns	nhp	Tonnage Disp.	Tonnage bm	Length ft in	Breadth ft in	Draught aft ft in	Draught fore ft in	Launched	Machinery
Baltic fleet										
Ships of the Line										
Oryol	84	450	3,713	2,385	202 8	51 8	23 6	20 9	1854	1858
Konstantin	78	450	3,697	2,631	215 0	53 2	23 0	21 6	1854	1858
Vyborg	72	450	3,505	2,496	215 0	51 8	23 0	21 6	1854	1856
Retvizan	81	500	3,823	2,641	215 10	52 8	23 1	21 7	1855	1857,
Gangut	81	500	3,814	2,659	212 0	53 8	23 1	21 7	1856	1857
Vola	81	500	3,814	2,659	212 0	53 8	23 1	21 7	1856	1857
Imperator Nikolai I	111	600	5426	3,469	233 6	58 3½	26 0	25 2	1860	1860
Sinop	135	800	5,585	3,813	242 2	59 6	25 10	24 2	1857	1860
Tsesarevich	135	800	5,563	3,821	241 6	60 0	25 9	24 5	1857	1860
Frigates										
Polkan	44	360	2,316	1,793	199 6	44 6	21 0	19 4	1853	1854
Askol'd	45	360	2,834	2,126	206 6	48 6	21 0	20 0	1854	1857
Il'ia Muromets	53	360	3,199	2,337	212 0	50 0	22 0	21 0	1857	1859
Gromoboi	53	360	3,199	2,337	212 0	50 0	22 0	21 0	1857	1858

POSTSCRIPT: THE RUSSIAN NAVY 1861

Name	Guns	nhp	Tonnage Disp.	bm	Length ft	in	Breadth ft	in	Draught aft ft	in	Draught fore ft	in	Launched	Machinery
Osliabia	45	360	2,958	2,280	230	0	46	6	20	6	18	6	1860	1860
Peresvet	51	450	3,837	2,921	251	0	50	0	22	4	20	4	1860	1860
General Admiral	70	800	5,669	4,386	305	0	54	8	23	6	22	1	1858	1859
Svetlana	40	450	3,188	2,458	229	7	47	10	21	6	18	6	1858	1858
Oleg	57	800	4,408	3,371	253	0	53	0	23	3	21	9	1860	1860
Alexander Nevskiy	51	800	4,562	3,315	272	0	51	0	23	6	21	6		1861
Dmitrii Donskoi	51	800	4,562	3,315	272	0	51	0	23	6	21	6		1861
Sevastopol	58	800	5,274	3,590	300	0	50	4	24	0	22	2		
Petropavlovsk	58	800	5,274	3,590	300	0	50	4	24	0	22	2		
Clippers														
Razboynik	6	150	615	548	152	0	27	10	12	11	10	11	1856	1856
Oprichnik	6	150	615	548	152	0	27	10	12	11	10	11	1856	1856
Strelok	6	150	615	548	152	0	27	10	12	11	10	11	1856	1856
Naezdnik	6	150	615	548	152	0	27	10	12	11	10	11	1856	1856
Dzhigit	6	150	615	548	152	0	27	10	12	11	10	11	1856	1856
Vsadnik	5	300	1,069	895	200	0	31	1	13	2	12	2	1860	1860
Abrek	5	300	1,069	895	200	0	31	1	13	2	12	2	1860	1860
Gaidamak	7	250	1,094	1,001	213	5	31	4	10	6	10	6	1860	1860
Zhemchug	7	350	1,585	1,154	250	0	30	9	15	6	13	2		
Almaz	7	350	1,585	1,154	250	0	30	9	15	6	13	2		
Izumrud	7	350	1,585	1,154	250	0	30	9	15	6	13	2		
Iakhont	7	350	1,585	1,154	250	0	30	9	15	6	13	2		
Corvettes														
Boyarin	11	200	885	762	163	4	31	1	14	0	12	4½	1856	1856
Posadnik	11	200	885	762	163	4	31	1	14	0	12	4½	1856	1856
Rynda	11	200	885	762	163	4	31	1	14	0	12	4½	1856	1856
Voevoda	11	200	885	762	163	4	31	1	14	0	12	4½	1856	1856
Novik	11	200	885	762	163	4	31	1	14	0	12	4½	1856	1856
Griden'	11	200	885	762	163	4	31	1	14	0	12	4½	1856	1856
Vol	11	200	885	762	163	4	31	1	14	0	12	4½	1856	1856
Medved'	11	200	885	762	163	4	31	1	14	0	12	4½	1856	1856
Kalevala	15	250	1,290	1,062	166	0	38	8	15	6	14	0	1858	1858
Baian	16	300	1,969	1,479	216	5½	36	0	18	2½	16	6¾	1857	1857
Bogatyr'	17	360	2,155	1,586	220	0	39	4	19	3	17	3	1860	1860
Varyag	17	360	2,156	1,609	225	0	39	8	19	3	17	3		
Vityaz'	17	360	2,156	1,609	225	0	39	8	19	3	17	3		
Gunboats			Light draught units											
		50	175		128	11	22	8	4	0	4	0	1855	1855
75 vessels	3	to	Deep draught units										to	to
		75	177		111	10	21	2	7	0	7	0	1856	1856
Tyulen'	1	40	215		119	9	19	0	5	3	4	9	1860	1860
Steamers														
Kamchatka	14	540	2,124	1,375	210	0	36	11	17	8	17	8	1841	1843
Olaf	14	400	1,796	1,203	198	0	36	2	15	4	15	4	1852	1852
Gremiashchii	4	400	1,501	1,126	190	0	36	0	13	6	13	0	1851	1851,
Smelyi	8	400	1,784	1,173	199	10	36	2	15	4	15	4	1858	1844
Groziashchii	4	400	1,500	1,103	190	0	36	0	13	6	13	0	1844	1843
Riurik	4	300	1,507	983	185	0	33	10	13	9¼	13	9¼	1852	1852
Khrabryi	8	300	1,450	975	185	0	33	2¼	15	2	14	11	1858	1844
Vladimir	5	350		758	187	0	29	0	13	6	13	6	1846	

White Sea flotilla

Steamer

Name	Guns	nhp	Tonnage	bm	Length ft	in	Breadth ft	in	Draught aft ft	in	Draught fore ft	in	Launched	Machinery
Solombala	8	240	1,180	1004	190	0	33	2	12	5	12	5	1859	1859

Name	Guns	nhp	Tonnage Disp.	bm	Length ft in	Breadth ft in	Draught aft ft in	Draught fore ft in	Launched	Machinery

Siberian flotilla

Gunboats

Name	Guns	nhp	Disp.	bm	ft	in	ft	in	ft	in	ft	in	Launched	Machinery
Morzh	2	80	464	394	149	1	22	10½	8	3	7	9	1860	1860
NN		60			130	0	25	0	8	0	8	0		
NN		60			130	0	25	0	8	0	8	0		

Black Sea flotilla

Corvettes

Name	Guns	nhp	Disp.	bm	ft	in	ft	in	ft	in	ft	in	Launched	Machinery
Zubr	11	200	885	762	163	4	31	1	14	0	12	4½	1856	1856
Buivol	11	200	885	762	163	4	31	1	14	0	12	4½	1856	1856
Rys	11	200	885	762	163	4	31	1	14	0	12	4½	1856	1856
Vepr'	11	200	885	762	163	4	31	1	14	0	12	4½	1856	1856
Volk	11	200	885	762	163	4	31	1	14	0	12	4½	1856	1856
Udav	11	200	885	762	163	4	31	1	14	0	12	4½	1856	1856
Sokol	9	220	1,017		164	0	32	4	14	4	14	0	1858	1859
Iastreb	9	220	1,017		164	0	32	4	14	4	14	0	1859	1859
Krechet	9	220	980		164	0	32	3	14	8	12	7	1860	1860

Notes: Clipper *Plastun* (*Razboynik* class launched in 1856) was lost off Gotland on 18 August 1860 (OS). Steamer *Otvazhnyi* (300 nhp launched in 1843) was struck from the list of the fleet on 8 April 1861 (OS).

Russian Navy 1861 sailing warships

Baltic fleet

Ships of the line

Name	Guns	Launched
Prokhor	84	Launched 1851
Andrei	84	Launched 1844
Imperator Pyotr I	110	Launched 1850
Vladimir	84	Launched 1851
Imperatritsa Aleksandra	84	Launched 1851
Ne Tron' Menia	84	Launched 1850
Krasnoi	84	Launched 1847
Pamiat' Azova	74	Launched 1848
Iezekiil'	74	Launched 1847
Velikii Kniaz' Mikhail	74	Launched 1852

Frigates

Name	Guns	Launched
Sysoi Velikii	60	Launched 1849
Vilagosh	60	Launched 1851
Kastor	44	Launched 1854
Borodino	60	Launched 1850
Narva	60	Launched 1846

Corvettes

Name	Guns	Launched
Kniaz' Varshavskii	20	Launched 1850
Smolensk	30	Launched 1850
Olivutsa	20	Launched 1844

Brigs

Name	Guns	Launched
Agamemnon	20	Launched 1849
Palinur	20	Launched 1850

Blockship

Avrora

White Sea flotilla

Brig

Name	Guns	Launched
Novaia Zemlia	16	Launched 1845

Notes: Ship of the line *Prokhor* serving as a gunnery training vessel. Year of launch year for *Imperator Pyotr I*, *Vladimir*, *Imperatritsa Aleksandra*, *Ne Tron' Menia*, *Velikii Kniaz' Mikhail*, *Kastor*, *Kniaz' Varschavskiy*, *Smolensk*, *Olivutsa*, *Agamemnon*, and *Palinur* is that of last repair. Frigate *Avrora* (44 guns launched in 1835) and brig *Antenor* (20 guns launched in 1836) were struck from the list of the fleet on 8 April 1861 (OS).

Appendices

A Russian and Swedish fleets in June 1714

Russian fleet on 20 June 1714 (1 July 1714)
Leferm (74) Commodore Sivers
Sv. Ekaterina (62) Peter I as Vice-Adm.
Viktoriia (62)
Gavriil (52)
Sv. Antonii (52)
Poltava (52) Commodore Shelting
Pernov (52)
Riga (52)
Rafail (52)
Fortuna (52)
Perl (50)
Armont (50)
Randol'f (50)
Oksford (50)
Esperans (48)
Arondel' (44)
Sv. Pyotr (32)
Samson (32)
Sv. Pavel (32)
Sv. Il'ia (32)
Landsdou (32)
Printsessa (20)
Natal'ia (18)
Diana (18)

Swedish fleet at Gangut 27 July 1714 (7 August 1714)
Prins Karl Fredrik (72) Schoutbijnacht Ankarstierna
Vastmanland (64)
Bremen (64) Admiral Wattrang
Stockholm (64) Schoutbijnacht Ehrensjiold
Fredrika Amalia (64)
Skane (62)
Sodermanland (56)
Pommern (56)
Öland (56) Vice-Adm. Lillje
Liffland (54)
Verden (54)
Halland (54)
Riga (54)
Goteborg (50)
Gottland (50)
Wachtmeister (50)
Reval (40)
Anklam (34)
Fenix (32)
Wollgast (28)
Falken (20)
Askedunder bomb
Strombolo bomb
Goya (18) brig
Pollux (16) brig
4 fire-ships

B Russian fleet on 6 May 1743 (17 May 1743)

Sv. Aleksandr (76)
Severnyi Oryol (66)
Revel' (66)
Slava Rossii (66)
Sv. Pyotr (66) Adm. Golovin
Ingermanland (66)
Osnovanie Blagopoluchiia (66)
Gorod Arkhangel'sk (54)
Kronshtadt (54)
Astrakhan' (54) Rear-Adm. Barsh
Azov (54)
Neptunus (54) Rear-Adm. Kalmykov
Severnaia Zvezda (54)
Sv. Andrei (54)
Rossiia (32)
Voin (32)
Samson mortar (14)
Iupiter mortar (10)
Mitau fireship (6)
Brilliant fireship
Tonein galiot
Lotsman galiot
Shturman galiot
Novaia Nadezhda hospital ship
Minerva yacht
Novyi Pochtal'on packet boat

Novaia Nadezhda, a hospital ship, was included in a line of battle 'to create impression on the enemy'.

C Russian and Swedish orders of battle on 13 May 1743

Russian fleet
Sv. Aleksandr (76) Rear-Adm. Kalmykov
Sv. Pyotr (66) Adm. Golovin
Severnyi Oryol (66)
Revel' (66)
Ingermanland (66)
Slava Rossii (66)
Osnovanie Blagopoluchiia (66)
Gorod Arkhangel'sk (54)
Kronshtadt (54)
Astrakhan' (54) Rear-Adm. Barsh
Azov (54)
Neptunus (54)
Severnaia Zvezda (54)
Sv. Andrei (54)
Voin (32)
Rossiia (32)
Samson (14) mortar
Iupiter (10) mortar
Mitau (6) fireship
Brilliant fireship
Tonein galiot
Lotsman galiot
Shturman galiot
Vest-Inzhi sloop
Minerva yacht
Novyi Pochtal'on packet-boat
Novaia Nadezhda hospital ship
S. Apostol Pavel (80) joined the fleet on 28 June after the cessation of hostilities.

Swedish fleet
Drottning Ulrika Elenora (84) Adm. von Utfall
Friheten (66) Commodore Stoldtz
Enigheten (72) Vice-Adm. Sjostierna
Drottningholm (42)
Goumlta 68
Hessen-Cassel (64) Commodore von Stauden
Prinsessan Sofia Charlotta (64)
Prins Vilhelm (64)
Vastmanland (62)
Fredrika Amalia (62)
Scaringne (62)
Pommern (60)
Stockholm (60)
Bremen (60)
Finland (56/60)
Verden (54)
Freden (42)
Jaramas (36)
Fama (32)
Karlberg (22)
Kristina (22)
Ekholmsund (26)
Castor (18)
Pollux (18)
Sjoumlkatten (6)
Thordon (6) mortar ship
Askedunder (6) mortar ship
Later, the newly completed *Fredrik Rex* (62) (Adm. of the Fleet Taub) joined the fleet.

D Baltic fleet Units Dispatched to the Arkhipelago Campaign 1768–74

First Arkhipelago Squadron dispatched from Kronshtadt 26.7.1769
Trekh Ierarkhov (66) 1765 flag to Admiral Orlov, Gen.-en-chef
Evstafii Plakida (66) 1763 flag to Admiral Spiridov
Sviatoi Ianuarii (66) 1763
Severnyi Oryol (66) 1763 converted into a 32-gun hospital ship at Portsmouth
Trekh Sviatitelei (66) 1765

Evropa (66) 1768
Rostislav (66) 1768
Nadezhda Blagopoluchiia (34) 1764
Grom bomb vessel
2 packet boats
4 pinks

Second Arkhipelago Squadron dispatched from Kronshtadt 9.10.1769
Sviatoslav (80) 1769 flag to Rear-Admiral Elphinston, originally assigned to First Squadron
Ne Tron' Menia (66) 1763
Saratov (66) 1765
Tver' (66) 1765 forced to return to Revel'
Afrika (32) 1768
Nadezhda (32) 1762

Third Arkhipelago Squadron dispatched from Revel' on 15.6.1770
Vsevolod (66) 1769
Sviatoi Georgii Pobedonosets (66) 1770 flag to Rear-Adm. Arff
Aziia (54) 1766

Fourth Arkhipelago Squadron dispatched from Revel' on 8.5.1772
Chesma (80) 1770 flag to Rear-Adm. Chichagov
Pobeda (66) 1770
Graf Orlov (66) 1770

Fifth Arkhipelago Squadron dispatched 21.10.1773
Sviatoi Velikomuchenik Isidor 1772 flag to Rear-Adm. Greig
Aleksandr Nevskii (66) 1772
Sviatykh Zhen Mironosits (66) 1771
Pavel (32) 1773
Natal'ia (32) 1773

E Armed Neutrality Squadrons 1780–2

Barents Sea Squadron under Rear-Adm. Khmetevskiy 1779
Viacheslav (66)
Preslava (66)

Mediterranean Squadron under Rear-Admiral Borisov 1780–1
Sviatoi Velikomuchenik Isidor (76)
Tvyordyi (66) in 1780–1
Aziia (66)
Patrikii (32)
Amerika (66)
Simion (32)
Slava Rossii (66) wrecked

Portuguese Squadron under Rear-Admiral Palibin 1780-81
Iezekiil' (78)
Deris (66)
Sviatoi Kniaz' Vladimir (66)
David Selunskii (66)
Spiridon (66)
Aleksandr (32/38)

North Sea Squadron under Admiral Kruz 1780–2
Sviatoi Velikomuchenik Panteleimon (74) in 1780
Sviatoi Nikolai (66)
Mariia (32) in 1781–2
Aleksandr Nevskii (66)
Tvyordyi (66) in 1782
Ingermanlandiia (66)
Simion (32) in 1782
Blagopoluchie (66)

Mediterranean Squadron under Rear-Admiral Sukhotin 1781–2
Sviatoi Velikomuchenik Panteleimon (74) in 1781–2
Ne Tron' Menia (66)
Evropa (66)
Voin (32/38)
Pamyat' Evstafii Plakida (66)
Mariia (32) in 1781–2
Viktor (66)

F Black Sea fleet in 1790

Ioann Predtecha Turkish prize (82)
Tsar' Konstantin (46)
Rozhdestvo Khristovo (78) flag to Adm. Ushakov
Fyodor Stratilat (46)
Ioann Bogoslov (46)
Sv. Troitsa (Soshestvie Sv. Dukha) (72)
Kazanskaya Bogoroditsa (46)
Soshestvie Sv. Dukha (44)
Bogoiavlenie Gospodne (72)
Navarkhiia (44)
Sv. Pavel (70)
Prepodobnyi Nestor (40)
Sv. Vladimir (70)
Makropleia (Sv. Mark) (36)
Mariia Magdalina (68)
Sv. Ieronim (34)
Preobrazhenie Gospodne (68)
Ioann Zlatoust (32)
Leontii Muchenik (58)
Grigorii Velikiia Armenii (16)
Sv. Georgii Pobedonosets (50)
Nikita Muchenik (20)
Sv. Andrei Pervozvannyy (50)
Sv. Nikon (18)
Sv. Nikolai (50)
Sergii Radonezhskii (18)
Aleksandr Nevskii (46)
Ioann Voinstvennik (6) storeship
Pyotr Apostol (46)

G Russian Squadron Dispatched to England in June 1795

The fleet under Vice-Admiral Khanykov comprised members of both the Kronshtadt and Revel' squadrons. It left Kronshtadt on 12 June 1795 and anchored in the Downs on 7 August.

Pamiat' Evstafii (74) flag to Vice-Adm. Khnayakov
Retvizan (66)
Nikanor (66)
Pyotr (74) flag to Rear-Adm. Thate
Filipp (66)
Venus (44)
Gleb (74)
Kronshtadt (44)
Sviataia Elena (74)
Arkhipelag (44)
Iona (66) flag to Rear-Adm. Makarov
Riga (44)
Mikhail (44)
Pimen (66)
Revel' (44)
Graf Orlov (66)
Narva (44)
Parmen (66)
Rafail (44)
Evropa (66)

H Russian Squadrons Dispatched to England in 1798

The fleet under the overall command of Vice-Adm. Makarov went to England in three separate divisions.

1st Division under Vice-Adm. Makarov himself left Kronshtadt in May and at the beginning of July joined with the squadron of Vice-Adm. Duncan (10 ships of the line, 2 frigates, 1 brig), who was the senior commander on station.
Elisabeta (74) (flag) 1795
Retvizan (66) 1783
Mstislav (74) 1785
Evropa (66) 1793

Boleslav (66) 1783
Narva (40) 1790
Dispich (or *Dispatch*) (20) cutter bought in England in 1796

2nd division under Vice-Adm. Thate left Arkhangel'sk in May and arrived at Nore in August.
Vsevolod (74) (flag) 1796
Pobeda (66) 1797
Severnyi Oryol (74) 1797
Schastlivyi (44) 1798
Isidor (74) 1795
Pospeshnyi (38) 1798
Aziia (66) 1796

3rd division under Rear-Adm. Kartsev departed Revel' on 20 August 1798, delayed due to severe storm damage.
Prints Gustav (74) (flag) Swedish prize built in 1758; captured in 1788, lost in transit
Sviatoi Pyotr (74) 1786; forced to return to Kronshtadt due to storm damage
Aleksei (74) 1790; delayed by storm damage
Sofiia Magdalina (74) Swedish prize built in 1774; captured in 1788, delayed by storm damage
Iziaslav (66) 1784; delayed by storm damage, repaired in England in 5.1789
Riga (44) 1790; delayed by storm damage

I Admiral Chichagov's Squadron to England, September 1799

Aleksandr Nevskii (74)
Sv. Ianuarii (66)
Mikhail (66)
Emgeiten (66)
Iona (66)
Five supporting frigates

J Black Sea Expeditionary fleet April, 1798

Sv. Pavel (82)
Zakharii i Elisavet (74)
Sv. Troitsa (76)
Bogoiavlenie Gospodne (72)
Sv. Pyotr (74)
Mariia Magdalina (68)
Sviatoi Kniaz' Vladimir (68) damaged in collision and forced to return to Sevastopol.
Grigorii Velikiia Armenii (50)
Nikolai (46)
Mikhail (48)
Navarkhiia Voznesenie Gospodne (40)
Soshestvie Sviatogo Dukha (44)
Kazanskaya Bogoroditsa (46)
Schastlivyi (36)
Aleksandr Nevskii (46)

K Ships assigned to the Mediterranean Theatre in 1807

Black Sea ships stationed at Corfu
Mariia Magdalina (74) 1799
Krepkii (54) 1801
Sviataia Paraskeva (74) 1799
Nazaret (46) 1800
Aziia (66) 1796 transferred to Black Sea fleet in 1800
Sviatoi Mikhail (50) 1796

Commodore Greig's 1804 Mediterranean Squadron
Sviataia Elena (74) 1785
Retvizan (62) 1790 Swedish prize
Venus (44) 1793 Swedish prize
Avtroil (24) 1789 Swedish prize (rowing frigate)

Vice-Admiral Seniavin's 1805 Mediterranean Squadron
Arkhangel Uriil (80) 1802
Sviatoi Pyotr (74) 1799
Moskva (74) 1799
Selafail (74) 1802
Iaroslav (74) 1799
Kildyuin (32)

Commodore Ignatyev's 1806 Mediterranean Squadron
Rafail (80) 1802
Skoryi (60) 1805
Tvyordyi (80) 1805
Legkii 38 1803
Sil'nyi (74) 1804
Shpitsbergen (32) 1805
Moshchnyi (66) 1805

Lesser warships purchased or otherwise acquired
Corvettes
Grigorii (24) 1788 (?) (BS) corvette, uncertain origin, listed only by R. C. Anderson
Dneper (18) (BS) corvette, uncertain origin, listed only by R. C. Anderson
Al'tsinoe (18) 1805 corvette, purchased in the Mediterranean by Seniavin
Pavel (18) 1804 (BS) corvette, converted at Kherson
Diomid (24) 1805 (BS) corvette, converted at Kherson
Kherson (24) 1805 (BS) corvette, converted at Kherson
Derzkii (28) 1806 corvette, purchased at Monte-Negro
Verona (22) 1806 corvette, purchased at Monte-Negro
Feniks (18) 1805 brig, Seniavin's squadron, purchased in England
Argus 12 1805 brig, Seniavin's squadron, purchased in England
Letun 12 1805 brig, Seniavin's squadron, purchased at Malta
Bogoiavlensk (16) 1806 brig, purchased in the Mediterranean
Oryol (16) brig, purchased in the Mediterranean
Aleksandr (16) 1804 (BS) brig
Bonasorte (16) 1799 (BS)brig
Ekspeditsion (16) poliaka captured from the French at Corfu in 1799
Zabiiaka (14) shebeck, French prize captured in 1806
Azard (14) shebeck, French prize captured in 1807

L Russian Ships Evacuated to England in 1812

Arkhangel'sk fleet under Vice-Admiral Crown
Nord-Adler (74) 1811
Prints Gustav (74) 1811
Ne Tron' Menia (74) 1809
Trekh Ierarkhov (74) 1809
Sviatoslav (74) 1809
Vsevolod (66) 1809, separated in transit, wintered in Norway, arrived in 1813
Saratov (66) 1809, grounded and destroyed at Sveaborg
Pobedonosets (64) 1809

Kronshtadt fleet under Admiral Thate
Khrabryi (120) 1808, erroneously listed as a 74 by Anderson
Smelyi (88) 1808 erroneously listed as a 74 by Anderson
Trekh Sviatitelei (74) 1810
Bystryi (44) 1807 frigate
Borey (74) 1807
Arkhipelag (44) 1811 frigate
Severnaia Zvezda (74) 1807
Sveaborg (36) 1809 frigate and Admiral Thate's flagship
Pamiat' Evstafii (74) 1810
Oryol (74) 1807
Kastor (36) 1807 frigate
Iupiter (74) 1812
Gonets (20) 1808 brig
Chesma (74) 1811
Poluks (32) 1812 frigate arrived in 1812
Sviatyk zhen mironosits (74) 1811
Venera (56) 1808 frigate

Select Bibliography

Anderson, R.C. *Naval Wars in the Baltic*, Robert Stockwell Ltd, London, 1910

Anderson, R. C. *Naval Wars in the Levant*, Princeton University, 1952

Andrienko, V. G. Prodazha Russkoy Eskadry Ispani in 1817–1818 ('The Sale of the Russian Squadron to Spain in 1817–18'), *Gangut* no. 39, St Petersburg, 2006

Bourchier, Lady (Jane) *Memoir of the Life of Admiral Sir Edward Codrington*, Longmans, Green, and Co., London, 1873

Bykhovsky, Israel Adolfovich *Petrovskie Korabely* [Peter's Shipwrights], Sudostroenie, Leningrad, 1982

Chernyshev, A. A. *Rossiiskii Parusnyi Flot: Spravochnik* [The Russian Sailing Fleet: Reference Book], Voennoe. Izdatelstvo, vols 1–2, 1997–2002

Cross, Anthony Glenn *By the Banks of the Neva: Chapters from the Lives and Careers of the British in Eighteenth-century Russia*, Cambridge University Press, 1977

Daly, John C. *Russian Seapower and 'The Eastern Question' 1827–41*, Naval Institute Press, Annapolis MA, 1991

Danilov, A. M. *Lineinye Korabli I Fregaty Russkogo Parusnogo Flota* [Ships of the Line and Frigates of the Russian Sailing Navy], Amalfeia, Minsk, 1996

Elagin, Capt. S. A.(ed.) *'Istoriya Russkogo flota'. Period Azovskiy'*, 1864 (History of Russian Navy. The Azov Period), Tipografiya Gogenfeldena i Ko, St Petersburg, 1875

Fincham, John *A History of Naval Architecture*, Whittaker and Company, London, 1851

Glete, Jan *Navies and Nations, Warships, Navies and State Building in Europe and America 1500–1860 vols I and II*, Almqvist & Wiksell International, Stockholm, 1993

Glete, Jan 'Den svenska linjeflottan 1721–1860: En översikt av dess struktur och storlek samt några synpunkter på behovet av ytterligare forskning,' ['The Swedish battle fleet, 1721–1860: An overview of its structure and size with some consideration of the need for further research.'] *Forum Navale*, no. 45 (1990)

Golovachev, V. F. *Deystviya Russkogo Flota v Voyne so Shvedami 1788–1790* ('Operations of Russian Fleet in the War with Sweden 1788-1790'), Tipographiya Morskogo Ministerstva, St Petersburg, 1873

Golovachev, V. F. *Istoriya Sevastopolya kak Russkogo Porta* (History of Sevastopol as a Russian Port), Izdanie Sevastopolskogo Odtela na Politekhnicheskoy Vystavke, St Petersburg, 1872

Gomm, Berhard, *Russische Kriegsschiffe 1856–1917*, 4 vols, Wiesbaden, 1989–2000

Grebenshchikova, G. A. *'Dvenadtsat' Apostolov'* (series 'Midel-Shpangout', no. 5 (10) 2003)

Grebenshchikova, G. A. *100-pushechnye korabli tipa 'Victory' v russko-shvedskoi' i napoleonovskikh voinakh* (100-gunned Ships of the 'Victory' Class), Izdatelstvo Ostrov, St Petersburg, 2006

Houghton, John *Ships of the Line and Frigates of the Navies of the World 1835–1840*, Melbourne, 1999

Hughes, Lindsey, *Russia in the Age of Peter the Great*, Yale University Press, New Haven and London, 1998

Ilyin, Lieutenant A. A. *Nauka Morskoy Artillerii* (Science of Naval Ordnance), 'V tipografii Shtaba Voenno-Uchebnykh Zavedeniy', St Petersburg, 1846

Jägerskiöld, Olaf *Den svenska utrikespolitikens historia, II:2, 1721–1792*, Stockholm, 1957

Krotkov, A. *Russkiy Flot v Tsarstvovanie Imperatritsy Ekateriny II in 1772–1783* [The Russian Navy in the Reign of Empress Catherine II], Tipografiya Morskogo Ministerstva, St Petersburg, 1889

Kuznetsov, L.A. 'Russkaya Eskadra dlya Ispanskogo Korolya' ['The Russian Squadron for the King of Spain'], *Gangut Magazine* no. 31 and 33, 2002–3

Lanitzki, Günter *Kanonendonner über Ostseewellen: der schwedisch-russische Seekrieg von 1788 bis 1790* [Cannon thunder over the Baltic Sea waves: the Swedish-Russian naval warfare from 1788 to 1790] Frieling, Berlin, 2002

Lehti, Aarni, and Karl Immonen *Porin Puiset Slotalaivat* [Imperial Sloops of War from Porin], Porin, 2006. (Available in PDF format from the Wikipedia site 'List of Russian steam frigates' at http://en.wikipedia.org/wiki/List_of_Russian_steam_frigates)

Mitchell, Donald W. *A History of Russian and Soviet Sea Power*, Andre Deutsch, London, 1974

Milyutin, D. *Istoriia Voyny 1799 Goda mechdu Rossiey i Frantsiey* [History of War between Russia and France], V Tiporgafii Imperatorskoy Akademii Nauk, St Petersburg, 1852–3

Munthe, Arnold *Flottan och ryska kriget, 1788–1790: Otto Henrik Nordenskjöld* [Fleet and Russian War, 1788–1790: Otto Henrik Nordenskjöld], Svenska sjöhjältar (Swedish sea heroes no. 7), Norstedt, Stockholm 1914–17

Oakley, Stewart P. *War and Peace in the Baltic 1560–1790*, Routledge, London and New York, 1992

Phillips, Edward J. *The Founding of Russia's Navy, Peter the Great and the Azov Fleet, 1688-1714*, Greenwood Press, Westport CT and London, 1995

Piechowiak, A. B, 'The Anglo-Russian Expedition to Holland in 1799', *The Slavonic and East European review*, 1962

Popov, A. A. Ingermanland, *Zapiski Uchenogo Komiteta Glavnogo Morskogo Shtaba* [Proceedings of the Scientific Committee of the Chief Naval Staff] Part 5, St Petersburg, 1835

Sapherson, C. A. and J. R. Lenton *Navy Lists from the Age of Sail Volume Six 1787–1791, The Russian Navy Comes of Age*, Partizan Press, Leigh on Sea, Essex, 1996

St Hubert, Christian and Boris Drashpil 'Main Shipyards, Engine Builders and Manufacturers of Guns and Armour Plate in the St Petersburg Area Up to 1917', *Warship International*, no. 4, 1985

Saul, Norman E. *Russia and the Mediterranean 1797–1807*, University of Chicago Press, Chicago and London, 1970

Saul, Norman E. 'The Russian Navy, 1682–1854: Some Suggestions for Further Study', *New Aspects of Naval History*, ed. Craig L. Symonds, Naval Institute Press, Annapolis, 1981.

Shaw, Stanford J. *Between Old and New: The Ottoman Empire under Sultan Selim III, 1789–1807*, Harvard University Press, Cambridge MA, 1791

Shirokorad, Alexander Borisovich *200 let parusnogo flota Rossii [1696–1891 gg.]* [200 Years of the Sailing Navy of Russia, Veche, Moscow, 2007

Sokolov, A. *Russkiy Flot pri Konchine Petra Velikogo* [Russian Fleet at the Death of Peter the Great], Zapiski Gidrograficheskogo Departamenta Morskogo Ministerstva, Tipografiya Morskogo Ministerstva, Part 6, St Petersburg, 1848

Storch, A. *Russland unter Alexander dem Ersten*, J. F. Hartknoch, St Petersburg and Leipzig, 1808

Turner, Eunice H. 'The Russian Squadron with Admiral Duncan's North Sea Fleet, 1795–1801', *The Mariner's Mirror* 49 (1963) 212–22

Veselago, General F. F. *Spisok Russkich Voennych Sudov, 1668–1860* [A List of Russian War Vessels from 1668 to 1860], St Petersburg, 1865

Von Pivka, Otto *Navies of the Napoleonic Era*, David & Charles Ltd, Newton Abbot, 1980

Zorlu, Tuncay *Innovation and Empire in Turkey, Sultan III and the Modernization of the Ottoman Navy*, Taurus Academic Studies, I. B. Tauris & Co. Ltd, London, 2008

Documents and Periodicals

Arkhiv grafov Mordvinovykh [Papers of Admiral Mordvinov], ed. by V. A. Bilbasov, vols 1–3, Tipografiya Skorokhodova, St Petersburg, 1901 (Data on the Black Sea fleet 1784–98)

Britain and Russia in the Age of Peter the Great, Historical Documents, document no.148, pp. 136–8, published by the School of Slavonic & East European Studies, London, 1998

Calendar of State Papers, Domestic Series (1699–1700)

Central Russian Naval Archive at St Petersburg

Great Britain, War Office *Armed Strength of Russia* HMSO, London, 1873, 1880, 1886

Istoriya Otechestvenogo Sudostroeniya (History of National Shipbuilding), ed. by a group of authors headed by I. D. Spasskiy, vol. I, Sudostroenie, St Petersburg, 1994

Materialy dlya istorii Russkogo flota [Materials for the History of Russian Navy] 17-volume compilation of Russian naval documents, St Petersburg, 1865–1904, vols I–IV ed. by Capt. S. A. Elagin, vols V–XV ed. by General F. F. Veselago, vols XVI–XVII by S. Ogorodnikov

Morskoi Sbornik [Sea Collection], St Petersburg, various years 1848–1914

O Sudakh Chernomorskogo Flota, Postroennykh so Vremeni Vstupleniya na Prestol Gosudarya Imperatora Nikolaya Pavlovicha [About the Ships Built Since the Time of Accession to the Throne of His Imperial Majesty Nikolay Pavlovich], St Petersburg, 1844

Pamyatnaya Knizhka Morskogo Vedomstva [Aide-Memoire of the Navy Office for the years 1853–1869]

Polnoe Sobranie Zakonov Rossiyskoy Imperii [Complete Collection of Laws and Regulations of the Russian Empire], ed. by M. M. Speranskiy, 45 vols, St Petersburg, 1830; vols 43–44, *Kniga Shtatov* (Book of Establishments), include naval establishments and regulations

Russkie Flotovodtsy. Admiral Ushakov ed. by R. N. Mordvinov, vols 1–3, Voenno-Morskoe Izdatelstvo Voenno-Morskogo Miniisterstva Soyuza SSR, Moscow, 1951–6

Russkie Flotovodtsy. M. P. Lazarev Dokumenty, ed. by A. A. Samarov, (vols 1–2) and K. I. Nikulchenkov (vol. 3), Voenno-Morskoe Izdatelstvo Voenno-Morskogo Ministerstva Soyuza SSR, Moscow, 1952–961

Sudostroenie [Shipbuilding, historical section], Leningrad and St Petersburg, various years 1974–96

Sundry Anecdotes of Peter the First, National Library of Scotland, Carmichael and Gordon Papers MS 109 by John Bell of Antermony

Uchenie Deystviyu Orudiyami [Exercises for the handling of guns], Naval Regulations, Naval Ministry, 1837

Zapiski Uchenogo Komiteta Glavnogo Morskogo Shtaba (1827–44) [Proceedings of the Scientific Committee of the Supreme Naval Staff], Chief of Naval Staff, 1828–44 (annual publication)

Unpublished Documents and Collections

Papers of General-Admiral Apraksin: unpublished

Papers of Peter I, (material discussed at the meetings with shipbuilders during the period of 10 December 1723–4 and February 1724): unpublished material, St Petersburg Naval Archives

Websites

www.rusnavy.com is the official English language website of the Russian Navy. Historical and biographical information from a Russian perspective may be found there.

www.fatruren.org/jan-erik.karlsson/wacht 1 .htm is a Swedish-language website with basic information on almost every Swedish warship built through the present, presented in Swedish alphabetical order.

www.voy.com/39735 Yener, Emir 'A Complete Turkish order of battle at the Battle of Navarino' (posted 21/1/2007) and 'Navarino Order of Battle – Ultimate Version' (posted 25/1/2007) Naval History in the Age Of Sail (1650–1815) [website] is one of the cited sources for the composition of the Ottoman and Egyptian participants in the battle of Navarino.

Index of Ship Names

Gun rating and date of launch is shown where known

Section I: The Seagoing Navy

Abbas-Abad 12 (1827) 317
Abel'tazh 14/18 281–2
Abo 12 (1809) 289
Adler (1705) 151
Adrianopol' 84/108 (1830) 298–9
Afrika 32 (1768) 147–8
— 32 (1811) 288–9
Agamemnon 20 (1834) 243
Agatopol' 60 (1834) 303–4
Agnets (*Lamgotes*) 24 263
Aiaks 20 (1829) 242
— 20 (1843) 244
— 16 (1820) 210
Aist 64 (1706) 257
Aiu-Dakh 8 310
Akhilles 16 (1819) 210
Aleksandr 66 (1786) 269
— 32/38 (1778) 172
— 16 282
— 16 283
— 12/16 291
— 4 (1825) 321
Aleksandr Nevskii 74/80 (1826) 226–7
— 74 (1787) 159
— 66 (1772) 132
— (*Sviatoi Aleksandr*) 48/50/52 (1787) 271
— (renamed *Vind-Khund*) 36 (1821) 202
Aleksandra 44/54 (1827) 235
— (1848) 246
Aleksei 74 (1790) 161
— 8 (1774) 281
— 291
Al'tsinoe 18 209
Alupka 2 (1842) 310
Amerika 66 (1773) 163
Amfitrida 44/52 (1832) 237
Amsterdam Galey 32 (1720) 149–50
Anadyr' (1853) 322
Anapa 84/108 (1829) 298
— 74 (1807) 285–6
Andrei 80/84 (1844) 223–4
— 8 (1817) 293
Andro 181
Andromakha 18 (1841) 307
Anna 44/54 (1829) 236
— 44 304
Antenor 20 (1835) 243–4
Apollon 32 (1740) 146
— (1821) 207
Apostol Andrei 50 (1786) 270–1
Apostol Pyotr (*Sviatoi Peter*) 36 (1696) 263
Araks 12 (1839) 318
Ardebil' 8 (1828) 318

Ardon 8 (1838) 318
Arfa 36 (1699) 260
Argonavt 12 (1838) 308
Argus 44 (1807) 198
— 44 (1813) 200
— 12 211–12
Ariadna 20 (1851) 307
— 16 (1808) 316
Arkhangel Gavriil 84/86 (1839) 300
— 66 (1749) 126
— 52/54 (1713) 134
— 38 (1787) 169–70
— (ex-*Vestnik*) 8 (1781) 281
Arkhangel Mikhail 52 (1713) 134
— 44 (1791) 168
— 32 (1748) 146–7
Arkhangel Rafail 66 (1745) 125
— 52/54 (1713) 134
— 44 (1791) 168
Arkhangel Uriil 80/76 (1802) 188
— 66 (1749) 126
Arkhipelag 60 (1829) 303
— 38/46 (1789) 170
— 44 (1811) 200
— 30 251–2
— 30 313
Arkhistratig Mikhail 64/72 (1800) 168
Armont (ex-*Ormonde*) 44/48/50 140
Arondel' (ex-*Arundel*) 44/48/50 140
Arsis 74/80 (1828) 228
— 74 (1816) 191
Astrakhan' 62/66 (1720) 122
— 66 (1756) 127
— 54 (1736) 136
— 20 (1784) 316
— 12 (1824) 317
Astril'd 8 (1699) 253–4
Atis 18 255
Avrora 44/56 (1835) 237–8
Avtroil 44 (1811) 200
— 44 (1819) 200–1
— 24 (1767) 252–3
Aziia 74 (1810) 286
— 66 (1773) 163
— 66 (1796) 167
— 54 (1766) 138
— 16 (1770) 264
Azov 74/80 (1826) 226
— 54 (1736) 136–7
— 16 (1770) 264

Baklan 38 (1789) 183
Baku 14 (1835) 318
— 12 (1821) 317
Baraban (*Trumel*) 26/36 (1699) 262
Beber (1705) 151
Begun 8 (1804) 212

Belka 8 (1808) 319
Bellona 44/54 (1830) 236
Berezan' 6/14 282
Berezino 74/80 (1830) 229
Berislav (renamed *Luka Evangelist*) 28/40 (1786) 277
Berlin 74 (1813) 191
Beskermer 50/56 (1784) 250
Bezboiazn' (*Sunderban, Sonderfres, Onberfrest*) 36 (1699) 261
Bir-Drager 3 (1703) 153
Blagodat' 130 (1800) 156
Blagoe Nachalo (*Gut-anfangen, Gut-begin, Desegel-begin*) 32/36 (1699) 261
Blagopoluchie (ex-*Pravitel'nitsa Rossiiskaia*) 66 (1741) 125
— 66 (1774) 163–4
Blagonamerennyi 20 (1818) 208
Bodryi 32 (1808) 205
Bogemiia 26 (1768) 180
Bogoiavlenie Gospodne 66 (1791) 270
— 34 (1798) 179
Bogoiavlensk 16 212
Bogoroditsa Pskovskaya 282
Boleslav 66 (1783) 165–6
Bol'sheretsk (1739) 321
Bomb no. 1 8 280
Bomb no. 2 7 281
Bomba 24 263
Bonasorte 16 313
Borey 74 (1807) 190
Boris 74 (1789) 161
Boris i Gleb 66 (1772) 132
Borodino 74/80 (1830) 229
— 74 (1850) 234
Brailov 44 (1836) 304
— 12 (1773) 279
Briachislav 38/46 (1785) 169
Brien 74/80 (1829) 229
— 74 (1813) 286
Brilliant 30 251
Britaniia 44/50 (1707) 140–1
Bukharest 12 (1770) 264–5
Bulinbruk (ex-*Sussex*) 46/50 (1704) 138–9
Burgas 60 (1832) 303
Bystryi 44 (1807) 198
— 12 (1833) 311

Cherepakha (*Shkhelpot*) 56/58 (1700) 258
— 8 (1833) 319
Chernyi Oryol (1791) 321–2
Ches'ma 84/92 (1849) 302
— 84/91 (1828) 298

— (ex-*Sviatoi Ioann Krestitel'*) 80/86 (1770) 120
— 74 (1811) 193
Chetvertyi 58 (1773) 274–5
Chetyrnadtsatyi (renamed *Perun* and *Amvrosii Mediolanskii*) 40/44 (1783) 276

Dansk-Ern 18/24 (1694) 251
David Selunskii 66 (1779) 133
Degas 14 (1704) 150
— 14 (1710) 262
Dekrondelivde (*De Kroon de Liefde*) 32 (1720) 150
Del'fin 62/64 (1703) 257
— 184
Delos 181
Derbent (renamed *Parizh*) 110/112 (1826) 293
— 64/66 (1724) 123
Deris' 66 (1772) 132
Derpt 28 (1704) 144
Derzkii 28 209
Desiatyi (renamed *Krym*) 44 (1779) 275
Deviatyi (renamed *Pospeshnyi*) 44 (1779) 275
Devonshir 52 (1714) 141
Diana 44/56 (1833) 237
— 54 (1852) 239
— 44 (1818) 200
— 18/34 (1823) 289–90
— 16/22 (1806) 207–8
— 18 (1711) 151
— 16 292
Diomid 20 (1831) 243
— 24 (1804) 289
Dionisii 8 (1817) 293
Dispach 18/20 (1795) 184
Dmitrii Donskoi 74 (1810) 286
— 66 (1771) 131–2
Dmitrii Solunskii 284
Donai 12 282
Donder (*Grom*) 6 (1716) 152
Dozhd' 16 (1834) 245
— 14 (1808) 213
Drezden 74 (1813) 191
Drotik 16 (1839) 309
Drozd 213
Dumkrakht 44 (1699) 259
— 32 (1707) 144
Dvenadtsat' Apostolov 120/130 (1841) 296
— 110 (1811) 285
Dvenadtsatyi (renamed *Strela* and *Ioann Voinstvennik*) 40/44 (1782) 275–6

Dvu-na-desat' Apostolov 100/108/112 (1788) 155
Dzhevan-Bulak 8 (1828) 317–18

Edinorog 36/44 (1699) 262
— 18 (1806) 206
Eingorn 8 254
Ekaterina 44/56 (1828) 236
— 2 (1823) 321
Ekspedition 16 314
Elena 36 (1825) 202
Elisaveta 74 (1795) 163
— 44/63 (1828) 235–6
— 16 292
— 4 (1821) 321
Emgeiten 84/94 (1828) 222
— (later *Kronshtadt*) 84 (1822) 188
— 62 (1732) 248
Emmanuil 64 (1824) 196
— 24/38 (1800) 179
Endimion 12 (1839) 308
Endrakht (*Endracht*) 32 (1719) 150
Enei 16 (1842) 308–9
Enos 60 (1831) 303
Eol 12 (1817) 214
Erivan 60 (1829) 303
— 12 (1827) 317
Esperans 40/50 (1698) 149
Etna 6 (1727) 152
Evangelist Mark (*Sviatoi Mark*) 20/22 (1773) 175
Evlampii 293
Evropa 66 (1768) 130
— 66 (1793) 167
Evstafii 44/48 (1817) 288
— 32 (1773) 171
Evva-Elenora 254
Evva-Katerina 10/14 254

Falk 20 255
— 14 (1705) 150–1
— 14 (1710) 262
— 8 254
Fanagoriia (renamed *Prepodobnyi Nestor*) 28/40 (1786) 277
Favoritka 16 (1723) 152
Femistokl 18 (1833) 308
— 16 (1839) 308
Feniks 20/22 (1811) 210
— 20 (1828) 242
— 18 211
— 14 (1705) 151
— 12 283
Feodosii Totemskii 44 (1798) 169
Fershampenuaz 74/82 (1833) 233
— 74 (1817) 194
Filipp 66 (1790) 166–7
— 24 (1788) 278
— 8 (1779) 281
Filoktet 20 (1834) 243
Finland 74/80 (1840) 230
— 74 (1814) 194
— 52/56 (1735) 248
Flag 40/52 (1699) 259
Fligel'-Fam (*Fligel' De Fam*) 28 (1704) 144
Flora 44/48 (1818) 288

— 44 (1839) 304–5
— 22 (1806) 208
Fortuna 48/50 (1696) 139–40
Fridemaker 80/88/90 (1721) 117–18
— 66 (1742) 125
Fridrikhh Reks 119
Fridrikhshtadt (90/96) 114–15
Frigate no. 1 20 (1798) 316
— 18 (1702) 141
Frigate no. 2 20 (1798) 316
— 18 (1702) 141–2
Fyodor 180
Fyodor Stratilat 46 (1790) 271

Gagara 38 (1789) 183
Gamburg 74 (1813) 191
Gangut 90/92 (1719) 114
— 84 (1825) 221
Ganimed 14 (1808) 215
Gavriil 100/110 (1802) 187
Gektor 36 (1817) 202
— 32 (1736) 146
— 26 (1781) 175
— 20 (1829) 242
Gelendzhik 12 (1831) 310–11
Gel'gomar 26/32 (1790) 253
Georgii Pobedonosets 283
Gerkules 48/50/52 (1699) 260
— 16 (1820) 316
Geroi 48 (1807) 197
Gleb 74 (1789) 161
Glubokii 10/12 (1827) 310
Gonets 20 (1808) 210
— 20 (1800) 212
— 20 (1818) 210
— 16 (1835) 309
— 14 (1829) 245
— 14 293
Gornostai I 8 (1807) 319
— *II* 8 (1808) 319
Gorod Arkhangel'sk 54 (1735) 136
— 54 (1761) 138
Goto Predestinatsiia (*Bozh'e Predvidenie*) 58 (1700) 258
Grad 10/16 (1831) 245
Graf Orlov 66 (1770) 131
— (renamed *Mikhail*) 66 (1791) 167
Graf Severnyi 12 284
Granat-Apol' 36 (1699) 260
Gremiashchii 32 (1762) 147
— 24 (1827) 209
Grigorii 180–1
Grigorii Bogoslov (ex-*Boristen*) 14/18 (1781) 278
Grigorii Velikiia Armenii 50 (1791) 273
— (ex-*Pchela*) 24/26 (1782) 278
Grom (*Donder*) 14 (1699) 262
— 14 (1783) 185
— 14 (1805) 320
— 10 (1765) 185
Gromovaia Strela (*Donderpeyl*) 14 (1699) 263

Iagudiil 110 (1800) 265
— 84/96 (1843) 301
— 50/52 (1715) 134

— 32 (1746) 146
Iakht-Khund 32 (1724) 145
Iamburg 14 (1704) 150
Ianus 12 (1814) 214
Iaroslav 74 (1784) 160
— 74 (1799) 162
Iaroslavets 36 (1784) 175
Iashcheritsa 14 (1808) 215
— 8 (1808) 317
Iason 24 (1815) 289
— 12 (1805) 290
— 12 (1850) 309
Iassy 14 (1770) 280
— 12 (1770) 265
Iastreb 20 (1789) 183
— 14 (1806) 210
— 14 (1808) 214
Ida 16 (1820) 210–11
Iezekiil' 74/80 (1847) 234
— 78 (1773) 158
— 74/80 (1826) 225–6
Ifigeniia 22 (1834) 306
Imperator Aleksandr 110/118 (1827) 218
Imperator Frants 110 (1821) 285
Imperator Pyotr I 110/118 (1829) 218–19
Imperatritsa Aleksandra 84/96 (1827) 221–2
Imperatritsa Anna 110/114 (1737) 115
Imperatritsa Ekaterina II 84/96 (1831) 299
Imperatritsa Mariia 84/96 (1827) 297
— 84/90 (1853) 302
Ingermanland 74/80 (1842) 231
— (ex-*Iezekiil'*) 74/80 (1844) 231–2
— 64/68 (1715) 121
— 66 (1735) 124
— 66 (1752) 126
Ingermanlandiia 66 (1773) 132
Ioann Bogoslov 74 (1783) 159
— 46 (1788) 271
Ioann Krestitel' (*Ches'ma*) 100/108 (1783) 154
Ioann Predtecha 66 312–13
Ioann Zlatoust 74/83 (1825) 287
— 32/36 (1791) 277
— (ex-*Taganrog*) 10/16 (1785) 278
Ioann Zlatoust Pervyi 80/86 (1751) 118–19
Ioann Zlatoust Vtoroi 66 (1749) 126
Iona 66 (1790) 166
— 24 (1788) 278
— 8 (1783) 281
Iozh (*Igel*) 40 (1700) 261
Isaak-Viktoriia 64/68 (1719) 122
Isidor 74 (1795) 162
— 74 268
Iunona 44/54 (1830) 236
Iupiter 10 (1755) 152
— 10 (1771) 185
— 6 (1715) 152
Ivan-Gorod 28 (1705) 142
Iziaslav 66 (1784) 167
Izmail 12 (1773) 279

Josif II (renamed *Rozhdestvo*

Khristovo) 80 (1787) 265–6

Kagul 44 (1843) 305
Kalipso 18 (1845) 307
Kamchadal (1849) 322
Kamchatka 28 (1817) 206–7
— (1829) 318
Kamen' (*Stein*) 44 (1699) 259–60
Kandiia 14 255
Karl-Konstantin 10 282
Karlskronvapen 34 250
Kastor 44/54 (1831) 237
— 36 (1807) 202–3
— 34/36 (1823) 202
— 18 (1829) 307
Kater no. 1 20 (1790) 183
— *no. 2* 20 (1790) 183
— *no. 3* 20 (1790) 183
Katsbakh 74/80 (1828) 228
— 74 (1816) 191
Kavaler (*Chevalier*) 32 (1737) 146
Kavkaz 20 (1784) 316
Kazan' (*no. 1*) 16 (1807) 316
— (*no. 2*) 16 (1816) 316
Kazanskaya Bogoroditsa 46 (1791) 272
Kazarskii 20 (1834) 243
Keko-Tavro 12 282
Khameleon 12 (1814) 214
Kherson 24 (1805) 289
Khobot 14 (1708) 152
Khotin 16 (1770) 264
Khrabryi 120 (1808) 187
— 84/86 (1847) 301–2
— 66 (1774) 164
Kildyuin 32 (1798) 201
Kinburn (renamed *Pokrov Bogoroditsy*) 28/40 (1786) 277
Kir Ioann (ex-*Fridrikhh Reks*) 80/86 (1762) 119
— 74 (1786) 161
Kisken 22/32 (1715) 251
Kizliar 20 (1785) 316
— 10/18 (1794) 319
Kliment Papa 18 284
Kniaginia Lovich 44/54 (1828) 235
— 44 304
Kniaz' Varshavskii 22/30 241
Kniaz' Vladimir 74 (1824) 192
Kola 26 (1806) 206
Kolokol (*Klok*) 42/46 (1697) 261
Kolym 12 (1819) 215
Komar 4 (1849) 318
Kommerstraks 14 255
Konduktor 282
Konstantin 44/48/58 (1844) 239
— 44/46 (1824) 200
— 4/8 (1777) 281
— 2 (1848) 320
Konstantsiia 22 181–2
Kopchik (1851) 247
Kopor'e 14 (1704) 150
Kotka 8 (1794) 182
Kovarna 60/54 (1845) 304
Krasnoi 84 (1847) 224
— 74/80 (1830) 229
— 74 (1816) 286
Krasnolsely 14 283

Krechet 20 (1789) 183
Kreiser 36 (1821) 202
— 32 (1751) 147
Krepkii 54 (1801) 274
Krepost' (*Zamok, Kastel, Stargeyt, Sitadel*) 46/52 (1699) 259
Kreyser 32 (1723) 145
Kronprins Gustaf-Adol'f 64 (1782) 249
Kronshlot 28 (1704) 144
— 54 (1738) 137
Kronshtadt 38/46 (1789) 170
Krotov (1834) 245
Kruis (*Kreiser*) 8 254
Krym 18 (1810) 289
Kulevchi 60/52 (1847) 304
Kul'm 74/90 (1828) 228
— 74 (1813) 286
Kur'er 16 (1783) 279
— 12 (1702) 148
— 12 (1831) 309
Kuril 4 (1842) 321
Kutsal-Mulim 8 (1794) 182

Ladoga (1820) 207
Landsdou (ex-*Noris*) 32/44 149
Lapominka 16 (1825) 242
Lastka (*Shval*) 50 (1709) 258
Lastochka 12/18 (1826) 310
— 16 (1838) 309
Lavrentii (1807) 291
Le Briun (ex-French *Brune*) 32 (1781) 313
Lebed' 38 (1789) 183
— 12 (1831) 247
Leferm (ex-*Le Ferme*) 62/66/70/74 (1700) 139
— 62/66 (1739) 124
Lefort 84/94 (1835) 224
Legkii 44 (1816) 198
— 44 (1819) 201
— 38 (1803) 201
— 32 (1773) 171
— 26 (1793) 279
— 10/12 (1835) 311
— 8 (1799) 182
Legma 6 (1790) 184
Leiptsig 110/118 (1816) 187
— 74/80 (1836) 230
Leontii Muchenik 62/66 312
Leshch 14 (1808) 213
Lesnoe 90 (1718) 114
— 74/80 (1829) 228–9
— 74 (1811) 286
— 66 (1743) 125
Letuchii 28 (1788) 183
Letun 12 212
Lev (*Lev s sableiu*) 36/44 (1699) 262
Lifartun (*Le Fortune*) 284
Liliia 34/36 (1699) 261
— 36 (1806) 289
Liman (1806) 293
Liubek 74 (1813) 191
Lizet (*Munker*) 16/18 (1708) 151
— 14 (1711) 262
Lizeta 16 (1806) 206
Lomonosov (1859) 319
London 54 (1707) 140

Los' (*Elk*) 14 (1808) 213
— 184
Lovkii 12 182
Luch 12 (1835) 311
Luks 14 (1705) 150
L'vitsa 26 255

Magubei-Subkhan 40 313
Maksim Ispovednik 74 (1788) 161
— 74 (1812) 286
Marl'burg 60/64 (1714) 140
Mangishlak 8 (1837) 318
Mariia 74 (1808) 286
— 44/54 (1827) 235
— 32 (1778) 172
Mariia Magdalina 66 (1785) 269
Mariia Magdalina pervaia 66 (1789) 269–70
Mariia Magdalina vtoraia 74 (1799) 267–8
Mars 10 (1771) 185
Mecheslav 66 (1783) 165
Mel'pomena 44/52 (1836) 238
— 22 (1806) 208
Menelai (renamed *Olivutsa*) 20 (1841) 306–7
Merkurii 44 (1815) 198
— 44 (1820) 198–9
— (*Merkurius*) 22/28/36 (1699) 261
— 22 184
— 20 (1808) 210
— 18/20 (1820) 290
Merkurius 32 (1740) 146
Messemvriia 60 (1840) 304
— 24 (1832) 306
Meteor 16 (1836) 245
Miach (*Bal*) 54/50 (1702) 260
Miana 8 (1828) 318
Midiia 60/54 (1843) 304
Mikhail (1820) 321
— 293
Mikhail Arkhangel 28 (1704) 142
Mikhail/Sviatoi Mikhail 74 (1798) 267
Mikono 181
Milo 181
Minerva 44 (1811) 288
— 32 181
Mingreliia 16/18 (1813) 290
Mirnyi 32 (1823) 205
— 20 (1818) 208
Mirotvorets (*Vredemaker*) 14 (1699) 263
Mitau 32 (1733) 145
Modon 16 (1770) 264
Mogileti 4/6 283
Moller 16 (1826) 241
Molniia 18/20 (1808) 215
— 16 186
— (*Bliksem*) 14 (1699) 262–3
— 14 (1829) 245
Moreia 16 (1770) 264
Moshchnyi 66 (1805) 195
Moskva 74 (1799) 162
— 64/68 (1715) 121
— 66 (1750) 126
— 66 (1760) 127
Mozdok 10 (1785) 319
— 10 (1795) 319–20

Mstislav 74 (1785) 160
Mstislavets 44 (1784) 169
Mukha 4 (1849) 319
Munker (*Mon Coeur*) 14 (1711) 262
Muravei 14 (1808) 213
— 6 (1821) 319
Nadezhda 32 (1762) 147
— 32 (1781) 173
— 24 (1828) 240
— 24 (1845) 241
— 10 (1766) 175
Nadezhda Blagopoluchiia 32/38 (1786) 174–5
— 34 (1764) 171
— 283–4
Nadyozhnyi 8 (1788) 183
Naktsiia 22 181
Narova 4 (1830) 246–7
Narva (ex-*Sviatoslav*) 74/80 (1829) 228
— 74/80 (1846) 232
— 60/64 (1714) 121
— 38/46 (1790) 170
— 28 (1704) 144
Natal'ia 66 (1754) 126–7
— 32 (1773) 171
— 18 (1711) 151
Navarin 20 254
Navigator 8 (1806) 213
Nazaret 44 (1800) 273–4
— 38 (unfinished) 179
Ne Tron' Menia 84/92 (1832) 222–3
— 74 (1809) 190
— 66 (1763) 128
— 66 (1780) 164
— 54 (1725) 135
Neark 12 (1840) 308
Neptun 18 182
Neptunus 70/72 (1718) 117
— 54 (1736) 136
— 54 (1758) 138
Nestor 20 (1835) 243
Neva 44/54 (1829) 236
— 32 (1808) 205
— 24/28 (1805) 203
— 20 (1816) 203
— 8 (1788) 182
Nikanor 66 (1789) 166
Nikita Muchenik (ex-*Pochtal'on*) 8 (1766) 281
Nikolai 74/81 (1816) 286
— 20 292
— 4 (1827) 321
— 2 (1847) 320
— (1822) 322
Nishtadt 56 (1721) 141
Nord-Adler 74/91 (1820) 287
— 78/80/88 (1729) 117
— 74 (1811) 190–1
Novaia Nadezhda 54 (1730) 136
Novaia Zemlia 6/16 (1819) 211
— 16 (1845) 244
— 2 (1838) 245
Novopavlovsk 16 (1770) 264
— 15 (1789) 280
Nyrok 10 (1839) 311

Odinnadtsatyi (renamed *Khrabryi*) 44 (1779) 275
Okhta 20 (1827) 242
Okhtenka 16 (1821) 211
Oksford (ex-*Tankerville*) 50 139
Olen' 14 (1808) 214
— 184
Ol'ga 44/54 (1827) 235
— (ex-*Messemvriia*) (renamed *Arkhiolo*) 24 (1829) 313
Olifant 32 (1705) 144
— 18 (1713) 252
Olimp 20 (1817) 210
Opyt 7/16 (1852) 310
— 14 (1806) 213
— 10 312
— 8 (1819) 215
— 4 (1843) 318
— (1847) 246
Oranienbaum 12 (1829) 246
— 12 (1849) 246
Orest 18 (1836) 306
Orfei 18/24 (1821) 290
— 16 (1845) 309
Oryol 84 (1854) 225
— 74/80 (1833) 230
— 74 (1807) 190
— 22 (1668) 315
— 16 212
Osnovanie Blagopoluchiia 66 (1735) 124
Ostrolenka 74/80 (1834) 230
Otkrytie 18/28 (1818) 207
Otvazhnost' 12/24 (1834) 240
Otvoryonnye Vrata (*Opon-de-Port*) 32/34/36 (1699) 261

Palamed 18 (1839) 308
Palinur 20 (1835) 244
Pallada 52 (1832) 239
Pamiat' Azova 74/86 (1831) 230
— 74 (1848) 232–3
Pamiat' Evstafii 84/108 (1830) 298
— 74 (1791) 162
— 74 (1810) 192
— 66 (1770) 131
Panagiia Apotogrilli 282
Panagiia Apotokofory 282
Panagiia Apotumengano 14/16 282
Panagiia Kaligati 8 282
Panagiia Popandi 282
Panagiia Turleni 10 282
Panagiya Turlyeni 12 284
Panteleimon 80 (1824) 287
— 66 (1786) 166
Pantelemon-Viktoriia 66 (1721) 122–3
Paraskeva 283
Paris 20 (1829) 242–3
— 20 (1843) 244
Parizh 120/130 (1849) 296
— 110 (1814) 285
Parmen 74/89 (1823) 287
— 66 (1789) 166
Paros 10 180
Patrikii 44 (1816) 198
— 44 (1819) 198
— 32/38 (1779) 172

Patrokl 20 (1831) 243
Pavel 32 (1773) 171
— 18 289
Pegas 22 (1826) 307
— 12 (1818) 215
Penderakliia 24 (1831) 306
Perl (ex-*Groote Perel*) 48/50 (1706) 140
Pernov 50/52 (1710) 133
Persei 16 (1841) 308
Perun 20/24 (1808) 215
— 16 (1842) 312
— 14 (1780) 185
Pervyi 32 (1771) 274
— 10 (1770) 280
Peterburg 28 (1704) 143
Petergof 32 (1808) 205
— 12 (1829) 246
— (1859) 322
Piatnadtsatyi (renamed *Legkii* and *Kiriil Belozerskiyy*) 40/44 (1783) 276
Piatyi (*Fifth*) 42 (1774) 275
Pilad 20 (1840) 306
Pimen 74/95 (1823) 287
— 66 (1789) 166
Piram 18 (1806) 206
Pobeda 66 (1770) 131
— 66 (1797) 167
— 16 180
Pobedonosets 64 (1809) 195
Pobeditel' 18 (1788) 185
Pobedoslav 74 (1782) 159
Pobedoslav-Dunaiskii 12 (1772) 279
Pochtal'on (renamed *Nikita Muchenik*) 20/24 (1766) 278
Podobnyi 7/12 (1826) 312
Podrazhislav 32/38 (1781) 174
Poliarnaia Zvezda 6 (1844) 246
Poltava 110 (1808) 285
— 84/90 (1820) 222
— 66 (1743) 125
— 66 (1754) 126
— 52/54 (1712) 133–4
Poluks 36 (1807) 203
— 32 (1812) 203
— 24 254
— 18 (1829) 307
Pomona 44/54 (1830) 236–7
— 24 (1817) 203
— 22 (1806) 208–9
Pomoshchnyi 38/40 (1788) 170
— 24 (1821) 204
— 20 181
Portsmut 54 (1714) 141
Pospeshnyi 44/52 (1821) 288
— 36/44 (1816) 201
— 36/38 (1798) 170
— 36 288
— 32 (1774) 172
— 32 (1793) 279
— 10/12 (1845) 311
Postoianstvo 12/24 (1834) 240
Poti 12 (1831) 311
Pozharskii 14 212
Pravyi 74/76 (1804) 285
Predpriiatie 24 (1823) 207
Premislav 34/42 (1785) 174

Preslava 66 (1772) 132
Priam 20 (1834) 243
Prints Aleksandr 12/14 282
Prints Evgenii 50 (1721) 141
Prints Gustav 70/74 (1758) 248–9
— 74 (1811) 191
Prints Karl 64 (1758) 248
Prints Oranskii (renamed *Korol'Niderlandskii*) 44/54 (1829) 236
Printsessa 18/20 (1714) 151–2
Printsessa Anna (renamed *Sviatoi Iakov*) 12 (1733) 148
Printsessa Elena 16/20 283
Prokhor 84 (1851) 224–5
— 74 (1823) 192
— 66 (1788) 166
Provornyi 44/48 (1820) 199–200
— 36 (1816) 201
— 20/22 (1773) 175
— 10/12 (1845) 311–12
Prozerpina 44/56 (1832) 237
Ptolomei 18 (1845) 308
Purga 4 322
Pyotr 74 (1790) 161
— 74 (1814) 194
Pyotr I i II 100 (1727) 115
Pyotr II 54 (1728) 136
Pyot Apostol 46 (1788) 271
Raduga 16 (1845) 246
— 14 (1818) 215
— 14 (1828) 244
— 8 (1806 (1816?)) 317
Rafail 80/82 (1802) 188
— 66 (1758) 127
— 54 (1724) 135
— 36/44 (1828) 305
Rak 14 254
Randol'f 50 138
Ratnyi (*Martial*) 110 (1802) 265
Razzhyonnoe Zhelezo (*Git eyzer*) 36 (1701) 258
Retvizan 74/80 (1839) 230
— 74 (1818) 191
— 62 (1783) 249–50
Revel' 68 (1717) 121–2
— 66 (1735) 124
— 66 (1756) 127
— 38/46 (1790) 170
— 16 (1824) 211
Richmond (ex-*Svivsten*) 44 149
Riga 54 (1729) 135–6
— 50 (1710) 133
— 38/46 (1790) 170
— 14 (1821) 211
Rodislav 66 (1782) 165
Rodos 60 247
Rossiia 120/128 (1839) 220
— 32 (1728) 145
— 32 (1754) 147
— 24 (1825) 204
— (renamed *Petergof*) 20 (1814) 203
Rostislav 110 (1817) 187
— 100/108 (1784) 155
— 84/90 (1844) 301
— 66 (1768) 130–1
Roza (*Rose*) 14 (1705) 151

Rozhdestvo Bogoroditsy 4/8 281
Rys' (*Lynx* or *Luks*) 44 (1699) 260

Samson 70 (1704) 257
— 32/34 (1711) 149
— 10/14 (1740) 152
— 10 (1758) 152
— 6 (1727) 152
Sankt Mikhail 54 (1723) 135
Sant Iakim 14 (1704) 150
Santorin 181
Saratov 100/108 (1785) 155
— 66 (1765) 129
— 66 (1809) 196
Sardar-abad 12 (1827) 317
Scchyogol 8 (1807) 319
Schastie (ex-*Generalissimus Rossiiskii*) 66 (1741) 124
Schastlivyi 44 (1798) 168–9
— 36 (1793) 277–8
— 32 (1774) 171–2
— 8 (1788) 183
Schooner no. 1 8 (1795) 280
— 8 (1826) 244
Schooner no. 2 8 (1795) 280
— 8 (1827) 244
Sedel'-Bakhr (*Sed-ul Bahir*) 42 313
Sed'moi (*Seventh*) (renamed *Kherson* and *Vasilii Velikii*) 42 (1777) 275
Selafail 84/96 (1840) 300
— 74 (1802) 189
— 50/52 (1715) 134–5
— 32 (1746) 146
Seniavin 16 (1826) 241
Sergii Radonezhskii 18/22 (1789) 280
Sevastopol' 14 292
Severnaia Zvezda 74 (1807) 190
— 54 (1735) 136
Severnyi Oryol 74 (1797) 162
— 66 (1735) 124
— 66 (1763) 128
— 66 (1787) 166
— 40 (1752) 180
— 184
Shagin-Girei 313
Sharlota 16 209
Shchyoglenok 14 (1808) 214
Shestnadtsatyi (renamed *Skoryi* and *Fedot Muchenik*) 40/44 (1783) 276
Shestoi 42 (1774) 275
Ship Sloop no. 1 20 (1779) 316
— no. 2 20 (1779) 316–17
— no. 3 20 (1789) 317
Shirokii 10/12 (1827) 310
Shlissel'burg 60/64/66 (1714) 121
— 54 (1751) 137
— 28 (1704) 143
Shpaga (*Degen*) 60 (1709) 257
Shpitsbergen 32 (1805) 206
— 2 (1838) 245
Shtandart 44/60 (1824) 288
— 28 (1703) 142
Sila (*Starkt*) 32/34/36 (1699) 261
Silistrilia 84/88 (1835) 299
Sil'nyi 74 (1804) 189–90
Simion i Anna 74 (1797) 267
Simion 32/38 (1779) 172

Sizopol' 60/54 (1843) 304
— 24 (1830) 306
Skorpion 60/62 (1709) 257
— 40/52 (1699) 259
Skoryi 74/81 (1818) 286–7
— 60/62 (1805) 195
— 12 (1845) 312
— 6 (1833) 311
Skuchnaia 10/14 (1845) 310
Slava 32/38 (1781) 173
— 16 180
Slava Ekateriny (renamed *Preobrazhenie Gospodne*) 66 (1783) 269
Slava Georgiia Pobedonostsa 8 284
Slava Rossii 66 (1774) 163
Slolvei 12/16 (1826) 310
Slon (*Oliphant*) 44 (1699) 260
Smelyi 88 (1808) 188
Smelaia 16 (1809) 309
Smirnyi 24 (1824) 207
Smolensk 74/80 (1830) 229–30
Snapop 12 (1837) 247
— 12 255
Sneg (*Snow*) 14 (1829) 244
Snuk 14 (1705) 151
Sobaka (*Treigun*) 44 (1699) 260
Sobol' 14 (1806) 210
Soedinenie (*Uniya, Einheit*) 30 (1699) 261
Sofiia Magdalina 74 (1774) 249
Sokol 44 (1699) 260
— 20 (1789) 183
— 16 (1783) 279
— 12/15 (1821) 293
— 8 (1804) 212
— 20 (1805) 212
Solombal 26 (1806) 206
Sopernik 11/12 (1826) 312
Soshestvie Sviatogo Dukha (ex-*Sviataia Troitsa*) 46 (1791) 271–2
Speshnyi 44/50 (1801) 197–8
— 32 (1813) 289
— 10 (1835) 311
Spiashchii Lev 70 (1709) 257
Spiridon 66 (1779) 132
Spiridon Trimifiiskii 6 281
Staryi Dub 70 (1705) 257
Staryi Oryol/Orel 80/82 (1709) 257
Stor-Biorn 26/32 253
Storfeniks (*Stora Feniks*) 32/34 (1708) 250
Straford (ex-*Wintworth*) 50 (1701) 139
Strakh (*Sshkrek*) 14 263
Strashnyi (*Terrible*) 14 (1788) 185
— 14 186
Strela (*Arrow*) 20 (1804) 212
— 16 (1811) 215
— 16 (1848) 246
— 15 (1822) 293
— 14 (1829) 245
Strel'na 12/14 (1831) 246
Struia 12 (1835) 311
Strus 44 (1699) 259
Stul 36 (1699) 261
Sulitsa (*Lants*) 60 (1709) 257
Sultan Makhmud 84/86 (1836) 300

Sveaborg 36 (1809) 201
— 32 (1808) 205
Sverchok 14 (1808) 214
Sviataia Aleksandra 34/38 (1790) 176
Sviataia Elena 74 (1785) 159
— 34/38 (1790) 176–7
— 28 284
Sviataia Ekaterina (ex-Prints Georg) 80/86 (1762) 119
— 66/70/74 (1721) 122
— 66 (1742) 125
— (renamed *Vyborg*) 60/64 (1713) 120–1
— 60 (not launched) 268
— 38 (1790) 176
— 34 (1792) 178
— 321
Sviataia Elisaveta 34 (1794) 178
Sviataia Mariia 34 (1794) 178
— 321
Sviataia Paraskeva 74 (1799) 268
Sviataia Tat'iana 283
Sviataia Troitsa 66 (1791) 270
Sviataia Velikomuchenitsa Varvara 66 (1745) 125
Sviatoe Prorochestvo 44 (1694) 141
Sviatoi Aleksandr 70/76 (1717) 116–17
— 38 (1790) 176
— 34 (1792) 177
— 8 (1766) 175
— 8 313
Sviatoi Aleksandr Nevskii 66 (1749) 126
— 66 (1762) 128
Sviatoi Andrei 78/80/88 (1721) 117
— 74 (1821) 192
— 54 (1737) 137
— 4/16 283
Sviatoi Andrei Pervozvannyy 80/86 (1758) 119
Sviatoi Antonii (Panduanskiy) 50/52 138
— 30 (1784) 276–7
Sviatoi Dmitrii Rostovskii 100 (1758) 116
Sviatoi Evsevii 100/108/112 (1790) 156
Sviatoi Evstafii Plakida 66 (1763) 128
Sviatoi Feodosii 30 (1784) 277
Sviatoi Fyodor 32 (1762) 171
Sviatoi Georgii 66 (1701) 257
Sviatoi Georgii Pobedonosets 110/118 (1829) 219–20
— 66 (1770) 131
— 66 (1780) 164
— 50 (1785) 270
Sviatoi Iakov 66 (1761) 127
— 16/32 (1711) 149
Sviatoi Ianuarii 66 (1763) 128
— 66 (1780) 164
Sviatoi Il'ia 30/32 (1714) 145
— 26 (1703) 144–5
— 12/26 (1703) 148
Sviatoi Isakii 54 (1740) 137
Sviatoi Kliment Papa Rimskii 80/86 (1758) 119
Sviatoi Kniaz' Vladimir 66 (1771) 132
Sviatoi Konstantin 38 (1790) 177

— 34 (1796) 178
Sviatoi Lavrentii 16 (1820) 211
Sviataia Maria 38 (1790) 177
Sviatoi Mark (ex-*Markopleya*) 36 313
Sviatoi Matvei 16 279
Sviatoi Mikhail 50 (1796) 273
— 32 (1758) 147
— 32 (1774) 172
Sviataia Natal'ia 66 (1727) 123
Sviatoi Nikolai 80/86 (1754) 119
— 66 (1774) 164
— 54 (1748) 137
— 46/50 (1790) 273
— 42/50 149
— 38 (1790) 177
— 34 (1796) 178–9
— 26 180
Sviatoi Nikolai I 283
Sviatoi Nikolai II 283
Sviatoi Nikolai III 16 283
Sviatoi Nikolai Belomorskiy 20 279
Sviatoi Nikolai Chudotvorets 100/108/112 (1789) 156
— 20 278
Sviatoi Nikon 18/22 (1789) 280
Sviatoi Panteleimon 54 (1740) 137
Sviatoi Pavel 84/90 (1794) 266
— 80/86 (1743) 118
— 80/86 (1755) 119
— 66 (1784) 269
— 34/38 (1790) 177
— (*Apostel Pavel*) 34 (1696) 263
— 32 (1710) 144
— (renamed *Arkhipelag*) 22 181
Sviatoi Pyotr 80/88 (1720) 118
— 74 (1786) 160–1
— 74 (1794) 266–7
— 74 (1799) 162–3
— (ex-*Ioann*) 66 (1741) 125
— 66 (1760) 127
— 32 (1710) 144
— 8 (1779) 281
Sviatoi Ravnoapostol'nyi Kniaz' Vladimir 100/112 (1788) 155–6
Sviatoi Sergii 66 (1747) 125–6
— 32 (1761) 147
Sviatoi Sergii Chudotvorets 20 278
Sviatoi Spiridon 18 284
Sviatoi Vasilii 18 284
Sviatoi Velikomuchenik Isidor 74 (1772) 158
Sviatoi Velikomuchenik Panteleimon 74 (1772) 158
Sviatoi Zotik Okhotsk ? (1806) 322
Sviatoslav 84/94 (1845) 301
— 80/86 (1769) 119–20
— 74 (1809) 190
— 66 (1781) 164–5
Sviatykh Zhen Mironosits 74 (1811) 193
— 66 (1771) 132
Svir' 16 (1806) 206
Svyatogo Dukha 12 (1702) 148
Sysoi Velikii 74 (1788) 161
— 74 (1822) 192
— 74 (1849) 233
Taganrog (renamed *Sviatoi Ieronim*)

30/34 (1785) 277
— 16 (1770) 264
Taganrogskaia 14 284
Taimalar 14 262
Tarantul 4 (1847) 318
Tavriz 12 (1827) 317
Telemak 20 (1828) 242
Tenedos 60 (1828) 303
Tezei 18 (1845) 308
Tikhvinskaya Bogoroditsa 44 (1799) 169
Tino 251
— 313
Tiz'ba 18 (1806) 206
Tol'skaya Bogoroditsa 74 (1799) 267
Topaz 8 (1806) 212–13
Torneo 32 (1808) 205
Trekh Ierarkhov 100/108 (1783) 154
— 84/90 (1838) 300
— 74 (1809) 190
Trekh Ierarkhov – Vasiliia Velikogo, Grigoriia Bogoslova, Ioanna Zlatousta (1765) 129–30
Trekh Sviatitelei – Petra, Aleksaya, Iony 66 (1765) 129
Trekh Sviatitelei 74 (1810) 193
— 74 (1819) 191–2
— 66 (1781) 165
Tretii 58 (1773) 274
Tri Riumki Dri Ryumor 26/36 (1699) 262
Tri Sviatitelia (Three Consecrators) 120/130 (1838) 295–6
Trinadtsatyi (renamed *Pobeda* and *Matvei Evangelist*) 42 (1782) 276
Triumf 28 (1704) 144
Tsar' Konstantin 74 (1779) 159
— 74 (1825) 192
— 74 (1837) 233
— 46 (1789) 271
Tsaritsyn 12 (1795) 316
Tserber 14 (1814) 215
Tserera 44/54 (1830) 237
Tsesarevich 44/52 (1841) 238–9
Tsesarevna (ex-*Bellona*) 44/58 (1841) 238
Tsvet Voiny 60/62 (1709) 258
— 32/34/36 (1699) 261
Turkmenchai 8 (1828) 318
Tver' 66 (1765) 128–9
Tvyordyi 110/118 (1819) 187
— 84/90/74 (1805) 188
— 66 (1774) 164

Uchenik (1841) 247
Ulis 20 (1843) 244
Uliss 20 (1828) 242
Ul'riksdal' 24 (1738) 251
Ungariia 26 (1766) 180
Unnamed 100/108/112 (not launched) 156
— 80 (4 ships, unfinished) 258
— 70 (2 ships, never launched) 258
— 66 (1758) 127
— 50 (1711) 133
— 48 (3 ships, unfinished) 259
— 48 (4 ships, unfinished) 259

— 48 (2 ships, unfinished) 259
— 38 (1699) 261
— 36 (never launched) 260
— 24 (unfinished) 262
— 16/18 262
— 16 (1784) 175
— 14 (1704) 150
— 14 (1780) 319
— 4 (1791) 184
— 2 (1834) 245
— 144
— (not launched) 170
— (2 ships, unfinished) 259
Unylaia 8 (1845) 310
Uraniia 24 (1820) 204
Uriil 84/96 (1840) 300–1
— 52 (1715) 134
Userdie 20 (1827) 242
Uspekh 24 (1839) 241
— 8 312

Vakhmeister 44/52/56 (1681) 247
— 32/46 (1732) 145
— 32 (1754) 147
Varakhail 66/68 (1800) 270
— 54 (1749) 137
— 54 (1752) 137–8
— 50/52 (1715) 135
Varna 84/96 (1842) 301
— 60 (1830) 303
Varshava 120/121 (1833) 295
Vecheslav 12 (1773) 279
Vein-Drager 3 (1703) 153
Velikii Galeas (1711) 263
Velikii Kniaz' 12 184
Velikii Kniaz' Konstantin 120/130 (1852) 296
Velikii Kniaz' Mikhail 74/86 (1827) 227–8
Venera (ex-*Skoryi*) 44/62 (1829) 236
— 48/56 (1808) 197
Venker (French privateer *Le Vainqueur*) 30 250
Venus 44/50 (1783) 252
Vernost' 24 (1834) 241
Verona 22 209
Vestenshliup (ex-*Bernhardus*) 12 254
Vestnik (renamed *Arkhangel Gavriil*) 30/32 276
— 29 (1786) 182
— 20 (1800) 212
— 12 (1813) 214
— 12 (1831) 309
— 12 (1841) 310
Vestovoi 44 (1822) 200
— 14 (1835) 309
— 8 175
Vesy 6 (1702) 263
Vezul 32 (1813) 289
Viacheslav 66 (1771) 131
Vifleem 38 (unfinished) 179
Vikhr' 14 (1829) 244–5
— 10 (1852) 246
Viktor 66 (1771) 131
Viktoriia (ex-*Vainqueur*) 40/60 139
Vilagosh 74 (1851) 234–5
Vind-Hund 32 (1724) 145

Vind-Khund (Borzoi) 36 (1823) 202
Vinkel'gak 62 (1703) 257
Vinogradnaia Vetv' (Veinshtok) 56/58 (1702) 260
Vladimir 84/92 (1833) 223
— *Sviatoi Vladimir/Kniaz' Vladimir* 66 (1787) 269
Vladislav 74 (1784) 160
Voin 32/38 (1778) 172
Voin (Warrior) 32 (1737) 146
— 32 (1804) 288
Vola 84/92 (1837) 223
Volga 8 (1806) 317
Volkhov 32 (1788) 182
— 16 (1806) 206

Voronezh 62 (1703) 257
Vos'moi (renamed *Ostorozhnyi*) 44 (1778) 275
Vostok (East) 28 (1818) 207
Vozmislav 32/38 (1783) 173
Voznesenie Gospodne (Navarkhiia) 40/46 (1790) 272–3
Vseslav 74 (1785) 160
Vsevolod 74 (1796) 162
— 66 (1769) 131
— 66 (1809) 196
Vtoraia Ekaterina 20 (1773) 175
Vtoraia/Farvater (1862) 322
Vtoroi 32 (1771) 274
— 10 (1770) 280

Vulkan 14 (1807) 320
— 14 (1817) 320
Vyborg 74 (1841) 233–4
— 54 (1729) 136
— 50 (1710) 133
Vysheslav 66 (1781) 165

Washington 72 (1796) 250

Zabiiaka 16 (1839) 309–10
Zachatie Sviataia Anna 66/74 (1800) 167–8
Zadornaia (1856) 246
Zakharii i Elisavet 99/100 (1747) 115–16

— 74 (1795) 267
Zapasnyi 181
Zefir 12 (1817) 214–15
Zeia 181
Zhavoronok 12/15 (1825) 310
Zhemchug 8 (1806) 212
Zhuravl' Steregushchii (Kroan Opvakht) 44 (1699) 260
Zhurzha 16 (1770) 264
Zmeia 8 (1808) 317
— 4 (1847) 318
Zvezda/Zolotaia Zvezda (Starn/Degoudestarn) 40/52 (1699) 259

Section II: The Inshore Navy

Admiral Lefort 328
Agamemnon 355
Aglaia 346, 347
Aist 331
Aleksandr 360
Aleksandr Makedonskiy 330
Aleksei 343
Amos 345
Amur 329
Anchous 331, 335, 337
Andrei 360
Andronik 345
Anguzhiguli 340
Anshtura 331
Anstiza 330
Antip 345
Antiparos 332
Apollo 329
Arcke des Verbondes 357
Arkanne 357
Arkhangel Mikhail 343, 344
Arkhip 344
Arnaut 355
Auza 336
Azard 326
Azartnaya 353

Baba 331
Bachan 340
Bagul 336
Bagulya 330, 331, 337
Baraban 331
Bardun 331
Bars 326, 337, 357, 358
Barsuk 353
Bavulo 340
Beglaia 340
Belaya 331
Bellona 324
Beluga 333, 336, 337
Bespokoinaia 353
Bezdelka 336
Biork 339
Björn Ernsida 325
Blagaia 333, 335
Blagoveshchenie 343
Blizko Ne Podkhodi 356
Blokha 356

Bochan 335, 337
Bodaya 332, 333
Bodraia 333, 336, 337, 339
Boelesht 355
Brongo 331
Bug 338, 344
Buian 353
Buinaia 336, 340
Buivol (Boul) 357
Butsefal 337
Byk (Oss) 357
Bystraia 325, 329, 332, 333, 335, 336

Captain A. A. Grott 328
Captain A. Bykovskiy 329
Captain A. Gasenius 329
Captain A. Veyde 328
Captain B. Pristav 328
Captain D. Inglis 328
Captain F. Bulart 329
Captain F. Hotunskiy 328
Captain Khotunskiy 329
Captain Oleshev 329
Captain P. Cunningham 329
Captain Prince I. Y. Trubetskoy 329
Captain Prince N. I. Repnin 329
Captain R. Bruce 329
Captain Shmidt 329
Captain V. Turlavil 328
Captain V. Ushakov 328
Captain Y. V. Bruce 329
Chagodoshcha 334
Chaika 340, 346
Chayka 331
Chechetka 336, 337, 339
Cheglik 340
Chekhonya 331
Chepura 346
Cherenok 340
Cherepakha 331, 336, 337, 339
Chernyy Drozd 339
Ches'ma 337
Chestnaia 329
Chizh 340

Dallarna 338
Dantan 331
Datulya 331

Del'fin 329, 330, 331, 335
Dem'ian 345
Derzkaia 353
Desna 338, 343
Diana 325, 329
Diatel 340
Dikii Byk (Auroks, Wilde Boul) 356
— 357
Dinamind 339
Dionisii 344, 345
Dmitriy 343
Dnestr 343
Dnieper 333, 358
Dobraia 329, 335, 337, 340
Dobychnaya 335, 337
Doezzhaia 340
Don 333, 335, 358
Dorofei 345
Drakon 326, 333, 336, 359
Drozd 331, 340
Drug 332
Dunzhelo 340
Dvina 332, 358

Edinorog 337, 359
Ekaterina 337
Ekho 347
Ekht 340
Elen 337, 339
Elen' 356
Elena 329
Elisaveta 343
Erofei 345
Ersh 331
Etekblas 339
Etna 359
Evdokim 345
Evridika 355

Fakel 347
Feniks 330, 336, 337
Feofan 345
Figura 336
Filin 331
Finlyadia 339
Fivra 331, 335, 336
Fokshany 336
Folpo 330

Foma 343
Fontanka 354
Forel' 331, 336
Fridrikhsgam 337, 339
Fyodor 345
Fyodor Stratilat 330

Gabora 331
Gaddan 338
Gagara 331
Galka 336
Gasbora 330, 336, 337
Gavun 331
Gektor 356
Gerasim 345
Giena 353
Gnevnaia 335
Gogol' 331
Golub' 330, 335, 337
Golubitsa 340
Gorishcha 331
Gorlitsa 340
Gota 331
Grach 331, 340
Gremiashchaia 359
Gremiashchii 357, 359
Grendulina 331
Grenok 331
Grigorii 360
Gripen 338
Grom 358, 360
Grom i Molniia 356
Gromkaia 353
Groza 353
Gus 331, 333, 346

Iakov 345
Iakutsk 348
Iaroslavl' 338
Iashcheritsa 353
Iasnaia 340
Iasson 345
Iastreb 336, 337, 353
Iaz 331
Il Fortunato 344
Illarion 343
Il'men' 333
Ingul 344

Ingulets 344
Iniia 339
Iosif 342
Iozh 353
Iput' 338
Irina 345
Irinarkh 346
Isaksha 336
Isidor 345
Iupiter 330
Iustin 345
Izhora 331, 336, 337, 339

Kaban 340
Kagarka 340
Kagul 336
Kambala 340
Kanona 331
Kanonerskii 354
Kaporotsul 340
Karakatitsa 331
Karas' 331, 333
Karneika 330, 336, 337, 340
Karostel' 331, 340
Karp 331
Kavaler Sviatoi Aleksandr 329
Kavaler Sviatoi Andrei 329
Kazan 338
Khitraia 332, 335
Khorek 353
Khornus 340
Khrabraia 334–5, 335
Khrabraia (ex-Legkaia) 359
Khristofor 360
Khval'naia 329
Kiliia 336, 343
Kipriian 346
Kir (ex-No. 8) 360
Kirill 360
Kit 326, 329, 336, 340
Kleopatra 343, 354
Klest 340
Klitemnestra 355
Klop 356
Kochet 340
Kolomar 330
Kolpitsa 340
Kolumba 330
Komar 356
Kometa 336, 337
Konoplianka 340
Konstantin i Elena 344
Konstantsiya 330, 336
Kopchik 331, 335, 339
Kopets 340
Koron 339
Korona 329
Korshun 353
Kostyl' 332, 333
Krabby 331
Krasnaia 340
Krasnaia Gorka 334
Krasnoperaya 331
Krepkaia (ex-Skoraia) 359
Krikun 353
Krokodil 331, 333, 336, 353, 358
Kronverk 334

Krot 353
Ksenofont (ex-No. 7) 359
Kuban' 344
Kulik 331, 334, 340
Kuropatka 340
Kyumen 346–7
Kyumen-Reka 337

Ladoga 331, 333, 336
Laks 331
Laksen 338
Langvila 330, 336
Laruzet 336, 339
Laskovaia 329
Lastka 331
Lastochka 334, 340
Lastovitsa 340
Laust 330
Lavalaktii 335
Lavrentii 345
Lebed' 331, 337, 339
Lefeb 356
Legkaia 325, 332, 335, 336
Lemnos 333
Leontii 345
Leopard 357–8
Leshch 331, 333, 336
Letuchaia 324, 333, 339
Lev 326, 329, 343, 357, 358
Lifliandiia 339
Lisitsa 336, 337
Liubov' 330
Lobra 340
Lofer 337
Lokh 340
Lomi 331
Losos 340
Lovkaia 341
Lyufer 337
Lyurik 336

Makarii 326
Makropleia 338
Malaya Neva 334
Malinovka 340
Manuil 345
Mariia 346
Mariia Magdalina 343
Mark 345
Mark-Antonii 354
Mavra 345
Medved' 326, 333
Medved' (Ber) 357
Melkovodnaia 331
Merkurii 335
Mikhail 344, 346
Minerva 324, 329
Minulo 340
Mir 337, 339
Miron 345
Modon 339
Mogilev 336, 358
Moika 354
Moisei 345
Mokkey 343
Moklets 331
Molniia 330, 358

Mologa 334
Monplezir 329
Moris 329
Morskaia loshad' 337
Morzh 340
Moskva 334, 335
Mukha 347
Musels 331
Mushula 331, 335, 339

Nadezhda 330, 332, 337, 339, 348, 355
Nadezhda Blagopoluchiia 344
Nadezhnaia 333, 336
Narova 333, 337
Nartiss 343
Narva 334
Nastupatel'noe (renamed Porazhaiushchaia) 341
Natal'ia 344
Natal'ia Dvina 333
Navaga 331
Neboiazlivyi 356
Nepobedimaia 330, 337, 358
Nepobedimyi 359
Nepokin' 341
Neposhchada 333
Nepristupnaia (ex-Ostorozhnoe) 359
Nerva 334
Netopyr' 331
Neva 333, 336, 340, 358
Neyshlot 337
Nezhnaia 340
Nikifor 360
Nikodim 343
Nikolai 343, 344
Nikon 345
Nordosten-Norden (Osten-Norden) 338–9
Novokuplennaia 344

Obnovlenie Khrama Rossii 344
Oboronitel'naia (ex-Okhranitel'noe) 359
Oden 326
Ognevaia 336
Oka 333, 334
Okhranitel'noe (renamed Oboronitel'naia) 341
Okhta 331, 336
Okun' 340
Olen' 346
Olifant (ter) 357
Olifant (renamed Buivol) 357
Olonets 358
Onega 331, 336
Orfei 355
Orn 338
Orsha 336
Oryol 326, 330, 334, 335, 336
Osa 353
Osetr 333, 336, 340
Osmotritel'naia 340
Oster-Gotland 339
Ostorozhnoe (renamed Nepristupnaia) 341
Ostraia 335, 337
Ovod 356

Pallada 346
Palmsherna 339
Palyulos 329
Parasim 331, 335, 339
Paris 329
Parizh 356
Paros 336
Parta 331
Patrikii 346
Pavel 342
Pavlin 337
Pchela 346, 353
Pegaia 339
Pegas 337
Pelikan 335
Penelopa 355
Peni 334
Perekhvat 340
Perepelka 336, 340
Perinaia Tiagota 329
Pernov 334, 336
Peterburg 333
Petergof 334, 335
Piglatsiia 335
Piskar' 340
Pitsa 331, 336, 339
Plamida 331
Planeta 336, 339
Plato 329
Pobeda 330, 344, 355
Pobezhdaiushchaia (ex-Letuchaia) 359
Polotsk 336
Popeshnaia 333
Popugai 336
Porazhaiushchaia (ex-Nastupatel'noe) 359
Postoianstvo 330
Potatuy 331
Poust 331
Prevoskhoditel'naia 329
Prigozhaia 340
Prilezhnaia 340
Principium 328
Priyatelnaya 329
Prokofii 343
Prolet 340
Promyshlennaia 335
Pronia 331, 336, 337
Prozerpina 325
Pustel'ga 334, 336, 339
Pyotr 342

Rak 331, 336, 339
Rayna 340
Raza 330
Razgenevannyi 356
Razumnaia 329
Remes 340
Repolov 335, 339
Riabchik 331
Riga 339, 358
Ritsa 331
Rodion 345
Rogvald 326
Rokhovo 355
Rossia 334
Rumba 331

Ryabets 340
Rys' 326

Saiga 336
Salamandra 330
Sal'pa 331
Samuil 345
Sarga 331
Savva 345
Sazan 331
Schastlivaia 332, 333, 336, 337
Seim 338
Seld 331
Sellan Vere 325
Selo Sarskoe 334
Semga 330, 331, 335
Sepa 330
Serditaia 353
Serdityi 356
Serdobol' 357
Serna 337
Seskar 334
Sestrebek 336
Severnyi Medved' 356
Sevriuga 340
Shchegol' 335
Shchegol' 330, 340
Shchuka 333, 336, 339, 340, 353
Sheksna 334, 335
Shereshpyor 340
Shoutbenakht B. E. de Lozier 328
Shubra 330
Shumnaia 353
Sig 331
Siiatel'naia 329
Simion 345
Sinitsa 340
Sklonnaia 329
Skobra 330
Skoraia 325, 335, 340
Skorpion 353
Skvorets 331, 340
Slava 344
Slavianka 331, 333
Slavnaia 332, 333, 335
Slolvei 336, 340
Slon 326, 337
Smelaia 333, 334, 335, 337, 339

Snigir 333, 336, 337, 340
Snov 338
Sofiia 355
Soika 331, 335, 339
Sokol 330, 331, 335, 336, 337
Solovaia 335, 339
Som 331
Sommers 333, 334
Sopka 359
Soroka 331, 336
Sova 340
Sozha 338
Spesivaia 332, 333
Spiashchii Lev 356
Stazh 353
Stepan (or *Stefaniy*) 360
Sterliad' 333, 336, 340
Strakh 330
Strashnaia 333
Strashnaya 332, 358
Strashnyi 356
Straus 331, 333
Strela 353, 358
Strizh 340
Sudak 331, 335, 339
Sukhum 344
Sverchok 356
Svetlaia 333, 335, 340
Sviataia Anna 329, 340
Sviataia Ekaterina 344
Sviataia Elisaveta 344
Sviatoi Aleksandr 340
Sviatoi Andrei 346
Sviatoi Feodosii Totemskii 344
Sviatoi Fyodor 340
Sviatoi Ioann 344
Sviatoi Nikolai 333, 335
Sviatoi Pavel 344
Sviatoi Pyotr 330, 344
Svir' 358
Svirepaia 330, 332
Svirepaia (ex-*Bystraia*) 359
Sviyaga 333
Svoilo 330

Taganrogskaia 343
Tarakan 356
Tarantul 353

Telemakus 329
Terpelivaia 329
Tigr 326, 358
Tikhvin 334
Tiligul 344
Timofei 344
Tit 345
Tiuters 334
Tobol 348
Tonina 331
Torneo 347
Torsar 333, 334
Tosna 331, 336, 337
Trana 338
Trekh Sviatitelei 344
Treska 330, 331, 336, 337, 339
Trofim 345
Troil 356
Troitskaia 335
Tsapkaia 340
Tsaplia 331
Tsederkreits 338
Tserera 346
Tsyvilsk 334
Turukhtan Kolpitsa 336, 337, 339, 340
Tver' 336, 338

Ubornaia 329
Uchtivaia 329
Udalaia 335, 336, 337
Uliss 329, 355
Umnaia 332, 333
Upovanie 330
Uringe 331
Ustritsa 336
Ustyuzhna 334
Utka 331, 335, 339, 346
Uzh 353
Uzhasnaia 326

Vakhmeister 342
Val'fish 331, 333
Valfisk 338
Vasfish 331
Vedraia 329
Venera 330
Venus 329
Vera 330

Vernaia 336
Veselaia 333, 335, 336, 340
Veter 329
Vice-Admiral Y. S. Lima 328
Vikhr' 353
Viktoriia 330, 333
Vil'manstrand 333-4, 337
Visla 331, 335
Vitebsk 358
Volga 331, 332, 333, 343, 358
Volk 326
Volkhov 333, 347
Vorobei 340
Voron 331, 333, 340
Vorona 336, 339
Voronaia 335, 339
Vulf 333, 334
Vuoksa 358
Vyborg 339
Vydra 330
Vyrezub 340

Yanos 329
Yastre 331

Zabavnaia 329
Zabiiaka 326, 353
Zadornaia 329
Zaiachii Beg 329
Zakharii 345
Zalet 340
Zhar 331, 335, 336
Zhavoronok 333, 334, 340
Zherekh 331
Zhuravl' 331, 334
Zhurzha 336
Ziablitsa 331, 340
Zlaia 332, 333, 353
Zlobnaia 341
Zmeia 330, 353
Zolotoe Iabloko 329
Zolotoi Oryol 329
— 330
Zuy 330, 335, 337
Zvezda 330

Section III: Russian Naval Auxiliaries

Abikhail 392
Abin 4 392
Abo 10 (1840) 382
Adler 2 392
Agrakhan (1723) 378
Ailla-Margarita 395
Akhangel Mikhail (1735) 368
Akhill 10 403
Akhiollo (1829) 389–90
Akhtapom (1771) 380
Akkerman 2 (1849) 387
Aland (1851) 382
Al'bertin 394
Aleksandr 8–18 393
— (1740) 377

— (1787) 389
— (1799) 363
— 364
— 377
— 391
— 398
Aleksandr Magnus (1723) 378
— (1726) 378
Aleksandr Nevskii (1716) 373
Aleksandra (1731) 363
Alfius 392
Al'ians 394
Allert 6 370
Alupka 2 (1842) 370
Amerika 12 390

Andrei 10 (1790) 403
Andromeda 4 391
Anna 364
— 399
Anna-Margarita 395
Anna-Mariia 364
— 377
Anna-Suzana 395
Apsheron (1723) 378
— (1727) 378
Aragva 2 (1849) 387
Ararat (1723) 378
Arkhistratig Mikhail 391
Astrabad (1723) 378
Astrakhan' (1723) 378

— (1729) 378
Astroliabiia 6–10 (1843) 370
Atlas (1806) 380–1
Avdot'ia 399
Azov 379

Babaev 10 (1764) 402
Baikal (1848) 388
Baklan (1741) 366
— 391
Baku (1719) 377
— 4 (1811) 383
Balaklava 4 (1851) 388
Beber (1732) 367
— (1806) 381

Begun (1803) 400
Belaia Gora 377
Belka 400
Berezan' 6 (1837) 386
— (1853) 370
Bir-Drager (1703) 367
Blagodat' 399
Blagoveshchenskiy (1703) 366
Boets 26–32 (1788) 380
Boris i Gleb (1765) 401
— (1808) 388
Boristen (1781) 401
Britta-Margarita 394
Bug 10–22 385–6
— 2 (1842) 387
— (1850) 370
Buivol 6 (1774) 364
— (1825) 398
— 401
Bukharest 12 (1770) 380
Bystryi 16 (1772) 372
Bzyb' 4 392

Chaika 6 (1825) 385
— (1806) 381
Chambers 396
Chapman 5–15 (1832) 386
— 395
Chechersk 401
Chepura (1741) 366
Cherepakha (1725) 376
— (1750) 363
— (1771) 380
— (1773) 379
— (1820) 384
Chernyy Byk (1725) 366
Chichagov (1764) 402

Dagerort (1725) 368
— (1736) 368
Dagestan (1723) 378
— (1726) 378
De Bir-Drager (17026) 366–7
Degog 395
Degop 367
Del'fin (1803) 400
— (1819) 400
Demovin (1727) 377
Der-Yung-Ioann 393
Derbent 12 (1842) 384
Desna 398
Deson 376
Devora 379
Dibel-Shley-Yung 394
Diomid (1804) 384
Dmitriy 393
— 399
Dnepr 4 (1838) 386
— 390–1
— 398
Dnestr 4 (1851) 388
Dob 4 392
Dobroe Namarenie (1789) 402
Domkrat (1806) 381
Don 6 (1829) 383
— (1776) 379
Donets 6 (1829) 383

— (1783) 364
Dora 6 393
Drofa (1779) 364
Dromader (1828) 398
Dub (1834) 398
Dubki (1725) 368
Dubrovka 398
Dunay 4 (1847) 387
— (1810) 384
Dutch buer No. 1 367
— *No. 2* (1819) 367
Dvina 10 (1852) 382
— 8 (1829) 381
— (1735) 376

Edinorog 22 (1759) 374–5
— (1703) 366
— 399
Efim 377
Einikkheit 396
Ekaterina (c. 1730) 368
— 379
Ekaterina-Magdalina 395
Ekateringof (1725) 368
Ekspeditsion 401
Elena 36–38 (1825) 389
— 390
Elenora (1730) 363
— 364
Elizabet-Ekaterina 364
Elisaveta 394
— 391
— 379
Emba 2 (1832) 383
Emmanuil 393
— 394
Ermak (1827) 388
Erpelei (1727) 377
Evdokiia 399
Evlampii 389
Evstafii 38 (1773) 375
Eynikhkeyt 394–5
Ezel' (1725) 368
— (1736) 368
— 378

Farvater 398
Feodosiia 14 (1853) 388
Feolog 379
Filadel'fiia 370
Filadel'fiia Pekst 393
Filipp 364
Fligel'-de-Fam (1726) 371
Fontanka (1822) 381
Fortuna (1727) 371
— 391
— 393
Frau Korneliia 395
Frau Margarita 393
Frau Zhanetta 393
Frigant 396
Fyodor (1790) 363
— 399

Gagan 4 (1827) 386
Gagara 391
Gagra 10 (1841) 387

Gapsal 4–12 (1834) 382
— (1854) 383
Gel'd-Sak (Sak-Drager) (1703) 367
Genrietta 395
Georgievskii (1703) 366
Georgii 6 (1861) 391–2
Gerkaniya (1723) 378
Gilyak 391
Gilyan (1723) 378
Girkaniia (1726) 378
Gizhiga (1844) 388
Gogland 22 (1765) 375
— (1720) 363
— 401
Golshtiniia (c. 1730) 368
Gorod Kazan' (1703) 366
Gostogai 4 392
Graf Khvostov 390
Gribsvald 394
Grigorii (1790) 403
— (1798) 384
— 364
— 377
Gunaki (1727) 377
Gus (1741) 366
Gustav-Adolf 396
Gut-Drager (1703) 366
— (1725) 376

Hofnung (1st) 394
— (2nd) 395

Iagudiil 379
Iakov 364
Ialta 8 (1840) 387
Ianus 393
Iaroslavl' 379
Iasashna (1787) 402
Iassy 12 (1770) 380
Ik-Gebe-Gevest (1704) 367
Impressa 395
Ingul 2 (1837) 386
— (1820) 384
Ingulets 10–22 (1826) 385
Ioann (1740) 377
— 364
— 391
Ioann Bogoslov (1790) 401
Iogan 394
Iogan-Frau-Mariia 395
Iogan-Sharlotta 391
Iosif (1790) 399
Iozh (1703) 366
Ipogrif (1790) 403
Irina 18 (1791) 404
Irkutsk (1834) 388–
Irtysh (1838) 389
— 392
Iunga Peters 395

Kaledoniia 392
Kambala (1771) 380
— (1820) 384
Kamel (1716) 373
Karakatitsa 398
Kargopol 22 (1750) 374
Karolina 394

Karolina-Frederika 394
Kars-Maker (1723) 363
Kasatka 390
Kaspiiskii Neptun (1723) 378
Kavkaz (1723) 378
— (1727) 378
Kazan' (1723) 378
— (1727) 378
Kem' (1846) 388
Ketti 392
Kherson (1805) 384
— 391
Kholmogory 26–32 (1786) 380
— 12 (1750) 374
Khrabryi 10 (1789) 403
Khvat 390
Kichkasy (1790) 399
Kiev 378
Kil' (1725) 368
Kildyuin 12 (1743) 374
— (1798) 380
— 375
Kiliia 4 (1849) 387
Kinburn 2 (1838) 386
Kir (1790) 403
Kishinev 2 (1851) 388
Kit 4 (1826) 386
— (1806) 381
— (1819) 384
— 398
Kniaz' Mikhail (1792) 380
Kodos 4 392
Kola 38 (1774) 375
— 12 (1742) 374
— (1831) 388
Kolpitsa (1785) 380
Kommerstraks 370
Konkordiia 395
Konstantin 396
Koren-Shkhern (1703) 366
Korneliia 377
Krasnaia Gorka (1748) 368
Krichev 398
Kron-Prints 394
Kronshlot (1766) 363
Kronshtadt (1731) 378
— (1766) 363
Krotkii 16 (1825) 381
Kuban' 4 (1837) 386
Kulik 390
Kuma (1837) 384
Kumik (1727) 377
Kura 7 (1852) 384
— 4 (1819) 383
— (1837) 384
Kur'er 6 (1703) 363
— (1727) 371
— 16 (1757) 372
— 16 (1761) 372
Kuropatka 400
Kuz'ma 364
Kvadrant 6–10 (1845) 370

Ladoga (1741) 367
Ladushka (1806) 381
Laima (1774) 379
Lang Dreyd 395

Lanzheron 4–8 393
Lapomink 22 (1762) 375
— 12 (1743) 374
Lasorser 6 376
Last-Drager (1704) 366
Lastka (1727) 371
Lava 4 392
Lavensar (1734) 368
Lavrentii (c. 1730) 368
Lebed' 12 (1750) 371–2
— 6 (1821) 384–5
— (1741) 366
— (1779) 364
Lebedka 390
Leto 390
Letuchii 16 (1766) 372
— 10 (1795) 372
Lev 22 (1759) 374
— (1816) 384
— 379
Libava 4 (1832) 381
Liberta 395
Lidiia (1825) 400
Liman 2 (1849) 387–
— (1806) 389
Loshak (1827) 398
Lots-bot nos.1, 2, 3, 8 (?, 1773, ?, ?) 369–70
Lots-Galiot (1704) 369
Lots-galiot no. 1 (1772) 369
Lotsman (1755) 369
Lovets 390
Lubianka 378
Luna 4 (1807) 383
Lyustikh (1704) 367

Mamay 4 392
Margarita 395
Mariia 6 (1819) 384
— (1740) 377
Menzula 6–10 (1845) 370
Meri 393
Merkurii (1727) 371
Merkurius (1732) 371
— 12 (1755) 372
— 364
Merkuriye 403
Mezen' (1819) 381
— (1833) 388
Mezha 398
Mikhail 364
— 396
Minerva 394
Mit Byurger 395
Molniia 389
Mologa 4 (1835) 382
Montetsello 392
Morzh 398
Moskva (1723) 378
— (1726) 378
— 379
Moskvoretskii (1722) 362
Mozas 364
Msta 4–12 (1840) 382
Mugan (1727) 377
Mukha 4 (1808) 383
Nadezhda (1825) 385

— 366
— 399
Naian 26–32 (1788) 380
Nargin 22 (1765) 375
— (1734) 368
Narva (1731) 378
Natal'ia (1703) 366
Navaga (1806) 381
Neman (1853) 382–3
Nepristupnyi 10 (1789) 403
Neptun 14 (1845) 370
— 395
Nerva (1734) 367
Nevka (1822) 381
Nikolai 363
— 377
— 399
— 364
— 391
— 396
— 398
— 399
Nikon (1789) 389
Nizhnyi Novogorod (1723) 378
Nordshtern 395
Nosorog (1827) 398
Novaia Dvinka 22 (1749) 374
— 12 (1742) 374
Novopostroennyi (1756) 368–9
Novyi Kronshlot 12–16 376
Novyi Kur'er (1733) 371
Novyi Pochtal'on (1736) 371
Nyrok 6 (1826) 385

Ob' 401
Observatorium 394
Oka 4 (1836) 382
Okhotsk (1739) 365
— (1805) 366
— (1836) 388
Olonets (1741) 363
Onega (1704) 366
— (1759) 376
— (1833) 388
Opyt 10 (1825) 385
Oryol (1703) 366
Osel 6 (1774) 364
Osetr (I) 4 (1806) 383
Osetr (II) 4 (1817) 383

Pallas (1787) 402
Paltus 398
Panov 10 (1764) 402
Pantikopey 391
Patriarkh (1704) 368
Pavel 391
Pavlin (1836) 400
Pchela 4 (1808) 383
— (1782) 401
Pechora 4 (1836) 382
Pelageia 4 391
Pelikan (1836) 400
Perfilii (1790) 363
Persei 4 391
Pervyi/(Pilot) (1726) 369
Pervyi Kaper 12–14 (1719) 376
Petergof (c. 1732) 368

Pinega 4 (1839) 382
Platon (1790) 399
Pochtal'on (1727) 371
— *(Nikita Muchenik)* 16 (1766) 372
Pocht-galiot 6 (1703) 363
Pocht-Gorn (1726) 371
Pocht-Wagen (1726) 371
Podobnyi 10 (1826) 385
Poliarnaia Zvezda (1766) 402
Polifem (1815) 381
Polotsk 14 402–3
Polumesiats (1703) 366
Popeshnyi 10 372
Portitsa 2 (1849) 387
Povrakul 22 (1749) 374
— 12 (1743) 374
Prepodobnyy Zosim (1750) 402
Priazhka (1822) 381
Primer 4 (1824) 385
Prints Aleksandr 13–24 (1716) 373
Prints Karl 394
Printsessa Anna (1722) 377
Prorok Daniil 364
Prut 4 (1849) 387
— (1813) 384
Pyotr 4 (1825) 383
— 377
— 391

Rak (1750) 363
— (1771) 380
— (1773) 379
— (1822) 398
Redut-Kale 6 (1827) 386
Renni 4 (1826) 385
— 2 (1850) 387
Repida 4 (1826) 385
Revel' (1731) 378
Revna 398
Revnitel' 10 (1825) 385
Riga (1731) 378
Rion 4 (1843) 387
— (1810) 384
Rozhdestvo Bogoroditsy 389
Ryashch (1723) 378
Rymnik 2 (1849) 337

Sagozan (1723) 378
Samson (1703) 366
— 376
Sankt-Peterburg (1726) 378
— 379
— (1803) 400
— (1819) 400
St Petersburg (1731) 378
Santa Anna 364
Saratov (1729) 378
Saturn 22 (1768) 375
Sekstan 6–10 (1845) 370
Selafail (1740) 377
— 379
Sergii 389
Seskar 369
— 378
Severnaia Zvezda (1703) 366
Shakhdag (1726) 378
Shakhdan (1723) 378

Sharlotta 4 391
Sharlotta-Karolina 394
Shlissel'burg (1741) 367
Shturman (1755) 369
Sil'nyi 10 (1789) 403
Simbirsk (1723) 378
— (1729) 378
Sirena 14 (1845) 370
Slava Rossii (1789) 402
Slon 22 (1758) 374
— 12 (1832) 386
— 6 (1774) 364
— (1825) 398
— 401
Smelyi 10 (1789) 403
— 390
Socha 4 (1839) 386–7
Sokol 12 (1750) 371
— 16 (1772) 372
— 10 (1794) 372
— (1803) 400
— 390
Sol 6 (1703) 363
Solntse (1703) 366
Solombal 24 (1782) 375
— 22 (1762) 375
Solombala (1832) 388
Solovetsk (1849) 388
Solovki 390
Sommers (1748) 368
Sopernik 10 (1826) 385
Sout-Drager (1703) 367
Sovatiy 378
Strel'na (1766) 363
Struia (1834) 400
Subashi 4 392
Sudzhuk-Kale 396
Sukhum-Kale 6 (1827) 386
— 2 (1842) 387
Sviataia Anna (1723) 378
Sviataia Ekaterina (1723) 378
Sviataia Elisaveta (1723) 378
Sviataia Nadezhda (1791) 366
Sviataia Natal'ia (1723) 378
Sviatoi Andrei (1759) 376
— 377
Sviatoi Andrei Stratilat 377
Sviatoi Diodor (1727) 378
Sviatoi Georgii (1776) 365
Sviatoi Iakov (1799) 363
Sviatoi Ioann (1788) 401
— 364
— 369
Sviatoi Ioann Krestitel' (1741) 373
Sviatoi Konstantin (1769) 365
Sviatoi Nikolai (1723) 378
— (1792) 380
— (1799) 366
— 363
— 391
Sviatoi Pavel 14 (1740) 372–3
— (1768) 365
— (1766) 377
— (1723) 378
— 375
Sviatoi Pavel 378
Sviatoi Pyotr 14 (1740) 372

— (1723) 378
— (1726) 378
— (1742) 377
— (1768) 365
— 364
— 378
Sviatoi Pyotra (1703) 366
Sviatoi Savvatii (1754) 376
Sviatoi Zosima 378
Svir' 4–12 (1839) 382
Svyatogo Kuzmy Svyatogradtsa (1765) 401
Syas (1704) 366

Taganrog 398
Tarantul (1771) 380
— (1779) 364
Temernik (1783) 365
Terek (1835) 383–4
Tmutarakan (1723) 378
Tonein (1740) 369
— 363
Tovi 379
Triton 14 (1835) 370
Tsaplia (1779) 364

Tsar' Konstantin 390
Tsaritsyn (1723) 378
— (1729) 378
Tsemes 4 393
Tseres 397–8
Tsitadel' (1766) 363
Tsvey Bruders No.1 394
— *No. 2* 395
Turukhtan Kolpitsa (1785) 380
Tver' 4–12 (1841) 382
Tvertsa 4–12 (1842) 382

Udaloi 390
Ulitka (1823) 398
Unter Nemung 392–3
Ural (1788) 383
— (1816) 381
— (1834) 383
Uriil 379
Urtemizh (1727) 377
Uspekh 8 (1826) 385
Ustyug 12 (1749) 374
Utka 2 (1819) 384

Valerian (1790) 399

Varakhail 379
Vasilii 363
— 398
Vater-Falk 12–14 (1719) 376
Vein-Drager (1703) 367
— (1726) 367
Vel'kom (1703) 367–8
Venera 22 (1768) 375
Verbliud 22 (1758) 374
— 6 (1774) 364
— (1827) 398
— 391
— 401
Vesna 390
Vetryanitsa (1806) 381
Vilgelmina 391
Vindava 6 (1832) 370
Vind-Khund 36–38 (1821) 389
Voinsliy (1703) 366
Vol (1806) 381
Volga 4–12 (1842) 382
— 4 (1811) 383
— 4 (1823) 383
— (1788) 383
Volik 10 401

Volkhov 4 (1835) 382
Vologda 22 (1749) 374
— (1734) 363
Vozobnovlennyi Okhotsk (1787) 365
Vtoroi/Shturman (1727) 369
Vulan 396
Vulkan (1723) 378
— (1727) 378

Yaik 4 (1823) 383
Yunge-Eduard 370
Yunge-Piter 363
Yunge-Tobias 364
Yungfrau Mariia 364

Zakharii (1755) 365
Zenzili (1727) 378
— 378
Zhaba (1823) 398
Zhuk (1822) 398
Zinait (1729) 378
Zinanoy (1723) 378
Zmeia (1825) 385

Section IV: The Russian Steam Navy

Abrek 5 (1860) 422
Aleksandr Nevskii 51 (1862) 413
Almak 7 (1861) 423
Arkhimed 48 (1848) 410
Askol'd 46 (ex-*Mariia*) (1854) 411
— 17 (1863) 421

Baba-Yaga 3 (1856) 427
Baian 161 (1857) 420
Balagur 3 (1855) 426
Bessarabiia 6 (1843) 424
Bogatyr' 28 (1836) 415
— 17 (1860) 420
Boyarin 11 (1856) 419
Bronya 3 (1856) 427
Buian 3 (1855) 426
Buivol 11 (1856) 419
Burun 3 (1855) 425
Burya 3 (1855) 426

Chayka 3 (1856) 427

Dmitrii Donskoi 51 (1861) 413
Domovoi 3 (1856) 426
Dozhd' 3 (1855) 425
Dym 3 (1856) 427
Dzhigit 3 (1856) 421–2

Gaidamak 7 (1860) 422–3
Gangut 84/90 (1825) 409
General Admiral 70 (1858) 412
Gerkules 10 (1831) 417
Gogol' 3 (1855) 426
Gornostai 2 (1863) 427
Grad 3 (1855) 426
Gremiashchi 4/11 (1851) 417
Griden' 11 (1856) 420
Grom 3 (1855) 426

Gromoboy 53 (1857) 411
Gromonosets 6 (1843) 424
Groziashchii 4/8 (1844) 417
Gul 3 (1856) 427

Iadro 3 (1856) 427
Iakhont 7 (1862) 423
Iastreb 9 (1860) 425
Il'ia Muromets 53 (1858) 411
Imperator Nikolai I 111 (1860) 408
Inei 3 (1856) 426
Iorsh 3 (1855) 426
Izumrud 7 (1862) 423

Kalevala 11/15 (1856) 420
Kamchatka 14/20 (1840) 415
Kartech' 3 (1856) 427
Khersones 4/6 (1843) 423–4
Khrabryi 4/10 (1844) 416–17
— 8 (1858) 418
Khvat 3 (1855) 425
Kolchan 3 (1856) 427
Kol'chuga 3 (1856) 427
Komar 3 (1855) 426
Konstantin 81 (1855) 410
Kopchik 3 (1855) 426
Kop'e 3 (1856) 427
Korshun 3 (1855) 426
Krechet 9 (1860) 425
Krym 4/6 (1842) 423

Legkii 3 (1856) 426
Likhach 3 (1855) 425
Luk 3 (1856) 427
L'vitsa 9 (1865) 425

Marevo 3 (1856) 427
Mech 3 (1856) 427

Medved' 11 (1856) 419–20
Metel' 3 (1856) 427
Molniia 3 (1855) 425
Moroz 3 (1856) 426
Morzh 2 (1860) 427

Naezdnik 3 (1856) 422
Novik 11 (1856) 419

Oboroten' 3 (1856) 427
Odessa 4/6 (1842) 423
Olaf 14/24 (1852) 418
Oleg 57 (1860) 413
Oprichnik 3 (1856) 422
Oryol 84 (1854) 410
Osa 3 (1855) 426
Osetr 3 (1855) 426
Osliabia 45 (1860) 413
Otliv 3 (1856) 426
Otvazhnyi 4/10 (1843) 416

Pamiat' Merkuriia 9 (1865) 425
Pantsir' 3 (1856) 427
Pchela 3 (1855) 426
Peresvet 51 (1860) 413
Petropavlovsk 58 (1865) 414
Pishchal' 3 (1856) 427
Plamya 3 (1856) 426
Plastun 3 (1856) 422
Polkan 44/45 (1853) 411
Poryv 3 (1855) 426
Posadnik 11 (1856) 420
Postrel 3 (1855) 425
Povesa 3 (1855) 426
Priboi 3 (1856) 426
Priliv 3 (1856) 426
Prokaznik 3 (1855) 426

Razboynik 3 (1856) 421
Retvizan 74 (1837) 410
Riurik 4/6 (1851) 418
— 6 (1870) 418
Roza 3 (1856) 427
Rusalka 3 (1855) 426
Rynda 11 (1856) 420
Rys' 11/12 (1856) 419

Sekira 3 (1856) 427
Sevastopol 58 (1864) 413–14
Shalun 3 (1856) 426
Shchegol' 3 (1855) 426
Shchit 3 (1856) 427
Shchuka 3 (1855) 426
Shkval 3 (1855) 426
Shlem 3 (1856) 427
Shmel' 3 (1855) 426
Sinop (ex-*Bosfor*) 135 (1858) 407–8
Smelyi 14/21 (1844) 417
— 8 (1858) 418
Sneg 3 (1855) 426
Sobol' 2 (1863) 427
Sokol 9 (1859) 424–5
Solombala 4/8 (1859) 418
Sorvanets 3 (1855) 426
Sterliad' 3 (1854) 425
Strelok 3 (1856) 421
Svetlana 40 (1858) 411–12

Tigr 4 (1858) 424
Tolcheia 3 (1855) 426
Treska 3 (1856) 427
Tsesarevich 135 (1857) 407
Tucha 3 (1855) 425
Turman 3 (1855) 425
Tyulen' 1 (1860) 427

Udav 11 (1856) 420

Varyag 17 (1862) 420–1
Ved'ma 3 (1855) 426
Vepr' 11 (1856) 419
Vikhr' 3 (1855) 425
Vityaz' (later *Skobelev*) 17 (1862) 421

Vladimir 2/5 (1845) 417
— 9 (1848) 424
Voevoda 11 (1856) 419
Voin 4/6 (1857) 425
Vol 11 (1856) 420
Vola 84/92 (1837) 409–10
Volk 11 (1856) 419

Volna 3 (1855) 426
Vsadnik 5 (1860) 422
Vyborg 74 (1841) 410
Vyiuga 3 (1856) 427
Vystrel 3 (1856) 427
Vzryv 3 (1856) 427

Zabiiaka 3 (1855) 425
Zarevo 3 (1856) 427
Zarnitsa 3 (1855) 426
Zhemchug 7 (1861) 423
Zubr 11 (1856) 419
Zvon 3 (1856) 427
Zyb' 3 (1855) 426

Picture Credits

Maps 33, 62, 83, 89 by Peter Wilkinson

National Maritime Museum: Frontispiece, no. PU8013; 34, no. BHC1951; 53, no. PZ0144; 59, no. PW4597; 61, no. B0681-H; 68, no. PZ3664; 75, no. A4816; 81, no. PX9319; 82, no. PW4628; 88, no. PW4672; 95, no. PW4710; 96 (right), no. BHC2889; 196, no. J3383; 198, no. J3923; 250, no. J3631; 253, no. J3924; 337, no. J7025

Sudstroenie magazine: 23, 122, 255, 266, 268, 272, 300, 174, 240 (bottom), 403, 408, 411, 413, 414, 426

From *Voennaya Encyclopedia*: 27, 37 (top), 40, 56, 57, 76, 107 (top), 108, 110, 187, 248

T. M. Matveeva, *Ubranstvo Russkikh Korabley*, Sudostroenie, Leningrad, 1979: 36, 37 (below), 71, 84, 100, 101, 107 (bbelow), 118, 134, 205, 218, 219, 226, 227, 249, 258 294, 296, 297, 327, 328, 330, 331

G. A. Grebenshchikova, *100-pushechnye korabli tipa* Victory, Ostrov, SPb, 2006: 41, 116–17, 154–5, 157

G. A. Grebenshchikova, *120-pushechnyy Korabl* Dvenadsat Apostolov, Gangut, SPb, 2003: 44, 45, 220, 297, 300

Central Naval Museum, St Petersburg) 77, 92, 93 (top), 94, 114, 149

Gangut magazine: 120, 135, 143, 176, 177, 178, 325, 326, 341, 350, 358, 253

A. A. Chernyshev, *Rossiyskiy Parusnyy Flot*, v. 1, Moscow, 1997): 165, 200, 234, 267; v. 2, 198, 352, 354, 355, 379, 368, 349 (below), 356 (left), 378

Russian Navy 1696–1996 (Moscow, 1996): 349 (top)

Briz magazine: 421